PENNSYLVANIA GERMAN PIONEERS

IN TWO VOLUMES

Volume II
1785–1808
Indexes

PENNSYLVANIA GERMAN PIONEERS

A Publication of the Original Lists of Arrivals
In the Port of Philadelphia
From 1727 to 1808

By

RALPH BEAVER STRASSBURGER, LL.D.
President of the Pennsylvania German Society

Edited by

WILLIAM JOHN HINKE, PH.D., D.D.

Second Printing
IN TWO VOLUMES

VOLUME II
1785 - 1808
INDEXES

Baltimore
GENEALOGICAL PUBLISHING CO., INC.
1980

Originally published: Norristown, PA, 1934
Reprinted, with permission of the
Pennsylvania German Society,
by Genealogical Publishing Co., Inc.
1001 N. Calvert St., Baltimore, MD 21202
1966, 1975, 1980, 1992, 2002
Publisher's Preface © 1966
by Genealogical Publishing Co., Inc.
Baltimore, Maryland
All Rights Reserved
Library of Congress Catalogue Card Number 66-23871
International Standard Book Number: Volume II: 0-8063-0881-8
ISBN Set Number: 0-8063-0882-6
Made in the United States of America

INTRODUCTION

The War of the Revolution brought all emigration from Europe to America to a stop. It also made all laws relating to immigration obsolete. The colonies were now independent states, with no king to swear allegiance to and no pope to fear. Hence new laws were necessary, which would take account of these new conditions.

ORIGIN OF THE LATER LISTS

With this background in view the later lists, beginning in 1785, can readily be accounted for. Shortly after the close of the War, when immigration again set in, the General Assembly of Pennsylvania passed, on April 8, 1785, the following statute:

An Act for establishing the office of Register of all German passengers, who shall arrive at the Port of Philadelphia, and of all indentures by which any of them shall be bound servants for their freight, and of the assignments of such servants in the city of Philadelphia.

Section I. Whereas, by several acts of assembly of the province of Pennsylvania, all masters of vessels, merchants and others, importing by land or by water any men or women passengers or servants are obliged within the space of twenty-four hours after their arrival, to make entry and give or cause to be given upon oath or affirmation to the officer for that purpose appointed, a true and just account of all the names of the servants and passengers so imported, which account the said officer should duly enter with the mayor of the city of Philadelphia, if such passengers were designed to be landed at Philadelphia. And that the said mayor should examine into the character and circumstances of such servants and passengers, and grant certificates containing the names of all the servants or passengers which he should judge fit to be landed; and that every indenture, whereby any such German passenger should be bound to serve his or her master or mistress, should be acknowledged before the mayor or recorder of the city of Philadelphia, and he keep an exact record thereof clearly expressing the province, county, city, borough or township wherein such master or mistress resides, and that the said mayor and recorder in the said city should in like manner keep

a record of the assignments of servants, therein expressing the places of the assignee's abode:

Section II. And whereas since the change of the government of Pennsylvania, the offices of mayor and recorder of the city of Philadelphia have been vacated, and the justices of the peace of the said city collectively, or any three of them by an act of this commonwealth, are empowered to do and perform certain special matters and things, formerly directed to be done and performed by the mayor, recorder and aldermen of the said city; but no provision has been hitherto made by law for registering the names of the German passengers, who shall arrive at the port of Philadelphia, and taking the acknowledgment of the indentures of such passengers as shall or may bind themselves servants for their freight: And whereas reason and justice require that the officer who is to execute so important a trust for foreigners, should be fully acquainted with their language, and able to converse with them.

Section III. Be it enacted and is hereby enacted by the Representatives of the Freemen of the Commonwealth of Pennsylvania in General Assembly met, and by the authority of the same, That an office for registering all German passengers who at any time hereafter shall arrive at the port of Philadelphia, and the execution of all such indentures by which any such passengers shall bind him or herself servants for their freight, shall be and is hereby established; and that a person understanding and speaking the English and German languages with ease and propriety, an inhabitant of the said city, in confidence and reputation with the public for his integrity and discretion, shall from time to time be appointed and commissioned by the president or vice-president in council, and being duly sworn to the true and faithful performance of the several duties required of him by this act, before the chief justice or any one of the judges of the supreme court of this state shall be the register of German passengers arriving in the port of Philadelphia, and by virtue of his said office, shall use and exercise all the powers and authorities of a justice of the peace for the city and county of Philadelphia, as far as the same shall be required for the support and efficacy of his office and the laws respecting the importation of German passengers and binding them out servants and not otherwise; and that the health officer having received from the captain of any vessel importing German passengers the list of their names, shall with his German interpreter review all the said passengers on board, men, women and children, and inquire whether any of them are superannuated, impotent or otherwise likely to become chargeable to the public, and make report thereof in writing to the said register, who if he approves thereof, shall enter the same in a book for that purpose to be kept by him, and transmit the original thereof to the office of the secretary of the supreme executive council and give his order and license to land such of them as are returned sound, without any defect in mind and body.

Section IV. And be it further enacted by the authority aforesaid, That all indentures of such German passengers, men, women and children, by which they shall be bound to serve, and all assignments of servants made within the said city shall be made and acknowledged before the said register or his lawful deputy and by him certified, and the full contents thereof entered and registered in the same manner, and to the same effect, as servants indentures and assignments of servants were heretofore by law made and acknowledged before the mayor of the city of Philadelphia, and by him registered; and that all persons whom it may concern shall be entitled to have a copy or abstract of such register.

Section V. And be it further enacted by the authority aforesaid, That the fees of the said register shall be the same as were usually taken by the mayors of the said city, until it shall be otherwise provided by act of assembly.* Passed April 8, 1785. Recorded L. B. No. 2, p. 522.

In order to carry out the provisions of this law, Col. Lewis Farmer was appointed as the first Register of German passengers. He served in this capacity from 1785 to at least 1804. The first health officer under the new law was John Jones.

According to this new statute but one list of the names of the passengers was required. It was to be handed by the captain of a ship to the health officer. With the list as a guide he was to examine, together with his interpreter, all the passengers of a ship, as to their physical and mental condition. The result was to be reported in writing to the Register of German passengers, who, if he approved, was to enter the same in a book and then transmit from time to time the original reports to the Secretary of the Supreme Council of the State.

According to a strict interpretation of the words of the law the Register of German passengers was to enter the report of the health officer into a book and transmit it to the Supreme Council. But as a matter of fact what the Register did transmit were the lists of the passengers. This appears clearly from three such letters, which we publish in this volume. (See pp. 14, 33, 40.).

CONTENTS OF THE LISTS

In accordance with these provisions only one list of passengers of each ship was made and preserved. It was the captain's list. But, although the law demanded only the names of the passengers to be handed in, many of the captains were pleased

* Statutes at Large of Pennsylvania, Vol. XI, 1782, pp. 602–604.

to give much more, to the great delight of posterity. No less than seventeen captains add the ages of the passengers (Nos. 342, 370, 412, 438, 439, 458, 460, 475, 480, 481, 485, 486, 490, 491, 497, 501, 505). Six captains gave the ages of the children only (Nos. 373, 389, 464, 487, 495, 499). Ten captains give the occupations of the passengers (Nos. 412, 458, 460, 475, 480, 485, 490, 491, 501, 505). Eleven captains give their places of birth (Nos. 428, 460, 480, 485, 486, 487, 490, 491, 497, 501, 505), in some cases, however, the names of the country or district merely, whence they came (Nos. 428, 460, 485, 505). Nine captains describe the personal appearance of the passengers, including their height, complexion, color of hair and eyes (Nos. 454, 460, 475, 480, 485, 490, 491, 501, 505). Two captains make reference to their baggage (Nos. 453, 475). Two give information about the passage money and the amount loaned to the passengers (Nos. 455, 471). Two captains state the number of persons in each family (Nos. 489, 495), and one captain includes in his report the contract made between him and his passengers (No. 469), a most welcome addition.

In general, we must conclude that these later lists are much more varied in contents than the lists before the year 1775.

Alongside of these actual lists of passengers, the State has preserved a number of other documents, which were considered of sufficient importance to be included in this volume. They are as follows:

In the first place, there are three letters of the Register of German passengers (Nos. 333, 350, 356), to which we have already referred. They are of importance because they bear evidence to the fact that not all the lists have come down to us. For example, in his letter of May 19, 1786 (No. 333), Col. Farmer transmitted lists, extending from June 20th to December 1785. In reality the eight surviving lists run from June 20th to October 29, 1785, and they do not contain 665 names, as stated in the letter, but only 642 names. This shows that one list or perhaps two are wanting.

Then there are several lists (Nos. 356, 386) that give the number of passengers brought over by various ships, but not the actual names of the people. These lists are of interest, because they prove that passengers came from many other ports besides those mentioned in the ordinary shiplists.

Again, there are four lists of persons (Nos. 336, 344, 345, 354), containing 77 names, of those who signed the oath of allegiance to the Commonwealth of Pennsylvania. They are a counterpart to the lists of signers of the oath of allegiance to the King of England in Volume I.

Finally, there is a list of French passengers (No. 406), who were aided by a grant of $1,500, voted by the Assembly. Of these various lists only the last (No. 406) had been printed before.

Most of the lists printed in this volume were published by the State of Pennsylvania, in the *Pennsylvania Archives,* second series, Vol. XVII. But there are many omissions in that publication. For some reason which is not apparent at present, none of the eight lists of the year 1785, none of the seven lists of 1791, none of the ten lists of 1792, nor two of the undated lists (Nos. 440, 441) were printed by the State, so that, together with the seven lists mentioned previously, there are 34 lists, containing 1,440 names, which appear for the first time in this work.

The statistics of the lists are of sufficient interest to be presented in full. We give in the following tabular statement the number of ships and passengers for each of the twenty-four years, for which the lists are preserved:

Years	Ships	Passengers	Years	Ships	Passengers
1785	8	639	1798	5	115
1786	6	224	1799	3	45
1787	4	352	Undated	6	323
1788	5	157	1800	5	158
1789	3	114	1801	7	90
1790	2	44	1802	10	643
1791	7	320	1803	8	763
1792	10	464	1804	11	1211
1793	10	239	1805	10	818
1794	10	352	1806	7	586
1795	9	282	1807	6	359
1796	17	805	1808	1	98
1797	5	62			
			Totals:	175	9263

This summary shows that we present in this volume 175 shiplists, with a total of 9,263 names. When we add these to

the 29,085 names, which are published in the first volume of this work, we get a total of 38,307 names, recorded in the shiplists. If we add the 77 names in the four lists of signers of the oath of allegiance (Nos. 336, 344, 345, 354), we get a grand total of 38,425 names. The actual number of passengers was, of course, much larger. The two lists, Nos. 356 and 386, add 3,146 other passengers, whose names have not been preserved.

When the American colonies became independent states, the ships sailing for America were no longer compelled to stop at an English port in order to secure clearance papers for American ports, but the ships came direct from the continental port, at which the passengers embarked. As in the preceding period most of the ships came from Holland. From Amsterdam came seventy ships and eight ships from Rotterdam (Nos. 339, 346, 361, 375, 402, 420, 450, 493). The other ports, from which the ships sailed, were as follows: Sixty ships from Hamburg, twelve ships from Bremen (Nos. 417, 430, 441, 442, 443, 444, 456, 458, 467, 482, 490, 498), seven ships from Tonningen in Denmark (Nos. 473, 478, 491, 492, 494, 501, 506), one ship from Copenhagen (No. 382), one ship from St. Thomas (No. 483), one ship from St. Domingo (No. 386), one ship from Lubeck (No. 476), one ship from London (No. 347) and one ship from Frederickstadt (No. 472), while in the case of twelve ships the port of departure is not given (Nos. 325, 328, 329, 330, 376 406, 413, 432, 439, 481, 485, 505).

TERMINATION OF LISTS IN 1808

As the lists of pioneers, preserved by the State of Pennsylvania, come to an end abruptly in the year 1808, the question naturally arises: Why do the lists stop in 1808?

In looking about for an adequate reason, we must remind ourselves, first of all, of the state of affairs in Europe at that time.*

In 1802, the peace of Amiens ended the War between France and England. But, when a commercial war was kept up even after the military operations had ceased, peace was not

---

* The following statements are based on *The Cambridge Modern History*, Vol. VII, New York, 1903; E. F. Heckscher, *The Continental System, an economic interpretation,* Oxford, 1922; R. L. Garis, *Immigration Restriction,* New York, 1927.

of long duration. War broke out again between the two countries in May 1803, and continued until the fall of Napoleon in
1815.

Upon the renewal of hostilities England seized all French
and Dutch vessels in British ports. In June 1803, the mouths
of the Elbe and Weser rivers were declared in a state of blockade and, in August 1804, this blockade was extended from the
Weser to the port of Brest on the French coast. Although this
blockade was annulled in 1805, it was renewed and further
extended in April 1806.

Napoleon, meanwhile, contented himself with arresting all
Englishmen on French soil, with occupying Hanover, which
belonged to the English royal house, with seizing Cuxhaven,
at the mouth of the Elbe, and closing the North Sea ports to
English trade. But he delayed more stringent measures until
he had humbled Prussia by his victories at Jena and Auerstadt
in October 1806. Then, when all of western Germany was under his control, he issued the famous Berlin Decree, from the
capital of his defeated foe, on November 21, 1806. It em-
braced four main points: (1) All the British isles were declared in a state of blockade and all commerce with them was
prohibited; (2) British subjects within French territory were
declared prisoners of war; (3) All trade in British goods was
prohibited and goods from England and her colonies were declared fair prizes of war, when captured; (4) Every vessel
from England or her colonies was refused access to any port
on the continent of Europe.

As far as the blockade of Great Britain was concerned it
was only a blockade on paper and hence a mere grandiose ges-
ture, for, as Lord Erskine remarked before Parliament: "Napoleon might just as well have declared the moon in a state of
blockade." Through the victory of Nelson at Trafalgar, on
October 21, 1805, the French fleet had been swept off the sea.
Hence France was powerless to enforce any blockade of England. But it imposed upon Europe a self blockade on land,
which, if it hurt France and her allies, was supposed to injure
Britain much more, and, by preventing her from disposing of
her goods, was intended to compel her to sue for peace.

The decree of the French emperor was answered on the part
of Great Britain by a number of orders in council, the most
important dated November 11, 1807. Through these orders

not only all enemy countries with their colonies, but also all places from which the British flag was excluded were declared in a state of blockade, trade in their products was prohibited and every vessel trading with these countries as well as its cargo was declared a fair prize.

Napoleon in turn answered these British measures with still harsher decrees, which interfered still more with the rights of neutrals. By the Second Milan decree, for example, promulgated on December 17, 1807, he ordered that any vessel which submitted to the British regulations (even against its will), which allowed an examination of its cargo, which made a call at an English port and paid duty there, should thereby forfeit the protection of its flag, as it had become English property and, as a consequence, was subject to seizure. The result was that there were no longer any neutrals. They were treated as Englishmen in disguise or as confederates of the English.

Meanwhile important events had taken place in America, which were destined ultimately to draw America also into the conflict.

In April 1805, an American vessel, the *Essex*, with a cargo from Barcelona, Spain, had landed at Salem, Massachusetts, had there discharged her cargo, paid duty on it, and, after having undergone some repairs, had reloaded the same cargo to transport it to Havana, Cuba. On her way she was seized by an English warship, taken to England and condemned as a fair prize, because, as the court contended, the intention had never been really to sell the goods in the States, but in Cuba. Hence she fell under the prohibition that neutrals could not trade with enemy colonies, on the contention that this trade was not open to them before the war and was now only made accessible to them through English naval victories. In other words, neutral trade was prohibited from profiting by English naval victories.

When the news of this decision reached America there was great indignation. Merchants throughout the nation and chambers of commerce called upon Congress to retaliate. Hence, in April 1806, a Non-importation Act was passed by Congress, by which most of the industrial products of Great Britain were excluded. This act did not come into force until November 1806, but was rescinded six weeks later.

Its place was taken, in December 1807, by an Embargo Act.

This was due to the so-called "Chesapeake affair." An English man-of-war stopped and searched the United States Frigate "Chesapeake," and removed from her four sailors, one, because he was a deserter from an English warship, the other three because when born they were British subjects.

In view of these high-handed actions of the combatants, America could do one of three things: It could resist the encroachments of the belligerents with all her might, or tamely submit to all of them, or, finally, withdraw from all oversea commerce. Jefferson, who was a Virginia country gentleman, and as such regarded agriculture as the highest work of man and believed that giving up all foreign commerce might be a blessing in disguise, chose the last of these alternatives, and persuaded Congress to close the ports of the United States to all foreign trade. As a result, from December 1807 to March 1809, all commerce with foreign countries ceased. This had no effect on the madness of the belligerents, but was ruinous to America. Especially the New England States resisted the law to a man and evaded it in every manner possible, so that, in March 1809, the embargo was lifted. Its place was taken by a non-intercourse law, which limited the prohibition to trade to France and England, but gave the President power to suspend the operation of the law in case England rescinded her orders in council or France revoked her decrees.

A few days after having signed this law Jefferson retired and Madison became President of the United States, in March 1809. He had hardly assumed the presidency when David Erskine, the English minister, offered to withdraw the objectionable orders in council. A series of notes were exchanged. In the first, Erskine offered to make reparation for the attack on the Chesapeake and return the three captured American sailors. In the second, he offered the withdrawal of the orders in council, if America would renew her intercourse with Great Britain, and in the third he named June 10, 1809, as the day on which the orders in council would be suspended, as far as American vessels were concerned. In view of these promises President Madison issued a proclamation, in which he announced that after June 10, 1809, commerce between the two countries would again be reopened. This proclamation was hailed with great joy by the commercial interests of the country. But, when these promises became known in England, the

British government promptly repudiated them and recalled her minister. This put Madison in the awkward plight of having to recall his proclamation and issue a new proclamation, by which all trade with England was again stopped.

Meanwhile Napoleon had retaliated on America by the Rambouillet decree of March 1810. By it every American vessel which had entered a French port since May 20, 1809, was ordered seized. The decree was not published till May 1810, by which time $10,000,000 worth of American goods had accumulated in French ports. These were seized and sold for the benefit of the French treasury.

All earlier acts having failed to bring the belligerents to their senses and respect the rights of neutrals, Congress tried another method of retaliation. On May 1, 1810, it passed the Macon bill, No. 2, which permitted American trade with the rest of the world and gave the belligerents until March 3, 1811, to rescind their orders and change their decrees, but threatened to put the non-intercourse act in force against that country which had not modified its rules of war.

When this law was submitted to Napoleon by his foreign minister Champagny, he considered it an excellent means whereby to draw America into the conflict on the side of France, by pretending to suspend his decrees and causing the United States to enforce the Non-intercourse Act against Great Britain only.

In carrying out this plan he ordered Champagny to notify the American minister that the decrees of Berlin and Milan would be revoked on November 1, 1810, if by that time Great Britain had rescinded her Orders in Council, or the United States had caused Great Britain to respect her rights. Madison, taking it for granted that the decrees of Napoleon had actually been revoked on November 1st, issued a proclamation on November 2nd, giving Great Britain three months' notice that, unless her Orders in Council were revoked by February 2, 1811, the Non-intercourse Act would be put into effect against Great Britain. When the day set arrived, Great Britain had not acted. Hence President Madison persuaded Congress to enforce nine sections of the Non-intercourse Act of 1809 against Great Britain.

Meanwhile Napoleon had rescinded his decrees on paper only, for after November 1, 1810, a number of American

vessels which appeared in French ports were seized. His explanation that while the decrees were repealed, as far as United States vessels were concerned, the municipal laws of French ports were still in force, was a mere subterfuge. Madison, however, accepted this explanation, because some of the American vessels coming direct from America had been released. He called Congress into special session in November 1811, complaining in his message that the repeal of the French decrees had not induced Great Britain to rescind her Orders, but that they were enforced more vigorously than ever before; that the ports of America were blockaded by English ships and that American rights were disregarded. As a result Congress prepared for war, by ordering the ranks of the regular army to be filled and calling for 50,000 volunteers.

Meanwhile France had issued a decree, on March 2, 1811, but not published until May 1812, by which it was ordered that the Berlin and Milan decrees were not to apply to American vessels. And, finally, on June 23, 1812, Great Britain rescinded her Orders in Council, as far as American vessels were concerned. But this last action came too late. Four days before, on June 19, 1812, Madison by proclamation announced that a state of war existed between the United States and England. The war lasted until Christmas 1814.

This review of some of the outstanding events leading up to the War of 1812 has shown that there were at least three causes for the stoppage of immigration into Pennsylvania. First, the decrees of France, establishing a Continental Blockade, and the English Orders in Council, prohibiting neutrals to trade with France and her colonies. Secondly, the various American acts of Congress, establishing a self-blockade of the United States and prohibiting all foreign trade, and thirdly, the War of 1812, which did not come to an end until 1814.

There was, however, still another cause for the cessation of the immigrant lists of Pennsylvania in 1808. It was the Constitution of the United States.

The ninth section of the first article of the Constitution provides that "the immigration or importation of such persons as any of the States, now existing, shall think proper to admit, shall not be prohibited by Congress prior to the year 1808, but a tax may be imposed on such importation not exceeding ten dollars for each person."

The framers of the Constitution intended originally to have this section apply to slaves exclusively. Thus Luther Martin, one of the members of the Constitutional Convention wrote to the Maryland Legislature:

"The design of this clause is to prevent the General Government from prohibiting the importation of slaves." *

The language of the Constitution is, however, vague enough to admit of another interpretation. Thus Mr. Iredell, later one of the Justices of the Supreme Court of the United States, declared before the legislature of North Carolina: "The committee will observe the distinction between the two words migration and importation. The first part of the clause will extend to persons who come into this country as free people, or as slaves bought. But the last part refers to slaves, because free people cannot be said to be imported. The tax, therefore, is only to be laid on slaves who are imported and not on free people who migrate." *

But while Judge Iredell limited the right of taxation to the importation of slaves, others contended that the language of the Constitution permitted Congress to tax voluntary immigrants as well as slaves. According to this interpretation of the Constitution Congress had power to legislate on the subject of immigration as well as the importation of slaves. This interpretation of the Constitution came ultimately to prevail through a long series of legal decisions.

Accordingly, on March 2, 1819, the first federal law on the subject of immigration was passed, which contained the provision that at the port of landing a full and complete report be made by the ship's officer to the custom authorities, which was to include a statement as to the name, sex, age and occupation of each passenger. This resulted in the first official statistics, prepared by the Federal Government, for the year ending September 30, 1820. By this law of Congress the keeping of immigration records passed from the states into federal control.

DOCUMENTS BROUGHT OVER BY PIONEERS

In the Introduction to the first volume of this work, the editor presented a series of documents, brought over by the pi-

* Garis, *Immigration Restriction*, pp. 60–61.

oneers. But, since this introduction was printed, a number of new documents have been discovered, which are of sufficient interest and importance to warrant their presentation by facsimile and their translation for the use of the general reader.

The most interesting of these documents is a Letter of Manumission and a permit to emigrate, issued by the Archbishop of Mayence to John Valentine Griesheimer, on April 28, 1730. It reads as follows : *

"We, by the Grace of God, Francis Lewis, Archbishop of Mayence, Chancellor and Elector of the Holy Roman Empire, Administrator of the Grand Master's Office in Prussia, Master of the German Order in Germany and France, Bishop of Worms and Breslau, Dean and Lord of Ellwangen, Count Palatine of the Rhine in Bavaria, Duke of Gulich, Cleve and Berg, Prince of Moers, Count of Veldentz, Sponheim, Marck and Ravenspurg, Lord of Ravenstein, Freudenthal, Cullenberg, etc. etc.,

"Herewith we let it be known that, Whereas our subject at Lampertheim, John Valentine Griesheimer, for himself, his wife and four children, namely Caspar, John, Anna Margaret and Jacob, has asked that we might be pleased, in view of the good fortune that awaits them elsewhere, graciously to release all of them from the serfdom, to which they are subject, graciously to grant their submissive petition and manumit and dismiss them,

"Therefore, they are herewith and by virtue of this letter, from now on and forever afterwards, released and freed from their serfdom, yet with this explicit reservation, that, if the above-mentioned John Valentine Griesheimer, his wife and children, shall sooner or later return and settle again in our lands or under our jurisdiction, in which we have inherited the right of serfdom, that they shall ipso facto be subject to their former serfdom and without further process shall be subservient unto us.

"In testimony of this our certificate of manumission our seal has been affixed. Given at Worms, April 28, 1730.

The Electoral Government of Worms.

(SEAL)   John Adam Schrenck, J. G. Gigant."

* See illustration, facing p. 66. Joseph Griesheimer landed at Philadelphia, August 21, 1730. See Vol. I, pp. 31–33.

From this document we learn that some form of serfdom existed in the archepiscopate of Mayence as late as the year 1730. It probably consisted merely in the payment of an annual tithe from the produce of flocks and fields to the sovereign. The last vestiges of serfdom did not disappear in Germany until after the wars of Napoleon, through the reawakening of the Spirit of Freedom in 1812.

Another interesting document is a Permit to emigrate, issued to Henry Gerhard Diener, on May 13, 1751, by the Prince of Isenburg and Buedingen. It reads: *

"We, by the grace of God, Wolffgang Ernest, Prince of Isenburg and Buedingen, etc., etc.,

"Herewith and by these presents make it known that, whereas Henry Gerhard Diener, born at Birstein, has submissively petitioned and requested, that we release him and his family from the claims to which they are subject to us and the County of Isenburg, and graciously permit him to leave our land, we graciously grant this submissive request;

"Therefore, by virtue of these presents we grant that the above-mentioned Henry Gerhard Diener, together with his family, may leave our land, move to another place and settle there.

"In testimony of which our secret printed Princely Seal has been affixed. Given at Birstein, May 13, 1751."

(SEAL)

Then we present a pastoral letter of recommendation, issued to Joseph Eberhard on his departure from Eych, in the Palatinate, on May 1, 1727. It reads as follows: †

"The bearer of this, Joseph Eberhard, born at Jaegersdorf, in Switzerland, has been a member of our church, Reformed according to the Word of God, as he proved by the observance of the external duties of our religion, by which we judge in the spirit of love, such as the diligent attendance upon the preaching of the Word, the reverent use of the Holy Communion

---

* See illustration facing p. 98. Henry Gerhard Diener landed at Philadelphia, Sept. 14, 1751. See Vol. I, p. 460.

† See illustration, facing p. 114. Joseph Eberhard arrived at Philadelphia, Oct. 16, 1727. As Michael Eberam (Vol. I, p. 16) is Michael Eberhardt (p. 17), so Joseph Eberam (Vol. I, p. 16), sick, must be this Joseph Eberhard.

and the Christian conduct of his life, as far as it is known to us;

"Therefore, the pastors and elders of the churches, to whom this letter is shown, are requested graciously to receive him as such and admit him, under their supervision, to their Christian fellowship. In testimony of which the present attestation is submitted. Eych, in the Electoral Palatinate, May 1, 1727.

N. Dieterici, Pastor."

Finally, we present two real passports. The first, dated October 15, 1723, was issued to Peter Reist. It reads as follows:

"The bearer of this, Peter Reist, born at Rhein Dürckheim, intending to travel to Rhein Dürckheim, within the episcopate of Worms, is departing from here, a place at which no pestilential plague, but, thank God, pure air prevails. Therefore, all places can allow him to pass and repass. Given the 15th day of October, 1723.

<table>
<tr><td>{ SEAL OF THE
{ CANTON OF BERN }</td><td>Attested by the chancellery at
Summiswald."</td></tr>
</table>

Viséed at Montbelliard, November 29th, 1723.*

The second passport, that of Andrew Loretz, issued to him at Chur, September 8, 1784,† has already been translated in the Introduction to Volume I, p. XXXVIII.

INDEXES IN THIS VOLUME

Finally, some words of explanation may be given about the Indexes, presented in this volume. They are as exhaustive as possible, so as to make the whole contents of this work readily accessible to the reader. It is hardly necessary to say that the greatest possible care has been used in the construction of the Indexes. To give only a single proof. After the Index of the Pioneers had been printed, every one of its more than 50,000 references was checked up with the printed lists, a work which took nearly three months to complete.

The most difficult index to prepare was the last, that of the pioneers, due to the many, and often contradictory, variants.

---

* See illustration, facing p. 82.
† See illustration facing p. 130.

Not every variant of a surname, found in the lists was given, because many of them are mere scribal monstrosities, that have no value. In selecting the names to be recorded in the index, the editor was guided by the following principles: Whenever a passenger himself signed his name, his spelling was adopted, as every man ought to be the best judge as to how to spell his name. There is only this exception to be made, that some of the passengers were so near the line of illiteracy, that they actually did not know how to spell their names. Some could not write their name twice in the same way. In that case the correct form of the name was given first in the index, followed by an asterisk, e. g., Schützer * (Shitzer), which means that the form Shitzer is actually found in the text, but that it should be spelled Schützer. If the passenger was unable to write his name, that form of his surname was placed first which comes nearest to the original. Thus, e. g., when the captain's list reads Hans Michael Verdus (I, 35), but the other two lists agree in reading Hans Michael Wiedner (pp. 36, 37), there can be no question that the latter is the correct form. Sometimes none of the various officials who wrote down the name understood it correctly, as e. g. when in list No. 10 all three clerks made an Irishman out of a German, by writing Johannes Mcinterfer. Fortunately his wife, or other relative, was on board, and in this case the clerk wrote Phronick Mickinturfer. That sounds more like a German name and hence the two names were entered under that form. The original was probably something like Meckendörfer, but as this is doubtful, the editor preferred not to guess. In other cases a guess can be ventured that has every probability in its favor. Thus we find on p. 346 Martin Oadt, p. 347, Marti Tienod, and p. 348, Martin Oats. The correct form must have been Martin Ott, under which it has been recorded, with a cross reference from Oadt to Ott.

Generally speaking the captains' lists have the least value, as far as the spelling of the names is concerned. They were in most cases written by men who had no knowledge of German and to whom German surnames were a mystery they could not fathom. They wrote down the names as they were pronounced to them, spelling them as they would spell English names. As a result there are hundreds of names that have such fantastic forms that they are unrecognizable. There are, however, some

exceptions among the ships' officers. Thus, e. g., list 41 A is written in a beautiful German script, with all names spelled correctly. As was emphasized in the introduction to volume I, the so-called captains' lists were not written by the captains. They considered such a menial task as preparing a list of their passengers beneath their dignity and would assign the task to one of the ship's officers, the first or second mate. List 50 A is signed by Tho. Petterlo, Mett. We are not at all surprised that the spelling of the names of passengers on his ship is just as poor as the spelling of mett for mate.

To give only a few examples of how names were misunderstood we may quote the following: One officer wrote Hendrick Sculps (p. 240). The clerk of the court at Philadelphia heard Henrich Schultz, (p. 243), which is no doubt correct. Another wrote Albert Uderstal (p. 591). The man himself signed Albert Otto Steg (p. 593). Still another put down the monstrous form Hans Jackop Struhgefier (p. 117). The man himself signed Hans Jacob Schreiber (p. 120). Again, we find the English looking name Jacob Rudolph Seymour (p. 301), but a glance at the next list shows that it should have been Jacob Riedesheimer (p. 302). Such wide divergences prove that the A lists must be used with great caution.

Sometimes the names are divided wrongly. One of the clerks wrote Johann William Engel (p. 549), a perfectly good German name, but the other two lists agree in the rarer name Johann Wilhelm Mengel (pp. 545, 547). One list gives the name Listen Walter (p. 106), the next shows that it was misunderstood for Lichtenwallner (p. 111). Such examples could be multiplied by the hundreds. They all show how difficult it is to make a reliable index of these contradictory forms.

If two lists agree they are generally followed, unless the form they present is inherently impossible. All German surnames have meanings, although some names are so old or have such a peculiar dialectical form that their etymology escapes us. Still the large majority of surnames has been analyzed and is duly entered in one of the many books on German family names.

Some of the variant surnames were not merged under one form of the name, because these variants represent geographical and dialectical differences. Thus, e. g., Müller, Möller and Miller are not to be regarded as identical. They represent dif-

ferent forms of the name as used in different parts of Germany, Müller is South German, Möller is used in the central districts and Miller in northern Germany.

The same is true of many Christian names. Johann and Johannes are popularly treated as two different names. They are often given to two boys in the same family. Hence they are kept apart in the Index. Only the graphical variants Joh., Johan and Johann are treated as identical.

A few general directions may help to locate in the index some names that appear in the lists.

Some names ought to begin with K, but they are actually found under C. Such names as Korn and Kuhl are occasionally written Corn and Cool, by the English clerks. Other names that should begin with T are found sometimes under D, and vice versa. Also, names beginning properly with B are found occasionally under P, as Pens for Bentz. However, there are cross-references, which will facilitate the finding of the name in the index. The names beginning with Sch presented the greatest difficulties in arranging them for the index. The following rules were applied:

> For Sh see Sch, as Shelling see Schelling.
> For Sl see Schl, as Slatter see Schlatter.
> For Sm see Schm, as Smith see Schmidt.
> For Sn see Schn, as Snyder see Schneyder.
> For Sw see Schw, as Swartz see Schwartz.

A few words are sufficient to call attention to the Index of Christian Names. It was added in order to assist persons in understanding the meaning as well as the variant forms of German Christian names, as found in the lists. Some of the variant forms, such as Kunrad and Oldrich, show that in popular speech many archaic forms survive. The etymology of the Christian names has been given wherever possible. Attention has also been called to the many saint names that are found among the Christian names.

With these introductory remarks it is hoped the indexes will prove to be a useful and sufficient key for the lists themselves.

WILLIAM J. HINKE

Auburn Theological Seminary,
Auburn, New York

TABLE OF CONTENTS

				PAGE
Lists of Ships				3–206
325.	June	20, 1785	Mynheer van Berckel	3
326.	Aug.	27, 1785	Adolph	3
327.	Aug.	29, 1785	Patsey Rutledge	6
328.	Sept.	5, 1785	Favourite	6
329.	Oct.	4, 1785	London Packet	11
330.	Oct.	11, 1785	Hamburgh	12
331.	Oct.	15, 1785	Betsy	12
332.	Oct.	29, 1785	Lydia	13
333.	May	19, 1786	Passengers for 1785	14
334.	Aug.	19, 1786	Candide	15
335.	Sept.	27, 1786	Patsey Rutledge	16
336.	Sept.	30, 1786	Signers of oath of allegiance	17
337.	Oct.	11, 1786	Nassau	18
338.	Oct.	17, 1786	Hannah	19
339.	Oct.	31, 1786	Dispatch	19
340.	Dec.	14, 1786	Bristol	22
341.	Apr.	5, 1787	Rosetta	22
342.	May	23, 1787	Patsey Rutledge	22
343.	Oct.	10, 1787	North America	24
344.	Sept.	24, 1787	Signers of oath of allegiance	25
345.	Oct.	5, 1787	Signers of oath of allegiance	27
346.	Oct.	14, 1787	Dorothea	28
347.	July	7, 1788	Le Brie	30
348.	Aug.	5, 1788	Mary	32
349.	Oct.	2, 1788	Laurel	32
350.	Nov.	5, 1788	Commerce	33
351.	Nov.	5, 1788	Amsterdam Packet	34
352.	Jan.	10, 1789	Patsey Rutledge	34
353.	Sept.	29, 1789	Philadelphia	34
354.	Sept.	30, 1789	Signer of oath of allegiance	35
355.	Oct.	1, 1789	Mary	35
356.	—.	—, 1789	Passengers for 1789	37
357.	Mar.	31, 1790	Philadelphia Packet	41
358.	Oct.	4, 1790	Mary	41
359.	Jan.	18, 1791	Philadelphia Packet	42
360.	June	30, 1791	Mary	42
361.	Aug.	10, 1791	Diana	42
362.	Aug.	23, 1791	Philadelphia Packet	44
363.	Sept.	12, 1791	Fair American	45
364.	Sept.	27, 1791	Pallas	46

PAGE

365. Oct. 22, 1791 Van Stophorst 47
366. Apr. 26, 1792 Philadelphia Packet 48
367. May 26, 1792 Patsey Rutledge 48
368. June 28, 1792 Union 48
369. June 29, 1792 America 49
370. Aug. 3, 1792 Catharina 49
371. Sept. 7, 1792 Rainbow 51
372. Sept. 8, 1792 Columbia 52
373. Sept. 22, 1792 Henricus 54
374. Sept. 22, 1792 Martha 55
375. Sept. 23, 1792 Fame 55
376. Feb. 9, 1793 Union 57
377. Mar. 8, 1793 Columbia 57
378. July 19, 1793 John 57
379. Aug. 16, 1793 Union 58
380. Sept. 17, 1793 Columbia 58
381. Sept. 25, 1793 Brothers 60
382. Sept. 27, 1793 Samuel 60
383. Oct. 4, 1793 Polly 61
384. Nov. 10, 1793 Peggy 61
385. Nov. 12, 1793 Jean 62
386. Nov. 25, 1793 Passengers from May to Nov. 62
387. Feb. 18, 1794 Apollo 67
388. Mar. 12, 1794 John 68
389. May 31, 1794 Columbia 69
390. June 3, 1794 Union 70
391. July 14, 1794 Brothers 71
392. Aug. 20, 1794 Holland 71
393. Aug. 25, 1794 Birmingham Packet 72
394. Nov. 6, 1794 Peggy 72
395. Nov. 10, 1794 Sarah 73
396. Nov. 12, 1794 Sophia Carolina 73
397. Jan. 2, 1795 John 74
398. Feb. 27, 1795 Livonia 74
399. July 7, 1795 Concord 74
400. Sept. 18, 1795 Rose 75
401. Oct. 5, 1795 Hamburgh Packet 76
402. Oct. 13, 1795 Thomas Chalckley 76
403. Nov. 17, 1795 Friendship 77
404. Nov. —, 1795 Mary 78
405. Dec. 15, 1795 Minerva 79
406. Jan. 13, 1796 French passengers 80
407. Mar. 29, 1796 Henry and Charles 81
408. Apr. 13, 1796 Molly 82
409. June 3, 1796 America 82
410. June 17, 1796 Harriot Baltimore 82
411. July 25, 1796 Harmony 83
412. July 30, 1796 Mary 83

PAGE

413. Aug. 19, 1796 Holland 85
414. Aug. 29, 1796 Voltaire 89
415. Oct. 15, 1796 Concord 89
416. Oct. 15, 1796 Bacchus 89
417. Oct. 19, 1796 Polly 90
418. Oct. 20, 1796 Mary 90
419. Oct. 24, 1796 America 90
420. Oct. 26, 1796 George 91
421. Oct. 31, 1796 Two Friends 93
422. Nov. 22, 1796 Enterprize 94
423. Feb. 12, 1797 Columbia 94
424. Feb. 13, 1797 Good Friends 94
425. Feb. 15, 1797 Peggy 95
426. Feb. 24, 1797 Unnamed ship 95
427. Mar. 16, 1797 Fair Hebe 96
428. May 4, 1798 America 96
429. Aug. 31, 1798 Pennsylvania 96
430. Oct. 31, 1798 Triton 98
431. Nov. 1, 1798 Pallas 98
432. Dec. 19, 1798 Columbia 98
433. Oct. 6, 1799 Fair American 99
434. Oct. 17, 1799 Boston Packet 99
435. Nov. 19, 1799 Amiable Creole 100
436. ——. —, —— Amiable Matilda 100
437. ——. —, —— Columbia 100
438. ——. —, —— Jean 102
439. ——. —, —— Nancy 103
440. ——. —, —— Patsey Rutledge 104
441. ——. —, —— Industry 105
442. Feb. 25, 1800 Juno 105
443. Mar. 27, 1800 Ocean 106
444. Aug. 19, 1800 Anna 106
445. Sept. 30, 1800 Tryphena 108
446. Dec. 3, 1800 Diana 108
447. July 3, 1801 Venus 109
448. July 11, 1801 Delaware 109
449. Sept. 8, 1801 New York 109
450. Sept. 19, 1801 Express 110
451. Sept. 30, 1801 Molly 111
452. Sept. 30, 1801 Lavinia 111
453. Nov. 5, 1801 Der Biedermann 111
454. Mar. 8, 1802 Polly 111
455. Aug. 20, 1802 Belvidere 112
456. Aug. 26, 1802 Urania 114
457. Sept. 7, 1802 Pennsylvania 115
458. Oct. 5, 1802 Maria 116
459. Oct. 6, 1802 Devotion 117
460. Oct. 6, 1802, Juno 120

PAGE

461. Oct. 12, 1802 Tom 120
462. Nov. 15, 1802 Jacob 121
463. Nov. 22, 1802 Union 123
464. June 22, 1803 Traveller 124
465. Sept. 5, 1803 Charlotte 125
466. Sept. 8, 1803 Fortune 127
467. Oct. 3, 1803 Urania 130
468. Oct. 7, 1803 Canton 130
469. Oct. 9, 1803 Commerce 131
470. Nov. 15, 1803 Favourite 135
471. Nov. 15, 1803 Pennsylvania 137
472. Feb. 21, 1804 Carolina 138
473. Mar. 19, 1804 Union 138
474. Apr. 17, 1804 Indostan 138
475. Aug. 11, 1804 Newton 140
476. Aug. 25, 1804 Leopard 144
477. Aug. 27, 1804 Rebecca 145
478. Sept. 10, 1804 Maria Elisabeth 147
479. Sept. 15, 1804 Atlantic 149
480. Sept. 19, 1804 Margaret 153
481. Nov. 3, 1804 Fortune 157
482. Nov. 3, 1804 Cato 160
483. Mar. 4, 1805 Antelope 161
484. May 7, 1805 Little Cherub 162
485. Aug. 26, 1805 Margaret 162
486. Sept. 5, 1805 Verny 169
487. Oct. 18, 1805 The Liberty 174
488. Oct. 18, 1805 Little Cherub 177
489. Oct. 26, 1805 Fair American 178
490. Nov. 30, 1805 Three Sisters 180
491. Dec. 6, 1805 Aeolus 181
492. Dec. 30, 1805 Johann Andreas 182
493. Apr. 30, 1806 Isabella 183
494. June 5, 1806 Kathrine 183
495. Aug. 3, 1806 Orlando 185
496. Oct. 22, 1806 Cordelia 187
497. Nov. 8, 1806 Atlantic 189
498. Dec. 1, 1806 Three Sisters 191
499. Dec. 11, 1806 Fair American 192
500. Apr. 2, 1807 Speedwell 193
501. May 8, 1807 Betsey 194
502. July 15, 1807 Isabella 195
503. Sept. 15, 1807 Frederick Augustus 196
504. Sept. 28, 1807 Mechanic 197
505. Dec. 3, 1807 William P. Johnson 198
506. Jan. 5, 1808 Three Sisters 204
Index of Captains 207
Index of Ships 215
Index of Ports 223
Index of Officials and Merchants 225
Index of Christian Names 229
Index of Pioneers 257

PENNSYLVANIA GERMAN PIONEERS

OFFICIAL LISTS OF PERSONS
ARRIVING IN THE PORT OF PHILADELPHIA

PRESERVED IN THE ARCHIVES OF THE
COMMONWEALTH OF PENNSYLVANIA AND
NOW PUBLISHED FOR THE FIRST TIME IN
THEIR ENTIRETY

Volume II

1785–1808

Indexes

LISTS OF PENNSYLVANIA GERMAN PIONEERS
1785–1808

[List 325] [List of Passengers of the Ship Mynheer van Berckel. Captain William Campbell. June 20th, 1785.]*

John Nich. Rodell	Yorick Fred. Corrman,
John Mich. Rodell	15 miles in the country
Alex^r. Hoofman	John Derick Foote
Johannes Hartost	Antoni Bella
Yohan de Rodell	Pauel Winders
Philip Jac. Rodell	Andreas Roush
Michael Wise	Fred. Carl Pastorius
Handerick Rodell	Matthaus Brochel &
Fred. Rodell	Spouse

Sworn before me John Jones, Health Officer
William Campbell.

[List 326] List of Passengers on board the Ship Adolph, Captain Matthew M. Clarkson, from Amsterdam, Viz., [August 27, 1785.]

Salm Christⁿ Helm	Jacob Burg
Anna Maria Krautworstin †	Hendrick Wagener
Peter Krautworstin	John Jacob Loos
Catharina Albertin	Johan George Schwingel
Anna Maria Voltzin	Joh. Schiefler
Xav. Veit	Johannes Creutz
Frederick Yager	Johann George Linksweiler
Andrew Wolf	Burgh Bresler
Francis Schmitt	George Linksweiler
Hendrick Thomas	Anna Cath^a Linksweiler, wife
Lawrence Weidler	Cath^a Stotin
Martin Voltz	Maria Magd^a Rumlin
George Pfaflin	Eva Rumlin
J. P. Zwingler	Joh. Ch. Smucker
John Jacob Rozenkrans	Ferdinand Schmucker

* Endorsement used as heading.
† The ending "in" should be dropped. It is the feminine ending in German.

3

Hend^k Schmucker
Hend^k Jacob Smucker
Hend^k Smucker
Appilunia Smucker, wife
Cath. El. Helmin
El^r Tedrin
Anna Maria Helmin
Eva Elis Helmin
Magdelena Dendelsteinin
Jacob Steiner
    the old man, gone to the Hospital.
Anna Cath. Steiner, wife
Fred^k Steiner
Hend^k Philip Steiner
Johann Philip Hamman
Maria M.   D^o
Catharina   D^o
Madlena   D^o
George Rahl
Joh. Adam Bracht
Anna M. Bracht
Adam Becker, dy'd on the passage
Catharina Becker
Johann Wm Bracht
Anna Cath^a Beckerin
J. Val. Eckel
Acada Eckel, wife
J. G. Bruining
Dorothea D^o, wife
Adam Hoffman
Appalona D^o, wife
Joh: Adam Willman
Elizabeth   D^o, wife
Conrad   D^o
Hend^k   D^o
Christ^n   D^o
Wilhelm   D^o
Maria   D^o
Johannes Schonberger

Chath^a Maria Wiedman, wife
Eliz. Cath. Schonberger
Elizabeth Schonberger
Appalona Schonberger
Cath^a Schonberger
Johann Nich^s Schonberger
Johannes Scherer
Fred^k Willem Marcus
Anna Cath^a Linksweiler
Johann Jacob   D^o
Elizabeth Ulrichin
George Schonberger
Peter Schonberger
Joha^s Kessler
Anna Cath. Kessler, wife
J. P. Faust
Maria Faust
Peter Lisman
Elizabeth Lisman
Ludwig Zieling
Johann Conr^d Willman
Martin Thiel
J. N. Backer
Johann Friederick
Catharina   D^o
John Friederick
Margareta Schafferin
G. Reer
J. Nich^s Koch
Conrad Rettinger
Adam Haak
Jacob Rettinger
Christiana Thielin
Eliz. Laubin
Eva. Gobbellsin
Cath^a Gobbellsin
Magdalena Schafferin
Johann Conrad Trott
Johann Thiel
Johann Bastian Sulion
J. Hendrick Geyt

George Schaffer

Car. Fred^k Wyngartner

John Adam Kolb

Anna B. Kolb, wife

Christiana Kolb

Elizabeth Kolb

Eva Kolb

Adam Kolb

John Adam Corber

Elizabeth Korber, wife

George Reeg

Cath^a Reeg, wife

Eliz. Kleinin

Peter Ulrick

Hend^k Hasenpluck

Michael Ewe

Martin Ruckert

Joh. Nich. Mutz

Joh. Wack

J. B. Kolb

Catharina Kolb, wife

Catharina Kolb

John Hend^k Kolb

Dorothea Kolb

Anna Clara Walterin

Peter Walter

Maria Sophia D^o, wife

Catharina   D^o

Eva   D^o

Elizabeth   D^o

Maria   D^o

Kunrad   D^o

Johann Fried^k Dietrich

Alexander Burgerd

Maria Christ^a Burgerd, wife

Hannah Burgerd

Nicholas Gebhart

———— D^o

Lawrence Jacky

Elizabeth   D^o

Ludwick Jacky

Lawrence Jacky

Hend^k Tromper

Johann Martin Hasmert

Antony Kleinin

Eliz. Schinckel

Carl Plannet

Jacob Wittmer

Abraham Verber

Margaret Burgin

Maria Cath. Burgin

Conrad Zeylin

Dorothea Fautz

Peter Smucker

Adam Liesman

Katrina Kisler

J. F. Wilen

A. M. Colbin

Jan Jacob Jacien

C. L. Jacien

J. A. Burghart

A. M. Hamman

Ev. C. Heiner

A. M. the Adolph

J. F. Kridel

Eliz^t Vidring

Philad^a 27th Aug. 1785

Sworn before me the 3rd Sepr 1785, John Jones, Health Officer.

Mat^w M. Clarkson.

[Endorsed:]

List of Passengers on board the Ship Adolph.

[List 327] List of Passengers on Board Patsy Rutledge, Wm Bell, Commander. [August 29, 1785.]

Mr Simpson	Jno Phillip Rops
Mr Danl Siebert	Nichlas Cruser
Jno Fred^k Hambing	Mich^l Blincaith
Jno Godfrey Light	Cora E. C. Blimke, child
Jno Alex. Bowers	Jno Waggoner
Jno Manuel Brant	Fred^k Bowell
Ch. Israel Chyson	Casp^r Mahon
Jno Baker	Cath. Elamatik [?]
Hanna Dorety	Magretta Dorety
Peter N. Cope	Benard Devoir
Marie Devore	Margery Devoir
Christian Han	Johan Devoir, child
Jno N. Lymp	William Devoir, child
Jno L. Gilkin	Jno Church Comeyoun
Hans C. Martin	Anna Catherina
Anna M. Martin	David Shutely
Hans Casp^r Martin, child	Thos. H. Blackwell
Anna Maria Baker	Johan Elija Blimke
Jno C. Baker, child	Total 37

I do hereby certify that the above is a true and just list of the names and number of Germans imported in the Ship Patsy Rutledge from Hamburgh. Witness my hand

W^m. Bell.

Sworn before John Jones, Health Officer.

[Endorsed:]

German Passengers on board Ship Patsy Rutledge, Capt. Bell, f^m Hamburgh. August 29th 1785.

[List 328] [List of German Passengers on Board the Ship Favourite, Captain Nicolaus Valans. Septr. 5th 1785.]*

BED STEADS	Jno Casper Rubert
Nos. 1 & 2.	Nich^s Fulmer
Jacob Fulman	Marg^t Cooperin
Margaret Fulman	

* Endorsement used as heading.

No. 3.
Geo. Casper Ruiter
Martin Ruiter
John Bartholomew Ruiter
Godfrey Ruiter
Anna Ruiter
Nich[s] Beyer

No. 4.
Conrad Ditman
Honor Ditman
John Ditman, sen[r].
Christopher Ditman
Martha Ditman
Catharina Ditman
John Ditman
John Wind

No. 5.
Nich[s] Schrater
Jerona Schrater
Gertrude Teichmannin
Catharine Hornin
John Filler

No. 6.
Chas. Gunther
Marg[t] Gunther
Elizabeth Gunther
Anna Maria Gunther
John Gunther
Chas. Gunther, jun[r].
Eva Gunther
Anna Maria Gunther
Dorothy Timmermannin

No. 7.
Andreas Bott
Anna Maria Bott
Mary Bott
Barbara Bott

Casper Bott
Anna Cath[a] Bott
John Bott

No. 8.
John Beyer
Molly Beyer
Barbara Beyer
William Beyer
Marg[t] Beyer
Magdalene Beyer
Nich[s] Vogler
Susanna Vogler
Anna Rudigerin

No. 9.
John Muller
Cath[e] Muller
John Muller, jun[r].
Hendrick Muller
Margaret Muller
John Beyer
Anna Beyer
Doria Beyer

No. 10.
John Beyer
Balthazar Beyer
Will. Beyer
Margaret Beyer
Cath[e] Beyer
Anna Maria Mullerin
John Beyer

No. 11.
John Paus
Kunigunda Pausin
Nich[s] Paus
Eva Pausin
Barbara Pausin

Gertrude Pausin
Jacob Kraushaar

No. 12.
Martin Ehrhard
Michael Eckhard
George Kunss
David Weber
Jacob Eller
Fred^k Schonhalz

No. 13.
Conrad Phropheter
Anna Louisa Phropheter
Anna Rosina Phropheter
Adam Riess
Eliz. Riess
Marg^t Riess
George Riess
John Faussen

No. 14.
Barbara Julchin
Christopher Remmich
Juliana Matthessin
Jacob Schlosser
Cath^e Weber

No. 15.
Leonard Jung
Anna Rosina Jung
Anna Marg^t Jung
Susanna Jung
Anna Maria Bernhardin
Barbara Jeckelin

No. 16.
Christopher Fersch
Cath^e Fersch
Cath. Fersch
Geo. Fersch
Nich^s Dunckel

Barbara Dunckel
Charles Dunckel
Nich^s Dunckel

No. 17.
Andreas Scherger
Magdalene Scherger
Kilian Scherger
Cath. Scherger
Barbara Scherger
Geo. Kraft
Christopher Arbort

No. 18.
Philip Arnold
Regina Arnold
Maria Elizab. Arnold
John Fred^k Arnold
Philip Jacob Arnold
John Philip Arnold
Eva Marg^t Markin
Eva Cath. Jungin

No. 19.
Geo. Ehrlich
Maria Sarah Ehrlich
Geo. Ehrlich, jun^r.
Paulus Ruckert
Adam Schumacher

No. 20.
Simon Steinmetz
Marg^t Steinmetz
Casper Steinmetz
Cath. Steinmetz
Jno Peter Guttman
Marg. Cath. Guttman
Anna Marg^t Guttman
Maria Ruckertin

No. 21.
Fred^k Moll

Elizab. Moll
Gerard Moll
Anthony Moll
Nich. Moll
Magdalen Moll
Regina Kaufmanin

No. 22.
Adam Schnellbacher
Maria Eliz. Schnellbacher
Geo. Schnellbacher
Philip Schnellbacher
Barbara Schnellbacher
Christina Schnellbacher
Anna Margaret Schnellbacher
Jacob Mercker
Maria Cath. Kissewelter

No. 23.
Philip Marck
Eva Cath. Marck
Geo. Marck
Mary Cath. Marck
Geo. Adam Marck
Henry Offenstein

No. 24.
Mich^l Schott
Cath. Schott
Conrad Schott
Dorothy Schott
Martin Gitz
Maria Magdal. Gitz
Henry Gitz

No. 25.
John Weichel
Marg^t Weichel
Jno Port
Maria Magdal. Port
Casper Port
Matthias Holzel

No. 26.
Nich^s Hertel
Marg^t Hertel
Michael Hertel
Nich^s Hertel, jun^r.
Geo. Hertel
Sarah Hertel
Joseph Wenger
Julius Jacob Hertel, an infant
    born 1st Sept^r.

No. 27.
Philip Korn
Jacob Schum
Nich^s Gebhard
Anna Gebhard
Geo. Eckel
Nich^s Weber

No. 28.
Geo. Horner
Anna Horner
Jno Horner
Jacob Horner
George Horner, jun^r.
Anna Marg^t Horner
Kunigunda Horner
Valentine Flegler
Eva Flegler
Dorothy Flegler
Nich^s Flegler

No. 29.
Martin Michel
Cath. Michel
Cath. Eliz. Michel
Anna Maria Michel
Geo. Adam Muller

No. 30.
Conrad Naas

Eva Maria Naas
Michael Naas
Cath. Naas
Anna Maria Naas
John Muller

No. 31.
Henry Hoffman
Geo. Koch
Geo. Lauer
Anna Cath. Hollebach

No. 32.
Geo. Graul
Rosina Graul
Christina Graul

No. 33.
Nich^s Diel
Cath. Diel
Jno Diel
Magdal. Diel
Adolph Diel
Conrad Diel
David Diel

No. 34.
Geo. Horn
Ottilia Horn
Geo. Horn, jun^r.
Casper Horn
Jacob Horn
Christian Horn
Godfrey Conrad
Cath. Conrad
Jno Conrad
Carlina Conrad

No. 35.
Geo. Würz
Eva Würz

Cath. Würz
Eva Eliz. Würz
Dorothy Würz
Matthias Würz
Geo. Würz
Philip Würz
Ottilia Würz

No. 36.
Henry Gottel
Philipina Gottel
Charlotta Gottel
Philipina Gottel, jun^r.
Christian Gottel
Frederica Gottel
Eliz. Gottel
Henry Gottel
Louis Gottel

No. 37.
Adam Gebhard
Susanna Gebhard
Susanna Gebhard, jun^r.
Geo. Gebhard
Anna Maria Gebhard
Michael Schuman

No. 38.
Geo. Saal
Anna Barbara Saal
Anna Marg^t Saal
Leonard Saal
Maria Cath. Saal
Michael Saal

No. 39.
Geo. Horn
Jacob Strein
Adam Strein
Geo. Bauman

No. 40.
Fred^k Gotz
Mary Gotz
Mary Gotz, jun^r.

No. 41.
Jno Brede
Engeltina Breda

No. 42.
None

No. 43.
Nich^s Wilhelm
Christoph Gath
Fred^k Poller
Fred^k Kram
Jno Schmutz

No. 44.
Barbara Cath. Lechin
Christina Kramers
Magdalene Pensin

No. 45.
Charles Roos
Jno Roos
Elizab. Roos
Eliz. Roos, jun^r.
Henry Hartman
Henry Muller

CABIN PASSENGERS

One a minister—
Christopher Gattes

Sworn before John Jones, Esqr.

Nicholas Vallance.

[List 329] A List of German Redemptioners on board the
London Packett, Thomas Truxton, Esqr, Commander, Viz.,
[October 4, 1785.]

Augustus Langebarth
Sofia, his wife
Henry, his son (a boy)
Johannas Ricketts
Charles Chorlsbourn
Casper Rithelberger

Jacob Polander
Jacob Frizon
George Barnett
Philip Bernhard
Benjamin Joel
Jowel Sap & Leon Elias

Sworn before me this Third Day of October, In the year of
our Lord One Thousand seven Hundred and Eighty five.
John Jones,
Health Officer.

[Endorsed:]
List of German Passengers on Board the Ship London
Packet, Thomas Truxton, Commander. October 4th 1785.

[List 330] A List of Passengers Names on board the Ship Hamburgh, Cap^n. William Paul. [October 11, 1785.]

Mr Boden	Hance Ernest Eggers
Mr Jno Lovenhagen	Jno Henry Martins
Mrs Sarah Lovenhagen	Andrew Henry Henninger
William Lovenhagen	Jno Jacob Sevenbaggs
Thomas Lovenhagen	Gottlip Herman Minca
Dorothy [Lovenhagen]	Anna Allhight Minca
George Mackie	Christian Fred^k Carl Mince
Henrick Ludwick Miller	Julias Aug^s Allbrink
Francis Joseph Helfrigh	Maria Eliz^t Allbrink
Maria Teresia Helfrigh	Jno Carl Allbrink
Maria Teresia Helfrigh, Junr.	Henery Vinsalous All[brin]k
Francis Joseph Helfrigh	Jno Fred^k Willfoot
Anna Cathrina Miller	Albright Striker
Henry Staffers	Yorick Cope
Anna Staffers	29

William Paul

Sworn before me the Eleventh day of October, 1785.

John Jones,
Health Officer.

[Endorsed:]

List of Passengers on Board the Hamburgh, Captn W^m. Paul.

[List 331] Philadelphia October 15th 1785. [List of Passengers on Board the Brig Betsy, from Amsterdam, Captn. Sam Dawson.]*

Sebastian Rub ⎫	Benjm^n Herr, Lancaster county
Mary Rub ⎪	
Mary Thielen ⎬ Germans	
Joal Swarts ⎪	
Jacob Neff ⎭	

I do certify the above list of Passengers on Board the Brig Betsey from Amsterdam to Be Just and True

Saml. Dawson.

* Endorsement used as heading.

Sworn before me this fifteenth Day of October 1785.

John Jones,
Health Officer.

[List 332] List of Names of the Passengers on board the Brig Lydia, Gardner Hammond, Commander, from Amsterdam. [October 29, 1785.]

No. 1.
Hans George Schrockhaus
Anthony Kuhn

No. 2.
Philip Flick
Anna Maria Flick ⎫
John Flick ⎪
Anthony Flick ⎬ Children
Lewis Flick ⎭
Christopher Crass
  Children:
Maria ⎫
Peter ⎬ Crass
Magdalena ⎭

No. 3.
Jacob Weygandt
Hanna Weygandt, his wife
John Hayser
Paul Merckle
Valentine Martinengo

No. 4.
Christopher Wiener
  Children:
Jacob ⎫
Christiana ⎬ Wiener
Christopher Vinninger
Juliana Vinninger,
  his daughter, with two children
Margaret Gesinder
Chulur Taubner

Nos. 5 & 6.
Frederick Schaffer
Sabina Schaffer
  Children:
Rosina ⎫
Catrina ⎪
Elizabeth ⎪
Frederick ⎬ Schaffer
Michael ⎪
Charles ⎪
Jacob ⎭
William Bichel
Jacob Agster

No. 7.
Andrew Uhler
Henry Tillich
Andrew Schaffer
Ulrich Loffler

No. 8.
Adam Schauer, his wife
Elizabeth do
  Children:
John Schauer
Jacob do
Susanna do
Catarina do
Rosina do

No. 9.
Samuel Thorwarth
Christopher do

Philip Thorwart
Christopher Hausser
Jacob Steinmetz

No. 10.
George Sigmann, his wife
Chartar Sigman
  Children:
Peter ⎫
Frederick ⎬ Siegman
George ⎪
Catarina ⎭

No. 11.
Hanna Crayser
Christiana Muller
Jacobina Ziegler
Jacob Labhahan
Catarina Streb
Christiana ⎫
Magdalena ⎬ Children
Jacob ⎭

No. 12.
Conrad Gern

Barbara Gern
  Children:
Christopher ⎫
Conrad ⎪
Cordula ⎬ Gern
John ⎪
Hanna ⎭

No. 13.
Bernard Rummel
Jacob Sauber
Daniel Becker
Michael Trunckel
John Raichoet

No. 14.
Michael Muselman, his wife
Barbara Muselman
  Children:
Eva Bar[bara]
Christiana d°
Michael Muselman
Jacob d°
Christiana d°
Catarina d°

Gardner Hammond [Captain.]
Sworn before me this twenty Ninth Day of October, In the year of our Lord One Thousand Seven Hundred and Eighty five.

John Jones,
Health Officer.

[Endorsed:]
List of Pass^{rs}. on Board the Brig Lydia, Gardner Hammond, from Amsterdam. October 29th 1785.

[List 333] [Letter of Lewis Farmer, transmitting lists of passengers, May 19th 1786.]
I beg leave to transmit to his Excellency the President, and the Honourable the Supreme Executive Council the Names of

German Passengers who arrived in this Port from May 11th 1785 to December following of the Same Year, being as appears by the Lists of the Different Captains Six Hundred and Sixty five, out of which Three hundred and Thirty were bound and Registered before me, I likewise assigned Sixty three Irish Passengers.

I have the Honour to be with the greatest Respect
Gentelmen
Your most Obedient
and
Very humble Servant
Lewis Farmer.

Philadelphia, May 19th 1786.

[Endorsed:]
1786, May 19th, from Colo Lewis Farmer, List of German Passengers.

Lewis Farmer.

[List 334] List of Passengers on board the Ship Candide, Capt. Lournois, from Amsterdam. [August 19, 1786.]

J. F. Weyland	Christn Bartje
Jos. Berenger	Christn Bartje
John Hufke	Johan Bartje
Lebreght Ken	Martin Kelder
Jacob Vey	Andw Longblood
F. Anthony	John A. Botty
J. Kinsel	Hendk Andre
Leonard Pering	Wm Clutland
Christian Reiswinar	Johan Heys
Cathart Reiswinar	Danl Heys
Chatharine Reiswinar	Wishard Thomas
Chria Reiswinar	Anty Reynard
Margt Bibeling	Nichs Riess
Susana M. Neugebran	Anthy Mariener
Fredk Snider	Wm Wieldinar
Adam Speck	Lewis Sneider
Philip Oakly	Abraham Dicks
Christn Bartje	Jacob Lehman
A. Maria Bartje	Peter Andreas

Christian Esby
Jacob Andreas
Peter Cloos
Wentzell Hoofman
Christian Hoofman
J. F. Hoofman
Christian Teresa ⎫
Johan Christoffr ⎬ Hoffman
Dorothy ⎭
Fredᵏ Berhard
Wilhelmina Hoffman
Christʳ Bull
Tick Lorman
Francis Stutt
Hans Fredᵏ Plumbok
John Wolter
Joˢ Greinar
Joˢ Arbor
Claus Lero
J. F. Dubbendorf
J. Manar

Carl Fredᵏ Brothak
J. F. Weynland
Ludwᵏ Kleywer
Jacob Abrams
Jacobus Vanden Booger
Maria Booger
Maria Booger
Johanna Hintein
Susann Hintein
A. Maria Hintin
Maria Sophia Klinger
Johan Gotlib
John Fredᵏ Kinderen
Maria Sophia Kinderen
Fredᵏ Loosky
J. Chas. Bittig
Henry Pikell
Hans Peters
Ludwig Rediken
J. Fredᵏ Vogniet
John Kepsky

Adriaan Laernoes [Captain.]

I do certify that in Conformity with the duty of my Office, I visited the within mentioned Vessel, at the proper place; & made the Inquiries directed by Law; & that they all appear to be in perfect Health both in body & Mind.

Philᵃ August 22ᵈ 1786.

Samˡ F. Jones,
Deputy Health Officer.

Sworn before me August 29ᵗʰ 1786.
Lewis Farmer, Register.

[Endorsed:]

List of Passengers on Board the Ship Candide, Capᵗ Adrian Laernoes, from Amsterdam. August 19ᵗʰ 1786.

[List 335] [List of Passengers on Board the Ship Patsey Rutledge, Capⁿ. Wᵐ Bell, from Hamburg. Septʳ 27ᵗʰ 1786.]*

* Endorsement used as heading.

Mr John Harpst

Mrs Harpst

John Vick

John Mart

J. Edmon Oehme

J. Chr^s König

Gotlib Eichler

Gottfriend Kennig

John Schenell

George Proskey

George Anders Ising

Francis Joseph Lewdwig

Nicholas Folcass

J. H. Crunburg

Christian Caws

Dorothy Caws

J. Friderik Caws

J. Ct. Caws

Hanna Cobbier

Hanna Nerner

Frederica Charles

Total of Passengers Emported in the Ship Patsey Rutledge, Wm Bell, Master, from Hamburg. Consisting of 21, in Num^{br} twenty one.

These are to certify that in Conformity with the Duty of my office, I have been on board the Ship Patsey Rutleg, William Bell, Master, in which were imported the People whose Names are herein written and upon Examination I find them to be in perfect Health

Sep^t ye 27th 1786.   James Brown,

Deputy Health Officer.

Sworn before me this Twenty-Seventh Day of September, 1786.

Lewis Farmer, Register.

[List 336] Record of persons names who have taken and subscribed the following oath of allegiance and fidelity before Jonathan Penrose, Esqr., agreeably to an act of assembly passed the fourth day of March One thousand Seven hundred & Eighty six:

[March 22, 1786—September 30, 1786]

Viz. We do swear or solemnly, sincerely and truly declare and affirm that we renounce and refuse all allegiance to George the third, King of Great Britain his heirs and successors, and that we will be faithful and bear true allegiance to the Commonwealth of Pennsylvania, as a free and independent state; and that we will not at any time do or cause to be done, any matter or thing that will be prejudicial or injurious to the freedom and Independence thereof; and we do further swear (or solemnly, sincerely and truly declare and affirm) that we never

have since the declaration of the Independence of the United States of America, voluntarily joined, aided, assisted or abetted the King of Great Britain, his Generals, fleets or armies, or their adherents (knowing them to be such) whilst employed against the said United States, or either of them.

1786 March 22	District of South^{wk} *	Affirmed	Joseph Bird
"	ditto	Oath	Samuel Muschell
"	ditto	O^e	John Cavan
"	ditto	O^e	George M^l Kegg
"	ditto	O^e	William Hubbard
"	ditto	O^e	Charles Smith
"	ditto	Oath	James Irvin
"	ditto	O^e	William Kemp
April 3	ditto	Affirmed	Joseph Williamson
19	ditto	Oath	Peter Young
May 8	ditto	O^e	William Gamble
"	ditto	O^e	John Gamble
July 22	ditto	O^e	Francis Moore
Septem^r 6	ditto	O^e	John Edgeworth
27	ditto	O^e	Ebenezer Call
30	ditto	Affirmed	John Bissell

Jon^{n.} Penrose {SEAL}

Inrolled in the Rolls Office for the State of Penn.
Commission Book N°. 1 Page 100.
Witness my hand and Seal of Office the 20th October 1790.
Math^{w.} Irwin.

[List 337] List of Passengers on Board the Ship Nassau, Josiah Hunt, Master. [October 11, 1786.]

Names:

Mr Apple, wife & son	Ludwick Jack
Jno Eatman, wife & 2 daugh^s	Henry Shrouder
Peter Salcon, wife & son	Tobias Shipherd
Fred^k Riderband	Adam Symons
George Paysel	Jⁿ Butcher
Jno Chirstian	Jⁿ Farrell
Wm Kennick	Jo^h Feyil
Mich^l Harpers	Joⁿ Suvers

* Southwark is now within the city limits of Philadelphia.

George Mack	Fred^k Shroud
Jo^n Rickard	Henry Snavell
Jo^n Martin	2 Cabin Passengers

These are to Certify that in Conformety with the Duty of my office I have been on board the Ship Nassau, Josiah Hunt, Master, in which were imported the People whose Names are herein written and upon Examination I find them to be in perfect Health.

Philadelphia, October ye 11th 1786.

James Brown,
Deputy Health Officer.

Sworn before me October 12th 1786.

Lewis Farmer, Register.

[List 338] A List of Passengers from Amsterdam in the Ship Hannah for Philadelphia. [October 17, 1786.]

Jacob Ob	Frederich Grime
Ludwick Steigelman	Phillip Carrel Wood
Daniel Steigelman	John Henner—wife—& child
George Miller	Jacob Fratschl
Carrel Henry Shwanigel	Georg Siegwald
Melcher Bang	John Henrich Kobel

These are to certify that in conformity with the Duty of my office I have been on board the Ship Hannah, Andrew Davis, Master, in which were imported the people whose names are herein written and upon Examination I find them to be in perfect health.

Philadelphia, October 17th 1786.

James Brown,
Deputy Health Officer.

Sworn before me this nineteenth day of October, 1786.

Lewis Farmer, Register.

[Endorsed:]

List of Passengers on Board the Ship Hannah, Captain Andrew Davis, from Amsterdam.

October 17th 1786.

[List 339] List of German Passengers on Board the Brig

Dispatch from Rotterdam, Capn Jn° Veder. [October 31ˢᵗ 1786.]*

Freights: Freights:

No. 1.

Matheus Bierenloven	dᵒ 1
Ludwig Vorlender	dᵒ 1
Wendel Pyroth	dᵒ 1
George Eyden	dᵒ 1
Johan David Maternus	dᵒ 1
Antoni Pullig	dᵒ 1
Joh. Jos. Bauman	dᵒ 1

No. 2.

Christoph Gerrecht with wife and four children	dᵒ 4
Eberhardina Christiana Lotteren	dᵒ 1

No. 3.

Adam Bantz	dᵒ 1
Franz Bangest	dᵒ 1
Mathis Cawein	dᵒ 1
Friederick Weinman	dᵒ 1
Georg Bernhard Steigelman	dᵒ 1

No. 4.

Christina Blankeinin	dᵒ 1
Philippina Fischerin	dᵒ 1
Elizabeth Blankenheimerin	dᵒ 1
Barbara Dollin	dᵒ 1

No. 5.

Jacob Kappes	dᵒ 1
Joseph Krigner	dᵒ 1
Georg Martin Regele	dᵒ 1
Johann Peter Schirab	dᵒ 1

No. 6.

Johannes Heinerich Muller	dᵒ 1
Johannes Wekerle	dᵒ 1
Johann Martin Horn	dᵒ 1
Jacob Höffer	dᵒ 1
Nicolas Hamburger	dᵒ 1

No. 7.

Susanna Lotsing	dᵒ 1
Anna Magdalena Teklenburgin	dᵒ 1
Amalia Teklenburgin	dᵒ 1

No. 8.

Martin Vogel	dᵒ 1
Wilhelm Striebel	dᵒ 1
Peter Steitz	dᵒ 1

No. 9.

Andreas Heerdt	dᵒ 1
Christoph Loh	dᵒ 1

No. 10.

Johann Christoph Lilly	dᵒ 1
Heinrich Peihl	dᵒ 1
Fredᵏ Reicheneker	dᵒ 1

No. 11.

Henirk Pieter Mallesie, with wife and four children	dᵒ 4½

No. 12.

Adam Dorsch with wife and two children	dᵒ 2½

* Endorsement used as heading.

Barbara Doshin   d° 1   Franz Kummelman   d° 1

No. 13.

Joh. Georg Nus, with
  wife and two children   d° 2½
Johann Adolph Winkler   d° 1

No. 14.

Michael Fliker, with wife
  and four children   d° 4½

No. 15.

Johann Henrich Henning   d° 1
Johan Georg Rindlaub   d° 1
Georg Heinerich Schwan   d° 1

No. 16.

Johann Heinerich Hörner   d° 1
Johann Phillip Hörner,
  with wife and three
  children   d° 3

     —

freights   64

Deze onderstaande zyn nog om het
getal der Persoonen die zig thans aan
boord bevinden te volbrenge—wyl
die boven staande 64 enkel en alleen
vragten zyn *

These certify that in Conformity with the duty of my office
I visited the Brig Dispatch, Jn° Veder, Master, on her arrival
at the place directed by Law; and upon examination, I found
the Servants imported in said Brig to be in good bodily Health,
& to appearance sound of Mind.
Phil^a. Octr 31st 1786.

                Jn° Jones, Health Officer.

The following are the names of the Children mentioned on
the other side:

Henrich Pieter ⎤
Johannes   ⎪
Willem Pieter   ⎬ Mallesie
Anna Maria   ⎦

Maria Sallemie ⎤
Margarieta   ⎬ Dorshin

Orchil Maria   ⎤
Maria Catharina ⎪
Maria Elizabeth   ⎬ Horner
Catharina   ⎪
Maria Dorothea ⎦

Maria Dorothea ⎤
Johan Christoph ⎪
Johan Michel   ⎬ Flikker
Anna Elizabeth   ⎦

Johan Georg Nus
The other child of Nus died near
  the Willemstad [Williams-
  town]

Johan Michel Erich   ⎤
Pieter Willem Andries ⎪
Catharina   ⎬ Garrecht
Orchille   ⎦

* This Dutch sentence means: "The above-named [64 freights] must yet be
increased by those who are on board. But the above-mentioned 64 alone are
freights." In addition there were 11 other persons, making a total of 75 persons.

Sworn before me this thirty-first Day of October 1786.

Lewis Farmer, Register.

[List 340] List of Passengers on Board the Ship Bristol, Capt. Earl. [Dec. 14th 1786.]*

John Rokir	Marg. Eliz. Durin
wife & child	Johana Sophia Barleater
Chris. Wm Sahn	Elisa Meyers

John Earle.
Sworn before me John Jones, Health Officer.

[Endorsed:]
Ship Bristol.

[List 341] [List of German Passengers on Board the Ship Rosetta from Amsterdam. Capn. Ede Corneliss. April 5th, 1787.]†

Jon. Jos. Terner	J. G. L. Benner
Fredr de Wein	

On the Ship Rosetta. Capn Ede Corneliss, from Amsterdam.
April 5th, 1787.

[List 342] List of Passengers on board Ship Patsey Rutledge, Wm Bell, Master, from Hamburgh, arrived on [23rd] May, 1787.

	Years		Years
Conrad Nics Sommer	40	John Christian Meyer	28
Andrew Peter Roos	32	Hinrich Gerhard Schalke	20
Anna Maria Roos	30	Meinhd Matth. Rabenau	28
John Andrew Paetz	28	Friederich Pietz	27
Herman Wida	32	John Chrin Peterssen	24
John Gottfried Hunger	32	Friederich Voss	18
Anna Christina Stunger	36	Hinrich Willm Sundberg	17
John Veizapff	36	Martn Ph. Peterssen	19
Carl Friederich Schmidt	31	Nichs Strent	18

* Note at end of list used as heading.
† Endorsement used as heading.

Years

Herman Died^k Becker	27	L. C. Sophia Friedleber	29
Christ^r Kiellmann	32	Marg^a Eliz^th Strüven	33
Christ^r Albert	69	Cath^a Corn^a Schmidt	19
Carl Ed^w Ahrend	28	Anna Cath^a Stacks	19
Christ^rr Adler	36	Lucia Eliz^th Schmidt	40
John George Heusler	35	Anna Cath^a Schultzen	38
Jens Jochim	40	Cath^a Eliz^th Siemonsen	39
John Gottf^d Jurgens	35	Cath^a Mª Wagener	38
Johan Jahnke	32	Anna Marg^a Zimmermann	27
Mathias Rieper	36	Anna Marg^a Erbs	22
Hans Mich^l Steffens	29	Cath. Eliz^th Frahms	23
Hans Casp^r E. Schomacker	34	Hanna Eliz. Kenning	24
Fried^k Albert Vaye	24	Anna Kocks	27
		Anna Christ^a Meyer	20
WOMEN		Anna Eliz^th Moller	25
Anna Eliz^th Baumann	28	Anna Meyern	20
Anna Maria Buck	28	Eliz^th Magd^a Meyer	25
Cath^a Marg^a Drenbargs	30	Eliz^th Sucken	45
Eliz^th Dammann	25	Anna Cath^a Seeman	27
Christ^n Cath. Eckhoff	16	Cath^a Marg^a König	24
Cath^a Eliz^a Gerken	34	Anna Marg^a D. Fransen	32
E. M. Dorothea Stelmers	28	Eliz^th Boden	25
Charl^o Eliz^th Hussen	21	Dor^a Lutkens	23
Anna Sophia Hammers	24	Dor^a Rosenbusch	23
Ch^n Gerduck Horns	29	Dor^a Marg^a Martens	18
C. C. W. Jasprams	36	A. C. E. Messen	30
Cath^a Marg^a Jahnken	37	Anna Maria Wohlers	19
Maria Eliz^th Köllner	44	Mrs Smith	
Anna Abel Lohsen	30	Juliana Smith	
Anna Cath^a Langloh	22	Child Smith	
Cath^a Marg^t Möller	46	—Jonas	20
Maria Mönings	34	Mr Ham	
Anna Marg^ta Nelling	31	Mr Hein	
Maria Eliz^th Rugen	38	Hinrich Kleinworth	

Sworn before me this Twenty fifth Day of May in the Year
of our Lord One Thousand Seven Hundred and Eighty Seven.

John Jones,
Health Officer.

[Endorsed:]

List of Passengers on Board the Ship Patsey Rutledge, Wm Bell, Master, from Hamburg. May 23rd 1787.

[List 343] A List of the Passengers on Board the Dutch Ship Nord America, Capt Tys de Haas, from Amsterdam. Viz., [October 10, 1787.]

Joseph Nyzel
Johannes Hornung
Casper Gryner
Adam Staaf
Adam Schwartz
Catharina Richterin
Georg Fey and his wife and two
   children under 4 years
Pieter Stark
Balthasar Mulder
Nic. Roth
Anna Maria Rothin
Jacob Hageman
Anna Maria Hagemanin
Christian Roth
Heinrich Roth
Greta Rothin
Anna Margreta Rothin
Margreta Rothin
Elisa Rothin
Susanna Rothin
Michial Roth
Nicolaas Roth
Edmer Raap
Casp. Jungert
Pieter Neuman
Nicolaas Knauf
Carl Swartz
Joh. Pauls
Dorethie Pauls
Joh. Georg Pauls
Joh. Hend. Pauls
Joh. Adam Pauls
Anna Maria Pauls

Daniel Phil. Buttinger
Elisabeth Fluckin
John L. Visser
Johannes Flucks
Frans Schaffer
Anna Maria Schäfferin
Heinr. Koch
Cath. Kochin
Elisab. Kochin
John Simons
Johannes Nagel
J. F. W. Jarkins
Maria Eva Jarkinsin
Johanna Margreta Jarkinsin
Maria Eva Jarkinsin
Susan. Doroth. Jarkinsin
Jacob Gucker
Fred. Gucker
Adam Segeler
C. W. Sander
J. M. Hildebrand
J. Ritbert
Jan Valentin
Soph. Dor. Wolffin
Corn. Stonfield
John. Jac. Wild
Daniel Andre
Hend. Hildenbrand
Engel . . . Nieuw Lander
Jacob Schwartz
J. P. Gruylig
J. W. Kumpf
. . . Vlag
P. Theobald, in the cabin

F. Hesshuyzen in D°   Wᵐ Mart. Wieland
J. M. Buchner   [Total] 72.
Johannes Seitz

Philadᵃ

Personally Came Capᵗ Tys de Haas Before me the Sub-
scriber, one of the Justices of the Peace for the City & County
of Philadelphia, and being duly Sworn did say that the above
is a true list of the names of Passengers brought into this Port
in the Ship North America of which he is Master & that none
of them are Convicts.
October the 10ᵗʰ 1787.

                                        Tys de Haas.

    Sworn before me
            William Rush.

[Endorsed:]

List of German Passengers on Board the Ship North America, Tys de Haas, from Amsterdam.
October 10ᵗʰ 1787.

[List 344] A list of the Names of Persons who took the
Oath and Affirmation of Allegiance to this State, passed the
fourth of March 1786. [September 24, 1787.]

March 15ᵗʰ Absalom Michener of Bristol township, Farmer, Philadᵃ County

Jacob Lukens of ditto, Miller

John Cochran of this City

18 Christopher Rapp of Bristol Township, Philadᵃ County, Farmer

James C. Fisher of Philadᵃ, Merchᵗ

March 21 Benjamin Gibbs of Philadᵃ, Merchant

April 5 Peter Beck of this City, Cordwainer

May 6 John Steedot of ditto, Tavernkeeper

June 6 Robert Worrell blacksmith, Oxford Township, Philadᵃ County

Septem 27ᵗʰ Isaiah Worrell, of ditto, Shopkeeper

October 5ᵗʰ David Lauck, of this City, Cooper

7 William West, Northern Liberties, Gentᵐ

9 Charles Wilstach, of

this City, Shopkeeper

Oct[r] 9 John Hallman of
this City, Cord-
wainer

10 John Case, of the
Northern Liberties,
Taylor

Jacob Krener, of this
City, Cordwainer

George Teace, of this
City, Tobacconist

Alexander Willson,
of the Northern L.,
tanner

Sante Steverong of
this City, Porter

John Barnes of
ditto, hatter

James Wallace of
ditto, Butcher

John George Mayer
ditto, Baker

Abraham Dull, ditto,
House Carpen[r]

Abraham Hartman
D[o], Labourer

Jn[o] Michael Barth,
ditto, Taylor

Joseph Warner, Jun[r],
ditto, boat builder

Christopher White,
ditto, Porter

Philip Reaver, ditto,
Breeches Maker

Henry Hildebrand,
ditto, House Car-
pent[r]

George Einwachter,
Labourer

Joseph Leyendecker,
ditto

John Wright, N.
Liberties, Barber

Frederick Anthony,
ditto, Labourer

Frederich Winkle,
ditto, ditto

Marden Cost, N.
Liberties, labourer

Joseph Pepper, ditto,
Carter

Charles Conrad, of
the N. Liberties, la-
bourer

Nathan Marpel, of
this City, Labourer

Mathias Champ, dit-
to, Labourer

Leonard Ron, ditto,
Carter

Conrad Bachman,
ditto, Taylor

John Kever, of this
City, Cordwainer

Henry Soust, ditto,
Tallow Chandler

James Cornish, ditto,
Turner

Jacob Endress, of the
N. Liberties, Carter

Edward Shandzey,
of this City, La-
bourer

William Higgins, of
the N. Liber., ditto

Elisha Crosby, of this
City, Hatter

Andrew Haney, of
this City, Hatter

Abraham Halter,
ditto, blacksmith

Jacob Baker, ditto, ditto

Andrew Martin, ditto, Labourer

William Kinnard, ditto, House Carpenter

Darby Dohana, ditto, ditto

Alexander McKinley, ditto

1787

April 14 George Ewart, of this City Gent^n

21 John Salter, Junr, ditto, Baker

Seal Witness my hand & Seal, Septem^r 24th 1787.

William Rush.

[Inro]lled in the Rolls Office for the State of [Pennsylvan]ia in Commission Book No. 1, Page 101.

Witness my hand and Seal of Office, the 20 October 1790.

Math^w Irwin.

M. A.

[Endorsed:]

Inrolled in the Rolls Office for the State of Pennsylvania in Commission Book No. 1, page 100.

Witness my hand and Seal of Office the 20th October 1790.

Math^w Irwin.

M. A.

[List 345] Letter of Samuel Wharton, transmitting Names of persons who have taken the oath of allegiance and fidelity.

October 5, 1787.

Sir:

The following Persons have made Oath before me agreeable to Act of Assembly passed the 4th day of March 1786, respecting Allegiance and Fidelity.

I am Sir

Y^r most h^{ble} Servant,

Saml Wharton.

1787

October 7, Norman (×) McCally, Labourer, in Shippen Street, District of Southwark, County of Philadelphia.

October 10, James Gamble, ——, Second Street, District of Southwark, in the County of Philadelphia.

October 10, Mark Collins, Captain of a Sea Vessel, District of Southwark, in the above County.

[Endorsed:]
Inrolled in the Rolls Office for the state of Pennsylvania in
Commission Book No. 1, Page 100.
Witness my hand and seal of office the 20ᵗʰ October 1790.
Mathʷ Irwin.

[List 346] List of German Passengers who Arrived at the
Port of Philadᵃ, in the Ship Dorothea, Severus Dalsted,
Master, from Rotterdam. October 14ᵗʰ 1787.

Carel Moeller
George Fredᵏ Arnold
George Epler
Jacob Stuckler
Jacob Kuntz
Joh. Heinrich Nischwitz
Jacob Volkel, his wife & 4 chil-
   dren, Vizᵗ
Maria Elisabeth Volkel
Joos Volkel
Johannes Volkel
Ludᵍ Volkel
Maria Volkel
Martin Kruger & 6 children, Vizᵗ
Anna Margretha Kruger
Maria Madelaina Kruger
Anna Christina Kruger
Johann Ludᵏ Kruger
Anna Elisabeth Kruger
Cathᵃ Elisabeth Kruger
Jan Philip Spelshus
Anna Christina Glaan & 2 chil-
   dren, Vizᵗ
Margeretha Glaan
Christina Glaan
Johan Peter Muller
Nicolaas Fritzgen
Johan George Weysz
Anna Catrut Liese
Johann Balthazar Dietz
Jacob Stumpf

Johann Schatz
Johan Henr. Sieppert
Joh. Rudolf Vos
Anna Christina Vos
Maria Margᵃ Haubergerin & 2
   children, Vizᵗ
Peter Hauberger
Johannes Hauberger
Anna Elizabeth Germanin
George Diederich Lex
Jacob Lex
Henrich Bretz
George Rosseler
Christiaan German
Johan Betz
Dorothea Betz
Wilhelm Betz
Jⁿ Jacob Richter
Johan Richter
Johann Bernd Rau
Johan Sahner
Nicolaas Fritz
Anna Maria Smit
Maria Dorothea Rau
Clara Schneider
Cathᵃ Welden
Charlotta Faulhaberin
Johan Jacob Hem
Johan Daniel Bohm
Johan Daniel Spenscheld
Jacob Ewi

J. Adam Nees
Hend. Phil. Dornek
Wilhelm Troll
Michel Fautz
Fredrik Miller
Johan Heymerdingen
Martin Herniker
George Jacob Rodel
Johan Nic. Probst
Christophel Ruckert
Hartman Ruckert
Magdalena Ruckert
Hartman Ruckert, Junr
Martin Schneider
Adam Lever
Magdalena Lever
Charlotta Hexamerin
Roeloff Hayenants
Ernst Fred^k Geyer
Isaac Solomons
Johan Carl Koller
Johann Conraad Godschalk
Peter Guthman
Marger^a Guthman
Philip Guthman
Nicolaas Guthman
Anna Guthman
Henrich Gutenberger
Adam Gutenberger
Carel Lud^k Wilh^m Albertus
Johan Hend^k Neereman
Johann Kolb
Peter Weber
Juliana Weber
Johann Henrich Weber
Johannes Weber
Kraft Weber
Johan Henrich Weber
Johan Fred^k Weber
Johan Henrich Knebel
Anna Elisabeth Knebel

Anna Gertrut Knebel
Susanna Knebel
Joh^a Jul^a Elis^th Buchenerin
Johann Joost Wunderlich
Cath^a Liese Wunderlich
Anna Liese Wunderlich
Johann Wunderlich
Joost Wunderlich
Maria Annetta Wunderlich
Conraad Knoch
Joh^a Elisabeth Knoch
Peter Wieth
Christina Wieth
Johan Henrich Birkborch
Anna Cath^a Birkborch
Johann Joost Birkborch
Mathias Baldt
Cath^a Baldt
Johannes Hesselbach
Anna Elsa Hesselbach
Johan Henrich Hesselbach
Herman Knoch
Peter Engel
Sevila Cath^a Engel
Christophel Joh^s Engel
Johann Philip Engel
Christian Engel
Jacob Engel
Philip Peter Engel
Maria Cath^a Engel
Anna Soph^a Bierman
Wid^w Scholten
Wilhelm Scholten
J. Carel Tob. Geyer
Cath^a Geyer
Henrich Geyer
Mathias Eeker
Johan Philip Eeker
Jacob Eeker
Fred^k Kroeg
Jacob Schinkel

Baltzer Martin
Johan Mich[l] Kayser
Nicolaas Voltz
Anna Maria Voltz
Anna Liese Voltz
Barbara Voltz
Engelica Voltz
Jacob Voltz
George Fleischouwer
Philip Hend[k] Schiekendantz
Johan George Hoffman
Johan Fred[k] Schatzig
Johan Mattheus Straub
Philip Wilhelm Boller
George Wilhelm Diehl
Sophia Kelly
Nelly Kelly
Magd[a] Christ[a] Regenstein
Johanna Regenstein
Henry Regenstein
Andries Schreuder
Daniel Bopp
Dorot[a] Bopp
Sophia Bopp
Carel Strohe
Mad[a] Strohe
Philips Jacob Strohe
Daniel Strohe

Daniel Bopp, Jun[r]
Salomea Bopp
Joh[n] Simon Joncker
Henrica Joncker
Hans Hen. Joncker
Henrica Joncker
Johann Henrich Joncker
Johann Elias Kirberger
Andreas Dorscheyner
Susanna Maria Germanin
Adam Rech
Henrich Strohn
Peter Bekker
Johannes Seitz
Abraham Schmutz
Coenraad Heyman
Johann Daniel Bonn
George Zeb
Johan Christ[n] Böhm
Jacob Götz
Peter Ulrich
M. Ulrich
Anna B. Nagelerin
The Rever[d] Petrus Heilbrun
The Rever[d] Johann Bapt[a] Heil-
brun
194 Passengers.

Johan Paulsen.
Sworn before me Lewis Farmer, Register.

[Endorsed:]
    List of German Passengers who Arrived in the Ship Dor-
othea, Captain Severus Dalsted, from Rotterdam at the Port
of Philad[a], Oct[r] 14th 1787.

[List 347] [A true and exact list of the passengers arrived in le Brie, a Barque from London, Capt. William Jung,
Philadelphia July 7th 1788.]*

* Note at foot of list used as heading.

Le Ministre et Docteur, Albert Fresne, sa fame Lidie, 2 enfans Albert et Albertine.

Jean Henry Visard, sa feme Madelaine, 3 enfans Abram Louis, Marie Anne et Marguerithe.

Abram Bourquin, sa feme Suzanne, 2 enfans Josue et Pierre Frederick.

Jean Pierre Villiot, sa feme Marie Salome, 3 enfans Jean Henry, Marie Anne, et Jean Geofroid.

Jean Jacques Villard, sa feme Susanne Marie, 7 enfans Marieanne, Suzane, Jacob, Marie, Jean Henri, Elisabeth, Louis.

Jacob Gossin, Madeleine sa feme 2 enfans Suzanne, Emanuel.

Abram Echeman, sa feme Anne, 2 enfans, Anne Catherine, Marguerithe.

David Frederick Gobat, sa feme Suzane.

Jean Pierre Sauvain, sa feme, Catherine.

Charles Frederick Dubois.

Daniel Girard.

Abram et Frederick Raiguel.

David Chevallier.

David Eche, sa soeur Suzanne.

David Pretre, sa soeur Catherine.

David Carnal.

Jean Opliguer.

Jean Zeller, sa femme Anne Marie, 5 enfans, Jean, Anne Marie, Frena, Anne, Barbe.

Jacob Senn, sa feme Elisabeth, 3 enfans Anne Marie, Jacob, Jean Henri.

Jean George Pfremmer, sa femme Anne, et Catherine.

Jean Scheffner, sa feme Anne, 1 enfant Catherine.

Jean Jacques Vaibel, sa feme Ursule, 5 enfans, Jacob, Martin, Catherine, Barbe et Frederick.

Jean Vaibel, sa feme Ursule, 3 enfans Jacob, Jean Noe, Villiame.

Martin Guetiguer

Martin Schaub

Frederick Toma

Johanes Frichi

Susanne Gerr

Maria Neuschvander

Abram Sauvain de Vinzestre [Winchester] en Virginie.

Abram Capitaine Marchand

Abram Saupi

Jean Pierre Complaire

David Sauvain

Elisabeth Guntzehauser

Edwd. Hawkins ⎫
James Cocheroft ⎬ Cabin Passengers
Mrs. Winship ⎭

[Endorsed:]
List of German Passengers who arrived at Philadelphia
from London July 7ᵗʰ 1788.

[List 348] List of Passengers on Bᵈ the Brig Mary, Kieran
Fitzpatrick, from Amsterdam, Aug. 5, 1788.

M. Kurtz and Wife	A. Margretha Scharfer
J. Frend	Margᵃ Ritzema
H. Masschert	J. C. Kuhl
J. C. Weidman	J. A. Schmidt
P. Zeg	Anna Mad. Scharfer
J. P. Comming	Anna Susana Scharfer
E. L. Bacsch	Angnita Scharfer
Eal Frish	Isach Melhinger
F. Nottenius	J. G. Melhinger
G. F. Alar	P. Call
S. Ohser	H. George Hermann
G. Wehlspach	John Berstiend & wife
G. E. Gramer	John Scharcaum
J. Allmendinger	J. Boie
J. D. Knapschneide	

[Endorsed:]
List of German Passengers who arrived in the Brig Mary
from Amsterdam. August 5ᵗʰ 1788.

[List 349] [List of German Passengers who arrived in the
Brig Laurel, from Amsterdam. October 2ᵈ 1788.]*

. . . Bahner	P. Leonard
Pr. Ansbach	. . . Graf
God. Ban	Simon Keppelar
A. Zultz	Wᵐ Lotman
Michael Ekker & son	Chrisⁿ Balk

* Endorsement used as heading.

Ch. Blisser
G. M. Smith
. . . Schaffer
P. Anspack

. . . Schutts & brother
Catharine Bonzin
J. Loftler

Brig Laurel from Amsterdam,
Nathaniel Ingraham,
Master.
          For
Co^l. Lewis Farmer.

[List 350] The following Passengers are arrived here from Amsterdam in the Schooner Commerce, Captn Casper Faulk. Nov. 5, 1788.

John Henrich Stiele
Elizabeth Catharina Stiele
Catharina Stiele
Aug. Carl Frederick Loeffler
Friederich Andreas Haase
John Matthys Sanders

John Ludwig Wernwag
Daniel Hummel
Jacob Kupper
Christian Haars
John Friederich Teutsch

I do Certify the Above being a True list of the Passengers, who Arrived in the Schooner Commerce.

Casper Faulk.

[Endorsed:]
List of German Passengers arrived in the Schooner Commerce, from Amsterdam. Nov. 5th 1788.

To his Excellency the President
          and
The Honorable the Supreme Executive Council
of the Commonwealth of Pennsylvania.
Gentelmen.
I beg leave to Transmit to your Honorable Board the List of German Passengers who Arrived at the Port of Philadelphia from July 7th to November 5th 1788.*

* The list itself has not survived.

I am Gentelmen
with the greatest Respect
your most Obedient
and very humble Servant
Lewis Farmer.

Philadelphia, November 22, 1788.

[List 351] List of Passengers on board the Ship Amsterdam Packet. William Campbell Morton.* [Novr. 5th 1788.]

Fredrik Wasts	Catrena Lemanning
Joanes Sadellor	Hendreck Wise
Daniel Bumpgardner	

[Endorsed:]
List of German Passengers who arrived in the Ship Amsterdam Packet, from Amsterdam, Novr. 5th 1788.

[List 352] A List of German Passengers Arrived at the Port of Philadelphia from Hamburg, on Board the Ship Patsey Rudledge, Wm Bell, Master [January 10th 1789.]

Baltzar Smith	Henry Kaihl
Jacob Alterman	Christian Treichel
Henry Alterman	

I do hereby Certify the Above to be a true List of all the Passengers on Board of the above mentioned Ship.

Wm Bell.

Philad^a January 10th 1789.

[Endorsed:]
List of German Passengers on Board the Ship Patsey Rudledge, Captn Wm Bell, from Hamburg, January 10th 1789.

[List 353] List of German Passengers who arrived at the Port of Philadelphia from Amsterdam, in the Brigantine Philadelphia Packet, Captain John Earl, Commander, September 29th 1789.

Johannes Brandhover	Johann Jacob Strohn
Sarah Brandhover	Johannes Yenny
Cristina Gertraut Strohn	

* Note at foot of list used as heading.

I do hereby Certify the above being a true List of the Passengers on Board the Above described Vessel. Wittness my hand the year & date above Written.

Jno. Earle.

[Endorsed:]
List of German Passengers on Board the Philadᵃ Packet. Captain John Earl, from Amsterdam. September 29ᵗʰ 1789.

[List 354] [Certificate of oath of allegiance and fidelity by A. D. Viaud. September 30, 1789.]

City of Philadelphia Ss.

To Matthew Irwin, Esquire, Recorder of Deeds for the City and County of Philadelphia.

I do hereby certify that Augustino Doinique Viaud, Mariner, aged Thirty Years, born at Bordeaux in the Province of Guienne in the Kingdom of France, Son of Daniel Viaud, Merchant of Bordeaux and Mary his Wife, & who came last from Corunna, in Biscay in the Kingdom of Spain to this City, personally appeared before me Samuel Powel Esquire Mayor of the said City on the Twenty Sixth Day of September in the Year of our Lord One Thousand Seven Hundred and Eighty Nine and voluntarily took and subscribed the Oath of Allegiance & Fidelity to the Commonwealth of Pennsylvania conformably to an Act of the General Assembly of the said Commonwealth passed the Thirteenth Day of March Aᵒ. Dⁱ. 1789. In Testimony whereof I have hereunto set my Hand and Seal this Thirtieth Day of September Aᵒ. Dⁱ. 1789.

Samuel Powel, Mayor.

[Endorsed:]
Inrolled in the Rolls Office for the State of Pennsylvania in Commission Book Nᵒ 1, Page 104.

Witness my hand and Seal of Office, the 20ᵗʰ October 1790.

Math. Irwin.

[List 355] [List of German Passengers on Board the Brigantine Mary, Captain Kirnen Fitzpatrick, from Amsterdam. October 1ˢᵗ 1789.]*

* Endorsement used as heading.

MEN

Carel Waggener
Henry Smith
Jacob Wise
Daniel Counts
Adam Heiler
Justine Hartnat
Lamburgh Road
Carrol Ludwigh Barngat
Lewdwight Mingh
Christian Frank
Jacop Berkelbach
Johanes Faner
Christian Fornhoaf
Johanes Waggener
Henerich Sheaffer
Peter Hoorst
Henerich Heaf
Adam Arnolds
Jacop Hornevius
Lewis Henery Bast
Jonna Peter Schit
Johan Jost Weber
Jacop Wast
Hendrich Wilhelm Zimerman
Johannes Miller
Johanes Sneider
Johannes Georg Hoffheintz
Johan Gorg Ebert
Johan Gorg Ebert, Swiss
Conrad Dederich

30

WOMEN

Johana Harknat
Jusina Benald
Ana Elizabeth Road
Maria Barncat
Ellizabeth Frank
Susana Craftin

Anna Magdelenia Find
Anna Maria Berkelbach
Elizabeth Horniavius
Elizabeth Cristiana Do
Ana Cathena Do   Do
Justinia Hart
Ellizabeth Zimerman
Anna Maria Miller
Anna Maria Hoffheintz
Anna Magdalena Ebert
Anna Maria Dederich

17

GIRLS

Christina Harknat
Anna Cristinia Harknat
Charlote Harknat
Anna Elizabeth Barncat
Philipina Barncat
Cristina Do
Fredericha Frank
Louise Sharp
Jacop Heneavis
Henerita Bast
Cristenia Buckle
Willemenia Shitz
Hennerotia Shitz
Carrolinia Weber
Willeminia ditto
Margarita Do
Henerita Do
Caterrinia Maria Do
Catherina Do
Louisa Sleifenbaum
Maria Do
Anna Maria Zimmerman
Anna Chatherina Miller
Anna Elizabeth Hoffheintz
Ana Catherrina Do
Elizabeth Ebert
Anna Magdelina Do

Catarenia Dederich
Philipina D⁰
Anna Margreta D⁰
Maria Cristina D⁰
Elizabeth D⁰
Justine Busserin

33

BOYS

Cristian Harknat
Carol Harknat
Honer Road
Hancrist Road
Lewdwight Toolat
Frederich Barncat
Philip Frank

Cristena Frank
Gottfried Shitz
John William Shitz
Frederich Henerich Weber
Johann   D⁰   D⁰
Friederich Earl Weber
Wilhelm Sleifenbaum
Anthon Sleifenbaum
Jacop Hoffhintz
Johanes Ebert
John Just D⁰
Jacob D⁰
Johan Gorg D⁰
Johanes Diderich
Sebastian D⁰
Johan Jacop D⁰
Laudwight Frank

I do hereby Certify the Above to be a true list.

K. Fitzpatrick.

[List 356] A List of Passengers for the year 1789.

			£	s	p
April	4th	Ship Therira three Passengers	o	1	6
	15	Brig Agnus from St Eustatia three do	o	1	6
	23rd	Brig Pomona from Jamaica two	o	1	o
	25	Ship Levant from Liverpool one	o	o	6
	28th	Brig Two Brothers from Dublin five	o	2	6
May	4th	Brig Catherine from Halifax Three do	o	1	6
	7th	Brig Molly from Antigua one Passenger	o	o	6
	11th	Sloop Hester from St Croix one	o	o	6
		Brig Sea Flower from Hispaniola Two	o	1	o
		Brig Hope from Kingston Six	o	3	o
		Ship Pigau from London Ten	o	5	o
	12th	Brig Live Oak from Kingston Ditto	o	5	o
		Ship Philadelphia from Charleston Nine	o	4	6
	13th	Ship Young Eagle from London Three	o	1	6
		Ship Grange from Liverpool one	o	o	6
	19th	Ship Commerce from Newry Four	o	2	o
		Ship Hannah from Barbados Five Passrs	o	2	6
		Ship Hamburgh from Cork Eleven	o	5	6

		£	s	p
	Brig Missouri from Burdeaux one	o	o	6
20th	Sloop Adventure from Halifax Four	o	2	o
21st	Brig Mariury from St Croix Three	o	1	6
22nd	Schooner Tryale from St Thomases Nine	o	4	6
25th	Brig Charleston from Charleston One	o	o	6
26th	Polaire St Agustus from Carthagena 119 Passengers	2	19	6
28th	Brig Peggy from Teneriffe One	o	o	6
	not Paid Isaac & Robt Wallne			
June 3rd	Sloop Polly from Boston one	o	o	6
	Sloop Jane from St Eustatia one Passr	o	o	6
5	Sloop Betsy & Ann from Barbados Four	o	2	o
6	Brig Union from Aux Cays one Passr	o	o	6
9th	Brig Polly from Cape Francois One	o	o	6
	Brig Fame from Kingston Thirteen	o	6	6
9th	Schooner Charlotte from Jamaica One	o	o	6
	Sloop Dolphin from Alexandria One	o	o	6
	Sloop Marian from St Eustatia Three	o	1	6
10th	Brig Louther from Kingston One	o	o	6
	Ship Nelley from Barbados Three	o	1	6
	Sloop Paragon from N. Providence One	o	o	6
	Sloop Lark * from St Thomases Five	o	2	6
12th	Ship Philadelphia from Charleston 27	o	13	6
15th	Sloop Susana from Antigua Two	o	1	o
	Brig Philadelphia from Charleston Sixteen	o	8	o
16th	Brig Cathirine from Halifax Eight	o	4	o
	Brig Ladie Watterstorf from St Croix Seven	o	3	6
23rd	Brig Sally from Nova Scotia Nine	o	4	6
	Brig Ecuna from Jamaica·One	o	o	6
24th	Brig Genteele from Port au Prince Four Passrs	o	2	6
25th	Schooner Friendship from Charleston Four	o	2	o
26th	Ship Conception from N. Orleans Sixteen	o	8	o
	Brig Nancy from Jamaica Two	o	1	o
	Sloop Nancy from Ditto Seventeen	o	8	6
29th	Sloop Hannah Teneriffe Seven Passrs	o	3	6
	Ship Elizabeth from Cork Eleven	o	5	6
	Brig Muntin from Antigua one Passr	o	o	6
	Brig Hope from Jamaica five	o	2	6
	Ship Patsy Rutledge from Havre de Grass one	o	o	6

* Name partly erased.

			£	s	p
	30th	Sloop Hannah from Wilmington 12	0	6	0
July	2nd	Brig Minerva from Jamaica Ten	0	5	0
	3rd	Sloop Exchange from Savana Five	0	2	6
	8th	Schooner Sally from N. Orleans Eight	0	4	0
	10th	Sloop Sally from Surinam Three	0	1	6
	13th	Brig Charleston from Charleston Sixteen	0	8	0
	14th	Brig Hetty from Charleston Three	0	1	6
	15th	Snow Experiment from Liverpool Two	0	1	0
	18th	Brig OConnel from Amsterdam Three	0	1	6
		Brig Hope from Port au Prince Four	0	2	0
	24th	Brig Live Oak from Jamaica Eleven	0	5	6
		Sloop Sally from Bermuda one	0	0	6
	29th	Sloop Two Betseys from Aux Cays Two	0	1	0
	30th	Schooner St Joseph from New Orleans 9	0	4	6
		Schooner Nancy from St Johns One	0	0	6
	31st	Brig Catherine from Halifax Two	0	1	0
Aug^t	3rd	Brig Cunningham from L. Derry 82	2	1	0
		Brig Havana from Nevry Fifty	1	5	0
		Schooner Polly from Cape Francois Two	0	1	0
		Sloop Hannah from Wilmington 11	0	5	6
		Ship Philadelphia from Charleston Sixteen	0	8	0
	4th	Brig Philadelphia from Charleston 19 Pass^{rs}	0	9	6
	5	Ship Betsy from L. Derry Eighty six Pass^{rs}	2	3	0
		Brig Ruby from Greenock Sixteen	0	8	0
		Brig Rose Croix from Port au Prince Two	0	1	0
	6th	Brig Dispatch from Antigua one	0	0	6
		Brig Ark from Jamaica Five	0	2	6
	9th	Schooner Charlotte from Jamaica one	0	0	6
	10th	Brig Ruby from Halifax one Pass^r	0	0	6
	17th	Brig John from St Martins one	0	0	6
		Ship Minerva from Nova Scotia Four	0	2	0
	24th	Brig Minerva from St Eustatia one Pass^r	0	0	6
	31st	Ship Sally from L. Derry Ninety-eight	2	9	0
Sept	2nd	Brig Sophia from Belfast Sixty one	1	10	6
		Ship Happy Return from L. Derry Seventy three	1	16	6
		Sloop Hope from New Orleans Fourteen	0	7	0
	4th	Ship Nancy from L. Derry one hundred & fifty three	3	16	6
	7th	Brig one Passenger	0	0	6

		£	s	p
	Brig Hetty from Charleston Six	0	3	0
9th	Sloop Hester from St Cruce Two	0	1	0
10th	Sloop Hester from Port au Prince one	0	0	6
15th	Brig Catherine from Halifax Two	0	1	0
	Sloop Betsy & Ann from Turks Islands One	0	0	6
	Schooner Commerce Three	0	1	6
	Schooner from Jamaica Four	0	2	0
16th	Schooner Fortune from Richmond Four	0	2	0
17th	Brig Adventure from Grinada Four	0	2	0
18th	Schooner Two Sisters from Port au Prince one	0	0	6
21st	Schooner Dolphin from Jacgumel Two	0	1	0
22	Sloop Dave from Bermuda one	0	0	6
	Ship Polly from Hull Two	0	1	0
	Brig Philadelphia from Charleston Eight	0	4	0
28th	Sloop Topahannock from Port au Prince One	0	0	6
	Ship Cyrus from Lisbon Three	0	1	6
	Ship Pigau from London Twelve	0	6	0
29th	Brig Rose from Windsor Two	0	1	0
	Brig Ruby from Halifax Eleven	0	5	6
	Ship Apolo from London Fourteen	0	7	0

£31" 13" 0

Omissions made and found by examining
the Entries & comparing them with this acc^t.
44 Passengers Head money since Jany^y 1st 1" 2" ..
1789

1310 Passengers at 6^s £32" 15" 0

To his Excellency the President and the Honorable the Supreme Executive Council of the Common Wealth of Pennsylvania.

Gentlemen:

I beg leave to transmit to your Honorable Board the List of German Passengers, who arrived at the Port of Philadelphia from January 10th October 1st in the present Year, and were permitted to land agreeably to Law,

I am Gentlemen with the greatest Respect
your most Obedient
and very humble Servant
Lewis Farmer,

Register of German Passengers.
Philadelphia November 14th 1789.

[List 357] List of German Passengers, who arrived at Philad[a] in the Ship Philad[a] Packet, from Amsterdam, John Earl, Master. March 31, 1790.

Elizabeth de Wilde	Philip Haman
Jacobina Faust	Wilhelm Bloede
Johanna Damess	Peter Gans, Cabin Passenger

[Endorsed:]
List of German Passengers on Board the Ship Philad[a] Packet, John Earl, Master. March 31[t] 1790.

[List 358] List of Passengers in the Brig Mary, from Amsterdam. Philadelphia 4th October, 1790.

George J. Wighterman †	Ph. Ernst Orth *
Wilhelmina Larin	Jos. Schreiber *
David Schneider	Adam Finck
Jonathan Schaaf	Joh. George Haselbach
Sam. Fried. Schoch	Johan Adam Holtzwand
Joh. Knautz	Christian Becker
Fried. Heitz	Joh. Jacob Haman
Joh. Jacob Schell	Joh. George Schnitz
Joh. G. Knecht with his wife &	Joh. Jacob Chur
three children viz[t]	Peter Wedel
John Dan—6 years	Joh. Ch. Blummer
Joh. God. 2 d[o]	Anna Christ[a]. Bertram
Anna Cath. 3 d[o]	Joh. Coenrad Rothhaar
Heinz Ernst Busch	David Israel
Johan Casp[r] Bertram	Christ. Heinz Borett
David Rind	Joh. F. Bottinger
Adam Rothhaas	Hans G. Laubengayer
Moses Nathan	George E. Kleinknecht *
Jan Kuyper	Casper Zollicofer
Lud. C. Kuhn	

I do hereby Certify the Above to be a True Return on Board the Brig Mary under my Command.

K. Fitzpatrick.

* Names crossed out.   † A Lutheran minister.

List of German Passengers on Board the Brig Mary, Cap[n] Fitzpatrick, from Amsterdam. Oct[r] 4th 1790.

[List 359] List of Passengers on Board the Ship Philadelphia Packet, Edward Rice, Master, from Amsterdam. Philad[a] January 18th 1791.

Maria Jacobs	John Godfreedom Marks
Henry Richards	Abr[m] Geerman
Susannah Kram	John Valintine
J. G. Myers, his wife & 2 children	Jacob Whitcomb
Barnard Driesbach & wife	

I do hereby Certify, that the above is a True List of Passengers on Board of the Above Ship under my Command.

Edward Rice.

List of German Passengers who Arrived in the Ship Phila Packet, from Amsterdam, Edward Rice, Master. Jan[y] 18th 1791.

[List 360] List of German Passengers who arrived in the Brigantine Mary, from Amsterdam, at the Port of Philad[a]. June 30th 1791, viz.

Stephanus Clauss	George Ernst Fries
Johannes Balde	Regina Dorothea Heringin
Johann Henry Balde	William Balde

I do hereby Certify the above being a True List of the Passengers on my Vessell above mentioned.

K. Fitzpatrick.

List of German Passengers in the Brigantine Mary, Kirnin Fitzpatrick, Master, from Amsterdam. June 30th 1791.

[List 361] A List of German Passengers on board the Ship Diana, Ozias Goodwin, Commander. [August 10th 1791.]

Henrick Jullig	George Peter	
Dorothea, his wife	Henrick	3 Childr[n]
	Parble	

Peter Grall
Barbara his wife
Catharina ⎤
George ⎥
Peter ⎬ 4 Childrn
Barbara ⎦
Daniel Guntar
Ann Margaret, his wife
Daniel ⎤
Hans Daniel ⎥
Catharine ⎥
Caroline ⎬ 7 Childrn
Hans Jacob ⎥
Hans William ⎥
Conrad ⎦
Francis Rame
Catharine, his wife
Frederick ⎤ 2 Childn
John Daniel ⎦
Daniel Stier
Catharine, his wife
Catharine Margt Rippart
George ⎤
Christian ⎥
Catharine ⎥
Elizabeth ⎬ 6 Childrn
Margaret ⎥
Sophia ⎦
Casper Hein
Margaret, his wife
Peter ⎤
Hans ⎬ 3 Childrn
Lewis ⎦
Jacob Snell
Sophia, his wife
Joh. Henry ⎤
Catharine ⎥
Hans Mary ⎬ 4 Childrn
Jacob ⎦

Peter Blanch
Dorothy, his wife
Sophia ⎤
Margaret ⎬ 3 Childrn
Magdalena ⎦
George Mori
Catharine, his wife
George, George Henry,
Peter, 3 Children
Daniel Weisborrn
Barbara, his wife
Laurens, their child
Magdalina Eidelmenin
Magdalina, her child
Christina Weisbornin
Margaret, her child
Michel Bauer
Catharine, his wife
Philip Jerry ⎤
Philip Jacob ⎥
Hans Michael ⎬ 5 Childrn
Catharine Debora ⎥
Hans Peter ⎦
Peter Durenburgh
Eliza, his wife
Solima ⎤
Philip ⎥
Jerry Frederick ⎬ 4 Childrn
Hans Jerry ⎦
Salima vander Gros
Urclina, her Child
Margaret Rippart
Lewis ⎤
Martin ⎥
George ⎬ 4 Childrn
Jacob ⎦
Christian Wolts
Catharine, his wife
Conrad Schmeltzer
Margaret, his wife

Christian ⎤
Catharine ⎥ 4 Childr[n]
Regina ⎥
Maretia ⎦
George Sisz
Anna Elizabeth, his wife
Hans Jerry ⎤
Catharine Eliza ⎥ 4 Childr[n]
Hans Jacob ⎥
Maria Magdalena ⎦
George Henry Mortel
Catharine, his wife
Martin Rapp
John George, his son
Peter Durenburgh
Margaret, his wife
Hans Jerry ⎤ Children
Magdalena ⎦
Joh. Gettinger
Johan, Filius
Fred[k] Granram
Carl Granram
Valentine Weindling
George Klein
George Wolf
Joh. Christ[n] Weirmuller
Christian Fritz
Nichol Harig
Johannes Jost

Nichol Hauter
Nicholas Schworer
Theobald Schmidt
Jacob Raith
Conrath Schultz
Johan Lewis Urban
Catharine Wagnarin
Joh. Justus Kersten
Charl Fred Hugeuin
Georg Liamur
Joh. Matthias Simon
Joh. Hoehn
Frantz Arforg
Carl Hend[k] Schmadhtahn
Joh. Leonard Bloeser
M. Schneider
Ph. Andermann
Georg Fred. Kranss
Dan. Fred. Ley
Loisa Linnerin
Susan Mortlen
Fred Brecheisen
Catharine, his wife
Fredrich ⎤
Catharine Eliza ⎥ 3 Childr[n]
Johan George ⎦
Barbara Weindling

140 Total

I do hereby Certify the within being a True List of the Passengers on Board my Ship Wittness my hand this tenth Day of August 1791.

Ozias Goodwin.

[Endorsed:]
List of German Passengers in the Ship Diana, Ozias Goodwin, Master, from Rotterdam. August 10th 1791.

[List 362] List of Passengers on Board the Ship Philadelphia Packett, from Amsterdam. [August 23rd 1791.]

Ph. Jac. Britz	J. J. Ham
Jacob G. Popie	Francisca Ham, wife
Jacob Stohr	Jacob Ham
I. Fred Fanholtz	Francisca Ham
Ant. Hartman	Barbara Ham
J. G. Hartzog	J. F. Habelmaker
Dem. Salamarna Hertzog, wife	J. S. Eder
George Hertzog	G. C. Lux
Frederick Hertzog	Elizabeth Herman
Coem Lutter	J. P. Eckhard—Cabin Passenger

I do hereby Certify the within Being a True List of the Passengers on Board my Ship, Witness my hand this Twenty third Day of August 1791.

Edward Rice.

[Endorsed:]
List of German Passengers in the Ship Philad[a] Packet, Edward Rice, Master, from Amsterdam. August 28th 1791.

[List 363] Passengers on board the Ship Fair American, Capt. Benjamin Lee, from Amsterdam. Arrived in Philadelphia 12 September, 1791.

Georg Ludwig Anschutz	Frantz Breiner
Catharina Elizabeth Anschutz	Friederich Weisäcker
Johann Georg Anschutz	Johan Martin Klein
Christian Anschutz	Maria Magdalina Schnukin
Elizabetha Anschutz	Margaritha Schnukin
Dorothea Anschutz	Peter Koch
Johann Jacob Anschutz	Johan Wilhelm Versbach
Johann Philip Anschutz	Wilhelm Versbach
Heinrich Jully	Conradt Lysinga
Catharina Barbara Jully	Jacob Herman Hein
Maria Magdalina Jully	Anna Catharina Hein
Heinrich Jully	Margaretha Philippina Hein
Adam Jully	Bernhart Hein
Johann Jacob Günther	Catharina Philipine Guntzing
Maria Barbara Günther	Johannes Elenberger
Jacob Günther	Maria Elenberger
Johannes Günther	Elizabetha Elenberger

Magdalena Elenberger
Friederich Henn
Friederich Jonas
Anna Maria Jonas
Johann Wilhelm Jonas
Philippus Jonas
Jacob Jonas
Anna Catharina Jonas
Juliana Jonas
Heronimus Ecker
Henrich Gölzen
Philipp Linder
Philip Bosler
Johan Jacob Hartmann
Christian Kutscher
Jacob Mesmer
Johannes Ginder
Elizabetha Ginder
Frederica Ginder
Anna Maria Ginder
Johanna Louisa Ginder
Johannas Ginder
Caspar Faller

Peter Faller
Anna Catharina Faller
Mietje Josephs
Gustave Frederic Goetz
Johan Christopf Geil
Johann Peter Diring
Adam Henrich
Jacob Friederich Roller
Johann Bernhardt Schuler
Johannes Gotfried Dieterich
Scintje Obisau
Carolina Christiana Gasner
Philip Schimper
Bernhart Schüller

CABIN PASSENGERS

Christopf Ludwig Alberty
Maria Catharina Alberty
Maria Dorothea Bronner
Johan Jacob Bronner
Christian Godfried Elsasser
Total 76

I do hereby Certify the above being a true List of all the Passengers on Board the Ship within Mentioned. Witness my hand this thirteenth Day of September 1791.

B. Lee.

[Endorsed:]
List of German Passengers in the Ship Fair American, Benj^m Lee, Master, from Amsterdam. September 12th 1791.

[List 364] [List of German Passengers in the Ship Pallas, Charles Collins, Master, from Amsterdam. Sepr 27th 1791.] *

Joh. G. Nertwig
Elisabeth Notwig
Joh. George Dickhout

Anna Clara Dickhout
Peter Bare, with wife & two children

* Endorsement used as heading.

Peter, Catharine
Casper Hill
John Hein. Strauel
Jacob Egternoel
Charles Borbishel
Nicholas Hoffman
Andrew Schneider
Cornelius Barthelmel
Abraham Kettler
. . . Dickman
John Muller
Cor. Gott. Saur
Joh. Hen. Hugel
G. Wm Hugel
Mart. Brouwer
John Morgenthael
John Cappers
John Cline
George Notting
Catharine Meyer
Mar. Strooms
Paul Smith
Philip Schmidt
Died. Petts

Andrew Egternoel
Nic. Leigle
Christian Cable, & wife Christian
    & Mary
Frederick Snyder
John Valentine Heir
Elizabeth Schmitt
John Ostreith
Joh. Peter Kern
Ant° Bousorum
Philip Stubenitzke
Gen. Schlicht
John Peter Blends
Maria Mutlerin
John Mason, with wife & two
    Children Mary, Joseph, George
    Michel
Andrew Sereros
Charles Egternoel
John Roon
Lamber Roberson
Barkont Butlinger, wife & daugh-
    ter. Mary, Margeretta
                            56

I do hereby Certify this to be a true list of the Passengers on Board the Ship Pallas under my Command, September 27th 1791.

Charles Collins.

[List 365] A List of Passengers Brought over in the Ship Van Stophorst from Amsterdam, James Porter, Master. [Octr 22^d 1791.]

John Wilm Stearag
John Conrad Brun
Fridrich Drusbe
John H. Rosenburg
Daniel Carbaum

Elizabeth Carbaum
Daniel Carbaum
Charles Carbaum
Maria Elizabeth Ditto
Maria Susanna Ditto

Maria Margareta Do   Addam Kepple
Simon Kepple

These are to Certify the above being a True List of the Passengers on Board my Ship. Philad^a. October 22^d 1791.

James Porter.

[Endorsed:]
List of German Passengers on Board the Ship Van Stuphorst, James Porter, Master, from Amsterdam. Octr 22^d 1791.

[List 366] List of German Passengers, who arrived in the Philadelphia Packet, Captain Edward Rice, from Amsterdam. Philadelphia April 26th 1792.

Henry Frantz Henstead   Tuniss Tunece
Jacobina Colpin   3.

[Endorsed:]
List of German Passengers, arrived April 26th 1791, Philad^a Packet, Edward Rice, Master.

[List 367] A List of Passengers by the Ship Patsey Rutledge, from Hamburg. Danl McPherson, Master. [May 26th 1792.]

Freidrich Willhelm Kungoldt   Carol Schumaker
Freidrich Ludwig Albert   Johann Dedrich Smith
Johann Christian Bartels   George Rex, his wife Maria &
Johann Christian Loehr   one child
Johann Christopher Lange   10

I do hereby Certify that the above are the Names of all the Passengers on Board the Vessell above Named. Philad^a May 25th 1792.

Danl McPherson.

[Endorsed:]
List of German Passengers Arrived May 26th 1792, Ship Patsey Rudledge, Daniel McPherson, from Hamburg.

[List 368] A List of Passengers & Servants by the Brig

Union, from Hamburgh. Arrived the 28th day of June, 1792.
Viz.

John Valentine Schellerd	Johan Francis Christian, 5 years
Martha Elizb Schellerd	old
Johann Jurgen Schellerd	Johan Henderick Daniel, 3 years
Peter Andre Langenhagen	old
Carl Harbermier	Johan Wilhelm Storck
Christian Adeler	Christo. Cloudy
Caterena Elizh Castirens	Christian Hendrich Loudiwick

I do hereby Certify, the above being a true list of the Passengers on Board the Brigt Union, arrived at the Port of Philada, June 28th 1792.

James Dryburgh.

[Endorsed:]
List of German Passengers arrived June 28th 1792, on Board the Brigantine Union, James. Dryburgh, Master.

[List 369] List of Passengers on board the ship America, William Campbell, Master, last from Amsterdam. Vizt. [June 29th 1792.]

Mrs. Pet. van Hage & 3 children	J. V. D. Muhler
Christn Strohm & wife	Anthony Regel
John Strohm	Caspar Zollinger & wife & 2 chil-
Barbara Strohm	dren
Elizabeth Strohm	. . . Benjamin
George Hoff & wife & 4 children	24 Passengers
J. E. D. Himroth	
Heronimus Lesh	

Philada 29th June 1792.

William Campbell.

[Endorsed:]
List of Germany Passengers, arrived June 29th 1792, on Board the Ship America, Wm Campbell, Master, from Amsterdam.

[List 370] A List of the People in the Ship Catharina, Capt

Hendrick Trautman, sailing from Hamburg, destined for Philadelphia, with Cabin Passengers. [August 3ᵈ 1792.]

Her. Berzy with his wife and child

Daughter, 26 years old

Hinrigette, 26 years old

Marsᵉ Ramon, with wife and son

Jacob Evers, 29 years old

Fridrik Oldrich Westfal

Johan Lonaun, 22 years old

Westfallen with wife and 4 children

Johan Hendrik Olsen, 24 years

Hendrik Tiel, 20 years old

Fredrik Scheÿver, with his wife

Stübbe with wife and 5 children

Lindemann with wife and 2 children

Anna Reimslach, 38 years

Johan Bonse, 28 years

Melgert Owans with wife and 2 children

Johan Schmelsen, with wife and 2 children

Johann Bauer, with wife

Danniel Witschief, with bride

Jochim Ritter, with wife and child

Johann Wittschif with bride

Johan Spares, with wife and 2 children

Hendrik Dirks, 32 years old

Michel Brom, 24 years old

Johan Gasau, 30 years old

Frans Bromsted, 22 years old

Johan Sommerfelt, 28 years old

Martien Tiel, and son 8 years

Margretha Casiens, with son 3 years

Paul Hüsing, 34 years old

Christiann Schroder, 42 years old

Johan Bohrmester, with wife and child 1 year

Cathrina Kromrom, 22 years old

Peter Pien, 28 years old

Jochim Puls, 37 years old

Christina Tempel, 32 years old

Hans Schultz, 25 years old

Johann Mosemann, 34 years

Johann Waggner, with wife and child

Carlel Dell, with wife

Peter Holtz, with wife

Jochim Törentz, with wife

Christina Wentzen, with 3 children

Peter Bokkendall, with wife and 2 children

Hans Beyter, with wife and child

Jochen Hagemann, with wife and 2 children

Jochen van Netten, 44 years old

Martin Scharffnat, 24 years old

Pilip Ekhart, 24 years old

Johan Reÿmers, 23 years old

Johann Krämer, 42 years old

Johann Hegt, with wife and 2 children

Jacob Schütt, 32 years old

Frank Schmitt, with wife and child

Jochim Pingel, with wife and 5 children

Claus Koppman with Wife and 5 Children

Clas Hipner, with his bride

Anna Chathrina Stiefers

Torbann, 20 years old
Helmke, with son 5 years old
. . . Beyter

Busch and brother
   Total 132 Persons.

[Endorsed:]

List of German Passengers, arrived in the Brigantine Catherine, Henry Trautman, from Hamburg, August 3ᵈ 1792.

[List 371] List of the Passengers on board the Ship Rainbow, Richard Salter, Master, from Amsterdam. [September 7ᵗʰ] 1792.

Henry Bart	Nichols Gudermuth
Cethnet Bart	Dority Gudermuth, a child
Casp. Kuhnzick	Johan Zittle
Ann Kuhnzick	Barbry Zittle
Cethnet Kuhnzick, a child	Johann Zittle
Barr Bart	Nicholas Zittle
Margret Bart	Elizᵗ Zittle
Catharine Bart	Geo. Zittle
Catharine Bart	Gartrute Zittle
Johan Bart	John Geo. Zittle, a child
Hirer Bart	William Walter
John Tungent	Margret Walter
Barbry Tungent	Susana Walter
Anne Lusarye Tungent	Jacob Walter
Catha. Tungent	Peter Walter
Susana Tungent	Johanes Walter, a child
Barbry Tungent	Michal Marten
Niclos Tungent, a child	Nicholas Burkhard
Nichols Guddermouth	Johanes Gudermuth
Catharine Gudermuth	Catharine Hartmannin
Hans Gudermuth	Lawˢ Schleising
Lawˢ Gudermuth	B. G. Schneck
Philip Gudermuth	John M. Senft

Philad. Sept. 7 1792.

Richᵈ Salter.

[Endorsed:]

List of German Passengers arrived in the Ship Rainbow, Richard Salter, from Amsterdam, September 7ᵗʰ 1792.

[List 372] Liste of all The Passenger on Boord The Ship Columbia, Capt. Wm Maley. [Septr. 8th 1792.]

Andres Hennisch
George Storck
Philipp Geist
Henric Nerthwein
George Neuzenhoeffer
Franz Dünne
Conrad Weigand
Conrad Ekard
Christian Fahler
George Weissenbach
Hartmann Scheer
John Schirmer
Anna Schirmer, his wife
Conrad Schirmer, his son
Fetter Emig
Ludwig Schenckel
Anna Elisabeth, his wife
Anna Catharina, his daughter
Kunigunda Simonin
George Albrecht
Henrich Albrecht
Catharina Müller
John Wernert Efort
Maria Magdalena, his wife
Gabriel Ament
Joseph Knobellach
Michel Dobler
Valentin Ekhard
Frederic Freutley
George Meyer
Christoph Brume
Wilhelmina Führ
Ludwig Riedy
Christina Schildin
Fetter Fischborn
Adam Schetzel

Adam Edner
John Boerner
Christina Dillemann
Elizabetha Dillemann
Catharina Rötterin
Elisabetha Heidlinger
Mathis Grünenwald
John Meyer
Anna Maria Meyer, his wife
John Adam, his son
Nicolaus Hetterich
Eva Elisabetha Hetterich, his wife
John Adam, his son
Caspar Werner
Margaretha Werner, his wife
Conrad Werner &
John Werner, his sons
John Lauk
George Preisach
Catharina Schallerin
Petter Werner
Philipp Strohe
John Hartmann
Barbara,* his wife
Anna Maria, his daughter
Elisabetha D^o
Barbara, D^o
Nicolas, his son
Margaretha, [his daughter]
Daniel Nast
George Renner
Dorothea Rieffenach
Philipp Emde
Wilhelm Köhler
George Nauer

* All these Barbaras are written Narbara, an impossible spelling.

Charlotta, his wife

Charlotta & ⎫
Barbara ⎭ his daughters

Jacob Nauer

Christina, his wife

Jacob, his son

Daniel Dau Nieda

Christoph Schmitt

John Schmitt

Barbara Hammin

Frederic Erbes

Magdalena Pfeiffer

. . . Beutemüller

Ferdinant Löwenstern

John Muller

Louisa Ellenberger

George Ludwig

George Ludwig, his son

Magdalena & ⎫
Catharina ⎭ his daughters

John Weiss

Maria Notenius

Gottliebe & ⎫
Frederica ⎭ her daughters

Henric Stuckard

Wendelina Dormick

Catharina Lesin

George Weimann

John Gast

Maria Eilferin

Jacob, her son

Carolina Hochstein

Jacob Schuster

Margaretha Baldin

Dorothea Röhrscheid

Petter Oxner

Frederica Schneider

Jacob Klein

Philipp Frey

John Oblinger

Barbara, his wife

Christian, his son, 13 yrs.

Barbara, his daughter, 12 yrs.

John, his son, 10 yrs.

Carle, D°, 8 yrs.

Jacob D°, 3½ yrs.

Lorenz Hoffmann

Louis Ducomma

Henrich Roulett

Frederic Pitsher

Barbara, his wife

Frederic, his son

Barbara, his daughter

Abraham, his son

Rudolph Pitsher

Maria Margretha, his daughter

Jacob Kauffmann

Jacob Hug

John Busser

Catharina, his wife

Jacob Felmy, her son

John Müller

Andres Müller

Jacob Müller

Jacob Gerster

John Gerster

Martin Gass

Henrich Scheffers

Christian Burger

Barbara Würtz

Elizabetha Keller

Michel Schnertzinger

Samuel Gentsch

Ludwig Koch

Frederic Geiler

Jacob Knapp

Michel Zeyley

Catharina Grüninger

Barbara Wucherin

Andres Barthels

Gustus Barthels
George Schiebelhuth
Henrich Diegenhart
Nicolas Shmitt
Frantz Petter Remmann
Jacob Wibbeling
Ludwig Minz

John Van Grunningen
159 Total

Conrad Seypert ⎫
John Keller ⎬ Americans
Jacob Frey ⎪
John Gottlieb Bergmann ⎭

[Endorsed:]
List of German Passengers arrived at the Port of Philadelphia, in the Ship Columbia, Wm Maley, Master, from Amsterdam. Septr. 8th 1792.

[List 373] List of Passengers on board the Brig Henricus, Capt. Martin Jager, from Amsterdam. Philadelphia Septbr. 22. 1792.

1 Johannes Theodorus Bartlam
2 George Shultz
3 Margaretha Shultz
4 Johannes Anspach
5 Cristina Sachsen
6 her child, 4 weeks old
7 Catharina Damen
8 Sebilla Damen
9 Godfrey Kerch
10 Johannes Smutz
11 Johannes Rude
12 Johannes Grebill
13 Nicolas Miller
14 Frederich Waldor
15 Christina Strickler
16 Johannes Reissendorff
17 Peter Riessendorff
18 Frederich Brandt
19 George Kraut
20 Philipp Dalen
21 Margaretha Dalen
22 Nicolaus Dalen
23 Barbara Herstein

24 Jacob Ebel
25 Jacob Nicholaas
26 Gertrout Eaberten
27 Philippine Zerwinna [?]
28 Christina Otenheimer
29 Margaretha Becker
30 Carl Hollenberger
31 Wilhelmina Hollenberger
32 Anna Bolman
33 Catharina Lefieber
34 Kaatje Lefieber, 11 years
35 Rooye van Aaken
36 Carolina Gotre
37 Alessius de Leistwitz
38 George Strickler
39 Bernard Spier
40 Christian Ernst Lax

Americans:
Johannes Herstein
August Braun
Wendel Serwin
Christ Schneider

Marten Jager.
[Endorsed:]
List of German Passengers arrived at the Port of Philadelphia, in the Brigantine Henricus, Martin Jaeger, from Amsterdam. Septr 22^d 1792. E.

[List 374] List of the Passengers on board Brig Martha,
Capt. Ebenezer Hoyt, from Amsterdam [Septr 22, 1792.]

Mr. Charles Schaubert
Charles Lewis Bauman
Heinrich Abelmann
Herman Diederich Benner

Franz Loose
5 Total

Bohl Bohlen, 1 American

Eben^r Hoyt.
[Endorsed:]
List of German Passengers, arrived at the Port of Philad^a,
Ebenezer Hoyt, Comander, from Amsterdam, in The Brig
Martha. Septe^r 22. 1792. E.

List [375] List of Passengers on Board the Ship Fame,
Capt. Alex^n Fraser, from Rotterdam [Sept^m. 23^d. 1792.]

Barbara Jungedins
Andrew Schusler
Elisa Schusler & two children
Nicholas Schleyger
Ann Margarett Schusler
Margarett Schusler
John Staff
John Frederick
Valentine Schusler
Elisa Godmaning
John H. Schlough
Andrew Zehn
Catherine Margarett Trunking
Catherine Uring
George Schiever
Christopher Hofnagel
Andreas Dieterick
John Beum & his wife Beum &
    one child

John Beyer
Casper Zeeler
John Quilman
Balzar Hartman
Valentine Beyer
John Beyer
John Heitznor & his wife & two
    children
Nicholas Jager & his wife &
    Anna Maria, one child
Dolly Woolmakerin
John Schaubergen
Christian Hofman
John Hofman
Nicholas Loresch & his wife &
    one child
Melchior Hock & his wife
Ann Margaretta Hock
Michael Hock

Henry Hock
Valentine Hock
Casper Hock
John Andrew Hock
John Zener & his wife
John Zener, Jn^{r.}
Ann Margaret Zener
John Philip Zener
Zigmond Zener
Catherine Zener
Eberharden Zener
John Zener
John Zener
Nicholas Jordon & his wife
Elisa Jordon
Ann Margarett Jordon
John Jordon
Dorothy Jordon
Susan Jordon
Henry Jordon
John Miechelen & wife
John Miechelen, Jn^r.
Christian Miechelen
Ann Junkin
John Mum
Valentine Vashold
Casper Vashold
Dorothy Vashold
Maria Vashold
Ann Richterin
Andrew Kreuilich
John Neuman
Margarett Burgedin & child
Catharina Kroning
Jacob Sleyger
William Euler
Ann Catherine Euler
Bender Schlauch & his wife

John Slauch
John William Slauch
John Riticher & wife
Catharine Riticher
John Riticher
Eva Evertine
Margarett Hartman
George Junger & wife
Barbara Junger
Casper Junger
John Sleyger & wife
Catharine Sleyger
Valentine Sleyger
Michael Henken
Andrew Selverk
John Adam Beum
Christian Bonnet
Eliza Moedine
Barbara Lossin & child
John Wytsel & his wife
John Wytzel
Conrad Wytzel
John Anton Brand
Conrad Kilmer
Antron Truppertin
John Ludewig Gephard
Christian Frederick
John David Kesler
Christopher Walker
Ludwig Simmons &
Eve, his wife
John Simmons
Ludwick Simmons
Peter Simmons
Melchior Simmons
Gabriel Simmons
Catharine Simmons
Total 131

[Endorsed:]
List of German Passengers, who Arrived at the Port of

Philad^a. in the Ship Fame, Alex^n. Frazer, Master, from Rotterdam. Septr. 23^d 1792. E.

[List 376] Passengers in the Steerage [on Board the Brig Union] Feby. 9 1793.

Cristian Schlichting
John Fredk. Bachmann
John Samuel Anters
Anne Catherine Kosters

Anne Jurgens

CABIN PASSENGER

Mr. Chas. Dachenhausen

[Endorsed:]
I do certify the within to be a True List of the Passengers on Board the Brig Union, Philad^a. Febry. 9th 1793. E.

James Dryburgh.

[List 377] List of Passengers from Amsterdam p^r Columbia, Capt Wm Maley, arrived March 8th 1793.

Fred^r. Ludewig Gutt
Sophie Salmia Gutt
Marie Charlotte Reinhard
Frederich Gutt

Elisabeht Charlotte Reinhard
Frederika Fucating
Louis Pignot

[Endorsed:]
List of Passengers on Board Ship Columbia, Wm Mailey, Comander, from Amsterdam. March 8th 1793. E.

[List 378] List of Passengers per the Ship John, William Wirtwel, Commander, from Amsterdam. July 19, 1793.*

H. v. Manierik ⎫
Charles v. Manierik ⎭ Americans
— Tustado
George Friederichs
Aime Brandt
Louis Mathew
Andrias Ellewin
Sophia Ellewin
Friederich Ellewin
Catharina Ellewin

Margaretha Ellewin
Johan Michael Ellewin
Johana Catharina Ellewin
Johan Gottlieb Richter
Anna Brussin
Franey Eyman
Ruticius Haake
Engel Everst
Johana Catharina Seyny
Hanna Mipers

* Endorsement used as heading.

Johana Maria Soutling
Hanna Margaretha Ehliman
Anna Maria Christiana Sybrand
Henriette Camphuysen
Wilhelmina Tysen
Gosse Scheles
Frunje de Ronde
Nicolaus Jacobus Bonirs
Peter Sables
Hendrich Worhy
Hendrich Hoige
Cornelia Ebbeling
Maria Schmit
Alida Korrich

Fried. Christelmyer
Friederich Ellerkamp
Ellisabeth Ellerkamp
Ellisabeth Ellerkamp
Johan Carel Muller
Friederich August Friederichson
Dorothea Catharina Friederich-
son
Johanna Friederichson
Friederich Augs. Friederichson
Caert Conraadt Friederichson
Adam Nickulus
Carl de Man Trotz
Engel Cathr. Friederichson

[List 379] Gentlemen Passengers on board the Brig Union Capit. Bell [August 16th 1793.]

Mr Laffert
— Molter
— Johnson, citizen of Newyork
— Oppelt
— Benade
— Heinze
— Caske
— Heine
— Gehbe
— Müller
— Frederic Saalig

— Braunschweiger
— Ruhl
Christian Gottlob Chalybaeus,
  shopman
Gottlieb Steuernagel, shoemaker
Frederic Gottlieb Lange, shoe-
  maker
Joh. Gottlieb Solbrig, printer
Charles Andrew Thalman,
  printer

[Endorsed:]

I do Certify, the above being a True List of the Passengers on Board my Vessell from Hamburg, Philadᵃ August 16th 1793.
Wᵐ Bell. E.

[List 380] List of Passengers on board Ship Columbia, William Maley, Mr, from Philadelphia. Sep. 17, 1793.

Joseph Faurie
Johann Friederich Just Fabritius
Johann Philip Nothnagel
Ludwig Nothnagel

James Borrowdale
Ann Rosetta Borrowdale, his
  wife
Johann Michel Nicolas

Philip Harig
Sabilla Harig, his wife
Catharina Salame Harig ⎤
Louisa Margaretha Harig ⎬
Maria Elizabeth Harig ⎦
             his children
Clement Rentgers
Catharina Rentgers, his wife
Wilhelm Rentgers ⎤
Christian Rentgers ⎮ his
Peter Rentgers ⎮ children
Catharina Rentgers ⎦
Henrich Schuster
Dorothea Catharina Schuster, his
  wife
Carolina Schuster ⎤
Friederich Schuster ⎮
Catharina Margar- ⎮
  itha Schuster ⎬ his children
Henrich Schuster ⎮
Christian Schuster ⎮
Louisa Schuster ⎦
Frantz Becker
Maria Johanna Becker, his wife
Carolina Elizabeth Becker ⎤
Anthon Jacob Becker ⎬
Gertruth Becker ⎦
             his children
Henrich Lauer
Anna Margaretha Lauer, his
  wife
Maria Sophia Lauer ⎤
Henrich Ludwig Baltser Lauer ⎮
Christian Lauer ⎬
Georg Ludwig Lauer ⎦
             his children
Georg Christian Ulrich
Maria Margretha Ulrich, his
  wife
Louisa Ulrich ⎤ his
Johann Jacob Ulrich ⎦ children

Philip Cramer
Louisa Cramer
Jacob Wolff
Reinelt Fons
Peter Grund
Hans Michel Keil
Christian Schram
Christina Klein
Elizabeth Trinkels
Philadelphia Susanna Jones
Elizabeth Folmer
Johann Ludwig Wilhelm Franke
Friederich Kortorel
Johann Friederich Wilhelm
  Chrinstin
Jan Pieters
Elizabeth Maria Pieters, his wife
Christina Pieters ⎤ his children
Laurens Pieters ⎦
Elizabeth Betts
Conraad Betts, her son
Christina Bergs
Hanna Lehmkiels
Johanna Miesander
Johanna Jansen
Jacob Frank
Sebilla Mühlenbach
Emanuel Friederich Schultz
Johann Peter Frohwein
Johann Henrich Lehrs
Georg Ludwig Riepenhausen
Christian Schiebe
Johannes Kurst
Michel Siebenlist
Juliana Muth
Maria Muth, her daughter
Jan Pistor
Andries Pistor
Johann Christopher Tack
Jacob Malambre
Johann Henrich Siemezing

Johann David Otto	Louis Dominique
Arnold Heins	Jacob Opp ⎫
Johann Mathias Metzger	Jacob Loesch ⎬ Americans
Gerritje Muller	John Bohlen ⎭

Wm Maley, capt.

[Endorsed:]
List of German Passengers Arrived in the Ship Columbia, Wm Maly, Commander, From Amsterdam. Septr 17th 1793. E.

[List 381] [List of German Passengers arrived in the Ship Brothers, Caleb Earl, Commander, from Hamburgh, September 25th 1793.]*

Philip Hendrik Bastrop	Louis Widerholt
Georgina Wolfeline Francoise	Louis Sigfrid
Lycklama Bastrop	John Winclear
Susana Maria Bastrop	John Stigman
Cristina Maria Bastrop	John Cruse
Marta Kinnema Bastrop	James Shults
Augustina Bastrop	Betse Allbring
Maria Neiman	Dally Beans
John Mann	

Philadelphia 25 Sept^r '93.

Caleb Earl.

The Above are Passengers on Board the Ship Brothers from Hamburgh.

[List 382] A List of Passengers on board of the Brigg Samuel, Benjamin G. Dexter, Master, from Copenhagen. Philadelphia, Sept. 27th 1793.

John George	Francis Merchel
John Hilem	

Benjamin G. Dexter.

[Endorsed:]
List of German Passengers arrived in the Brigg Samuel, B. Dexter, Commander, from Coppenhagen, Septr 27th 1793. E.

* Endorsement used as heading.

[List 383] Brig Polly, James Dryburgh, Capt., from Hamburg. Oct. 4, 1793.

STEERAGE PASSENGERS

Johaan Blume
Philipp Baltaasar
Johann Nonn
Carl Benecke, senior
Julius Benecke, junior

Wilhelm Hanniball
Johann Loey
Andreas Gronau

CABIN PASSENGER

Georg Diederich Wünning

[Endorsed:]
List of German Passengers on Board the Brig Polly, James Dryburgh, from Hamburg, October 4ᵗʰ 1793. E.

[List 384] List of the Passengers on board the Ship Peggy, John Elliot, Mastʳ from Amsterdam. Nov. 10, 1793.

Jos. Gnied Doornauwer
Pierre Jos. Porteur
Jas du Boir
Leon Engelbert
Corl Peters
Adrian Churvest
Corn. Wm. Englehart
Wesselman Ting & son
Mallk King
Joseph Helzel
Van Offen
Antji Caspers
Johan Boller
Elizabeth Bollerin
Jol Mallhert
Jol Kiser
Adam Berstroser
Micl Rings
Joh. Rol
Jacob Hodel
Jacob Krautt

Petan Korrel
Fried Hottz
Heinz Bedtlof
Jacob Selzer
David Strolm
Valent Eszevein
Jacob Tyd Goart & wife
Johan Scliffer & wife
Philip Hess
Carl Crom
Joh Rau
Philip Von Dessen
Hinz Smith
Crom Vonder Beek
Godf. Burnsel
M. Meyer
D. Schumacher
Frans Becke
Magdaline Ligte
Benjamin Here
Hein. Mollinger

[Endorsed:]
List of German Passengers on Board Ship Peggy, Jnº Elliot, from Amsterdam. Novʳ 10ᵗʰ 1793. E.

[List 385] A List of Passengers by the Ship Jean, Dan¹ Mc-
Pherson, Master, from Hamburg. Philadelphia, 12ᵗʰ Novᵇʳ
1793.

George Hinrich Burght   Elizabeth Myer

                              Dan¹ McPherson.

[Endorsed:]
List of German Passengers arrived in the Ship Jean, Daniel
McPherson, from Hamburg, 12ᵗʰ Nov 1793. E.

[List 386] List of the Number of Passengers who Arrived
from the Island of Sᵗ Domingo, since the disturbance there.
Vizᵗ

			[PASSEN-GERS]
1793			
May	15ᵗʰ	Sloop Driver, Robᵗ Wilson, from Port au Prince	7
"	"	Schooner Industry, M. Lewis, Cape N. Moul	1
"	"	Sloop John Vanvohis, Cape Francois	1
"	27	Schooner Frankling, Tallman, D⁰	11
"	"	Schooner Good Intent, G. Atkinson Jeremie	7
"	18	Brig Good Hope, Hill Simons L'Ogan	32
"	"	Brig Jason, David Ross, Port au Paix	20
"	21ˢᵗ	Brig Sally, Edwʳ Allen, Sᵗ Marks	2
"	"	Sloop Fanny, David Young, Cape Francois	3
"	"	Brig Polly, John Charnock, D⁰	4
"	"	Brig Jamina & Fanny, T. Conkling, D⁰	4
"	"	Brig Sally, John Cochran, D⁰	15
May	25	Ship Arathusa, John McClintock, D⁰	12
"	"	Brig Harriot, James Bently, Port au Prince	9
"	27	Ship Rising Sun, A. Lory D⁰	24
"	"	Brig Nymph, Thomas Webb D⁰	9
"	30	Schooner Fair Lady, Goffigan D⁰	25
"	31	Ship Betsey, Read Reading D⁰	36
June	1ˢᵗ	Schooner Two Brothers, Isaac Philips D⁰	9
"	"	Schooner Hope, Thomas Child D⁰	4
"	5	Schooner Tryall, Robᵗ Kennedy, Cape Francois	6
"	"	Sloop Wealt & Polly, John Hughes, Sᵗ Domingo	5
"	6ᵗʰ	Brig Portland, Wᵐ Pratt, Sᵗ Marks	5

1793

"	7	Schooner Isabella, James McKever, Cape Francois	3
"	11	Brig Aurora, Edwd Smith, Port au Prince	1
"	"	Brig Susannah, Jno Allison L'Ogan	4
"	12	Schooner Willing Maid, Wm Wallace, Cayamet	7
"	"	Brig Hiram, G. Childs, Cape Francois	5
"	13	Brig Harmony, James Dunphy, Port au Prince	2
"	"	Ship Diana, A. Cain, Cape Francois	33
"	17	Schooner Betsey, Wm Nash D^o	13
"	18	Brig Alfred, John Sheehan, Port au Prince	4
"	"	Sloop Sally, A. Bartlet, Cape Francois	5
"	20	Brig Experiment, Saml Smith D^o	1
"	21	Schooner Colly, Simon Digby, St. Domingo	7
"	25	Schooner Betsey & Hannah, Jos. Tolford	1
"	28	Schooner Two Sisters, Capt. Post, Port au Prince	2
"	29	Schooner Alex^r, Thomas Norris, Cape Francois	3
July	3	Schooner Betsey, Benjn Wheeler D^o	6
"	8	Schooner Juno, E. Hamblin D^o	17
"	"	Schooner Industry, Wm Trislin D^o	6
"	"	Schooner Eagle, Lloyd Jones D^o	28
"	"	Brig Nancy, Chas Quandril D^o	6
"	"	Brig Active, Wm Waters D^o	76
"	9	Brig Hazard, C. Coggshell D^o	14
"	10	Brig Hope, Joseph Pool D^o	14
"	12	Brig La Jeanne Sophia, Caseraugh D^o	34
"	13	Sloop Louisana, James Philips, Cape Francois	6
"	15	Pilot Boat Delaware from Sea D^o	11
"	17	Schooner LaLoger, N. Martin D^o	17
"	22	Sloop Sally, Wm Edger D^o	18
July	22	Sloop Driver, Robt Wilson, Port au Prince	7
"	24	Sloop Amelia, Wm Wilson, Cape Francois	32
"	"	Brig Nally, Joseph Smith D^o	55
"	"	Ship America, Gillis D^o	53
"	"	Schooner Linnet, G. Wallington D^o	6
"	24	Schooner Charming Betsey, Ja^s Art D^o	124
"	26	Schooner Betsey, W. Willis, St Marks	13
"	27	Brig Tryton, Wm Ridgway, Cape Francois	12
August	2	Sloop William, Capt. La Sage D^o	25
"	5	Sloop Rainbow, Isaac Mackey D^o	44

				[PASSEN-
1793				GERS]
"	6	Brig Lydia, Sam¹ Rinker	Dᵒ	51
"	"	Sloop Nancy, Ralph Clark	Dᵒ	26
"	7	Brig Mary, James Rush	Dᵒ	99
"	"	Schooner Dolphin, Wᵐ Watson	Dᵒ	68
"	9	Sloop Venus, Robᵗ Smith	Dᵒ	20
"	13	Brig Mary & Joseph, Capᵗ Labosser	Dᵒ	38
"	"	Schooner Industry, Lewis	Dᵒ	16
"	15	Brig Theadoria, Joseph Vansise, Port au Prince		2
"	16	Schooner America, R. Rightington, Cape Francis		24
"	19ᵗʰ	Sloop Jenney, E. Webb, from Cape Francois		22
"	20	Brig Hannah, G. Connell, Sᵗ Domingo		5
"	22	Sloop Nautilus, Thomas Jones, Jeremca		3
"	23	Sloop Sally, Andʷ M. Combe, Port au Prince		5
"	"	Schooner Farmer, David Radney	Dᵒ	5
"	26	Schooner Rodner, Thomas Horton, Sᵗ Domingo		22
"	27	Schooner Allice, W. W. Waymouth	Dᵒ	10
"	29	Schooner York, L. Baily, Port au Prince		4
"	30	Sloop William, Wᵐ Canby, Sᵗ Domingo		10
"	31	Sloop Polly, James Houston, Cape N. Moul		2
Septʳ	2	Sloop Haskins, from Cape Francois		6
"	3	Sloop Sally, Obed Samon, from Gonave		15
"	4	Sloop Polly, James Hodge, Cape Francois		54
"	6	Brig Molly, B. Razor, Sᵗ Domingo		37
"	7	Sloop Ranger, David Welber, Sᵗ Domingo		13
"	20	Brig Tryphena, James Wilson, Sᵗ Domingo		17
"	"	Sloop Wincey, James Crowner, Sᵗ Domingo		1
"	21	Schooner Andʷ, Stephen Homer	Dᵒ	3
"	23	Schooner Kelly, Port au Prince	Dᵒ	19
Octʳ	4ᵗʰ	Sloop Lavina, S. Church, Sᵗ Domingo		23
Octʳ	4ᵗʰ	Sloop Commerce, I. Massey	Dᵒ	16
"	8	Brig Nohe's Ark, James French	Dᵒ	26
"	10	Sloop Sally, Wᵐ Hess	Dᵒ	26
"	29	Schooner Isabella, Stoy, Port au Prince	Dᵒ	4
Nov	4	Brig Sally, A. W. Trusdal, Sᵗ Marks		8
"	6ᵗʰ	Brig Sally, John Cochran, from Sᵗ Domingo		24
"	7	Brig Baron de Carondelet, Joseph Conklin		13
"	11	Schooner Good Intent, T. Davis, Sᵗ Domingo		4
"	"	Ship Swanwick, John Cassin	Dᵒ	5

[PASSEN-
GERS]

1793
"   "   Snow Mercury, Robt Clay, with Prisoners from
            Jamaica   7
"   "   Sloop Union, John Wallace, from Port au Prince   3
"   "   Ship Rebecca, Benjn Wayet, Cape Francois   103
"   "   Schooner Industry, Joseph Pool, S^t Do   4
"   12   Brig Ruth, George Usher, St Domingo   6
"   25   Brig Ranger, Capt Patten   D°   6
                                                        ———
                                          Total   1836

CITIZENS OF THE UNITED STATES

From the Western Country by way of New Orleans

[PASSEN-
GERS]

May   6th Schooner Industry, S. Antony   7
June   15   Snow Alexander, V. Lamarry   30
Augs^t 16   Pilot Boat Swift from Sea, taken out of the petit
            Demecrat   24
"   20   Schooner John, a Prize   13
"   22   Brig Eliza, A. Bennet   11
"   Schooner Betsey, Betterton   10
Novr 13   Brig Chance, A. Oswald   6

FROM GEORGIA

July   5th Brig Peggy, Morrison   9
"   "   Schooner Lively, R. Green   5

FROM SOUTH CAROLINA

May   4th Schooner Eagle, Loyd Jones   9

FROM SOUTH CAROLINA

May   13   Brig Georgia Packet, E. Burrows   2
"   31   Schooner Peggy, S. Kelly   4
June   5th Brig Aurora, M. Strong   8
July   22   Schooner Peggy, S. Kelly   21
"   "   Brig Georgia Packet, E. Burrowes   25

[PASSEN-
GERS]

Septr 3 Schooner Peggey, S. Kelly   11
  "   9 Schooner Venus, John Thompson   12
Novr 16 Ship Delaware, James Art   20

FROM NORTH CAROLINA

May   5th Sloop Susannah, E. Mitchell   9
July   22 Brig Carolina, S. Carpenter   10
Septr 11 Brig Fortune, Chas Grice   8
  "   28 Schooner Polly, Joseph Britt   2

FROM NEW YORK

May   11th Schooner Waymouth, Lamander   2

FROM BOSTON

May   24 Schooner Maria, John Hills   2
Augt 30 Sloop Nancy, E. Lowe   2

FROM BERMUDA

July   20th Sloop Speedwell, Darrell   1
Novr 9   Schooner Recovery, Fortisque   1
  "   20 Brig Sally, P. Odlin   2

FROM LONDON

Novr 6th Ship Pigou, Loxley   4
  "   "   Ship Wm Penn, Ja^s Josiah   5

FROM SCOTLAND

Novr 11th Ship Fame, Joseph Holbrook   7

FROM FRANCE

Novr 12th Ship Van Staphorst, Lowe   4
                                                            ——
          Total amount of citizens   286

Citizens of the United States, I have given up the duty, ever
since I have been in Office, but it seems to require the Legislature to say all Citizens of the United States, shall be exempt
from paying any duty. The mode I have followed, has been

to make the Captains return the names of all passengers, and record them, but where there are Citizens take no pay, for I think it is hard for any person going out of his State into another to be obliged to pay when he returns: The Law says all passengers from beyond Sea; but this Law was passed so early as the year Twenty nine, when it was Impossible to foresee the intercourse between State and State, or of People going down the Ohio, and coming by way of New Orleans to this City. It may fall into the hands of Some Officer that may take the advantage of the Words of the Law, to the Injury of the Citizens.

[Endorsed:]
Account of Passengers arrived in the Port of Philadelphia from 15 May to Nov 25 1793 incl.
Examined two copies   J. Trimble.

[List 387] [List of German Passengers arrived in the Ship Appollo, C. Fitzpatrick, from Amsterdam. Febr^y 18th 1794. E.] *

Johann Friederich Rohde, chief miner and Maria Sophia, née Vietor, his wife

Mr. Carl Reinhard Gottfried Staudinger

MAIDSERVANTS:

Louise Frederike Scheuber
Maria Catharina Kaun

CHILDREN

Georg Friedrich Heinrich
Johann Dietrich Ernst Valentin
Johannette Catharina Elisabette
Georg Ludwig Theodor
Ehrgott Ferdinand Wilhelm
Mariane Friederike Henriette
Carolina Christina Elisabette
Heinrich Friederich Segnerus

MINERS:

Georg Daniel Klug
Philip Christian Kraushaar
Matheus Hüster
Maria Elisabette, his wife
Anna Elisabette, his child

———

J. C. Ruler
Joseph Shian
Eliza Clevley
Magret Engle
Stephen Biebl
Michael Kolman

SISTERS-IN-LAW

Henriette Maria Vietor
Gertraud Elisabette [ditto]
Candidate: Ludwig Ernst Andreas Eigenbrodt

* Endorsement used as heading.

Mich¹ Mante
J. G. Jager
Mich¹ Joler
Joh. Hels
J. J. Bury

Frederick Reach
Cristiana Reach, wife
Philipina Reach, child
Jean F. Lautinger

[List 388] List of Passengers of Ship John, William Whitewell, Mʳ, from Amsterdam, March 12, 1794.

Johan William Welker
Johann Vogel
Francis Ambrust
John Jager
Johann Ungar
Daniel Pieper
David Koonig
Andreas Bosdorff
Johann Gecke
Anthony Krigler
Frederick Holtz
Heinrich Bieleveld
Johann Kuyper
Johann Kas
Dominica Steinwyk
Johann Tepo
Johann Herbst
Maria Magdalina Herbst, his
  wife
Maria Magdalina Herbst ⎫
Johannes Herbst   ⎬
Johannes David Herbst ⎭
              his children
Helena Paapen
Anna Maria Hullenbrug
Johannes Hartman
Matje Hartman, his wife

Maria Termaaten
Anna Luggins
Elisa Feis
William Steinberg
Maria Weegenaar
Jurian Keppelaar
John Friedrik Godmann
John F. Obernhauser
Agata Obernhauser, his wife
Maria Elizabeth ⎫
Jan |
Friederik   ⎬ his children
Willem |
Simon   ⎭
Catharina Viege
Christina Maasin
Dorothia Muthin
Eliz. Hullenbrug
John Müller
Agnes Monsieurin
Maria Anna Verylie
Georg Nicholas
Johann Caspar Werschiede
Anthony Kollebern
Conraad Hyde
Jacob Sauerheben, American

[Endorsed:]
List of German Passengers arrived at the Port of Philadᵃ,
Wᵐ. Whitewell, Commander, from Amsterdam. March 12ᵗʰ
1794. E.

[List 389] List of Passengers on board the Ship Columbia Capt. Wᵐ Maley, bound to Philadelphia. May 31, 1794.

Nᵒ NAMES OF PASSENGERS

1 John Dorneck
  Anna Magaretha Dorneck
  Heinrich Jacob Dorneck, 13 yrs.
2 John Michel Klapthor, 13 yrs.
3 Magdalena Klapthor, 9 yrs.
4 P. W. Eichbaum
  Jane Eichbaum
  Charlotte Eichbaum
  Arnold Eichbaum, 8 yrs.
  Wilhelmina Eichbaum, 4 yrs.
  William Eichbaum, 6 yrs.
  Elizabetha Eichbaum, 2 yrs.
5 John Swetman
6 Nicolaus Fertner
  Catharina Fertner
  Ludwig Fertner, 12 yrs.
7 Mattis Fertner
  Elizabetha Fertner
8 George Fertner
9 Louis Fertner
10 Basilius Fertner
11 Elizabetha Fertner
12 John George Friederich
   M. Magdalena Friederich
   Nicolaus Friederich, 5 yrs.
   Philipp Friederich, 3 yrs
   Ludwig Friederich, 1 yr.
13 John Carl Martin
14 John Conrad Koch
15 Friedrich Hoffman
16 John Peter Schäzel
17 John Adam Müller
18 A. Dorothea Müllerin
19 John Adam Muller
20 Conrad Ebel
21 Balthaser Spiess
22 Michel Bub
23 Catharina Kifferdorffin
24 Anna Maria Veitin
25 A. Catharina Kochin
26 Jacob Seyboldt
27 Dorothea Körberin
28 Heinrich Wastgau
29 John Riebel
   C. Maria Riebel
30 John Friederich Eickhoff·
   George Eickhoff, 11 yrs.
   Conrad Eickhoff, 10 yrs.
31 Eberhard Eickhoff
32 Johanna Bell
33 Margaretha Hellt
34 Catharina Weingartin
35 Henriette Sussanna Frölich
36 John Gottlob Kursner
37 Johanna Sophia Kohlslates
38 Maria Elizabetha Staal
39 John Gade
40 Christian Zauerling
41 John Beutel
42 John Caspar Mattis
   Dorothea Mattis
   Friederich Christian, 11 yrs.
   Philipp Heinrich, 9 yrs.
43 Andreas Bush
   A. Regina Bush
44 Carl Eberle
   Catharina Eberle
   Friedrich Eberle, 1 yr.
45 Wilhelmina Kirchnerin
46 George Andreas Eberle
47 Henrich Jacob Eberle
48 Gerrit Kemp

49 Henrich Joseph Diederich
50 Catharina Ewig
51 Henry Vaucker
52 Peter Bewyr, 12 yrs.
53 Abraham Bewyr, 10 yrs. dead
56 Adolph Marx
    Catharina Marx
    Christiana Marx, 11 yrs.
    Andreas Marx, 8 yrs.
    Jacob Marx, 6 yrs.
    Gertruth Marx, 2 yrs.
57 Augusta Waldberg
58 Catharina Shaefferin
54 Anna Bewyr, 11 yrs.
54 Margaretha Bewyr, 9 yrs.

59 Clara Mollen
60 Sophia Klinkel
61 Catharina Korbin
62 Friederich Muller
63 Carl Kniess
64 George Datt
65 Casper Rielman
66 Philip Rittner
67 John Volk
68 George Christ Kohler
69 Lorenz Otto
70 Justuz Christ Stockman
71 John Jacob Krall

72 John Humler
    Maria Humler
73 Peter Lazer
    Catharina Lazer
74 Ludwig Enterz
    Margaretha Enterz
75 Margaretha Holzin
76 Wilhelmina Kniestin
77 John George Kniest
    Johanna Christiana
    Carolina Kniest, 3 yrs.
    Dorothea Kniest, 2 yrs.
78 A. Elizabeth Diehn
79 Wilhelm Leonard
80 Jacob Geller
81 Franz Meyerhoff
82 Martha Helena Rubenthal
    Johannes Rubenthal, 8 yrs.
    Andreas Rubenthal, 6 yrs.
    Christiana Rubenthal, 3 yrs.
    Nicolaus Friedinger
    J. W. Hoffman
    Annatje Schensema
    Richard Crown
    George Haas
    David Gerad
    Catharina Gerad
    Geertruyde Soeter

          Total 128.

[Endorsed:]

List of German Passengers on Board Ship Columbia, William Maley, Master, from Amsterdam. Arrived May 31st 1794. Received August 25th 1795, a List of German Passengers from 9th of February 1793 to 7th of July 1795.

          Lewis Farmer, Regr.

[List 390] List of German Passengers arrived at the Port of Philadelphia, of the Brig Union, Capt. Folger, from Hamburg. June 3 1794. E.] *

* Endorsement used as heading.

John Henerich Idie

Baldice Goldner

Willm Foyte

Hendrich Dewbeck

Johan Henrick Maruse

Fridrick Brown

Goerg Fridrick Newde

C. L. Jonderman

Elisbeath Jonderman, his wife

Cristian Jonderman, daughter

Louvise Charlote Melig

Joseph Demant

Henry Roberts

George Perkens

Edward Perkens

Martha Perkens

[List 391] Passengers in the Ship Brothers of Philadelphia, last from Hamburg to Philadelphia.   July 14th, 1794.

C. E. Ewald

P. A. Tietjens

A. H. Kohn

J. H. Möller

P. H. Varon

F. C. Schmidt

J. C. Musculus

Philadelphia July 14th 1794.   Caleb Earl.

[Endorsed:]

List of Passengers arrived in the Ship Brothers, Captn Caleb Earl, from Hamburg. July 14th 1794. E.

[List 392] List of Passengers on Board the Ship Holland, Capt C. Franklin, J^r from Amst^m. [August 20th 1794.]

CABIN PASSENGERS

Muller Prevot Jn^r & Ar. de Vogel

F. de Fresnaye

Van Kestel

Isaac W. Bartels

STEERAGE PASSENGERS

William Follendorff, Newlander,

Lebart Hayler

Hans Jaco[b] Thiman

Anth. Buckman & wife

Joseph Hullebrade & wife

Christ. Benedickt

Juliana Wertmans

Catharina Follendorff

Anne Maria Gottliebs

Peter Platz & wife

Wilhelmina Ostendorff

Anne Maria Johansing

Ant. Hurtgen

Hein. Schilling

Maria Foncke Gortz, with 2 children

Johannes Gortz

Catharina Aildens

Carl Lud. Burch

Ch. Miller

J. J. Conrad

J. L. Menger

Maria Opman

J. W. Greimel

C. H. Cordes

J. H. Fensch

Anth^y Henricks

Carl Sartorius

J. C. Ilmen

Cornelius Van den Weldenberg

J. H. Siebert

Louis Baultin

Anne Cath. Metger

John Kerres

Hend^k Busch

Daniel Cobet

Ab^r. Cobet

John Klyn

C. Andrewsen

[Endorsed:]

List of German Passengers arrived in Ship Holland, Cristopher Franklin, from Amsterdam. August 20th 1794. E.

[List 393] Passengers in Ship Birmingham Packet, from Hamburgh, George Lockyer, Philad. Aug. 25th. 1794.

CABIN PASSENGERS

Monsr Barthoud

Mad^m Berthoud

Mons. Derochea

Mons. Terascou

Mons. Journell

Mons. Berthoud

Gothilf Nicolas Lutzens

Christiana Wilhelmina Lutzens

Susana Barbery Lutzens

Francis Gothilf Lutzens

Lud. Henrick Von Storich

Henerick Hock

Johan Strauble

Christian Luders

Frederick Bode

Rudolph Bode

Carolina Bode

Jos. Frey

Barb^a Frey

Christiana Frey

Gustavus Witt

Catherine Witt

Johan Witt

Cath. Baumanin

[Endorsed:]

List of German Passengers, Capt George Lockyer, in the Ship Birmingham Packet. from Hamburg. August 25th 1794. E.

[List 394] List of Passengers Names on board the Ship Peggy, John Elliott, Master, from Amsterdam. Nov. 6, 1794.

John ⎫
Elizabeth ⎬ Hammon
Abraham ⎫
Angel ⎬ Cohan

John Swiers

Antonio Honius

John Ritz

Zwanan Vigal

Peter ⎫
Margaret ⎬ Erlinghurst
Godfred Reinhart
Magnus Stultz
Jasper Kraft
Tedric Frake
Casper Helliquest
Henry Lipper
Christian Kopping
Fedrick Rosenthal
Henry Eggell Hanio

Dan¹ Holstein
Francis Dessalaur
Francis Van Tilhas
Matthias De Koning
Willm Aulhorn
Gustaf Wetekind
Thos ⎫
Elinora ⎬ Woodsand
Elizabeth ⎭
Simon Kepler
Jacob Elderst

John Elliot.

[Endorsed:]
List of German Passengers, arrived in Ship Peggy, Jn° Elliott, Master, Novr. 6th 1794. E.

[List 395] List of the Passengers on Board of the Brigantine Sarah from Hamburgh. [Novemb. 10, 1794.]

Lewis Bourdillon & 2 children
Alexander Crom
Jean Louis Duby
Jean Salomon Fazy
Antoine Charles Cazenove

Jeane Antoine Cazenove
André Jerret
David Gandou
David Martin
Jacob Buffle

Philadelphia Novem^b 10, 1794.

Daniel May.

[Endorsed:]
List of German Passengers arrived from Hamburg, Brigantine Sarah, Daniel May, Captn. Novr 11th 1794. E.

[List 396] [List of German Passengers in the Ship Sophia Carolina, Peter Ehler, Commander, from Hamburg, arrived Novr 12th 1794.] *

Mr. Tohmas Leuffer, wife and one son
Mr. Eckstein, wife, son, two daughters
Mr. G. H. Lüers

Mr. I. Iden
Mr. F. J. Rahn
Mr. A. Scheel
Mr. F. Schleicherd

13

* Endorsement used as heading.

Philadelphia Novem^r 12th 1794.

Peter Ehler.

[List 397] Passengers in the Ship John of Philadelphia from Amsterdam. [Jany. 2^d 1795.]

Mr. Stunie with wife & six children	Mr. Ludwig
Mr. A. Zony	Mr. Kraz
Mr. Meyer	Mr. May
	Mr. Newman

Philad. Jan 2^d 1795.

Wm Whitwell.

[Endorsed:]
List of German Passengers arrived from Amsterdam, Ship John, W. Whitwel, Capt. Jany. 2^d 1795. E.

[List 398] List of the Passengers on Board the Ship Livonia, from Amsterdam, Feby 27th 1795.

Christian Brand

Jonnis Frederick & his wife & two children

Philadelphia, Feby 27th 1795.

[Endorsed:]
List of Passengers, Ship Livonia, Jas. Parker, from Amsterdam. Feb. 27. 1795. E.

[List 399] Names of the Passengers on board the Concord from Hamburg to Philadelphia, July 7, 1795.

Mrs. Jeanne Elizabeth Malet Prevost
André ⎫
Henry ⎬ her children
André Louis ⎭
Mr. Peter Galline
Miss Francis Gay
Mr. Zacharie Fauguelvey, called Laroche

Doctor Heinrich Zolfers & wife
Johann Gottfried Gadecke
Johann Friedrich Wilhelm Neumann
John Dohrn
Lorois Houssage
Louis Cr. Houssage Lepine
Louis René Houssage
    three bros. & their servant

Henry Gallon

August H. Schmid, wife & two children

Johann George Hummel, his wife Anna Maria & his son

Christian Hummel

Christian Friederich Ludwig Küster

George Pickelmann

Lion Mussina

Levy Hirsch

Soren Royen

John Stone, seaman of the United States

Captⁿ William Campbell, citizen of the United States

[Endorsed:]

List of Passengers, Ship Concorde, John Thompson, from Hamburg July 7th 1795. E.

[List 400] Passengers on board the Rose from Hamburg, Capt. John Meaney. Sepr. 18, 1795.

H. Newman

Mary Newman

Jn° Newman

Martin D°

Felton D°

Henry Christ

Jn° Lefart

Peter Speitzel

Jn° Ritkar

Hans Adam Miller

Jence Venan

Ursela Kriegeren

Barbara Kesliener

Margaret Speitzel

Efferen Tigerin

Mich^l William

Gorgon Fred. Bumach

Robt Steinnberk

Jn° Intellinger

Gabriel Zelinger

Moses Quin

Philip Lagam

Simon Newman

Benjamin Wolfe

Betsey Stone

Christian Stettly

George Bourben

Godfrey Keller

Jn° Jacobs

Henrich Bremer

Abm Markel

Henry Eckart

Jn° Fritch

Henry Baker

Edwd Clarke ⎫
William Clark ⎪
Jn° Belk ⎬ Cabin
Francis Marshall ⎭

Mary Enar

Amamuel Enar

Charles Enar

Jn° Newman

Septemb^r 18th 1795.

John Meaney.

[Endorsed:]
Brig Rose from Hamburg, Captⁿ. John Meaney. 42 Passengers.

[List 401] List of Passengers from Hamburgh, in Hamburgh Packet, Caleb Earl, Master. Oct. 5, 1795.

CABIN PASSENGERS

R. Camppell
Rebecah Camppell & child
P. S. Schild
Elizebeth Lants
Annah Hezhald

STEERAGE PASSENGERS

Louis Emanuel de la Flechére
Johann Jacob Seidel, doctor
Friederich Gottlieb Segel, clerk
Johann Heinr. Georg Sax, servant

Johann Ernst Droy, cooper
Johann Michael Delken
Anna Maria Delken
Elsi van Leuvel
Ludolph Heinr. Ludewig Kiegel
Johann Jacob Lents
Johannes Mecke   } joiners
Johann George Leytman
Johann Heinr. Nurenberg, baker
Heinrich Siegmon Zucker, miller
Friederich Knorr, miller

Philadelphia Octr 5th 1795.   Caleb Earl.

[Endorsed:]
Ship Hamburg Packet, Caleb Earl, Captⁿ, from Hamburg. 21 Passengers. Oct. 5, 1795.

[List 402] Names of the Passengers on Board the Ship Thomas Chalckley, from Rotterdam, Capt. Robert Rice. Oct. 13, 1795.

Jon. Henrick Stiever
Johanns Miller
Jacob Kern
Joseph Crumber
Jon Coenraied Berkman
Sophiea Berkman
August Ludwick Hark
Louis Hark
Fredrick Konfleur
Jon. Fill Graftt
Johanes Bruyn

Fredrick Sevonboom
Hendrack Diearman
Cathⁿ Elisbeth Frielang
Liena Ludica
Julina Wieling
Maria Roenes
Rebecca Velveriss
George Bloodhart
John Mesner
Hendrick Donnett
Fredrik Fiering

Jan. David Benter

Jan. Fredrick Sckierer

John Harps

Jurien Roode

Anna Kurter

Mielie Roode

Michel Antony Prie

William Dieckman

Carieliena Oarn

William Hendrick

Peter Hausen

Fredrick Stratsburg

Lotte Kempers

Elisebeth Kloss

Johana Everstene

Jacob Scutts

Eva Maria Scutts

Jacob Frederick Scutts

Jacob Williams

Johan Wilhelm Oartan

Peter Niewill

Gerard Persons

Jacob Rubbel

Fredrica Rubbel

Earnst Leamen

Jur. Jacob Keatrer

Cathirina Keatrer

Eliseabeth Van Orn

Mathias Everstine

Jon. Hendrick Bearin Boom

Hendrick Rintrop

Elisabeth Rintrop

Carolina Rinetrop

Fredrick Rinetrop

Hendrick Rinetrop

John Conrad Hubner

Margriatha Trapp

Daneal Allen

Philip Clien

Christinea Clien

Johana Gutte

John Allof

Gasper Booms

Gasper Hierman

Gorit Frieser

Johannes Bolb

Jan Newinghuzen

Mariea Molendel

Arnoldes Niewinhuzen

Jacobus Hutchinssen

David Pristore

Johanes Selb

Joh. Bridenban

John Necklos Koutz

Fredrich Stoner

Ch. Charlotte Meyer

Philad\u00aa October 13, 1795.   M. McPherson.

[Endorsed:]
Ship Thomas Chalklay, from Rotterdam, Capt\u207f Robert Rice.
78 Passengers.

[List 403] List of the Passengers on board the Brig Friend-ship, Nathan Clarke, Master, from Amsterdam. Nov. 17, 1795.

Doctor of Med. & D.D. J. De Jongh

Christian Westfahlen, his wife and two children

C. A. F. Otto, his wife and three children

Elizabeth Seibel & child

Johan Nickel, his wife and two children

Johan Ulrich Ammer, his wife & six children

Henrich Schroeder, his wife & child

Michael Faust, his wife & three children

Christian Moller, his wife & child

Barbara Gass & child

Johan Peter Blankard, his wife & child

Daniel George Schaffer, his wife & two children

Anna Gabriels

Johan Geenan

Nicholas Schreb

Conrad Kratz

Cornelle Casaly

Leonard Evers

Anna Elizabeth Durmans

Caspar Henkel

Johan Michael Lehr

Conrad Fryberger

Johan Justus Wiel

Johan Jacob Hermani

Johan Frans Pflaume

Anna Elizabeth Dalhoff

Johan Christoph Rhode

Jan Berler

Johan Jacob Vander Biechelaar

Johan Christian Nagel

Johan Godfried Pflag

Maria Kegelin

Johannas Kerkhuis

Klaas Peters

Harman Henkel

Total 67

Philadelphia, Novr 17, 1795.   Nath. Clark.

[Endorsed:]
Brig Friendship from Amsterdam. Captn Nathan Clark. 67 Passengers. Nov. 17, 1795.

[List 404] The Names of Passengers on board the Brig Mary from Hamburgh to Philadelphia, Wm Bell, Master. Nov. 1795.

CABIN PASSENGERS	[STEERAGE PASSENGERS]
Jonathan Reynolds	Michael van Kuk and wife
Andrew Benade	Heinrich Danker and wife
Christian Fried^r Schaaf	Conrad Kreuser
Madame Schaaf	Christian Gottlob Paulus
Johann Fried^r Rudolphi	Christian Samuel Michael
David M. Michael	Johann Gottfried Pietsch
Charles Moelien	Christoph Lupach
Carl Ludwig Schmid	Gottlieb Byhan

Mathias Friesel
Henrich Matthiesen
Johann George Zwickel
Carl Kayne
Johann Koelling
Henrich Poppe
Johann Schomermel
Henrich Meitzel
Johann Gottfred Kaelbel
Carl Gottleben
Philip Jacob Volmer
Carl Witte
Christoph Brichmann
Henrich Wigand
Christian Fried^r Blume
Christian Heinrich Malchowff
Benjamin Angst

Johann Huppe
Johann Christoph Suvermann
Johann Gasper Frisch
Johann Gottlob Schwartz
Friech. Wilhelm Herzog
Johann Adam Kreyn
Johann Carl Weiss
Andrew Uhle
Friedrich Uhle
Georg Bernhard Schramm
Johann Conrad Phillip Geiger
Johann August Geiger
Phillip Gottlob Frank
Friedrich Wilhelm Meyer
Christina Friederica Seybottin
Anna Peterson

Wm Bell.

[Endorsed:]
Brig Mary from Hamburg, Capt. William Bell. 50 Passengers. Nov 1795.

[List 405] List of Passengers on Board the Brig Minerva from Hamburgh, James Snell, Mast^r. [December 15th 1795.]

Johan Jacob Behn
And. Duchêne
Georg Yoder Horst
Gerlach Läf
Jacob Dillman
Anmaria Dillmanin
Christian Bender
Johannes Peter Schreiber
Maria Catriena Schreiberin
Heinrich Ahlmann
Johannes Schrey
Johannes Daub

Maria Margreta Daubin
Dillmanus Daub
Friedrich Beking
Jacob Christoph Schnurer
And. Pitstäch
Daniel Schöner
Johannes Birckellbach
Heinrich Rittner
Henry Louis Martander
Margretha Carolina Elisabetha
   Strasern
Johann Brasilius Möller

Philad^a December 15th 1795.   James Snell.

[Endorsed:]
Brig Minerva from Hamburg. Capt⁺ James Snell. 23 Passengers.

[List 406] An Account of Money, Food & Cloathing, distributed amongst the necessitous French Emigrants by the Commissioners named in the act of the Legislature of Pennsylvania, pass'd the 13th of January 1796, granting Fifteen hundred Dollars for that purpose.

Francis, a child, deserted
Morand & child, husband absent
Ducasse, three children, widow aged
Marten Garnier, woman pregnant
Fleur Delys & wife, infirm
Chevernet, two women
Delame, wife & 2 children, infirm
Clastner & son, aged
Niel & wife, infirm
Regal, man
Sophia Polier, a young woman
Felicite & 3 children, lying in.
Widow Paquot & daughter
Widow Darey, woman & child
J. Savoye, wife & 3 children, blind
Yaya & 3 children, sick
Widow Belleyarde, daughter & grand child
Constance, woman
Combilaire, widow & 3 children
Prestet, widow & daughter
Pestel, man aged
Jean Lewis, man sick
Sophia & child
Caroline, woman
Abzira, ditto
Coquigny, woman & 2 children

Francois Laurent, orphan child
Sanitte, woman
Henn, man sick
Houen, three children
Luise, a child
Sylvie, woman
Angele, married child
Justine, woman
Adelaide Andre & mother
Nanon & Charlotte, woman
Rosalie, ditto
Froment, man
D'Owrle, woman
Claire & Zayre, ditto
La Voche, ditto
Dan Sauream, man
Faick, wife & 3 children
Madelain, and two children
Mane Modat, ditto,
Fourtunce, woman & child
Gartang, & two children
Romaine Launay, woman
Francois Lersel, destitute & 3 children
——————————, sick man
Belzan, aged man
Souchet, ditto, woman
Sauvage, woman & 2 orphans
Dermarets, ditto, blind
Mallerive
Jourdan, sick man

Groullat	Dierre
Lamourout, woman & daughter, blind	Laborde
	Dubran
LeGrard, sick woman	Leger, old woman, lame
Maillard	Guegnim
Aunay	Marie
Cockburn, aged man	Ducror
Savoye	Graciena
Banecourt	Guvoin
Gerard	Carnois
Bellevie	Olivier, old man & infant
La Feve	Saxie, widow, sister & 5 children
Guibert	Gue, ditto & 6 children
Michand, sick man	Marquet
Constant	Lafleur
Blanchard	Auberste
Boudier, old woman & grandchild	Trebert
Guerrier	Liberté
St Rosin	Fanbon
Durien	Lamotté
Vocart	Thorren
Rene	Charlotte
Froite	Rose Geman, man & wife, aged
Berard	Bedane, aged
Laurent	Corneille Juene, a woman
Ann	Corneille

The whole number of Persons relieved are about two hundred & twenty Persons.

Amount of bills for cloathing, bedding, etc.	£317. 10. 6
Ditto Ditto Ditto for bread	41. 7. 8
Ditto Ditto Ditto " wood	31. 11. 11
Ditto of money distributed at different times & paid for sundry necessaries	171. 19. 11
Total received of the State Treasurer	£562. 10.

[List 407] List of Passengers on Board the Ship Henry & Charles from Hamburgh. [March 29, 1796.]

Catherine Claussen   Nicholas Bowers

Philadᵃ March 29ᵗʰ '96.   Benjamin Slade.

[Endorsed:]
Ship Henry & Charles from Hamburg. Capᵗⁿ Benjamin Slade. 2 Passengers. Mar. 29, 1796.

[List 408] Passengers on Board the Brig Molly, Wᵐ Campbell, Master, from Hamburgh. Vizᵗ [April 13ᵗʰ 1796.]

Joh. Bodel

April 13ᵗʰ 1796.

[Endorsed:]
Brig Polly from Hamburg Capᵗⁿ Robᵗ Campbell. One Passenger. April 13, 1796.

[List 409] A List of Passengers on Board the Ship America from Hamburgh, Capᵗ James Ewing. Viz [June 3ᵈ 1796.]

Christian Martin Oldenburg
Maria Elizabeth Oldenburg
Henrich Oldenburg
Christiana Oldenburg
Ludwick Graff
Lois Wernick
Geᵒ Frederick Reguel
Christopher Roller

Johan H. Buercke
George Plumstock
Christian Ramskart
Ludwig Frieds
Margaret Frieds
Andrew Zeifs
Edward Boyson

Philadᵃ June 3ᵈ 1796.

[Endorsed:]
Ship America from Hamburg, Capᵗⁿ James Ewing. 15 Passengers. June 3, 1796.

[List 410] A List of passengers on Board of the Ship Harriot Baltimore, Thoˢ W. Norman, Master. [June 17, 1796.]

Fedrick Moller
Fedrick Harrshoff

Christen Less

Philadelphia June 17, 1796.   Thomas W. Norman.

[Endorsed:]
Ship Harriott from Hamburg. Captⁿ Thos W. Norman. 3 passengers.

[List 411] A List of Passengers on board the Ship Harmony from Hamburgh, July 25, 1796.

Joh. Gobhard Cunow	John Otto
Benigna Sophia Cunow	Weigan Miller
Augusta Henrieta Cunow	Fred^k Long
Carolina Louise Cunow	Frederick Clear
Johanna Lehmann	John Glassmann
Johann Caspar Freytag	Just. H. Vaspar
Johann Christian Ebbeke	John Long
Johann Gottlable Rentner	William Gilland
Joseph Metzler	Christian Denny
Jean Baptist Chambaud	Anna Denny & three children
Gustav Zeekendoff	John Wall
Ludewig Krumbharr	John Young
Louis Marquis Rangoree	Christian Sholtz
Johan Nyromeen Geetze	Frederick Goodry
Louis Willmans	Benjamin Ganny
Cristopher Ceke	Gunther Walspan
Carl Gastell	George Walsh
Charlotte Philippine Cunow	John Walsh
Henry Streider	John Fakeenner
Hannah Streider	William Gillihan
Hannah Dillon	

Philad^a July 25th 1796.   Ja^s Moore.

[Endorsed:]
Ship Harmony. James Moore, Captⁿ, from Hamburg. 44 Passengers. July 25 1796.

[List 412] Passengers on board the Brig Mary, Capt Earl, from Hamburgh, July 30, 1796.

	AGES		AGES
William Hippenstiel, farmer	46	Ann Justina Hippenstiel	17
Ann Sophia Hippenstiel	43	Mary Elisabeth Hippenstiel	13

John Weber, farmer 30
Mary Elisth Wolf 24
Conrad Bald, farmer 28
Anna Sophia Bald 28
Frederic Bald, farmer 24
Christina Bald, and one child,
  6 mos. old 22
Jost Flemmer, farmer 22
Ann Gertrout Koenig 22
John Jost Menn, smith 36
Ann Mary Menn, and one
  child, 1 yr. 29
Elisabeth Menn 19
Philip Menn, farmer 18
John George Menn, farmer 17
Ann Catharine Menn 12
John Henry Menn 12
George William Menn 7
Jost Henry Menn 5
John Jost Dickel, farmer 23
Mary Cath. Weyand 18
Jost Aflerbach, smith 22
John Henry Greve, farmer 34
Ann Elisabeth Greve 30
Mary Elisabeth Greve, 50
Jost Strackbein, farmer 47
Ann Mary Strackbein 43
Mary Elisabeth Strackbein 21
Jost Henry Strackbein, farmer 18
Valentine Strackbein, farmer 15
Catharine Strackbein 12
John Jost Strackbein 5
Christoph Raff, farmer 21
John Ulrich Frank, farmer 20
Philip Widman, farmer 18
Philip Mayer, farmer 20
John Ulrich Kusmaul, farmer 18
Frederic Segfried, farmer 20
George Spies, farmer 26

Elisabeth Spies, and one child,
  one month 26
Ludwick Strackbein, tailor 30
Richard Stremmel, farmer 35
Elisa Gertrout Stremmel 36
Ann Gertrout Stremmel 20
Ann Catharine Stremmel 18
Caspar Spies, tailor 50
George Spies, farmer 22
Philip Spies, farmer 20
Henry Eckart, farmer 19
Pens Bauman, farmer 19
John Jost Voelkel, farmer 27
Mary Catharine Voelkel, and
  one child, 1 mth old 26
George Sasmanshaus, farmer 22
George Walter, smith 26
Sophia Schreckegast 22
Philip Strackbein, farmer 36
Ann Gertrout Strackbein 37
Christian Strackbein, farmer 16
Ann Elisabeth Strackbein 14
Catharine Strackbein 12
Elisabeth Strackbein 10
Daniel Strackbein 8
John Henry Strackbein 6
John Jost Strackbein 3.
George Lud. Henk, wheelwr. 32
Ann Mary Henk 25
Mary Elisabeth Henk 50
Ann Gertrout Henk 24
Ann Elisabeth Henk 14
John George Henk 11
John Jost Henk 8
John Henry Henk 7
Philip Henk 4
Jost Bald, farmer 36
Ann Mary Bald 33
Ann Sophia Bald 20

Mary Elisabeth Bald	12	Mary Catharine Rudolph	18
John Jost Bald	9	Christian Rudolph	16
Louisa Jost, and one child, 2		Abraham Rudolph	14
yrs.	6	Mary Ann Rudolph	7
Jacob Gladen, farmer	28	Francis Rudolph	5
Mary Gladen	28	George Deiniger	37
John Gladen	5	Regine Deiniger, with 2 chil-	
Philip Miller, smith	26	dren	24
Elisabeth Miller	23	William Deiniger	16
George Koch	40	Catharine Deiniger	14
Mary Lienda Koch	40	Michael Deiniger	12
Jost Henry Koch	11	Lena Elisa Deiniger	18
Elisabeth Koch	7	Mr. Joseph Donatt & his Lady,	
Jacob Rudolph, carpenter	50	Cabin Passengers	
Ann Mary Rudolph	48		

Philadelphia, July 30th, 1796.   Benjn Earle.

[List 413] List of the Passengers on board the Ship Holland, Christoph Francklin, Junior, Commander. Aug. 19, 1796.

Crentien Achenback	Jean Henry Beitzel
Adolph Arenholtz	Catherine Beitzel
Anne Marie Ahrenholtz	Marie Catherine Beitzel
Antoine Bluhm	George Bandholtz
Justine Bluhm	Catharine Bentfern
Daniel Bard	Guillaume Baldt
Jean Born	Regine Elisabeth Baldt
Justine Born	Fredrique Foebel
Jean Beltz	Catherine Baldt
Sophie Beltz	Susette Baldt
Jean Beltz	Jean Henry Baldt
Anne Elisabeth Beltz	Anne Marie Baldt
Krafft Beltz	Guillaume Baldt
George Beltz	Jean Henry Baldt

Jean Josse Baldt
Dietrich [Baldt]
Jean Eckhardt
Catharine Eckhardt
George Eckhardt
Marie Eckhardt
Sophie Eckhardt
Jean Engel
Jean George Foebel
Anne Marie Foebel
Fredric Föbel
Conradine Foebel
Fridrique Fœbel
George Fredric
Jean Nicholas Fischer
Jean Friebe
Anne Marie Friebe
M. Catherine Friebe
Jean George Friebe
Jean Henry Friebe
Chretien Friebe
Jean August Frank
Jean Föbel
Catherine Föbel
Chrétien Friedrich
Catherine Friedrich
Jean Friedrich
Catherine Friedrich
Jean George Friedrich
Guillaume Friedrich
Henry Franck
Marie Franck
Henry Franck
Jean Franck
Catherine Frank
Madelon Franck
Anne Franck
Elisabeth Franck
Fredric Guillaume Fischbach
Elisabeth Fischbach
Fredric Föbel

Madelon Föbel
Jaques Grote
Jean Jaques Gärther
George Grube
Chrétien Horchler
Henriette Horchler
Charlotte Horchler
Adolph Horchler
Chrétien Hencke
Marie Elisabeth Hencke
Maria Catherine Hencke
Anne Marie Hencke
Jean Josse Hencke
Chrétien Hencke
Jean George Hencke
Jean George Hencke, senior
Elisabeth Hencke
Jean Hencke
Madelon Hencke
Catherine Hencke
George Hencke
Jean George Hencke, junior
Chrétien Hencke
Chrétienne Hencke
Jean Hencke
Louise Hencke
George Daniel Hencke
Jean Josse Junge
Catherine Jung
Elisabeth Jung
Jean Jung
Daniel Jung
George Jung
Henry Jung
Marie Jung
Philipp Kahm
Henry Kauffmann
Chrétienne Kellerin
Valentin Lepold
Marie Elisabeth Lepold
Anne Marie Lepold

Valentin Lepold

Jaques Lepold

Jean Lepold

Jean Philipp Lepold

Jean Leibe

Jean Lepold

Louise Lepold

Valentin Lepold

George Lepold

Charles Lepold

Chrétienne Lepold

Louise Lepold

Anne Elisabeth Müllerin

Henry Meyer

Conrad Metzger

Daniel Metzger

Jaques Metzger

Jean Miesse

Jean Müller

Piérre Pfeil

Chrétien Pfeil

Anne Marie Pfeil

Guillaumette Pfeil

Anne Elisabeth Pfeil

Daniel Pfeil

Conrad Pfeil

Madelon Pfeil

Catherine Pfeil

Georg Petry

Jean Henry Pheil

Marie Gertrude Pheil

Marie Elisabeth Pheil

Jean Pheil

Jean Josse Pheil

Elisabeth Gertrude Pheil

Catherine Elisabeth Pheil

Marie Margarethe Pheil

Jean Jost Risstein

Jean Reinhard

Bernard Rath

Marie Rath

Marie Rath

Marie Elisabeth Rath

George Henry Rath

Anne Marie Rath

Nicolas Rath

Conrad Riehl

Catherine Riehl

Jean Riehl

George Adam Riehl

Catherine Riehl

Jaques Risstein

Catherine Risstein

Christine Risstein

Gottlob Schultz

—— Schweinitz

Chrétien Sassmann

Marie Sassmann

Josse Sassman

Elisabeth Sassmann

George Sassmann

Gertrude Sassmann

Anne Marie Saltzmannin

Frederic Sassmannshausz

Anne Marie Sassmannhaus

George Guill^{me} Sassmannhausz

George Henry Schreckegast

Sophie Schreckegast

Marie Elisabeth Schreckegast

Floriane Schreckegast

George Schreckegast

Daniel Schreckegast

Krafft Schneider

Marie Elisabeth Schneider

Josse Schneider

Josse Schmidt

Catherine Schmidt

Jaques Schmidt

Marie Elisabeth Schmidt

Marie Schmidt

Justine Schmidt

Guillaumette Schmidt

George Spiess
Jaques Saltzmann
Henry Joseph Schmidt
Josse Stänger
Jean Josse Schneider
Margarethe Schneider
Jaques Schneider
Louis Schneider
George Schneider
Christine Schneider
Louise Schneider
Justine Schneider
Marie Schneider
Adam Stegmüller
Anne Stegmüller
Jean Henry Schneider
Elisabeth Schneider
August Sander
Jean Schneider
Catherine Schneider
George Schmidt
François Spiess
Catherine Spiess
George Spiess
Krafft Spiess
George Spiess
Guillaume Schneider
Catherine Schneider
Louise Schneider
Chrétienne Schneider
George Schneider
Chrétien Schneider
Elisabeth Marie Schneider
Guillaumette Schneider
Elisabeth Schneider
Jean Schneider
Jean Thum
Anne Elisabeth Thum
Guillaume Vogel
Dorothee Voogel
Krafft Völckel

Marie Catherine Völckel
George Völckel
Philipp Völckel
Anne Elisabeth Völckel
Florentine Völckel
Marie Catherine Völckel
Josse Weber
Catherine Weber
Catherine Weber
Jean Weber
Marie Elisabeth Weber
Jean Henry Wiedersprecher
Anne Elisabeth Weberinn
Krafft Wied
Justine Wied
François Wied
Chrétien Wied
Sophie Wied
George Wied
George Wunderlich
Jean Wagner
Marie Gertrude Wagner
Marie Wagner
Jean Chrétien Wagner
Jean Conrad Wagner
Marie Catherine Wuchbohrin
Jean Wunderlich
Pierre Weber
Anne Weber
Henry Wulff
Anne Wulff
Elisabeth Wulff
Jean Wulff
Jean Wulff
Krafft Weber
Marie Pheilin
—— Friedlin
Harriot King

CABIN PASSENGERS

Mr Loss

Madam Loss
Mr Loss, snr
Mr —— Bielfield

Mr Holbecker
Mr Holbeck
Napper Tandy, Esqr

[List 414] Passengers by the Ship Voltaire, Ezra Bowen, Master, from Hamburg. [August 29, 1796.]

Joseph Douey
Gabriel Brehant
Leon Masan
John F. Gianque
Henry Mayerhoff

Jacob Hebb & Wife
Frederic Damisch
Frederic Gotlieb Friz
Andrew Zeimer
Noel Simson

Philadelphia 29 August, 1796.   Ezra Bowen.

[Endorsed:]
Captn Ezra Bowen, with German Passengers from Hamburg. Aug. 29, 1796.

[List 415] List of Passengers per Ship Concord, John Thompson, Master, from Amsterdam [15th Octr 1796.]

John W. Godfrey of Philada
Fredrich Habel ⎤
Julian Robreacht ⎦ Servts to do
Rochus Sylva
Maria Christina Sylva
Hermanus Josephus Sylva
Maria Thereza Sylva

Betramus Josephus Reus
Maria Dorothea Reus
Hermanus Josephus Reus
Antonius Reus
Anna Maria Elisabeth Reus
Mathieu De Prez

Philada 15th Octr 1796.   John Thompson.

[Endorsed:]
Captn Jno Thomson, with German Passengers, from Amsterdam. Oct. 15, 1796.

[List 416] Pasrs on Bd the Ship Bacchus from Hamburgh, Philada, 15th October, 1796. Richard George.

Augusta Maria Fischer, the mother

Friederica Augusta Amalia Boetzsch, born Ficher

Albertine Henrietta Carolina   Adolph Ficher
   Ficher   Johann Boetzsch
Johana Augusta Adolphina Ficher   Ernst Neumann
Augusta Sophia Juliana Ficher   Henry Moellinger
Friederich Fischer   Johannes Guth
Carl Fischer

[Endorsed:]
Richard George, Captn with German Passengers from Hamburg, 1796. Oct 15, 1796.

[List 417] List of Passengers on board the Brig Polly from Bremen. [Oct. 19, 1796.]

Mr. Thos H. Pratt   Will. Erpson
Jno. Metzger   Bart^w Orron

Phil^a Oct. 19, 1796.   William Campbell.
   Sworn 24th Oct^r '96. rec^d 3/.

[Endorsed:]
Capt^{tn} Wm Campbell with German Passengers from Bremen. Oct 19, 1796.

[List 418] List of Passengers p^r Ship Mary, S. Parker, Mast^r [Oct 20, 1796.]

Colonel More de Pontgebeau   Mr Johan Venbleck.

Philadelphia 20th Octr 1796.   Samuel Parker.
   Sworn 20th Octr 96.

[Endorsed:]
Captn Saml Parker, with German Passengers from Hamburg. Oct. 20, 1796.

[List 419] A List of passengers on board the Ship America, Capt James Ewing, from Hamburg. [October 24, 1796.]

L. C. B. Orleans   Nicholas Mascard
Peter Bodevain   William Leamford
Mr. Denion   Alexander Joseph Lefever

Harmon Saxe   Mathias Dembrouiskie
John East

Philadelphia, October 24, 1796.   James Ewing.

[Endorsed:]
Captn James Ewing, with German Passengers from Hamburg. Oct. 24, 1796.

[List 420] List of Passengers on board Ship George, of Portland, Francis Waite, M^r. from Rotterdam. Oct. 26, 1796.

Peter Casper Kimpel
Anna Gertruth Kimpel
Johann Abram Kimpel
Johann Arnold Jansen
Herinrith Sarton
Andrew Hegenbein
Wilhelm Jansen
Johanna Amend
Cornelia Cremer
Christiana Trossenberg
George Walter
Alida Walter
Mathias Walter
Peter Walter
Alida Walter
Elizabeth Mamme
Carolina Dan Streven
Maria Simons
Catharina Sanders
Henericus Hehmann
Maria Magdalena
Samuel Hehmann
Nathaniel Hehmann
Christoph Ott Kamptz
Christoph Clausen
Catharina Elizabeth
Adam Keb
Elizabeth Keb
Mina Keb

Simon Abraham
Abraham Blumhost
Wilhelm Roemer
Gertruth Roemer
Gertruth Roemer
Rulophs Sohmiths
Isaac Testhe
Anna Gertruth
Wilhelmina Testhe
Isaac Testhe
Daniel Testhe
Johannes Testhe
Anna Catharina
Peter Orth
Catharina Orth
Catharina Orth
Brigita Orth
Stephen Orth
Anton Friebaldt
Anna Gertruth Friebaldt
Ary Questro
Helena Questro
Anna Christina Nippes
Abram Nippes
Daniel Nippes
Wilhelm Nippes
Anna Catharina Nippes
Martin Wansther
Thomas Hesthsthin

Catharina Hesthsthin
Frona Hesthsthin
Wilhelm Hesthsthin
Dorir. Hesthsthin
Elizabeth Cirokler
Johannes Denom
Helena Meyerin
Ludwig Gumder
Peter Valth
Catharina Groth
Lorentz Demeer
Elizabeth Forss
Anna Catharina Franck
Maria Graeffin
Anna Rau
Maria Catharina Hoohstin
Anna Catharina Hoohstin
Wilhelmina Hoohstin
Catharina Brook
Anna Catharina Brook
Hanna Brook
Carl W. Brook
Anna Eliz. Knipping
Anna Mary Knipping
Jacob Knipping
Catharina Danitkers
Anna Elizabeth Schroader
Gertruth Schroader
H. Cath. Kruins
Christina Ludwig Meyer
Helena Meyer
Carolina Meyer
Cecilia Meyer
Johann Friederith Schroeder
Philipp Neuhoft
Friederith Huth
Heinrith Schwatter
Carolina Schreiber
Theodor Schreiber
Anna Maria Vogel
Alida Maria Vogel

Johannes Rhimhare
Johannes Zeller
Johannes Roth
Anna Gertruth
Rahel Roth
Johann Gottlieb Roth
Sarah Roth
Anna Catharina Roth
Johannes Roth
Anna Maria Roth
Anna Charlotta Roth
Hartmann Teusfer
Freiderich Bremicker
George Michel Futting
Anna Elizabetha
Peter Johannes Futting
Johanna M. Futting
Johann H. Futting
Maria Catharina Futting
Peter Ilfer
Catharina Stephans
Elizabeth Doos
Joh. H. Plade
Anna Juliana
Johann Christophel Plade
Joh. Heinrich Plade
Joh. Geo. Plade
Arnoldus Plade
Anna Maria Plade
Gertruth Plade
Abraham Levi
Johannes Meyners
Helena Meyners
Lamerdje van Kleve
Conrad Marx
Gerhardus Marx
Matthew J. Weingarten
Johann Schniell
George F. C. Friese
Walter Betker
Heinrich Klein

Hertzog Levi
Sauter Philipp
Maria Elis. Legin
Arnold Karthause
Joseph Starck
Johann G. Leigues
Elizabeth Leigues
Johanna Elizabetha Leigues
Catharina Leigues
Carl Alexander Leigues
Johann W. Leigues
Johannes Leigues
Johann Ludwig Joseph Hausen
Anna Stramann

Johann George Fickkelie
Clasina Ratenmacher
Elizabeth Becker
Petronella Boos
Wilhelm Boos
Peter Libert
Anna Wilhelmina Libert
Johann Gottlieb Libert
Anna Wilhelmina Libert
Barbara Aubie
Herrmann Hoommel
Christian Pinsel
Engelina Pinsel

Philadelphia Octo^r 26th 1796.

Francis Waite.

[Endorsed:]
Captⁿ Francis Waite, with German Passengers from Rotterdam. Oct. 26, 1796.

[List 421] A List of Passengers on board the Ship Two Friends, from Hamburg, Viz. Oct. 31, 1796.

Johan Fredk. Wille
Charles Henry Ferdinand
Joachim Valentine Benthin
Wm. Maufsin
Fredk. Wm. Otto
Johan Fortart
Christopher Hamermann
Charles Christ. Baxman
John Joderm Prit
Wm. Peter Parits
David Johnn
Zacharias Bricham
Frederick Christoph Brisehot
John David Moeller
John Barman

John Peter Sawer
Charles Fredk. Klana
John Henry Schlotsman
Christopher Frederick Dietent
Adam Charles Stichet
John Stichet
Michael Hutter
Charles Schaltser and wife
John Prinfinger
Christ. Fredk. Huna
Henry Schwatz and wife and 3
   children
Joseph Dominick Millant
Andreas Zimdecker
John Henry Homberg

Moritz Henry Koepper, wife &   Henry Koenig
one child

Caleb Hathaway.

31st October, 1796.

[Endorsed:]
Captn. Hathaway, with German Passengers from Hamburg. Oct. 31, 1796.

[List 422] A List of Passengers on board the Ship Enterprize from Hamburgh, my Self Master, Viz. [Nov. 22. 1796.]

Francis Bruno   Joseph Dayor
Bernard Brant   Franz Dayor
Joseph Fiekert   M. Rouwer
Peter Dayor

Philadelphia 22. Novbre 1796.

Thomas Norris.

[Endorsed:]
Captn Thos Norris, with German Passengers from Hamburg. Nov. 22, 1796.

[List 423] List of Passengers pr. Ship Columbia from Amsterdam, Capt. Reuben Mason. Feb. 12, 1797.

Godfrey Smith, American   Martin Wagenaar
George Neuman   Carl Gersing
Marianna Veryly, ditto   Margaretha Gersing
Anthon Knesius   Carolina Gersing
Eady Crown, ditto   Anthon Gersing

Philadia 12 Febr 1797.

Reuben Mason.

[Endorsed:]
Captn Reuben Mason, with German Passengers from Amsterdam. 12 Feb. 1797.

[List 424] A List of Passengers on board the Ship Good Friends, John Smith, Master, from Hamburg, Viz. [Feby. 13, 1797.]

Ignace Lobez   Mr Gasse
Mr Geinly

Philadelphia Feby. 13th. 1797.

Jno. Smith.

[Endorsed:]
Capt John Smith, with German Passengers from Hamburg.
Feb. 13, 1797.

[List 425] A List of Passengers on board the Brig Peggy
from Amsterdam. Viz. [Feb. 15, 1797.]

Jacob Downe   Wm Stock
Peter Couper   John Preyra

Philad^a 15th Feb. 1797.

David Hardie.

[Endorsed:]
Captⁿ David Harde with German Passengers from Amsterdam. Feb. 15, 1797.

[List 426] [Capt. Joseph Johnston with German Passengers from Amsterdam. Feb. 24, 1797.]*

Lamberdus ⎱ Veldo   Gerrit   ⎱ Neukamp
Susanna   ⎰   Henrica   ⎰
Hermanus   ⎱ Schols   Anna Rippe
Catherina ⎰   Jan   ⎱ Coidou
Johanes   ⎱ Rees   Johanna   ⎰
Catherina ⎰   Carel   ⎱ Flaeg
Casper   ⎱ Sauerland   Regina   ⎰
Maria   ⎰   Henrica   ⎱ Alterman
Engel   ⎤   Sophia   ⎰
Anna   ⎬ Nipman   Peter Schurman
Peeter   ⎦   Renier   ⎱ Geener
Johanna Schiling   Maria   ⎰
Jan   ⎱ Schilling   Otto Kuper
Anna   ⎰   Christian ⎱ Pinsel
Wilhelmus ⎱ Rath   Englia   ⎰
Maria   ⎰

* Endorsement used as heading.

Nicolas ⎤
Dorothea ⎦ During

Geertruy Appeldoorne

Maria   ⎤
Elisabeth ⎬ Moolekamp
Catherina ⎦

Elisabeth Muller

Casper Cause

Wernart ⎤
Philipine ⎦ Wiseman

Everhard Gerdorf

Anna Vos

Philad^a 24th Feb. 1797.

Joseph Johnston.

[List 427] List of Passengers on board Brig^t Fair Hebe, Phinias Eldridge, Master, from Amsterdam. [16th March 1797.]

J. L. Winchins   J. Maria Sara Winchins

Philad^a 16th March, 1797.

Phin^s Eldridge.

[Endorsed:]

Captⁿ Phineas Edridge, with German Passengers from Amsterdam. 16th March 1797.

[List 428] List of Passengers on board the Ship America from Hamburgh, David Hardie, Master. May 4, 1798.

John Hooffman of N. York

Fridrich Montmolling, Philadelpia

Lewis Divernois, from Swisserland

G. J. Farne, from Swisserland

Francis Meissonin   D^o

Miss Fabry, young lady from Swisserland

Francis Sanday, from Swissland

Charles Gaurden   D^o

John Ellice, Phila.

Mathews Weever, d^o

Philadelphia, May the 4th [1798].

David Hardie.

[Endorsed:]

List of German Passengers, arrived in the Ship America, David Hardie, Master. May 4th 1798.

[List 429] List of the German Passengers on board the Ship Pennsylvania, Dav^d Williamson, Master, from Hamburgh. [August 31st 1798.]

Andreas Dotter
Margaretha Elhartin
Fredrick Schwelger
Christian Dᵒ
Johan Henrick Neil
Carl Wilhelm Westpalen
J. F. Sander
Sousanna Fietcherin
Cathrina Franzin
Maria Eliz. Dᵒ
Maria Dᵒ
Johannes Fein
Daniel Lange
Jacob Bonacker
Henrich Reiter
Susanna Dᵒ
Henrich Dᵒ
Frans Bargo
Jacob Philips
Elizabeth Philipsen
Jacob Kelser
Christian Jostedt
Anna Maria Schneiderin
Joh. Henrich Jung
Anna Maria Dᵒ
Jacob Benen
Elizabeth Berner
Emericus Dᵒ
Maria Anna Dᵒ
Johan Wilhelm Berner
Maria Catharina Dᵒ
Bernhard Beigel
Maria Eliz. Dᵒ
Jurgen Henrich Dᵒ
Maria Cath. Tresbachin
Anna Margᵗ Dᵒ
Frans Schutt
Cathrina Dᵒ
Anna Maria Dᵒ
Mannes Lime

Johannes Fiscal
Anna Maria Dᵒ
Johannes Gassauer
Cathrina Dᵒ
Maria Dᵒ
Elizabeth Dᵒ
Peter Dᵒ
Daniel Dᵒ
Elizabeth Beckerin
Johannes Groth
Maria Eliz. Dᵒ
Anna Maria Dᵒ
Anna Eliz. Dᵒ
Johan Jurgen Dᵒ
Johannes Dᵒ
Jacob Winter
Maria Cath. Dᵒ
Anna Margᵗ Volmerin
Maria Cath. Kellerin
Elizabeth Richstein
Johann Philip Dᵒ
Philip Capann
Cath. Eliz. Dᵒ
Joh. Nichˢ Schum
G. C. Lachenmeyer
Joh. Bilderback
Sophia Dᵒ
Johan Kepple
Johann Peter Lach
Maria Eliz. Dᵒ
Anna Maria Tresbachin
Cathrina Dᵒ
Johan August Rothe
John G. Bissen
Johannes Lach
Andreas Somberty
—— in the Cabbin——
Mʳ Philipson
Miss Dᵒ

I certify the within, & above is a true list of the German Passingers, on Board the Ship Pennsylvania, which I command. Chester 26th Aug 1798.

David Williamson.

[Endorsed:]
List of German Passengers arrived in the Ship Pennsylvania, David Williamson, Master, August 31st 1798.

[List 430] List of Passengers on board the Ship Triton from Bremen. Zacharias Spilcker, Master. [Oct. 31, 1798.]

Sebastian Gester —— Mumme
Nicolaus Hake

Philadelphia, Oct. 31, 1798.

Zachs Spilcker.

[Endorsed:]
List of German Passengers, arrived in the Ship Triton. Zacharias Spilker, Master. Novr 1st 1798.

[List 431] List of passengers on board the Brig Pallas, Henry Hutchinson, Master, from Hamburg. [Nov 1st 1798.]

Frederick Henning Stahl   Ferdinand Schmiedt
Anthony Henry Podmann   Christian Holm

Philadelphia, Novembr 1st 1798.

Henry Hutchison.

[Endorsed:]
List of German Passengers, arrived in the Brig Pollas, Henry Hutchinson. Novr 2d 1798.

[List 432] Ship Columbia, Henry Lelar, Master. Dec 19, 1798.

Michael Gurts   Fried. Kaum
Elias Kappeler   John Peter Friedriks
Gerrit Hahn   John Georg Wirth
Samuel Guthle   John Fries
Erhard Koller   John H. Koll

John F. Mensing
John George Kocher
Ant. Engelhard
Mich. Sensowkc
Jacob Bender

Ant. Schade
R. C. Kosterman
John Braschloss
Dan. Backer
Wm. Ten Katen

[Endorsed:]
List of German Passengers, arrived in the Ship Columbia, Henry Lelar, Master. Decr 19th 1798.

[List 433] List of Passengers on board the Ship Fair American from Hamburg. John C. Brevoor, Master. Oct 6, 1799.

Mr John T. Spies
M^s Johanna Peterman & 6 children
Mr Wilhelm Muller
Widow J. G. Frank
Geo. Frank
Johann Geo. Stolle
Elizabeth, Maria & Jacobina Troll

CABIN PASSENGERS

Carl Hopfeldt
Louisa Kenberg
Christian Winckler
Gustaf Heinrich Dalman
Gideon Hellwig
Johan Ludwig Eberhard
Myndert Hinrich Brahms
Johannes Frank

[Endorsed:]
List of German Passengers, arrived in the Ship Fair American, John C. Brevoos, Master. Octr 6th 1799.

[List 434] Names of the Passengers on Board the Boston Packet, Huling Cowperthwait, Master, from Hamburg. Oct. 17, 1799.

George Gotz & his wife
Fred. Böckel & his wife
George Vobell & his wife
Wilhelm Smidt & his wife
David Gentech
Gott. Weidner
Joh. Wassermann
Hen. Beck

John Kurtz
Martin Reif
Hen. Teyen
Jacob Dantzebecker & his wife
—— Beck
—— Beck
—— Beck
H. Musse

John Meyer   —— Möller
Jos. Barthen   Joh. Guillich

Philad^a 17, October 1799.

                              Huling Cowperthwait.

[Endorsed:]
List of German Passengers, arrived in the Ship Boston
Packet, Huling Cowperthwait, Master. Octr 17th 1799.

[List 435] List of Passengers on board the Brig Amiable
Creole, Phinias Eldridge, Master, from Hamburgh. Nov.
19, 1799.

Alloys Miller   Johann Daniel Muller
Christian Frederick Lange   Pierre Cenas
Casper Lange   Gasper Verdal
Sophia St. Emelia Lange   G. W. R. Hogerdorn
Christian Ludwk. Lange

[Endorsed:]
List of German Passengers, arrived in the Brig Amiable
Creole, Phinias Eldrige, Master, Novr 19th 1799.

[List 436] Passengers in the Brig Amiable Matilda,
Michael Burke, Master. [Undated.] *

Daniel Godlob Strabe   Jacob Schwartzstrauber
Daniel Schwartzstrauber   Johannes Dihring

[Endorsed:]
Brig Amiable Matilda, Captn Michael Burk, from Hamburg, 4 passengers.

[List 437] [List of Passengers in the Ship Columbia from
Amsterdam, Captn. William Maley, 149 passengers.]† [Un-
dated.]

---

* This list and five others that follow (Nos. 436–441), all undated, have been
placed here, at the end of the eighteenth century, rather than with the year 1796,
as was done in Vol. XVII of the *Pennsylvania Archives,* second series.
  † Endorsement used as heading.

Hind. Jager	
Catrina Jager	
Gottlieb Jager	
Ferd. Jager	N^{ro} 1
Frantz Jager	
Wilhelmina Jager	
Fred. Wilh. Ibach	
Magdalena Ibach	
Tresia Ibach	
Frantzsisca Ibach	
Gottlieb Ibach	N^{ro} 2
Ferdenand Ibach	
Giedion Ibach	
Justaf Ibach	
Biniamin Hütz	
Margreta Hütz	
Hindraieta Hütz	
Carlina Hütz	
Joh. Peter Hütz	N^{ro} 3
Carl Hütz	
Ab^{rm} Kornbusch	
Joh. Lindeman	
Christian Jeger	
Danil Kühn	
Peter Bond	
Ab^{rm} Wolfers	N^{ro} 4
Peter Horsberg	
Adam Zeiseler	
Engel Tesche	
Catrina Tesche	
Helena Hasenclever	
Peter Heller	N^{ro} 5
Lodewig Estinghausen	
Wilhelm Hemmerichs	
Johannes Mayweg	
Isack Mayweg	
Wilhelm Mayweg	
Wilhelm Drucks	N^{ro} 6
Jacob Henn	
Johannes Bäcker	

Arnold Muller	
Bernadus von Kempen	
Alidar von Kempen	
Elisabeta von Kempen	N^{ro} 7
Raegus von Kempen	
Biniamin Schlieper	
C. Hind. von Lehn	
Carl Ibach	
C. Doretha Ibach	
Fredr. Dort Ibach	
Carl Fred. Ibach	
Carl Lürters	
C. Wilhilmina Lüters	N^{ro} 8
Dorth. Lüters	
Wilhelmina Lüters	
Jana Lüters	
Dort. Drucks	
Wilhelm Hammes	
C. Margreta Hammes	
Abramina Hammes	
Gottlieb Hammes	N^{ro} 9
C. W. Hammes	
Joh. Peter Hammes	
Ab^{rm} Eicher	
Johannes Hammes	
Wilhelmina Hammes	
Carlina Hammes	
Lowisa Hammes	N^{ro} 10
Wilhelm Hammes	
Ab^{rm} Berger	
Arnold Crau	
Wilhelm Berteram	
Margreta Berteram	
Dort Berteram	
Joh. Hiersfeld	N^{ro} 11
Catrina Marg. Hiersfeld	
Gottlieb Kuhler	
Andreas Wilhelm	
An. Catrina Wilhelm	N^{ro} 12
Elisabeta Wilhelm	

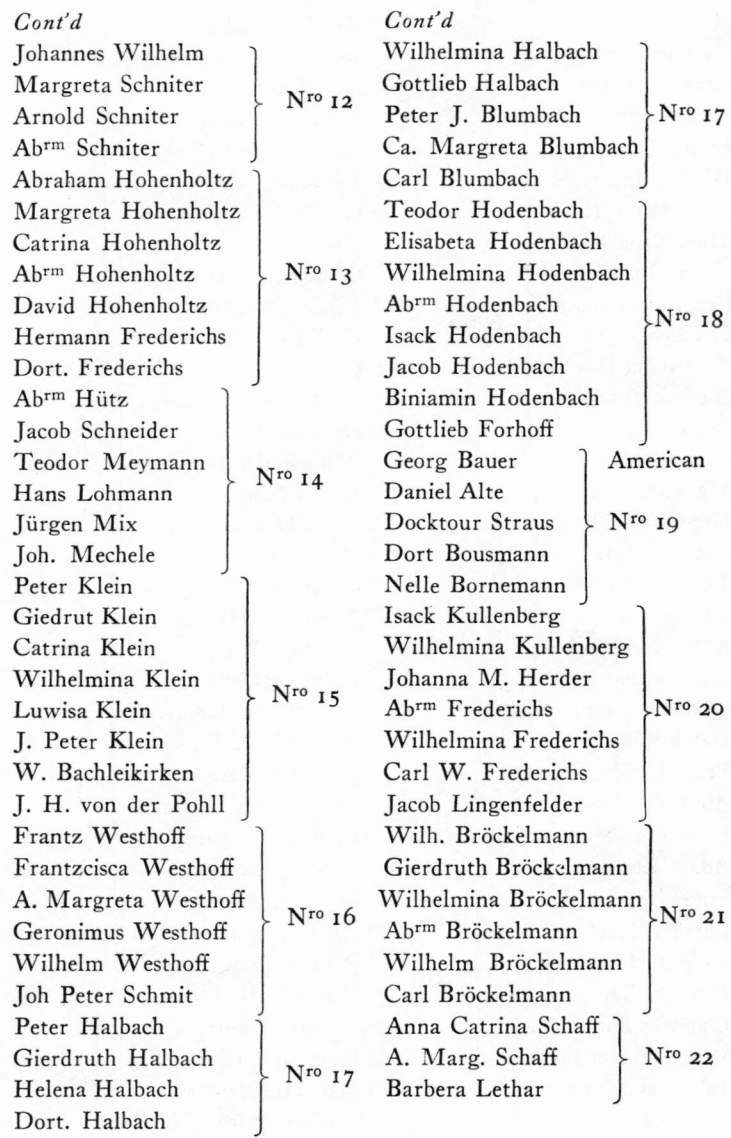

Cont'd

Johannes Wilhelm
Margreta Schniter
Arnold Schniter
Ab^rm Schniter
} N^ro 12

Abraham Hohenholtz
Margreta Hohenholtz
Catrina Hohenholtz
Ab^rm Hohenholtz
David Hohenholtz
Hermann Frederichs
Dort. Frederichs
} N^ro 13

Ab^rm Hütz
Jacob Schneider
Teodor Meymann
Hans Lohmann
Jürgen Mix
Joh. Mechele
} N^ro 14

Peter Klein
Giedrut Klein
Catrina Klein
Wilhelmina Klein
Luwisa Klein
J. Peter Klein
W. Bachleikirken
J. H. von der Pohll
} N^ro 15

Frantz Westhoff
Frantzcisca Westhoff
A. Margreta Westhoff
Geronimus Westhoff
Wilhelm Westhoff
Joh Peter Schmit
} N^ro 16

Peter Halbach
Gierdruth Halbach
Helena Halbach
Dort. Halbach
} N^ro 17

Cont'd

Wilhelmina Halbach
Gottlieb Halbach
Peter J. Blumbach
Ca. Margreta Blumbach
Carl Blumbach
} N^ro 17

Teodor Hodenbach
Elisabeta Hodenbach
Wilhelmina Hodenbach
Ab^rm Hodenbach
Isack Hodenbach
Jacob Hodenbach
Biniamin Hodenbach
} N^ro 18

Gottlieb Forhoff
Georg Bauer   American
Daniel Alte
Docktour Straus
Dort Bousmann
Nelle Bornemann
} N^ro 19

Isack Kullenberg
Wilhelmina Kullenberg
Johanna M. Herder
Ab^rm Frederichs
Wilhelmina Frederichs
Carl W. Frederichs
Jacob Lingenfelder
} N^ro 20

Wilh. Bröckelmann
Gierdruth Bröckelmann
Wilhelmina Bröckelmann
Ab^rm Bröckelmann
Wilhelm Bröckelmann
Carl Bröckelmann
} N^ro 21

Anna Catrina Schaff
A. Marg. Schaff
Barbera Lethar
} N^ro 22

[List 438] A List of Passengers by the Ship Jean, Capt. Daniel McPherson, from Hamburg. [Undated.]

	AGES		AGES
Adolph Hoofenagel	51	George d⁰	1½
Anna Maria, wife	46	Johannas Gordon	37
Anna Barbra	18	Anna Margreta, wife	34
Anna Sabina	16	Anna Margreta [d⁰]	13
Adolph Hoofenagel	13	Elizebath [d⁰]	11
Johannes d⁰	11	Lova [d⁰]	7
John Adam d⁰	8	Johannas [d⁰]	1½
Barbra Elizabeth	6	Johan Andreas Vernike	
Johannas Echart	45	Carol Christian Blume	
Elizabeth d⁰	44	Johan George Vrick	
Anna Sabina [d⁰]	20	Christian Lambe	
Schalota [d⁰]	18	Gotlib Ernst Graff	
Elizabeth [d⁰]	16	Johan Daniel Paulie	
Johannas [d⁰]	14	Hieronimus Nicolas Heilman	
Catrina [d⁰]	12	Carol Beulow his Lady & one son	
Conerada [d⁰]	6	Didrich Beulow & his Ladey	
Justus [d⁰]	5	Mʳ Cyprian Willmer	
Daniel Stenger	40	Christian Nicolas Phemoler	
Anna Sophia, wife	35	Francies Mayerhoof	
Catrina d⁰	15	Peter Malow	
Johannas d⁰	13	Allexander Malow	
Daniel d⁰	9	Mʳ Livingston, a citizen of New	
Fritz d⁰	5	York	

[Endorsed:]
Ship Jane from Hamburg, Captⁿ Daniel McPherson, 51 Passengers.

[List 439] List of Passengers Imported in Ship Nancy, Wᵐ Wallace. [Undated.]

	AGES		AGES
Simon Ideling	27	John Peter	24
Jacob Stinebroff	24	Thomas Paulcher	27
Frederick Tryer	26	Jacob Lassaul	29
Lawrence Klyne	22	Christian Berkman	26
Gasper Hoofman	20	Michael Jacob	20
John Prince	28	John Bedsheller	23
Tobias Hackerman	36	Henry Mire	20

	AGES		AGES
Michael Shole, Senr	63	Philip Trap	23
Michel Shole, Junr	26	Peter Masmer	21
Christopher Mire	17	John Grossnickle	21
Anthony Englebert	27	Francis Hackerman	28
Hendrich Hemper	42	Michael Mire	29
Christian Switzer	20	Martin Mire	23
John Eyhault	39	Martin Springley	36
Hendrick Nikerick	32	George Shewler	30
Jacob Mire	27	Jacob Cloates	22
John Houselbeck	25	William Cerst	27
Nicholas Robertus	29	Philip Bens	27
George Painter	26	Casper Mans	20
John Mire	24	Michael Kemperly	26
George Machly	37	Jacob Beck	25
Aaron Housneck	43	Philip Kevell	27
Jacob Switzer	23	Jacob Frank	30
Nicholas Onas	38	Thomas Rush	20
Joseph Mire	25	John Howes	18
David Shydeaker	24	Jacob Adolph	19
Ulrich Shydeaker	20	Martin Snider	31
Hans Shydeaker	15	Andrew Ringer	17
Jeremiah Rhode	48	Mellcher Bulman	58
Matthias Leazer	24	Jacob Easterly	22
Andrew Kashly	15	John Kowler	16
George Roisler	39	John Kashneate	33
Jacob Reece	49	Jacob Pavelich	28
Matthew Reece	17	Martin Mire	15
John Meyminger	55	Johan Hitsellbeck	36
Michael Robb	16	In all 73	
Yust Terr	23	73 [men] 36.6 [women & chil-	
Philip Hiner	20	dren]	
Conrad Pletz	28		

[Endorsed:]
List of Palatines imported in Ship Nancy, Wm Wallace.

[List 440] [List of Passengers on Board the Ship Patsey Rutledge, who were in the Spinnhouse in Hamburg. Taken in comp^y with the Health Officer & Interpreter. Undated.] *

* Endorsement used as heading.

Mathias Reeper
Charles Erdman Arnt
John Jonica
A. Cath. Longloch
Fred. Albert Faiay
Christian Adler
Jens Jochan
J. Geo. Fred. Hausler, convict
Hance Casper Shoemaker,
  d° branded
Jos. Godfrey Jorgins, convict,
  branded
Christ. Albert, 69 years old,
  branded
John Michael Stephen, convict,
  branded
Eliz. Shucks
Cath. Marg. Joncan
A. Eliz. Bowman
Eleonora Mayer
A. Marg. Erbst
A. Eliz. Hening
Cath. Eliz. Simon
Cath. Cornalia Smith
Maria Eliz. Colinarr
Cath. Shultz

Engel Mada Herman
Christina Gaul
Cath. Marg. Counish
Cath. Marg. Trimbach
Margarite Eliz. Strum
Eliz. Tamnach
Christina Sophia Eckosh
Corlina Sastra
A. Eliz. Miller
Cath. Margaretha Wagner
A. Carolina Simon
Anna Laussin
A. Cath. Mayer
Marg. Nelling
Cath. Marg. Miller
Maria Mannin
A. Sophia Hamerin
A. Cath. Maria Stocks
Maria Buchin
A. Marg. Kochin
Marg. Eliz. Reubin
Anna Mayerin
Eliz. Smith
Dorothea Franzin
Marg. Zimmerman
Catherina Eliz. Meffs

[List 441] Passengers by Snow Industry, from Bremen.
Viz. [Undated.]

William Spickwall, man
Johanna Dinnee ⎫
Anna Maria Holm ⎬ woman
                ⎭

Robert Miller, Master.

[Endorsed:]
Snow Industry, from Bremen, Captⁿ Robert Miller, 3 Passengers.

[List 442] List of passengers on board the Brig Juno, John Philip Albers, Master, from Bremen, Viz. [Feby 25th 1800.]

John Georg Selbert
Barbara Selbert, his wife
Caspar Selbert ⎫
Adam Selbert ⎭
    children of the above
Maria Selbert, sister of J. G. Sel-
bert

Valentin Apple
Margaretha Apple, his wife
Elisabeth Elgedin
Catharine Kochin
John Adam Fuss

[Endorsed:]
List of German Passengers, arrived in the Brig Juno, John
Philip Albers, Master, Feby 25th 1800.

[List 443] List of 16 German Redemptioners on board the
Sc^r David L'Hommedieu from New York, who were pas-
sengers in the Brig Ocean, Cap^n Markau, from Bremen for
Philad^a. Wreckd on Long Island. Consignd to John Miller,
Junr. March 27, 1800.

Henry Schlag
Anne Marg^t Schlag, his wife
Anne Marg. Schlag, daughter
Anne Savine Schlag, idem
Mich^l Schlag, Son
Fred^k Handschuh
Marg^t Handschuh, his wife
And^w Handschuh, their son

Jean Adam Handschuh, d^o
Eliz^a Handschuh, their daughter
Cath^e Handschuh, idem
Guilm^e Handschuh, Son
Mich^l Jordan
Cath^r Jordan, his wife
Valentine Khunrich
Dorethe Khunrich

Philad^a 27 March 1800.

Jno Miller, Jr.

[Endorsed:]
List of German Passengers, arrived on the Brigantine Ocean,
Beren Markau, Master, March 27th 1800.

[List 444] [List of German Passengers, arrived in the Ship
Anna, Jan Jurgens, Master. Aug^st 19th 1800.] *

Joh. Diedr. Nenstiel, with wife &
    4 children
Andreas Nenstiel
Joh. Andr. Mitz

Joach. Friedr. Krickel
Joh. Andr. Maurer, with wife &
    3 children
Hinr. Muller

* Endorsement used as heading.

Carl Sam. Prentzel
Joh. Jac. Walter
Joh. Andr. Schmidt
Franz Schachamayr
Joh. Valt. Unger
Friedr. Dittmer
Joh. David Papst
J. G. D. Fiedler
John Godfrey Daniel
Marcus Jacob
Friedr. Krick
J. C. Hoffmann
Peter Hinr. Ottmer
Pierre P. Ignou, with wife & 2 children
C. T. Hannibal Sulter
Gerh^d. Hinr. Lange
Joh. Ludw. Metsch
Moses Nathan
Abraham Isaac
Ernst Friedr. Schumann
Jonas Isaac
Conrad Reuter
Conrad Weyl
Gottf^d Fichtner, with wife and one child
Rosina Senfen, with her child
Johann Christ. Weise
Mart. E Gottf^d Scheffler
Christ. Heinr. Kuch
Johann. Ramm, with his wife and one child
Joseph Reitzenbohn
Franz Spitzer
Jonas Heinemann, with his wife
Wilhelm Preppernau
Johann Christ. Saltzmann
Carl Ludw. Czolbe
Joh. Fischer
Kauf^m. Isaac Beyfusz

Gottf^d Schafer
Peter Linck
M. J. Ettenhofer
Joh. Jac. Weber
Joh. Marquard
Friedr. Marquard
Johann Seidel
Joh. Heinr. Weber
Carl Friedr. Mercier
Franz Adolph Wilke
Joh. Hen. Schlotke
Joh. Georg Gottf^d Müller
Heinr. Georg Wagner
Carl Fried. Wolm
Joh. Wilh. Walter
Joh. H. Lienau
Christ. Muller
Christ. Ludw. Krieger
Georg Krafft
Joh. Henr. Tieger
Joh. Fried. Hohmann
C. F. Krister
Carl Schlimmer
Valentin Volkel
Louis Volkel
Gottf^d M. Steckmar
J. L. Krinckhorn
J. G. Dolle
Nathan Gerson
J. H. Henning
Christ. Vollmer
Anna Dorothea Klockmann
Christ. Schultz
Joh. Henr. Lange
F. Gottl. Pflug
Johann Pohl
Heinr. Wilhelm Wilking
Johann Jacob Welck
Johann Jacob Halle
Wolf Simon

Jette Mosen
Salomon Jacob
Aron Abraham
Georg P. Heiland, with wife and
three children
Joh. Christ. Petsch
Levy Hirsch
Heinr. Knorre
Joh. Casp. Kolbe
Fried. Augt Schultz, with wife
Joh. Fried Krahl
Abrah. Hertz

Joh. Math. Reich
Joh. Henr. Moller
Joh. Henr. Lapp
Christ. Hülsmann
Michael Pasch

CABIN PASSENGERS

Mr. Louis David Girard
Mr. Joh. Henr. Lange
Mr. Pierre Reaud
Mr. Joh. Carl Hecht.

The above are the Passengers on board the Hamburg Ship
Anna. Commanded by Captain Jurgens.

[List 445] List of Passengers in the Brig Tryphena, Thomas
Arnold, Master, from Amsterdam. [Sept 30th 1800.]

Bapt Loro
Mich. Lagni
J. B. Longenatto
Lucca Messa
Anto. Poggi
B. Mulinari
A. L. Lange
P. J. Priesterback
Jacob Lessie
Ch. Korfes
Hub. Radermacher
J. D. Suer Richd
J. Mehelars

Hendric van Henning, 5 yrs.
Jan Schmidt, Sarah, 3 yrs.
Joh. Bayer
Christfer Rumpth, Sophia 3 y.
Doroth. Eisnin
Marth. Elis. Reistin
Wilhelm Wachterholt
Chrisn. Brandin
M. C. Salion
Maria Leer
T. Van Wyngarde, Peter 6 y.
J. H. Crolus, Henry Fredk.

Philada Sept 30th 1800.

Thomas Arnold.

[Endorsed:]
List of German Passengers, arrived in the Brig Tryphenia,
Thomas Arnold, Master. Sept 30th 1800.

[List 446] Names of the Passengers on Board the Ship
Diana, Wm Hess, Master, from Bremen. [Decbr 3d 1800.]

Eimer Boerman & his wife Anna   Sophia Boerman, sister to Eimer
Catharina & Kichgy Boerman,   Boerman
  children

Philadelphia, Decb^r 3^d 1800.

Wm Hess.

[Endorsed:]
List of German Passengers, arrived in the Ship Diana, William Hess, Master. Novr 3^d 1800. [!]

[List 447] A List of Passengers on board the Brig Venus, from Hamburg, Ja^s Stevenson, Master. [July 3, 1801.]

Taylor White   Henry Keil
William Johnson   Godhart Jaseon & wife
Christian Wiett

Philad^a July 3^d 1801.

Ja^s Stevenson.

[Endorsed:]
List of German Passengers on Board Brig Venus, James Stephenson, Commander, from Hamburg. July 3^d 1801. 6 Passengers.

[List 448] List of Passengers on Board the Brig Delaware from Hamburg. July 11, 1801.

Mr Stinefield   Mr Mehia
Mr Smith   Boy Christian Jones

German Passengers.
Phila^d July 11th 1801.

Ja^s Dunphy.

[Endorsed:]
Brig Delaware from Hamburg. July 11, 1801.

[List 449] List of Passengers of the Ship New York of New York from Hambro, John Seaward, Master. Sept. 8, 1801.

Mr Alexander Latouche   Mr Joachim Green
Mr Georg Erich   Mr Friedrich Kiesling

Mr Peter Schmidt
Heinr. Fortmann
Pieter Sharp
Georg Mecke
Friedrich Schumann
Matthias Kiehn
Joh. Christ Lehmann
Georg Schuster
Carl Schaaf
Friedrich Becher
Maria Becher
Jacob Becher
Johan Becher
Alexander Weber
Anna Weber
Johann Messerschmidt
Conrad Müller
Conrad Weber
Heinrich Rang
Johan Rang
Maria Rang
Jost Rang
Johan Becker
Magdalena Becker
Mattheus Reuter
Anna Reuter

Magdalena Schmitt
Johan Schmitt
Magdalena Schmitt
Johan Pezel
Anna Pezel
Johan Schmitt
Catharina Schmitt
Johan Schmitt
Daniel Spiess
Maria Spiess
Maria Spiess
Anna Spiess
Johan Spiess
Johan Jost Spiess
Wilhelm Spiess
Jacob Schmitt
Catharina Schmitt
Maria Becher
Maria Schmitt
Joh. Christ Schmitt
Anna Schmitt
Catharina Schmitt
Johannes Schmitt
Peter Kollhagen
Friedrich Kleiss

Philadelphia 8th Sept. 1801.

Jno. Seaward.

[Endorsed:]
List of German Passengers, arrived at the Port of Philad^a from Hamburg, in the Ship Newyork, Cap^n. John Seaward. Sepr. 8th 1801. 55 Passengers.

[List 450] Brig Express, Capt Garden, from Rotterdam. Sept. 19, 1801.

Hendrik Sann
Johanna Sann
Johan Pieter Sann
Barnendina Sann
Adam Sann

George Sann
Johanna Sann
Jacoba Sann
Maria Sann
Johanna Sann

[Endorsed:]

List of German Passengers, arrived in the Brig Express, Cap^n Resolve Gardner, from Rotterdam. Septr 19th 1801. 10 Passengers.

[List 451] Passengers in the Brig Molly, Benj^m Huggins, from Hamburgh.

George Frederick Miller,
   wife Margaret & two children

30th Septr 1801, Philadelphia.

B. Huggins.

[List 452] Passengers Names on board the Ship Lavinia, Captn Tristam Gardner, from Hamburg. [Sept. 30th 1801.]

Catharina Wiegand	Martin Föller
Johann Heinr. Fischer	Joh^n Henrich Ungewickell
Christ^n Phillip Beuschel	Gottlieb Boramann
Joh^n Samuel Beech	Willm Mauber

Philad^a Sept 30th 1801.

T^m Gardner, Junr.

[Endorsed:]

List of German Passengers, arrived in the Ship Lavinia, Tristram Gardner, Master, from Hamburg, Sepr 30, 1801. 8 Passengers.

[List 453] List of Passengers on board Der Biedermann. [Novr. 5th 1801.]

Joh. Willhelm Humel ⎤ 1 trunk	Bouchardt Steimetz, 1 trunk
Anna Magaretha Humel ⎦ 1 kit	Frantz Peter Maanke, 1 trunk
Joh. Gotthardt Meyer, 1 trunk	H. C. D. Willhelm Graach, 1 kit

[Endorsed:]

List of German Passengers, arrived at the Port of Philad^a, Ship Bliderman, Capt. Bereson, from Hamburg. Novr. 5th 1801. 6 Passengers.

[List 454] [List of German Passengers, arrived in the Port

of Philad^a in the Brig Polly, Capⁿ Müller, from Hamburg.
March 8th 1802.] *

J. F. Leffler	5 feet 4 inch. high, brown complexion, black hair.
H. Rude	5 feet 6 inch. high, brown complexion, black hair.
J. C. Miller	5 feet 3 inch. high, fair complexion, dark hair.
C. D. Buchholz	5 feet 2 inch., fair complexion, gray hair.
Lewis Combe	5 feet 4, black hair, dark complexion.

NB. All Prussian measure.

[List 455] List of the Passengers on Board the Ship Belvidere, John Dorson, Master, bound to Philadelphia from Amsterdam. Aug. 20, 1802.

NAMES OF PASSENGERS	PASSAGE MONEY	MONEY ADVANCED	TOTAL DEBT
Valentin King, 15 guineas at 12 gulden	fl.180	fl.34.5	fl.214.5 †
Johannes Erbt "	180	22.5	202.5
Michael Kneisel "	180	36.5	216.5
Conrad Kneisel "	180	36.5	216.5
Margareta Mullerin "	180	25	205
Jacob Jung "	180	36	216
Wm Juste "	180	36.5	216.5
Philip Weber "	180	37.5	217.5
Frantz Linde "	180	32.5	212.5
Michael Schäffer "	180	21.10	201.10
Johan Hasselbach "	180	33.10	213.10
Andries Schäffer "	180	20	200
George Jung "	180	40	220
his wife "	180	24	204
Jacob Hoks "	180	34	214
Peter Linnekam "	180	34.10	214.10
Wilhelm Heppel "	180	32.10	212.10
Peter Fratemacher "	180	31.10	211.10
Johan Bucher "	180	16.8	196.8
his wife "	180	16.8	196.8
Carolina Bucherin "	180	16.8	196.8
Rebecca Bekkenbachin "	180	35.10	215.10

* Endorsement used as heading.
† The passage money was figured in Dutch guilders or florins (fl.).

NAMES OF PASSENGERS		PASSAGE MONEY	MONEY ADVANCED	TOTAL DEBT
Jacob Hasselbach	"	fl.180	fl.37.10	fl.217.10
Andries Flick	"	180	33.10	213.10
Christian Acker	"	180	33.10	213.10
Jacob Nell	"	180	35.10	215.10
Margart Hasselbachin	"	180	37.10	217.10
Catharina Hasselbachin	"	180	37.10	217.10
Jacob Jung	"	180	33.10	213.10
his wife	"	180	23.10	203.10
Wilhelm Spies	"	180	37.10	217.10
his wife	"	180	23.10	203.10
Andreas Guttenberger	"	paid 144		
Nicol Held	"	180		180
Wilhelm Stroch	"	180	9.10	189.10
Bernard Krebs	"	180	12.10	192.10
John Adam Rothenmilk	"	180	35.10	215.10
Isaac Kalker	"	180		180
Philip Sauer	"	180	33.10	213.10
Clementz Smeltz	"	180	39.10	219.10
Jacob Beckerbach	"	180	35.10	215.10
George Romer	"	180	33.10	213.10
Anton Schroder	"	180	33.10	213.10
Joseph Völker	"	180	35.10	215.10
Martin Eller	"	180	9.	189.
Moses Wolf	"	180	6.10	186.10
Salomon Joseph	"	180	3.10	183.10
Henr. Pfeffer	"	180	37.10	217.10
Joh. Trauts	"	paid 144		
Joh. Fried. Ulrich	"	180	16.10	196.10
Joh. Bauseman	"	180		180
Johanna Jonin	"	180	12.6	198.6
Joseph Kusett, paid to the capt.		144		
Andr. Nase D° D°		144		
Christ Taarts		180		180
Philip Taarts		180		180
Johannes Krautman		180	33.10	213.10
Valentin Krautman		180	35.10	215.10
Joh. Lud. Renne paid fl.66		168		102
Johanna Manfrez		180		180
Wilhelmina Punnekach		180		180

NAMES OF PASSENGERS	PASSAGE MONEY	MONEY ADVANCED	TOTAL DEBT
Joh. Öllich	paid fl.144		
Fried. Ziegler	paid 144		
Hend. Burkhard	180		180
Wilhelm Harms	180	6.10	186.10
Died. Koch	180	3.18	183.18
Hend. Jacob	180	9.12	189.12
Fred. Adolf	180	9.10	189.10
Johannes Faust	180		180
Philip Thorter	180		180
Godfried Massenger	180		180
Joh. Carl Schadel	180	6	186
Hend. Otterste	180	6	186
Jacob Valet	180	6	186
Fried. Michte	180	6	186
Wilhelm Kreis	180		180
Adam Miller	180		180
Johan Duckhardt	180		180
Hend. Drister	180	14	194
Frans Tilbrey	180	16	196
A. Durheimer	not paid 144		
John Riebel (Newlander)	free		
his wife	paid 144		
	fl.14460	fl.1497.5	fl.14739.5

[Endorsed:]
List of German Passengers on board Ship Belvedere, John Dorson, Master, from Amsterdam, arrived at the Port of Philadelphia, August 20th 1802. 86 Passengers.

[List 456] List of Passengers who are still on the Urania. [August 26th 1802.]

Andreas Totter	Johann Ziegeler
Anna Maria Totter, née Röhrig	Johann Ziegeler
Johann Adam Totter	Anna Margaretha Ziegeler
Christiana Totter	Catharina Ziegeler
Carolina Friderica Limbertin	Hinrich Walter
Catharina Weissmantel	Joseph Brand

Sebastian Reinig
Nicolaus Scheel
Johann Georg Müller
Johan Caspar Wenzell
Peter Selpert
Rosina Selpert, née Roth
Hanne Eva Selpert
Jacob Selpert
Johannes Hofmann
Magdal. Hofmann, née Brückner
Johann Georg Hofmann
Christina Hofmann
Anna Sabina Hofmann
Jost Heinrich la Roche
Anna Maria la Roche, née Formaldinn
Nicolaus la Roche
Johann Fritzius
Gertruda Fritzius, née Meinhardinn
Johann Fritzius
Conrad Fritzius
Margaretha Fritzius
J. G. Fritzius
Eva Cath. Fritzius, née Jordan
Nicolaus Leibold
Anna Cathar. Leibold née Heinicken
Johann Georg Leibold
Elisabeth Zehnern
Catharina Zehnern, née Steinbach
Elisabeth Zehnern

Johann Schüssler
Margarat Elis. Schüssler, née Werner
Anna Barbara Schüssler
Anna Martha Schüssler
T. G. Barthelemy
Barthel Schlag
Mariane Schlag, née Barthelemy
Georg Friedrich Schlag
Johannes Schlag
Johannes Kaufmann
Hinr. Kaufmann
Conrad Euler
Johannes Reinig
Maria E. Reinig, née Maulinn
Johann Adam Müller
Anna Mar. Müller, née Kesslerinn
Anna Maria Müller
Johann Müller
Johann Röhrig
Anna Margar. Röhrig, née Birksin
Jacob Euler
Michael Wirth
Eva Wirth, née Künreich
Catharina Wirth
Adam Schmidt
Margaretha Jarges, née Scheit
Catharina Müllerin
Anna Margaretha Mullerin
Jacob Müller
Traugott Jarges

[Endorsed:]

List of German Passengers on Board the Brig Urania, Captain W^m. Geersen, from Bremen, arrived at the Port of Philadelphia, August 26th 1802. 71 Passengers.

[List 457] List of Passengers on B^d the Ship Pennsylvania from Hamburg. Capt. Peter Yorke. Septr 7, 1802.

L. A. Hecksher
Fr. Berg
Charles Seller
John Muller
Henry Dornham
Herman Machol
Jos A. Manguzer
Peter von Metz
Philip Bloom

Lewis Snell
Mrs. Snell
Lewis Snell, boy
Johst Snell, boy
Anna Sophia Snell
John Reamer
Mrs. Reamer
Henry, a boy

Philadelphia Septr 7th 1802.

Peter Yorke.

[Endorsed:]
List of German Passengers, arrived at the Port of Philad^a
in the Ship Pennsylvania from Hamburg, Peter Yorke, Master,
Septr. 7th 1802. 17 Passengers.

[List 458] List of the Passengers in the Brig Maria, Capt
David Hardie, Master, from Bremen to Philadelphia. Oct. 5,
1802.

[NAME AND OCCUPATION]	AGES	[NAME AND OCCUPATION]	AGES
Siemon Christian Bolze, barber	22	Zacharias Ullrich, none	52
John W. Friedr. Stedler, tailor	20	Gerhard Henry Burger, none	34
John Friedr. Wolleben, none	26	Christoph Teichmuller, farmer	20
Lorenz Spillner, none	18	Margaretha Zimmermann,	
Friedr. Lasch, none	15	none	18
Caspar Erb, farmer	19	John Henry Kerstenbrug, none	44
Elisabeth Fischer	41	Siemon Samhard *	
John Fischer, Sr. coachman	40	Amalia Do	
John G. Fischer, weaver	17	Henrich Samhard	
Catharina Fischer	11	Louise Do	
Cristian W. Fischer	2	Christ. Oppermann, tailor	45
Jacob Anspach, none	56	Cath. Do	26
Henrich Ehlers, farmer	25	Conrad Do	15
Andreas Eckhard, none	28	Elisabeth Do	13
John Willers, none	26	Maria Do	4
Daniel Wiedemann, none	26	Conrad Schaefer, butcher	31
John Henry Weitzel, none	18	Elisabeth Do	26
John Hanfling, farmer	45	Louise Do	5

* Paid their passage in full.

[NAME AND OCCUPATION]	AGES
John Schaefer	2
Charles Denecke, millright	47
Elisabeth Denecke	48
Anna Martha Dᵒ	21
John Christoph, Dᵒ, millright	20
Catharina Dᵒ	13
Henriette Dᵒ	11
Jacob Nuckell, farmer	40
Maria Cath. Dᵒ	14
John Friedr. Dᵒ	13
Christian Dᵒ	7
John Dᵒ	4
Andreas Diederich, cooper	20
William Schau, tailor	36
Charles Guth, gardner	35
Nicolaus Helmstead, none	26
Adam Rodelsberger, turner	21
Henry Heitgress, baker	20
John Andrew Holtz, none	45
Friedr. Andrew Holtz	15
Anthony Schmith, barber	19
Albert Pisch, waiter	23
Charles Schmith, barber	19
Charles Peterson, waiter	21
Andrew Hister, none	23

[NAME AND OCCUPATION]	AGES
Henry Schroeder, farmer	23
John Danser, none	25
John Andrew Baker, soap-boiler	21
Joh. Burke, barber	33
Gottfried Sailor, cooper	28
Christopf Ludʷ Notnagel, shoemaker	19
Charlotte Elers	26
George Schmith, tailor	46
Anne Cath. Dᵒ	32
Maria Dᵒ	13
Johanne Dᵒ	5
Elisabethe Dᵒ	1
Henrich Kayser, gardner	45
John Begener, stonecutter	22
Henrich Nebeling, turner	45
Anne Cath. Dᵒ	47
Samuel Dᵒ	10

CABIN PASSENGERS

William Geisse
Frantz William Geisse
Doctor C. Christ. Gerlach and
   wife Christine

Philadelphia, October the 5ᵗʰ 1802.

David Hardie.

[Endorsed:]
List of German Passengers on Board Brigantine Maria,
Captain David Hardie, from Bremen, arrived at the Port of
Philadelphia, October 5ᵗʰ 1802. 81 Passengers.

[List 459] [List of German Passengers arrived at the Port
of Philadᵃ in Ship Devotion, Captain Wᵐ Waters, from
Amsterdam. October 6th 1802.] *

Peter Orellig
Fredk. Brodbeck

Carl Theodor Breuning
Joh. Melch. Trimple

* Endorsement used as heading.

Joh. Jac. Schiser
Joh. Schafer, his wife and child
Christian Fred. Stanger & daughter
Joh. Fred. Volck
Wilh. Weinel
Peter Traut
Walter Kewitz
Joh. Horn
Daniel Toller
Joh. Litzemberger
Jac. Geissler
Casp. Coenr. Ludwig
Heinr. Dietz
Hein. Vinct. Ludwig
Andreas Zemba
Martin Scham
Christian Schnitzel
Christian Usenberg
Heinr. Bentz
George Jos. Seil
Johs. Jas. Luckler
Heinr. Israel
John Geo. Kuster
John Balth. Werlin
Joh. Geo. Kler
John Tamlong
Hernie Guntrum
Joh. Gott¹ Wils. Hunter
Georg Fred. Rachel
Joh. Chri. Brenner
Heinr. Bortheld Bohrz
Phil. Jacob Wolsey
Augᵗ Orth
Adam Weiltz
Johann Michl Geisendorfer
George Michˡ Lorentz
Joh. Berkenhauer
George Adam Gentle
Joh. Muller

Martin Engel
Joh. Schnitzel
Jacob Brodbeck
Frantz Gittinger
John Mumm
Jacob Dupuit
Neck. Peters
Casper Graft
Wilch. Heinr. Scriba
Heinr. Kleyn
Joh. Beirt
Fredᵏ Martin Reis
Joh. Joah Wideling
John Diet. Wideling
Christian Hoffman
Philip Chr. Greyder
John Gat. List
Casper Hanch
Joh. Geo. Hickler
George Leonh. Schaffer
George David Hartman
Frantz Schnitter
Jan Van Brink
Joh. Goft Arnold
Joh. Dav. Kaufman
Turkis Hattelsman
Wilh. Hassel
Georg Jacob Hassel
Joh. Jacob Winkebah
Joh. Brukhafer
Joh. Geo. Kellner
John Fredᵏ Schober
Isaac Vorman
Chr. Kum
Jacob Swever
Geo. Heil
Jan. De Bert
Philip Burke
Natye Alters
Fred. Wilch. Kopper

Joh. Veil

Peter Hargel & wife Maria

Jacob Storm, wife & four child[r].

Medestus Schmidt & wife

Joh. Georg Drufild

Theobald Litchtemberger

Andreas Simon

Jacob Weigand

Gottl. Glose

Albert Kergar

Benjamin Hahn

Joh. Heinr. Ott

Jac. Fred. Henne

Joh. Fred. Tranch

Joh. Euselin

Isaac Wilch. Wolete

Fred Voght

Heinr. Meyr

Fred Wilch. Grosz

Georg Wilch. Lutze

August Gerke

Ulf. Stroemberg

Balth. Mallerchon

Nicola De Val

Christian Haar

Anton Ternos

Mathias Thomas

Peter Noll, his wife & five child[r].

Georg Rhan, his wife & five child[r].

Cath. Ebelin & two children

Heinr. Schutter, his wife & four child[r].

Nicolas Weinert, wife & two child[r].

Dorothea Neithman

Ernestine Weinert

Agnes Konrin

Barbara Mackin

Arthar Ebelin

Anna Laube

Jan Dirk Benjwort

Cath. Wohnfiedt

Maria Aul

Elizabeth Van Ahlen

Jacob Bul, his wife & three child[r].

Susanna Van Busen

P. Wilch. Krugman

Elisa Grotnover

Christ[n] Flick

Benjamin Siloz

Johndre Welzet

Philip Hassinger

Franck Vellin

Joh. Schiffeld

Jacob Stein

Jos. Kuhns

Joh. Fred. Schick

Francis Limtich

Andreas Schreher

Adolf Katterfeld

Carl Ludw. Wischneske

Leonh. Gunter

Martin Lanbe

Jacob Mich

Wilh. Fager

Jacob Gagel

Coenir Hoenig

Joh. Berg

Jacob Schwartz

Jacob Becker

Fredk. Wilh. Seibald

Jacob Bauer

Jacob Hachstors

Johannes Pfeau

Jannett De Viz

Susanna Stein

Peter L. Freidersdorf

Martin Zink

186 passengers

[List 460] Report of Alien Passengers on board the Hamburgh Ship Juno, of which H. H. Wolters is Master, arrived at the Port of Philadelphia in the State of Pensilvania, on the 6 Day of Oct^b 1802, from Hamburg.

J. Breithaupt, aged 22 years, born in Saxony, merchant, middle sized, round face, blue eyes, common nose, dark brown hair.

Erich Tants, aged 30 years, born in Hanover, farmer, long and strong, fresh faced, blue eyes, sharp nose, yellow hair, well shaped otherwise.

Herm. H. Wolters.

[Endorsed:]

List of German Passengers, arrived in the Ship Juno, Cap^n Herman H. Walter, from Hamburg, October 6th 1802. 2 Passengers.

[List 461] List of Passengers p^r the Ship Tom, Capt F. P. C. Permeir, Master, from Hamburgh, arrived Oct. 12, 1802.

Johann Philip Schnell
Jacob Stacher & wife
Johan Schneider & wife
Anna Elizabeth Baldt
Johannes Klippert & wife, did not come in the ship
Frederick Knuppel & Chris^n Klippert
C. Aeric Klippert
Henry Christ^n Klippert
Johann Geo. Stertzing & wife and Jost Henrich, small child
Debus Baldt & wife & small child
Johannis Volckel and wife
Maria Magdalena Schmidt
Elizabeth Becker
Samuel Hiller
Johannes Gessener & wife
Anne & Catharine Gessener
Johann Henrich & Louisa
Maria Elizabeth
Johan Geo. & Johan Jost

Peter Moller & wife
Geo. Christian Burger & wife
Anna Maria
Anna Martha & Johannes
Johan Henrich Grupe
Anthoni Rath
Anna Margaretta Grosien
Johan Matheas Schneider
Johan Henrich Schneider
Anna Catharina Schneider
Ludwig Schneider & wife
Elizabeth & Catharine
Johann Heinrich & Johannes
Johan George Reymann
Johan Henrich Gessener & wife
Johan Jost & Johann Henrich
Johann Christ [Gessener]
Catharina & Christina
Johann Jost Schnell & wife
Anna Elizabeth [Schnell]
Johann Jost Schneider & wife
Elizabeth

Jost Henrich Henchell
Johann Conrad Ritter & wife
Henrich Gotze & wife
Henrich & Wilhelm Gotze
Johann Geo. Hohmann
Philip, their son
Johann Durfeldt
Kasemir Hesse
Margaretta Schneider

Maria Elizabeth Schneider
Dirck Gossen
David Thimm
Gerhard Wieler
Johann Dridger
Johann Gundelach
Johann Gotfried Bosse
Samuel Stob
Valtin Wahm

Making in the whole 87.

[Endorsed:]
List of German Passengers, arrived the Port of Philad[a] in the Ship Tom, Capt. Francis Peter Christian Permer from Hamburg. October 12th 1802. 87 Passengers.

[List 462] List of Passengers p[r] the Ship Jacob, Capt[n] John Moore, from Amsterdam, consigned to Wharton P. Lewis. Nov. 15, 1802.

Hartman Neeff
George Chr. Wagely
George Lindberger
—— Lowiery
Peter Endey
Joseph Thup
Jacob Urban Weyts
Henry Reuter
John Meyer
Caspar Zweigele
William Klief
Jacob Scheibe
H. Myer
Michael Harg
George Vitz
Christian Kroh
Henry Christ. Martin
Benjamin Terry
Martin P. Wachter
John Henry Giese

John Gottfred Geyer
John Adam Herer
—— Wiesenback
—— Wiesenback
—— Wiesenback
Dieterson Sommer
Wilhelmine Sommer
Jacob Fredrick Boehmer
Peter R. Olgaate
Gievan Gaeome Olgaate
Martin Hartey
—— Antoniede
Henry Jansen
John Eckstein & wife
John Leder
John Peter Alls. Soltzer
Anna L. Leinkuhl
John Wolfgang Staal
Fred[k] Hellwig
John Fred[k] Steysemann

Jacob Fred^k Meyer
Charles Storll
Herman Crul
Mich^l Meuliman
John Holler
August John
Samuel Booher & wife
Antoni Ringold
Joseph Mellman
Philip Mergether
John Michael Sebald
Charles Bookenhagen
Henry Myer
Mathias Toon
Lona van Eonsonn
Henry Suchnitz
John Buchmann
Matth^s Lambrechts
Isaac Jacobs
Hector Klein & wife
John E. Sewening
Salomon Philip
John Henry Pickel
John Henry Schultz
Joseph Rune
Abraham Gometz Palyetso
J. D. Daniel
Henry Muller
William Jansen
Niclaas Schipper
Henry Batmann
Maria F. Fick
John Koch
Frederick Unguer
—— Bergmann
August David Ehrick
Jacob Leeber
Frantz Joseph Dierchs
Johanna Steiner
Gottlieb Snyder

Johanna de Neith
John Henry Pohn
Fred^k Gessner
Chr. Emanuel Vogele
Herman Runkhorst
J. Eberhard Klymar
Conrad Kramer
G. Reyntzer
Willhelmina van Gieler
Gertruit Everhauser
Andrew Looman
—— Eller
Jacob David
John Paul
G. K. Gross
Anton K. Rook
Anna Schelvieck
Frantz Roier
William Melius
Philip Kuhner
George Fred^k Pabst
Anthony Nagel
Henry Toking
Jacob Gresemeyer
Martin Ombony
Christ. Henry Denn
F. C. Daneger
Michael Stiezel
Frederick Myer
Philip Van Zypher and wife
B. Hamer
Charles Lautiere
Maria Iannphe Lautiere
George Lauer
—— van Zurdiogh
Pierre Moutermann
John Wolters
William Driesman
Peter Zieserson
Antonie Roemer

Teri Isaace
W. J. Lampas
Paul Hoeflick
John Zeitler
Chas. Bachman
R. F. Kniper
Jacob Backer
John Crey Runk
Philip Toll
John Leander
John Decker
Casper Ross
Gerret Ross
John Andrew Marlack
—— Hemeleyk
J. G. Grievogel
J. F. Grievogel
Maria Holeman
Mertje Koppe

Frantz Burbarth
Sebastian Herman
Carolina Scholtmann
Naatge Kıoon
Jansey Nebling
Chr. Nothengsieler
F. Raner
F. Leesenberg
—— Vandenburg
George Schmoltz
Peter Meng
Paul Boysobo
George Dill
Henry Kurt
Engelbrecht Schierbaum
G. F. Boyer
Chaˢ Clisore
W. Neotvogel
Caroline Lukenberg

Total 161, one died.

John Moore.

[Endorsed:]
List of German Passengers, Arrived at the Port of Philadelphia, in Ship Jacob, John Moore, Commander, from Amsterdam. Philadᵃ November 17ᵗʰ 1802. 161 Passengers.

[List 463] List of Passengers on board the Brig Union, Jonas Warren, Master, from Hamburg. [November 22, 1802.]

John Dandelot
Charles Weymann
Jacob Keller

Moses Jacobs
James Wagner

Philadelphia 22ᵈ November 1802.

Jonas Warren.

[Endorsed:]
List of German Passengers, arrived on the Brig Union,

Cap^n James Warren, from Hamburg, at the Port of Philad^a
November 22^d, 1802. 5 Passengers.

[List 464] List of Passengers on Board the Ship Traveller,
Captain George Billups, from Amsterdam. June 22, 1803.

Hans Adam Sallete	Martin Keller
Elisabeth Sallete	Eva Keller
Heinrich Sallete	Martin Keller
Anna Barbara Sallete	Helena Keller
Anna Maria Sallete	Henerich Keller
Elisabeth Sallete	Anna Maria Keller
Hans Adam Salate	Wernard Schop
Frederick Sallate	Anna Schop
Ursala Sallete	Christoph Schop, 11 y^r
Dorcas Rude	Anna Schop, 8 y^r
Elisabeth Rude	Johannes Weber
Friederick Rude	Hans Adam Weirtz
Dorus Rude	Margareth Weirtz
Johannes Rude, 12 y^r	Heinrich Weirtz
Johann Jacob Rude, 10 y^r	Heinrich Schop
Elisabeth Rude	Ursula Schop
Barbara Rude, 13 y^r	Jacob Schop
Heinrich Rude	Hans Jacob Buser
Maria Rude	Barb. Buser
Rummeyer Reyenhause	Johannes Rolle
Magdalena Reyenhause	Jacob Rolle
Hans Jacob Tounnen	Jeronimus Rolle
Anna Tounnen	Ulrich Wagenaar
Martin Tounnen	Andreas Wagenaar
Trina Tounnen	Johannus Schude
Heinrich Lotze	Martin Buser *
Elisabeth Lotze	Martin Tuchter *
Heinrich Lotze	Fredirick Tounner *
Friederich Moller	Heinrick Kreyeveller
Hans Jacob Reyginaas	Nicolaus Snyder
Barbara Reyginaas	Hans Jacob Kriller
Hans Jacob Reyginaas	Christian Hagelaar
Elisabeth Reygenaas, 13 y^r	Fritz Rude
Trina Reygenaas, 12 y^r	Barbara Weber
Christoffel Reyginaas, 9 y^r	Heinrich Lutenecker *

Peter Sichmund, cook
Chatarina Sichmund
Johann Sichmund
Carl Henristo
Garret Hienrich Teyle
Johann Martin Eitel
Barend Brunder
Christ Fried. Bozito
Johann Stortz
Philip Heird
Joh Fr. Bach
Fried. Becker
Carl Jacob Beinarde
T. M. Betist
Philip Heterish
Barand Minne
Joh. Jac. Theimser
F. L. Reineke
Joh. Carl Crombholts *
G. L. Schelfer
Rud. Reidbrock
Joh. W. Kleist
Casper Heintzler
Laurentz Kirteling
Frants Joseph Bince
Joh. Christ. Ehrenfreid Locknill
Frants Pott
Cath. Pott
Joh. Fry

F. Nestler
Partricius Abt Sager
Philip Krum
Nicolaus Klyn
Everen Degenfield
Georg Baner
Georg Reichmann
Geirts Lieve Borts
Joh. F. Philipson
J. Ch. Gerkels
C. F. Schusler
Johanna Jacoba Lindrot
Peter Christiaan
Fr. Glockner
Joh. Th. Zunein
Joh. And. Kliberg
Joseph Stop
Gerret Krugh
Barthold Laar
Jacob Heyberger
Jacob Harsel & his Wife & two
 Children
Johann Anton Schreuder
Johanne Bursch
Johannes Martins
Engeline Gesine Brourver
Willem Roelof Brourver
Nancy Barlles

Memorandum:

The five Passengers in the foregoing List marked thus * did not come on board the Ship.

George Billups.

[Endorsed:]

List of German Passengers who arrived at the Port of Philad^a in the Ship Traveler, Cap^n George Billups, from Amsterdam. June 22^d 1803. 137 Passengers.

[List 465] List of the Passengers on Board the Ship Charlotte, Whereof Thomas Horton is Master, from Hamburg, Septr 5, 1803.

CABIN PASSENGERS

Adam Drocker

Johannes Glaucer, wife and two children

STEERAGE PASSENGERS

Ludwig Harpell, wife and five children

Frederick Harpell, wife and four children

George Frittz, wife and one child

Peter Smith

Frederick Seller

Christian Estricker, wife and four children

Christian Raw

John Burkolt

Conrad Wilpley

Alias Danhaur

Christian Keane

George Cook and wife

Martin Wilpley

Christian Wilpley

George Neysinger

George Simberman

George Rickell

Jacob Wiker

Peter Hartline

Adam Laybolt

Johannes Bandele

Johan Riley

Godleip Schwarts

Matthews Prizer

Hendrick Bender, wife and one child

Conrad Cabell

Wilhelm Mardoff

George Striker

George Dippele

Wilhelm Banghirt

Henry Jordan

Christopher Koffman

John Wilt

Jacob Nestle

Jacob Poorbalt

Christian Poorbalt

Christopher Princekoffer

Jacob Shine

Christian Koffman

Wilhelm Woolf

Johan Estricker

Frederick Rickell

Frederick Cunsman

Martin Fullbrake

Conrad Blank

Bernard Horgg

Gabriel Englehart

Peter Hausenbeck

Johan Harm

Tobias Swink

Christopher Apell

Charles Straup

Martin Jacobson

Peter Byder

Johan Peterson

Frederick Keppell

John Rockholt

Henry Lavenfort, wife and two children

Christian Gaadyard

John Danhaur

Johan Riddle

Christian Vandell and

Jacob Poies, wife and three children

Ninety Six Passengers

[Endorsed:]

List of German Passengers, arrived at the Port of Philad^a,

in Ship Charlotte, Tho[s] Horton, Commander, from Hamburgh, Sept[r] 5th 1803. 102 Passengers.

[List 466] List of the Passengers on board the Ship Fortune, Caleb Earl, master, from Hamburg. Sept. 8, 1803.

N[o] 1 Joh[n]. Heinr. Fried. Thym
2 Jacob Kohl
3 Joh[n]. Benj[n] Zeibig
4 Joh[n] Christ[n] Danicke
5 Joseph Niwatel
6 Fried[k] Tierking
7 Joh[n]. And. Carpo
8 Christian Kuntz
9 Hans Gath
10 Elias Hertz
11 Johannes Seip
Anna Catharina do, his wife
Anna Catharina do ⎫
Johannes do ⎬ children
Johann Peter do ⎭
12 John George Bohm
Margaretha C. Seipen, do, his wife
Joh[n]. Peter, his son
13 Johann Vulgarn
14 Leopold Muller
15 Ellinger Motig
16 Franz Konig
18 Peter Muller
Anna Catharina, his wife
Martha Wilhelmina ⎫ children
George ⎭
19 Heinr. Conrd. Her[n]. Schrader
20 Joh[n]. Christ[n]. Wilh[n]. Jager

21 Arnold Hesse
Maria Margaretha, his wife
Eberhard ⎫
Christoph ⎬ children
Catharina ⎪
Johannes ⎭
22 Adam Seip
Jacobine do, his wife
Joh[n] Fried[k] ⎫ children
Albertus ⎭
23 Leopold Rudolph
Anna Catharina, his wife
Anna Elisabeth ⎫
Caspar ⎬ children
Anna Maria ⎪
Maria Catharina ⎭
24 Jacob Friesen
25 Johannes Gerke
Anna Maria, née Bunkerdren, his wife
Maria Gertrut ⎫
Anna Maria ⎬ children
Johannes ⎪
Marianne ⎭
26 George Ludwig Althaus
Christina, his wife with one child
27 George W[m]. Reimschneider
28 Maria Schutter ⎫ two sisters
Elizabeth Schutter ⎭
30 Just. Heinr. Holdinghausen

George, do., his son

32 George And^r. Steidelmuller

33 Carl Baumgarten

34 Christian Hinze

35 Friedrich Kuntze

36 Johannes Wetter

37 Jacobus Han
Maria Gertrude, née
Gerke
Mathias Han ⎱
Anna Catharina Han ⎰
children

38 Joachim Heinr. Maack

39 Gottlieb Nitscko

41 Fried^k. Hupfenstiel
Maria Elisabet, his wife
Johann Jost, their son

42 Joh^n Kraff Goebels
Magdelena, his wife

43 Johannes Franck
Magdelena, his wife

44 Hinrich Bode
Louise, his wife

45 Joh^n Hinr. Franck
Louise ⎫
Joh^n Ludwig ⎬
Maria Elizabeth ⎭
children

46 Joh^n Hinr. Frank
Catharina, his wife

47 Jurgen Schneider
Gerdruth, his wife
Jacob ⎫
Johannes ⎬children
Anna Elisabeth ⎪
Catharina ⎭

48 Louise Schneidern
Anna Margaretha, her
sister

49 Joh^n. Willh^m. Roth

Catharina, his wife

50 Johannes Debes
Rosina, his wife
Freiderica ⎫
George Heinrich ⎬
Maria Catharine ⎭
children

51 Joh^n. Jurg^n. Weber
Maria Elisabeth, his wife
Maria Magdalene ⎫
Johan Jurgen ⎬
Wilh. Christian ⎭
children

52 Elias Kirschtein
Catharina Sneider, his
bride

53 Jost Berchelbach
Christina Imhofin, his
bride

54 Ludwig Richstein

55 Heinr Kramer
Maria Gert^{de} Webern,
his bride

56 Jurgen Kessler

57 Joh^n Philip Lange
Maria Gertrude, his
mother

58 Johannes Martin
Anna Elis^h Schmidtin, his
bride

59 Joh^n. Jost Roth
Louise Rodepiller, his
wife
John Hinrich ⎫
Ludwig ⎬ children
Fritz ⎪
Herman ⎭

60 Joh^n. Jost. Rodepiller
Catharina, his wife
Maria Elisa ⎱ children
Anna Elise ⎰

61 Magdalena Weilin
    Jacob Weil, her brother
62 Hinrich Boden
63 Hinrich Blumenstiel
64 John. George Afterbach
65 John. Danl. Eckel
66 Johannes Weiss
    Christina, his wife
67 Joh Christ Weber
68 Friedk Messerschmidt
    Maria Elisa, his wife
    Maria Elisa, his daughter
69 Jers. Messerschmidt
    Johannes   ⎤ his brothers
    Joh Hinrich ⎦
70 Carle Buck
    Anna Maria Buckin
    T. Weber, a child
    Wilhelne Buckin
71 Ludwig Schmidt
    Bernhardt   ⎤
    John. Christn. ⎦ his brothers
    Johannes
    Anna Maria Elisa ⎤
    Dorothea   ⎦ his sisters
72 John. Danl. Pfeiffer
73 Wilhelm Saure
    Anna Catharine, his wife
    his children:
    Henrietta Friderica
    Anna Maria
    Elisabeth
74 John. Ludw. Bremer
    Maria Cathna, his wife
    Catharina Elisa ⎤
    Catharina   ⎥ chil-
    Joh. Ludwig   ⎥ dren
    Anna Elisa   ⎦
75 Joh. Hinr. Schmidt
    Catharina, his wife

Ludwig   ⎤
Johannes   ⎥
Anna Catharina ⎦ children
76 Joh. George Bremer
    Maria Elisa, his wife
    John. Peter ⎤
    Joh. George ⎥ children
    Anna Elisa   ⎥
    Anna Maria ⎦
77 Gertrud Jacobs   ⎤
    Matthias Jacobs ⎦ brother & sister
78 Johannes Rischstein
    Louise, his wife
    Catharina Elisa ⎤
    John. Jacob   ⎥
    Johannes   ⎥ children
    Christiana   ⎥
    John. Jost   ⎦
79 Catharina Elisa Diesbach
    Anna Elisa Diesbach, her child
80 Anna Elisab. Groth
    Jacob Spies, a child
81 Peter Otto
    Cath. Elisa Frarikin, his bride
82 Michel Berger
    Sybilla, his wife
    Conrad   ⎤ children
    Anna Maria ⎦
83 Joh. Gottlieb Schlichteweg
84 Victor de Ville
    Elizabeth, his wife
84 John. Gottfd Newmann
86 Joh. Conrd. Schaul
87 François Serrurier
88 Johan Junkhaus

[Endorsed:]

List of German Passengers, Arrived in Ship Fortuna, Caleb Earl, Master, from Hamburgh, at the Port of Philadelphia. September 8th 1803. 202 Passengers.

[List 467] Names of Passengers who arrived here with the Brigg Urania, Captn Wilh^m. Geersen, from Bremen.* Oct. 3, 1803.

Hermann Sammler, with 2 children
Mathias Zacharias
Johann Georg Kraul
Johann Jost Feyring
Reinhard Drescher
Catharina Jungerin
Johann Daniel Born
Casp^r Lorenz, with wife & 3 children
Joseph Bubeck, with wife & 4 children
Dorothea Ulrich, with 3 children

[Endorsed:]

List of German Passengers, arrived at the Port of Philad^a, Wm Geersen, Commander, from Bremen, in the Brig Urania, October 3^d 1803. 24 Passengers.

[List 468] A List of Cabin Passengers on Board Ship Canton, Thos. Wills, Master, from Amsterdam. October 7, 1803.

Mr Prediger & sister
Mrs Prediger, wife
Mr Schryver
Mr Everts & 2 servants
Mr Teleken & servant
Mr Pletts & wife
Mr Boon
Mr Van Enst & clark
Mr Beeresteen
Mr Roberts & 2 little bros.
P. F. C. Haller
G^o Rap
C. Muller
G^o Myer
C. Walker
F. Walker
J. Smith
F. Ely
―― Jasper
Jon. Rap
Mr. Prediger's man
Black Gridle

Philad^{ia} 7, October 1803.

Thos. Wills.

* The heading, which is in German, in the original, reads: "Nahmen der Passagiere welche mit der Brigg Urania, Capt. Wilh^m Geerson, von Bremen, alhier angekommen."

[Endorsed:]

A List of Passengers on Board Ship Canton, Captain Tho[s] Wills, from Amsterdam, arrived in Port of Philad[a] October 7, 1803. 30 Passengers.

[List 469] [List of German Passengers arrived at the Port of Philad[a], Nathaniel Ray, Cap[t], from Amsterdam, Ship Commerce, Oct[r]. 9th 1803. 235 Passengers] *

We, the undersigned, I, Nathan Ray, Captain of the Ship Commerce, on the one part, and we passengers on the other part, accept and obligate ourselves hereby as persons of honor.

On the first part, We passengers, in order to undertake our voyage hence to Philadelphia in North America with the above-mentioned Captain Nathanael Ray, are obligated to behave ourselves quietly and as good passengers during the voyage, and to be fully satisfied with the food below specified, agreed upon between the Captain and ourselves, and as regard water and further provisions, to comply with regulations the Captain shall find necessary, in view of contrary winds and the requirements of a long voyage.

In the second place we agree to pay our passage with the following stipulations:

Those who are in position to settle (for the passage money) in Amsterdam, to pay for one person whether man or woman,

(Children under 4 years old being free)

From 4 to under 14 years six and one-half guineas;

From 14 years and older thirteen guineas.

Those who cannot settle here but will settle in America, to pay

(Children under 4 years being free)

From 4 to under 14 years seven and one-half guineas;

From 14 years and older fifteen guineas.

Those who pay their passage in America shall be bound to produce it within 10 days. No passenger shall be allowed to leave the ship in America without knowledge of the Captain, especially such as have not yet settled for their passage. If one of the passengers dies on the voyage, the family of such a person shall be obligated to settle for his passage, if he dies beyond the middle point of the voyage hence. But if he dies on

---

* Endorsement used as heading.

this side of the middle point the loss shall be to the account of the Captain.

On the other part, I, Captain Nath. Ray, obligate myself to convey faithfully the undersigned passengers to Philadelphia in North America, if God grants a prosperous voyage, to furnish them with the necessary conveniences on the ship, and further to provide the food hereinbelow specified. For this conveyance the above-mentioned passage money must be paid to me. Distribution shall be made daily among these passengers, to wit, to one full passage, (a half passage in proportion, and for children nothing) :

Sunday. A pound of beef with barley.

Monday. A pound of flour, and a pound of butter good for the whole week.

Tuesday. A half-pound of bacon, cooked with peas.

Wednesday. A pound of flour.

Thursday. A pound of beef with potatoes.

Friday. One half-pound of rice.

Saturday. Peas, a pound of cheese and six pounds of bread for the whole week, and one half-pound of bacon.

A quart of beer and a quart of water per day. Vinegar also is to be taken along on the ship, not only to keep the same clean, in order to insure good and fresh air, but also for the refreshment of the passengers.

Since beer sours during the voyage and is very harmful to the health of passengers, only enough beer for a part of the voyage will be taken along, and when this is gone a double portion of water will be given. Half of the water will be supplied for cooking. Each morning a small glass of Holland gin * and each week now and then some vinegar.

We promise to fulfill all the above-mentioned and to this end bind our persons and property as of right.

Done at Amsterdam the . . . . 179.

Heinrich Botzin	Elisab. (✕) Hunsinger
Matis Gissi, and wife	Margred Hunziger
Hans Jakob Gissi	Durs Rudy, and wife
Danjel Wagner, and wife	Jakob Rudy
Johannes Hunziger, and wife	Anna (✕) Ruthe

* Called by its French name "Genever = *genièvre,* from the Latin *juniperus.*

Durs Rudy

Jacob Wäber and wife

Jacob Wäber

Johannes Wäber

Christian Wäber

Marya Wäber

Daniel Hofman, and wife

Anna Hofman

Elisabet Hofman

Daniel Hofman

Heinrich Graff and his wife

Elisabetha Graff

Anna Barbara Graff

Hans Jacob (X) Muller

Ana Maria (X) Muller

Heinerich Mangold, and wife

Heinrich (X) Mangold

Hans Gass, and wife

Hans Jacob Gass

Cathrina (X) Schop

Anna (X) Gas

Martin (X) Mathery

Jacob Böchin

Jacob Marttin

Heinrich Marttin

Jacob Hoch

Adam Bärli

Benedict (X) Berger, and .wife

Ann Maria (X) Gass, stepchild
of Berger

Barbara (X) Berger

Elisabeth (X) Berger

Hans Jacob Gass

Anton Baermann

Hans Jacob Grinder

Hans Jörik Gass

Hans Jacob Gruber, & wife

Marti Gruber

Anna Maria Gruber

Elisabeth (X) Gruber

Anna (X) Gruber

Christen Mützenberg, & wife

Catharina (X) Mützenberg

Johannes (X) Binger, & wife

Maria (X) Binger

Johannes (X) Binger

Conrad (X) Binger

Hans Jacob (X) Binger

Hans Ulrich (X) Binger

Christian (X) Binger

Wernhar Spitteler

Bernard Herges

Michael Käufer, & wife

Andereas Bernhard, & wife

Jacob (X) Bernhard

Johan Joseph Harriges

Ulrich Schmidt

Hans Bessener, and wife

Fried. (X) Bessener

Matthes (X) Bessener

Hans (X) Bessener

Hans Ulrich (X) Ishe, & wife

Hans Ulrich (X) Ishe, & wife

Johanes Ischü

Hans Jacob Ischi

Maria (X) Iche

Frederich (X) Iche

Paul Carl Hen, & wife

Catrina (X) Sweitzer

Bernhart Schweitzer

Adam Tshudi, & wife

Hans Georg (X) Thomme

Johannes (X) Thomme

Elisabeth (X) Thomme

Anna (X) Thomme

Samuel Gerster & wife

Johanes Gerster

Adam Schaub & wife

Hans Jacob (X) Schaub

Barbara (X) Schaub

Anna (X) Schaub

Martin (X) Schaub

Johans Schopp
Hans Jurge (✕) Hasseler
Anna (✕) Sehn
Hans Jacob Fribuger, & wife
Johannes (✕) Freiburger
Hans Jacob (✕) Freiburger
Jacob Schaffner
Heinrich (✕) Rüthi, & wife
Anna Rudy
Johannes (✕) Ruthi
Johannes Egger
Jacob Andereg, & wife
Magdalene Hohl, stepda. of
  Jacob Andereg
Georg Benedict Kienzle
Michael Glass
Johannes (✕) Riet
Johann Rosenstellner
Joh. Andreas Beck
Peter Kroneburger
Michael Walsch
Adam Bernhard
Catharina Bernhardin
Adam Briegel
Peter Rees
Philip Heinrich Blum, and wife
Nikolaus Mang
Johan Gurg Petri
Friederich (✕) Burghoff
Friderich Burckhardt
Daniel Anspach
Johann Georg Brauch
Philip Jacob (✕) Bauer, &
  wife
Friedrich Kramlich
Jacobina (✕) Muller
Anna Maria (✕) Schmeltzer
Jacob Meyer
Deimel Burgesser
Johannies Speck

Niedarth Speck
Katrin Speckin
Nicolaus Kuhlenkampff
Nicolaus Kuhlenkampff
Lorrens Salade
Aric Hal [Holl]
Carl Heuche
Georg Adam Klaudt
Georg Reidt
Georg Phillip Euler
Johann Hein
George Heinrick Runckel
Conrad Bingemann
John Nicolaus (✕) Keuffer
Franz (✕) Noffeneyer, & wife
Barbara (✕) Noffeneyer
Magdalena (✕) Noffeneyer
Egbert Dursch and wife
Philipp Wiedemann
Lanard Wiedmann
Antoine Jacheld
Joseph Greenond
J. H. Koesteyn, & wife
Johann David Deeg
Gutman Liber
Peter Siebold
Johann Christoph^r Gottlieb
  Schleich
Dafid Gidaud
Jacob Eggart
Georg Friderich Schäufele
Georg Friedrich Diem
Joh. Georg Weimann
Carl Haermbstaedt
Dhomas Walter
Franz Stumm
Fillab Majer
Johan Lindestiegel
Philip (✕) Stoppel
Conrad Lampe

Lucas Eggermann
Johann Jacob Wagner

Andreas Kretz
Johan Henrych Rickers

I certify, that Captain Nath^n Ray of the Ship Commerce from Amsterdam has entered 235, Two hundred thirty five, Passengers in my Office, October 9th 1803.

Wm Allen, Collector of Head money,
City of Philadelphia, Lewis Farmer Esqr, Register
of German Passengers

[List 470] List of Passengers on board the Ship Favourite, John Alfton, Master, from Amsterdam. Nov. 15, 1803.

Jacob de Harts Becket
Blassius Slekmeyer, and wife
Joseph Bible
Johannes Schlorser
B. Hummel, and wife
Joseph & Maria Hummell, minors
Francis Wessells
Maria Landman
Carl Fred. Erdman
Peter Boekhoart
Gerrit A. Lenden
Johannes Streignagle
Jacob Hannig
Jan Plankman
Dirk Pompies
Braun Hieman
Marus Kolen
Johan George Huisman
Joseph Pomplier
Christiana Spier
Joseph Brocheck
Jacob Luts
Wilhelm Hulsenberg
Anth^y Herbold
Fred Lafava
Aaron Philips

Michael Herns
Ludoff Otte
B. Dolman
Henrick Pothoff
Christiana Salveyler
Barend Beerends
Jacob Moses
Jacob Epsteiner
Pieter Groenwood
Jan Barner, and wife
C. Sauten
Joh. Gerh. Sauten
Barend Everet
Jan Jacob Dobler
Joh. George Eberlein
Senf Mois. Schiff
Kaufman Isaac Bayje
Joseph Robeson
Jacoba Lobe
Magdalen Reiter
Anna Elisab. Trock
Christian Corneleise
Jacob Van Achten
Jan Hendrick Keuberen
Jan Land
Johannes S. Smitt
John Jurel [?]

John George Girke
M. A. Welnagle
Coenra^d Sorbel Broun
Peter Flaning
Carl Ehlers
—— Schumman, girl
Johanna Schnap
Piper Seel
Wilhelmina Bos
Cath. Hive
Conraad Kehl
Johan Jacob Schedel
Johan C. Kunso
Philip S. Jurken
Henry Richman
G. Berg
Hend. de Jong
Isaac Walter
John Van Mausorn
B. Vinden Becht
Fred Boene
John C. Kerber
John Pieterse
Maria Weithard
John Wilh. Keldwick
John Renit
Maria de Lernn
Usyer Poplak
A. Wolf
Janna Kagee
John Priester, and wife
Wilhelm H. Priester ⎫
Jacob Priester ⎬
Maria C. Priester ⎭
Ehric Winter
H. Homberg, and wife
H. Homberg ⎫ minors
A. Homberg ⎭
Maria N. Regnier
Jacob Gaiman, and wife
Engel Raddemaus

M. Warnick
Hend. Kraamer
Jacob Kuntrell
Wm. Fred. Hink
Johan Scheligs
Johannes Kuller, and wife
Rosina W. Kuller
Johanna Kuller
Philipina Kuller
George Scholder, and wife
John Scholder ⎫
George Scholder ⎬ minors
Eva Scholder ⎪
Andrew Scholder ⎭
Jacob Wirtman
Frederik Gutman
Nic. van Morvont
Cath. Ertel
Barb. Ertel
Fred Ertel
Jacob Ertel
George A. Doll
Lamb Koener
Hend. Williams
Roger Toutenhoofd, and wife
Magdel. Toutenhoofd ⎫ minors
Cath. Toutenhoofd ⎭
Joh. Dubrommer
Otto Van Wingaarde
H. Better
Grutge Van Tellage
S. L. Couteret
Dort Hoffman
Jan Magel Fet
Eva Sebina Fet
Johanette Fet
John Peter Fet
Johanna Fet
Margretta Fet
Catharina Fet
Ludwick Leiner

Anthony Fetts
Philip Ulmer

CABIN PASSENGERS

Frederick Dorn
John Hamman

Jacob Diehl
Van der Namen
Elizabeth de Young
Rosetta de Young
Dr. Hoffman

Philadelphia the 15th of November 1803.

John Alftan.

[Endorsed:]
List of German Passengers, arrived at the Port of Philadᵃ, John Alften, Capᵗ, from Amsterdam, Ship Favorite, Novʳ 15th 1803. 153 Passengers.

[List 471] List of the Passengers on Board the Brig Pennsylvania. [Nov. 15, 1803.]

	FREIGHTS	PASSAGE MONEY	MONEY ADV.	TOTAL
Justus Walter	1	164.10		164.10
N. Dingelwein	1	164.10	15	179.10
Elisah Krebsin	1	164.10	25	189.10
Helena Krebsin	1	164.10	25	189.10
Adam Risinger, and Wife	2	329	50	379
Philip Bechtel	1	164.10	25	189.10
Adam Gerenstein, 9 yrs.	½	82.5	10	92.5
J. G. Voegt	1	164.10	25	189.10
Johan Seltenreich	1	164.10		164.10
Engell Walter	1	164.10		164.10
Herm. Olyslage	1	164.10		164.10
Friderick Coster	1	164.10		164.10
Abraham Coster	1	164.10		164.10
Frederick Heintz	1	164.10		164.10
Anna Cornelisse	1	164.10		164.10
Catharine Schmit	1	164.10		164.10
Carl Opitz	1	164.10	2.10	167
Fred. Jac. Vander Huvell	1	164.10		164.10
Joh. W. Krugman	1	164.10		164.10
Jeduir Fricke	1	164.10	2.10	167
Godf. Schumacker	1	164.10		164.10

	FREIGHTS	PASSAGE MONEY	MONEY ADV.	TOTAL
Phillip Frolick	1	164.10	12	176.10
John Ab. Winter	1	164.10		164.10

CABIN PASSENGER

M. Mackie
30 Guil⁸ paid here fr. 240   360

[Endorsed:]
List of German Passengers Peter F. Moody, with German Passengers from Amsterdam.

[List 472] [List of German Passengers arrived at the Port of Philadᵃ from Fredericstad, Febrʸ 21, 1804, Ship Carolina.] *

P. F. Courvoisier Sandoz, a Swiss   C. G. Schneider, Dᵒ
C. Fisher, a German   William Rosen, Dᵒ

Philad.ᵃ 21st Feb.ʸ 1804.

Th. Moore.

[List 473] List of German Passengers on Board the Brigantine Union, Capⁿ Hanse, from Tonningen, arrived at the Port of Philadelphia, March 19ᵗʰ 1804.

Charles Seager   John Sneider

[List 474] [List of German Passengers Arrived at the Port of Philadᵃ in the Ship Indostan, Captain John Green, from Hamburgh. April 17ᵗʰ 1804.]†

Gottfried Wilhelm Philip   Joh. Andr. Brandt
Carl Philip   Wolmer Julius Heinr. Meyer
Christ. Gottl. Schmidt   Johann Wilschütt
Joh. Carl Philip Klein   Joh. Friedᶜʰ Meisch
Joh. Wilhelm Röting   Heinr. Überhoff
Joh. Casper Everling   Nicol. Adolph Suck
Michael Küsner   Peter Becker
Hans Nicolaus Kros   Frantz Becker
Christ. Nitscher   Jacob Hampf

* Endorsement used as heading.
† Endorsement used as heading.

Joh. Joachim Stoltze
Joh. Heinr^ch Harthmann
Joh. Herrman Schaeffer
Georg Weidemann
Ernst Müller
Joh. Joachim Günther
Christ^n Grünberg
Joh. Hinr. Alm
Hinr. Munsenheimer
Anton Rasch
Joh. Eberhard Wehhagen
Gottl. Strahlheimer
Joh. Krafft Wunderlich
Joh. Christ. Schultz
Joseph Korff
Joh. Dav. Peter Mittelstaedt
Anton Christ. Schröder
Wilhelm Keyser
Jurgen Died^ch Bellmann, dead *
Joh. Fried^ch Breege
Elias Salomon Pappenheimer
Joh. Anson
Christ. Rühle
Joh. Christ. H. Lanckau
Joh. Nicolaus Beyer
Jacob Marsch
Herman Mich. Bosseck
Joseph Ublond
Benjamin Kann
Joh. Bernh^d Stöltzner
Joh. Hinr^ch John
Nicolaus Beyersdorff
Jean Frans Pinard
Joh. Adam Proebster
Luis Alexander
Sam. Hinrich Kroll
Georg Pappler
Jacob Gerson
Paul Hoffmann
Joh. v. Bergen

Christ. Gottl. Weis
Fried^ch Holtz
Joh. Christ. Holtz
Thomas Hoffmann
Joh. David Borst
Joh. Albert Billhoch
Moses Levy
Wolff Isaac
Levy Kohn
Jacob Siemon
Joh. Claus Pfeil
Bernh^d Krüger
Joh. Hein^ch Schmidt
Dettloff Joenicke
Joseph Ahrends
Fried^ch Gottfr. Fuhrmann
Benjamin Samoel
Fried^ch Kadwitz
Peter Nicol. Lippert
Joh. Gottl. Tüppel
August Müller
Joh. Christ. Schmoch
Samoel Wessel
Christ. Emmerling
Ephraim Munthau
Lasch Johannsen
Joh. Joseph Claus
Hinr. Andr. Schulenburg
Jürgen Mich. Lutjohan
Carl Wilh. Trewill
Joh. Hinr. Balstad, dead *
Christ. Jac. Dreyer
Joh. Fried^ch Holte
Joh. Fried. Zahn
Jochim Lange, dead *
Fried^ch Müller
Asmus Hein. v.Münden
Heinr. Roth
Jürg. Hein^ch Schultz
Bernh^d Kantzler

* Name crossed out.

Carl Krauss
Casper Fahts
Joach. Carl Kronstüber
Egerath Franck
Joh. Gottl. Lungwitz
Heinr. Rotjeroth
Joh. Andr. Gehres
Heinr. Werkentin
Fried^{ch} Alexander Grund
Aug. Fried^{ch} Rehlmann
Jacob Meyer
Joh. Gottfr. Herschelmann
Heinr. Löhr
Joseph Wilh. Berber
Joh. Christ. Grassmann
Joh. Philip Thiel
Georg Fried^{ch} Quedenfeldt
Peter Fühles
Joh. Gottl. Müller
Joh. Hinr. Kreutzburg
Joh. Herm. Krüger
Aug. Christ. Hesse
Carl Fried^{ch} Niculai

MARRIED WOMEN

Anna Cath. Maria Müller
Anna Cath. Günther
Anna Munsenheimer
Jeanette Rasch
Cath. Margar. Wehhagen
Cath. Elisabeth Wunderlich
Juliana Schultz

Bergitta Christina Keyser
Maria Margar. Breege
Friederica Carol. Christ. Kroll
Maria Cath. Hoffmann
Anna Maria Dosch
Maria Dorothea Schmoch
Maria Elisabeth Rotjeroth
Henrietta [Rotjeroth]
Barbara Elisab. Ottoin
Margaretha Elisab. Winkelmeyer
Anna Sophia Kollen
Wilhelmina Christ.^l Grund
Anna Margar. Blumen

CHILDREN

Anna Juliana Hinrietta Günther
Joh. Hinr. Munsenheimer
Joh. Fried^{ch} H. Wehhagen
Joh. Hinr. Wehhagen
Johanna Maria Christ. Wehhagen
Gottl. Fried^{ch}. Conrad Schultz
Maria Magdalena Breege
Johann Christ. Wilhelm Breege
Anna Kroll
Maria Kroll
Wilhelm Hoffmann
Johannes Hoffmann
Herman Wilh. Martinssen
Maria Cath. Lena Rotjeroth
Christ. Jacob Hesse
Carl Hesse.

[List 475] Manifest of Passengers on board the Brig Newton, John Riley, from Hamburg, addressed to Messrs Nicklin & Griffith. Aug. 11, 1804.

NAMES	OCCUPATIONS	AGES	HEIGHT	BAGGAGE
Henry Pressell	saddler	28	5.10 ft.	1 trunk
his wife	saddler	24	5	"

NAMES	OCCUPATIONS	AGES	HEIGHT	BAGGAGE
G. A. Simon	saddler	24	5 ft.	no luggage
T. E. A. Janna	grocer	26	5.4	1 trunk
G. Fischer	shoemaker	18	5.4	no luggage
his wife	"	18	5	do
H. Butz	no trade	18	5.4	do
Joseph Nagle	no trade	22	5.4	do
G. A. Siebert	miller	38	5.5	bag
G. A. Whilimack	weaver	34	5.4	"
G. Tausch	farmer	30	5.6	
A. D. Schiele	blacksmith	21	5.6	bag
A. Siligman	no trade	15	5	
G. Comeke	chairmaker	43	5	
C. Jardins	distiller	36	5.8	bag
L. Knuppel	carpenter	18	5	
H. Bauer	butcher	28	5	
H. Kruger	clerk	37	6	
A. Lueke	clothmaker	25	5	
G. F. Weyrick	sockmaker	26	5.6	
Franz Hoffman	tailor	45	5.8	
J. W. Emeke	farmer	30	5.4	
P. H. Minan	shoemaker	24	5.4	
J. J. Betz	tailor	19	5.4	bag
H. G. Porch	turner	23	5	do
J. C. Becker	blacksmith	24	5.8	do
D. Heigening	watchmaker	30	5.8	nothing
J. Maul	farmer	24	5.5	do
G. Stahd	farmer	29	5.5	bag
J. J. Sahn	farmer	36	5.4	nothing
W. G. Lückel	carpenter	20	5.8	bag
G. Lauber	farmer	21	5.5	do
P. Saemanshaus	farmer	20	5.5	nothing
J. Hummerhaus	farmer	26	5.5	bag
J. H. Beltys	carpenter	30	5.8	nothing
E. Bantzs	tailor	22	5.8	"
J. Buch	miller	21	5.6	"
H. Beitzel	tailor	21	5.4	"
H. F. Ehlers	tailor	29	5.2	trunk
Cammassasea	no trade	19	5.4	bag
Hauff	no trade	19	5.5	bag
B. Bestells	shoemaker	25	5.4	

NAMES	OCCUPATIONS	AGES	HEIGHT	BAGGAGE
F. Keimh	carpenter	27	5.4 ft.	trunk
H. Kligenburg	tailor	21	5	no luggage
E. Reiter	locksmith	29	5.3	bag
J. Schmidt	no trade	38	5.8	ditto
J. Reiter	tailor	25	5.8	ditto
J. H. Hahs	locksmith	20	5.8	ditto
J. Fisher	farmer	31	5.9	ditto
his wife	farmer	20	5	
F. Schewetzer	butcher	32	5.8	d°
J. Baltzer	weaver	22	5.8	ditto
C. Fucks	linen weaver	25	5.6	trunk
L. Fucks	ditto	23	5.6	nothing
L. G. Bornin	maidserv^t	27	5.6	ditto
J. H. Wahl	tailor	19	5.5	bag
J. Jockeln	serv^t woman	51	5	nothing
Joh^s Wahl	boy	11		
E. Sheiden	maidserv^t	22	5	trunk
A. Leickle	farmer	30	5.6	nothing
J. G. Netz	farmer	30	5.6	chest
his wife	ditto	31	5	
his 2 children		7 & 4 years		
Lud. Netz	farmer	40	5.4	chest
his wife	"	35	5	
his child		10		
his sister	serv^t maid	36	5	
P. Spies	farmer	49	5.4	chest
his wife	"	39	5	
his 8 children		21. 19. 17. 15. 13. 11. 9. 4 years old		
G. Ruhs	farmer	36	5.4	1 chest
his wife	"	40		
his 2 children		12 & 14 years		
P. Fucks	saddler	32	6	nothing
his wife	"	40		
his 3 children		17, 6 & 3½ years		
M. Banz	farmer	48	6	1 trunk
his wife		40		
his 6 children		25. 14. 13. 10. 8. 7 years		
J. Donners	farmer	32	5	1 trunk
his wife		24	5	

NAMES	OCCUPATIONS	AGES	HEIGHT	BAGGAGE
P. H. Braun	farmer	32	5.8	nothing
his wife		29	5	
his sister		19	5	
J. G. Mohle	shoemaker	29	5.2	
his wife		34		
his 2 children		4 yrs & 18 weeks		
J. Boehm	farmer	28	5.8	bag
his wife				
J. C. Eulers	carpenter	32	6	no luggage
his wife		33	5	
his 3 children				
H. C. Bertels	shoemaker	30	5	
his wife		29		
his 2 children				
C. Donnier	tailor	29	5.6	trunk *
his wife		24		
his 1 child		4		
his sister		15		
H. Kuhn	carpenter	26	5.6	1 trunk
his wife		20		
A. Gungheim	shoemaker	31	5.8	2 trunks † coarse linen
his wife		30		
his 2 children		4 & 1½ yrs		
Jus^n Sasmannhous	farmer	36	5	trunk
his wife		34		
his 2 children		12 & 8 yrs		
G. Strachbein	farmer	36	5.6	bag
his wife		29		
his 2 children		7 & 1½ yrs.		
A. E. Strachbein	farmer	31	5.4 ft.	
his 1 child		4½ years		
G. H. Trite	farmer	16	5	
his sister	maidservant	19	5.2	
Just Trite	farmer	45	6	chest
his wife		35		
his 5 children		19. 16. 13. 4. 1 years old		

* 160 ells of coarse linen for family use.
† Also 40 ells of coarse linen.

NAMES	OCCUPATIONS	AGES	HEIGHT	BAGGAGE
E. F. Huster	tallowchandler	44	5.4	chest
his wife		33	5	
G. Kummerer	farmer	31	6	chest *
his wife		29	5	
his mother		61	5	
his 3 children		12, 6, 4 yrs.		
M. Kelmer	farmer	40	5.6	
his wife		27		
his 1 child		7		
G. Wahl	farmer	37	5.5	
his wife		27		
J. Schume	farmer	30	5.2	
his wife		30	5.	
his 1 child		3		
P. Nelling	farmer	44	5.8	trunk †
his wife		28	5	
his mother		70		
his 4 children		14, 13, 6, 4 yrs.		
Leid Radeboch	farmer	27	5	no baggage
his wife		25	5	
his 2 children		3 & 1½ yrs.		
A. M. Schmitter	farmer	42	5 ft.	
1 Child		9		
Riemenshider	no trade	21	5.4	trunk
Mary Klein	maidservt	22	5	
Andw Wannbolt	cook	28	5	
W. Turmer	cabin passenger			2 trunks 1 portmanteau
Mr. Rochkendorf & Lady	Do			4 trunks
J. Malcolm	Do			2 trunks

1 Package addressed to collector, preventative for the fever.

[List 476] Passengers on board the Brig Leopard, Pigot Shaw, Mr, from Lubeck. [August 25th 1804.]

Frederick Hartel	John Wesch
Jacob Bolts	Levi Solomon

* Also 400 ells of coarse linen.
† About 90 ells of linen.

David Balba
Ludwick Ressing
Norbert Boltz

Henry Reichel
George Drummer

Philad^a, 25th Augt 1804.

Pigot Shaw.

[Endorsed:]
List of German Passengers on Board the Brig^t Leopard, Captain Piggot Shaw, from Lubeck, arrived in the Port of Philad^a, August 25th 1804.

[List 477] List of Passengers, landed at The Lazaretto, from on board Rebecca, Captⁿ David Low, from Amsterdam. Aug 27, 1804.

John Loliger
Jacob Banger & wife
Janette D°
Elijah D°
Trena D°
Jacob D°
Claus Bater & wife
Samuel D°
Anna Mira D°
Jacob Gross & wife
Hannah D°
Jacob Alt & wife
Jacob Atz & wife
Jacob Breitenster & wife
    a child D°
Jacob Switzer
Martin Vogl
Jacob Schude & wife & child
Casper Schafner
Jacob Gerster
Johanes Gerster
Johans Frisher
Lun^d Bey
Jacob Schwitzer
Anna Marga^t D°
Johannes D°

Ursele D°
Hance Jacob D°
Hanst Gristy & wife
Hance Jacob D°
Manuel Crist D°
Henrich D°
John Bey & wife
Nicol. Borey
Jacob Kreger
John Ulgersh
John Burkerd
Jacob Schneder & wife
Jacob D°
Tur Atz
Henery Burgy
Henery Schaub
John Ott
Jacob Buster
Jacob Schwitzer & wife
Jacob D°
Nicholas D°
Margret D°
Hannah D°
Jacob Erb & wife
Peter Segrest D°
Matth^s D°

Hann. M. D°

Reningen D°

Catherine D°

Henil D°

Martin Schudy & wife

Elizbeth D°

Marthi D°

Henery Haffelfinger & wife

Anna Maria D°

Anna D°

Margret D°

H. Rudy & wife

Bernr. Bartar

Barbara Barter

Johannes D°

Anna Mira D°

Jacob Huser

Henery Mangold & wife

Hannah D°

Barbara D°

Martin D°

Jacob Wagner & wife

Jacob Burgy & wife

Jacob D°

Magret D°

Maria D°

Hanes Jac. Schnieder & wife

Frena D°

Anna D°

Maria D°

Nichola D°

Nicholas Mischile & wife

Martin Moschizer & wife

Anna D°

Martin D°

Sucor D°

Jacob Haffilfinger & wife

Bascher Haffilfinger

Peter Thom & wife

Jacob D°

Johannes D°

Fred D°

Johannes Hasly & wife

Jacob D°

John Jacob Gas & wife

Jacob D°

Elisabeth D°

Jacob Moria & wife

Barbara D°

Jacob D°

Anna D°

Salem D°

Hans Georg Grieder & wife

Anna D°

Hans Jacob Walter & wife

Marie Weber

Jacob Schaub & wife

Widow Schaub

Henery Schaub Linttos

Henery Schaub & wife

Barbara D°

Henry D°

Jacob D°

Daniel Reis

Francs Fridrich

Henery Huser & wife

Jacob Strub & wife

Catharine River

Elizabeth D°

Cath. D°

Adam Grieder & wife

Jacob Grieder & wife

Hans Schaub & wife

Martin D°

Marie D°

David D°

Cath^n D°

Hanns D°

Heinz Schaub & wife

Henery D°

Elisabeth D°

Marie D°

Barbara Schaub
Anne D°
Jacob Gas
Anna D°
Jacob D°
Jacob Heartman & wife
Hein^r. Thommas
Joseph Ring & wife
Widow Hanner
Antony Matter
Nicole Michle & wife
Regina D°
Magrete D°
Daniel D°
Jacob D°
Catherine D°
J. J. Ditman & wife
Jacob Weber
M. E. Smith
Fredrick Fenchel
John Minner
Magret Minner
Henery Albrite & wife
Daniel D°
Magret D°

John Roland
Arnold German & wife
Frederick D°
Conrath Markly
Mr. Eyerman
Henery Hafer & wife
Francis Lautherbach
Francis Grove
Ar. Kolman
Fr^d. Gauble
G. Witmeyer
B. Folger
Jacob Attz
Anto. Kretcher & wife
Anna Schob D°
Anna Cath^r D°
Christane D°
Catherine D°
Sam Evert
Jacob Baab & wife
Elizbeth Poppel
Lud. Eppelschier
M. Zimmer

Aug 27 1804

[Endorsed:]
List of Passengers per Ship Rebecca, remain [?] Aug, 27, 1804.
To be returned to Lewis Farmer, when copied for the health officer.

[List 478] List of Passengers on board the Ship Maria Elisabeth, Capt. Henry Hutchison, from Tonningen, Septr 10, 1804.

Wilhelm Frederick
Anna Maria, his wife
Elisabeth, daughter
Johannes, son
Jacob Weber

Elisabeth, his wife
Christian Koster, stepson
Everhard Weber, his son
Elisabeth Weber, his daughter
Johannes Otto

Conrad Rehorhn
Elisabeth, his wife
Frederic, his son
Charlotte Pebler
George Pebler, her son
William Brensill
Margaret, his wife
Johann Gothard
Anna Gothard, his wife
Ludewig Schmidt
Jacob Brumps
Andreas Schroder
Just Bode
Anna Elisabeth, his wife
Christian, son
Catharina, daughter
Herrman Bode
Anna Elisabeth, his wife
Anna Elisabeth Wiele
Kraft Wiele, her son
Catharine Elisabeth, her daughter
Johannes Marbacher
Caroline, his wife
Christina, his daughter
Johan Georg, his son
Francisca, his daughter
Carl, his son
Valentine, his son
Carolina, his daughter
Anna Maria, his daughter
Conrad Wigham
Veit Wigham
Luise Schuemaker
Maria Lismannhausen
Christian Wike
Elena Elich
J. H. Wike
Catharina, his wife
Johann Christn, his Son

J. Frederic Wike
Catharina Wike
Johann H. Bode
Christina Moller
Maria Magdalena, her daughter
C. Louise, her daughter
Anna Elisabeth, her daughter
G. Henrich Moller, her son
Catharina Reuter
Catharina Müller
Catharina, her daughter
Louise Ruter
J. Christian, her son
J. Ludewig, her son
Jurgen Schneider
K. Luise Schneider
Anna Catharine Schneider
Georg Amelius Zimmer
Michael Klingelhover
Eve Weber
Johannes Peltz
Elisabeth Weber
Johann Henrich, her son
Johannes, her son
Gottlieb Steidling
Andreas Grim
Catharine, his daughter
Philippina Jacobine, his daughter
Henrietta, his daughter
Christian Ludwig, his son
George Vennil
Barbara, his wife
Christoph Balbach
Sebastian Snatz
Adam Ruhde
Joseph Steicherwald
Philip Lentz
Isaac Simson
Caspar Libmann
J. C. Wolff

Magdalena Wolff, his wife
George Petershall
Johann Turching
Johann George Hellmann
Joseph Hertzberger
Catharina Kessler
Just. H. Kessler, her son
Anna Margaretha, her daughter
Johannes, her son
Catharine Messerschmidt
Anna E. Messerschmidt, her daughter
Christina, her daughter
Johann Frederic, her son
Anna Barbara, her daughter
Johann Just, her son
Friederich Benfer
Maria Elizabeth, his wife
Johannes Fregalius
Mr. C. H. Willigmann ⎫
" Helveti ⎪
" Vincent Linau ⎬ cabin passengers
" J. J. Hagen ⎪
" J. F. E. Jahnke ⎭
J. Feldentropf
Jonathan Eash

Maria Magdelena Eash
Christian Wurfel
Johannes Ceyfert
Elisabeth, his wife
Barbara, his daughter
Johannes, his son
Elisabeth, his daughter
Eve, his daughter
Nicholas, his son
Johannes, his son
Lorentz, his son
Johann F. Buchanner
Helena, his wife
Johann Quick
Anna E. Quick, his wife
George, his son
Martha, his daughter
Anna Catharine, his daughter
Johann Nicolas Hartzel
Johann Georg, his son
Philip Schmit
Elisabeth, his wife
Peter, his son
Catharine, his daughter
Philip, his son
Jacob, his son

Philada. Septr 10, 1804.

[List 479] List of Passengers p. Ship Atlantic, Elihu Doty, Master, from Amsterdam. [Septr 15th 1804.]

John Hoernle
Elizabeth, his wife
Joseph ⎫
Madaline ⎬ children
George Bentell
Katharine, his wife

John George ⎫
Fredericka ⎪
Anna Maria ⎪
Johanna ⎬ children
John Friderich ⎪
Israel ⎪
Katy ⎭

George Boehringer
Katharine, his wife
Johann, his child
John Konzelman
Dorothy, his wife
Frederik ⎱ children
John George ⎰
George Wild
Maria, his child
Thierry Federbush
Elisabeth, his child
George Velte
E. Katharine, his wife
E. Katy ⎱ children
George ⎰
Gottlieb Schurle
Eliz\a, his wife
Gotlief, his child
Matthew Rein
Lucina, his wife
Katharine ⎱ children
Jacob ⎰
Jacob Scholle
Margaretta, his wife
Jacob ⎫
Margarette ⎪
Salome ⎬ children
Matthew ⎪
Gottlieb ⎪
Elizabeth ⎭
Frederick Brown
Barbara, his wife
Phillipina, his child
Elias Wilhelm
Regina, his wife
Christian Frederick ⎫
John Jacob ⎪
Johanna ⎬ children
Gottlieb ⎭
George Holterreich

Johanna, his wife
John Georg ⎫
John Jacob ⎬ children
John ⎭
Barnard Duurwachter
Elizabeth, his wife
Elizabeth ⎱ children
Wilhelmina ⎰
Jacob Wohlgemuth
Margaret, his wife
John Jacob ⎱ children
Christian ⎰
John Langenbacher
Katharine, his wife
George Jacob ⎫
Gottlieb ⎬ children
Catharine ⎭
Theophilus Knodel
Elizabeth, his wife
Conrad, his child
Jacob Zimmerman
Jacob, his child
Matthew Henning
Agnes Henning, his wife
Gaspar Goetz
Frederica, his wife
Katharine ⎱ children
Frederica ⎰
David Stipper
Rosina, his wife
Ferdinand Haug
Eliza, his wife
Mathew Kleine
Jacob, his father
Katharina, his wife
Ludowick ⎫
Jacob ⎪
Jacobina ⎬ children
Christina ⎪
Dorothea ⎭

Christian Velte
Katharine, his wife
Frederica, his child
David Hurlebans
Eliza, his wife
Sophia ⎤
Eliza ⎬ children
Barbara ⎦
David Schaefer
Margaretta, his wife
Christine ⎤ children
Katharine ⎦
Jacob F. Wyngartner
Christina, his wife
Jacob ⎤
Margaretta ⎢
Friderich ⎬ children
George ⎢
Godfrey ⎢
Michael ⎦
Joseph Bonnet
Katy, his wife
Katharine ⎤
John ⎢ children
Frank ⎢
David ⎦
James Baker
Rosina, his wife
Phillip Jacob ⎤ children
Rosina ⎦
John Bamesberger
Frederica, his wife
John, his child
Christopher Leicht
Dorothea, his wife
Ludowig ⎤
Andreas ⎢
Dorothy ⎬ children
Gottlieb ⎢
Christopher ⎦

Christina Rapp
Rosina, her child
Widow Veltes
Mary Katy, her daughter
Regina Zeller
Regina, her daughter
Widow Bochringer
Philip Jacob, her child
Susanna Rosdannen
Maria ⎤
Peter ⎢ children
Magdalen ⎢
Margaret ⎦
Magdalen Leicht
Magdalen, her child
John Frederich Reichert
John Holterreich
Frederick Gerne
Gottlob Ruff
Thierry Knodel
Jacob Sunder
John Kappel
George Schmidt
John Reichart
Joseph Gotterwa
Eliz. B. Hoerlin
Christina Buchinrotten
Magdalen Eisel
Katy Weison
Margaret Voiten
Magdalen Kehrweger
Dolly Spael
Elisa M. Imler
Mary E. Lautenschlager
Mary M. Russonbrod
Jane F. Knorn
George Russenbrod
Mary A., his wife
John ⎤ children
Michael ⎦

George Wagner
Anna Mary, his wife
Anna ⎱ children
Jacob ⎰
Jacob Wohnle
Katy, his wife
Katy ⎫
John G. ⎬ children
Anna Mary ⎭
James Smith
Johanna, his wife
John F. ⎫
Regina ⎬ children
Jacobina ⎭
Barbary Knapper
Margaret ⎱ children
Gottlieb ⎰
Wentell Herman
Margaretta, his wife
Stephen Renz
Anna Barbara, is wife
Anna Barbara ⎱ children
Anna Maria ⎰
James Krail
Mary, his wife
John G. ⎱ children
Margaret ⎰
William Hinger
Phillipina R., his wife
Lewis Eppele.
Margaret, his wife
Lewis ⎱ children
Jacob ⎰
George Schule
Maria Agnes, his wife
Anna M. ⎫
John G. ⎪
John Adam ⎬ children
Anna Maria ⎪
John Jacob ⎭

Mathew Reiff, Sen.
Anna Maria, his wife
Maria Agnes ⎫
John ⎬ children
Anna M. ⎭
Matthew Reiff, Junr
Maria M., his wife
John George, his child
John Mutchler
John G. ⎱ children
Christine K. ⎰
Jacob Muckenfuss
Anna, his wife
Regina ⎱ children
Anna B. ⎰
Ferdinand F. Schule
Mary A., his wife
Jacob Reiff
Anna B. Herman
John Herman
Anna, his wife
John G. ⎫
Anna ⎪
Maria B. ⎬ children
Anna M. ⎭
Theophilus Schuler
Jacob F. Schuler
Lawrence Lewis
Dorothy Keison
Katherine Haller
Jacob ⎫
Juliana ⎪
Charlotta ⎬ children
Johanna ⎭
Francis Blanck ⎱
Regina Bamesberger ⎰
John Merle ⎫
Christian Voehle ⎪
Diederich Feierbush ⎬
J. G. Kauker ⎭

George M. Schmied ⎫
Chris^t Staitman ⎪
Anna M. Stygerin ⎬
Lewis F. Haugmayer ⎭
Total 257.

The above Passengers are all Steerage Passengers and all from the Dutchy of Wurtenburg in the German Empire.

Augustin Le Moine, from Liege
Christian Fokke, from Hanover
Lucius Herman, Madgeburg

Israel Solomon ⎫
Isaac E. Israel ⎪
Abr. E. Israel ⎪
L. M. Goldsmidt ⎬ Holland
Moses Jacobs ⎪
Rosina Jacobs ⎭

The above are steerage Passengers [not from Wurtenberg.]

Jacobey Desey ⎫
Ary Van Holy ⎬ Holland
Theodorus A. Brongers ⎭
Total 269.

The last three are cabin Passengers.

Elihu Doty.

[Endorsed:]
List of German Passengers, who arrived at the Port of Philad^a in the Ship Atlantick, Elihu Doty, Master, from Amsterdam. Sepr. 15th 1804.

[List 480] Report of alien passengers on board the Ship Margaret, of which E. C. Gardner is Master, arrived at the Port of Philadelphia in the State of Pennsylvania, on the 19th day of September, 1804.*

J. Kirn, wife, 2 children, 29, Wirtemberg, blacksmith, 5½ ft., dark brown hair.

G. Reichard & his wife, 27, Ashberg, farmer, 5½ ft., dark brown hair.

Lewis Weiss, wife, 1 child, 26, Vaihingen, butcher, 5½ ft., dark brown hair.

John Winter & his wife, 43, Vaihingen, weaver, 5½ ft., dark brown hair.

Israel Bader, wife, 2 children, 27, Oberhausen, weaver, 6 ft., dark brown hair.

Caspar Humel, wife, 4 children, 36, Ehningen, distiller, 6 ft., dark brown hair.

* Two columns, "Country from whence they have come," all from Wirtemberg, and "To what nation they belong," all Germans, are omitted.

John Shertler, wife & 3 children, 54, Markgröningen, farmer, 6 ft., grey hair.

Jacob Benzenhöfer, wife, 2 children, 34, Shondorf, farmer, 6 ft., black hair.

Michael Conradt, wife, 7 children, 50, Ludwigsburg, weaver & silk dyer, 6 ft., brown hair.

David Rückenbrodt, wife, 2 children, 30, Malmsheim, weaver, 5½ ft., flaxen hair.

Henry Lenz, wife, 4 children, 43, Beutelspach, farmer, 5½ ft., dark brown hair.

William Geissendörfer, wife, 1 child, 24, Stuttgard, musician, 6 ft., flaxen hair.

Frederic Emhard, wife, 1 child, 35, Möhringen, tailor, 6 ft., flaxen hair.

Charles Kiehnle, wife, 1 son, 61, Egenhausen, geometer, 5½ ft., dark brown hair.

Conrad Grabenstein, wife, 4 children, 55, Wallheim, farmer, 6 ft., dark brown hair.

Christoph Epting, wife, 1 child, 25, Bissigheim, cooper and brewer, 6 ft., flaxen hair.

Godfrey Villinger, & his wife, 27, Beningheim, soap-boiler, 5½ ft., flaxen hair.

Wm Hartstein, wife, 2 children, 40, Unterhausen, stonecutter, 5½ ft., dark brown hair.

George Leuze, wife, 3 children & mother-in-law, 39, Ehningen, farmer, 5½ ft., black hair.

Godlieb Kaiser, wife, 1 child, 26, Beilstein, merchant, 5½ ft., dark brown hair.

Jacob Eheman, wife, 5 children, 40, Shornbach, farmer, 6 ft., flaxen hair.

David Humel, wife, 7 children, 43, Ehningen, tobacco box-maker, 6 ft., dark brown hair.

Peter Häfelin, wife, 1 child, 34, Nordheim, shoemaker, 5½ ft., red brown hair.

Jacob Herman, 6 children, 44, Genkengen, farmer, 5½ ft., black hair.

Martin Herman, 3 children, 43, Genkengen, shoemaker, 6 ft., dark brown hair.

George Burghard, wife, 7 children & 1 maid-servant, 43, Oberaichen, farmer, 5½ ft., yellow brown hair.

George Kiess, wife, 5 children, 52, Möhringen, farmer, 5½ ft., dark brown hair.

Christian Riesh, wife, 2 children, 31, Heimerdingen, shoemaker, 6 ft., brown hair.

Joshua Vaihinger, wife, 7 children, 52, Feldbach, farmer, 6 ft., black hair.

Frederic Gross, wife, 6 children, 40, Oberaichen, farmer, 6 ft., brown hair.

Christoph Mohl, wife, 5 children, 58, Phullingen, farmer, 5½ ft., grey hair.

Leonhard Ulmer, wife, 5 children, and 1 maid servant, 40, Möhringen, farmer, 5½ ft., black hair.

George Biechteler, wife, 5 children, 42, Grönenbach, stocking weaver, 5 ft., black hair.

Leonhard Staiger, wife, 4 children and 1 maid servant, 39, Möhringen, weaver, 5½ ft., black hair.

Thomas Ulmer, wife, 1 child, 68, Möhringen, shoemaker, 5 ft., grey hair.

George Bertsh, wife, 5 children, 45, Unterhausen, cooper, 5½ ft., yellow hair.

George Walz, wife, 1 child, 28, Möhringen, farmer, 6 ft., black hair.

W^m. Klermundt & wife, 41, Calw, farmer, 5 ft., brown hair.

Michael Bühl, his wife, mother, sister, and 4 children, 44, Mussberg, farmer, 6 ft., dark brown hair.

George Keppeler, wife, 4 children, 55, Pfullingen, farmer, 5½ ft., grey hair.

Frederic Wolfer, wife, 5 children, 39, Markgröningen, farmer, 5½ ft., brown hair.

Jacob Lüllich, wife, 1 child, 25, Rielingshausen, farmer, 5 ft., flaxen hair.

Jacob Hohenstein & wife, 35, Lowehausen, Prussia, miller, 6 ft., brown hair.

John de Young, 30, Medembleck, Holland, military officer, 6 ft., light complexion.

Dederic Heydorn, 19, Pyrmont, Waldeck, printer, 5½ ft., brown hair.

Frederic Stroh, 22, Sachsenheim, tailor, 5 ft., flaxen hair.

Christoph Sholl, 22, Graben, tailor, 5 ft., flaxen hair.

Michael Bässler, 21, Strempfelbach, farmer, 6 ft., dark brown hair.

J. Jacob Geiger, 54, Bissingen, carpenter, 6 ft., dark brown hair.

Frederic Henninger, 29, Ludwigsburg, stonecutter, 5½ ft., dark brown hair.

Frederic Friz, 18, Rielingshausen, weaver, 5 ft., dark brown hair.

J. G. Hausburg, 28, Halle, stocking weaver, 5½ ft., brown hair.

Ernst Lewis Gaier, 34, Markgröningen, shepherd, 6 ft., brown hair.

Daniel Trippel, 31, Markgröningen, butcher, 5½ ft., dark brown hair.

Daniel Brenner, 25, Beutelspach, farmer, 5 ft., dark brown hair.

Lewis Gruis, 28, Heilbrunn, clerk, 4 ft., flaxen hair.

Lewis Burkhard, 21, Ludwigsburg, weaver, 5 ft., flaxen hair.

Jacob Reuk, 21, Enzweihengen, carpenter, 5½ ft., flaxen hair.

C. Adam Belz, 18, Ludwigsburg, tailor, 5½ ft., flaxen hair.

Frederic Joost, 18, Ludwigsburg, rope-maker, 5 ft., yellow hair.

G. Godlob Zimmerman, 23, Ludwigsburg, shoemaker, 5 ft., flaxen hair.

G. Frederic Buchhalter, 20, Ludwigsburg, baker, 5½ ft., brown hair.

J. Frederic Schäfer, 25, Shornbach, weaver, 6 ft., flaxen hair.

J. George Kurz, 20, Grossashbach, cooper, 5 ft., black hair.

G. Adam Tresz, 19, Grossashbach, baker, 5½ ft., brown hair.

John Klein, 24, Westhof, Hesse, architect, 5½ ft., flaxen hair.

Gottlieb Lillich, 20, Rielingshausen, weaver, 5½ ft., yellow hair.

J. Godlieb Götz, 20, Grossachsenheim, glass-maker, 5½ ft., brown hair.

Christian Ernst, 22, Fellbach, farmer, 5½ ft., black hair.

John Heim, 34, Möhringen, weaver, 5½ ft., yellow hair.

Jacob Hofmeister, 21, Fellbach, farmer, 6 ft., black hair.

J. Michael Riesch, 24, Heimerdingen, farmer, 6 ft., black hair.

C. Godfrey Phäler, 18, Ludwigsburg, turner, 5½ ft., brown hair.

Felix Trumpeter, 60, Braunau, Bavaria, clerk, 5½ ft., grey hair.

Anton Mözel, 18, Homburg, Zweibrücken, bookbinder, 5½ ft., grey hair.

Juda Bair Levy, 16, Kreuznach, clerk, 5½ ft., flaxen hair.

Regina Shöllin, 48, Snaith, 4½ ft., black hair.

Catharine Krämerinn, 40, Möhringen, 5 ft., black hair.

Charlotte Neuserinn, 34, Möhringen, 5½ ft., brown hair.

Elizabeth Schwäglerinn, 50, Gerhardstadten, 5 ft., black hair.

Frederica Dobelmann, 20, Ludwigsburg, 4½ ft., dark brown hair.

Godlieb Heim, 37, Möhringen, weaver, 5½ ft., yellow hair.

Anna Mary Armstrong, 28, Gottenborg, Sweden, 5 ft., flaxen hair.

Mary Armstrong, 12, Gottenborg, Sweden, 4 ft., flaxen hair.

Wm. van der Veen, 20, Breuckelen, Holland, doctor, 4½ ft., brown hair.

Tobias Jacob Ezechiel, 18, Amsterdam, Holland, 4½ ft., brown hair.

John Lehle, 33, Markgröningen, butcher, 6 ft., black hair.

David Jung, 24, Möhringen, joiner, 6 ft., flaxen hair.

David Villinger and wife, 27, Beningheim, soap-boiler, 5 ft., flaxen hair.

John Armbrust, wife, 2 children, 28, Benosen, schoolmaster, 5 ft., brown hair.

Burkhard, widow, 3 children, 50, Grossachsen, 5 ft., black hair.

Two hundred & Seventy Passengers.

[Endorsed:]

List of German Passengers, arrived in the Port of Philadelphia pr. the Ship Margaret, E. C. Gardner, Master, from Amsterdam. Septr 19th 1804.

[List 481] List of Passengers p. Ship Fortune. [Nov. 3, 1804.]

	AGES		AGES
Henry Renck, drowned	48	Henry Kuessling	44
Maria Renckinn	46	Anna Eliz. F. Kuessling	36
J. J. Renck	18	J. C. Charles Kuessling	11
John Renck	14	Frederica Kuessling	8
Anna Elis. Renck	10	—— Kuessling, dead	1
Margaret Renck	5	Henry Groteyahn	32
Eliz. Opringen	40	Sophia Groteyahn	28
Caspar Larber	36	—— Groteyahn	2
Gertrude Larber	32	Jacob Hartman	36
—— Larber ⎱ twins	1½	Maria E. Hartman	31
—— Larber ⎰	1½	Peter Hartman	7
Melchior Larber	28	Cath. Hartman	5
Elisabeth Larber	27	Jn° George Hartman	2
—— Larber	1	Eliza Hartman	½
Frederick Wilhausen	55	Cath. Petrien	30
Anna Marg. Wilhausen	45	Wilhelmina Leitert	4
Henry W. Wilhausen	19	J. C. F. Leitert, dead	
George F. Wilhausen	16	Carolina Leitert, dead	
Marg. Charles Wilhausen	12	—— Leitert, dead	
John Christ Wilhausen	10	—— Leitert, dead	
William Wilhausen	8	Jacob Adam	
Caroline Wilhausen	4	John P. Stauss, dead	
—— Wilhausen, dead	1	Eliz. Staussen, dead	
John Christ Kummer	33	Johannes Rotte	29
Dorothy Elis. Kummer	38	Catherine A. Rotte	29
John Geo. Kummer	16	Henry Rotte	4
Saml Wm Kummer	12	William Rotte	2
John F. Kummer	4	Peter Ricker	..
John Dan. Kummer	31	Hannah Eliz. Rickeren	40
Charlotte Kummer	35	Henry Ricker	18
Hannah M. Kummer	13	Catherine Ricker	7

AGES

AGES

Henry Kohlhauer	33	John Kohlhauer	27
Cath. Eliz. Kohlhauer	27	Mar. Cath. Kohlhauer	30
Eliz. Becker	48	Anna Elis. Kohlhauer	7
John Kohlhauer	6	Peter Kohlhauer	5
Peter Kohlhauer	3	Conrad Kohlhauer	2
Catherine Lotsen	54	J. G. Weil	27
Peter Henry Lotsen	24	Anna M. Weil	31
Annette Lotsen	16	Juliana Bohenin	22
John Jost Goldman	26	William Weil	8
Eliz. Goldman	26	Maria Cath. Weil	5
Sophia Goldman	56	Cath. Elis. Weil	2
—— Goldman	6	Johann E. E. Shuhman, dead	
Peter Reshek	34	Anna Cath. Shuhman	34
Sophia Resheken	36	Christ. Shuman	9
Margaret Resheeken	14	Christina Shuhman	6
Jacob Kessler	38	Henry Drolsbach	42
John F. Lotz dead		Christina Drolsbach	41
Philippina Kessler	31	C. A. Salbein	46
Anna M. Lotzen	36	—— Drolsbach	12
Phillip Kessler	8	—— Drolsbach	8
John F. Lotz	4	—— Drolsbach	6
Maria C. Kondey	30	—— Drolsbach	4
Anna E. Kondey	11	—— Drolsbach, dead	1
John Geo. Kondey	7	Maria Elis. Greiss	39
—— Kondey	11 mos.	Anna M. Greiss	16
Carolina Helden	38	Catherina Greiss	14
Felix Hy Helden	20	Jost Muller	42
Conrad Heldt, drowned	17	Anna Marg. Muller	39
John P. Heldt	2	John Muller	19
Christ. Hahn	45	Jonas Muller	17
Susannah Folkin	45	Cath. Elis. Muller	15
Hann Wilh. Hahn	15	Sophia Muller	13
Peter Deisel	27	Jacob Muller	11
Catherine Deisel	18	John P. Schneider	39
Christian Pfaff	30	Peter Schneider	14
Caterina Pfaff	32	Ludwig Schneider	7
Cath. Pfaff, dead	1½	John S. Fuchs	45
Anna M. Pfaff	12	Anna E. Fuchsen	43
Cath. Elis. Pfaff	9	J. Jost Fuchs	20
Henry Pfaff	5	J. Henry Fuchs	19

	AGES		AGES
J. G. Fuchs	15	Cath. Schmidt	11
Eliz. Fuchs	12	J. Martin Schmidt	6
John Fuchs	10	Casper Heipel	
Catherine Fuchs	5	Christina Heipel, dead	
Simon Fuchs	3	—— Heipel	
Conrad Seip	39	—— Heipel	
Maria E. Seipen	28	—— Heipel	
Maria C. Greasman, dead		Conrad Frendt	40
Anna Elis Seip	7	Dorothy Frendt	38
John Seip	4	Carolina Frantzen	37
Peter Reinhard	44	J. George Frendt	15
Eliz. Reinharden, dead		Conrad Frendt	11
Peter Reinhard	22	—— Frendt	1
Anna Elis. Reinhard	16	John Otteherdendorp	40
George Henry Reinhard	15	Eliz. Otteherdendorp	
Anna Reinhard	13	Conrad Otteherdendorp	5
John Hoffman	47	Conrad Becker	20
Susanna Hoffman	41	Eliza Lamp	
Conrad Hoffman	17	Daniel Meyer	28
John Hoffman	13	Daniel Neieman	28
Henry Hoffman	10	Anna Eliz. Netz	14
Anna Cath. Hoffman	7	Adam Netz	9
Anna Maria Hoffman	3	John Christ. Kulp	32
John Henry Stahl, dead		Wilhelmina Kulp, dead	
Maria E. Stahl	30	Christian Lechner, dead	30
John Stahl		Anna M. Lechner	30
—— Stahl, dead		Henry Boehm	22
—— Stahl, dead		Anna E. Boehm	
John Henry Conrad	27	Nicholas Schneider	36
Magdalena Conrad	28	Anna M. Schneider	26
—— Conrad	2½	Jacob Schneider	5
Peter Frantz	44	—— Schneider, dead	3
Christian Newart	29	—— Schneider, dead	1
M. C. Newarten	25	Jacob Reinbein	29
—— Newarten, dead	½	Henry Charles Gese	24
John Henry Schmidt	52	John Phillip Klotz	24
Anna Eliz. Schmidt	42	Gustavus Bruch	24
Anthony Schmidt, drowned	19	Frederica Bruchen	20
Ludwig Schmidt	17	Christian Nesster	30
John Schmidt	13	Vincent Schazenhuber	26

	AGES		AGES
Yorick Wagoner	28	Christ. Aug. Kleinrath, dead	
Jacob Wagoner	25	Gerlach Heusge	
John Wohlfeel	28	Charles Frederich Schmidt	36
John Christ. Seitler	30	Caspar Muller	25
John Herm. Kreins	28	Freiderich Weisener	22
Hinrich Dohrman, dead		Hinrich Walter	48
Heinrich Gunther	28	Johannes P. Honnis	19
Alexander Levi	27		
Leopold Abraham	28	CABIN PASSENGERS	
Jacob Himmelman	40	George Vollberth	
Jacob Legnor	36	Christ. Nienaber	
John Val. Boder	20	Henry Heatherley	
Susman Hertz	22	John Hubbard	
John Jost Marcs	20	Timothy Lane	
John Christ. Ries	33	Ferdinand Muller, doctor of the	
Samuel Weibel	36	ship	
Frederich Merich	23	Captain Morse has entered &	
John George Buch	32	paid for two hundred & twenty	
Charles Ph. Kratz	20	five Passengers	

[List 482] List of 38 Passengers, arrived in the Ship Cato, Captn Levi Barden, from the River Jade near Bremen. Philadelphia, 3 November, 1804.

John Frederick Gerhard Nieman *	J. Anthony Grobe
	Eckard Muller
John Ludwig Hencke	John Gunter
John Christoph Muller	John Gotlieb Bogener, Prussia
Christiana Sophia Eleanora Muller (wife)	Henry Graff, Prussia
	Frantz Mühlberger
John Frederick Muller (child)	Frederick Loschenkohl
Louis Muller (child)	John F. Freese, Denmark
Henry Keiser	John Died. Michaelis
John Wm Smith	Lorenz Breitenbach
Geo. Tippenhouer, Prussia	Elizabeth Breitenbach (wife)
Joseph Schmider	Peter do (child)
Frederick Lubeck	William do (child)
Henry Grobe	Henry do (child)

* The persons after whose name no place name is given are all marked as coming from Germany.

John Breitenbach (child)
Frederick Goeb
Ernst Fred. Knauff
Abraham Berend Cohen, Hamburg
Christopher Reider, Switzerland
—— Fisher
—— Wheeler

Simon Becker
Rudolph Giese
Frederick Gerkis
Gerkis (wife)
Gerkis (child)

[Endorsed:]
Philad^a 3 Novr 1804, for Levi Barden, Captn. H. J. Hutchins.

[List 483] List of Passengers on board the Sch^r Antelope, James Church, Master, from St Thomas. [March 4, 1805.]

David Dryler
—— Jahrhaus
Gerhard Simons
John Bardesrosin
—— Sterheld
—— Dingler
—— Miller
—— Beck
—— Fisher
Barbary Elwangerin
C. Rossinbergen
A. B. Richer
C. Ottin
—— Volmer
C. Volmerin
J. Volmer
George Koch
John Koch
—— Wichler
——Wichlerin
—— Baisch
Christ^n Bausset
Henry Bausset
Mary Bausset
Emanuel Bausset

—— Veigner
Catharina Veignerin
Christiana Veignerin
Frederich Veigner
Michael Veigner
—— Harmen
Daniel Hamma
Godfrey Hamma
Barbary Harmen
—— Dobler
A. Maria Doblerin
Elizabeth Doblerin
Cath. W. Kohlerin
Cath^n Kohlerin
—— Breining
Johana Breigning
John Breigning
Magdalin Breminger
Johann Breminger
Christiana Breminger
Jacob Keitzler
Jacob Keitzler
Frederick Keitzler
Jacob Keitzler
Job Keitzler

Johanna Keitzlerin	—— Hoerchinger
A. Maria Keitzlerin	J. F. Maergle
Fredericka Keitzlerin	—— Schaekrer
—— Forchel	—— Moerchel
Maria Forklen	J. F. Harma
S. Forklin	Margaret Hamma
F. Forklin	Ann Maria Hamma
Eve Forklin	Magdalina Hasel
—— Wormer	Godfrey Hoestz
Cath. Wormerin	John Geo. Hoetz
Mag. Wormerin	—— Ritter
Fredericka Leibharden	Barbary Ritterin
Fredericka Leibharden	Maria Ritterin
J. S. Vander	Fred^k Rittar
Catharine Ott	Barbary Rittera
Peter Ulrich	Dorotha Ritterin
—— Maergle	Godfrey Ritterin
—— Baum	M. Deuschelin
—— Schuhler	Jacob F. Deuschlin
—— Kober	C. F. Deuschelin
—— Freidenberger	—— Scheidler
—— Albrecht	John Scheidler
—— Kresch	Eve Scheidler
—— Kohl	

[Endorsed:]
List of German Passengers, who arrived at the Port of
Philad^a on the Schooner Antelope, James Church, Commander,
from St. Thomas. March 4th 1805.

[List 484] A List of the passengers in the ship Little Cherub,
Daniel Brewton, Master, from Amsterdam. May 7, 1805.

CABIN PASSENGERS	STEERAGE PASSENGERS
Gibbs West	Christopher Neunhoessure
Branco Deiong & son	George Snyder

[Endorsed:]
May 7, 1805. Little Cherub.

[List 485] Report of alien Passengers on Board the Ship

Margaret, of which Edward C. Gardner, [Captain]. Arrived at the Port of ———— in the State of ———— on the day of ———— [Aug 26, 1805.]

NAMES OF PASSENGERS	AGES	PLACE OF NATIVITY	OCCUPATION	DESCRIPTION OF PERSON
Jacob Geyger	36	Wurtemburg	farmer	brown & tall
Elizabeth Geyger	34			
J. A. Librant	39	Wurtemburg	farmer	light
Rosina Librant	34			
Andras Librant	12			
Frederica Librant	9	Containing		
Ludwic Librant	6	one family		ordinary
Jacob Librant	3			
Edward Librant	2 months			
Solomon Woolf	35			
Elizabeth	30			
George	9			
Johannas	3	Wurtemburg	farmer	ordinary
Magdaleina	1½			
Solomon	½			
Michael Libely	43			
Maria	45			
Michael	19			
Joseph } Wife &	17	Wurtemburg	farmer	ordinary
Christian } Children	8			
Maria	6			
Louisa	3			
Casper Byrer	39			
Rosina	39			
Frederick	13	Wurtemburg	farmer	ordinary
Gotlope	2½			
Johannas	¾			
Joseph Geyger	31	Wurtemburg	farmer	6 feet 6
Anna	30			inches
Margaret Desting	17	Wurtemburg	servant maid	ordinary
Johann Senable	29			
Regina	22	Wurtemburg	shoemaker	very light
Frederich	¾			

NAMES OF PASSENGERS	AGES	PLACE OF NATIVITY	OCCUPATION	DESCRIPTION OF PERSON
Johan G. Specht	44			low stature,
Margaret	48			with a hump
K. Margaret	20			on his back
Catharine	18	Wurtemburg	wine gardener	
Gotlieb	16			
David	12			
Abraham	5			
Michael Binenger	67			
Sabina	55			
Anna Maria	28	Wurtemburg	house carpenter	ordinary
Frederica	25			& large
Sabina	18			
Adam Librant	19	Wurtemburg	stone mason	light
Paul Frank	45			
Barbara	42			
Regina Barbara	18			
John George	12	Wurtemburg	farmer	low stature,
Frederich	5			old & dark
Avelhart	3			
Christina	3			
Froneca	2			
George Miller	25	Wurtemburg	butcher	tall & light
Frederich Miller	13	Wurtemburg	servant boy	light
George F. Frank	45			
Margaret	38			
Feronaca	12			
Christina	10	Wurtemburg	farmer	ordinary
G. Frederich	6		wine dresser	stature &
Elizabeth	3½			dark
Christianan	2			
Jacob Lible	25			
Christina	21	Wurtemburg	farmer	light
Johannas	2			
Christoph Bower	35			
Christiana	28	Wurtemburg	farmer	light
Johan Ludwich	5			
Christina	3			
Johan George Schillinger	32			
Maria Barbara	28	Wurtemburg	farmer	dark
Elizabeth	5			
Johannas	3			

NAMES OF PASSENGERS	AGES	PLACE OF NATIVITY	OCCUPATION	DESCRIPTION OF PERSON
Jacob Spingler	38			
Agnes	38			
Barbara	41			
Godfried	13			
David	10	Wurtemburg	farmer	dark
Jacob	7			
Barbara	9			
Gotliep, born on board				
Catharine Sneper	18	Wurtemburg	servant maid	light
George Schambacher	36			
Margaret, wife	35			
Jacob	12			
John George	10	Wurtemburg	farmer	ordinary
Margaret	8			
Johannas	3			
Catharine	2			
Christian Zerwick	20	Wurtemburg	butcher	ordinary
George F. Wagner	35			
Magdalana, wife	27			
Johanna Catharine	3½	Wurtemburg	blacksmith	dark
David	1			
George Wolfley	16	Wurtemburg	butcher	
Abraham Biser	42			
Christianne	45			
Abraham	18			
Gotlib	17			
Christianna	15			
Auguste	12	Wurtemburg	cooper	light & tall
Gottfried	10			
Carolina	8			
Johan	3½			
Frederica	2			
Johannas Rap	35			
Maria Catharine	22			
Johannas	5	Wurtemburg	farmer	light
Maria Juliana	3			
Anna Moss	50	Wurtemburg	gentle woman	large & black
Frederick Tapilots	25	Wurtemburg	baker	light

NAMES OF PASSENGERS	AGES	PLACE OF NATIVITY	OCCUPATION	DESCRIPTION OF PERSON
Mathew Seemuller	34			
Magdalena	38			
Elizabeth	11	one family		
Henrica	3½	Wurtemburg	tailor	dark
Gotlope	1			
Sarah, born on board				
Joseph Spicer	34	Wurtemburg	tailor	dark
Elizabeth, wife	38			
Jacob Amand	44	Wurtemburg	farmer	dark
Magdalina, child	3½			
Johannas Kirklinger	24			
Anna Maria	28			
Anna Catharine	17	Wurtemburg one family	weaver	light
Johan Frederich	15			
Frederich	1			
Godfried Rich	21	Wurtemburg	farmer	dark
Johannas Wiedman	42			
Barbara	43			
Leonard	13	——	——	—
Barbara	3			
Johannas	1			
Johannas Bidle	42			
Anna Maria	50	Wurtemburg	vine dresser	dark
Johan	19			
Johan Snider	45			
Christianna	45			
Charles	14			
John Freder[ick]	12½	Wurtemburg	butcher	dark
John Gotlieb	11			
Christan	2			
Malchior Crener	32			
Rosina	29	Wurtemburg	farmer	dark
Elizabeth	1			
Johan G. Schruntz	60	Wurtemburg	tailor	dark
Charlotta, wife	45			
David Silhart	44			
Elizabeth	28			
Catharine	3½	——	——	—
Gotfry Maga, born on board				

NAMES OF PASSENGERS	AGES	PLACE OF NATIVITY	OCCUPATION	DESCRIPTION OF PERSON
Jacob Voley	42	Wurtemburg	baker	light
Jacob, son	17			
Johan Kortz	44			
Barbara	34			
Barbara	9	Wurtemburg	tailor	**dark**
Johannas	5			
Jacob	2			
Godfried Beam	35	Wurtemburg	weaver	light
Anna Maria	39		midwife	
Christoph	12			
Johannas	7			
David	3½			
Maria	2			
Jacob Libelie	25	Wurtemburg	shoemaker	light
Johan Eikeholt	23	Wurtemburg	stone mason	light
David Eikholt	20			
Johan Beam	42			
Elizabeth	39			
John George	10	Wurtemburg	farmer	light
John Jacob	7			
Anna Barbara	½			
Adam Vernin	56			
Lousia	52			
Anna Maria	18	Wurtemburg	farmer	
Margaret	16			
Daniel	15			
George Richenbach	44			
Magdalene	33			
George	14	Wurtemburg	weaver	light
Johannas	4			
Leonard Michle	27	Wurtemburg	weaver	light
George M. Fogaler	36			
Rosine	31			
Wilhelmina	12			
Hendrich	10	Wurtemburg	goldsmith	tall & dark
Godlieb	8			
Johan	6			
Louis	2½			
Jefferson, born on board				

NAMES OF PASSENGERS	AGES	PLACE OF NATIVITY	OCCUPATION	DESCRIPTION OF PERSON
Jacob Dingler	36			
Louisa	42	Wurtemburg	tailor	tall & dark
Frederica	6			
George Minden	34	Wurtemburg	cooper	light
Anna	32			
Gotlieb Werner	38	Wurtemburg	stone mason	dark
Catharine	35			
Dorothy	3½			
Johan George Mose	18	Wurtemburg	weaver	light
Johan Abaler	17	Wurtemburg	blacksmith	light
Thomas Siler	24	Wurtemburg	farmer	light
Barbara Siler	18	Wurtemburg	maid	light
Johan Wolmer	36	Wurtemburg	baker	dark
Philip Simon	18	Wurtemburg	barber	light
Johan Lise	22	Wurtemburg	vine dresser	dark
Catherine Kanetruwar	42	Wurtemburg	servants	light
Christiana, daughter	12			
Johan F. Wise	36	Wurtemburg	tailor	dark
Frederich Schible	21	Wurtemburg	clerk	light
Abraham Sundle	43			
Julianne	40			
Johann	13	Wurtemburg	farmer	dark
Jacob	9			
Henrica	4			
Catharine	1			
Johan Wiedman	53			
Michael	21	Wurtemburg	potter	dark
Johan	19			
Anna Maria Schohen	26	Wurtemburg	servant maid	dark
Johannas Meyer	24	Wurtemburg	carpenter	dark
Johan Numer	20	Wurtemburg	farmer	dark
John G. Bentz	47			
Elizabeth	49			
Catharine	18	Wurtemburg	shoemaker	dark
Jacob	13			
John	7			
August Armfelt	31	Wurtemburg	apothecary	light
Joh. Lousey	29	Wurtemburg	butcher	dark
Luis Linder	21	Wurtemburg	millright	light

NAMES OF PASSENGERS	AGES	PLACE OF NATIVITY	OCCUPATION	DESCRIPTION OF PERSON
Adolph Strous	21	Wurtemburg	clerk	dark
Johan Ried	21	Wurtemburg	silversmith	dark
Jacob May	30	Wurtemburg	stone mason	dark
Emanuel May	22	Wurtemburg	stone mason	dark
Hendrich Lindler	36			
Anna	46			
Johannas	13	Wurtemburg	farmer	dark
Anna	11			
Joseph Olhi	29		distiller	
		Wurtemburg	&	dark
Elizabeth	26		farmer	
P. F. Graff	24	Wurtemburg	merchant	light
Edward Klinsmith	17	Wurtemburg	stone mason	light
George Levern	29	Wurtemburg	farmer	dark
F. F. G. Dobliner	22	Wurtemburg	goldsmith	dark
Willm Conoly	20	Ireland	weaver	tall & dark
Nancy Conoly	24	Ireland	weaver	tall, round visage

[List 486] Passengers in Ship Verny, Captn Elisha King, from Amsterdam [Septr 5, 1805.]

NAMES		PLACE OF BIRTH	YEARS
Johan Augustin		Gemhoffen	36
Phillipine Augustin Jahninn		Feltzkirchen	42
Henri Hecker		Hoesten	36
Gottlieb Johan Lichtenecker		Frankfurth	30
Frederika	his wife	Hanau	30
Phillip Hock		Rendel	29
Jacob Aull		Dusseldorff	18
Johan Everich		Dillsum ⎱ Issenburg	30
Anna Maria Achtzehterin	his wife	Dillsum ⎰	24
Joseph Baden		Rhein Breitbach	32
Anna Maria Baden	his wife	Haren, Westphalen	29
Friederich Baden	his son	Rhein Breitbach	11
Johan Frederich Herlinger		Stargard	33
Friederika	his wife	Stargard	23
Charlote Herlinger	his child	Amsterdam	8d.
Johannes König		Feldbach	30

NAMES		PLACE OF BIRTH	YEARS
Christina Frederika Wessner	his wife	Feldbach	31
Heinrich Hettinger		Rheineck	44
Catharine	his wife	Betigheim	36
Heinrich Hettinger	his child	Betigheim	13
Lorenz Hettinger	his child	Betigheim	12
Christina Eva	his child	Betigheim	11
Bernhard	his child	Betigheim	8
Mathias	his child	Betigheim	6
Johanes Winterradt		Pfaltz	46
Maria van Derlinden	his wife	Miegen, Grafschaft	38
Phillip Winterradt	his child	Pfaltz-Rafenstcin	16
Johanes Winterradt	his child	Pfaltz-Rafenstein	9
Conrad Krugeli		Mandelsheim	40
Johanes Janssen		Emerich	38
Johana Janssen	his wife	Emerich	40
Johanes Janssen	his child	Emerich	13
Johanes Bernhard Siegemann		Sandebeck	24
Elizabeth Siegemann	his wife	Sandebeck	26
Elisabeth Siegemann	his child	Paderborn	1
Gottlieb Heninger		Ludwigsburg	25
Peter Hildebrandt		Hardehausen	22
Elizabeth Hildebrandt		Munster	19
David Hann		Gross Hebbach	50
Maria Magdelena	his wife	Gross Hebbach	52
Catharina Barbara	his child	Gross Hebbach	24
Johana Augusta	his child	Gross Hebbach	22
Catharina Magdelena	his child	Gross Hebbach	13
Johan Gaspar Methe		Rohdra	50
Anna Elizabeth Kratzenbergen		Zunstersbach	49
Anna Maria Knollin		Wallroth	28
Michael Friederich Strasinsky		Elbing	26
Johana Wilhelmina Constanz	his wife	Preus Minden	26
Carl	their child	Preus Minden	10 months
Jacob Link		Gross Gotha	24
Joseph Mohr		Alten Krautheim	28
Andreas Stahl		Marbach	27
Johan Christoph Müller		Werdenhausen	44
Anna Franziska	his wife	Kassel	38
Catharina Margretha	his child	Hofgeismar	13
Anna Catharina	his child	Hofgeismar	12

NAMES		PLACE OF BIRTH	YEARS
Johan Heinrich	his child	Hofgeismar	9
Johan Martin	his child	Hofgeismar	8
Dorethea Elisabeth	his child	Hofgeismar	6
Johan Conrad	his child	Hofgeismar	4
Christoph Phillip	his child	Hofgeismar	1
Johan Michael Brigel		Haubersbronn	35
Maria Rosina	his wife	Geisingen	32
Johan Georg	his child	Geisingen	8
Joseph	his child	Geisingen	6
Anna Catharina	his child	Geisingen	1
Christoph Friederich Neff		Feldbach	23
Matheus Glauner		Feldbach	22
Matheus Friederich Schmidt		Feldbach	21
Johan Christoph Pauli		Ludwigsburg	35
Dorothea Helena Pauli	his wife	Ludwigsburg	33
Charlota	his child	Ludwigsburg	16 mos.
Matthis Friederich Maille		Feldbach	47
Catharina Barbara	his wife	Feldbach	50
Catharina Barbara	his daughter	Feldbach	25
Mathias Friederich	his son	Feldbach	22
Johanes	his son	Feldbach	21
Friederika	his daughter	Feldbach	19
Walburga	his daughter	Feldbach	15
Maria Magdelina		Feldbach	12
Friederich Hauser		Feldbach	31
Eva Margreth Ehningerinn		Strumpfelbach	21
Christina Barbara Seiseram		Kemnath	24
Carl Flor		Hildesheim	18
Adolph Harzfeld		Heidingsfeldt	28
Jung Michael Stark		Schneid	52
Michael	his son	Schneid	19
Jacob Friederich	his son	Schneid	15
Margretha	his daughter	Schneid	12
Christoph Graff		Genningen	36
Johanes Krehl		Minsingen, auf der Alp	38
Michael Kramer		Rauchingen	52
Johana Jäckle		Heimerdingen	23
Johana Jüngling		Marbach (am Neker)	20
Christian Schneider		Stoltzenberg	25
Friederich Kohler		Schweiberlingen	36

NAMES		PLACE OF BIRTH	YEARS
Joseph Steibel		Frankfurth	24
Carl Wankel		Fulda	34
Phillip Jäger		Willofs	24
Christian Kring		Heyger Seelbach	27
Anna Catharina	his wife	Rottenbach	24
Johanes Heinrich Eichert		Heyger Seelbach	27
Joost Heinrich Eichert		Heyger Seelbach	24
Jacob Bauer		Beningen	38
Johanes Winter		Oberarschel	25
Jacob Frey		Offenburg	26
David Krauter		Ungeheurhof	27
Michael Herlein		Feurbach	45
Catharine	his wife	Feurbach	47
Melgior	his son	Feurbach	16
Anna Margarethe	his daughter	Feurbach	24
Johan Phillip	his son	Feurbach	13
George Phillip	his son	Feurbach	11
Michael Müller		Detter	33
Christina	his wife	Detter	38
Burkardt	his son	Detter	5
Andreas	his son	Detter	3
Andreas Kessler		Weissenbach	42
Margretha	his wife	Weissenbach	45
Johan Michael	his son	Weissenbach	7
Anna Margretha	his daughter	Weissenbach	18
Catharina Elisabeth	his daughter	Weissenbach	15
Dorothea	his daughter	Weissenbach	10
Maria Catharina	his daughter	Weissenbach	4
Margretha	his daughter	Weissenbach	1
Andreas Kessler	his son	Weissenbach	14
Johan Stephan Diehl		Seikenhoff	28
Elisabeth Thomasin	his wife	Seikenhoff	22
Margretha Thomasin		Seikenhoff	28
Heinrich Becker		Manheim	32
Paul Wolf		Manheim	36
Michael Wolf	his son	Manheim	17
Johan Heinrich Kring		Heygerseelbach	40
Elisabeth	his wife	Heygerseelbach	30
Ludwig	his child	Heygerseelbach	12

NAMES		PLACE OF BIRTH	YEARS
Anna Maria	his child	Heygerseelbach	10
Christian	his child	Heygerseelbach	8
Johan Heinrich	his child	Heygerseelbach	6
Anna Margretha	his child	Heygerseelbach	4
Catharina	his child	Heygerseelbach	6 mos.
Heinrich Muller		Langenbach	43
	his wife	Langenbach	24
	his child	Langenbach	2½
Joost Neeb		Marienburg	22
Christ Neeb		Marienburg	26
Johanes V. Treupel		Heygerseelbach	23
	his wife	Heygerseelbach	24
Christian Mak		Gross Aspach	19
Johan George Mak		Gross Aspach	24
Jacob Wirth		Gross Aspach	22
Daniel Wirth		Gross Aspach	19
Jacob Wilhelm Dechant *		Nassau Weilburg	22
Georg Friederich Fechting		Waldangelbach	36
Peter Schmidt		Ober Mollau	28
Johan Röhnisch		Frankfurth	45
Sophia Duesing		Hanover	28
Ludwig Donath		Eichenstreuth	18
Heinrich Becker		Manheim	32
Maria Schulenberg		Lipstadt	23
Christop Knodel		Detisheim	24
Johan Georg Rösch		Henningen	45
Regina	his wife	Henningen	43
Christoph Kogel	son-in-law	Henningen	18
Barbara Rosch	his daughter	Henningen	15
Jacob	his son	Henningen	5
Anton Meyerle		Monheim	28
Gerhard Müller		Nassau Diehlenburg	28
Ludwig Friederch Hägeli		Unterturkheim	20
Jacob Heker		Schweiberdingen	48
Elisabeth	his wife	Schweiberdingen	48
Catharina	his daughter	Schweiberdingen	24
Elisabeth	his daughter	Schweiberdingen	20

* A Reformed minister. See *Fathers of the Reformed Church*, Vol. III, p. 175.

NAMES		PLACE OF BIRTH	YEARS
Anna Maria	his daughter	Schweiberdingen	15
Conrad	his Son	Schweiberdingen	12
Eva Elisabeth Bauer		Markgröningen	23
Jacob Friederich Müller		Vaihingen	24
Tobias Bühler		Ottisheim	17
Jung Conrad April		Ertenbach	32
Eva Catharina	his wife	Ertenbach	32
Catharina	his child	Ertenbach	1 yr. 6 mos.
Johan Stephan Weipert		Enzweihingen	19
George Michael Plessing		Holinwarth	47
Anna Margretha	his wife	Holinwarth	36
Anna Maria Catharina	his daughter	Holinwarth	21
Johana Cristina	his daughter	Holinwarth	13
Maria Magdalena	his daughter	Holinwarth	11
Johan Daniel	his son	Holinwarth	6
Johanes Nagel		Durlach	19
Joseph Steibel		Frankfurth	18
Conrad Jäckle		Heimerdingen	23
Maria Bartels		Embden	29
	her child	Embden	4
Conrad Vogt		Hessenkassel	34
Christian Lorenz Allich		Heilbron	32
August Fickardt		Dettmolt	27
Carl Montfort		Zell	36

[List 487] On Board the American Ship The Liberty, Captain Sidney H. Burrough, from Amsterdam to Philadelphia, sailed from the Texel, August 4th, 1805. [Arrived in Philadelphia October 18, 1805.]

PASSENGERS OVER 14 YEARS OF AGE IN THE CABIN	CHILDREN UNDER 14 YEARS	THEIR NATIVE PLACES	UNDER WHICH GOVERNMENT
Mr. Hasseler	4	Aarau	Swiss
Mrs. Hasseler		Aarau	Swiss
Magdalena Gysin, servant		Aarau	Swiss
Mr. Zöller		Emendingen	Baden
Mr. Müslin		Bern	Swiss
Mr. Chaillet		Murten	Swiss
Mr. Tschiffely		Bern	Swiss

PASSENGERS OVER 14 YEARS OF AGE	CHILDREN UNDER 14 YEARS	THEIR NATIVE PLACES	UNDER WHICH GOVERNMENT
David Fred Tschiffely		Bern	Swiss
Mr. Neuhaus		Gals	Swiss
Mr. da Coste		Lyons	France
Mr. Blanchard		Chambery	France

IN THE STEERAGE

Madame Gex	5	Vevey	Swiss
Anthon Gex, son		Vevey	Swiss
Mr. Obussieur		Lausanne	Swiss
Mr. Albert		Lausanne	Swiss
Mrs. Albert		Lausanne	Swiss
Mr. Marcel	3	Lausanne	Swiss
Mrs. Marcel		Lausanne	Swiss
Mr. Riss	3	Deitingen	Swiss
Mrs. Riss & 2 sons		Deitingen	Swiss
Mr. Gostely		Bern	Swiss
Mrs. Gostely		Bern	Swiss
Mr. Thoman		Hollstern	Swiss
Mrs. Thoman		Hollstern	Swiss
Mr. Vöghly		Pratten	Swiss
Mrs. Vöghly		Pratten	Swiss
Mr. Dreyer		Bern	Swiss
Regina, his daughter		Bern	Swiss
Two sons		Bern	Swiss
Mr. Schurch	4	Summiswald	Swiss
Mrs. Schurch		Summiswald	Swiss
Mr. Mundweyler		Danicken	Swiss
Mr. Wirz	3	Gelterkinden	Swiss
Mrs. Wirz		Gelterkinden	Swiss
Mr. Ziegler	4	Unterranseen	Swiss
Mrs. Ziegler		Unterranseen	Swiss
Mr. Suther	4	Diepflingen	Swiss
Mrs. Suther		Diepflingen	Swiss
Two sons		Diepflingen	Swiss
Joh. Jenny	1	Diegten	Swiss
Mrs. Jenny		Diegten	Swiss
Mrs. Schwyzer	2	Lausen	Swiss
Jacob Jenny	2	Gelterkinden	Swiss
Mrs. Jenny		Gelterkinden	Swiss

PASSENGERS OVER 14 YEARS OF AGE	CHILDREN UNDER 14 YEARS	THEIR NATIVE PLACES	UNDER WHICH GOVERNMENT
IN THE STEERAGE			
Mrs. Imhoff	3	Aristorg	Swiss
Mr. Zärlin	1	Diepflingen	Swiss
Mrs. Zärlin		Diepflingen	Swiss
Mr. Gerster	3	Gelterkinden	Swiss
Mrs. Gerster		Gelterkinden	Swiss
Mr. Gräffelin	4	Hollstern	Swiss
Mrs. Graffelin		Hollstern	Swiss
Mrs. Freyvogel	4	Gelterkinden	Swiss
Mr. Hug	3	Siesach	Swiss
Mrs. Hug		Siesach	Swiss
Mr. Gerber	3	Zunsgen	Swiss
Mrs. Gerber		Zunsgen	Swiss
Two sons		Zunsgen	Swiss
One daughter		Zunsgen	Swiss
Mr. Schaub		Mattens	Swiss
Mr. Bury		Gelterkinden	Swiss
Mr. Weber		Ormanlingen	Swiss
Mr. Frey		Siesach	Swiss
Mrs. Frey		Siesach	Swiss
Two sons		Siesach	Swiss
Mrs. Hirbin		Gelterkinden	Swiss
Mrs. Handschin		Rykenbach	Swiss
Mr. Bossard		Herrissau	Swiss
Mr. Frickert		Gelterkinden	Swiss
Mr. Künzly		Leonberg	Wurtemberg
Mr. Bauman		Menznau	Swiss
Mr. Winckelblech		Basel	Swiss
Mr. Martin		Liestal	Swiss
Mrs. Martin		Liestal	Swiss
Two sons		Liestal	Swiss
Three daughters		Liestal	Swiss
Mr. Lewisohn		Berlin	Prussian
Mr. Colmar		Brestenberg	Swiss
Mr. Rubin		Thun	Swiss
Mr. Schmidt		Aarau	Swiss
Mr. Bundt		Herrissau	Swiss
Mr. Lippoldt		Dornburg	Saxen Weimar

PASSENGERS OVER 14 YEARS OF AGE	CHILDREN UNDER 14 YEARS	THEIR NATIVE PLACES	UNDER WHICH GOVERNMENT

IN THE STEERAGE

Mr. Dalmazo		Turin	Piemont
Dr. Daller		Lausanne	Swiss
Mr. Salathe		Seltesberg	Swiss
Mr. Schwickert		Baknan	Wurtemberg
Mr. Lüthi		Langnau	Swiss
Mr. Kindt		Pest	Hungarian
Mr. Kuhn		Degersheim	Swiss
Mr. Manhart		Pfefficken	Swiss
Mr. Niehans		Bern	Swiss

SINGLE GIRLS WITHOUT
THEIR PARENTS

Catharine Wachter		Bötzberg	Swiss
Susanna Stubacher		Lampenberg	Swiss
Marg. Derghard		Amsterdam	Holland

BY THE SAILORS

Peter Halbout		Guernsey	England
James Vivent		Guernsey	England
Wm. Braun			United States

Total of passengers: 162

Male Passengers over 14 Years of Age	75	
Female ditto ditto	33	
Children under 4 Years of Age	20	
Ditto from 4 to 14 Years	34	162

Certified the above to be a True list of the Passengers.
Philadelphia October 18th 1805.

> for Capn. S. H. Burrough.
>   Laurn Heiron, Junr
>   Second-mate.

[Endorsed:]

List of German Passengers, arrived in the Port of Philada, Ship Liberty, from Amsterdam. October 18th 1805.

[List 488] List of the Steerage Passengers, on board the Ship the Little Cherub, Daniel Brewton, Master. [Oct. 18, 1805.]

Joh. Phil. Pogert, wife & two children
Conrad Looner & his wife
Magdalena Retzin
Josua Beck
Carl Otten
Johann Haefele, wife & three children
Christian Kirn, wife & three children
Jacob Ekelsberger
Johan Trompeter, wife & seven children
Jan Hend^k Richter & wife
Joseph Simmering & wife
Andreas Hutter
Bernhard Schwager
J. Reinh^d Schmidt
Wilhelm De Cludt
Heinrich Fischer
Wilhelm Roth
Ludwig Schaber
Friedrich Flugfelder
Abr. Bedinger
Hein^r Wies, wife & daughter
Joseph Ritsekky, wife & 2 children

Johan Abt, wife & one child
Hein^r Abt, wife & two sons
Hein^r Abt, wife, 4 daughters and 2 sons
Christoph Hörtel, wife & child
Georg Loorer, wife & child
Engelh^d Auderich, wife & 2 children
Ernst Freundt, wife & child
George Adam Dies
Widow Werle & two Sons
Wendel Titus, wife & 4 children
Thomas Kegel & son
Fried^r Klein
Hein^r Donias
Ignaz Diebold
Christian Thoma
Samuel Martin
Fried^r Weiland & his wife
Sebast. Himmelsbacher
Johann Millich
J. A. Morian

CABIN PASSENGERS

Henry Frind
Lewis Querne

Daniel Brewton.

[Endorsed:]
List of German Passengers, arrived in the Port of Philadelphia, Ship Little Cherub, from Amsterdam, October 18th 1805.

[List 489] List of passengers on Board the Ship Fair American, Jesse Fraley, Master from Amsterdam to Philadelphia. [October 26th, 1805.]

NAMES OF FAMILIES	NUMBER OF PERSONS	NAMES OF FAMILIES	NUMBER OF PERSONS
Fred^k Henning	4	David König	6

NAMES OF FAMILIES	NUMBER OF PERSONS	NAMES OF FAMILIES	NUMBER OF PERSONS
Tobias Silber	1	Bal. Berdsch	3
Albrecht Ruff	1	Christ. Rall	3
Jacob Dorwarth	4	Martin Rebstock	7
Jacobina Knodelin	2	Jacob Rentz	6
Conrad Hähnlen	9	Michael Wittler	4
David Kant	3	Joh. Waltz	1
Eberhard Eberschwein	4	Jacob Wittel	3
Catharina Schafferin	6	Martin Fluth	7
Mathias Trautwein	6	Jacob Lillich	6
Simon Durwächter	2	Jacob Lipp	3
Geo. Wagner	2	Geo. Fred^k Schmid	3
Joh. Hunn	3	Jacob Hummel	5
Gotlb. Klett	7	Elias Entz	1
Elizabeth Thorwarth	4	John Entz	1
Peter Flach	3	Geo. Jäger	1
Christ. Vogt	4	Mich. Hagmann	5
Saml Etter	5	Jacob Knodel	10
Margarethe Bessan	5	Mich. Wolfangel	1
Godfrey Riesch	5	Jacob Casper	1
Adam Reichard	4	Jacob Rentz	1
Christ. Käsmann	4	Conrad Bahnmuller	2
George Keppeler	6	Ph. C. Lex	7
Matthias Speidel	7	Gutin	1
David Hainle	5	Eichacker	1
Henry Schwartz	5	Jacob Busch	1
George Schwitte	10	John Fisher	1
Jacob Geissel	2		
Joh. Geo. Bläher	4		253
Joh. Kährer	6	Died With the Small pox	
Joh. Stump	7	6 children	6
Mich. Shehrer	7		
Jacob Horr	4	remaining on Board	249
Jacob Bruchlacher	5		Persons
George Haidt	6		

[Endorsed:]

List of German Passengers, arrived in the Port of Philadelphia, Ship Fair American, from Amsterdam, October 26th 1805.

[List 490] Report of Alien Passengers on board the American Ship Three Sisters of Bremen, burthen 200 tons or thereabouts, owned in Bremen by Geo. W. Trahn & others, H. C. Haesloop, Master, from Bremen—Arrived 30 November, 1805.

[*Name, age, place of nativity, occupation, height, complexion.*]

John Chr. Mengel, 25, Bettelhausen, farmer, 5 ft. 6 in., light complexion.

Catharine Mengel, 24, Bettelhausen, farmer, 5 ft., black hair.

Johannes Muller, 30, Fischenbach, farmer, 5 ft. 6 in., dark complexion.

Catharine Lise Muller, 28, Fischenbach, farmer, 5 ft., fair complexion.

John H. Muller, 6, Fischenbach, 2½ ft., fair complexion.

Conrad Senger, 30, Bloorbach, farmer, 5 ft. 8 in., fair complexion.

Catharine Sengar, 28, Bloorbach, farmer, 5 ft. 2 in., fair complexion.

Carl Sengar, 2, Bloorbach, 2 ft., fair complexion.

Johannes Benfer, 48, Fischenbach, farmer, 5 ft. 10 in., dark complexion.

Ann Lise Benfer, 50, Fischenbach, farmer, 5 ft. 5 in., dark complexion.

John Chr. Benfer, 20, Fischenbach, farmer, 5 ft. 6 in., dark complexion.

John Benfer, 13, Fischenbach, farmer, 4 ft. 2 in., fair complexion.

William Weber, 50, Sassenhausen, farmer, 5 ft. 5 in., dark complexion.

Anna Lise Weber, 41, Sassenhausen, farmer, 5 ft. 5 in., dark complexion.

George Weber, 22, Sassenhausen, farmer, 5 ft. 6 in., fair complexion.

Maria Anneleese Weber, 19, Sassenhausen, farmer, 4 ft. 6 in., fair complexion.

Anna Christiana Weber, 19, Sassenhausen, farmer, 5 ft. 5 in., fair complexion.

Maria Cath^a Weber, 24, Sassenhausen, farmer, 5 ft. 5 in., fair complexion.

Carl Speck, Senr, 56, Laasfe, weaver, 5 ft. 10 in., fair complexion.

Wilhelmina Speck, 32, Laasfe, 5 ft. 4 in., fair complexion.

Carl Speck, son, 18, Laasfe, baker, 5 ft. 10 in., fair complexion.

Christian Speck, 16, Laasfe, 5 ft. 8 in., fair complexion.

Fred^k Speck, 3, Laasfe, 2 ft. 6 in., fair complexion.

Frederica Speck, 6, Laasfe, 3 ft., fair complexion.

John Bruch, 32, Laasfe, mason, 5 ft. 5 in., fair complexion, br. hair.

Dorothea Bruch, 36, Laasfe, 5 ft. 8 in., fair complexion, br. hair.

Anna Catharina Bruch, 3, Laasfe, 2 ft. 6 in., fair complexion.

Margareth Weber, 13, Sassenhausen.

John Jost Diederick, 48, Riestein, farmer & weaver, 5 ft. 4 in., dark complexion.

Louisa Diederick, 47, Barfeld, 5 ft. 3 in., dark complexion.

John Diederick, 24, Barfeld, farmer, 5 ft. 6 in., fair complexion.

John Ust. Diederick, 13, Barfeld, farmer, 4 ft., fair complexion.

Christian Diederick, 17, Barfeld, farmer, 5 ft. 6 in., fair complexion.

John E. Heyn, 31, Laasfe, painter & glazer, 5 ft. 10 in., dark complexion.

Catharine Lise Heyn, 28, Laasfe, 5 ft., dark complexion.

Catharine Lise Heyn, 2, Laasfe, 2 ft. 6 in., fair complexion.

George Weber, 28, Bettelhausen, shoemaker, 6 ft., fair complexion.

Danˡ Zacharias, 26, Elsoff, tailor, 5 ft. 6 in., fair complexion.

Charlotte Germeyer, 22, Laasfe, 5 ft., fair complexion.

Maria Schneider, 24, Sassenhausen, 5 ft., fair complexion.

Victor Kesler, 23, Berlenburg, clerk, 5 ft. 6 in., fair complexion.

Carl Werner, 23, Laasfe, baker, 5 ft. 6 in., fair complexion.

Fredᵏ Hirschberg, 23, Laasfe, farmer, 5 ft. 6 in., fair complexion.

Gabriel Senner, 23, Bettelhausen, farmer, 5 ft. 6 in., fair complexion.

Anna Cathᵃ Spiesen, 17, Bettelhausen, 5 ft. 4 in., fair complexion.

J. Pulferich, 30, Steinbach, hunter & waiter, 5 ft. 7 in., fair complexion.

John H. Hoffman, 25, Wilsdorf, coachman, 5 ft. 8 in., fair complexion, brown hair.

Jacob Wolf, 22, Laasfe, weaver, 6 ft., fair complexion.

John Eckell, 28, Barfeldt, farmer, 5 ft. 6 in., dark complexion.

Geo. Hʸ Hublitz, 28, Barfeldt, tailor, 5 ft. 8 in., dark complexion.

John Vobel, 21, Barfeldt, farmer, 5 ft. 2 in., fair complexion.

Anthony Vobel, 22, Barfeldt, farmer, 5 ft. 3 in., fair complexion.

Elizabeth Vobel, 24, Barfeldt, farmer, 5 ft. 3 in., fair complexion.

Justina Vobel, 25, Barfeldt, 5 ft. 4 in., dark complexion.

Joseph Hilker, 25, Munster, joiner, 5 ft. 5 in., fair complexion.

Bernard Nebe, 20, Wehr, joiner, 5 ft. 5 in., fair complexion.

Philip Nebe, 23, Wehr, joiner, 5 ft. 7 in., fair complexion.

Martin Cappe, 28, Wilsdorf, farmer, 5 ft. 2 in., dark complexion.

Joseph Peter, 29, Bordeaux, waiter, 5 ft. 6 in., dark complexion.

Maria Eliza Burnin, 24, Schwarzenau, 5 ft., dark complexion.

Jacob Benner, 25, Wevenbach, miller, 5 ft. 6 in., dark complexion.

[Endorsed:]

A List of German Passengers, arrived at the Port of Philadᵃ Novʳ 30ᵗʰ 1805, from Bremen.

[List 491] Report of Alien passengers on board the American Ship Aeolus of Portsmouth N. H., burthen 272 Tons or there abouts, owned by Messrs Samˡ & Wᵐ Hale of Portsmouth

N. H., Jacob C. Treadwell, Master. From Tonningen in Denmark. Arrived in the Delleware River of Sixth Day of Dec. 1805.

[*Name, age, place of birth, nationality, occupation, size, complexion.*]

Frederick Belou, 24, Hurnhut, Saxony, joiner, tall & thin, fair hair & light complexion.

Abraham Reimer, 27, Dantzig, Prussia, millright, rather small, dark hair.

Jacob Reimer, his brother, 28, Dantzig, Prussia, millright, middling size.

John Roy, 18, Elbing, Prussia, clerk or storekeeper, light hair, fair complexion.

Clauss Dick, 22, Einlage, Prussia, farmer, middling size, dark hair.

J. George Fraulich, 28, Hurnhut, Saxony, blacksmith, rather small & slim, fair complexion.

John Hartnock, 26, Hurnhut, Saxony, tailor, light hair, rather small.

Magnus Huttin, 42, Christiansfelten, Denmark, cabinet maker, black hair rather tall & slim.

Gotlop Hebener, 44, Gnaudun, Saxony, butcher, large & portly, black hair, dark complexion.

Christian Britz, 39, Hurnhut, Saxony, farmer, tall & dark complexion.

George Irmer, 32, Gnadunfelt, Prussia, baker, rather short & thick.

Philadelphia 7th December, 1805.

Jacob C. Treadwell.

[Endorsed:]
A List of German Passengers, arrived at the Port of Philadª, Decr 7th 1805, from Tonningen. Passenger List p. Aeolus.

[List 492] Report of my Ship Johann Andreas, belonging to Hambro [Hamburg] from Tönningen, arrived yᵉ 30, Decr 1805.

Mr. Nicol. Louis	Casper Elstner ⎤ children
Mrs. Caroline Louis	Johannes Elstner ⎦
Mr. Daniel Scheel	Levin Ancker
Nicolaus Bünning	Frieder. Kuneke
Joseph Elstner	Margaretha Harmsen ⎤ my wife
Elisabeth Elstners	H. Hinrich Harmsen ⎦ and child

Jacob Hinr. Harmsen.

[Endorsed:]

A List of German Passengers, arrived at the Port of Philad[a],
December 30th 1805, from Tonningen.

[List 493] List of the Passengers arrived in the Brig Isabella, John Edwards, Master, from Rotterdam, on the 30th
April, 1806.

Philip Liye, wife & three children	Henry Bark
Thomas Suindener, wife & daughter	William P. Rury
	Jacob Mire
Jacob Inhoop, wife & one daughter	Antonello Bemant
Herman H. Hackman	Frederick Tunisse
Jacob Bark	Anthony Stoel
John E. Lewis	Matthew Andresson
	Matthew Engeler

In all twenty two persons.
Philad[a] 1st May 1806.

John Edwards.

[Endorsed:]
A List of German Passengers, arrived at Philad[a] May 1st,
1806, in the Brig Isabella, Capt. John Edwards, from Rotterdam.

[List 494] Report and Manifest of the Cargo laden on
board of the Brig Kathrine, whereof John Lawrence is Master,
which Cargo was taken on board at Tonningen, burthen
153, 63/95 tons, built at . . . in the State of Connecticut and
owned by James Keith, Merchant at Alexandria, as per Register granted at Alexandria, the 26th day of July, 1804 and bound
for Philadelphia. [June 5, 1806.]

STEERAGE PASSENGERS

Isaac Christian Zupmann	Gaspar Legwin
Johann Friedrich Braemer	Friedrick Luste
Heinrich Friedrich Begner	Niels Madzen
Heinrich Hettman	Andreas Lincke
Godfried Grouse	Michel Schilling

Wilhelm Lindt
Jacob Byli
Carel Waulke
Carel Libhard
Christjan Heinrich Peters
Johannes Batz
Friedrich Bindel
Jacob Eruch
Jacob Thumann
Heinrich Ehele
Evrard Strom
Heinrich Ihnizen
Heinrich Peters
Christjan Jacobi
Wolfgang Schneyder
Coenraad Schmidt
Sebastjan Nasgigt
Jacob Baum
Johann Godfried Lange
Godfried Ramler
Johann Mirch
Carel Richter
Jacob Ditmer
Caspar Natchem
Elias Vouner
Jacob Israel
Daniel Lintz
George Koch
Johann Nitz
Andries Bond
Godlieb Vedet
Jacob Koch
Morritz Binder
Dit^ch Kruxxe
Johann Nievühre
Friedrich Zepprich
Michael Ruil
Joseph Weisz
Jacob Abraham
Claudius Ziehmer
Adam Luwig

Friedrich Pahnke
Friedrich Petersen
George Bansch
Barbara, his wife
Catharina, daughter
Christoph, son
Heinrich, son
Heinrich Laurence, son
Daniel Schmidt
Anna Christjana, wife
Bernard, son
Johs., son
Maria Catharina, daughter
Johann Justus
Christina Elisabeth, wife of Johann Justus
Johann Coenrad, son
Reinhard, son
Coenrad, son
Maria Catharina, daughter
Christjan, son
—— Brandt
Sophia Dorothea, wife
Jacob Heinrich
Heinrich Hinfeldt
Andreas Huberti, his brother
Elisabeth, wife
Maria, daughter
Katharina, daughter
Barbara, daughter
Friedrich Heller
Johann Kruxxe
Daniel Harpe
H. Roger
Leopold Knie
Christina, wife
Charlotte, daughter
Carel, son
Leopold, son
Harms Staeglich
Charlotte, his wife

Carolina, daughter A. Brommer
Auguste, son Andrew Bendig
Valentin Rutter John Thierman

[Endorsed:]
Returns of German Passengers October and Dec. 1805 and January 1806—Received June 5th, 1806.

[List 495] List of Passengers with their Lugage & other Articles, on board the Ship Orlando, Daniel S. Stellwagen, Master, from Amsterdam, bound for Philadelphia. [Aug. 3, 1806.]

Henry Gass, with wife & four child^n, oldest 15 years
Henry Martin, single man
John Dagen, with wife & two child^n, oldest 15 years
Jacob F. Beck, with wife & one small child
John G. Beck, single man
John J. Gass, a single man
Fr. Inhoff, single man
Anna Schafner, servant woman to F. Inhoff
Christian Steinmetz, single man
Henry Hanshew, single man
Fred^k Hanshew, single man
Danl Ricker, with wife & 3 child^n, oldest 10 years
Fred^k Gass, single man
J$^{no.}$ J. Freyvogel, with wife & 4 child^n 18, 16, 14, 9 years
P. Kulp, with wife & two small child^n, 1 born at sea
Margaret Singley, single woman
Michael Singley, with wife & one small child
Rosina Singley, single woman
John Schnearley, single man
Jacob Halfadle, with wife & one small child
Anthony Kammen, single man
John Stout, with wife & 3 small child^n, one born at sea
G. A. Yung, with wife & 4 child^n 13, 12, 6, 2 years
Adam Ehrhard, with wife & 4 child^n 14, 12, 7, 3½ years
John Lull, single man
Henry Ebner, single man
Fred^k Rubins, single man

John Slisell, single man
Fred[k] Fisher, single man
Usilla Halfadle, single woman
Ch[r] Loter, with wife
Philip Brown, single man
Leon[d] Schnievly, single man
Barbara Caufman, single woman
Charles Streamer, single man
Conrad Anne, single man
Jacob Welper, single man
Chr. F. Knutz, with wife & one child, 2 years
John Lenger, single man
John L. Rian, single man
G. F. Blume, single man
Ch[n] Kneariem, single man
John Feltman, single man
Jn[o] P. Michaels, single man
John Hendricks, with wife
F. Essick, single man, the ship's doct[r]
Anthony Priesdecke, single man
John Kreamer, single man
Ch[r] Kuntentwine, single man
P. Krousenburger, single man
Joseph Chneidle, single man
John J. Alkewhen, single man
G. F. Verner, single man
John C. Ufferman, single man
Sophia Sauerkamp, single woman
Eliesa Stock, with son, a widow woman
Tonina Stock, single woman
Adrina Brillenburg, single woman
N. Reckard, & wife
G. L. Smith, single man
Mary Dickerling, single woman
Anna Dickerling, single woman
Mary Driden, single woman
Jn[o] Deger, with wife & one small child
Julian Jansen, single woman
W[m] Rider, single man
John H. Meat, single man
Henry Saga, with wife & two child[n], 13 & 1 years old

One hundred & Nineteen Passengers making ninety Eight full freights or Ninety Eight drawing full Allowance of Provissions & Water &c.

Dan¹ S. Stellwagen.

August 3ʳᵈ 1806.

[Endorsed:]

A List of German Passengers, arrived at Philadᵃ, August 3ʳᵈ 1806, in the Ship Orlando, Capᵗ Daniel S. Stellwagen, from Amsterdam.

[List 496] List of Passengers on board Ship Cordelia from Amsterdam, Calvan Delano, Master. [Oct. 22. 1806.]

Conrad Ruther
Lewis Fowle
Ferdinand G. Evans
Godfry Minock
Martin Martin
Mary Martin, wife
Salamy Martin
Jacob Martin
Johannas Martin
Maria Martin
Barbara Martin
Elizabeth Martin
Fidela Souder
Elenor Souder
Mary Souder
Joseph Souder
Feronaga Souder
Jacob Souder
Jacob Rudey
Henrick Anneshansly
Anna Anneshansly
Salama Anneshansly
Hendrick Anneshansly
Anna Anneshansly
Jacob Anneshansly
Anna Anneshansly
—— child Henry
Fred. Draes

Hendrick Ursburg
Hendrick Lideritz
Casper Freidle
Barbara Freidle
Barbara Freidle
Maria Freidle
Rachel Freidle
Elizabeth Freidle
Anna Freidle
Cordelia Freidle
John Buny
Mary Buny
Jacob Werber
Mary Hansinger
Magdalena Temple
Anna Wooser
Christopher Wankmiller
Christiana Wankmiller
Rachel Wankmiller
Johan Stabler
Magdalena Stabler
John Stabler
Christiana Stabler
George Woolf
Fred. Dresel
Fred. Pfirsich
John M. Lesig
Barbara Fulmerin

Fred^r A. Erkert

Johann Hamscher

Charles Maysenhölder

Johan Vogel

George Jacoby

William Waltz

Bernard Henricks

John Eckert

Valentin Hobbert

John Peterman

John Grötzinger

John Kügele

Fred Kügele

George T. Smith

Joseph Swartz

Fred Osterloh

Mary Osterloh

Louisa Osterloh

Charles Osterloh

Julian Osterloh

Albri Osterloh

Christopher Glasser

John Siegworth

Anthony Armpriester

Jacob Woolf

Michael Woolf

George Sanger

Fred Diesel

Dorothy Sanger

Valentine Hoger

Thomas Hoger

John T. Fry

Goodly Raisch

Christian Raisch

George Lermon

Michael Stoltz

Isaac Woolf

Abraham Woolf

Fredrick Woolf

Fredrick Rosendal

Maria Rosendal

Jacob Neif

Jacob Kramer

John M. Wilt

John Weyman

John Fr. Doberer

William Shanger

Rebecca Shanger

Jacob Justter

William Kramer

Anna Kramer

Catharin Kramer

Mary Kramer

Christian Kramer

William Kramer

Jacob Kramer

Christian Neif

Dorothy Neif

Catharin Nief

Christian Nief

Jacob Nief

Christopher Keysers

Christena Keysers

Margaret Keysers

Abraham Keysers

Catharin Keysers

Eve Wolfsin

Charlotta Strumfer

William Strumfer

John Strumfer

Michael Günther

Christian Günther

Barbara Günther

Regena Günther

Margaret Günther

Catharin Günther

Hannah Günther

Rosena Günther

Jacob Günther

Joan Waltz

Elizabeth Waltz

Catharena Waltz

Christiana Waltz
Abraham Young
Abraham Woolf
Christiana Woolf
Abram Woolf
Christiana Woolf
Elizabeth Woolf
Barbara Woolf
Michael Waltz
Regena Waltz
Michael Stiger
Margaret Stiger
Johanna Stiger
John G. Stiger
John G. Wacker
William Ulmer
Johanna Stopster
John G. Günther
Anne W. Günther
Eve R. Günther
Cathareen Günther
Johanna Günther
Elizabeth Günther
Samuel Günther
Abraham Matzger
Dorotha Matzgar
Fred. Matzgar
Hansch Matzgar

Johannas Matzgar
George Matzgar
Jacob Matzgar
Simeon Rebman
Catharin Rebman
Anna Rebman
Catharin Rebman
Agguth Rebman
Dorothy Rebman
Joseph Rebman
Casper Rebman
Barbara Rebman
Magdalena Rebman
Christena Rebman
John Rebman
Simeon Rebman
Jacob Schleiss
Christena Feit
Fred Wurster
Fred. Feit
Mary Feit
Johannas Feit
Charles Feit
Hersch Leib
Samuel Jacobs
Meirs Samuel
John Smith

Philadelphia 22ᵈ October, 1806.   Calvin Delano.

[Endorsed:]
    A List of German Passengers, arrived at Philadᵃ, Octoʳ 21ˢᵗ
1806, in the Ship Cordelia, Capᵗ Calvin Delano from Amsterdam.

[List 497] List of Passengers on board the ship Atlantic,
Capt. G. W. Burbank, from Amsterdam. [Nov. 8, 1806.]

NAMES & PLACES OF BIRTH	AGES	NAMES & PLACES OF BIRTH	AGES
Jacob Selzer, Freinzheim	46	Anne Marie	43

NAMES & PLACES OF BIRTH	AGES	NAMES & PLACES OF BIRTH	AGES
Jacob	21	Magdalena	2
Christina	19	and an infant born at sea	
Ludwig	17	Charlotte	
Charlotte	11	Phillip Strackbein, Witgen-	
Joh. Adam	7	stein	24
Catharina	3½	Christina	30
Carl	½	John Philip	1
Andreas Bauer, Paffen-		Georg Missen, Witgenstein	33
schwabenheim	48	Anna Maria	24
Catharina	47	and an infant born at sea	
Joh. Phillip	21	John George	
Christian	21	Adam Friedrich Kopp,	
Elisabeth	13	Neckerweyhingen	39
Johannes	12	Christina Magdalena	34
Christine	9	Joh. Friedrich	13
Samuel	7	Justina Margaret	4½
Johann Chr. Kleinjung,		Peter Dionis von Franz,	
Mühlheim	29	Coeln	30
Clara Anna Sophia	30	Caspar Joseph von Stein,	
Catharina Carolina Sophia	3	Trier	29
and an infant born at		Phillip Heinrich Oertel,	
sea		Strasburg	24
Georg Dreisbach, Wittgen-		Johann Conrad Fleischmann	
stein	40	Culmbach	29
Margaretha	32	Johannes Maysenhoelder	
Georg	20	Stugard	21
Catharina	18	Jacob Heppler, Eslingen	23
Anna Marie	15	Joh. Wilhelm Berg, Rhein-	
Marie Elisabeth	13	breitenbach	29
Johann Heinrich	11	Johann Schaub, Listhal	28
Elisabeth Gertraud	8	Jasper Hesse Goemann,	
Anton	6	Wiener	44
Margaretha	3	Theodor Webner, Raths-	
Georg Heinrich	1	kirchen	25
George Heinrich Dreisbach,		Gottfried Knecht, Solingen	48
Witgenstein	24	Christian Triebel, Schleu-	
Marie Magdalena	23	singen	25
Johannes George	1	Gottfried Lindemuth, Eis-	
Phillip Dickel, Witgenstein	26	leben	23
Christina	23	Franz Schaeffer, Paterborn	20

NAMES & PLACES OF BIRTH   AGES   NAMES & PLACES OF BIRTH   AGES

Conrad Simon, Milsongen   23   Cassimer Heinrich Seifert,
Peter Jacob Loehr, Hitten-   Murhardt   24
    hausen   25   Johann Christian Negele,
Friederich Peter Loehr,   Spiegelberg   18
    Walhalwen   22   Christoph Wilhelm, Stim-
Peter Jacob Kettering, Her-   plebach   25
    mersberg   24   Friedrich Idler, Stimplebach 27
John Jacob Kettering, Her-   John Georg Knecht, Gabel-
    mersberg   18   berg   20
Walter Walter, Walhaven   24   Conrad Birkle, Osweiler   20
Michel Wild, Salstadt   22   Valentin Hobert, Vach   28
Simon Schoeffer, Gerhards-   Wilhelm Haltmann, Disburg 22
    born   19   Debora Wissels, Wesp   22
Phillip Gillerd, Jestwesler 23   John Dirk Borkink, Borelno 23

[Endorsed:]

A List of German Passengers, arrived at Philad^a, Novr 8th 1806, in the Ship Atlantic, Capt. George W. Burbanck, from Amsterdam.

[List 498] List of Passengers on board the Ship Three Sisters, [Capt. Herman] Haesloop, from Bremen [Dec. 1, 1806].

Thomas Magnus Streck   Anna Catarina Hoehn
Maria Streck   Johann Christopf Hoehn
Carolus Magnus Streck   Christopf Hoehn
Ferdinand Mowritz Streck   Catarina Hoehn
Alexander Magnus Streck   Maria Elizabeth Hoehn
Carolina Blandina Streck   Hendrich Junghin
Helena Clarissa Streck   Anna Elizabeth Junghin
Louisa Wilhelmina Streck   Hendrich Junghin
Maria Amelia Streck   Wilke Zimmermann
Johann Gotlieb Koutge   Martin Fincken
Anna Koutge   Alheid Fincken
Anna Rachel Koutge   Diedrich Fincken
Eleonora Constantina Koutge   Gewerd Fincken
Anna Carolina Koutge   Peter Bergheiser
Sophia Hedewig Mumsen   Anne Elizabeth Bergheiser
Albrecht Burghard Mumsen   John Jacob Bergheiser
Johann Hoehn

[Endorsed:]

A List of German Passengers, arrived at Philad^a, December the 1st 1806, in the Ship Three Sisters, Capt. Herman Haasloop, from Bremen.

[List 499] List of the Passengers on board the American Ship Fair American, Captn J. Fraley, bound for Philadelphia. [December 11, 1806.]

Jacob Schaal and wife
Hans George Schaal
Rosina Schaal
Gottfried Schaal
Friederick Schaal
Michael Pertsch and wife
Jacob Keller and wife
Hans George Mahle and wife
Christian Mahle, 18 years
Dorothea Mahle, 16 years
Hans George Mahle, 13 years
Elizabeth Mahle, 12 years
Matthias Larier and wife
Noa Larier, 11 years
Lydia Larier, 8 years
Hans George Stohs and wife
Maria Agnes Stohs
Carl Stohs
Fried. Pfeil and wife
Gotefried Pfeil
Ludwig Pfeil
Christina Kurtz
Fried. Nachtrup and wife
Chatharina Nachtrup
Joh. Adam Nachtrup
Joshua Fried. Nachtrup
Dorothea Nachtrup
Barbara Nachtrup
Gottlob Jacob Muller
Johannes Layer and wife
Eva Schalin Layer
Fried. Buler and wife

Carl Fried. Seybold
Johannes Pertsch
Johann Gross and wife
Christian Gross
Christiana Romen
Abraham Frieschknecht and wife
Michael Scholköpf and wife Margarethe
Rosina Scholköpf
Joh. George Scholköpf
Anna Maria Scholköpf
Mattheas Palmer and wife
Feit Handel
Henrich Christ Schremman
Maximilliam Obermey
Margareth Sehiffelin
Johannes Schiffelin
Andreas Schiffelin
George Schiffelin
George Frail
Simon Frail
Joh. Fried. Dizler
Michael Schuler and wife
Joseph Daiger
Frantz Kauffman
Jacob Konig
Joseph Newbert
Christian Raul
Joh. Fried. Kleinjung
Anna Kleinjung
Carolina Bastert
Joseph Sampson & wife

Fried. Weisbeck
Joh. Ant. Bader
Gottlieb Kussman
Christian Glink
John Ernst Hubert
Johannes Chevalier
Johannes Kuhnel, wife
  Margareth
Christopher Frederick Unkel
Joh. Adam Unkel
Casper Rall
Johanna Elisab. Roelofs
Maria Wilh. Kroesen
Joh. George Schuh
Daniel Beck
Maria Adrina Cornman
Jacob Wagner
Carl August Frostdorp

Johanna Marie Frostdorp
Mattheus Kranenburg
Arnold Felder
Jacob Kern
George Schastler
Fried. Wilh. Mierman
Bernh. Imthurn
Christ Lehman & wife
Nicholas Lehman
Daniel Lehman
Henry Jacob Hafner, wife
Daniel Hafner
Christoph Wolff
J. G. Schallenmiller
J. M. Stöther
Jacob Mun
Johannes Cannape
Fried. W. Wolters

Jesse Fraley.

[Endorsed:]

A List of German Passengers arrived at Philad[a] December the 11th 1806, in the Ship Fair American, Capt Jesse Fraley, from Amsterdam.

[List 500] List of Passengers in the Ship Speedwell, Captn Thos Wills, Master, from Amsterdam. [April 2, 1807.]

Louisa Tallam
Frederika Tallam
Rosina Tallam
Christina Tallam
Manette Maneuvre
Salomé Bauer
John Fisser

John Rynders
Vincent Godt
Baptist Büsser
John Büsser
John Baptist Büsser
John Peschalett
Peter A. Laubie

Thos. Wills.

[Endorsed:]

A List of German Passengers, arrived at Philad[a], April 2, 1807, in the Ship Speedwell, Capt. Thomas Wills, from Amsterdam.

[List 501] Report and Manifest of the Cargo laden on board the American Schooner Betsey, whereof James Foster is master, burthen one hundred 8 13/95 tons, built at Wells, State of Massachusetts, bound to Philadelphia, which Cargo was taken on board at Tonningen. [May 8, 1807.]

[Name, occupation, age, place of nativity, complexion]

George Miller, farmer, 40, Nassau, Light Complexion
Eleanor Miller, 40, Nassau, Light Complexion
Christian Miller, 14, Nassau, Light Complexion
John Miller, 11, Nassau, Light Complexion
Francis Miller, 8, Nassau, Light Complexion
George Miller, 3, Nassau, Light Complexion
Catherina Miller, 13, Nassau, Light Complexion
Daniel Harman, blacksmith, 37, Bremen, Light Complexion
Elizabeth Harman, 29, Bremen, Light Complexion
Elizabeth Harman, 11, Bremen, Light Complexion
Maria Harman, 7, Bremen, Light Complexion
Jacob Harman, 3, Bremen, Light Complexion
Daniel Harman, 3, Bremen, Light Complexion
Antonio Shafer, carpenter, 38, Nassau, Light Complexion
Mary Shafer, 33, Nassau, Light Complexion
Maria Shafer, 8, Nassau, Light Complexion
Caterina Shafer, 6, Nassau, Light Complexion
Johanna Shafer, 1, Nassau, Light Complexion
Christina Shafer, 26, Nassau, Light Complexion
Powell Lowman, miller, 32, Bremen, Light Complexion
Elizabeth Lowman, 35, Bremen, Light Complexion
Henry Lowman, 6, Bremen, Light Complexion
Hannah Matherwatson, 60, Bremen, Light Complexion
Maria Allis, 30, Bremen, Light Complexion
Henry Allis, 12, Bremen, Light Complexion
Barbary Allis, 5, Bremen, Light Complexion
Nicholas Allis, 2, Bremen, Light Complexion
Johannes Folk, farmer, 29, Hamburg, Dark Complexion
Hannah Folk, 24, Hamburg, Light Complexion
Frederick Holtsman, weaver, 26, Hamburg, Light Complexion
Maria Holtsman, 25, Hamburg, Light Complexion
Elizabeth Ryer, 20, Bremen, Light Complexion
Maria Bayman, 20, Bremen, Light Complexion

Johanna Frash, tailor, 22, Bremen, Light Complexion
Christian Kensinger, tailor, 34, Bremen, Light Complexion
Daniel Harcker, tailor, 20, Bremen, Light Complexion
Emanuel Stick, tailor, 24, Bremen, Light Complexion
Conrad Rashpaker, tailor, 19, Bremen, Light Complexion
Christian Brinley, tailor, 22, Hamburg, Light Complexion
Joseph Laman, baker, 40, Bremen, Light Complexion
Adam Plebb, baker, 22, Hamburg, Light Complexion
John Niman, baker, 26, Hamburg, Light Complexion
Andrew Helser, baker, 19, Hamburg, Light Complexion
John Sherhult, baker, 25, Hamburg, Light Complexion
John Christon, butcher, 21, Hamburg, Light Complexion
John Mark, butcher, 30, Hamburg, Light Complexion
Letmon Jonass, butcher, 22, Hamburg, Light Complexion
Christian Arperman, gunsmith, 19, Bremen, Light Complexion
Andrew Leabo, gunsmith, 40, Bremen, Light Complexion
Jacob Niman, blacksmith, 25, Hamburg, Dark Complexion
Valantin Teckler, shoemaker, 26, Hamburg, Light Complexion
Michael Gute, carpenter, 45, Hamburg, Light Complexion
John Mainsult, carpenter, 28, Hamburg, Light Complexion
Gotlip Fiers, brewer, 30, Hamburg, Light Complexion
Bernit Hime, weaver, 27, Hamburg, Light Complexion
Lafel Seamon, 22, Hamburg, Light Complexion
Elias Hinaman, 19, Hamburg, Light Complexion
Joseph Meyer, 25, Hamburg, Light Complexion
Solomon Swabber, 19, Hamburg, Light Complexion
Lapil Church, 19, Hamburg, Dark Complexion
Christian Fritz, 29, Bremen, Light Complexion
David Frost, 28, Hamburg, Light Complexion
John Selia, 18, Hamburg, Light Complexion
Francis Smith, 28, Hamburg, Light Complexion
Johanna Fannil, 40, Bremen, Light Complexion
Elderick Shaniembar, 20, Hamburg, Light Complexion
John Coltin, 14, Hamburg, Light Complexion
John Watinburg, 31, Hamburg, Light Complexion
John Folk, 48, Bremen, Light Complexion
Christian Offman, 44, Hamburg, Light Complexion
    Ship Stores
8 Barrells beef

[List 502] List of the passengers on board the Brig Isa-

bella from Amsterdam. [Roger Crane, Master. July 15, 1807.]

John Chrˢ. Rynhardt
Geert Van Forstenberg
William Van Beek
Chrhˢ. Fruitin
Fried. Karl Kroll
Conrad Eberhardt
Daniel Eise
Konrad Linken
Maria Augᵉ Linkin
George Motter
Philip Fisher
Jnᵒ. J. Aboult
Wilh. Berg
George Bruckman
Christian Alfey
John Schliegel
Wilh Gotl. Granter
John Sᵗ Balster
Peter Seytfert
Anthony Kampf
Peter Rausenbach
George Hartman
Nich. Schliegel

Nick. Bohne
John Meitler
John George Meiller
Ferdinand Happel
Jnᵒ Chrs. Prentler
Chriˢ. Katke, with wife and five
    children
John George Baden
Fried. Ludw. Ach
Joseph Borcorni
Fried. Ludw. Ende
John Jacob Heionker
Philip Fried. Hahnlin
George Hogeban
Wilh. Schnauber
Carl Ogg
Wynlen Matterman
Carolina Trautin
George Reick
Christopher Huttz
George Sanderson
Christopher Schmerham
John Genau

Roger Crane.

[Endorsed:]

List of German Passengers, arrived at the Port of Philadᵃ, the 15ᵗʰ July, 1807.

[List 503] List of Passengers on board Ship Frederick Augustus, Capt. Robinson Potter, from Amsterdam. [Septʳ 15, 1807.]

—— Moehlin, with wife & four
    children
Adrianus Newenhart
Matthias Schroeder
Deidrick Yanson
Henery Beise

Abraham Schacht
Jacob Minion
Abraham Van der Linden
Henry Ponder
—— Herr & his wife
—— Laform & son

Lena Schuld   —— Kumel & wife
D. B. Mullen & son & servant   J. N. Care
    girl   Diederick Cuns Baker
—— Passavant & wife

Philadelphia 15, Sept\[^r] 1807:   Robinson Potter.

[Endorsed:]
A List of German Passengers arrived at the Port of Philad\[^a],
the 15\[^th] September, 1807.

[List 504] List of Passengers on Board the Ship Mechanic,
V. Bagley, Master, from Amsterdam. [Sept. 28, 1807.]

John D. Thiele   George Everling
Frederick Schuh   Anton Meyer
Rosina Schuh   Frederick Meyer
Frederick Schuh   Gerrit Willms
David Schuh   Jan Reichenocker
Gottleib Schuh   Jacob Reichenocker
Emanuel Schuh   George Fisler
Frederick Schuh   Sophia Fisler
Auguste Schuh   Jacob Zopse
Lewis Kleinsmith   Catharine Beckling
William Christ   Maria Beckling
Lewis Christ   Jan Gotle
Maria Ishen   Rosina Gotle
Jan Buller   Christophe Gotle
Jan Winel   Louisa Gotle
Gotleib Factorius   Maria Gotle
Henri Most   Louisa Gotle
Henri Arnold   Carolina Gotle
Jacob Saefried   Henry Gotle
Frederic Teininger   Abraham Fallung
Gotleib Gross   David Fallung
William Muller   Catharine Fallung
Gotleib Muller   Frederic Burdermann
Charles Harte   Frederic Dageler
Henry Harte   Daniel Ritter
George Krauter   Frederic Tenkerney
William Brundt   Jan Fischer

Christe Kuntz
Catharine Kunz
Maria Kunz
Henri Kunz
Anthon Kunz
Elisabeth Eppelshein
Charles Blum
William Heinmetz
Jost Heindorf
Maria Heindorf
Catharine Heindorf
Henri Heindorf
Jan Schultheis
Christiana Schultreis
Carolin Schultheis
Carl Shoebur
Peter Shoebur
Elisabeth Shoebur
Leonard Shoebur
Maria Shoebur
John Barsch

Elisabeth Barsch
Henry Barsch
William Kraut
Jacques Agterman
Wilhelmine Schroeder
Charlotte Kleinhousen
Christiana Breiner
Catharine Eichhacker
Maria Kunsman
William Schepplein
Henry Merklein
Lewis Hange
August Hange
August Hange
Sophia Hange
Catharine Boge
Angel Boge

CABIN PASSENGERS

Joh. A. Zeigler
Denois Laroche

Val. Bagley.

[Endorsed:]
A List of German Passengers, arrived at the Port of
Philadᵃ, the 28th Septʳ 1807.

[List 505] Report of Alien Passengers on Board the Ship
William P. Johnson, of which Moses Wells is Master, arrived at the Port of Philadelphia in the State of Pennsylvania
on the Third of December in the Year of our Lord One Thousand Eight hundred and Seven.

[*Name, age, place of nativity, allegiance, occupation, appearance.*] *

John Swarzentruber, wife & 1 child, 31, Waldeck, Elector of Hessia,
farmer, middle sized, black hair & grey eyes.
H. J. Martin, wife & 3 sons, 52, Canton Basel, Republic Switzerland,
farmer, middle sized, black hair & grey eyes.

---

* Two columns are omitted, one headed "Freights," containing the number 1
for every adult and ½ for every child, the other headed "Country from whence
they come," containing in every case "Holland" or "ditto."

Lewis Steingötter, 19, Hein, Prince Esenburg, farmer, small sized, flaxen hair & grey eyes.

Godlieb Bunger, 34, Oldenburgh, Prince Oldenburgh, distiller & farmer, middle sized, flaxen hair & grey eyes.

Philip Krocker, 24, Günsheim, Prince Darmstadt, baker, middle sized, black hair & grey eyes.

Christian Wismatt, 25, Oberrode, Prince Primate, baker, middle sized, black hair & grey eyes.

J. Cath. Deboldin, 23, Idigheim, Prince Würzburg, baker, middle sized, black hair & grey eyes.

Mary ·Teunissen, 19, Rotterdam, King Holland, servant girl, middle sized, red hair & grey eyes.

Fredrick Ramspott, 20, Roden, Prince Waldeck, farmer, middle sized, flaxen hair & blue eyes.

John Haeppe, 30, Hessia, Prince Hessia, farmer, middle sized, black hair & grey eyes.

Bastian Koehl, 25, Federsheim, Empire France, miller, middle sized, flaxen hair & grey eyes.

John Shmall, 26, Hanau, Prince Hessia, baker, middle sized, flaxen hair & grey eyes.

Balthazar Striegel, 41, Bieberach, King Wirtenburg, hatter, middle sized, brown hair & blue eyes.

Catharine Smoke, 34, Hamburg, Empire Germany, servant girl, middle sized, flaxen hair & blue eyes.

Caspar Leonhard, wife & 2 children, 42, Canton Zürrich, Republic Switzerland, brickmaker, middle sized, black hair & grey eyes.

C. Lindeman, wife & 3 children, 39, Bishweiler, Republic Switzerland, cooper, middle sized, flaxen hair & blue eyes.

M. Shafner, wife & 1 child, 30, Maulburgh, Republic Switzerland, farmer, middle sized, flaxen hair & grey eyes.

Joseph Erhard, 28, Rodersdorf, Republic Switzerland, farmer, middle sized, black hair & grey eyes.

Jacob Wolf, 33, Witgenstein, Count Witgenstein, farmer, middle sized, flaxen hair & blue eyes.

Henry Aflerbach, 25, Witgenstein, Count Witgenstein, carpenter, middle sized, flaxen hair & grey eyes.

Margareth Michels, 27, Günstadt, King Holland, servant girl, middle sized, black hair & black eyes.

Anthony Sholze, 23, Nauenburgh, Prince Hessia, clerk, middle sized, brown hair & grey eyes.

Henry Spate, 21, Nauenburgh, Prince Hessia, saddler, middle sized, flaxen hair & grey eyes.

William Oesterling, 18, Mehrenhausen, Prince Waldeck, tanner, middle sized, flaxen hair & grey eyes.

Fred. Wm Graf, 22, Niederwarholdern, Prince Waldeck, tanner, middle sized, flaxen hair & blue eyes.

Gerhard Benjn Witstach 18, Amsterdam, King Holland, clerk, middle sized, brown hair & black eyes.

Toby Shönheit, 21, Türingen, Empire of Germany, clerk, middle sized, brown hair & brown eyes.

J. Christian Krug, 21, Lützen, Empire of Germany, butcher, middle sized, brown hair & brown eyes.

L. Mundhenk, wife & 2 children, 29, Pyrmont, Prince Waldeck, shoemaker, middle sized, flaxen hair & grey eyes.

Henry Mundhenke, 32, Pyrmont, Prince Waldeck, gardner, middle sized, flaxen hair & grey eyes.

Lewis Mundhenke, 20, Pyrmont, Prince Waldeck, shoemaker, middle sized, flaxen hair & grey eyes.

Joseph Grabe, 19, Lügde, Empire of Germany, locksmith, middle sized, black hair, grey eyes.

John Wm Zügel, 21, Murhard, King of Wirtemberg, butcher, middle sized, brown hair & blue eyes.

John Gotlieb Krail, 22, Sulzbach, King of Wirtemburg, butcher, middle sized, flaxen hair & blue eyes.

John David Hofman, 23, Eidmanhausen, King of Wirtemburg, butcher, middle sized, brown hair & blue eyes.

Lewis Laitenberger, 23, Kaltenwesten, King of Wirtemburg, butcher, middle sized, flaxen hair & blue eyes.

Andrew Mädenfind, 23, Unterwiederstädt, Prince of Dessau, miner, middle sized, flaxen hair & grey eyes.

Andrew Brabender, 20, Rheinbreitbach, Empire of Germany, miner, middle sized, brown hair & grey eyes.

John Peter Graef, 27, Seinaltkirchen, Empire of Germany, Ironsmelter, middle sized, brown hair & brown eyes.

Joseph Beinarseck, 30, Bohemia, Empire of Germany, smith, middle sized, flaxen hair & blue eyes.

C. Guterman & son, 44, Dickheim, Empire of France, smith, middle sized, black hair & brown eyes.

George Steiner, 23, Gutach, Empire of Germany, baker, middle sized, black hair & brown eyes.

John Pickel, 24, Lintz, Empire of Germany, tinker, middle sized, flaxen hair & blue eyes.

John Jacob Bauer, 25, Marbach, King of Wirtenberg, butcher, middle sized, flaxen hair & blue eyes.

John Shwegler, 25, Witzenhausen, Elector of Hessia, gardner, middle size, black hair & grey eyes.

Geo. Jost, 24, Offenbach, Prince Primas, baker, middle size, black hair & black eyes.

Geo. Fred. Blum & wife, 33, Marbach, King of Wirtenberg, weaver, middle size, flaxen hair & blue eyes.

Juliana Stieflin, 26, Sulzbach, Wirtenberg, servant girl, middle size, flaxen hair & blue eyes.

Jacob Dentler, 15, Bentelsbach, Wirtenberg, no trade, middle size, flaxen hair & blue eyes.

John Fred. Heess, 14, Shnaid, Wirtenberg, no trade, middle size, flaxen hair & brown eyes.

Eliz. Voll, 40, Kornwestheim, Wirtenberg, middle size, flaxen hair & blue eyes.

& six children

C. Henry, 17	Henrietta, 10
Jn. Henry, 14	Jn. Fred., 4
Jn. Godlieb, 12	Sophy Eliz., 2

John Fred. Walter, 57, Eslingen, Wirtenberg, blacksmith, middle size, black hair & grey eyes.

Godlieb Göckeler, 15, Shnaid, Wirtenberg, no trade yet, middle size, brown hair & blue eyes.

J. G. Volmar, 15, Shnaid, Wirtenberg, no trade yet, middle size, flaxen hair & blue eyes.

Godfrey Sandsenbacher, 23, Maubach, Wirtenberg, butcher, middle size, flaxen hair & blue eyes.

Mathew Pleisz, 21, Steden, Wirtenberg, carpenter, middle size, brown hair & brown eyes.

Godlieb Chr. Gramer, 20, Ludwigsburg, Wirtenberg, needlemaker, middle size, brown hair & brown eyes.

Geo. Fredric Thum, 38, Backnang, Wirtenberg, woolen weaver, middle size, flaxen hair & grey eyes.

Jn. Leonhard Kirchner, 35, Rodenburgh, Bavaria, skin-dresser, middle size, flaxen hair & grey eyes.

C. Cath. Benzenhäferin, 17, Stungardt, King Wirtemberg, servant girl, middle size, brown hair & grey eyes.

Juliana Frizin, 36, Backnang, King Wirtemberg, servant girl, middle size, flaxen hair & blue eyes.

Fred. Leyer & wife, 23, Breunigsweiler, King Wirtemberg, linen weaver, middle size, flaxen hair & blue eyes.

John Shaubel, 24, Marbach, King Wirtemberg, locksmith, middle size, brown hair & blue eyes.

George Shaubel, 22, Marbach, King Wirtemberg, turner, middle size, brown hair & blue eyes.

Christian Banshaff, 36, Cornwestheim, King Wirtemberg, gardner, middle size, black hair & grey eyes.

Matthew Leible, 24, Hösselwardt, King Wirtemberg, shoemaker, middle size, flaxen hair & grey eyes.

John Jacob Fisher, 19, Kronbach, King Wirtemberg, shoemaker, middle size, brown hair & grey eyes.

John Wacker, 18, Hosselwardt, King Wirtemberg, tailor, middle size, dark hair & blue eyes.

Jnº Chr. Klotz, wife & 1 child, 38, Marbach, King Wirtemberg, tailor, middle size, black hair & blue eyes.

Henry Chs. Eckhardt, 19, Marbach, King Wirtemberg, soapboiler, middle size, dark hair & brown eyes.

Eb. Ch. Bauer & wife, 37, Marbach, King Wirtemberg, butcher, middle size, brown hair & grey eyes.

Burkh. F. Vogel, 23, Fishingen, King Wirtemberg, butcher, middle size, black hair & black eyes.

Geo. Fred. Hausser, 22, Marbach, King Wirtemberg, butcher, middle size, flaxen hair & blue eyes.

John Mozer, 22, Steden, King Wirtemberg, butcher, middle size, brown hair & blue eyes.

Charles Halwadt, 26, Ecksten, King Prussia, shoemaker, middle size, flaxen hair & blue eyes.

Getrud Richtern, 38, Manheim, Emperor of France, woman cook, middle size, brown hair & grey eyes.

John Godf. Wörlein, 35, Nördlingen, King of Bavaria, butcher, middle size, brown hair & grey eyes.

Chr. Gold. Gscheidle, 21, Grosshohren, King of Wirtemberg, butcher, middle size, black hair & black eyes.

Wiegand Kurtz, 20, Diddeshausen, Elector of Hessia, carpenter, middle size, flaxen hair & grey eyes.

J. F. Kock, 33, Hameln, Elector of Hanover, butcher, middle size, brown hair & grey eyes.

Catharine Seizin, 24, Ludwigsburg, King of Wirtemberg, servant girl, middle size, brown hair & grey eyes.

J. C. Mohr & two children

M. H. Winkel, wife & 1 child, 40, Eisnith, King of Prussia, baker, middle size, black hair & grey eyes.

Aug. Ferdinand Rainmann, 32, Berlin, King of Prussia, turner, middle size, black hair & black eyes.

Michel Hofstetter, 25, Nordlingen, King of Wirtemberg, merchant, middle size, flaxen hair & grey eyes.

Jo. Geo. Shaetter, 23, Carbach, Elector of Hessia, tailor, middle size, flaxen hair & grey eyes.

John Henry Kesling, 18, Hande, Elector of Hessia, no trade yet, middle size, brown hair & grey eyes.

John Wilhelm, 25, Arau, Rep. Switzerland, butcher, middle size, flaxen hair & blue eyes.

Henderietta Wesselmann, 24, Behsten, King of Prussia, servant girl, middle size, flaxen hair & blue eyes.

C. Van der Au, wife & 1 child, 37, Fulda, Emperor of Germany, tutor, middle size, black hair & black eyes.

Dorothea Smith, 24, Amsterdam, King of Holland, servant girl, middle size, flaxen hair, blue eyes.

Godf. Henry Volkmar, 30, Goslar, Emperor of Germany, coppersmith, middle size, flaxen hair, blue eyes.

Chr. Lewis Frank, 25, Koenigsbrun, King of Wirtemberg, locksmith, middle size, black hair, black eyes.

Jacob Knoes, 28, Rüsselheim, Elector of Hessia, baker, middle size, flaxen hair, blue eyes.

Jacob Smith, 33, Dirkheim, Emperor of Germany, baker, middle size, brown hair, grey eyes.

Bernard Müller, 23, Würzburg, Emperor of Germany, suspender-maker, middle size, black hair, black eyes.

Jacob Vyl, 12, Amsterdam, King of Holland, no trade yet, small size, black hair, brown eyes.

John Gavelt, 29, Amsterdam, King of Holland, clerk, middle size, flaxen hair, blue eyes.

Philip Wm. Hartel, 29, Göttingen, Emperor of Germany, bookbinder, middle size, brown hair, blue eyes.

John Aug. Borstoff, 20, Magdeburg, King of Prussia, carpenter, middle size, brown hair, blue eyes.

Dorothea Mundhenk, 22, Pyrmont, Prince of Waldeck, seamstress, middle size, flaxen hair, blue eyes.

Mary Chr. Humannsen, 20, Usingen, Emperor of Germany, seamstress, middle size, black hair, blue eyes.

Godlieb Hammer   10 ⎫
Christina Hammer   12 ⎬ Schnaid, King of Wirtemberg, no trade yet.
Godfrey Hammer   8 ⎭

R. Frederika Tochterman   32 ⎫
Frederika d°   12 ⎪ Marbach, King of Wirtemberg, middle
Conrad Tochterman   8 ⎬ size, brown hair, blue eyes.
Godfry Tochterman   7 ⎭

Frederika Cressmann, 32, Marbach, King of Wirtemberg, middle size, brown hair, blue eyes.

John Staufer, 27, Laiselheim, Emperor of France, miller, middle size, brown hair, brown eyes.

Henry Staufer, 28, Laiselheim, Emperor of France, miller, middle size, brown hair, brown eyes.

Henry Zucher, 25, Delfeld, Emperor of France, miller, middle size, brown hair, brown eyes.

John Winklar, 21, Horn, King of Holland, farmer, middle size, flaxen hair, blue eyes.

Nicolaus Shaub, 20, Listhal, Republic of Switzerland, servant, middle size, brown hair, brown eyes.

Susan Shaub, 22, Listhal, Republic of Switzerland, servant girl, middle size, brown hair, brown eyes.

Peter Smith & wife, 32, Montebauer, Emperor of Germany, doctor, middle size, black hair, grey eyes.

CABIN PASSENGERS

Ferdinand Temme, 46, Brunswick, Elector of Brunswick, professor of learning, middle size, brown hair, grey eyes.

John Rudolph Grote, wife and two children, 50, Osnabruck, Emperor of Germany, merchant, middle size, flaxen hair, grey eyes.

Christian Heydorn, 20, Pyrmont, Prince of Waldeck, watchmaker, middle size, brown hair, black eyes.

[Endorsed:]
A List of German Passengers, arrived at the port of Philad^a. Decr 3rd 1807.

[List 506] List of Passengers on board the Ship Three Sisters, Capt. Haesloop, from Tonningen [Jan. 5, 1808.]

Johannes Limpert   Catharine Lempert, his wife

Catharine, their daughter

Peter ⎤
George ⎦ their sons

Friedr. Wilhelm Beimbrecht
Henr. Auge
Maria Sophia Auge, his wife

Mar. Fried. ⎤
Wilhelmina ⎬ their daughters
Henriette ⎦

J. Valentin ⎤
Reinhardt ⎥
Heinrich ⎬ their sons
Christian ⎦

Melchior Wahl
Anna Clara Wahl, his wife
Heinrich, their son
Kunigunte, their daughter
Johannes Krug
Anna Webern Krug, his wife
Elisabeth, their daughter
Elisabeth Kluben
Nicholaus Matheus
Conrad Jaeger
Augustin Ghion
Dominico Marete
Geo. Balista Zenore
Jean Ghio
Johann Andreas Schaub
Friedr. Wilhelm Seucke
Johann Friedr. Seucke
George Richter
George Koch
Hein. Keil
Anna Margar Keil, his wife
Gertrude, their daughter
Johann Muller
David Hirschfeld
Johann Dunckel
Johann Georg Speiss
  & his wife
G. Carl Zeidler

Benjamin Bickenback
Wendeling Baumgarten
Carlo Balck
Friedr. Maertens
August Maertens
Heinr. Brandes
J. H. Machle
Johann Schmidt
Johannes Feillmann
Hennr. Freiderike, his wife
Hanchon, their daughter

Carl ⎤
Wilhelm ⎬ their sons
Friedr. ⎦

Johann Ignatz Wegener
Christine Ganisen
Casper Lindguist
John Georg Unger
Wilhelm Brandt
Carl Ludwig Eifert
Henr. Albert Hartmann
Georg Heine
Joh. Hinr. Ohm
Christian Seitz
Andreas Hoffman
Catharina Stucker
Hinrich Moller
Anna Catharina, his wife
Elisabeth, their daughter
Cl. Gottlieb, their son
Wilhelm Hanche
Maria Catharina, his mother
Heinrich, his son
Catharina, his daughter
Anna Cordes
Johann Dan¹ Haacke
Otto Heinr. Heinsemann
Joh. Conrad Lahrs
Herman Klamp
John Hinr. Reuter
Christian Nool

Henrich Frietag

August Muller

—— Numsen

—— Went

—— Luhne

Doctor Dode

Friedrich Stenzenberch

Joh. Dottler Saxe

Arnd Harms

Joach^m Grevismuhl

Nicholas Schroder

two infant Children

CABIN PASSENGERS

E. Spanhooft

J. J. Reeve

J. Jacob Cuhn

D. Carl Bade

Johann Melcher,
in behalf of Capt. Harm. Haesloop.

[Endorsed:]

A List of German Passengers, arrived at the Port of Philad^a., the 5th January, 1808.

INDEX OF CAPTAINS

Abercrombie, James
Sept. 19, 1743   I, 340, 341, 342
Sept. 9, 1749   I, 396
Sept. 14, 1751   I, 456
Sept. 23, 1752   I, 484
Sept. 24, 1753   I, 545, 547, 548
Oct. 16, 1754   I, 636, 638, 640
Adams, James
Aug. 24, 1749   I, 390
Albers, John Philip
Febr. 25, 1800   II, 105
Alfton (Alftan), John
Nov. 15, 1803   II, 135
Allan, James
Dec. 11, 1739   I, 273, 274
Sept. 27, 1740   I, 276, 277, 278
Sept. 29, 1741   I, 300, 301, 302
Allen, James
Sept. 5, 1751   I, 453
Alterhand, Capt., see Tran, Arthur
Anderson, Thomas
Nov. 10, 1743   I, 352
Armstrong, Capt.
(Sept. 19, 1749)   I, 409
Armstrong, Thomas
June 21, 1774   I, 757
Arnold, Thomas
Sept. 30, 1800   II, 108
Arnott, Thomas
Oct. 13, 1747   I, 366, 368
Sept. 15, 1748   I, 377, 379, 380
Sept. 14, 1749   I, 400
Aug. 28, 1750   I, 438
Sept. 21, 1751   I, 465
Sept. 15, 1752   I, 478
Sept. 28, 1753   I, 563, 565, 566
———, 1754   I, 675
Sept. 26, 1764   I, 692
Oct. 10, 1768   I, 721
Oct. 13, 1769   I, 726
Oct. 1, 1770   I, 729
Sept. 17, 1771   I, 733
Auchterlony, Patrick
Oct. 10, 1752   I, 494

Bagley, Val.
Sept. 28, 1807   II, 197
Ball, John
Oct. 11, 1733   I, 134, 135, 136

Ballendine, J.
Oct. 7, 1749   I, 419
Barden, Levi
Nov. 3, 1804   II, 160
Barnes, Theophilus
Oct. 16, 1752   I, 496
Baron, John
Jan. 16, 1775   I, 762
Beal, Capt.
(Sept. 19, 1749)   I, 409
Beech (Beach), Henry
Sept. 20, 1738   I, 225, 227, 229
Bell, Thomas
Sept. 23, 1741   I, 293, 294, 295
Bell, William
August 29, 1785   II, 6
Sept. 27, 1786   II, 16
May 23, 1787   II, 22
Jan. 10, 1789   II, 34
Aug. 16, 1793   II, 58
Nov. —, 1795   II, 78
Benn, James
Sept. 29, 1733   I, 130, 133
Benn, John
Oct. 21, 1761   I, 683
Bereson, Capt.
Nov. 5, 1801   II, 111
Billups, George
June 22, 1803   II, 124
Boswell, Benjamin
Nov. 9, 1749   I, 426
Bowen, Ezra
Aug. 29, 1796   II, 89
Brady, Thomas
Sept. 13, 1749   I, 399
Brevoor, John C.
Oct. 6, 1799   II, 99
Brewton, Daniel
May 7, 1805   II, 162
Oct. 18, 1805   II, 177
Brodrick, Thomas
Oct. 26, 1754   I, 661, 662, 663
Brown, John
Sept. 16, 1748   I, 383, 384
Sept. 14, 1754   I, 595, 597, 598
Brown, Patrick
Nov. 10, 1767   I, 719
Dec. 7, 1773   I, 757
Brown, Robert
Oct. 7, 1743   I, 348, 349, 350

Sept. 2, 1749   I, 394
Aug. 18, 1750   I, 433
Browning, Henry
Sept. 26, 1749   I, 411
Bryson, Andrew
Dec. 4, 1771   I, 738
Sept. 27, 1773   I, 752
Sept. 30, 1774   I, 758
Budden (Buden), Richard
Aug. 27, 1739   I, 257, 258, 261
Bull, Capt.
Oct. 31, 1771   I, 735
Bull, John
Sept. 24, 1737   I, 175, 176, 177
Burbank, George W.
Nov. 8, 1806   II, 189
Burke, Michael
Undated   II, 100
Burrough, Sidney H.
Oct. 18, 1805   II, 174

Campbell, Hugh
Aug. 21, 1750   I, 435
Aug. 25, 1751   I, 450
Sept. 27, 1752   I, 488
Campbell, William
June 20, 1785   II, 3
June 29, 1792   II, 49
Apr. 13, 1796   II, 82
Oct. 19, 1796   II, 90
Carr, Matthew
Nov. 10, 1764   I, 702
Carter, John
Oct. 31, 1737   I, 194, 195, 196
Castle, Capt.
Oct. 19, 1772   I, 742
Castle, Richgate
Sept. 5, 1751   I, 452
Caton, James
Sept. 21, 1765   I, 707
Cheesman, Thomas
Sept. 7, 1748   I, 372, 374, 375
Chilton, William
Sept. 30, 1740   I, 279, 280, 281
Church, James
Mar. 4, 1805   II, 161
Clapp, John
Dec. 4, 1764   I, 703
Clarke, Nathan
Nov. 17, 1795   II, 77
Clarkson, Matthew M.
Aug. 27, 1785   II, 3
Clymer, Christopher
Sept. 28, 1733   I, 126, 129
Clymer, William
Sept. 5, 1730   I, 34, 35, 36
Coatam, Thomas
May 30, 1741   I, 292
Sept. 2, 1749   I, 393

Aug. 31, 1750   I, 442
Sept. 16, 1751   I, 462
Sept. 22, 1752   I, 482
Sept. 28, 1753   I, 559, 560, 562
Oct. 22, 1754   I, 651, 653
Collins, Charles
Sept. 27, 1791   II, 46
Cook, James
Sept. 29, 1769   I, 726
Sept. 19, 1771   I, 735
Corneliss, Ede
Apr. 5, 1787   II, 22
Coultas, James
Aug. 17, 1729   I, 23, 25, 26
Coultas, John
August 23, 1728   I, 17, 19
Cowie (Cowey), James
Sept. 3, 1742   I, 323, 324, 325
Sept. 2, 1743   I, 334, 336, 338
Cowperthwait, Huling
Oct. 17, 1799   II, 99
Craigie (Craiges, Craigs), James
Sept. 11, 1729   I, 27, 29, 30
Cranch, John
Oct. 26, 1741   I, 313, 314, 315
Crane, Roger
July 15, 1807   II, 196
Creagh, James
Sept. 25, 1749   I, 410
Crockatt, David
Sept. 27, 1727   I, 10, 11
Sept. 11, 1728   I, 21, 22
Sept. 18, 1732   I, 71, 75, 77
Cunningham, William
Oct. 7, 1751   I, 473
Curson, Robert
Sept. 23, 1732   I, 83, 86
Cusack, Martley
Sept. 24, 1742   I, 330
Sept. 30, 1743   I, 347

Dalsted, Severus
Oct. 14, 1787   II, 28
Davidson, John
Nov. 4, 1766   I, 713
Davies (Davis), John
Oct. 2, 1727   I, 14, 15
Davies, John
Oct. 16, 1727   I, 16, 17
Davis, Andrew
Oct. 17, 1786   II, 19
Dawson, Samuel
Oct. 15, 1785   II, 12
De Grove, Adolph
Oct. 2, 1749   I, 417
De Haas, Tys
Oct. 10, 1787   II, 24
Delano, Calvin
Oct. 22, 1806   II, 187

Demster, George
Dec. 24, 1772   I, 744
Dexter, Banjamin G.
Sept. 27, 1793   II, 60
Dorson, John
Aug. 20, 1802   II, 112
Doty, Elihu
Sept. 15, 1804   II, 149
Doyle, John
Oct. 21, 1754   I, 645, 647
Duncan, James
Nov. 24, 1773   I, 756
Dunlop, Capt.
Sept. 27, 1752   I, 489
Dunlop, Colin
Aug. 29, 1730   I, 31, 32, 33
Dunphy, James
July 11, 1801   II, 109
Durell, George
Dec. 22, 1744   I, 358
Dryburgh, James
June 28, 1792   II, 49
Febr. 9, 1793   II, 57
Oct. 4, 1793   II, 61

Earl, Benjamin
July 30, 1796   II, 85
Earl, Caleb
Sept. 25, 1793   II, 60
July 14, 1794   II, 71
Oct. 5, 1795   II, 76
Sept. 8, 1803   II, 127
Earl, John
Dec. 14, 1786   II, 22
Sept. 29, 1789   II, 34
Mar. 31, 1790   II, 41
Edgar, James
Nov. 5, 1764   I, 700
Edwards, John
Apr. 30, 1806   II, 183
Ehler, Peter
Nov. 12, 1794   II, 73
Eldridge, Phinias
Mar. 16, 1797   II, 96
Nov. 19, 1799   II, 100
Elliot (Elliott), John
Nov. 10, 1793   II, 61
Nov. 6, 1794   II, 72
Ellis, Thomas
Sept. 8, 1753   I, 509, 510, 511
Ewing, James
June 3, 1796   II, 82
Oct. 24, 1796   II, 90
Ewing, John
Sept. 27, 1752   I, 491
Sept. 14, 1754   I, 591, 592, 593
Eyres, Richard
Oct. 3, 1770   I, 730

Faulk, Casper
Nov. 5, 1788   II, 33
Fisher, Joseph
Oct. 14, 1731   I, 54, 56
Fitzpatrick, C.
Febr. 18, 1794   II, 67
Fitzpatrick, Kieran (Kirnen)
Aug. 5, 1788   II, 32
Oct. 1, 1789   II, 35
Oct. 4, 1790   II, 41
June 30, 1791   II, 42
Folger, Capt.
June 3, 1794   II, 70
Ford, William
Nov. 30, 1730   I, 37, 38
Forster, Ralph
Oct. 27, 1764   I, 696
Foster, James
May 8, 1807   II, 194
Fraiser (Frazer), George
Oct. 19, 1736   I, 167, 168
Fraley, Jesse
Oct. 26, 1805   II, 178
Dec. 11, 1806   II, 192
Francklin, Michael
Sept. 21, 1731   I, 47, 51, 53
Franklin, Christopher
Aug. 20, 1794   II, 71
Aug. 19, 1796   II, 85
Fraser, Alexander
Sept. 23, 1792   II, 55

Gardner, Edward C.
Sept. 19, 1804   II, 153
Aug. 26, 1805   II, 163
Gardner (Garden), Resolve
Sept. 19, 1801   II, 110
Gardner, Tristam
Sept. 30, 1801   II, 111
Geerson, William
Aug. 26, 1802   II, 115
Oct. 3, 1803   II, 130
George, Richard
Oct. 15, 1796   II, 89
Gill, Robert
Oct. 3, 1768   I, 720
Oct. 22, 1773   I, 754
Sept. 29, 1774   I, 758
Gladman, Thomas
May 28, 1742   I, 320, 321
Goad, John
Sept. 26, 1753   I, 555, 556, 557
Goodman, Walter
Sept. 11, 1738   I, 212, 213, 215
Sept. 3, 1739   I, 264, 267, 270
Dec. 3, 1740   I, 286, 287, 288
Goodwin, Ozias
Aug. 10, 1791   II, 42

Govan, John
Oct. 25, 1748   I, 386, 387, 388
Gray, John
Sept. 26, 1732   I, 93, 94, 95
Gray, Thomas
Oct. 7, 1765   I, 708
Green, John
Apr. 17, 1804   II, 138
Grove, John
Oct. 23, 1752   I, 499

Haesloop, Herman C.
Nov. 30, 1805   II, 180
Dec. 1, 1806   II, 191
Jan. 5, 1808   II, 204
Hall, James
Oct. 9, 1747   I, 365
Hamm, Peter
Nov. 7, 1754   I, 665, 668, 669
Hammond, Gardner
Oct. 29, 1785   II, 13
Hanse, Capt.
Mar. 19, 1804   II, 138
Hardie, David
Febr. 15, 1797   II, 95
May 4, 1798   II, 96
Oct. 5, 1802   II, 116
Hardie, Robert
Oct. 29, 1774   I, 760
Hardy, Alexander
Oct. 26, 1767   I, 717
Hargrave, Charles
Sept. 30, 1732   I, 96, 97, 98
Harle, Ralph
Sept. 1, 1736   I, 154, 157, 159
Harmsen, Jacob Hinr.
Dec. 30, 1805   II, 182
Harrison, Robert
Febr. 7, 1738   I, 251, 253, 254
Hassleton, William
Oct. 17, 1750   I, 446
Hathaway, Caleb
Oct. 31, 1796   II, 94
Hawk, Samuel
Oct. 26, 1768   I, 723
Hazelwood, Capt.
Nov. 30, 1750   I, 449
Hess, William
Dec. 3, 1800   II, 108
Hill, Arthur
May 31, 1773   I, 747
Hill, William
Sept. 18, 1727   I, 7, 9
Hodgeson, John
Sept. 30, 1727   I, 13
Hodgson, George
Oct. 30, 1738   I, 243, 244, 245

Honor, Ruben
Nov. 22, 1752   I, 507
Hope, Alexander
Sept. 16, 1738   I, 216, 218, 219
Horton, Thomas
Sept. 5, 1803   II, 125
Houston, George
Oct. 28, 1738   I, 240, 242, 243
Howell, John
Sept. 10, 1737   I, 173, 174
Hoyt, Ebenezer
Sept. 22, 1792   II, 55
Huggins, Benjamin
Sept. 30, 1801   II, 111
Hunt, Josiah
Oct. 11, 1786   II, 18
Hunter, Richard
Oct. 15, 1766   I, 711
Dec. 10, 1771   I, 739
Hutchinson (Hutchison), Henry
Nov. 1, 1798   II, 98
Sept. 10, 1804   II, 147
Hyndman, William
Oct. 17, 1749   I, 424

Ingraham, Nathaniel
Oct. 2, 1788   II, 33

Jackson, Joseph
Sept. 25, 1754   I, 600, 601, 603
Jager, Martin
Sept. 22, 1792   II, 54
James, Michael
Aug. 30, 1749   I, 391
Jefferys, Richard
Sept. 14, 1751   I, 458
Johnson, George
Nov. 19, 1771   I, 736
Johnston, George
Dec. 3, 1772   I, 744
Oct. 1, 1773   I, 753
Johnston, James
Sept. 30, 1772   I, 739
Johnston, Joseph
Febr. 24, 1797   II, 95
Jones, Amos
Oct. 23, 1754   I, 659
Jones, Stephan
Aug. 15, 1774   I, 758
Jung, William
July 7, 1788   II, 30
Jurgens, Jan
Aug. 19, 1800   II, 106

Kenneway, Charles
Sept. 23, 1752   I, 486
Kerr, George
Nov. 5, 1764   I, 699

Keys, William
Sept. 1, 1769 — I, 725
King, Elisha
Sept. 5, 1805 — II, 169

Lasly (Lesley), John
Oct. 23, 1754 — I, 655, 656, 658, 659
Lattimore, Wm. Copeland
July 27, 1771 — I, 733
Lawrence, Capt.
Nov. 10, 1756 — I, 682
Lawrence, John
June 5, 1806 — II, 183
Lawson, George
Sept. 7, 1748 — I, 376, 377
Lee, Benjamin
Sept. 12, 1791 — II, 45
Lee, Edward
Aug. 27, 1733 — I, 113, 114, 115
Lelar, Henry
Dec. 19, 1798 — II, 98
Lickley, John
Sept. 19, 1753 — I, 536, 537, 538
Lockyer, George
Aug. 25, 1794 — II, 72
Lournois (Laernoes), Adriaan
Aug. 19, 1786 — II, 15
Low, David
Aug. 27, 1804 — II, 145
Loxley, Benjamin, Junr.
June 4, 1773 — I, 747
Loyd, Thomas
May 15, 1732 — I, 57, 58
Lumsdaine, Capt.
Nov. 20, 1741 — I, 318, 319
Lyon, Charles
Nov. 1, 1755 — I, 681, 682
Lyon (Lion), John
Oct. 2, 1753 — I, 576, 578, 579

Maclane (Malane), William
Dec. 12, 1754 — I, 671, 672, 673
Maley, William
Sept. 8, 1792 — II, 52
Mar. 8, 1793 — II, 57
Sept. 17, 1793 — II, 58
May 31, 1794 — II, 69
Undated — II, 100
Markau, Capt.
Mar. 27, 1800 — II, 106
Marshall, James
June 28, 1735 — I, 151, 152
Sept. 9, 1738 — I, 209, 210, 211
Marshall, William
Nov. 23, 1763 — I, 687
Mason, John
Aug. 25, 1742 — I, 322
Sept. 5, 1743 — I, 339
Nov. 2, 1744 — I, 356

Sept. 15, 1749 — I, 404
Aug. 28, 1750 — I, 439
Sept. 24, 1751 — I, 467
Oct. 4, 1752 — I, 492
Sept. 24, 1753 — I, 538, 540, 543
Mason, Reuben
Febr. 12, 1797 — II, 94
May, Daniel
Nov. 10, 1794 — II, 73
McPherson, Daniel
May 26, 1792 — II, 48
Nov. 12, 1793 — II, 62
Undated — II, 102
Meaney, John
Sept. 18, 1795 — II, 75
Merchant (Marchant), Samuel
Aug. 26, 1735 — I, 152, 153, 154
Sept. 16, 1736 — I, 162, 164, 165
Miller, John, Jr.
Mar. 27, 1800 — II, 106
Miller, Robert
Undated — II, 105
Milner, Richard
Nov. 25, 1763 — I, 687
Mirion, John, see Davies, John
Mitchell, Robert
Sept. 27, 1749 — I, 414
Montpelier, Daniel
Oct. 16, 1751 — I, 475
Oct. 20, 1752 — I, 497
Moody, Peter F.
Nov. 15, 1803 — II, 138
Moore, James
July 25, 1796 — II, 83
Moore, John
Sept. 26, 1752 — I, 487
Sept. 17, 1753 — I, 531, 532, 534
Sept. 30, 1754 — I, 604, 606, 607
Nov. 15, 1802 — II, 121
More, Th.
Febr. 21, 1804 — II, 138
Morris, James
Oct. 11, 1732 — I, 99, 100, 101
Morse, Capt.
Nov. 3, 1804 — II, 160
Morton, William Campbell
Nov. 5, 1788 — II, 34
Muir, William
Sept. 11, 1749 — I, 397
Aug. 25, 1750 — I, 436
Sept. 16, 1751 — I, 463
Sept. 22, 1752 — I, 481
Sept. 26, 1753 — I, 550, 552, 553
Sept. 30, 1754 — I, 609, 610, 612
Müller, Capt.
Mar. 8, 1802 — II, 112
Nevin, James
Oct. 3, 1753 — I, 585, 586, 587

Nicholas, Daniel
Oct. 17, 1749   I, 422
Nicholson, Clement
Aug. 15, 1750   I, 431
Norman, Thomas W.
June 17, 1796   II, 82
Norris, Thomas
Nov. 22, 1796   II, 94
North, George
Sept. 21, 1742   I, 327, 328
Aug. 30, 1743   I, 332, 333

Olive, Thomas
Oct. 16, 1741   I, 310, 311, 312
Ord, George
Sept. 10, 1770   I, 729
Osborne, Peter
June 17, 1771   I, 733
Apr. 30, 1773   I, 746
Osmond (Osman), John
Sept. 19, 1765   I, 706
Oct. 13, 1766   I, 710
Oct. 5, 1767   I, 713
Oct. 29, 1770   I, 731
Nov. 3, 1772   I, 743
Aug. 3, 1773   I, 748
Oct. 31, 1774   I, 761
Oxman, Lazarus
Sept. 4, 1728   I, 20, 21

Parish, George
Oct. 4, 1751   I, 472
Nov. 3, 1752   I, 504
Sept. 11, 1753   I, 518, 519
Parker, James
Febr. 27, 1795   II, 74
Parker, Samuel
Oct. 20, 1796   II, 90
Parrett, John
Sept. 21, 1732   I, 78, 81, 82
Patton, William
Oct. 25, 1738   I, 233, 235
Paul, William
Oct. 11, 1785   II, 12
Paynter, Edward
Sept. 5, 1738   I, 198, 200, 202
Sept. 3, 1739   I, 265, 267, 270
Paynter, Lovell
Nov. 25, 1740   I, 282, 283, 285
Percy, Hugh
Aug. 16, 1731   I, 39, 41, 42
Aug. 11, 1732   I, 59, 63, 64
Aug. 17, 1733   I, 106, 110, 111
Aug. 30, 1737   I, 168, 170, 171
Aug. 27, 1739   I, 256, 258, 261
Dec. 3, 1740   I, 289, 290, 291
Permeir (Permer), Francis Peter C.
Oct. 12, 1802   II, 120
Peter, James

Sept. 18, 1773   I, 749
Phillips, Jacob
July 27, 1738   I, 197, 198
Pickels, Wm.
Dec. 8, 1773   I, 757
Pickeman, Robert
Oct. 8, 1744   I, 352, 353
Pipon, Joshua
Jan. 8, 1739   I, 250, 251
Pittcairne, John
Nov. 8, 1752   I, 506
Oct. 3, 1753   I, 581, 582, 584
Porter, James
Oct. 22, 1791   II, 47
Porter, Robert
Sept. 19, 1764   I, 690
Aug. 24, 1765   I, 703
Oct. 18, 1766   I, 712
Potter, Robinson
Sept. 15, 1807   II, 196
Potts, William
Oct. 9, 1775   I, 762

Randolph, John
Oct. 19, 1749   I, 420
Ray, Nathaniel
Oct. 9, 1803   II, 131
Reason, James
Sept. 26, 1743   I, 343, 344
Reid (Ried, Reed), Daniel
Aug. 28, 1733   I, 116, 119, 120
Sept. 23, 1734   I, 142, 145
Rice, Edward
Jan. 18, 1791   II, 42
Aug. 23, 1791   II, 45
Apr. 26, 1792   II, 48
Rice, Robert
Oct. 13, 1795   II, 76
Richey (Richy), Capt.
Sept. 10, 1753   I, 512, 513, 515
Ricks, Thomas
Aug., 1747   I, 363
Riley, John
Aug. 11, 1804   II, 140
Robertson, John
Jan. 13, 1767   I, 713
Febr. 24, 1772   I, 739
Robinson, Henry
Nov. 4, 1767   I, 719
Robinson, James
Oct. 13, 1764   I, 694
Ross, Charles
Oct. 21, 1754   I, 643, 645
Ross, John
Oct. 22, 1754   I, 648, 650
Russel, James
Sept. 5, 1748   I, 371
Sept. 15, 1749   I, 402
Aug. 13, 1750   I, 429

Sept. 16, 1751	I, 460
Sept. 19, 1752	I, 479
Sept. 14, 1753	I, 521, 523
Sept. 30, 1754	I, 613, 616, 618

Salter, Richard
Sept. 7, 1792	II, 51

Seaward, John
Sept. 8, 1801	II, 109

Seix, James
Nov. 19, 1753	I, 589, 590

Shaw, Pigot
Aug. 25, 1804	II, 144

Slade, Benjamin
Mar. 29, 1796	II, 82

Smith, Charles
Nov. 1, 1763	I, 685
Aug. 8, 1764	I, 688
Sept. 9, 1765	I, 705
Sept. 23, 1766	I, 708
Oct. 6, 1767	I, 715
Oct. 26, 1768	I, 722
Oct. 24, 1769	I, 728
Nov. 23, 1770	I, 732
Nov. 25, 1771	I, 737
Oct. 16, 1772	I, 740
Oct. 25, 1773	I, 755

Smith, George
Oct. 7, 1755	I, 677, 678, 679

Smith, John
Febr. 13, 1797	II, 94

Snell, James
Dec. 15, 1795	II, 79

Spencer, George
Sept. 26, 1749	I, 413

Spilcker, Zacharias
Oct. 31, 1798	II, 98

Spurrier, John
Sept. 28, 1749	I, 416
Sept. 25, 1751	I, 469
Nov. 2, 1752	I, 501
Oct. 1, 1754	I, 626, 629, 633
Oct. 29, 1767	I, 718

Stanfell, Francis
Sept. 20, 1764	I, 691

Stedman, Charles
Oct. 8, 1737	I, 188, 191, 192
Nov. 9, 1738	I, 245, 246, 247
Oct. 2, 1741	I, 303, 305, 306

Stedman, John
Sept. 10, 1731	I, 42, 45, 46
Sept. 11, 1732	I, 66, 68, 69
Sept. 18, 1733	I, 121, 124, 125
Sept. 12, 1734	I, 136, 140, 141
Sept. 26, 1737	I, 178, 180, 182
Oct. 27, 1738	I, 236, 238, 239

Steel, Hugh
Sept. 19, 1749	I, 407
Aug. 11, 1750	I, 426

Sept. 9, 1751	I, 455
Sept. 15, 1753	I, 526, 527, 529

Stellwagen, Daniel S.
Aug. 3, 1806	II, 185

Stephanson, George
Aug. 29, 1770	I, 728

Sterling, Walter
Sept. 9, 1738	I, 204, 205, 207

Stevenson, Capt.
Dec. 11, 1744	I, 357

Stevenson, James
July 3, 1801	II, 109

Sutton, James
Oct. 19, 1772	I, 742
Apr. 30, 1773	I, 746
Sept. 21, 1773	I, 751

Tait, James
Sept. 15, 1748	I, 382

Thompson, John
July 7, 1795	II, 75
Oct. 15, 1796	II, 89

Thompson, Thomas
Oct. 5, 1737	I, 184, 185, 186

Thomson, Alexander
Oct. 12, 1741	I, 307, 308, 309

Thomson, John
Nov. 3, 1750	I, 447

Tiffin, William
Sept. 24, 1747	I, 364

Tran, Arthur
Sept. 29, 1753	I, 568, 570, 571

Trautman, Hendrick
Aug. 3, 1792	II, 50

Treadwell, Jacob C.
Dec. 6, 1805	II, 182

Trump, John
Sept. 29, 1753	I, 573, 574 575

Truxton, Thomas
Oct. 4, 1785	II, 11

Turpin, Robert
Sept. 25, 1732	I, 87, 89, 91

Tymperton, Constable
Oct. 17, 1732	I, 101, 104, 105

Valans (Vallance), Nicolaus
Sept. 5, 1785	II, 6

Veder, Jno
Oct. 31, 1786	II, 20

Vitery (Vettrey, Vitrey), Wm.
Sept. 3, 1739	I, 264, 267, 270
Sept. 23, 1740	I, 274, 275

Wadham, John
Aug. 13, 1750	I, 428

Waire, Capt., see Wier, James

Waite, Francis
Oct. 26, 1796	II, 91

Wallace, William
  Undated   II, 103
Wallace, William
  Sept. 20, 1738   I, 226, 227, 229
Wallis (Wallace), Thomas Edward
  July 27, 1770   I, 728
  Nov. 23, 1773   I, 756
Ware, Charles
  Oct. 12, 1738   I, 231, 232, 233
Warren, Jonas
  Nov. 22, 1802   II, 123
Waters, William
  Oct. 6, 1802   II, 117
Weems, William
  Nov. 7, 1741   I, 315, 316
Wells, Moses
  Dec. 3, 1807   II, 198
Whitewell (Whitwell), William
  Mar. 12, 1794   II, 68
  Jan. 2, 1795   II, 74
Wier (Waire), James
  Sept. 23, 1751   I, 466
  Sept. 30, 1754 I, 620, 622, 624
Wilkie, William
  Sept. 29, 1750   I, 445
Wilkinson, Thomas
  Oct. 25, 1746   I, 362

Williamson, David
  Aug. 31, 1798   II, 96
Wills, Thomas
  Oct. 7, 1803   II, 130
  Apr. 2, 1807   II, 193
Wilson, John
  Sept. 19, 1738 I, 221, 222, 224
Wilson, William
  May 29, 1735 I, 146, 149, 150
  Sept. 26, 1741 I, 296, 297, 299
  Sept. 30, 1743   I, 346
  Oct. 20, 1744   I, 355
  Sept. 27, 1746   I, 359, 361
  Sept. 12, 1750   I, 443
Wirtwel, William
  July 19, 1793   II, 57
Wolters (Walter), Herm, H.
  Oct. 6, 1802   II, 120
Wood, Lyonell
  Dec. 6, 1738   I, 248, 249

Yorke, Peter
  Sept. 7, 1802   II, 115
Younghusband, Charles
  Oct. 5, 1763   I, 684
  Oct. 20, 1764   I, 695

INDEX OF SHIPS

Adolph
Aug. 27, 1785   II, 3
Adventure
Sept. 23, 1732   I, 83, 86
Sept. 25, 1754   I, 600, 601, 603
Adventure Galley
Oct. 2, 1727   I, 14, 15
Aeolus
Dec. 6, 1805   II, 181
Albany
Sept. 4, 1728   I, 20, 21
Sept. 2, 1749   I, 394
Alexander & Anne
Sept. 5, 1730   I, 34, 35, 36
Allen
Sept. 11, 1729   I, 27, 29, 30
America
June 29, 1792   II, 49
June 3, 1796   II, 82
Oct. 24, 1796   II, 90
May 4, 1798   II, 96
America, Brig
July 27, 1771   I, 733
Amiable Creole
Nov. 19, 1799   II, 100
Amiable Matilda
Undated   II, 100
Amsterdam Packet
Nov. 5, 1788   II, 34
Anderson
Aug. 21, 1750   I, 435
Aug. 25, 1751   I, 450
Sept. 27, 1752   I, 488
Ann
Sept. 28, 1749   I, 416
Ann Galley
Sept. 27, 1746   I, 359, 361
Sept. 23, 1752   I, 486
Anna
Aug. 19, 1800   II, 106
Antelope
Mar. 4, 1805   II, 161
Apollo
Febr. 18, 1794   II, 67
Atlantic
Sept. 15, 1804   II, 149
Nov. 8, 1806   II, 189
Aurora
Oct. 8, 1744   I, 352, 353

Bacchus
Oct. 15, 1796   II, 89

Bannister
Oct. 21, 1754   I, 645, 647
Barclay
Sept. 14, 1754   I, 595, 597, 598
Belvidere
Aug. 20, 1802   II, 112
Bennet Galley
Aug. 13, 1750   I, 428
Betsey (Betsy)
Sept. 19, 1765   I, 706
Oct. 13, 1766   I, 710
Oct. 26, 1768   I, 723
Betsey, Brig
Dec. 4, 1771   I, 738
Oct. 15, 1785   II, 12
Betsey, Schooner
May 8, 1807   II, 194
Betsie (Betsey), Snow
Aug. 27, 1739   I, 257, 258, 261
Beulah
Sept. 10, 1753   I, 512, 513, 515
Birmingham
Aug. 25, 1794   II, 72
Boston
Nov. 10, 1764   I, 702
Boston Packet
Oct. 17, 1799   II, 99
Bristol
Dec. 14, 1786   II, 22
Britannia
Sept. 21, 1731   I, 47, 51, 53
Sept. 26, 1764   I, 692
Oct. 26, 1767   I, 717
Oct. 3, 1770   I, 730
Sept. 18, 1773   I, 749
Brotherhood
Nov. 3, 1750   I, 447
Brothers
Aug. 24, 1750   I, 436
Sept. 16, 1751   I, 463
Sept. 22, 1752   I, 481
Sept. 26, 1753   I, 550, 552, 553
Sept. 30, 1754   I, 609, 610, 612
Sept. 25, 1793   II, 60
July 14, 1794   II, 71

Candide
Aug. 19, 1786   II, 15
Canton
Oct. 7, 1803   II, 130
Carolina
June 4, 1773   I, 747

Febr. 21, 1804	II, 138	*Crawford*	
Carterel		Oct. 26, 1768	I, 722
Dec. 11, 1744	I, 357	Oct. 24, 1769	I, 728
Catharine		Nov. 23, 1770	I, 732
Oct. 19, 1772	I, 742	Nov. 25, 1771	I, 737
Apr. 30, 1773	I, 746	Oct. 16, 1772	I, 740
Sept. 21, 1773	I, 751	Oct. 25, 1773	I, 755
Jan. 16, 1775	I, 762	*Crown*	
Aug. 3, 1792	II, 49	Aug. 30, 1749	I, 391
Catharine, Brigantine		*Cullodian*	
July 27, 1738	I, 197	Oct. 15, 1766	I, 711
Catharine, Snow			
May 28, 1742	I, 320, 321	*David L'Hommedieu*	
Cato		Mar. 27, 1800	II, 106
Nov. 3, 1804	II, 160	*Davy*	
Chance		Oct. 25, 1738	I, 233, 235
Nov. 1, 1763	I, 685	*Delaware, Brig*	
Aug. 8, 1764	I, 688	July 11, 1801	II, 109
Sept. 9, 1765	I, 705	*Der Biedermann*	
Sept. 23, 1766	I, 708	Nov. 5, 1801	II, 111
Chance, Snow		*Devotion*	
Nov. 10, 1756	I, 682	Oct. 6, 1802	II, 117
Charlotta		*Diana*	
Sept. 5, 1743	I, 339	Aug. 10, 1791	II, 42
Charlotte		Dec. 3, 1800	II, 108
Sept. 5, 1803	II, 125	*Dispatch, Brig*	
Charming Betty		Oct. 31, 1786	II, 20
Oct. 11, 1733	I, 134, 135, 136	*Dolphin, Brig*	
Charming Molly		Aug. 29, 1770	I, 728
Oct. 22, 1773	I, 754	May 31, 1773	I, 747
Sept. 29, 1774	I, 758	*Dorothea*	
Charming Nancy		Oct. 14, 1787	II, 28
Oct. 8, 1737	I, 188, 191, 192	*Dragon*	
Nov. 9, 1738	I, 245, 246, 247	Sept. 30, 1732	I, 96, 97, 98
Chesterfield		Sept. 26, 1749	I, 413
Sept. 2, 1749	I, 393	Oct. 17, 1749	I, 422
Christian		*Duke of Bedford*	
Sept. 13, 1749	I, 399	Sept. 14, 1751	I, 458
Clementina		*Duke of Wirtenberg*	
Dec. 7, 1773	I, 757	Oct. 16, 1751	I, 475
Columbia		Oct. 20, 1752	I, 497
Sept. 8, 1792	II, 52		
Mar. 8, 1793	II, 57		
Sept. 17, 1793	II, 58	*Eastern Branch*	
May 31, 1794	II, 69	Oct. 3, 1753	I, 585, 586, 587
Febr. 12, 1797	II, 94	*Edinburgh*	
Dec. 19, 1798	II, 98	Sept. 5, 1748	I, 371
Undated	II, 100	Sept. 15, 1749	I, 402
Commerce		Aug. 13, 1750	I, 429
Oct. 9, 1803	II, 131	Sept. 16, 1751	I, 460
Commerce, Schooner		Sept. 19, 1752	I, 479
Nov. 5, 1788	II, 33	Sept. 14, 1753	I, 521, 523
Concord		Oct. 2, 1753	I, 576, 578, 579
July 7, 1795	II, 74	Sept. 30, 1754	I, 613, 616, 618
Oct. 15, 1796	II, 89	*Elizabeth*	
Cordelia		Aug. 27, 1733	I, 113, 114, 115
Oct. 22, 1806	II, 187	Oct. 30, 1738	I, 243, 244, 245
Countess of Sussex		*Elizabeth, Billander*	
Oct. 7, 1765	I, 708	Sept. 5, 1751	I, 452

Elliot
  Aug. 24, 1749   I, 390
Endeavor, Snow
  Nov. 10, 1743   I, 352
Enterprise, Snow
  Dec. 6, 1738   I, 248, 249
Enterprize
  Nov. 22, 1796   II, 94
Europa
  Nov. 20, 1741   I, 317, 318, 319
Express, Brig
  Sept. 19, 1801   II, 110

Fair American
  Sept. 12, 1791   II, 45
  Oct. 6, 1799   II, 99
  Oct. 26, 1805   II, 178
  Dec. 11, 1806   II, 192
Fair Hebe
  Mar. 16, 1797   II, 96
Fame
  Nov. 24, 1773   I, 756
  Sept. 23, 1792   II, 55
Fane
  Oct. 17, 1749   I, 424
Favourite
  Sept. 5, 1785   II, 6
  Nov. 15, 1803   II, 135
Forest
  Oct. 10, 1752   I, 494
Fortune
  Sept. 8, 1803   II, 127
  Nov. 3, 1804   II, 157
Fox, Snow
  Oct. 12, 1738   I, 231, 232, 233
Francis & Ann
  May 30, 1741   I, 292
Francis & Elizabeth
  Sept. 21, 1742   I, 327, 328
  Aug. 30, 1743   I, 331, 332, 333
  [Sept. 19, 1749]   I, 409
Frederick Augustus
  Sept. 15, 1807   II, 196
Friendship
  Oct. 16, 1727   I, 16, 17
  Sept. 20, 1738   I, 225, 227, 229
  Sept. 3, 1739   I, 264, 267, 270
  Sept. 23, 1740   I, 274, 275
  Oct. 12, 1741   I, 307, 308, 309
  Nov. 2, 1744   I, 356
  Nov. 19, 1753   I, 589, 590
  Oct. 21, 1754   I, 642, 643
Friendship, Brig
  Nov. 17, 1795   II, 77

General Wolfe
  Dec. 10, 1771   I, 739
George
  Oct. 26, 1796   II, 91

Glasgow
  Sept. 9, 1738   I, 204, 205, 207
Good Friends
  Febr. 13, 1797   II, 94
Good Hope, Snow
  Sept. 29, 1753   I, 573, 574, 575
Good Intent
  Nov. 9, 1749   I, 426
  Oct. 23, 1754   I, 655, 656, 658
Grampus, Brigantine
  Nov. 4, 1767   I, 719

Halifax
  Sept. 22, 1752   I, 482
  Sept. 28, 1753   I, 559, 560, 562
  Oct. 20, 1754   I, 651, 653
Hamburgh
  Oct. 11, 1785   II, 12
Hamburgh Packet
  Oct. 5, 1795   II, 76
Hamilton
  Oct. 6, 1767   I, 715
Hampshire
  Sept. 7, 1748   I, 372, 374, 375
Hannah
  Oct. 17, 1786   II, 19
Harle
  Sept. 1, 1736   I, 154, 157, 159
Harmony
  July 25, 1796   II, 83
Harriot Baltimore
  June 17, 1796   II, 82
Henricus
  Sept. 22, 1792   II, 54
Henrietta
  Oct. 22, 1754   I, 648, 650
Henry & Charles
  Mar. 29, 1796   II, 81
Hero
  Oct, 27, 1764   I, 696
Holland
  Aug. 20, 1794   II, 71
  Aug, 19, 1796   II, 85
Hope
  Febr. 24, 1772   I, 739
  Dec. 3, 1772   I, 744
  Oct. 1, 1773   I, 753
Hope, Galley
  Aug. 28, 1733   I, 116, 119, 120
  Sept. 23, 1734   I, 142, 145

Indostan
  Apr. 17, 1804   II, 138
Industry
  Undated   II, 105
Isaac
  Sept. 27, 1749   I, 414
Isabella
  Apr. 30, 1806   II, 183
  July 15, 1807   II, 196

Jacob
Oct. 2, 1749 — I, 417
Nov. 15, 1802 — II, 121
Jamaica Galley
Febr. 7, 1739 — I, 251, 253, 254
James Goodwill
Sept. 27, 1727 — I, 10, 11
Sept. 11, 1728 — I, 21, 22
Janet
Oct. 7, 1751 — I, 473
Jean
Nov. 12, 1793 — II, 62
Undated — II, 102
Jeneffer
Nov. 5, 1764 — I, 699
Johann Andreas
Dec. 30, 1805 — II, 182
John
July 19, 1793 — II, 57
Mar. 12, 1794 — II, 68
Jan. 2, 1795 — II, 74
John, Brig
Oct. 19, 1736 — I, 167, 168
John & Elizabeth
Nov. 7, 1754 — I, 665, 668, 670
John & William
Oct. 17, 1732 — I, 101, 104, 105
Johnson Galley
Sept. 18, 1732 — I, 71, 75, 77
Joyce
Nov. 30, 1730 — I 37, 38
Judith
Sept. 15, 1748 — I, 382
Juno
Jan. 13, 1767 — I, 713
Juno (Brig)
Febr. 25, 1800 — II, 105
Oct. 6, 1802 — II, 120

Kathrine, Brig
June 5, 1806 — II, 183
Ketty, Snow
Oct. 16, 1752 — I, 496
King of Prussia
Oct. 3, 1764 — I, 694
Oct. 9, 1775 — I, 762

Laurel
Oct. 2, 1788 — II, 32
Lavinia
Sept. 30, 1801 — II, 111
Leathley
Sept. 19, 1753 — I, 536, 537, 538
Le Brie
July 7, 1788 — II, 30
Leopard
Aug. 25, 1804 — II, 144
Leslie
Oct. 7, 1749 — I, 419

Liberty
Oct. 18, 1805 — II, 174
Little Cherub
May 7, 1805 — II, 162
Oct. 18, 1805 — II, 177
Livonia
Febr. 27, 1795 — II, 74
London, Billinder
Jan. 8, 1739 — I, 250, 251
London Pacquet (Packet)
Sept. 29, 1769 — I, 726
Sept. 19, 1771 — I, 735
Oct. 4, 1785 — II, 11
Louisa, Snow
Nov. 8, 1752 — I, 506
Oct. 3, 1753 — I, 581, 582, 584
Lowther, Snow
Oct. 14, 1731 — I, 54, 56
Loyal Judith
Sept. 25, 1732 — I, 87, 89, 91
Sept. 3, 1739 — I, 265, 269, 272
Nov. 25, 1740 — I, 282, 283, 285
Sept. 3, 1742 — I, 323, 324, 325
Sept. 2, 1743 — I, 334, 336, 338
Lydia
Dec. 11, 1739 — I, 273, 274
Sept. 27, 1740 — I, 276, 277, 278
Sept. 29, 1741 — I, 300, 301, 302
Sept. 19, 1743 — I, 340, 341, 342
Sept. 24, 1747 — I, 364
Oct. 19, 1749 — I, 420
Lydia, Brig
Oct. 29, 1785 — II, 13

Margaret
Sept. 19, 1804 — II, 153
Aug. 26, 1805 — II, 163
Maria, Brig
Oct. 5, 1802 — II, 116
Maria Elizabeth
Sept. 10, 1804 — II, 147
Marlborough
Sept. 23, 1741 — I, 293, 294, 295
Martha, Brig
Sept. 22, 1792 — II, 55
Mary
Sept. 26, 1732 — I, 93, 94, 95
Sept. 29, 1733 — I, 130, 133
June 28, 1735 — I, 151, 152
Oct. 20, 1796 — II, 90
Mary, Brig
Aug. 25, 1742 — I, 322
Aug. 5, 1788 — II, 32
Oct. 1, 1789 — II, 35
Oct. 4, 1790 — II, 41
June 30, 1791 — II, 42
Nov. —, 1795 — II, 78
July 30, 1796 — II, 83

Mary, Galley
Sept. 7, 1748   I, 376, 377
Mary & Sarah
Oct. 26, 1754   I, 660, 662, 663
Mechanic
Sept. 28, 1807   II, 197
Mercury (Mercurius)
May 29, 1735   I, 146, 149, 150
Minerva
Oct. 29, 1767   I, 718
Oct. 10, 1768   I, 721
Oct. 13, 1769   I, 726
Oct. 1, 1770   I, 729
Sept. 17, 1771   I, 733
Sept. 30, 1772   I, 739
Minerva, Brig
Dec. 15, 1795   II, 79
Molley (Molly)
Sept. 30, 1727   I, 12, 13
Sept. 10, 1737   I, 173, 174
Oct. 16, 1741   I, 310, 311, 312
Molly, Brig
Apr. 13, 1796   II, 82
Sept. 30, 1801   II, 111
Molly, Snow
Oct. 26, 1741   I, 313, 314, 315
Montague
Dec. 8, 1773   I, 757
Morning Star, Brig
Dec. 24, 1772   I, 744
Mortonhouse
Aug. 23, 1728   I, 17, 19
Aug. 17, 1729   I, 23, 25, 26
Muscliffe Galley
Dec. 22, 1744   I, 358
Mynheer van Berckel
June 20, 1785   II, 3
Myrtilla
Sept. 21, 1765   I, 707

Nancy
Sept. 20, 1738   I, 226, 227, 229
Aug. 31, 1750   I, 442
Sept. 16, 1751   I, 462
Sept. 27, 1752   I, 491
Sept. 14, 1754   I, 591, 592, 593
Undated   II, 103
Nancy, Brigantine
June 21, 1774   I, 757
Nancy & Sucky
Sept. 1, 1769   I, 725
Nassau
Oct. 11, 1786   II, 18
Neptune
Oct. 25, 1746   I, 362
Sept. 23, 1751   I, 466
Sept. 24, 1751   I, 467
Oct. 4, 1752   I, 492
Sept. 24, 1753   I, 538, 540, 543

Sept. 30, 1754   I, 620, 622, 624
Dec. 12, 1754   I, 671, 672, 674
Oct. 7, 1755   I, 677, 678, 679
Neptune, Snow
July 27, 1770   I, 728
Nov. 23, 1773   I, 756
New York
Sept. 8, 1801   II, 109
Newton
Aug. 11, 1804   II, 140
Norris
May 15, 1732   I, 57, 58
North America
Oct. 10, 1787   II, 24

Ocean, Brig
Mar. 27, 1800   II, 106
Oliver
Aug. 26, 1735   I, 152, 153, 154
Orlando
Aug. 3, 1806   II, 185
Osgood
Sept. 29, 1750   I, 445

Pallas
Nov. 25, 1763   I, 687
Sept. 27, 1791   II, 46
Nov. 1, 1798   II, 98
Patience
Sept. 16, 1748   I, 383, 384
Sept. 19, 1749   I, 407
Aug. 11, 1750   I, 426
Sept. 9, 1751   I, 455
Sept. 15, 1753   I, 526, 527, 529
Patience & Margaret
Oct. 25, 1748   I, 386, 387, 388
Patsey Rutledge
Aug. 29, 1785   II, 6
Sept. 27, 1786   II, 16
May 23, 1787   II, 22
Jan. 10, 1789   II, 34
May 26, 1792   II, 48
Undated   II, 104
Patty & Peggy
Oct. 29, 1774   I, 760
Peggy
Sept. 24, 1753   I, 545, 547, 548
Oct. 16, 1754   I, 636, 638, 640
Nov. 10, 1793   II, 61
Nov. 6, 1794   II, 72
Febr. 15, 1797   II, 95
Pennsylvania
Nov. 1, 1755   I, 681, 682
Pennsylvania (Brig)
Aug. 31, 1798   II, 96
Sept. 7, 1802   II, 115
Nov. 15, 1803   II, 137
Pennsylvania Merchant
Sept. 10, 1731   I, 42, 45, 46

Sept. 11, 1732   I, 66, 68, 69
Sept. 18, 1733   I, 121, 124, 125
Pennsylvania Packet
Oct. 3, 1768   I, 720
June 17, 1771   I, 733
Apr. 30, 1773   I, 746
Phebe
Oct. 19, 1772   I, 742
Philadelphia Packet
Sept. 29, 1789   II, 34
March 31, 1790   II, 41
Jan. 18, 1791   II, 42
Aug. 23, 1791   II, 44
Apr. 26, 1792   II, 48
Phoenix
Sept. 30, 1743   I, 346
Oct. 20, 1744   I, 355
Sept. 15, 1749   I, 404
Aug. 28, 1750   I, 439
Sept. 25, 1751   I, 469
Nov. 2, 1752   I, 501
Nov. 22, 1752   I, 507
Oct. 1, 1754   I, 626, 629, 633
Plaisance, Pink
Sept. 21, 1732   I, 78, 81, 82
Pleasant
Oct. 11, 1732   I, 99, 100, 101
Polly
Sept. 19, 1764   I, 690
Aug. 24, 1765   I, 703
Oct. 18, 1766   I, 712
Polly, Brig
Oct. 4, 1793   II, 61
Oct. 19, 1796   II, 90
Mar. 8, 1802   II, 112
President
Sept. 27, 1752   I, 489
Prince of Wales
Nov. 5, 1764   I, 700
Princess Augusta
Sept. 16, 1736   I, 162, 164, 165
Priscilla
Sept. 11, 1749   I, 397
Sept. 12, 1750   I, 443

Queen Elizabeth
Sept. 16, 1738   I, 216, 218, 219
Queen of Denmark
Oct. 4, 1751   I, 472
Nov. 3, 1752   I, 504
Sept. 11, 1753   I, 516, 518, 519

Rachel
[Sept. 19, 1749]   I, 409
Rainbow
Sept. 7, 1792   II, 51
Ranier
Sept. 26, 1749   I, 411

Rawley
Oct. 23, 1752   I, 499
Rebecca
Aug. 27, 1804   II, 145
Recovery
Oct. 23, 1754   I, 659
Recovery, Brigantine
Oct. 31, 1771   I, 735
Restauration
Oct. 9, 1747   I, 365
Richard & Elizabeth
Sept. 28, 1733   I, 126, 129
Richard & Mary
Sept. 26, 1752   I, 487
Sept. 17, 1753   I, 531, 532, 534
Sept. 30, 1754   I, 604, 606, 607
Richmond
Oct. 5, 1763   I, 684
Oct. 20, 1764   I, 695
Robert & Alice
Sept. 11, 1738   I, 212, 213, 215
Sept. 3, 1739   I, 263, 267, 270
Dec. 3, 1740   I, 286, 287, 288
Sept. 24, 1742   I, 330
Sept. 30, 1743   I, 347
Rosanna
Sept. 26, 1743   I, 343, 344
Rose
Sept. 18, 1795   II, 75
Rose, Snow
Sept. 10, 1770   I, 729
Rosetta
Apr. 5, 1787   II, 22
Rowand
Sept. 29, 1753   I, 568, 570, 571
Royal Union
Aug. 15, 1750   I, 431

Saint Andrew, Galley
Sept. 12, 1734   I, 136, 140, 141
Sept. 26, 1737   I, 178, 180, 182
Oct. 27, 1738   I, 236, 238, 239
Oct. 2, 1741   I, 303, 305, 306
Oct. 7, 1743   I, 348, 349, 350
Sept. 9, 1749   I, 396
Aug. 18, 1750   I, 433
Sept. 14, 1751   I, 456
Sept. 23, 1752   I, 484
Saint Mark
Sept. 26, 1741   I, 296, 297, 299
Saint Michael
Sept. 8, 1753   I, 509, 510, 511
Sally
Nov. 4, 1766   I, 713
Oct. 5, 1767   I, 713
Nov. 10, 1767   I, 719
Oct. 29, 1770   I, 731
Nov. 3, 1772   I, 743

Aug. 3, 1773 — I, 748
Oct. 31, 1774 — I, 761
Sally, Brigantine
Oct. 17, 1750 — I, 446
Sally, Snow
Aug. 15, 1774 — I, 758
Samuel
Aug. 16, 1731 — I, 39, 41, 42
Aug. 11, 1732 — I, 59, 63, 64
Aug. 17, 1733 — I, 106, 110, 111
Aug. 30, 1737 — I, 168, 170, 171
Aug. 27, 1739 — I, 256, 258, 261
Dec. 3, 1740 — I, 289, 290, 291
Samuel, Brig
Sept. 27, 1793 — II, 60
Samuel & Elizabeth
Sept. 30, 1740 — I, 279, 280, 281
Sandwich
Nov. 30, 1750 — I, 449
Sarah
Sept. 20, 1764 — I, 691
Sarah, Brigantine
Nov. 11, 1794 — II, 73
Shirley
Sept. 5, 1751 — I, 453
Sophia Carolina
Nov. 12, 1794 — II, 73
South Carolina
Nov. 12, 1794 — II, 73
Speedwell
Sept. 25, 1749 — I, 410
Apr. 2, 1807 — II, 193
Squirrel, Snow
Oct. 21, 1761 — I, 683
Success, Brigantine
Nov. 25, 1763 — I, 687

Thane of Fife, Snow
Nov. 7, 1741 — I, 315, 316
Thistle
Sept. 19, 1738 — I, 221, 222, 224
Thistle, Billender
Oct. 28, 1738 — I, 240, 242, 243
Thistle of Glasgow
Aug. 29, 1730 — I, 31, 32, 33
Thomas Chalckley
Oct. 13, 1795 — II, 76
Three Sisters
Nov. 30, 1805 — II, 180
Dec. 1, 1806 — II, 191
Jan. 5, 1808 — II, 204
Tom
Oct. 12, 1802 — II, 120
Townsend (Townshend)
Oct. 5, 1737 — I, 184, 185, 186
Traveler
June 22, 1803 — II, 124
Triton

Oct. 31, 1798 — II, 98
Tryall, Snow
Dec. 4, 1764 — I, 703
Tryphena
Sept. 30, 1800 — II, 108
Two Brothers
Oct. 13, 1747 — I, 366, 368
Sept. 15, 1748 — I, 377, 379, 380
Sept. 14, 1749 — I, 400
Aug. 28, 1750 — I, 438
Sept. 21, 1751 — I, 465
Sept. 15, 1752 — I, 478
Sept. 28, 1753 — I, 563, 565, 566
———, 1754 — I, 675
Two Friends
Oct. 31, 1796 — II, 93
Two Sisters, Snow
Sept. 9, 1738 — I, 209, 210, 211
Tyger
Nov. 19, 1771 — I, 736

Union
Sept. 27, 1773 — I, 752
Sept. 30, 1774 — I, 758
Union, Brig
June 28, 1792 — II, 49
Febr. 9, 1793 — II, 57
Aug. 16, 1793 — II, 58
June 3, 1794 — II, 70
Nov. 22, 1802 — II, 123
Mar. 19, 1804 — II, 138
Urania
Aug. 26, 1802 — II, 114
Oct. 3, 1803 — II, 130

Van Stophorst
Oct. 22, 1791 — II, 47
Venus, Brig
July 3, 1801 — II, 109
Vernon, Bilander
Aug., 1747 — I, 363
Verny
Sept. 5, 1805 — II, 169
Virtuous Grace
Sept. 24, 1737 — I, 175, 176, 177
Voltaire
Aug. 29, 1796 — II, 89

William
Oct. 31, 1737 — I, 194, 195, 196
William P. Johnson
Dec. 3, 1807 — II, 198
William & Sarah
Sept. 18, 1727 — I, 7, 9
Windsor
Sept. 26, 1753 — I, 555, 556, 557
Winter Galley
Sept. 5, 1738 — I, 198, 200, 202

INDEX OF PORTS

Aberdeen I, 317

Amsterdam I, 174, 185, 195, 235,
316, 417, 642, 645,
655, 661, 665, 703
II, 3, 12, 13, 15, 19,
22, 24, 32, 33, 34,
35, 41, 42, 44, 45,
46, 47, 48, 49, 51,
54, 55, 57, 60, 61,
67, 68, 70, 71, 72,
74, 77, 89, 94, 95,
96, 100, 112, 117,
121, 124, 130, 131,
135, 138, 145, 149,
157, 162, 169, 174,
178, 185, 187, 189,
193, 196, 197

Berwick on Tweed I, 713

Boston I, 37, 57

Bremen II, 90, 98, 105, 106, 108,
115, 116, 130, 180, 191

(Charleston), S. C. I, 153

Copenhagen II, 60

Cowes I, 16, 29, 41, 63, 78, 85, 89,
94, 119, 145, 149, 157,
164, 170, 175, 180, 185,
205, 209, 235, 238, 242,
244, 246, 251, 275, 295,
299, 309, 322, 326, 330,
333, 338, 339, 342, 345,
346, 351, 353, 355, 356,
357, 382, 384, 390, 391,
393, 394, 398, 399, 400,
404, 408, 410, 414, 416,
419, 420, 424, 426, 434,
435, 436, 439, 442, 443,
445, 447, 449, 450, 452,
455, 456, 465, 466, 467,
472, 473, 475, 478, 479,
481, 482, 491, 492, 497,
504, 506, 507, 509, 515,
519, 529, 534, 536, 543,
550, 555, 562, 571, 575,
579, 581, 590, 593, 597,
607, 612, 618, 624, 633,
645, 648, 659, 674, 685,
690, 696, 699, 701, 702,
703, 705, 706, 708, 710,
712, 713, 718, 719, 722,
729, 731, 732, 733, 735,
736, 738, 740, 744, 749,
753, 755, 761

Deal I, 13, 17, 22, 25, 35, 75, 100,
110, 200, 218, 257, 261, 270,
281, 285, 288, 302, 312, 315,
328, 413

Dover I, 9, 31, 45, 56, 104, 114,
167, 174, 195, 213, 227,
229, 276

Falmouth I, 11, 375, 762

Fredericstad (now Fried- II, 138
richstadt, Schleswig,
Germany)

Gosport I, 640, 642, 655, 679

Hamburg I, 504, 509, 519, 538,
573, 589, 600, 671,
757
II, 6, 16, 22, 34, 48, 50,
58, 60, 61, 62, 70, 71,
72, 73, 74, 75, 76, 78,
79, 81, 82, 83, 89, 90,
93, 94, 96, 98, 99,
100, 102, 104, 108,
109, 111, 112, 115,
120, 123, 125, 127,
138, 140

Jade River, near Bremen II, 160

Leith, Scotland I, 363, 365, 368,
370, 389

Lisbon (Portugal) I, 711, 726, 728,
729, 730, 735,
739, 756, 757,
760

London I, 135, 152, 197, 249, 250,
274, 320, 352, 364, 376,
447, 681, 682, 694, 707,
720, 725, 728, 733, 738,
739, 742, 746, 747, 751,
757, 758, 762
II, 30

Lubeck (Germany) II, 144

Orkney Isl. I, 361, 453

Plymouth I, 15, 68, 97, 124, 128,
133, 140, 191, 222,
232, 396, 484, 499,
549, 600, 651

Poole, in Dorsetshire I, 358

Portsmouth I, 20, 371, 380, 402,
422, 428, 429, 431,
458, 469, 486, 487,
488, 494, 496, 501,
523, 566, 585, 661,
665, 683, 684, 687,
691, 713, 717, 721,

Rotterdam

723, 726, 743, 748, 752, 754, 758

I, 7, 10, 13, 14, 16, 17, 20, 21, 23, 27, 31, 35, 39, 42, 45, 47, 54, 59, 66, 75, 78, 83, 89, 94, 97, 100, 104, 110, 114, 119, 124, 128, 133, 136, 145, 149, 154, 162, 167, 170, 175, 180, 191, 200, 205, 209, 213, 218, 222, 227, 232, 238, 242, 244, 246, 251, 256, 257, 263, 264, 270, 274, 276, 279, 283, 286, 290, 292, 295, 297, 302, 306, 308, 311, 314, 318, 322, 323, 327, 330, 332, 334, 339, 341, 343, 346, 349, 352, 355, 356, 357, 359, 362, 363, 365, 366, 370, 371, 374, 377, 382, 384, 386, 390, 391, 393, 394, 396, 397, 399, 400, 402, 404, 407, 410, 411, 413, 414, 416, 419, 420, 422, 424, 426, 428, 429, 431, 433, 435, 436, 438, 442, 443, 445, 447, 449, 450, 452, 453, 455, 456, 458, 462, 463, 465, 466, 467, 469, 472, 473,

475, 478, 479, 481, 482, 484, 486, 487, 488, 489, 491, 492, 494, 496, 497, 499, 501, 506, 507, 513, 523, 529, 534, 538, 545, 550, 555, 559, 565, 568, 576, 581, 585, 591, 595, 604, 609, 616, 620, 626, 636, 648, 651, 659, 675, 677, 683, 684, 685, 687, 688, 690, 691, 692, 695, 696, 699, 701, 702, 703, 705, 706, 708, 710, 712, 713, 715, 717, 718, 719, 721, 722, 723, 726, 728, 729, 731, 732, 735, 736, 737, 740, 743, 744, 748, 749, 752, 753, 754, 755, 758, 761, 762

II, 20, 28, 44, 55, 76, 91, 110, 183

St. Christopher   I, 292
St. Domingo   II, 62
St. Thomas   II, 161
Shields (England)   I, 417
Tingmouth (now Teign-   I, 703
 mouth, Devonshire,
 England)
Tonningen, Denmark   II, 138, 147,
 (now Tönning,   182, 183,
 Schleswig, Ger-   194, 204
 many)

INDEX OF OFFICIALS AND MERCHANTS

Allen, William, Esqr. Justice, Mayor   I, 45, 47, 159, 165, 171, 177, 182, 192, 196, 202, 235, 239, 245, 270, 275, 288, 312, 333, 339, 342, 354, 356, 358, 362, 370, 371, 380, 394

Allen, William Collector of Head Money   II, 135

Asheton, Ralph, Esqr. Counsellor   I, 55, 57, 111, 120, 125, 165, 168, 171, 174, 182, 186, 196, 197, 202, 215, 219, 224, 233, 249, 319

Attwood (Atwood), William, Esqr. Counsellor, Mayor   I, 362, 370, 371, 380

Barclay, Gilbert Merchant   I, 687

Beneset (Benezet), Daniel Merchant   I, 638, 640, 643, 646, 656, 662, 663, 668, 669, 684, 690

Bond, Phineas Health Officer   I, 581, 681

Bond, Thomas, Dr. Health Officer   I, 311, 318, 512, 516, 521, 525, 530, 536, 545, 550, 555, 558, 568, 573, 576, 581, 595, 600, 604, 608, 613, 620, 626, 636, 641, 645, 648, 651, 659, 665, 675

Bringhurst & Mifflin, Messrs. Merchants   I, 742

Brooke, Henry Counsellor   I, 38, 39, 100, 152

Brown, James Health Officer   II, 17, 19

Bryan, George Justice   I, 710, 736, 737, 748

Charles, Robert Clerk of Council   I, 25, 29, 32, 34, 39, 41, 42, 45, 47, 51, 54, 56, 57, 58, 62, 66, 68, 71, 78, 81, 83, 87, 89, 93, 96, 99, 100, 101, 104, 106, 110

Christie, James Merchant   I, 738, 745

Claypole, George Alderman   I, 38, 39

Coxe, William Justice   I, 703

Coxe & Furman, Messrs. Merchants   I, 756

Cuningham & Nesbit Messrs. Merchants   I, 711

Duché, Jacob Mayor   I, 683, 684, 695, 707

Duncan & Co. Merchants   I, 760

Farmer, Lewis, Col. Register   II, 15, 17, 19, 30, 34, 40, 70, 135, 147

Fisher, Joshua Merchant   I, 733, 746, 749, 757

Fisher, William, Esqr. Mayor   I, 756

Fitzwater, George Counsellor   I, 129

Franklin (Franklyn), Benjamin Justice   I, 529

Gibs & West, Messrs. Merchants   I, 725

Gibson, John Justice, Mayor   I, 719, 738, 742, 743, 744, 746, 747, 751

Gordon, Patrick Lieutenant Governor   I, 39, 41, 42, 45, 47, 51, 54, 55, 57, 58, 62, 65, 68, 70, 75, 78, 81, 83, 87, 89, 92, 96, 99, 100, 101, 104, 106, 110, 111, 115, 120, 125, 129, 133, 136, 141, 145, 150, 152, 154

Graeme, Thomas, Dr. I, 278, 281, 318,
Counsellor, Health 394, 396, 512,
Officer 516, 521, 525,
530, 536, 545,
550, 555, 558,
568, 573, 576,
581, 595, 600,
604, 608, 613,
620, 626, 636,
641, 645, 648,
651, 659, 665,
675, 681

Greenway & Rundle, I, 575
Messrs.
Merchants

Griffits, Thomas, I, 38, 39, 41, 42,
Esqr. 45, 47, 55, 57,
Mayor 62, 136, 141,
145, 165, 174,
177, 186, 192,
196, 197, 207,
215, 219, 224,
229, 233, 235,
251, 254, 261,
270, 278, 281

Hamilton, Andrew I, 38, 39, 68, 70,
Recorder 229, 270

Hamilton, James, I, 333, 350, 361,
Esqr. 391, 393
Counsellor, Governor

Harrison, Henry I, 683
Justice

Hartley, William I, 411

Hasel (Hasell, Has- I, 38, 39, 41, 42,
sell), Samuel 54, 62, 66, 68,
Mayor 70, 75, 78, 81,
83, 89, 104,
111, 115, 125,
129, 133, 159,
174, 186, 192,
215, 224, 229,
242, 249, 251,
261, 270, 281,
285, 292, 295,
299, 309, 312,
321, 330, 333,
342, 345, 388,
390

Hillegas, Michael I, 649, 651
Merchant

Hopkinson, Thomas, I, 363, 364
Esqr.
Counsellor

Howell, Samuel I, 706, 707, 710,
Merchant 713, 720, 723,
731, 743, 748,
754, 758, 761

Humphreys, James, I, 735, 754
Esqr.
Justice

Hunter, Richard I, 739
Merchant

Irwin, Matthew II, 18, 27,
Rolls Officer 28, 35

James, Abel I, 681, 682, 694
Merchant

James & Drinker, Messrs. I, 694
Merchants

Jansen, Derick, I, 51, 54, 159
Esqr.
Counsellor

Jones, Isaac, I, 685, 687, 690,
Esqr. 692, 699, 700,
Justice, Mayor 717, 719, 720,
725, 726, 728,
729, 730, 732,
733, 738, 739

Jones, John I, 757,
Merchant, II, 3, 5, 6, 11,
Health Officer 12, 13, 14,
21, 22, 23

Jones, Samuel F. II, 16
Health Officer

Keppele (Kepplee, I, 519, 537, 578,
Kepler), Henry, 579, 601, 603,
Sr. 622, 624, 672,
Merchant 673, 742, 746,
751

Keppele, Henry, Junr. I, 761
Merchant

Keppele & Steinmetz, I, 742, 746,
Messrs. 751, 762
Merchants

Langhorne, Jeremiah I, 278
Counsellor

Lawrence, John, I, 702, 705, 710,
Esqr. 711, 713
Mayor

Lawrence (Lau- I, 51, 141, 150,
rence), Thomas 159, 165, 168,
Counsellor, Mayor 171, 196, 215,
219, 224, 251,
254, 275, 362,
419, 420, 422,
424, 425, 426,
428, 429, 431,
433, 435, 436,
438, 442, 443,
444, 534, 542,
548, 708,

Logan, James, Hon. I, 159, 165, 171,
President of Council 177, 182, 186,
192

Maddox, Joshua, I, 302, 333, 345,
Esqr. 350, 368, 384,
Counsellor 390, 391, 397,
399, 400, 402,
404, 407, 410,
411, 413, 414,
456, 460, 466,

473, 487, 489,
491, 492, 494,
496, 497, 504,
507, 511, 515,
519, 523, 534,
553, 571, 583,
607, 650, 653

Martin, David   I, 447
Rector of Academy
Mease & Callents,   I, 758
Messrs.
Merchants
Mifflin, John, Esqr.   I, 590
Justice
Mifflin, Samuel   I, 691, 706, 708,
Justice   713, 723, 731,
   732, 735, 754
Miller, Peter,   I, 739, 744, 757,
Esqr.   758, 761
Justice
Morris, Anthony,   I, 235, 239, 242,
Esqr.   245, 254
Counsellor, Mayor
Morris, Robert Hunter   I, 659
Governor
Neave, Richard, Junr.   I, 747
Merchant
Neill, Henry   I, 758
Merchant
Palmer, Anthony,   I, 202, 363,
Esqr.   364, 368
President
Parker, Richard   I, 726
Merchant
Pemberton, James   I, 728
Merchant
Penn, John   I, 725
Proprietary
Penn, Richard   I, 745
Proprietary
Penrose, Jonathan   II, 18
Peters, Richard   I, 675
Secretary
Peters, William,   I, 467, 557, 562,
Esqr.   566, 579, 587,
Justice   663, 683, 688,
   694
Plumsted, Clement,   I, 51, 54, 55, 57,
Esqr.   159, 168, 171,
Counsellor, Mayor   174, 177, 182,
   215, 219, 224,
   229, 233, 235,
   245, 249, 251,
   254, 281, 288,
   321, 322, 352,
   446, 447, 449,
   450, 452, 453,
   455, 456, 458,
   460, 462, 463,

465, 469, 537,
672, 673
Powel, Samuel,   I, 762
Esqr.   II, 35
Mayor
Read, Charles,   I, 100, 104, 111,
Esqr.   115, 120, 125,
Counsellor   133, 141, 145,
   150, 152, 154,
   159
Rhoads, Samuel, Esqr.   I, 760
Mayor
Ritchie, Robert   I, 751, 752, 758
Merchant
Roberts, Edward   I, 129, 274
Counsellor, Mayor
Robinson, Septimus,   I, 333, 338, 339,
Esqr.   342, 344, 350,
Counsellor   354, 357, 358,
   361, 380, 384,
   575, 679, 682
Ross, John   I, 713, 719, 757
Merchant
Ruecastle, Robert   I, 688, 690, 691,
Merchant   699, 703, 705
Rundel, Mr.   I, 702
Merchant
Rush, William   II, 25, 27
Justice
Searle, James   I, 701, 703
Merchant
Shervel & Salter, Messrs.   I, 719
Merchants
Shippen, Edward,   I, 354, 356, 357,
Esqr.   358, 416, 479,
Mayor   481, 482, 484,
   486, 499, 501,
   506, 742
Shoemaker, Benjamin,   I, 345, 354, 357,
Esqr.   368, 371, 380,
Counsellor   388, 400, 411,
   470, 515, 532,
   534, 542, 565,
   566, 586, 605,
   607, 615, 618,
   629, 633, 678,
   679, 684, 685,
   687, 692, 695
Shoemaker, Samuel   I, 633, 684, 685,
Merchant, Mayor   687, 692, 695,
   717, 720, 721,
   726, 729
Shute, Atwood, Esqr.   I, 682
Justice
Stedman, Alexander   I, xxxvi, 472,
Merchant   473, 475, 527,
   529, 546, 548,
   552, 553, 560,
   562, 582, 583,

597, 610, 611, 653

Strettell (Strethill), I, 321, 322, 325,
Robert, Esqr.   328, 330, 338,
Counsellor, Mayor   354, 356, 357,
                      362, 364, 371,
                      380, 390, 393,
                      475, 478, 658
Taylor, Abraham,   I, 288, 309, 322,
Esqr.   325, 330, 333,
Counsellor   338, 345, 352,
                      361, 364, 375
Thomas, George,   I, 197, 207, 215,
Hon.   219, 223, 233,
Lieutenant Governor   247, 254, 261,
                      270, 274, 285,
                      288, 295, 309,
                      316, 325, 330,
                      333, 339, 342,
                      344, 345, 350,
                      353, 361
Till (Tell), William, I, 306, 315, 316,
Esqr.   321, 322, 328,
Counsellor   330, 338, 339,
                      342, 344
Tinker,   I, 593
Governor of Rhode Island
Trimble, J.   II, 67
Port Officer
Turner, Joseph,   I, 330, 361, 364,
Esqr.   375
Counsellor
Viney, Jacob   I, 762
Merchant

Warder, Jeremiah   I, 682, 726,
Merchant   735, 747
Wharton, Samuel   II, 27
Justice
White, Robert, Capt. I, 730
Merchant
Wilcocks, John   I, 728, 756
Merchant
Willing (Welling),   I, 417, 589, 590,
Charles, Esqr.   593, 598, 603,
Mayor   612, 618, 624,
                      633, 640, 643,
                      647, 670
Willing, Thomas,   I, 696, 712, 713,
Esqr.   715, 718, 722,
Justice   728, 729, 733,
                      740, 753
Willing & Morris,   I, 696, 709, 712,
Messrs.   713, 715, 718,
Merchants   722, 728, 729,
                      732, 733, 735,
                      736, 737, 738,
                      739, 740, 744,
                      753, 755
Wood, Samuel, Esqr.   I, 593
Captain
York, Thomas, Esqr.   I, 463
Justice
Young, James, Esqr.   I, 749, 751, 755
Justice
Zachary, Lloyd, Dr.   I, 311
Health Officer

INDEX OF CHRISTIAN NAMES

The entries under each name consist of three items: (1) The correct German form of each name is placed in the first line. If it is not followed by a page reference it means that it does not occur in the lists. (2) The variants of each name follow. Those that are marked by an asterisk (*) were written by English clerks. (3) The explanations of the names, given in parentheses, were added by the editor. Only one or at most two references are given with the principal form of each name. It seemed useless to add more.

The following abbreviations are used:

Ar. Aramaic
AS. Anglo-Saxon
Dt. Dutch
E. English
Fr. French
G. German
Gr. Greek
Hebr. Hebrew
It. Italian
LG. Low German
MHG. Middle High German

OHG. Old High German
ON. Old Norse
Pers. Persian
Pg. Portuguese
Sp. Spanish
Sw. Swedish

acc. according
abbr. abbreviation
Bibl. Biblical
cf. confer, compare
contr. contraction

d. died
der. derived
dial. dialectical
dim. diminutive
esp. especially
fem. feminine
fest. festival
fr. from
gen. genetive
lit. literally
masc. masculine
prob. probably
transl. translation

A. MASCULINE NAMES

AARON   I, 227
Aron,* Aran *
(Bibl. name. Meaning uncertain)

ABRAHAM   I, 19
Abram,* Aberham,* Abrahamm
(Bibl. Name; fr. Hebr. ab, father, and ram, exalted; hence: Of exalted parentage)

ABSALOM   II, 25
(Bibl. name; fr. Hebr. ab, father and shalom, peace)

ACHILLES   I, 583
(Gr. name of three martyred saints. Meaning uncertain)

ADAM   I, 11
Atam, Adamm, Adtam, Atem, Aadam
(Bibl. name; fr. Hebr. adhama, earth; hence, the earthy one)

ADOLF   I, 181
Adolph, Atolph, Adolff, Adolffe *
(Bishop of Osnabruck, d. 1224; fr. OHG. Athaulf, lit. noble wolf, i e., noble hero)

ADRIAN   I, 719
Adrianus   II, 196
(Fr. form of Hadrian; name of several Popes; lit. one from the city Hadria)

AEMILIUS
Amelius   II, 148
(Lt. Name; prob. fr. aemulare, to be zealous; hence, the zealous one)

AENEAS
Eneas, Ennos,* Enoas * I, 163, 165
(Gr. name; meaning uncertain)

AERIC   II, 120
Aric   II, 134
(Meant for Erich)

AGATIUS   I, 546
(Prob. meant for Achatius, perhaps derived fr. Hebr. Ahaz, abbr. fr. Jehoahaz, Jehovah has held)

ALBERT   I, 145
Lt. Albertus, Alberth, Alberdt
(From OHG. Atalberaht, shining as to nobility, i. e., of noble race)

ALBINUS   I, 170, 172
(Name of several saints; transl. of German Weiss, i. e., White)

ALBRECHT   I, 20
Albrächt, Albreght,* Albrit,* Allbrecht, Albright *

(From OHG. Atalberaht; the same as Albert, of noble race)

ALEXANDER I, 125
Allexander, Alexanter, Alicksantter, Allecsande'r, Elexander,* Alixander* (Name of Pope Alexander I, who died as martyr. Gr. name, warding off men, i. e., the defender)

ALEXANDRE I, 593
(Fr. form of Alexander)

ALFRED
Elfreth* I, 596
(AS. Aelfred, fr. aelf, elf, and read, counsel, lit. an elf in counsel, i. e., a good counsellor)

ALIAS II, 126
Alies I, 111
(Meant for Elias, see I, 111, 112)

ALOYSIUS
Alessius II, 54
Alloys II, 100
(Saint in Roman calendar; Lt. name, from Louis, Ludwig)

ALPHONSE I, 593
It. Alphonso I, 595
(Fr. and It. names, from OHG. Adalfuns, funs, ready, adal, noble race)

AMAMUEL II, 75
(read prob. Emanuel)

AMBROSIUS I, 412
Ambrossius, Ambros
(Name of famous church father; Gr. name, lit., the immortal, or, the divine)

ANASTASIUS I, 64
Annastasius
(Name of Catholic saint; his festival on Apr. 27. Gr. name, the one risen again, through baptism)

ANDRÉ I, 407
Andree I, 688
(Fr. of Andrew)

ANDREAS I, 13
Andtreas, Anderes, Andares, Andries, Andrias, Antreas, Antress, Antres, Andterreas, Andereas,* Andareas,* Andaris,* Andreuss,* Anders,* Andrus,* Andrew* (Name of Gr. saint, meaning the manly)

ANSELMUS I, 375
(Name of famous medieval theologian; from Gothic as, god, and helm, helmet, i. e., God is protector, or the protection of the gods)

ANTOINE I, 592
(Fr. for Anthony)

ANTONELLO II, 183
(It. dim. of Antonio)

ANTONIO II, 194
(It. of Anthony)

ANTONIUS I, 102
Anton, Anthoni, Antony,* Anthony,* Antonias, Antonnius, Andonius, Anthonius, Andönius, Andon
(Name of famous saint, Antonius of Padua, 1135–1231; Roman name, meaning perhaps the headman)

ANTREAS I, 590
Anttres, Antres, Antries, (phonetic spelling of Andreas)

ARNDT I, 155
Arnt, Arend, Arent,* Arnd, Arant* (contr. of Arnold)

ARNOLD I, 277
Arnolt, Arnholt, Arnoltz, Lt. Arnoldus
(Bishop of Soissons, d. 1087, Aug. 15; OHG. Arnoald, fr. arn, eagle, and wald, woods; hence, the eagle of the woods)

ARNST* I, 676
(see Ernst)

ARTHUR
Arthar II, 119
(An English name, perhaps of Welsh origin, so Webster)

ARY II, 153
(Meant perhaps for Erich)

ASMUS I, 180
Assmes, Ashmes, Aschemus, Asimus, Aschmes, Assmess
(Abbr. of Erasmus)

AUBRIGHT* I, 280
(Meant for Albright, Albrecht, see the latter)

AUGUSTINUS I, 65
Augustin, Augustyn,* Augusten* (Name of church father, Augustin, bishop of Hippo, d. 430; Lt. name, fr. augustus, exalted)

AUGUSTUS I, 33
August
(Lt. augustus, exalted, revered)

AUSTUS I, 382
(Meant for Augustus, cf. E. Austin)

AVELHART II, 164
(Meant perhaps for Eberhard, due to confusion of r and l; or fr. Abelard)

BALLENTIN I, 519
(Meant for Valentin)

BALSAZAR I, 438
Balsatzar,* Baltsatzer,* Balsatzer,

Balsatzor,* Balsathar,* Balzasar, Balzazar,* Balzasor (Bibl. name, fr. Babyl. Bel-shar-usur, O Bel protect the king. Identified with Balthasar)

BALSTER I, 99, 282
(Contr. of Balthasar)

BALTHASAR I, 76
Balthaser, Baltheser, Baldasar, contr. Baltzar,* Balzer, Baltzer, Balsher, Balsar, Balser, Bollser,* Balthas, Baldas, Baltes,* Baltus,* Baldice,* Baltz, Baldt.
(Acc. to tradition one of the three wise men. His bones are said to have been brought from Milan to Cologne, in 1164. Supposed to be derived fr. Balsazar, Belsazar)

BAPTISTE
Bapdhiste I, 746
Baptist II, 193
Baptista II, 30
(Fr. form of [John, the] Baptist)

BARDEL I, 36
(Abbr. of Bartholomaeus)

BARNABAS
(Bibl. name; Aram. meaning perhaps son of prophecy)

BAREND II, 125
Barent
(Meant for Berndt, Bernhard)

BARNARD II, 42, 150
(Meant for Bernhard, E. Bernard)

BARNET * I, 19
(Meant for Barndt, Bernhard)

BARNHARD I, 145
(See Bernhard)

BARTHOLD I, 60
Bartolt, Bartholt, Bortheld
(Variants of Berthold, OHG. Berahtold, famous ruler)

BARTHOLOMÄUS I, 385
Bartholomeus, Bartolomeus,* Batholomes, Bathelmus,* Bartholomay, Bartholme, Bartholome, Bartlome, Bartlyme, E. Bartholomew,* abbr. Barthel, Bartell, Bardel, Bartel, Bahrtel, Bardell, Bartol *
(Hebr. name, son of Tolmai; patron of tanners and butchers; festival, Aug. 24)

BASILIUS II, 69
(B. the Great, bishop of Caesarea, d. 379; Gr. name, the royal; festival, June 14th)

BASTIAN I, 69
Bastion,* Basion,* Basston,* Passions *
(Abbr. of Sebastian)

BAULUS I, 90
Baullus, Bawl
(Meant for Paulus, Paul)

BEDER I, 305
Better
(Meant for Peter)

BELSAZAR
(See Balsazar)

BENDER II, 56
(Hardly a personal name; prob. a name of trade; cf. Fassbender, barrel maker)

BENEDICT I, 65
Benedictus, Bennedictus, Benedicktus, Benedick,* Benetick,* Bendict,* Benedigt,* Benedice,* Benddeck, Bendich, Bändicht
(Name of founder of Benedictines, his festival March 21. Lt. name, fr. bene and dictus, lit. well said, i. e., the blessed)

BENJAMIN I, 691
Beniamin, Benia *
(Hebr. name. Son of the right hand)

BENTZ I, 428
(Contr. of Bernhard, or of Vincens)

BERNDT I, 46
Bernd, Bernt, Behrnt
(Contr. of Bernhard)

BERNHARD I, 33
Bernhart, Bernhardt, Lt. Bernhartus,* Bernharth, Bernard,* Bernerd,* Bernart, contr. Berndt, Bernt, Bernd,* also Barnt, Barnard, Barend, Barnet, Banhart,* Bern *
(Fr. OHG. Berinhard, bold as a bear)

BERTHOLF I, 237
Berdolf I, 239, 240
(OHG. Berahtolf, famous wolf)

BERTRAM
Berdtram I, 281
Lt. Bertramus II, 89
Bardtram
(Fr. OHG. rhaban, hram, raven, and beraht, famous, hence, famous raven)

BESIEGER I, 353, 354
(German form of Victor)

BLASIUS I, 416, 455
Blassius, Blaziers *
(Regarded as abbr. of Basilius, St. Blasius, was bishop of Sebaste, in Armenia, d. 316 as martyr)

BODO I, 678
(Abbr. of Bothmar, fr. OHG. Bodemar, famous commander)

BONGRAD I, 653

Bengard
(Abbr. of Pancratius)
BOUCHARDT   II, 80, 111
(Meant for Burckhardt)
BRANCO   II, 162
BRASILIUS   II, 79
(Meant for Basilius)
BRAUN   II, 135
(Surname, used for Christian name)
BURCKHARDT   I, 737
(OHG. Warder of the castle)

CAERT   II, 58
(Meant prob. for Cort, contr. of
Conrad)
CARL   I, 36
Carle, Carel,* Coral,* Carlen,
Corol,* Lt. Carolus, Fr. Carrelle,
Carle
(Fr. OHG. charal, karl, the (free)
man cf. Kerl, E. churl)
CARSTEN *   I, 538
Casen,* Kasen *
(Low German form of Christian)
CASIMIR   I, 355
Cassimir,* Casimör, Cassmir, Cas-
mire, Casmer *
(Fr. Polish Kazimierz, Giver of
peace)
CASPAR   I, 29
Casper, Caspers, Casbar, Casber,
Chasper, Caspart, Cashper, see also
Kaspar
(Acc. to legend one of the three wise
men. From Pers. Kansbar, treasurer)
CASTEN   I, 509, 511
Caston
(Dial. form of Carsten, LG. of
Christian)
CHARLES   I, 594
(Fr. form of Karl, also E. transl.)
CHRÉTIEN   II, 86
(Fr. of Christian)
CHRISTIAN   I, 30
Christiyan,* Christyan,* Christen,
Christan,* Christane, Christgan,
Cristian,* abbr. Christ. Lt. Chris-
tianus
(Fr. Christ, a Christian, see Acts
11:36)
CHRISTMAN   I, 104
(Dim. of Christian)
CHRISTOPHORUS   I, 244
Christopher,* Christofer, Christofel,
Christophel, Christopfel, Christoph,
Christoff, Christof, Christop,*
Christopf, Christolf *
(Name of saint, appears in legend in

6th century. Gr. name, the bearer of
Christ)
CHURCH *   II, 8
(Meant most likely for Jurg, dial.
form of Georg)
CLAUDIUS   II, 184
Claudt, Fr. Claude
(Lt. name, fr. claudus, lame)
CLAUS   I, 499
Clas   II, 50
(Abbr. of Nicklaus, see Nicolaus)
CLEMENS   I, 20
Clement, Clements, Clementz,
Clemence *
(Lt. clemens, merciful)
COBUS   I, 401
(Abbr. of Jacobus)
COLLAS *   I, 165
Colaus   I, 443
(Abbr. of Nicholas)
COLMAN   I, 710
(See Kolman)
CONRAD   I, 19
Conradt, Conrat, Conratt, Conrath,
Connrath, Conraet, Conerard,*
Coenraad,* Conraat,* Connard,*
Conraed,* Coneradt,* Conrod,*
Conerat,* Conrade *; see also Kon-
rad
(OHG. Kuonrat, giving bold coun-
sel)
CONSTANTINUS   I, 322
Constantin
(Fr. Lt. constans, firm, faithful)
CORD   I, 510
Cort *   I, 538
(Stands for Kurt, abbr. of Conrad)
CORNEILLE
Cornelle   II, 78
(Fr. form of Cornelius)
CORNELIUS   I, 65
Dt. Corneelis, Cornelis   I, 145
(Name especially frequent in diocese
of Cologne; head of Pope Cornelius
venerated in Minster of St. Cor-
nelius at Aix-le-Chapelle; fr. Lt.
cornu, horn, hence, strong or hard as
a horn)
CRAFT   I, 668
(See Kraft)
CRATES   I, 40
(Prob. abbr. of Pancratius)
CRISPIN   I, 84
(Name of saint, d. 287, at Soissons,
patron of cobblers, fest. Oct. 25. Fr.
Lt. crispus, having curly hair)
CRONOMUS   I, 88
(Stands for Geronimus, form of
Hieronymus)

CUNRADT   I, 390
Cunrad, Cunrath, Coonrod *
(Older form of Conrad)

CUNS   II, 197
(Meant for Kuntz, dim. of Conrad;
also used as family name)

CYPRIAN   II, 103
(Bishop of Carthage, d. 258; Lt.
name, the man from Cyprus)

CYRIACUS   I, 686
(Saint, fest. Aug. 8; Gr. name, belonging to the Lord; also used as
family name)

DANIEL   I, 56
Daniell, Dannill,* Daniehl, Danniel,
Dangel, Danniegel, Danel
(Hebr. name; my judge is God)

DARIUS   I, 170
(Gr. name, der. fr. Persian; lit. pos-
sessing wealth)

DAVID   I, 25
Davidt, Davit,* Daviet,* Davith,
Dauvit, Daviedt, Dafid, Davyd,
Dowid
(Hebr. name, the beloved)

DEBT   I, 206
(Prob. abbr. of Theobald)

DEBUS   II, 120
(LG. form of Theus, contr. of Mattheus)

DEEST   I, 279
(Variant of Ties, contr. of Matthias)

DEGENHART   I, 141
(OHG. Theganhard, lit. the hardy
young hero, cf. Degen, sword, hero)

DEIDRICK *   I, 528
Deitrick,* Dedrick,* Dedrich
(Variant of Dietrich)

DEIMEL   II, 134
(Prob. a family name, used as a
Christian name, fr. Deimling, Tom
Thumb)

DEIS   I, 352
Deys, Dues
(Variant of Thies, Theis; contr. of
Matthias)

DENOIS   II, 198
(Prob. meant for Denis, Fr. of
Dionysius)

DEOBALD   I, 204
Deobalt, Debalt, Deowalt, Debolt
(Variant of Theobald)

DEPELT   I, 11
(Variant of Theobald)

DERRICK   I, 14
Derick   II, 3

(Meant for Dirck, or E. equivalent
for Dirck, see I, 158, 160)

DETTLOFF   II, 139
(OHG. Theudulf, the wolf among
the people)

DEWALD   I, 94
Dewalt, Dewaldt, Diewald, Diewalt
(Variant of Theobald)

DHOMMES   I, 33
Dommes
(Variant of Thomas)

DIBOLT   I, 702
Diebolt
(Variant of Theobald)

DIDER   I, 691
Diter   I, 329
(Abbr. of Diederich, Dietrich)

DIDIER   I, 471
Diedier, Didie
(Fr. for Desiderius)

DIEBOLDT   I, 761
Diebold, Diebolt, Dieble,* Diewalt
(Variant of Theobald)

DIEDERICH   I, 8
Didrich, Diedrick *
(Variant of Dietrich)

DIEL   I, 388
Diehl
(Contr. of Dietel, dim. of Dietrich)

DIELMAN   I, 25
Diellman, Lt. Dielmanus, Dilmanus
(Kosename, or pet name; der. fr.
Diel, dim. of Dietrich)

DIERICH   I, 52
Dirick
(Contr. of Dietrich; E. Derrick)

DIETER   I, 15
Diether, Diter, Dietter
(OHG. Teuthar, the people's
army)

DIETERSON   II, 121
(Son of Dieter, or Dietrich)

DIETMAR   I, 452
(OHG. Theudemar, famous among
the people)

DIETRICH   I, 98
Dieterich, Dettrich, Ditrich, Diterich,
Dietherich, Diethrich, Detrick,*
Diedrich, Diederich, Didrich, Dide-
rich, Deidrick,* Tiderich, Titrich
(OHG. Theudorich, the ruler
among the people)

DILMAN   I, 23
Dilmanus, Dillmanus, Dilmanis
(Variant of Dielman)

DIONYSIUS   I, 647
Dionisius
Fr. Dionise, Dionis, abbr. Nycius
(belonging to the god Dionysius)

DIRCK I, 18
Dirk, Dierk, Dirch, Dirick *
(LG. form of Dietrich; E. Derrick)
DOBIAS I, 14
(Variant of Tobias)
DOMINICUS I, 372
Dominick II, 93
It. Dominico II, 205
(St. Dominick, the founder of the Dominicans, 1170–1221, was much venerated in Germany; Lt. name, fr. dominus, hence, belonging to the Lord)
DOMINIQUE I, 453
(Fr. of Dominicus)
DOMMES I, 34
Domas, Doms *
(Variants of Thomas)
DONIUS I, 406
Donis
(Abbr. of Antonius)
DORUS II, 124
(Abbr. of Theodorus)
DOWIES I, 232, 352
(Meant for Dobias, Tobias)
DRIES I, 541
(Abbr. of Andries, Andreas)
DURST I, 164
Dorst,* Durs, Dort *
(Fr. MHG. türren, to dare, hence, daredevil)

EBERHARD I, 228
Eberhart, Eberhardt, Everard,*
Evrard,* Everhard, Ewerhart,
Ewerhardus
(OHG. Eburhard, strong as a wild boar)
EBERT I, 408
Eberth, Evart *
(Contr. of Eberhard)
ECKHARD
Ekhart I, 411
Echart,* Eckard, Eckart
(OHG. Agihard, strong with the sword)
EDMER II, 24
(Prob. meant for Edmund)
EDMUNDUS I, 422
Edmund, Edmond, Edmon
(AS. Eadmund, the protector of property, cf. G. Vormund, guardian; at least once a mistake for Erdmann, see pp. 383, 385)
EDWARD II, 26
(AS. Eadward, the ward or guardian of property)
EGBERT II, 134

(OHG. Agabert, famous with the sword, cf. E. bright, G. prächtig)
EGIDIUS I, 21, 378
Egydius, Egieties, Egidi
(Gr. name, fr. aegis, the shield of Zeus, hence, holder of shield, i. e., protector. St. Aegidius d. about 725, in the Provence; fest. Sept. 1st)
EHLER I, 510, 512
Ellers, for Ehlers
(Fr. OHG. Agelhar, sword of battle)
EHRENFRIED I, 461
(The protector of honor, OHG. era, honor and fridu, protection, cf. G. einfriedigen, to fence in)
EHRGOTT II, 67
(Sentence name: Honor God)
EIMER II, 109
(If correct, a surname; der. fr. OHG. Agemar, famous, mar, with the sword, agi)
EITEL I, 378
Eytel
(MHG. îtel, the only one)
ELDERICH
Elderick II, 195
(Fr. OHG. Alderich, the old ruler)
ELFRETH * I, 596
(See Alfred)
ELIAS I, 33
Ellias,* Elleias, Alies,* Elija *
(Hebr. name, Elijah, my God is Jehovah)
ELISAUS I, 64, 65
Eliseaus
(Lt. form, used in Vulgate, of Elisha; Hebr. name, God has saved)
ELLINGER II, 127
(Prob. surname, used as Christian name; fr. Ehling, patronymic of Adalo, abbr. of Adalhard, of strong race)
EMMANUEL I, 446
Emanuel, Emanuell
(Variant of Immanuel)
EMMERICH I, 302
Emerich, Emrich, Emericus, Emric,*
Emig *
(OHG. Ermanrih, the powerful ruler; fr. the It. Amerigo, America is derived; hence, America is a German name)
ENEAS I, 163
(See Aeneas)
ENGEL I, 390
Engell, Engle *

(Abbr. of one of the following names)

ENGELBERT   I, 299
Engelberd, Engelbertt, Engelberth
(OHG. Angelberht, bright as an angel; popular etymology)

ENGELBRECHT   II, 123
(Variant of Engelbert)

ENGELHARDT   I, 416
Engelhart
(OHG. Angilhart, strong as an angel; popular etymology)

ENGELWIRD   I, 616
(From a surname; lit. the inn-keeper of the angel. There was the figure of an angel over the door of the inn)

ENNREICH   I, 149
(Stands prob. for Ernreich or Ehrenreich, rich in honor)

ENOCH *   I, 474, 749
(Hebr. name, meaning prob. the dedicated one)

EPHRAIM *   I, 539, 541
Ephrahim
(Hebr. name, the fruitful one)

ERASMUS   I, 52
Errasmus,* Erazamus *
(Gr. name, fr. erasmios, beloved)

ERDMANN   I, 439, 578
Erdman
(Der. fr. Hartmann, Artmann, Erd-mann, the strong man)

ERHART   I, 374
Erhardt, Erhard, Ehrhardt
(OHG. Erhart, strong in era, honor)

ERICH   I, 512
Erick,* Aeric *
(Euarix, the guardian [cf. Lt. rex] of ewa, law)

ERNST   I, 25
Ernestus, Ernest,* Arnst *
(OHG. Arnust, the determined war-rior)

ESAIAS   I, 382
(Hebr. name, Isaiah, Jehovah has delivered. Only the Lt. form fr. Vul-gate occurs, not usual G. form, Jesaias)

ESAU   I, 71
Isau
(Hebr. name, the red-head)

ESRA   I, 67
Ezra
(Aram. name; abbr. of some name like Azariah; Jehovah has helped)

ETIENNE   I, 362
(Fr. for Stephan)

EWALD   I, 469
Ewalt, Ehwalt
(OHG. Ehwald, the protector, wald, of ewa, the law)

EWERHARDUS   I, 693
Everhard *
(Variant of Eberhard)

EZECHIEL
Ezekiel *   I, 349
Etielle, Etzielle   I, 350, 351
(Hebr. name, the strength of God)

FABIAN   I, 759
(Lt. name, fr. Fabius, the cultivator of faba, the bean)

FALKERT *   I, 16
(Prob. meant for Volkhart; OHG. Fulchard, strong among the people)

FALLENDIN   I, 86
Faldin
(Variant of Valentin)

FEIT   II, 192
Feyt *
(Variant of Veit)

FELDEN   I, 33
Feldin, Felde
(Variant of Valentin)

FELIX   I, 13
Fellix, Felicks *
(Fr. Lt. felix, prosperous, happy; a Swiss saint)

FELTEN   I, 30
Felton, Felter,* Felte *
(Variants of Valentin)

FERDINAND   I, 409
Fertinantt, Lt. Ferdinandus
(OHG. Fridenand, bold in giving protection)

FIDELIS   I, 742
Fiteli
(Lt. name, fidelis, the faithful)

FILBERT   I, 711
(OHG. Filibert, very famous; fili, cf. viel, much)

FILIBUS   I, 650
Filbs, Filbs, Fillibs, Filib, Filb, Fillip, abbr. Fill
(Variants of Philip)

FINCHENT *   I, 20
(See Vincent)

FLORIAN   I, 228
(Name of martyr, who died May 4, 304. Lt. name, fr. florians, he who flourishes)

FRANCISCO   I, 760
Fransisco
(Sp. of Francis)

FRANCK   II, 119

(Lt. Francus, a Frank, a German
tribe, which settled at the Rhine,
named fr. franca, the javelin, their
favorite weapon)

FRANCO   I, 760
(It. of Francis)

FRANÇOIS   I, 163
(Fr. of Francis)

FRANTZ   I, 13
Fransz, Franz, France,* Francis,*
Lt. Fransciscus
(Franciscus, latinized form of
Frank, Frantz, contr. of Franciscus)

FRIEDRICH   I, 21
Friederich, Friderich, Fridrich,
Frederich, Frietderich, Fritrich, Frittrich, Fredrich,* Frederick,* Frederik,* Fredrick,* Fradrick,* Frederic,* Lt. Friedericus, contr. Fritz
(OHG. Rich in protection; or ruler
of peace)

FRIK   I, 325
(Meant for Friedrich)

FRITZ   I, 378
(Contr. of Friedrich)

FYT *   I, 192
Fight,* Feyt *
(Meant for Veit)

GABRIEL   I, 52
Gaberiel, Gabril,* Jabryel *
(Hebr. name; the mighty man of
God)

GALLUS   I, 393, 434
(Name of the founder of St. Gall,
Switzerland, d. 627; fest. Oct. 16; in
Lt. gallus means cock)

GASPAR   I, 762
Gaspard, Gasper
(Fr. forms of Casper)

GEBHARD
Gebhart   I, 493
(OHG. Gebahard, strong in giving
or hospitality)

GEERT   II, 196
(Dt. form of Gerhard)

GEOFROID   II, 31
(Fr. of Godfrey, Gottfried)

GEORG   I, 20
Geörg, Görg, Gorg, Gerg, Gurg,
Jarig,* Jerich, Jerch, Jerige,* Jer-
rick,* Gerich,* Jorich, Jörg, Jereck,*
Jerick,* Yearig,* Yerg,* Yorg,
Yorick *
(St. George, venerated since the
Crusades, fest. Apr. 23. Gr. name,
the tiller of the earth)

GERHARD   I, 25
Gerhart, Gerhardt, Gerort, Gerdt,

Gerrard,* Gerard,* Lt. Gerhardus
(OHG. Garehard, strong with the
spear)

GERLACH   I, 404, 571
(OHG. Gerolah, playing with the
spear; cf. German, the spearman)

GERONIMUS   II, 102
(cf. It. Geronimo = E. Jerome, see
Hieronymus)

GERRET   II, 125
Gerrit, Gerdt, Geirts, Gorit
(Dt. forms of Gerhard)

GEWERD   II, 191
(Dial. form of Gebhard)

GIDEON   I, 105
Giedion
(Hebr. name; the one who cuts
down, namely enemies)

GILBERT   I, 107, 111
(OHG. Gisalbreht, famous as a
hostage)

GILLES
Geles   I, 51
Gile,* Gilli, Giles,* Yilles
(Fr. forms of Aegidius, Gidius,
Gilius, E. Giles)

GILLIAN   I, 106
Gelian,* Gylyan
(Variant of Kilian *)

GISBERTUS   I, 51
Gisbert, Gysbert,* Giesbert
(Same as Giesebrecht, famous of
spear)

GLAUS *   I, 189
(Meant for Claus; abbr. of Nicklaus, Nicholas)

GODFRIED   I, 490
Godfriet,* Godfrid
(Variant of Godfrey, Gottfried)

GOGHAM *   I, 241
(Meant for Jochem, variant of
Joachim)

GOMEZ
Gometz   II, 122
(Sp. name)

GORG   I, 322
Görg, Gorgon   II, 75
(Variants of Georg)

GOTTFRIED   I, 52
Gottfriedt, Gottfrit, Gottfrith,* God-
fried, Godfrey *
(OHG. Godafrid, the protection of
God)

GOTTHARD   I, 742
Gotthardt, Godhart,* Godhert
(OHG. Gotahard, strong as God)

GOTTHELF
Gothilf   II, 72
(Sentence name: Help oh God)

GOTTHOLD I, 759
(OHG. Godavald, the ruler of God, but changed through popular etymology into: God is gracious)

GOTTLIEB I, 277
Gotlieb, Gottlib,* Gotlip,* Godlieb *
(OHG. Godolef, born of God, lieb = leip, one who is left; changed through popular etymology)

GOTTLOB II, 79
Godlob, Gotlope *
(The praise of God)

GRAFF I, 514
Kraff
(OHG. gravo, judge, director)

GRAFFT * I, 645
Graft *
(Variant of Kraft)

GREGORIUS I, 141
(Name of many saints, especially Pope Gregory, the Great, d. 604. Gr. name, the watchful one, fr. egeirein, to watch)

GUILIELMUS I, 725
Guiliam I, 123
(Lt. of William, Wilhelm)

GUILLAUME I, 731
(Fr. for William, Wilhelm)

GUNTHER II, 83
Gunder *
(OHG. Gundahar, the battle army)

GUSTAF II, 99
Gustav, Justaf, Lt. Gustavus (fr. gunt, battle, and staf, staff, hence battle-staff, cf. Fallstaff)

GUSTUS II, 54
(Variant of Justus)

GUTMAN II, 134
(Perhaps not a Christian name, but a surname, transposed)

HADOLF I, 483
(Prob. meant for Adolf)

HAGEN I, 501, 660
(Abbr. fr. Hangarich, the ruler of the dwelling; hagen, a dwelling surrounded by a thorn hedge, cf. The Hague)

HANCRIST II, 37
(Contr. of Johan Christian)

HANDERICK II, 3
(Variant of Hendrick, Heinrich)

HANICKEL I, 67
Hanicle
(Contr. of Johann Nicholas)

HANNES I, 11
Hanes, Hance,* Hansh *
(Abbr. of Johannes)

HANNIBAL II, 107
(Phoenician name of famous general; Baal is gracious)

HANS I, 9
Hanns, Hansen, Hance,* Hantz,* Hanse,* Hens *
(Abbr. of Johannes)

HARMON * I, 144
(Meant for Herman)

HARMS II, 184
(Contr. of gen. of Hermann)

HARTMANN I, 374
Hartman, Hardtman
(OHG. Hartmann, strong man)

HARTWIG I, 382
(OHG. Harduwig, strong in battle)

HAUBRICH I, 401
Houbrig,* Hobrick *
(OHG. Huguberht, bright in thought)

HECTOR I, 320
(Gr. name; holding fast)

HEINI I, 740
Heiny, Hein
(Swiss dim. of Heinrich)

HEINICKL I, 300
(Contr. of Heinrich and Nicholas)

HEINRICH I, 11
Heinrig, Heynrich, Henrich, Henrick, Hennrich, Henerich, Hendrich,* Hendrick,* Hendryk,* Hindrig, Hyndrick,* Hendri,* Hanrich,* Handerick, Henerick *
(OHG. Hangarih, the chief of the house)

HEINZ II, 41
Hinz
(Dim. of Heinrich)

HELFFER I, 631
(Der. fr. Helffrich, OHG. Chilperich, the helpful ruler)

HELMAN I, 710
(OHG. Hildemann, Man of battle, changes to Hillmann, Hellmann)

HENDRIK I, 407
Hendrick, Hendric, Hendricus, Hendrix *
(Dt. forms of Heinrich)

HENIRK II, 20
(Meant for Hendrik)

HENNING II, 98
(Patronymic of Henn, Hein, Heinrich, hence, son of Henry)

HENRI I, 32
Hanri
(Fr. of Henry)

HENRICH * I, 12
Henrick, Henerick, Henricus
(Variants of Heinrich)

HERBERT   I, 143
Herberd, Herber
(OHG. Hariberaht, famous in the
army)
HERMANN   I, 95
Herrmann, Herman, Harman, Lt.
Hermanus, Hermans,* abbr. Manus
(OHG. Hariman, man of the
army)
HEROLD
Harolt *   I, 508
(OHG. Chariwalda, ruler of the
army)
HERSCH   II, 189
Hirsch
(Jewish name; derived from name
of house, which showed the figure
of a deer)
HERTZ   I, 663
Hartz
(Jewish name; same as preceding
name)
HERTZOG   II, 93
(A surname, reversed)
HIERONYMUS   I, 86
Hieronimus, Heronimus, Hirieon-
imus, Hironimus, Hyronimus, Hier-
onemus,* Heironimus, Hironymus,
Geronimus,* Jeronimus *
(Name of famous church father, d.
at Bethlehem, 430. Gr. name, the
one who has a holy name)
HILDEBRAND   I, 330
(OHG. Hildibrand, a flame [sword]
in battle)
HIPOLITO   I, 761
(Pg. for Hippolitus, name of martyr
in 3rd century; Gr. name, loosening
horses)
HISBERT *   I, 29, 30
(Meant for Gisbert)
HONORIUS   I, 745
Honor, Honer
(Lt. name, the honorable)
HUBERICH   I, 282
Hubrig, Houbrick,* Hobrick *
(OHG. Hugiberaht, bright in
thought)
HUBERT   I, 492
Hubertus
(OHG. Hugibert, bright in mind,
or thought)
HUMBERT
Humber   I, 405
(OHG. Hunbraht, famous as a giant,
cf. Hüne, giant)
HUNTER *   I, 247
(Prob. meant for Humbert)

IGNATIUS   I, 410
Ignatzius, Ignathius, Ignathes, It.
Ignacio   I, 711
Fr. Ignace   II, 95
(Name of famous church father; Lt.
the fiery)
IMMANUEL   I, 443
Emmanuel, Emanuel
(Hebr. name; God with us)
ISAAC   I, 284
Isaak, Isac, Isak, Isack, Isach, Isa
(Hebr. name; he laughs)
ISAQUE   I, 723
(Fr. of Isaac)
ISAI   I, 71, 75, 77
(Perhaps meant for Esau)
ISRAEL   I, 437
(Hebr. name; explained as warrior
of God)

JABEZ   I, 421
(Hebr. name; explained I Chron.
4:9, as born in pain)
JACOB   I, 11
Jakob, Jacop, Lt. Jacobus, also prob.
Jacho   I, 247
(Hebr. name; the heelcatcher, fr.
aqeb, the heel)
JACQUES   I, 196
Jaques,* Jaque *
(Fr. forms of Jacob)
JAMES   II, 151
(E. transl. of Jacob)
JAN   I, 322
Jann, Jaen
(Dt. of John)
JARIG   I, 480
Jarrick
(Meant for Georg)
JASPER *   I, 703
(Dial. form of Kaspar)
JEAN   I, 95
(Fr. for John)
JEFFERSON   II, 167
(born on board of ship)
JENCE   II, 75
(Perhaps for Jahns, contr. of Jo-
hannes)
JEORG   I, 133
Jerg, Jereg, Jerig, Jerick,* Jerige,*
Jerrick *
(Variants of Georg)
JEREMIAS   I, 379
Jeremia, Jeremiah, Jerrimias,* Jere-
mya,* Jerimy *
Fr. Jeremie   I, 721
(Hebr. name. He whom Jehovah has
appointed)

JERICH I, 35
Jerige,* Jerick,* Jerik,* Jereck,*
Jerrick,* Jerig,* Jeri *
(Variants of Georg)

JEROME I, 673
(Fr. and E. form of Hieronymus;
sometimes a mistake for Jeremias,
see I, 175, 176)

JERONIMUS II, 124
(See Hieronymus)

JERRY II, 43
(Meant for Jerg, see Georg)

JOACHIM I, 315
Jochim, Jochem, Joackim *
(Hebr. name. Same as Jehoiachim,
Jehovah has raised up)

JOBST I, 452
(Contr. of Jodocus)

JOCHMUS I, 336
Jochamus, Jochem, Jochim, Jockem,*
Jogen
(Variants of Joachim)

JODOCUS I, 502, 749
abbr. Jost and Jobst
(St. Jodocus, from Bretagne, France,
d. as hermit 669; venerated in south
Germany. Gr. name; fr. yos, arrow,
hence, holding arrows)

JOEL I, 498, 761
(Hebr. name; Jehovah is God)

JOGEN I, 505
(Perhaps meant for Jochem, Joachim)

JOHANN I, 9
Johan, Joan,* John *
(Hebr. name; Jehovah is gracious;
same as Johannes)

JOHANNES I, 9
Johanes, Johans, Johnes, Johanas,*
Johannis,* Johanis,* Lt. Joan-
nes I, 482
(Hebr. name; Jehovah is gracious;
same as Johann)

JOHANICKEL I, 404
(Contr. of Johann and Nicholas)

JOHANNRICH I, 706
Johenrich
(Contr. of Johann and Heinrich)

JONAS I, 436
(Lt. form of Jonah, used in Vulgate.
Hebr. name: dove)

JONATHAN I, 159
(Hebr. name. Jehovah has given)

JÖRG I, 12
Jorg, Jorick,* Jorich, Jörge
(Variants of Georg)

JOSEPH I, 9
Josebh, Josef, Lt. Josephus

(He increases; He is Jehovah)

JOSIAS I, 411, 507
(Lt. form of Josiah. Hebr. name.
Jehovah supports)

JOST I, 20
Joest,* Joost *
(Contr. of Jodocus, or sometimes of
Justus)

JOSUA I, 359
Fr. Josue I, 708
E. Joshua II, 155
(Hebr. name. Jehovah is salvation)

JOWEL II, 11
(Meant for Joel)

JUAN I, 761
(Sp. of John)

JUDA II, 156
(Hebr. name. Meaning doubtful; explained as the one praised)

JÜLCH I, 448
(Dial. form of Julius)

JULIUS I, 402
Jullius, Juilis,* Jullus, Jülch
(Name of 1st bishop of Le Mans,
d. about 400. Lt. name: Jovilius, belonging to Jove, or Jupiter)

JUNGHANS I, 334
(The B list, p. 332, shows that his
name was Hans Meier, Junior)

JURG * I, 10
Jurgh,* Jurig, Jurich,* Jourge,*
Jurrig,* Jurge,* Jurgeck *
(Variants of Georg; phonetic spel-
lings)

JURIAN II, 68
(Meant for Jurgen, form of Georg)

JUSTICE I, 31
Justes
(Meant for Justus)

JUSTINUS I, 265
Justin
(Christian philosopher and martyr
d. about 166. Lt. name, der. fr.
justus, the just)

JUSTUS I, 51
Just, Jusdus, Justes, Justice
(Lt. name; the just)

KARL I, 158
Karll, Karle
(OHG. Charal, the (free) man; cf.
G. Kerl and E. churl; see also Carl,
E. Charles)

KASEMIR II, 121
(See Casimir)

KASPAR I, 30
Kasper

(Acc. to legend one of the three wise men; see also Caspar)

KILIAN I, 457
Killian, Gillian
(Scotch missionary; bishop of Würzburg, d. as martyr 689. Celtic name)

KLAUS I, 286
Klas, Klaas
(Abbr. of Nicklaus, Nicholas)

KOLMAN I, 710
Colman
(From ON. kollir, helmet, hence, the man of the helmet)

KONRAD I, 691
Konrat, Konradt, Korrad, Kuhnroth
(OHG. Chuonrath, bold in counsel; cf. G. kühn; see also Conrad)

KRAFT I, 425
Krafft, Craft, Graft
(Abbr. fr. perhaps Kraftheri, the strength of the army)

KREIMAN I, 280, 281, 282
Crymon *
(Meant perhaps for Cayman, a saint who appears in the martyrologies)

KRISTEN * I, 30
(Meant for Christian)

KUNRAD I, 302
Kunradt, Kuhnroth
(Older form of Konrad, Conrad)

KUNTZ
Kuns I, 397
(Dim. of Konrad, also used as family name, see p. 693)

LAMBERTH I, 507
Lamber,* Lt. Lampertus, Lamberdus
(OHG. Landoberht, famous or bright in the land; same as Lambrecht)

LAMBRECHT I, 504
Lamburgh *
(OHG. Landoberht, famous or bright in the land)

LANHART I, 33
(Variant of Leonhart)

LARS I, 201
Lasch * II, 139
(Sw. of Laurentius)

LAURENTIUS I, 445
Laurenzius, Laurentz, Laurenz, Laurents,* Laurens, Lawrentz,* Lowrence,* Lawrence,* see also Lorentz
(Name of saint, martyr in 3rd century. Lt. name, the man fr. Laurentum, Italy)

LAUX I, 759
(Contr. of Lucas)

LAZARUS I, 153
Lazerus,* Lazrus *
(Hebr. name; der. fr. Eleazar, God has helped; same as G. Gotthilf)

LEBART II, 71
(Meant for Lebolt, Leopold, with exchange of r for l)

LEBRECHT I, 735, 750
Leberecht, Lebreght
(Sentence name: Live right)

LEBS I, 114
(Abbr. of Philips)

LEITEL I, 380, 507
Lydel
(Der. fr. Leuthold; OHG. Liutoald, ruler of the people)

LEMMILL I, 739
(Dim. of Lambrecht)

LENHART * I, 313
Lehnhart, Lenhard, Lenert, Lenord *
(Variants of Leonhard)

LEON II, 61
(Abbr. of name like following)

LEONHARD I, 69
Leonhart, Leonhartt, Leonharth, Leohnhard, Leonerd,* Leonthart, Leonart,* Leonard,* Länhart, Lenhart, Lenhard, Lehnhart, Leendert,* Lionhard,* Linnard,* Linhard, Lienhart, Linnert, Löhnhart
(Usually transl. Strong as a lion)

LEOPOLD I, 36
Leopoldt, Leobold, Lt. Leboldus
(OHG. Liutbald, bold among the people)

LEVI II, 144
Levy
(Hebr. name. The attendant of the temple)

LEWDWIGHT II, 36
(Meant for Ludwig)

LEWIS II, 152
(Meant for Fr. Louis)

LIBORIUS
Lyborius I, 155, 158
Liworius, Liber
(Bishop of Le Mans, in 4th century, venerated especially in North Germany)

LIEB I, 717
(Abbr. of Liebolt, OHG. Liutbald, bold among the people)

LIND I, 394
(Abbr. of Linder, OHG. Lindher, lit. the dragon of the army)

LINHARD I, 480

Linnhart, Linhart, Linnert, Linard *
(Variants of Leonhard)

LODWICK * I, 360
Lodowick,* Lodawick,* Lodewick,*
Lodwich *
(Variants of Ludwig)

LÖNHARD I, 33
(Variant of Leonhard)

LORENTZ I, 33
Lorenz, Lorens, Lohrentz, Lorrentz,
Lorance,* Loerens,* Larrance,*
Loretz
(Derived fr. Laurentius)

LORIAN * I, 425
(Prob. meant for Florian)

LOSKER I, 399
(Doubtful name)

LOTHARIUS I, 583
Lothar, Lotharus
(OHG. Chlodochar, famous in the
army)

LOUIS I, 51
Luis, Loui
(Fr. of Ludwig)

LUCAS I, 51
It. Lucca II, 108
Lucka *
(Lt. name. The man of the town of
Lucca)

LUCIUS II, 153
(Latinized form of Lutze, dim. of
Ludwig, OHG. Chlodowich, famous
in war)

LUDOLF I, 536, 537
Ludolff, Ludoff, Ludolph
E. Ludolphus
(OHG. Chludulf, famous wolf)

LUDOWIGH * I, 10
Ludewig,* Ludowick *
(Variants of Ludwig)

LUDWIG I, 13
Lutwig, Ludewig, Lutwick,* Lodwig,* Lodwich,* Loudwick,* Lodwick,* Lewis *
(OHG. Chlodowich, famous in war)

LUNZY * I, 450
(If correct, der. fr. Lunz, a dim. of
Lundbert, famous as to woods)

LUTHERICH I, 12, 13
(read Ludwig)

LUTHERUS I, 582, 583
(read Lotharius)

LYDEL I, 380
(See Leidel)

MAGNUS I, 380
(Name of early Christian mission-
ary, d. about 750; Lt. name, the
Great; but occasionally it exchanges

with Manus, see pp. 629, 635, an
abbr. of Hermanus)

MALICHA * I, 172
(Perhaps meant for Melchior)

MANNES I, 710
Manus, Mainus
(Abbr. of Hermanus)

MANUEL I, 760
(Sp. abbr. of Immanuel)

MARCELLUS I, 727
(Name of Pope Marcellus I, d. 309.
Lt. dim. of Marcus)

MARCUS I, 94
Markus, Marckus,* Markes,* abbr.
Marx, Marks,* Mark
(Name of St. Mark, the Evangelist,
fest. Apr. 25. Lt. name, son of
Mars)

MARIUS I, 20
(Lt. name)

MARO I, 757
(The cognomen of Vergil, Publius
Vergilius Maro)

MARQUARD
abbr. Quardt I, 297
(From ward, guardian, and mark,
boundary)

MARQUIS II, 83
(Stands perhaps for Marcus)

MARTIN I, 9
Mardtin, Mardin, Marthin, Martten,
Marten, Marden, Martein, Mar-
tain,* Martine,* Martyn,* Mardien,
Marty, Marte, Marti, Mardi, Mer-
ten, Mertin,* Merdin *
(Name of St. Martin, bishop of
Tours, d. about 400; Lt. name, be-
longing to the god Mars)

MARTZOLF I, 730
(Germanized form of Marcellus)

MARUS II, 135
(Meant prob. for Marcus)

MARX I, 13
(Contr. of Marcus)

MATTHÄUS I, 328
Madtheus, Matheus, Matteus, Mat-
theus, Mathäus, Mathaus, Matthaus,
Matthes, Mattes, Mates, Mathes, E.
Matthew
(Hebr. name. Gift of God)

MATTHIAS I, 56
Mathias, Mathais, Mattheis, Ma-
theis, Madteis, Mattdes, Mathis,*
Matias,* Matis,* Mattys,* Mathys,*
Mattis, Maddis, Madhias
(Gift of Jehovah; same as Mat-
theus, in meaning)

MATTHIEU
Mathieu I, 455

Mattieu, Matieu
(Fr. for Matthew)
MATZ I, 131
(Contr. of Mattheus)
MAURITZ* I, 642
(Lt. Mauricius, prob. fr. Maurus, the Moor; Fr. Maurice; the leader of the Theban legion, suffered martyrdom about 300 A.D.; see also Moritz)
MAX I, 498
(Abbr. of Maximilian)
MAXIMILIAN I, 719
Maximilianus
(The apostle of Noricum, martyr under Diocletian; der. fr. maximus, the greatest)
MEINHARD II, 22
Myndert II, 99
(OHG. Maginhard, strong in power)
MEIRS II, 189
(Jewish name; distinguished)
MELCHIOR I, 105
Melcher, Melcker,* Melchier,* Melker,* Melger, Melgior, Melichor, Meliger, Mellcher,* Milcher
(acc. to medieval legend one of the three wise men; Hebr. name. King of light)
MELGERT II, 50
Melger
(Meant for Melcher, Melchior)
MEYER I, 44
(Fr. Lt. major, cf. major domo, the manager of an estate)
MICHAEL I, 11
Michel, Michell, Michal, Michall,* Michale, Michele, Michelle, Michle, Michiel,* Migiel,* Migel, Michgel, Mickell,* Meichal, Meichel
(Hebr. name. Who is like God)
MICHAELO I, 421
Michaele
(It. of Michael)
MODESTUS II, 119
Medestus
(Roman saint, Lt. name, the modest)
MORITZ I, 104
Morritz, Morris*
(Germanized form of Mauritius)
MOSES II, 41
It. Mose, Mosi
(Hebr. name, explained as one drawn fr. the water, fr. Hebr. mashah, to draw; more likely fr. Egyptian mesu, child)

NATHAN II, 107
(Hebr. name; abbr. of Nathaniel, gift of God)
NATHANAEL I, 321
Nathaniel I, 143
(Hebr. name. Gift of God)
NICKEL I, 311
(Abbr. of Nicolaus)
NICODEMUS I, 418
(Bibl. name; Gr. the victor of the people)
NICOLAUS I, 288
Nicholas, Nichlaus, Nichlos,* Nicklaus, Nicklos, Nicklas, Niklas, Niclas, Niclaes, Nicolas,* Nicolaas,* Nickolas, Nickelaus, Nickelas, Nicollas,* Niklos, Nichols,* Nigelas, Niglaus, Nigglaus, abbr. Nickel, Nickell,* Nicel*
Fr. (Nicolas) Nicola I, 729
(Bishop of Myra, in Lycia, in 4th century; Gr. name. The victor of the people)
NIEDHART
Niedarth II, 134
(OHG. Nidhard, strong in nît, battle fury)
NIELS II, 183
Neals
(Sw. abbr. of Cornelius)
NOAH I, 650
Noa
Fr. Noé II, 31
(Hebr. name, explained as rest-giver, a popular etymology)
NOËL II, 89
(Fr. name. fr. Lt. natalis, birthday, that of Jesus is meant, Dec. 25th)
NÖLCHEN I, 478
(Nölcken, dim. of Arnold)
NORBERT II, 145
(Saint, archbishop of Magdeburg, 1126-1134; fr. Nordbert, famous Norseman)
NYCIUS I, 740
(Abbr. of Dionysius)

OLDRICH II, 50
Oellrig,* Olerick,* Olrige, Olrig
(OHG. Uodalrich, hence Oldrich is the older form of Ulrich)
OSWALD I, 52
Oswalt,* Ohswald,* Ostwald*
(OHG. Ansowald, the divine ruler, or, perhaps, strong as a god)
OTTO I, 129
Otho
(The apostle of Pommerania, Otto,

bishop of Bomberg; OHG. Audo, abbr. of Audoperth, or a similar name; famous in possessions)

PALZER I, 631
Paltser,* Poltzer *
(Meant for Baltzer, abbr. of Balthasar)
PANCRATIUS I, 441
(Youthful Christian, beheaded under Diocletian; Gr. name; allpowerful)
PASSIONS I, 85
(Prob. meant for Bastian, abbr. of Sebastian)
PATRICIUS
Partricius II, 125
Patrick I, 143
(Lt. name of St. Patrick)
PAULUS I, 75
Paullus, Pallus,* Palus,* Baulus, G. Paul, Fr. Paule
(Der. fr. Lt. paulus, little)
PENS II, 84
(Prob. meant for Bentz, dim. of Bernhard)
PERHART * I, 30
(Meant for Bernhart)
PETERS I, 160
(Son of Peter)
PETRUS II, 30
Peter, Peder, Petter, Pedter, Pöeter, Peeter,* Beder, Better, Sp. Pedro
(Gr. name, fr. petra, rock)
PHILIPPUS I, 104
Philip, Philips, Phillippus, Philib, Philibs, Philipp, Phillip, Philb, Phylype
Fr. Philippe I, 746
(Gr. name; Lover of horses)
PIERRE I, 95
Piere, Pier
(Fr. for Peter)
PIETER I, 29
Piter,* Peiter *
(Dt. forms of Peter)
PIETRO
Pitro I, 711
Pitre
(It. forms, properly Pietro, of Peter, Sp. Pedro)
PILUS I, 449
(Prob. abbr. of Theophilus, Gr. name, lover of God)
PIPER II, 136
(Usually a family name; lit. the piper)

POLTZER * I, 177
Poltser *
(Meant for Baltzer, contr. of Balthasar)
POWELL I, 241
(Meant for Paul)

QUARDT I, 297
Quard
(Abbr. of Marquardt, the guardian of the boundary)
QUIRINUS
Querinus I, 717
(Lt. name; fr. quiris, lance, the one who hurls the lance)

RALPH * I, 217, 249
(Meant for Rudolph; E. Ralph, a contr. of Rudolph)
RAYNARD * I, 10
(Meant for Reinhard)
REICHARD I, 644
Reichardt, Reichart, Reicher, Richart,* Richard *
(OHG. Richhart, strong as a ruler)
REIMER I, 678
Reymer, Reimar
(OHG. Raginmar, famous as a counsellor)
REINHARD I, 359
Reinhardt, Reinhart, Rainhart, Rheinhardt, Raynard,* Reynard,* Rinhart,* Rinehart,* Rinard *
(OHG. Raginhart, strong as a counsellor)
REINHOLD I, 94
Reinholt, Rhineholt,* Reinelt,* Rynholl *
(OHG. Raginwald, ruling by counsel, the ending hold, gracious, due to popular etymology)
REMIGIUS I, 459
(Saint, bishop of Rheims, d. 535; Lt. name, fr. remex, -igis, oarsman)
RENIER II, 95
(Perhaps for Reiner, contr. of Reinhard)
RENINGEN II, 146
(Patronymic of Ragan, abbr. of Raganhar, counsellor of the army)
REYMUND I, 326
Remund, Reymound,* Roumand,* E. Raymund
(OHG. Raginmund, guarding counsel)
RICHARD I, 708
(Fr. of Reichard)

ROBERT I, 360
Rubert,* Lt. Robertus
(OHG. Hruodperht, bright with
fame; cf. Ruprecht)

ROCHUS II, 89
(Saint Rochus of Montpellier, d.
1327; Roch, abbr. of Hrohhart,
strong in battle cries; same as
Rückert, German poet)

ROELOFF II, 29
Roloff, Roelof, Roolof, Ruluf, Ru-
lophs
(Contr. of Rudolf)

ROGER II, 136
(Prob. meant for Rotger)

ROLANDT I, 450
Roland *
(OHG. Hrodlant, the fame or glory
of the land)

RONYARD * I, 80
(Prob. meant for Reinhard)

RÖTTGER I, 505, 710
Rotger
(OHG. Hrodgar, the glorious spear)

RUBEN I, 707
(Hebr. name, Reuben; explained:
Behold a son, a popular etymology)

RUDI I, 249
Rude, Rudy, Rudey,* Ruthy *
(Swiss dim. of Rudolph)

RUDOLF I, 19
Rudolff, Rudolph, Rutolff, Rutolph,*
Rodolph,* Rudulph,* Rodolp *
(OHG. Hrodulf, lit. the wolf of
fame, i. e., the famous wolf)

RUFINUS I, 372
(Lt. name, der. fr. rufus, redhead)

RULOPHS II, 91
Ruluf * I, 47
(Contr. of Rudolf)

RUPERT
Rupertus I, 322
Rubert, Rubertus
(OHG. Hruotberht, one bright with
fame; same as Ruprecht)

RUPRECHT I, 422
(OHG. Hruotberht, bright with
fame; same as Rupert)

RUTICIUS II, 57
(May be meant for Rüdiger,
Rotger)

RYNHARD * I, 648
(Meant for Reinhard)

SALOMON I, 393
Sallamon, Solomon, Salmon *
(Hebr. name; Maker of peace)

SAMSON I, 472

(E. form of G. Simson; Hebr.
name; the little sun)

SAMUEL I, 14
Samuell,* abbr. Sam II, 147
(Hebr. name; lit. heard of God, i. e.,
asked for of God)

SANDER I, 433
(Stands for Xander, abbr. of Alexander; also used as surname, see
pp. I, 491, 494)

SCIPILO I, 15
(Perhaps intended for Scipio)

SEBALD * I, 41
Sebalt, Sebaldt
(Der. fr. Seibold, Siebold: OHG.
Sigibald, Bold in victory)

SEBASTIAN I, 36
Sebästian, Sebastyan, Sepastian *
(St. Sebastian died as martyr under
Diocletian; Gr. name, fr. sebastos,
the honorable)

SENF II, 135
(Jewish name)

SEVERINUS I, 431
(St. Severinus was bishop of Cologne, d. about 400; Lt. name, der.
fr. severus, severe)

SEYBERTH I, 429
(Same as Siebert, fr. OHG. Sigi-
peraht, famous in victory; cf. G.
Sieg, victory)

SIEBERT
abbr. Siep I, 501, 719
(OHG. Sigiperaht, famous in victory)

SIEGESMUND I, 755
Sigmund, Siegmund, Siegmundt,
Siegmon *
(OHG. Sigimund, one who guards
victory)

SIEGFRIED I, 479
Siegfriedt
(OHG. Sigifrid, one who protects
victory)

SILAS
Seilas * I, 479
(Bibl. name, der. fr. Lt. Silvanus,
the woodsman)

SILVESTER I, 385
Silvestor *
(Name of Pope Silvester I, d. 325;
fr. Lt. silva, the woods, hence,
woodsman)

SILVIUS I, 415
(Lt. name, fr. silva, woods, hence,
woodsman)

SIMÉON I, 66, 407
(Fr. form of Simon)

SIMON I, 26

Siemon, Simmon, Lt. Simonus, Simonius, abbr. Simm
(Hebr. name; heard, i. e., of God)
SIRACH   I, 442
(Sirach, in Hebr. Ben Sira, the author of the Book of Ecclesiasticus; also used as surname, see I, 719)
STANISLAUS   I, 727
(From Slavic stan, camp, and slawa, glory, hence, the glory of the camp)
STEPHANUS   I, 234
Stephannus, Stephan, Stephen, Stefanus, Stefan, Stefen, Steffan, Stefahn, Steffen, Stefen,* Staffa,* Stafen,* Staffen,* Steven
(Bibl. name, first Christian martyr, fr. Gr. stephanos, crown)
STOFFEL   I, 492
Stofel
(Abbr. of Christoffel, Christopher)
SUCOR   II, 146
(Jewish name, same as Sacher, abbr. of Zacharias, Jehovah remembers)
SUSMAN   II, 160
(Prob. a Jewish family name, meant for Süssmann)

TAMUS   I, 503
(Phonetic spelling of Thomas)
TATCIUS   I, 457
(Meant perhaps for Tacitus, fr. Lt. tacitus, silent)
TETRICH   I, 229
Tedric   II, 73
(Meant for Diedrick, variant of Dietrich)
TEWALT *   I, 10
Tebalt
(Variants of Theobald)
THEBUS *   I, 382
(Variant of Theus, abbr. of Mattheus)
THEIS   I, 436
Teys *
(Abbr. of Mattheis, Matthias)
THEOBALD   I, 315
Teobald,* Teobalt, Theobalt, Tebald,* Tebalt,* Tebelt,* Tewald, Tewalt,* Thiebalt, Deobald,* Dibolt, Diebolt, Dewald, Dewalt, Dewaldt, Diewald, Diewalt
(OHG. Theudobald, bold among the people)
THEODOR   I, 475, 708
Theodorus   I, 357
(Gr. name. Gift of God)

THEOPHILUS   I, 244
(Bibl. name, Gr. A lover of God)
THIEBALT   I, 355
(Variant of Theobald)
THIEL   I, 352
Tiel, Thiels,* Diel
(Contr. of Dietel, dim. of Dietrich)
THIELMAN   I, 164
Thielmannus   I, 191
(Dim. of Thiel, which is der. fr. Dietrich)
THIERRY   II, 150, 151
(Fr. equivalent of Dierich, a contr. of Dietrich)
THOMAS   I, 34
Tomas, Tohmas, Tamus, Dhommes, Dommes, Domas, Doms
(Name of apostle Thomas, fest. Dec. 21. Der. fr. Hebr. tôam, the twin)
TICK   II, 16
(Prob. meant for Dirck)
TIDERICH   I, 10
Tieterich, Titrick *
(Variants of Dietrich)
TILMAN   I, 443
Tielman,* Lt. Tilemannus I, 341
(Variants of Thielman and Dielman)
TIMOTHEUS
Timothy *   II, 160
(Bibl. name, Gr. fearing God)
TOBIAS   I, 9
Thobias, Tohbias, Tobies,* Towias, Towies
(Hebr. name, Tobijah, Jehovah is good)
TONICUS *   I, 7
(Abbr. of Antonius)
TONIS *   I, 676
(Abbr. of Antonius)
TORRES   I, 434
Tores
(Prob. meant for Dors, Durs)
TOWIAS   I, 496
Towies
(Variants of Tobias)
TRAUGOTT   I, 750, 757
(Sentence name, late pietistic formation. Lit. Trust God)
TÜNGES   I, 495
Tönges   I, 679
(Der. fr. Antonius, with nasalized pronunciation)
TUNISS   II, 48
(Meant for Tonis, abbr. of Antonius)
TUR   II, 15
(Prob. meant for Durs)

UDRY *   I, 19
Uldry,* Uldrick *
(Variants of Ulrich)
UHLAND   I, 114
(OHG. Odolland, prob. fr. Odol-
nand, bold as to home, i. e., bold in
the defense of the home)
ULDRICH   I, 29
Uldrick,*   Ulderick,*   Uldric,*
Ueldrick,*   Uldery,*   Uldry,*
Woldrich *
(Older forms of Ulrich, OHG.
Uodalrich, ruler of landed estates)
ULI   I, 19
Ully, Uhly, Uhli
(Swiss dim. of Ulrich)
ULRICH   I, 11
Uhlerich,   Uhllerich,   Uhlrech,*
Uhlrich, Uhlrick,* Uhlrigh,* Ule-
rich, Ulerick,* Ulric,* Ulrick,* Ul-
righ,* Ullrech, Ullrich, Ullerich,
Ullerick,*   Ullerig,*   Ullwrick,*
Urick,* Urik,* Urig,* Urigg,* Wil-
righ *
(OHG. Uodalrich, ruler of landed
estates)
URBAN   I, 278
(Name of Pope Urban I, d. as
martyr 230, patron of vintagers, der.
fr. Lt. urbanus, refined, polished)
URIK *   I, 80
Urick,* Urig,* Urigg *
(Meant for Ulrich)

VALENTIN   I, 308
Lt. Valentinus, Vallentinus, Vallen-
thien, Vallentin, Valtein, Valantine,*
Valentine,*   Valendine,*   Velten,
Veltin, Velthen, Valten, Valtin, Wal-
lendin, Weltin
abbr. Valt   I, 712
(Name of bishop of Terni, mar-
tyred in 273, patron of palsied, fest.
Febr. 14. From Lt. valens, strong,
healthy)
VEIT   I, 90
Veith, Viet,* Fyt,* Vitus *
(Name of saint, d. 303, fest. June
15. Meaning uncertain, perhaps fr.
Lt. vita, life; It. Guido, E. Guy)
VELTEN   I, 26
Velthen, Veltin
(Variants of Valentin)
VENDAL *   I, 54
Vendell,*   Vendael,*   Vindael,*
Vindle *
(Meant for Wendel)
VICTOR   II, 129

Victtor
(Name of martyr)
VILLIPS   I, 41
(Meant for Philips)
VINCENS   I, 17
Vincents,   Vincentz,   Vincent,*   Lt.
Vincentius, Vinsintzius, Vinsent *
(Name of martyr, d. 304, at Sara-
gossa, fest. Jan. 22. Lt. vincens, con-
quering, conqueror)
VINSALOUS   II, 12
(Meant for Wenzeslaus)
VIRECH *   I, 22, 23
Veery *
(Prob. meant for Ulrich, Ulry)
VITUS   I, 276
(See Veit)

WALLENDIN   I, 495
(Variant of Valentin)
WALLES   I, 471
(Meant prob. for Baldes, Bal-
thasar)
WALRAD   I, 304
Wolrath, Wolraht
(OHG. Waldorad, ruling by coun-
sel)
WALTHER   I, 299
Welder   I, 24
(OHG. Waldhar, ruling the army)
WALTHART   I, 165
(OHG. Walhart, strong as a ruler)
WEIGAND   I, 400
Weigan
(Part. form, OHG. Wigand, the
fighting man, the warrior; same as
Wiegand and Wiand)
WEINBERT   I, 473, 507
(OHG. Winipreht, famous as a
friend, same as Weinbrecht)
WEIRICH   I, 170
Weyrich, Wirich *
(OHG. Wigirich, the ruler in
battle)
WELTIN   I, 174
Welten, Welder *
(Variants of Valentin)
WENDEL   I, 21
Wendell, Wendal, Wennell, Wen-
tell, Windel, Wenell, Winnale *
(OHG. Wandalus, the Vandal)
WENDELING   II, 205
(Patronymic of Wendel, hence the
son of Wendel)
WENZEL   I, 648
Wentzel, Wentzell *
abbr. Wentz
(Abbr. of slav. Wenzeslaus, the
glory of the crown)

WERNER   I, 394
Warner, Wernhar,* Wernner,
Wernel, Wernart,* Wernert,* Wer-
nard,* Vernor *
(OHG. Warinheri, one who is a
tower or protector in battle)
WESSELMAN   II, 61
(Der. fr. Wessel, like Wetzel a dim.
of Warinheri, now Werner)
WEYBRECHT
Weybegt   I, 458
(OHG. Wigbert, famous in battle)
WEYMAR   I, 356
(OHG. Wigmar, famous in war)
WIAND   I, 675
Wyant, Wyan,* Weyan *
(OHG. part. Wigand, the fighting
man, the warrior)
WIEGAND   I, 705
(OHG. part. Wigand, the warrior)
WIENAND
Winantus   I, 673
Wynant *
(OHG. Wignand, daring in battle)
WIEPERTUS   I, 296
Wibbertus, Webbertus   I, 298, 299
(OHG. Wigberth, famous or shin-
ing in battle)
WIENERT   I, 484
(OHG. Winihart, strong as a
friend)
WIL   I, 718
Will
(Abbr. of Wilhelm)
WILBERT   I, 423
(OHG. Willaperht, he who is dis-
tinguished by his will)
WILHELM   I, 11
Willhelm, Wilhellem, Wilhelmens,
Wülhelm
Dt. Willem, Wilm, Wellem, Welm,
Lt. Wilhelmus; E. William
(OHG. Willahalm, the willing or
ready protector; helm cf. helmet)
WILKE   II, 191
(Dim. of Wilhelm)
WILLEM   I, 9
Wilm, Wilms, Wellem, Welm
(Dt. forms of William)
WISHART
Wishard   II, 15
(OHG. Visichard, strong in wis-
dom)
WOLDRICH *   I, 240
(Meant for Uldrich, Ulrich)
WOLF   I, 412
Wolff, Woolf *
(Abbr. of Wolfgang, stalking the
wolf)

WOLFARTH   I, 696
(OHG. Vulfhard, strong as a wolf)
WOLFGANG   I, 653
Wolffgang
(OHG. Wolfgang, one who walks
after the wolf)
WOLMER   II, 138
(OHG. Waldomar, famous as a
ruler)
WOLRICK *   I, 109
(Meant for Ulrich)

XANDER
Sander *   I, 433
(Abbr. of Alexander)
XAVER   II, 3
abbr. Xav.
(Name of St. Francis Xavier, Span-
ish Jesuit missionary, 1506–1552)
XTIAN   I, 17
(Read Christian)
XTOPHEL   I, 17
(Read Christophel)
XTOPHER   I, 17
(Read Christopher)

YEARIG *   I, 284
Yerack *
(Meant for Georg)
YERG   I, 11
Yerich,* Yerigh,* Yerke,* Yerrick *
(Meant for Jerg, Georg)
YILLES   I, 17
(See Gilles)
YIRK *   I, 15
(Meant for Jerg, Georg)
YOHAN   II, 3
(Meant for Johan)
YORG   I, 34
Yorick *
(Meant for Jorg, Georg)
YOST   I, 367
(See Jost)
YSACH   I, 632
Ysah
(Meant for Isaac)
YUST   II, 104
(See Just, Justus)

ZACHARIAS   I, 38
Zachrias, Zachary *
(Hebr. name, Zachariah, Jehovah
has remembered)
ZACHARIE   II, 74
(Fr. form of Zacharias)
ZIGMOND *   II, 56
(Meant for Sigmund)

B. FEMININE NAMES

ABEL   I, 131
(Abbr. of Apollonia)
ABRAMINA   II, 101
(Der. fr. Abram)
ADELAIDE   II, 80
(Fr. of G. Adelheit, OHG. Adal-
haid, of noble kind or rank)
ADOLPHINA   II, 90
(Der. fr. Adolph)
ADRINA   II, 186, 193
(Prob. meant as fem. form of
Adrian)
AGATA   II, 68
Agate, Acada *
(Gr. name, fr. agathos, good)
AGNES   II, 68
Agnis,* (nasalized) Angnita,   II, 32
also prob. Anganea, Anganias
(Gr. name, fr. hagnos, holy, pure)
AHLHEID   II, 191
Alheid, Allhight
(Contr. of Adelheit)
AIME   II, 57
(Fr. name, beloved, darling)
ALBERTINE   II, 31, 90
(Der. fr. Albert)
ALCE   I, 23
(Meant for Else, abbr. of Elisabeth)
ALIDA   II, 58, 91
Alidar
(Prob. a contr. of Adelaida; cf.
Ahlheid and Adelheid)
ALLENA   I, 55, 85
(Perhaps meant for Helena, pro-
nounced Elena; cf. E. Ellen)
AMALIA   II, 20, 89
(Abbr. of Amalheid, of an indus-
trious nature)
AMARYLLIS   I, 55
(Gr. name)
ANALIS   I, 23
Anlis,   Anlies,   Anelies,   Anlias,
Anneleiss
(Contr. of Anna and Elisa)
ANGEL   II, 72
(Meant for Engel)
ANGELE   II, 80
(Fr. name)
ANMARIA   II, 79
(Contr. of Anna Maria)
ANNA   II, 120
Ann, Anne
(Hebr. name. Grace)
ANNE   II, 31
(Fr. name)
ANNABAERT   I, 44
(Contr. of Anna and Bertha)

ANNATJE   II, 70
Antji   II, 61
(Dt. dim. of Anna)
ANNELEESE   II, 180
Anlis
(Contr. of Anna and Elisa)
ANNETTE   II, 158
Annetta
(Dim. of Anna)
ANTONIA
Antonie   II, 122
(Der. fr. masc. name, Antonius)
APOLLONIA   I, 55
Ablonia,   Apalonia,   Aploney,
Aplonia,   Appellona,   Appellonia,
Appilunia,   Apploney,   Appollona
(Belonging to the god Apollo)
AUGUSTA   II, 70
Auguste
(Der. fr. Augustus)
AUGUSTINA   II, 60
Augustin   II, 169
(Fem. form of Augustin)

BARBARA   II, 11
Barbera, Barber, Barberry, Barbary,
Barbra
(Gr. name, the foreigner)
BARBE   II, 31
(Fr. form of Barbara)
BARBEL   I, 43
Barbella, Barbil
(Dim. of Barbara)
BARVIL   I, 80
(Meant for Barbel, dim. of Bar-
bara)
BEATA   I, 148
Beat
(Fem. of Beatus, the first apostle
to Switzerland, d. 112 A.D.)
BENIGNA   II, 83
(Fem. of Benignus, disciple of
Polycarp and apostle of Burgundy.
Lt. name, kind or benign)
BERNHARDINA
Barnendina   II, 110
(Fem. form of Bernhard)
BETSEY   II, 75
(Dim. of Elisabetha)
BETSILA   I, 24
(Meant for Elisabetha)
BLANDINA   II, 191
(A martyr at Lyons under Mark
Aurelius, in 177; Lt. name,
blandus, caressing)
BOBLE   I, 84
(Meant for Barbel)

BRIGITA   II, 91
   Bergitta   II, 140
   (Name of famous Swedish saint, d.
   1344; E. Bridget; Norse form of
   Bertha)

CÄCILIA   II, 92
   Cecilia, Sicilia
   (St. Cecilia was martyred about
   230; Lt. name, caecus, blind)
CARITAS   I, 123
   (Lt. name; Charity)
CAROLINA   II, 46
   Caroline, Carrolinia, Carlina, Cor-
   lina
   (Der. fr. masc. name, Carl)
CARTROUT   I, 139
   Catrut
   (Meant for Gertrude)
CATHARINA   II, 21
   Catharine, Caterena, Catarine, Ca-
   trina, Catrin
   (Gr. name, fr. katharos, pure; see
   also Katharina)
CHLOE
   Clove   I, 43
   Cleovea, Cleophe   I, 147, 148
   also Gluf   I, 103
   (Bibl. name, Gr.)
CHRISTIANNA   I, 73
   Christiana, Christian
   (Contr. of Christine and Anna)
CHRÉTIENNE   II, 86
   (Fr. of Christine)
CHARLOTTA   II, 10
   Charlotte
   (Fem. of Charlot, dim. of Charles)
CHRISTINA   II, 22
   Christine, Chrystien, Cristinia,
   Cristina
   (Fem. of Christian)
CLAIRE   II, 80
   (Fr. of Clara)
CLARA   II, 28
   Klara
   (Lt. name, fr. clarus, famous)
CLARISSA   II, 191
   (Der. fr. Clara)
CLASINA   II, 93
   (Perhaps the fem. form of Claus,
   abbr. of Niclaus)
CLEOVEA   I, 147
   Cleophe
   (See Chloe)
CONRADA   II, 103
   Conrade
   (Fem. of Conrad)
CONRADINE   II, 86
   (Der. fr. Conrad)

CONSTANCE   II, 80
   (Fr. of Constantia)
CONSTANTINA   II, 191
   (Fem. of Constantin)
CORA   II, 6
   (Der. fr. Lt. cor, heart)
CORDELIA   II, 187
   (Der. fr. Lt. cor, heart)
CORDULA   II, 14
   (Dim. of Lt. cor, heart)
CORNELIA   II, 23, 58
   Cornalia
   (Fem. form of Cornelius)
CREDLE   I, 84
   (Meant for Gretel, dim. of Mar-
   garetha)
CRETE   I, 44
   Creeto
   (Meant for Grethe, abbr. of Mar-
   garethe)
CRISPINA
   Crispin   I, 84
   (Fem. of Crispin)

DEBORA   II, 91
   (Hebr. name; the bee)
DIANA   I, 190
   (Name of Greek goddess)
DOLLY   II, 55
   (If correct, dim. of Dorothea)
DOMINICA   II, 68
   (Lt. name; the mistress; fem. of
   Dominicus)
DORCAS   II, 124
   (Gr. name; transl. of Tabitha, the
   roe)
DORIA   II, 7
   (Prob. abbr. of Theodora)
DOROTHEA   II, 21
   Dorothy, Dorothia, Dority, Thor-
   odea, Thoredea
   abbr. Dorte   I, 242
   (Gr. name; Gift of God)
DOROTHEE   II, 88
   (Fr. of Dorothea)

EADY   II, 94
   (May perhaps be Ida)
EBERHARDINA   II, 20
   (Fem. of Eberhard)
ELENA   II, 148
   (Read Helena; Elena also It.
   form)
ELEONORA   II, 105, 131
   Eleanor, Elinora
   (Gr. name, the merciful, fr. eleos,
   mercy)
ELISA   II, 22
   (Abbr. of Elisabeth)

ELISABETH II, 24
(Hebr. name. My God has sworn)
ELIZA II, 56
(E. form of Elisa)
ELSA II, 29
Else, Ells
(Contr. of Elisabeth)
EMILIA
Amelia, Emelia II, 191, 100
abbr. Melia, Mela I, 49, 85
(Fem. of Aemilius)
ENGEL II, 96
Engele I, 73
(Same as masc. name)
ENGELICA II, 30
(Der. of Engel, the angelic)
ENGELINA I, 93, 127
Engeline, Engeltina
(Also fr. Engel)
ERNESTINE II, 119
(Fem. of Ernest)
ESTHER I, 127
Ester, Easter, Hester I, 49
(Bibl. name, usually connected with
Gr. asther, star)
EVA II, 3
Eve, Even, Efa, Epha
(Hebr. name; explained as [mother
of] life)

FELICIA I, 132
(Fem. form of Felix, happy)
FELICITÉ II, 80
(Fr. of Felicity)
FERINA I, 28
Ferona I, 190
(Variant of Verena)
FERONICA I, 135
(Variant of Veronica)
FIDELA II, 187
(Fem. form of Fidelis)
FLENY I, 40
(Perhaps for Freny, with exchange
of l for r; contr. of Verena)
FLEUR II, 80
(Fr. for Flora)
FLORA I, 139
(Lt. name, the blooming one)
FLORENTINE II, 88
(Der. prob. fr. Florus, Flora)
FLORIANE II, 87
(Fr. name; der. fr. Florianus, saint
and martyr, who died 230)
FRANCISCA II, 45
Frantzisca, Franscisca, Franciscos
(Fem. form of Franciscus)
FRANÇOISE II, 60
(Fr. name; fem. of François)

FRANEY II, 57
(Prob. contr. of Verena)
FRANICK I, 80
Fraunek I, 123
(Variants of Veronica)
FREENICK I, 24
Frenech, Feronica, Frenee
(Variants of Veronica)
FRENA I, 44
(Variant of Verena)
FREYJA I, 144
(Perhaps intended for Frida)
FRIEDERIKE II, 67
Frederica, Friederica, Frederika,
Frederike, Friderica
(Fem. form of Friederich)
FRONIK I, 81
Froneca, Frauneck
(Variants of Veronica)
FRUNJE II, 58
(Perhaps Dt. dim. of Veronica)

GARTRUTE II, 51
(Variant of Gertrud)
GEORGINA II, 60
(Fem. form of Georg)
GERRITJE II, 60
(Dt. dim. of Margaret)
GERTRUD I, 127
Gertraud, Gertraut, Gertrowte,
Geertruyde, Gertrauth, Gertrude,
Gertrout, Gertruda, Gertrudt, Ger-
trut, Gertruth, Gertrouy, Gerduck,
Ketruid
(OHG. Gertraud, the lover of
spears)
GERDUCK II, 23
(Meant for Gertrud)
GLUF I, 103
(Prob. meant for Clove, Chloe)
GOTLIVEN I, 80
(Intended for Gottliebe, fem. form
of Gottlieb)
GOTTLIEBE II, 53
(Fem. form of Gottlieb)
GRETHA I, 60
Greta, Greda, Kreta, Grete
(Abbr. of Margaretha)
GRUTGE II, 136
(Meant for Gretchen, dim. of Mar-
garet)
GUILLAUMETTE II, 87
(Fr. name, dim. of Guillaume)

HANNA I, 132
Hannah, Hanne
(Hebr. name; Grace)
HANNCHEN

Hanchon II, 205
(Dim. of Hannah)
HARRIOT II, 88
(Fr. form of Henrietta)
HEDWIG
Hedewig II, 191
(OHG. Hathuwic, the one who fights in battle)
HELENA II, 68
(Gr. name; prob. the shining one, fr. helios, sun)
HENRICA II, 30, 95
(Fem. form of Heinrich)
HENRIETTA
Henriette II, 69
Heneretta, Hinrigette
(Dim. and fem. form of Heinrich)
HESTER I, 49
Hestar
(Meant for Esther)
HINRIGETTE II, 50
(Meant for Henrietta)

INGLE I, 139
(Read Engel)
ISABELLA I, 55
(Sp. Isabel, form of Elisabeth)

JACOBA II, 135
(Fem. form of Jacob)
JACOBINA II, 14
Jacobine, Jacob Benia (!)
(Fem. form of Jacob)
JANE II, 151
(Meant for Fr. Jeanne)
JEANNE II, 74
(Fr. form of Jane)
JEANETTE II, 140
Jannett II, 119
(Dim. of Jane, cf. Jenny)
JETTE II, 108
(Abbr. of Henriette)
JOHANNA II, 30
Johana, Joanna
(Fem. form of Johann, John)
JOHANNETTE II, 67
(Dim. and fem. form of Johann; cf. Jeanette)
JOHANEVA I, 49
(Contr. of Johanna and Eva)
JUDITH I, 24, 61
Judit
(Hebr. name, the Jewess)
JULIANNA I, 156
Juliana, Juliane, Julianne, Julian
(Contr. of Julia and Anna)
JUSTINA II, 83
Justine, Justinia
(Fem. form of Justinus)

KATTJE II, 54
(Dt. dim. of Katharina; cf. G. Kätchen)
KATHARINA II, 184
Katharine, Kathrine, Katrina, Katterrena, Katrena, Katherina, dim. Katy
(Gr. name; the pure. Of the saints, esp. St. Catharine of Siena, d. 1380)
KATY II, 149
(Properly Käthi, dim. of Katharine)
KILIANA I, 62
(Fem. form of Kilian)
KUNIGUNDA II, 7, 9
Kunigunte
(Meaning uncertain, either bold in battle, or, one who battles for the clan)

LAMERDJE II, 92
(Dt. dim. apparently fr. Lammert, Lambert)
LAODICEA I, 108
(Really not a woman's name, but that of a church in Asia Minor)
LENA II, 197
(Abbr. of either Helena or Magdalena)
LEONA I, 44
(Fem. form of Leon)
LONA II, 122
(Perhaps meant for Leona)
LIENDA II, 85
(Contr. of Rosalinda)
LIESE II, 29
Lise
(Contr. of Elisabeth)
LINA I, 28
(Abbr. of Carolina)
LISABETH I, 148
Lisbetha, Lisbet, Lysbet, Lisbat, Lizaberth
(Abbr. of Elisabeth)
LOTTE II, 77
(Abbr. of Charlotte)
LOUISA II, 8
Louise, Luisa, Luise, Luiss, Loisa, Luwisa
(Fem. form of Louis)
LUCIA II, 23
Lucy
(Lt. name, fr. lux, light; prob. the shining one)
LUCINA II, 150
(Der. fr. lux, light; Roman goddess of the day)
LUCRETIA I, 43
(Lt. name, fem. form of Lucretius,

the one who gains possessions; cf. lucrative)

LUWIS I, 157
(Phonetic spelling of Louise)

LYCKLAMA II, 60
(Unknown meaning)

LIDIE II, 31
(Fr. form of Lydia)

LYDIA II, 192
(Bibl. name, cf. Acts 16:14; fr. the province of Lydia, in Asia Minor)

MADELAINE II, 31
Madelen, Matelin, Madaline, Madelaina, Matelina, Mettlina, Maudlin
(Fr. form of Magdalene)

MADELON II, 86
(Fr. name. der. fr. Madelaine)

MAGDALENA II, 13
Magdalene, Magdalenia, Magdalen, Magdelin, Madelina
(From the city Magdala)

MANETTE II, 193
(Fr. name)

MARDLING I, 153
(Meant for Magdalene)

MARGARETHA II, 59
Margaritta, Margaretta, Margarett, Margaret, Margret, Margarite, Margrit, Margat, Maretia, Margery
(Gr. name; prob. margaris, pearl)

MARGUERITHE II, 31
(Fr. of Margaret)

MARIA II, 30
Marie, Marye, Marya, Maree, Marrea, Mary
(Of uncertain meaning; perhaps fat)

MARIANNA II, 94
Marianne
(Contr. of Marie and Anna)

MARIEANNE II, 31
(Fr. form of Marianne)

MARTHA I, 75
(Bibl. name; Aram. the mistress)

MARYLIS I, 28
Marilis, Marelis, Merreles
(Contr. of Marie and Elisa)

MATJE II, 68
Mietje
(Dt. dim. of Margaret)

MELIA I, 49, 50
Mela
(Abbr. of Amelia)

META I, 28
Maeta
(Abbr. of Margaretha)

MIELIE II, 77

Millia I, 73
(Abbr. of Emilia)

MIETJE II, 46
Mertje II, 123
(Dt. dim. prob. of Margaret)

MINA
Menea I, 40
(Abbr. of Wilhelmina)

MIRE I, 80
Mirea I, 86
(Occur in both cases with Anna, meant prob. for Anna Marie)

MOLLY II, 7
(If correct, pet form of Mary)

MORET I, 24
(Perhaps intended for Margaret)

MOTLEY I, 40
(Prob. for Madelaine, Maudlin)

NANCY II, 126
(Name of Irish girl; pet form of Anna)

NANON II, 80
(Fr. name, dim. of Anna, cf. G. Nanne)

NAATGE II, 123
Natye II, 118
(Dt. name; dim. of Anna)

NELLY II, 30
Nelle; prob. also Neals I, 40
(Abbr. of Cornelia)

OLIVE I, 151
(G. form Olivia, an olive branch)

ORCHIL II, 21
Orchille
(Meant for Ursula)

ORSULA I, 151
Orsel, Ossel, Orstel
(Variants of Ursula)

OTTILIA II, 10
Otilia
(Dim. of Otto, OHG. Audila, rich in possessions)

PARBLE II, 42
(Meant for Barbel, dim. of Barbara)

PAULINA I, 103
(Lt. name; der. fr. Paulus, the little)

PERCY I, 108
(Fem. name; possibly meant for Bertha)

PETRONELLA II, 93
(Der. fr. Petrus)

PHILADELPHIA II, 59
(Name of one of the seven churches of Asia Minor; perhaps influenced by Philadelphus)

PHILIS I, 24, 28
Phillis
(Intended perhaps for Felicia; not Phyllis, which is not German)

PHILIPPINA II, 20
Philipina, Philippena, Phillipina, Phillipine
(Fem. form of Philippus)

PHRONICK I, 28
(Variant of Veronica)

PSALMA I, 108
(Perhaps meant for Salma, Selma)

RAHEL II, 92
Rachel II, 187
(Hebr. name; the ewe lamb)

REBECCA II, 76
(Hebr. name; meaning uncertain)

REGINA II, 8
Regine
(Not the Lt. regina, queen, but cf. OHG. Ragino, contr. of Reinhard; hence, the counsellor)

REGULA I, 147
(Lt. name, fr. regula, rule, hence, the orderly one)

ROMAINE II, 80
(Fr. name, from Lt. Romanus, fem. Romana, the Roman lady)

ROSALIE II, 80
(Fr. name; the rose-like)

ROSELVA II, 51
(Prob. meant for Rosalie)

ROSETTA II, 58, 137
(Dim. of Rosa, the little rose)

ROSINA II, 8
Rossina, Rosena
(Lt. form, belonging to the rose)

SABINA II, 103
Savine
(Lt. name, from the people of the Sabines)

SALAME II, 59
Salme, Salem, Salm, Salmia, Sallemia
(Variants of Salome)

SALOME II, 150
Solomia, Salomea, Salima, Solima, Salame, Salume
(Hebr. name, the peaceful)

SCINTJE II, 46
(Prob. Dt. form of Cynthia)

SARAH I, 49
(Hebr. name, the princess)

SELMA I, 50
Salma
(Abbr. of Anselma)

SHARLOT I, 80
(Variant of Charlotte)

SEVILLA II, 29
(Intended for Sibylla)

SIBYLLA I, 132
Sabilla, Sebilla, Sevila, Seville, Sibela, Sivilla, Sibila, Sybilla
(Lt. name, the Sibyl, one who gives oracles)

SICILIA I, 50
(Read Cecilia)

SILIGE I, 61
(Read perhaps Cecilia)

SOLOMIA I, 49
(Read Salome)

SOPHIA II, 16
Sofia, Soffia
(Gr. name; wisdom, i. e., the wise)

SUSANNA II, 10
Susana, Susannah, Susanah, Susean, Susan
(Hebr. name, the lily; E. dim. Suky, used as ship name)

SUSETTE II, 85
(Fr. name; dim. of Susanna)

SUZANNE II, 31
(Fr. form of Susanna)

SYLVIE II, 80
(Fr. form of Sylvia)

THERESA II, 12, 16
Teresia, Teresa, Tresia, Thereza
(Gr. name; the huntress)

TONINA II, 186
(Abbr. of Antonina)

TRINA II, 124
Trena
(Abbr. of Catharina)

TURKIS II, 118
(Read prob. Dorcas)

URCILLA I, 138
Ursilla
(Variants of Ursula)

URSELINA II, 43
Urclina
(Der. fr. Ursula)

URSULA II, 124
Ursella, Ursilla, Ursela, Ursley, Ursul, also Orsell
(Lt. name; little bear)

URSULE II, 31
(Fr. form of Ursula)

VAITA   I, 49
(Fem. form of Veit; correctly Vita,
cf. Eva, life)
VERENA   I, 147
Frena, Frenee, Freina
(Lt. name, the one who causes rev-
erence)
VERONICA   I, 49
Phronick, Fronik, Feronica
(Name of legendary saint; Gr.
name, fr. Gr. Beronike, dial. form
of Pherenike, lit. carrying off vic-
tory, hence, the victorious)

WALBURGA   II, 171
(From burg, protection and wala,

the dead, i. e., giving protection to
the dead)
WENDELINA   II, 53
(Belonging to Wendel)
WILHELMINA   II, 18
(Fem. form of Wilhelm)
WILLEMINA   II, 36
Willemenia
(Dt. form of Wilhelmina)
WOLFELINE   II, 60
(Fem. form of Wolf. dim., little
wolf)

ZAÏRE
Zayre   II, 80
(Fr. name)

C. DOUBTFUL NAMES

ACHIOR	I, 434	FLENY	I, 40
AGGUTH	II, 189	FOGLIN	I, 495
(Read perhaps August)		FONCKE	II, 71
ANSPEL	I, 7		
		GAEOME	II, 121
BARKONT	II, 47	GEIRTS	II, 125
BASCHER	II, 146	GESINE	II, 125
BEVEL	I, 37	GIBBS	II, 162
BOTIS	I, 508	GIEVAN	II, 121
(Fr. name)		GOFT	II, 118
BUSTNIP	I, 68	GOODLY	II, 188
CANESH	I, 94	HANDLESS	I, 85
CATHART	II, 15	HENIL	II, 146
CETHNET	II, 51	HIRER	II, 51
CHARTAR	II, 14		
CHULUR	II, 13	IANNPHE	II, 122
COEM	II, 45		
COENIR	II, 119		
CREDELASS	I, 85	JANSEY	II, 123
CURLA	I, 67	JEDUIR	II, 137
		JERONA	II, 7
DARBIE	I, 143	(Possibly Jerome)	
DORBIE	I, 143	JOSSE	II, 86
DUMAT	I, 144	(Read perhaps Joseph)	
(Woman's name)			
		KICHGY	II, 109
EDAR	I, 445	KINNEMA	II, 60
EDEME	I, 746	KONGUR	I, 80
EFFEREN	II, 75		
(Woman's name)		LAFEL	II, 195
EGERATH	II, 140	LAPIL	II, 195
EGGELL	II, 73	LASCH	II, 139
(Read perhaps Engel)		(Read perhaps Lars)	
EGRAM	I, 38	LEARMER	I, 232
EKEL	I, 31, 33	LEID	II, 144
ENDICK	I, 123	LETMON	II, 195
EVAN	I, 15	LEVIN	II, 182
EVEREN	II, 125	LIEVE	II, 125

THE END

INDEX OF PIONEERS

For the rules adopted in the selection and arrangement of the names see the discussion in the Introduction to this volume.

AAKEN
Rooye, van   II, 54
AAL (AAHL, EHEL)
  Johann Wilhelm
  (Wilhelm)   I, 576, 578, 580
  Johannes   I, 750
ABALER
  Johan   II, 168
ABBRITER
  Jacob   I, 741
ABEL (AABEL, ABLE, AUBEL)
  Aⁿ Elisabetha   I, 156
  Hans Adam   I, 87, 90, 91
  Hans Georg
  (Hans Jerig) I, 83, 86, 88, 90, 92
       667, 669, 671
  Johann Jacob   I, 87, 90, 91
  P. Matheas   I, 504
  Steffan (Stophel)   I, 667, 669, 671
ABELMANN
  Heinrich   II, 55
ABENDSCHONN (ABENTSHON, read ABENDSCHOEN)
  Christian   I, 424
  Reinholt   I, 424
  Samuel Henry   I, 424
ABERHOLT
  Abraham   I, 10
ABERLE (ABERLEE)
  Conradt Israel   I, 437
  Hendrich   I, 10
ABERLY (read ABERLE)
  Jnᵒ Jacob   I, 741
  Rudolph   I, 147, 150, 151
ABERT
  Peter   I, 464
ABEZANT
  Anna Marya   I, 24
ABIARIUS
  Johan. Hen.   I, 234
ABIN see AMEND
ABLE see ABEL
ABLEN (ABLIN)
  Andrew   I, 20, 21
ABLEY (IBELIEY, IBLIEY)
  Elizabet   I, 118
  Hans Adam   I, 118

  Hans Migel   I, 118
  Maria Pitter   I, 118
  Michiel
  (Michael, Migeel) I, 116, 120, 121
  Resina   I, 118
ABOULT
  Jnᵒ J.   II, 196
ABRAHAM
  Aron   II, 108
  Jacob   II, 184
  Leopold   II, 160
  Simon   II, 91
ABRAMS
  Jacob   II, 184
ABT
  Heinʳ   II, 178
  Johan   II, 178
ABZIEGER
  Paul   I, 711
ABZIRA
  ——   II, 80
ACH
  Fried. Ludw.   II, 196
ACHABACH see ACHEBACH
ACHE
  Hermannus   I, 483
  Johann Ludwig   I, 483
  Johannes Jacob   I, 484
ACHEBACH (ACHABACH)
  Johann Kraft   I, 731
  Mathaus (Matthias)   I, 643, 644
  Philib (Philip)   I, 666, 668, 670
ACHEN
  Johan Henrich   I, 755
ACHENBACH (AUCHENBAUGH, AGENBACK, HUBACK, HOE-BACK)
  Johannes   I, 560, 561, 563
  John Rudolff
  (Hendᵏ Adolph) I, 222, 223, 225
  Michael   I, 222, 223, 225
ACHENBACHER
  Hans Jerg   I, 410
ACHENBACK
  Crentien   II, 85
ACHER see ACKER

ACHTEN
Jacob, Van   II, 135
ACHTUNG (AGTUNG)
Johannes   I, 378, 380, 381
ACHTZEHTER
Anna Maria   II, 169
ACKER (ACHER, ACOER, OCHER)
Caspar   I, 714
Christian   I, 677, 678, 679
                              II, 113
Ezechiel   I, 349, 350, 351
Georg   I, 428
Hendrick   I, 88, 90, 92
Jacob   I, 184, 186, 187
Johan George   I, 405
Johann Georg
  (Johannes Jerick) I, 559, 561, 562
Philip Jacob   I, 88, 90, 92
ACKERMAN (ACCERMAN, ACK-
  ERMANN, ACKHERMAN, AK-
  ERMAN, HACKERMAN)
Christoff   I, 429
Frantz (Francis)   I, 227, 229, 231
Hans Georg   I, 736
Jacob   I, 436, 527
Johan Wendel   I, 445
Johann Georg   I, 445
Michel (Meichel, Michael) I, 35, 36
Nickella   I, 382
Paul   I, 735
Stephan (Stephen) I, 236, 238, 239
Tobias   I, 227
ACKERT   (ASKERITT,   ACKER-
  ITT)
Conrad (Conraat)   I, 252, 253, 255
Heinrich   I, 252, 253, 255
ACKHORDEN
Anna Maria   I, 28
Magdelina   I, 28
ADAM (AADAM)
Anthony   I, 314, 315
Carel   I, 259, 261
Caspar   I, 755
Catharina   I, 108, 109
Ernst Christoph   I, 521, 524
Hans Jacob   I, 531, 533, 535
Hartmann
  (Hartman)   I, 373, 374, 375
Jacob   I, 604, 606, 607
                              II, 157
Joan Emmerich   I, 714
Johan (Johann)   I, 403, 762
Johann Georg   I, 698
Johann Henrich
  (Hendrick) I, 107, 111, 112, 466
Johannes (Johan)   I, 283, 284, 285
                              366, 368
                              373, 374, 375
Johannes Adam   I, 496

Martin   I, 257, 260, 262
Michel (Mich.)   I, 256, 259, 261
Peter   I, 485
Philip   I, 420
ADAMI (ADAM)
Henrich   I, 317, 318, 319
ADAMS
Adam   I, 464
Hans   I, 451
Jacob   I, 421
Nicholas   I, 8
ADELER
Christian   II, 49
H. George   I, 481
ADELHYT
Willem   I, 346
ADELMANN (ADELMAN)
Hans Michael   I, 507
Wilhelm   I, 444
ADEST
Falkert   I, 16
ADICH (ATTICK)
Jorg Petter (Petter) I, 265, 268, 271
ADISCH (ABBITSCH)
Johan Martin
  (Martin)   I, 605, 607, 608
ADLER
Christian   II, 23, 105
Johannes   I, 752
(See also ATTLER)
ADOLPH (ADOLF)
A. M.   II, 5
Fred.   II, 114
Jacob   I, 227; II, 104
Johannes   I, 591, 592, 594
ADOLPHAT error for OTT
ADRIAN
Christian   I, 497
ADTELBERGER (ADLEBERGER)
Hans Jerg (John)   I, 527, 528, 530
Philip   I, 527, 528, 530
AELBRAGT
Joseph   I, 8
AESCHER
Christian   I, 722
AESCHLIMAN   (AESCHLIMANN,
  ESELMAN, ESLAMAN)
Christian   I, 732
Hans (Johannes)   I, 629, 632, 635
Peter   I, 629, 632, 635
AFFERLINE
Appolona   I, 85
AFFLEBER
Johann Ludwig   I, 754
AFLERBACH (AFFLERBACH)
Henry   II, 199
Johan Daniel   I, 710
Johan Henrich   I, 731
Jost   II, 84

AFTERBACH
Johⁿ George II, 129
AG
And. I, 503
AGEDER (EIGENTER)
Anna Kreta I, 50
Dorothia I, 50
Henriks I, 50
Johannes (Johan) I, 47, 52, 53
Katherina I, 50
Ludwig I, 50
Magdelena I, 50
Margerita I, 49
AGH error for HAAG
AGRICOLA
Ludwig I, 684
AGSTER
Jacob II, 13
AGTERMAN
Jacques II, 198
AGUNTIUS
Ludwig I, 502
AHANER see AHNER
AHLBACH (OHLBACH)
Anna Dumat I, 144
Anna Eliz. I, 144
Anna Margret I, 144
Gerderuth Margreta I, 144
Joanis Gerard I, 144
Joanis Peter I, 144
Joanis Wilhelm I, 144
Johan Wilhelm I, 143, 145, 146, 478
Zachrias (Zacharias) I, 143, 145, 146
AHLBORN (AHLLBORN, ALBORN)
Carol (Ernest) I, 574, 575, 576
Christoffel I, 573, 574, 575
AHLEM
Johan Jacob I, 464
AHLEMANN
Johann I, 747
AHLEN
Elizabeth Van II, 119
AHLES (AHLAS)
Johann Caspar (John
Caspar) I, 297, 298, 299
Peter I, 397
AHLMANN
Heinrich II, 79
AHNER (AHANER, ANER)
Felix I, 148
Hs. Ulric I, 147, 148
Johan Ulrich I, 147, 149, 150
Joseph I, 476
Margareth I, 148
Verena I, 148
AHREND
Carl Ed^w II, 23
AHRENDORFF see ARNDORFF

AHRENDS
Joseph II, 139
AHRENHOLTZ (ARENHOLTZ)
Adolph II, 85
Anne Marie II, 85
AHRENS (ARRENT, ARNST)
Christian I, 517, 518, 519
Hans Henry (H.
Henry) I, 517, 518, 519
Johann Heinrich I, 509, 510, 511
AILDENS
Catharina II, 71
AKERS (ECKERT)
Henry (Henrich,
Henrey) I, 99, 100, 101
ALAR
G. F. II, 32
ALBER
Joseph I, 360, 362
ALBERÄCHT see (ALBRECHT)
ALBERS (ALLBES)
Johann Henrich
(Hendrick) I, 681, 682
ALBERT (ALBERTH, ALBERD,
HALBERT, PLUER)
Adam I, 204, 206, 207
Anna Katherin I, 50
Bastian I, 266, 269, 272
Christian II, 105
Christina Barbara I, 50
Christoph (er) I, 458; II, 23
Freidrich Ludwig II, 48
Johan Frantz
(France) I, 266, 269, 272
Johan Jacob I, 523, 525
Johann Michel I, 89, 91, 92
Johann Philipp I, 507
Johannes (Johanes,
Johan) I, 47, 51, 53, 412
627, 630, 633
John George I, 173, 174, 250, 251
Katharina I, 49
Lorentz I, 627, 630, 633
Mr. II, 175
Mrs. II, 175
Sophia Katherin I, 50
Wilhelm I, 508, 628, 631, 635
William I, 266, 269, 272
ALBERTHAL
Johann Nickel I, 715
Nickellas I, 703
ALBERTI
Casimir Bernhard I, 716
Catharina II, 3
Johann Philipp
(John Philip) I, 672, 674
(See also ALBERTY)
ALBERTUS
Carel Lud^k Wilh^m II, 29

ALBERTY
Christopf Ludwig II, 46
Maria Catharina II, 46
ALBIRGER
Johan Christ I, 479
ALBRECHT (ALBRIGHT, AL-
BRETH, ALBERÄCHT)
Anna I, 73
Antonius (Antoni) I, 102, 105
Barbara I, 74, 103, 148
Christiana I, 74
Christoph I, 438, 446
Cristina I, 62
David I, 517, 518, 520
Eva I, 62
Georg (George, Gerich,
Jerig) I, 102, 104, 105
490; II, 52
Hans I, 103
Hans George I, 340
Hans Jacob I, 393
Heinrich (Henrich) I, 399; II, 52
Jacob I, 60, 64, 65, 74, 303
305, 306, 743
Johann Georg
(John George) I, 173, 174
Johannes (Johannis) I, 72, 76, 77, 340
359, 447, 471
Johannes Matthias I, 189, 192, 194
Johans I, 490
John I, 55
Joseph I, 9
Leonard I, 715
Levit (Levy) I, 301, 302, 303
Lodawick I, 74
Magdalena I, 61
Maria I, 62
Maria Magdalena I, 190
Maria Margareta I, 190
Metalina I, 74
Michiel I, 62
Nicolaus I, 718
Peter I, 103
Philip I, 496
Wilhelm I, 545, 547, 549
—— II, 162
(*See also* ALLBRECHT)
ALBRIGHT (read ALBRECHT)
Jacob I, 717
ALBRIGHTBERGER error for AL-
BRECHT BIRCKERT
ALBRITE (read ALBRECHT)
Daniel II, 147
Henery II, 147
Magret II, 147
ALDER (read ALTER)
Johannes I, 404
ALDHAUS *see* ALTHAUS

ALDORFFER (ALLDORFER, AL-
TERFER, read ALTDORFER)
Frederick I, 60, 64, 65
Friederich
(Frederick) I, 106, 110, 112
ALDORPHIA (read ALTDORFER)
Henrack I, 344
ALEBERGER
Antries I, 502
ALEN
Johannes I, 325, 326
ALEXANDER
Luis II, 139
ALFEY
Christian II, 196
ALGEIR (read ALLGEIER)
Jeremiah I, 719
ALGYER (ALGEYER)
Hans Michael I, 451
Johannes I, 425
ALHER (ALBER)
Mathias I, 526, 528, 530
ALIZON
George I, 729
ALKEWHEN
John J. II, 186
ALLAN
Johann Adam I, 460
ALLBRECHT (read ALBRECHT)
Georg Adam I, 457
ALLBRING
Betse II, 60
ALLBRINK
Henery Vinsalous II, 12
Jnᵒ Carl II, 12
Julias Augˢ II, 12
Maria Elizᵗ II, 12
ALLDORFER *see* ALDORFER
ALLEMAN (ALAMAN, ALEMAN)
Hermon (Harm.) I, 536, 537, 538
Johan Christian
(Christⁿ) I, 536, 537, 538
Johan Friedrich
Christian I, 536, 537, 538
ALLEMAND
Jean Jaque (John) I, 592, 593, 594
ALLEN
Daneal II, 77
Peter I, 676
ALLER
David I, 485
Jacob I, 393
Johan Jacob I, 545
Johann Peter (Petter) I, 401, 479
Johannes (Hannes) I, 609, 610, 612
ALLES
Abraham I, 423
Johan Jacob I, 423

ALLEX (ALEX)
Michael   I, 526, 528, 530
ALLHELM
Godfried Willhelm   I, 504
ALLICH
Christian Lorenz   II, 174
ALLIMAN
Dorst   I, 485
ALLIMANG
Jacob   I, 369, 370
ALLIS
Barbary   II, 194
Henry   II, 194
Maria   II, 194
Nicholas   II, 194
ALLMAN
Henrich   I, 696
John   I, 695
ALLMENDINGER
J.   II, 32
ALLOF
John   II, 77
ALLPP
Bernhart   I, 490
ALLSCHBACH (read ALLSPACH)
Johann Davit   I, 487
ALLSPACH
Jacob   I, 691
Johannes Georg   I, 710
(*See also* ALSBACH *and* ALS-PACH)
ALLTSTATT (ALSTADT)
Anna Judith   I, 24
Hans Merten (Martin)   I, 24, 26
ALM
Joh. Hinr.   II, 139
ALMAN
Stephan   I, 406
ALMBACH
Friedrich   I, 435
ALMERS
Henry   I, 320, 321, 322
Rosina   I, 320
ALS
Adam   I, 737
ALSBACH
Henrich   I, 686
(*See also* ALSPACH *and* ALL-SPACH)
ALSPACH (ALTSPACH, ALSBACK)
Madeis (Mathews)   I, 212, 213, 215
Reinhart (Renhert)   I, 213, 215
ALSTATT
Jost   I, 763
ALSTER
Conradt   I, 500
ALT
Jacob   II, 145
Johannes   I, 217, 219, 220

Matheas   I, 600
Michael   I, 474
Vallentin (Valentin)   I, 234, 235, 236
ALTBOTER
Cunrath   I, 407
ALTDÖRFER *see* ALDORFER *and* ALTORFER
ALTE
Daniel   II, 102
ALTEFRIED
Jnº Geo.   I, 731
ALTENBERGER
Johanes (Joh.)   I, 179, 181, 183
ALTENDORFF
Anderas   I, 474
ALTER
Georg Friederich   I, 512, 514, 515
Georg Heinrich   I, 512, 514, 515
Johann Christian   I, 453
Johann Jacob   I, 512, 514, 515
ALTERMAN
Henrica   II, 95
Henry   II, 34
Jacob   II, 34
Sophia   II, 95
ALTERS
Natye   II, 118
ALTHART (ALTHURT)
Lorentz (Lawrence)   I, 642, 644
ALTHAUS (ALDHAUS, ALTOUS, HALDHOUSE, HANDHUYZE, ALTHOUS)
Abraham (Abram)   I, 47, 51, 53
Arnd   I, 424
Christian   I, 720
Christina   II, 127
Erasmus   I, 403
George Ludwig   II, 127
Henry   I, 382
Johan (Gerg (Wm)   I, 237, 239, 240
Johan Krist (Johan Christⁿ)   I, 237, 238, 240
Johannes (Johan)   I, 237, 238, 240
Johannes   I, 403
ALTHENN (ALTHEN, ALDEN)
Peter   I, 340, 341, 343
ALTHERR
Fridrich   I, 689
Joseph   I, 484
ALTHÖL
Joh. Nicklas   I, 507
ALTHOUS *see* ALTHAUS
ALTIG
Johanes   I, 489
ALTIK
Daniel   I, 399
ALTLANDT (ALTLAND)
Jacob   I, 163, 165, 167

ALTMAN
 Anthon I, 405
 Jacob I, 405
 Jorg I, 405
 Wilhelm I, 405
ALTOMUS (ALTHOMUS, AL-
 DAMOS)
 Johann Friederich
 (Fredrick) I, 276, 278
 Peter I, 276, 277, 378
ALTORFER (ALDORFF)
 Lenhart I, 332, 333, 334
ALTRITH
 Michael I, 472
ALTRUTH
 Christoph I, 424
ALTSCHUH
 Jerg I, 698
ALTVATTER
 Jacob I, 691
 Johan Friederich I, 709
ALTZ
 Johann Michael I, 686
ALWINE
 Hans Jacob I, 304
ALWOHN (ALBON, ALLWOHN)
 Gotthardt
 (Gothard) I, 615, 617, 619
 Lorentz I, 615, 617, 619
AMACHER (APEMAKER)
 Michel (Michael) I, 592, 593, 594
AMAND
 Jacob II, 166
 Magdalina II, 166
AMANDUS
 Jacob I, 155, 158, 160
AMAUS
 Ludwig I, 687
AMBORN (HOMBORN)
 Christoffel (Christolf) I, 55, 56, 57
AMBROS
 An Maria I, 157
AMBROSE
 Peter I, 699
AMBROSI (AMBROSE)
 Matheis (Mathies) I, 99, 100, 101
AMBRUST
 Francis II, 68
AMBRUSTER
 Christian I, 468
 Matheis I, 468
AMECKER
 Paul I, 713
AMELON
 Christoff I, 538
AMEND (AMENDT, AMENT)
 Gabriel II, 52
 George (Jurigh) I, 341, 342, 343
 Jerg Elias (Elias) I, 221, 222, 224

Johanna II, 91
Johann Georg I, 69, 70
Johann Philip I, 341, 342, 343
Johannes I, 341, 342, 343
AMHYSER
 Caspar I, 382
AMMAN (AMAND, AMON)
 Hans Uhlrig (Ulric) I, 147, 150, 151
 Jacob I, 417, 665, 668, 670
 Johanes (Hannes) I, 643, 644
AMMEN (OMMEN)
 Durst I, 392
 Philip I, 392
AMMER
 Johan Ulrich II, 78
AMMICH
 Hans I, 447
AMMON
 Adam I, 476
 Jacob I, 31, 33, 34
AMMS
 Petter I, 401
AMOES
 Peiter I, 675
AMON (AMENT)
 Ernest I, 348, 350, 351
 Hans Gerg I, 349, 350, 351
AMPEL
 Lorentz I, 433
AMREIN (AMERING)
 John Henry
 (Johan Hendirkc) I, 652, 654
AMWEG (AMWÄG, AMWIGH)
 Hans Marden
 (Martin) I, 179, 181, 183
 Johann Samuel I, 722
 John Michael I, 27
 Leonhart (Linhart) I, 27, 29, 30
 Magdelina I, 28
ANCHEMENTER
 Petter I, 714
ANCKER
 Levin II, 182
ANDEREAS, ANDERASS, see AN-
 DREAS
ANDEREG
 Jacob II, 134
ANDERICH (ANDERECK)
 Christian I, 134, 136
ANDERMANN
 Ph. II, 44
ANDERS (ANDER, ANDERAS,
 ANDREAS, ANTERS)
 Adam I, 372
 Anna I, 138, 139
 Baltzer I, 137, 141, 142
 George
 (Jurge) I, 136, 137, 139, 140, 142
 Jacob I, 478

John Samuel II, 57
Marcus I. 353, 354
Maria I, 138
Michael (Michel) I, 179, 181, 183
Paulus I, 478
Urcilla I. 138
(*See also* ENDERS)
ANDICH
Wilhelm Zacharias I, 199, 201, 203
ANDONI (ANTHONY)
Jacob I, 724
Johanes Bet.
(Peter) I, 378, 380, 381
Lorenz I, 698
Paulus I, 167, 168
(*See also* ANTHONI)
ANDRAE (ANRA, ANDRE)
Adelaide II, 80
Christian I, 441
Daniel II, 24
George Friederich I, 551, 552, 554
Hend^k II, 15
Johann Nicolaus I, 318, 319
ANDREA
J. Peter I, 456
ANDREAS (ANDEREAS, AN-
DERAS, ANDERASS, ANDRAS,
ANDRES)
Christian I, 621, 623, 625
Friederich
(Frederick, Fred^k) I, 610, 611, 613
G. Michael
(Jerg Nicolaus) I, 621, 623, 625
Jacob II, 16
Johann Adam (Adam) I, 59, 63, 64
Johann Philipp I, 355
Joh. Wendel I, 757
Johannes I, 472
Martin I, 419
Matthias I, 16
Michael I, 57, 58
Oswald I, 610, 611, 613
Peter II, 15
Rudolph (Rudolf) I, 31, 33, 34
ANDRESSON
Matthew II, 183
ANDREW
—— I, 320
ANDREWSEN
C. II, 72
ANDRIJE
Matheas I, 493
ANDRIOLER (ANDRIOLA)
Johannes I, 600, 602, 603
ANER *see* AHNER
ANGEBRANT (ANGUBRANT,
ANKENBRANTT)
Christoph I, 31, 32, 33

ANGEL
Philip Carl I, 335, 336, 338
ANGELBACH *see* UNCKELBACH
ANGELBERGER
Philipp I, 122, 125, 126
ANGELE II, 80
ANGENE
Theobalt I, 522, 524
ANGER
Gerg Fridrich
(Geo. Fredrick) I, 642, 644
Nickel I, 156, 159, 161
ANGERMAYER
Adam I, 490
ANGEULY
Henry I, 486
ANGNE
A^n Catharina I, 157
ANGNY
Dewalt I, 363
ANGST
Benjamin II, 79
Daniel I, 379, 380, 382
Hans Henry
(Ulrich) I, 252, 253, 254
Johan Jacob (Jacob) I, 628, 631, 634
Marcus (Mark) I, 522, 525
ANGSTED (ANNGSTED)
Gorge (Geroge) I, 127, 128, 129
Johannes I, 128
ANHORN
Johan Phillippus I, 467
ANNE
Conrad II, 186
ANNER (ANARD)
Hans I, 252, 254, 255
ANNESHANSLY
Anna II, 187
Henrick (Hendrick) II, 187
Jacob II, 187
Salama II, 187
ANNEWALLT
Fallendhin I, 683
ANSBACH
Pr. II, 32
ANSCHUTZ
Catharina Elizabeth II, 45
Christian II, 45
Elizabetha II, 45
Dorothea II, 45
Georg Ludwig II, 45
Johann Georg II, 45
Johann Jacob II, 45
Johann Philip II, 45
ANSEL
David I, 476
ANSON
Joh. II, 139

ANSPACH (ANSPAG, ANSPACK)
Anspel I, 7, 8
Daniel II, 134
Henrich Jacob
(Jacob) I, 205, 206, 208
Jacob II, 116
Johann Friederich I, 715
Johannes II, 54
P. II, 33
Wilhelm I, 323, 324, 326
ANSPACHER (ANSPAG)
Hans Jerch I, 8, 9
ANSSEL
Peter I, 489
ANSTATT
Johann Georg I, 367, 369
Johannes I, 410
ANSTEIN
Hans Georg I, 468
ANTEL
Peter I, 507
ANTERS see ANDERS
ANTES (ANDIS)
Johan Friederich I, 372
Wilhelm I, 307, 308, 309
ANTGER (APGARD)
Johannes
(Joanis Peter) I, 143, 145, 146
ANTHEIS
Wilhelm (William) I, 672, 673, 674
ANTHON see ANTON
ANTHONI (ANTHONY, ANTONI,
ANTONIE)
Adam I, 724
Frederick II, 26
F. II, 15
Georg Hans I, 440
Jacob I, 404, 440, 585, 586, 588, 724
Johannes I, 304, 305, 306
Nicholas I, 697
Paulus I, 300, 301, 303
ANTON (ANTHON)
Frantz I, 440
Michael I, 358
ANTONIEDE
—— II, 121
ANZEMILLER
Joseph I, 484
APEL, APELL see APPEL
APFEL (APEL, APFFEL)
Apalonia I, 104
Christian I, 740
Johann Casper
(Casper) I, 377, 379, 381
Pieter (Johann Peter) I, 102, 105, 106
Wendel I, 694
APGARD see ANTGER
APP
Christian I, 475

Michael I, 485
APPACH (ABACH)
Johannes Christoph I, 536, 537, 538
APPEL (APEL, APELL, APPELL)
Apalonia I, 104
Christian I, 695
Christopher II, 126
Elizabeth I, 38
Elleias I, 695
Geo. I, 694
Henrich I, 72, 76, 78
Johann Adam I, 411
Johann Jacob I, 715
Johannes I, 412
Joh. I, 179
Jonas I, 720
Regula I, 147
Thomas I, 411
Wilhelm I, 340, 341, 343
(See also APPLE)
APPELDOORNE
Geertruy II, 96
APPENZELLER
Jacob I, 469
APPLE (APLE)
Andrew I, 185
Clara I, 131
Henrich (Henry) I, 72, 76, 78
Henry I, 736
Margaretha II, 106
Mr II, 18
Peter I, 131, 133, 134
Valentin II, 106
APRIL
Catharina II, 174
Eva Catharina II, 174
Jung Conrad II, 174
ARBEITER
Joh. Abraham I, 452
ARBENGAST
Georg I, 451
Johannes I, 461
ARBOR
Jos II, 16
ARBORT
Christopher II, 8
ARCULARIUS
Henrich I, 747
Philip Jacob I, 747
AREND (ARENDT, ARENTH)
Barth. I, 452
Jacob I, 390
Jacobus I, 689
Johann Wilem I, 419
Peter I, 689, 757
(See also ARNDT)
ARENHOLTZ see AHRENHOLTZ
ARENSBERGER
Peter I, 357

ARFORG
Frantz II, 44
ARIES (AERIES)
Pierre I, 352, 354
ARLDNOLD (read ARNOLD)
Hans Jerig I, 8
ARMBREAST see ARMBRUSTER
ARMBRUSTER (ARMBREAST,
ARMBRUST, AMBRISTER
ARMPRIESTER)
Anthony II, 188
Christoff
(Cristofell) I, 199, 201, 203
Gabriel I, 487
Hanns Jurg (Hans Jerg,
John Gerrit) I, 637, 638, 640
Jacob I, 491
John II, 156
John Godhart (Godhert) I, 314, 315
(See also ARMRESTER)
ARMENBETER
Feder I, 724
ARMFELT
August II, 168
ARMGAST
Hans I, 410
Michael I, 411
ARMINGEON (ARMESON)
Pierre I, 526, 527, 529
ARMRESTER (ARMRISTER, read
ARMBRUSTER)
Anthon I, 367, 369
ARMSHEINER (ARMSMER)
Johann Nicolaus
(Nichs) I, 628, 631, 634
ARMSTRONG
Anna Mary II, 156
Mary II, 156
ARNBÜHL
Johannes I, 485
ARNDORFF (AHRENDORFF)
Philip Henrich I, 577, 578, 580
ARNDT (ARND, ARNT, ARNTH,
ARAND, ARANT, ARENT)
Abraham I, 44
Anna Katrina I, 117
Anna Margrit I, 117
Anna Maria I, 118
Carl I, 521, 524
Catrina I, 45
Charles Erdman II, 105
David I, 45
Feldin I, 382
Hartwig I, 382
Henrich I, 465
Herman (Harman) I, 116, 119, 121
Jacob I, 45
Johann Berndt (Barent) I, 43, 46
Johannes Theis I, 726

John Conrad I, 749
Maria I, 44
Migerl I, 118
Peter (Pitter) I, 116, 119, 121
ARNET
Jacob I, 10, 12
ARNOLD (ARNOLDT, ARNOLT)
Christof I, 478
Conrad I, 432
Frietrig I, 686
Georg I, 185, 186, 187
Georg Friederich I, 185, 186, 187
George Fredk II, 28
Henri II, 197
Jacob, Senior I, 367, 368
Jacob, Junior I, 367, 368
Jacob I, 752
Jacob Friedrich I, 727
Joh. Goft II, 118
Johann Gorg
(George) I, 243, 244, 245
Johann Nichelaus
(Joh. Nichs) I, 564, 565, 567
Johannes, I, 276, 277, 278, 421
John Fredk II, 8
John Philip II, 8
Jörg I, 513, 514, 516
Lorentz (Lawrence) I, 656, 657, 659
Maria Elizab. II, 8
Martin I, 322
Matheus (Mathias) I, 637, 639, 640
Michael I, 454
Nicholas I, 709
Peter I, 421, 457
Philip II, 8
Philip Jacob II, 8
Regina II, 8
Wilhelm
(William) I, 421, 656, 657, 659
ARNOLDS
Adam II, 36
ARNOLDUS
Jno I, 740
ARNOUL
Jean Pierre I, 468
ARRNNOS (AMMOS, HAMMER)
Jacob I, 290, 291, 292
ARNSTERGER
Johan Adam I, 706
ARPERMAN
Christian II, 195
ARRIS
J. Adam I, 494
Johannes I, 494
ARZT (ARTS, AARTS, ARTES)
Joannes I, 85
Johann Jacob I, 469
Johannes I, 84, 85, 86, 87

ASH
  Nicklas (Nichᵃ)   I, 595, 597, 599
ASHELMAN   (HESHLEMAN, HESSLEMAN)
  Wilhelm (Ulrich)   I, 610, 611, 613
  (*See also* AESCHLIMANN)
ASCHENBRENNER   (ASHEN-BRANDER)
  Urban (Orbinos)   I, 290, 291
ASHMAN
  J. Henry (John Henry) I, 646, 647
ASKERITT *see* ACKERT
ASPECK (ASBECKE)
  Christian   I, 185, 186, 187
ASPER
  Johannes (Johan, John) I, 232, 233
ASSELOER
  Johannes   I, 675
ASSUM
  Johann Peter   I, 493
ASTIMER
  Matthias   I, 754
ASWALT *see* OSWALD
ATERHOLT (ODERHOLT, read ADERHOLD)
  Christian   I, 509, 510, 511
ATTLER (read ADLER)
  Rheinhardt   I, 26
ATZ
  Jacob   II, 145
  Tur   II, 145
ATTZ
  Jacob   II, 147
AU
  C. Van der   II, 203
  Christafur   I, 660
  Fredrick   I, 660
  Gerick   I, 660
  Johannes Henrich   I, 700
AUBEL (AUBLE, AUBY)
  Jacob   I, 304, 306, 307
AUBERSTE
  ——   II, 81
AUBERTIEN (OBERDICE)
  Pierre (Piere, Peter) I, 258, 260, 263
AUBIE
  Barbara   II, 93
AUCH (AUG)
  Jacob   I, 605, 606, 608
AÜCHELE (EIGEL)
  Hans Geo.
    (Hans Jerg)   I, 661, 662, 664
AUDERICH
  Engelhᵈ   II, 178
AUEN (AVEN)
  Johannes Casper
    (Casper)   I, 532, 533, 535
AUER (AWE, OUER, AWER)
  Anthony   I, 744

Elias   I, 573, 574, 575
Franciscus   I, 471
Gorg Deobalt   I, 436
Johannes   I, 523, 525
AUGE
  Christian   II, 205
  Heinrich   II, 205
  Henriette   II, 205
  Henr.   II, 205
  J. Valentin   II, 205
  Mar. Fried.   II, 205
  Maria Sophia   II, 205
  Reinhardt   II, 205
  Wilhelmina   II, 205
AUGEN
  Margreth   I, 60
  Elisabeth   I, 60
AUGENSTEIN
  Casper   I, 465
  Hans Georg   I, 476
  Johannes   I, 476
AUGMON
  Frany   I, 80
AUGUSTIN
  Johan   II, 169
  Johann Hironimus   I, 714
AUGUSTINUS
  Christoph Heinerich   I, 713
AUHAGEN (AUHAUGE, OHAGE)
  Christofel (Chrisᵗ)   I, 589, 590
  Conrad   I, 589, 590, 591
AUL (AULL)
  Jacob   II, 169
  Maria   II, 119
AULEBAKER
  Andreas   I, 169, 170, 172
AULHORN
  Willᵐ   II, 73
AULLENBACHER   (OULEN-BACHER, OULBACHREN)
  Andreas   I, 122, 125, 126
  Anlies   I, 123
  Maria   I, 123
AUMAN (AMMON)
  Daniel   I, 559, 560, 562
AUMÜLLER (AUMILLER, OMILLER)
  Conrath (Conrad) I, 656, 657, 658
  Johannes   I, 656, 657, 658
  Johann Georg   I, 451
  Philip Counrath   I, 429
AUNAY
  ——   II, 81
AURANDT (AURANT)
  Joh. Jacob   I, 752
  Johannes   I, 577, 579, 580
AUSHENECH (ESHRICH)
  Henry (Hendrick) I, 556, 557, 558

AWERT (EBERT)
Hans Philip   I, 296, 297, 299
AX
Johannes   I, 340, 341, 342
AXE
Ludwick   I, 760
AXER
Christian   I, 403
Michel   I, 330

BA . . .
Nickl   I, 699
BAAB
Jacob   I, 363; II, 147
BAART
Philip Jacob   I, 232
BAAS (AS)
Filb (Filp, Philip)   I, 610, 611, 613
BAB
Nicklas   I, 406
BABEMEYER
Elizabeth   I, 40
Friederich
(Fredrick, Fredk.)   I, 39, 41, 42
BABST *see* PABST
BACH (BAACH, BACHY, BECK,
BOCK)
Adam
(Hans Adam)   I, 225, 228, 230
Andreas   I, 725
Bartle (Bartholme) I, 225, 228, 230
Henry (Henrich)   I, 667, 669, 671
Hs. Gerg   I, 446
Johan   I, 355
Joh. Fr.   II, 125
Johann Michael, (John
Nicjlus, Nickel)   I, 257, 260, 262
Johann Nickel   I, 731
Johann Nicol
(Hans Nichl*)   I, 601, 602, 603
Johann Peter   I, 396
Johannes   I, 717
Michael Jacob   I, 717
Michel   I, 498
Philip Wilhertz   I, 432
Zacharias   I, 504
BACHART
George   I, 417
BACHER
Hans Georg   I, 408
Salmon   I, 405
BACHHOFFEN (BAKHOFFER)
Hans George   I, 508
Johan Jorg   I, 508
BACHLEIKIRKEN
W.   II, 102

BACHMAN (BACHMANN, BACK-
MAN, BOCHMAN)
Andreas   I, 327, 329
Chas.   II, 123
Conrad   I, 460, 733
II, 26
Felix   I, 252, 253, 255
Hans   I, 252, 254, 255
Heinrich (Henrich) I, 252, 253, 255,
420, 472, 702
Jacob   I, 332, 333, 334, 522, 524
Johan Christian I, 574, 575, 576
Johan Jacob   I, 522, 524
Johannes   I, 545, 547, 653, 654
John Fredk.   II, 57
Julius Christoph   I, 399
Lorentz   I, 522, 524
Ludwig   I, 659, 752
BACHRACH (BACKRACK)
Samuel   I 678, 679, 681
BACHRODT
Nicklaus   I, 752
BÄCHTEL (PIETHEL)
Abraham (Abram) I, 264, 267, 270
BACK (read BECK)
George Danl.   I, 24
Hans Jacob   I, 509
Johan Jacob   I, 276, 277, 278
Johann Henry
(John Hendrick) I, 276, 277, 278
Johann Wilhelm   I, 276, 277, 278
Johans Georg   I, 458
Philip Jacob   I, 24
BACKASTOS (BAKERSOOL)
Hans Jerick
(Hans Ulrich)   I, 348, 350, 351
BACKER (read BÄCKER)
Dan   II, 99
Jacob   II, 123
Johannes
Johann Michel   I, 169, 170, 172
J. N.   II, 4
Philip   I, 169, 170, 172, 484
Vallentin   I, 485
(*See also* BÄCKER, BAKER and
BECKER)
BÄCKER
Dilmanis   I, 685
Johan Deis   I, 402
Johann Engell   I, 684
Johann Michael (Michel) I, 501, 684
Johannes   II, 101
Johannes Michael   I, 484
BACSCH
E. L.   II, 32
BADE
D. Carl   II, 206
BADEN
Anna Maria   II, 169

Friederich II, 169
John George II, 196
Joseph II, 169
BADENHAINER
Johann Christ I, 401
BADENHAMER (BADENHANER,
BAUDENHEIMER)
Johann Peter
(Peter) I, 568, 570, 572
BADENHEIMER
Chrisⁿ I, 676
Johann Wilhelm I, 466
BADER (BAWDER, BATTER,
PATER)
Andras
(Andreas) I, 212, 214, 216
Christoph (Christof,
Christopher) I, 31, 32, 33
Christopher I, 250, 251
Hans Gerg (Jorg) I, 485, 494
Israel II, 153
Joh. Ant. II, 193
Johan Gerg I, 427
Johann Georg
(Jn° Geo.) I, 649, 650
Johannes I, 507
Laurence (Lawrence) I, 72, 76, 78
Matteas I, 494
Peter I, 522, 524
Phillip Jacob I, 356
BAEKER
Arnst I, 676
Chrisⁿ I, 676
Philip I, 676
Theis (Teys) I, 676
Tonis I, 676
BAER (BAIR)
Jacob I, 13
Johannes I, 346
Johannis I, 18, 19
BAERMANN
Anton II, 133
BAERNS
Andries I, 13
BAFFENMAYER
Mathäus I, 433
BAGER
John George I, 499
BÄHLER (BÜHLER, LEGHTNER,
BENNER, FYBAYLOR)
Jerg Ernst
(Jurig Arnet) I, 265, 268, 271
Johan Vit
(Johan Figt) I, 265, 268, 272
BAHLSDORF
Johann Friederich I, 742
BAHN
Johan Henrich
(Henrick) I, 47, 51, 53

BAHNER
—— II, 32
BAHNMULLER
Conrad II, 179
BÄHR
Jacob I, 14
Johann Jacob I, 408
Johannes I, 596, 598, 599
BAHRET (BARRET)
Balthas (Baldus) I, 209, 211
BAIDEMANN
Simon Peter I, 702
BAIER see BEYER
BAINE see BEEN
BAIR see BAER
BAISCH
Friderich I, 491
Gorg Friederich I, 470
Jacob I, 491
—— II, 161
BAKER
Anna Maria II, 6
Diederick Cuns II, 197
George (Jerick) I, 545, 547, 549
Hans Georg I, 188
Henry II, 75
Henry George
(H. George) I, 573, 574, 575
Jacob I, 347; II, 27
James II, 151
Johanes I, 467
Jn° II, 6
John Andrew II, 117
Jn° C. II, 6
Michael I, 497
Nicklas I, 347
Phillip Jacob II, 151
Rosina II, 151
Yerick (read Georg) I, 451
(See also BECKER)
BAKHOFFER see BACHHOFFEN
BALACK (PAALT, BARTH)
Aⁿ Catharina I, 157
Johan Jacob I, 155, 158, 160
BALBA
David II, 145
BALBACH
Christoph II, 148
BALBIERER (BALBIRER)
John Ditter (Han Peter) I, 642, 644
Philliebs I, 431
BALCH (BOLCH, BOLK)
Andreas I, 539, 541, 543
BALCK
Carlo II, 205
BALD
Ann Mary II, 84
Anna Sophia II, 84
Christina II, 84

Conrad II, 84
Elias I, 237
Frederic II, 84
John Jost II, 85
Jost II, 84
Margaretha II, 53
Mary Elisabeth II, 85
(*See also* BALDT)
BALDE
Johann Henry II, 42
Johannes II, 42
William II, 42
BALDESBERGER (BURSBEGER, BALDSBERGER)
Hans George I, 428
Peter I, 246, 247, 248
BALDT
Anna Elizabeth II, 120
Anne Marie II, 85
Catharine II, 29, 85
Debus II, 120
Dietrich II, 86
Guillaume II, 85
Jean Henry II, 85
Jean Josse II, 86
John Adam I, 563
Mathias II, 29
Regine Elisabeth II, 85
Susette II, 85
BALDUF (BALTOF, read BALDAUF)
Johan Peter I, 576, 578, 580
(*See also* BALLDAUF)
BALEUR
Jacob I, 452
BALK
Chris^n II, 32
BALLDAUF (EIGENDENSEIM)
Johan Dietdrich (Johan Died^k) I, 601, 602, 603
BALLENBERGER
Johann Jeremias I, 753
BALLIET (BALIET, BALIETT, BULIUT)
Baullus (Paulus) I, 213, 215
Joseb I, 421
BALLMAN (BOLLMAN, BULLMER)
Johan Nike (Janis Nickell) I, 265, 269, 272
Joh. Adam (Adam) I, 265, 269, 272
BALLMER
Jacob I, 740
BALMAS
Piere I, 455
BALME (BALD)
Jaques (Jacob) I, 526, 527, 529
BALMER (PALMER)
Carl Diedrich (Carl) I, 60, 64, 65

Christian I, 60, 64, 65
Jacob I, 231, 232, 233
Jerg Michel (Michael) I, 231, 232, 233
Michael I, 185, 186, 187
BALMSTROM
Christian I, 718
BALSAM
Peter I, 435
BALSCHBACH (BALTSBACH)
Jorg I, 454
Peter (Petter) I, 59, 64, 65
BALSTAD
Joh. Hinr. II, 139
BALSTER
John S^t II, 196
BALT
Johanes I, 8
BALTAASAR
Philipp II, 61
BALTHAUR (BOLTHAWER)
Joh. Andres I, 517, 518, 519
BALTISBARGER (BOLTISBERGER, POLDESBERGER, read BALDESBERGER)
Hendrick I, 331, 333, 334
BALSTER
Johan Leonhardt I, 423
BALTZ (PAULSE)
Johann Gorg (Johs. Yerick) I, 72, 76, 77
John Georg I, 760
Katharine I, 73
BALTZAER
Caspar I, 487
BALTZEL
Carl I, 686
Georg Jacob I, 686
Jacob I, 686
——— I, 754
BALTZER
Jacob I, 484
J. II, 142
Philip I, 716
Thomas (Dhomas) I, 227, 229, 231
Wiellm (Wielm, Wilhelm) I, 614, 616, 619, 741
BALTZLY (BANTZLER, PANTZLY, BALTZLE, BALZLY, WALTZEL)
Christoff (Christian) I, 629, 632, 636
Petter (Peter) I, 629, 632, 636
BAMBERGER (PAMBERGER)
Henry (Hendrik) I, 264, 267, 271
BAMESBERGER
Frederica II, 151
John II, 151

Regina   II, 152
BAN
  God.   II, 32
BANDEL
  Michel   I, 689
BANDELE
  Johannes   II, 126
BANDER
  Jnᵒ Geo.   I, 740
BANDHOLTZ
  George   II, 85
BANECOURT
  ———   II, 81
BANER
  Georg   II, 125
BANG
  Melcher   II, 19
BANGER
  Elijah   II, 145
  Jacob   II, 145
  Janette   II, 145
  Trena   II, 145
BANGEST
  Franz   II, 20
BANGHIRT
  Wilhelm   II, 126
BANHER
  Samuel   I, 497
BÄNINGER (PENINGER)
  Hans Jacob   I, 252, 254, 255
  Ulrich   I, 252, 254, 255
BANNADURER (BANTOR)
  Christen (Christ)   I, 677, 679, 680
BANNER (PANNER)
  Christian   I, 559, 561, 562
  Hans Jerg   I, 443
BANNKAUF (BANKAULF)
  Anton (Anthony)   I, 55, 56, 57
BANNOT (PANOCH)
  Johann Peter   I, 667, 669, 671
BANSCH
  Barbara   II, 184
  Catharina   II, 184
  Christoph   II, 184
  George   II, 184
  Heinrich   II, 184
  Heinrich Laurence   II, 184
BÄNSCHE (BAUSCH, BOEMSH)
  George (Georg)   I, 137, 141, 142
BANSHAFF
  Christian   II, 202
BANTLI (BANTLIE)
  Jacob   I, 336, 339
BANTLION
  Christoph Friederich   I, 475
  Georg Wilhelm   I, 475
BANTZ (BANCE, BANZ)
  Adam   II, 20
  E.   II, 141

Friederich   I, 720
  Jacob   I, 250, 251
  M.   II, 142
BÄNTZLER
  Friedrich   I, 692
BANUTZ
  Johann Jacob   I, 400
BAPP
  Johan Rudolf   I, 720
BAPTISTA
  Joannes   I, 739
BAPTISTE
  Jean   I, 735
BAPTISTO
  John   I, 728
BÄR (BER, BEHR)
  Caspar   I, 365
  Christoffel   I, 363
  Christophel   I, 346
  Elias   I, 462
  Hans Jacob   I, 434
  Hans Rudolff   I, 364
  Henry   I, 398
  Jacob   I, 332, 333, 334, 398
  Jeremias   I, 402
  Johann Heinrich   I, 710
  Johannes   I, 332, 333, 334, 398
  Melcher   I, 346
  Melchior   I, 346
  Philipp Jacob
    (Philip Jacob)   I, 677, 679, 680
  Rudolf   I, 398
  (*See also* BAER, BARE *and* BARR)
BARAL (BARRAL)
  Jaque (Jaques)   I, 646, 647
  Jaques (Jacob)   I, 646, 647
  Johan Christoph
    (John Christoff)   I, 646, 647
  Johan Jacob   I, 646
BARB
  Jacob   I, 676
BARBEL
  Anna   I, 67
  Maria   I, 67
BARBEZAT (BURBASA)
  Jaque (Jack)   I, 592, 593, 594
BARCH
  Danˡ   I, 716
BARCHELL
  Andreas   I, 430
BARCHMANN
  Christ. Sam.   I, 431
BARD (BAAR)
  Daniel   II, 85
  Franc (Francis)   I, 592, 593, 594
  Wilhelm (William)   I, 592, 593, 594
BARDECK
  George   I, 742

BARDESROSIN
John II, 161
BARDON
Jacob I, 696
BARE (BEAR)
Catharine II, 47
G. Peter (George) I, 568, 570, 572
Jarig
(George, Jarrick) I, 99, 100, 101
Peter II, 46, 47
Samuell I, 12
BAREBLE
Anna I, 209
BARESTEIN (BARSTAYN, PAAR-
STEYN)
Matthes I, 87, 90, 91
BARETH
Michael I, 421
BARGO
Frans II, 97
BARK
Henry II, 183
Jacob II, 183
BARKEL (BECKEL, BERG)
B. Christian
(Barthelo^m Christ^n) I, 672, 673,
674
BARLE
Michael I, 452
BARLEATER
Johana Sophia II, 22
BÄRLEY (BÄRLI)
Adam II, 133
Heinrich I, 738
BARLING (BARLIN, BERLIN, BAR-
LY)
Abraham I, 246, 247, 248
Georg Frederik I, 246, 247, 248
Hans Jacob (Jacob) I, 246, 247, 248
BARLLES
Nancy II, 125
BARMAN
John II, 93
BARNCAT (BARNGAT)
Anna Elizabeth II, 36
Cristina II, 36
Frederich II, 37
Maria II, 36
Philipina II, 36
BARNER
Jan II, 135
Johannes I, 420
BARNES
John II, 26
BARNETT
George II, 11
BARNEXA
Franco I, 760

BARNGAT
Carrol Ludwigh II, 36
BARNITEL
Johann Adam I, 728
BARNSTEIN
Andres I, 525
BAROMO
Jonas I, 711
BARON (BARRON)
Hans Philip I, 370
Jaque (Jacob) I, 526, 528, 529
Jean I, 353, 354
Matthias (?) I, 370
Nickolas I, 492
BARR (BAAR, BÄR, BEAR, BEER)
Bart. Rudolf (Barthol.) I, 273, 274
Blassius
(Blatious, Blaziers) I, 286, 287,
288
Hans I, 273, 274
Hans Martin I, 258, 260, 263
Heinrich (Hend^k) I, 273, 274
Jacob I, 162, 164, 166
Johannes (Hans) I, 591, 592, 594
BARS (BOARS)
Johannes
(Johanis, Johannys) I, 47, 51, 53
BARSCH
Elisabeth II, 198
Henry II, 198
John II, 198
BART
Barr II, 51
Catharine II, 51
Cethnet II, 51
Henry II, 51
Hirer II, 51
Jacob (Jacobes) I, 116, 120, 121, 398
Johan II, 51
Juliane Catherine I, 148
Margret II, 51
(*See also* BARTH)
BARTAR *see* BARTER
BARTEL
Anderas I, 689
BARTELME *see* BARTHELME
BARTELS (BARTOLS, BARTHALS)
Heinrich Christophel
(Friederich Henrich) I, 509, 510,
511
Isaac W. II, 71
Johann Christian II, 48
Maria II, 174
BARTENBACH (BARDENBACH)
Johannes I, 621, 623, 625
BARTER (BARTAR)
Anna Mira II, 146
Barbara II, 146

Bernr. II, 146
Johannes II, 146
BARTH (PARTH, PART)
Aⁿ Catharina I, 157
Johann Jacob I, 155
Johann Ludwig I, 409
Johannes I, 9, 421
Jn° Michael II, 26
Marthin
(Hans Martin) I, 257, 260, 262
Michael I, 421
Peter I, 323, 325, 326
Philipp I, 701
Zacharias I, 38, 39
BARTHEL (BARTLE)
Jacob I, 287, 288, 289
(*See also* BARTTEL)
BARTHELME (BARTELME, BAR-
TELMEH, BARTHELMEH)
Filib (Philip) I, 205, 206, 208
Jacob I, 198, 201, 202
Johanes I, 8
Johann (Johanis) I, 204, 206, 208
(*See also* BARTHOLOMAE)
BARTHELMEL (read BARTHEL-
MEY)
Cornelius II, 47
BARTHELMEY
Johann Wendel I, 695
BARTHELMY
Sebastian I, 371
T. G. II, 115
BARTHELS
Andres II, 53
Gustus II, 54
BARTHEN
Jos. II, 100
BARTHMES
Johan Adam I, 456
Philipus I, 347
BARTHOLOMAE (BARTHOLOMA,
BARTHOLEMY, BARTOLE-
MOW)
Carl I, 761
Johann Nicolaus I, 546, 548, 550
Michael I, 761
Peter I, 293, 294, 296, 761
(*See also* BARTHELME *and* BAR-
THOLOMEW)
BARTHOLOMEW
Christina I, 123
Mattias (Mathias) I, 243, 244, 245
BARTHOLOMUS
Benedick I, 67
BARTHOLT
G. Adam I, 437
BARTHOUD
Mad^m II, 72
Monsr II, 72

BARTJE
A. Maria II, 15
Christⁿ II, 15
Johan II, 15
BARTLAM
Johannes Theodorus II, 54
BARTLEMAN (BARTHOLOMA)
Adam I, 667, 669, 671
BARTMAN (BARTTMAN)
Johan Georg I, 256, 258, 261
Johan Michel I, 256, 258, 261
Johann Matteas
(Mathias) I, 256, 258, 261
Johannes Adam
(Adam, Johann) I, 661, 662, 664
BARTOLMES
Peter I, 347
BARTRAM
Jn° Henry I, 748
BARTRUFF
Andereas I, 484
BARTTEL
George Adam I, 437
BARTTLER (BAUCHLER, BACH-
LER)
Conrad (Conraat) I, 252, 253, 255
BARTZ (BARTS)
Johann Friedrich I, 234, 235, 236
BASERMANN
Friederich I, 746
BASHIDOCH
Christian I, 747
BASLER (BAASLER, BOOSSER)
Friedrich I, 99, 100, 101
Jacob I, 448
Johannes I, 448
Joseb I, 448
J. Godlop
(John Godlep) I, 672, 673, 674
Peter I, 448
Ulrich I, 99, 100, 101
BASS
Johan Nicol I, 456
BASSEL (BASEL)
Conrad I, 328
Johan Georg (Jerig) I, 155, 158, 161
BASSELER (BOSLER)
Michael (Michal) I, 586, 587, 588
(*See also* BASSLER)
BASSERER *see* BESER
BASSERMANN (BASERMAN)
Michael I, 373, 374, 376
Siegmund (Simon) I, 378, 379, 381
BASSING
Matteis I, 339
BASSLER
Friedrich I, 426
Michael II, 155

BAST (BASST)
Anna Maree — I, 80
Davit — I, 421
Gerg (Jurig) — I, 78, 81, 82
Henerita — II, 36
Jacob Henrich — I, 755
Johanas — I, 80
Johann Adam — I, 474
Johann Michael — I, 421
Johann Michel — I, 714
Lewis Henery — II, 36
Vallentin — I, 433
BASTEN, von
Joh. Herm. — I, 182, 184
BASTERER (BASTER)
Philipp (Philip) — I, 614, 616, 618
BASTERT
Carolina — II, 192
BASTIAN
Adam — I, 24
Andres — I, 491
Andrew — I, 24
Anna — I, 73
Elizabeth — I, 73, 74
Geo. — I, 685
Herman — I, 74
Johann Georg — I, 730
Jo. Heinrich — I, 730
Johan Jacob — I, 748
Johann Nickolaus — I, 750
Johannes — I, 71, 76, 77
Jonas — I, 491
Lorentz (Lawrence) — I, 71, 76, 77
Maria — I, 73
Matelina — I, 73
Matheis — I, 471
Michel — I, 421
Theobalt — I, 739
BASTROP
Augustina — II, 60
Cristina Maria — II, 60
Georgina Wolfeline Françoise
  Lycklama — II, 60
Marta Kinnema — II, 60
Philip Hendrik — II, 60
Susana Maria — II, 60
BATE (BALD)
Johann Jacob — I, 700
John Adam
  (Johannes Arnt) — I, 560, 561, 563
BATER
Anna Mira — II, 145
Claus — II, 145
Samuel — II, 145
BATH
John Atam — I, 420
BATHENFELD
Philipp — I, 438

BATICH
Johan Jacob — I, 443
BATMANN
Henry — II, 122
BATRAM
Hans Caspar — I, 504
BATT
Michael — I, 728
BATTEFELT (BATTENFELD)
Hans Adam — I, 438
Johannes — I, 438
Justus — I, 744
(*See also* BATHENFELD)
BATTEIGER
Johann Valentin — I, 718
BATTENBERG
Hermanus — I, 408
BATTER
Hans Georg — I, 487
BATZ (POTTS)
Johann Georg — I, 415
Johann Peter — I, 436
Johann Reinhart
  (John Rinehard) — I, 555, 556, 557
Johannes — I, 753; II, 184
Michael — I, 360, 361
BÄTZ (BEATS)
Adam — I, 68
Cathrina — I, 68
Johann Görg (Jerich) — I, 66, 69, 70
Magdalena — I, 68
Maria — I, 68
BAUB
Tobias — I, 497
BAUCH (BOUGH, BUCK)
Hans Georg
  (Hans Enger) — I, 226, 229, 231
Hendrich
  (Hendrick, Henry) — I, 266, 269, 272
Johinrich — I, 752
Thomas — I, 431
BAUDEMONT
Andre — I, 445
BAUER (BAUR, BAWER, BOUER,
  BOUR, BOWER)
Adam — I, 66, 403
Andreas — I, 122, 125, 126; II, 190
Barbara — I, 68
Caspar — I, 496
Catharina — II, 190
Catharine Debora — II, 43
Catherine — I, 123; II, 43
Christian (Chris[n]) — I, 176, 177, 178, 621, 623, 625; II, 190
Christine — II, 190
Conrad — I, 614, 616, 619, 690
Deobald — I, 347

Eb. Ch. II, 202
Elisabeth II, 190
Eva Elisabeth II, 174
Georg II, 102
Hanns I, 490
Hans Georg I, 418
Hans Martin I, 89, 91, 92
Hans Michael II, 43
Hans Peter II, 43
Helena I, 74
Henrich I, 432
Henry I, 702
H. II, 141
Jacob (Jacho) I, 246, 247, 248, 421,
470, 502, 522, 524
II, 119, 172
Johann II, 50
Johann Adam I, 470
Johann Bernhard I, 490
Johann Christoffel
(Christopher) I, 40, 41, 42
Johann Friederich I, 513, 514, 516
Johann Georg I, 449, 705, 759
Johan Henrich I, 504
Johann Konratt I, 470
Johann Jacob I, 485
Johann Jost I, 506
Johann Martin
(Martin) I, 72, 76, 77
Joh. Math. I, 758
Johann Michael
I, 317, 318, 319,
512, 514, 515
Johann Nickel
(Johan Nicklaus) I, 204, 206, 208,
593, 594
Johan Paul
(John Paul) I, 317, 318, 319
Johan Peter I, 204, 206, 208,
513, 514, 516
Joh. Phillip II, 190
Johan Thebald I, 487
Joh. Ulrich I, 432
Johannes
(Johanes) I, 402, 415, 480, 717
II, 190
John Jacob II, 201
Jn° Philip I, 743
Joseph Peter I, 442
Kilian I, 500
Margaretta I, 73
Maria I, 123
Martin I, 409, 724
Mathias I, 317
Michael
(Michel) I, 195, 196, 197, 256,
259, 262, 346
II, 43
Moritz I, 489

Nicklas
(Nicholas) I, 595, 597, 599
Nicolaus
(Johan Nichl.) I, 303, 305, 306
Philip I, 432
Philip Jacob II, 43, 134
Philip Jerry II, 43
Salomé II, 193
Samuel II, 190
Sebastian I, 367, 369
Susanna I, 73
Thomas I, 195, 196, 197, 591,
593, 594
Valentin I, 689
(*See also* BAUR *and* BOWER)
BAUERDT (BOWERS)
Henrich I, 332, 333, 334
BAÜERLE
Johann Conrath I, 457
Johann Ludwig I, 399
BAUERMAN
Michel I, 461
BAUERSACHS
Hans Michel I, 432
Paulus I, 738
BAUERSCHMIDT (BAUER-
SCHMID)
Jacob I, 491
BAUINGER
Heinerich I, 434
BAULTIN
Louis II, 72
BAUM
Carl Ludwig I, 698
Hans Jacob I, 476
Henry I, 698
Jacob I, 169, 171, 172, 390;
II, 184
Jerg Simon I, 454
Johan I, 693
Johan Adam I, 356
Johann Georg I, 741
Johann Jacob I, 443
Johann Philippus
(John Philip) I, 373, 374, 375
Johannes I, 169, 171, 172, 433
Pfilb (read Philip) I, 433
—— II, 162
BAUMAN (BAUMANN, BAUM,
BAWMAN, BOWMAN, BOU-
MAN)
Abraham I, 409, 501
Albert I, 16
Albreght I, 17
Andreas (Adereas) I, 596, 598, 599
Anna I, 24
Anna Eliz^th II, 23
Anna, Jr. I, 24
Anna Margareta I, 191

Balthas I, 491
Betsila I, 24
Caspar (Grosper) I, 55, 56, 57
Cath. II, 72
Charles Lewis II, 55
Christian I, 677, 679, 680
Christina I, 191
Conrad I, 677, 679, 680
Daniel I, 476
Elizabetha I, 190
Friederich Wilhelm I, 732
Georg I, 472, 746
II, 10
Georg Adam
(Yerick Adam) I, 384, 386
Georg Christoph I, 507
Georg Jacob I, 715
Gottlieb I, 409
Hans Conrad I, 474
Hans Jacob
(Jacob) I, 188, 191, 193
252, 254, 255
Hans Jerrick I, 7
Henrick I, 54
Jacob (Jacobus) I, 14, 15, 24, 25, 26
142, 145, 146
252, 254, 255
322, 362, 398
498
Jacob, Jr. I, 362
Joh. Jos. II, 20
Johann I, 408
Johann Georg I, 408, 480, 687
Johan Jacob I, 494, 498
Johann Martin I, 732
Johannes
(Johanes) I, 189, 192, 194, 263
267, 270, 408, 418
582, 583, 584
Johenrich (Henry) I, 71, 76, 77
Leonhart I, 499
Michel I, 357, 753
Mr. II, 176
Pens (read Bentz) II, 84
Peter I, 364, 396
Thomas I, 750
Walter
(Walthart) I, 163, 165, 166
BAUMBERGER
Carl I, 367, 368
BAUMER (BAWINER, BAWMER, BÖMMER)
Henry (Heinrich) I, 205, 206, 208
Johan Adam I, 205, 206, 208
Johan Peter I, 205, 206, 208
Rudolph
(Roedolph) I, 252, 253, 255
BAUMGÄRDTNER (BAUMGERT-

NER, BAUMGARDNER, BOOM-GARDNER, BUMGARNER)
Christ (Christopher) I, 24, 26, 27
Daniel II, 34
Gottfriet I, 424
Hans Michel I, 60, 64, 65
Henry I, 331, 333, 334
Johan Fridrich I, 72, 76, 78
Johan George
(Hans Jorig) I, 162, 164, 165
Johann Peter
(Johans Petter) I, 195, 196, 197
Johannes I, 427
John I, 60, 64, 65
Matheis I, 249, 250
Rudolph I, 163, 165, 166
Simon I, 419
Ursley I, 24
Valtin
(Valentine) I, 179, 181, 183
BAUMGARTEN
Carl II, 128
Hubert I, 492
Wendeling II, 205
BAUMGIRTEL (BOOMGIRDLE)
Johan Erhart
(John) I, 373, 374, 376
BAUMONK
Hans Geo. I, 699
BAUR (BAUER, BOWER)
Bernhard I, 456, 755
Christian I, 493
George Henry
(Jurg) I, 539, 541, 543
Hans Atam I, 714
Jacob I, 460
Johann Georg I, 442
Johannes I, 341, 342, 343
Linhard I, 690
Ludwig I, 431
Martin I, 545, 547, 549
Michael
(Michel) I, 546, 547, 549, 727
Moritz I, 489
Moses I, 512, 514, 515
Simon I, 512
Steffan I, 414
(*See also* BAUER *and* BOWER)
BAURMEISTER (BOHRMISTER)
Heinrich
(Jn° Henry) I, 589, 590, 591
BAUS
Hans I, 499
Hans Adam I, 404
Johannes I, 752
BAUSCH
Gabriel I, 527, 529, 530
Johann Adam I, 697
Johan Henrich I, 698

BAUSCHAR
Johann Daniel   I, 413
BAUSEL
Jacob   I, 9
BAUSEMAN
Joh.   II, 113
BAUSHER
Jno. Lud.   I, 719
BAUSMANN (BAUSMAN)
Andreas   I, 702
Johann Michel   I, 382
Johann Peter   I, 366, 368
Lorentz   I, 363
Philipps Jacob   I, 702
Willhelm   I, 363
(*See also* BOUSMAN)
BAUSSER (BOUSER, BEASLER, BEWSER)
Anna Catherina   I, 128
Anna Elisabehta   I, 127, 128
Anna Maria   I, 128
Christian   I, 126, 129
Daniel   I, 127
Esther   I, 127
Jacob   I, 127
Magdalena   I, 128
Matheus (Matthes)   I, 126, 129
Mathis (Matthes)   I, 126, 129
BAUSSET
Christ^n II, 161
Emanuel   II, 161
Henry   II, 161
Mary   II, 161
BAUSUM
Johannes   I, 465
Lorentz   I, 430
Philippus   I, 465
BAUT
Jn° Christopher   I, 749
BAWMAN *see* BAUMAN
BAWNGWAR
Henry   I, 369, 370
BAXMAN
Charles Christ.   II, 93
BAY
Jacob   I, 738
BAYDEMANN
Johan Henrich   I, 715
BAYER (BAYR, BEIER, BEIR)
Andres (Andras)   I, 198, 200, 202
Friederich   I, 759
Georg Friedrich   I, 447
Jacob   I, 21, 23
Joh.   II, 108
Johann Adam   I, 428
Johann Ewald   I, 416
Johan Georg Fridrich   I, 472, 491
Johann Phillipps   I, 198, 200, 202
Johann Ulrich   I, 739

Johannes   I, 517, 519, 520
Martin   I, 198, 200, 202
Philippus   I, 346
(*See also* BEYER)
BÄYERLEIN
Jacob   I, 693
BAYJE
Kaufman Isaac   II, 135
BAYLY
Nicholas   I, 28
BAYMAN
Maria   II, 194
BAYR *see* BAYER
BEACH
John Adam   I, 699
BEAM
Anna Barbara   II, 167
Anna Maria   II, 167
Christoph   II, 167
David   II, 167
Elizabeth   II, 167
Godfried   II, 167
Johan   II, 167
Johannas   II, 167
John George   II, 167
John Jacob   II, 167
Jno. Wm.   I, 719
Maria   II, 167
Michael   I, 487
BEANS
Dally   II, 60
BEARRER
Jacob   I, 436
BEAUFORT
Gaspar   I, 762
BEAUJACQUE
Frantz Carl   I, 708
BEAVENAN
Anton   I, 406
BEAVER (PROUVA, BRUA)
Dieble (Debalt)   I, 300, 301, 302, 303
Hans Geo.   I, 300
Hans Jacob   I, 300, 301
Peter   I, 303
BEAGLESON
Johanna   I, 24
BEAR
Anna Maria   I, 37
Bernhart   I, 359
Frena   I, 80
Hans Jacob   I, 37, 38, 39
Hendrick   I, 37
John   I, 37, 38, 39
Madelen   I, 80
Maria Barbra   I, 38
BEBEL
Philip   I, 412
BEBERTZ (BEVERT, BEUERILES)
Johanes

(Johan, Johanis) I, 266, 269, 272
BEBIGHAUSEN *see* BIBIGHAUS
BECHEL
Christo   I, 517
BECHER (BAKER, BEGER)
Christopher   I, 711
Friedrich (Fredᵏ)   I, 609, 611, 612
                                II, 110
Hans Jorg   I, 225, 228, 230
Jacob   II, 110
Johan   II, 110
Johann Andreas   I, 455
Johann Marthin
  (Martin)   I, 188, 191, 193
Maria   II, 110
Philip   I, 701
(*See also* BECKER)
BECHLER (BEGLER)
Peter   I, 628, 631, 634
Simon   I, 628, 631, 634
BECHOLDT (BECHDOLD, BECK-
  HOLT,   BECHOLT,   BECH-
  OLTT)
Hans Jerg (Hans
  Jorg)   I, 194, 196, 197
Hennrich (Henry) I, 221, 223, 224
(*See also* BECHTOLDT)
BECHT
B. Vinden   II, 136
BECHT
Jacob   I, 450
BECHTEL (VECHTEL, PRITEL,
  BECHTLE, BEGTEL)
Hans Georg   I, 347
Jacob   I, 194, 195, 196
Joh. Georg Fried.   I, 733
Jorg   I, 19
Laurence   I, 97
Peter   I, 481
Philip   II, 137
Samuel   I, 347
BECHTLER
Anna Magdelena   I, 144
Anna Maria   I, 144
Eliz.   I, 144
Maria Barbara   I, 144
BECHTLUF   (PECKLUF,   PEK-
  LUFF, PECTLOF)
Eliza   I, 79
Tobias   I, 79, 81, 83
BECHTOLDT (BECHTOL, BECH-
  TOLD,   BECHTOLT,   BACK-
  HOLZ,   BACKHOLT,   BECK-
  HOLT)
J. George (Joh.
  Jurg)   I, 564, 565, 567
Johann Georg   I, 564, 566, 567
Johannes (Johanis) I, 199, 201, 203
Veit (Vide)   I, 226, 228, 230

BECK (BECKH, BEK, BACK, PECK,
  BEECK)
Abraham   I, 458
Adam   I, 478, 652, 654
Andreas (Andereas) I, 282, 284, 285
                        360, 361, 458
                             522, 525
Anna Barbel   I, 117
Anna Catherine   I, 128
Anna Katrina   I, 117
Antony   I, 128
Bernhard (Bern-
  hart)   I, 522, 525, 690
Blasius   I, 462
Burckhart   I, 366
Christian   I, 752
Christoph (Chris-
  topher)   I, 384, 386, 732
Daniel   I, 642; II, 193
Debolt   I, 440
Engelina   I, 127
Frantz   I, 740
Georg Heinrich
  (Henʸ)   I, 649, 650
Georg Peter   I, 689
Hans Conrad   I, 369, 370
Hans Jerg   I, 490
Hans Michal   I, 502
Hen.   II, 99
Henry   I, 748
Jacob   I, 199, 201, 203
                        213, 214, 216
                  376, 377, 414, 480
                                II, 104
Jacob F.   II, 185
Jerg Wilhelm   I, 722
Johan   I, 436
Joh. Andreas   II, 134
Johan Christian Heinrich I, 413
Johann Christoph I, 531, 533, 535
Johann Friedrich (Fri-
  derich, Frid-
  rich)   I, 346, 432, 478, 749
Johann Georg (Johan
  Jerg, Johan Jorg,
  Johan Jurg)   I, 234, 448, 458
                  488, 540, 542, 544
                        585, 587, 588
Johann Henrich   I, 128, 415
Johann Jacob   I, 373, 374, 375
                             521, 524
Johan Loretz   I, 697
Johann Ludwig (John
  Ludawick)   I, 555, 556, 557
Johan Marcus   I, 459
Johann Martin   I, 393
Johann Thommas   I, 508
Johan Wilhelm
  (Johann Wilh.) I, 155, 158, 160

276, 277, 278
Johannes (Johanes) I, 283, 284, 286
420, 564, 566, 567
627, 630, 633
Jnº Adam I, 716
John G. II, 185
Jörig (Georg) I, 314, 315
Josua II, 178
Martin I, 546, 547, 549
Mathias (Matheus,
Matheis, Matthes) I, 127, 129, 130
155, 158, 160
Peter II, 25
Samuel I, 425
Stephan I, 426
Weyrich I, 414
Yerick (Georg) I, 451
—— II, 99, 161
(*See also* BECKH *and* BACK)
BECKE
Frans II, 61
BECKEL
Jnº Peter I, 696
BECKENBACH (BECKEBACH,
BECKEBAG)
Adam I, 474
Caspar I, 474
Georg Adam I, 474
Georg Leonhardt I, 474
Johann Georg I, 474
BECKENHAUB (BAKENHAUPT)
Hans Adam (Adam) I, 620, 622, 625
BECKER (BEGGER, BEKKER,
BAKER, BACKER)
Adam I, 256, 259, 262
II, 4
Anna I, 118
Anna Cathª II, 4
Anthon Jacob II, 59
Arnolt (Arnold) I, 622, 624, 626
Bernhart I, 336, 337, 339
Carolina Elizabeth II, 59
Casper I, 615, 617, 620
Catharina II, 4
Christian I, 402, 750
II, 41
Conrad I, 568, 570, 572, 763
II, 159
Conradt (Coenraad) I, 258, 260, 263
Daniel I, 465; II, 14
Elizabeth II, 93, 97, 120, 158
Ernst I, 402
Fillib (Philip) I, 450
Frantz I, 340, 341, 342
II, 59, 138
Frederick (Fredrick) I, 116, 119, 121
Friederig (Fredrick,
Fried.) I, 282, 284, 285, 330
II, 125

Friedrich Christian I, 305, 306
Gabriel I, 709
George (Gorg) I, 258, 260, 263, 445
Gertruth II, 59
Gorg Ernst I, 444
Gottlieb I, 701
Hannes I, 335, 336, 338
Heinrich (Henrich,
Hennrick) I, 199, 201, 203, 310
312, 313, 501
II, 172, 173
Henrich Wilhelm (Yer-
rick Wilhelm) I, 582, 583, 584
Herman Diedᵏ II, 23
J. C. II, 141
Jacob (Johan) I, 287, 288, 289
303, 382, 403
610, 611, 613
621, 624, 626
II, 119
Johan II, 110
Johan Adam I, 401
Johann Daniel I, 494
Johan Dieterich
(Didrick) I, 283, 284, 285
Johann Friederich I, 750
Johann Gorg (Jurig) I, 610, 611, 613
Johann Henrich
(Johann Heinrich) I, 507, 751
Johann Jacob I, 402, 492, 736, 748
Johan Nickel I, 683
Johann Philipp I, 401, 726
Johann Velten I, 698
Johann Wilhelm
(William) I, 335, 336, 338, 642
644, 656, 657, 658
Johannes I, 84, 86, 87
336, 337, 339
352, 354, 418
419, 438, 487
465, 615, 617
620, 730, 759
Johannes Mattes I, 398
Johannes Peter I, 686
Jnº Lud. I, 756
John Peter I, 436
Joseph Herman
(Johan) I, 89, 91, 92
Lodwich (Ludnᵏ) I, 170, 171, 173
Lorens I, 169, 171, 172
Magdalena I, 189
II, 110
Margaretha II, 54
Maria Johanna II, 59
Martin I, 296, 298, 299, 706
Mathias (Matheas) I, 402, 581
581, 584
Michael (Michel) I, 258, 260, 263
686, 696

Migler I, 118
Nicolaus (Nicholas) I, 415, 735
Peter (Petter) I, 266, 269, 272
283, 284, 285
412, 415, 629
632, 635, 736
II, 30, 138
Philip I, 622, 624, 626
Philip Peter I, 402
Rudolph I, 303
Simon II, 161
Stinkee (read Trinka) I, 28
Theobald I, 488
Velten (Felte) I, 27, 29, 30,
258, 260, 263
Wendel I, 415
Wilhelm (Willem,
Wm.) I, 569, 571, 572
629, 632, 635
684, 738, 744
Wilhelm Jost
(Willm Yaost) I, 282, 284, 285
Wilhelm Ludwig I, 305, 306
BECKERBACH
Jacob II, 113
BECKET
Jacob de Harts II, 135
BECKLEY (BEGLY, BEYBY,
BECKLY)
Christian I, 317
Daniel (John
Daniel) I, 317, 318, 319
Godlieb I, 450
BECKLIN (BÖCKLE, BOCKLY,
BÄCKLE, BÄCKHLE, BERKLY)
Barbara I, 60, 61
Christoph I, 59, 63, 64
Hans Jacob I, 59, 63, 64
Henrich I, 61
Kathrina I, 61
Matteus (Mathias) I, 59, 63, 64
Ullrich I, 59, 63, 64
BECKLING
Catharine II, 197
Maria II, 197
BECKMAN
Johannes I, 733
BED
Henry I, 503
BEDANE
—— II, 81
BEDERRI (PEDRE)
Johann Bern (Bernhardt,
Johan Barnard) I, 257, 260, 262
BEDINGER
Abr. II, 178
BEDSHELLER
John II, 103

BEDTLOF
Heinz II, 61
BEECH
Joh[n] Samuel II, 111
BEEGE (BEEK)
Jacob I, 383, 385
BEEK
Crom Vonder II, 61
William Van II, 196
BEEN (BAINE)
Hendrick I, 237
Rudolf I, 13, 14
BEENIGER (PINEGAR, BENNE-
GAR)
Martin I, 265, 268, 271
BEENSLY
Jacob I, 432
BEER (BARE)
Abraham I, 167, 168
Georg I, 97
Hans Ulrich I, 97, 98, 99
Johannes I, 467, 741
Peter I, 307
(*See also* BEHR and BER)
BEERENDS
Barend II, 135
BEERESTEEN
M[r] II, 130
BEERETT *see* BERRET
BEERGER *see* BERGER
BEESSEL
Wendal I, 493
BEETEL
Andreas I, 96
BEGARI (BEGGARI, PECKARY)
Vinsintzius (Vincent) I, 512, 514, 515
BEGENER
John II, 117
BEGER
Jabez I, 421
BEGNER
Heinrich Friedrich II, 183
BEGTEL
Hans Jerg I, 347
BEGTHOLT
Phillips I, 430
BEGTOLL
Dirck I, 17
BEHELING
Johan Jacob I, 750
BEHL
Leonhart I, 476
BEHLER (BELER)
Conrad I, 420
John Michael I, 305, 306
Vallentin I, 420
BEHLERDT (BEELERTH)
Johan Jacob I, 59, 63, 64

BEHN (BEHEN, BOHM)
  Conrad (Coneradt) I, 71, 75, 77
  Johan Jacob II, 79
  Johannes I, 57, 58
  Katharine I, 72
  Maria Christiana I, 74
BEHR
  Jacob I, 449, 686, 704
  Martin I, 707
  Philipp I, 707
  Samuel I, 14, 704
BEHRINGER (BERINGER, BERN-
  EGER, BERNIGER)
  Elias I, 244, 245
  Hans Georg
    (Yerick) I, 236, 238, 239
  Heinrich I, 443
  Paulus I, 346
  Stephen (Steffann) I, 237, 238, 239
BEHSE (BESEN)
  Jobst Hinrich I, 516, 518, 519
BEICHEL (BEICHGEL)
  Jost I, 661, 663, 664
BEIER (BEYER)
  Andreas I, 46, 47
  Catrina I, 44
  Christoff (Christophel) I, 43, 46
  Hendrick I, 44
  Jacob I, 734
  Jerick I, 44
  Johann Philip
    (Johann Phipp) I, 43, 46, 47
    335, 336, 338
  Margarite I, 44
  Maria I, 44
  (*See also* BEYER)
BEIGEL
  Bernhard II, 97
  Hans Jerik I, 20
  Jacob I, 20
  Jurgen Henrich II, 97
  Maria Eliz. II, 97
BEIL
  Balser I, 179, 181, 183
  Johan Henrich I, 496
BEILER (BILER, PILER)
  Anna I, 190
  Barbara I, 190
  Christopher I, 190
  Elizabeth I, 190
  Ferona I, 190
  Jacob I, 188, 192, 193
  Maria I, 190
  Vincent I, 248, 249, 250
BEILSTEIN
  Jnº Geo. I, 723
BEIMBRECHT
  Friedr. Wilhelm II, 205

BEINARDE
  Carl Jacob II, 125
BEINARSECK
  Joseph II, 200
BEINDER
  Hans Adam I, 8
BEINN
  Christophel I, 752
BEIRITSCH
  Peter I, 705
BEIRT
  Joh. II, 118
BEISBEKER
  Johan I, 401
BEISE
  Henery II, 196
BEISEL (BEISELL, BEISSEL)
  Barbella I, 109
  Gerg Petter I, 390
  Hans Jacob I, 109
  Hans Peter
    (Peter) I, 106, 109, 110, 112
  Johann Pätter I, 416
  Nickolaus I, 396
  Peter I, 482
  Susannah I, 107
BEISER
  Jacob I, 363
BEITELMAN (BEIDELMAN, BEY-
  DELMAN, BYDLEMAN, BEY-
  DELMANN, MEIDELMAN)
  Dettrich (Titrick) I, 31, 33, 34
  Elias (Ellias) I, 31, 33, 34
  Felden (Feld. Velde) I, 31, 33, 34
BEITENMAN (BEITTENMAN)
  Georg Friederigh I, 443
  Hans Jerg I, 443
  Johan Jacob I, 443
BEITLER
  Dorothea I, 139
BEITRATT (BEITRAT, BIEDERT)
  Hans Jacob I, 162, 164, 166
BEITTEL
  Jacob I, 488
BEITZ
  Diebolt I, 702
BEITZEL (BELTZER, BELTZEER,
  BEIZEL)
  Catherine II, 85
  H. II, 141
  Jean Henry II, 85
  Johan Henrich I, 382
  Johannes I, 188, 191, 193
  Maria Magdalena I, 189
  Marie Catherine II, 85
BEK, BEKH *see* BECK
BEKER *see* BECKER
BEKING
  Friedrich II, 79

BEKKENBACH
  Rebecca   II, 112
BEKRIN *see* BECKER
BELER
  Francis   I, 710
BELERTH
  Maria   I, 60
BELIS (LIES, PUTES)
  Johann Konrad
    (Conrad)   I, 559, 561, 563
BELITS (BELITZ)
  Larance (Lorentz)   I, 20, 21
BELK
  Jn°   II, 75
BELL
  Henericus   I, 7
  Johanna   II, 69
BELLA
  Antoni   II, 3
BELLE (BELLY)
  John (Pier Jean)   I, 593, 595
BELLER
  Christian   I, 62
BELLEVIE
  ——   II, 81
BELLEYARDE
  ——   II, 80
BELLMAN (BEELMAN)
  Jurgen Died^ch   II, 139
  Melchior (Mellcher) I, 227, 229, 231
BELOU
  Frederick   II, 182
BELSCHER (BLESSER)
  Michel (Michael)   I, 35, 36
BELSNER (BELSER, PELTZNER)
  Simon   I, 96, 98
BELTENTORFFER
  Jacob   I, 382
BELTYS
  J. H.   II, 141
BELTZ (BELZ, PELZ, PELTZ)
  Anne Elisabeth   II, 85
  C. Adam   II, 156
  George   II, 85
  Georg Michael   I, 489
  Herman   I, 391
  Jean   II, 85
  Johan Jacob   I, 489
  Johann (John)   I, 589, 590
  Johann Michael   I, 736
  Johan Petter (Peter) I, 556, 557, 558
  Krafft   II, 85
  Sophie   II, 85
  (*See also* PELTZ)
BELZAN
  ——   II, 80
BELZHUBER
  Melcher   I, 490

BEMANT
  Antonello   II, 183
BEMER
  Christ^n   I, 676
  Hendrick   I, 676
  Johannes   I, 676
  Peter   I, 676
BENADE
  Andrew   II, 78
  ——   II, 58
BENALD
  Justina   II, 36
BENCE
  Andrices   I, 286
BENCK (BINCK, PINCK)
  Johann Philib (Johann
    Philibbus, John
    Philip)   I, 297, 298, 299
BENCKLER
  Johann Jacob   I, 716
BENCKNER
  Leonhard   I, 691
BENDER (BENDTER, BENTER,
    PAINTER, BINDDER)
  Ambrosius   I, 414
  Bastian   I, 703
  Caterina   I, 28
  Christian   II, 79
  Conradt   I, 446
  Elias Nickel (Elias
    Nicholas)   I, 222, 223, 225
  Eve   I, 40
  Friedrich   I, 420
  Georg (George,
    Jerg)   I, 59, 63, 65, 227
                    229, 231, 684, 703
  Georg Adam   I, 96, 97, 98
  Georg Michael
    (Jurig Mich.) I, 265, 268, 271
  Hans Adam   I, 97, 98
  Hans Gorg (Hans Jerg) I, 39, 41, 42
  Hans Jacob   I, 12, 13
  Hanns Philip   I, 437
  Hendrick   II, 126
  Henry   I, 724
  Henry, Junr   I, 404
  Hisbert (read Gisbert) I, 27, 29, 30
  J. Nickolas   I, 500
  Jacob   I, 222, 223, 225
                              II, 99
  Jacob Nicklas   I, 222, 223, 225
  Jan David   II, 77
  Johan   I, 406
  Johan Adam (John
    Adam)   I, 280, 281, 282
  Johan Beder   I, 446
  Johann Conrad (Con-
    rad)   I, 615, 617, 619
  Johan Georg, Junr   I, 459

Johan Henrich I, 708
Johann Ludwig I, 503
Johan Melcher I, 359
Johan Petter I, 446
Johann Philib (Johan
Philip) I, 642, 644
Johann Wilhelm I, 704
Johannes (Johanes) I, 340, 341, 342
347, 404, 459
615, 617, 619, 703
Johannes, Jr. I, 340, 341, 342
Joseph I, 458
Katrina (Kathrina) I, 60, 61
Leonhardt I, 488
Ludewig I, 464
Maria I, 61
Martin I, 457, 642, 644
Nicolaus I, 627, 630, 634
Paulus I, 382
Peter (Joan Peter) I, 311, 312, 313
Rupertus I, 322
Sebastian I, 688
Valentin I, 423
BENDERS
Christof I, 19
BENDIG
Andrew II, 185
BENDLER (BEUDLER, BINDLER)
Christian I, 59, 63, 65
Elisabeth I, 61
John I, 59, 63, 64
Susanna I, 61
BENECKE
Carl, Senior II, 61
Julius, Junior II, 61
BENEDICT (BENDICT, BENE-
CICK)
Christ II, 71
Ditterich (Titrick) I, 209, 211
Johan Jacob I, 330
Melchior I, 413
BENEN
Jacob II, 97
BENER
Christoff I, 426
Ludwich I, 706
BENESET (BASKER, BUKOO)
Johanes (Johannes) I, 596, 598, 599
BENFER
Ann Lise II, 180
Friederich II, 149
Johannes II, 180
Johann Gorg I, 710
John II, 180
John Chr. II, 180
Maria Elizabeth II, 149
BENGEL (BINGEL)
Andereas I, 620, 622, 624
Daniel I, 20

Johann Adam I, 700
Johan Daniel (Daniel) I, 20, 21
Johann Henrich I, 329
Joh. Lenhart
(Leonard) I, 627, 630, 633
BENGTEL
Barbra I, 117
BENI
Abraham I, 7
BENIGHOFF (BENNIGHOFF)
Ehrenfried I, 461
Johan Philipp I, 461
Johann Vallentin I, 461
BENISH
J. Christian I, 480
BENIX (PANIX)
Henry (John Henry) I, 569, 571, 573
BENJAMIN
——— II, 49
BENJWORT
Jan Dirk II, 119
BENKER
Xtopher I, 17
BENNECH
Credleless I, 85
Merreless I, 85
BENNER (BENDER)
Bastian (Bastyan,
Bestian) I, 237, 238, 240
Carl I, 737
Dangel (Daniel) I, 425, 710
Hans Gerg I, 736
Hennerich I, 424
Herman Diederich II, 55
J. G. L. II, 22
Jacob II, 181
Johan Christ I, 467
Johan Peter I, 433
Johan Philib I, 436
Johannes I, 340, 341, 342, 424
646, 647, 710, 735, 737
Lutwig I, 424
Marten I, 737
Peder (Peter) I, 237, 239, 240
BENNITES
Simon I, 85
BENNZ see BENTZ
BENOIT
Humber I, 405
BENS, BENSCH see BENTZ
BENSE
Johanes I, 17
BENSINGER
Anthon I, 346
BENSLE
Johann Carle I, 452
BENTE
Lodowick I, 16

BENTELL
  Anna Maria   II, 149
  Fredericka   II, 149
  George   II, 149
  Israel   II, 149
  Johanna   II, 149
  John Friderich   II, 149
  John George   II, 149
  Katharine   II, 149
  Katy   II, 149
BENTER *see* BENDER
BENTFERN
  Catharine   II, 85
BENTHIN
  Joachim Valentine   II, 93
BENTZ (BENCE, BENS, BENNZ, BENZ, PENS, PENTS)
  Antreas   I, 287, 288
  Carl   I, 500
  Catharine   II, 168
  Christian   I, 421
  Elizabeth   II, 168
  Gorg Jacob (Ereh Jocb)   I, 195, 196, 197
  Heinr.   II, 118
  Jacob   I, 407
          II, 168
  Jeorg Heinrich   I, 500
  Jorg   I, 407
  Johann Christ.   I, 569, 570, 572
  Johann Christoph   I, 480
  Johann Davyd   I, 740
  Johann Ludwig   I, 407
  Johann Philipp (Philip)   I, 227, 229, 231
  Johannes (Johanes)   I, 89, 90, 92, 466, 744
  John   II, 168
  John G.   II, 168
  Lenhart   I, 96, 98
  Michael (Mickell)   I, 88, 90, 91
  Philip   II, 104
  Verena   I, 148
BENTZIGER
  Bartlyme   I, 428
BENTZINGER
  Joseph   I, 365
BENZENHAFER
  C. Cath.   II, 201
BENZENHOFER
  Jacob   II, 154
BER (BARR, BERR)
  Daniel   I, 397
  Gorg Wilhelm   I, 744
  Hans Conratt (Hans Conradt)   I, 596, 598, 599
  Hans Jorg   I, 725
  Hans Michell (Hans Mich[1])   I, 596, 598, 599

  Johann Jacob   I, 418
  Johannes   I, 397, 596, 598, 599
  Nickel   I, 725
  Peter   I, 440
  (*See also* BÄR, BARE and BEHR)
BERARD
  ———   II, 81
BERBER
  Joseph Wilh.   II, 140
BERBERICH (BERGERING)
  Johann Philipp   I, 513, 514, 515
BERBISDORFF, von
  Georg Friedrich   I, 21
BERCH
  Bernhart   I, 439
BERCHELBACH
  Jost   II, 128
BERCHER
  Jacob   I, 434
BERCKEL
  Jacob   I, 690
BERCKELBACH
  Johann George   I, 755
BERCKHÄUSER (BERKHEISER, BERKSHEIRS)
  Wilhelm   I, 556, 557, 558
BERCKHYSER (PERHAWSER, PERKHAYSER)
  Johanes (Johannes Ties)   I, 277, 278, 279
BERDSCH
  Bal.   II, 179
BERENGER
  Jos.   II, 15
BERENSTECHER
  Andreas   I, 462
BERFUS
  John Jogen   I, 505
BERG
  Andres   I, 448
  Ernst   I, 732
  Fr.   II, 116
  G.   II, 136
  Jacob   I, 448, 727
  Joh.   II, 119
  Joh. Wilhelm   II, 190
  Johann Fillib   I, 754
  John   I, 697
  Wilh.   II, 196
  (*See also* BERGH)
BERGDOLL
  Isaac   I, 741
BERGEL (PERTZELL, BERKEL)
  H. Jacob (Hans Jacob)   I, 258, 260, 263
BERGEN
  Joh. v.   II, 139
BERGENSLOTT
  Jerig Frederick   I, 20

BERGER (BEERGER, BERGHER)
Ab^rm II, 101
Andreas I, 500
Anna Maria II, 129
Barbara II, 133
Benedict II, 133
Caspar (Casper) I, 199, 201, 203
Christoph
(Christoff) I, 236, 238, 239
Conrad II, 129
Elisabeth II, 133
Georg I, 62, 497
Hans I, 428
Jacob I, 546, 548, 550
Jaque (Jaques) I, 526, 527, 529
Joerg Wilhelm I, 352, 354
Johann Adam I, 432
Johan Arnt (John
Adam) I, 672, 673, 674
Johan Christian I, 352, 354
Johann Friedrich I, 502
Johann Jost I, 642, 644
Johan Philippus I, 467
Johannes (Johan) I, 205, 207, 208
Kasper I, 739
Matheas I, 439
Michael (Michel) I, 440
II, 129
Peter I, 279, 280, 281
Sybilla II, 129
BERGERHOFF
Johannes I, 322
BERGES (BARTJES)
Michel (Michael) I, 378, 380, 381
BERGH
Frederick D. I, 20
Leonerd I, 62
Peter Denk I, 20
Veltin I, 62
BERGHAN
J. Friederich I, 505
BERGHEIMER (BERGHERMER)
Salome I, 61
Susanna I, 61
Wilhelm (Wihlm) I, 59, 63, 65
BERGHEISER
Anne Elizabeth II, 191
John Jacob II, 191
Peter II, 191
BERGHER see BERGER
BERGMAN (BERGMANN, BARG-
MAN, BERKMAN)
Balthasar I, 621, 623, 625
Carl Anton I, 455
Christian I, 227, 229, 231, 690
Christohf I, 324, 325, 327
Friedrich I, 685, 759
Jacob I, 685
Johan Gorg

(Georick) I, 216, 218, 219
Johann Michael I, 690
John Gottlieb II, 54
—— II, 122
(See also BERKMAN)
BERGS
Christina II, 59
BERGSTRÖSSER (BERGSTROS-
SER, BERGSTRASER)
Johann Görg (Johann
Gorg, Gerich) I, 43, 45, 46
BERGTOLD (BERGTOHLT, BERG-
TOLL)
Anna I, 117
Elisabet I, 117
Josef I, 396
BERGTOLL (BARTOL)
Peter I, 384, 386
(See also BERGDOLL)
BERHARD
Fred^k II, 16
BERIAN
Maria Margrat I, 241
BERIE (BEEREY, PUREY)
Joseph I, 257, 260, 262
BERINGER (BERRINGER, BER-
IGER)
Bartholomeus
(Bartholomew) I, 629, 633, 636
H. Nicklas I, 481
Nicklaus I, 540, 542, 544
Peter (Petter) I, 457, 627, 630, 634
BERKEL (BERKLEY, BIRKEL)
Anna Barbara I, 131
Barbara I, 132
Catherina I, 132
Dorothea I, 131
Hans Jacob I, 131, 132, 133, 134
Jacob I, 131, 133, 134
Maria Magdalena I, 132
BERKELBACH
Anna Maria II, 36
Jacop II, 36
BERKENHAUER
Joh. II, 118
BERKMAN
Christian II, 103
John Coenraied II, 76
Sophiea II, 76
BERLER
Jan II, 78
BERLETT (BARLET, BARLIT)
Anna I, 79
Johan Wolff
(Hans Woolf) I, 79, 82, 83
BERLIB
Andreas I, 469
BERMES (BÄRMAS)
Johannes I, 336, 337, 339

BERN (BARND)
Georg Augustus
(Augustus) I, 275, 276
Peter I, 376, 377
BERNAHT (read BERNHART)
Hans Jacob I, 451
BERNARD (BERNART)
Conrad I, 758
Jacob I, 609, 610, 612
Joseph I, 493
(*See also* BERNHARD)
BERNAUER
Johan Jacob I, 437
BERNDHEISELL
John I, 60, 64, 65
Wendel I, 60, 64, 65
BERNDT
Jacob I, 714
BERNE (BEARNE)
Wilhelm I, 88, 90, 92
BERNER
Elizabeth II, 97
Emericus II, 97
Johan Wilhelm II, 97
Maria Anna II, 97
Maria Catharina II, 97
BERNET
Nich^s I, 727
BERNGARDT (BERNGARDTS,
BARNGARDT, BERGANT)
Hans Peter
(Hans Pieter) I, 188, 191, 193
BERNHARD (BERNHARDT, BERN-
HART, BERNHARTT)
Adam I, 488, 725
II, 134
Andereas II, 133
Anna Maria II, 8
Carol (Carral) I, 521, 524
Caspar I, 702
Catharina II, 134
Christian I, 404, 473
Christopher I, 205, 207, 208
Dangel I, 752
Georg I, 714
Hans Heinrich I, 13
Henrich (Henry) I, 293, 295, 296
Jacob I, 293, 294, 295, 667, 669, 671
686; II, 133
Johann Georg I, 390
Johann Ludwik (Ludwig) I, 643, 645
Johann Petter (Jn° Peter)
I, 296, 298
299, 643, 645
Johan Stefan
(Johann Staffen) I, 185, 186, 187
Johann Thomas I, 593, 595
Johannes I, 480, 492
Joseph I, 491

Jurg (Georg) I, 356
Martin I, 399
Matheis I, 432
Nicklas I, 487
Philip II, 11
Teoboldus I, 501
Ulrich I, 451
Wendel I, 714
Wilhelm I, 702
BERNHARDI
Christian I, 439
BERNINGER
Henrich I, 701
Nicklas I, 444
BERNÖLLER
Henrich I, 685
BERNTHEUSEL
Johann Martin I, 391
BERNTZ (BARNTZ)
Johannes (Johanis) I, 198, 200, 202
BEROTH (PARROTT)
Frantz Luthwig I, 198, 200, 202
BERRET (BEERETT, BERETH)
Anna I, 61
Casper I, 62
Henrich I, 60, 64, 65
Henry I, 62
Johanes I, 8
John I, 62
BERRINGER *see* BERINGER
BERSCH
Johann Andres I, 455
Johannes I, 410
BERSCHMAN
Claus I, 391
BERSTIEND
John II, 32
BERSTROSER (read BERGSTROS-
SER)
Adam II, 61
BERSY
Johann Jacob I, 482
Johann Ludwig I, 482
BERT
Jan. De II, 118
BERTELS
H. C. II, 143
BERTERAM
Dort II, 101
Margreta II, 101
Whilhelm II, 101
(*See also* BERTRAM)
BERTHOLT
Gebhart I, 493
BERTHOLT de (BERTHOLD,
BARTHOLD)
Johann Philipp
(Johan) I, 185, 186, 187
Thomas I, 444

BERTHOUD
Mad^m II, 72
Mons. II, 72
BERTRAM
Anna Christ^a II, 41
Johan Casp^r II, 41
BERTSCH (BERTSH)
Balthas I, 742
George II, 155
Hans Jurg I, 470
Jacob I, 422, 677, 678, 680
Johan Cunrad I, 714
BERTSCHI
Issac I, 702
BERY
Christoph I, 472
BERZY
Her. II, 50
Hinrigette II, 50
BESA (BISSA)
Philip I, 243, 244, 245
BESCHER
Matdes I, 382
BESCHLER
Christian Ernst I, 690
BESER *see* BESSER
BESIKER (BESSAKER)
Jacob I, 78, 81, 82
BESINGER (BESENAR)
Andreas (Andrias) I, 116, 120, 121
BESMER
Johann Christoph I, 426
BESSAN
Margarethe II, 179
BESSENER
Fried. II, 133
Hans II, 133
Matthes II, 133
BESSER (BESER, BISSER)
Benddeck
(Conrade, Bendeck) I, 264, 268, 271
Christoff I, 97, 98, 99
Simon I, 97
BESSERER (BESERER, BASSORER)
Johann Christoph
(Joan Crist) I, 287, 288, 289
BESSINGER
Phi. Jacob I, 730
BEST
Johann Georg
(Hans Yerrick) I, 652, 653
Johann Mates I, 722
Johannes I, 734
Willhelm
(William, Willm) I, 199, 201, 203
BESTELLS
B. II, 141
BESTENHOLTZ (RESTENHOLTZ)
Jacob I, 249, 250

BETER, BETHER *see* PETER
BETHMANN
Johann Ludwig I, 758
BETIS
Conrad I, 684
BETIST
T. M. II, 125
BETKER
Walter II, 92
BETLER (PEPLER)
Freiderich
(Fredrick) I, 656, 657, 659
BETSCHEN (PETER)
Caspar (Casper) I, 55, 56, 57
BETSCHLER (BEDSHELLER)
Johannes (John) I, 227, 229, 231
BETTER
H. II, 136
BETTINGER (BEDINGER)
Johan Martin I, 546, 547, 549
BETTS
Conraad II, 59
Elizabeth II, 59
BETZ
Christian I, 435
Dorothea II, 28
Friedrich
(Frederick) I, 621, 623, 625
Hans Jerg (Jerge) I, 372, 453
Jerg Friedrich I, 741
J. J. II, 141
Johan II, 28
Johann Christjan I, 706
Johann Daniel I, 458
Johan Friedrich I, 741
Johann Georg
(George) I, 556, 557, 558
Johann Jost I, 743
Johann Ludwig I, 691
Johann Urbahn I, 691
Johann Willhelm
(Willm) I, 283, 284, 285
Martin I, 489
Matthias I, 372
Wilhelm II, 28
BETZALT
Friderich I, 418
BETZEL (BETZELL, PETZELL)
Gottfriedt (Godfried) I, 213, 215
BETZER (PESSERT)
Haman I, 279, 281, 282
BETZLER
Georg I, 439
BEUEL (BEIEL, BEUELL)
Simo (Siemonis) I, 143, 145, 146
BEUERLE (BEYERLY)
Johann Phillip (Philip) I, 649, 651
BEUGEL
Mattheis I, 489

BEUL
 Michel I, 395
BEULOW
 Carol II, 103
 Didrich II, 103
BEUM
 Berteram I, 478
 John II, 55
 John Adam II, 56
 Mrs. II, 55
BEUSCHEL
 Christⁿ Phillip II, 111
BEUSCHLEIN (BEUSCHLEINN, BIESLIN)
 Andres (Andreas) I, 409, 627, 630
  634
 Casper I, 503
BEÜSER
 Friderich I, 748
BEUST
 Anna Maria I, 144
BEUTEL
 John II, 69
BEUTEMULLER
 —— II, 53
BEUTHLER (BEUTTLER)
 Hans Christ I, 394
 Hans Uhlerik I, 482
BEVER see BEWER
BEWER (BEVER, BEEBER, BEWYR)
 Abraham II, 70
 Anna II, 70
 Christina I, 103
 Dorothy I, 103
 Gerg I, 451
 Jacob I, 103, 724
 Lawrence
  (Lorentz, Lowrens) I, 264, 268, 271
 Margaretha II, 70
 Peter II, 70
BEY
 John II, 145
 Lunᵈ II, 145
BEYDELER (BADLER)
 Johannes (Jan) I, 14, 15
BEYER (BAYER, BIER)
 Albinus (Albert) I, 169, 170, 172
 Andreas (Anderas) I, 43, 46, 47, 365
 Anna I, 73, 74
  II, 7
 Anna Rosina I, 49
 Balthazar II, 7
 Barbara II, 7
 Caspar I, 736
 Cathrina (Katharina) I, 72, 123
  II, 7
 Christ. Selma I, 50
 Deowalt (Ewald) I, 156, 159, 161

 Doria II, 7
 Dorothea I, 50
 Elizabeth I, 50
 Friedrich I, 741
 George I, 366
 Hans Melchior I, 155, 158, 160
 Hans Michael I, 428
 Jacob I, 21, 50, 237, 238
  239, 297, 298
 Jan Jacob I, 199, 201, 203
 Johan Nicklas I, 294, 295
 Joh. Nicolaus II, 139
 Johann Adam (Hans Adam) I, 47,
  51, 53, 122, 125, 126
 Johann Christoph I, 72, 76, 77
 Johann Georg I, 195, 196, 197
 Johann Jacob I, 47, 51, 53,
  335, 336, 338
 Johann Leonhard I, 310, 311, 312
 Johannes (Johanes) I, 217, 219, 220
  256, 259, 261, 429
 Johannes Jacobus I, 478
 John II, 7, 55
 John Philip I, 394
 Joseph I, 48, 52, 53
 Leonhardt I, 714
 Magdalene II, 7
 Margaret I, 124; II, 7
 Maria I, 44
 Molly II, 7
 Nicklas
  (Nicholas, Nickel) I, 277, 278, 279
  425
  II, 7
 Peter (Petter) I, 170, 171, 173
 Philip I, 198, 200, 202
 Philip, Junʳ I, 199, 201, 203
 Stephan I, 403
 Susan I, 68
 Valentine
  (Vallenthin, Faldin) I, 71, 75, 77
  759; II, 55
 Walles I, 471
 William II, 7
BEYERLE (BEYERLIE, BEYERLY)
 Andres (Adreas) I, 246, 247, 248
 Dieter I, 728
 Frederick I, 760
 Jacob I, 476, 498
 Johann Jacob I, 97, 98, 99
  736
 Johann Michael I, 36, 37
 Johannes I, 683
BEYERMEISTER
 Johann Friedrich I, 693
BEYERSDORFF
 Nicolaus II, 139
BEYFUSZ
 Kaufᵐ Isaac II, 107

BEYGHART
Josep   I, 409
BEYL (BIELLE)
Henry   I, 367, 368
Johan Peter   I, 365
Johanes (Johannes)   I, 628, 631, 634
Rudolff   I, 9
BEYLSTEIN
Johann Wendel   I, 464
BEYRER
Johann Conrad   I, 454
Johann Friderich   I, 706
Joseph   I, 506
BEYSELY
Jacob   I, 365
BEYTENMAN
Hans Jerg   I, 443
BEYTER
Hans   II, 50
——   II, 51
BEZENGREEN
Eliza   I, 80
BEZNER (BESTNER)
Samuel   I, 585, 586, 587
BIBELING
Marg^t II, 15
BIBER
Anthoni   I, 406
BIBIGHAUS (BIBIGHAUSE, BE-
BIGHAUSEN)
Daniell (Dangel)   I, 237, 239, 240
Johan Jost (John Yost)   I, 367, 369
Johannes   I, 731
Jurig (Georg)   I, 237
BIBLE
Joseph   II, 135
BIBLER
Johann Frantz   I, 457
BIBR
Johannes   I, 506
BICHEL (BIALLE)
Eberhart   I, 439
Ludwig Joseph
(Loadwick)   I, 240, 242, 243
William   II, 13
BICHER (BIGCHER, PIGGER)
Peter (Petter)   I, 615, 617, 619
BICHLER
Fillib   I, 358
Jacob   I, 358
Simmon   I, 710
BICK (PICK)
Johann Georg   I, 532, 533, 535
BICKEL (BICKELL, PICKEL,
PICKLE)
Christoph   I, 94, 95, 96
Georg Felte
(Jerricks Felder)   I, 94, 95, 96
Hans   I, 364

Johan Philip   I, 94
BICKENBACK
Benjamin   II, 205
BICKES (PIECK)
Johann Georg   I, 234, 235, 236
BICKRER see BRICKER
BIDELYOUNG
Philip   I, 496
BIDERMAN
Hans Casp.
(Hans Casper)   I, 582, 583, 584
BIDLE
Anna Maria   II, 166
Johan   II, 166
Johannas   II, 166
BIDMER
Christian   I, 448
BIEBEL
Hans Adam   I, 449
BIEBER (BEABER)
Andereas   I, 403
Dewald   I, 357
Felden   I, 724
Hans Nickel   I, 406
Henrich   I, 463
Jacob   I, 403, 406
Jerg   I, 357
Johann   I, 357
Johannes   I, 463
Michel   I, 463
Nicol   I, 724
Ulrick   I, 700
(*See also* BIBER *and* BIEWER)
BIEBL
Stephen   II, 67
BIEBLER
Friederich   I, 457
BIECHELAAR
Johan Jacob Vander   II, 78
BIECHELER (PIGELER)
Johannes (Jn⁰)   I, 637, 639, 641
BIECHTELER
George   II, 155
BIEDEKOPP (KAPP)
Wilhelm
(William Peter)   I, 591, 592, 594
BIEDENBÜNDER (BENER)
Johannes
(Johannes Peter)   I, 383, 385
BIEDIGER (BEIDINGER, BUI-
DICER)
Hans Adam   I, 169, 171, 172
Peder (Peter)   I, 169, 171, 172
BIEDMAN
Nicklas   I, 402
BIEG
Iohann Philip   I, 472
Stephann   I, 472

BIEGBIE
  Geo.   I, 317
BIEGEL
  Wilhelm Henrich   I, 697
BIEHL (BIEHEL, BUHL)
  Daniel   I, 629, 635
  Gurg Wendel   I, 21
  Hans Jacob   I, 21
  Johann Philip   I, 390
  Petter (Peter)   I, 628, 632, 635
BIEHLER (BIELLER)
  Anthony   I, 213, 214, 216
  Paul   I, 701
BIEHN
  Johann Conrad   I, 425
  Johannes
    (Johanes, Hannis) I, 264, 267, 270
BIEL
  Johannes Lutwig   I, 435
  Johannes Wilhelm   I, 435
BIELER (MILLER, BIELDER)
  Davit (David)   I, 263, 267, 270
  Johann Mardin
    (Hans Marⁿ)   I, 264, 267, 270
  Michel   I, 391
BIELEVELD
  Heinrich   II, 68
BIELFIELD
  Mʳ ――――   II, 89
BIEN
  Petter   I, 488
BIENER
  Caspar   I, 683
BIENTELHEIMER
  Conradh Friederich   I, 702
BIER
  George   I, 502
  Peter   I, 377, 378, 379, 381
BIERBAUER
  Henrich   I, 488
BIEREN
  Dieterich, von   I, 505
BIERENLOVEN
  Matheus   II, 20
BIERKENBEYL
  Christian   I, 676
BIERMAN
  Anna Sophᵃ   II, 29
BIERR
  Hans Nickel   I, 697
BIETCH
  Davit   I, 464
  Michael   I, 464
BIETIGHOFFER
  Johan Philipp   I, 491
BIETTEL (BIETEL)
  Nicolaus   I, 179, 181, 183
BIEWER read BIEBER

BIGHT
  Hans Georg   I, 508
BIGLER (BIEGLER)
  George   I, 474
  Hans Jacob   I, 449
  Johannes   I, 423
  Martin   I, 474
  Marx (Marcus)   I, 127, 129, 130
  Michel   I, 292, 293
BIHL (BAYLE)
  Michel (Michael)   I, 386, 388, 389
BIHLMEIER (BEYLMEYER)
  Johann Leonhardt
    (Leonard)   I, 48, 52, 54
BIKER (BRICKER)
  Christan   I, 80
  Eliz.   I, 81
  Peter   I, 79, 82, 83
BIKLER
  Christian   I, 15
BILDERBACK
  Joh.   II, 97
  Sophia   II, 97
BILDHOUS
  John Jacob   I, 357
BILDMAN
  Christoph Samuel   I, 390
  Jacob   I, 479
BILE
  Michel   I, 445
BILFINGER (BELFINGER)
  Peter   I, 585, 587, 588
BILGER
  Johan Ludwig   I, 469
BILLER
  Christoff Fridrich   I, 499
BILLHEIMER (BILDHEYMER)
  Hans Michael   I, 646, 647
  Johanes   I, 438
BILLHOCH
  Joh. Albert   II, 139
BILLIGER (PELIGER)
  Daniel   I, 93, 94, 95
  Johann Friderich   I, 463
BILLING
  Abraham   I, 482
  Siegfried   I, 479
BILLINGESLEBEN (BILSINGLE-
    BEN)
  Johan Heinrich   I, 509, 510, 511
BILLMAN (BIELMAN, BULLMAN,
    PULLMAN)
  Christian (Hans) I, 246, 247, 248
  Hanns Davidt
    (David)   I, 162, 164, 165
  H. Dewalt   I, 484
BIMMER (BAMAN)
  Thomas   I, 627, 630, 634

BIMMERSDÖRFFER
Johannes   I, 434
BINCE
Frants Joseph   II, 125
BINCKLI (BINCKLIE)
Jacob   I, 744
Johann Peter   I, 447
BINCKLY *see* PINCKLEY
BINDEL
Friedrich   II, 184
BINDENBERGER
Conrad   I, 761
BINDER
Albrecht Friedrich   I, 358
Hans Jacob   I, 446
Hans Jerg   I, 328
Jacob   I, 328
Johann Friedrich   I, 446
Johann Philipp   I, 358
Marttin   I, 428
Morritz   II, 184
Mose (Mosi)   I, 327, 329
BINDSCHÄDLER (BINDSCHED-
LER)
Casper   I, 344, 345
Susanna   I, 147
BINENGER
Anna Maria   II, 164
Frederica   II, 164
Michael   II, 164
Sabina   II, 164
BINER
Michael   I, 424
BING (BIN)
Anderas (Andres)   I, 198, 201, 202
Jacob   I, 198, 200, 202
Peter   I, 484
BINGEL *see* BENGEL
BINGEMANN
Conrad   II, 134
BINGER
Christian   II, 133
Conrad   II, 133
Hans Jacob   II, 133
Hans Ulrich   II, 133
Johannes   II, 133
Maria   II, 133
BINGLEY (PINGLEY, PINKLEY)
Hans Michel   I, 152, 153, 154
BINGMANN (BINGMAN)
Conrad   I, 698
J. Jost (Joost)   I, 614, 616, 618
BINIGER
Peter   I, 457
BINKLER (BENKELKER)
Johannes   I, 24, 25, 26
BINNER
Johann Adam   I, 501

BINTNAGEL (BINNEAGLE, PINT-
NAGLE)
Johannes   I, 89, 91, 92
BINTZ
Johan Christoffel   I, 692
Jnⁿ Eberhard   I, 649
BINTZEL
Jacob   I, 763
Johannes   I, 391
BIRCK
Johann Gorg   I, 495
BIRCKELBACH (BIRCKELLBACH)
Johann Jost   I, 731
Johannes   II, 79
BIRCKENMEYER (BURGEMEYER)
J. George (Han Geo.) I, 665, 668, 670
BIRCKENSTOCK (PERKER-
STOCKS)
Jost   I, 221, 223, 224
BIRCKER
Andres   I, 423
BIRCKERT (ALBRIGHTBERGER,
BIRKEL, BERKIT)
Johann Friederich Albrecht
(John Fredrick)   I, 652, 654
John Albrecht Henry
(John Albright Hendrick)
   I, 652, 654
BIRCKI
Johann Jacob   I, 707
BIRCKLE
Ludwig   I, 465
BIRD
Joseph   II, 18
BIRGER
Adam   I, 369, 370
BIRHEIM (WIRHIME)
Johan Conradt
(Conrad)   I, 677, 678, 680
BIRKBORCH
Anna Cathᵃ   II, 29
Johan Henrich   II, 29
Johann Joost   II, 29
BIRKELBACH
Johann Georg   I, 755
BIRKENBERG
Abraham   I, 492
BIRKENBEYLY
Gerhart   I, 436
BIRKI
Katherina   I, 49
BIRKINGBEY
Christian   I, 401
BIRKLE
Conrad   II, 191
BIRLE
Wolfgang   I, 97
BIRRO
Martin   I, 450

BIRSON
Hans Philipus I, 405
BIRSTÄDT
Jochem I, 747
BIRSUNG (PEIRSON)
Lorentz (Lowrans) I, 213, 215
BISCHANTZ (PEESHANCE)
Johan Thomas
(Thomas) I, 620, 622, 624
BISCHOFF (BISCHOF, BISHOF, BUSCHOF, BISHOP)
Ann Catherine I, 320
Barbel I, 43
Conrad I, 691
Davidt I, 320, 321, 322
Frantz (Fransz) I, 367, 368
Frantz Michel I, 367, 369
George
(Johannes Jerick) I, 560, 561, 563
Henrich
(Hendrick) I, 106, 110, 112
Jo. Mich. I, 704
Johann Jacob I, 367, 368
Johannes I, 43, 46, 47
(Johann, Johanes) I, 256, 259, 261
373, 374, 375
476
Joseph I, 169, 171, 172
Matheis (Mathes) I, 367, 369
Peter (Petter) I, 290, 291
William (Willem) I, 221, 222, 224
289
BISCHON (BISHON)
Guilliam I, 303
Hans Martin I, 476
BISECKER
Anna Mare I, 80
Conrad I, 365
BISER
Abraham II, 165
Auguste II, 165
Carolina II, 165
Christianna II, 165
Frederica II, 165
Gotlib II, 165
Gottfried II, 165
Johan II, 165
BISH (BESH)
Sebastian (Bastian) I, 185, 186, 187
Theob^d I, 729
BISHON *see* BISCHON
BISHOPBERGER (PISHOPBERGER)
Jacob I, 512, 514, 515
BISS
Johann Gerg I, 716
Nich^s I, 739
BISSACOR (read BISECKER)
Anna Mare I, 80

BISSAHR
Sebastian I, 407
BISSELL
John II, 18
BISSEN
John G. II, 97
BISWANGER
Peter I, 31, 32, 33
BITILION
Abraham I, 474
BITINGER
Andres I, 463
BITSSERKER
Uhllerich I, 434
BITTENBENDER (BENEBENDER)
Christoffel I, 358
Johann Conrath I, 236, 238, 239
BITTER
Johann Jacob I, 462
BITTERLEY (PEATERLY)
Hans Michel (Jacob) I, 275, 276
BITTIG
J. Chas. II, 16
BITTMAN
Johann Philipp I, 701
BITTNER
Casper I, 31, 32, 34
Martin I, 292, 293
BITTORFF (PETORF)
Johann Caspar
(Casper) I, 677, 678, 680
BITZER
Johannes I, 445
Ludwig I, 445
Mattheis I, 496
Michel I, 495
BIZANOR
Jacob I, 80
BLACHER
Nicholas I, 718
BLACK
W^m I, 756
BLACKWELL
Thos. H. II, 6
BLADER
H. Nicklas I, 428
BLADMAN
Christopher I, 331
Hans Ulderick I, 331, 333, 334
BLÄHER
Joh. Geo. II, 179
BLAICH
Christian I, 448
BLANCH (read BLANCK)
Dorothy II, 43
Magdalena II, 43
Margaret II, 43
Peter II, 43
Sophia II, 43

BLANCHARD
Mr.   II, 175
——   II, 81
BLANCKENBERG
John Melchior   I, 718
BLANCKENBILLER (BLANKEN-
BULLER)
Johan Georg
(Jurg)   I, 678, 679, 681
BLANK (BLANCK)
Christian (Cristian) I, 116, 119, 121
473
Conrad   II, 126
Davit (David)   I, 652, 654
Francis   II, 152
Hans   I, 473, 485
Hans Michael   I, 451
Jacob   I, 485, 704
Jerick (George)   I, 546, 547, 549
Nickolas   I, 485
BLANKARD (BLANKART)
Johan Peter   II, 78
Johann Ernst   I, 517, 519, 520
BLANKEIN
Christina   II, 20
BLANKENHEIMER
Elizabeth   II, 20
BLANKENHORN
Friedrich   I, 442
BLASER (BLÄSER)
Anna Barbara   I, 131
Anna Gertruda   I, 131
Anna Margaretha   I, 132
Catherina   I, 132
Christian   I, 130, 133, 134
Hans Jerg (Jorg)   I, 472
Hans Matz   I, 131
Johan Adam   I, 131
Johannes Jacob   I, 435
Maria Magdalena   I, 132
Nicolaus   I, 131
Peter   I, 257, 260, 262
(*See also* BLASSER)
BLASIN
Anna   I, 117
BLASSER (BLASER)
Hans   I, 442
Peter   I, 257, 260, 262
BLATT
Johann Bernhardt   I, 466
BLATTENBERGER (PLATTEN-
BERGER, PLATENBERGER)
Johannes   I, 340, 341, 343
BLATTNER (BLADNER, BLAT-
NER)
Anna Maria   I, 49
Georg Michel   I, 50
Hans Michael
(Michel)   I, 47, 51, 53

Katherina   I, 49
Maria Katherina   I, 49
Michael (Mich.)   I, 265, 268, 271
BLÄTZ (BLITZ)
Andtras (Ands)   I, 589, 590, 591
BLATZER
John Georg   I, 472
BLAUCH
Hans   I, 448
BLAWAMI
Catrina   I, 189
BLECHER
Johan Jost   I, 401, 754
Johann Wienert   I, 484
Johannes (Hannes) I, 666, 668, 670
John Conrad   I, 482
Jost William (Joost
Willem)   I, 237, 239, 240
Wilhelm   I, 666, 668, 670
BLECHOR (read BLECHER)
Andereas   I, 455
BLECK
Fillip   I, 487
BLECKER
Johan Henrich
(Joh. Henry)   I, 613, 616, 618
BLEIBTREU
Friedrich   I, 167, 168
BLEICH (BLEIG)
Hans Michel
(Hans Mich.)   I, 597, 598, 600
Johan Friederick
(Fredrick)   I, 585, 586, 587
BLEICHERODT (KLYKROOT)
Heinrich Christop   I, 527, 528, 530
BLEICKENBACHER (BLEYGEN-
BACHER)
Johan Peter   I, 656, 657, 658
BLEIER (BLYARD)
Hans Atem (Hans
Adam, Jo. Adam.) I, 621, 622, 625
BLEIGESTAUFER
Hans   I, 364
BLEIKER (BLIECKER)
Johann Jacob   I, 546, 547, 549
Johan Jost   I, 675
BLEINIGER
Willhelm   I, 688
BLEISTEIN (BLINSTEIN, PLY-
STAIN)
Abraham (Abm)   I, 609, 611, 613
BLENDS
John Peter   II, 47
BLESCH
Jonas   I, 736
Joseph   I, 716
BLESINGER
Antoni   I, 471

BLESSING (BLESING, BLASS-
INGER)
Jacob   I, 605, 606, 608
                       620, 622, 624
BLEULER (BLEILER)
Caspar   I, 147, 150, 151
Catherine   I, 149
Hs. Hend.   I, 149
Hs. Jacob   I, 149
BLEY
Johanes   I, 429
BLEYMEYER (BLEYMEIER)
Marttin   I, 418
Paulus   I, 442
BLICHER
Hendrick (Hanrich)   I, 47, 51, 53
BLICHLE (BLICKLY)
H. Adam (Adam)   I, 656, 657, 658
BLICKENSTORFFER   (BLICKEN-
STERFFER, BLIECKENSTORF-
FER, BLICHENDERFFER)
Christian   I, 569, 570, 572
Jacob   I, 384, 386
Jost   I, 569, 570, 572
BLIKLY (BLEAKLY)
Johanes   I, 497
Martin   I, 360, 361
Matheus (Matheas) I, 360, 361
BLIM (PLIM)
Daniel   I, 485
Henrick
(Henrich, Hendrick) I, 23, 25, 26
BLIMKE
Cora E. C.   II, 6
Johan Elija   II, 6
BLIN
Johann Paul   I, 762
BLINCAITH
Mich[1]   II, 6
BLINTZINGER
Johann Georg   I, 454
BLISSER
Ch.   II, 33
BLITZ
Johannes   I, 692
Paulus   I, 540, 542, 544
Phillipp   I, 709
BLOAT
John   I, 496
BLOCH
George   I, 456
Johanes   I, 456, 712
Michael   I, 456
BLOCHER (PLOCHER,
PLOUGHER)
Johanes   I, 584
Matheus   I, 471
Mattheis (Mathies,
Mathias)   I, 551, 552, 553

Michael   I, 583, 584
BLOCK
Jno Henry   I, 726
BLODEL
Johann Dieter   I, 702
BLOEDE
Wilhelm   II, 41
BLOEMEN
Jaen   I, 21
BLOESER
Joh. Leonard   II, 44
BLÖKINGER
Johannes   I, 494
BLOM
J. Peter   I, 478
John Peter, Senior   I, 478
BLONK
Hans Jacob   I, 392
BLOODHART
George   II, 76
BLOOM
Philip   II, 116
(*See also* BLUM)
BLOSER
Christian   I, 471
BLOSS
Conrad   I, 327, 329
Georg Conradt   I, 421
Jacob   I, 438
Peter   I, 709
BLOSSER
Christian   I, 443
BLOY
Jacob   I, 290
BLUIGNER
Peter   I, 459
BLUM (BLUHM, BLOOM, PLUM)
Anthoni   I, 462
Antoine   II, 85
Charles   II, 198
Frantz (Frans)   I, 35, 36
Geo. Fred.   II, 201
Henrich   I, 723
Jacob   I, 79, 82, 83
Johann Jacob   I, 464
Johannes   I, 688
John   I, 20
Justine   II, 85
Philip   I, 689
Philip Heinrich   II, 134
(*See also* BLUME)
BLUMBACH
Ca. Margreta   II, 102
Carl   II, 102
Peter J.   II, 102
BLUME
Carol Christian   II, 103
Christian Fried[r]   II, 79
G. F.   II, 186

Johann II, 61
Johann Görg I, 390
BLUMEN
Anna Margar. II, 140
BLUMENSCHEIN (BLOMESCHYN,
PLUMENSTEIN)
Daniel I, 605, 606, 608
Johann Henrich I, 395
Johannes I, 437
Vallentin I, 464
BLUMENSTIEL
Hinrich II, 129
BLUMER (PLUNER)
Christopher I, 493
Johan Jerick (J.
George) I, 545, 547, 549
BLUMHARD (BLOOMHART)
Johannes I, 605, 607, 608
BLUMHOST
Abraham II, 91
BLÜMLER
Johann Gottlieb I, 716
BLUMMER
Joh. Ch. II, 41
BLYGER (PLYGER)
Jacob I, 167, 168
BOAMINING
Margt I, 210
BOB (POP)
Johan Bernhartt I, 627, 630, 633
Johan Georg (Jurg) I, 627, 630, 633
John Enrich (John
Henry) I, 316, 317
BOBE
Godlieb I, 441
BOBELL
Jacob I, 720
BOBENHEISSER (BOBENHUYZEN,
BOBENHYZER, BOBEN-
HEUSER)
Andreas I, 205, 206, 208
Johanes (Johan) I, 205, 206, 208
BOCE
Henry I, 420
BOCHIN
Jacob II, 133
BOCHRINGER
Philip Jacob II, 151
Widow II, 151
BOCK (BACK, BUCK)
Conrad I, 726
Daniel I, 421
Elizabeth I, 49
Georg Peter (Yerrick
Peter) I, 595, 597, 599
Georg Philipp I, 507
Hans Michel I, 50
Jacob I, 420
Johan Henrich I, 352, 353

Johann Michell I, 443
Johannes I, 258, 260, 263, 455
656, 657, 658
John Andreas I, 545, 547, 549
Leonard I, 47, 50, 51, 53
Maria Elizabeth I, 50
Maria Katherine I, 50
Maria Salina I, 50
BÖCKEL (BOCKEL, BEKEL)
Fred II, 99
Johannes I, 458, 621, 623, 625
Tobias (Dobias) I, 179, 180, 183
BOCKING
Richard I, 304
BÖCKLE (BÖCKHLE, BUKLEY)
Gottlieb I, 696
Jacob I, 596, 598, 599
(See also BECKLIN)
BÖCKNEY
Reichart I, 305, 306
BOCKRANTZ (POCKRANZ)
Ludewig Wilhelm I, 517, 518, 519
BOCKREIKER
Israel I, 705
BOCKS (BOOKS)
Hans (John) I, 162, 164, 166
BODANER (BOATAMAYER)
Johanes I, 526, 528, 530
BODE
Anna Elisabeth II, 148
Carolina II, 72
Catharina II, 148
Christian II, 148
Frederick II, 72
Herrman II, 148
Hinrich II, 128
Johann H. II, 148
Johann Peter I, 521, 524
Just II, 148
Louise II, 128
Rudolph II, 72
BÖDEKER
Arnold I, 746
BODEL
Jacob I, 717
Joh. II, 82
BODEN
Elizth II, 23
Hinrich II, 129
Mr II, 12
BODER
John Val. II, 160
BODEVAIN
Peter II, 90
BODMER (BETTERMAN)
Ulrich (Ulrey) I, 99, 100, 101
BODOMER
Philip I, 422

BODT
Hans Philipp I, 717
BOECKENER (BÜCKENER, PECK-
ONER)
Johan Nickel I, 276, 277, 278
BOEHLER
Elizabeth I, 320
Peter I, 320
BOEHM BÖHM, BÖM, BOM)
Anna E. II, 159
Conradt I, 431
Erhart I, 407
Ernst I, 439
Henry II, 159
J. II, 143
Jacob I, 346
Joannes I, 367, 369
Johann Adam I, 522, 524
Johan Christ[n] II, 30
Johan Daniel II, 28
Johann Phillips, Senr I, 337, 339
Johann Phillips, Junr I, 335, 337, 339
Johann Reichardt I, 420
John George II, 127
Joh[n] Peter II, 127
Margaretha C. Seipen II, 127
Nicolaus I, 500
Paulus I, 478
Peter I, 237, 238, 239
Sam I, 237
BOEHMER
Jacob Fredrick II, 121
BOEHRINGER
George II, 150
Johann II, 150
Katharine II, 150
BOEKH (BOOKH, BECK)
Jacob I, 227, 229, 231
BOEKHOART
Peter II, 135
BOENE
Fred II, 136
BOERMAN
Anna II, 109
Catharina II, 109
Eimer II, 109
Kichgy II, 109
Sophia II, 109
BOERNER
John II, 52
BOES see BOSSE
BOETZSCH
Friederica Augusta Amalia II, 89
Johann II, 90
BOGAREY
Barbarey I, 79
BOGE
Angel II, 198
Catharine II, 198

BOGENER
John Gotlieb II, 160
BOGER (BIEGER, BIGGER,
BOGHER, BÖGER)
Andreas I, 509, 510, 511
Eva I, 61
Hans Paulus I, 60, 64, 65
Henrich Conrad I, 746
Immanuel I, 443
Johan Philip (Fil.) I, 60, 64, 65
Joseph Jo[s] I, 637, 639, 641
Justina I, 62
Martin I, 43, 45, 46
Mathias I, 62
Michiel I, 62
Philip I, 667, 669, 671
BOGERISS (BECHERER)
Simon I, 234, 235, 236
BOGERT (BOCKER)
Nicholas I, 16
Nickel I, 84, 86, 87
Peter I, 356
BOGUS
Jacob I, 468
BOHEN
Juliana II, 158
BOHL (BOLE)
Conrad I, 649, 650
BOHLANDER (BOLANDER, BOH-
LENDER)
Johann (Johan
Adam) I, 656, 657, 658
Johannes (Hannes) I, 655, 657, 658
Philips Henrich I, 726
BOHLEN
Bohl II, 55
John II, 60
BOHLER (BOLLER, BEHLER,
BÖHLER)
Jacob I, 569, 571, 572
Nicolaus I, 710
Paulus I, 551, 553, 554
Tomas I, 413
BOHLICH (BOHLIG)
Johan Georg (Hans
George) I, 672, 673, 674
BÖHM see BOEHM
BÖHMER (BOHMER, BÖMER)
Conrad I, 716
Friedrich I, 716
Johan Adam I, 466
Johann Christ. I, 401
Johann Henrich
(Henry) I, 568, 570, 572
Johann Michael I, 545, 547, 549
Johann Peter I, 401, 438
Johann Philippus I, 466
Johann Wilhellm (John
William) I, 568, 570, 572

Johannes   I, 396, 401, 438
Maria Eliz.   I, 144
BOHN (BON)
    Johann Baltzar   I, 359, 361
    Johannes   I, 359, 361
    Philips (Philip)   I, 359, 361
    Wendel (Wentell)   I, 194, 195, 196
BOHNE
    Johan Jacob   I, 329
    Johanes   I, 329
    Nick.   II, 196
BÖHNER   (BOHN,   BOONER,
    BOHNER)
    Adam   I, 155, 158, 160
    Andreas   I, 410
    Burckhart   I, 360, 361
    Johann Conradt (Con-
        radt)   I, 383, 385
    Johann Gottfriedt   I, 366
BÖHNET
    Tobias   I, 749
BOHR
    Johann Adam   I, 398
    Johann Friederich   I, 397
BÖHRINGER (BIERINGER, BER-
    INGER)
    Adam   I, 384, 385
    Andreas   I, 384, 385
    Carl   I, 759
    Joseph   I, 471
BOHRMANN
    Bastian   I, 485
BOHRMESTER
    Johan   II, 50
BOHRN
    Peter   I, 430
BOHRZ
    Heinr Bortheld   II, 118
BOHTE
    Hinrich Julius   I, 517, 519, 520
BOIE
    J.   II, 32
BOIR
    Jas du   II, 61
BÖKEL (BIEGEL, BECKEL)
    Anna   I, 156
    Friderich (Frederick) I, 155, 158, 160
BOKKENDALL
    Peter   II, 50
BOLANDER (POLANDER)
    Johann Nickel   I, 316, 317
BOLB
    Johannes   II, 77
BOLCH
    Johan Adam   I, 542, 544
BOLEY (POLAY, POLEY)
    Anthony   I, 702
    Johann Carl   I, 702
    Johannes (Hannes)   I, 665, 668, 670

BOLIG
    Johan   I, 540
BÖLL
    Johann Peter   I, 713
BOLLAND
    Madheis   I, 403
BOLLBACH (BULBACK)
    Johann Adam (Johan
        Adm)   I, 601, 602, 603
BÖLLE (BERLIE)
    Johannes   I, 18, 19
BOLLENBACHER   (BULIPACKER)
    Johann Abraham
        (Abraham)   I, 283, 284, 285
BOLLENIGER
    Heinrich   I, 508
BÖLLER (BOLLER, BILLER)
    Elizabeth   II, 61
    Hans Martin   I, 221, 223, 224
    Jacob   I, 411
    Johan   II, 61
    Philip Wilhelm   II, 30
BOLLICK
    John   I, 727
BOLLINGER   (BOLINGER,   BÖL-
    LINGER, BULINGER)
    Christoph (Christopher)   I, 263
                               267, 270
    Jacob   I, 449, 522, 524
BOLLON (BOWLONG)
    Anna   I, 74
    Conrath (Conradt)   I, 71, 75, 77
    Elizabeth   I, 73
BOLMAN
    Anna   II, 54
BOLSCHNER
    Johann Wolfgang   I, 718
BOLTZ (POLTZ, BOLTS, PULTZ,
    FOLTZ)
    Georg   I, 620, 622, 624
    Jacob   II, 144
    Johann Jacob   I, 485
    Johannes Michael
        (Michel)   I, 195, 196, 197, 301
                               302, 303
    Norbert   II, 145
BOLZE
    Siemon Christian   II, 116
BOMBACH (BOMBOCK)
    Gorg (Jerick)   I, 289, 290, 291
BOME
    Johan Jacob   I, 330
BOMWARD (BONWART, BANG-
    WART)
    Hans Michell (Hans
        Michael)   I, 591, 593, 594
BON (BONN)
    Johann Daniel   I, 754; II, 30
    Johan Seilas   I, 479

Johannes I, 448
Johannes Petter I, 479
Joseph I, 684
Nicolaus I, 448
BONACKER
Jacob II, 97
BOND
Andries II, 184
Peter II, 101
BONDELI (BONDLIECK)
Sigmund (Sickmont) I, 555, 556, 558
BONE
Johanes I, 501
Philip I, 746
BONEBLUST
J. Christian I, 492
BONER see BONNER
BONET
Hans Michal I, 429
BONGART (BOMGART)
Bastian I, 335, 337, 338
BONGHART
Anna I, 117
BONI (BONY, PONNE)
Andres (Andrus) I, 27, 29, 30
Hans Michael I, 720
Hendrick I, 273, 274
Joanna Margaret I, 28
Simon I, 720
BÖNIG
Johann Dieterrich I, 750
(See also BÖNNIG)
BÖNING (BENE, RENE)
Reinhart (Reynard, Hans
Rinerd) I, 236, 238, 239
BONIRS
Nicolaus Jacobus II, 58
BONJOUR (PUNCHOER)
Andreas (And^w) I, 637, 638, 640
BONN see BON
BONNART
Henry I, 685
BONNER (BÖNNER, BONER)
Caspar (Jasper) I, 283, 284, 286
Hans Jacob I, 244, 245
Rudolph I, 72, 76, 78
BONNET
Christian II, 56
David II, 151
Frank II, 151
Jean (John) I, 526, 528, 529
Johan Peter (John
Peter) I, 185, 186, 187
John II, 151
Joseph II, 151
Katharine II, 151
Katy II, 151
BONNETT (BONET, BUNETT)
Jacob I, 113, 765

Jaques I, 114, 115
(See also BUNNETT)
BONNEWITZ
Hans Johann I, 405
BÖNNIG
Johann Jeremias I, 750
Philipp I, 751
BÖNNIGHOFF (BEINIGHOFF,
BINNIGHOFF)
Johannes I, 546, 547, 549
BONSE
Johan II, 50
BONTAUX
Joseph I, 498
BONTZ (BONZ, BANTS)
Catharine II, 33
Hans Virech (Hans Veery) I, 22, 23
BOOCH (BOOG, read BUCH)
Hans I, 197, 198
Jerik I, 20
BOOCHER (read BUCHER)
Dietrich I, 97
BOOGER
Jacobus Vanden II, 16
Maria II, 16
BOOHER
Samuel II, 122
BOOKE
Nicolas I, 485
BOOKENHAGEN (read BUGEN-
HAGEN)
Charles II, 122
BOOKIUS (BOCKIUS, BOCKEJUS)
Johannes (Johanne) I, 297, 298, 300
BOOM
Jon. Her.drick Bearin II, 77
BÖOMER (BEHMER)
Friderich I, 576, 578, 580
BOOMS
Gasper II, 77
BOON
M^r II, 130
BOOR
Johann Mich. I, 398
BOORLINGER
Peter I, 15
BOORS (BOERS)
Gisbertus (Gysbert) I, 47, 51, 53
Henderick I, 468
BOOS
Johan Kilian I, 762
Johannes (Johan) I, 205, 207, 208
Nicolaus I, 701
Petronella II, 93
Wilhelm II, 93
BOOSER
Lenhart I, 392
BOOTS
Jacob I, 487

BOPENMEIER
Stephan I, 327, 329
BOPP (BOP)
Daniel II, 30
Dorot^a II, 30
Hans Georg I, 726
Johann Capar (Conrad) I, 649, 650
Johann Jacob I, 436
Johannes I, 340
Salomea II, 30
Sophia II, 30
(*See also* BOB)
BORAMANN
Gottlieb II, 111
BORBISHEL
Charles II, 47
BORCHART (BUCHER, BUR-
CHART)
Peter I, 199, 201, 203
BORCORNI
Joseph II, 196
BORD
Nigglaus I, 431
BORDILI
Johann David I, 718
BORDON
Nich^s I, 747
BORELL (BORELLE)
Abraham I, 546, 548, 550
Mathaus I, 747
BORET (BOORET, BURRET)
Jorg Michael
(Michal) I, 226, 228, 230
BORETT
Christ. Heinz II, 41
BOREY
Nicol. II, 145
BORGER (BORGER, BURGER)
Hans Nicklas (Johannes
Nicholas) I, 560, 561, 563
Hendrick I, 735
BÖRGERES
Filipus I, 330
BORGFELD (BORGFIELD)
Henry (Henery) I, 516, 518, 519
BORIS
Lawrence I, 711
BORISCHT
Johanes I, 501
BORKART
Mich. I, 455
BORKINK
John Dirk II, 191
BORLEMAN
Jean Dieter I, 15
BORMAN
Daniel I, 15
Jacob I, 526, 528, 529
Nicolaus I, 763

BORN (BORNN, BURN)
Andres (Andereas) I, 233, 235
Barbell I, 242
Conrad I, 562
Goerg (Joerg,
Yerick) I, 289, 290, 291
Hans Adam I, 241
Jean II, 85
Johann Daniel II, 130
Justine II, 85
L. G. II, 142
Ludwig (Ludwick) I, 175, 176, 177
Michael (Michall) I, 240, 242, 243
Philip I, 478
Vallentin I, 444
BORNEMANN
Nelle II, 102
BÖRNER (BORNER)
Johann Adam I, 444
Johann George I, 427
BORNHÜTTER (BOURNHEKER)
Johann Gerlach I, 577, 578, 580
BORNTRÄGER
Martin I, 714
BOROCKER (BORAKA, BROKE)
Michael I, 310, 311, 312
BOROVI
Georgius I, 367, 369
BORR
Johann Mattes I, 398
BORROWDALE
Ann Rosetta II, 58
James II, 58
BORSCH
Friedrich I, 732
BORST (BOARST)
Johann Bernhard I, 711
Joh. David II, 139
Michael (Michl) I, 23, 25, 26
BÖRSTLER (BIRSTLER, PERST-
LER)
Hans Georg (Hans Jerig) I, 91, 92
Jorg (Jurg) I, 615, 617, 620
BORSTOFF
John Aug. II, 203
BORTLE (BARTEL)
Nicolas (Nicolaus) I, 84, 86, 87
BORTLEHR
Johan I, 709
BORTNER (PORTERNER)
Balser (Pauley) I, 84, 86, 87
Hanna Mela I, 85
Jacob I, 85
Merreles I, 85
BORTS
Geirts Lieve II, 125
BORTT (PORT)
Petter (Peter) I, 324, 325, 327

BORTZ (BORZ)
Gorg I, 699
Hans I, 406
Ludwig I, 13
BOS
Wilhelmina II, 136
BOSCH
Conradt I, 400
Dietrich (Diedrick) I, 383, 385
Jacob I, 497
Johan Daniell I, 446
Johan Jacob I, 446
Johann Michael, Jun' I, 446
Johanes I, 502
Willhelm I, 409, 473
BOSCHUNG (BOSHUNG,
BUSHUNG)
Anna Barbara I, 50
Barbera I, 49
Christina I, 50
Hans I, 47, 51, 53
Hans Philip I, 50
Johann Nicklaus I, 104, 105
Magdalena I, 50
BOSDORFF
Andreas II, 68
BOSER (POSSER)
Hans Jerg I, 490
Johannes I, 332, 333, 334
Mattheis I, 490
BOSERMAN (BOSERMANN, BAS-
SELMAN)
Johan Friedrich I, 390
Nicolaus (Nicholas) I, 646, 647
BOSHARDT (BOSHART, BUS-
HART)
Andreas I, 366
Heinrich I, 415, 435
Joh. Jacob (Jacob) I, 555, 556, 557
BÖSINGER (BUSINGER)
Johann Peter I, 729
Johannes I, 155, 158, 161
BOSLER (BOSLLER, BAASLER,
BOSSLER, BUSLER)
Henrich I, 96, 98
Johann Wilhelm (Hanse
Wm) I, 240, 242, 243
Kattarina Barball I, 242
Maria Barbara I, 242
Philip II, 46
BOSMAN
Hen. I, 536
BÖSMER
Hans Jerg I, 426
BÖSS (BOOS)
Christian I, 592, 593, 594
Jacob I, 759
Johannes I, 316, 317

BOSSART (BOSHAAR, BOSHART,
BOSSARD, BOSSERT)
Hans Henry I, 348, 350, 351
Jacob I, 146, 149, 150
Mr. II, 176
BOSSE (BOES, POES)
Johann Christoffel I, 749
Johann Gotfried II, 121
Johannes I, 366, 368
Ludwig (Lutwick,
Luturg) I, 212, 214, 215
BOSSECK
Herman Mich. II, 139
BOSSEL
Heinrich I, 709
BOSSER (BOSART, OSER)
Christopher I, 331, 332, 334
Philip I, 279, 280, 281
BOSSERMAN
Samuel I, 528, 530
BOSSERDT (BOSSART, BOSSERD,
BOSCHART, BOSSERT, BUS-
SARD, POSSART)
Anna I, 148, 151
Balsatzar I, 147, 149, 150
Bernard (Bernhart) I, 304, 305, 306
Caspar I, 148, 151
Eliza, Elizabeth I, 147, 190
Eve I, 28
Felix I, 252, 254, 255
Hans (Ulrich) I, 252, 254, 255
Heinrich (Hendryk) I, 148, 151, 152
Jacob I, 27, 28, 29, 30, 252, 254, 255
Johannes
(Johanes) I, 28, 559, 561, 562
Marilis I, 28
Michael I, 470
Rodolph I, 148
Susanah I, 28
BOSSIG
Uldrig I, 746
BOSSONG (BOSSENG)
Debalt (Theobald) I, 564, 565, 567
BOTH *see* BOTT
BOTHGISS
Heinrich I, 704
BOTHMAN (BOTTMAN)
Georg
(Bothman) I, 516, 518, 519
BOTHNER
Ludwig I, 169, 170, 172
BOTT (BOTH, BOHT, BOTE, POT)
Andreas II, 7
Anna Catha II, 7
Anna Maria II, 7
Barbara II, 7
Casper II, 7
Henrick I, 74
Hermanus I, 335, 337, 338

Johann Balthasar
(Johan Belser) I, 71, 76, 77
Johann Emrich I, 336, 337, 339
Johann Hennrich
(John Hend^k) I, 373, 374, 375
Johann Jonas
(John Jonas) I, 373, 374, 375
Johann Martin I, 497
Johannes I, 614, 616, 618
John II, 7
Mary II, 7
Peter I, 335, 337, 339
Ursilla I, 73
BÖTTGER
Johann Matheus I, 743
Johann Wilhelm I, 479
BOTTINGER
Joh. F. II, 41
BÖTTLE
Michel I, 9
BOTTSY
Yerrick I, 596
BOTTY
John A. II, 15
BOTZ (BOOS, TROULST)
George Davit
(Jurich Geo.) I, 246, 247, 248
BOTZIN
Heinrich II, 132
BOUCHY
Johanes I, 406
BOUDIER
—— II, 81
BOURBEN
George II, 75
BOURDILLON
Lewis II, 73
BOURGHELL
Josep I, 746
BOURQUIN
Abram II, 31
BOURQUIN
J. I, 753
Josue II, 31
Pierre Frederick II, 31
Suzanne II, 31
BOUSH
John Mich I, 286
BOUSMANN (read BAUSMAN)
Dort II, 102
Henry I, 433
BOUSORUM
Ant° II, 47
BOUTH
Henry I, 500
BOUTHEROT (BUDINOT, BUT-
NER)
Abram (Abraham) I, 592, 593, 595
Davit (David) I, 592, 593, 595

BOUTON (BUTTONG)
Jan Daniel (Dan) I, 256, 258, 261
BOVERN
Eliza I, 766
BOWELL
Fred^k II, 6
BOWER (BOUER, BOUR, read prob.
BAUER)
Andreas I, 501
Anna I, 124
Baltaser I, 418
Christian I, 527, 528, 530
Christiana (Christina) II, 164
Christoph (Christoff) I, 481
II, 164
Conrad I, 469
Diterich· I, 527, 528, 530
F. Peter I, 500
George Henry (George Henrick,
Jeorge Henrich) I, 637, 639, 640
Hans George I, 451
Hans Michel I, 328
Henry (Hendrick) I, 555, 556, 558
Johan Ludwich II, 164
Johanes I, 450
Margaret I, 124
Michael I, 451, 501
Stephan I, 501
Ulrich I, 348
BOWERS
Jn° Alex. II, 6
Nicholas II, 81
BOWMAN
A. Eliz. II, 105
Jacob I, 555
BOYER
G. F. II, 123
Nicholas I, 759
BOYNEBURG
Johann Wilhelm I, 715
BOYSOBO
Paul II, 123
BOYSON
Edward II, 82
BOZITO
Christ Fried. II, 125
BRABECKH
Mardi I, 417
BRABENDER
Andrew II, 200
BRACHT
Anna M. II, 4
Joh. Adam II, 4
Johann W^m II, 4
BRÄCHTBÜL (BRÄCHTBÜLL,
BRECHBEL)
Christian I, 629, 632, 635
BRACK *see* PRACK
BRACKLOHR

Friederich I, 724
BRACKMANN
Johan Conrad I, 749
BRADFORD
Mathew I, 28
BRADTFISCH
Johann Georg I, 728
BRAEMER
Johann Friedrich II, 183
BRAGHER (BRAGER)
John George
(George) I, 637, 639, 641
BRAHL (BRALL, BRAUL)
Joh. Ludwig I, 517, 518, 519
BRAHMS
Myndert Hinrich II, 99
BRAITLIGER
Ulrich I, 475
BRALLION
John Manvell I, 80
BRÄMER (BREMEN)
Jacob I, 589, 590, 591
BRAMMEREL
Johannes Christianus I, 433
BRAND (BRANDT, BRANT)
Aime II, 57
Andreas I, 732
Anna Margaret I, 84
Bernhard (Bernard) I, 470; II, 94
Christian II, 74
Christian Carl I, 422
Christine II, 108
Friedrich
(Frederick) I, 621, 623, 626
721; II, 54
Hans Hermon
(Herman) I, 517, 518, 520
Hans Wilhelm I, 72, 76, 78
Jacob I, 397, 457
Joachim Jacob I, 762
Joh. Andr. II, 138
Johann Christen I, 422
Johann Monb. I, 422
Johann Theis
(Matthias) I, 568, 570, 572
Johannes
(Johans) I, 156, 159, 161, 752
John Anton II, 56
Jn⁰ Manuel II, 6
Joseph II, 114
Jost (Joost) I, 263, 267, 270
Martin I, 323, 324, 326
Michael (Michell) I, 83, 86
Otto Carol I, 505
Rossina I, 60
Samuel I, 59, 63, 64
263, 267, 270
Simon I, 486
Sophia Dorothea II, 184

Wilhelm (Wm) I, 216, 218, 219
II, 205
——— II, 184
BRANDEL (BRENDEL)
Hans Jorg (Hans Jerick) I, 209, 211
Johan Phillip I, 209, 211
John Hendrick I, 210
BRANDENBURG (BRONDENBURG,
BRANDEBURGER)
Johan Andonges
(Anthony) I, 279, 280, 281
BRANDENBURGER
Jacob I, 713
Willem Henrich I, 479
BRANDER (BRANNER)
Johann Diederich
(Johan Peter) I, 189, 192, 194
BRANDES
Heinr. II, 205
BRANDFASS
Conrad I, 517
BRANDHOVER
Johannes II, 34
Sarah II, 34
BRANDMÜLLER (BRANDMILLER)
Johann I, 320, 321, 322
BRANDNER
Andreas I, 431
BRANDSTETTER
Friedrich I, 691
BRANG
Johann Jacob I, 430
BRANHOLTZ *see* BRUNHOLTZ
BRANTS (BRONST, BROUGH)
Hans Michael I, 226, 228, 230
BRASCHLOSS
John II, 99
BRATTLER
Hans Michael I, 706
Johann Jacob I, 706
BRATZ
Georg I, 360, 362
BRAUCH
Johann Georg II, 134
BRÄUCHLE
Joachim I, 489
BRAUCHLER (BRAUGLER)
Johan Theobald
(Dewald) I, 313, 314, 315
BRAUENFELDER
Matdeis I, 352
BRAUER
Andreas I, 442
BRAUN (BROWN)
Andreas (Andereas) I, 399, 486, 700
Anna Margaretha I, 132
Anthoni (Anthony) I, 653, 654
August II, 54
Bastian I, 401

Catherina I, 132
Conrad I, 700, 721
Cornelius I, 732
Daniel I, 432
Georg Conradt
  (Jurg Conrad) I, 513, 514, 515
Georg Friedrich I, 512, 514, 515
Georg Lenhardt I, 399
Georg Michael I, 399
Gottfried
  (Gottfriet) I, 234, 235, 236
Hans I, 441
Hans Martin I, 130, 133, 134
Henrich I, 416
Jacob I, 482, 498, 521, 523
Johann Burckhard
  (Burkhard) I, 377, 379, 381
Johan Engel
  (Engle) I, 569, 571, 573
Johann Friedrich I, 487
Johann
  Georg (Yerrick) I, 487, 492, 513
    514, 515, 532
    534, 535, 582
    583, 584
Johann Jacob I, 132, 439, 454
Johann Matthaus I, 512, 514, 515
Johann Michael I, 700
Johann
  Peter (Pater) I, 307, 308, 309
    401, 569, 571
    573
Johan Wendel I, 226, 229, 231
Johannes I, 498, 707
Johannes Engelbert
  (John Engel) I, 296, 298, 299
Maria Christina I, 132
Maria Elizabeth I, 131
Marteine I, 522, 525
Martin I, 686
Michael I, 687
Peter
  (Johann Peter) I, 335, 336, 338
P. H. II, 143
Valenthin (Wallendin) I, 495, 703
Wm. II, 177
Wolffgang (Woolf) I, 209, 211
BRÄUNICH (BRAUNIG)
Georg Heinrich I, 730
Hans Michaell I, 470
BRAUNS
Peter I, 403
BRAUNSBERG
Johann Georg I, 443
BRAUNSCHWEIGER
—— II, 58
BRAUNWALD (BANGWALT)
Jacob I, 591, 592, 594

BRAUSS (BRAUS)
Andreas I, 500
Görg I, 496
Hans Adam I, 237, 238, 240
Merck Adams I, 237
BRÄUSSER
Johann Henrich I, 752
BRÄUTIGAM (BRIDEGAM)
Joachim Andereas I, 505
Johann Daniel (Dan.) I, 681, 682
Paulus I, 531, 533, 535
BRAYMOYER
Thomas Henry I, 364
BRECH
Adam I, 335, 336, 338
George I, 449
BRECHBILL (BRECHBUHLL,
  BRECHBIL, BRECHBIEL,
  BRAKEBILL)
Anna I, 61
Benedict I, 104, 105
Christian I, 221, 222, 224
Hans I, 104, 105
Hans Pieter I, 104, 105
Henry I, 221, 222, 224
Jacob I, 104, 105
Johannes (John) I, 59, 63, 65
Wendell I, 59, 63, 65
BRECHBÜEHLER (BRECHBELLER)
Abraham I, 629, 632, 636
BRECHEISEN
Catharine II, 44
Catharine Eliza II, 44
Fredrich II, 44
Johan George II, 44
BRECHER
Johan Nicol I, 35
BRECHLE
Hans Jerg I, 360, 361
BRECHNER
Johann Chrisⁿ I, 731
BRECHT
David I, 50
Johan Tieterich
  (Johan Diedrick) I, 652, 654
BRECHTEL (PRECHTEL)
Johann Georg I, 688
BREDA
Engeltina II, 11
BREDE
Jnº II, 11
BREDER
Michael I, 555
BREEGE
Johann Christ. Wilhelm II, 140
Joh. Friedᶜʰ II, 139
Maria Magdalena II, 140
Maria Margar. II, 140

BREHANT
  Gabriel   II, 89
BREIDBACH
  Nicolaus   I, 698
BREIDENBACH   (BREIDERBACH,
    PREIDENBACH)
  Johann Filip   I, 390
  Johannes   I, 656, 657, 659
  (*See also* BREITENBACH)
BREIEL (PRAIEL)
  Peter   I, 293, 294, 296
BREIGNING *see* BREINING
BREILINGER
  Peter   I, 451
BREINER
  Christiana   II, 198
  Frantz   II, 45
  G. Michael   I, 499
BREINIG (BREYNICH)
  Jerg   I, 422
  Johannes   I, 527, 528, 530
  Marx   I, 474
BREINING
  Johana   II, 161
  John   II, 161
  ——   II, 161
BREIS
  Johan Henrich   I, 390
BREISACH
  Mich¹   I, 417
BREISCH
  Jacob   I, 696
  Joseph   I, 695
BREIT (BREAD)
  Ludwig   I, 317, 318, 319
BREITENBACH (BREITEBACH)
  Elizabeth   II, 160
  Henry   II, 160
  Johannes   I, 363, 717
  John   II, 161
  Lorenz   II, 160
  Peter   II, 160
  Valentin   I, 717
  William   II, 160
BREITENBÄCHER   (BRITEN-
    BÜCHER)
  Abraham   I, 706
  Balthas   I, 705
BREITENFELD   (BREITTEN-
    FELTD)
  Johann Benedicktus
    (Benedik Dues)   I, 510, 512
BREITENGROSS
  George   I, 135
BREITENHERDT (BRIDLEHEART)
  Johann Christoph I, 539, 541, 543
BREITENSTER
  Jacob   II, 145

BREITHAUPT
  J.   II, 120
BREITINGER (BREYDINGER)
  Adam   I, 661, 662, 663
BREITSCHEIDT
  Emmanuel   I, 446
BREITSCHIETT
  Valentin   I, 481
BREITSCHWERD
  Mattheus   I, 485
BRELING
  Dorothy   I, 40
BREM (BREEM, PRIM, PRIMM)
  Georg Christophel   I, 461
  Henrich   I, 282, 284, 285
  Jacob   I, 282, 284, 285
BREMAUER   (PREMAUER, BRE-
    MAUR)
  Johann Casbar
    (J. Casper) I, 184, 185, 187
BREMER
  Anna Elisa   II, 129
  Anna Maria   II, 129
  Catharina   II, 129
  Catharine Elisa   II, 129
  Christopher I, 536, 537, 538
  Georg Henrich   I, 728
  Henrich   II, 75
  Joh. George   II, 129
  Joh. Ludwig   II, 129
  John Peter   II, 129
  Leonhart   I, 485
  Maria Cathⁿᵃ   II, 129
  Maria Elisa   II, 129
  Wilhelm   I, 517, 519, 520
  (*See also* BREMMER)
BREMICH (BREMIG, PREMICH)
  Johann Adam   I, 689
  Matthew   I, 689
  Mich¹   I, 689
BREMICKER
  Freiderich   II, 92
BREMINGER
  Christiana   II, 161
  Johann   II, 161
  Magdalin   II, 161
BREMMER
  Jnᵒ Henry Christian   I, 749
  (*See also* BREMER)
BRENCKERT
  Johannes   I, 710
BRENDLE   (BRENDTLE, BREND-
    LEY)
  Andreas   I, 465
  Hans Fredrich   I, 462
  Phillipp (Philip) I, 582, 583, 584
BRENDLINGER
  Conradt   I, 476
  Joseph   I, 476

BRENER
Hans Jacob   I, 485
Simon   I, 472
BRENGEL (BRINGEL)
Christian   I, 169, 170, 172
                          629, 632, 635
Jacob   I, 629, 632, 635
Rudolph   I, 706
BRENHAUER
Johann   I, 431
BRENHOLTZ (BRENHOLTS)
Anna   I, 153
Christian   I, 152, 153, 154
BRENNEISEN (BRINSINS)
George Michl   I, 35
Hans Veltin   I, 36
Jerg Michel   I, 36
BRENNEMAN
Daniel   I, 698
Jacob   I, 700
BRENNER (BRENNER, BRANDER)
Adam   I, 513, 515, 516
Appellonia   I, 108
Barbara   I, 109
Charlotte   I, 109
Daniel   I, 559, 560, 562; II, 155
Frantz Petter   I, 720
H. George   I, 497
Hans Caspar
   (Gasper)   I, 107, 111, 112
Hans Jacob   I, 485
Hans Philipp   I, 408
Joh. Chri.   II, 118
Johann Gerhardt
   (Hans Gerhardt) I, 195, 196, 197
Ludwig   I, 720
Philipp Adam   I, 408
BRENSILL
Margaret   II, 148
William   II, 148
BRENTZ
Jacob   I, 724
Johann Jacob   I, 484
BRENTZER (PRINCER)
Christian   I, 282, 284, 285
BRENTZINGER (BRENTZIGER)
Johann Adam   I, 460
Johan Christoph   I, 439
BRESER
Johann Henrich   I, 507
BRESLER (BRESZLER)
Burgh   II, 3
George   I, 421
Georg Adam   I, 704
Jerg Simon   I, 421
Nicklas   I, 421
Philip Jacob   I, 694
BRESSLAUER (BRESLAUER)
Johannes   I, 662, 664

BRETHEICH (BRETNIGHT)
Johann Henrich
   (Hend^k)   I, 387, 388, 389
BRETZ
Henrich   II, 28
Henry   I, 433
Jacob   I, 339
Ludewig   I, 433
Philipp   I, 355
Wendel   I, 433
Wilhelm   I, 339
BREUER
Johannes   I, 719
BREUN (BRUN)
ETIENNE
   (Stephen)   I, 527, 528, 530
BREUNING
Carl Theodor   II, 117
Johan Philipps   I, 493
BREUNINGER (BREUINGER)
Anna Maria   I, 132
Baltzer (Walter) I, 131, 133, 134
Barbara   I, 209
Eliz^th   I, 210
Gottlieb (Joh^s Godlief) I, 209, 211
Hans Jacob   I, 132
Hans Martin   I, 209, 211
Margaretha   I, 131
———   I, 698
BREY
Hans George   I, 185, 186, 187
BREYHAN
Hans George   I, 505
BREYMEYER
Johann Georg   I, 489
BREYVOGEL
Joh. Peter   I, 356
BRICHAM
Zacharias   II, 93
BRICHMANN
Christoph   II, 79
BRICKER
Anna Barba   I, 81
Eliza   I, 81
Jacob   I, 450
Peter   I, 83
BRIDEBACH   (read   BREITEN-
   BACH)
Johann Michael   I, 698
BRIDENBAN
Joh.   II, 77
BRIEFF
Frietrich   I, 748
BRIEGEL (BRIGEL)
Adam   II, 134
Anna Catharina   II, 171
Johan Georg   II, 171
Johan Michael   II, 171
Joseph   II, 171

Maria Rosina II, 171
BRIEGNER (BRICKNER)
Gottlieb (Godlip) I, 275, 276
BRIELL (BRIEHLL, BRIEL)
Johann Henrich
(Hendrich) I, 653, 654
Johann Herman
(Herman) I, 653, 654
Marttin (Martin) I, 653, 654
BRIGEL see BRIEGEL
BRIGHTBYLE
Anneleiss I, 241
BRIKNER
Nicklaus I, 423
BRILL
Henrich I, 413
BRILLENBURG
Adrina II, 186
BRIMMER (BRIMER)
Hanns
Gorg (Jurig) I, 116, 119, 121
BRINHARTT (BRILHARTT)
Peter (Petter) I, 163, 165, 166
BRINK
Jan Van II, 118
BRINKER (BRINCKER)
Andreas I, 151, 152
Conrad I, 151
Hans I, 151
Hans Georg I, 661, 662, 664
Henry I, 434
Hyndrick I, 151
Jacob I, 151
Regula I, 151
BRINKMAN
Friederick I, 430
BRINLEY
Christian II, 195
BRINTZIGHOFER
Caspar I, 490
BRIO (PRIO, RIO)
Abram (Abraham) I, 300, 301, 302
Jacob I, 300, 301, 302
BRISEHOT
Frederick Christoph II, 93
BRITBILL
Anna I, 103
Benedick I, 102
Hans I, 102
Hans Pieter I, 102
Jacob I, 102
Maria I, 103
BRITZ
Christian II, 182
Ph. Jac. II, 45
BRITZIUS (BRETZIUS, BREITIUS,
BRÜTZIUS, BRETIG)
Christian I, 706
Jacob I, 379, 380, 382

Johan Adam
(Adam) I, 628, 631, 635
Johann Wilhelm I, 436
BROBECK (read BRODBECK)
Hans Rude I, 392
Heinr. I, 392
Heironimus I, 417
Mardi I, 417
BROBST (BROPTS, PROPTS)
Barbara I, 108, 109
Johann I, 107, 111, 112
Michael (Michal) I, 107, 111, 112
BROCHECK
Joseph II, 135
BROCHEL
Matthaus II, 3
BROCK (BRACK)
Anna I, 117
Cristina I, 118
Fridric I, 118
Madlena I, 118
Rudolf (Rudolph) I, 116, 119, 121
Vallentin I, 472
BRÖCKELMANN
Abrm II, 102
Carl II, 102
Gierdruth II, 102
Wilhelm II, 102
Wilhelmina II, 102
BROD (BRODT)
Paulus I, 399
Samuel I, 522, 524
BRODBECK (BRODBÄCK, BRODT-
BECK, BROBECK, BROD-
BECKH)
Adam I, 392
Claus (Cloyce) I, 275, 276
Fredk. II, 117
Georg Friderich I, 582, 583, 584
Hans Jerg I, 420
Hinerich (Henry) I, 275, 276
Jacob II, 118
Johan I, 476
Johan Michel I, 585, 587, 588
Johannes (Johanes) I, 475, 476
Martin I, 476
BRODER (BREEDER, BRODER)
Johann Nickell
(Nickell) I, 283, 284, 285
Wendel I, 355
BROGLI
Fiteli I, 689
BROKHART
Christian I, 483
Johannes I, 483
BROLLAR
Hestar I, 80
BROM
Michel II, 50

BROMBACH
  Conrad   I, 708
  Johan Melchior   I, 482
  Johannes   I, 708
BROMER (BROMMER)
  A.   II, 185
  Willhelm   I, 761
BROMSTED
  Frans   II, 50
BRONGERS
  Theodorus A.   II, 153
BRONHOLTZ *see* BRUNHOLTZ
BRÖNING
  Caspar   I, 429
  (*See also* BRÜNING)
BRONK
  Hendrick   I, 445
BRONNER
  Adam   I, 414
  Johann Jacob   I, 371; II, 46
  Johann Peter   I, 372
  Maria Dorothea   II, 46
  (*See also* BRUNNER)
BROOK
  Anna Catharina   II, 92
  Carl W.   II, 92
  Catharina   II, 92
  Hanna   II, 92
BROOKER
  Jacob   I, 275
BROSER
  Hans Jaco¹   I, 246
BROSIUS
  Johann Abraham   I, 330
  Johann Georg
    (Georigh)   I, 277, 278, 279
  Johann Heinrich   I, 383
  Johan Nicklaus   I, 330
BROSS
  Hans Jerg   I, 526, 528, 529
  Johann Conrat   I, 427
  Johann Nickel   I, 427
BROSSMAN (BROSMAN, PROSS-
  MAN)
  Frantz (Francis)   I, 265, 268, 271
BROST (BRUST)
  Andonius
    (Anthony)   I, 387, 388, 389
  Christian   I, 406
BROTHAK
  Carl Fredᵏ   II, 16
BROTHELL
  John Jurigh   I, 88
BROTSMAN (BRATZMAN,
  BROATSMAN)
  Friederich
    (Fredrick)   I, 240, 242, 243
  Jacob Hendrick   I, 241
  Maria Barbara   I, 242

Urian Adam   I, 241
Yogham Fredrick   I, 241
BROUN (read BRAUN)
  Bastⁿ   I, 676
  Coenraᵈ Sorbel   II, 136
  Peter   I, 676
BROUNMILLER (BROWNMILLER,
  BROUMILLER)
  Johannes (Joannes)   I, 256, 258, 261
BROUNWART (BROWNWAART,
  BROWN WART)
  Anna   I, 74
  Julian   I, 73
  Mathias   I, 71, 75, 77
BROURVER
  Engeline Gesine   II, 125
  Williem Roelof   II, 125
BROUWER (read BRAUER)
  Mart.   II, 47
BROWBAK
  Adam, Junior   I, 392
  Adam, Senior   I, 392
BROWN (BROWNE, BRAUN)
  Andreas   I, 700
  Barbara   II, 150
  Burgard   I, 667
  Christian   I, 498
  Christopher (Christ,
    Christop)   I, 23, 25, 26
  Conradt (Conraet)   I, 195, 196, 197
  Frederick (Fridrick)   II, 71, 150
  George   I, 480, 500
  Hans Jacob   I, 592
  Jacob   I, 413, 498
  Johannes (Johannis,
    Johanes)   I, 212, 214, 215, 498, 749
  Lena   I, 67
  Martin   I, 231, 452
  Melchior   I, 372
  Michael (Michel)   I, 179, 181, 183
  Philip   II, 186
  Phillipina   II, 150
  Rudolph (Roland)   I, 87, 90, 91
  (*See also* BRAUN *and* BROUN)
BRUA (PROAU)
  Lorentz
    (Lowrens)   I, 264, 268, 271
BRUBACHER (PRUBACHER,
  BROWBACKER)
  Abraham   I, 397, 609
  Christian   I, 698
  Jacob   I, 403, 609, 611, 612
  Johanes   I, 397
  Johann Jacob   I, 609, 611, 612
BRUCH (BRUG, BROOK)
  Anna Catharina   II, 180
  David   I, 176, 177, 178
  Dorothea   II, 180
  Gustavus   II, 159

Herrmanus   I, 340, 341, 343
Johann Jost   I, 753
Johan Mathais (Mates,
   Matheis)   I, 155, 158, 160
John   II, 180
Thomas (Thoˢ)   I, 287, 288, 289
BRUCHEN (read BRUCH)
Frederica   II, 159
BRÜCHER
Johannes   I, 748
BRUCHLACHER
Jacob   II, 179
BRÜCKBAUER (BRICKBAUR)
Johannes   I, 335, 337, 339
BRÜCKEL (BRIGEL)
J. J. (Jacob)   I, 621, 623, 625
BRÜCKER (BRUCKER, BRICKER,
   BRUKER, PRICKER)
Anna   I, 190
Barbara   I, 190
Friederich   I, 391
Hans   I, 190
Hans Peter   I, 209, 214
J. Jacob   I, 482
Jacob   I, 212, 213, 215, 422
Johan Michael   I, 379, 380, 382
Johannes   I, 320, 321, 322
Julius   I, 521, 523
Mary Barbara   I, 320
Mich.   I, 422
Peter   I, 188, 192, 193
BRÜCKERT
Christoph   I, 693
Jacob   I, 693
Matthäs   I, 447
BRUCKHAUSEN
Johann Adam   I, 698
BRUCKMAN (BRUKMAN, BRICK-
   MAN)
George   II, 196
Johann Valentin
   (Valentine)   I, 667, 669, 671
BRUDER
Johan Georg   I, 495
Matheis   I, 497
BRUDERLE
Jacob   I, 163
BRUG *see* BRUCH
BRUGHLY
Matheas   I, 498
BRUINING
Dorothea   II, 4
J. G.   II, 4
BRUKER *see* BRUCKER
BRUKHAFER
Joh.   II, 118
BRUKHOLDER
Ullrich   I, 687

BRULASHER
Jacob   I, 17
BRUMBACH
Johann Jacob   I, 443
Johannes Henrich (Joh.
   Heinrich)   I, 620, 622, 624
BRUMM (BRUM, BRUME, BRUN)
Christoph   II, 52
Heinrich Philipp   I, 547, 549
Philip Jacob   I, 546
BRUMPS
Jacob   II, 148
BRUN (BRAUN)
Steffe (Stephen)   I, 205, 206, 208
BRUNCKS von (BRUNKS von)
Anthon Bartholo-
   maus   I, 517, 518, 520
BRUNDER
Barend   II, 125
BRUNDLE
Matheus   I, 439
BRUNDT
William   II, 197
BRUNER *see* BRUNNER
BRUNGART
Mardin   I, 484
BRUNHOLTZ (BRUNNHOLTZ,
   BROWNHOLTZ, BRONHOLTZ)
Dewald   I, 596, 598, 600
Frantz   I, 433
Ludwig   I, 372
BRÜNING (BRUNING)
Caspar   I, 429
Johann   I, 490
Stoffel   I, 429
BRUNINGER (BRUNNINGHER)
Anna Melia   I, 50
Barbara   I, 49
Hans Adam   I, 50
Veith   I, 47, 51, 53
BRUNN (BRUN)
Henrich Zum
   (Hendᵏ)   I, 609, 611, 612
Johann Daniel
   (Daniel)   I, 154, 158, 160
John Conrad   II, 47
Matteas   I, 347
BRUNNER (BRUNER)
Anna   I, 148
Appollona   I, 55
Caspar   I, 404, 439
Caterina Lisbet   I, 28
Conradt (Conrad)   I, 344, 376, 377
Cristof   I, 405
Felix   I, 97, 98, 99
Frantz   I, 459
George (Jurich,
   Ulrich)   I, 252, 253, 255
Hans   I, 344, 345

Hans Conrad I, 344, 345
Hans Jacob (Jacob) I, 54, 56
Heinrich (Henrich,
Hendryk) I, 56, 147, 150, 252
253, 255, 348
350, 351, 392
Hiroimus (Jeremiah) I, 564, 565, 567
Hs. Ulric I, 148
Jacob I, 18, 19, 332, 333, 334, 414
Jeremiah I, 55
Jeremiah Michael I, 55
Johan Henrich I, 155, 158, 161
Johannes I, 27, 661, 662, 664
John Hendrick I, 28
Joseph I, 27, 29, 30
Margaret I, 55
Margreeden I, 55
Melchior I, 436
Paulus I, 155, 159, 161
Peter I, 395, 396
Philip I, 434
Sophia I, 55
Wolf Henrich I, 55
BRUNO
Francis II, 94
BRUNS
Peter I, 504
BRUNSHOLTZ (PRINTZHOLTZ,
read BRUNNHOLTZ)
F. Adam I, 429
Jörg Jacob I, 429
BRUNT
Henry I, 756
BRUSEL (RUSSELL)·
Johann Philipp
(Philip) I, 621, 623, 625
BRUSS
Anna II, 57
BRUST
Adrian I, 726
Johan Christoffel I, 411
Johan Conrat I, 411
Thomas I, 726
BRUYN
Johanes II, 76
BRYZELIUS (PRYZELIUS)
Paul Daniel I, 320, 321, 322
Regina Dorothea I, 320
BUB
Henrich I, 383
Jacob I, 499
Jerg I, 711
Michel II, 69
BUBACK (POOBAGH)
Michael I, 653, 654
BUBECK
Joseph II, 130
BÜBEL
Johan Daniel I, 431

BUBER (BÜBER)
Conrath I, 372
Peter I, 263, 267, 270
BUBIKOFER (BYBYKOFFER)
Joseph I, 610, 611, 613
BUBINGER (BOBINGER)
Florian I, 225, 228, 230
BUCH (BUCK, BUKH, BUECK,
BOCK, BUK)
Hans I, 677, 678, 680
Hans Gerg
(Jurg) I, 20, 21, 225, 228, 230
J. II, 141
Jacob I, 677, 679, 680
Johann Phillipp I, 503
Johannes I, 332, 333, 334
366, 368, 559
561, 562, 755
John Caspar (Caspar,
Gaspar) I, 656, 657, 659
John George II, 160
Jorch Michel (Jurick
Mich¹) I, 212, 214, 215
Maria II, 105
Michael Friedrich I, 508
Michal I, 718
(*See also* BOOCH *and* BUGH)
BUCHAKER (BUCKAKER)
Valentine I, 367, 369
BUCHANNER
Helena II, 149
Johann F. II, 149
BÜCHELL
Johann David I, 438
BUCHENER
Joha Julᵃ Elisᵗʰ II, 29
BUCHER (BOUCHAR, BOUCHER,
BOUGER, BOUGHER)
Bardell I, 266, 269, 272
Benjeaman I, 153
Carolina II, 112
Caspar I, 434
Christian I, 153
Christiana I, 153
Conrad I, 434
Hans I, 152, 153, 154
331, 332, 334
Hans Peter I, 272
Hans Ulrich I, 79, 82, 83, 384, 386
Heinerich
(Hendryk) I, 148, 384, 386
Jacob I, 147, 148, 252, 253, 255
Johan (John) I, 152; II, 112
Johan Baltes I, 360, 362
Johann Engel I, 467
Johann Henrich I, 467
Johann Michael I, 327, 329
Niclaus I, 17
Peter (Petter) I, 266, 269, 272

BÜCHERT
Paul I, 722
BUCHHALTER
G. Frederic II, 156
BUCHHAMER
Johan I, 403
BUCHHECKER
Andreas I, 704
BUCHINROTTEN
Christina II, 151
BÜCHLE (BICKLER)
Jacob I, 526, 528, 530
BUCHLER (BÜCHLER, BEIGHLER, BIGLER)
Andreas I, 124
Anna I, 123, 124
Elizabeth I, 124
Lenhard I, 697
Maria I, 123
Marx (Marcus) I, 129, 130
Matthaus I, 122, 125, 126
BUCHMAN (BUCHMANN, BUOCHMAN, BOOKMAN)
Adam I, 410
Hans Jurg I, 715
Jacob I, 332, 333, 334, 355, 440
John II, 122
Martin I, 440
Matthias (Matias) I, 646, 647
Philip I, 711
BUCHMÜLLER
Johannes I, 741
BUCHNER (BUGNER)
J. M. II, 25
Johann Henrich (Henry) I, 568, 570, 572
Johann Martin (Martin) I, 568, 570, 572
Johannes (John) I, 568, 570, 572
Martin I, 570
BUCHOLTZ (BUCHHOLZ)
C. D. II, 112
Johan Adam I, 372
BUCHS
Jacob I, 469
BUCHTEL
Johannes I, 522, 525
BUCHTER
Johannes I, 395
BUCHY (BÜCHIE)
Rudolff I, 335, 337, 338
BUCK (BÜCK, read prob. BUCH)
Anna Maria II, 23, 129
Carle II, 129
Hans Balthas I, 438
Isaac I, 480
Johan Jacob I, 294, 295
Martin I, 438
Wilhel^{ne} II, 129

BUCKBECK
Christoff I, 439
BUCKE
Philip I, 403
BUCKEL (BÜCKEL, BÜCKELL)
Friedrich I, 417
Georg Adam I, 752, 753
Jacob I, 471
Johannes I, 286, 287, 289
Lönhart I, 474
BUCKENMEYER (BUCKEMIER)
Friederich (Phed.) I, 236, 238, 239
BÜCKHARD (BICKHARD)
Johann Daniel (Anthony) I, 643, 645
BUCKI
Jacob I, 347
BÜCKING
Dieterich Wilhelm I, 731
BUCKLE
Cristenia II, 36
BUCKMAN
Anth. II, 71
BÜCKS (BUCS)
Jacob I, 469
Peter I, 428
BÜCKSELL
Philippus I, 430
BUCS see BUCKS
BUDA
Heinerich I, 393
Johan Lutwig I, 393
BUDEMAN (PATEMAN, PUTEMAN)
Isaac (Isace) I, 559, 561, 563
BUDERSWAG (BOTESHWAY)
Wenzel (Wentzel) I, 646, 648
BUDINOT see BOUTHEROT
BUEB (BOUHA, BUB)
Christoph (Chris.) I, 232, 233
Hans I, 232
Philip Jacob I, 232, 233
Philip Jacob, Junr I, 232
BUERCKE
Johan H. II, 82
BUEYS (BUSS)
Janis I, 118
Jurig Adam I, 118
Lodwick I, 118
Mairs Margrita I, 118
BUFFEL (BEIFLE, BUFFELL)
Paulus (Paul, Peiter) I, 212, 213, 215
BUFFLE
Jacob II, 73
BUGAR
Margrit I, 81
BUGH (read BUCH)
Anna Maria I, 117

Martin I, 438
BUGNER
Christian I, 322
BÜHL (BUHLL, BUL)
Jacob II, 119
Johann Wilhelm
(Wilhelm) I, 577, 578, 580
Michael II, 155
Peter I, 304, 305, 306
BÜHLER (BUHLER, BULER,
BEULER)
Andreas I, 761
Anna Maria I, 144
Christian I, 485
Conrad (Johan
Conradt) I, 652, 654
Fried. II, 192
Jacob I, 732
Johann David
(David) I, 179, 181, 183
Johann Jacob I, 695
Martin I, 694
Peter (Petter) I, 527, 528, 530
Tobias II, 174
Ulrich I, 143, 145, 146
BUHLMAN (BULMAN)
Gerhard (Gerrit) I, 581, 582, 584
Mellcher II, 104
BÜHLMAYER (BILLMAYER)
Jacob I, 88, 90, 92
BÜHRLE (BÜHRLI, BEERLIE)
Melchior I, 349, 350, 351
BUHZER
Traugott Leberecht I, 750
BÜKLE
Johann Adam I, 458
BULER *see* BÜHLER
BULGREN
Frena I, 80
BULINGER *see* BULLINGER
BULL (read BUHL)
Christ^r II, 16
BULLER (BÜLLER)
Jan II, 197
Johannes I, 13, 14
BULLIG (BILLIG)
Johann Arnold I, 130, 133, 134
BULLINGER (BULLENGER, BU-
LINGER)
Christ^n I, 175, 176, 178
Elizabeth I, 73, 74
Hans Martin I, 71, 75, 77
Henrich (Hend-
rich) I, 199, 201, 203, 358
Jacob I, 175, 177, 178
Johann Martin I, 71, 76, 77
BULMAN *see* BUHLMAN
BUMACH
Gorgon Fred. II, 75

BÜMBEL
Baltzer I, 471
BUMBGARDNER *see* BAUM-
GÄRDTNER
BUNDRIGG (BUNTREE, BUN-
DRY)
Nicholas I, 307, 308, 309
BUNDSSTEIN (PUNTSTEIN,
STEIN)
Rainhart (Rein-
hard) I, 622, 624, 626
BUNDT
Mr. II, 176
BUNETT
Christina I, 767
Jacob I, 765
Johan Simon I, 767
Margret I, 767
Mary I, 766
Susanna I, 767
BUNGER
Godleib II, 199
BUNNING
Nicolaus II, 182
BÜNTZ (BINTZ, BENSS)
Anna Maria I, 242
Hans Georg (Hans Gerig,
Hansheria) I, 240, 242, 243
Hans Petter I, 241
Kattarina Barbal I, 242
BÜNTZEL
Johannes I, 522, 524
BUNY
John II, 187
Mary II, 187
BURBACH
Philipp I, 735
BURBARTH
Frantz II, 123
BURCH *see* BURG
BURCHARDT (BURCHART,
BURCHHARDT, BORGHAD,
BURGHARD)
D. Dieterich I, 684
Israel I, 462
J. Leonhart
(Leonard) I, 629, 632, 635
Jacob (Jakob) I, 628, 631, 634
Martin I, 440
Simon I, 461
(*See also* BURCKARD *and*
BURCKHARD)
BÜRCKARD (BURKART, BOR-
GART, BURKERT)
Hennrich I, 344, 345
Jacob I, 426
BURCKERT
Johans I, 716

BÜRCKH
  Jacob   I, 448
BURCKHARDT   (BURCKHARD,
  BURCKHART, BORKHART)
  Casper   I, 683
  Friderich   II, 134
  Georg Jacob (Jurig
    Jacob)   I, 264, 268, 271
  Hans Georg   I, 423
  Jacob   I, 472
  Johann   I, 508
  Johan Georg   I, 459, 761
  Johannes   I, 540, 542, 544
  Simon   I, 459
  (*See also* BURGHARD *and* BURK-
    HARD)
BÜRCKHLE   (BÜRCKLE,   BERK-
    LEY)
  Lorentz
    (Lawrence)   I, 589, 590, 591
BURCKI (BURKIE)
  Catrina   I, 190
  Christian   I, 188, 192, 193
  Jacob (Jacop)   I, 116, 119, 121
BURCKNER
  Peter   I, 322
  (*See also* BURGENER)
BURDERMANN
  Frederic   II, 197
BÜRELL
  Andoni   I, 499
BURG (BURCH)
  Carl Lud.   II, 71
  George Ludwig   I, 399
  Jacob   I, 736; II, 3
  Johan Christian   I, 496
  Nickolas   I, 445
BURGEDIN
  Margarett   II, 56
BURGENER
  Peter   I, 322
BURGER (BÜRGER)
  Andereas   I, 363
  Anna   I, 135
  Anna Maria   II, 120
  Anna Martha   II, 120
  Christian   II, 53
  Daniel   I, 257, 260, 262
  Geo. Christian   II, 120
  George Philip (Jurg
    Philip)   I, 540, 544
  Gerhard Henry   II, 116
  Hans   I, 350, 351
  Hans Michel   I, 35, 36
  Hans Peter   I, 359
  Henry   I, 249, 250
  Joachim   I, 314, 315
  Johann Christian
    (Christian)   I, 178, 180, 182

  Johan Michel   I, 501
  Johan Simon (Siemon)   I, 540, 544
  Johannes   II, 120
  Margaretha   I, 135
  Martin   I, 35, 36, 513, 514, 516
  Mathias   I, 244, 245, 383, 385
  Michael   I, 461
  Nicholas   I, 134, 136
  Philip   I, 135
  (*See also* BURGHER)
BURGERD
  Alexander   II, 5
  Hannah   II, 5
  Maria Christᵃ   II, 5
BÜRGESSER
  Deimel   II, 134
  Otto   I, 596, 598, 600
BURGHALTER   (BURGHOLDER,
    BURKHALDER,   BURCHAL-
    TER)
  Anna Barbara   I, 128
  Anna Catharina   I, 128
  Anna Magdalena   I, 128
  Barbara   I, 127
  Christian   I, 629, 632, 636, 707
  Elizabeth   I, 128
  Ester   I, 61
  Hance Peter   I, 128
  Hans   I, 629, 632, 636
  Jacob   I, 707
  Johannes   I, 707
  Margaretha   I, 128
  Ulrich (Ullrich,
    Uhlrich)   I, 60, 64, 65, 127
                       129, 130, 629
                            632, 636
BURGHARD   (BURGHART,
    BURCKHART, BURKART)
  Frantz (Frans)   I, 609, 612
  George   II, 154
  George Philip   I, 542
  Hans Jerich (Jurgh)   I, 88, 90, 91
  J. A.   II, 5
  Johann Friderich   I, 88, 90, 92
  Johan Georg
    (Hans Jurg)   I, 266, 269, 272
  Johan Nicklas
    (Nicholas)   I, 293, 294, 296
  Michael   I, 609, 611, 612
  Philip   I, 266, 269, 272
  Simon   I, 542
  (*See also* BURKHARD *and* BUR-
    GERD)
BURGHER   (HELBURGER,   BUR-
    RIER, BURGCHER)
  Hans Jacob   I, 482
  Jacob   I, 264, 267, 271
  Philip   I, 264, 267, 271
  Samuel (Sam)   I, 264, 267, 271

Ulrich (Ullerig) I, 214, 216
BURGHOFF
  Friederich II, 134
BURGHT
  George Hinrich II, 62
BÜRGI (BURGI, BURGER, BER-
  GER, BURK)
  Hans Rudi (Hans) I, 249, 250
  Henry I, 249, 250
  Margaret II, 5
  Maria Cath. II, 5
  Michael I, 507
BURGING
  Peter I, 710
BURGRETT
  Mickel I, 289
BURGSTAHLER
  Joseph I, 500
BURGY
  Henery II, 145
  Jacob II, 146
  Magret II, 146
  Maria II, 146
BURKE
  Joh. II, 117
  Philip II, 118
BURKERD
  John II, 145
BURKHARD (BORKHARD, BURCK-
  HARD, BURKHART)
  Anna I, 123
  Carolus I, 122, 125, 126
  Cathrina I, 123
  David l, 121, 124, 125
  Elizabeth I, 123
  Hans I, 121, 124, 125
  Heinrich I, 415
  Hend. II, 114
  Lewis II, 156
  Nicholas II, 51
  Paulus I, 122
  —— II, 156
BÜRKIE (BURCKIE, WERKIE)
  Michael (Meisel,
    Meischeiel) I, 627, 630, 634
BURKOLT
  John II, 126
BURMAN
  Johannes I, 720
BURN
  Eliz. I, 80
  Jacob I, 80
  Maria Eliza II, 181
BURNSEL
  Godf. II, 61
BURR
  Friederich
    (Frederick, Fred[k]) I, 605, 606, 608

BURSCH
  Johanne II, 125
BÜRY (BURY, BIRY, BIRI)
  Christian I, 59, 63, 65
  Gertrauth I, 61
  Hans Baltzer I, 740
  J. J. II, 68
  Mr. II, 176
BUS *see* BUSCH
BUSCH (BUS, BUSH, BUSS, PUSS)
  A. Regina II, 69
  Andreas II, 69
  Anna I, 67
  Cathrina I, 67
  Dionisius I, 734
  Eliza[t] I, 79
  Georg Conrad I, 762
  Hannes (John) I, 387, 388, 389
  Hanns Georg
    (Hans Jurg) I, 605, 606, 608
  Hans Michael I, 652
  Heinz Ernst II, 41
  Henrich (Hend[k]) I, 387, 388, 389
    II, 72
  Herman, im I, 510
  Jacob I, 605, 606, 608, 702
    II, 179
  Johann Daniel I, 365
  Johann Frantz I, 700
  Johann Georg I, 474
  Johan Gunder I, 654
  Johann Jost I, 753
  Johann Henrich I, 753
  Johan Jacob I, 66, 69, 70
    162, 164, 166
  Johan Martin I, 390
  Johan Michael
    (Michell) I, 116, 120, 121
    283, 284, 286
  Johann Nickel I, 371
  Johann Paul I, 390
  Johan Philip I, 365
  Johannes I, 467, 643, 645
  Ludewig I, 521, 523
  Maria Margrita I, 118
  Peter I, 643, 645
  Sebastian I, 348, 349, 351
  Willhelm I, 753
  —— II, 51
BUSCHFELD (BOFFELT, BOS-
  VELD)
  Joan Hend. I, 237
  Johan Jost
    (Johan Joost) I, 237, 239, 240
BÜSCHLER
  Johann Ludwig I, 486
BUSEL
  Johannes I, 685

BUSEN, van
Susanna   II, 119
BUSER
Barb.   II, 124
Hans Jacob   II, 124
Heinrich   I, 391
Martin   II, 124
BUSH *see* BUSCH
BUSHART
Adam   I, 289
BUSHON
Andreas   I, 660
BUSING
Eieffa   I, 117
BÜSINGER
Johann Peter   I, 729
BUSKEY
Nicholas   I, 660
BUSMAN (BUSSMAN)
Andreas   I, 536, 537, 538
Hans Henry
(John Henery)   I, 537, 538
Henry   I, 536, 537, 538
(*See also* BOSMAN)
BUSS *see* BUSCH
BUSSART
Andereas   I, 415
BUSSE
Heinrich Wilhelm   I, 749
BUSSEL
Christian Ludwig   I, 748
BUSSER
Baptist   II, 193
Catharina   II, 53
Hans   I, 392
Johannes   I, 721
John   II, 53, 193
John Baptist   II, 193
Justine   II, 37
BUSSLER
Heinrich   I, 738
BUSSY
Hans Uhlleryg   I, 416
BUSTER
Jacob   II, 145
BUSTH
Michael   I, 493
BUTCHER
Jn   II, 18
BUTEFISCH
Johann Conradt   I, 503
BÜTEKOFER (BOTIKOFER)
Nicklaus (Nicholas)   I, 151, 152
BUTH
Peter   I, 390
BÜTLER (BITTLER)
Johannes   I, 155, 158, 160
BUTLINGER
Barkont   II, 47

Margeretta   II, 47
Mary   II, 47
BÜTSCHE
Gregorius   I, 522, 525
BÜTTEL (BETTEL)
Andtreas   I, 502
Christoff (Chrtstn)   I, 540, 542, 544
Hans Jorg   I, 503
BUTTERFASS (BUTERFAS)
Daniel   I, 199, 201, 203
Mattheus   I, 336, 337, 339
BUTTERWEK   (BOTTERWECK,
BUTTERWICK)
Johannes (Hans)   I, 304, 305, 306
BUTTINGER
Daniel Phil.   II, 24
BUTTMAN
Eberhart   I, 485
BÜTTNER (BÜDTNER)
Gottfriedt   I, 435
Hans Gorg   I, 702
Hans Michel   I, 363
Hennrich   I, 363
Johann Carl   I, 748
Johan Christoph   I, 502
Joseph   I, 596, 597, 599
Michel   I, 699
BUTZ (POTTS, PUTZ)
H.   II, 141
Johann Gorg   I, 716
Johannes   I, 491
John Henry   I, 347
Peter   I, 246, 247, 248
646, 647
BÜTZEL
Adam Michael   I, 720
BYDER
Peter   II, 126
BYERLEY
Casper   I, 660
BYHAN
Gottlieb   II, 78
BYLE
Eveles   I, 242
BYLI
Jacob   II, 184
BYRER
Casper   II, 163
Frederick   II, 163
Gotlope   II, 163
Johannes   II, 163
Rosina   II, 163
BYSHALL
Jacob   I, 413

CAAREL (read CARL)
Casper   I, 437

CABEL (CABLE)
Christian II, 47
Daniel I, 437
Hans I, 394
Mary II, 47
CABELL (CABBELL)
Conrad II, 126
Nicolaus I, 715
CACHELLER (CALLER)
Martin I, 666, 668, 670
CACHO
Jacob I, 744
CAFFARAL (CAUFFEREL)
Paul I, 526, 527, 529
CAFFROTH
Peter Wilhelm I, 371
CAHLER
Jno. Jacob I, 85
Jno. Jerack I, 85
CALB (CALEB)
Martin I, 20, 21
CALL
Ebenezer II, 18
P. II, 32
CALLER (CARLO)
Michell I, 176, 177, 178
CAMBECK
Jacob I, 401
CAMELL
Bernhard I, 143
Joas I, 760
John I, 143
Patrick I, 143
CAMERSON
John I, 143
CAMMASSASEA
—— II, 141
CÄMMERER (CAMMERER, KAM-
MERER)
Andreas I, 184, 186, 187
Dietrich I, 476
Johann Ludwig I, 155, 158, 161
(See also KÄMMERER)
CAMMERLICH
Johann Fridrich I, 750
CAMMERON
Daniel I, 143
CAMORE
Theobald I, 268
CAMPBIN (read KAMP)
Maria Magdelina I, 28
CAMPE
Franc Carel, von I, 506
CAMPHUYSEN
Henriette II, 58
CAMPING (read KAMP)
Magreta I, 40
CAMPPELL
R. II, 76

Rebecah II, 76
CANKLOOTS (KONGETZ)
Albrecht Wolff
(Woolf) I, 66, 69, 70
CANNAPE
Johannes II, 193
CANTZLER
Anthony I, 546, 548, 550
CANZ
Johann Jacob I, 442
CAP (CAPP)
George Fyt I, 189, 192, 194
Georg Martin I, 191
(See also CAPP)
CAPANN
Cath. Eliz. II, 97
Philip II, 97
CAPELL
Charles I, 756
CAPP (CAAP)
Georg Fridrich
(Fridrich) I, 67, 69, 70
Michael I, 67, 69, 70
CAPPE
Martin II, 181
CAPPERS
John II, 47
CAPPES (CAPES)
Henrich
(J. Heinrick) I, 621, 623, 625
CAQUELIN (CACKELIE)
Didie (Diderich) I, 162, 165, 166
Jean (Hance) I, 163, 165, 166
Sebastien I, 162, 165, 166
CAR (KAR)
Catherina I, 43
Christian I, 45
Creeto I, 43
Gerich Hendrich I, 45
Heinrich I, 44
CARBAUM
Charles II, 47
Daniel II, 47
Elizabeth II, 47
Maria Elizabeth II, 47
Maria Margareta II, 48
Maria Susanna II, 47
CARBER (CARVER, GERBICK)
Simon (Simeon) I, 527, 528, 530
CARE
J. N. II, 197
CAREL (CAAREL, read CARL)
Caspar I, 437
Dewald I, 271
Hans Michael I, 507
CARGES
Philipp I, 500
CARIE
Dorbie I, 143

CÄRIUS
Peter   I, 701
CARL (CARLE, CAREL, CARREL, KARL)
Christopf   I, 485
Conrad   I, 50
Elizabeth   I, 50
Esaias   I, 372
Georg   I, 472
Georg Andereas   I, 467
Georg Martin   I, 454
Hans Joseph
(Hans Michael)   I, 162, 164, 165
Henry   I, 474
Jacob   I, 48, 52, 53
Johanes   I, 243, 244, 245, 660
Jo[hann]   I, 739
Johann Jacob
(Jacob)   I, 384, 386, 401
Johann Kasber   I, 384, 386
Johannes Wilhelm   I, 753
Maria Magdalina   I, 49
Nicholas (Nicolaus)   I, 661, 662, 664
Simon (Simeon)   I, 66, 69, 70
   162, 164, 166
   660
(*See also* CAAREL *and* CAREL)
CARMANE
Anthony   I, 473
Johanes   I, 473
CARNAL
David   II, 31
CARNE
Jarrick   I, 100
CARNOIS
————   II, 81
CAROLINE
————   II, 80
CAROLUS
Johans   I, 760
CARPO
John And.   II, 127
CARR
Jno   I, 753
CARTER
William   I, 143
CARTMAN
Isaac   I, 706
CASALY
Cornelle   II, 78
CASE
John   II, 26
CASIENS
Margretha   II, 50
CASKE
————   II, 58
CASMAN (KUSMAN, read prob. KÄSMANN)
Margaret   I, 43

Ruluf (Roolof)   I, 43, 46, 47
CASNER
Philip   I, 685
CASPAR (CASPER)
Jacob   II, 179
Valentin (Valantine)   I, 383, 385
(*See also* KASPAR, KASPER)
CASPERS
Antji   II, 61
CASSEL (CASTLE)
Christian   I, 213, 215, 216
CASSELER (CASSLER, CASSEL)
Wilhelm (William)   I, 576, 578, 580
CASSER (CASSAR, CASERN)
Alexander   I, 122, 125, 126
Anna   I, 123
Johan   I, 123
Magdalena   I, 123
Mathias   I, 123
CASTIRENS
Caterena Elizh   II, 49
Johan Francis Christian   II, 49
Johan Henderick Daniel   II, 49
CASTLE
Jillis   I, 16
Johannes   I, 16
CATO
John   I, 592
CAUFMAN, CAUFFMAN, KAUFMAN, KAUFFMAN   *see*
CAUSE
Casper   II, 96
CAVAN
John   II, 18
CAWEIN
Mathis   II, 20
CAWS
Christian   II, 17
Dorothy   II, 17
J. Ct.   II, 17
J. Friderik   II, 17
CAZENOVE
Antoine Charles   II, 73
Jeane Antoine   II, 73
CAZO
Hermanus   I, 726
CEIL (read KEIL)
Johan Henrich   I, 731
CEKE
Cristopher   II, 83
CENAS
Pierre   II, 100
CERBER (read KERBER)
Henry   I, 328
CERST
William   II, 104
CEYFERT (read SEYFERT)
Barbara   II, 149
Elisabeth   II, 149

Eve II, 149
Johannes II, 149
Lorentz II, 149
Nicholas II, 149
CHAILLET
Mr. II, 174
CHAILLOT
Nicola I, 754
CHALYBAEUS
Christian Gottlob II, 58
CHAMBAUD
Jean Baptist II, 83
CHAMP
Mathias II, 26
CHAPLIN
Mr. I, 20
CHAPPELLE (CHAPPEL)
Eberhart I, 455
Jean Pierre (Peter) I, 526, 527, 529
Jeremie I, 526, 527, 529
CHARLES (CHARLE)
Claude I, 201, 203
Frederica II, 17
CHARMELY
Simon I, 403
CHARTIER
Joseph I, 405
CHASER
Joseph I, 689
CHASROOD
Nicholas I, 16
CHEIL (KIELL)
Christofel
(Christopher) I, 653, 654
CHEVALLIER
David II, 31
Johannes II, 193
CHEVERNET
—— II, 80
CHIRNY (SHERNEY)
Johanes (Johannes) I, 585, 587, 588
CHNEIDLE
Joseph II, 186
CHONRATH (read CONRAT)
Johann Nicolaus I, 394
CHORIST
Valentine I, 754
CHORLSBOURN
Charles II, 11
CHRESMAN
Nicholas I, 16
CHRESTIEN (CHRISTIAN)
Jean François
(Francis) I, 163, 165, 166
CHRINSTIN
Johann Friederich Wilhelm II, 59
CHRIS see CRESS
CHRISBACK
Michael I, 450

CHRISMAN
Mathias I, 687
CHRIST (CRIST, KRIST)
Anna I, 60
Balthasar I, 686
Ernst Wilhelm I, 712
Eva Catherina I, 127
Georg Simeon
(Georg Simon) I, 173, 174
Hans Adam I, 330
Henry II, 75
Jacob I, 59, 63, 64, 127, 129, 130
Johann Gorg I, 330, 467
Johann Leonhardt I, 431
Johann Phieliepps I, 460
Johannes I, 18, 20
Lewis II, 197
Magdalena I, 127
Marcus I, 127, 129, 130
Maria I, 80
Nickolaus (Nicholas) I, 373, 374, 375
Philipps Conradt I, 734
William II, 197
CHRISTBAUM
Johann I, 467
CHRISTEIN (CHRISTIN)
Christian I, 471
Hans Jerg I, 471
Peter I, 471
CHRISTELMYER
Fried. II, 58
CHRISTIAN (CHRISTIAAN, CHRISTEN)
Anna I, 67
Carl Friedrich Daniel I, 503
Catharine I, 67
Eva I, 67
Friederich (Fred^k) I, 390, 628, 631 634
Gottfried (Gotfrey) I, 265, 268, 271
Hans I, 274
Hendrich (Hendrick) I, 66, 67, 69, 70
Jerick I, 67
Jo. (Jn°) I, 708; II, 18
Johann Gerg
(Joh. Jurg) I, 585, 587, 588
Johann Michael I, 509
Johannes I, 717
John Wilhelm
(Johan William) I, 656, 657, 658
Ludwig (Ludewig) I, 585, 587, 588
Magdalen I, 67
Margaret I, 67
Maria I, 67
Peter II, 125
Philip I, 335, 336, 338
Rudolff (Rudolph) I, 79, 82, 83
Salme I, 67

CHRISTIANSEN
Johann (Johan)   I, 601, 602, 603
CHRISTIN see CHRISTEIN
CHRISTLER
John Jacob   I, 156, 159, 161
CHRISTMAN   (CRISTMAN,
CHRISTMANN)
Charles   I, 687
Daniel   I, 34, 35, 36
Frantz   I, 724
Henrich   I, 317, 318, 319
Jacob   I, 163, 165, 167
Johann Georg   I, 734
Johann Philipp   I, 419
John Jorg Paulus   I, 705
Johan Michael   I, 394
Matthias   I, 687
Michel (Michal)   I, 379, 380, 382
                          384, 386
CHRISTNER
Hans   I, 732
CHRISTON
John   II, 195
CHRISTY (CHRISTI)
Hanns Jerg   I, 477
Hans (Johan)   I, 274, 275
Rudolph   I, 445
CHRON
Nicklos   I, 15
CHRUY
Johann   I, 617, 619
CHRYPFEIUS
Johann Petter   I, 696
CHUR
Joh. Jacob   II, 41
CHURCH
Lapil   II, 195
CHURVEST
Adrian   II, 61
CHYSON
Ch. Israel   II, 6
CIDER
Hance Yarah   I, 344
CIEWITS (read KIEWITT)
Hans Peter   I, 408
CINKEL
Conrad   I, 502
CIROKLER
Elizabeth   II, 92
CLAAR (GLASS)
Winantus
(Antus)   I, 672, 673, 674
CLAAS (CLAUS)
Michael (Mich¹)   I, 677, 678, 680
CLAIN (read KLEIN)
Martin   I, 451
Mathias   I, 289
CLAIRE
———   II, 80

CLAITHER
Chris. Stein   I, 237
CLAP (CLOP, KLAP)
Johann Ludwig   I, 12
Jörg Valentin   I, 12
Joseph   I, 10, 12
Jurg   I, 10
Ludowigh   I, 10
Peter   I, 301, 302, 303
CLARK (CLARKE)
Edwd   II, 75
William   II, 75
CLASS (CLAAS)
Johannes (John)   I, 637, 639, 641
CLASSEN
Engelbert   I, 754
CLASTNER
———   II, 80
CLAUBOUGH
Martin   I, 704
CLAUDE
Pitro   I, 729
CLAUDY (CLODY)
Martin (Mark)   I, 232, 233
Vallentin   I, 453
CLAUS (CLAUSS)
Conrath   I, 371
Georg   I, 442
Hans Michael   I, 508
Johan Herman   I, 371
Joh. Joseph   II, 139
Johan Teys   I, 495
Johannes   I, 358, 442, 495, 684
Leonhart   I, 479
Mathias   I, 256, 259
Stephanus   II, 42
CLAUSSEN
Catharina Elizabeth   II, 91
Catherine   II, 81
Christoph   II, 91
CLAUSSENIUS
Wilhelm   I, 425
CLAUSER (KLAUSSER)
Henry   I, 445
Jacob   I, 348, 350, 351, 445
Mathias (Matteas,
Matthias)   I, 256, 259, 261
Peter   I, 348
CLAUTSCH
Jacob   I, 721
CLEAR
Frederick   II, 83
CLEH (KLEY)
Johann Nickel
(Hans Nichall)   I, 266, 269, 272
CLEIS (CLEISS)
Hans Jorg   I, 405
Johan Daniel   I, 737
CLEM see KLEMM

CLEMENT
Johann Henrich   I, 707
CLEMENTS (CLEMENS, CLEM-
ENTZ)
Jn⁰ Michˢ   I, 752
Johann Peter   I, 421
Michel   I, 213, 215
Nickelaus
(Nicklos, Nicholas) I, 378, 379, 381
Vallantin
(Valentine)   I, 621, 623, 625
CLEVLEY
Eliza   II, 67
CLEWER (CLEVER)
Conrad   I, 84, 86, 87
Mardin   I, 355
CLICK
Baldos   I, 94
CLIEN (read prob. KLEIN)
Christinea   II, 77
Philip   II, 77
CLINE (read KLEIN)
Anthony   I, 736
Jeremiah   I, 721
John   II, 47
(*See also* KLEIN)
CLISORE
Chaˢ   II, 123
CLOATES
Jacob   II, 104
CLODER (CLODDER)
Jacob   I, 221, 223, 224
CLOSS (CLOS, CLOOS)
Christian   I, 496
Johann Henrich   I, 465
Johann Theobald   I, 509
Melchior
(Leonard)   I, 204, 206, 207
Peter   II, 16
CLOSSE
Hans Jerg   I, 394
CLOSSHEIM
Johannes   I, 340
CLOSSMEYER
Johannes Peter   I, 495
CLOTER
Francˢ   I, 760
CLOUDY
Christo.   II, 49
CLOW
Jacob   I, 707
CLUDT
Wilhelm De   II, 178
CLUND
Anna Margritta   I, 144
CLUTLAND
Wᵐ   II, 15
CNUBER
Jacob   I, 468

COALE (COAL, read KOHL)
Anna   I, 38
Leonard   I, 37
COATS
Christian   I, 358
COBBEL
Daniel   I, 706
COBBIER
Hanna   II, 17
COBET
Abʳ   II, 72
Daniel   .II, 72
COBIS (CABBAS)
Caspar (Casper)   I, 556, 557, 558
COBLENTZ
Jacob   I, 730
COBLET
Christoff   I, 447
COCH (COGH, read KOCH)
Anna Catrina   I, 28
Jurg   I, 10
COCHEROFT
James   II, 32
COCHET
Georg Dietrich   I, 723
Isaac   I, 723
Johann Isac   I, 723
COCHRAN
John   II, 25
COCK
Michael   I, 99
COCKABETER
Anna   I, 73
COCKBURN
——   II, 81
COELUS
Johannes   I, 482
COGER
Jacob   I, 19
COGGER (COKER, KOKER)
Eveles   I, 241
Michall   I, 241
Peter (Petter)   I, 240, 242, 243
COHEN (COHAN)
Abraham   II, 72
Abraham Berend   II, 161
Angel   II, 72
COIDOU
Jan   II, 95
Johanna   II, 95
COIST *see* KOST
COLB *see* KOLB
COLINARR
Maria Eliz.   II, 105
COLLAR
Maria   I, 80
COLLEP
Peter   I, 431

COLLER
Henry   I, 431
COLLINS
Mark   II, 27
COLMAR
Mr.   II, 176
COLP
Jacobina   II, 48
(*See also* KOLB)
COLTIN
John   II, 195
COMB
Hannah   I, 84
COMBE
Lewis   II, 112
COMBILAIRE
——   II, 80
COMEKE
G.   II, 141
COMEYOUN
Anna Catherina   II, 6
Jn⁰ Church   II, 6
COMMENS (COMENS)
Christian   I, 310, 311, 313
COMMING
J. P.   II, 32
COMPLAIRE
Jean Pierre   II, 31
COMPO
Peter   I, 486
COMÜLDER (COMMELLDER)
Johan Hendrik
(Jn⁰ Henry)   I, 589, 590, 591
CONATEN
Anna Eve   I, 79
CONNET (KONNET)
Joseph   I, 645, 647
CONOLY
Nancy   II, 169
Willᵐ   II, 169
CONRAD (CONRADT, CONRAT,
CONRATH)
Carl Ferdinand   I, 753
Carlina   II, 10
Cath.   II, 10
Charles   II, 26
Christian   I, 629, 632, 635
Conrad   I, 363
Erhardt   I, 683
Friederich   I, 404
Georg (George,
Yerick)   I, 179, 181, 183
283, 284, 285
402
George Magnus (Gorge Magnus,
Jurg Manus)   I, 629, 632, 635
Godfrey   II, 10
Hans   I, 415
Hans Leond.   I, 67, 69, 70

Hans Martin   I, 288, 289
Henrich   I, 402
J. J.   II, 71
Jacob   I, 179, 181, 184
283, 426, 702
Jn⁰   II, 10
Johan Friedrich   I, 461
Johann Georg   I, 521, 524
Johan Henrich   I, 443
Johann Jacob
(Jacob)   I, 176, 177, 178
Johann Michael   I, 427
Johann Michael   I, 753
Johann Peter   I, 367, 368
Johan Steffen
(Hans Stephen)   I, 188, 191, 193
Johannes   I, 412, 487
John Henry   II, 159
Jost (Jurs)   I, 559, 561, 562
Magdalena   II, 159
Mathias   I, 757
Michael (Michel)   I, 483; II, 154
Nicklas   I, 427
Paul   I, 709
Pether   I, 750
Ully   I, 415
Wilhelm   I, 486, 487
——   II, 159
(*See also* CUNNERAD *and* CON-
RAD)
CONRADI (CONRADE)
Caspar   I, 430
Hans Martin   I, 286, 288
Johannes   I, 709
CONSE
Christian   I, 724
CONSELMAN (CONSLEYMEN)
Barthlemeus   I, 310, 311, 313
CONSTANT
——   II, 81
CONSUL
Etienne   I, 362
CONTICK
Durst   I, 445
CONTONO
Jons   I, 760
CONVER
Christian Carel   I, 455
Henrich (Hendrick)   I, 387, 388, 389
Johann Petter   I, 508
CONVIRE
Francoi   I, 363
COOBLE
Hans   I, 13
COOK
George   II, 126
Jn⁰   I, 738
COOLER
Fridrich   I, 102

COOLL (read KUHL)
Johann Olrich   I, 766
Maria   I, 767
Mathies   I, 767
Solmey   I, 766
COOLMAN (read KUHLMAN)
Francis   I, 732
COOPE
Joost   I, 14
COOPER
Georg   I, 449
Marg^t   II, 6
COOPMAN
Johannes   I, 18
COOS
Christian   I, 276, 277, 278
COPE
Peter N.   II, 6
Yorick (Georg)   II, 12
COPENHAVER (COPEHAVER)
Barbara   I, 67
Catharina   I, 67
Maria   I, 67
Michael   I, 66, 69, 70
Rosina   I, 67
Wolff (Woolf)   I, 66, 69, 70
COPFIRS
Margret   I, 117
COPIA
Joh. Nicolaus   I, 382
Sigmund   I, 469
COPPY
Uhllerik   I, 415
COQUIGNY
——   II, 80
CORBER
Elizabeth   II, 5
John Adam   II, 5
(*See also* KÖRBER)
CORBO (CARBO)
Jean (Johan)   I, 184, 185, 187
CORDES
Anna   II, 205
C. H.   II, 72
CORELL (CORRELL, CURREL)
Daniel   I, 204, 206, 207
Johan Jacob (Johann
Jacob, Jacob)   I, 297, 298, 300
Johannes   I, 297, 298, 300
   318, 319, 397
(*See also* KORREL)
CORMAN (CORRMAN, CORNMAN)
Conradt   I, 318, 319
CORN (read KORN)
Henry   I, 503
Nich°   I, 14
CORNAR
Anna   I, 124
Paulus   I, 124

Salumi   I, 124
CORNEILLE
——   II, 81
CORNELISSE (CORNELEISE, read
CORNELIUS)
Anna   II, 137
Christian   II, 135
CORNELIUS (CORNEILUS)
Elizabeth   I, 108
J. Jacob (Johan)   I, 601, 602, 603
Lawrence   I, 109
Petter   I, 107, 111, 112
Vronicke   I, 109
CORNGIBEL
Johann   I, 429
CORNGIBER
Vallentin   I, 444
CORNHAS (CORNHES)
Johannes   I, 522, 525
CORNISH
James   II, 26
CORNMAN
Maria Adrina   II, 193
CORRELL
Johann Adam   I, 419
CORRMAN
Yorick Fred.   II, 3
CORSINI (CORSENEZ)
Johann Friedricus
Franciscus   I, 589, 590
CORT (COURT, CORD)
Christoff (Christ^n)   I, 517, 519, 520
Christoff, Junr   I, 517, 519, 520
Ernst   I, 516, 518, 519
CORTERN
Henrich   I, 691
COST
Marden   II, 26
COSTE
Mr. da   II, 175
COSTER (CÖSTER)
Abraham   II, 137
Friderick   II, 137
H. Henry
(Hans Enert)   I, 536, 537, 538
Lorentz   I, 652, 654
COTT (GOTT, COOT)
Johan Conradh (Johan
Conrath, Conrad)   I, 601, 602, 604
COTTRINGER
John   I, 725
COTZ (read prob. GÖTZ)
Christoph   I, 468
COUGHLY (COCKLEY)
Henry   I, 331, 332, 334
COULER
Margarit   I, 123
COUMAND
Hans Philip   I, 304

Walrad I, 304
COUN
Hans I, 66
COUNISH
Cath. Marg. II, 105
COUNTS (read KUNTZ)
Daniel II, 36
COUPER
Peter II, 95
COURPENNING
Hendrick I, 458
COURSE
Henry I, 747
COURTEUER
Joseph I, 405
COUSSE (GROSS)
Andereas
(Andreas) I, 156, 159, 161
COUTERET
S. L. II, 136
COUTTIEZ
Jean I, 469
COUTS see KAUTZ
COUWALD (COWALT)
Nicklas (Nicholas) I, 276, 277, 278
COWELL
Ann Eliza I, 766
Anna Catrina I, 766
Conreet I, 766
Savena I, 766
CRABLE
Hans Erick I, 12
Michell I, 12
CRAFT (read KRAFT)
Susana II, 36
CRAM
Elizabeth I, 67
CRAMER (KRAMER, CREMER)
Daniel I, 488
Johann Helffer I, 628, 631, 634
Johannes Peter I, 353, 354
Lorentz I, 628, 631, 634
Louisa II, 59
Philip II, 59
(See also KRÄMER)
CRÄMM
Johan Tönges I, 699
CRANESTER (KRANISTER)
Johannes
(Johanis) I, 199, 202, 204
CRAPY
Peter I, 407
CRASLER see KRESLER
CRÄSMANN (CROSMANN,
CHRESSMAN)
Johann George I, 276, 277, 278
CRASS
Christopher II, 13
Magdalena II, 13

Maria II, 13
Peter II, 13
CRASSEN (CRASSAN)
Carel I, 304
Jeorg I, 422
CRATSAR (read KRATZER)
Anna I, 80
CRATZ see KRATZ
CRAU (read prob. GRAU)
Arnold II, 101
CRAYSER
Hanna II, 14
CREASMAN
Maria I, 60
CREBIL (CREEPLE)
Jakob (Jacob) I, 23, 25, 26
(See also KREBIEHL)
CREBLER
Achior I, 434
Jacob I, 434
CRECA
Philte I, 324
CREESH
Georg I, 469
CREESTE
Christian I, 406
CREETOR
Moret I, 24
CREFF (CREEF, read GRAEF)
Jacob I, 408
Philipp Jacob I, 408
Sebastian I, 7
CREINER (read GREINER)
Andereas I, 404
Johanes I, 523, 525
Martin I, 35, 36
CREITZ
Jacob I, 420
CREMER
Conrad I, 425
Cornelia II, 91
Johann Friedrich I, 415
(See also CRAMER and KRÄMER)
CRENER
Elizabeth II, 166
Malchior II, 166
Rosina II, 166
CRENTZER (GRENSER,
GRANSER)
Peter (Peiter) I, 287, 288, 289
CRESS (KRESS, CRESSE, CHRIS)
Jacob I, 287, 288, 289
Jeorge Philip (Jurich, Jurich
Philip) I, 287, 288, 289
Johann Henrich I, 499
CRESSE (CHRIS)
Matteas (Mathias) I, 244, 245
CRESSEL
Christoff I, 363

CRESSMANN (CRESMAN, CREES-
MAN)
Frederika   II, 204
Hans Adam   I, 314, 315
Johan Henrick   I, 327, 329
CRETEL
Hans Michael   I, 489
CREUCAS (KRIMUS)
Jacques (Jacb)   I, 195, 196, 197
CREUSUMER (CHRIESMERG)
William (Wm.)   I, 66, 69, 70
CREUTZ (CREYTZ, KREUTZ)
Christophorus Theophilus
(Christian)   I, 244, 245
Dewalt   I, 521, 523
Johann Daniel (Dan-
iel)   I, 377, 379, 381
Johann Gorg   I, 693
Johann Hinrich (John
Henry)   I, 569, 570, 572
Johannes (John)   I, 569, 571, 573
                              II, 3
Philip   I, 318, 319
Tilman   I, 443
Wilhelm   I, 495
CRICK
John Conrad   I, 712
CRIES
Johannes   I, 731
CRIGHBAN
Credle   I, 241
CRILING see GREULING
CRIMM (read GRIMM)
Peter   I, 496
CRINSTON
Hans Ulrich   I, 35
CRIPSIZER
Even Boble   I, 85
Hanna Margrett   I, 85
Hanna Mela   I, 85
Hannah Boble   I, 85
CRISON
Isaac   I, 21, 22
CRISPIN (CRISSBY)
Joseph   I, 586, 587, 588
CRISSTA
Maria   I, 79
CRIST
Henrich   II, 145
Johannes   I, 307
Manuel   II, 145
CROFF
Jacob   I, 660
CROLL
Martin   I, 660
CROLUS
Henry Fred[k]   II, 108
J. H.   II, 108

CROM
Alexander   II, 73
Carl   II, 61
(See also CROMM)
CROMBACH
Johan Conrath   I, 693
Johannes   I, 693
CROMBHOLTS
Joh. Carl   II, 125
CROMER
Frederick (Fred[k]) I, 175, 176, 177
CROMM
Antonias   I, 699
Henrich   I, 699
Johan Theis   I, 684
CRON (CROWN read KRON)
Henrich (Hend[k])   I, 373, 374, 376
Johannes   I, 221, 223, 224
Lorentz   I, 296, 298, 299
Martin   I, 179, 181, 183
Simon Jacob   I, 307, 309, 310
CRONBACH
Leonhardt (Leon-
hart)   I, 155, 158, 160
CRONEBERG
Johann Wilhellem   I, 466
CRONEMAN
Leon[d]   I, 760
CRONENBERG
Hermanus   I, 503
CRONENBERGER
Friederich   I, 761
Johann Peter   I, 761
Philippes   I, 323, 325, 326
CRONMILLER
Johann Martin   I, 490
CRONRO (CRONRAW)
J. Henry (Johannes
Henrich)   I, 577, 578, 580
CROO (read KROH)
Henry   I, 16
CROP (CROOPE, CROPE, CROPP)
Casper (Gasper)   I, 331, 332, 334
George   I, 468
Rosina   I, 28
CROSBY
Elisha   II, 26
CRÖSSMANN, (CRÖSMAM, CROSS-
MAN, GREESMAN)
Georg (Dirick)   I, 24, 26, 27
Henrich (Henr[k])   I, 176, 177, 178
Johan Georg (Johannes
Dirick)   I, 24, 26, 27
Johan Henrich (John
Hendrick)   I, 286, 287, 288
Marya   I, 24
Philip Balthaser (Philip
Balter)   I, 286, 287, 288

Niklos   I, 17
(*See also* GROSSMAN)
CROUSE (read KRAUSS)
Johannes   I, 12
CROW (read KROH)
Ludwick   I, 660
CROWN
Eady   II, 94
Richard   II, 70
CROY (COY)
Lorenz Friedrich   I, 539, 541, 543
CROYTER (CROITER, read KREU-TER)
Jacob   I, 176, 177, 178
CRUL (read CROLL)
Herman   II, 122
CRUM (CROMM, CRUMM, CRAMM)
Johann Frentz (Francis)   I, 569, 571, 572
Johannes (John)   I, 569, 571, 573
Paulus (Paul)   I, 569, 571, 573
CRUMBER
Joseph   II, 76
CRUNBURG
J. H.   II, 17
CRUSE
John   II, 60
CRUSER
Nichlas   II, 6
CRUSIUS
Georg Ludwig   I, 683
CRUYSMEYER (CRYSMEYER)
Simon   I, 209, 211
CRYBILE
Christian   I, 16
Jn°   I, 16
CUHN (read KUHN)
J. Jacob   II, 206
CULMAN
Jacob   I, 734
Johan Burckhardt   I, 701
Johannes   I, 690
Philips (Philip) I, 277, 278, 279, 717
CUMM (KOWN)
Johann Adam Simon (Adam Simon)   I, 116, 120, 121
Johan Christoff (Christoph, Crostpffel)   I, 116, 120, 121
(*See also* KUM)
CUMP
George   I, 414
CUNCKEL (KONKEL, KANKEL)
Andreas (Anderreas, Anderas)   I, 627, 631, 634
Peter   I, 627, 631, 634
CUNIUS
Johann Jacob   I, 419
Philips (Philip)   I, 205, 206, 208

CUNKEL
George   I, 444
CUNNERAD (read CONRAD)
Friedrich Jacob   I, 433
CUNNINGHAM
Mary   I, 23
CUNOW
Augusta Henrieta   II, 83
Benigna Sophia   II, 83
Carolina Louise   II, 83
Charlotte Philippine   II, 83
Joh. Gebhard   II, 83
CUNRAD (CONRED, CONRAD, CUNRATT, CONRADT)
Christian   I, 629, 632, 635
Daniel   I, 492
Henrich (Henry)   I, 300, 301, 302
Johannes   I, 492
(*See also* CONRAD)
CUNSMAN
Frederick   II, 126
CUNTZ (CONCE, COONES, KUNTZ)
Catharine   I, 67
Eva   I, 67
Frantz   I, 431
Gerg   I, 716
Hans   I, 67
Hans Görg   I, 66, 69, 70, 712
Hans Michael   I, 423
Jacob   I, 156, 159, 161
Johann Henrich   I, 435
Johan Jacob   I, 9
Johann Niclaus (Nickel) I, 328, 426
Johannes (Johanes)   I, 37, 38, 39
Lorentz   I, 347
Ludwig   I, 628, 631, 634
Mathis   I, 715
Michael   I, 440
Nick.   I, 420
Theobalt   I, 431
William   I, 382
(*See also* KUNTZ)
CUNTZER (KINSER)
Nickel   I, 31, 33, 34
CUNTZMAN (CUNTZELMAN, KUNTELMAN)
Johann Jacob (Jacob) I, 592, 593, 594
Philipp Jacob   I, 716
CUNY
Beniamin   I, 399
CUONRAD (read CUNRAD, CONRAD)
Johan Engl   I, 467
CURFES (KURFES, COURFAS)
Christoph (Christn) I, 585, 586, 588
CURNERT
Johan Philip   I, 35

CURR
Heinrich   I, 454
Johan Georg   I, 453
CUSHWA (CUSCHWAH)
Isau (Isua, Isai)   I, 71, 75, 77
CYRIACI
Samuel   I, 686
CZOLBE
Carl Ludw.   II, 107

DACHENHAUSEN
Mr. Chas   II, 57
DAGELER
Frederic   II, 197
DÄGEN (read DEGEN)
Jacob   I, 275, 276
John   II, 185
Peter   I, 414
DAGENBECK   (DAGENBAG,
DAGEABACK)
Martin   I, 244, 245
DAHLETH
Marx   I, 442
DAHLHEIMER (DALHEYMER)
Bernherd
(Bernernd)   I, 205, 207, 209
DAHLMANN
Peter   I, 501
DAHMER
Johann Jost   I, 744
DAHN
Phillipp   I, 411
DAICHLER
Johannis   I, 490
DAIGER
Joseph   II, 192
DALEN
Margaretha   II, 54
Nicolaus   II, 54
Philipp   II, 54
DALHOFF
Anna Elizabeth   II, 78
DALICK (DALIK)
Vallentin   I, 621, 623, 625
DALLER
Dr.   II, 177
DALMAN
Gustaf Heinrich   II, 99
DALMAZO
Mr.   II, 177
DALWIG
Daniel   I, 257, 260, 262
DAMAN
John   I, 749
DAMBELLER
Jnᵒ Henry   I, 752

DAMEN
Catharina   II, 54
Sebilla   II, 54
DAMESS
Johanna   II, 41
DAMISCH
Frederic   II, 89
DAMMEL (DAMER)
Johan (John)   I, 637, 639, 641
DAMMANN
Elizth   II, 23
DAMMER   (DAMER,   TAMER,
TAMAR)
Christopher   I, 359, 361
Johan Balthasar   I, 359, 361
Johannes   I, 359, 361
John   I, 637, 639, 641
DAMPF
Wilhelm Friedterich   I, 744
DAMSER
Christan   I, 425
DANBACH
Jacob   I, 20
DANDELOT
John   II, 123
DÄNDERICH
Johann Jacob   I, 412
Johannes   I, 412
DANECKER (DANEGER)
F. C.   II, 122
Jacob Bernard   I, 454
DANENHAUER   (DANEHAUER,
DANHAUR,   DANNAHAWER,
DANNENAUER)
Abraham   I, 188, 189
Alias (Elias)   II, 126
Anna Maria   I, 189
Hans Georg (Jerg) I, 188, 360, 361
John (Jnᵒ)   I, 705; II, 126
Maria Dorothea   I, 189
Urcilla   I, 189
DANICKE
Johⁿ Christⁿ   II, 127
DANIEL (DANIELL)
Adam   I, 212, 214, 215
J. D.   II, 122
Jacob   I, 438
Johann Henrich (Henry) I, 314, 315
John Godfrey   II, 107
DÄNIG
Johan Henrich   I, 114, 115
D'ANION   (DANION,   DE AVA-
SONG)
Jean Louis (John Lew)   I, 93, 95
DANITKERS
Catharina   II, 92
DANKER
Heinrich   II, 78

DANLER
Hans   I, 79, 82, 83
Velley   I, 79
DANN (KAM)
Henrich (Henry)   I, 627, 630, 634
DANNCKHER
Jacob   I, 428
DANNEFELTZER (DANNENFEL-
SER, DANNFELTZER, DANNE-
FELD)
Dewalt   I, 487
Görig   I, 702
Johan Wendel   I, 335, 336, 338
DANNER
Abraham   I, 712
Allexander   I, 392
Christian   I, 503
Christoffer   I, 322
Dietrich   I, 331
Henrick   I, 364
Johann Uhland   I, 114, 115
Mardin   I, 400
Michel   I, 331, 494
Nickel   I, 391
Stephan   I, 683
DANNERINBORGEN
Michael (Michell)   I, 451
DANNEWALD (DAMEWALD)
Christian   I, 327, 329
DANNEY (TANNEUGH, TANNY,
TANYN)
Johan Adam (Hans
Adam)   I, 266, 269, 272
Johann Jacob   I, 266, 269, 272
Ludwig (Lodowich,
Ludwick)   I, 266, 269, 272
Philip (Phillip)   I, 266, 269, 272
DANNHÖFFER (DANHAVER)
Arnolt (Arnold)   I, 643, 645
DANNINGER
Jacob Friederik   I, 491
DANNWOLF
Friedrich   I, 471
DÄNNY (DEINIE, DEYNE)
Hans Michael (Mich[1])   I, 244, 245
DANSER
John   II, 117
DANSIUS
Johannes   I, 416
DANTIUS
Johann Valentin   I, 505
DANTZEBECKER (DANTZE-
BECHER, TANZENBECKER)
Jacob   II, 99
Johann Ludwig (Lud-
wig)   I, 677, 678, 680
Thomas   I, 677, 678, 680
DANZEL
Hans   I, 423

DAPPELLER
Barbara   I, 148
DÄPPEN (TEPPE)
Christen (Christian)   I, 163, 165, 166
DAFPER
Christian   I, 382
DARAHN (TARRAR)
Jorg (George)   I, 296, 298, 299
DARAND
Geo. Peter   I, 304
DÄRENDINGER (DERINGER)
Johannes   I, 667, 669, 671
DAREY
Widow   II, 80
DARM
Daniel   I, 405
DARTO
Michael   I, 347
DASCHER (DASHER)
Johann Christian   I, 169, 171, 173
DASER (DASAR, DASSER)
Agatius (G. A.)   I, 546, 548, 550
Paulus   I, 546, 548, 550
DASONS
Francis   I, 143
DÄSTERR
Johan Jacob   I, 403
DATISMAN
Johann Jacob   I, 399
DATT
George   II, 70
DÄTTWYLER
Martin   I, 392
DATZ
Adam (Johan Adam)   I, 581, 582, 584
Johan Better (Sebas-
tian)   I, 581, 582, 584
DAUB
Dillmanus   II, 79
Johann   I, 685
Johannes   I, 750; II, 79
Maria Margreta   II, 79
Peter   I, 205, 207, 208
Reinhart   I, 372
William (Wilhelm)   I, 204, 206, 208
DAUBENBERGER
Johann Jacob   I, 457
Valentin   I, 457
DAUBENSPECK (TOWASPECK)
Johan Jacob   I, 155, 158, 160
DÄUBER (DAUBERR)
Andon (Antone)   I, 643, 645
Bastian   I, 718
Friedrich   I, 369, 370
Georg Christoph (Yer-
rick Chris.)   I, 609, 610, 612
Georg Michael   I, 513, 514, 516
Johann Abraham   I, 461
Johann Ernst   I, 718

Peder (Peter) I, 378, 380, 381
Wilhelm I, 369, 370
DÄUBLER
Mathias Friderich I, 748
DÄUBLIN
Christian I, 448
DAUDERMAN
David I, 339
DAUERNHEIM (DAUERHEIM)
Johannes I, 643, 645
DAUM
Georg I, 684
Philibs I, 312, 313
DAUMENLANG
Jacob I, 430
DAUMER
Henry I, 430
Johann Ulrich I, 430
DAUMILLER
Tobias I, 468
DAURSCHAUER
Jacob I, 359
DAUSMAN
Daniel I, 691
DAUTTEL
Jacob I, 360, 362
DAVID
Jacob II, 122
Joseph I, 672
DAYBENER
Henry I, 754
DAYOR
Franz II, 94
Joseph II, 94
Peter II, 94
DEANE (DANE)
Hans Jericke I, 93
Michael I, 93
DEBALT (TEBOLT, DEBALD)
Jacob I, 199, 201, 203
John George I, 440
DEBELBESIN (DEBELBISSEN, DEIBELBESIN)
Casper I, 50
Elizabeth Margarita I, 49
Hans I, 48
Hans Georg (Hans George) I, 48, 52, 53
Hans Michel (Hans Michl) I, 48, 52, 53
Magdelena I, 49
DEBERTSHÄUSER
Henrich I, 685
Jacob Friedrich I, 397
DEBERWELL
Ludwig I, 509, 510
DEBES
Friderica II, 128
George Heinrich II, 128

Johannes II, 128
Maria Catharine II, 128
Rosina II, 128
DEBOLD
J. Cath. II, 199
(See also DEBALT)
DEBONG (DIBONG)
Lorentz (Lawrence) I, 225, 228, 230
DEBUS (DAWIS, DEWYS)
Daniel I, 349, 350, 351, 449
Jacob I, 349
Lodwick I, 349, 350, 351
DECHAN
Friederich I, 498
DECHANT
Jacob Wilhelm II, 173
DECHER (DECHERT)
Johann Georg I, 620, 622, 624
Johann Peter (Joh. Peter) I, 620, 622, 624
DECK (DEK)
Anna I, 139
Anna Barbara I, 139
Johan Hend^k I, 139
Johannes I, 139
Mathes (Matheis) I, 156, 159, 161
Nicklaus (Nicholas) I, 137, 141, 142
Simon I, 199, 201, 203
DECKER
Casper I, 232
Fred. I, 700
Georg Michael I, 526, 528, 530
Henry I, 459
Johann Henrich I, 465
Johann Jacob I, 310, 312, 313, 496
Johann Jorg I, 465
Johannes (John) I, 465; II, 123
Michael I, 522, 524
Rudolf (Roedolph) I, 252, 253, 255
Wendel I, 721
Willhelm (Wilhelm) I, 585, 587, 588
DECREIFF
Herman I, 356
(See also DEGREIFF)
DEDERER
Albrecht I, 457
Johann Ludwig (Luterich) I, 12, 13
DEDERICH
Anna Margreta II, 37
Anna Maria II, 36
Catarenia II, 37
Conrad II, 36
Elizabeth II, 37
Maria Cristina II, 37
Philipina II, 37
DE DIE (DAWDIE)
Abraham I, 591, 592, 594
Isacque I, 723
Jean I, 708

Jean Pier I, 708
Josue I, 708
DEDIGMAN (TADIGMAN, TADIGSMAN)
Anna Maria I, 127, 128
Maria Barbara I, 127, 128
Maria Catherina I, 128
Philip (Filbs) I, 127, 129, 130
DEEG (TECK, DEG)
Andreas I, 586, 587, 588
Friederich (Fredrick) I, 586, 587, 588
Johann David II, 134
Michael I, 506
DEER
Stephan I, 455
DEFERN (DEVEHERN, DE VEHRN)
J. Friederich I, 517, 518, 520
DEG
Georg I, 698
DEGEN (DEEGEN)
Georg Vallentin I, 693
Hans I, 392
Jacob I, 750, 751
Johann Ludwig I, 699
Johannes I, 390
DEGENFIELD
Everen II, 125
DEGENHART
Henrich Friderich I, 452
DEGER
Jno II, 186
DEGHE
Edar I, 445
DEGREIFF (DE GREIFF, DE-CRAFFT)
Carl I, 546, 548, 550
DEH (THEA)
Joan Nicolaus (Nicholas) I, 667, 669, 671
DEHN
Jerg Henrich I, 740
DEIBLE
Jacob I, 393
DEILE (THEYLE)
Fridrich (Fredk) I, 605, 606, 608
DEILL
Henrich Daniel I, 462
DEIMER (TIMOR)
Johan Simon (Simon) I, 277, 278, 279
DEIMLING (TIMELING)
Jacob Ludwig I, 645, 647
DEIN (DIEN)
Andreas (Anderas) I, 614, 616, 618
DEINIGER (DEININGER)
Catharine II, 85
George II, 85
Johann Michael I, 452
Lena Elisa II, 85

Michael II, 85
Regine II, 85
William II, 85
DEINIUS (DINIUS)
Jacob I, 705
John I, 705
DEIONG
Branco II, 162
DEISEL
Catherine II, 158
Peter II, 158
DEISERT
Georg Peter I, 694
DEISINGER (TIESINGEN)
Barthel I, 383, 385
Henrich (Hendk) I, 383, 385
DEISMAN
Ludwig Henrich I, 745
DEISS (DEIS, DISE, TICE)
Johannes (Joanis) I, 293, 294, 295
Michael I, 476
Peter I, 293, 294, 295
DEISSMILLER
Johan I, 728
DELAME
—— II, 80
DELATTER (DELADER, DE-LAUDER)
David I, 304, 305, 306
DELB
Isach Leboldus I, 156, 159, 161
(See also DELP)
DELBIG
Casimir I, 751
DELCHER
Johannes I, 430
DELCKAMP (DELCAMP)
Henrick Christoph (Henry Chrs) I, 589, 590, 591
DELISS
Albert I, 735
DELITZ (DELIZ)
Ernst (Augt. Ernest) I, 516, 518, 519
DELKEN
Anna Maria II, 76
Johann Michael II, 76
DELL
Carlel II, 50
DELLER
Johann Gerg I, 413
DELLINGER (TILLINER, TILLINGOR)
Jacob I, 113, 114, 115, 766
Philipp I, 439
Veltin I, 399
DELMER
John I, 143
DELP (DELB, DELPP)
Conrad (Conrath) I, 180, 182, 184

Gerg Petei   I, 546, 547, 550
J. Nicklas   I, 395
Johann Gorg (Hunderick)   I, 240, 242, 243
Johannes (Hannes)   I, 646, 647
DELYS
Fleur   II, 80
DEMANCHE
Heary   I, 453
DEMAND (DEMANDT, DEMANT, DEMAN)
Conrad   I, 615, 617, 619
Johannes   I, 756
Joseph   II, 71
DEMARER
Louis   I, 747
DE MARS
Jan   I, 322
DEMBROUISKIE
Mathias   II, 91
DEMER (DEMEER)
Georg Ludtwig (Ludwig)   I, 180, 182, 184
Lorentz   II, 92
DEMLER
Johann George   I, 479
Peter   I, 470
DEMMEL
Jacob   I, 740
DEMUTH
Johannes   I, 471
DENAR
Christian   I, 660
DENCKER
Jacob   I, 428
DENDELSTEIN
Magdelena   II, 4
DENECKE
Anna Martha   II, 117
Catharina   II, 117
Charles   II, 117
Elisabeth   II, 117
Henriette   II, 117
John Christoph   II, 117
DENGLER
Andreas   I, 753
Jacob   I, 436
DENIG (DENICK)
Johann Peder (Peter)   I, 378, 379, 381
Johannes (John)   I, 576, 578, 580
DENION
Mr.   II, 90
DENN
Christ. Henry   II, 122
DENNER
Henricus   I, 762
Jnº Henry   I, 731

DENNINGER
Jacob   I, 455
DENNSCHERZ
Lorenz Joseph   I, 503
DENNY (DENEY)
Anna   II, 83
Christian   II, 83
Joh. Bernhart (Jan Burn)   I, 297, 298, 300
DENOM
Johannes   II, 92
DENSTRELL
David   I, 470
DENTLER
Jacob   II, 201
DENTZEL
Johann Henrich   I, 709
DENTZER
Hans Michael   I, 446
DENTZLER (TANTZLER)
Abraham   I, 148
Jacob   I, 146, 148, 149, 150
Margareth   I, 148
Rodolph   I, 148
DENYE
Pieter   I, 749
DENZEL
Johann Georg   I, 731
DEOBAD (read DEOBALD)
Simon Peter   I, 710
DEOBALT (DOBALTH, DEWALD)
Michel (Michal)   I, 205, 207, 208
DEÖRR see DÖRR
DÉPRÉ
Jacque   I, 702
DER see DERR
DERBER (DARBEER)
Engele   I, 73
Pieter (Peter)   I, 72, 76, 78
DERDTER (DORTER)
Petter (Peter)   I, 615, 617, 619
DEREMOT
Jacob   I, 427
DERETINGER
Durst   I, 406
DERFFENBECHER
Caspar   I, 416
DERGHARD
Marg.   II, 177
DERLINDEN
Maria, van   II, 170
DERMARETS
   II, 80
DE ROCHE
Abraham   I, 708
DEROCHEA
Mons.   II, 72

DERR (DER, TERR, THER)
Conrad I, 436
Georg Michel I, 399
Henrich I, 716
Johann Georg I, 694
Yust I, 227; II, 104
DERRICK
Simon I, 236
DERSCH (DURSCH)
Deys (Matthias) I, 642, 644
DERST (DERSCH)
Abraham I, 347
Friederich Adam
(Fredᵏ) I, 665, 668, 670
Johann Paul (Paul) I, 102, 105, 106
DERTING
Johann Adam I, 487
DERTWA
Peter I, 719
DESCH, (DES, TASH, TEST)
Gorg (Georg) I, 178, 180, 183
Johann Philip (Philip) I, 314, 315
Nicolaus (Nicholas) I, 665, 668, 670
DESCHER
Petter I, 452
DESCHLER (ESLER)
Johann David
(Daffid) I, 116, 120, 121
Johannis I, 497
DESCHNER
Johann Egydius I, 410
Jörg I, 707
DESEY
Jacobey II, 153
DESLOCH (TESLO)
Jerg (George) I, 592, 593, 594
DESSALAUR
Francis II, 73
DESSEN
Philip, von II, 61
DESSLER
Hans Adam I, 304
DESTER
Jacob I, 189, 192, 193
Johann Jacob
(Jacob Jr.) I, 189, 192, 193
DESTING
Margaret II, 163
DETINGER (DUTON, DUTON-GEN)
Abram I, 595, 597, 599
DETLOFF
Jochim Heinrig I, 504
DETMOLDER * (TETMOLDER)
Johann I, 718
DETTIS (DITTIS, DITESS)
Tobias I, 225, 228, 230
DETTMER (DETEMER)
Hans Michell (Michl) I, 18, 19

DETTWEILER (DETTWEILLER, DEDWILLER, TEDWEILER)
Jacob I, 610, 611, 613
Johan I, 759
Johannes I, 724
Jost I, 698
Melchior I, 163, 165, 166
DEUBER
Johann David
(David) I, 560, 561, 563
DEULL
Georg Anthon I, 449
Johann Henrich I, 456
DEUSCHLIN (DEUSCHELIN)
C. F. II, 162
Jacob F. II, 162
M. II, 162
DEUSS (THYS)
Johann Daniel I, 531, 533, 535
DEUSSINGER (TEYSINGER)
Fried. (Fredrick) I, 656, 657, 658
DEUTSCH (TEUTSCH)
Georg Adam I, 718
Henry I, 468
Johⁿ Friederich II, 33
Johann Philipp I, 457
DEUTSCHENBACH (TEUTCHEN-BACH)
Johann Adam I, 677, 678, 680
DEUTSCHER * (TEUTTSCHER, DEITSHER, THEUSCHER)
Anna Barbara I, 131
Christophel I, 131
Jacob I, 131
Johan[na] Barbara I, 132
Johann Peter (Peter) I, 130, 133, 134
Johannes I, 130, 133, 134
Susanna Elizabeth I, 132
DE VIGNAIR
Michelle I, 735
DEVIL
Johann Leonᵈ I, 704
DEVITTUS
Anton I, 428
DEVOIR (DEVORE)
Benard II, 6
Johan II, 6
Margery II, 6
Marie II, 6
William II, 6
DEWALD (DEWALDT, DEWALT)
Caspar I, 363
Friederich I, 734
Hans Jerg I, 359
Henrich I, 709
Jacob I, 521, 523
Johannes (John) I, 358, 496
Leonhart I, 348, 349, 351
P. Ludwig I, 457

DEWBECK
 Hendrich II, 71
DEWESS
 Johan Henrich I, 114, 115
DEWETTEN
 Joannes I, 459
DEWO (TEVO, DIBO)
 Conrad I, 629, 632, 635
DEXHEIMER (DEXHEYMER,
 DECKSHEIMER)
 Daniel (Dan¹) I, 665, 668, 670, 688
 Johann Ludwig I, 688
DEXTER
 Johan Matteus I, 353, 354
DEYERLING (BYERLING)
 Johann Michael
 (John Michel) I, 387, 388, 389
DEYLINGER
 Caspar I, 480
DEYNEN
 Johannes I, 102, 104, 105
DEYS (TEY)
 Johannes I, 378, 380, 381
DHÄMER
 Hinrich Michael I, 726
DHOM
 Bennedictus I, 403
DIBEL *see* DIEBEL
DICHTERMÜLLER
 Kilian I, 457
DICK
 Adam I, 213, 215, 216
 Clauss II, 182
 Friderich I, 404
 George I, 445
 Jacob I, 447
 Johann Peter I, 433
 Johann Philip I, 402
 Nicklas I, 447
 Peter (Petter) I, 629, 632, 635, 676
 Phillip I, 433
DICKE
 Henrich I, 738
 Hermanus I, 738
DICKEL (DICKELL, DICKOL,
 DÜCKEL)
 Charlotte II, 190
 Christina II, 190
 Georg Adam I, 701
 John I, 758
 John Jost II, 84
 Magdalena II, 190
 Peter I, 615, 617, 619
 Phillip II, 190
 Werner I, 615, 617, 619
DICKER (DICKERT, DÜCKER)
 David I, 307
 Johann Baltzer I, 577, 578, 580

DICKERHOFF
 Frederik I, 472
DICKERLING
 Anna II, 186
 Mary II, 186
DICKERT
 Johannes I, 355
DICKES
 Johann Vallenthin I, 702
DICKHOFF (DYCKHOFF)
 Bernard (BERNT) I, 179, 181, 183
DICKHOUT
 Anna Clara II, 46
 Joh. George II, 46
DICKMAN
 —— II, 47
DICKS
 Abraham II, 15
DIDEL (DITTEL)
 Hans Adam I, 245, 246, 247
DIEDERICH (DIEDRICH, DIED-
 RICK, DIDRICH)
 Andreas II, 117
 Christian II, 181
 Hans Adam I, 456
 Henrich Christof
 (Henry Chris.) I, 573, 574, 575
 Henrich Joseph II, 70
 Johan Jacop II, 37
 Johann I, 484
 Johannes (Johˢ) I, 221, 223, 224
 601, 602, 603
 II, 37
 Johannes Peter I, 427
 John II, 181
 John Jost II, 180
 John Ust. II, 181
 Leonhart (Leonard) I, 551, 552, 554
 Louisa II, 181
 Michael (Michel) I, 628, 632, 635
 Nicholas (Nickelas) I, 376, 377
 Sebastian II, 37
 Wilhelm I, 427
DIDIER
 J. I, 731
DIEARMAN
 Hendrack II, 76
DIEBALT (THEBOLD)
 Johann George I, 307, 308, 309
DIEBEDORFFER (DIEBEDORVER,
 SEIBEDORFER)
 Henry I, 332, 333, 334
DIEBEL (DIBEL, DÜFEL)
 Johan Mattes I, 691
 Velentin (Valentin) I, 180, 182, 184
DIEBERT
 Johann Georg I, 695
DIEBLER
 Johannes I, 755

DIEBOLD (DIEBOLT)
Hans   I, 410
Hans Michel   I, 268, 271
Ignaz   II, 178
DIECKENSCHIEDT (DIECKEN-
SCHIET)
Christoffel   I, 355
Diellman   I, 356
DIECKMAN
William   II, 77
DIEDS
Wilhelm   I, 676
DIEFENBACH (DIEFFEBACH)
B.   I, 700
Jno Philb   I, 752
DIEFFENBACHER
Caspar   I, 430
Conrat   I, 696
Johann Martin
(John Adam)   I, 185, 186, 187
DIEGENHART
Henrich   II, 54
DIEHL (DIEL, DIHLL, TIEL, TILL)
Adolph   II, 10
Alexander (Alexanter)   I, 28, 30
Bernhart   I, 372
Carl   I, 256
Cath.   II, 10
Christian   I, 642, 644
Conrad   II, 10
David   II, 10
Eberhard   I, 614, 616, 619
Georg (Jurg)   I, 615, 617, 619
Georg Philip
(Philip)   I, 628, 631, 634
George Wilhelm   II, 30
Hans Adam   I, 256, 259, 261
Hans Conrad
(Hans Konrad)   I, 615, 617, 620
Hans Jacob   I, 31, 32, 33
Hans Michel   I, 9
Jacob   I, 307, 308, 309, 727
   II, 137
Johann Casper
(Casper)   I, 556, 557, 558
Johann Daniel   I, 256, 259, 261
Johann David
(Johan Debt)   I, 204, 206, 207
Johan Fill   I, 459
Johann Friederich   I, 684
Johann Georg   I, 494
Johann Nicolaus   I, 684
Johann Peter   I, 283, 284, 286
Johann Phylips   I, 622, 624, 626
Johan Stephan   II, 172
Johann Wilhelm   I, 723
Johannes (Hannes)   I, 43, 45, 46
283, 284, 286
372, 732

Jno   II, 10
Jost (Joost)   I, 263, 267, 270
Magdal.   II, 10
Martin (Mardin)   I, 569, 571, 572
Matthias (Matheas)   I, 643, 645
Nichs   II, 10
Peter   I, 714
Philib   I, 402
Simon Peter   I, 330
Wilhelm (Wm.)   I, 204, 206, 208
Wyan   I, 13
DIEHLBAUER (DEHLBAUER, TIL-
BOUER)
Han (Hann,
Johanis)   I, 266, 270, 273
DIEHLBECK
Johann   I, 487
DIEHM (THEEM)
Hans Adam   I, 539, 541, 543
DIEHN
A. Elizabeth   II, 70
DIELBOHNN (POON)
Johann (Dewaile)   I, 293, 294, 296
DIELE
Johann Gottfried   I, 447
DIELEBACH
Beder   I, 448
DIEM (DIM)
Christian   I, 551, 552, 553
Georg Friedrich   II, 134
H. Adam   I, 474
Johan Adam   I, 409
Peter   I, 506
(*See also* DIHM)
DIEMER (DEMER, TIEMER)
Andreas   I, 440
Jacob   I, 712
Johann Georg
(Yerrick)   I, 609, 611, 613
Johann Jacob
(John Jacob)   I, 286, 287, 288
John Christoff (Christl,
Johan Christn)   I, 601, 602, 603
DIENER
Caspar (Casber)   I, 666, 668, 670
Henrich Gerhardt   I, 460
Johannes   I, 444
Peter   I, 521, 524
DIENIUS
Nicklas   I, 420
DIER
Jacob   I, 210
DIERCHS
Frantz Joseph   II, 122
DIERENBERGER
Hans Jerg   I, 442
DIERRE
———   II, 81

DIERSEN
J. Adam   I, 457
DIERSTEIN
Hans   I, 396
DIES
George Adam   II, 178
DIESBACH
Anna Elisa   II, 129
Catharina Elisa   II, 129
DIESBERGER
D. Carl Gottlieb   I, 428
DIESCH
Mattias   I, 471
DIESEL
Fred.   II, 188
DIESS
Fred.   I, 726
DIESSINGER
John Henry   I, 684
DIETENT
Christopher Frederick   II, 93
DIETER (DIEDER, DIETHER)
Catharine   I, 73
Elizabeth   I, 73
Hans Jerg   I, 13
Jacob   I, 475
Johann Michel   I, 71, 76, 77
Johann Stephan
(Stephan)   I, 564, 566, 567
Johannes   I, 71, 76, 77
Jorg (Jorick)   I, 28, 30
Michael   I, 360, 362
Peter   I, 716
Susana   I, 73
DIETERICH (DIETRICH, DIETE-
RICK, DIEDRICH)
Adam   I, 717
Adam Lorentz   I, 678, 679, 680
Andreas   II, 55
Andreas Gabriel   I, 480
Ann   I, 40
Casper   I, 717
Christoph   I, 704
David   I, 365, 441
Diebolt   I, 482
Elias   I, 359
Fred.   I, 755
Georg Hans   I, 483
Heinrich (Henry)   I, 734, 743
Isaac (Isac)   I, 283, 284, 286
Jacob   I, 245, 246, 247
     483, 491, 707
Johan Adam
(Johann Adam)   I, 383, 385
Johann Bernhard   I, 704
Johann Fried[k]   II, 5
Johann Jacob   I, 493, 722
Johann Lutwig   I, 719

Johan Michgel
(Johan Misael)   I, 373, 374, 375
Johann Wolfgang
(John Wolpgan)   I, 652, 653
Johannes (Johannis,
John)   I, 39, 40, 41, 42, 471
Johannes Gotfried   II, 46
Michael   I, 479
Nickolas   I, 420
Peter   I, 648, 650, 690
Philibs (Philip)   I, 621, 623, 625
Stoffel   I, 707
DIETERLE
Johann Jacob   I, 760
DIETEWIG
Johann Stephan   I, 422
DIETHOFF
Gottfried Heinrich   I, 735
DIETMAR
Heinrich   I, 446
DIETZ (DIEZ, DITZ, DOTZ,
DUETZ, TIETZ)
Andreas   I, 430
Anless (Anna Elisa)   I, 241
Friedrich (Fred[k])   I, 677, 678, 680
Georg Christof   I, 513, 514, 516
Georg Friedrich   I, 605, 606, 608
Gottfried   I, 425
Hans Georg (Uriah)   I, 240, 242, 243
Heinrich (Henrich)   I, 684; II, 118
Johann Balthazar   II, 28
Johan Caspar
(Casper)   I, 605, 606, 608
Johann Christopher   I, 731
Johann Conradt   I, 502
Johan Friedrich   I, 402
Johann Georg (Jurg)   I, 513, 514, 516
Johann Jacob
(Jacob)   I, 240, 242, 243
     294, 295, 296, 723
Johan Jost   I, 684
Johan Nickel   I, 430
Johann Phylips   I, 622, 624, 626
Johannes   I, 403, 754
Johannes Michael
(Michael)   I, 386, 388, 389
John Adam   I, 493
Jonas (Johannes)   I, 386, 388, 389
Martin   I, 457
Michael (Michel)
     I, 240, 242, 243
     638, 639, 641
Petter   I, 241
Philip   I, 715
Thomas   I, 513, 514, 515
Uhllerik (Woldrich)   I, 240, 242, 243
Wilhelmus   I, 401
DIETZEL
J. Henry   I, 456

DIEWES (DIEWOS, DIBOS)
Johannes I, 401
Johanrich (Johan Christ., Christian) I, 276, 277, 278
DIGEL
Jacob I, 495
DIGER (BICKERT)
Christoff (Christophel) I, 646, 647
DIGLER
Simon I, 406
DIHM (THIEM)
Adam I, 627, 630, 634
Andreas I, 531, 532, 534
Hans Adam I, 627, 630, 634
Hans Dhomas I, 502
Johan Lorentz I, 754
Johann Peter (Peter) I, 556, 557, 558
Petter I, 502
Thomas I, 627, 630, 634
(*See also* DIEHM)
DIHRING
Johannes II, 100
DIKHANS
Balzasor I, 488
DILBRANER (TILLBONER)
William (Wilhelm) I, 564, 565, 567
DILGARD
Baulus (Paulus) I, 367, 369
DILIER
Franciscus I, 479
DILL (TIEL)
Adam I, 175, 177, 178
Adolph I, 714
Georg Albrecht (Yerrick Albright) I, 551, 553, 554
George II, 123
Johan Michel (Michael) I, 130, 133, 134
Johannes Philipp I, 564, 565, 567
Jonas I, 706
Nicklaus I, 393
DILLINGER (DIELINGER)
Hans Wolf I, 18, 19
Henry Wilhelm (Werhelm) I, 18, 19
DILLMANN (DILLMAN, DILLEMANN)
Anmaria II, 79
Christina II, 52
Elizabetha II, 52
Gerg Fridrich (Fred^k) I, 677, 678, 680
Hans Georg I, 464
Hans Jorg (Hans Geo^e) I, 175, 176, 177
Henrich Jacob (Hans Jac^b) I, 175, 176, 178
Jacob II, 79
DILLON (DILON)
Hannah II, 83

Nicola I, 405
DILS
Jacob I, 479
Moritz Wilhelm I, 479
Peder I, 478
DIMOT (TIMOUT, TYMOET)
Johans Hubrig (John Hubrig) I, 279, 280, 281
DINCK
Peter I, 440
DINCKEL
Michael I, 503
DINDORFF
Johan Jacob I, 521, 523
DINGELWEIN
N. II, 137
DINGER
Johan Peter (Peter) I, 622, 624, 626
DINGES (DINGIS, TINGES)
Fillipp I, 403
J. Peter I, 464
Jacob I, 307, 308, 309
Johannes I, 445
Michel (Michael) I, 420, 643, 645
DINGLER
Frederica II, 168
Jacob II, 168
Johan I, 517, 519, 520
Louisa II, 168
—— II, 161
DINIUS
John I, 705
DINNEE
Johanna II, 105
DINSMAN
Michael I, 676
Theis I, 676
DINTELSBECK (TENDELSPECH, TENDELLPECK
Friedrich (Frederick) I, 83, 86
DIPPEL
Johann Hermann I, 430
Johann Nicolaus I, 694
Johann Peter (John Peter) I, 573, 574, 575
DIPPELE
George II, 126
DIPPSBERGER
Ernst Jacob I, 441
DIR (DEER, read prob. DERR)
Hans Michel (Michael) I, 637, 639, 640
Matthaus (Mathias) I, 637, 639, 640
DIRE (PERITER)
Joan (John, John Peree) I, 592, 593, 595
DIRING
Johann Peter II, 46

DIRKS
Hendrik II, 50
DIRNER (TUNER, TURNER)
Anthony I, 652, 654
Hans Jacob (Jacob) I, 653, 654
DIRR (read prob. DERR)
Georg (Hans George) I, 96, 97, 98
Michael (Michel) I, 96, 97, 98
DIRSTEIN (DIERSTEIN)
Michel I, 59, 63, 64
Samuel I, 471
DISCHARDT
Johann Henrich I, 727
DISCHER
Johann Conrad I, 741
Simon I, 689
Wilhelm I, 432
DISCHLER
Hans Georg I, 439
DISCHONG (DICHONG, DISHON)
Diedrich Wilhelm I, 478
Mattis (Matthias) I, 563, 565, 566
Wilhelm I, 563, 565, 566
DISINGER
Eberhart I, 683
DISPION (DISPIONIT)
Jacob (Johan Jacob) I, 250, 251
DISSLER (DISSELER, TISSLER, TISELER)
Hans (Hance) I, 163, 165, 166
Hans George I, 516, 518, 519
DITERIG
Hans I, 442
DITHART (DIEDER)
Maddeis (Matthias) I, 378, 380, 381
DITLOH (DEADLO, DIEDELA)
Daniel (Danail) I, 628, 631, 635
DITMAN (DITTMAN)
Catharina II, 7
Christopher II, 7
Conrad II, 7
Honor II, 7
J. J. II, 147
Johann Heinrich I, 755
Johannes I, 731
John II, 7
Loudwick I, 31, 32, 33
Martha II, 7
DITTENHÖFFER (DÜTTENHÖF-FER, TITENHAVER)
Johan Paulus (Paulus) I, 31, 33, 34
DITTMER (DITMER)
Friedr. II, 107
Jacob II, 184
Johannes I, 601, 602, 604
DITZ *see* DIETZ
DIVERNOIS
Lewis II, 96

DIWALL
John I, 414
DIZLER
Joh. Fried. II, 192
DÖBELE (DÖBEL, DOBELY)
Fridrich (Friedrich) I, 358
Georg Martin I, 513, 514, 515
Jacob I, 508
Rudolf I, 508
DOBELER
Jacob I, 427
DOBELMANN
Frederica II, 156
DOBERER
John Fr. II, 188
DOBLEN
Hans Gerg I, 358
DOBLER (DÖBLER, DÖBELER)
A. Maria II, 161
Elizabeth II, 161
Jan Jacob II, 135
Jodocus I, 502
Johann Nicolaus I, 727
Jorg (Jerg, George) I, 59, 63, 64
Leonhart I, 59, 63, 64
Lorentz I, 445
Mattheus (Mathys) I, 244, 245
Michel II, 52
—— II, 161
DOBLINER
F. F. G. II, 169
DOCHMAN
Henry I, 358
DOCHTERMAN (DOUGHTER-MAN)
Andreas I, 348, 350, 351
Jacob Friederich I, 348, 350, 351
DOCK
Balthasar I, 400
Hans Michael I, 492
Henrich I, 400
Johann Mattheus I, 727
DOCKWADEL (DOCKUSBADEL)
Georg Friedrich
(Fredᵏ) I, 605, 606, 608
DOCTOR (DOCKTER)
Hans George I, 482
Martin I, 482
DODE
Doctor II, 206
DODERER (DODDERE)
Hans Ulrick I, 18
Johan Georg I, 19
DOERBAUM
Johannes I, 686
DOGENER (DOGANER, POGNER, POGENER)
Aran (Aron, An-dreas) I, 113, 114, 115, 765

Catrina I, 766
DOHANA
Darby II, 27
DOHL *see* DOLL
DOHR (DEHR, DOOR)
Jelles (Jelles, Juilis) I, 59, 63, 65
DOHRMAN
Hinrich II, 160
DOLDT (DULDT)
Joh. Philip (Phillip) I, 143, 145, 146
DÖLIKER (TELICKER)
Hans Jerg (Hans Geo.) I, 646, 647
DOLL (DOHL)
Barbara II, 20
Casper I, 257, 260, 262
Christoffel (Christopher) I, 257, 260, 262
Frieterig I, 422
George A. II, 136
Gorg (Geo.) I, 683, 695
Hans Michael I, 327, 329
Jacob I, 730
Johan Christian I, 169, 171, 172
Johan Nickel (Johan Nickell) I, 266, 269, 272
Johan Peter (Peter) I, 169, 171, 173
Johannes (Joanis) I, 293, 294, 295, 475
Marte I, 475
Philip I, 257, 260, 262
Sebastian (Sabastian) I, 256, 259, 261
DÖLLE (DOLLE)
Henrich I, 720
J. G. II, 107
DOLLENDORP
Wm I, 749
DOLLINGER (DÖLLINGER)
Georg Philipp I, 200, 202, 204
Martin I, 236, 238, 239
DOLLMAN (DOLMAN, DOLLMANN)
B. II, 135
Casper I, 539, 541, 543
Johann Mattheus I, 706
DÖLPSTER
Peter I, 461
DOMAS (read THOMAS)
Peter I, 233
DOMINGO
Juan I, 761
DOMINIQUE
Louis II, 60
DOMME (DOMMI, DOMIE)
Anna Barbara I, 37
Christina I, 37
Hans I, 484
Jacob I, 392
Johannes I, 324, 325, 326
Joseph I, 37, 38, 39

DOMMEN (TOMME, DOMEN)
Jacob I, 212, 214, 216
Johan Kasper I, 494
DONAT (DONATT, DONATH)
Herman I, 685
Johannes Jacob I, 496
Joseph II, 85
Ludwig II, 173
DONBACH
Hans Jacob I, 21
DONGES
Conradt I, 499
Engel Wirth I, 499
Johann Philipp I, 752
DONGSHEN
Johan I, 479
DONIAS
Heinr II, 178
DONIWAND
Oyn I, 143
DONNER
Andereas I, 393
Hans Everard I, 531,533
DONNERS
J. II, 142
DONNETT
Hendrick II, 76
DONNIER
C. II, 143
DONSELT
Johan Zacharias I, 716
DOOPEL
Hans Woolf I, 102
DOOR *see* DOHR
DOORNAUWER
Jos. Gnied II, 61
DOOS
Elizabeth II, 92
DORÉ
Antoine I, 729
DOREST
Casper I, 23, 25, 26
DORETY
Hanna II, 6
Magretta II, 6
DÖRFFLING
Johann Adam I, 420
DÖRFFLINGER (DERFLINGER)
Barbara I, 132
Friderich I, 131, 133, 134, 409
Johannes I, 585, 587, 588
Margaretha I, 131
DÖRGES (DURGESS)
Jurgen Henrich (Jorgan Herrick) I, 574, 575, 576
DORHEIMER *see* DORSCHHEIMER
DÖRING
Georg Eberhart I, 500

DORMAN (THORMAN)
J. Karsten (Kasen) I, 536, 537, 538
DORMEYER
Andereas   I, 493
Jacob   I, 405, 493
Joab   I, 493
Michael   I, 406
Samuel   I, 405
DORMICK
Wendelina   II, 53
DORN (DOHRN, DORNN)
Caspar   I, 421
Frederick   II, 137
Jacob   I, 652, 654
Johan Henrich   I, 754
Johannes   I, 460
John   II, 74
DORNBACH
Johan Deis   I, 352, 354
Johan Henry (Joh.
  Henrich)   I, 352, 354
Johannes   I, 352, 353
DORNBERGER
Adam   I, 586, 587, 588
DORNECK (DORNEK, DORNECH)
Anna Margaretha   II, 69
Heinrich Jacob   II, 69
Hend. Phil.   II, 29
Johann Jerg   I, 686
John   II, 69
DORNER (DÖRNER, TORNER)
Henrick   I, 234
Jacob   I, 503
Johann Henrich   I, 756
Thomas   I, 290, 291
DORNHAM
Henry   II, 116
DORNIG
Henry   I, 346
DORNWIND
Fredrich   I, 546, 547, 549
DÖRR   (DEORR,   TERR,   TOAR,
  TEHR, TÖRR)
Adam   I, 714
Conrath   I, 697
Georg (Geo.)   I, 217, 219, 220
Hans George   I, 365
Hennrich   I, 759
Johann Adam I, 397, 596, 598, 599
Johann Christian   I, 523, 525
Johann Friederich   I, 737
Johann Henrich   I, 323, 324, 326,
                      666, 668, 670
Johann Jost   I, 378, 380, 381
Johannes   I, 341, 342, 343, 692
Michell   I, 93, 95
Peter   I, 701
Sebastian   I, 21, 23

DORSCH (DÖRSCH, DORSH)
Adam   II, 20
Johan Friederich   I, 734
Margarieta   II, 21
Maria Sallemie   II, 21
DORSCHEIMER
Jacob   I, 701
Martin   I, 652, 654
DORSCHEYNER
Andreas   II, 30
DORST
Hans Casper (Hans
  Gaspar)   I, 212, 214, 215
Johannes   I, 686
DORTWEILER (DARTWILLER)
Daniel   I, 406
Martin   I, 406
Nicolaus   I, 406
DÖRTZBACH (DIRTZIBACH)
Ferdinand (Johan Ferdi-
  nand)   I, 246, 247, 248
DORWARTH
Jacob   II, 179
(See also THORWARTH)
DOSCH (DOSH)
Anna Maria   II, 140
Barbara   II, 21
Christoph   I, 507
Hans George   I, 508
Hans Mich. (Mich[1]) I, 627, 630, 633
Hans Philip   I, 501
Johann Michael   I, 539, 541, 543
Michael   I, 727
DOSER
Johann Martin   I, 491
Michael   I, 491
DOSH see DOSCH
DÖSS
Bernhart   I, 702
DOSSER
Daniel   I, 442
DÖST
Gerhart Peter   I, 371
Johann Nicolas   I, 371
DOSTMAN
Johan Martin   I, 507
DOTTER   (DÖTTER,   DETTER,
  TOTTER)
Andreas   II, 97, 114
Anna Maria   II, 114
Christian   I, 576, 578, 580
Christiana   II, 114
Johann Adam   II, 114
Martin   I, 418
Mattis   I, 418
Nicolaus   I, 418
DOTTINGER
Jonas   I, 753

DOTTWEILER
Christoph Didrich I, 714
DOUDEMAND
Jn⁰ Bapdhiste I, 746
DOUDNET
Wilhelm I, 714
DOUEY
Joseph II, 89
DOUTREMER
Gilli I, 748
DOWNE
Jacob II, 95
D'OWRLE
——— II, 80
DRACH (TROOGH)
Andres I, 502
Petter I, 502
Rudolf (Rudolph) I, 614, 616, 618
DRACHSEL (DRACHSELL, TRACK-
SEL, TRACHSEL, TRECHSELL)
Abraham I, 406
Anna Maria I, 108
Catharina I, 108
Daniel I, 110
Hans Bernhardt (Bern-
ard) I, 107, 111, 112
Johan Peter I, 169, 170, 172
Johannes I, 168, 170, 172
John George I, 691
Peter (Petter) I, 107, 110, 111, 112
DRACKER (DRAGER)
Johann Adam I, 737
Ludwig (Lodwick) I, 383, 385
DRAES
Fred II, 187
DRAP (TRAP)
Philip I, 227, 229, 231
DRAPET
Jean I, 439
DRARBACH (TRARBACH)
J. Adam I, 456
Jacob I, 456
Mich. I, 456
DRASS see DROSS
DRAUGH (DRAUG)
Rudolph I, 31, 32, 33
DRAUT see TRAUTH
DRAUTMAN
Hans George (Hance
George) I, 162, 164, 166
DRAYER see DREHER
DREBBERT
Justus I, 500
DREER (DREAR)
Hans Mich¹ I, 715
Johann George I, 437
DREHER (THREHR, THRER,
THREER)
Andreas I, 715

Davidt I, 308, 309
Georg (Dirick) I, 23, 25, 26
Hans Georg I, 395
Jacob I, 490
Johan Jeorg (Geo.) I, 269, 272, 457
Johanes
(Johannes) I, 204, 206, 208, 697
Juliana I, 23
Sebastian I, 480
DREIBELBISS
Johann Jacob I, 93, 94, 95
DREICHLER (DRAICHLER,
DRYGHLER)
Daniel (Daniell) I, 221, 222, 224
DREIGLER
Johanes (Michel) I, 179, 181, 183
DREISBACH (DREYSBACH)
Anna Marie II, 190
Anton II, 190
Catharina II, 190
Elisabeth Gertraud II, 190
Georg II, 190
George Heinrich II, 190
Johann Adam I, 340, 341, 343
Johann Heinrich II, 190
Johann Jost I, 340, 341, 343
Johannes George II, 190
Mardin I, 437
Margaretha II, 190
Marie Elisabeth II, 190
Marie Magdalena II, 190
Martinus I, 473
Simmon I, 340, 341, 343
DRENBARGS
Catha Marga II, 23
DRENIEL
Johann Ernst I, 697
DRESBACH (TROESTBACH)
Henrich I, 666, 668, 670
DRESCH
Rudolff I, 721
DRESCHER (DRESHER)
Christopher I, 137, 141, 142
George (Georg) I, 137, 141, 142
Maria I, 139
Reinhard II, 130
Rosina I, 139
DRESEL
Fred. II, 187
Gooder I, 310
DRESS
Andres I, 685
Conrad I, 360, 362
DRESSER (TRESCHER)
Johan Nicolaus (Nicho-
las) I, 646, 647
DRESSLER (DRESLER, TRESLER)
Andreas I, 502
Johann Andreas I, 399

Johan Henrich I, 329
Johann Jerg I, 395
Johan Peder (Peter) I, 256, 259, 261
DREXEL
Antoni I, 727
DREXLER
David I, 734
Frantz Petter I, 742
DREYDEL (DRYDEL, TREYTEL)
Michel (Michael) I, 297, 299, 300
DREYER (DRYER)
Christ. Jac. II, 139
Johan Jurick I, 266
Mr. II, 175
Regina II, 175
DREYMAN
Johan Henrich I, 748
DRIDEN
Mary II, 186
DRIDGER
Johann II, 121
DRIES (DRIESCH)
Andreas I, 130, 133, 134
Anna Maria I, 131, 132
Barbara Elizabeth I, 132
Cornelius I, 130, 133, 134
J. S. O. I, 432
Jn. Adam I, 130, 133, 134
Maria Barbara I, 132
Peter I, 130, 133, 134
DRIESBACH
Barnard II, 42
DRIESMAN
William II, 122
DRIESSLER
Peter I, 724
DRILL
Jacob I, 718
DRINKEL (TRENKLE, ZINGLE,
ZINKLE)
Christoff (Chris-
topher) I, 246, 247, 248
Stephen (David) I, 246, 247, 248
DRION
Johann Michaell I, 475
DRISTER
Hend. II, 114
DROCKER
Adam II, 126
DROG (THROOG)
Hans Diebolt (Hans Theo-
bald) I, 231, 232, 233
DROGO
Anna I, 103
Maria Katrina I, 103
DROLINER *see* DROLLINGER
DROLLINGER (DROLLING, DRO-
LINER)
Adam I, 226, 228, 230

Eberhard I, 226, 228, 230
Hance Michel I, 344
DROLSBACH
Christina II, 158
Henry II, 158
—— II, 158
DROM *see* DRUMM
DRONAH
Jan I, 723
DROPENSTAD (DROPENSTOD,
BROPTENSTAD)
Diedrich I, 516, 518, 519
DROQUET
Isaac I, 687
DROSS (DRASS, DRAST)
Johann Peter (Peter) I, 179, 181, 183
DROUTNER
Gerick I, 660
DROWTWINE
Annis I, 79
DROY
Johann Ernst II, 76
DRUCK (DRÜCK)
Johann Görg I, 310, 311, 312
Johan Petter I, 397
DRUCKENBRODT
Andreas I, 689
DRUCKMILLER (TRUCKIN MIL-
LER)
Peter I, 513, 514, 516
DRUCKS
Dort. II, 101
Wilhelm II, 101
DRUFILD
Joh. Georg II, 119
DRUMBERG (TRUMBERG,
DROONBERG)
Daniel (Jan Daniel) I, 199, 201, 203
DRUMHELLER (TRUMHELLER)
Han Leonard (J. Leon-
hart) I, 661, 663, 664
DRUMM (DRUM, DROM)
Johan Adam (Adam) I, 169, 171, 172
Johan Simon I, 330
Phillips (Philip) I, 204, 206, 207
Simon I, 257, 260, 262
DRUMMER
George II, 145
DRUSBE
Fridrich II, 47
DRÜSCHEL
Andres I, 468
DRUZ
P. F. I, 732
DRYBLER
Johan Steffen I, 479
DRYER *see* DREYER
DRYLER
David II, 161

DU —
Johanes Petter — I, 401
DUBBENDORF
J. F. — II, 16
DUBEL (DOUBLE)
Johan Morritz (Johan
Maurice) — I, 305, 306
DUBENDORFFER (DÜBEN-
DÖRFER, DIEBENDERF)
Abraham — I, 148
Allexand. — I, 7, 9
Anna — I, 148
Rodolph — I, 148
DUBERNOCK
Joseph — I, 717
DUBIER (DEBEER)
Joseph — I, 667, 669, 671
DÜBINGER
Bernard — I, 348, 350, 351
DUBKE (DOBGEN)
Johannes, van — I, 137, 141, 142
DUBO
Abraham — I, 102, 105
Anna — I, 103
Philip — I, 102
DUBOIS
Charles Frederick — II, 31
DUBRAN
—— — II, 81
DU BRET
J. B. — I, 754
DUBROMMER
Joh. — II, 136
DUBS (DUPS, TOOPS, TUPS)
Hans — I, 332, 333, 334
Hans Jacob — I, 162, 164, 166
Hans Jost (Johann) — I, 162, 164, 165
Heinrich (Hendrick) — I, 23, 25, 26
155, 158, 160
Jacob — I, 97
Oswald — I, 436
DUBY
Jean Louis — II, 73
DUCASSE
—— — II, 80
DUCHAND
Francis — I, 757
DUCHENE
And. — II, 79
DUCHMANN *see* TUCHMANN
DÜCKEL *see* DICKEL
DUCKHARDT (DÜCKHERDT,
DICKERT, DÜCKER)
Johan — II, 114
DÜCKER (DICKER, DICKERT)
Johann Baltzer — I, 577, 578, 580
DÜCKHERDT
Peter — I, 489

DUCKWELL (DUCKWEEL, DUCK-
WEELA)
Rudolph — I, 175, 176, 178
DUCOMMA
Louis — II, 53
DU CORBIER
Jean Pierre — I, 522, 524
DUCROR
—— — II, 81
DUENSCHMAN
Michel — I, 402
DUESING *see* DÜSSING
DUESTO
Jean — I, 363
DUETZ *see* DIETZ
DÜFEL *see* DIEBEL
DUFF
Johannes — I, 508
DUFFEYDAL (DUFFYDAL, DIF-
FITAL)
Johannes — I, 373, 374, 375
DÜFFORDT
Jacob — I, 697
DUGRAVE
Johan — I, 405
DUHIN (DEER)
Henrich Harman (Henry
Arent) — I, 509, 510, 511
John Friederich — I, 509, 510, 511
John Heinrich — I, 509, 510, 511
DUHMANN
Hans Adam — I, 712
DÜHMER
Johan Michael — I, 704
DUKANY
Jacob — I, 714
DULL (read DOLL)
Abraham — II, 26
DULLMAYER (DALLMEYR,
TURMEYER)
Nicholas — I, 546, 548, 550
DULLNICK
Mattheus — I, 476
DULON (DILON, DELO)
Pierre (Petter) — I, 163, 165, 166
DUMBALD (DUMBALDT)
Abraham (Aberham) — I, 167, 168
Ernst Friderich — I, 167, 168
DUMERNICHT (DOMINICK)
Casp. David (Cas-
per) — I, 217, 219, 221
DUMM (DUM)
Johann Jorg — I, 431
Johann Valtin — I, 690
DUMMEN
Joseph — I, 409
DUMMER
Johanes — I, 417

DÜMMIG (TIMMICK)
Peter (Petter) I, 538, 540, 543
DUNCKEL (DUNKELL)
Barbara II, 8
Charles II, 8
Johann II, 205
Johannes (Joannes) I, 31, 32, 33
Nich[s] II, 8
DUNCKER
Johann Christian I, 757
DUNCKI (DUNCKY, DUNCKEL, DÜNKI)
Heinrich (Hendrich) I, 253, 254, 255
Jacob I, 252, 254, 255
Melichor (Melger) I, 252, 254, 255
DUNDIER
Jacob I, 308
DUNKELBERG
Clemens I, 20
DUNNE
Franz II, 52
DUNSCHMAN (DUNSMAN)
Johan Dheis I, 401
Johannes Peder (John Peter) I, 279, 282
Paulus (Baulus) I, 279, 280, 281
DUNTER
Peter I, 494
DUNTZ (DUNTS)
Jorg Michel (Hans Mich[1]) I, 189, 192, 194
DUPARK
Clement I, 140
DUPEE
Flora I, 139
Margaret I, 140
Odoren I, 139
DUPONT
Gorg I, 724
DUPOY
Conrad I, 21
DUPS *see* DUBS
DUPUIT
Jacob II, 118
DÜRCK (TURK)
Friedrich I, 582, 583, 584
DUREN
Durst I, 391
DURENBURGH
Eliza II, 43
Hans Jerry II, 43, 44
Jerry Frederick II, 43
Johan II, 44
Magdalena II, 44
Margaret II, 44
Peter II, 43, 44
Philip II, 43
Solima II, 43

DURETSCH (DURETCH)
Dionysius (Dionise) I, 645, 647
DURFELDT
Johann II, 121
DURHEIMER
A. II, 114
DURIEN
——— II, 81
DURING (DURIN)
Dorothea II, 96
Marg. Eliz. II, 22
Nicolas II, 96
DÜRINGER
Hans I, 429
DURMANS
Anna Elizabeth II, 78
DURNAY (TURNY, TURNAH)
Daniel (Danill, Danil) I, 289, 290, 291
DURON (TUROLF)
Andereas (Andreas) I, 649, 650
DÜRR
Anderas I, 438
Christian I, 489
George Piter I, 398
Johann I, 697
Johan Georg I, 477
Johann Ulrich I, 469
Johanes I, 414
Leonard I, 683
Lorentz (Laurence) I, 21, 23, 483, 697
Michael I, 481
Sebastian I, 21, 23
Valentin I, 683
DURRENBERGER
Christopf I, 440
DURSCH
Egbert II, 134
DURST (TURST, DIERST)
Conrad I, 199, 201, 203
George (Georg) I, 297, 298, 300
J. Jacob (John Jacob) I, 622, 624, 626
Johan Peder I, 689
Lowrance I, 450
DÜRSTLER (DORST)
Georg Adam (Geo. Adam) I, 636, 638, 640
DURWACHTER (DUUR-WACHTER)
Barnard II, 150
Elizabeth II, 150
Simon II, 179
Wilhelmina II, 150
DURY (DURIE, DERRIE)
Jacob I, 226, 228, 230
Jorg (Jurk) I, 131, 133, 134

DUSSING (DUSING, DUSIN, DUESING)
Hans Michel   I, 655
Nicholas   I, 652, 653
Sophia   II, 173
DÜTERIE
Jereg   I, 490
DÜTT (DOET)
Johannes   I, 585, 586, 587
DÜTTE (DUTE)
David   I, 475
Hans George   I, 475
DUTTINGER (DETINGER, TOT-TINGER)
Johannes   I, 209, 211
DUTWEILER
Felix   I, 483
DUVAL
Daniel   I, 405
DUVINGER
Killian   I, 414
DUY
Johann Christian   I, 433
Johann Friedrich   I, 433
D'VEAU (de WUE)
Pieter (Piter)   I, 167, 168
DYCKER
Nicholas   I, 659
DYCKHOFF see DICKHOFF
DYER
Eliz. Catherina   I, 210
Maria   I, 210
Maria Dorothy   I, 210
DYWEL
Matheas   I, 491

EABERTEN (read EBERT)
Gertrout   II, 54
EAGEL (EEGEL read IGEL)
Bernhart (Bernard)   I, 637, 638, 640
EAGER
Johann Friedrich   I, 450
EAKERS (YEEKS, HYXES)
Johan Henry (Henrick)   I, 217, 219, 220
Nicklas (Nicolas)   I, 217, 219, 220
EARP (read ERB)
Jacob   I, 660
EASH see ESCH
EAST
John   II, 91
EASTBACH
Johan   I, 449
EASTERLY
Jacob   II, 104

EATMAN
Jno   II, 18
EATTER (ETER, read ETTER)
Hans Georg   I, 348, 349, 351
EBBEKE
Johann Christian   II, 83
EBBELING (read EBELING)
Cornelia   II, 58
EBBERLI
Veronica   I, 60
EBBLY (read EPPLE)
Martin   I, 476
EBBY
Henrich   I, 59, 63, 64
EBECHE (EBECHEE, ENDIKE)
Christo (Christian)   I, 517, 518, 520
EBEL
Conrad   II, 69
Jacob   II, 54
EBELE (EEBELE)
Johann Towias   I, 496
EBELIN (read prob. EBELING)
Arthar   II, 119
Cath.   II, 119
EBENER
Hans Georg (Hance Jerack)   I, 93, 94, 95
Johann Jacob   I, 366
Matheas   I, 493
EBERAM
Joseph   I, 16
Michal   I, 16
EBERDECKER
Hans   I, 307
EBERHARD (EBERHART, EBER-HARDT, EBERTH, EVER-HARD)
Albrecht (Albreght)   I, 198, 200, 202
Andon   I, 737
Andreas (Andereas)   I, 545, 647
Anna   I, 210
Balthasar   I, 761
Barbara   I, 148
Christian   I, 209, 211, 355, 693
Conrad   II, 196
Elias   I, 394
Frederik (Frittrich)   I, 169, 171, 172, 482
Georg (George)   I, 418, 762
Georg Martin   I, 750
Godfrid   I, 167, 168
Gottlieb (Godlief)   I, 198, 200, 202
Hans   I, 394
Hans Caspar   I, 445
Hans Jerg   I, 366

Heinrich I, 440
Jacob I, 17, 466, 545, 547, 549
Johan Ludwig II, 99
Johan Nickel I, 372
Johanes I, 348, 350, 351, 477
Johann Thomas
(Tho.) I, 236, 238, 239
Johan Wendel I, 367, 368
Johenrich (Johan
Henrich) I, 367, 368
Jorg Christian I, 411
Martin I, 751
Michel I, 17
Paulus I, 355
Philipp I, 432
Regula I, 148
Thomas I, 237
Verena I, 147
EBERHAUF (EHRHOF, HEROW)
Johan Michael I, 545, 547, 549
EBERLE (EBERLY, EBERLIE,
EBERLI)
Adam I, 437
Barbara I, 61
Bartel I, 22, 23
Carl II, 69
Catharina II, 69
F. Conrad I, 478
Friedrich II, 69
Georg Christoph I, 551, 552, 554
Georg Ludwig I, 683
Georg (Georch) Michael I, 478
George Andreas II, 69
Hanns Jacob I, 485
Heinrich (Henrick) I, 11, 61
Henrich Jacob II, 69
Hieronymus
(Heronimus) I, 188, 191, 193
J. George I, 500
Jeremias I, 485
Johann Georg I, 486
Johannes I, 424
Sebastian I, 22, 23
Simon I, 574, 575, 576
EBERLEIN
Joh George II, 135
EBERLIE *see* EBERLE
EBERLIN
Israel I, 491
EBERLING (ABLING)
Ludwig (Lodw^k) I, 384, 386
EBERLY *see* EBERLE
EBERMANN (ABERMANN, ABRA-
MAN)
Conrade I, 93, 94, 95
Elizabeth I, 73
Hans Jacob I, 93, 94, 95
Johannes I, 72, 74, 76, 77
Maria I, 74

Michael I, 93, 94, 95
EBERNICHT (EBNIE)
J. Friederich
(Frederick) I, 601, 602, 604
EBERSCHEIDT (ELVERSITE)
Friederich (Frederick) I, 37, 38, 39
Margret I, 38
EBERSCHWEIN
Eberhard II, 179
EBERSOHL (EBERSOLL, EBER-
SHOLL)
Abrahm I, 11
Carl I, 546, 548, 550
Jacob I, 686
Johannes I, 264, 268, 271
Jost (Joost) I, 263, 267, 270
Pedter (Petter,
Peter) I, 263, 267, 270
EBERSORT (EBBERGAULT, EB-
BERSAULT)
Jacob I, 638, 639, 641
EBERT (EBERTH)
Anna Magdalena II, 36
Carl Philipp I, 733
Elizabeth II, 36
Georg I, 686
George Adam I, 485
Hans Jerg (Hans
Georg) I, 47, 51, 53
Hans Michel I, 47, 51, 53
Hans Philip I, 296, 297, 298
Jacob I, 372; II, 37
Johann
(Johannes) I, 378, 379, 381,
602, 604
Johann Adam I, 400
Johan Gorg II, 36, 37
Johann Jacob I, 432
Johan Just (Johan
Jost) I, 378, 379, 381
Johann Michael I, 87, 89, 91
Johann Nicolaus (Nickel) I, 461
Johann Philip I, 461
Johanes II, 37
John Just II, 37
Marcell I, 727
Mathias I, 372
EBERTS
Johanes I, 409
EBI
Jacob I, 359
EBLER (ABELER, ABEL)
A^n Elisabetha I, 156
Eberhart (Eber-
hardt) I, 155, 158, 161
EBNER
Henry II, 185
ECHART, ECHERT *see* ECKHART

ECHE
David   II, 31
Hans Marti   I, 438
Suzanne   II, 31
ECHEMAN
Abram   II, 31
Anne   II, 31
Anne Catherine   II, 31
Marguerithe   II, 31
ECHTERNACH
Christian   I, 722
Mattheus   I, 415
ECK (ECKH)
Joseph   I, 428
Matthias   I, 485
ECKART, ECKARDT *see* ECK-
HART
ECKEBRET
Johann Daniel   I, 505
ECKEL (ECKELL)
Acada   II, 4
Adam   I, 707
Geo.   II, 9
Georg Peter   I, 488
Henrich   I, 412
J. Val.   II, 4
Johann Anthon   I, 448
Johann Hermann (John
Herman)   I, 296, 298, 299
Johann Philipp   I, 448
Johannes   I, 413, 701
John   II, 181
John Dan[l]   II, 129
Peter   I, 750
ECKENBERGER
Adam   I, 715
Jacob   I, 714
Johannes   I, 762
ECKENROTH
Henrig   I, 340
ECKER (EKER, ECKARTS)
Abraham   I, 225, 228, 230
Andereas   I, 422, 569, 571, 573
Christian   I, 301, 302, 303
Christopffel
(Christophel)   I, 189, 192, 194
Christopher   I, 317
Heronimus   II, 46
Johanes (Hans,
Jann)   I, 551, 552, 554
Johann Philip   I, 304, 305, 306
Martin   I, 476
Peter   I, 301, 302, 303
Phillipp   I, 697
ECKERT
Conratt (Conrad)   I, 39, 41, 42
Jerimias (Jeremiah)   I, 649, 650
Johann Peter   I, 413
Johannes   I, 328, 481

John   II, 188
Joseph   I, 394
Lenhardt   I, 711
ECKET (EKET)
Christian   I, 327, 329
ECKFELDT
Jacob   I, 689
ECKH *see* ECK
ECKHARD (ECHART, ECHERT,
ECKARD, ECKART, ECK-
HART)
Aberham   I, 477
Andereas (Andrew
Lawrence)   I, 574, 575
Andreas   II, 116
Anna Sabina   II, 103
Carl   I, 692
Catharine (Catrina)   II, 86, 103
Conerada   II, 103
Conrad   II, 52
Conrad Henrich   I, 390
Daniel   I, 455
Elizabeth   II, 103
Frantz   I, 684
George   I, 760; II, 86
George Adam   I, 427
George Wilhelm
(Jurian)   I, 340, 342, 343
Hans George   I, 477
Henry   II, 75, 84
Henry Chs.   II, 202
J. P.   II, 45
Jean   II, 86
Johann Jacob   I, 412
Johann Ludwig   I, 431
Johann Wilhelm   I, 753
Johannas   II, 103
Johannes Wilhelm
(Hans W[m])   I, 601, 602, 603
Justus   I, 702; II, 103
Marie   II, 86
Michael   II, 8
Philip   II, 50
Schalota   II, 103
Sophie   II, 86
Valentin   II, 52
ECKHOFF
Christ[n] Cath.   II, 23
ECKLER
Johann Henrich   I, 89, 90, 92
ECKLY
John Diterich   I, 508
ECKMAN
Hans Jacob   I, 7
Johanes   I, 8, 9, 419
ECKNER
Hans Felix   I, 345
ECKORD (ECKFORD)
Margaretta   I, 55

Philip   I, 55, 56, 57
Susanna   I, 55
ECKOSH
  Christina Sophia   II, 105
ECKROTH (ELZEROOT)
  Johann Wilhelm   I, 340, 342, 343
ECKSTEIN
  Johannes   I, 736
  John   II, 121
  Mr.   II, 73
EDANS
  Hans Asher   I, 268
EDEBBERGER
  Francis   I, 454
EDEBORN (EDERBORN)
  Peter   I, 376, 377
EDEL
  Jost   I, 481
  Rudolf   I, 485
EDELMAN
  Anna Maria   I, 127
  Baltasar   I, 127
  David   I, 127, 129, 130
  Filib Jacob (Philip) I, 126, 129
  H. Peter   I, 481
  Hans   I, 662, 664
  Hans Adam   I, 481
  Hans Gerg   I, 395
  Hans Peter   I, 395
  J. George   I, 481
  Johann Adam   I, 437
  Johan Geo.   I, 662, 664
  Johannes (Hannes)   I, 481, 661
                        662, 664
  John   I, 712
  John Adam (Jo.
    Adam)   I, 620, 622, 625
  Margaretha   I, 127
  Peter (Piter) I, 36, 395, 661, 662, 664
  Vallentin   I, 395
EDENBORN (EDENBURN, EDIN-
    BOURN)
  Martin   I, 297, 298, 299
EDER
  J. S.   II, 45
EDERLY
  Christopher   I, 455
EDESMAN (EDISMA)
  Johan (Johannes)   I, 18, 19
EDGEWORTH
  John   II, 18
EDINGER (ETTINGER)
  Abraham   I, 628, 631, 635
  Johann Philip
    (Philip)   I, 180, 182, 184
  Melchior   I, 696
  Wolfarth Reinhard   I, 696
EDLINGER
  Davit   I, 454

EDNER
  Adam   II, 52
EDZEBELL
  Maurice   I, 304
EEBELE see EBELE
EEKER
  Jacob   II, 29
  Johan Philip   II, 29
  Mathias   II, 29
EERLMAN
  Lutwig   I, 407
EERZUM
  John Jacob   I, 622
EFORT
  John Wernert   II, 52
  Maria Magdalena   II, 52
EGART
  Adam   I, 414
EGE (EGI, AEGIE, EGER)
  Adam   I, 646, 647
  Bernhart (Ber-
    nard)   I, 226, 228, 230
  Friderich (Fredᵏ) I, 677, 679, 680
  Hans Jerg   I, 477
  Jacob   I, 226, 228, 230
  Johann Jacob   I, 477
  Johan Michel
    (Michal)   I, 226, 228, 230
  Simon   I, 646, 647
EGEL
  Johannes   I, 719
  Jnº   I, 753
  Jnº Geo.   I, 753
EGELBERGER
  Friederich   I, 20
EGEMAN
  Johann   I, 698
EGEN (EGAN)
  Christoff
    (Christian) I, 243, 244, 245
  Johann   I, 504
EGENBERGER
  Josef   I, 360, 361
EGENER
  Joh. Mathys   I, 14
EGENSCHNELLER
  Hans Georg   I, 502
EGER
  Philipp Jacob   I, 413
EGERT
  George Michael   I, 496
  Johann Georg   I, 747
  Johan Henrich   I, 414
EGGART
  Jacob   II, 134
EGGER
  Johannes   II, 134
EGGERMANN
  Lucas   II, 135

EGGERS
Hance Ernest II, 12
EGGLER
Ullrich I, 442
EGLI (EGLE, EGELY)
Jacob I, 508
Joh. Marttin I, 585, 586, 587
Marx I, 363
Philip I, 737
EGLIN
Leonhard I, 714
EGOLFF (EGOLFFE)
Johanes (Johannes) I, 360, 361
Michael I, 360, 361
Michael, Jun[r] I, 360, 361
EGTERNOEL
Andrew II, 47
Charles II, 47
Jacob II, 47
EGY
Rudolf I, 508
EHELE
Heinrich II, 184
EHELLER
Hans Jerg I, 488
EHEMANN (EHEMAN)
Hans Jerg (Hans
Georg) I, 184, 186, 187
Jacob II, 154
EHHALT
Matthes I, 522, 525
EHLERS
Carl II, 136
H. F. II, 141
Henrich II, 116
EHLIMAN
Hanna Margaretha II, 58
EHLY (ELEY, EHLY, ELLY)
Christians I, 88, 90, 91
Hans David I, 88, 90, 91
EHM (RAHM)
Peter I, 531, 533, 535
EHMAN
Andres I, 737
EHMIG
Christian I, 761
EHNINGER
Eva Margreth II, 171
EHNTZWEITH
Vallentin I, 430
EHRENDFRIED
Johann Gerg I, 750
EHRENFEUCHTER (EHRNFEICH-
TER, EHRENFEICHTER)
Friderich (Friede-
rich) I, 258, 260, 263
EHRENHART (ERNHARDT,
ERENHART)
Christopher I, 71, 75, 77

Jacob (Hans
Jacob) I, 204, 206, 207
Joh. Philip I, 356
Johannes I, 356
Katharina I, 73
Maria I, 74
EHRENSPERGER
Hans Ullrich I, 392
EHRESMANN
Andres I, 704
Georg Jacob I, 481
EHRET
Christoph I, 704
EHRHALT (EYHAULT)
Johannes (John) I, 227, 229, 231
EHRHARD (EHRHART, ERHARD,
ERHART)
Adam II, 185
Heinrich I, 710
Johan I, 400
Johann Carl I, 545, 547, 549
Martin II, 8
Niclaus (Nich[s]) I, 596, 598, 599
Valledin I, 503
EHRHEIM (EEHRHEIM, EIHR-
REM)
Johan Henrich
(Henrick) I, 642, 644
Johannes I, 642, 644
EHRIG *see* ERRICH
EHRICK
August David II, 122
EHRING
Samuel I, 409
EHRLICH
Geo. II, 8
Geo. jun[r] II, 8
Maria Sarah II, 8
EHRMAN (EHRMANN)
Hans Jorg I, 472
J. Andereas
(Andreas) I, 551, 553, 554
Johans I, 457
Josef I, 458
Michael I, 721
Willhelm I, 442
EHRNFEUCHTER (ERNFEIGTER)
Christoph (Chris-
tophel) I, 645, 647
EIBACH
Bartlome I, 486
EICH
Christoph I, 413
Henrich I, 691
Joh. Nickel I, 413
EICHACKER
——— II, 179
EICHART
Christian I, 400

EICHBAUM
Arnold II, 69
Charlotte II, 69
Elizabetha II, 69
Jane II, 69
P. W. II, 69
Wilhelmina II, 69
William II, 69
EICHEDE
Hans Peter I, 405
EICHELBERGER
Friederich I, 21
Hans Jerg (Jurig) I, 116, 120, 121
Julian I, 117
EICHELBURNER (EIGLEBOUR-NER, IGLEBOURNER)
Daniel I, 217, 219, 220
EICHELY (EYGLE)
Jacob I, 596, 598, 600
EICHER (EYEGER)
Ab^rm II, 101
Christian I, 609, 611, 613
Jacob I, 716
Johannes
(Hannes) I, 609, 611, 612
EICHERT
Johanes Heinrich II, 172
Joost Heinrich II, 172
Michael I, 15
EICHHACKER
Catharine II, 198
EICHHOLTZ (EICKHOLTZ, EYCHOLTZ)
Adam I, 418
Friderich I, 360, 362
Johann Jacob I, 169, 171, 172
Johann Martin I, 418
EICHHORN (EYKHORN)
Jacob I, 348, 350, 351
EICHLER (EYCHLER)
Augustus Sieg-friedt I, 621, 623, 625
Conrad I, 509, 510, 511
Gotlib II, 17
Hieronimus I, 509, 510, 511
EICK
Jacob I, 339
EICKHOFF
Conrad II, 69
Eberhard II, 69
George II, 69
John Friederich II, 69
EIDELMEN (read prob. EDEL-MANN)
Magdalina II, 43
EIDIER
Franciscus I, 451
EIER
Catharina I, 67

EIFERT
Carl Ludwig II, 205
EIGELBERGER
Gorg Bastian I, 464
EIGENBRODT
Ludwig Ernst Andreas II, 67
EIKHOLT (EIKEHOLT)
David II, 167
Johan II, 167
EILER
Adolf I, 339
EILFERIN
Jacob II, 53
Maria II, 53
EILSHEIMER (EILSAMER, EYGELSHEYMER)
Bernhart (Bern-hard) I, 678, 679, 680
EILTING
Martin I, 471
EIMANN
Jacob I, 397
EIN
Jeriam I, 66
EINIGER (EININGER)
Barbara I, 109
Catharina I, 109
Hans Adam I, 109
Hans Lehnard (Hans Lenard, Leonard) I, 107, 111, 112
Johanes I, 692
Maria Crete I, 108
EINSEL
Johann Ludwig I, 459
EINWÄCHTER (EINWACHTER)
George II, 26
Joh. Georg I, 741
EIRN
Clement I, 8
EISCHLY
Johannes I, 427
EISE
Daniel II, 196
EISEL
Magdalen II, 151
EISELE
Ludwig I, 446
EISELEN
Johann Conrad I, 760
EISELMAN (EISELEMAN, ESEL-MAN)
Benedict (Benedick) I, 66, 69, 70
Magdalina I, 44
EISELY
Lorian I, 425
EISEMAN (ISEMAN, EYSEMAN)
Barbella I, 109
Cathrina I, 109
Hans Kaspar

(Gasper) I, 106, 111, 112
Hans Wolff I, 106, 110, 112
Maria Crete I, 108
EISEN (EISSEN, LISA, LISSEY)
Carel (Cale) I, 93, 94, 95
Johan Kall (Johan Cal-
frick) I, 295, 296
EISENBEIS
Johann Georg I, 468
EISENHARDT (EISENHARD)
Andreas I, 471
Conradt I, 475
EISENHAUER (JOSSHOWER,
ISAN HOWER)
Hans Nicol (Hans
Mich¹) I, 317, 318, 319
Joh. Jacob I, 564, 566, 567
Johan Peder I, 317, 319
Johannes I, 317, 319
John I, 317
EISENHUTH
Henrich I, 593, 594
EISENMANN (EISENMAN, ISSE-
MAN)
Hans Georg I, 405
Ja. Nicklas I, 405
Johan Georg I, 721
Petder I, 405
EISENMENGER (EISENMÄNGER)
Georg I, 478
Johann Henrich I, 457
Kilian I, 478
Nicolaus I, 403
(*See also* EYSENMENGER)
EISGE (ESGE, ISAY)
Michel (Mich¹) I, 596, 597, 599
EISINBERG (read EISENBERG)
Hans George I, 451
EISNERT (HISENER)
Melcher (Milker) I, 539, 541, 543
EISNIN (read EISEN)
Doroth. II, 108
EITEL
Johann Martin II, 125
EITENMÜLLER (LEIDENMILLER)
Johann Nickolaus I, 621, 623, 626
EKELMAN
Johan I, 452
EKELSBERGER
Jacob II, 178
EKI
Antony I, 400
EKKER
Michael II, 32
EKMAN
Hans Jacob I, 7
Johanes I, 8
Peter I, 457

EKRON (ECRON)
Daniel I, 310, 311, 313
Johann Jacob I, 310, 312, 313
ELAMATIK
Cath. II, 6
ELDERST
Jacob II, 73
ELEE
Eve Tabaek I, 28
ELERS
Charlotte II, 117
(*See also* EHLERS)
ELGART
Jacob I, 754
ELGEDIN
Elisabeth II, 106
ELGERTH
Johannes I, 744
ELHART
Margaretha II, 97
ELIAS
Johan I, 487
Leon II, 11
ELICH
Elena II, 148
ELICK
Andres I, 12
ELIE
Nichol (Nickiel) I, 198, 200, 202
ELLENBERGER (ELENBERGER)
Christian
(Christiaen) I, 264, 267, 271
Elizabetha II, 45
Johannes II, 45
Louisa II, 53
Magdalena II, 46
Maria II, 45
Niclaus (Nicolas) I, 263, 270
Peter I, 396
Ullrich I, 396
ELLER
Carl I, 763
Christian I, 365
Henry I, 362
Jacob II, 8
Johann Georg I, 690
Johan Jacob I, 743
Johannes Joerg (Johannes
Gorg, John) I, 279, 281, 282
John I, 748
Ludwig I, 762
Martin II, 113
Michael I, 346
—— II, 122
ELLERKAMP
Ellisabeth II, 58
Friederich II, 58
ELLEWIN
Andrias II, 57

Catharina II, 57
Friederich II, 57
Johan Michael II, 57
Johana Catharina II, 57
Margaretha II, 57
Sophia II, 57
ELLICE
John II, 96
ELLIG
John Mich. I, 751
ELLING
Conrad I, 355
ELLINGER (ELINGER)
Johan Gorg
(Henrick) I, 217, 218, 220
ELLSCHEID
Conrad I, 436
ELS
Johann Henrich I, 690
ELSASS
Georg Jacob I, 713
ELSASSER
Christian Godfried II, 46
ELSER
Petter I, 416
ELSTNER
Casper II, 182
Johannes II, 182
Joseph II, 182
ELSTNERS
Elisabeth II, 182
ELWANGER
Barbary II, 161
ELY
F. II, 130
EMBICH
Christoph I, 491
EMBS (EMS)
Johan Jorg I, 307, 308, 309
Vallentin I, 307, 308, 309
EMDE
Philipp II, 52
EMEKE
J. W. II, 141
EMERICH
Nickell I, 452
EMERT (EMMERT)
Henrich (Hein-
rich) I, 678, 679, 681
EMEYER (EICHENMOYER)
Andreas Jacob (And^r
Jacob) I, 673, 674, 675
EMHARD
Frederic II, 154
EMICH (EMIG)
Dorothy I, 102
Fetter II, 52
Jacob I, 102
Johan Conrath I, 750

Johann Philipp I, 347
Johannes (Hans) I, 102, 104, 105
Nicholas I, 102
EMINGER
Gorg I, 722
EMMEL (EMMELL)
Johann Hartmann
(Hartman) I, 589, 590, 591
EMMER
Petter I, 487
EMMERICH
Johan Georg I, 487
(*See also* EMRICH)
EMMERLING
Andres I, 423
Christ. II, 139
EMMERT (EMERT)
Andreas I, 396
George I, 732
Johann Gorg Fredrig I, 89, 91, 92
Johann Philipp I, 36
Michael I, 88, 90, 92
Philip I, 297
Wendel I, 704
(*See also* EMERT)
EMMINGER
Elias I, 468
EMRICH (EMMRICH, EMERICK,
EMMERICK)
Andreas I, 703, 754
Anthoni I, 432
Carol (Carl,
Carrel) I, 582, 583, 584
George Friederich I, 487
Herman I, 582, 583, 584
Jacob (Yerrick) I, 387, 388, 389
Johann Friedrich I, 396
Johann Nickel I, 205, 207, 208
Johann Peter (Johan
Peter) I, 646, 648
Johann Theobald I, 726
Johannes I, 709
Jos. I, 724
ENAR
Amamuel (Emanuel) II, 75
Charles II, 75
ENAR
Mary II, 75
ENCK
Hanns Petter I, 455
Johann Jacob I, 703
END (ENDT, ENDE)
Fried. Ludw. II, 196
Jacob I, 666, 668, 670
Johannes I, 367, 368
(*See also* ENDT)
ENDER (ENDTER)
George I, 320, 321, 322
Johanes I, 409

ENDERLY
Abraham   I, 441
ENDERS (ENTERS, ENDES)
Conrath (Conrad)   I, 614, 616, 619
Ernst   I, 392
Hans Georg   I, 347
Johan Peter (John
   Peter)   I, 279, 280, 281
Johan Wil.   I, 718
Johann Philips   I, 699
Johannes   I, 414
Lorentz   I, 629, 633, 636
(*See also* ENTERS)
ENDEY
Peter   II, 121
ENDI
Jacob   I, 365
ENDLER
Philipp Adam   I, 173, 174, 175
ENDLICH
Johann Melcher   I, 710
ENDNER (VENDNER)
Isaac (Philip
   Jacob)   I, 551, 553, 554
ENDRES (ENDRESS)
Conradt   I, 500
Jacob   II, 26
Johann Michel   I, 539, 541, 543
Johannes   I, 409, 503
Michel   I, 716
Thomas   I, 627, 630, 633
Zacharias   I, 709
ENDT
Catharina   I, 123
Daniel   I, 122, 125, 126
Endick   I, 123
Johan Peter   I, 460
Valentine (Johan V.) I, 122, 125, 126
ENES
Johan   I, 729
Philib   I, 474
ENGEL (ENGELL, ENNGEL, EN-
GLE, INGLE, INGLIE)
Andreas   I, 441
Carl (Carles)   I, 373, 374, 376
Christian   II, 29
Christophel Joh[a]   II, 29
Conrad   I, 423
Georg Adam
   (Adam)   I, 605, 606, 608
Gorg (Geo.)   I, 184, 185, 187
Hans Christoff   I, 573, 574, 575
Henrich (Henr[k]) I, 176, 177, 178, 308
Jacob   I, 356, 358, 412
     II, 29
Jean   II, 86
Johann Conrad
   (Conrade)   I, 265, 268, 271
Johann Fridrich (Johann

Friehich)   I, 283, 284, 285
Johan Henrich
   (J. Herman)   I, 378, 380, 381
     517, 518, 519
Johann Jacob   I, 748
Johan Kasper
   (Casper)   I, 378, 379, 381
Joh. Peter (Peter)   I, 293, 294, 296
     378, 379, 381
Johann Philip   II, 29
Johann Wilhelm
   (Wilhelmus)   I, 378, 380, 381
Johannes
   (Johanes)   I, 373, 374, 376, 747
Ludewig   I, 434
Lydel (Eitel)   I, 378, 380, 381
Magret   II, 67
Maria Cath[a]   II, 29
Martin   II, 118
Matheis   I, 734
Peter   I, 205, 206, 208
     II, 29
Philib   I, 482
Philip Henrich   I, 693
Philip Peter   II, 29
Sevila Cath[a]   II, 29
Uhlrich
   (Ulrich)   I, 629, 632, 636
Wendel   I, 721
——   II, 24
ENGELBERT (ENGELBERTH,
ENGELBRET, ENGLEBERT)
Antonius
   (Anthony)   I, 227, 229, 231
     II, 104
Johannes   I, 686
Leon   II, 61
ENGELBRECHT
Martin   I, 470
ENGELER (ENGELAR)
Adam   I, 21
Jost   I, 420
Matthew   II, 183
Ullerig   I, 21
ENGELFRIED (ENGELFRIDT)
Heinrich   I, 760
Johann Wilhelm   I, 531, 533, 535
ENGELHART (ENGELLHARD,
ENGELHARD, ENGLEHART)
Andreas   I, 258, 260, 263
Ant.   II, 99
Corn. Wm.   II, 61
Gabriel   II, 126
George   I, 442
Johann Fridrich   I, 546, 548, 550
Johann Jacob   I, 696
Sophia   I, 67
Thomas   I, 731

ENGELMAN (ENGELLMANN,
   ENGELMANN)
  Jacob   I, 310, 312, 313
  Jacob, Junr.   I, 310, 312, 313
  Jeremias Ludwig   I, 488
  Johann Andreas   I, 474
  Joh. Willhelm (Han
    William)   I, 293, 294, 295
ENGELS (INGLIS)
  H. Peter (Hans
    Peter)   I, 596, 597, 599
  Peter   I, 652, 654
ENGEROST
  Phillippe   I, 757
ENGERSBACH
  Johann Wilhelm   I, 499
ENGERT
  Johann Adam   I, 750
  Philip   I, 18
ENGLAND (ENGLEND)
  Christoff (Chris-
    topher)   I, 72, 76, 77
  Maria   I, 73
ENGLER
  Johann Jacob   I, 419
ENGLERT (ENGLERTH)
  Hans Christoph   I, 438
  Hans Jurg   I, 503
  Johann Georg   I, 476, 494
  Michael   I, 495
  Ulrich   I, 22
ENKISCH
  Jacob   I, 455
ENSLIN
  Gotthold Frid.   I, 759
ENSLY
  Johan Melchior   I, 509
ENSMINGER (HANSMINGER,
   HANSMENGER, ENTZMIN-
   GER)
  Anna Creett   I, 241
  Anna Marrian   I, 241
  Catharina   I, 108, 109
  Cristian   I, 241
  Davidt   I, 441
  Friderik   I, 463
  Hans Nickel
    (Nicolas)   I, 240, 242, 243
                621, 623, 625
  Hans Philip   I, 109
  Henrich (Hen-
    drick)   I, 109, 317, 318, 319
  Johannes   I, 522, 524
  Kattarina   I, 241
  Loadwick   I, 241
  Nicolas   I, 109
  Peter (Pedter)   I, 107, 111, 112
ENTENMANN
  Hans Martin   I, 463

ENTERS (ENDERS, ENTERZ)
  Johann Georg (Johan
    Yerick)   I, 383, 385
  Ludwig   II, 70
  Margaretha   II, 70
ENTTIGER
  Johannes   I, 490
ENTZ
  Elias   II, 179
  John   II, 179
EONSONN
  Lona, van   II, 122
EPGERT (EBGENT)
  Fritz (Frist)   I, 279, 280, 281
EPPELMANN (EBELMAN)
  Johan Georg   I, 335, 336, 338
  Johannes   I, 397
EPPELSCHIER
  Lud.   II, 147
EPPELSHEIN
  Elisabeth   II, 198
EPPLE (APPLE, EPELE)
  Andreas (Andrew)   I, 185, 186, 187
  Jacob   I, 446; II, 152
  Johann Jerg
    (Yerick)   I, 283, 284, 286
  Lewis   II, 152
  Margaret   II, 152
  (*See also* EPPLI)
EPPLER (EPLER)
  Andreas   I, 489
  Bartolomeus   I, 445
  George   II, 28
  Hans   I, 169, 170, 172
  Jerg Adam   I, 366
EPPLI (APELY)
  Hans   I, 252, 253, 254
EPPLING
  Friederich   I, 697
  Gottfried   I, 697
EPSON
  Johan George   I, 455
EPSTEINER
  Jacob   II, 135
EPTING
  Christoph   II, 154
ER
  John   I, 19
ERB (ERBE)
  Anna   I, 190
  Caspar (Casper)   I, 614, 616, 618
                  II, 116
  Catherine
    (Catrina)   I, 190; II, 146
  Christian
    (Christ)   I, 155, 158, 160, 190
  Christophel   I, 190
  Claus (Glas)   I, 189, 192, 193
  Friederich   I, 399

Hann. M. II, 146
Hans Rudolf (Hance
  Rudolph) I, 163, 165, 166
Henil II, 146
Henry I, 751
Jacob I, 190; II, 145
Johanes
  (Johan, Hans) I, 189, 192, 193
Matth^s II, 145
Peter Segrest II, 145
Reningen II, 146
ERBACH
Balthes I, 372
Lorentz I, 355
ERBE
Hans I, 391
ERBEN
Johann Adam I, 452
Philips Henrich I, 323, 325, 326
ERBES
Frederic II, 53
ERBOLT
Hans Georg I, 472
ERBS
Anna Marg^a II, 23
ERBSHUSER (ERBSFUSER, HERB-
  SHEYSER)
Johannes I, 677, 679, 680
ERBST
A. Marg. II, 105
ERBT
Johannes II, 112
ERCHENBRECHT (JERGEN-
  BRIGHT)
Hans Georg (Hance) I, 93, 95
ERDEN (ERDE)
Christian, von I, 296, 298, 299
Johann Adam (Johan
  Adam), von I, 296, 298, 299
Johannes
  (Johanes), von I, 296, 297, 299
ERDMAN (ERDMANN)
Carl Fred. II, 135
Joh. I, 79
Johann Jacob I, 59, 64, 65
Johann Justus I, 179, 181, 183
Martin I, 456
ERDMAYER
George I, 372
ERDROTH
Johann Zacharias I, 395
ERFFURT (SERFORD, ERFORD)
Anthony I, 205, 206, 208
ERGOTT
Christian I, 265, 268, 271
ERHART (ERHARD, ERHARDT)
Casber I, 693
Daniel I, 468
Dietrich I, 440

Peter I, 440
Hinrig I, 453
Johann Georg I, 468
Johann Henrich I, 256, 259, 261
Johannes I, 307, 308, 309
Joseph II, 199
Mich^l I, 717
Wilhelm I, 307, 308, 309
ERICH (ERIG, ERICK, IHRIG)
Bastian (Baltus) I, 527, 528, 530
Georg II, 109
Jacob I, 736
Jno Geo. I, 753
Johan George I, 399
Johannes I, 661, 663, 664
John Conrad I, 711
Thomas I, 411
ERKERT
Fred^r A. II, 188
ERLENBACH (ELLABACK)
Johann Henrich
  (Hend^k) I, 383, 385
ERLENHEISER
Jno I, 696
Johannes I, 696
ERLEWYN (ERLEWYNE, ERL-
  WEIN)
Andreas (Andries) I, 39, 41, 42
Ann I, 40
Carols August I, 347
ERLINGER
Geo. I, 722
ERLINGHURST
Margaret II, 73
Peter II, 73
ERMAN
Johan Petter I, 490
ERMEL
Johannes I, 314, 315
ERMENTRAUDT (ERMAN-
  TROUD)
Johan Friedrich I, 256, 259, 261
  601, 602, 604
Johan Phillip
  (Philipus) I, 256, 259, 261
Johannes (Johanes) I, 256, 259, 261
ERMOLT (ARMOLT, ERMOLD)
Anthony I, 373, 374, 376
Joh. Pet. I, 755
Johann Georg I, 709
ERNIGH (ERNY)
Anna I, 68
Friederich I, 67, 68, 69, 70
Maria I, 68
ERNSPERGER (ARNSPARGER)
Jerg Henrich (Georg
  Hendrick) I, 189, 192, 194
ERNST (ERNSTE)
Adam I, 409

Anton   I, 739
Christian   I, 754; II, 156
Frantz Heinrich   I, 517, 518, 520
Georg Adam
  (Jurg Adam)   I, 292, 293
Hans Michel (Hans
  Michael)   I, 257, 260, 262
Jerg   I, 363
Jerg Balthas   I, 492
Joh. Jacob   I, 491
Johan Conrath   I, 195, 196, 197
Johann Georg   I, 694
Johan Wendel (Johans
  Ventel)   I, 195, 196, 197
John Frederic   I, 707
Ludwich   I, 454
Mardin (Hance Martin) I, 93, 95
Michel   I, 471
Nicolaus   I, 726
Peter   I, 378, 380, 381
ERPSON
Will.   II, 90
ERRHART (HERHERARD, HER-
ART)
Christian
  (Christiaen)   I, 264, 267, 271
ERRICH (read EHRICH)
Conrad   I, 457
ERSAME
Simon   I, 184, 186, 187
ERTEL
Barb.   II, 136
Cath.   II, 136
Fred   II, 136
Jacob   II, 136
Vallendin (Wallendin,
  Valentin)   I, 258, 260, 263
ERTINGER
Burghart   I, 410
ERTZBERGER
Jacob   I, 720
ERTZNER (BELSENER)
Johan Simon
  (Simon)   I, 279, 281, 282
ERUCH
Jacob   II, 184
ERYNSTEIN
Eliza.   I, 23
ESBOD
Simon   I, 365
ESBY
Christian   II, 16
ESCH (EASH)
Daniel Henrich   I, 305, 306
Hennrich (Henrick) I, 643, 645
Jacob   I, 477
Johann Adam   I, 745
Johan Gorg   I, 431
Jonathan   II, 149

Maria Magdelena   II, 149
Michael David   I, 759
Michel   I, 477
ESCHAUER (ISHENAVER)
Leonhard   I, 527, 528, 530
ESCHBACH   (ESHBAGH, ESH-
BAY)
Johann Heinrich
  (Henrich)   I, 198, 200, 202
Simon   I, 423
ESCHBACHER   (ESHBACHER,
ESHBACKER)
Andereas   I, 355
Christian   I, 396, 397
Christophel   I, 190
Eliza   I, 190
Peter   I, 188, 191, 193
ESCHELMAN   (ESCHELMANN,
ESLMAN, ISHELMAN, ESHEL-
MAN)
Better (Pitter) I, 116, 119, 120
Barbra   I, 117
Christian (Cristian) I, 116, 119, 120
Henrich   I, 18, 19
Jacob   I, 24, 26, 118, 397
Johan Albrecht   I, 400
Johannes (Johan)   I, 47, 51, 53
Peder (Pitter)   I, 116, 118, 397
ESCHENBACH (ESHENBACK)
Andreas (Andrew)   I, 274, 275
ESCHENFELTER
Phillips Jacob   I, 331
ESCHER (ESHER)
Gabriel   I, 722
Johann Conrad   I, 706
Johan Jacob   I, 722
ESCHMAN
Johanes   I, 722
ESDAN
Philip   I, 310
ESEL (EZLE, YSEL)
Reinhold (Rynholl) I, 93, 94, 95
ESHE (HESHE, EST)
Christian   I, 180, 181, 184
ESHWYN
Nickolas   I, 474
ESKUGEN   (ESCOGEN,   ESKU-
SEN)
Johannes   I, 213, 214, 216
Peter (Jan
  Pieter)   I, 213, 214, 216
ESLEY (ESLING, ESLIN)
Johan Georg (Jerig,
  John Yerk)   I, 283, 284, 286
ESLINGER
Christian   I, 408
Hanes Jerg   I, 427
ESMAN (NEASMAN)
Vallentin   I, 316, 317

ESPENSCHIED
  Jacob   I, 701
ESPER (ESBER)
  Hans Michael
    (Michael)   I, 615, 617, 620
ESPICH
  Johann Rudolph   I, 420
ESPING
  Philip (Phillip)   I, 143, 145, 146
ESSER
  Johann Georg   I, 481
ESSEWEIN
  Johannes   I, 428
ESSIG (ESSICH, ESSICK, ESSIK, ESIG)
  Baltazar   I, 372
  Christoff
    (Christoph)   I, 614, 617, 619
  F.   II, 186
  Hans Michael   I, 162, 164, 166
  Jerg Abraham
    (George)   I, 162, 164, 166
  Johann Willhelm
    (Willm)   I, 283, 284, 286
  Ludwig (Chas.
    Ludewik)   I, 316, 317
  Rudolff
    (Rudolph)   I, 162, 164, 166
  Wendel   I, 404
ESSY
  J. Conrad   I, 469
ESTER (HESTER)
  Anna   I, 117
  J. Ludwig
    (Lodowick)   I, 559, 561, 563
ESTEUE
  Michel   I, 735
ESTINGHAUSEN
  Lodewig   II, 101
ESTRICKER
  Christian   II, 126
  Johan   II, 126
ESZEVEIN (read ESSWEIN)
  Valent   II, 61
ETELMAN (read EDELMAN)
  Adam   I, 395
ETELWEIN (read EDELWEIN)
  Georg   I, 725
ETIENNE
  Jean Jaque   I, 708
ETSCH
  Christopf   I, 419
ETSPERGER
  Johann Wilhelm   I, 693
ETTE (ETTING)
  Johann Vallendein   I, 516, 518, 519
ETTEL
  Sebastian   I, 717

ETTENHOFER
  M. J.   II, 107
ETTER (ETER)
  Daniel   I, 322
  Georg Henrich   I, 441
  Hans George   I, 440
  Hans Philips   I, 483
  Jerg   I, 697
  Johan Christoffel   I, 490
  Johannes   I, 153, 154
  Margat   I, 153
  Sam^1 II, 179
ETZWEILLER (ELSWILER)
  Hs. Georg   I, 344, 345
EULEN
  Johannes   I, 409
EULENBER
  Johannes Krist   I, 478
EULER (EYLER)
  Adam   I, 307, 308, 309
  Ann Catherine   II, 56
  Conrad   II, 115
  Georg Phillip   II, 134
  Jacob   II, 115
  Johan Gorg   I, 184, 185, 187
  Philipp   I, 488
  William   II, 56
EULERS
  J. C.   II, 143
EULERT
  Johannes   I, 430
EULL
  Joh. Jacob   I, 743
EURICH
  Conrath   I, 709
  Johann Gorg   I, 709
EUSELIN
  Joh.   II, 119
EVA
  Johann Adam   I, 652, 654
EVALT
  Frans Peter   I, 601
EVANS
  Ferdinand G.   II, 187
EVAR
  Bartholmae   I, 482
EVELANDT (EVELAND)
  Jacob   I, 74
  Maria   I, 74
  Martin   I, 74
  Nicolas   I, 72, 76, 77
  Regina   I, 73
EVER
  Canesh   I, 94
EVERET
  Barend   II, 135
EVERHART *see* EBERHARD
EVERHAUSER
  Gertruit   II, 122

EVERICH
 Johan II, 169
EVERLING
 George II, 197
 Joh. Casper II, 138
EVERS
 Jacob II, 50
 Leonard II, 78
EVERST
 Engel II, 57
EVERSTENE (EVERSTINE)
 Johana II, 77
 Mathias II, 77
EVERT
 Martin I, 737
 Sam II, 147
EVERTINE
 Eva II, 56
EVERTS
 Mr II, 130
EVIE
 Andries I, 18
EVIGHER
 Christopher I, 517
EWALD (EVALDT, EWALT)
 Agnes I, 123
 C. E. II, 71
 George Adam I, 395
 Jacob I, 218, 219, 221
 Johannes I, 123
 John I, 516, 518, 519
 Ludwig I, 122, 125, 126
 Maria I, 123
EWART
 George II, 27
EWERS
 Johan I, 484
EWERT (EBERT)
 Johannes
  (Johanis) I, 200, 202, 204
EWI (EWE)
 Jacob II, 28
 Michael II, 5
 (*See also* EWY)
EWIG
 Adam I, 74
 Andres I, 19
 Benedict I, 469
 Catharina II, 70
 Christian I, 184, 185, 187, 474
 Hans Jurg I, 74
 J. Adam I, 468
 Johannes I, 71
 John I, 716
 Nicolaus (Nicolas) I, 71, 76, 77
 Wilhelm I, 474
EWY, EVY
 Elizabet I, 60
 John I, 61

 Kathrina I, 61
 Lisbetha I, 61
 Mergretha I, 61
EXELL
 Christo. I, 14
EYB (EIBE, GIBE)
 Jacob Michel
  (Jacob) I, 113, 114, 115, 765
EYCHELEN (EGLING)
 Barbara I, 43
 Hans Adam
  (John Adam) I, 43, 46
EYCHLER *see* EICHLER
EYCHOLTZ *see* EICHHOLTZ
EYCK
 Johann Jacob I, 339
EYDAM
 Christian I, 367, 368
EYDEN
 George II, 20
EYDMEYER
 Johannes I, 473
EYER
 Hans I, 358
 Mardin I, 416
EYERMAN
 Christoff I, 433
 Mr. II, 147
EYG (EGG)
 Rudolff
  (Rudolph) I, 147, 150, 151
EYGENBROD
 Austus I, 382
EYGER (EYGR)
 Christian I, 403
 Johannes Mattes I, 13
EYGLE
 Philip I, 649
EYHAULT
 John II, 104
EYLER
 Henry
  (Henrick) I, 665, 668, 670
 Jacob I, 759
 Johann Jacob I, 371
EYMAN (EYMANN)
 Franey II, 57
 Ullrich I, 697
EYRICH
 Andreas I, 502, 729
 Johann Philip I, 539, 541, 543
 Matheas I, 432
 Michael I, 432
EYROH
 Michael I, 491
EYSELOHR
 Johann Paulus I, 417
EYSEMANN (ISEMAN)
 Georg (Jurg) I, 585, 587, 588

EYSEN (EYSIN)
An Margreth I, 156
Jacob I, 155, 158, 160
Susana Maria I, 156
EYSENBREIT (ISINGBRID)
Peter I, 551, 552, 553
EYSENHAAR (WYSHAAR, WIESHAR)
G. Philip (Philip) I, 627, 630, 633
EYSENMAN
Hans Michel I, 364
EYSENMENGER
Henrich I, 469
J. Balth. I, 458
Peter Henrich I, 457
EYSTER
Johann Philibus I, 465
EYTEL
Johann Bernhart I, 485
EZECHIEL
Tobias Jacob II, 156

FAAS (FAASS, FAASE)
Christian I, 445
Johann Gorg
(Jurig) I, 199, 201, 203
Johann Philib I, 199, 201, 203
Johannes I, 67, 69, 70
FABER (FAVER)
Christian I, 718
Frantz Nicolaus I, 403
Hans Adam I, 195, 196, 197
Hans Jacob I, 195, 196, 197
Henrich I, 403
Jacob I, 718
Johan Caspar (Jan
Casber) I, 655, 657, 658
Johanes I, 490
Johann Henrich I, 412, 460
Michiel (Michael) I, 113, 114, 115
765
Valledien I, 718
FABION
Joseph I, 310, 311, 312
FABOR
Babor I, 767
Michal I, 767
Sarah I, 766
FABRICIUS (FABRITZIUS, FABRITIUS)
Johan Christian I, 751
Johann Friederich Just II, 58
Johann Henrich I, 693
FABRY
Miss II, 96

FACIUNDUS (FACKIUNDAS, FACUNDUS, FAGONDUS, FAXINDUS)
Ferdnand (Ferd.) I, 605, 607, 608
Gottlib Heinrich I, 526, 528, 529
Hans Conratt I, 528, 529
John Frederick I, 526
FACKENTHAL
Philipp I, 330
FACKERT
Philibus I, 353, 354
FACKLER (FACKHLER)
Adam I, 189
Barbara I, 189
Hans George I, 446
Hans Jacob I, 188, 191, 193
Johann Christoph I, 420
Johann Wendell I, 686
Magdalena I, 189
FACMEYER
Johanes I, 498
FACTORIUS
Gotleib II, 197
FACTS
Hans I, 17
FACUNDUS *see* FACIUNDUS
FAEGLER
Ludowick I, 637
FAETZET
Pierre I, 746
FAGER
Wilh. II, 119
FAGLY
Anna Barbara I, 766
FÄGULE
Marti I, 425
FAHL (FALL)
Diedrich I, 340, 341, 342
FAHLER
Christian II, 52
FAHNEN
Michel I, 498
FAHR (FÄHR)
Hans Ullrich I, 391
Johannes I, 453
FAHRENCORN
Andw I, 749
FAHRION (FARION)
Friderich (Fredrick) I, 199, 201, 203
FAHRMAN
Johann Henrich I, 723
FAHRNE
Joseph I, 448
FAHRNER
Jacob I, 449
FAHTS
Casper II, 140
FAIAY
Fred. Albert II, 105

FAICK
——   II, 80
FAJON
Jn°   I, 739
FAKEENNER
John   II, 83
FAKLER
Hans Adam   I, 418
FALCK (FOLCK, FOLK, FOLKE)
Hans Gorg
  (Jarrick)   I, 99, 100, 101
Jacob   I, 169, 170, 172
Jerg   I, 539, 541, 543
Johan Phillipp   I, 416, 717
Johannes   I, 412
Lutwig   I, 447
Simon   I, 452
FALCKENHAHN
Samuel   I, 430
FALKENSTEIN
Ludwig (Lodowyck)   I, 360, 362
FALKEYSEN
Hans Lux   I, 198
FALLER
Anna Catharina   II, 46
Caspar   II, 46
Johan Joseph   I, 113, 765
Peter   II, 46
FALLIÉZ
Mathieu   I, 748
FALLUNG
Abraham   II, 197
Catharine   II, 197
David   II, 197
FANBON
——   II, 81
FANDRICH
Christoph   I, 742
FANER
Johanes   II, 36
FANHOLTZ
I. Fred   II, 45
FANNER
Felix   I, 348
Henry   I, 348
FANNIL
Johanna   II, 195
FANTH
Johannes   I, 762
FANTZ (FAWNTZ)
Gerg (Georg)   I, 96, 98, 99
FARN
Abraham   I, 8
FARNE
G. J.   II, 96
Petter   I, 448
(*See also* FARNI)
FARNER
Johanes   I, 407

FARNI (FARNIE, FARNY)
Abraham   I, 168, 170, 171
Anna Elizabeth   I, 144
Cathrine   I, 144
Christian   I, 143, 145, 146
Hans Jacob   I, 463
Jacob   I, 265, 268, 271, 727
Joseph   I, 727
Peter   I, 722
FARRELL
Jn   II, 18
FARRINGER
Debalt   I, 441
Johan Nicklas   I, 484
FASEL (FÄSAL)
Jerg Jacob   I, 453
Johann Christop   I, 749
FASHAUS
Johan Henrich   I, 692
FASNACHT
Johan   I, 430
FASS (VASS)
Johann Jerg (Johan
  Jurg)   I, 378, 380, 381
Nickel   I, 432
FASSBENDER (FASSBENDLER)
Johann Jacob   I, 336, 337, 339
FASSENACHT
Johan Adam   I, 412
Johann Conrath   I, 412
FAUCH (FAUCK, FACK, FAUG)
Catharina   I, 108
Wilhelm Jacob (Philip Jacob,
  Jacob)   I, 596, 597, 599
FAUGUELVEY
Zacharie   II, 74
FAULHABER
Charlotta   II, 28
FAULHAFFER   (FOULER, FOL-
  HAVER)
Markus (March,
  Mark)   I, 245, 246, 247
FAULSTICH (FAULSTEG)
Balthasar
  (Baltzer)   I, 614, 616, 618, 747
FAURIE
Joseph   II, 58
FAUSS (FAUS)
John   II, 8
John Adam (Hans
  Adam)   I, 595, 597, 599
FAUSSER (FOUSER)
Conrad (Hans
  Conrad)   I, 585, 586, 588
FAUST (FAWST, FOUST)
Abraham   I, 257, 259, 262
Anton   I, 329
Henry   I, 314
J. P.   II, 4

Jacobina II, 41
Johann Franciscus I, 709
Johan George I, 257, 262
Johann Peter I, 113, 114, 115
709, 765
Johan Philip
(Fillibs) I, 113, 114, 115, 765
Johannes I, 170, 171, 173, 373
374, 375; II, 114
John George I, 327, 329
Maria II, 4
Michael (Michel) I, 577, 578, 580
II, 78
Nickel I, 432
Peter I, 327, 329, 356
Philips I, 688
Reighart I, 314
(*See also* FOUST)
FAUTH (FAUT, FOUT, FOUTH)
Hans Jerg (Hans
Jurig) I, 232, 233
Jacob I, 704
Valthin I, 736
FAUTZ (FAUTS, FOUTZ)
Christian I, 443
Dorothea II, 5
Matheas (Mathias) I, 597, 598, 600
Michel II, 29
Theevia I, 233
FAUTZER (FAUSTER, FAUTER)
George Michael
(Mich[1]) I, 595, 597, 599
FAVON (FAVIAN)
Jerig Mich (Georg Michel,
Jarrick Mich) I, 100, 101
Michael I, 100
FAWST *see* FAUST
FAY
Johann Conrath I, 495
FAYSS (FAYST, FAEIZ)
Adam I, 560, 561, 563
FAZLER (FAILSTER)
Martin (Martain) I, 555, 556, 557
FAZY
Jean Salomon II, 73
FECHER
Wiegand I, 705
FECHTHELM (FIGHTHELM)
Johann Friederich (John
Frederick), von I, 286, 287, 288
FECHTING
Georg Friederich II, 173
FECK
Friedrich Frantz I, 711
FECKELY
Godfrey I, 741
FECKSER (FIXER)
Johann Nicolaus I, 539, 541, 543

FEDER (FETER)
Helena I, 44
Katrina I, 44
Michel (Michal,
Michail) I, 43, 44, 45, 46
FEDERBUSH
Elisabeth II, 150
Thierry II, 150
FEDERHAFF (FERDERHAUF)
Balthas I, 442
Johann Georg (Hans
Georg) I, 526, 529, 530
Johan Friederich I, 527
FEDEROLF (FEDEROLPH)
Peter I, 32, 33, 34
FEECK (FEACK)
Johann Georg (Han
Geo.) I, 665, 668, 670
FEELLER
Uhllerich I, 393
FEERER
Hans Caspar I, 363
FEES
Friederich I, 481
FEESSER (FISER, FUSER)
Johanes Theis (Johan Ties,
John Tys) I, 279, 280, 281
John Tys I, 279
FEGER
Johann Henrich I, 456
Johan Michel I, 500
FEGERT
Jacob I, 466
FEGHTERN
Susanna I, 72
FEGLEAR (read FEGLER)
Jacob I, 80
FEGLEY (FEGLY, FEGELIN,
FIGLE, FIGLEY, FOGLIE)
An Catharine I, 157
Anna I, 117
Anna Maria I, 118
Barnard (Hans
Lennert) I, 117, 120, 121
Catrina I, 118
Catharina Margreth I, 156
Christina I, 108
Eva Maria I, 108
Hans Jurick I, 118
Henrich (Hans
Henrick) I, 117, 120, 121
Jacob I, 107, 108
Johan Peter (Hans
Peter) I, 155, 158, 160
Madlena I, 117
Mathis (Matayias) I, 117, 120, 121
FEHL (FEHLE, FEELT)
Georg Vallentin I, 451
Henry (Hendrich) I, 199, 201, 203

Johann Philipp
(Philip)   I, 213, 214, 216
FEHLER (FELER)
Hans Adam   I, 240, 242, 243
FEHNEL (FAHNEL, FANEL)
Johan Philipp
(Philip)   I, 581, 582, 584
FEHR (VEER)
Christoph   I, 526, 528, 529
Jacob   I, 252, 253, 255, 414
Johan Bernhard   I, 408
Johannes   I, 500
Sebastian   I, 234
FEHRING
Jnᵒ Diet.   I, 700
FEHRLEY (VENY)
Caral (Carl)   I, 582, 583, 585
FEHRLINGER
Johan Vallentin   I, 479
FEICHTNER
Christoffel   I, 492
FEICK
Johann Gorg   I, 457
FEICKERT
Wilhelm   I, 696
FEIDIG
Anderes   I, 409
FEIERABEND
Johan   I, 745
FEIERBUSH
Diederich   II, 152
FEIG
Jnᵒ   I, 749
FEILLEIN
Jülch   I, 448
FEILLER
Johanes   I, 506
FEILLMANN
Carl   II, 205
Friedr.   II, 205
Hanchon   II, 205
Hennr. Freiderike   II, 205
Johannes   II, 205
Wilhelm   II, 205
FEILTER
Hans Erick   I, 13
FEIN
Johannes   II, 97
FEINAUER (FEINNAUER, FYN-
HAUR)
J. Joseph   I, 605, 606, 608
FEINER (FINER)
Jacob   I, 642, 644
FEINST
Johannes   I, 738
FEIOCK
Jacob   I, 691
FEIRING
Matheis   I, 759

FEISS (FEIS)
Elisa   II, 68
Peter (Petter)   I, 546, 547, 549
FEIT
Charles   II, 189
Christena   II, 189
Fred.   II, 189
Johannas   II, 189
Mary   II, 189
FEITZ
Uhllerik   I, 494
FEL see FELL
FELBACH
Wilhelm Ernst   I, 736
FELBAUM (FELLBAUM)
Conrad   I, 346
Hans Adam   I, 346
FELBER
Hans Jerg   I, 453
FELDEN (FELTON)
Mattias (Mathias) I, 266, 270, 273
FELDENTROPF
J.   II, 149
FELDER
Arnold   II, 193
FELDFLIEGEL (FLEEGEL, FLI-
GEL)
Johan Vallentin
(Johan)   I, 234, 235, 236
FELDICH
Herman   I, 748
FELDMOYER
Johannes   I, 366
FELENKEUSER
Johann Henrich   I, 700
FELER (FEELER, FELLAR)
Anna   I, 79
Melcher (Melker) I, 78, 81, 82
FELICITE
———   II, 80
FELIER
Kattarina   I, 242
FELIX (FEELIX)
Johannes   I, 724
Martin   I, 724
Nicolaus (Nicholas) I, 652, 654
Stefanus   I, 724
FELKER
Anna Barbara   I, 139
Hans Georg   I, 139
Johan Jacob   I, 79
Maria Eva   I, 139
Maria Sarah   I, 139
FELL (FEL)
Caspar   I, 492
Warner   I, 735
FELLE
Nicklas   I, 363

FELLENBERGER
Johann Niclas I, 403
FELLENTZER
Johannes I, 522, 524
FELLER
Hans Jerg I, 526, 527, 529
FELLMAN (FOLLMAN, VELL-
MAN)
Jacob I, 155, 158, 160
FELMI (FELME, FELM, FELMY)
Abrahm (Ab^m) I, 595, 597, 599
Jacob II, 53
FELTBERGER (FETTBERGER)
Friederich I, 335, 336, 338
FELTE (FELTI, VELTE)
Bastian I, 232, 233
Peter I, 378, 380, 381
FELTMAN (FELTMANN)
Antoni (Anthony) I, 286, 287, 288
Johan Kilian I, 452
Johannes I, 697
John II, 186
FELTON
Henry I, 715
FELTZ
Hans I, 482
FENCHEL (FENCHELL)
Fredrick II, 147
Jacob I, 410
FENDERER
Gottfried I, 420
FENDTNER
Johann Friedrich I, 486
FENGEL
Gorg I, 402
FENN (FINN)
Johann Salomon I, 576, 578, 580
FENNIMA
Peter I, 16
FENSCH
J. H. II, 72
FENSLER
Geo. Casper I, 185
FENSTERMACHER (FINSTER-
MACHER, FINSTERMAKER)
Christian I, 307
Jacob I, 205, 206, 208
Mathias I, 204, 206, 207
Philip I, 169, 171, 173
Wilhelm (Johan
Willem) I, 204, 206, 207
FENTZ
Heinrich I, 727
FERBER
Hans Adam I, 461
Jacob I, 730
Johann Jacob I, 356
Johan Wilm I, 461
Philipp I, 441

FERDIG see FERTIG
FERDINAND
Charles Henry II, 93
FERER
Jno Gerg I, 706
FEREY
Maria I, 139
FERMAN
Henr. I, 516
FERNANTZ
Simon Peter I, 430
FERNSER
Philip I, 7
FERNSLER (FERNSSLER)
George Casper I, 185, 186, 187
Madtheus I, 22
FERRER
Johann Rudolf I, 508
FERSCH
Cath^e II, 8
Christopher II, 8
Geo. II, 8
FERSCHBACH
Jost I, 478
FERSTER
Michel I, 443
FERTIG (FERDIG, FERDIGH)
Andreas (Anderas) I, 627, 628, 630
631, 633, 634
Hans I, 502
Johan Christoffel I, 726
Peter I, 373, 374, 375
FERTNER
Basilius II, 69
Catharina II, 69
Elizabetha II, 69
George II, 69
Louis II, 69
Ludwig II, 69
Mattis II, 69
Nicolaus II, 69
FESBELY
Matteas I, 432
FESLAR
Orrla I, 80
FESSLER (FESELER, FESSELER)
Henrich (Henrick) I, 107, 111, 112
Johan Albrecht I, 512, 514, 515
Johann Andreas
(Andreas) I, 512, 514, 515
Johann Heinrich I, 711
Johann Jacob I, 711
Maria I, 108
Maria Crete I, 108
FESTINGER
David I, 649, 650
FETER (FETHER)
Johann Bernhar I, 363
Johann Peter I, 363

Ludwig I, 689

FETH (FET, read FETT)

Andreas
(Andereas) I, 627, 630, 633
Catharina II, 136
Eva Sebina II, 136
Jan Magel II, 136
Johanette II, 136
Johanna II, 136
John Peter II, 136
Margretta II, 136

FETHERCOILE
David I, 659

FETSCH
Caspar I, 729

FETTER
Anna Margarett I, 24
George I, 511
Hans Henry I, 512
Heinrich I, 510
Henry I, 628
Jacob I, 24
Joanna I, 44
Richd. I, 24

FETTERLE
Fredrick I, 545

FETZ (FETTS)
Anthony II, 137
Heinrich I, 434

FETZER
Andereas I, 480
Gerg I, 458
Johann Heinrich I, 687
Ludwig I, 448
Matthaus I, 458
Michael I, 480

FEUCHT
Hans Jerg I, 399

FEUERSTEIN (FEYERSTEYN,
FEIERSTEIN, FÜERSTEIN)
Georg Philipp I, 585, 586, 588
Johannes I, 430
Nicholus, Jun. I, 546, 548, 550
Nickell I, 546, 548, 550

FEY (FEIT)
Fred. I, 747
George II, 24
Johann Gorg (Han
Geo.) I, 667, 669, 671
Johan Michel I, 314, 315
Johan Wilhelm
(Wilhelm) I, 313, 314, 315
Mark I, 143
Nicol I, 347
Tobias I, 414
Vallentin I, 465

FEYE
Niclas (Nicholas) I, 217, 218, 220

FEYERBAGH
Henry I, 357

FEYL (FEYIL)
Johan I, 234; II, 18

FEYLY
Johanes I, 493

FEYRING
Johann Jost II, 130

FEYSEG
Jno I, 16

FEYSER
Johan Peter (Joh.
Peter) I, 352, 354

FICCUS (FIKUS)
Jost (Josph) I, 194, 196, 197
Peter I, 194
(*See also* FICKUS)

FICHER
Adolph II, 90
Albertine Henrietta Caro-
lina II, 90
Augusta Sophia Juliana II, 90
Johana Augusta Adolphina II, 90

FICHTER
Heinrich I, 738
Johann Leonhard I, 741
Lutwig I, 761

FICHTL (FIECHEL, read FICH-
TEL)
Ignathius
(Ignatius) I, 545, 547, 549

FICHTNER
Gottfᵈ II, 107

FICK
Johann Henrich I, 435
Maria F. II, 122

FICKARDT
August II, 174

FICKE (FAKEY)
Gottfriedt
(Godfrid) I, 671, 673, 674

FICKEL (FIKLE)
Michael (Michal) I, 143, 145, 146

FICKKELIE
Johann George II, 93

FICKUS (FICUS, VYKUS)
Valentine (Valentyn) I, 24, 25, 26
(*See also* FICCUS)

FIDE
Christian I, 16

FIECHGUS, FISCHKUS *see* FISCUS

FIEDLER (FIDLER, FIETLER)
Carl Gottlob I, 748
Christian Heinrich
(Hendrick) I, 636, 638, 640
Hans Michael I, 10, 11
J. G. D. II, 107
John (Jno) I, 646, 648
Philipp I, 367, 368

Vallentin   I, 433
FIEHL (FIEL)
Christoffel   I, 356
Johan Michael   I, 652, 654
Ip.   I, 355
Rudolff   I, 356
FIEHMAN (FEMAN)
Casper (Caspar)   I, 31, 32, 33
FIEKERT
Joseph   II, 94
FIENG
Augustin   I, 508
FIERING
Fredrick   II, 76
FIERS
Gotlip   II, 195
FIERSLER
Maria Catrina   I, 28
Philip (Phillip Michael)   I, 27, 30
FIESS (FEES)
Christian   I, 449
Johan David   I, 585, 586, 588
FIESSLER
Johan Jost   I, 401
FIESTEN
Hans Martin   I, 477
FIESTER
Gretha   I, 60
FIETCHER
Sousanna   II, 97
FIG (FEID)
Albracht   I, 179, 181, 183
FIGENEL
David   I, 720
FIGENER (FYGNER)
Andreas   I, 573, 574, 575
FIGHTMYER
Frederick   I, 741
FIGLIEY, FIGLIEN *see* FEGLEY
FILBERT
Samuel   I, 169, 170, 172
FILGER (FELGER)
Johann Henrich (John Henry)   I, 569, 571, 572, 736
FILIPIPI (read FILIPPI)
Johannes   I, 442
FILLER
Balsatzar   I, 444
Jacob   I, 15
John   II, 7
Michael   I, 672, 673, 674
FILLIBS (FÜLLIBS, PFHILLIPS)
Johan   I, 379
Johan Georg (Johannes Jerick)   I, 560, 561, 563
(*See also* PHILIP)
FILLINGER
Lutwig (Ludwick)   I, 200, 202, 204

FILTZINGER (FELSINGER)
Anderas (Andres)   I, 216, 218, 220
FILTZMEIER (FILTZNEYOR)
Johann Adam   I, 184, 186, 187
FIMPEL
Hans Jerg   I, 502
Johannes   I, 502
FINCK (FINK)
Adam   I, 693; II, 41
Alexander (Alex^r)   I, 646, 647
Alheid   II, 191
And^w   I, 694
Conrad   I, 297, 298, 300
Daniel   I, 409
Diedrich   II, 191
Gewerd   II, 191
Heinrich   I, 364
Johann Gerlach   I, 699
Johan Henrich (Johan Henry)   I, 677, 678, 680
Johan Nickel (Nichol)   I, 169, 171, 172, 204, 206, 208
Martin   II, 191
Michel   I, 474
Peter   I, 409, 677, 678, 680
Philip   I, 441
Thobalt (Tabald, Theobel)   I, 213, 214, 216, 323
FINCKY (FINKEY)
Jacob   I, 344, 345
FIND
Anna Magdelenia   II, 36
FINGER (FINGAR)
Maria Mattelina   I, 55
Peter   I, 396
FINKBEIN
Hans Georg   I, 499
FINSELER
Johannes   I, 757
FINSICK
Hans Adam   I, 539, 541, 543
FINTER
Hans Michel (Michel)   I, 184, 186, 187
FIOL
Jerg   I, 697
FIRNHABER
Jacob Nicolaus   I, 752
Johannes   I, 752
FIROHR (VIEROR)
Lenhart (Leonard)   I, 48, 52, 54
FIRRUMSLER
Matthias   I, 21
FISCHBACH (FISHBACH, FISHBACK)
Cathrina   I, 143
Elisabeth   II, 86
Frederic Guillaume   II, 86

Hans Jacob I, 143, 145, 146
Johann Walther
 (John Walder) I, 297, 298, 299
Johannes Joseph
 (Jost) I, 559, 561, 562
FISCHBORN
Adam I, 355
Andonius I, 355
Fetter II, 52
Johann Balthasar I, 355
FISCHEL (FICCEL, FISCHELL,
 FISSEL, FISCAL)
Anna Maria II, 97
Hanvinen I, 323
Johan I, 326
Johannes, Senr I, 323, 325, 326
Johannes I, 324, 325, 326
 II, 97
Kilian (Kilien) I, 323, 324, 326
FISCHER (FISHER)
Andreas I, 752
Ann I, 40
Anna Lydia I, 108
Anna Maria (Marrea) I, 84, 109
Augusta Maria II, 89
Bastian I, 604
C. II, 138
Carl II, 90
Caspar I, 473
Catharina I, 210; II, 116
Christ Peter I, 279, 280, 281
Christian
 (Christen) I, 406, 522, 525
Christian W. II, 116
Christoph I, 440
Conrad I, 692
Daniel I, 483, 592, 593, 594
David I, 84, 86, 87, 452
Elisabeth II, 116
Fleny I, 40
Francis I, 712
Frantz I, 481
Friederich (Fred^k) II, 90, 186
F. Reinhart (Fred-
 rick Reinhard) I, 656, 657, 659
G. II, 141
Geo. I, 686, 692
Georg Adam I, 415
Georg Bastian I, 504
Georg Henrich I, 723
Georg Ludwig I, 732
George I, 517, 518, 520
George Friedrich I, 394
Handless I, 85
Hans Jacob I, 109
Hans Jerg (Jorg,
 George) I, 395, 420, 552, 553
 554

Hans Mardi I, 348, 349, 351
Hans Melchor I, 344, 345
Hans Rutolph I, 415
Heinrich (Henrich) I, 423; II, 178
Henrich Ulrich
 (Ullerich) I, 60, 64, 65
J. II, 142
Jacob I, 15, 423, 435, 441
 471, 526, 527, 529
Jacob Friedrich I, 489
James C. II, 25
Jan II, 197
Jean Nicholas II, 86
Joh. II, 107
Johann David I, 517, 518, 520
Johann Friedrich
 (Frederick) I, 509, 510, 511, 536
 537, 538
Johann Gorg I, 710
Johann Gottfridt I, 748
Johann Heinrich
 (Hendrick) I, 107, 111, 112, 681
 682; II, 111
Johann Jacob
 (Jacob) I, 279, 280, 281, 459
Johan Michael (Hans
 Michell) I, 37, 38, 39
Johan Nicklaus
 (Nickel) I, 194, 196, 197, 204
 206, 207, 704
Johann Peter I, 628, 631, 634, 694
Johann Philip I, 677, 679, 680, 681
 682
Johann Ulerich I, 462
Johan Wilhelm
 (William) I, 107, 111, 112
Johannes
 (Joannes) I, 39, 41, 42, 256
 258, 261, 344 345
 425, 452, 508
 740
John (Jno) I, 718, 756
 II, 116, 179
John G. II, 116
John Jacob II, 202
Joseph I, 684
Jost D. I, 420
Jurg Johannis
 (Young Hance) I, 344, 345
Jurge I, 415
Kathrina (Katterrena) I, 62, 85
Lorentz I, 451
Ludewig (Lodowick,
 Ludwick) I, 551, 552, 554
Magdalen I, 210
Maria I, 61
Martin I, 741
Mattheis I, 718

Michael
  (Michel)   I, 363, 415, 490, 604
                              606, 607
Nicholas (Nicklas,
  Hans)   I, 264, 268, 271
Peter (Peder)   I, 423, 448, 666, 669
                              671, 722
Philipp   I, 423, 500; II, 196
Philippina   II, 20
Remund   I, 606, 607
Simon   I, 698
Susannah   I, 109
Theobald   I, 714
Thomas   I, 471
Ulriche   I, 485
Wilhelm (Wᵐ)   I, 175, 177, 178
Yerick   I, 451
——   II, 161
  (*See also* FISSER)
FISCHKUS, FISHKES *see* FISCUS
FISCUS (FISCHKUS, FIECHGUS)
  Friederich   I, 336, 337, 339
  Gerhardt
    (Gerhart)   I, 335, 337, 338, 356
FISELING
  Anna Barbara   I, 15
FISER (FISAR, FISEIR, FIZEER)
  Nickel, (Nickell)   I, 31, 32, 34
  Susanna   I, 67
  Wendel (Vendael)   I, 66, 69, 70
FISHBACH *see* FISCHBACH
FISLER
  Barvil   I, 80
  George   II, 197
  Sophia   II, 197
FISSEL (FESEL)
  Phillip Marti
    (Martin)   I, 237, 238, 239
FISSER (FISSHER)
  John   II, 193
  Jost D.   I, 420, 675
FISSLER (FISLER)
  Felix   I, 79, 81, 82
  Joh. Jacob   I, 497
  Johann Georg   I, 497
  Johann Michael   I, 497
FISSNAND
  Johan Peter   I, 56, 57
FISTER *see* PFISTER
FISTERER
  Gottfried   I, 745
FISTLER
  Michael   I, 441
FITHEIM (FYTHYM)
  George   I, 194, 196, 197
FITINCHER
  Nicklas   I, 759

FITTERER
  George   I, 335, 337, 339
FITTERLING
  Veit   I, 502
FITTING
  Johann Caspar   I, 494
  Johann Peter   I, 461
  Johann Philipp   I, 740
FITZ
  Johan Peter   I, 426
FITZLER
  Johann Jacob   I, 489
FIXE
  Adam   I, 429
FLACH
  Andreas   I, 410
  Hans   I, 410
  Johan Mades   I, 752
  Ludwig   I, 421
  Mades   I, 451
  Peter   II, 179
FLACHER
  Christian   I, 434
  Hans Jacob   I, 425
FLACHS (FLACH, FLAX)
  Hans Philip   I, 636, 638, 640
FLAEG
  Carel   II, 95
  Regina   II, 95
FLAIT
  Johanes   I, 499
FLAK
  Lucas   I, 365
FLAMER
  Francis   I, 719
FLAMERFELD (FLOMERFIELD)
  Gerderuth   I, 144
  Zacharias   I, 143, 145, 146
FLANING
  Peter   II, 136
FLAUM
  Johannes   I, 365
FLAX *see* FLACHS
FLEBACHER (FLUBACKER)
  Hans   I, 275, 276
  Jacob   I, 275, 276
FLECHÈRE
  Louis Emanuel, de la   II, 76
FLECK (FLECKE, FLEEK)
  Connrath
    (Conradt)   I, 246, 247, 248
  Henry (Hendrick) I, 582, 583, 584
  Johann Jacob
    (John Jacob)   I, 301, 302, 303
  Johan Wilhelm   I, 736
  Peter   I, 460
  Vallentin   I, 523, 525

FLECKSTEIN
Christian   I, 693
FLEGLER
Dorothy   II, 9
Eva   II, 9
Nich^s   II, 9
Valentine   II, 9
FLEISCHER (FLEISHER,
  FLESHER, FLISHER)
Baltzer (Baltzer)   I, 387, 388, 389
Heinrich   I, 503
Johannes   I, 450, 539, 541, 543
Peter   I, 503
(*See also* FLEISER)
FLEISCHMAN (FLEISCHMANN)
Jacob   I, 418
Johann Conrad   II, 190
Johan Martin   I, 460
FLEISCHOUWER
George   II, 30
FLEISER (HESSER, read
  FLEISCHER)
Jacob   I, 59, 63, 64
FLEKSTEIN
Friederich   I, 483
FLEMER (FLEMMER)
Johan Henrich   I, 353, 354
Jost   II, 84
FLENDER (FLANDER, FLINTER)
Daniel   I, 568, 570, 571
Johannes   I, 297, 298, 300
FLETTER
Michael   I, 627, 630, 633
FLEUR
Christoph   I, 453
Dominique   I, 453
FLEURE (FLURE, FLORIEY)
Hanliey   I, 117
Johannes   I, 116, 119, 120
Joseph (Josaph) I, 116, 119, 120
Maria   I, 117
FLEURY (FLEWIES)
Pierre (Perce)   I, 93, 95
FLEXSER (FLEXER)
Hans Philipp   I, 162, 164, 165
FLICHMAN (FLOHMAN)
Johannes   I, 307, 308, 309
FLICK (FLECK, PFLECK)
Andries   II, 113
Anna Maria   II, 13
Anthony   II, 13
Christ^n   II, 119
Gerlach   I, 467
Henrich   I, 688
Jn° Christ^n   I, 740
Johann Adam   I, 709
Johan Filibus   I, 467
Johan Henry (Johan
  Hendrick   I, 234, 235, 236

Johann Merden   I, 467
Johanes Petter (Johann
  Petter)   I, 467, 540, 542, 544
Johann Wilhelm   I, 728
John   II, 13
Lewis   II, 13
Philip   II, 13
FLICKINGER (FLICKIGER,
  FLÜCKIGER, FLOCKINGER)
Andres (Andris)   I, 79, 82, 83
Johannes   I, 27, 29, 30
Peter   I, 522, 524
FLICKRER (FLICKERR, FLYCKIN-
  NER, FLYKINNER)
Laodicea   I, 108
Ulrich (Olerick)   I, 107, 111, 112
FLICKSTÖRFER (FLICKES-
  TERVER)
Johannes   I, 396
Ullrich   I, 396
FLICKWIR
Gotthard David   I, 742
FLIDIGER (FLETIKER, FURRLER)
Hans   I, 246, 247, 248
FLIEHMANN (FLIEHMAN)
Friedrich   I, 717
Jacob   I, 415
FLIGER *see* PFLÜGER
FLIKKER (FLIKER)
Anna Elizabeth   II, 21
Johan Christoph   II, 21
Johan Michel   II, 21
Maria Dorothea   II, 21
Michael   II, 21
FLIMER *see* FLINDER
FLIN
Peter   I, 738
FLINDER (FLIMER)
Johannes   I, 666, 669, 671
FLINSPACH (FLINCBACK,
  FLINTSHBACK)
Anthoni (Anth^s,
  Anth^y)   I, 265, 268, 271
Johann Philipp (Hans
  Philip)   I, 551, 552, 554
Melchior   I, 551, 553, 554
FLOCKINGER *see* FLICKINGER
FLOHRI (FLOR)
Adolff (Adol)   I, 667, 669, 671
FLOMERFIELD *see* FLAMERFELD
FLOR (FLOOR, FLORER)
Ann   I, 7
Carl   II, 171
Leonhart
  (Lenhard)   I, 265, 268, 271
FLORANS (FLOWERES)
Conrad (Conrade) I, 265, 268, 271
Mich.   I, 265

FLORIG
Christian   I, 359
FLORIN (FLORY)
George (Han
Geo.)   I, 667, 669, 671
Johanes (Hannes)   I, 667, 669, 671
FLORIS (FROLUS)
Michael   I, 268, 271
FLOUGAR
Jacob   I, 344
FLOWR
Johan George   I, 430
FLUBACHER (FLUBECHER)
Hans   I, 392
Jacob   I, 738
(*See also* FLUMBACHER)
FLUCK (FLUK)
Elisabeth   II, 24
Johannes   I, 355
John Adolph   I, 505
FLUCKS
Johannes   II, 24
FLUG (FLUGH)
Jacob   I, 430
Philip   I, 356
FLUGFELDER
Friedrich   II, 178
FLUMBACHER
Johan   I, 738
FLUTH
Martin   II, 179
FLYDER
Mich[1]   I, 747
FOBEL (FOEBEL)
Anne Marie   II, 86
Catherine   II, 86
Conradine   II, 86
Fredric   II, 86
Fridrique   II, 85
Jean   II, 86
Jean George   II, 86
Madelon   II, 86
FOBSINGAREN
Maria   I, 44
FOCHT (FOGHT)
Georg Henrich   I, 714
Stephan   I, 742
FOCK
Anna Cathrine   I, 144
FODEL
Johan Jorg   I, 413
FOEGELMAN *see* VOGELMANN
FOELIX
Michael   I, 455
FOESIG (FASSIG)
Philipp Jacob (Philips
Jacob)   I, 621, 623, 625

FOGALER (read perhaps VO-
GELER)
George M.   II, 167
Godlieb   II, 167
Hendrich   II, 167
Jefferson   II, 167
Johan   II, 167
Louis   II, 167
Rosine   II, 167
Wilhelmina   II, 167
FOGEL *see* VOGEL
FOGELER *see* VOGLER
FÖGLE (FOGLE, read VÖGLE)
Adam   I, 697
Frid.   I, 717
FOGLEMAN *see* VOGELMAN
FOGLIE *see* FEGLEY
FOHL (FÖHL)
Andereas   I, 409
Hans Michel   I, 328
FOKKE
Christian   II, 153
FOLBER (FULBERT, FULPER)
Micl. (Michael)   I, 296, 298, 299
FOLBERG
Johan Willem (Johan
Willhelm)   I, 276, 277, 278
FOLCASS
Nicholas   II, 17
FOLCK
Baltas   I, 477
Christoph   I, 477
J. George   I, 395
Johanes   I, 418
(*See also* FOLK *and* VOLCK)
FOLCKS
Hans Jer.   I, 14
FOLENWEIDER
Jacob   I, 398
(*See also* WOLLENWEIDER)
FOLGER
B.   II, 147
FOLK
Hannah   II, 194
Johannes   II, 194
John   II, 195
Susannah   II, 158
FÖLKER
Johan Peter   I, 437
FOLKNER
Johannes   I, 490
FOLL (FULL, FÖLL)
Andreas (And.)   I, 536, 538
Martin   I, 414
FOLLEN
Fillib   I, 491
FOLLENDORFF
Catharina   II, 71
William   II, 71

FÖLLER (FOLLER)
Johannes   I, 444
Martin   II, 111
FOLMER (FORMER)
Elizabeth   II, 59
Jost   I, 340, 341, 342
Ludwig   I, 522, 525
FOLMER see also VOLLMER
FOLOCK
Peter   I, 16
FOLTZ (FOLS, FOULTZ, FOTZ)
Conrad   I, 522, 525
Friedrich   I, 736
Hans Jerg   I, 442
Johann Michel   I, 301, 302, 303
Johannes   I, 372, 760
Mates (Matteas)   I, 296, 297, 299
Peter   I, 427
FONAU (FANAW)
J. Martin   I, 585, 586, 587
FONDEIN (FONTIN)
Jacob
(Diedrich)   I, 615, 617, 620
FONRON
Charlos   I, 660
FONS
Reinelt   II, 59
FONSTOCK (FANSTICK)
Caspers
(Gaspar)   I, 667, 669, 671
FOOKS see FUCHS
FOOTE
John Derick   II, 3
FORBRINGER
Michael   I, 440
FORCH (FÖRCH, FÖRG, FERCH,
FIRK)
Joanes   I, 331
Johann (Johan)   I, 652, 653
Johann Georg (Joh.
Jurg)   I, 585, 586, 588
Johannes   I, 212, 214, 215
FORCHEL
———   II, 162
FORDENBACH (FURTENBACH)
Johann Philip   I, 536, 537, 538
FORDENE see FORTINEUX
FORDTENBACHER
Willhelm   I, 506
FORHOFF
Gottlieb   II, 102
FORKLEN (FORKLIN)
Eve   II, 162
F.   II, 162
Maria   II, 162
S.   II, 162
FORNER (FARNER)
Martin (Adam)   I, 383, 385

FORNNOFF   (FORNHOAF,
FOUNEG)
Christian   II, 36
Johann Georg
(Jerig)   I, 539, 541, 543
FORRAIN
Maria Eliza.   I, 55
FORRER
Jno. (Johannes)   I, 16, 17, 609
                              611, 612
FORSCH (FERSH)
Johan Adam
(Johannes Adam) I, 560, 562, 563
Martin   I, 685
FORSHBERGE
Nicolaus   I, 422
FORSS
Elizabeth   II, 92
FORST
Hennrich
(Hendryk)   I, 147, 150, 151
FORSTENBERG
Geert, Van   II, 196
FÖRSTER (FORSTER)
Benedictus
(Benedik)   I, 621, 623, 625
Conrath   I, 356
George   I, 701
Godfried (Gotfred)   I, 589, 590
Hans   I, 358
Hans Henry   I, 503
Hans Mich. (Hans)   I, 11, 12
Jacob   I, 412
Johann Andreas   I, 573, 574, 575
Johann Friederich   I, 385
Johan Jacob   I, 304
Johann Martin   I, 423
FORTART
Johan   II, 93
FORTINAUX (FORTNEUX, FOR-
TINEH, FORTINE, FORTINER,
FORDNE)
Francis   I, 169, 171, 172
Jacob   I, 316, 317
Jean Henri (Hen-
drick)   I, 31, 32, 33
Malicha   I, 169, 171, 172
Michel   I, 169, 171, 172
Samuel   I, 324, 325, 326
FORTMANN
Heinr.   II, 110
FORTNEY (FORDNEY)
David (Davit)   I, 266, 269, 272
FORTTMEIER (FORTMAYER)
Johann   I, 545, 547, 549
FOSS (FÖSS, FOLKS, VOSS)
Hen. Wm.   I, 536
Johann Phillippus
(Philip)   I, 568, 570, 572

Johannes
  (J. Wilhelm)   I, 537, 538
  Michel   I, 366
FOSSLER (FASELER, FAYSTER)
  Casper   I, 527, 528, 530
FOST (FOOST)
  Daniel   I, 352, 354
  Johan Philip   I, 352, 354
FOSTER
  Joh. Georg   I, 391
FOSTERHAVE
  Evan   I, 15
FÖTSCH
  Joseph   I, 760
FOULKE
  Georg   I, 737
FOULQUIER (VOLKE)
  Jean Jaq. (Jean Jaqe,
    Hans Jacob)   I, 605, 606, 608
FOURTUNCE   II, 80
FOUST (read FAUST)
  Anna Catrina   I, 766
  Anna Eliza   I, 766, 767
  Johan Hendrick   I, 767
  Johan Peter   I, 767
  Johanes   I, 767
  John Adam   I, 766
  John Hendrick   I, 767
  John Jacob   I, 766
  Matelina   I, 767
  Micol   I, 767
FOUX (read FUCHS)
  Merix   I, 12
FOW
  Jacob   I, 275
  Johannes   I, 275
  Ulrich   I, 237
FOWLE
  Lewis   II, 187
FOX
  Adam   I, 676
  Henrich   I, 676
FOYTE
  Willm   II, 71
FRAHMS
  Cath. Elizth   II, 23
FRAIL
  George   II, 192
  Simon   II, 192
FRAKE
  Tedric   II, 73
FRANCES
  Michell   I, 13
FRANCHIE
  Barnabie   I, 143
FRANCK (FRANK, FRANCKH)
  Andreas
    (Andareas)   I, 156, 159, 161
                           706, 747

Anna (Anne)   I, 67; II, 86
Anna Catharina   II, 92
Anna Millia   I, 73
Avelhart   II, 164
Barbara   II, 164
Catherine
  (Catharina)   II, 86, 128
Christian   II, 36
Christiana (Christina)   II, 164
Chr. Lewis   II, 203
Cristena   II, 37
Davit   I, 454
Egerath   II, 140
Elizabeth   II, 36, 86, 164
Ferdinand   I, 636, 638, 640
Frederich   II, 164
Fredericha   II, 36
Froneca (Feronaca)   II, 164
G. Frederich   II, 164
Geo.   II, 99
George (Gerg)   I, 649, 650, 741
George F.   II, 164
Hans Adam   I, 454
Hans Bernhardt   I, 477
Hans Marttin   I, 502
Henry   II, 86
J. G.   II, 99
Jacob (Johann
  Jacob)   I, 130, 133, 134, 227
           265, 268, 271; II 59, 104
Jean   II, 86
Jean August   II, 86
John Hinr.   II, 128
John Ludwig   II, 128
Joh. Michael   I, 513, 514
Johann Adam   I, 437, 690
Johann Conradt (Johannes
  Conrad)   I, 55, 56, 57
Johann Daniel (Johan
  Dan1)   I, 601, 602, 603, 698
Johann Georg
  (George)   I, 649, 650
Johann Henrich
  (Henrich)   I, 666, 668, 670
Johann Jobst   I, 452
Johann Ludwig Wilhelm   II, 59
                             516, 751
Johann Nicklas   I, 690
Johann Peter   I, 398
Johann Stephan   I, 371
Johann Teobaldt   I, 731
Johann Valentin   I, 732
Johan Wilhelm   I, 96, 97, 98, 397
Johannes
  (Johan)   I, 222, 223, 225
                283, 284, 286, 731
                           II, 99, 128
John George   II, 164

John Ulrich II, 84
Laudwight II, 37
Louise II, 128
Madelon II, 86
Magdelena II, 128
Margaret II, 164
Maria Elizabeth II, 128
Maria Sophia I, 131
Marie II, 86
Michael (Michl) I, 398, 637
Paul II, 164
Peter I, 649, 650
Philip I, 66, 69, 70
II, 37
Phillip Gottlob II, 79
Regina Barbara II, 164
FRANCKENBERGER (FRANKBER-
GER, FRANCKEBERGER)
Conrad (Con-
radt) I, 155, 158, 161
Johannes I, 156, 159, 161
FRANCKENFELT
Simon I, 391
FRANCKFURTHER (FRANCK-
FURTER, FRANKFORDER)
Caspar I, 371
Gerhart
(Gerhard) I, 628, 631, 635
Henrich I, 740
FRANCKHAUSER (FRANK-
HAUSER)
Johannes I, 20
Michael I, 449
FRANER (FRENNER, FRINER)
Johanes (Joannes,
Hans) I, 252, 254, 255
FRANGER
Nicklas I, 415
FRANK see FRANCK
FRANKHOUSEN (FRONKHOUSEN,
FRANKER)
Hans Peter
(Peter) I, 349, 350, 351
FRANKHUYSE
Johannes I, 18
FRANTZ (FRANTS, FRANS,
FRANZ)
Abraham I, 369, 370
Anna I, 60
Anna Marga D. II, 23
Barbara I, 60
Beder I, 369, 370
Carolina II, 159
Cathrina II, 97
Christian, Junr I, 59, 63, 64
Christian, Senr I, 59, 63, 64
Debalt I, 440
Dorothea II, 105
Elizabeth I, 61

Erasmus
(Assmes) I, 266, 269, 272
Eva I, 60
Frans Baltzar
(Frans Baster) I, 14, 15
Georg Michael I, 395
George I, 454
Henrich (Henn-
rich) I, 180, 182, 184
378, 380, 381
Henry (Henrick) I, 369, 370
Isaac I, 706
Jacob I, 212, 213, 215
244, 245, 464
Johann Christ.
(John Christ.) I, 279, 280, 281
Johann Jacob I, 700
Johann Wilhelm I, 700
Johannes I, 167, 168
269, 272
John I, 61
Jost Henrich I, 700
Judith I, 61
Ludwig I, 185, 186, 187
Magtalena I, 60
Maria II, 97
Maria Eliz. II, 97
Michel (Michiel) I, 14, 61
Paul I, 169, 171, 172
Peter II, 159
Peter Dionis, von II, 190
Philib I, 464
Veronica I, 61
FRARIK
Cath. Elisa II, 129
FRARRY
David I, 440
FRASCH (FRASH)
Jacob I, 446
Johanna II, 195
FRATCHER
Jno Henry I, 749
FRATEMACHER
Peter II, 112
FRATSCHL
Jacob II, 19
FRÄTZ
Christian I, 359
Johan Niclaus I, 367, 368
FRAUENFELDER (FRANFELDER,
FRAENFIELDER)
Hans George (Hans
Ulrich) I, 551, 552, 554
Jacob I, 721
Joseph I, 331
FRAUENSTADT
Petrus I, 456
FRAULICH
J. George II, 182

FRAUNK
  Michel   I, 237
FRAUWALDER
  Jacob   I, 352
FRAWINGER
  Hans Jacob   I, 393
FRAY *see* FREY
FREBLE
  John   I, 736
FRECH
  Johann Conrad   I, 470
  Johan Philip   I, 500
FRECHTNICHT   (FREECH-
    NIGHT)
  Rudolph   I, 536, 537
FRECK *see* FRICK
FREDELSCHIP *see* SCHIPP
FREDERICHS
  Ab^rm   II, 102
  Carl   II, 102
  Dort.   II, 102
  Hermann   II, 102
  Wilhelmins   II, 102
FREDERICK (FREDERICH, FRED-
    RICK,   FRIEDRICH,   FRID-
    RICH, FREDRICK, FREDERIK,
    FRIEDERICH)
  Andereas
    (Andres)   I, 199, 201, 203
  Anna Maria   II, 147
  Barbary   I, 40
  Christian   I, 185, 186, 187
                            II, 56
  Elisabeth   II, 147
  George   II, 86
  George Adam   I, 502
  Hans Georg   I, 184, 186, 187
  Jacob   I, 462
  Jerg Migel   I, 159, 161
  Jerick   I, 210
  Johann Georg   I, 88, 90, 92
  Johannes
    (Joanis)   I, 226, 228, 230
                            II, 147
  John   II, 55
  Jonnis   II, 74
  Philip   I, 209, 211
  Steven   I, 7
  Wilhelm   II, 147
  Zacharias
    (Zachrias)   I, 151, 152
  (*See also* FRIEDRICH)
FREE (FRIE, read FREY)
  Hans Jacob   I, 273, 274
  (*See also* FREY)
FREEMAN
  Abraham   I, 43, 45, 46
  Barbara   I, 139
  Catrina   I, 139

  Hend^k   I, 387
  Jacob   I, 139
FREESE
  John F.   II, 160
FREGALIUS
  Johannes   II, 149
FREIBURGER (FRIBUGER)
  Hans Jacob   II, 134
  Johannes   II, 134
  Lutwick   I, 697
FREIDAG *see* FREITAG
FREIDEL *see* FREIDLE
FREIDENBERGER
  ———   II, 162
FREIDERSDORF
  Peter L.   II, 119
FREIDLE   (FREIDEL,   FREYTLE,
    FRYTLE)
  Anna   II, 187
  Anna Veronica   I, 139
  Barbara   II, 187
  Casper   II, 187
  Cordelia   II, 187
  Elizabeth   II, 187
  Maria   II, 187
  Maria Ingle   I, 139
  Petter (Peter)   I, 137, 141, 142
  Philip   I, 139
  Rachel   II, 187
FREIND *see* FREUND
FREINDEL
  Johann Christian   I, 446
FREINE
  Philipps   I, 455
FREIS
  Johan Frantz   I, 428
FREISCHTZE
  Frantz   I, 749
FREITAG (FREIDAG, FRIETAG)
  Henrich   II, 206
  Johann Martin   I, 456
  Nicklaus
    (Nicholas)   I, 222, 223, 225
  (*See also* FREYTAG)
FREITENBERGER   (FREYDEN-
    BERGER)
  Konrat (Conrad)   I, 643, 644
FRELIGH *see* FRÖLICH
FREMBES
  Johann Peter   I, 508
FREMHABER (FREIHABER, FER-
    NABER)
  Johan Christoph I, 539, 541, 543
FRENDT   (FREND,   read   prob.
    FREUND)
  Conrad   II, 159
  Dorothy   II, 159
  J.   II, 32

J. George II, 159
——— II, 159
FRENER
Caspar I, 252, 253, 255
FRENGER (TRINGER)
Johann Nickel I, 304, 305, 306
FRESE (FRIESSEN)
Ehler (Ellers) I, 510, 512
FRESEN (FREESEN)
Johan Jost I, 276, 277, 278
FRESNAYE
F., de II, 71
FRESNE
Albert II, 31
Albertine II, 31
Lidie II, 31
FRETSER
Mathias I, 598
FRETTER (FRODER)
Henrich
(Henry) I, 615, 617, 620
FRETTLER
Caspar I, 407
FRETZ (FRETS, FRITZ)
Hanns Martin (Hanse
Martin) I, 240, 242, 243
Ludwig (Lod-
wick) I, 551, 552, 554
FREÜLLER (VRYLER)
Jost I, 221, 223, 224
FREUND (FREUNDT, FREIND)
Ernst II, 178
Jnᵒ Henry I, 688
Johann
Friedrich I, 512, 514, 515
Johannes
(John) I, 569, 570, 572, 689
Stefan I, 689
Willhelm I, 706
FREÜTLEY
Frederic II, 52
FREVEL (VREVEL)
Johannes Her-
manus I, 352, 353
Jost (Joost) I, 352, 353
FREY (FRY, FREYS, FRIES, VRY)
Andreas I, 106, 110, 112, 122
125, 126, 209, 211
437, 513, 514
515, 652, 654
Anna I, 210
Anna Barbara I, 148
Anna Maria I, 108
Appellonia I, 107
Barbᵃ II, 72
Barbella I, 107
Catharina Barbara I, 107
Christian I, 108, 711
Christiana II, 72

Christophel I, 124
Christopher
(Christoph) I, 24, 25, 26, 109
Clementz I, 468
Conrad (Conradt) I, 88, 90, 91
137, 141, 142
Elizabeth I, 109, 148
Eve I, 108
Francis I, 711
Fredrick I, 275
Hans I, 275, 276
Hans George (Hans
Jerg) I, 232, 233, 437
447
Hans Jacob
(Jacob) I, 652, 654
Hans Peter I, 106, 108, 110, 111
Hans Rudy I, 396
Hans Ulrich I, 23, 25, 26
Heinerich (Henrich,
Henerich) I, 341, 342, 343
708, 709
Hendrik (Hendrick,
Hendryk) I, 148, 210, 483
J. George I, 496
Jacob I, 103, 147, 150, 210, 234
369, 370, 414, 447, 469
499, 637, 638, 640
II, 54, 172
Johan Conrad
(Conrad) I, 643, 644
Johan Dietter
(Fredrick) I, 205, 207, 208
Johaneva I, 49
Johann Gorg I, 347
Johann Martin I, 738
Johann Philipp I, 727
Johannes
(Johanis) I, 47, 52, 53, 76, 78
369, 370, 522, 525
610, 611, 613
Jos. II, 72
Maria I, 210
Maria Crete I, 108
Maria Salma I, 107
Martha I, 210
Martin I, 707
Mettelina I, 109
Michael I, 738
Mr. II, 176
Mrs. II, 176
Nicholaus I, 50
Peter I, 610, 611, 613
Philippus (Philip) I, 621, 623, 625
II, 53
Susan I, 123
Tobias I, 8, 9
Valentine I, 108
Wendel I, 479

FREYBERGER
  Andreas   I, 693
  Jacob   I, 636, 638, 640
  Johannes   I, 693
FREYDEL (FRYDELE)
  Christoph   I, 521, 524
FREYDINGER
  Peter   I, 189, 192, 194
FREYER
  Georg Paul   I, 730
  Heinrich   I, 730
FREYHOFER
  Ulrich   I, 335, 337, 338
FREYLING (FRYLING, FREY-
  LANG)
  Johan Casbar
    (Gaspar)   I, 642, 644
  Johanes
    (Joanis)   I, 226, 228, 230
                  642, 644
FREYLY
  Abraham   I, 509
  Christian   I, 495
FREYMAN (FREEMAN, FREMAN,
  FREYMANN)
  Gorge (George,
    Jurig)   I, 256, 259, 261
  Jacob   I, 360, 362
FREYMILLER
  Joseph   I, 410
FREYMUHT
  Johann   I, 743
FREYS (FRACE, FRAIS)
  Johan Friderich
    (Fredk)   I, 293, 294, 295
  Johan Henrich
    (Henrich)   I, 256, 259, 262
FREYSINGER
  Daniel   I, 418
  Ludwig Fridrich
    (Ludwick)   I, 637, 638, 640
FREYTAG (FRYDAG)
  Erhardt   I, 760
  Friderich   I, 760
  J. August   I, 517, 518, 520
  Johann Caspar   II, 83
  Johann Georg   I, 709
  Johann Henrich   I, 754
FREYVOGEL
  Jno J.   II, 185
  Mrs.   II, 176
FRIBUGER *see* FREIBURGER
FRICHI (read FRITSCHI)
  Johanes   II, 31
FRICK (FRECK, FRICKH, FRIK,
  FRIKH, VRICK)
  Bernhart   I, 476
  Caspar   I, 273, 274
  Conrad (Konrad)   I, 66, 69, 70, 691

Daniel   I, 691
Frantz   I, 742
Friedrich Wilhelm
  (Fredk Wm)   I, 613, 616, 618
Georg Fridrich   I, 758
George   I, 659
Gertrouy   I, 67
Hans   I, 364
Henrich   I, 759
Jacob   I, 124, 332, 333
              334, 744
Johan George   II, 103
Johan Jacob   I, 716
Johan Peter   I, 724
Johann Nickelas   I, 715
Johannes   I, 273, 274, 450
              457, 458
Ludwig   I, 273, 274, 476
Michael (Michel)   I, 476, 498
FRICKE
  Jeduir   II, 137
FRICKER
  Anthoni   I, 434
  Gallus   I, 434
  Johannes   I, 434
FRICKERT
  Dangel   I, 759
  Mr.   II, 176
FRICKHEFFER
  Jno   I, 744
  Jno Jost   I, 744
FRID *see* FRIED
FRIDLI
  Andres   I, 472
FRIDRICH *see* FRIEDRICH
FRIDTEL (FREDEL)
  Bernd (Barn-
    hard)   I, 265, 268, 271
FRIEBALDT
  Anna Gertruth   II, 91
  Anton   II, 91
FRIEBE
  Anne Marie   II, 86
  Chretien   II, 86
  Jean   II, 86
  Jean George   II, 86
  Jean Henry   II, 86
  M. Catherine   II, 86
FRIEBELE
  Christoph   I, 761
  Urban   I, 436
FRIED (FRID)
  Christian   I, 437
  Hans Gerg
    (George)   I, 175, 177, 178
  Jacob   I, 480, 485
FRIEDBURG
  Ludwig Jacob   I, 329

FRIEDERICHS (FRIEDRIKS)
George II, 57
Joannes Andreas I, 574, 575, 576
John Peter II, 98
FRIEDERICHSON
Caert Conraadt II, 58
Dorothea Catharina II, 58
Engel Cathr. II, 58
Friederich August II, 58
Johanna II, 58
FRIEDINGER
Nicolaus II, 70
FRIEDLAND
Ludwig I, 464
FRIEDLE (FRIDELE, FRIDDELE, FREIDLE, FRIDLEY, FRIEDLY, FRIENDLY)
Anna Maria I, 73
Barbara I, 131
Elizabeth I, 132
Hans Georg I, 48, 50, 52, 53
Heinrich I, 474
Jacob I, 74
Johan Conradt I, 457
Johann Michael I, 457
Lawrence I, 50
Ludwig (Lodawick) I, 71, 76, 77
Maria I, 74
Maria Francisca I, 74
Michael I, 130, 133, 134
Solomia I, 49
FRIEDLEBER
L. C. Sophia II, 23
FRIEDLIN
—— II, 88
FRIEDRICH (FRIDRICH, FRIEDERICH, FRIEDERICK, FRIEDTERICH)
Bastian I, 413
Catherine II, 4, 86
Chrétien II, 86
Francs II, 146
Guillaume II, 86
Heinrich (Henry) I, 586, 587, 588
J. Jost I, 465
Jean II, 86
Jean George II, 86
Johann I, 415; II, 4
Johann Adam I, 759
John II, 4
John George II, 69
Jorich Bernhart I, 485
Josephus (Joseph) I, 531, 533, 534
Jurg Willhelm I, 457
Ludwig II, 69
M. Magdalena II, 69
Michel I, 481

Nicolaus II, 69
Philipp II, 69
FRIEDS
Ludwig II, 82
Margaret II, 82
FRIEH, VRIE *see* FRÜH
FRIELANG
Cath^n Elisbeth II, 76
FRIEM (PRIEM, BREM)
Johan Peter (Peter) I, 256, 259, 262
FRIER
Christian I, 15
FRIES (FRIESS, FRIS, VRIS)
Casber I, 701
George Ernst II, 42
Hans Melchior I, 106, 110, 112
Hans Michel I, 501
Jacob I, 178, 180, 182, 205 206, 208, 628, 631 634, 642, 644
Johan Christian I, 506
Johann Jacob (John Jacob) I, 556, 557, 558
Johann Simon I, 221, 223, 224
Johann Wilhelm I, 473
Johannes (Johann) I, 221, 223, 224, 706
John II, 98
Jno Philip I, 723
Jorg (Jurg) I, 629, 632, 635
Martinus I, 473
Michael (Michel) I, 221, 223, 224, 462
Rudolf I, 415
Samuel I, 384, 386
FRIESCHKNECHT
Abraham II, 192
FRIESE
George F. C. II, 92
Jacob II, 127
FRIESEL
Mathias II, 79
FRIESEN *see* FRIESE
FRIESER
Gorit II, 77
FRIESTNER
Johannes I, 437
FRIETAG *see* FREITAG
FRIETHRICK (read FRIEDRICH)
Bastian I, 413
FRIETT (read FRIED)
Balthes I, 489
FRIETZ *see* FRITZ
FRIEZNOR
Carle I, 294
FRIND (read FREUND)
Henry II, 178

FRIOTH
Abraham   I, 508
FRISCH (FRISH)
Carl   II, 32
Christian   I, 397
Johann Gasper   II, 79
Johann Michael   I, 754
FRISCHKORN
Andreas   I, 500
Leonhart   I, 688
FRISCHMUTH
Johann Daniel   I, 709
FRISHER
Johans   II, 145
FRISON
Jacob   I, 439
FRIT (FRITH)
Anganea   I, 61
Peter   I, 60, 64, 65
FRITILAUF
Johans   I, 497
FRITLEY
Alexdr   I, 15
FRITSCH (FRITCH)
Jacob   I, 178, 180, 182
Johannes   I, 698
Jn⁰   II, 75
Philip   I, 178, 180, 182
FRITZ (FRIETZ, FRIZ, FRITTZ, FRIETZ, FRETZ)
Balsatzar (Baltzar)   I, 656, 657, 659
Christian   II, 44, 195
Christoff   I, 427
Conrad   I, 372
Frederic   II, 155
Frederic Gotlieb   II, 89
George   II, 126
Hans   I, 19
Hans Jerg   I, 445, 498
Hans Uhllerick (Hans Geo.)   I, 243, 244, 245
Hardtman   I, 472
Heinrich   I, 471
Jacob   I, 10, 11, 390, 642, 644
Johan Adam   I, 276, 277, 278
Johan Christ   I, 269, 272
Joh. Jacob   I, 727
Johann Sebastian (Bastian)   I, 615, 617, 619
Johannes (Johan)   I, 404, 601 602, 603
Juliana   II, 202
Michael   I, 447
Nicolaas   II, 28
Philip   I, 276, 277, 278, 729
FRITZE
Johann Andreas   I, 739

FRITZGEN
Nicolaas   II, 28
FRITZINGER
Ernst Heinrich   I, 743
Johannes   I, 743
FRITZIUS
Conrad   II, 115
Eva Cath.   II, 115
Gertruda   II, 115
J. G.   II, 115
Johann   II, 115
Margaretha   II, 115
FRITZLEN
Johann Georg   I, 758
FRIZON
Jacob   II, 11
FROCH
Jacob   I, 99
FROCHTNIGHT (FROCHTE-NICHT)
Thomas   I, 516, 518, 519
FROHMAN
Michael   I, 359
FROHWEIN
Johann Peter   II, 59
FROITE
——   II, 81
FROKE
George   I, 310
FROKMAN
Georg   I, 452
FRÖLI (FROLICK, FRÖLLI)
Hans Jacob (Jn⁰ Jacob)   I, 249, 250
Henry   I, 434
FRÖLICH (FRELICH, FROLIG, FROELICH, FROLLICH, FRO-LICK)
Anna Lysbet   I, 241
Anna Maria   I, 23
Christian (Christian)   I, 240, 242, 243
Hans Michael (Michel)   I, 23, 25, 26
Henriette Sussanna   II, 69
Jacob   I, 507
Johann Andonius   I, 723
Johann Daniel   I, 199, 201, 203
Johann Gottlieb   I, 500
Johan Henrich (Henrick)   I, 289, 290, 291
Johan Marti (John Martin)   I, 173, 174, 175
Johannes   I, 507
Philip   I, 714; II, 138
FRÖMBDLING (read FREMDLING)
Benjamin   I, 691
Christian   I, 691

FROMENT
—— II, 80
FROMM (FROM, FROOM, FRUM)
Friederich I, 169, 170, 172
Joh. Conradt
(Conraadt) I, 273, 274
Mardin I, 492
Walter I, 696
FRONFELDER (FRONFILDER,
FRANFILDER)
Felix I, 253, 254, 255
FRONHEUSER (FRONHEISER)
Johann Craft
(Grafft) I, 666, 668, 670
FROSCHAUER (FROSHORN)
Hans Jerg I, 93, 94, 95
FROST
David II, 195
Laurens I, 758
FROSTDORP
Carl August II, 193
Johanna Marie II, 193
FROWENFELDER see FRAUEN-
FELDER
FRÜH (FRIEH, FREE, VRIE)
Conrad I, 495
Georg I, 340, 342, 343
Henrich
(Hendrick) I, 162, 164, 166
Jacob I, 162, 164, 166
Lorentz (Lohrentz,
Lorance) I, 162, 164, 166
Nicklas (Niclos,
Nicholos) I, 162, 164, 166
FRUITIN
Chrh[s] II, 196
FRUTCHE (FRUSCHTHI, FRUT-
ZUY)
Johann Friterich I, 398
Johann Petter
(Peter) I, 678, 679, 681
FRÜTRANCK
Jacobus I, 501
FRUTZ
Christian Wilhelm I, 721
FRY (read FREI)
Jacob I, 738
Joh.[ann] II, 125
John T. II, 188
FRYBERGER
Conrad II, 78
FRYDAG see FREYTAG
FRYER (FREYRE, FREY, read
FREIER)
Jacob I, 727
John Henr. I, 517, 518, 520
FUCATING
Frederika II, 57

FUCHS (FUCKS, FOOKS, FOOKES,
FOOX, FUX, FOX)
Anna E. II, 158
Anna Margreth I, 80
Anthon I, 727
C. II, 142
Catherine II, 159
Christian I, 413
Christoph I, 277, 278, 279
Conrad (Cunradt) I, 355, 473
Dewalt I, 440
Dielman I, 433
Eliz.[abeth] II, 159
Friedrich I, 419
Friedrich Hubertus I, 371
Georg Peter I, 539, 541, 543
George Henry
(Yerrick) I, 387, 388, 389
Hans Casper I, 539, 541, 543
Hans Jeorg
(Jerg) I, 343, 345, 596, 598, 600
Henrich I, 698, 702, 703
J. G. II, 159
J. Henry II, 158
J. Jost II, 158
Jacob I, 21, 22, 256
259, 261, 290
291, 356, 417
Johan Adam I, 234, 335, 337
339, 401
Johann Andreas I, 433, 702
Johann Frantz I, 79, 81, 83, 748
Johann Friederich I, 461, 489
Johann Gottfried I, 470
Johann Henrich I, 401, 714
Johan Michael I, 754
Johann Nicol I, 736
Johan Peter I, 356
Johann Wilhelm I, 371, 426
Johannes I, 156, 159, 161
365, 366, 368
449, 759
John II, 159
Jn⁰ Peter I, 752
John S. II, 158
Joseph I, 458
Jost I, 327, 329
L. II, 142
Leonhart
(Leonard) I, 344, 345, 348
350, 351
Martin I, 233
Marx I, 13
Matthias I, 277, 278, 279
Michael Caspar I, 458
P. II, 142
Peter I, 702, 718
Philipp Jacob I, 720
Philipps Heinrich I, 712

Philips   I, 433
Simon   II, 159
Ulrich   I, 440
Wilhelm   I, 722
(*See also* FOUX)
FÜCHTHORN
Johan Michael   I, 347
FÜCHTNER
Georg Martin   I, 741
FUCKEROTH (FUCKROTH, FO-
    KERALL)
Eleanor   I, 110
Godfrey   I, 110
Hans Adam   I, 107, 111, 112
Jacob   I, 110
Jerick   I, 110
Juliana   I, 108
Maria   I, 108
Philip   I, 110
FUCTIG (FURCTIG)
Adam   I, 331
Hans Adam   I, 331
FUEH
Chris.   I, 234
Johan Adam   I, 234
FÜERSTEIN, FEIERSTEIN, *see*
    FEUERSTEIN
FUES (FUESS, FUOSS)
Cornelis   I, 758
Johannes   I, 581, 583, 584
FÜHLES
Peter   II, 140
FUHR (FUR, FURE, FÜHR)
Christopher   I, 758
Georg William (Jurig
    William)   I, 266, 270, 273
Gerhardt   I, 436
Johann Lehnhart   I, 323, 325, 326
Johannes   I, 540, 542, 544
Wilhelmina   II, 52
FÜHRER (FORER)
Christian   I, 629, 632, 635
Daniel   I, 629, 632, 635
Killian   I, 482
FÜHRLING (VERILING, VERIT-
    ING)
Georg (George,
    Jerick)   I, 560, 561, 563
FUHRMANN (FURMAN, FUHR-
    MAN)
Chris^n   I, 735
Fried^ch Gottfr.   II, 139
Georg Philipp (Jacob
    Philip)   I, 189, 192, 194
Jacob   I, 393
Johann Daniel   I, 691
Johannes   I, 697
John   I, 699

Juliana   I, 191
Paulus   I, 317, 318, 319
Stephan   I, 423
FUHRSBACH
John Christ   I, 700
FULKER
Carl   I, 143
Johann (Johanis)   I, 79, 81, 83
FULLBRAKE
Martin   II, 126
FULLER * (VULLER)
Dorothy   I, 123
FULLEWILER
Rudolff   I, 683
FULLMAN (FULMAN)
Jacob   II, 6
Jno Geo.   I, 695
Margaret   II, 6
FULMER (FULLMER)
Barbara   II, 187
Jost   I, 367, 368
Nich^s   II, 6
FULTS
Henrick   I, 12
FUMEL (PHUNELE, ISHEMELL)
Philip   I, 287, 288, 289
FUNCK (FUNK)
Abraham   I, 363
Anna   I, 210
Benedick   I, 477
Carl   I, 481
Conrad   I, 296, 298, 299
Fritrich (Frederik) I, 130, 133, 134
George (Jorg) I, 313, 314, 315, 398
Hans (Hanns)   I, 13, 449
Heinrich (Hendrick) I, 209, 211
Joann (John)   I, 180, 182, 184
Johan Adam   I, 744
Johann Peter   I, 362
Johannes   I, 397
Jost   I, 434
Martin   I, 188, 191, 193
                           449, 738
Michael   I, 365, 691
Peter   I, 429
Rudy   I, 738
Sammuel   I, 707
———   I, 131
FUNCKBOHNER (FUNKBONER,
    FUNKLOHNER)
Conrath   I, 497
Hans Jacob (Jacob) I, 551, 552, 553
FÜNFER
Caspar   I, 379
FÜNFROCK
Michel   I, 450, 730
Staffan   I, 730

FURCH
Andres   I, 751
FURET
Philip   I, 362
FURKELL (FURKILL, VORKEL)
Johann Georg   I, 89, 91, 92
FURNY
Hans Adam   I, 369, 370
FURRA
John   I, 23
FURRER (FURER)
Christian   I, 448
Jacob   I, 447
Linhart (Leonard)   I, 252, 253, 255
FÜRST
Jacob   I, 757
Johann (Johannes)   I, 296, 298, 299
                       755
FÜRSTLER
Hendrich   I, 453
FÜRSTNER
Christo.   I, 417
FURTULY (FURLLY, FORTENA)
Jonas (Jonnas)   I, 324, 325, 327
FUSCH
Christian   I, 477
FÜSCHER
Johan Michel   I, 751
FUSE
John   I, 289
FUSELBACH
Matheis   I, 738
FÜSS (FÜS, FUSS, FUS)
Johann Theis
   (Joh. Thys)   I, 564, 565, 567
John Adam   II, 106
Magdelena   I, 44
Maria   I, 45
Nicklas (Nicholas)   I, 43, 46, 47
FÜSSER
Johannes   I, 719
FÜSSLER
Tomas   I, 453
FUT
Johan Peter   I, 304
FÜTTER
Stephanus   I, 717
FUTTING
Anna Elizabetha   II, 92
George Michel   II, 92
Johann H.   II, 92
Johanna M.   II, 92
Maria Catharina   II, 92
Peter Johannes   II, 92
FUX *see* FUCHS
FUYST
Andreas   I, 317

GAAB (KOAP)
Christoph
   (Christophel)   I, 656, 657, 658
GAADYARD
Christian   II, 126
GAAL
Georg Adam   I, 476
GAAR (CHARS)
Andreas   I, 87, 89, 91
Johan Adam   I, 87, 89, 91
GABB
Johann Georg   I, 455
GABEL (GABELE)
Con^d   I, 746
J. Peter   I, 481
Johan Friderich (Joen,
   Fredrich)   I, 257, 259, 262
Johan Philip (Philib,
   Pfilib)   I, 257, 259, 262
Johannes   I, 363, 627, 631, 634
Maria   I, 73
Peter   I, 72, 76, 78
Philip Henry   I, 521, 523
GABER
Johannes   I, 659
GABORY
Pier   I, 735
GABRIEL
Johann Carl   I, 706
Johannes   I, 725
GABRIELS
Anna   II, 78
GACHON
Johannes   I, 496
GACK (KACK, GAK, KOK)
Johann Jorg (John
   George)   I, 622, 624, 626
Johann Just (John
   Joost)   I, 622, 624, 626
Ludewig (Ludwig)   I, 622, 624, 626
GACKENBACH (GACKBACH)
Eckerlle (Carlle,
   Carel)   I, 387, 388, 389
Johann Henrich   I, 349, 350, 351
Johannes   I, 387
GADE
John   II, 69
GÄDECKE (GADECKE)
Johann Gottfried   II, 74
Johannes   I, 748
GAGE
Augusten   I, 746
GAGEL
Jacob   II, 119
GAHNAT
Eberhard   I, 474
GAHRAUS
Georg Adam   I, 742

GÄHRINGER
Jorg (Jerg)   I, 522, 525
GAIER *see* GEIER
GAIMAN
Jacob   II, 136
GAISEL
Christian Tobias   I, 502
GAKLY
J. Friederich   I, 499
GALL
Christoph   I, 509, 510, 511
Johann Friedrich   I, 409
Joseph   I, 485
GALLATER
Michael   I, 428
GALLE
Benedictus   I, 698
Friederich   I, 690
GALLER
Dorothia   I, 28
Sam¹ (Samuell)   I, 27, 29, 30
GALLINE
Peter   II, 74
GALLMAN
Hans Rudolph   I, 398
Jacob   I, 475
Joseph   I, 416
Mattheus (Maddes)   I, 398
GALLOE
Peter   I, 723
GALLON
Henry   II, 75
GALLY
Christian   I, 455, 459
Jacob   I, 459
GÄLT
Martin   I, 726
GALTE
Peter   I, 741
GALVIN
Simon   I, 503
GAM (AAM)
Jerick Leohart
(Leonard)   I, 84, 86
GAMBACH
Johann Philip   I, 335, 336, 338
Johannes   I, 335, 336, 338
GAMBER
Georg Michael   I, 437
Johann Henrich   I, 437
Johannes (Johannas)   I, 99, 101, 423
   433
GAMBERT
Wilbert   I, 423
GAMBLE
James   II, 27
John   II, 18
William   II, 18

GAMBLER
Andereas   I, 421
GAMBOLD
Hector   I, 320
GAMEL
John   I, 143
GAMPFFER
Johann Gottfried   I, 705
GAMPLER
Michael   I, 450
GANBER
Hermanus   I, 685
GANDER
Jacob   I, 667, 669, 671
GANDOU
David   II, 73
GANGLOFF
Jacob   I, 452
GANGWYER
Jacob   I, 11, 12
GANISEN
Christine   II, 205
GANN (GAN, KAAN)
Caspar   I, 596, 598, 599
Christoph
(Christopal)   I, 596, 598, 600
Fridrich   I, 442
Johannes   I, 442
Thomas   I, 442
GÄNNSLEN
Johannes   I, 346
GANNY
Benjamin   II, 83
GANS (GANNS)
Frantz Henrich   I, 367, 368
Johan George   I, 437
Johan Nickel   I, 437
Peter   I, 473; II, 41
GANSEL (GÄNSEL)
Salomon   I, 393
Vallentin   I, 685
GANSHOR (GANSH)
Peter Mathes   I, 653
GANSHORN
Hans Görg   I, 437
GÄNSLE (GÄNSSLI)
Gärg   I, 470
Jacob   I, 346
Johan   I, 720
GANTER (GANTHER, GANTTER,
GUNTER)
Ewalt (Ewald)   I, 378, 379, 381
Kilian   I, 433
Wilhelm   I, 546, 547, 549
GANTNER
Michael   I, 490
GANTSON
Anless   I, 241

GANTUS (GANTUSS, GANDUS)
Frantz (Jʳ)   I, 601, 602, 603
GANTY (CANDIE)
Jean (John)   I, 283, 285, 286
GANTZ (GANS, JANTZ)
Friedrich   I, 759
Gorg   I, 686
Heinrich
(Hendrich)   I, 252, 254, 255
Jacob   I, 686
Johann Georg   I, 694
GÄNTZLER
Phillippus Jacob   I, 719
GARAUS
Carl   I, 693
GARBEL (GARBELL)
Ephraim Benedigt   I, 539, 541, 543
GÄRBER (GARBER, CARBER)
Johann Fridrich   I, 470
Johannes   I, 394, 509
Michael   I, 527, 528, 530
GARDNER (GARTNER, GORD-NER)
Friederich
(Frederick)   I, 162, 164, 166
Hans George   I, 500
Johannes   I, 122, 125, 126
Maria   I, 123
Michael   I, 498
GAREIN
Wilhelm   I, 489
GARNER
Hans George
(Jorg)   I, 397, 438
GARNIER
Marten   II, 80
GARNUR
Johan Christian   I, 276
GARRECHT
Catharina   II, 21
Johan Michel Erich   II, 21
Orchille   II, 21
Pieter Willem Andries   II, 21
Veit   I, 502
GARSING
Abrahm   I, 447
GARSTER
Henry   I, 392
GARTANG
——   II, 80
GARTE
Jacob   I, 753
GÄRTHER
Jean Jacques   II, 86
GARTMAN
Jacob   I, 508
GÄRTNER (GARTNER, GARTH-NER, GARDNER)
George   I, 504

Hans Michael   I, 418
Hans Peter (Hans
Pedder)   I, 48, 52, 53
Heinrich   I, 730
Jacob   I, 294, 295, 296
Jerg   I, 348, 349, 351
Johann Wilhelm   I, 371
John Adam   I, 505
Margerita   I, 49
Peter   I, 707
GARTOM
Felix   I, 423
GÄRTTLER (GÄRTLER, GANT-LER)
Johann Joachim   I, 505
Johann Jorge
(Jnº Geo.)   I, 589, 590, 591
GASAU
Johan   II, 50
GASEL (GAZELL)
Johan Michel   I, 194, 195, 197
GASHA
Gabriel   I, 733
GASNER
Carolina Christiana   II, 46
GASS (GAS)
Ann Maria   II, 133
Anna   II, 133, 147
Barbara   II, 78
Elisabeth   II, 146
Fredrich (Fredᵏ)   I, 10, 12
    II, 185
George   I, 497
Hans   II, 133
Hans Jacob   I, 392; II, 133
Hans Jorik   II, 133
Henry   II, 185
Jacob   I, 10, 12
    II, 146, 147
Johann Georg   I, 449
John Jacob   II, 146
John J.   II, 185
Martin   II, 53
GASSAUER
Cathrina   II, 97
Daniel   II, 97
Elizabeth   II, 97
Johannes   II, 97
Maria   II, 97
Peter   II, 97
GASSE
Mʳ   II, 95
GASSER (GOSSER, GOSER)
Christian   I, 601, 602, 604
Friederich   I, 498
Hans Atam   I, 89, 90, 92
Johan Jacob   I, 390
Joseph (Jos.)   I, 601, 602, 603

GASSINGER
Johan Georg   I, 454
GASSMANN (GASSMAN, GOS-
MAN)
Benjamin   I, 706
Johannes (Hans, Jn⁰) I, 250, 251
Philipp   I, 449
GASSNER (CASSNER, GASNER)
Casper   I, 341, 342, 343
Marthin   I, 57, 58
GAST (KAST)
Jacob   I, 393
Johan Christijan (Joh.
Christ.)   I, 677, 679, 680
Johann Nickl (Johan-
nickl)   I, 677, 679, 680
Johannes   I, 692
John   II, 53
GASTELL
Carl   II, 83
GATH
Christoph   II, 11
Hans   II, 127
GATTES
Christopher   II, 11
GATTUNG
Johann Heinrich   I, 500
GAUBLE
Frᵈ.   II, 147
GAUER
Johann Nickal   I, 346
GAUFF (GAUF, GOUF, KAUF,
KAUFF)
Ditrich (Pieter)   I, 66, 69, 70
Margaret   I, 68
Peter   I, 68
Philip   I, 283, 284, 286
Wilhelm   I, 304, 305, 306
GAUFFRES (GOFRIES)
Jean (John)   I, 226, 228, 230
GAUGER (COUGER)
Georg Nicolaus
(Nichlos)   I, 163, 165, 167
Johann Conrath
(Conerard)   I, 163, 165, 167
Johann Georg (Hans
Jerich)   I, 66, 69, 70
GAUL (GAULL)
Christian   I, 734
Christina   II, 105
Joh. Marthin   I, 732
Joh. Theobalt   I, 730
John Adam   I, 340, 342, 343
Johann Ulrich   I, 113, 115, 766
Johannes   I, 703
GAURDEN
Charles   II, 96
GAUSS
Friederich   I, 446

Jacob   I, 707
Johann Georg   I, 446
GAUTIER (GOUTIER, GOODIER)
Jacques (Jacob)   I, 526, 527, 529
Pierre (Peter)   I, 526, 528, 529
GAVELT
John   II, 203
CAVET
Henri   I, 746
GAWFF (read GAUFF)
Hans   I, 413
GAY
Francis   II, 74
Jacob   I, 704
GAYDON
Jean Henri   I, 685
GEBBARD (GELBERT)
Nickls (Nicklas)   I, 296, 297, 299
GEBAUER
Gottfried   I, 746
GEBER
Daniel   I, 50
Henrick, Sr.   I, 47, 51, 53
Jacob   I, 517
Johannes (Hendrick,
Junr.)   I, 47, 51, 53
Johenrich
(Johannis)   I, 47, 51, 53
Katherina   I, 49, 50
Maria   I, 50
Sarah   I, 49
GEBHARD (GEBHARDT, GEB-
HART, GEBERTH, GEBERD,
GEBERT)
Adam   II, 10
Andres (David Andreas,
Andreas)   I, 667, 669, 671
Anna   II, 9
Anna Maria   II, 10
Conrad (Conrat)   I, 390, 412
Friedrich (Frederick) I, 43, 45, 46
George   II, 10
Gottfriedt
(Godfrid)   I, 620, 622, 624
Hans Jacob   I, 488
Heinrich
(Henrich)   I, 485, 614, 616, 619
Johann Adam
(Johan Adam)   I, 646, 648
Johann Heinrich   I, 513, 514, 515
Johanes (Johannes)   I, 627, 630
633, 689
John George
(Johan Geo.)   I, 646, 648, 689
John Ludewig   II, 56
Joseph   I, 422
Melchior   I, 412
Michael
(Michail)   I, 43, 45, 46

Nicholas (Niclas) I, 367, 369
  II, 5, 9
Peter I, 297, 298, 300
Philip I, 204, 206, 208
Susanna II, 10
—— II, 5
GECK (GEK)
 Georg Henrich I, 751
 Henrich
  (Hendrick) I, 102, 105, 106
 Johan Jacob I, 522, 524
GECKAN
 Jacob I, 234
GECKE
 Johann II, 68
GECKELER (GEKELLER)
 Joh. Peter I, 327, 329
 Johannes I, 462
GEEBER
 Johanes I, 406
GEEBS (GIABS)
 Abraham I, 376, 377
GEEIK
 Hans Ad. I, 235
GEENAN
 Johan II, 78
GEENER
 Maria II, 95
 Renier II, 95
GEER *see* GEHR
GEERMAN
 Abr^m II, 42
GEES
 Georg I, 440
GEESSLER (GEESSELER read
 GIESELER)
 Henry I, 508
 Jacob I, 472
GEETZE
 Johan Nyromeen II, 83
GEFELLER (GFELLER, FELLER)
 Adam I, 189, 192, 193
 Barbara I, 190
 Johannes I, 185, 186, 187
GEGNER
 Martin I, 707
GEHARD (read prob. GERHARD)
 Johannes I, 689
GEHBE
 —— II, 58
GEHR (GEER)
 Felden I, 14
 Johannes I, 483
GEHRES (GERES, GEERES)
 Joh. Andr. II, 140
 Simon I, 256, 259, 262
GEHRIG (GERICK, GERIG,
 GEHRICH)
 Adam I, 453

Albert I, 660
H. Adam I, 481
J. Philip I, 463
Joachim I, 435
Leonard I, 660
GEHRINGER
 John Georg I, 471
GEIB (GEIBE, GYB)
 Johann Conrad I, 367, 369
GEIBE (GYBB, GYB)
 Ludewig (Lodowich,
  Ludwick) I, 256, 259, 261
GEIBEL (GIBEL)
 Jacob I, 615, 617, 619
GEIDLINGER
 Conrad I, 421
GEIER (GAIER)
 Ernst Lewis II, 155
 Johannes I, 167, 168
GEIGENBERGER
 Christof I, 419
GEIGER (GEYGER, GAYGER,
 GEGER)
 Anna I, 210
 Barbara I, 189
 Bernhard I, 688
 Christian I, 188, 191, 193
 Friederich (Fred) I, 290, 291, 292
 Georg I, 424
 Hans I, 210
 Hans Jacob I, 257, 260, 262
 Henrich I, 732
 J. Jacob II, 155
 Jacob I, 221, 223, 224, 328
  346, 460, 732
 Johann August II, 79
 Johann Conrad Phillip II, 79
 Johann Friderich
  (Fredrick) I, 387, 388, 389
 Johan Heinrich I, 398
 Johann Michael I, 506
 Johann Paul I, 169, 170, 172
 Johannes I, 96, 97, 98, 453, 652, 654
 John Geo. I, 695
 Mattias (Mathias) I, 209, 211
 Paul I, 424
 Tatcius I, 457
 Wilhelm I, 96, 189
GEIGLE
 Jacob I, 471
GEIL
 Johan Christopf II, 46
 Vallentin I, 402
GEILER
 Frederic II, 53
 Johannes I, 506
GEILERT
 Mardin I, 522, 524

GEIMER (GEIMMER, GAYMER,
    KEYMER)
  Adam   I, 676
  Christian (Christ.) I, 629, 632, 636
GEINER
  Thomas   I, 454
GEINLY
  Mr   II, 95
GEINSER (KEYSLINGER)
  Philip Peter
    (Pfilip Peter)   I, 383, 385
GEISEL (GEISELL, GEISSELL,
    GEYSEL, GYSELL)
  Conrad   I, 615, 617, 619
  Herman   I, 615, 617, 619
  Jacob   II, 179
  Johannes   I, 615, 617, 619
  Paul   I, 217, 218, 220
GEISENDORFER
  Johann Michl   II, 118
GEISER (GEISSER, GYSER)
  Christof   I, 327, 329
  Hans   I, 473
  Johannes
    (Nickles)   I, 240, 242, 243
  Mariles Pitt   I, 241
  Peter (Hans
    Petter)   I, 240, 242, 243
  Yoghan Cristan   I, 241
GEISLER (GEISSLER, GYSLER)
  Christian   I, 240, 242, 243
  Jacob (Yerrk)   I, 596, 598, 599
                  II, 118
  Johanes (Johannes) I, 645, 647
  Johann Georg   I, 474
  Karl   I, 743
  Kattarina   I, 242
  Thomas   I, 501
GEISS (GEIS, GEYST, GISE,
    KEYS)
  Gerg Adam   I, 546, 548, 550
  Henrich (Hendrick) I, 652, 654
  Johann Adam   I, 468
  Johan Gorg
    (Georg)   I, 170, 171, 173
  Johann Peter
    (Peter)   I, 303, 305, 306, 403
  Johannes   I, 468, 493
  Peter   I, 702
  Philipp Jacob   I, 471
GEISSE
  Francis   I, 742
  Frantz William   II, 117
  William   II, 117
GEISSELMANN (KEYSLEMAN)
  Johan Michael
    (Mich¹)   I, 222, 223, 225
GEISSENDORFER
  William   II, 154

(*See also* GEISENDORFER)
GEISSERT
  Melchior   I, 448
GEISSHEINER
  Johann Peter   I, 762
GEISSINGER (GEISSIGER)
  Adam   I, 395
  Carl   I, 711
  Johann Caspar   I, 399
GEIST (GIST, KYCT)
  Christoph   I, 277, 278, 279
  Fred. Willem   I, 412
  Gottlieb   I, 717
  Hanns Jacob (Hans
    Jacob)   I, 609, 610, 612
  Jan Gorg (Geo.) I, 300, 301, 302
  Johann Henrich
    (Henrick)   I, 217, 219, 220
  Michl (Michael) I, 297, 299, 300
  Nicholas (Nicklas) I, 300, 301, 302
  Philipp   II, 52
GEISTWEIT
  Johannes   I, 467, 712, 755
GEITLING
  Johannes   I, 712
GELBACH
  Frantz   I, 399
  Fridrich (Friederich) I, 399
GELBERDT
  Friederich   I, 695
GELBEREE
  Johann   I, 432
GELE (KEBEL)
  Johan Matteas
    (Mathias)   I, 387, 388, 389
GELESEN (GILESZ)
  Elizabeth   I, 49
  Geles (Giles)   I, 47, 51, 53
  Gertrowte   I, 49
  Helena   I, 49
GELESSENER
  Mannes   I, 710
GELISEN
  Johannes   I, 422
  Nycklaes   I, 422
GELLER (GILLER, KELDER)
  Christoffel   I, 324, 325, 327
  Jacob   II, 70
  Martin   I, 59, 64, 65
GELLINGER (GILLINGER, GIL-
    LANGER)
  Simon   I, 84, 86, 87
GELTLACH (KELBACH)
  Johannes (Joh.) I, 180, 182, 184
GELTZ
  Hans George   I, 438
GEMAN (GEEMAN)
  Anna   I, 61
  Bendich (Benedigt) I, 59, 63, 65

Christian (Chretian)   I, 59, 63, 65
Rose   II, 81
GEMANDT
  Christoph Martin   I, 695
GEMBERLING   (GENBERLIN,
  GAMBERLEN, KEMPERLIN)
  Jacob   I, 704
  Johan Carl
  (Charls)   I, 621, 623, 625
  Johan Paul   I, 621, 623, 625
  Johann Peter   I, 264, 268, 271
GEMBLER
  Hanns Petter   I, 395
  Hans Michael   I, 395
GEMITA
  Conrat, van   I, 387
GEMLICH (GEMLING)
  Jacob   I, 154, 158, 160
GEMMER
  Johan Adam   I, 402
GEMSTER
  Johannis   I, 480
GENAU
  John   II, 196
GENEMS
  Jnᵒ Jacob   I, 745
GENHEIMMER
  Johann Georg   I, 487
GENNER
  Hans Georg   I, 462
GENNETT
  Jnᵒ   I, 752
GENSEL
  Jacob   I, 692
GENSEMER   (GESMER,   KENSI-
  MER)
  Gerge Daniel
  (Danil)   I, 226, 228, 230
  Hannes (Hanrich,
  Joanis)   I, 226, 228, 230
GENSLI (GENSLY)
  Conrad   I, 477
  Matthias   I, 199, 201, 203
GENTECH
  David   II, 99
GENTES
  Daniel   I, 750
GENTLE
  George Adam   II, 118
GENTSCH
  Samuel   II, 53
GEORG (GEORGE)
  Henrich   I, 427
  Jacob   I, 705
  Johann Conrad   I, 646, 647
  Johanns   I, 717
  John   II, 60
  Michel   I, 702
  Stophel   I, 591, 593

GEORGI (GEORGY)
  Henrich   I, 717
  Johann Christoph   I, 466
GEPHARD *see* GEBHARD
GERADWOLL
  Hans   I, 410
GERAHN (ERASH)
  Friedrich (Fredrick)   I, 274, 275
GERANKE (GERANGE, GERANG)
  Joh. Jurgen   I, 517, 518, 520
GERARD (read GERHARD)
  Catharina   II, 70
  David   II, 70
  Nicholas (N.)   I, 163, 165, 166
  ——   II, 81
GERBER
  Adam   I, 413
  Anna   I, 143, 144
  Felix   I, 559, 560, 562
  Hans   I, 188, 191, 193, 433
  Hans Christian
  (Christian)   I, 245, 246, 247
  Hans Jacob
  (Jacobes)   I, 116, 120, 121
  Hans Jerick   I, 118
  Hans Mich.   I, 460
  Jacob (Jacobs)   I, 118, 527, 528, 530
  Jan   I, 118
  Johann Adam   I, 348, 349, 351
  Johann Christian   I, 740
  Johannes   I, 156, 159, 161
    327, 329, 441
  Joseb   I, 441
  Jost Paul Kuhnroth   I, 419
  Maria Barbra   I, 118
  Michel   I, 143, 145, 146
  Mr.   II, 176
  Mrs.   II, 176
  Philip   I, 703
GERBRICH (GERBERIG)
  Andreas (Anderas)   I, 627, 630, 634
  Hans   I, 503
  Michel   I, 458
  Petter   I, 458, 627, 630, 634
GERCKENHAUSER   (KERKE-
  HOUSER)
  Jacob   I, 107, 111, 112
  Maria Crete   I, 108
  Mattelina   I, 109
  Susanah   I, 108
GERCKHARDT (YERKHARF)
  Vallendin (Valentine)   I, 314, 315
GERDING
  Henrich   I, 742
GERDNER
  Jacob   I, 436
GERDORF
  Everhard   II, 96

GEREBEL (read GREBEL)
Anna   I, 117
GERENSTEIN
Adam   II, 137
GERES (KERESH)
Johan Carel (John
Karl, Carle)   I, 266, 269, 273
GERGE
Johan Maties   I, 427
GERGERICH
Hans   I, 481
GERHARD   (GERHARDT,   GER-
HART)
Abram   I, 432
Christoph   I, 495
Conrad   I, 753
Conrat   I, 329
Daniel   I, 486, 725
Diterich (Dieter,
Titreak)   I, 627, 631, 634
Eytel   I, 465
Fritrich
(Frederik)   I, 256, 259, 261, 694
Georg Michael   I, 479
H. George   I, 455
Henrich   I, 155, 158, 160
                                    439, 467
J. Nicklas (Nickles,
Nicholas)   I, 628, 631, 634
Jacob   I, 297, 298, 300, 529
Johan   I, 279
Johann Peter   I, 695
Johan Wilhelm
(William)   I, 205, 206, 208
Johannes   I, 478
Johannes Peter   I, 724
Jorg Thomas   I, 688
Kathrina   I, 60
Lenhart (Linard, Lini-
herd)   I, 282, 284, 285
Maria   I, 61
Maria Catharina   I, 157
Martin (Merdin)   I, 59, 63, 64
Mergreed   I, 60
Peter   I, 257, 259, 262
William   I, 256, 259, 261
GERI (GEIRI, KEERE, GERRHY,
GERRY)
Hans Adam   I, 264, 268, 271
Jacob   I, 264, 268, 271
GERING
Andreas   I, 498
Baltes   I, 18
GERIS
Peder   I, 330
Philip   I, 330
GERISCH
Nickel   I, 699

GERKE
Anna Maria   II, 127
August   II, 119
Johannes   II, 127
Maria Gertrut   II, 127
Marianne   II, 127
GERKELS
J. Ch.   II, 125
GERKEN
Cath^a Eliz^a   II, 23
GERKIS
Frederick   II, 161
——   II, 161
GERLACH
Andres (Andreas)   I, 589, 590, 591
Balser   I, 102, 104, 105
C. Christ.   II, 117
Christine   II, 117
Hanns Görg (Jurg) I, 628, 631, 635
Herman   I, 614, 616, 618
Johann Heinrich   I, 424
Johannes   I, 614, 616, 618
Maria   I, 103
Nicolaus (Niclaus) I, 431, 576, 578
                                        580
Wendell   I, 60, 64, 65
GERLIGH (read prob. GERLING)
Frantz (Franz)   I, 367, 369
GERLING
J. Jacob   I, 464
GERLINGER
Ludwig   I, 750
GERMAN (GERMANN)
Adam   I, 395, 699
Anna Elizabeth   II, 28
Arnold   II, 147
Christian   II, 28
Cristoffel   I, 432
Daniel   I, 358
Frantz   I, 358
Frederick   II, 147
Hans   I, 364
Johan Konrath   I, 737
Johan Leohnhart   I, 395
Johan Ludwig (John
Ludwig, Ludwick) I, 293, 294, 295
Johann Peter   I, 359, 361
Susanna Maria   II, 30
GERMERDUNG (CARMETON)
Friederich   I, 323, 325, 326
GERMEYER
Charlotte   II, 181
GERN (KERN)
Barbara   II, 14
Christopher   II, 14
Conrad   II, 14
Cordula   II, 14
Hanna   II, 14
Jacob   I, 244, 245

Johannes I, 686
John II, 14
GERNANDT (GERNAND)
Bastian I, 424
George I, 180, 182, 184
GERNDT
Johan Henrich I, 397
GERNE
Frederick II, 151
GERNER
Johan Matthes I, 438
GERNERDT
Johannrich I, 706
GERNET
Johann Christian I, 697
Johannes I, 697
GERNHART (GERNHARDT, GERNHERD, GERMERTT)
Henrich (Henry) I, 205, 207, 208
GERR (read GEHR)
Susanne II, 31
GERRECHT
Christoph II, 20
GERRETT
Peter I, 405
GERRINGER (GERING)
Baltus I, 18, 19
Bastian (Bestian) I, 652, 653
Jacob I, 455
Nicklas (Nicholas) I, 652, 654
Thomas (Thos) I, 205, 207, 208
GERRO (GERRA)
Joseph I, 363
Piero I, 363
GERSCHHEIMER
Filips I, 693
GERSHWILLER
Andereas I, 410
GERSING
Anthon II, 94
Carl II, 94
Carolina II, 94
Margaretha II, 94
GERSON
Jacob II, 139
Nathan II, 107
GERST
Dewald I, 427
Friederich I, 427
Johann Nickel I, 415
John I, 722
Michel I, 730
GERSTENMEYER (GERSTE-MEYER)
Johan Gorg (Hans Jurg) I, 531, 533, 534
GERSTER (KASTER)
Caspar (Casper) I, 384, 386

Hans Jerg (Hance George) I, 162, 164, 166
Jacob II, 53, 145
Johanes II, 133, 145
John II, 53
Mr. II, 176
Mrs. II, 176
Samuel II, 133
GERTER (GERTERT)
Johannes I, 383, 385
GERTH (GIRT)
Hans George (Hansier) I, 198, 201, 203
GERTHNER (GERTNER)
Georg (Jerik) I, 20, 21
GERTSCH (GERS)
Johannes (Johan) I, 221, 222, 224
GERTZ
Johann Phillipp I, 322
Johann Seyberth I, 429
Johannis I, 430
GERVINUS
Görg Friedrich I, 322
GERWIG (GIRBICK, GERBICK)
J. Lenhart (Leonard) I, 527, 528, 530
GESCHWIND (GESCHWINDT, GESWINT)
Eberhart I, 184, 186, 187
Johannes I, 347
GESE
Henry Charles II, 159
GESELL (GESSEL, GESEL)
Jerg Ludwig I, 12, 14
Johann Leonhard I, 341, 342, 343
Johann Michael I, 402
John Georg I, 758
Michal I, 676
Peter I, 357
Wilhelm (Willem) I, 151, 152
GESINDER
Margaret II, 13
GESS
Fridrich I, 382
Johann Matthess I, 359
GESSNER (GESSENER)
Anne II, 120
Catharina II, 120
Christina II, 120
Fredk II, 122
Johan Adam I, 409
Johann Christ II, 120
Johan Geo. II, 120
Johan Henrich II, 120
Johan Jost II, 120
Johannes I, 378, 380, 381 468; II, 120
Louisa II, 120
Maria Elizabeth II, 120

GESTER
Sebastian II, 98
GETSON
Maria I, 103
GETT
Johannes (Josent) I, 194, 195, 196
GETTEL (KETTEL, GETTELL, GÖTTEL, GEHTEL)
Christina I, 132
Johann Jacob I, 131, 133, 134
Johanna Margaretha I, 132
Johan Peter I, 131, 133, 134
Margaretha I, 132
Peter I, 132
Sarah I, 131
GETTINGER
Johan (Joh.) II, 44
GETTLING
Wilhelm I, 443
GETTS (GOTZ, GETS, KETS)
Bermard I, 124
Christina I, 123
Conraad I, 102, 105
Elizabeth I, 124
Fredrick (Frederick) I, 122, 125, 126
Johan I, 124
GETZ
Christian I, 498
Martin I, 393
GETZELMAN
Christopher I, 559, 560, 562
GEULING
Jeorg I, 442
GEWINNER
Johann Friedrich I, 466
GEX
Anthon II, 175
Madame II, 175
GEYER (GAYER)
Catha II, 29
Conrad I, 661, 663, 664
Ernst Fredk II, 29
Georg Paul I, 391
Hans Casper (Casper) I, 604, 606, 607
Hans Michall I, 482
Henrich II, 29
J. Bastian (Bastian) I, 646, 647
J. Carel Tob. II, 29
Johann Adam I, 353, 354, 391, 507
Johann Balthaser I, 463
Johan Besieger I, 353, 354
Johann Casper I, 531, 532, 534
Johan Conrad I, 412
Johann Erhard I, 734
Johann Friedrich I, 451
Johann Henrich I, 412

Johan Jacob I, 531, 532, 534
Johann Petter I, 755
Johann Wilhelm I, 411
John Gottfred II, 121
John Jacob I, 173, 174
Philip I, 551, 553, 554
Wolf Caspar I, 412
(*See also* GUYER)
GEYGER
Anna II, 163
Elizabeth II, 163
Jacob II, 163
Joseph I, 582, 583, 585; II, 163
Michael I, 43, 46, 47
(*See also* GUYGER)
GEYHER
Gottlieb I, 710
GEYLER
Andereas I, 481
Mathais I, 481
GEYMAN (GYMAN, HIEMAN)
Johanes (Johann, Johannes) I, 628, 631, 634
Hans Jacob I, 79, 82, 83
GEYSER (JAYSER, KYSER)
Johann Georg I, 497
John Jacob I, 497
GEYT
J. Hendrick II, 4
GHIO
Jean II, 205
GHION
Augustin II, 205
GIANQUE
John F. II, 89
GIBBS (GIBS, GIPS)
Alexander I, 363
Benjamin II, 25
Johann Nickel (Nicholas) I, 626, 630, 633
GIBE
Andries I, 767
Catrina I, 766
Elizabeth I, 767
Marlina I, 767
Micoll I, 767
GIBLER
Jorg Michel I, 409
GICH
Jacob I, 693
(*See also* GIEG)
GICK
Henrich I, 693
GIDAUD
Dafid II, 134
GIEB
Jno Jacob I, 744
GIEBELER
Christgan I, 443

GIEBELHAUS
Erhard I, 722
GIEDELMANN
Johannes I, 706
GIEG (GIEGH)
Adam I, 627, 630, 633
Baltzer I, 540, 542, 544
Heronimus I, 627, 630, 634
GIELBERT *see* GILBERT
GIELER
Willhelmina, van II, 122
GIELMAN (KELMAN, KIELMAN)
Henry (Henery) I, 629, 632, 635
GIERSBACH
Johann Jost I, 465
GIES
Johannes I, 466
GIESE (GIESI)
Jacob I, 391
John Henry II, 121
Rudolph II, 161
GIESSLER, (KISLER, GERSLER, KISNER, KAISLER)
Davidt (David) I, 569, 570, 572
Henry (Henery, Henrick) I, 289, 290, 291
Johann Conrad I, 586, 587, 588
GIHL (GIHLL, GIL, KNIEL)
Christoffel (Christop[1]) I, 614, 616, 618
Johann Henrich I, 700
Johann Thomas I, 686
GILBERT (GIELBERT, GILBERTH)
Andreas I, 506
Anthoni (Anthony) I, 71, 76, 77
Baltzer I, 348
Bernhart I, 348, 418
H. Bernhart I, 443
Hans Jacob I, 443
Hans Jerg I, 443
Henry I, 347
Jacob I, 418
Johann Colaus I, 443
Johann Georg I, 443, 506
Johan Jacob I, 371
Johann Philipps I, 712
Johannes I, 454, 627, 630, 633
Jorg I, 689
Matteis (Mattias) I, 185, 186, 187
Wendal (Wendel, Vindle) I, 610, 611, 613
GILD (GILTT, GILLOK)
Killian (Philean) I, 331, 333, 334
GILDNER (GILTNER)
Conrad I, 646, 648
Frantz (Frans) I, 205, 207, 208
GILESZ *see* GELESEN

GILKIN
Jno L. II, 6
GILLAND
William II, 83
GILLERD
Phillip II, 191
GILLI
Geo. I, 729
GILLIHAN
William II, 83
GILLINGER
Jacob I, 348
GILLION (GILLIOM, GARLEGILLON)
Charle (Chaley) I, 199, 201, 203
Jan I, 199
GILLIONA
Peter I, 508
GILLMANN (GILMAN)
Daniel I, 310, 311, 312
Johan Adolph I, 493
GIMPEL (GIMBEL)
George Thomas I, 504
Peter I, 676
GIMPERLE (HEMPERLY)
Michael I, 227, 229, 231
GINÄHLE
Christoph I, 704
GINDER (GINTHER, GINTER)
Anna Maria II, 46
Elizabetha II, 46
Filleb (Philip) I, 363
Frederica II, 46
Henrich I, 405
J. Rudolph I, 405
Johan Caspar I, 486
Johanna Louisa II, 46
Johannes (Johannas) I, 732; II, 46
GINSBERG
Johann Georg I, 685
Johannes Engel I, 685
Johannes Peter I, 685
GINTER *see* GÜNTER
GINTNER
Augustinus I, 395
Hans Michael I, 418
Johannes I, 383, 385
GIR
Johan Balthes I, 340
GIRARD
Daniel II, 31
Louis David II, 108
GIRARDIN (GERARDIN, GERRARDIN)
Jacob I, 378, 380, 381
Peter I, 378
GIRKE
John George II, 136

GISCH (KISH)
Mattes (Mathias) I, 122, 125, 126
GISS (GYSEN)
Jacob I, 66, 69, 70
Johann Conradt I, 410
GISSELBRECHT
Johannes Michael I, 453
GISSI (GISSE, GISSY, KEESEY)
Conradt I, 305, 306
Hans Jakob II, 132
Jacob I, 56
Johan Wendel I, 56
Matis II, 132
GISSLER (GISLER, GESLER, GEIZLER)
Anna I, 117
Hans Adam I, 212, 214, 215
GIST
Johann Gorg
(Georg) I, 179, 181, 184
GISTERER
Christoph I, 489
GITTELMAN (GIDELMAN)
Johann Jacob I, 335, 336, 338
GITTING
Johan I, 443
GITTINGER
Frantz II, 118
GITZ
Henry II, 9
Maria Magdal II, 9
Martin II, 9
GLAAN
Anna Christina II, 28
Christina II, 28
Margeretha II, 28
GLACH
Johann Filbert I, 711
GLADEN
Jacob II, 85
John II, 85
Mary II, 85
GLADFELDER
Gaspar I, 331
GLADING
Abraham I, 707
GLAIS
Hans Philip I, 102, 105
GLANTZ (GLANCE)
Anna Margreate I, 85
Anton I, 734
Hance Micalle I, 85
Hieronymus (Jerimy) I, 84, 86, 87
Marrea Medl. I, 84
GLÄSENER
Jacob I, 685
Johann Henrich I, 685

GLASER (GLASSER, GLÄSSER, GLÄZER)
Carl (Carol) I, 384, 386
Christian I, 400
Christopher II, 188
Friederich (Johan
Fred^k) I, 585, 587, 588
Jacob I, 409
Jacob Friedrich I, 480
Johann I, 699
Johan Johanes I, 586, 587, 588
Johan Nickel (Jan
Nikel) I, 266, 269, 273
Johann Philip (Philip) I, 20, 21
Johannes I, 442
Leonhart (Lenhart) I, 169, 171, 172
Nicoles I, 725
Stephan (Stepha) I, 225, 228, 230
GLASS (GLAS, CLAS)
Abraham I, 437
Eva I, 123
Friederich I, 122, 125, 126
Hans Jacob I, 470
Johanes I, 494
Maria I, 103, 124
Martin I, 411
Michael II, 134
Phillib I, 702
Rosina I, 124
Sophia I, 127
GLASSBRENNER (GLASBRENNER)
Conrat (Connard) I, 99, 100, 101
Johann Fridrich I, 432
Johann Georg (Gorg) I, 59, 63, 65
GLASSLER
Johanes I, 500
GLASSMANN
John II, 83
GLÄSSNER
Johann Wilhelm I, 466
GLATTLY (CLATLEY, KLATLEY)
Felix I, 252, 254, 255
Henry (Henrich) I, 252, 253, 255
GLAUCHER (GAUCER)
Johannes II, 126
Peter I, 582, 583, 584
GLAUFLIEGEL
Christian I, 760
GLAUNER
Matheus II, 171
GLAUR
Barbara I, 148
GLECKNER see KLÖCKENER
GLEIM (KLEYM, CLIME)
Carl I, 667, 669, 671
Elizabeth I, 40
Jacob Christian I, 391

Johann Michael
  (Michiel)   I, 39, 41, 42
Susean   I, 40
GLESS
Adam   I, 701
GLEYSLER
Hans George   I, 483
GLICK *see* GLÜCK
GLIMPF (KLIMPH)
Johann Abraham (John
  Abraham)   I, 672, 673, 674
GLINK
Christian   II, 193
GLISSER
Balzazar   I, 400
GLOCKNER
Fr.   II, 125
GLÖKIL
Uhllerik   I, 484
GLÖKLER
Johan Peter   I, 719
GLOSE
Gottl.   II, 119
GLOSSER
Jacob   I, 445
GLOTZ (LOOS)
Johannes   I, 720
Ludwig (Lodowick) I, 246, 247, 248
GLÖTZEL
H. Uhllerik   I, 452
GLÜCK (GLICK)
Conrad   I, 421
Georg Peter   I, 408
Johann Philips
  (Philip)   I, 656, 657, 658
Johannes I, 656, 657, 658, 695, 717
Petter   I, 382
GLUG (LOOCK, read KLUG)
Jerg Jacob (Jacob) I, 293, 294, 295
GLUKNER
Charles   I, 746
GMEINBAUCH (MINEBOWER,
  read GEMEINBAUER)
Johann Wolfgang (Hans
  Wolph)   I, 652, 653
GMINDER (MINDER, GELINDER)
Hans Martin   I, 531, 533, 534
Johann Georg   I, 531, 533, 534
GNÄGE (QNÄG)
Johanes   I, 327, 329
GNÄRR
Leonhardt   I, 489
GNÄSCHELER
Anthon Henrich   I, 757
GNÖDLER
Hans Jerg   I, 446
GOART
Jacob Tyd   II, 61

GOB
Philip   I, 455
GOBAT (GOWBA)
Abraham   I, 591, 592, 594
David Frederick   II, 31
Suzane   II, 31
GÖBEL (GOBELL, GOBBELL, GO-
  BEL)
Anna Maria   I, 118
Antoniey   I, 118
Barbara   I, 118
Cath^a II, 4
Conrath (Conrad) I, 218, 219, 221
Eva   II, 4
Georg   I, 506
Hans Jerg (Je-
  rick)   I, 116, 118, 120, 121
Henrich   I, 88, 90, 91
Herrmann (Johannes Har-
  man)   I, 559, 561, 562
J. Davit (David)   I, 642, 644
Johann Adam (John
  Adam)   I, 386, 388, 389
Johan Henry (Hen-
  rick)   I, 217, 219, 220
Johann Jacob   I, 443
Johann Nickel   I, 398
Jurig Adam   I, 118
Madlena   I, 118
Moritz (Mauritz)   I, 642, 644
Petter (Peter) I, 637, 638, 640
—   I, 398
GÖBELER
Christian Matheis   I, 401
Johann Jacob   I, 466
GOBRECHT (GABRECHT)
Johann Christian I, 517, 518, 520
Johann Christoph I, 517, 518, 520
GOCKELER
Godlieb   II, 201
GODFRIED (GODFREY)
John W.   II, 89
Peter   I, 310, 311, 312
GODMAN
Elisa   II, 55
John Friedrik   II, 68
GODSCHALK
Johann Conrad   II, 29
Johan George   I, 359, 361
GODT
Vincent   II, 193
GÖDTEL
Johannes   I, 413
GOEB
Frederick   II, 161
GOEBELS
John Kraff   II, 128
Magdelena   II, 128

GOEDEKE (GOEDAKE)
Hans Georg (Georg) I, 59, 63, 65
GOEMANN
Jasper Hesse II, 190
GÖER
Peter I, 346
GOETZ
Frederica II, 150
Gaspar II, 150
Gustave Frederic II, 46
Hans Geo. I, 697
Jost I, 721
Katharine II, 150
(*See also* GÖTZ)
GOHL
Conrad I, 500
Elias I, 500
GOHN (COEN, JOHN, KOEN)
Adam I, 221, 223, 224
Fielip (Philip) I, 222, 223, 225
Johannes (Johan) I, 221, 223, 224
GOHNAUER (GOEHNAUR, GOCH-
NAUER)
Christian I, 60, 64, 65
Jacob I, 60, 64, 65
Kathrina I, 61
GÖHR
Hans Michael I, 382
GOHRMANN
Hans Jacob I, 459
GOLB (read COLB)
Philip I, 701
GOLDE (COLTE, COLT)
Jacob Samuell I, 736
Johann Gottfriedt I, 536, 537, 538
John Godfry I, 537
Niclaus Samuel I, 736
GOLDEBERGER
Hans (John) I, 232, 233
GOLDMAN
Eliz. II, 158
John Jost II, 158
Sophia II, 158
—— II, 158
GOLDNER
Baldice II, 71
Hans Jacob I, 349, 350, 351
GOLDSMIDT
L. M. II, 153
GOLL
Balthas (Baltzer) I, 627, 631, 634
GÖLLMAN
Johann Georg I, 726
Johann Leonhard I, 752
GÖLLNITZ
Johann Christian I, 480
GOLLSTADT (GOLDSTAD, GOLL-
STÄD)
Christian I, 517, 519, 520

Rudolph I, 517, 518, 519
GOLTER
David I, 685
GOLTZ (GOLZ)
Hans Peder I, 423
Henrich II, 46
GOMB
Frantz I, 726
GOMER (GOMMER)
Christstofel (Chris-
tiper) I, 173, 174, 175
Johans Adam I, 173, 174, 175
GOMPF (KHUMPH)
Johann Dietrich I, 592, 593, 595
GONDERMAN
Johan Jakob I, 467
Johan Wilhelm I, 352, 353
Johannes Engel I, 435
(*See also* GUNDERMAN)
GÖNNER(GONNER)
Johan Georg I, 462
Marcus I, 418
GONS
Jacob I, 7
GONTERT
Johannes I, 495
GONTZLER
Johann Conradt I, 391
GOOD (GOEDT, GOODE)
Felix I, 12
Henry I, 332, 333, 334
Jacob I, 258, 260, 263
Jn. Chris[n] I, 753
Johannes I, 304, 347
Petter I, 13
Samuell I, 13
GOODBROOD (GOODBROD,
GOODBROAD)
Barbary I, 40
George I, 41
Lodwich (Lodw., Lud-
wig) I, 39, 41, 42
GOODKNECHT
Hans Michael I, 492
GOODMAN
Jacob I, 404
Philip I, 404
GOODNIGHT
Gerick I, 660
GOODRY
Frederick II, 83
GORANSLO
Jor Adam I, 417
GORDON
Anna Margreta II, 103
Elizabeth II, 103
Johannas II, 103
Lova II, 103

GÖRES
Johann Phillip   I, 483
GÖRG (GEORG, GORGH, JERICH, JURG)
Christina   I, 60
Jacob   I, 246, 247, 248
Johann Jost   I, 495
Leonhart (Leonard)   I, 205, 206, 208
Michel (Michiel)   I, 59, 63, 64
Simon   I, 699
Thorodea   I, 60
GORGS (GÖRGES)
Johan   I, 724
Johannes David   I, 427
GÖRIG (GORICK, YERICK)
Johann Philipp
(Philip)   I, 71, 76, 77
Johannes (Hannes)
                          I, 596, 597, 599
Margeritta   I, 73
GORMAN
Johann Adam   I, 395
GORSCH
Jacob   I, 718
GÖRTLER
Jacob   I, 715
GORTNER
Peter   I, 143
GORTZ
Johannes   II, 71
Maria Foncke   II, 71
GOSCHA
Peter   I, 400
GÖSEL
Johann Lenerdt   I, 474
GOSH
Martin   I, 392
GOSNER
Fridrich   I, 393
GOSPORT (GASPERT, GÖSPER)
Nicklas (Nicholas)   I, 601, 602, 604
Vallentin (Valentine)
                          I, 622, 624, 626
GOSS (GASS, GOSSEN)
Carl   I, 399
Dirck   II, 121
Johan Adam (John Adam)   I, 286, 287, 288
Johann Gorg (Johan Geo.)   I, 655, 657, 658
Johann Kraft   I, 522, 524
Stephan   I, 481
GOSSER
Christian   I, 412
GOSSIN
Emanuel   II, 31
Jacob   II, 31

Madelaine   II, 31
Suzanne   II, 31
GOSSLER
Georg Adam   I, 391
Philip Reinhart   I, 371
GOSTELY
Mr.   II, 175
Mrs.   II, 175
GOT (GOULD)
George   I, 592, 593, 594
GOTHARD (read GOTTHARD)
Anna   II, 148
Johann   II, 148
GÖTHELL
Johann George   I, 505
GÖTHING
Johanes   I, 483
GOTLE
Carolina   II, 197
Christophe   II, 197
Henry   II, 197
Jan   II, 197
Louisa   II, 197
Maria   II, 197
Rosina   II, 197
GOTLIB (read GOTTLIEB)
Johan   II, 16
GOTRE
Carolina   II, 54
GÖTS see GÖTZ
GÖTSCHY
Anna   I, 147
Barbara   I, 147
Beat.   I, 148
Esther   I, 147
Henrdryk   I, 146
Magdalena   I, 148
Mauritz   I, 148
Rodolph   I, 148
GÖTTELL (GOTTEL)
Adam   I, 691
Charlotta   II, 10
Christian   II, 10
Eliz.   II, 10
Frederica   II, 10
Henry   II, 10
Louis   II, 10
Peter   I, 691, 692
Philipina   II, 10
(See also GETTEL)
GOTTENER (GOTENER, GORDNER)
Peter   I, 185, 186, 187
GOTTER
Uhllerich   I, 359
GÖTTERT
Valentin   I, 760
GOTTERWA
Joseph   II, 151

GOTTFRIED (GODFREID)
Georg (Jurich)   I, 213, 214, 216
Johan Georg   I, 759
GÖTTGEN
Johannes   I, 460
Ludwig   I, 626, 630, 633
GÖTTLE
Hans Georg   I, 499
GOTTLEBEN
Carl   II, 79
GÖTTLICH (GETLICK, GITLICK)
Henrich (Hendrick)   I, 287, 289
Johannes (Johans)   I, 287, 289
GOTTLIEBS
Anne Maria   II, 71
GÖTTMANN
Johann Philipp   I, 698
Nicholas   I, 747
Wilhelm   I, 468
GOTTSCHALCK (GOTSHALK,
GOTCHALK)
Christoff   I, 369, 370
GOTTSCHALCK
Joachim   I, 444
Joh. Geo.   I, 516
Johan George
(Johan Georg,
John Jurg)   I, 283, 284, 286
Nicolaus   I, 329
Philip Jacob   I, 481
GOTTSCHALL
Davit   I, 707
GOTTSKIND
Philip   I, 234
GOTTWALT (GOTWALT, GOT-
WALTS, GOTTWALS)
Johan Adam
(Adam)   I, 257, 260, 262
Johann Bardel   I, 477
Johann Jacob   I, 469
Johannes   I, 217, 219, 221
GÖTZ (GOTZ, GÖTS)
Andreas   I, 489
Balthas   I, 476
Christgan   I, 752
Fred^k   II, 11
George   II, 99
Hans Jacob   I, 425
Hans Jerg (Hans
Georg)   I, 188, 191, 193
J. Godlieb   II, 156
Jacob   I, 724; II, 30
Johann Adam   I, 564, 566, 567
Johann Andreas
(Andreas)   I, 667, 669, 671
Johann Baltaser
(Baltzer)   I, 564, 566, 567
Johan Leonhart   I, 468
Johann Michael   I, 713

Johan Petter   I, 355
Johann Philipp   I, 711
Johannes   I, 452
Jurg   I, 513
Leonhard   I, 762
Mary   II, 11
Nikel   I, 696
Peter   I, 684
Phillipp   I, 723
Vallenthin   I, 752
(See also COTZ)
GOTZE
Henrich   II, 121
Wilhelm   II, 121
GÖTZELMAN
J. Jacob   I, 501
Johannes   I, 501
GÖTZENTORFF (GETSINDORF,
KELSENDORF)
Wilhelm (William,
Wilm)   I, 200, 202, 204
GÖTZINGER
Friedrich   I, 394
GOUCHER (GOUGER)
Frans   I, 722
Hendrick   I, 8
GOULSTET
Christian   I, 517
GOURDAIN
Jean   I, 746
GOUTSEN
Solome   I, 62
GOUW
Hans Nichell   I, 266
GOVERNOR
Yerick   I, 237
GRAACH
H. C. D. Willhelm   II, 111
GRÄB
Johan Peter   I, 732
GRABE
Joseph   II, 200
GRABEMAN
Philip   I, 443
GRABENSTEIN
Conrad   II, 154
GRÄBER
Johann Philipp   I, 752
Johannes (John)   I, 357, 395, 412
                           555, 556, 558
Leobold (Theobald)   I, 268, 271
GRABERTH
Hanns Jerg   I, 714
GRACIENA
———   II, 81
GRACK
Conrad   I, 444
Johannes   I, 443

Nicolaus
(Nicholas) I, 218, 219, 221
GRAE
Velde I, 17
GRAFF (GRAF, GRÄF, GRAAFF,
GREF, GREFF, GRAVE)
Albrecht (Albert,
Albrake) I, 175, 176, 177
Anna Barbara II, 133
Anthony I, 464
Christian I, 396
Christoffel
(Christoff) I, 21, 424, 532
533, 535; II, 171
Christoph, Junior I, 424
Conradt (Con-
raad) I, 258, 260, 263
Elisabetha II, 133
Fred. Wm. II, 200
Geo. Adam I, 690
George (Gorg) I, 21, 22
Gotlib Ernst II, 103
Hans Georg
(Hans Jerg) I, 66, 69, 70
162, 164, 166, 359
Hans Peter I, 426
Heinrich (Henrich,
Hendᵏ) I, 609, 610, 612
II, 133, 160
Jacob I, 175, 176, 177
365, 449, 637
639, 641, 755
Johann Adam I, 693
Johan Anthon
(Anthᵒ) I, 649, 650
Johann Balthaser I, 721
Johann Casper I, 311, 312, 313
Johann Christoph I, 21, 22
Johann Friedrich I, 461
Johann Gorg I, 693
Johann Henrich I, 473, 539, 541
543, 755
Johana Jacob I, 310, 312
313, 690
Johann Michel I, 313, 314, 315
Johann Peter I, 721
Johan Sebastian I, 35, 36, 37
Johann Simon
(Simon) I, 324, 325, 327
Joh. Wilhelm I, 461
Johannes I, 311, 577, 579, 581
John Peter II, 200
Joseph I, 546, 548, 550
638, 742
Ludwick II, 82
Maria II, 92
Martin I, 310, 311, 312
Mattheis I, 412
Michael I, 96, 98, 99, 488

P. F. II, 169
Petter (Pedter,
Peter) I, 185, 186, 187
Philipp I, 488, 735
Philipps Daniel I, 752
Sebästian
(Bastian) I, 9, 162, 164, 166
———— II, 32
(*See also* CREFF)
GRAFFELIN
Mr. II, 176
Mrs. II, 176
GRAFFENPERGER
Ignatius I, 749
GRAFFERT
Christoffel I, 335, 337, 338
Phillip Peter I, 356
GRAFT (read KRAFT)
Casper II, 118
Jon. Fill II, 76
GRAHN
Martin I, 737
GRAHUM
Hans Adam I, 304
GRAIM
Johann Adam I, 706
GRALL
Barbara II, 43
Catharina II, 43
George II, 43
Johann Adam I, 412
Peter II, 43
GRAMER (read CRÄMER)
G. E. II, 32
Godlieb Chr. II, 201
Jnᵒ I, 741
GRAMES
Friedrich I, 752
GRAMLICH (GRAMLIG)
G. Henrich I, 481
Gorg I, 709
Hans Adam I, 408, 453
Johann Georg I, 485
Thomas I, 479
GRAMLY
Vallentin I, 408
GRAMM (GRAM, GRAN)
Cornelius I, 732
Johann I, 742
Johannes I, 470, 564
565, 567
Leonard I, 716
Peter I, 704
Wilhelm I, 732
(*See also* CRÄMM)
GRAMMER
Jacob Friedrich I, 763
GRANDADAM (GRANTADAM)
Adam I, 405

François I, 406
GRANGE
Andre, de I, 407
GRANGET (GRENSHET)
Adrian I, 719
Joan (Johan) I, 225, 228, 230
GRANOBEL
Jacob I, 340
GRANRAM
Carl II, 44
Fred^k II, 44
GRANTEMEIR (GRANTEMIER, GRINDELMEYR)
Philip I, 532, 533, 535
GRANTER
Wilh. Gotl. II, 196
GRÄSCH
Hans I, 421
GRASMEHER
Johann Gottfried I, 745
GRASMUCK
Johann Caspar I, 391
GRASS
George I, 491
Jacob I, 484
Ludwig I, 483
Michael I, 484
GRÄSSEL (GRESEL)
Jacob I, 652, 654
Matthis I, 717
GRÄSSLE
Christoph I, 454
GRÄSSLER
Johan Fritrich I, 505
GRASSMANN (GRASSMAN)
Joh. Christ. II, 140
Simon I, 418
GRÄTZ (GRÄZ, GRATZ)
Andreas I, 465
Christian I, 482
Phalatine (Valentin) I, 16
GRATZE
Jacob I, 406
GRATZIGER
Andres I, 734
GRAU
Christian I, 455
Frans I, 304, 305, 306
Gerlach I, 694
Jerg (Hans Jurg) I, 605, 607, 608
Johann Konrath (Conrad) I, 569, 570, 572
Leonard (Löhnhart, Löhhard) I, 31, 32, 33
(*See also* CRAU)
GRAUEL (GRAUL, CRAUL, KRAUL, GRÄUELL, GRAWL)
Christina II, 10
Geo. II, 10

Jacob I, 411
Johann George (Yerick) I, 236, 238, 239
Johann Michael (Michel) I, 113, 114, 115, 154, 158, 160, 765
Johannes I, 709
Peter I, 283, 284, 285, 459
Rosina II, 10
Sibila Elisabeth I, 156
GRAUER
Johannes I, 395
GRAUFEUS (GRAWIUS)
Johannes I, 84, 86, 87
GRAULICH
Jacob I, 621, 623, 625
GRAUS (GRAUSS)
Jacob I, 508
Jerg I, 473
Johannes I, 703
Nicklas I, 759
Wilm (William) I, 622, 624, 626
GRÄUTTLER
Johanes I, 475
GRAVAN (GRAWAN)
Georg Friderich I, 763
Johann Jacob I, 763
GREASMAN
Maria C. II, 159
GREB (KREBB)
Christ Henrich (Christian) I, 568, 570, 571
Johann Deis (Mathias) I, 568, 570, 571
GREBER (GRAVER)
Hans I, 393
Hieronimus I, 365
Leobald I, 264
GREBILL (CREBIEL, CREBIELL)
Andres I, 690
Johannes II, 54
Pedder I, 690
GRECH
John Philip I, 493
GRECKENBERGER
Georg Adam I, 476
GREEM, CRIM *see* GRIMM
GREEN
Jn° Geo. I, 723
Joachim II, 109
GREENAWALT, GREENWALD *see* GRÜNEWALD
GREENBLAT
Hans Jacob I, 392
Martin I, 392
GREENEMEYER
George I, 367, 369
GREENO
Apploney I, 153

GREENOND
Joseph II, 134
GREER (CREEAR)
Jacob I, 521, 524
GREESMAN (CRÖSSMAN)
Dirick (Georg) I, 24, 26, 27
Johannes Dirick
(Johan Georg) I, 24, 26, 27
Marya I, 24
GREIB (GRIPE)
Jacob I, 126, 129
GREIFFENSTEIN (GREYFFEN-
STEIN, GREIFFESTAND)
Johann Michael I, 512, 514, 515
Johannes I, 666, 668, 670
Nickolas I, 499
GREIM
Adam I, 450
Sebastian I, 450
GREIMEL
J. W. II, 71
GREIN
John I, 750
Peter I, 420
GREINER (GREINAR)
Friderich I, 730
Jacob I, 476, 730
Johannes (Johannis) I, 426, 445
II, 16
(*See also* CREINER)
GREIS (GREISS)
Anna M. II, 158
Catharine II, 158
Johan Bernd I, 467
Johannes Ernst I, 401
Maria Elis. II, 158
GREISER (GRAISER, GRAIZER)
Anna I, 209
Anna Eva I, 209
Hans Jerich I, 209, 211
Maria Christina I, 209
Susannah Catharina I, 209
GREISSELL
Hannes I, 724
GREITER
Casper I, 428
GRELL (GREL)
Henrich I, 473
Johan Wilhelm I, 468
GRENDELMEYER
Ursula I, 147
GRENTIER (KRAN)
Jean (Hannes) I, 678, 679, 681
GRESEL (GESEL)
Fillib (Philip) I, 653, 655
GRESEMEYER
Jacob II, 122
GRESHER
Wilhelm I, 387

GRESS (GREESS)
Jacob I, 646, 648
Johann Mardin I, 401
Johannes I, 369, 370, 697
Peter I, 705
GRESSER
Friederich I, 355
GRETT (CREATE, CREAT)
Andereas (Andres) I, 405
Johanes I, 405
GRETTER
Georg Michael I, 454
Johann Jacob I, 480
GRETZINGER (GRIETZINGER)
Christian I, 475
Conrad I, 476
Hans Jerg •I, 343, 345
GREULICH (GRAYLIGH)
Frantz I, 341, 342, 343
GREULING (GRILLING, GEM-
LING)
Peter I, 296, 297, 299
GREUTHER
Jacob I, 711
GREUTZ
Henrich I, 495
GREUTZER (CREUTZER, CREU-
SER, SCRIVER, KREITZER)
Andreas
(Andreas) I, 246, 247, 248
Peter I, 246, 247, 248
GREVE
Ann Elisabeth II, 84
John Henry II, 84
Mary Elisabeth II, 84
GREVISMUHL
Joachm II, 206
GREYDER
Philip Chr. II, 118
GRIBELER
Johann Lutwig I, 407
GRIDLE
Black II, 130
GRIEB
Josias I, 411
GRIEBEL
Frantz I, 407
GRIEBEN
Johannes Benedictus I, 686
GRIEDER (GRIETER, GRIDER,
GRIEDY)
Adam II, 146
Anna II, 146
Friederich (Fred-
erick) I, 162, 164, 166
Jacob II, 146
Hans Georg II, 146
Hans Jacob I, 162, 164, 166

Martin   I, 162, 164, 166
249, 250
GRIEDIMER
Christian   I, 370
GRIEGER *see* KRIEGER
GRIELL
Carolus Gottlob   I, 735
GRIENE (GREEN)
Pierre (Berring)   I, 592, 593, 594
GRIESEMER (GRISIMER)
Valtein (Velde)   I, 31, 32, 33
GRIESER
Anthoni   I, 440
GRIESINGER (CRESINER)
Johann Jacob
(Johannes)   I, 106, 111, 112
GRIESS (GRIES)
Jacob   I, 423
Johann Carl
(Johan Carel)   I, 596, 597, 599
Johannes   I, 492
GRIESSE
J. Johannes   I, 482
GRIEVOGEL
J. F.   II, 123
J. G.   II, 123
GRIFFE (GRIFFI)
Samuel   I, 88, 90, 92
GRIMB
Johannes   I, 433
GRIME
Frederich   II, 19
GRIMLER (KRIMLER)
Heinrich Augustus
(Augustas)   I, 628, 631, 634
Jacob   I, 392
GRIMM (GRIM, GRIME, KRIM)
Adam   I, 316, 317
Andreas   I, 155, 158, 160
II, 148
Carl (Carell)   I, 316, 317
Casper Heinrich   I, 506
Catharine   II, 148
Cha⁵   I, 705
Christian Ludwig   II, 148
Conradt   I, 615, 617, 619
Erhardt   I, 459
Georg (Jerrig,
Jurg)   I, 316, 317, 615
617, 619
Gregorius   I, 642, 644
Hans   I, 690
Hans Jacob (Johannes
Jacob)   I, 287, 288, 289
Henerich (Henrich)   I, 176, 177, 178
Henrietta   II, 148
Jacob   I, 283, 284, 285
Johann   I, 441
Johan Conradt   I, 156, 159, 161

Johann Egidius   I, 21, 22
Johan Heinrich   I, 441
Johan Hend^k   I, 188
Johann Jerg   I, 122, 125, 126
Johannes   I, 221, 223, 224
287, 288, 615
617, 619
Martin   I, 221, 223, 224
Philip   I, 378, 380, 381
Philippina Jacobine   II, 148
Vallentin (Feltin)   I, 283, 284, 285
(*See also* CRIMM)
GRIMMEL
Godfrey Werner   I, 749
GRINDER
Hans Jacob   II, 133
GRINDLER
Christoff   I, 428
Philipp Jacob (Philip
Jacob)   I, 596, 598, 600
GRINEUS
Simon Conrad   I, 370
GRING
J. Henry   I, 465
GRISSE
Johan Jacob   I, 408
GRISSLER
Johann Peter   I, 733
GRIST
Marey   I, 80
GRISTY
Hance Jacob   II, 145
Hans   II, 145
GRIZET
Louis   I, 446
GRO (CROW)
Carli (Carl)   I, 283, 284, 285
GROATS (GROOTS, RUDSH)
Hendrick   I, 331, 333, 334
GROB (GROP, GRUB, GROOP)
Hans Jacob   I, 273, 274
Heinerich (Henry,
Hend^k)   I, 273, 274, 332
333, 334, 415
Israel   I, 691
Jacob   I, 431, 725
Johan Adam   I, 357
Johanis (Johanes)   I, 328, 357, 415
Johann Carl
(Karl)   I, 116, 120, 121
Joh. Jacob   I, 689
GROBE
Henry   II, 160
J. Anthony   II, 160
GROBERGER
Daniel   I, 406
GRÖBIL (KIBLE)
Peter (Petter)   I, 527, 528, 530

GROBLER
Carl Friederich   I, 505
GRÖBS
Georg Friedrich   I, 713
GRODION (GOOTJAR)
Heinrich   I, 510, 511, 512
GROENWOOD
Pieter   II, 135
GROFF (GROF)
Abraham   I, 327, 329
Hans   I, 391
Hans Peter   I, 391
Jacob   I, 391, 426
Johann Christoph   I, 22
Peter   I, 426
GROFFE
Hans Jacob   I, 426
GROH
Georg Friedrich   I, 427
Johann Leonhard   I, 436
Johann Simmon   I, 423
GRÖHMANN (GROOMAN)
Johan Christoff
(Christiper)   I, 173, 174
GRÖLI
Linhart   I, 434
GRÖLL (GROLL)
Johannes   I, 709
Niclaus   I, 762
GROLLER (GOLLER, KOBLER, KOOLER)
Hans Jacob
(Jacob)   I, 175, 176, 177
GROMBEIN (GROTTENBENGER)
Jorg Adam   I, 638, 639, 641
GROMME
Friedrich   I, 726
GROMP (GROP)
Johann Carl   I, 116, 120, 121
GRONAU
Andreas   II, 61
GRONDT
Hanna   I, 123
Jerg Adam
(Jerick)   I, 122, 125, 126
GRÖNER (GRONER, GRONERS)
Andreas   I, 751
Johann Adam (Jan
Adam)   I, 213, 214, 216
GRONINGER (GRONNINGER)
John Michael   I, 704
Lawrence   I, 704
Leonhardt   I, 422
Paulus   I, 467
GROS
Salima, vander   II, 43
Urclina, vander   II, 43
GROSCH (GROSH)
Conrath   I, 372

Peter   I, 689
Valentin   I, 336, 337, 339
GROSCOST
Philip   I, 31, 32, 34
GROSIEN
Anna Margaretta   II, 120
GRÖSINGER (GRISSINGER)
Johan Georg
(John Yeer[k])   I, 526, 528, 529
Yerrick   I, 528
GROSJEAN
Jacob   I, 472
GROSNICKEL
Petter   I, 363
GROSS (GROS, GROOS, GROOTZ)
Adam   I, 403
Andreas   I, 156, 159, 160
Anna Cathrine   I, 144
Christian   I, 189, 192, 194
441; II, 192
Christoph (Christoff)   I, 394, 638, 639, 641
Fellix   I, 332, 333, 334
Fred Wilch.   II, 119
Freya Cathrina   I, 144
Friderich
(Frederic)   I, 454; II, 155
G. K.   II, 122
George   I, 189, 192, 194, 348
Gotleib   II, 197
Hannah   II, 145
Hans Conrad (Hans
Kurick)   I, 332, 333, 334
Henrich   I, 709
Henry   I, 495
Isaac   I, 526, 528, 530
Jacob   I, 494; II, 145
Johanes   I, 79, 339, 405
406, 425
Johann   II, 192
Johann Adam   I, 449
Johann Anderes   I, 493
Johann Casper   I, 144, 526, 528, 529
Johan Christian   I, 493
Johann Daniel   I, 703
Johann Friederich   I, 497
Johan Gerg   I, 499
Johan Henry   I, 144
Johann Jacob   I, 667, 669, 671, 698
Johann Peter   I, 143, 145, 146
Johan Philip   I, 144, 395
Johann Wilhelm   I, 143, 145, 146
John Heinrich   I, 509, 510, 511
Leopoldt Valentin   I, 478
Michael (Michl.)   I, 83, 86
Paulus   I, 478
Philip (Pilipus)   I, 649, 650
Philip Christian   I, 667, 669, 671
Philipp Hennrich   I, 499

Philips Daniell I, 586, 587, 588
Simon I, 317, 318, 319
Sophia Margaret I, 143
Teobalt I, 317, 318, 319
GROSSGLAUS (GROSSCLASS)
Johan Georg I, 691
Michael I, 559, 561, 562
GROSSHART (GROSSHARD)
Adam I, 737
Johann Hennrich I, 715
GROSSKOPF (GROSKOPF, GROSS-
KOPFF)
Jacob I, 335, 337, 338
Johann I, 454
GROSSMAN (GROSMAN)
Michael (Michell,
Mich.) I, 301, 302, 303
(*See also* CRÖSSMANN)
GROSSNICKLE
John I, 227; II, 104
GROTE
Jacques II, 86
John Rudolph II, 204
GROTEYAHN
Henry II, 157
Sophia II, 157
—— II, 157
GROTH
Anna Eliz. II, 97, 129
Anna Maria II, 97
Catharina II, 92
Johan Jurgen II, 97
Johannes II, 97
Maria Eliz. II, 97
GROTHEIM (GROTHEIN)
Andrew
(Andereas) I, 517, 518, 520
GRÖTHER
Johan Georg I, 418
GROTNOVER
Elisa II, 119
GRÖTZINGER
John II, 188
GROULLAT
—— II, 81
GROUNDBERG (GROUNDER-
BERG, KREENBERG)
Casper I, 516, 518, 519
GROUNDLER
Paulus I, 449
GROUSAAM
Melchior I, 122
GROUSE
Godfried II, 183
GROVE
Francis II, 147
Johannes Frans
(Frants) I, 373, 374, 376

GROW
Peter I, 423
GROWS (read KRAUS)
Madlena I, 118
GRUB (CRUP, GROUB, GROAB,
KRUB)
Andereas (Andres,
Anderas) I, 628, 631, 634
Christian I, 213, 214, 216
Debalt I, 488
Henry I, 363, 415
Jacob I, 204, 206, 208
Johan Gorg (John
Yerrick) I, 581, 583, 584
Johann Jacob I, 323, 325, 326
Johann Peter
(Peter) I, 556, 557, 558
582, 583, 584
GRUBE (GRUB)
George II, 86
Jacob I, 441, 747
Johann Daniel
(Dan) I, 256, 259, 261
Peter (Petter) I, 256, 259, 261
GRÜBEL
Peter Philipp I, 356
GRUBER
Anna I, 135; II, 133
Anna Maria II, 133
Anthony I, 652, 654
Elisabeth II, 133
Friedrich I, 513, 514, 515
Georg Philip I, 752
Hans Jacob II, 133
Hans Peter (Peter) I, 134, 136
Henrich I, 96, 97, 98
Jacob I, 400
Johann Joachim I, 753
Johannes I, 237, 238, 239
Martin (Marti) I, 135; II, 133
Nicklas (Nickell,
Nickel) I, 289, 290, 291
Philipp Ernst I, 88, 90, 92
Philipp Peter I, 752
Wilhelmus Jacobus I, 400
GRUBERT
Jacob I, 675
Wilhelm I, 675
GRUCK
Henrich Wilhelm I, 700
GRUEL
Marcus I, 396
GRUG (read KRUG)
Jacob I, 459
GRUI *see* GRUY
GRUIS
Lewis II, 156

GRÜLL
  Gottfried (Gott-
    friedt)   I, 159, 161
GRULLMAN
  Hans Jacob   I, 364
GRUMBACH
  Godfrey   I, 706
  Hans Peter   I, 348, 349, 351
  Jacob   I, 423
GRUMBACHER (CROMBACKER)
  Hans   I, 116, 119, 120
GRUMMET
  Christophel Ludewig   I, 504
  Johann Casper
    Friederich   I, 504
GRÜN (GRUEN, GRIN)
  Adam   I, 531, 533, 534
  Georg Simon   I, 736
  Hans David   I, 359
  Johan Henrich   I, 415
  John   I, 143
  Martin (Mardin)   I, 391, 497
  Michel (Michael) I, 231, 232, 233
  Paul   I, 684
  Vallentin   I, 325, 326
GRÜNAU (CRONOVAR, CRONO-
  WAS)
  Andereas (Andreas,
    Andriss)   I, 556, 557, 558
GRUNBERG
  Christⁿ   II, 139
GRUNBERGER
  Andreas   I, 237
GRUND (GRONT)
  Adam   I, 638, 639, 641
  Friedᶜʰ Alexander   II, 140
  Peter   II, 59
  Wilhelmina Christˡ   II, 140
GRUNDELL
  ——   I, 424
GRUNER (GRÜNER, KRONER)
  Durs   I, 473
  Johann Dietrich   I, 96, 98
  Johann Georg   I, 96, 98
  Johan Kolman   I, 347
  J. George (Han
    Geo.)   I, 665, 668, 670
GRÜNEWALD   (GRUNEWALT
  GREENAWALD, GREENWALD
  Abraham   I, 277
  Fredrick   I, 461
  Hans   I, 360, 362
  Hans Filb   I, 407
  Hieronimus   I, 627, 630, 633
  Jacob   I, 301, 302, 303, 734
  Joseph   I, 363
  Mathis   II, 52
  Migel   I, 709
  Niclaus   I, 736

Peter   I, 419
GRÜNINGER
  Catharina   II, 53
GRUNNINGEN
  John, Van   II, 54
GRUNTZGE
  Philipp   I, 721
GRÜNZWEIG
  Gottfried   I, 419
GRUPE
  Johan Henrich   II, 120
GRUSIUS
  Nicklas   I, 404
GRUVE (GROEFF)
  Anna   I, 210
  Hans   I, 210
  Peter   I, 210
  Veronica   I, 210
GRUY (GRUI)
  Christophel   I, 615
  Johann   I, 617, 619
  Michael   I, 615, 617, 619
GRUYLIG
  J. P.   II, 24
GRYDELBACH
  Dielmanus   I, 408
GRYNER
  Casper   II, 24
GRYS
  Johannes   I, 676
  Martyn   I, 676
GRYSING
  Jacob   I, 410
GSCHEIDLE
  Chr. Gold.   II, 202
GUBLER (GUBELER)
  Chrisⁿ Mathias   I, 676
  Hans Jacob   I, 398
  Peter   I, 637
GUCK
  Johan Stefan   I, 734
GUCKEL
  Johannes   I, 444
GUCKER (GÜCKER, KECKER)
  Adam   I, 330
  Christian   I, 44, 330
  Fred.   II, 24
  Jacob   I, 760; II, 24
  Johan Bartel   I, 43, 45, 46
  Johann Jacob   I, 340, 341, 343
  Johannes Henrich I, 340, 341, 343
  Katrina   I, 43
  Laurence   I, 44
  Peter   I, 531, 532, 534
GUCKERT (KOOCKHART)
  Sebastian
    (Sabastian)   I, 256, 259, 262
  Simon   I, 710

GUCKES (KOEKS)
Hans   I, 750
Johannes
  (Johan)   I, 205, 207, 208
GUDERMUTH   (GUDDER-
  MOUTH)
Catharine   II, 51
Dority   II, 51
Hans   II, 51
Johanes   II, 51
Laws   II, 51
Nichols   II, 51
Philip   II, 51
GÜDTNER
Johan Samuel   I, 723
GUE
——   II, 81
GUEGNIM
——   II, 81
GUERRIER
——   II, 81
GUERY
Mathieu   I, 452
GUETIGUER
Martin   II, 31
GÜFI (CEAVY)
Philip Lutwig   I, 88, 90, 91
GUGENHAN
Daniel   I, 508
Johan Georg   I, 508
GUGEST
Michael   I, 371
GUIBERT
——   II, 81
GUILLICH
Joh.   II, 100
GUILLOMONS
Piere   I, 509
GUIT (GUITE)
Nicholas   I, 760
GUITE
Peter   I, 711
GÜLBERTH
Christoph   I, 506
GÜLCHER
Dewalt   I, 695
GULDEN
Gallus   I, 393
GULICH
Johannes Clemens   I, 713
GÜLLAM (KEELHAM)
Andreas   I, 348, 350, 351
GÜM (KYM)
Christian   I, 89, 91, 92
GUMDER
Ludwig   II, 92
GUMEDEN
Beder, von   I, 407

GUMERINGER
Jacob   I, 500
GUMLER
Hans   I, 392
GUMMY
Johannes   I, 732
GUMPP (GUMP)
Johann Georg
  (Hans Jorig)   I, 72, 76, 78
GUNDACKER (GONDAKKER)
Johan Michel (John
  Michael)   I, 297, 298, 299
GUNDE (CONTEE)
Hans (Hance)   I, 27, 29, 30
GUNDEL
Hans Wolff   I, 683
GUNDELFINGER
Hans   I, 448
GÜNDER (GUNDER)
Georg Christoffel   I, 504
Gylyan   I, 428
J. Peter   I, 444
GUNDERMAN
Johannes   I, 435
GUNDERUM (CONTERON)
Jorg Lips (Yerrick
  Philip)   I, 582, 583, 584
GÜNDLACH (GUNDELACH)
Johann   II, 121
Johann Georg (Jo.
  George)   I, 621, 623, 625
GÜNDNER
Jacob   I, 498
GUNDRY
Michel   I, 735
GUNGHEIM
A.   II, 143
GUNKEL (GUNCKEL, GUNCKELL,
  KUNKEL, KONKELL)
Balthasar   I, 89, 91, 92
J. Michael   I, 412
Johan Georg
  (Geo.)   I, 217, 219, 220, 750
Johannes   I, 217, 218, 219, 220, 221
Peter   I, 509, 510, 511
  (*See also* KUNCKEL)
GUNN (CRAN, COON)
Hans Georg (Hans
  Jerick)   I, 209, 211
Hans Michael   I, 210
Veronica   I, 210
GUNST
Isaac   I, 428
GUNT
Anna Maria   I, 49
Hans Georg   I, 48, 50, 52, 53
Jacob   I, 48, 52, 53
Johanis   I, 50
Maria Elizabeth   I, 50

GÜNTER (GUNTAR, GUNTHER, GÜNTHER)
Ann Margaret II, 43
Anna Cath. II, 140
Anna Juliana Hinrietta II, 140
Anna Maria II, 7
Anne W. II, 189
Anthon I, 672, 673, 674
Barbara II, 188
Caroline II, 43
Caspar I, 222, 223, 225
Catharin
(Cathareen) II, 43, 188, 189
Chas. II, 7
Christian I, 459; II, 188
Conrad I, 378; II, 43
Daniel II, 43
Elizabeth II, 7, 189
Eva II, 7
Eve R. II, 189
Georg (Jorg) I, 222, 223, 225, 686
Hannah II, 188
Hans Daniel II, 43
Hans Jacob II, 43
Hans William II, 43
Heinrich (Henrich) I, 25, 26
II, 160
Jacob I, 711; II, 45, 188
Johann Heinrich (Jnº
Henry) I, 649, 650
Joh. Joachim II, 139
Johann Jacob II, 45
Johanna II, 189
Johannes I, 732; II, 45
Johannes Petter I, 72, 76, 78
John II, 7, 160
John Friederik I, 504
John G. II, 189
Leonh. II, 119
Margᵗ II, 7, 188
Maria Barbara II, 45
Michael I, 378, 379, 381
II, 188
Peter (Pether) I, 222, 223, 225
Regina II, 188
Rosena II, 188
Samuel II, 189
Wendel I, 724
GUNTRUM
Hernie II, 118
GÜNTTERT
Johannes I, 734
GUNTZEHAUSER (GUNTZEN-
HAUSER, GUNTZERHAUSER)
Elisabeth II, 31
Jacob I, 442
Reinhart I, 391
GUNTZING
Catharina Philipine II, 45

GÜRD
Christian I, 328
GURDNER (GURTHNER)
Christian I, 442
Johannes I, 605, 606, 607
GURTS
Johannes I, 21, 22
Michael II, 98
GUSH
Conrad I, 480
GUSMAN
Abraham I, 458
GÜSSEMAN (GEESEMAN)
Johan Georg
Wilhelm I, 313, 314, 315
GUSTAV
Carl I, 428
GUTCHREL
Michel I, 714
GUTDÄNDER
Wendell I, 696
GUTE
Michael II, 195
GUTEKUNST
Hans Jerg I, 446
Michael Friederich I, 712
GUTELIUS
Johann Peter I, 443
GUTENBERGER (GUTTENBER-
GER)
Adam II, 29
Andreas II, 113
Henrich II, 29
GUTERMAN
C. II, 200
Johann Henrich I, 460
GUTH (GUT, GUTT)
Caspar (Kasper) I, 147, 150, 151
Charles II, 117
Conrad I, 521, 523
Debalt (Deobald) I, 204, 206, 207
Felix I, 12, 13
Frederich II, 57
Fredʳ Ludewig II, 57
Hans I, 365
Hans Michel I, 13
Hendrick (Hendrik) I, 31, 33, 34
Jacob I, 60, 64, 65, 327, 329
462, 497, 705
Johan Georg I, 497
Johan Michael I, 497
Johannes II, 90
Lohrentz (Lorenz) I, 221, 222, 224
Peter (Peder) I, 13, 14, 628, 631, 635
Samuel I, 13, 14
Sophie Salmia II, 57
Susanna I, 61
——— II, 179

GUTHARD (GUTHART)
Henrich — I, 169, 170, 172
GÜTHING
Johannes Henrich — I, 408
Ludwig — I, 756
GUTHLE
Samuel — II, 98
GUTHMAN (GUTMAN, GUT-MANN, GUTTMAN)
Anna — II, 29
Anna Margᵗ — II, 8
C. — I, 728
Frederik — II, 136
Jnº Peter — II, 8
Johan Conrath — I, 340
Johan Geo. — I, 340, 342
Johann Rudolff — I, 340, 342, 343
Johan Stephan (John Stephan) — I, 246, 247, 248
Johan Willm — I, 340, 342, 343
Marg. Cath. — II, 8
Margerª — II, 29
Nicolaas — II, 29
Peter — I, 347, 428; II, 29
Philip — I, 162, 164, 166
— II, 29
GUTIGE (SHADIKE)
Henr. Christo — I, 516, 518, 519
GÜTINGER (HORTINGER)
Hans — I, 331, 332, 334
Jacob — I, 398
GUTKNECHT
Christian — I, 400
GÜTSELL (GOTTSE)
Johann Gorg (Johan Geo.) — I, 601, 602, 603
GUTTE
Johana — II, 77
GUTTENBURG
Johann Casbar — I, 690
GÜTTING (GUTTIN)
Andres — I, 732
Johann Peter — I, 507
Johannes Henrich — I, 484
GUTTINGER
Rudolph — I, 434
GUVOIN
—— — II, 81
GUYER (read GEYER)
Jacob — I, 508
GUYGER (GYGER read GEIGER)
Hans Jerick — I, 8
Johanes Hendk — I, 8
GYBERT (GYBART)
Barnet — I, 44
Catrina — I, 44
Eliz. — I, 44
Godlieb — I, 44
Julian — I, 44

Mathias — I, 44
Sabina — I, 44
GYS
Magdalena — II, 174
GYSINGER
Caspar — I, 755

HAACKE
Johann Danˡ — II, 205
HAAF (HAFF)
Peter — I, 677, 678, 680
HAAG (HAAGH, HAG, HACK)
Andreas — I, 499
David (Davith) — I, 373, 374, 376
Geo. — I, 689
Hans Casper — I, 502
Hans Jerg (Yerich) — I, 373, 374, 375
Hans Michael — I, 84, 86, 87
Heinrich (Henry) — I, 627, 631, 634
Jacob — I, 463, 507
Johan Tobias — I, 470
Michel (Michael) — I, 591, 593, 594
Valenthein — I, 397
HAAGE
Hans Jork — I, 718
HAAGER
Gottfried — I, 718
HAAK
Adam — II, 4
Hans Dirk — I, 18
Hans Georg — I, 499
HAAKE
Ruticius — II, 57
HAALLING (HALING)
Michel (Michall) — I, 163, 165, 167
HAAN (HANN)
Abraham — I, 189, 192, 193
Henry — I, 449
Jacob — I, 564, 566, 567
Johanes — I, 396
Johann Valentine (Valantine) — I, 189, 192, 193
HAANECAM (HANNEKAM)
Joseph — I, 586, 587, 588
HAAR
Christian — II, 119
Johann Adam — I, 731
HAARS
Christian — II, 33
HAARTZ
Jeorg Emig — I, 357
John Adam — I, 357
HAAS (HAS, HASS)
Albrecht — I, 93, 94, 95
Andreas — I, 432

Caspar   I, 628, 631, 634
Christian   I, 498
Fridrich
  (Friederich)   I, 198, 201, 203
George   II, 70
Gerlach   I, 743
Gorg Henrich (Jorg
  Henrich, Henry)   I, 614, 617, 619
Gorg Michel   I, 424
Hans George   I, 390
Hans Peter   I, 314, 315
Hartman   I, 628, 631, 634
Jacob (George)   I, 406, 697
Jacob Ullrich   I, 678, 679, 680
Johan   I, 652, 653
Johan Abraham
  (Abraham)   I, 282, 284, 285
Johann Georg   I, 490, 569, 570, 689
Johann Jacob
  (Jacob)   I, 568, 570, 572
Johann Konnrat   I, 465
Johan Kraft   I, 425
Johann Michael   I, 491
Johan Nickel   I, 731
Johann Peter   I, 313, 314, 315
Johann Philipp   I, 722
Johannes (Johanes)   I, 227, 229, 231
       313, 314, 315
       452, 507, 560
       561, 563, 683
John Henry (Johan
  Hendrick)   I, 653, 654
Ludwig (Lodwick)   I, 31, 32, 33
       595, 597, 599
Martin   I, 637, 639, 641
Mathis   I, 482
Michel   I, 751
Oswald   I, 410
Peter (Petter)   I, 167, 168, 689, 751
Philipp Carl (Phil-
  lip Carel)   I, 383, 385
Philips (Philip)   I, 296, 298, 299
HAASSE
  Conrad   I, 737
  Friederich Andreas   II, 33
  Otto   I, 452
HAASSLER (HASSELER)
  Abraham   I, 434
  Jacob   I, 434
HABACHER (HABACKER, HA-
  BAKER)
  Jerg   I, 450
  Johannes
    (Johannis)   I, 264, 267, 270
  Peter   I, 221, 222, 224
HABARAKER (HABERACHER)
  Johans   I, 7, 10

HABBECKER (HABEGR, HAPE-
  GER)
  Anna   I, 189
  Catrina   I, 189
  Christian   I, 188, 191, 193
  Hans Jacob   I, 188, 191, 193
  Joseph   I, 188, 191, 193
  Magdalena   I, 190
  Maria   I, 190
HABEL
  Fredrich   II, 89
  Geo.   I, 761
HABELMAKER
  J. F.   II, 45
HABER
  Jacob   I, 441
  Jerg   I, 498
  Philip   I, 415
HABERLING (HABERLIN)
  Adam   I, 441
  Christian Fridrich   I, 418
HABERLY (GIVERLY)
  Godfried
    (Godfricht)   I, 526, 527, 529
  Rutolph   I, 415
HABERMAN
  Henry   I, 440
HABERMEHL
  Ambrosius   I, 412
HABERSOOT (HABERSOD)
  Johannes   I, 335, 337, 338
HABERSTICH (HABERSTÜCH)
  Christian   I, 493
  Jacob   I, 493
  Michel   I, 318, 319
  Peter   I, 442
HABIGHT
  Christian Henry   I, 505
HABTÜGEL
  Johan Michael   I, 688
HACHEN
  Anthony   I, 450
  Julius   I, 450
HACHENBERG
  Joh. Peter   I, 700
  Johann Diterich   I, 718
HACHENBURGER
  Reinhart   I, 436
HACHMAN
  Jacob   I, 48, 52, 53
HACHSTORS
  Jacob   II, 119
HACKEHR
  Jacob   I, 365
HÄCKEL
  Andreas   I, 707
HACKENSHMIT (HACKETSMITT,
  HAKENSMITH)
  Conrath (Conrad)   I, 258, 260, 263

HACKER
Christoph I, 500
Georg I, 463
Hans Adam I, 416
HACKERMAN
Francis II, 104
Tobias II, 103
HACKERT
Frantz Petter I, 690
HACKMANN (HÄCKMAN,
HAACKMAN)
Abraham (Ab^m) I, 609, 611, 612
Elisabeth I, 157
Henrich I, 527, 528, 530
Herman H. II, 183
Johann Jacob I, 684
Johannes I, 395, 397
Peter I, 16
Rudolff I, 155, 158, 160
Ulerich I, 397
HADNER
Daniel I, 724
HADORN
Johannes (John) I, 280, 281, 282
HAEFELE
Johann II, 178
HAEN
Jacob I, 496
HAEPPE
John II, 199
HAER
Wilhelm I, 143
HAERMBSTAEDT
Carl II, 134
HAES
Peter I, 676
HÄFELIN
Peter II, 154
HAFER (HAFFER)
Hans Jorg I, 399
Henery II, 147
Johann Gorg I, 429
HAFFELE (HEFLEY, HAFFELEE)
John Carl (Johans
Carol) I, 195, 196, 197
HAFFELFINGER (HAFFIL-
FINGER)
Anna II, 146
Anna Maria II, 146
Bascher II, 146
Henery II, 146
Jacob II, 146
Margret II, 146
(*See also* HAFNENFEGER)
HAFFENTRAGER
Conrad I, 698
HAFFERKAM (HAFERKAM, HAF-
FERCAM)
Anthon (Anthonius) I, 577, 578, 580

HAFFERSTOCK
Jno Philip I, 705
Tobias I, 705
HÄFFNER (HAFNER, HAFFNER,
HÖFFNER)
Albertus I, 694
Christian I, 430, 704
Conrad I, 431
Daniel II, 193
Friederich
(Fredrick) I, 383, 385, 698
Georg Peter
(Jurg Peter) I, 677, 678, 680
George I, 498
H. George
(Hans Yerr^k) I, 596, 598, 599
Hans Jacob I, 344, 345
Henrich I, 409
Henry Jacob II, 193
Jno Geo. I, 696
Johann Jacob I, 457
Johann Philipp I, 493
Johannes I, 431
Lorentz I, 415
Matheis I, 447
HÄFNENFEGER (HALFELLFIN-
GER, read HAFFELFINGER)
Mard. (Marting) I, 275, 276
HAG
Jacob I, 507
Johann Michael I, 469
HÄGE (HAGE)
Hans I, 11
Hans Jacob I, 482
Johannes Gottfried I, 711
Pet., van II, 49
HAGELAAR
Christian II, 124
HAGELBERG
H. Zacharias I, 504
HÄGELE
Hanns Jerg I, 470
(*See also* HÄGELI)
HAGELGANS
Johann Sigmund I, 493
HÄGELI
Ludwig Friederch II, 173
HAGEMAN (HAGEMANN)
Anna Maria II, 24
Jacob II, 24
Jochen II, 50
HAGEN
Christian I, 450
J. J. II, 149
HAGENBACH
Hans Jerg I, 695
HAGENBUCH (HAGABUCK)
Andreas I, 189, 192, 193
Magdalena I, 190

Philipp Jacob I, 474
HAGENMÜLLER (HAGENMIL-
LER)
Christian Ernst I, 55, 56, 57
HAGER (HEGER, HAGHER)
Kilian . I, 414
Philip I, 341, 342, 343
William I, 708
HAGGY
Hans I, 10
HAGMANN (HACKMAN)
Mich. II, 179
Petter I, 16, 17
HAGNER (HACKNIR)
Friedrich (Fredrick) I, 383, 385
Johannes I, 495
Vallendin I, 491
HAGY (HAKIE)
Johannes (Joannes) I, 273, 274
Noah (Louis) I, 648, 650
HAHN (HAN, HAAN, HANN)
Andereas I, 410, 487
Anna Catharina II, 128
Benjamin II, 119
Catharina Barbara II, 170
Catharina Magdelena II, 170
Christian I, 386, 388, 389, 461
II, 6, 158
David I, 522, 524; II, 70
Domas I, 359, 361
Friederich Maximilian I, 719
George I, 736
Gerrit II, 98
Hann Wilh. II, 158
Jacob I, 410, 425, 475, 711
Jacobus II, 128
Jo. Pettder
(Peter) I, 559, 560, 562
Johana Augusta II, 170
Johann Maximilian I, 761
Johann Peter
(John Peter) I, 387, 388, 389
609, 610, 612
Johannes (Johanes) I, 256, 259, 262
359, 361, 474
666, 668, 670
Joseph I, 405, 496
Ludwig (Ludewig) I, 39, 41, 42
Maria Gertrude II, 128
Maria Magdelena II, 170
Mathias II, 128
Michael (Michel) I, 256, 259, 262
263, 267, 270
469
Nicklaus I, 683
Peter I, 357, 447
Peter Philipp I, 356
HAHNLEN (HAHNLIN)
Conrad II, 179

Philip Fried. II, 196
HAHS
J. H. II, 142
HAIDT
George II, 179
HAILE
Adam I, 293
HAIN (HAAN, HEHN)
George Michael I, 496
Henry (Heinrich) I, 622, 624, 626
HAINIG
G. Leopold I, 504
HAINLE
David II, 179
HAINTZ
Michael I, 716
HAIRS
Jacob I, 376
HAISCH
Hanns Jerch I, 394
HAITEBERGER
Johan Georg I, 490
HAKE
Nicolaus II, 98
HAL
Aric II, 134
HALBACH
Dort. II, 102
Gierdruth II, 102
Gottlieb II, 102
Helena II, 102
Peter II, 102
Wilhelmina II, 102
HALBER
Uhllerich I, 328
HALBERSTATT
Michal I, 521, 523
HALBON
Edeme I, 746
HALBOUT
Peter II, 177
HALDEN
Abraham, ab der I, 435
HALDER
Reynard (Richard) I, 24, 26
HALEWYN
Jan I, 743
HALFADLE
Jacob II, 185
Usilla II, 186
HALL
Egram I, 37, 38, 39
Henrich I, 469
Henry I, 204
Jacob I, 37
Robert I, 746
Sophia I, 38
HALLE (HEIALA, HÄLLE)
George Casper I, 305, 306

Johann Jacob II, 107
HALLEMAN (HIERLYMAN)
Felix I, 332, 333, 334
HALLER
Andreas I, 649
Barbara I, 147
Catherina I, 108, 109
Charlotta II, 152
Christian I, 344, 345
Christina I, 108
Dorothea I, 109
Elizabeth I, 148
Gabriel I, 234
Heinrich (Hendrich) I, 107, 109, 111
112, 435
J. Friederich
(Jacob Fredᵏ) I, 596, 597, 599
Jacob I, 344, 345, 384, 385, 508,
661, 662, 664; II, 152
Johanna II, 152
Juliana II, 152
Katherine II, 152
Matteis I, 493
P. F. C. II, 130
Peter (Petter) I, 107, 111, 112, 498
Philip I, 371
HALLIFAS
Hans George I, 429
HALLING (ALLEN)
Andreas Nicolaus
(And. Nicholas) I, 681, 682
HALLITSCHKE
Christian I, 757
HALLMAN
John II, 26
HALM
Johannes I, 427
Michel I, 695
Petter I, 702
HALS
Johann Georg I, 733
HALSHAULS *see* ALTHAUS
HALTE
Christian I, 396
HALTEMEYER
Davit I, 502
Hans George I, 502
Ludewigh I, 502
HALTER (HOLDER)
Abraham II, 26
Casper (Casparus) I, 209, 211
Hans Jacob I, 210
Martin (Hans Marthel) I, 209, 211
HALTERMEYER
Johanes I, 507
HALTIN
Anna Barbara I, 128
HALTMANN
Wilhelm II, 191

HALTSBIELDER
Stephen I, 18
HALWADT
Charles II, 202
HAM *see* HAMM
HAMAN *see* HAMMAN
HAMBACH
Henrick I, 432
HAMBING
Jnᵒ Fredᵏ II, 6
HAMBRECHT (AMBREGHT,
HAMBREET, AMBRIGHT,
HAMBREGHT)
Adam I, 237, 238, 239
Conrad (Conrat) I, 237, 239, 240
Johannes (Hans) I, 237, 238, 239
Viet(Fyt) I, 237, 238, 239
HAMBURGER
Michael I, 429
Nicolas II, 20
HAME
Erech Adam I, 194
HAMEL
Jacob I, 419
HAMER *see* HAMMER
HAMERICH (HAMRICKE, HAM-
RICK)
Amaryllis Eliza I, 55
Clara I, 55
Hans Jerg (John Yerke) I, 54, 56, 57
Margaretta I, 55
Paul I, 55
HAMERMANN
Christopher II, 93
HAMM (HAM)
Barbara II, 45, 53
Davit I, 410
Francisca II, 45
Hans Jerich (Hans Gerg) I, 35, 36, 37
J. J. II, 45
Jacob II, 45
Johann Daniel (John
Daniel) I, 373, 374, 376
Johann Jacob I, 521, 523
Mathias I, 748
Mʳ II, 23
Valentin I, 711
HAMMA
Ann Maria II, 162
Daniel II, 161
Godfrey II, 161
Margaret II, 162
HAMMACHER
Johann Adam (John
Adam) I, 279, 281, 282
Johann Huberich
(Hubrig) I, 279, 281, 282
HAMMAN (HAMAN)
A. M. II, 5

Balzasor (Balzer) I, 314, 315
Catharina II, 4
Friederich (Fred^k) I, 565, 566, 568
Friedrich Wilhelm I, 466
Jacob I, 402
Jeorg I, 427
Johann David I, 372
Joh. Jacob II, 41
Johann Philip II, 4
John II, 137
Madlena II, 4
Maria M. II, 4
Peter I, 400, 741
Philip I, 741; II, 41
Thomas (Thos.) I, 31, 33, 34
HAMMAND
Erasmus I, 273
HAMMEL (HERMEL, HAMMELL)
Johan Henrich (Joan
Hendrick) I, 39, 41, 42
Phillippus Martin I, 422
HAMMEN (HAMEN, HAMMER)
Balthasar I, 752
John Valentin I, 335, 336, 338
HAMMER (HAMER)
A. Sophia II, 105
Andreas I, 540, 542, 544
B. II, 122
Catherina I, 131
Christina II, 204
Friederich (Fred^k) I, 373, 374, 375
Georg Friederich I, 687
Godfrey II, 204
Godlieb II, 204
Hans Melcher I, 412
Hans Michael I, 130, 133, 134
Henry I, 396
Jacob I, 373, 375, 376
Johann Frantz I, 366, 368
Johann Görg I, 421
Johan Petter I, 479
Johannes I, 72, 76, 471
Melcher I, 463
Reinhart (Rinhart,
Rinehart) I, 27, 29, 30
Susan I, 28
Wilhelm I, 452
HAMMERLE
Hans Jacob I, 411
HAMMERS
Anna Sophia II, 23
HAMMERSMITH (HAMER-
SHMIT)
Philip I, 532, 533, 535
HAMMERSTEIN (HAMMER-
STEYN)
Jacob I, 614, 616, 618
HAMMES
Abramina II, 101

C. Margreta II, 101
C. W. II, 101
Carlina II, 101
Gottlieb II, 101
Joh. Peter II, 101
Johannes II, 101
Lowisa II, 101
Wilhelm II, 101
Wilhelmina II, 101
HAMMETER (HAMERTER)
Johann Sebastian I, 539, 541, 543
HAMMON (read HAMMAN)
Elizabeth II, 72
John II, 72
HAMPE
Andreas I, 749
HAMPF
Jacob II, 138
HAMSCHER
Adam I, 521, 523
Anton (Anthony) I, 387, 388, 389
Johann II, 188
Johannes I, 745
HANAUER
Johannes I, 78
HANBACH
Ulrich I, 304
HANCH
Casper II, 118
HANCHE
Catharina II, 205
Heinrich II, 205
Maria Catharina II, 205
Wilhelm II, 205
HANCKER
Isack I, 289
HANCKSTEIN *see* HANSTEIN
HAND (HANDT, HANT)
Hans Georg I, 454, 502
Hennrich I, 339
Johann Nicolaus (Johan
Nich^s) I, 601, 602, 604
Peter I, 456
HANDEL
Feit II, 192
Johan Adam I, 757
HANDSCHUH (HANDSHY, HAN-
SHEW)
And^w II, 106
Cath^e II, 106
Eliz^a II, 106
Fred^k II, 106, 185
Guilm^e II, 106
Henry I, 392; II, 185
Jacob I, 433
Jean Adam II, 106
Marg^t II, 106
Mrs. II, 176

HANDWERCK (HANDWERK,
   HANTWERK, HANDWERCH)
  Hans Georg   I, 159, 161
  Henry (Henrick) I, 266, 270, 273
  Johannes   I, 421
  Nicholas (Niclaus) I, 266, 270, 273
HANDWERCKER
  Peter   I, 346
HANE
  Johann Petter
   (Peter)   I, 173, 174, 175
HANEBACH
  H.   I, 718
HANENGRATH (HANNEGRAFT)
  Jacob   I, 653, 655
HÄNER
  Johannes   I, 684
  (*See also* HANNER)
HANES
  Conrad   I, 478
  Daniel   I, 659
HANEY (HÄNEY)
  Andrew   II, 26
  Philip   I, 421
HANF (HOUGH)
  Hans Georg   I, 532, 534, 535
HANFLING
  John   II, 116
HANFSTEIN
  Matheis   I, 471
HANG
  Hans Martin   I, 484
  Paulus   I, 330
HANGE
  August   II, 198
  Lewis   II, 198
  Sophia   II, 198
HANIO
  Henry Eggell   II, 73
HANMÜLLER
  Christoph   I, 704
  Johann Jacob   I, 704
HANN *see* HAHN
HANNE
  John Philip   I, 402
HANNER (HÄNNER)
  Johan Jost   I, 684
  Johannes   I, 720
  Widow   II, 147
HANNEWALT (HANOVELT)
  Andreas   I, 222, 223, 225
HANNIBALL
  Wilhelm   II, 61
HANNIG (HANICH)
  Hannes   I, 419
  Jacob   II, 135
HANNOLD
  Kraft   I, 471

HANRATH (HANRADE)
  Henry (Hendricus) I, 287, 288, 289
HANS
  Barbary   I, 40
  George   I, 40
  Hanis   I, 40
  Jacob   I, 66, 69, 70
  Johann Henrich   I, 346
  Johann Michael   I, 762
  Johann Peter (Peter) I, 283, 284, 286
  Michiel   I, 40
  Wendel   I, 457
HANSBERGER
  Peter   I, 16
HÄNSEL (HENTZEL)
  Johann Lorentz
   (Lorince)   I, 256, 259, 261
HANSELMANN
  Hans Jerg   I, 394
HANSEN (HANSSON)
  Johan Heinrich Eberhard I, 510, 511
HANSEY
  Hans   I, 275
  Hans Jacob   I, 275
HANSHEW *see* HANDSCHUH
HANSI
  Jacob   I, 276
HANSINGER
  Mary   II, 187
HÄNSLER
  Henrich Jacob   I, 485
HANSTEIN (HANCKSTEIN,
   HANSTON)
  Johann Ludwich
   (Lodwick)   I, 294, 295, 296
HAPFFER
  Christhian   I, 467
HAPP (HAP)
  Philip   I, 373, 374, 375
HAPPEL (HAPPELL)
  Ferdinand   II, 196
  Hennrich   I, 701
  Ludwig   I, 88, 90, 91
HAPPES
  Georg   I, 473
HARBACH
  Jacob   I, 695
  Johannes Peter   I, 741
HARBERMIER
  Carl   II, 49
HARBYN
  Margaret   I, 102
  Pieter   I, 102
HARCKER
  Daniel   II, 195
HÄRDEL
  Johann Adam   I, 503

HARDERT (HARDER)
Johann Martin (Johan
  Mart^n)   I, 601, 602, 604
HARDT (HARD, HART)
Frid.   I, 716
HARDTEN (HARTEN)
Elizabeth   I, 320
Johann Georg   I, 320, 321, 322
HARDTMANN   (HARDTMAN,
  HARDMAN,   HARTMAN,
  HARTMANN)
Abraham   II, 26
Adam (Atam)   I, 384, 386, 492
Anna Maria   II, 52
Ant.   II, 45
Balzar   II, 55
Barbara   II, 52
Casper   I, 31, 33, 34
Catharine   II, 51, 157
Christian   I, 407
Christ^n Ludwig   I, 517
Christoph   I, 480, 716
Conrad   I, 324, 325, 327, 574, 575
Eberhart   I, 522, 525
Elisabetha   I, 74; II, 52
Eliza   II, 157
Frantz   I, 403
Frantz Thomas   I, 692
Friederich
  (Frederick)   I, 60, 64, 65, 522, 525
Georg   I, 500, 753; II, 196
George David   II, 118
Geo. Henry   I, 692
George Jacob   I, 372
Hans Adam   I, 702
Hans George
  (Jurg)   I, 225, 228, 230, 492
Hendrick (Henrich) I, 8, 10, 355, 408
Henr. Albert   II, 205
Henry   II, 11
Herman   I, 170
Jacob   II, 157
Johann   I, 746
Johann Adam   I, 205, 207, 208, 753
Jno George   I, 756; II, 157
Johan
  Heinrich   I, 414, 465, 743
          II, 139
Johann Jacob   I, 739; II, 46
Johann Matthias   I, 723
Johann Michel   I, 472
Johan Nickel   I, 723
Johan Philip
  (H. Philip)   I, 661, 663, 664
Johann Theodor   I, 714
Johann Wilhelm   I, 723
Johanes   I, 418, 432, 503
          512, 627, 630, 634, 755
          II, 68

John   I, 753; II, 52
Joseph   I, 348, 349, 351
Katharine   I, 72
Laurence   I, 71, 75, 77
Margaretha   II, 52, 56
Maria   I, 72
Maria E.   II, 157
Matje   II, 68
Matthes   I, 418
Michel   I, 372, 460
Nicolas   II, 52
Paulus   I, 414, 522, 525
Peter   I, 423, 444, 696; II, 157
Philipp Leonhart   I, 715
Philips   I, 744
Rossina   I, 61
Salomon (Solomon) I, 559, 561, 562
Tobias   I, 732
Ulrich (Ulrick)   I, 283, 284, 285
Wilhelm   I, 522, 525
HARDTSTANG (HORSTONG)
Johann Wilhelm
  (Joh. Wm.)   I, 564, 566, 567
HARF (HARFF)
Johann Balthaser   I, 642, 644
Johannes   I, 642, 644
HARG
Michael   II, 121
HARGEL
Maria   II, 119
Peter   II, 119
HARGESHEIMER
Andony   I, 403
Michel   I, 403
HARHAUSEN (HARHOUSE)
Johan Peter (John
  Peter)   I, 280, 281, 282
HARIG
Catharina Salome   II, 59
Louisa Margaretha   II, 59
Maria Elizabeth   II, 59
Nichol   II, 44
Philip   II, 59
Sabilla   II, 59
HARK
August Ludwick   II, 76
Louis   II, 76
HARKMAN
Jurigh   I, 88
HARKNAT
Anna Cristinia   II, 36
Carol   II, 37
Charlote   II, 36
Christina   II, 36
Cristian   II, 37
Johana   II, 36
HARLAS (HALASS, HARLASH)
Philip   I, 199, 201, 203

HARLOFF
Joachim I, 505
HARM
Johan II, 126
HARMA
J. F. II, 162
HARMAN (HARMEN)
Barbary II, 161
Daniel II, 194
Elizabeth II, 194
Georg I, 62
Jacob I, 660; II, 194
Maria II, 194
Nichl. I, 237
—— II, 161
HARMANY
Willm I, 282
HARMS
Arnd II, 206
H. Hinrich II, 182
John Nich^s I, 749
Margaretha II, 182
Wilhelm II, 114
HARMSDORFF (HERMSDORFF)
Joan Carl (Jo.
Charl.) I, 620, 622, 625
HARNEWALD (HANNAVALL,
HANNEWALD)
A^n Elisabeth I, 156
Johans (Johannes) I, 154, 158, 160
HARNISCH (HARNISS)
Anna I, 80
Heinerich I, 434
Samuel I, 79, 82, 83
HARPE
Daniel II, 184
HARPELL
Frederick II, 126
Ludwig II, 126
HARPERS
Mich^l II, 18
HARPS
John II, 77
HARPST
John II, 17
M^rs II, 17
HÄRPSTER (HÖRPSTER, HARPS)
Michael I, 310, 311, 313
HARR
Conradt (Conrad) I, 586, 587, 588
HARRIGES
Johan Joseph II, 133
HARRIS
Peter I, 699
HARSCH
Martin I, 479
HARSEL
Jacob II, 125

HARSHOFF
Fedrick II, 82
HÄRSHY (HARSHE, HERSHEE)
Christian I, 341, 342, 343
HART (HARD, HARDT)
Geo. Mich^l I, 694
Georg Wielelm
(Wilhelm) I, 581, 583, 584
Hans I, 347
Johann Jacob (John
Jacob) I, 387, 388, 389
Johan Philips I, 336, 337, 339
Lorentz I, 336, 337, 339
Johan Wilhelm I, 408
Justinia II, 36
Michel I, 498
Nichol I, 725
HARTE (HARTEY)
Charles II, 197
Henry II, 197
Martin II, 121
HARTEL
Frederick II, 144
Philip W^m II, 203
HARTENSTEIN (HARDASTEIN)
Lutwig (Ludwig,
Lodwick) I, 276, 277, 278
HARTER
Andres I, 331
HARTH (HARTT)
Johann Vallenthin I, 367, 369
Nicklas I, 330
Sebastian I, 738
HÄRTHER
Georg I, 404
HARTIG
Carl Heinrich I, 755
HARTING
Peter I, 412
HARTKOPFF
Joachim I, 748
HARTLIEB
Hans Gorg I, 414
HARTLINE
Peter II, 126
HARTMAN *see* HARDTMANN
HARTMANS
Jean (John) I, 552, 553, 555
HARTMEYER
Math^s I, 706
HARTNAT
Justine II, 36
HARTNOCK
John II, 182
HARTOST
Johannes II, 3
HARTRANFT (HERTTERANFFT)
Abraham I, 138
Barbara I, 138

Georg   I, 138
Johann Georg   I, 496
Maria   I, 138
Melchior   I, 138
Rosina   I, 138
Tobias   I, 137, 140, 142
HARTSOE
Baltser (Poltzer)   I, 175, 177, 178
HARTSTEIN
Wm   II, 154
HARTTAFFEL (HARTAFFEL)
Robert   I, 360, 361
HARTTING
Christian   I, 444
HARTUNG (HARTONG)
Johan Conrath
  (Conrade)   I, 256, 258, 261
Johann Phillipp   I, 704
Jörg Philb   I, 414
Paulus   I, 479
HARTWEG (HARTWAY)
Georg (Jurg)   I, 629, 632, 636
Vitus (Tituas)   I, 275, 276
HARTWICH
Henrig   I, 412
HARTZEL
Henry   I, 449
Johann Georg   II, 149
Johann Nicolas   II, 149
HARTZOG *see* HERTZOG
HARWICK (HARWICK, ERWIG)
Anna Maria   I, 72
Jacob   I, 73
Johannes   I, 71, 75, 77
Nicollus   I, 73
Paulus   I, 73
HARZ
Jacob   I, 471
HARZER
Jacob   I, 734
HARZFELD
Adolph   II, 171
HAS *see* HAAS
HASE
Johann Friedrich   I, 198, 200, 202
Johan Marten   I, 408
HASEL
Magdalina   II, 162
HASELBACH
Joh. George   II, 41
HASELE (HESLY)
Elias (Alies)   I, 107, 111, 112
Erasmus   I, 109
Maria Crete   I, 109
Susanah   I, 108
HASENCLEVER
Francis Caspar   I, 745
Helena   II, 101

HASENPLUCK
Hendk   II, 5
HASHAR (HASHARE, HASSHAR)
Hendrich   I, 546, 548, 550
HASLER (HASSLER)
Hans Jacob   I, 392
Jacob   I, 392
John   I, 709
Michael   I, 378, 380, 381, 417
Sepastian   I, 392
HASLY
Jacob   II, 146
Johannes   II, 146
HASMAN
Jacob   I, 93
HASMERT
Johann Martin   II, 5
HASPELHORN
Ludewig   I, 413
HASS *see* HAAS
HASSEL
Georg Jacob   II, 118
Wilh.   II, 118
HASSELBACH
Catharina   II, 113
Jacob   II, 113
Johan   II, 112
Margart   II, 113
Nicklas   I, 390
HASSELBÄCHER   (HASSEL-
   BERGER)
Johann Gorg (John
   Yerrick)   I, 582, 583, 584
Philipes   I, 462
HASSELBERGER
John   I, 722
Fillip (Pillip, Phillip) I, 266, 269, 272
HASSELER
Christian   I, 396
Hans Jurge   II, 134
Mr.   II, 174
Mrs.   II, 174
HASSELWANGER   (HASELWON-
   GER, HASSELWANGER)
Johannes (Joanes) I, 258, 260, 263
HASSER (HOSHER, HOSSER)
Abram (Abraham)   I, 301, 302, 303
Christian   I, 301, 302, 303
HASSINGER
Johann Jacob   I, 382
Johannes   I, 382
Philip   II, 119
HATHER
Henry   I, 635
HATSLIN
Jacob Benia   I, 81
HATT *see* HEYT
HATTELSMAN
Turkis   II, 118

HATTSEBIELLER
  Staffen   I, 19
HATZ (HATTS, HATS)
  Georg (Jung Geo.,
    Jurigh)   I, 246, 247, 248
  Peter   I, 676
HAUBENSACK
  Daniel   I, 442
HAUBER
  Jacob   I, 471
  Johann Michael   I, 523, 525
  Ullrich   I, 398
HAUBERGER
  Johannes   II, 28
  Maria Marg^a   II, 28
  Peter   II, 28
HAUBERT (HAUBERD)
  Johan Fillib   I, 456
  Peter   I, 456, 685
HAUCH (HAUKH, HAUK, HOUG)
  Barbara   I, 123
  Jacob   I, 266, 269, 272, 394, 463
  Johann Petter   I, 266, 269, 272
  Michael (Mich^l)   I, 596, 598, 599
  Rudolff (Rudulph) I, 162, 164, 166
HAUCK (HAUK, HOAK)
  Adam   I, 539, 541, 543
  Andreas   I, 724
  Bärnhardt   I, 416
  Blasius   I, 416
  C. G.   I, 732
  Christian   I, 122, 125, 126
  Hans Jerg (Jerick) I, 122, 125, 126
  Hans Michel   I, 417
  Hans Petter   I, 194, 196, 197
  Jacob   I, 93, 94, 95, 327, 329, 697
  Jerick   I, 124
  Johann Dietrich   I, 693
  Johann Filib   I, 752
  Johann Heinrich   I, 437
  Joh. Lieb   I, 717
  Johan Petter   I, 686
  Johann Valatin   I, 686
  Johannes
    (Johanes) I, 656, 657, 659, 697, 740
  Lorentz   I, 436
  Martin   I, 740
  Michael   I, 492
  Rudolf   I, 359
HAUDENSCHILD   (HAUDEN-
    SCHILT)
  Hans Michel   I, 423
HAUDT (HAÜDT)
  Johan Georg   I, 689
  Johann Georg   I, 488
HAUEL
  John   I, 735
HAUENSTEIN
  Conrad   I, 704

Geo. Jacob   I, 704
Henrich   I, 432
HAUER   (HAUHER,   HAWER,
    HOWER)
  Anthony   I, 464
  Bernhart   I, 464
  Christoff (Christoph)   I, 464
  Hans Michel (Hans
    Michll)   I, 194, 195, 197
  Jacob   I, 194, 195, 197, 464
  Jerg   I, 491
  Johans Michel   I, 194, 195, 197
  Johans Nicklaus
    (Nicolaus)   I, 620, 622, 625
  Michael   I, 498
HAUF (HAFF, HAUFF, HAUFE)
  Georg   I, 556, 557, 558
  Johann Henrich
    (Heinrich)   I, 621, 623, 625
  Johan Petter (Johan
    Peter)   I, 667, 669, 671
  Michael   I, 399
  ————   II, 141
HAUG (HAUGH, HACK, HOGH)
  Eliza   II, 150
  Ferdinand   II, 150
  Georg Friederich   I, 427
  Georg Heinrich   I, 722
  Gorg (Jurigen)   I, 176, 177, 178
  Johan Wilhelm (Joh.
    Wilh.)   I, 352, 354
  Marti   I, 498
  Ruprecht   I, 422
HAUGENDOBLER
  Nicolaus   I, 445
HAUGMAYER
  Lewis F.   II, 153
HAUHER see HAUER
HAUN (HOUNE)
  Heinrich (Henrich) I, 621, 623, 625
  Johann Christian   I, 621, 623, 625
  Johann Peter (Peter) I, 621, 623, 625
HAUNSCHILNT (HAVENSHILDT)
  Johan Daniel (Jn°
    Died^k)   I, 589, 590, 591
HAUPT (HAUBT)
  Johan Henrich   I, 722
  Johann Nicholas (Johann
    Nickel)   I, 283, 284, 286
                     614, 616, 618
  Johann Philipp   I, 443
  Johannes   I, 614, 616, 618
  Michell   I, 399
  Philipps   I, 420
  Samuel   I, 614, 616, 618
  Sebastian (Bastian) I, 205, 206, 208
HAUPTMANN
  Heinrich   I, 365

HAUS (HAUSS, HAWES, HOUSE)
Christian I, 707
Georg I, 440
Johanes I, 451
Johann Michael I, 464
Philip I, 451
HAUSAMEN (HAUSAM, HOU-SAM)
Anthon I, 686
Johannes I, 104, 105
Wilhelm I, 483
HAUSBURG
J. G. II, 155
HAUSEN
Johann Ludwig Joseph II, 93
Peter II, 77
HAUSENBECK (HOUSELBECK)
John I, 227; II, 104
Peter II, 126
HAUSER (HÄUSER, HAUSSER, HAWSER, HOUSER)
Aberham (Abram) I, 393, 471
Carl I, 677, 678, 680
Christoff I, 410
Christopher II, 14
Conrad I, 436
Felix I, 248, 249, 250, 435
Friederich II, 171
Geo. Fred. II, 202
Hans Jacob I, 273, 274, 331
333, 334, 484
Hans Jerg I, 459, 506
Heinrich (Hendrich) I, 252, 253, 254
Jacob I, 209, 211, 398, 449, 480, 688
Jerg Marten I, 420
Johan Balthaser I, 696
Johann Conradt I, 424
Johann Henrich (John Hend.) I, 592, 593, 594
Johann Lönhardt (Leonard) I, 646, 648
Johann Martin I, 425
Johannes I, 348, 349, 351
410, 435, 449, 490
Joseph I, 409
Killian I, 474
Maria I, 189
Martin I, 13
Mathias (Maddes) I, 66, 69, 70, 470
Peter I, 293
Rudi I, 435
Uhllerik I, 485
HAUSHALTER (HAUSHOLDER, HOUSHALTER, HOUSE-HOLDER)
Christian I, 693
Georg Simon I, 704
Hans Adam (Johan Adam) I, 265, 268, 272

Henry I, 474
Lorentz I, 500
HAUSIHL (HOUSIE, HOUSIER)
Friederich I, 637, 639, 640
John Friederich (Jno. Frederick) I, 637, 639, 640
HAUSKNECHT (HOUSNECK)
Aaron II, 104
Ernst (Aaron) I, 227, 229, 231
Jacob I, 725
Johan Christian I, 317, 318, 319
HAUSLEITHER
Johann Martin I, 507
Christoph I, 649, 650
Georg Jacob I, 760
J. Geo. Fred. II, 105
Philipp Conrad I, 727
HAUSLER (HEYSLER, HYSLER)
Johannes I, 649
HAUSMANN (HOUSMAN)
David I, 488
Eva I, 103
Conrad (Conrade) I, 256, 259, 261
Georg Jacob (Jacob) I, 620, 622, 625
Jacob I, 335, 337, 338
Johann Christoffel I, 362
Joh. Conrad I, 546, 548, 550
Johann Jacob I, 711
Johann Philip I, 422
Johannes I, 426
Joseph I, 426
Maria I, 103
Paulus I, 426
HAUST
Herman I, 415
HAUSWIRTH (HAUSSWIRTH, HOSTWERT)
Abraham. I, 246, 247, 248
Christian I, 667, 669, 671
Jacob I, 474
HAUTER
Nichol II, 44
HAUTZ (HAUDS, HAUTS, HOUTS)
Lorentz (Lawrence, Lorents) I, 226, 228, 230
Philip I, 31, 33, 34
Philip Peter I, 721
HAUTZEL
Christ Jan I, 700
HAUTZENBIELER
Hans Jorg I, 445
HAUX (HONKS)
Theodorus Frid. I, 526, 528, 529
HAVERLENE
Hance Felter I, 85
HAVERVASS (HAVERWASS, HOW-ERVASS)
Anna Barba I, 55

Henrich   I, 55, 56, 57
Margaretta   I, 55
Margaretta, Junr.   I, 55
Philippena   I, 55
HAWER *see* HAUER
HAWES
   Peter   I, 293
HAWFFMAN
   Hans   I, 427
HAWKINS
   Edwd.   II, 32
HAWLY
   Durst   I, 391
   Hans   I, 391
HAY
   Conrad   I, 440
HAYD *see* HEYD
HAYDE (IDE)
   Johann Georg
      (Georg)   I, 199, 201, 203
HAYENANTS
   Roeloff   II, 29
HAYER *see* HEYER
HAYL
   Georg Schütterlin, von I, 411
HAYLER
   Lebart   II, 71
HAYN
   John Nicklas   I, 413
HAYNS
   Johan Marti   I, 394
HAYSER
   Johannes   I, 711
   (*See also* HEYSER)
HAYSH
   Hans   I, 451
HAYWIGH
   Pieter   I, 104, 105
HEAF
   Henerich   II, 36
HEANZ
   Anthony   I, 431
HEARTMAN (read HARTMAN)
   Jacob   II, 147
HEATHERLEY
   Henry   II, 160
HEATTEMAN
   Peter   I, 491
HEBB *see* HEPP
HEBBLER
   Jacob   I, 366
HEBEISEN (HEBEYSEN)
   Johannes   I, 501
   Martin   I, 731
   Philip   I, 366
HEBEL
   Johannes   I, 436
HEBENER
   Gotlop   II, 182

HEBERLING (HABLING)
   Johannes   I, 84, 86, 87
HEBIGT (read HABICHT)
   Johan Christoph   I, 746
HEBLING (HEBLIN)
   Nicholas   I, 539, 541, 543
HEBRECHT (HEBREIGHT, EBER-
      ICK)
   Henry (Henderick) I, 331, 332, 334
HEBTING
   Christian   I, 498
HECHELMAN
   Michael   I, 399
HECHLER (HEIGHLER, EYGLER,
      EYLER)
   Georg (Jerg)   I, 621, 623, 625
   H. George (Hans
      Jerr^k)   I, 595, 597, 599
   Martin   I, 596, 597, 599, 600
   Nicholas   I, 308
HECHT (HEGT, HEGHT)
   Anthoni (Anthony) I, 614, 617, 619
   Jacob   I, 410
   Johann   II, 50
   Joh. Carl   II, 108
   Peter   I, 614, 616, 618
HECK (HACKH, HAKH, HICK)
   Andreas
      (Andros)   I, 496, 559, 561, 563
   Anna Catherine   I, 128
   Christoffel   I, 378, 379, 381
   Daniel   I, 522, 524
   Elizabeth   I, 40
   Eva Maria   I, 127
   Hans Barthel   I, 532, 533, 535
   Jacob   I, 441
   Johann Daniel (Daniel) I, 652, 654
   Johan Jacob   I, 128
   Johan Jost (Yoost) I, 127, 129, 130
                       I, 601, 602, 603
   Lodwick (Ludwig)   I, 40, 41, 42
   Mary   I, 40
HECKART (ECKKART)
   Johannes (Hans) I, 378, 379, 381
HECKEL
   Friedrich   I, 707
HECKEMAN
   Hildebrand   I, 330
HECKENDORN   (HECKENDON,
      HEGENDORN)
   Daniel (Daniell,
      Dannill)   I, 162, 164, 166
   Hans, Senior   I, 162, 164, 166
   Hans, Junior   I, 162, 164, 166
   Jacob   I, 426
HECKENLEIB (HICKENLUBER)
   Andreas (And^w)   I, 637, 639, 640

HECKER (HÄKER, HEKER,
　ECKER)
　Andereas I, 408
　Anna Maria II, 174
　Catharina II, 173
　Conrad II, 174
　Elisabeth II, 173
　Henry (Henri) I, 364; II, 169
　Jacob II, 173
　Johann Egidius I, 467
　Johan Jacob I, 341, 342, 343
HECKERT (HECKER)
　Frans (Frantz) I, 154, 157, 160
　Mar Margreth I, 156
HECKMAN (HECKMANN, HICK-
MAN)
　Albrecht I, 513, 514, 516
　Andreas I, 323, 325, 326
　Hans Adam I, 481
　Jn° Adam I, 695
　Johann Adam I, 395
　Johann Nickelaus I, 723
　Johann Peter I, 382
　Melcher I, 425
　Nicklas I, 481
　Sebastian I, 709
HECKSHER
　L. A. II, 116
HECTOR
　Friderick I, 739
HEDERIGH (HADRACH)
　Niclaus I, 323, 325, 326
HEDINGA
　Johannes I, 716
HEDINGER (HEPINGER)
　Martin (Mardin) I, 513, 514, 516
HEDLY
　Leonhart I, 485
HEDRICH (read HEYDRICH)
　Johann Henrich I, 687
HEEGY
　Jacob I, 470
HEEN (HAN)
　Jacob I, 199, 201, 203
HEER
　Jacob I, 738
　Willm I, 7
HEERBURGER (HEARBURGER)
　Johannes I, 96, 97, 98
HEERDT
　Andreas II, 20
HEFA
　Johan I, 690
HEFFEIN
　Johan Friedrich I, 731
HEFFNER (HEFFENER)
　Johan I, 503
　Johann Dierk I, 356
　Johann Georg I, 408

　Lorentz I, 503
　Nickel (Nicholas) I, 233, 235
HEFFTERICH
　Andreas I, 521, 523
HEFRAN
　Anna Maria I, 241
HEFT (HEFFT, HOOFT)
　Anna Elizabeth I, 209
　Anna Maria I, 209
　Catherina I, 209
　George (Georg) I, 179, 180, 183
　Hans Windal I, 209, 211
　Philip I, 178, 180, 182
HEGELLE (HAGLE)
　Adam I, 73
　Anna I, 74
　Apolonia I, 73
　Elizabeth I, 74
　Tobias I, 71, 75, 77
HEGEN
　Johan Henrich I, 465
HEGENBEIN
　Andrew II, 91
HEGENDORN (HACKADORE, read
HECKENDORN)
　Martte (Martin) I, 175, 176, 177
HEGENSTILL
　Johannis I, 692
HEGENSWEILLER (HEGENZ-
WEILLER, HECETSWILDER)
　Hans Ullrich I, 332, 333, 334
HEGER (HAGER)
　Andreas I, 727
　Christoph I, 692
　Frantz Honorius I, 745
　Hermanus I, 397
　Johann Ludwig I, 188, 191, 193
　Jonathan I, 156, 159, 161
　Vallentin I, 359
HEGI
　Hans Jergi (Georg) I, 96, 98
　Jacob I, 96
　John I, 96
　Nicklas I, 440
HEGLER
　Barbara I, 144
HEGNER (HAGENER)
　Peter (Petter) I, 290, 291
HEHL
　Friedrich I, 760
HEHLHOFFER
　Fridrich I, 729
HEHMANN
　Henericus II, 91
　Maria Magdalena II, 91
　Nathaniel II, 91
　Samuel II, 91
HEHR
　Rudolph I, 684

HEIBERGER
  Ullrech   I, 740
HEIBLY
  Jacob   I, 418
HEICHEL
  Leonhart   I, 438
HEIDELBACH
  Henrich   I, 487
  (*See also* HEYDELBACH)
HEIDER
  Jacob   I, 29
  Johan Jacob   I, 441
HEIDLE (HEYDLE)
  Hans Jerg (Hans
    Jurg)   I, 605, 607, 608
HEIDLINGER
  Elisabetha   II, 52
HEIDRICH   (HEIDERICH,
    HEITERICH, HYDERICK)
  Abraham   I, 256, 259, 261
  Christopher   I, 701
  John Nicklas (Nich.) I, 256, 259, 261
HEIDSCHUH (HEYTSHOE)
  Jacob   I, 18, 19
HEIDT (HEYDT, HEART)
  Johann Michell   I, 539, 541, 543
HEIER (HIER)
  Hans Casper   I, 740
  Leonhart (Lenhart) I, 175, 176, 177
  Lorentz   I, 726
HEIFER
  Johannes   I, 697
HEIGENING
  D.   II, 141
HEIGES (HEIGIS)
  Jerg   I, 446
  Johan Gerg (George) I, 649, 650
HEIL (HAYL, HEILL, HEYL)
  Geo.   II, 118
  Georg Adam (Georg) I, 97, 98, 99
  Hans Jerg (Hans Gerg) I, 97, 98, 99
  Johannes   I, 499
  John Christian   I, 509, 510, 511
  Jorg   I, 499
HEILAND
  Georg P.   II, 108
HEILBRUN
  Johann Bapt^a   II, 30
  Petrus   II, 30
HEILBRUNER
  Georg Fridrich   I, 431
  Johan Fridrich   I, 431
HEILER (HEMLER)
  Adam   I, 71, 75, 77
                                         II, 36
HEILIGAS
  Frederick   I, 7
HEILIGER
  Johann Filip (John Philip) I, 287, 289

HEILMAN (HEILLMAN, HEILL-
    MANN)
  Christian   I, 559, 560, 562
  Hieronimus Nicolas   II, 103
  Jacob   I, 436
  Johannes   I, 88, 90, 92, 409
  Marthin   I, 88, 90, 92
HEIM
  Godlieb   II, 156
  Hans Jorg   I, 476
  Johann Friderich   I, 179, 181, 183
  John   II, 156
  Lorentz (Lorance) I, 198, 200, 202
  Michael   I, 488
  Willem   I, 31, 33
HEIMBACH (HEMBACH)
  Adam   I, 628, 631, 635
  Johannes   I, 759
  Mattes   I, 340
  Peter   I, 413
HEIMBERGER
  Georg Thomas   I, 457
HEIME (HIME)
  Bernit   II, 195
  Jacob   I, 226, 228, 230
  Paulus (Paul)   I, 225, 228, 230
HEIMER
  Johann Friderich   I, 330
HEIMLICH
  And^w   I, 747
HEIN
  Anna Catharina   II, 45
  Bernhart   II, 45
  Casper   II, 43
  Christoffel   I, 310, 312, 313
  Hans   I, 10;   II, 43
  Jacob Herman   II, 45
  Johann   II, 134
  Johannes   I, 465
  John Ernst   I, 505
  Lewis   II, 43
  Margaret   II, 43
  Margaretha Philippina   II, 45
  M^r   II, 23
  Paul   I, 10, 12
  Peter   I, 256, 259, 261
                                         II, 43
  Simon (Johan Simon) I, 310, 311, 313
HEINBERGER
  Jacob   I, 466
HEINDEL
  Johan Adam   I, 360, 361
HEINDORF
  Catharine   II, 198
  Henri   II, 198
  Jost   II, 198
  Maria   II, 198
HEINE
  Georg   II, 205

—   II, 58
HEINECKE
  Johann Adam   I, 493
  Johann Michael   I, 493
HEINEMANN
  Jonas   II, 107
HEINEN (HINNA)
  Gasper   I, 331, 333, 334
  Hans Henrich   I, 331, 333, 334
HEINER (HINER)
  Ev. C.   II, 5
  Matthias (Andreas) I, 620, 622, 624
  Philipp (Philip)   I, 227, 229, 231
                                II, 104
HEINICKEL (HEYKILL)
  Christoph   I, 532, 533, 535
HEINIG
  Hans   I, 391
HEININGER (HEINIGER, HEM-
    MINGER)
  Georg Friederich   I, 532, 533, 535
  Anna Barbara   I, 49
  Jacob   I, 426
  Johan Christoffel   I, 167, 168
  Johann Jacob   I, 712
  Johannes   I, 426
  Ullerich   I, 425
HEINISCH (HEINISH)
  Henry (Hendrick)   I, 652, 653
  Philip   I, 347
HEINLE
  Michel   I, 431
HEINLEIN
  Matthias   I, 645, 647
HEINLEN (HEINLIN)
  Davit   I, 409
  Matthes   I, 409
HEINLER (HEMBLER, HITNER)
  Andreas   I, 71, 75, 77
  Barbara   I, 73
HEINMETZ
  William   II, 198
HEINOLDT (HEINNOLDT, HAIN-
    HOLL)
  Johann Friederich I, 195, 196, 197
HEINRICH (HENRICH, HENE-
    RICH, HENDRICH, HENDRICK,
    HENDRICKS)
  Adam   I, 416
  Baltaser   I, 715
  Burckhart   I, 454
  Christian (Chris.)   I, 236, 238
                            239, 328
  Christoph (Christofer) I, 32, 33, 34
  Diana   I, 190
  Jacob   I, 102, 105, 106, 113,
                       114, 115, 765
                                II, 184
  Jerg (Gerich)   I, 43, 45, 46

Johann Görg   I, 465
Johan Nickel   I, 461
Johannes   I, 461, 465
Jurgen   I, 40, 42
Ludwig   I, 475
Martin   I, 459
Mattheis   I, 331
Michael   I, 446
Wendel (Vindle)   I, 189, 192, 194
HEINS
  Adam   I, 501
  Arnold   II, 60
  Friedrich   I, 471
  John   I, 707
HEINSMAN   (HEINSEMANN,
    HEYNSMAN, HINNSMAN)
  Anthony   I, 144
  Catherine   I, 144
  Jerg (Jurgen)   I, 143, 145, 146
  Johan Heinrich   I, 143, 145, 146
                       564, 565, 567
  Johanes (Joanis) I, 143, 145, 146
  Joseph   I, 144
  Maria Magdalena   I, 144
  Otto Heinr.   II, 205
  Susanna   I, 144
HEINTZ (HEINZ, HEYNZ, HENTZ)
  Abraham   I, 205, 207, 208
HEINTZ (HENTZ, HEYNZ)
  Andreas   I, 328, 704
  Christianus   I, 422
  Emanuel   I, 495
  Frederick   II, 137
  Jacob   I, 688, 730, 751
  Joh. Christoph (John
    Christopher)   I, 656, 657, 658
  Johann Friederich   I, 716,
  Johann Hennrich
    (John Henrich)   I, 577, 578, 580
  Johann Jacob   I, 496
  Johann Ludwig   I, 38, 39
  Johann Marx
    (Marks)   I, 204, 206, 208
  Johan Philip (Philip) I, 204, 206, 208
  Johann Wilhelm   I, 460
  Johannes   I, 362, 465
  Jost   I, 685
  Martzolf   I, 730
  Wendel   I, 716
HEINTZE (HEINZE)
  Peter   I, 435
  —   II, 58
HEINTZELMAN   (HEYSELMAN)
  Hans Jerg   I, 586, 587, 588
HEINTZLER
  Casper   II, 125
HEIONKER
  John Jacob   II, 196

HEIPEL
  Casper II, 159
  Christina II, 159
  —— II, 159
HEIR
  Burchard I, 743
  John Valentine II, 47
HEIRD
  Philip II, 125
HEISCH
  Hans Jerg I, 486
  Salomon I, 460
HEISEL (HEUSEL, HEYSEL)
  George
    (Jurg, Georg) I, 605, 606, 607
  Jacob I, 383, 385
HEISER (HEISSER, HEYSER)
  Adam I, 231, 232, 233
  Conrad I, 655, 657, 658
  Henrich I, 717
  Joh. Jacob I, 714
  Johann Adam I, 464
  Johannes I, 655, 657, 658
  (*See also* HEYSER)
HEISLER (HEYSLER, HEISSLER)
  Johan Kuns I, 397
  Magaret I, 10
  Peter I, 383, 385
HEISS (HAIS, HEIS, HESS)
  Barbara I, 189
  Catrina I, 189
  Dorothea I, 189
  Hans Jerg (Hans
    Georg) I, 188, 191, 193
  Hans Jorg (Hans Georg,
    Jun.) I, 188, 191, 193
  Jn° Chris (Johann
    Christof) I, 661, 662, 663
  Johann Dieterich I, 696
  Johan Heinrich
    (Henrich) I, 188, 191, 193
  Matthias I, 431
  Nickel (Michael) I, 293, 294, 296
  Reichart I, 421
  Wendel I, 696
HEIST
  Bartholome I, 451
  Johann Adam I, 468
  Johann Georg I, 468, 469
  Johann Henrich I, 494
  Johann Peter I, 395
  Johan Philip I, 395, 437
  Nickel I, 395
  Wilhelm I, 734
HEISTER (HEYSTER)
  Andreas I, 582, 583, 584
  Nicolaus (Nicolas) I, 642, 644
  Peter I, 441

HEIT (HEID, HIET)
  Andrea I, 180, 182, 184
  Jacob I, 464
  Johanes (Johannes) I, 147, 150, 151
  Martin I, 698
HEITGRESS
  Henry II, 117
HEITZ
  Fried II, 41
HEITZMANN
  Hans Gerg I, 498
HEITZNOR
  John II, 55
HEKENTURM
  Martin I, 468
HELBERY
  Christian I, 304
HELD (HELDT, HELT)
  Carolina II, 158
  Conrad II, 158
  Felix Hy II, 158
  Georg Diedrich
    (Diterich) I, 180, 181, 184
  Gorg Fridrich I, 693
  Hantz Jacob I, 410
  Johann Andreas I, 459
  Johann Henrich
    (Henry) I, 569, 570, 572
  Johan Leonhard I, 475
  Johannes Peter I, 564, 566, 567
  John P. II, 158
  Joseph I, 483
  Ludewig I, 410
  Nicol II, 113
  Willhelm I, 401
HELDER (HELTER)
  Johann Jacob (Jacob) I, 628, 631, 634
HELDI (HALEDU, HEUERLEY)
  Hans Adam I, 266, 269, 272
HELDMANN (ELTMAN)
  Johannes I, 666, 668, 670
HELFER
  Christophel I, 103
  Jacob I, 712
  Maria I, 103
HELFERT (HELFORD, HELFURT)
  John I, 60, 64, 65
  Margrath I, 62
  Maria I, 61
HELFFENSTEIN (HELFENSTINE,
  HELFENSTYN)
  Nicklas (Michael,
    Nichel) I, 257, 260, 262
  Peter I, 659
HELFRIGH
  Francis Joseph II, 12
  Maria Teresia II, 12
HELHOFF (KELGHOFER)
  Christian (Christ.) I, 629, 633, 636

HELICK
  Phillipp I, 734
HELL (HÖHL)
  Hans Michel I, 429
  Jacob I, 721
  Johanes I, 410
  John Jacob I, 721
  Pfillib I, 721
HELLEBRAN
  Connard I, 99
HELLENTHAL
  Johann Andoni I, 339
HELLER (HALLER, HILER)
  Bernhart (Barnt) I, 526, 528, 530
  Christoph
    (Stoffel) I, 198, 200, 202, 459
  Friderich Samuel I, 723
  Friedrich II, 184
  Georg Heinrich
    (Henrich) I, 672, 673, 674
  Heinrich I, 459
  Jacob (Jacobus) I, 495, 660
  Johann Ludwig I, 585, 587, 588
  Johannes Michal I, 407
  Killian I, 755
  Ludwig Wilhelm
    (Ludwig Wm) I, 605, 607, 608
  Peter II, 101
  Rudolph I, 18, 19
  Simon I, 198, 200, 202
  Zacharias I, 323, 325, 326
HELLERICH (HELRICH, HELL-
  RICH, HELLEBRICH)
  Christoff I, 615, 617, 619
  Jacob I, 615, 617, 619
HELLERMANN (HELLERMAN)
  Elias I, 646, 648
HELLING
  H. Nickolas I, 435
HELLIQUEST
  Casper II, 73
HELLMAN
  Bastian I, 481
  Jacob I, 718
  Johann George II, 149
  Peter I, 481
HELM
  Anna Maria II, 4
  Cath. El. II, 4
  Eva Elis II, 4
  J. Frantz I, 720
  Jacob I, 687
  Johann Friederich I, 709
  Johan Jacob
    (J. Jacob) I, 480, 661, 662, 663, 664
  Salm Christn II, 3
  Wilhelm I, 676
HELMBOLD
  George Christophel I, 734

HELMKE
  —— II, 51
HELMOLD
  Georg Ludwig I, 757
HELMSTÄTTER (HELMSTÄTLER,
  HELMSTETER)
  Johann Adam I, 677, 679, 680
HELMSTEAD
  Nicolaus II, 117
HELPES (HELPFISH, HULPES)
  Joh. Jacob
    (J. Jacob) I, 563, 565, 567
HELS
  Joh. II, 68
HELSENBECK *see* HESSELBACH
HELSER
  Andrew II, 195
HELTZEL (HELZEL, HELTSELL)
  Christoffel I, 135
  Eva Catherine I, 135
  George Frederich I, 429
  Hans Jacob I, 135
  Hans Michal I, 429
  Joseph II, 61
  Maria Dorothea I, 135
  Nicholas (Nicolas) I, 135, 136
HELVETI
  Mr. II, 149
HELWIG (HELLWIG)
  Adam I, 397
  Carlen I, 390
  Friederich (Fredk) I, 307, 308, 309
    II, 121
  Gideon II, 99
  Johann Jacob I, 433
HEM
  Johan Jacob II, 28
  Johannes I, 717
HEMB
  Han Jacob (Nichs) I, 615, 617, 619
HEMBELMAN
  Vallentin I, 402
HEMBELMANN
  Gerg I, 715
HEMBD (HEMBT)
  Cassmir I, 721
  Johann Nickel I, 487
HEMELEYK
  —— II, 123
HEMELRIGHT (read HIMMEL-
  REICH)
  Johan Nicol I, 303
HEMERLIN
  August I, 684
HEMMELE (HEMMLE)
  Christian I, 415
  Frantz I, 415
HEMMERICHS
  Wilhelm II, 101

HEMMERSBACH (HENNERS)
Johann Georg
(Joh. Yerrick)   I, 581, 582, 584
HEMMING
Rudolf   I, 434
HEMMLER
Christian   I, 410
HEMPEL (HEMBEL)
Gottlob   I, 740
Johan Christoffel   I, 448
HEMPELE (HIMBERLER)
Anthony   I, 185, 186, 187
HEMPER
Hendrich   II, 104
HEMRIER
Johann   I, 727
HENCHE
Johannes   I, 394
(*See also* HENDCHE)
HENCHELL
Jost Henrich   II, 121
HENCKE
Anne Marie   II, 86
Catherine   II, 86
Chrétien   II, 86
Chrétienne   II, 86
Elisabeth   II, 86
Georg Heinrich
Valentin   I, 195, 196, 197
George   II, 86
George Daniel   II, 86
Jean   II, 86
Jean George   II, 86
Jean Josse   II, 86
John Ludwig   II, 160
Louise   II, 86
Madelon   II, 86
Maria Catherine   II, 86
Marie Elisabeth   II, 86
HENCKEL (HENKEL, HINKELL,
HINCKELE)
Casper   I, 540, 542, 544
II, 78
Christoph   I, 750
Georg Henry (Hans
Jurig)   I, 265, 271
Harman   II, 78
Heinrich   I, 677, 678, 680
Johannes   I, 560, 561, 563
John Davit   I, 508
Michael   I, 412
Philip   I, 407
HENCKELS (HANKLER)
Pietter (Peter)   I, 153, 154
HENDCHE
Simon   I, 394
HENDRICK
Johanes (John)   I, 455, 569, 570, 572
Martin   I, 304

Mathias   I, 694
William   II, 77
HENDRYTROK (KENEYDROK)
Peter (John Peter)   I, 672, 673, 674
HENEAVIS
Jacop   II, 36
HENEY
Patrick   I, 143
HENGEL
Georg Friederich   I, 490
Simon   I, 683
HENGER
Lorentz   I, 416
HENGERER (HINGERER,
HINGER)
Danel (Daniel)   I, 637, 638, 640
Johann Melchior   I, 287, 288, 289
HENGSD
Michel   I, 416
HENK (HENKE)
Ann Elisabeth   II, 84
Ann Gertrout   II, 84
Ann Mary   II, 84
George Lud.   II, 84
Godfrey   I, 18, 20
John George   II, 84
John Henry   II, 84
John Jost   II, 84
Mary Elisabeth   II, 84
Philip   II, 84
HENKEN
Michael   II, 56
HENKENIUS
Johann Henrich   I, 488
Peter Bernhard   I, 488
HENLE (HENLY)
Johan Sigmund
(Sigmont)   I, 217, 218, 220
HENLEIN (HENLEN)
Jerich Casper   I, 304
Johannes   I, 415
Michael   I, 323, 325, 326
HENLY
Henry   I, 492
HENN (HEN)
Friederich   II, 46
Jacob   II, 101
Joachim   I, 402
Johan Jacob   I, 352, 354
Johann Peder   I, 352, 354
Johannes   I, 496
Johannes Burckhardt   I, 737
Matheis   I, 353, 354
Paul Carl   II, 133
———   II, 80
HENNE (HENE)
Jac. Fred.   II, 119
Moritz   I, 478

HENNEBERGER (HENEBERGER)
Hans Melchior
  (Hans Meligor) I, 185, 186, 187
  John I, 59, 63, 64
  Valentine I, 184, 185, 186
HENNEL (HAINEL)
  Jacob I, 127, 129, 130
HENNEMAN
  Johann Philipp I, 417
HENNER
  Johannes Andonyus I, 494
  John II, 19
HENNIG
  Johannes Nickel I, 427
  Johannes Peter I, 427
HENNIGER (HEMMINGER)
  Anna Maria I, 49
  Conrat I, 51
  Hans I, 497
  Hans Michel I, 48, 52, 53
HENNING (HENING)
  A. Eliz. II, 105
  Agnes II, 150
  Balzar I, 454
  Fred^k II, 178
  Hieronimus I, 344, 345
  J. H. II, 107
  Johann Henrich
    (Henry) I, 536, 537, 538
    II, 21
  Matthais Wilhelm I, 501
  Matthew II, 150
  Hendric, van II, 108
HENNINGER (HENINGER)
  Andrew Henry II, 12
  Frederic II, 155
  Gottlieb II, 170
  Johann Gorg I, 686
HENNISCH
  Andres II, 52
HENNY (HENNEY, HANEY)
  Fritrich I, 427
  Johann Georg
    (Johan George) I, 560, 562, 563
HENRICH
  Adam I, 7; II, 46
  Christian I, 328, 505
  Hans Paul I, 492
  Hans Peter I, 457
  Johann I, 707
  Johann Adolf
    (Adolf) I, 179, 181, 183
  Johann Friederich
    (John Frederik) I, 296, 298
    299, 695
  Johann Georg I, 418, 465
  Johannes I, 317, 318, 319, 465

HENRICHEL, (HENRIGEL,
  HENRIGL)
  Baltzer I, 732
  Christian Ludwig I, 732
  Johan Jacob I, 732
HENRICHS (HENRICH, HENRIG)
  Johannes I, 626, 630, 633
  Peter I, 627, 630, 633
HENRICI
  Hyronimus I, 739
HENRICK
  Conrad I, 716
  Hanis I, 116
HENRICKS (HENDRICKS)
  Anth^y II, 72
  Bernard II, 188
  John II, 186
HENRISTO
  Carl II, 125
HENRITZY
  Christoffel I, 715
HENRY (HENDRICK)
  Christoph I, 509
  Gerhart (Gerard,
    Gerit) I, 212, 214, 215
  Joh. Abraham (Jan
    Abram) I, 212, 214, 215
  Jost I, 467
  —— II, 187
HENSCHLER
  Rudholf I, 477
HENSE (HENCE, HENSSE)
  Burchart (Burget) I, 666, 668, 670
  Johan Hentery I, 754
HENSEL (HENSELL, HENSSEL)
  Bernerd (Barnet) I, 18, 19
  Johann Jost (Johan
    Jost) I, 286, 287, 288
  Petter (Peter) I, 301, 302, 303
HENSINGER (HENTZINGER)
  Johannes (Hans) I, 526, 528, 530
HENSLY (HUSLEY, HOUSLEY)
  Jochaim (Joachim) I, 252, 253, 255
HENSTEAD
  Henry Frantz II, 48
HENTZ *see* HEINTZ
HENZY
  Christoffel I, 397
HEPP (HEBB, HEP)
  Bernhardt I, 420
  Hs. Stephan I, 420
  Jacob II, 89
  Jerg I, 420
  Johannes I, 733
  Paulus I, 532, 533, 535
HEPPE
  Johan Dietrich I, 733

HEPPEL (HIPLE)
Johann Nicolaus
(John Nick)   I, 287, 288, 289
John Henry   I, 412
Melchor   I, 412
Wilhelm   II, 112
HEPPENER (KEPNER)
Johannes   I, 559, 561, 563
HEPPENHEIMER
Andreas   I, 359
HEPPLER
Jacob   II, 190
HEQUEDAS
Jabryel   I, 760
HERB (HERP, HIRB)
Johan Michael   I, 310, 312, 313
Mrs.   II, 176
Peter   I, 407
HERBEL (HARPEL, HORPELL)
Jeremias (Jeremiah) I, 621, 623, 625
Johann Peter   I, 292, 293
Johans (Johannes)   I, 35, 36
HERBER
Johan Adam   I, 347
Johann Nickel   I, 427
Johannes   I, 330
Peter   I, 330
HERBERGER (HERRBERRGER)
John Philip   I, 268
Petter   I, 701
HERBERTH
Johannes   I, 355
HERBERTS   (HORBERTS, HER-
BERTZ)
Hendrich (Henrick)   I, 48, 52, 53
HERBIG
Jacob   I, 397
HERBOLD (HERBOLT)
Anna Barbell   I, 242
Anth^y   II, 135
Hans   I, 241
Hans Adam   I, 241, 443
Jacob   I, 241
Leonhardt (Lenh^d)   I, 265, 268, 272
Nicolas   I, 241
Powell   I, 241
HERBST
Johann   II, 68
Johann David   I, 454
Johann Georg (Hans
Geo.)   I, 649, 650
Johann Henrich   I, 750
Johan Nickol   I, 690
Johannes   II, 68
Johannes David   II, 68
Maria Magdalina   II, 68
HERBSTER
Christoph   I, 760
Davit   I, 430

Mardin   I, 393
HERBY
Lazarus   I, 697
HERDE (HERDTE)
Casper   I, 257, 260, 262
Josua Caspar   I, 359
Rudolph   I, 359
HERDEL
Johann Henrich   I, 712
Phillip   I, 501
HERDER
Johanna M.   II, 102
(*See also* HERREDER)
HERE
Benjamin   II, 61
HERER
Johan   I, 17
John Adam   II, 121
HERFORD
Christian   I, 358
HERGES
Bernard   II, 133
HERGET (HERGEDT)
Friedrich   I, 372
Johan Henrich   I, 417
Petter   I, 438
HERGLE (LERGA)
Conradt (Conrad)   I, 217, 219, 220
HERGUTH
Johannes   I, 522, 524
HERHOLT
G. Henry   I, 504
HERIGER
Jeremias   I, 459
Joanes Yirk   I, 15
HERING (HERRING, HÖRING)
Conrad   I, 720
Friederich   I, 475
Jacob (Joh. Jacob)   I, 564, 565, 567
Johann Friederich   I, 472
Johan Henrich   I, 455
Johann Jorg
Christoffel   I, 576, 578, 579
John Godfried
(Godfrid)   I, 592, 593, 595
Ludewig (Lodowich) I, 621, 624, 626
Philip Wendel   I, 455
Regina Dorothea   II, 42
HERK
Albertus   I, 676
HERLE (HERLY)
Jacob Hendrich   I, 545, 547, 549
HERLEIN
Anna Margarethe   II, 172
Catharine   II, 172
George Phillip   II, 172
Johan Phillip   II, 172
Johannes   I, 551, 553, 554
Melgior   II, 172

Michael II, 172
HERLIEMAN (HEXLEMAN)
Sebastian I, 310, 312, 313
HERLINGER
Charlote II, 169
Friederika II, 169
Johan Frederich II, 169
HERM
Gerg David I, 741
HERMAN (HERMANN, HERR-
MANN)
Anna II, 152
Anna B. II, 152
Anna M. II, 152
Barbara I, 128
Catherina I, 128
Catherine (Barbara) I, 128
Christian I, 482, 501
Conradt (Conrad) I, 665, 668, 670
David I, 470
Dewald I, 128
Elizabeth II, 45
Engel Mada II, 105
Frantz I, 712
Friedrich I, 628, 632, 635
Gottlob (Goodloop) I, 282, 489
H. George II, 32
Hance (Peter) I, 128
Hans Adam I, 406
Hans Jerg I, 730
Hans Ludwick I, 724
Heinrich (Henry) I, 440, 706
J. Henry I, 495
J. Nicolas I, 358
Jacob I, 21, 22, 127
128, 129, 130, 372
471, 628, 632
635, 645, 647
II, 154
Jerg (Gerg) I, 367, 369
Jno Wm I, 712
Johan (Johann) I, 692, 763
Johan Filib I, 367, 368
Johan Georg I, 340, 440
Johan Heinrich I, 725
Johann Leonhart I, 72, 76, 78
Johann Peter
(Peter) I, 667, 669, 671
Johan Thiel I, 488
Johannes (John) I, 57, 58, 340, 366
367, 368, 378, 379
381, 488, 491, 621
623, 626, 637, 639, 640
II, 152
John G. II, 152
John George I, 712
Joseph Lorentz I, 758
Lucius II, 153
Ludwig I, 421

Margaretta II, 152
Maria B. II, 152
Martin I, 610, 611, 613
II, 154
Michel (Michal,
Johan Mich[1]) I, 605, 606, 607
Nickel I, 442
Peter I, 304
Samuel I, 481
Sebastian II, 123
Simon I, 488
Wendel (Wentell) I, 450; II, 152
HERMANI
Johan Jacob II, 78
HERMANUS
Johannes I, 401
HERMON see HERMAN
HERNER (HERNNER)
Daniel I, 332, 333, 334
Henrich I, 226, 228, 230
Joseph I, 269
HERNIKER
Martin II, 29
HERNS
Michael II, 135
HEROLDT (HERALDE, HERALD,
HEROLT)
Georg Christoph I, 343, 345
Johan Earah I, 344
Peter I, 660
HEROULD
Jeorg Michael I, 395
HERPEL (HERBEL)
Johan Philip (Phillip) I, 383, 385
HERPLY
Christoph I, 418
HERR
Benjmn II, 12
Hans Jacob I, 394
Johann Martin I, 425
Johannes I, 167, 168
718, 727
Ludwig Johann
(Ernst) I, 104, 105
Peter I, 459
Philip I, 409
Silvester (Silvestor) I, 383, 385
Willem I, 9
—— II, 196
HERRBERGER
Petter I, 701
HERREDER (read HERDER)
Andreas I, 412
Johannes I, 412
HERRGERÖDER
Johannes I, 114, 115
HERRIGER
Hans Erick I, 12
Johann Lenhard I, 495

HERRMANN *see* HERMAN
HERSCH *see* HIRSCH
HERSCHBERGER (HERSPERGER)
Adam I, 719
Casber I, 396
Henrich I, 723
Jacob I, 396
Johannes (Hannes) I, 609, 611, 612
HERSCHELMANN
Joh. Gottfr. II, 140
HERSCHFENGER
Johan Lorentz I, 372
HERSCHLER
Johann Georg I, 751
HERSHEE *see* HÄRSHY
HERSMAN
Uldrich I, 286
HERSTEIN
Barbara II, 54
Johannes I, 753; II, 54
HERSTER
Andereas I, 411
HERT *see* HIRTH
HERTEL (HERTELL)
Geo. II, 9
Hans Gorg I, 408
Josebh I, 698
Jorg Michael I, 708
Julius Jacob II, 9
Lenhart I, 481
Marg^t II, 9
Michael II, 9
Nich^s II, 9
Peter I, 734
Sarah II, 9
HERTER (HERTHER)
Andreas I, 445
Johannes I, 425
Martin I, 470
Nicholas I, 545, 547, 549
— I, 719
HERTLEIN (HERDLEIN, HERDLIN,
HERDYLN, HARTLEIN)
Hans Michael I, 173, 174
Michael I, 173, 174
HERTZ
Abraham II, 108
Andreas I, 423
Elias II, 127
Johannes (Johann) I, 628, 631, 634
Michael I, 727
Susman II, 160
HERTZBERGER (HERSBERGE)
Anna I, 190
Barbara I, 190
Christian I, 188, 192, 193
Joseph II, 149
Peter I, 190

HERTZEL (HERTZELL, HART-
SELL, HIRTZELL, HURTZELL)
Barbr. I, 79
Catarrina I, 79
Christen I, 80
Conrad (Conradt) I, 248, 249, 250
Hans I, 448
Hans Jerg I, 7, 10
Hans Leonhart
(Lenard) I, 79, 82, 83
Henrich (Hendrich) I, 79, 82, 83
Jacob I, 248, 249, 250
Jacob, Junr (Jacob) I, 248, 249, 250
Jerg (Yorg, Geo.) I, 32, 33, 34
Ludwig (Loudwick) I, 32, 33, 34
Matteas (Mathias,
Matthias) I, 258, 260, 263
Paulus (Pallus) I, 78, 81, 82
Ulrick (Urigg) I, 8, 79
HERTZER
Hans Jost I, 448
HERTZLER
Jacob I, 396
Johannes I, 448
HERTZOG (HERZOG, HARTZOG)
Andreas I, 432
Connradt I, 444
Dem. Salamarna II, 45
Friech. Wilhelm II, 79
Friederich
(Frederick) I, 296, 298, 299
II, 45
Gorg (George) I, 407
II, 45
Hans Nickel I, 465
Hans Pett. I, 492
J. G. II, 45
Johan Wilhelm I, 440
John Nickl I, 683
Levi II, 93
Philip I, 212, 214, 215
HERWAGEN
Henrich I, 702
HERWARD
A^n Catharina I, 157
HERWIG
Hans Michael I, 696
HERZELS
Hans Jer.
HESS (HES, HEESS, HESSE, HIS)
Abraham I, 293, 294, 295
Aneria I, 242
A^n Elisabeth I, 157
Augusdin I, 750
Balsatzar I, 468
Christian I, 442
Christopher I, 699
Daniel I, 456
Dhommes (Dommes) I, 31, 33, 34

Erasmus I, 436
Friederich Wilhelm I, 741
Hans Uhlerik I, 473
Henrich (Hendrick) I, 31, 33, 34
Henry I, 497
Isaac I, 411
Jacob I, 258, 745
Jeremias
(Jerrimias) I, 31, 32, 33
Jnᵒ Tobias I, 749
Johann Daniel I, 755
Johann Friedrich I, 531, 533, 535
Johan Georg
(Johan Gerg) I, 240, 242, 243
Johan Jacob I, 484
Johann Martin I, 688
Johann Ludwig I, 411
Johann Nicolaus I, 411
Johann Peter
(Petter) I, 15, 401, 716
Johannes I, 155, 159, 161
419, 725, 753
Johannes Conrad
(Johann Counrad) I, 559, 561, 563
John Fred. II, 201
Matthias I, 452
Nicklaus I, 412
Philip II, 61
Theobald I, 727
HESSE
Arnold II, 127
Aug. Christ. II, 140
Carl II, 140
Catharina II, 127
Christ. Jacob II, 140
Christoph II, 127
Eberhard II, 127
Jacob I, 348, 350, 351
Johannes I, 753
II, 127
Kasemir II, 121
Maria Margaretha II, 126
Vallentin (Valentine) I, 221, 222, 224
HESSELBACH (HESSELBACK,
HESSELBECK)
Anna Elsa II, 29
Johan Henrich II, 29
Johannes II, 29
Johannes Diterich
(John) I, 227, 229, 231
HESSELING (HERSLING)
Harmanus (Hermanes) I, 274, 276
HESSER
Johann Conrad I, 498
Johann Friderich I, 88, 90, 92
HESSHUYZEN
F. II, 25
HESSLER (HESLER)
Has. Heinrich I, 738

Michael I, 494
Petter I, 701
HESTER
Jacob I, 551, 552, 554
HESTERMAN (HUTERMAN)
Peter I, 232, 233
HESTHSTHIN
Catharina II, 92
Dorir. II, 92
Frona II, 92
Thomas II, 91
Wilhelm II, 92
HESWILER
Hance Yarah I, 344
HETLER
Hans Jerg I, 442
HETRICH (HETRECH, HETRICK,
HETRIG, HETTERICH, HET-
ERIG, HETTRICH, HETERISH)
Anna Margret I, 767
Carol (Coblin) I, 113, 114
115, 765
Catrina I, 767
Elizabeth I, 766
Eva Elisabetha II, 52
George I, 360, 362
Jacob (George) I, 546, 547, 549, 572
Jnᵒ Chaˢ I, 700
Johan Henrick I, 767
Johann Jacob I, 413
Johannes I, 217, 218, 220
John Adam II, 52
John Onst I, 767
Nicolaus II, 52
Philip
(Philipus) I, 582, 583, 584
II, 125
William I, 767
HETSCH
Vallendien I, 729
HETTERICH *see* HETRICH
HETTERLING
Susanna I, 156
Wilhelm I, 155, 158, 160
HETTICH
Johann Henrich I, 421
HETTINGER
Adam I, 408, 472
Bernhard II, 170
Catharine II, 170
Christina Eva II, 170
Heinrich II, 170
Lorenz II, 170
Mathias II, 170
HETTMAN
Heinrich II, 183
HETTMANSPERGER
Andereas I, 734

HETZ
  Philippus   I, 466
HETZEL
  George Frederich   I, 429
  Hans Michal   I, 429
  Henrich   I, 474
  Jacob   I, 466, 704
  Johanes   I, 499
  (*See also* HÖTZEL)
HETZER (HÖTZER, HETTSER)
  Hans Michael   I, 169, 170, 172
  Johan Dan.   I, 234
  Johan Filip
    (Philip)   I, 106, 111, 112
HETZLER
  Johan Balthasar   I, 394
HEU (HAY, HEY)
  Albrecht   I, 470
  Carle   I, 470
  Hans   I, 463
  Johan   I, 463
  Johan Carl (Johan
    Carle)   I, 266, 269, 272
  Linnert   I, 392
  Peter   I, 323, 325, 326
HEUBERGER (HEYBERGER)
  Andreas   I, 347
  Jacob   II, 125
HEUCHE
  Carl   II, 134
HEUCHER (HIGGHER)
  Christofel   I, 324, 325, 326
HEUDEKEL
  Hans Jerg   I, 491
HEUER
  Kunrad   I, 714
HEÜGOLD
  Johann Martin   I, 460
HEUN (HAINE, read HEYN)
  Johann Bastian
    (Bastian)   I, 569, 571, 572
  Johann Peter (Johannes
    Peter)   I, 560, 561, 563
HEUNMEYR
  Thomas   I, 328
HEUSCHKEL (HEUSCHKELL,
  HEUSCHKEHL)
  Beniamin   I, 441
  Johan Christoph   I, 441
  Johan Michael   I, 441
HEUSER
  Johann Christ   I, 700
HEUSGE
  Gerlach   II, 160
HEUSLER
  Christian   I, 446
  John George   II, 23
HEUSS
  Georg Caspar   I, 404

HEVERT
  John   I, 601
HEXAMER
  Charlotta   II, 29
HEYDE
  Johann Henrich   I, 708
HEYDECKER (SHYDENKER, SHY-
  DEAKER)
  David   I, 227
  Hans   I, 227
  Johan Georg   I, 320, 321, 322
  Ulrich (Uhllerich) I, 227, 229, 231
HEYDEL
  Johanes   I, 463
HEYDELBACH
  Jerg Wilhelm   I, 359
HEYDENREYD
  Johannes   I, 391
HEYDERICH (HYDENREICH)
  Anderas   I, 707
  Anna   I, 210
  Hannah   I, 210
  Johan Hendrick   I, 209, 211
HEYDERING
  Casper   I, 18
HEYDERSH
  Henry   I, 423
HEYDORN
  Christian   II, 204
  Dederic   II, 155
HEYDRICH (HEIDRICH, HEY-
  DERICH, HEYDTRICH, HEI-
  TRICH, HEDRICK, HEYDRIG)
  Abraham   I, 138
  Balthasar
    (Baldthasar)   I, 137, 140, 142
  Carol   I, 360, 361
  Caspar   I, 137, 140, 142, 360, 361
  Christoff
    (Christopher)   I, 138, 213, 215
  Eva   I, 138
  George (Georg)   I, 137, 140, 142
    360, 361
  Henrich Nickel   I, 715
  Johan Gerg (Jan
    Jurich)   I, 212, 214, 215
  John Adam   I, 327, 329
  Petter   I, 213, 215
  Rosina   I, 138
  (*See also* HEDRICH)
HEYDRICKS
  Kasper   I, 19
HEYDT (HEYD, HAYD, HEYT)
  Abraham   I, 212, 214, 216
  Conrad   I, 212, 214, 216
  Heinrich   I, 330
  Johan Christian   I, 501
  Johann Jacob   I, 480
  Johannes   I, 453

Philipp I, 486
Pieter (Peter) Junr. I, 212, 214, 216
HEYER (HEIER)
Andreas I, 726
Davit Henry I, 505
Friederick
(Fredrick) I, 582, 583, 584
George I, 234
Johan Friderich I, 341, 342, 343
Johan Georg
(Jurig) I, 256, 259, 261
Johann Peter I, 371
Lorentz I, 726
Michael I, 726
Vallandien I, 341, 342, 343
(*See also* HEIER)
HEYGIS
Johan Peter I, 459
Vallentin I, 446
HEYL (HEYLL, HEYEL, HOYLE)
Baltzer I, 421
Barbra I, 61
Christianus I, 758
Friedrich I, 477
George (Georg) I, 60, 64, 65, 430
Georg Thomas (Jurig
Thos) I, 265, 268, 272
Hans Thomas I, 265, 268, 272
Henrich (Henrick) I, 265, 268, 271
Jacob I, 497
Johan Adam I, 447
Johann Conrad I, 698
Johann Georg I, 698
Johann Henrich I, 496, 698
Johann Jacob I, 294, 295, 698
Johannes I, 290, 291, 444, 576, 578, 580
Jonas I, 390
Michael I, 705
Petter (Peiter) I, 212, 214, 215
Walter I, 715
HEYLER (KALLER)
Adam I, 348, 349, 351
Johannes I, 733
Michael I, 459
HEYLMANN (HEYLMAN, HAIL-
MAN, HEYLEMAN)
Antres (Andres,
Andreas) I, 155, 158, 160
Conrad I, 482
Hans Adam I, 209, 211
Johann Peter
(Petter) I, 59, 63, 65
Maria Elisabeth I, 157
Martin I, 697
HEYLY (HILIE, HAYLIE)
Frederik (Dedrich) I, 226, 229, 231
HEYMANN (HEYMAN, HIEMAN)
Coenraad II, 30

Geo. I, 698
Herman (Hemon) I, 283, 284, 286
Isaac I, 744
Johann Henrich I, 564, 566, 568
Johan Philipp (Joh.
Philip) I, 564, 565, 567
Wolfgang Nicolaus I, 683
HEYMERDINGEN
Johan II, 29
HEYN
Catharine Lise II, 181
Friederich I, 747
John E. II, 181
HEYNE
John Christopher I, 320, 321, 322
HEYNDEL
Christoph I, 411
HEYNEMANN (HEYNEMAN, HE-
NEMAN)
Johann Henrich I, 415
Johannes I, 536, 537, 538
HEYR (HOYR, HEIR)
Johannis (Johannes) I, 560, 561, 563
HEYROM
Dominicus I, 736
HEYS
Dan1 II, 15
Johan II, 15
HEYSER (HAYSER, HEISER,
HEISSER)
Carol (Carolo,
Carle) I, 266, 269, 272
Casper (Caspar) I, 180, 182, 184
Conrad I, 655, 657, 658
Henry I, 421
Johannes (Hannes) I, 655, 657, 658
John II, 13
J. I, 502
Peter I, 464
HEYSHE
Willhelm I, 400
HEYSINGER
Hans Fill I, 7
HEYSLER
Johannes I, 649
HEYSTER
Joh. Jorg I, 353, 354
HEYSY
Hans Georg I, 468
HEYTZMAN
J. Hans I, 411
HEZELAR
Elizth. I, 81
HEZHALD
Annah II, 76
HIBLER
Johann Georg I, 684
HIBSCHER
——— I, 480

HICKER
 Leonhard (Leondr)   I, 22, 23
HICKLER
 Joh. Geo.   II, 118
HICKMAN (HECKMAN, HIKMAN)
 Johan Adam (J.
  Adam)   I, 661, 663, 664
 Johan Peter   I, 677, 679, 680
 Peter   I, 482
HIDEBRUNER (read HILDEBRUN-
  NER)
 Wolf   I, 660
HIEBER
 Michael   I, 722
HIEBNER
 Georg Milcher   I, 523, 525
HIEMAN
 Braun   II, 135
 Jacob   I, 399
HIERBER
 Philips   I, 427
HIERMAN (read HERMAN)
 Gasper   II, 77
HIERONYMUS (HIRONIMUS,
  HYRONIMUS)
 Johann Balthaser   I, 367, 368
 Johann Frantz   I, 367, 368
 Peter   I, 156, 159, 161
HIERSFELD
 Catrina Marg.   II, 101
 Joh.   II, 101
HIESTAND (HIESTANT, HIE-
  STANDT, HISTANT)
 Henrich (Henry)   I, 610, 611, 613
 Jacob   I, 16, 17, 484
 Johan   I, 48, 52, 53
 Johannes   I, 16, 17, 732
HIG
 Diewald   I, 455
HIGHLER (HIGLER, HIGHLEY)
 Anthony (Anthon)   I, 184, 186, 187
HIGGINS
 William   II, 26
HIHGERT
 Frantz   I, 461
HIKENLEIBLY (HIKELYFER,
  HICKELYOER)
 Jacob   I, 637, 638, 640
HILD (HILT)
 Andreas   I, 756
 Georg (Gorg, Jurg)   I, 614, 616, 618
HILDENBRANDT (HILDEBRAND,
  HILLEBRANT, HILTEN-
  BRANDT HILTENBRANTT,
  HÜLDENBRAND)
 Adam   I, 440
 Andreas   I, 470
 Catrina   I, 139

Christoffel
 (Christ)   I, 287, 288, 289
 Conr.   I, 699
 Elizabeth   II, 170
 Friedrich   I, 617, 619
 Hannes   I, 332
 Hend. (Henry)   II, 24, 26
 J. M.   II, 24
 Jacob   I, 460
 Johan Jacob   I, 139
 Johannes   I, 453
 John Elizabet   I, 139
 Michael (Michel)   I, 237, 238, 239
 Peter   II, 170
 Wilhelm   I, 277, 278, 279
HILDESHEIMER
 Johan   I, 234
HILEM
 John   II, 60
HILGERD (HILGERT)
 Hendrick   I, 748
 Johann Jacob   I, 366, 368
HILKER
 Joseph   II, 181
HILL
 Casper   II, 47
 Jacob   I, 293, 294, 295
HILLEBRANT *see* HILDEBRAND
HILLEBRECHT (ELBRICHT, ELE-
  BRICHT)
 Casper   I, 536, 537, 538
HILLEGAS (HELLIGAS, HILLI-
  GAS)
 Adam   I, 60, 64, 65
 Georg Albrecht   I, 360, 362
 Joh. Friederich   I, 9
 Leopold   I, 35, 36
HILLER
 Jacob   I, 707
 Johannes   I, 526, 528, 530
 Joseph   I, 394
 Samuel   II, 120
HILLIGER (HELIGER)
 Peter   I, 622, 624, 626
HILLINGER
 Henry   I, 439
HILLSINHEISER (HELLSINHEI-
  SER, HELFEYSEN)
 Martin   I, 568, 570, 572
HILPOTT (HILLIPOTT, FILLI-
  POTT)
 Adam   I, 34, 35, 36
HILTENBEITTEL
 Johann Adam   I, 418
HILTENBRANDT   *see*   HILDE-
  BRAND
HILTNER
 Johann Wilhelm   I, 540, 543
 Michel   I, 538

HILTSHER
J. Friederich   I, 504
HILTZBECK (HILTZEBECK, HITS-
   BERG)
Jurg Fredk   I, 513, 514, 515
HILTZHEIMER (HILSHEIMER)
Jacob   I, 371
HIME *see* HEIME
HIMELRIGH (read HIMMEL-
   REICH)
Johannes   I, 422
HIMMELBERGER (HIMELBER-
   GER, HENNEBERGER)
Jerg   I, 409
Valentine
  (Vallentin)   I, 184, 186, 187
HIMMELMAN
Jacob   II, 160
HIMMELREICH   *see*   HEMEL-
   RIGHT
HIMMELSBACHER
Sebast.   II, 178
HIMROTH
J. E. D.   II, 49
Johann Georg (Johannes
  Jerick)   I, 559, 561, 563
Simon Ludwig   I, 479
HINAMAN (read HEINEMAN)
Elias   II, 195
HINCK (HINK)
Johann Matthias   I, 748
Wm. Fred.   II, 136
HINCKE (HENCKE)
Casper   I, 605, 606, 608
HINCKEL (HINKEL, HINKELL,
   HINCKLE, HENKEL)
Christian   I, 314
Conrad   I, 382
Hans Lenart   I, 404
Johan George (Johan
  Geo.)   I, 656, 657, 658
Johanes   I, 728
John Vallentin (Johan
  Felt)   I, 656, 657, 658
HINCKENAUER
Johann Petter   I, 422
HIND
Philip   I, 440
HINDENLANGS (HINELAND)
Wallendin
  (Valatine)   I, 592, 593, 594
HINDER (KINDER)
Hans Adam   I, 199, 201, 203
HINDERLE
Sebastian   I, 723
HINDERLEUTHNER (INDERLYD-
   NER)
Hans Casper   I, 237, 238, 240

HINDERSHIT
John Georg   I, 403
HINDERSTEIFF (HENDERSTIEF)
Caspar   I, 677, 678, 680
HINER *see* HEINER
HINFELDT
Andreas Huberti   II, 184
Barbara   II, 184
Elisabeth   II, 184
Heinrich   II, 184
Katharina   II, 184
Maria   II, 184
HINGER
Frederick   I, 636
Phillipina R.   II, 152
William   II, 152
HINKER
Christopher   I, 537
HINNBORGER
Adam   I, 396
HINNE (HINA)
Jacob   I, 252, 253, 255
HINRICH
Hans Michel   I, 456
HINRICHS
Daniel   I, 364
HINSCH
Johannes   I, 468
Philip   I, 365
HINSEY
J. Henry (Henery)   I, 536, 537, 538
HINTEN (HINTEIN, HINTIN)
A. Maria   II, 16
Johanna   II, 16
Susann   II, 16
HINZE
Christian   II, 128
HIPGE
Johann Jacob   I, 494
HIPNER
Clas   II, 50
HIPPE (HIEPPE, HIPP)
Christian   I, 517, 519, 520
Hans Georg   I, 486
HIPPEL
Fridrich   I, 704
HIPPENSTIEL
Ann Justina   II, 83
Ann Sophia   II, 83
Mary Elisabeth   II, 83
William   II, 83
HIPSCHER
Mattheis   I, 471
HIRNEISEN
Hans Jerg   I, 477
Michell   I, 477
HIRNI
Juhans   I, 494

HIRNSCHALL (HIRNSCHAEL)
Thielman (Tiel-
man) I, 162, 164, 166
HIRSCH (HIRSH, HERSCH,
HERSH)
Conrath
(Conrad) I, 280, 281, 282, 425
Frederick I, 502
Friedrich (Fred.) I, 472, 734
Jacob I, 546, 548, 550
Johan Leonhardt I, 708
Johannes I, 276
John Henry I, 713
Levy II, 75, 108
Martin I, 400
Philib (Philip) I, 257, 259, 262
Simon I, 276, 277, 278
HIRSCHBERG
Fredᵏ II, 181
HIRSCHBERGER
Christian I, 397
Dan¹ I, 730
HIRSCHFELD (HIRSCHFELDT)
David II, 205
Friederich I, 695
HIRSCHI (HERSI)
Christian I, 263, 267, 270
HIRSCHLAG
Johann I, 710
Johannes Michel I, 698
HIRSCHMANN (HIRSCHMAN)
Andreas I, 476
J. G. E. I, 710
Johann Adam I, 476
Johannes I, 735
Matheus I, 476
Ulrich I, 476
HIRSHNER (HERSCHERRN)
Johannes I, 296, 298, 299
HIRT (HIRTH, HERT, HERTH,
HIERD, HIERDT, HERTT,
HIRTT)
Anna Barbara I, 49
Anna Maria I, 49
Feligi (read Felix) I, 483
Georg I, 307, 308, 309
Hann Martha I, 210
Hennerich I, 329
Jacob I, 307, 308, 309, 480
Johann Adam I, 352, 353
Johann Christoph I, 531, 533, 535
Johann Martin I, 694
Johann Melchior
(Melchor) I, 677, 679, 680
Johannes (Hans) I, 237, 238, 239
Maria Elizabeth I, 49
Maria I, 209
Matteus (Mathias) I, 237, 238, 240
Nicklas I, 430

Steffan I, 469
Vaita I, 49
HIRTER (HIERT)
Johan Adam I, 352, 353
HIRTZEL
Melcher I, 328
HISLE (HIRSLE, HISSLE)
Susannah Catrina I, 28
Valentine Perhart I, 27, 30
HISLEY
Hans I, 15
HISSARD
Jean I, 731
HISSING (HISSONY)
Baltsatzor (Baltser) I, 264, 268, 271
HISTANT see HIESTANT
HISTER see HÜSTER
HITE (read HEID)
Anna Christina I, 131
Anna Elizabeth I, 132
Peter I, 130, 133, 134
HITMAN
Hans Georg I, 457
HITNER
Hans Adam I, 531
HITSCHNER (HITSNER)
Peter I, 531, 533, 535
HITSELLBECK
Johan II, 104
HITTEL
Nickellas I, 703
HITTER
Michell I, 660
HITZ (HITTS)
Heinrich I, 332, 333, 334
Johannes I, 692
Sebastian I, 730
HITZER
Samuell I, 471
HITZLER
Sip (Sep, for Joseph) I, 719
HIVE
Cath. II, 136
HOAK see HAUK
HOAR (HOARR, HOOR)
Jacob I, 545, 547, 549
HOBACH (HOBBACH, HOBACK)
Diettrich (Peter) I, 323, 324, 326
Michael I, 751
HOBBACHER (HOOBER)
Johann Michael (John
Michael I, 556, 557, 558
HÖBEL
Christoph Adam I, 328
HOBER
Jacob I, 659
Johannes I, 659
Peter I, 659

HOBERT (HOBER, HOBBERT)
Hendrich (Hend^k)   I, 273, 274
Valentin   II, 188, 191
HOBLER
Abraham   I, 234
Hans George   I, 397
Jacob   I, 459
HÖBLICH
Anthonius   I, 356
HÖBLING (HEBLING)
Peter   I, 540, 542, 544
HOCH (HOGH, HOG, HOOG, HOOGH, HOK)
Annabaert   I, 44
Christian (Christ^n) I, 621, 623, 625
Jacob   I, 18; II, 133
Johan Christ (Johan
Christian)   I, 609, 610, 612
Johann Georg   I, 476
Johan Lienhart   I, 716
Johann Petter   I, 717
Johannes   I, 621, 623, 625
Lind   I, 394
Lorentz   I, 418
Maria   I, 123
Thomas   I, 551, 553, 554
HOCHGENUG (HOOGINUNK)
Länhart (Länhartt,
Leonard)   I, 32, 33, 34
HOCHHEIMER
Georg Ludwig
(Lodowick)   I, 681, 682
HOCHLANDER (HOGLANDER, SLOTSUNDER)
Hans Michael   I, 198, 200, 202
HOCHMAN (HOGHMAN)
Jacob   I, 15
HOCHRYTTER (PREITER)
George (Geo.)   I, 665, 668, 670
HOCHSCHILD
A^n Elisabeth   I, 157
HÖCHST
Johann Joerg   I, 687
Johannes   I, 693
HOCHSTÄD
Dewald   I, 346
HOCHSTÄTTER (HOCHSTETTER, HOCHSTADLER, HOSTEDLER)
Christian   I, 407
Jacob   I, 246, 247, 248
Nicklaus   I, 407
HOCHSTEIN
Carolina   II, 53
HOCHSTENBACH
Johannes   I, 353, 354
HÖCHSTRASSER
Jacob   I, 715
Paulus   I, 523, 525

HOCHZIG
Hans George   I, 395
HOCK, (HÖCK, HAAK, HOOK, HOOCK)
Andreas   I, 199, 201, 203
               265, 268, 271
Ann Margaretta   II, 55
Casper   II, 56
Geo.   I, 716
Esra   I, 67
Hans George   I, 450
Henrich (Henerick,
Henry)   I, 614, 616, 619
              II, 56, 72
Johan Cunrad   I, 412
Johann Friederich   I, 412
Johan Jacob
(Jacob)   I, 378, 379, 381
Johann Philipps   I, 429
Johannes (John)   I, 23, 25, 26
Johannes   I, 468, 759
John Andrew   II, 56
John Jacob   I, 19
John Michael (Han
Michel)   I, 642, 644
Martin   I, 258, 260, 263
Mathias (Mattias) I, 258, 260, 263
Melchior   II, 55
Michael   II, 55
Phillip   II, 169
Stephen   I, 66
Valentine   II, 56
HÖCKER (HOCKER, HOKER)
Georg Wilhelm I, 257, 260, 262
Simon Henrick I, 304, 306, 307
Wilhelmus   I, 305
HÖCKERT (HOOKERT)
George Wilhelm I, 510, 511, 512
Johann   I, 711
HÖCKHLEN
Jacob Friderich   I, 738
HOCKNER
Hans Adam   I, 399
HODEL
Jacob   II, 61
HODELE (HODELY, HODOLY)
Nicklas (Nicholas) I, 243, 244, 245
HODENBACH
Ab^rm   II, 102
Biniamin   II, 102
Elisabeta   II, 102
Isack   II, 102
Jacob   II, 102
Teodor   II, 102
Wilhelmina   II, 102
HOEHN
Anna Catarina   II, 191
Catarina   II, 191
Christopf   II, 191

Johann (Joh.) II, 44, 191
Johann Christopf II, 191
Maria Elizabeth II, 191
HOENIG (HOENICH)
Coenir II, 119
Philip Abrahamm I, 689
HOERCHINGER
—— II, 162
HOERLE (HOORLE)
Anna I, 67
Curla I, 67
Eliz. B. II, 151
Hendrich I, 67
HOERLI
Jerich I, 67
Johannes I, 66, 67, 69, 70
Margaret I, 67
HOERNLE
Elizabeth II, 149
John II, 149
Joseph II, 149
Madaline II, 149
HOETTINGER (HODENAR)
Andereas
(Andreas) I, 373, 374, 376
HOETZ (HOESTZ)
Godfrey II, 162
John Geo. II, 162
HOFE
Conrad, im I, 441
HOFELEN
Johann Jacob I, 704
HOFF (HOAF, HOOF)
Anna Barbara I, 107
Christina I, 109
Conrad I, 470
France I, 456
Friderich Conrath I, 716
George II, 49
Hans Dider I, 691
Hans Jacob I, 106, 110, 112
Hans Michael I, 508
Johan Atam (John) I, 37, 38, 39
Johann Georg (Hans
Geo.) I, 656, 657, 658, 704
Johann Jacob I, 753
Johannes I, 453
Johannes Henrich I, 691
Johenrich I, 728
Lorentz (Laurence) I, 31, 33, 34
Magel I, 704
HOFF (HOOFF)
Henricus
(Henereches), de I, 323, 325, 326
HOFF (HOFE, HOOFF)
Benedicht, im I, 450
HOFF
Marty, im I, 433

HOFFACKER (HOFFECKER)
Filib I, 691
Hans I, 398
Jacob I, 740
Johann Michael I, 88, 90, 92
Michel I, 691
Ullry I, 398
HOFFBAUER (HOFFBAUR, HOFF-
BERGER)
Christian I, 596, 597, 599
HÖFFELBAUER (HEFELBOWER,
HEIFELBOWER)
Georg Balthas (Yerick
Baltus) I, 383, 385
Philipp (Philip) I, 383, 385
HÖFFER (HAEFFER, HAFER,
HÖFER, HOFFART, HOFFERT)
Anna Margaret I, 28
Anna Margaret, Junr. I, 28
Christian I, 28
Gideon I, 102, 105, 106
Hans I, 236, 238 239
Hermanus I, 335, 337, 339
Jacob II, 20
Johan Henrich I, 353, 354
Johannes I, 494
Johannes Wilhelm I, 576, 578, 580
Jorick I, 27, 29, 30
Kattarina Dorte I, 242
Matthias
(Mates) I, 335, 337, 338, 756
Rosina Dorte I, 242
Rudolph I, 459
HOFFERT (HOFFNER)
Lorentz I, 513, 514, 516
HOFFHEINTZ (HOFFEINTZ)
Anna Catherina II, 36
Anna Elizabeth II, 36
Anna Maria II, 36
George I, 464
Jacop II, 37
Johann Adam I, 688
Johann Danngel I, 688
Johan Jacob I, 465
Johannes Georg II, 36
HÖFFLER
Cunrad I, 470
HOFFMAN (HOFMAN, HOFFMAN,
HOFMANN, HOFFMANN)
Adam I, 199, 201, 203
II, 4
Andreas (Andrew) I, 37, 38, 39, 740
II, 205
Anna I, 138; II, 133
Anna Cath. II, 159
Anna Margaret I, 143
Anna Maria I, 132; II, 159
Anna Sabina II, 115
Appalona II, 4

Balthasar (Balser)   I, 136, 140, 141
Barbara   I, 138
Bartolomeus   I, 508
Bastian
    (Sebastian)   I, 513 514, 516
Burckhardt (Porchas)   I, 12, 13
Caspar (Casper,
    Gasper)   I, 226, 229, 231, 469
Christian   I, 232, 469, 492
    II, 16, 55, 118
Christian Teresa   II, 16
Christina   II, 115
Christoph
    (Christopher)   I, 96, 97, 98 138
    359, 361, 472
Chs.   I, 506
Conrad (Cunradt)   I, 397, 727
    II, 159
Daniel   I, 264, 267, 270, 621
    623, 625; II, 133
David   I, 132, 343
Dorothy (Dort)   II, 16, 136
Dr.   II, 137
Elizabeth   I, 190; II, 133
Eva Catherina   I, 131
Frantz Jacob   I, 720
Franz   II, 141
Fred^k Berhard   II, 16
Friedrich (Friederich, Frederick,
    Fredrick)   I, 189, 190, 192, 193, 418
    430, 689, 710, 723, 745
    II, 69
Friedrich Wilhelm   I, 724
Georg (Gerg, Gorg, George, Gorge,
    Jorg, Jurg)   I, 136, 140, 141, 198
    200, 202, 413, 417
    433, 509, 620, 622
    625, 723
Georg Ludwig   I, 422
Hans Georg (Gerg,
    Jorg)   I, 31, 33, 34, 365, 417
Hans Henrich
    (Hendrick)   I, 143, 145, 146
Hans Lenord   I, 12, 13
Hans Michel (Hans
    Mich.)   I, 100, 101
Hans Peter (Hans
    Beter)   I, 113, 114, 115, 765
Hans Philip   I, 305, 306
Hans Uhllerik
    (Ulrich)   I, 252, 254, 255
Heinrich (Henrich, Hendrick,
    Henry, Henerick)   I, 12, 237, 238
    240, 252, 253, 254
    509, 676
    II, 10, 159
Henrich Adam   I, 523, 525
J. C.   II, 107
J. W.   II, 70

Jacob
    (Jacobus)   I, 131, 133, 134, 232
    233, 234, 235, 236
    345, 372, 390, 419
    506, 510, 615, 617
    620, 676, 736
Johann Adam   I, 335, 337, 338, 409
Johann Andreas
    (And.)   I, 600, 602, 603
Johann Baltzer
    (Balster)   I, 282, 284, 285
Johann Bernhardt   I, 714
Johan Burkhart   I, 399
Johan Christoff   II, 16
Johann Daniel   I, 337, 437, 465
Johann Dietrich   I, 453
Johann Egidius
    (Egitias)   I, 185, 186, 187
Johann Georg
    (Jorg)   I, 16, 17, 494
    582, 646, 647
    II, 30, 115
Johann Henrich (Johan
    Hend.)   I, 237, 239, 240, 473
    512, 514, 515, 756
Johann Jacob
    (Jacob)   I, 577, 578, 580
    684, 686
Johan Martin   I, 390
Johann Michael (Joh.
    Michel)   I, 102, 104, 105
    404, 474
Johan Nicklas (Nicolaus,
    Nicholas)   I, 484, 655, 656, 658
Johan Petter (Hans
    Peter)   I, 96, 98, 198, 200
    202, 257, 260, 262
    267, 270
Johann Phillipps (Hans
    Philip)   I, 487, 652, 653
Johann Theis   I, 478
Johann Vallentin   I, 470
Johannes (Joannes,
    Hannis)   I, 31, 33, 34, 263
    267, 270, 279, 280
    281, 336, 337, 339
    424, 513, 514, 516
    697; II, 115, 140
Johannes Cobus   I, 401
Johannes Daniel   I, 336, 337, 339
Johannes
    Henrich   I, 340, 341, 343, 401
Johanes Jerig   I, 88, 90, 92
Johannes Mattias   I, 690
Johannes Michgel   I, 372
Johannes Wilhelm (Joh.
    Willhelm)   I, 296, 298, 299
John   II, 55, 159
John David   II, 200

John H. II, 181
Joost I, 237
Justinus (Justin) I, 265, 268, 271
Lorenz II, 53
Magdal. II, 115
Maria Cath. II, 140
Maria Magdalena I, 132
Martin (Johann Martin,
Mardin) I, 263, 267, 270, 691
Mathias
(Mattheis) I, 188, 191, 193
Michael
Michal) I, 366, 470, 488, 502
564, 565, 567, 595
597 599
Nicklas (Nicholas) I, 346, 736
II, 47
Paul I, 492, 666, 668, 670
691; II, 139
Peter I, 264, 297, 298, 299, 470
Philibs (Fillibs,
Philip) I, 297, 299, 300, 335
337, 338, 482, 540
542 544, 551, 552
554
Reichard (Richart,
Reicher) I, 390, 642, 644
Rosina I, 138
Rudolph I, 419, 507
Susanna I, 138; II, 159
Thomas II, 139
Ursula (Urcilla) I, 138
Vallentin (Velthen,
Felthen) I, 522, 524, 728
Wentzell II, 16
Wilhelm (William) I, 413, 418, 423
II, 140
Wilhelmina II, 16
HOFFMANING (HOFMINING)
Elizabeth I, 40
Jacob I, 40
Katrena I, 40
Scipilo I, 15
HOFFNER (HOFNAR, HOFFNAR)
Hanns Jerg
(Jurick) I, 116, 120, 121
Orstel I, 117
HOFFSTÄDLER (HOFSTEDLER,
HOFSTETTER, HOCHSTÄT-
TER, HOCHSTETTLER)
Christian I, 414
Jacob I, 155, 158, 160
Mᵃ Eva I, 156
Mᵃʳ Catharina I, 156
Michel II, 203
HOFFSTATT
Johan Petter I, 698
HOFIUS
Joh. Theodor I, 708

HÖFLICH (HÖFFLIG, HOEFLICK)
Conradt I, 355
Jacob I, 359
Johan Pfillib I, 356
Paul II, 123
HOFMAN see HOFFMAN
HOFMEISTER
Albrecht I, 486
Jacob II, 156
HOFNAGEL
Christopher II, 55
HÖFTLINGER (HEFLINGER, HOF-
TER)
Andereas I, 677, 679, 680
HOGARD (HOEGER)
Antoine (Atwan) I, 591, 592, 594
HOGEBAN
George II, 196
HÖGER (HOGER)
Johann Carl I, 480
Johan Michael I, 706
Thomas II, 188
Valentine II, 188
HOGERDORN
G. W. R. II, 100
HOGNON
Francois I, 407
HÖH (HOH)
Frantz I, 714
Hans Adam I, 503
Johann Gorg I, 502
Johann Simon I, 714
Nicklaus I, 493
Simon I, 714
Vallentin I, 714, 762
HOHENHOLTZ
Abraham II, 102
Catrina II, 102
David II, 102
Margreta II, 102
HOHENSCHILT
Johann Adam I, 159, 161
HOHENSTEIN
Jacob II, 155
HOHL (HÖHL)
Johannes I, 605, 606, 608
Magdalene II, 134
Matthaus (Matheas) I, 360, 361
Pfellib I, 721
HÖHLER (HEHLLER)
Johann Gottfried I, 576, 578, 580
HOHLSTEINER (HOLSTEYNER)
Georg Michael I, 66, 69, 70
Maria I, 67
Simon Peter I, 66, 69, 70
HOHMANN
Joh. Fried. II, 107
Johann Geo. II, 121
Philip II, 121

HÖHN
Georg Friedrich   I, 425
HÖHNEISS
Bernhardt   I, 490
HOHWERDER *see* HUBERTER
HOIGE
Hendrich   II, 58
HOKS
Jacob   II, 112
HOLANDER
Gerrick   I, 660
Hans Jacob   I, 428
HOLBECK
Mr   II, 89
HOLBECKER
Mr   II, 89
HOLBEIN   (HOLBE,   HOLBEN,
HOLBY)
Balthasar
(Silvester)   I, 185, 186, 187
Johan Jacob   I, 328
HOLBER (HOLBE)
Conrath (Conraed)   I, 184, 185, 187
Johann Michael   I, 719
HOLBY
Johannes   I, 448
HOLDEINTZ
Hans Jerg   I, 451
HOLDEMAN
Hans   I, 15
HOLDER
Alexander   I, 457
Jacob   I, 506
Johann Martin   I, 506
HOLDERBAUM
Johan Peter   I, 456
HOLDINGHOUSEN
Eliza Maria   I, 143
George   II, 128
Johann Henrich   I, 713
Just. Heinr.   II, 127
HOLDT
Hans Adam   I, 331
HOLEMAN
Maria   II, 123
HOLL (HÖLL, HELL, HEELL)
Abraham (Jan
Abram)   I, 190, 213, 214, 216
Andreas   I, 213, 214, 216
Anna   I, 62
Barbara   I, 61, 62, 190
F. Philip   I, 437
Georg (Jurg)   I, 615, 617, 619
Gottlieb   I, 62
Hans (Johannes,
Hanes)   I, 188, 191, 193
Hans Wendel
(Wendell)   I, 59, 63, 65
Isaac   I, 188, 191, 193

Johan Nicklas (Jan Nichol
J. Nickolas)   I, 212, 214, 216, 437
Johan Petter   I, 496
Johannes   I, 384, 386
Kathrina   I, 62
Maria   I, 62
Peter   I, 292
Rosina   I, 62
Wernel (Wennel,
Vindle)   I, 188, 191, 193
HOLLAND
Johann Christian   I, 721
Johan Ernst   I, 504
HOLLEBACH   (HOLLENBACH,
HOLENBACK)
Anna Cath.   II, 10
Christoph   I, 468
Johan Georg   I, 539, 541, 543
John Melchior   I, 690
Michael   I, 539, 541, 543
Nicholas   I, 539, 541, 543
HOLLENBERGER
Carl   II, 54
Wilhelmina   II, 54
HOLLER (HALLER)
Barbara   I, 127
Jacob   I, 546, 548, 550, 712
John   II, 122
Maria Magdalena   I, 127
Nickollas·
(Nicolaus)   I, 179, 181, 183
Simon   I, 401
HÖLLERMAN (HALLERMAN)
Adam   I, 621, 623, 625
Jacob   I, 469
HOLLICH
Johann Michael   I, 432
HOLLINGER (HOLINGER)
Jacob   I, 156, 159, 161
Jacob   I, 175, 176, 178
HOLLSCHEITT (HOLSCHEYT)
Johannes   I, 532, 533, 535
HOLLSTEIN
Michael   I, 473
HOLLY
Andres   I, 448
Michel   I, 448
HOLM
Anna Maria   II, 105
Christian   II, 98
Johann Nicolaus   I, 437
HOLPASCH (read HOLZBACH)
Johann Peter   I, 401
HOLSBACHER
Andres   I, 9
HOLSCHUH (HOLTZSHOE)
Hans Michal   I, 286, 287, 288
HÖLSEL *see* HÖLTZEL
HOLSINGER *see* HOLTZINGER

HOLST (HUST)
Friedrich
(Fredrick) I, 636, 638, 640
HOLSTEIN
Dan[1] II, 73
Hendrick I, 27
HOLSTEINER (HOLSTIENDER)
Johannes Leonhart I, 21, 22
HOLSTEN (HOLSTON)
Conrad I, 730
Margret I, 38
Maria Brabra I, 38
HOLTE
Joh. Fried[ch] II, 139
HOLTER (HOLTHER)
Hans Adam I, 457
Johan (John) I, 674, 675, 676
HOLTERREICH
George II, 150
Johanna II, 150
John II, 150, 151
John Georg II, 150
John Jacob II, 150
HOLTSPAN
Andrew I, 8
HOLTZ (HOLZ)
Friedrich (Frederick) II, 68, 139
Friedr. Andrew II, 117
Hans George I, 246, 247, 248
Jacob I, 373, 374, 375, 474
Johan Adam I, 438
Joh. Christ. II, 139
Johann Michael I, 734
Johannes (Jn°) I, 130, 378, 380, 381
743
John Andrew II, 117
Margaretha II, 70
Peter II, 50
Willhelm I, 399
HOLTZAPFEL (HOLTZAPFELL,
HOLTSAPFEL, HOLSTAFFLE,
HOLTSAFFLE, HOLTZAPPEL)
Anna Barbara I, 49
Anna Barbara Katermena (?) I, 49
Erasmus (Erazamus) I, 48, 52, 53
Friederich
(Fredrick) I, 655, 656, 658
Hans Leonard (Hans
Lenhart) I, 48, 52, 53
Heinrich I, 684
HOLTZBENDER (HOLZBENDER,
HOLSLENARD)
Nicklas I, 307, 308, 309
HOLTZEDER (OLLSELLER)
Allena Marger I, 85
Appolona I, 84
David I, 84, 86, 87
Hance Peter I, 85
Margeratt I, 84

Marrea Boble (Barbara) I, 85
HÖLTZEL (HOLZEL, HOLSEL, HEL-
SEL)
Johann Heinrich I, 460
Johann Philipp I, 430
Johann Tobias (John
Tobias) I, 373, 374, 375
Matthias II, 9
Philip Swendel (Phillip
Vendell) I, 373, 374, 375
HOLZER (HOLTZER)
Hans George I, 485
Johan Jacob I, 762
Johann Jörg I, 430
HOLTZHAUSER (HOLTZHAUS-
SER, HOLTZHAUSEN)
Abraham I, 621, 623, 625
Caspar I, 39, 41, 42
Didrich (Dieterich) I, 621, 623, 625
Frederick I, 687
Martin I, 488
HOLTZINGER (HOLTSINGER)
Barbara I, 55
Jacob I, 55, 56, 57
Jerg I, 470
Magdalena I, 49
Rudolph I, 48, 52, 53
HOLTZMANN (HOLTZMAN,
HOLTSMAN)
Andreas I, 684
Frederick II, 194
Heinrich I, 432
Joest Hendrich I, 545, 547, 549
Maria II, 194
HOLTZMER (HOLTZNER)
Johannes I, 235, 236
HOLTZ-SHOE (read HOLZSCHUH)
Hans George I, 482
Jn° Geo. I, 752
HOLTZWAND
Johan Adam II, 41
HOLTZWARTH
Andreas I, 741
HOLWER
Christoff I, 346
HOLY
Ary, Van II, 153
HOMAN
Johannes (Johan) I, 217, 219, 220
Michael (Mich[l]) I, 666, 669, 671
HOMBERG
A. II, 136
Christian I, 491
H. II, 136
John Henry II, 93
HOMBERGER
Jacob I, 147
HOMBERT
Johannes I, 467

HOMENEY (HUBENY)
John Yergen I, 310, 312, 313
HOMERICK
Peter I, 676
HOMMEL (HOOMMEL)
Herrmann II, 93
Johannes (John) I, 637, 639, 641
HOMMER (HOMER)
Johann Jacob I, 401
Peter I, 478
HOMRIGHAUSEN
Johannes I, 382
HONEGGER
Hans Jacob I, 392
HONEST
Michl I, 18
HONETHER
Johannes I, 243
HÖNGÄRTNER (HENKER)
Christen (V. Christen,
Christian) I, 559, 561, 562
HÖNICK (HÖNIG, HONIK, HON-
ING, HONNIG)
Anna Catrina I, 766
Jacob I, 483, 697
Jerg (Gerg,
Jurich) I, 264, 267, 270
Johann Georg I, 88, 90, 92
Johannes I, 335, 336, 338, 503
Marilos I, 766
Nicklas (Nicholas) I, 264, 270
HONIUS
Antonio II, 72
HÖNNER
Johann Jorg I, 495
Sebastian I, 539, 541, 543
HÖNNETZ (HÖNNTZ)
Jacob I, 363
Johann Filb I, 727
HONNIG *see* HÖNICK
HÖNNINGER (HENNINGER)
Johann Friederich I, 739
Simon I, 169, 170, 172
HONNIS
Johannes P. II, 160
HONNOLD
Hans Jorg I, 435
HONSACRE *see* HUNTZICKER
HONSTEIN
Joseph Fridrich I, 754
HÖNYSEN (HONEYSEN)
Jacob I, 551, 552, 554
HOOFENAGEL *see* HUFNAGEL
HOOFMAN (read HOFFMAN)
Alex^r II, 3
Christian II, 16
Gasper II, 103
J. F. II, 16

John II, 96
Wentzell II, 16
HOOGSTADT (read HOCHSTADT)
Hans I, 14
HOOHST
Anna Catharina II, 92
Maria Catharina II, 92
Wilhelmina II, 92
HOOT *see* HUT
HOOVER
Andreas I, 210
Frantz I, 462
Jacob I, 462
HOOZER
George I, 450
HOP
Hans Georg (Hans
Yerrick) I, 551, 552, 553
Peter I, 390
HOPBACK
John Jacob I, 27, 29, 30
Magdelina I, 28
HOPENGARTNER
George I, 502
HOPF (HOPFF)
Adam I, 412
Heinrich I, 704
Johann Caspar
(Casper) I, 585, 586, 588
Johann Phillip I, 366
Johannes I, 462, 585, 586, 588
HOPFELDT
Carl II, 99
HÖPFER (HÖPFFER)
Johannes (John) I, 637, 639, 640
Stephan I, 707
HOPMAN (HOPMANN, HOPE-
MAN)
Hans Jacob I, 252, 253, 255
Jacob I, 252, 253, 255
Johann Friederich
(Fred.) I, 681, 682
Johan Just (Uste) I, 681, 682
HOPP
Frantz I, 716
HOPPACHER (HOBACH)
Adam I, 556, 557, 558
HOPPE
Johan Gottlob I, 446
HÖPPENER (HÖPNER, HIPNER)
Georg Casper I, 536, 537, 538
HÖPPLER (HABLER)
Johann Caspar (Casper) I, 383, 385
HÖR
Johann Peter I, 709
HÖRAUFF
Andreas I, 502

HORBACH (HORBAGH, HER-
  BACH)
Johann Peter   I, 313, 314, 315
Peter   I, 763
HORBERGER
Jacob   I, 419
HÖRCH
Simon   I, 403
HORCHLER
Adolph   II, 86
Charlotte   II, 86
Chrétien   II, 86
Henriette   II, 86
HOREIN
Leonhart   I, 365
Tohbias   I, 423
HÖRERS
Johannes   I, 741
HORGER (HORGHER)
Hanns Jerg   I, 13
Joseph   I, 410
HORGG (HÖRG)
Bernard   II, 126
Johan Petter   I, 395
HÖRING (HERING)
Johann Gorg   I, 437
Johann Ludwig   I, 468
Johanes   I, 468
Philip Wendel   I, 455
HORLACHER   (HORRLACHER,
  HURLOCHER)
Christoph   I, 454
Frenech   I, 44
Gottfried
  (Godfret)   I, 240, 242, 243
Hans Georg (Hance
  Jurg)   I, 130, 133, 134
Hans Michael   I, 43, 46, 47
Hendrick   I, 15
Joh. Carl (Carolo)   I, 15
Johan David   I, 489
Margareta   I, 241
Maria   I, 44
HÖRMAN   (HÖRRMAN, HERRE-
  MAN)
Johan Jacob   I, 722
Michel   I, 585, 587, 588
HORN (HORNE, HORNN)
Adam   I, 724
Andreas (Andreuss)   I, 84, 86, 87
Casper   II, 10
Catharine   II, 7
Christian   II, 10
Christopf
  (Christoph)   I, 484, 540, 542, 544
Frans   I, 468
Frederick
  (Friederich)   I, 173, 174, 175

George (Geo.
  Jurg)   I, 539, 541, 543; II, 10
George Frederik   I, 429
Hagen   I, 501
Hans Georg   I, 429, 712
Heinrich (Henricus)   I, 717, 732
Jacob   I, 469; II, 10
Johann Georg   I, 737
Johann Martin   II, 20
Johan Migel   I, 753
Johann Peter (John
  Peter)   I, 556, 557, 558
Johann Philipp   I, 399, 730
Johann Stephanus   I, 503
Johannes (Joanis,
  Johanes)   I, 293, 294, 296, 429
                  540, 542, 544, 717
                              II, 118
Johannes Henrich   I, 435, 696
Michael   I, 747
Ottilia   II, 10
Philipp Jacob   I, 501
Sebastian   I, 538, 541, 543
Ulrich (Ullerich)   I, 179, 181, 183
HORNÄFFER
Ernest   I, 505
J. Andereas   I, 505
HORNBERGER
Christian   I, 276, 277, 278, 443
Hans Bartel (Hans
  Bardel)   I, 35, 36, 37
Jacob   I, 99, 100, 101
Johan Carl (John Carl) I, 35, 36, 37
Johan Heinrich   I, 730
Johan Jacob   I, 276, 277, 278
Johan Peter   I, 276
HORNECKER
Rudolph   I, 364
Uhllerik   I, 364
HORNER (HÖRNER)
Anna   II, 9
Anna Margt   II; 9
Caspar (Casper)   I, 249, 250
Friedrich   I, 445
George (Georg)   I, 501; II, 9
H. Albert   I, 535
Hans Michel   I, 539, 541, 544
Heinrich   I, 445
Jacob   I, 249, 250; II, 9
Johann Christian   I, 329
Johann Heinerich   II, 21
Johann Jacob   I, 502, 752
Johann Melcher   I, 502
Johann Phillip   II, 21
Johans (Jno)   I, 502; II, 9
Kunigunda   II, 9
Maria Catharina   II, 21
Maria Dorothea   II, 21
Maria Elizabeth Catharina   II, 21

Nicolaus I, 445
Orchil Maria II, 21
Walter (Valtin,
  Valentine) I, 627, 630, 634
HORNEVIUS (HORNIAVIUS)
Ana Cathena Cristiana II, 36
Elizabeth II, 36
Elizabeth Cristiana II, 36
Jacop II, 36
HORNGACHER
Jeremias I, 443
HORNIG
Franciscus Josephus I, 167, 168
HORNIGER
Isaac I, 660
HORNISSER
Georg Michael I, 504
HÖRNLIN
Hans Jacob I, 406
HORNS
Chn Gerduck II, 23
HORNUNG (HORNING, HORNIG)
Georg Ludwig (Georg) I, 59, 64, 65
Johann Melchior
  (Milchior) I, 681, 682
Johann Wendel
  (Winkell) I, 292, 293
Johannes II, 24
Leonhard I, 748
HORNY
Bentz I, 428
HÖRPEL
Johan Gorg I, 412
HORR
Jacob II, 179
Johann Leonhardt I, 721
HORRESTER
Jacob I, 13
HORSBERG
Peter II, 101
HÖRSCH (HORSCH, HORSH)
Barbara I, 49
Friedrich I, 483
Joseph I, 50
Michel I, 48, 52, 53
Peter I, 50
HORST (HORRST, HOORST)
Georg Yoder II, 79
Johan Elias I, 455
Joh. Nickel I, 694
Johann Wilhelm I, 360, 362
Ludwig I, 435
Peter II, 36
Wendel I, 335, 337, 338
HORSTER
Johannes Christian I, 735
HORT (HORTT)
Johannes I, 405

Lodwick I, 716
Peter I, 488
HORTEL
Christoph II, 178
HORTER
Johann Valtin I, 693
HORTHE
Jean Gaspard I, 738
HÖRTHLER (HITLER)
Georg (George) I, 638, 639, 641
HORTIG
Johannes I, 493
HOS (HOOS, prob. HAAS)
Philip I, 231, 232, 233
HOSCHAR (HOSCHARR)
Hans Petter I, 407
Henrich I, 407
Theobalt I, 407
HOSHAUER, (HOSHIER, HOS-
  HEAR)
Lorentz I, 301, 302, 303
HOSINGER
Philipp I, 592
HOSLINGER
Philip I, 594
HOSNER
George I, 409
HOSP
Christoph I, 545, 547, 549
HOSSLER
Henry I, 490
HOSTE (HOOSTE)
Dorst (Dort) I, 55, 56, 57
HOSTEIN (HORSTEIN, HOSTAIN)
Hans Nicholas I, 318, 319
HOSTER (HORSTER)
Johann Wilhelm I, 307, 308, 309
HOSTETTER (HOSTEETTER)
Anna I, 61
Barbara I, 61
John I, 61
Maria I, 60
Oswald I, 59, 63, 65
Ulrich I, 407
Veronica I, 61
HOSUER
Marten I, 12
HOTHEM
Johannes I, 732
HOTTEL
Anna I, 67
Curle I, 67
Hendrich I, 67
Jerich I, 67
Johannes I, 66, 67
Margaret I, 67
HOTTEMAN (HOOTMAN)
C. Friederich I, 533, 535
Christn I, 531

HOTTENBACH (HOTTEBACH)
Hans Michel   I, 485
Jacob   I, 404
Johan Georg   I, 485
Peter   I, 487
HOTTENBACHER
G. Friedrick   I, 506
HOTTENSTEIN
Davidt   I, 500
Jacob   I, 499
HÖTZ (HOTTS, HOTTZ)
Andreas   I, 440
Danniell   I, 660
Fried.   II, 61
Gorg Carl (Carl)   I, 378, 379, 381
J. Friedrich
(Fredrich)   I, 378, 379, 381
Johann Adam   I, 395
HÖTZEL
Andreas   I, 500
Daniel   I, 499
HOTZINGER
George   I, 440
HÖTZLER
Johan Gorg   I, 464
HOUBLY
Joseph   I, 102
HOUEN
———   II, 80
HOUER
Jacob   I, 13
HOUGH *see* HAUCH
HOUP
Barnard (Barn^d)   I, 175, 176, 177
HOURG
Jacob   I, 232
HOUSE *see* HAUS
HOUSEHOLDER *see* HAUSHALTER
HOUSER *see* HAUSER
HOUSEWART,   HOUSEWORT,
HOUSWETT, HOUSWET
Jacob   I, 113, 114, 115, 765
HOUSHT
Jacob   I, 365
HOUSIER *see* HAUSIHL
HOUSMAN *see* HAUSMAN
HOUSNECK *see* HAUSKNECHT
HOUSSAGE
Lorois   II, 74
Louis René   II, 74
HOUSWETT (read prob. HOUSE-
WART)
Anna Lies   I, 767
Anna Marie   I, 767
Barbara   I, 767
Caspar   I, 767
Cradell   I, 767
Jacob   I, 767
Maria   I, 766, 767

HOUSWIRD
Michael   I, 400
HOVEN
Hein, von   I, 505
HOWES
John   II, 104
HOY
Andreas   I, 432
Friedrich   I, 718
Hans Jerrick   I, 7
Jacob   I, 691
John   I, 709
HOYDEN (HEYDON)
Melchor (Melcher)   I, 55, 56, 57
HOYER
Peter Ludewig   I, 459
HUB (HÜB, HOOP)
Augustus   I, 457
Johann Georg   I, 457
Johan Sebastian   I, 316, 317
Peter   I, 691
HUBACH (HOEBACK)
Jacob   I, 222, 223, 225
HUBACKER
Jacob   I, 732
John George   I, 691
HUBBARD (read HUBERT)
John   II, 160
William   II, 18
HUBELE (HOUBELY)
Catrina   I, 189
Eva   I, 189
Frederick (John
Fredk)   I, 349, 350, 351
Jacob   I, 188, 191, 193
HUBEN
Peter, von   I, 716
HUBENER (HUBNER, HÜBENER)
Christoffel
(Christoph)   I, 577, 579, 580
Henrich   I, 421
HUBER   (HOOBER,   HUOBER,
HÜBER, HOEBER)
Adam   I, 714
Alce   I, 23
Andreas (Anderas)   I, 614, 616, 618
Balthasar (Baltzar)   I, 189, 192, 194
Casper   I, 686
Christian   I, 78, 81, 82, 96, 98
610, 611, 613
Conradt
(Conrad)   I, 490, 546, 548, 550
Felix   I, 252, 253, 254
Frans   I, 462
Friedrich   I, 355, 553
George   I, 509, 725
Gerg Friedrich   I, 684
Hans   I, 78, 81, 82
Hans Heinrich   I, 331, 332, 334

Hans Jacob
(Jacob)   I, 225, 228, 230
    327, 329
Hans Jerg (Jorg)   I, 13, 416, 424
Hans Martin   I, 80
Hans Ullrich (Hans
Ulrich)   I, 23, 25, 26, 304,
    305, 306, 345
Hans, von   I, 434
Hans Wendel
(Hans Windel)   I, 551, 552, 554
Hans Yerick   I, 451
Heinickl (John Nicklas,
Joh. Nicklas)   I, 297, 298, 300
Heinrich (Hendryk,
Henry)   I, 146, 149, 150, 364, 398
Heiny   I, 415
Jacob   I, 14, 80, 364, 398, 462
    471, 609, 610, 612
Johan Adam   I, 431
Johann Frantz   I, 456
Johann Georg   I, 424, 438, 713
Johann Jacob   I, 435
Johan Martin   I, 490
Johann Michael   I, 320, 321, 322
    435, 462
Johannes   I, 19, 93, 95, 96, 417
    614, 616, 618, 716
John Mich[s]   I, 722
Jorg   I, 347
Kasper   I, 398
Lawrence   I, 719
Ludwig   I, 327, 329, 689
Michel, von   I, 723
Nickel   I, 714
Paulus   I, 744
Peter   I, 513, 514, 515
Philap Titter   I, 327, 329
Philipp   I, 714
Rudolf   I, 364, 398
Simmon Leitel   I, 507
Wilhelm (William)   I, 162, 164, 166
HUBERT (HUBER, HOOPER,
HUBBERT)
Andreas   I, 307, 308, 309
Caspar   I, 495
Christian   I, 48, 52, 53
Daniel   I, 48, 52, 53, 307, 308, 309
George (Jurgen)   I, 307, 308, 309
Henrich   I, 423
Johann Adam
(Adam)   I, 205, 206, 208
John Ernst   II, 193
Mich[1] (Michael)   I, 661, 663, 664
Theoph.   I, 472
HUBERTER (HOHWERDER)
Valentin   I, 307, 308, 309
HUBERTI
Andreas   II, 184

Barbara   II, 184
Elisabeth   II, 184
Katharina   II, 184
Maria   II, 184
HUBERTZ
Antres   I, 708
HÜBLER (HOBLER)
Abraham   I, 349, 350, 352
Anna   I, 767
Anna Barbara   I, 766
Anna Maria   I, 767
Frances   I, 767
Jacob (Johan
Jacob)   I, 176, 177, 178
HUBLITZ
Geo. H[y]   II, 181
HUBLY
Mathis   I, 391
HÜBNER (HIEBNER, HUBENER,
HUBNER)
Anna   I, 139
Christoph
(Christoffel)   I, 138, 180, 182, 184
David   I, 136
George (Georg)   I, 136, 140, 141
Hans   I, 137, 139, 141, 142
John Bern[d]   I, 749
John Conrad   II, 77
Ludewig
(Lodwich)   I, 265, 268, 271
Maria   I, 137, 139
Melchior   I, 136, 139, 140, 141
HUBRICH (HOOVERICH)
Michael (Michal)   I, 225, 228, 230
HÜBSCHER (HIPSCHER)
Albrecht   I, 471
Mattheis   I, 47
HÜBSCHMAN (HIPSCHMAN)
Gerhardt   I, 179, 181, 183
HUBSER (HUPSON)
Uhlerick (Ulrich)   I, 233
HUBY
Friederich   I, 356
HUCK
Andreas   I, 430
HUCKABACK
Casper   I, 236
HUDERE
Michael   I, 470
HUEBER
Jacob   I, 406
Lisabeth   I, 148
Rodolph   I, 148
HUELLER
Simon   I, 676
HUENIG (HEYNING)
Daniel   I, 243, 244, 245
HUESELMAN (HISLAR)
Daniel   I, 117, 120, 121

HUFER (HUFAR)
Barbary   I, 80
Franey   I, 80
Johannes   I, 697
HUFF (HUF)
Hans Georg   I, 421
Johann Philipp   I, 714
Johannes   I, 413
Philip   I, 723
Phillip Petter   I, 438
Vallentin   I, 356
HUFFSHMIT (read HUFSCHMID)
Peter   I, 449
HUFKE
John   II, 15
HUFNAGEL (HOOFENAGEL)
Adolph   II, 103
Anna Barbara   II, 103
Anna Maria   II, 103
Anna Sabina   II, 103
Barbra Elizabeth   II, 103
Frantz Henrich   I, 522, 525
Johan Christian   I, 522, 525
Johannes   I, 493; II, 103
John Adam   II, 103
HUG
Hans   I, 415
Jacob   II, 53
Johannes   I, 331, 332, 334
Joseph   I, 433
Michael   I, 426
Mr.   II, 176
Mrs.   II, 176
HÜGEL (HUGEL)
Christian   I, 500
G. W[m]   II, 47
Joh. Hen.   II, 47
Johannes   I, 444
Lodwig (Ludwick)   I, 102, 105
HÜGET (HUGETT, HUGGET)
Frantz Carle   I, 205, 207, 208
Petter (Peter)   I, 169, 171, 173
HUGEUIN
Charl. Fred.   II, 44
HUGLY
Adam   I, 424
HUGO (HUGOV)
John Daniel
(Johannes Dan[ll])   I, 559, 561, 563
HUGUELET (HUGELET, HUGLE)
Abram (Abraham)   I, 591, 592, 594
Charles   I, 591, 592, 594
HUHN (HUN, HOUN, HUNN)
Joh.[ann]   II, 179
Johann Anthonius
(John Anthon)   I, 577, 578, 580
Johann Daniel   I, 404
Johann Gerlach   I, 404

Johan Nickel   I, 355
Johann Valendin   I, 356
HUI (HOUY)
Hans Ulerich   I, 84, 86, 87
HUIBES
Paule   I, 363
HUISMAN
Johan George   II, 135
HULBUES (HULBUS)
Christ[l]   I, 676
HULBUS
Peter   I, 675
HULCKERT
Hans Jacob   I, 474
HULL
Thomas   I, 400
HULLEBRADE
Joseph   II, 71
HULLENBRUG
Anna Maria   II, 68
Eliz.   II, 68
HÜLLER (HULER)
Johan Simon
(John Simon)   I, 279, 281, 282
HULSENBERG
Wilhelm   II, 135
HULSMANN
Christ.   II, 108
HULTS see HOLTZ
HULTZLER
George   I, 439
HUMANNS
Mary Chr.   II, 204
HUMBERT
Adam   I, 716
Friedrich   I, 475
Johann Georg   I, 610, 612
Philipp Jacob   I, 475
Wilhelm   I, 445
HUMBOLD
Christian   I, 400
HUMLAND
Jacob   I, 304
HUMLER
John   II, 70
Maria   II, 70
HUMMEL (HUMELE, HUMEL, HUMBEL, HUMBLE)
Adam   I, 71, 76, 77
Anna Magaretha   II, 111
Anna Maria   II, 75
B.   II, 135
Caspar   II, 153
Christian   II, 75
Christoff   I, 480
Daniel   II, 33
David   II, 154
Elias   I, 487
George   I, 399

Gorg Philipp I, 344, 345
Hannes Jacob I, 344, 345
Jacob II, 179
Johan Chrisn I, 675
Johann George II, 75
Johan Gerhart
 (Gerhard) I, 569, 570, 572
Johan Heinrich I, 487
Joh. Willhelm II, 111
Johannes
 (Johannis) I, 360, 361, 417
Joseph II, 135
Maria II, 135
Thomas (Tomas) I, 156, 159, 161
HUMMER (HUMER)
Jacob I, 676
Jnᵒ Wᵐ I, 755
Johan George I, 469
HUMMERHAUS
J. II, 141
HUMMERLE
Hans Jurch I, 450
HUMRICH
Johannes Henrich I, 495
Petter I, 401
HUN see HUHN
HUNA
Christ. Fredk. II, 93
HUNDT (HUND, HULD)
G. Mich. (Gorch
 Nicl) I, 601, 602, 604
Michael I, 503
HUNGEL
Phillip I, 384
HUNGER
John Gottfried II, 22
HUNGERBERER (HUNGERBALT)
Davit (David) I, 610, 611, 613
HÜNNER (HUNER)
Kraftt I, 416
Willhelm I, 478
HUNOLT
Mattheis I, 466
Wilhelm I, 466
HUNROF
Maria Catrina I, 139
HUNSAM
Johannes I, 102
HUNSICKER (HUNSECKER,
 HUNTSEKER, HUNSEKER,
 HUNSICER, HUNSINGER,
 HUNTZICKER, HUNTSINGER,
 HUNTZEKER, HONSACRE,
 HUNZIGER)
Abraham I, 240, 242, 243
Anna I, 44
Creeta I, 241
Daniel I, 628, 631, 633
David I, 539

Elisab. I, 44; II, 132
Frena I, 44
Hannes I, 44
Hartman (Martin) I, 43, 45, 46
Jacob I, 127, 129, 130, 704
Johann Georg I, 418
Johannes (Joannes,
 Johann) I, 79, 81, 82, 176
 177, 178, 212, 214
 215, 378, 379, 381
 II, 132
Margred II, 132
Meyer I, 44
Peter I, 240, 242, 243
Simon I, 176, 177, 178
Thomas I, 628, 631, 635
Ursul I, 44
Valendine I, 61
HUNSLMAN
Jerick I, 118
Margrita I, 118
HUNTER
Joh. Gottˡ Wils. II, 118
HÜPBISH (HIPTSCH)
H. Michal
 (Michael) I, 637, 639, 641
HUPFENSTIEL
Friedᵏ II, 128
Johann Jost II, 128
Maria Elisabet II, 128
HUPPE
Johann II, 79
HÜPPEL (HUPPEL, HIPPELL)
Jacob I, 367, 368
Johannes I, 204, 206, 207, 376, 377
HUPPER
John Henry I, 748
HÜRCHE (KENKE)
Johannes I, 340, 341, 342
HURLEBANS
Barbara II, 151
David II, 151
Eliza II, 151
Sophia II, 151
HURRELMAN (HARLEMAN)
Gerdt (Garet) I, 574, 575, 576
HÜRSTMAN
Peter I, 700
HÜRTER (HARTER)
Gorg (Geo.) I, 301, 302, 303
HURTGEN
Ant. II, 71
HUSCH (HUSH)
Vallentin I, 371
Vallentin, Junʳ I, 371
HUSER (HOUSER)
Anna I, 144
Christian I, 143, 145, 146
Henery II, 146

Jacob II, 146
Johan Jacob I, 460
Johanna I, 144
Niclaus I, 144
HUSGEN (HISGEN, HUTZGEN)
Johan Martin I, 736
Johann Theis
(Mathias) I, 569, 570, 572
HUSING
Paul II, 50
HUSS (HUS)
Charl⁰ Eliz^th II, 23
Hans Peter I, 15
J. Friederich I, 480
Johan Georg I, 750
Johann Jacob
(Fredrick) I, 199, 201, 203
Johannes I, 495
HUSSELICH
Bernard I, 103
Michael I, 103
Susan I, 103
HUSSEY
Martha I, 320
Robert I, 320
HUSSUNG (HOSONG, BUSSUNG)
Jacob I, 629, 632, 635
Johan Gorg I, 484
Stoffel I, 492
HÜSTER (HISTER, HUSTER, HÜSTERR)
Andrew II, 117
Anna Elisabette II, 67
Daniel I, 180
E. F. II, 144
Johannes I, 89, 91, 92
John Fried^k I, 405
Jost I, 180, 182, 184
Maria Elisabette II, 67
Matheus II, 67
HUT (HUTH, HOET, HOOT)
Casper I, 21
Friederith II, 92
George I, 568, 570, 572
Jacob I, 335, 337, 338, 453
Johann Georg I, 367, 368
Joh. Samuel I, 479
Johannes I, 7, 9, 397, 444
Michael I, 458
Michal I, 358
Valentin I, 458
HUTCHINSSEN
Jacobus II, 77
HÜTER (HETER)
Andreas (Anderas) I, 628, 631, 635
Casper (Caspar) I, 178, 180, 182
Jerg Peter I, 457
HUTHMACHER (HOUTMACHER)
Jacob I, 734

Melcher I, 232
HUTIER
Herman I, 675
HÜTIG
Johan Andreos I, 455
Philip Ludwig I, 373, 374, 375
HÜTTENLOCH
Andres I, 522, 525
HUTTER
Andreas II, 178
Christian I, 266, 269, 272
Michael II, 93
HUTTIN
Magnus II, 182
HÜTTNER
Friederich I, 688
Hans Jerg
(Hans Georg) I, 169, 170, 172
HUTZ (HUTTZ)
Abʳᵐ II, 102
Biniamin II, 101
Carl II, 101
Carlina II, 101
Christopher II, 196
Hindraieta II, 101
Joh. Peter II, 101
Margreta II, 101
HÜTWOHL
Matthais (Mathias) I, 379, 380, 382
HUTZLERN
Johannes I, 480
HUVELL
Fred. Jac., Vander II, 137
HUVIGH (HYVIGH)
Barbar I, 103
Pieter I, 102
HUY
Johann Fridrich I, 762
Paulus (Poolos) I, 289, 290, 291
HUYET
Michel I, 419
HYBLER
Josephus I, 722
HYDE
Conraad II, 68
HYDEL (HEIDELL)
Simonn (Simon) I, 649, 650
HYDER (HEIDER)
Andreas I, 451
Hance Michl.
(Hanns Michel) I, 23, 25, 26
Katherine I, 23
HYER
Nich. I, 747
HYL (read prob. HEIL)
Johan Nicklas I, 330
HYLMAN (read HEILMAN)
Jerick I, 237

HYPE
  Henrich   I, 283
HYTTEL (HITTEL)
  Georg Michael   I, 199, 202, 203
HYX (HECKS)
  Johann Gorg
    (Joan Georg)   I, 184, 185, 187

IACHOF (FATH)
  Fridrich
    (Friedrich, Jacob)   I, 376, 377
IBA
  Caspar   I, 423
IBACH (YBACH)
  C. Doretha   II, 101
  Carl   II, 101
  Carl Fred.   II, 101
  Ferdenand   II, 101
  Frantzsisca   II, 101
  Fred. Wilh.   II, 101
  Fredr. Dort   II, 101
  Giedion   II, 101
  Gottlieb   II, 101
  Jacob   I, 482
  Justaf   II, 101
  Magdalena   II, 101
  Tresia   II, 101
ICHE
  Frederich   II, 133
  Maria   II, 133
ICKRATH
  Johannes   I, 339
IDELING
  Simon   I, 226
                                         II, 103
IDEN
  Mr. I.   II, 73
IDIE
  John Henerich   II, 71
IDLER
  Friedrich   II, 191
  Jacob   I, 706
IGELSBACH   (YSLSBACH,   ISLS-
  BACH)
  Johann Christoffel
    (Christophel)   I, 122, 125, 126
  Sarah   I, 123
IGNOU
  Pierre P.   II, 107
IHLE (IHL, ELE, EYLE)
  Hans Jorg (Hans
    Yerrick)   I, 652, 654
  Johann Jorrg (George)   I, 649, 651
  Johann Michael   I, 508
  Johannes   I, 652, 654

IHMME
  Frantz   I, 501
IHNIZEN
  Heinrich   II, 184
IHRICH (IHRIG)
  Gottlib   I, 457
  Johann Lenhardt   I, 752
  Johann Michel   I, 737
  Johann Peter   I, 737
  Johannes   I, 737
  Petter   I, 397
IHRINGER
  Philipp   I, 457
IKART
  Michl   I, 14
ILESHEVER
  France Joseph   I, 210
  Ludewick   I, 210
ILFER
  Peter   II, 92
ILGENFRITZ
  Appellonia   I, 190
  Hans Georg   I, 190
  Johann Gorg (Hans
    Georg)   I, 189, 192, 193
  Johann Leonhard
    (Hans Leonard)   I, 652, 654
ILGER (ILGAR)
  Johann Georg
    (Johan Geo.)   I, 600, 602, 603
ILGES
  Johann Paul   I, 435
ILLIG (ILLICK)
  Andreas   I, 13
  Hans Rudolf   I, 96, 98
  Johann Phillip (Johan
    Phillipp)   I, 264, 268, 271
ILMEN
  J. C.   II, 72
IMBOTTY
  Johan Adam   I, 478
IMBSWEILLER
  Peter   I, 419
IM BUSH (IM BUSS, IN BUSS)
  Herman   I, 510, 512
IMHOF (IMHOFF, IMMHOFF)
  Christina   II, 128
  Johannes   I, 297, 298, 300
  Mrs.   II, 176
IMLER (EMLER)
  Anna   I, 135
  Catherina   I, 135
  Elisa M.   II, 151
  Isack Marcus (Erreck
    Mens)   I, 93, 94, 95
  Johan   I, 135
  Ludwig   I, 135
  Sabina   I, 135
  Wilhelm   I, 134

IMMEL (EMMEL)
Johannes
(Johanes) I, 292, 293, 642, 644
Leonhard I, 66, 69, 70
Michael I, 66, 69, 70
IMMENHAUSER (IMENHEYSER)
Adam I, 373, 374, 375
IMMICH (IMICH)
Georg Friederich I, 711
Jerg I, 420
IMTHURN
Bernh. II, 193
INÄBNIT
Peter I, 487
INCLEV
Pitre I, 726
INDER
Jacob I, 461
INDORFF
Killian I, 364
INFELD
Joseph I, 508
INGEBRAND
Adam I, 367, 368
INGELHOFF
Nicklas I, 503
INGOLD (ENGOLD, INGAN)
Andereas (Andreas) I, 559, 561, 562
Pieter I, 124
INHOFF
Fr. II, 185
INHOFT
Hans Jacob (Hans
Jacᵇ) I, 176, 177, 178
INHOOP
Jacob II, 183
INKLEREE
Jno. Casper I, 24
INNEBERGER (LINEBERGER)
Michael I, 656, 657, 658
INSUL
Wendel I, 428
INTELLINGER
Jnᵒ II, 75
IRMER
George II, 182
IRVIN
James II, 18
ISAAC (ISACK)
Abraham II, 107
Barbara I, 68
Fredrick I, 68
Jacob I, 68
Jonas II, 107
Teri II, 123
Wolff II, 139
ISCH (ISH)
Nicklos I, 79
Petter I, 405

ISCHI (ISHE)
Hans Jacob II, 133
Hans Ulrich II, 133
Maria II, 197
ISCHLER
Ludwig I, 708
ISCHU
Johanes II, 133
ISELE
Blasius I, 455
ISELLER (EISLER, ISLLER, ISSEL-
LER)
Davit (David) I, 595, 597, 599
Hans George I, 398
ISEMANN
Philipp I, 754
ISENRING
George I, 737
ISERLOH (YSERLOH, YSERLOCH)
Christian I, 446
Johan Otto (Hans
Otho) I, 216, 218, 219
Johann Peter
(Jon Peter) I, 185, 186, 187
ISING
George Anders II, 17
ISINGER
August I, 685
ISLER
Anna I, 147
Catherine I, 148
ISLEWOOD
Leona I, 44
ISRAEL
Abr. E. II, 153
David II, 41
Elias (Helias) I, 672, 673, 674
Heinr. II, 118
Isaac E. II, 153
Jacob II, 184
ISSENBURGER
John Henry I, 712
ISSENER
J. Adam I, 468
ITSCHNER (ETSNER)
Jacob I, 649, 650
ITZBERGER
Theobald I, 691

JAAC
Killian I, 441
JACHELD
Antoine II, 134
JACIEN
C. L. II, 5
Jan Jacob II, 5

JACK
  Ludwick   II, 18
JACKE
  Abraham   I, 162, 165, 166
JÄCKEL   (JACKEL,   JÄCKLE,
  JAKELE, JECKEL, JEGEL)
  Abraham   I, 136, 140, 141
  Anna   I, 138
  Balthasar (Baltzer) I, 136, 137, 138
                140, 141, 142
  Barbara   II, 8
  Caspar   I, 137, 140, 142
  Christopher
    (Christian)   I, 137, 140, 142
  David   I, 137
  George   I, 136, 140, 141, 393
  Hans Heinrich I, 137, 140, 142
  J. Baltasar   I, 395
  J. George (Joh. Jurg) I, 564, 566, 567
  J. Henry (Joh.
    Hend^k)   I, 564, 566, 567
  Jeremias   I, 137, 140, 142
  Maria   I, 138
  Matthias (Matias) I, 137, 140, 142
  Regina   I, 138
  Rosina   I, 138
  Susannah   I, 138
JACKES
  Johann Philb   I, 487
JÄCKLE   (JAKLY,   YAKLEY,
  JÄCKLER, JEGLY)
  Andereas   I, 488
  Conrad   II, 174
  Friedrich   I, 522, 525
  Hans Ulrich I, 348, 350, 351
  Johana   II, 171
JACKS
  Johann Michael I, 276, 277, 278
JACKY
  Elizabeth   II, 5
  Lawrence   II, 5
  Ludwick   II, 5
JACOB (JAKOB)
  Abraham   I, 696
  Christian   I, 702
  Daniel   I, 362
  Georg Henrich   I, 727
  George Adam   I, 739
  Hans   I, 162, 164, 166
  Hans Görg (Hans
    Georg) I, 300, 301, 302, 727
  Hans Michel I, 546, 548, 550
  Henry (Hend.)   I, 423
                 II, 114
  Johann Fillib   I, 712
  Johann Martin I, 531, 532, 534
  Johannes I, 390, 428, 478
  Marcus   II, 107

  Michel (Michael) I, 227, 229, 231
                  II, 103
  Nicklaus   I, 440
  Phillipp   I, 445
  Salomon   II, 108
  Stephen (Stafen) I, 162, 164, 166
JACOBI (JACOBE)
  Adam   I, 426, 474
  Christ. Hinr. (Christian
    Henry) I, 672, 673, 674
  Christjan   II, 184
  Johann (Jacob) I, 527, 528, 530
  Johann Michel   I, 522, 524
  Johann Nickel   I, 522, 524
  Johann Peter   I, 522, 524
  Maria   I, 122
  Matheis   I, 426
  Petter   I, 426
  Philip Jacob   I, 386
  Phillib   I, 507
  (See also JACOBY)
JACOBS
  Gertrud   II, 129
  Hans Jacob   I, 204
  Isaac   II, 122
  Jno II, 75
  Maria   II, 42
  Matthias   II, 129
  Moses   II, 123, 153
  Philip   I, 204, 206, 207
  Rosina   II, 153
  Samuel   II, 189
JACOBSON
  Martin   II, 126
  Nicholas   I, 742
JACOBY   (JAKOBY,   JACOBIE,
  JACOBI)
  Abraham Stoffel   I, 759
  Christoffell
    Wendell I, 226, 228, 230
  Conrad   I, 695
  Ernst   I, 581, 582, 584
  George   II, 188
  Jacob   I, 426
  Johann Jacob   I, 390
  Jost   I, 437
  Peter   I, 296, 298, 299
  Sebastian
    (Sabastian) I, 266, 269, 272
JACQUART
  Friedrich   I, 496
  Johann Carl I, 546, 548, 550
  Johann Petter   I, 725
JAEBLIN
  Hans   I, 698
JAGEL
  Bernhart   I, 468

JÄGER (JEGER, JAEGER, JAGER, YAGER)
Andreas   I, 492, 693
Anna Maria   II, 55
Baltzer   I, 444
Catrina   II, 101
Christian   II, 101
Conrad   II, 205
Conradt   I, 546, 547, 549
Dieterick   I, 697
Ferd.   II, 101
Frantz   II, 101
Frederick   II, 3
George (Jorg)   I, 701
   II, 179
Gottlieb   II, 101
Heinr. (Hiney, Hind.)   I, 275, 276, 701
   II, 101
J. G.   II, 68
Jacob   I, 420
Johann Christ   I, 737
Joh. Christ[n] Wilh[n]   II, 127
Johann Görg   I, 323, 325, 326
   646, 647
Johann Hartman (Johann Hartmann, Hertman)
   I, 600, 602, 603
Johann Simon (John Simon)   I, 551, 552, 554
Johan Wilhelm   I, 402, 676
Johannes (Johanis, John)   I, 199, 201, 203
   335, 336, 338, 699
   II, 68
Lenhart (Leon[d], Leonhardt)   I, 156, 159, 161
Martin   I, 500
Nicholas   II, 55
Peter   I, 137, 141, 142
Phillip   II, 172
Vallentin (Valentine)   I, 646, 647
Wilhelmina   II, 101
JÄGI (JAGI, YAKI)
Christian (Cresten)   I, 194, 196, 197
Johann   I, 104, 105
JAHBLER
Johan   I, 415
JAHN
Johan Zacharias   I, 506
Johannes   I, 412
Phillipine Augustin   II, 169
JAHNKE
Cath[a] Marg[a]   II, 23
J. F. E.   II, 149
Johan   II, 23
JAHRHAUS
———   II, 161

JAND (JANT, YAND)
Melchior (Melcher)   I, 213, 215, 216
JANNA
. T. E. A.   II, 141
JANNEL
Martin   I, 442
JANS
Frans   I, 397
Wilhelm   I, 198, 200, 202
JANSEN (JANSON, JANSSEN, JANSOHN, YANSON)
Bernhart (Barnard)   I, 323, 324, 326
David   I, 687
Deidrick   II, 196
Henry   II, 121
Johann Arnold   II, 91
Johanna   II, 59, 170
Johanes   II, 170
Jorg Wilhelm   I, 687
Julian   II, 186
Peter   I, 531, 533, 534
Wilhelm   II, 91, 122
JANTZ (JANZ, JANTZE)
Frantz   I, 372
Hans (Hance)   I, 629, 632, 635
Hans George (Hans Yerrick)   I, 581, 583, 584
Jacob   I, 686
Johan Vihlib (Philip)   I, 390
JAQUEPIE (Jackpie)
Jean (John)   I, 591, 592, 594
JAQUEY
Jacob   I, 660
JARDINS
C.   II, 141
JARGES
Margaretha   II, 115
Traugott   II, 115
JARKINS
J. F. W.   II, 24
Johanna Margreta   II, 24
Maria Eva   II, 24
Susan. Doroth.   II, 24
JASEON
Godhart   II, 109
JASPER
John William   I, 719
———   II, 130
JASPRAMS
C. C. W.   II, 23
JAUCH
Andreas   I, 500
Christian   I, 577, 578, 580
Johann Conrad (Conrad)   I, 645, 647
JAUSS (JAUS, YAUSE)
Gerg Friderich   I, 491

Johann Christian
  (Christian)   I, 596, 598, 600
Johannis   I, 732
Martin   I, 526, 528, 529
JAUZY (YONSER, YOUTZEE)
Berhart (Bernard)   I, 264, 267, 271
JAVET
Henry   I, 746
JAXTHEMER
Johann Philips   I, 395
JAYSER (JEISER)
Engelhart   I, 450
Friederich   I, 348, 349, 351
Jacob   I, 155, 158, 160
Johann Georg   I, 497
Johann Joachim (John
  Yoham)   I, 556, 557, 558
Wilhelm Gottlieb   I, 500
JECK
Johann Georg   I, 508
JEGNER (YEGENER)
Hans Henrich
  (Johannes)   I, 71, 75, 77
Katharina   I, 72
JEHLE
Ulrich   I, 419
JEIDLER
Thomas   I, 487
JENIEG (JANIGH, REINARD)
Christian   I, 199, 201, 203
JENNY
Jacob   II, 175
Joh.   II, 175
Mrs.   II, 175
JENSEL (GINSEL)
Friederich   I, 526, 528, 529
Michel   I, 442
JENTES (BONDAS, JANTUS)
Elias   I, 629, 632, 635
JENTZ
Gorg Martin   I, 727
JERGEN (JARGON, JERGON)
Hans   I, 699
Mathias (Matthias,
  Marthiy)   I, 99, 100, 101
JERGER (JARGER, YONGER)
Martin   I, 35, 36
JERLING (GERLING, GEROULT)
Johan Lenhart
  (Lengart)   I, 178, 180, 182
John Asmus (Joh.
  Aschemus)   I, 178, 180, 182
JERMAN (IREMAN
Hans Jerich   I, 209, 211
Maria Marg^t   I, 209
JERRET
André   II, 73
JESEL (JESLE)
Ulrich   I, 627, 630, 633

JESERANG (JESRAN)
Bartholmi
  (Bartholome)   I, 265, 269, 272
Gorg Michel (Jerick
  Mickell)   I, 265, 269, 272
JETTER (JEDER, JÖDDER, YET-
  TER)
Johan Andreas   I, 360, 362
Johann Michael
  (Michael)   I, 649, 650
Johannes   I, 365, 551, 552, 554
John Jacob   I, 417
Martin   I, 693
JEYTER
Gottlieb   I, 409
Johannes   I, 409
JIERDAN (JIERDON, JORDAN)
Jean (Jan, Johan)   I, 226, 228, 230
JOAN
Joachim   I, 357
JOB
George   I, 234
JOCHAN
Jens   II, 105
JOCHEM (JOCHIM, JOGEM)
Andreas   I, 155, 158, 160
Anna Maria   I, 156
Fred.   I, 693
George (Jerich,
  Jurg)   I, 199, 201, 203
Jens   II, 23
Margreth   I, 156
Michael   I, 155, 158, 160
JOCHLIE (YUCHLI)
Bandicht
  (Benedictus)   I, 163, 165, 166
JOCK (JOAC, YOAK)
Martin   I, 265, 268, 272
JOCKEL
Henrich   I, 724
J.   II, 142
JODER (YODER)
Christian   I, 329
Daniel   I, 698
Jacob   I, 329, 473
JOEL (YOEL)
Benjamin   II, 11
Johann Heinrich   I, 492
JOENICKE
Dettloff   II, 139
JOERG
Johannes   I, 688
JOH
Johann Adam   I, 395
Johann Jacob   I, 395
Johan Jerg (Johan
  Georg)   I, 184, 185, 187
Joha. Johan   I, 715

Johann Michel I, 395
Peter (Petter) I, 662, 663, 664
JOHANSEN (JOHANSING)
Anne Maria II, 71
Lasch II, 139
JOHE (JOHO)
Johannes (Joh⁸) I, 209, 211
Susanna I, 210
JOHN (JOHNN)
August II, 122
Caspar I, 137, 141, 142
David II, 93
Joh. Hinr^ch II, 139
Johanna II, 113
JOHNS (JONNAS)
Fillep (Filber) I, 323, 325, 326
JOHNSON
William II, 109
—— II, 58
JOHST
Carel I, 703
JÖKE (JÖK, DECK)
Andreas I, 234
Hans Adam
(Johannes) I, 234, 235, 236
JÖKY
Johann Jörg I, 158, 160
JOLER
Mich¹ II, 68
JOLLGO
Johann Fridrich I, 328
JOMEL
Paul I, 448
JONAS (JONNAS, JONASS)
Anna Catharine II, 46
Anna Maria II, 46
Engel I, 390
Friederich II, 46
Jacob II, 46
Johann Wilhelm II, 46
Johannes I, 390
Juliana II, 46
Letmon II, 195
Philippus II, 46
Simon I, 323, 325, 326
—— II, 23
JONCAN
Cath. Marg. II, 105
JONCK
Peter I, 508
JONCKER
Hans Hen. II, 30
Henrica II, 30
Johann Henrich II, 30
Joh^n Simon II, 30
JONDERMAN
C. L. II, 71
Christian II, 71
Elisbeath II, 71

JONES
Christian II, 109
Philadelphia Susanna II, 59
JONG (JONGH)
Adam I, 676
Andreas I, 676
Christian I, 676
Hend., de II, 136
Henrich I, 676
J., de II, 77
Peter I, 676
Wilhelm I, 676
JONGER
Jacob I, 406
JONICA
John II, 105
JORAM
Joseph I, 453
JORAY (ZORA)
Abraham I, 591, 592, 594
JORDAN (JORDON, YORDEN, YORDE, JORDEL)
Adam I, 474
Ann Margarett II, 56
Anna Elizabeth I, 132
Cath^r II, 106
Dorothy II, 56
Elias I, 652, 654
Elisa II, 56
Geo. Christian I, 517
Hans George I, 131
Henry II, 56, 126
J. Friederich I, 517, 518, 520
Jacob I, 470
Johannes I, 130, 131, 133
134, 483
John II, 56
Melchior I, 637, 639, 641
Mich¹ II, 106
Nicholas II, 56
Susanna (Susan) I, 131
II, 56
JORDANNUS
J. Marius I, 20
JORDTE
Ullrich I, 397
JORDY
Johan Georg I, 733
JORENBERGER (ERNBERGER)
Johan Henry (Johan
Hend^k) I, 276, 277, 278
JÖRENS (JORNS)
Konradt Heinrich
(Conr H.) I, 589, 590, 591
JÖRG (JORCH, JORG, GEORGE)
Hans Peter I, 661, 663, 664
Johan (Johannes) I, 32, 33, 432
Johann George
(Jorg) I, 569, 570, 572

Johann Henrich I, 743
Johanes (John) I, 569, 570, 572
JORGER (JURIGHER)
Johann Veit I, 88, 90, 92
JORGINS
Jos. Godfrey II, 105
JORHOLTZ
Frantz Wilhelm I, 460
JOSEPH (JOSEP)
Georg Hennrich I, 456
Israel I, 678, 680
Peter I, 731
Salomon II, 113
JOSEPHS
Mietje II, 46
JOST (JOOST, JOUST, YOST)
Caspar (Casper) I, 627, 630, 634
Conrath I, 405
Frantz (France) I, 283, 284, 286
Frederic II, 156
Geo. II, 201
Hans Caspar
(Casper) I, 106, 110, 112
Jacob I, 7, 9, 18, 20, 763
Johann Conrad
(Conrad) I, 178, 180, 182, 461
Johan Gerg I, 521, 524
Johan Nickle I, 429
Johannes (Joanis) I, 204, 206, 208
II, 44
Leobold (Leopald) I, 225, 228, 230
Louisa II, 85
Martin I, 441
Michel I, 390
Nicholas (Nicklaus) I, 234, 441, 736
Peter I, 168, 170, 172
204, 206, 208
Simon (Simeon) I, 539, 541, 543
JOSTEDT
Christian II, 97
JOTTER (JOTHER, YOTTER)
Catharina I, 157
Christian I, 329
Conrad I, 363
Hans Petter I, 395
Johanis I, 395
Jost I, 359
JOUGNAL
Davit I, 508
JOUNGER
J. Daniel I, 495
JOURDAN
——— II, 80
JOURNELL
Mons. II, 72
JUD
Johann Engel I, 685
Johannes I, 685
Johannes Jacob I, 686

JUDÄ (JUDE)
Nicklaus (Nichlos) I, 163, 165, 166
Philipps Carl I, 455
JUENE
Corneille II, 81
JULIEN
Peter I, 701
JULIUS
Henrich I, 367, 368
Jacob I, 372
JULLIG (JULICH)
Barbara (Parble) II, 8, 42
Dorothea II, 42
George Peter II, 42
Henrick II, 42
JULLY
Adam II, 45
Catharina Barbara II, 45
Heinrich II, 45
Maria Magdalina II, 45
JUNCHFER
Jacob I, 491
JUNCK(JUNCKEN)
Jacob I, 462
JUNCKEN (JONCKEE)
Johann Ernst I, 531, 532, 534
Johann Henrich I, 531, 532, 534
JUNCKER
Jacob I, 359, 483
Michel I, 427
JUND (JUNDT, YUNDT)
Andres I, 459
Hans Gorg (Hans
Geörg) I, 405, 451
Jacobus I, 438
JUNG (JUNGCK, JUNK, YOUNG)
Abraham I, 402, 465
II, 189
Adolf I, 314
Andreas I, 749
Anna (Ann) I, 74; II, 56
Anna Cathrine I, 143
Anna Marg^t II, 8
Anna Maria I, 144; II, 97
Anna Rosina II, 8
Balthasar I, 461
Bernhart I, 526, 528, 530
Burchardt I, 749
Carl (Carle) I, 304, 305, 306
Catherine II, 86
Christian I, 225, 228, 230
696, 727
Christofel I, 419
Christopher Hendrick I, 241
Conrad (Conrath) I, 356, 495
Daniel (Dan^1) I, 750; II, 86
David I, 500; II, 156
Egidius I, 698

Elisabeth
(Elizabeth, de) I, 73, 144
II, 86, 137
Eliza Cathrine I, 143
Engelbert I, 408
Eva Cath. II, 8
Fertinantt I, 421
Fredrick Jacob I, 241
G. A. II, 185
Gabriel I, 316, 317
George II, 86, 112
George Adam I, 437
Gerrick I, 660
Gogham (Joachim) I, 241
Hans Adam I, 359
Hans Georg (Jerg) I, 365, 432, 440
Hans Peter I, 400
Harmon I, 144
Henrich (Hendrick,
Henry) I, 240, 242, 243
II, 86
Isaac I, 400, 447
J. George I, 493
Jacob I, 465, 734
II, 112, 113
Jean II, 86
Johan I, 74
Johan Adam I, 401
Johan Conrad I, 754
Johann Engel (Joh.
Engel) I, 576, 578, 579
Johann Gorg (Johan
Geo.) I, 601, 602, 603, 720
Johan Henrich I, 72, 76, 77, 443
577, 579, 581
II, 97
Johann Jacob I, 699
Johann Leonhard I, 425
Joh. Martin
(Mardien) I, 564, 565, 567
Johann Michel I, 692
Johann Nickel
(Nick⁸) I, 387, 388, 389
427, 435
Johan Peder (Johann
Peter) I, 323, 324, 326, 353
354, 495, 564
565, 567
Johan Philippus I, 413
Johan Tunges I, 495
Johan Wilm I, 402
Johannes (John) I, 113, 114, 115, 143,
145, 146, 340, 341
343, 347, 397, 439
443, 480, 564, 566
567, 626, 630, 633
681, 682, 703, 765
II, 83
Johannes Engelberth I, 467

Johannes Petter
(Peder) I, 401, 435
Johannes Wilhelm
(William) I, 568, 570, 571
John, de II, 155
Leonhart (Leonard) I, 425
II, 8
Lorentz I, 702
Ludwig I, 522, 524
Madlin I, 242
Marcus I, 89, 91, 92
Maria Gerderuth I, 144
Marie II, 86
Matheus I, 89, 91, 92
Melchior (Melcher) I, 465
Michael (Michel) I, 314, 315
750, 751
Nickelas I, 323, 325, 326
Peter I, 307, 308, 309, 699
II, 18
Philip I, 432, 759
Reinhard (Reinhardt) I, 10, 11, 359
Rosetta, de II, 137
Susanna II, 8
Uriah Jacob I, 241
Vallendin
(Valantine) I, 188, 192, 193, 358
Wendell I, 419
Wilhelm I, 358
JUNGBLUD
Johannes I, 415
Nichlaus I, 303, 305, 306
JUNGE (YOUNGE)
Fellone I, 12
Jean Josse II, 86
Johan David I, 426
Michael I, 426
Peter I, 426
JUNGEDINS
Barbara II, 55
JUNGER
Barbara II, 56
Casper II, 56
Catharina II, 130
George II, 56
Johan Paul (Paul) I, 378, 379, 381
JUNGERT
Casp. II, 24
JUNGHEN (JUNGHENN, JUNK-
HAN, JUNGHEM)
Anna Elizabeth II, 191
Conrad I, 672, 673, 674
Hendrich II, 191
Johan Herman
(Herman) I, 189, 192, 193
Johannes I, 642, 644
JÜNGLING
Jacob I, 476
Johana II, 171

JUNGMAN (JUNGMANN)
Conrad I, 35
Johann Caspar I, 453
Johann Ditrich I, 57, 58
JÜNGST
Henrich I, 709
Johannes (Johannis) I, 577, 579, 580
596, 598, 599
JUNKHAUS
Johan II, 129
JUREL
John II, 135
JÜRG
Mich. I, 715
JURGENS
Anne II, 57
John Gottf^d II, 23
Willm I, 7
JURKEN
Philip S. II, 136
JUSONG (JUSANG)
John Andereas (Johann Andreas,
John Andreas) I, 601, 602, 604
JUST (JUSTE, JOST, SHUST)
John Aug. I, 749
Lenard (Leonard) I, 246, 247, 248
Phillips (Philip) I, 297, 298, 300
JUSTE
W^m II, 112
JUSTTER
Jacob II, 188
JUSTUS
Christina Elisabeth II, 184
Christjan II, 184
Coenrad II, 184
Johann II, 184
Johann Coenrad II, 184
Maria Catharina II, 184
Reinhard II, 184
JUTZ
Antoni I, 690
JUTZNER (JUSTLER)
Christian I, 521, 524
JUTZY
Peter I, 359

KABEL
Johan Michel I, 394
Sebastian I, 523, 525
KACHEL (KAGEL, KÄGEL, KAG-
GELL)
Hans Andreas I, 444
Heinrich I, 705
Johann Conrad I, 546, 548, 550
Jurg Philip I, 540

KACHELRIESS (KAHELRIES, CO-
CHELRISE)
Nicolaus (Nicholas) I, 173, 174
KACHER
Hans Gorg I, 724
KACHLER
Johan Georg I, 705
KADWITZ
Fried^ch II, 139
KAELBEL
Johann Gottfred II, 79
KAEMER
George I, 422
KAFFENBERGER
Georg Niclas I, 736
KAFFER (KAFER, CAFFER)
Matteas (Mathias) I, 277, 278, 279
Vincent I, 184, 186, 187
KAFFEROTH (GAFFEROT)
Ernst Wilhelm I, 532, 533, 535
KÄGY (KAGEE)
Janna II, 136
Rudolph I, 698
KAHL (KAHEL, KAILE)
Johannes (Joanis) I, 293, 294, 295
Jorg Fielpp I, 542, 544
KÄHLE (KILIE)
Friederich (Johann
Fridrich) I, 526, 528, 530
KÄHLER (KEHLER)
Johann Simon (John
Simon) I, 672, 673, 674
KAHM
Philipp II, 86
KAHN (KAM)
Ludewig (Ludwig) I, 614, 616, 618
KAHRER
Joh. II, 179
KAIHL
Henry II, 34
KAISER (KEYSER)
Adam I, 701
Godlieb II, 154
Johanis
(Johannes) I, 677, 679, 680
KALBACH (GALLBACH)
Filib (Filb, Philip) I, 297, 298, 300
KALBFLEISCH
Johann Henrich I, 359, 361
Johannes I, 693
KALCHAUFER
Martin I, 716
KALCKBRENNER (KOLKBRENER)
Christian I, 672, 673, 674
KALCKLÖSER, KALCKGLESER,
KALKLIESER, KALCKGLÖ-
SER)
Agnis I, 28

Caspar I, 465
Christophel
(Christopher) I, 27, 29, 30
Emanuell I, 27
Henerich I, 465
Jacob I, 27, 29, 30
Johann Hendrick (John
Hendrick) I, 27, 29, 30
Maria I, 28
KALKER
Isaac II, 113
KALL
Joh. Gorg I, 353, 354
Johan Willen (Johan
Willm) I, 353, 354
KALLADIE (KALLADAY, GAL-
LETE)
Jacob I, 222, 223, 225
KALLEMEYER
Johan Gorg I, 503
KALLENBERGER
Johannes I, 497
KALTBEKER
Johan Adam I, 719
KALTEISEN
Johan Georg I, 439
KALTER
Johann Mardin I, 414
KALTMILLER (KOLTMAN)
Jacob I, 648, 650
KALTREUTER (KALTRITER,
KALDRITER)
Jurgen (Hans
George) I, 307, 308, 309
Peter I, 307, 308, 309
Philip I, 307, 308
KALTSCHMIDT
Johannes Gerhardt I, 734
KAMB (read KAMP)
Paulus I, 683
KAMBECK
Jacob I, 676
KAMM (KAMP, COMB)
Adam I, 756
Hans Georg I, 513, 514, 516
KAMMAN (KAMMEN)
Anthony II, 185
Frantz I, 486
KÄMMER (KAMMER)
Daniel (Dangel) I, 725
Friedrich I, 483
J. Peter I, 459
Michel I, 730
Peter I, 724
KÄMMERER
Bastian I, 476
Jacob I, 474
Johan Gorg I, 729

Nickel I, 696
Peter I, 476
KAMP (CAMP)
Daniel I, 408
Davit I, 408
Hans Jorg I, 408
Johann Adam
(Adam) I, 294, 295, 296
(*See also* CAMB, CAMPIN and
KAMB)
KAMPER
Valentin I, 718
KAMPF (KAMPFF, KEMPF)
Anna Maria I, 108
Anthony II, 196
Catharina I, 109
Christian I, 107, 111, 112
Frederick I, 109
Gilbert I, 107, 111, 112
Hans Melcher I, 546, 547, 550
Hans Peter I, 109
Johann Christoph I, 710
Johann Conradt
(Conrad) I, 107, 111, 112
KAMPMAN
Johan Petter I, 486
Johann Wilhelm I, 486
KAMPTZ
Christoph Ott II, 91
KANDER (CANTER, KANTEN)
Hans Jacob I, 84, 86, 87
Katterrena I, 85
Marrea Martine I, 85
KANETRUWAR
Catherine II, 168
Christiana II, 168
KANN
Benjamin II, 139
Michael I, 451
KANT
David II, 179
KANTZ (KANZ)
Jacob I, 422
Johann Martin I, 478
Johannes (H.
Johannes) I, 610, 611, 613
Michael I, 422
KANTZLER
Bernhᵈ II, 139
KAPFFENBRENER
Johann Paullus I, 692
KAPP (KAP)
Andreas I, 87
Johannes (Johanes) I, 274, 275
Michael I, 462
KAPPE
Johannes I, 465
KAPPEL (KAPEL)
Andoni (Antoni) I, 335, 337, 338

Hans Jorg   I, 464
John   II, 151
KAPPELE
Jacob Ludwig   I, 475
KAPPELER
Elias   II, 98
KAPPES (KAPPIS)
Balds   I, 688
Gottfried   I, 479
Jacob   II, 20
John Georg   I, 470
KAPPLER (KAPLER, KÄPPLER)
Abram   I, 700
Andereas   I, 477
Hans Martin   I, 96, 98
Sebastian   I, 448
KAPPUS
Peter   I, 747
KAPS
Joh. Ernst   I, 706
KÄRCH (KARCH, KERCH, KARG)
Gorg   I, 367, 368
Johann Peter (Jan
Peter)   I, 213, 214, 216
Johannes   I, 649, 650
(*See also* KARG)
KARCHER (KÄRCHER, KARGHER,
KARGER, KERCHER)
Abel   I, 131
Anna Catherina   I, 132
Christoph Jacob
(Christopher)   I, 551, 552, 554
David (Davidt)   I, 130, 131, 133, 134
Jerg Friderich   I, 366
Johan Martin
(Martie)   I, 226, 229, 231
Johannes   I, 646, 647
John Nicklas   I, 487
Jost   I, 456
Ludwig Henrich   I, 559, 561, 563
Michel (Michal)   I, 225, 228, 230
Phillipp
(Philip)   I, 301, 302, 303, 419
Reinhardt Diedtrich   I, 555, 556, 558
KARG (KARGH)
Jacob   I, 477, 697
Johann Leonhart   I, 503
Joseph   I, 477
Leonhard   I, 727
Martin   I, 481
Michael   I, 480
KARL (CAREL, CARREL, KARLE)
Fridrig (Fredrick)   I, 226, 228, 230
Hans Peter
(H. Peter)   I, 661, 662, 664
Jacob   I, 661, 662, 664
Johan Helman   I, 710
Johan Kasber (John
Casper)   I, 384, 386

John Jacob   I, 710
KARLI (KARLE, CARLO, KARLEE)
Hans (Hendrick)   I, 188, 191, 193
Hans Leobald   I, 264
Joseph   I, 189
KARNAGEL (CARNAGAL)
Georg Adam (Yerick
Adam)   I, 384, 386
KARNER
Jacob   I, 431
KARP
Peter   I, 721
KARR
Jerg   I, 507
KARST (KAARS, CAARS)
Jacob   I, 122, 125, 126
Margaret   I, 123
Wilhelm (William)   I, 227, 229, 231
KARSTMANN (GORTMAN)
Daniel   I, 307, 309, 310
KARTER
Hans Jerg   I, 345
KARTHAUSE
Arnold   II, 93
KARTZ
Jacob   I, 411
KARWIN
Georg Philipp   I, 692
KAS (KASS)
Frederich   I, 715
Johann   II, 68
KÄSCHSTER
Johann Michal   I, 328
KASE (KEES)
Dewald (Table)   I, 93, 94, 95
KASHLEY
Andrew   I, 227
KASHLY
Andrew   II, 104
KASHNEATE
John   II, 104
KASHNETZ (CASTNITZ)
Hans (Joanns,
Johannes)   I, 169, 171, 172
Hans Jerg (Hans
Geoe)   I, 169, 171, 172
(*See also* KASTNITZ)
KASKE
George   I, 320, 321, 322
KASMANN
Christ.   II, 179
KASPAR (CASPAR)
Johan Peder (John
Peter)   I, 280, 281, 282
(*See also* CASPAR)
KASSEL (KASEL)
Jan Adam (J. A.)   I, 293, 294, 295
Johannes   I, 17

Jorg Peter I, 716
Yilles (Gilles) I, 17
KASSENBERGER
Georg Ludwig I, 457
KASSLER
Ludwig I, 430
KAST (KOST, CAST)
Frederick I, 513, 514, 515
Georg (Yerick) I, 383, 385
Hans Jerg I, 462
Johann Martin I, 446
Thomas I, 409
KASTNER (CASSNAR)
Adam I, 383, 385
KASTNITZ (KASHNEATS, KASH-
NEATE)
Johannes (John) I, 227, 229, 231
(*See also* KASHNITZ)
KATEN
Wm., Ten II, 99
KATKE
Chris. II, 196
KATTERER
Anthony I, 497
KATTERFELD
Adolf II, 119
KATTERMANN (KATTERMAN,
CATTERMAN)
Davit I, 485
Filipp (Philip) I, 596, 597, 599
Hans Jacob I, 237, 238, 239
Hans Wylight I, 237
KATYMAN
Melchior I, 499
KATZ (CATTS, KOTZ, KARTZ)
Georg I, 761
Hans Conradt I, 393
Jacob I, 411, 684
Johann Jacob
(Jacob) I, 577, 578, 580
Martin I, 411
Michel (Michael) I, 232, 233, 477
Peter I, 684
Stephan I, 477
KATZENBACH (KATZEBACH)
Jo. Hennrich I, 501
Johann Mattheis I, 726
KATZENBACHER
Kon. I, 413
KATZENMEYER (KAZENMYRER,
KATZENMYERER)
Peter I, 560, 561, 563
KATZENSTEIN
Hans George I, 331
KAUCHER
Michael I, 470
KAUF (KAUFF)
Henry I, 317
Johann Daniel I, 722

KAUFER
Hans Henrich I, 484
Michael II, 133
KAUFFELD (CONFELD, CAUF-
FELD, CAWFELD, KAWF-
FELD)
Christopher I, 204, 206, 208
George I, 362
Johannes I, 362
Nicklas I, 362
KAUFFLER (KOFFEL)
Anna (Eliza) I, 190
Hans I, 188
Hans (Henry,
Henrich) I, 188, 191, 193
KAUFMAN (KAUFFMANN,
KAUFFMAN, CAUFMAN,
KAUFMAN)
Anna Maria I, 189
Augustus I, 305, 306
Barbara I, 189; II, 186
Carl Heinrich Jacob
(Carel Hend^k) I, 609, 610, 612
Christian I, 360, 362, 407
435, 448, 718
Christoff (Stophel) I, 677, 678, 680
Frantz II, 192
Friderich I, 328
Geo. (George) I, 662, 664
Godlib I, 445
Hanes I, 19
Hans I, 304
Hans Jacob I, 188, 191, 193
Hans Philip I, 304
Heinrich (Henry) I, 14; II, 86, 115
Jakob I, 407, 409, 462, 485, 521
524, 698, 710; II, 53
Johan (Hans) I, 107, 111, 112
Johan Adam I, 365
Johann Anderes I, 234, 235, 236
Johan Conrath I, 695
Joh. Dav. II, 118
Johann Jacob I, 691
Johan Jerg (Jurg) I, 226, 228, 230
Johann Michel (Johan
Michael) I, 652, 654
Johannes I, 360, 361, 435, 474
628, 631, 635; II, 115
John Reinhard I, 697
Joseph I, 404, 754
Peter I, 407
Regina II, 9
Sallomon I, 434
Samuel I, 396
Valentin I, 704
KAUHER
Jacob I, 471
KAUKER
J. G. II, 152

KAULBACH (KULBACH)
Frantz Wilhelm I, 352, 354
Henry I, 495
KAULITZ (COULAS)
Johann Urbahn (John
Arban) I, 574, 575
KAUM
Fried. II, 98
KAUMANN (KOWMER)
Johannes (John) I, 556, 557, 558
KAUN (KAN, KON)
Anna Maria I, 119
Catharina I, 108
Dorothea I, 109
Efa Barbra I, 118
Hendrick I, 109
Johannes I, 109
Margrita I, 118
Maria Catharina II, 67
Michal I, 109
Nicolaus (Nicholas) I, 107, 111, 112
KAUPP (CAUP)
Christian I, 232, 233
KAUPT
Philip I, 399
KAUSLER (KAUSSLER)
Michael (Mich¹) I, 615, 617, 620
KAUTZ (KAUZ)
Christian I, 494
Diterich I, 431
Hans Georg (Görg) I, 491, 506
Hans Henry (J. Henry) I, 642, 644
Jacob I, 491, 492
Johann Jacob I, 545, 547, 549
Johannes I, 494
Joseph I, 451
KAUTZMAN (KAWTZMAN)
Hans Adam I, 432
Hans Gorg I, 454
Jacob I, 418
Johann Heinrich I, 432
Philip I, 437
KAYNE
Carl II, 79
KAYSER (KEYSER)
Carl I, 408
Friedrich (Fredᵏ) I, 649, 650
Henrich II, 117
Johan Mich¹ II, 30
Johannes I, 687
Lorentz (Lorens) I, 179, 181, 183
Martin I, 526, 528, 529
Sebastian I, 446
Uhlrich I, 734
KEANE (read prob. KÜHN)
Christian II, 126
KEANIG (KEANICH, read prob.
KÖNIG)
Andereas I, 430

Carol I, 430
Jacob I, 445
KEARSTUTER
Martine I, 13
KEATRER
Cathirina II, 77
Jur. Jacob II, 77
KEB
Adam II, 91
Elizabeth II, 91
Mina II, 91
KEBEL
Jacob I, 706
KEBELRING
Christian I, 753
KEBLER (KIEBLER)
John Peter (Johan
Peter) I, 646, 647
Peter I, 705
KEBLLE (KEBELL, CAVEL,
CABAL)
Barbara I, 67
Filbs (Philip) I, 66, 69, 70
Maria I, 67
KECK (KEG, KEGG)
Antreas I, 698
Carl Wilhelm I, 732
George I, 167, 168
George M¹ II, 18
KEEGER
Christopher I, 747
KEEN
Hans Georg I, 407
KEENER (KUNNER)
Friederich (Fred-
rick) I, 559, 560, 562
KEEPER
Friederich I, 434
Melchior I, 434
KEES
Peter I, 585, 587, 588
KEESEY (KERSEY, KERZEY)
Anna Barbara I, 55
Catharina I, 55
Conrad I, 55
David Vincent I, 55
Jacob I, 54, 56
John Vendal I, 54
Ulrick I, 55
KEESLER
Jacob I, 737
KEFFER
Jerg Adam I, 714
KEGEL (KEGELL, KEGILL)
Lenhart I, 88, 90, 91
Maria II, 78
Thomas I, 430; II, 178
KEGENHOWER
Jacob I, 18

KEGEREIS
  Michael   I, 496
KEGG
  George M¹   II, 18
KEHL
  Conraad   II, 136
  Jacob   I, 705
  Johannes   I, 710
  Sebastian   I, 701
KEHLE
  Pillib Jacob   I, 487
KEHLER
  Matheas   I, 415
  Michel   I, 19
KEHM
  David   I, 422
KEHR (KEHER, KHERR)
  Abraham   I, 646, 647
  Friederich   I, 323, 324, 326
  Johannes   I, 509, 510, 511
KEHRWEGER
  Magdalen   II, 151
KEIL (KEYL)
  Anna Margar.   II, 205
  Gertrude   II, 205
  Hans Michel   II, 59
  Heinrich (Henry)   II, 109, 205
  Johan Carle   I, 20, 21
  Johann Conrad (Con-
    rad)   I, 667, 669, 671
  Johann Henrich   I, 686
  Johan Jacob   I, 418
KEILER
  Mich¹   I, 17
KEILHAUER
  Johann Georg   I, 753
  Phillib Martin   I, 744
KEILINGER
  Johan Adam   I, 424
KEIM
  Aschmes (Casper)   I, 293, 294, 296
  F.   II, 142
  Jacob   I, 178
  Michel   I, 20, 21
KEIN
  Ludwick   I, 170, 171, 173
KEINADT
  Jacob   I, 494
  (*See also* KEINODT)
KEINARTH (KEYNERT)
  Johannes (Johann)   I, 649, 650
KEINEL
  Johann Philip   I, 484
KEINER   (KIENER,   KEYNER,
    KUNER)
  Johannes (Tahns)   I, 257, 260, 262
  Ludewig (Lodwick)   I, 591, 592, 594
  Melcher (Melichior)   I, 257, 260, 262

KEINGAR (KENOR)
  Hans   I, 677, 678, 680
KEINODT
  Michael   I, 366
KEIPPER (KIPER)
  Jacob   I, 292, 293
  Johanes   I, 292
  Johann Casper   I, 702
KEISER (KEYSER, KISER)
  Agnis   I, 24
  Andˢ   I, 460
  Christoph   I, 93, 94, 95
  Hans Michal   I, 144
  Henry   II, 160
  Jacob   I, 460
  Johanna   I, 144
  Johannes   I, 143, 145, 146
  Jol   II, 61
  Juliana   I, 144
  Magritt   I, 81
  Maria Cathrine   I, 144
  Michel   I, 695
  Susan   I, 79
  Velten (Welder)   I, 24, 26
  (*See also* KEYSER)
KEISON
  Dorothy   II, 152
KEITER (KEITTER, KEYDER)
  Johannes   I, 90, 91
  Michel Ludwig (Michal
    Ludwig)   I, 585, 586, 588
  Peter   I, 88, 90, 91
KEITZLER
  A. Maria   II, 162
  Frederick   II, 161
  Fredericka   II, 162
  Jacob   II, 161
  Job   II, 161
  Johanna   II, 162
KEIYFER
  Laurence   I, 102
KELB (KEELB)
  Hans Jerige (Hans Erick)   I, 12, 13
KELCHER
  Johan Jacob   I, 745
KELCHNER (KELYENAR)
  Hans Georg (Hans Gorg,
    Hans Jerick)   I, 43, 45, 46
  Michael   I, 122, 125, 126
KELCHOFFNER
  Diebolt   I, 716
KELDER
  Barbra   I, 118
  Catrina   I, 117
  Martin   II, 15
KELDRIEN, KELDRIN *see* KELDER
KELDWICK
  John Wilh.   II, 136

KELGENNA (KELGENAR)
Crete I, 44
Frederick I, 44
KELHEVER (KELHOVER, KILL-HAVER)
Benjamin I, 429
Hendrick I, 24, 26
KELL (KEEL, SHÄLL)
David (Davit) I, 324, 325, 327
Johann Christ. (Johan
Christ) I, 352, 353
KELLER (KELER, KEYLER)
Andreas I, 384, 386, 397
Anna Maria II, 124
Anthony I, 282, 284, 285
Barnard I, 116, 119, 121
Carl (Charles) I, 35, 36
Caspar (Casper) I, 249, 250
Chrétienne II, 86
Christian I, 556, 557, 558
667, 669, 671
Christoffel (Christoph) I, 493, 694
David I, 409
Elizabetha II, 53
Eva II, 124
Frederick I, 705
Georg (Jerg,
Jarrich) I, 99, 100, 101, 742
Godfrey II, 75
Hans I, 761
Hans Conrath
(Conrad) I, 147, 150
Hans Jacob I, 163, 165, 166
347, 425, 497
Hans Jörg (Hans
Jurg) I, 447, 497, 678
679, 681
Hans Michael I, 131, 132, 133, 134
Heinrich
(Henry) I, 252, 253, 255, 707
II, 124
Helena II, 124
Jacob I, 167, 168; II, 123, 192
Johann Christophel I, 722
Johann Georg I, 436
Johann Henrich
(Henry) I, 205, 206, 208, 436
Johan Leendt I, 21, 22
Johan Peter
(John Peter) I, 387, 388, 389
Johann Reinhart I, 405
Johann Vallentin
(Johan Valentin) I, 646, 647
Johannes I, 99, 100, 101, 163
165, 167, 221, 223
224, 386, 388, 389
393, 569, 571, 572
621, 623, 625, 689
John I, 711; II, 54

John Heinrich I, 509, 510, 511
Joseph I, 195, 196, 197
221, 222, 224
L. Wilhelm I, 480
Margrita I, 117
Maria I, 139
Maria Cath. II, 97
Martin I, 275, 700; II, 124
Mathias (Matheas) I, 148, 421
Nicolaus (Nickelas) I, 335, 337, 338
Peter I, 744
Valentin I, 422
Wendel I, 416
KELLNER (KÄLLNER)
Joh. Geo. II, 118
Johann Peter I, 410
KELLY
Nelly II, 30
Sophia II, 30
KELMAN
Jno Henry I, 749
KELMER
M. II, 144
KELSER
Jacob II, 97
KEM
Joseph I, 761
KEMMERER (KEMMER)
Johannes I, 615, 617, 619
KEMMLER (CIMBLER)
Hans Jacob (Jacob) I, 344, 345
KEMP (KEMPF)
Conrad I, 646, 647
Gerrit II, 69
Mathias I, 689
William I, 745; II, 18
KEMPEN
Alidar, von II, 101
Bernardus, von II, 101
Elisabeta, von II, 101
Raegus, von II, 101
KEMPER
Henrich
(Hendrick) I, 227, 229, 231
Joh. Jacob (Jacob) I, 293, 294, 296
KEMPERLING
Johannes I, 714
KEMPERLY
Michael II, 104
KEMPERS
Lotte II, 77
KEMPF (KEMPFF)
Christian I, 431
Henry I, 569, 571, 572
Johann (Johan) I, 667, 669, 671
Johann Gerhart I, 728
Johann Thies I, 728
John I, 569

KEN
Lebreght II, 15
KENBERG
Louisa II, 99
KENCKEL
Jacob I, 710
KENDEL (KENDELL)
Hans Jacob (Jacob) I, 378, 379, 381
Jacob I, 705
KENDER
Bastian I, 501
KENEY (GENEY, KNEY)
Ferdinand I, 545, 547, 549
KENNEL
Joseph I, 463
KENNEL (KENNDEL, KENIL)
Johann Rutolf
(Rudolph) I, 384, 386
Peter I, 369, 370
KENNELY
Jacob I, 462
KENNEMAR (KENAMA)
Jacob I, 93
Stephen (Staffen) I, 93, 94, 95
KENNER
Conrad (Conradt) I, 243, 244, 245
KENNIG (KENNICK)
Gottfriend II, 17
Wᵐ II, 18
KENNING
Hanna Eliz. II, 23
KENSINGER (KINSINGER, KEYN-
SINGER)
Anna Barbara I, 24
Christian II, 195
Frenee I, 24
KENT
Matteas I, 346
Nicolaus I, 94, 95, 96
KENTSCH (KIRSCH)
Johannes I, 645, 647
KENTTNER
Geo. I, 694
KENTZEL (KENSEL, KENSELL)
Jacob I, 212, 214, 216
Joseph I, 212, 214, 216
KENTZING
Marguerit I, 148
KENTZLER
Baltz I, 466
KEPLER
Simon II, 73
KEPLINGER
Hans Georg I, 417
KEPNER (KEPPNER, KEPLER)
Johann Jacob I, 513, 515, 516
KEPPELAAR (KEPPELAR)
Jurian II, 68
Simon I, 591, 592, 594; II, 32

KEPPELER (KEPLER, KEPNER,
KEPPNER, KEPPELAAR,
KEUPPLER)
George II, 155, 179
KEPPELL
Frederick II, 126
KEPPLE
Addam II, 48
Johan II, 97
Simon II, 48
KEPPLINGER (KÖPPLINGER,
KEPLINGER, CAPLINGER)
Johannes (Johanes,
Joannes) I, 31, 33, 34
Leonhart (Leonard) I, 31, 33, 34
Martin (Hans Martin) I, 72, 76, 78
KEPSKY
John II, 16
KEPSTER
Matthäus I, 506
KERBER (KERBEL)
Geo. Michael
(Jork Michel) I, 246, 247, 248
Jacob I, 695
John C. II, 136
(*See also* GERBER)
KERCH
Godfrey II, 54
Jacob I, 403
Samuel I, 403
KERCHER
Johann Philip I, 330, 356
KERCHNER
Andreas I, 423
KERCKHOFF (PERKHOFF)
Urban I, 277, 278, 279
KEREL
Nicklas I, 505
KERG
Jnᵒ Henry I, 709
KERGAR
Albert II, 119
KERHARTEN
Margarett I, 81
KERKENER
Elizabeth I, 68
KERKES
Christina I, 49
Wilhelm I, 48, 52, 53
KERKHUIS
Johannas II, 78
KERLINGER
Johannes I, 438
KERLS (KALLS)
Wilhelm I, 517, 519, 520
KERN (KERNE, KEARN)
Abraham I, 48, 52, 53
Carl Balthasar
(Baltus) I, 386, 387, 389

Conrad I, 234, 628, 631, 634
Elizabeth I, 49
Friedrich
  (Frederik) I, 367, 369, 500
Georg (George, Jerg,
  Jurg) I, 178, 180, 183
    226, 228, 230
Georg Adam I, 500
Georg Michael I, 476
Gertrowte I, 50
Hans I, 398
Hans George I, 425
Hans Jacob I, 253, 254, 255
Henry I, 79
Jacob I, 396, 614, 617, 619
    II, 76, 193
Johann Adam I, 433
Johan Nickelas I, 461
Joh. Peter II, 47
Johan Simon I, 348, 349, 351
Johann Tomas
  (Thos) I, 169, 170, 172
Johannes I, 50
Jost I, 711
Karl (Carl) I, 155, 158, 160
Katherina I, 49
Leonhardt I, 349, 350, 351
Magdilen I, 79
Margaret I, 81
Mathias (Matheas) I, 614, 617, 619
Mattheus (Mattheis) I, 367, 368, 471
Michl I, 14
Nicolaus (Nicholas) I, 79, 82, 83
Urik Willm I, 80
Vallentin I, 399
Verena I, 147
KERNER
  Martin I, 730
KERNIG
  Michael I, 231
KERR (KER, KEER)
  Christian
    (Cristian) I, 116, 119, 120
  Coenraad I, 18
KERRES
  John II, 72
KERSCH
  Mattheus I, 405
KERSCHER (KERSHER)
  Johann I, 510, 511, 512
  Mathias I, 510, 511, 512
KERST (KIRST, GERST)
  Johannes I, 335, 336, 338
KERSTEN
  Joh. Justus II, 44
KERSTENBRUG
  John Henry II, 116
KERTCHER
  Andereas I, 446

KERTS (GÜRTZ)
  Johannes I, 532, 533, 535
KERVER (CARVER)
  Nicolaas (Nicolas,
    Nicholas) I, 24, 26
KESE (KISSY)
  Heinrich I, 746
  Jacob I, 162, 164, 166
KESHIT
  Kasper I, 20
KESLIENER
  Barbara II, 75
KESLING
  John Henry II, 203
KESNOSER
  Conreet I, 766
  Johan Yerck I, 766
  Kertroudt I, 766
KESSELL (KESSEL, GESELL)
  Anna Barbara I, 28
  Christina Margaret I, 28
  George I, 718
  Hans I, 79, 82, 83
  Jacob I, 703
KESSELRINCK
  Georg Ludwig I, 686
KESSINGER (CASINGER)
  Andres (Andrew) I, 194, 196, 197
  Johann Georg
    (Hance Georg) I, 194, 196, 197
KESSLER (KESSELER, KESLER,
    KISLER)
  Andreas I, 331; II, 172
  Anna Cath. II, 4
  Anna Margaretha II, 149, 172
  Casper (Gasper) I, 344, 345, 469
  Catharina II, 149
  Catharina Elisabeth II, 172
  Christopher I, 705
  Dorothea II, 172
  Friederich I, 727
  Georg Wilhelm I, 701
  Gorg Peter I, 701
  Hans Abraham
    (Abram) I, 301, 302, 303
  Hans Jacob
    (John Jacob) I, 243, 244, 245
  Jacob II, 158
  Johann Adolf
    (Adolf) I, 564, 565, 567
  Johann Ernst I, 763
  Johan Gorg I, 740
  Johann Georg I, 745
  Johann Leonhardt I, 449, 661, 662, 664
  Johan Michael II, 172
  Johann Peter I, 686
  Joh. Philip
    (Johann Philips) I, 564, 565, 567
  Johannes I, 426, 452, 702

II, 4, 149
John David II, 56
Jurgen II, 128
Just H. II, 149
Katrina II, 5
Leonard (Johann
Leonhardt) I, 397, 661, 662, 664
664, 737
Margretha II, 172
Maria Catharina II, 172
Michel (Mich¹) I, 384, 386
Peter I, 737
Philippina II, 158
Phillip II, 158
Victor II, 181
KESTBOHRER
Wilhelm Chroph I, 489
KESTEL
——, van II, 71
KESTELIPSGER
Francys I, 116
KETCH (CLASE)
John Nicklas (Nickle) I, 316, 317
KETERING
Christoff I, 706
KETTEMAN (KETTEMANN)
Andrew I, 692
Christoph I, 427
Johann Georg I, 427
Johannes I, 344, 345
KETTENRING (KETTERING)
Frans I, 691
Hans Adam
(Adam) I, 290, 291
Johann Jacob I, 705
John Jacob II, 191
Michael I, 705
Peter Jacob II, 191
KETTERER (HITTERER)
Hans Michel I, 585, 586, 588
Heinrich I, 715
Johan Carl (Hans) I, 585, 586, 588
KETTERLE (KETTLE, CETTLER)
Wendel (Winnale,
Wennell) I, 93, 94, 95
KETTLER
Abraham II, 47
KETTMAN
Christoph I, 474
KETTNER (KATNER)
Feronica I, 135
Georg Michel (George) I, 134, 136
Henrich Adam I, 135
Johan Henrich I, 135
Johann (Johannes) I, 134, 136
Maria I, 135
KEUBEREN
Jan Hendrick II, 135

KEUFFER
John Nicolaus II, 134
KEULER
Daniel I, 463
Johan Henrich I, 401
Johannes I, 463
Valten I, 17
KEUNING
Jacob I, 266
KEUPPLER see KEPPELER
KEVELL
Philip I, 227; II, 104
KEVER
John II, 26
KEWGH
Adam I, 362
KEWITZ
Walter II, 118
KEYLBACH
Christoph I, 408
KEYSE
Conradt I, 304
KEYSER (KAISER)
Andreas (Anderas) I, 551, 552, 554
Anna Melia I, 49
Bergitta Christina II, 140
Ekhart I, 411
Feronica I, 49
Godfrey I, 691
Gurg (Jerick) I, 289, 290, 291
Henry (Hendrick) I, 276, 277, 278
Jacob I, 276, 277, 278
336, 337, 339
344, 345, 346
Johann Christian I, 540, 542, 544
Johann Conradt I, 688
Johann Georg I, 444
Johann Michel
(Nickel) I, 310, 311, 313
Johan Nickel I, 711
Johanes
(Johannes) I, 622, 624, 626, 717
Leonhart I, 411
Magdelena I, 49
Nicolas I, 15
Paulus I, 79, 82, 83
Philip I, 748
Rudy (Roday) I, 344, 345
Ulrich (Vrich) I, 48, 52, 53
Valentin I, 430, 628, 631, 634
Wilhelm II, 139
KEYSERS
Abraham II, 188
Catharin II, 188
Christena II, 188
Christopher II, 188
Margaret II, 188
KEYSLINGER
Phillip Peter I, 383

KEYTEL (CIDELE)
George (Jerick)   I, 538, 540, 543
Peter (Pieter)   I, 538, 540, 543
KHUNRICH
Dorethe   II, 106
Valentine   II, 106
KIBELINGER
Philip   I, 484
KIBLER (KIEBLER)
Georg   I, 454
Matthaus   I, 497
KICHLER (KIGELAR)
Johann Gurg
(Joh. Jurg)   I, 564, 565, 567
Johannes   I, 277, 278, 279
KIDERER
Johann Georg   I, 470
KIEFFER (KIEFER, KEEFFER,
KEFFER, KIFER, KIFFER,
KÜFER)
Abraham   I, 378, 379, 381
Andres   I, 730
Byle   I, 213
Casper   I, 378, 379, 381
Daniel   I, 295, 296
Elisabeth   I, 60
Friedrich
(Friderick)   I, 59, 63, 64
175, 177, 178
Jacob   I, 59, 62, 64, 65, 691
Jerg   I, 322
Joh. Jacob   I, 727
Johann Leonhardt   I, 59, 63, 65
Johanes   I, 406, 752
Lena   I, 62
Lorentz (Laurenz)   I, 104, 105
Maria   I, 60, 61
Marx   I, 355
Michel   I, 717, 751
Nickolas   I, 441
Peter (Petter)   I, 213, 215, 295, 296
Valentin   I, 184, 186, 187
Wendal (Wendel)   I, 387, 388, 389
KIEGEL
Ludolph Heinr. Ludewig   II, 76
KIEHL (KEIL, THIEL)
Johan Georg
(Hans Jerg)   I, 236, 238, 239
Ludwig   I, 723
KIEHN
Johannes   I, 407
Matthias   II, 110
KIEHNER (KIHNER)
Gottfried   I, 737
Hans Jacob   I, 471
KIEHNLE
Charles   II, 154
KIEL (KEEL)
Johannes Henrich   I, 755

Peter   I, 615, 617, 619
KIELMANN (KIELMAN)
Christ^r   II, 23
Johann Martin   I, 585, 586, 588
KIELNECKER
Johann Paulus   I, 452
KIENER
Adam   I, 10
Hans   I, 10
Wm.   I, 10
KIENLE (KUNLY)
David (Davidt)   I, 551, 552, 554
KIENTZ
Mathis   I, 483
Michael   I, 410
KIENTZEIN
Hans Martin   I, 446
KIENZLE
Georg Benedict   II, 134
KIEPORT
Daniel   I, 304
KIES (KISS, KIESS)
Caspar (Casper)   I, 604, 606, 607
George   II, 154
Henrich   I, 715
Johan Carl   I, 715
Johan Fridrich   I, 480
Johann Jacob   I, 393
KIESECKER (KEISACKER)
Johan Ernst
(Johan Adam)   I, 383, 385
Philip   I, 539, 541, 543
KIESEL (KIESSEL, KISSLE)
Hance Urick   I, 27
Hans Jacob (Hans
Jorg, John Jacob)   I, 27, 29, 30
Johann Heinrich   I, 502
KIESLING
Mr Friedrich   II, 109
KIEST (KIEF)
Hertz (Hartz)   I, 661, 663, 664
KIEWITT *see* CIEWITS and KÜ-
WIT
KIFFERDORFF
Catharina   II, 69
KIFIE
Jean Jaque
(Johan Jacob)   I, 666, 668, 670
KILGUS
Friederich   I, 497
KILIAN (KILON, KILLIAEN,
KEULIAN, KILLIAN)
Andreas (Andreuss)   I, 84, 86, 87
Caspar   I, 408
Henrich (Henry)   I, 37, 38, 39
Johannes (Hanias)   I, 282, 284, 285
Matheus   I, 310, 312, 313
Michael   I, 414

KILL
Peter   I, 396
KILLE
Felde   I, 19
KILMER (KILNER, KILLINOR)
Conrad
  (Conraad)   I, 24, 25, 26
               II, 56
KILSENLANDER (KITSEN-
  LANDER, KITSINTANDER)
Anna Barbara   I, 28
Christian   I, 27, 29, 30
KIMBER (GIMPER)
Henry (Henrich)   I, 576, 578, 580
KIMMEL
Adam   I, 457
Georg   I, 468
Jacob   I, 457
Johann Jacob   I, 436
Johann Nicolaus
  (Johannes)   I, 609, 610, 612
Johann Philippi   I, 457
Valtin   I, 457
KIMMERLEN (KIMMERLIN)
Hans Martin   I, 463
Johannes   I, 463
KIMPEL
Anna Gertruth   II, 91
Johann Abram   II, 91
Peter Casper   II, 91
KINANSO
Juan   I, 761
KINBERG
John Valentine   I, 749
KINCKER (KINGER, KENOR)
Johannes (Johan Christoph,
  Christoph)   I, 677, 678, 680
KIND (KINDT)
Johann Jörrig   I, 419
Johann Nickel
  (John Nich[s])   I, 384, 386
Johann Nicklas
  (Nicholas)   I, 378, 380, 381
Martin   I, 419
Mr.   II, 177
KINDER
Philip   I, 451
KINDEREN
John Fred[k]   II, 16
Maria Sophia   II, 16
KINDIGH (KINDIGE)
Mardtin (Martine)   I, 13, 14
KINDLISHBERGER
Uhllerick   I, 406
KING
Harriot   II, 88
Mallk   II, 61
Valentin   II, 112

KINN
Marrea   I, 84
Marrea Barber   I, 84
Marrea Margett   I, 84
KINNARD
William   II, 27
KINNER (KINER)
Adam   I, 11
Hanes   I, 11
Ulrich   I, 11
KINSEL
J.   II, 15
KINSINGER (KEYNSINGER, KEN-
  SINGER)
Abraham   I, 24, 26
Anna Barbara   I, 24
Frenee   I, 24
KINTER
Anth.   I, 237
KINTZ (KINSS)
Hans   I, 491
Joseph   I, 491
Michael   I, 451
Philip   I, 56, 57
KINTZEL (KINSLER)
Johan Adam (Hans
  Adam)   I, 244, 245
Johann Christoph
  (Chris.)   I, 236, 238, 239
KINTZER (KINSER, KINZER)
Jacob   I, 178, 180, 182
Johann Jacob   I, 170, 171, 173
Johan Nicklas
  (Johan Nic.)   I, 234, 235, 236
KINTZI
Johannes   I, 741
KINTZINGER
Johann Christoph   I, 395
KIPP
Johann Henrich   I, 487
Johannes   I, 582, 583, 584
Michel   I, 420
KIPPENBERG
M. Frederik   I, 504
KIPPING
Anna   I, 28
Johannah   I, 28
Johannes   I, 27, 29, 30
Sivilla   I, 28
KIPSIER
Ulrich   I, 231
KIRBACH (KIERBACH)
Anna Maria   I, 144
Christian   I, 279, 280, 281
Freyja Cathrine   I, 144
George Wilhelm   I, 279, 280, 281
Jorge Wilhelm   I, 281
Simon   I, 143, 145, 146

KIRBE
  Michel   I, 394
KIRBERGER
  Johann Elias   II, 30
  Marie Cather.   I, 148
KIRCH
  Hennrich (Henrich)   I, 367, 368
  Jacob   I, 390
KIRCHBISCHEN
  Johannes Petter   I, 495
KIRCHER (CHENIKER, SERCHER)
  Johan Adam (Adam)   I, 316, 317
  Johannes   I, 463
  Willhelm   I, 701
KIRCHHART
  Andon   I, 403
KIRCHHOFF (KIRCHOFE)
  Christoph   I, 10, 12
KIRCHHOFFER
  J. Peter (John
    Petter)   I, 577, 579, 581
KIRCHNER
  Adam   I, 371
  Friederich   I, 464
  Görg (Jorg)   I, 421, 744
  J. George   I, 464
  J. Leonhard   II, 201
  Johann Andreas   I, 719
  Johannes (Johan)   I, 48, 52, 53
  Paulus (Paul)   I, 199, 201, 203
  Wilhelmina   II, 69
KIRCHSETTEN
  Christoph   I, 724
KIRKHOFE
  Christophel   I, 217
KIRKLINGER
  Anna Catharine   II, 166
  Anna Maria   II, 166
  Frederich   II, 166
  Johan Frederich   II, 166
  Johannes   II, 166
KIRMANN
  Gorg   I, 451
KIRN
  Christian   II, 178
  J.   II, 153
KIRSCHBAUM
  J. Adam   I, 458
  Johann Michael   I, 751
  Johan Filepes   I, 432
KIRSCHENMANN
  Johan Christian   I, 715
KIRSCHER
  Gerort Philibb   I, 444
KIRSCHMAN
  Hans Mart.   I, 480
KIRSCHNER (CRISNER, KIRSH-
    NER)
  Ann   I, 40

Barbary   I, 40
Elizabeth   I, 40
Johann Gorg (John
  George)   I, 39, 41, 42, 371, 429
Johannes
  (John)   I, 113, 114, 115
                              749, 765
Martin (Mertin)   I, 40, 329
KIRSCHTEIN
  Elias   II, 128
KIRSHEYER
  Eberhard   I, 695
KIRSTOHBER
  Petter   I, 495
KIRT
  Jacob   I, 714
KIRTELING
  Laurentz   II, 125
KISAUER
  Jnⁿ Henry   I, 691
KISECKER (KIESECKER)
  Hans   I, 627, 630, 633
KISKOLT
  Sebastian   I, 486
KISLING
  Jacob   I, 425
KISSEL
  Andereas   I, 486
KISSELBERG
  Andereas   I, 475
KISSEWELTER
  Maria Cath.   II, 9
KISSNER
  Jacob   I, 757
KISTLER (KUSTER)
  Jacob   I, 179, 181, 183
  Johannes   I, 184, 186, 187
KISTLING
  Christoph   I, 494
KISTNER (KEESNER, KISNER)
  Heinrich
    (Hendrick)   I, 246, 247, 248
  Johan Georg   I, 517, 518, 519
  Johann Leonhaar
    (Leonard)   I, 662, 663, 664
  Johann Philip
    (Philip)   I, 79, 82, 83
  Johannes   I, 717
  Martin   I, 661, 663, 664
KITCHIN
  Philip   I, 55
KITSMILLER (KETS MILLER)
  Johannes   I, 18, 19
KITTWEILER
  Hans Rudolf   I, 416
KITZ
  Johann Georg   I, 390
KLAAS
  Melcher   I, 205

KLAGES
  Johann Valentin   I, 371
KLAMM
  Georg Michal   I, 699
  Jacob   I, 699
KLAMP
  Herman   II, 205
KLAMPERT (KLAPPER)
  John Henry
    (J. Henry)   I, 573, 574, 575
KLANA
  Charles Fredk.   II, 93
KLAPPERT (KLAPPER)
  Friederich
    (Friderich)   I, 297, 298, 300
  Johann Herman   I, 684
  Johannes   I, 684, 738
KLÄPPINGER (KLUPINGER)
  Johann Georg
    (Georg)   I, 179, 180, 183
KLAPTHOR
  John Michel   II, 69
  Magdalena   II, 69
KLAR (KLÄR, KLÄRR)
  Christophel   I, 403
  Friderich   I, 402
  Jacob   I, 488
  Rudolph   I, 492
KLAS (KLASS)
  Johann Michel   I, 428
  Simon   I, 699
KLASES
  Peter   I, 469
KLATZ
  Johann Peter   I, 717
KLAUDT
  Georg Adam   II, 134
KLAUSER
  Anna Maria   I, 28
  Hans Joreck (Hans
    Jorick, Hance Jorick)   I, 27, 30
  (*See also* CLAUSER)
KLAWER
  Michael   I, 360, 362
KLEBER (CLEVER)
  Jerg Balthas
    (Yerick Baltus)   I, 383, 385
KLEBSATTEL   (CLIPSADLE,
  CLIPSADELL)
  Andreas   I, 113, 114, 115, 766
  Frantz   I, 119, 121
KLEE (GLEE, KLEH, KLEEH)
  Georg   I, 454
  Georg Adam
    (George Adam)   I, 649, 650
  Jacob   I, 696
  Michael   I, 419
  Nickel (Johan
    Nickell)   I, 204, 206, 207

  Theobald (Deobald)   I, 204, 206, 207
  (*See also* CLEH)
KLEHAS
  Arnold   I, 424
KLEHR (CLAIR)
  Caspar (Casper)   I, 376, 377
  Stephanus   I, 234
KLEIBER
  Georg   I, 714
  Henrich   I, 714
KLEIDERLEIN
  Georg   I, 732
KLEIKAM (KLITHAM)
  Johann Conrad   I, 574, 575, 576
KLEIM
  Adereas   I, 503
  Johan Peter   I, 443
  Michael   I, 410
  Peter   I, 390
KLEIN (KLINE, KLEYN, KLYN,
  CLINE, KLYNE, KLEINE)
  Adam   I, 725
  Andreas   I, 464, 513, 514, 516
  Andrew Hinen   I, 241
  Anna Rosin   I, 79
  Antony   II, 5
  Bastian   I, 264, 268, 271
  Bernhart   I, 300, 301, 303
  Casper   I, 419
  Catharina   I, 109; II, 102
  Christian
    (Chris[n])   I, 264, 268, 271, 676
  Christina   II, 59, 150
  Conrath   I, 521, 523
  Daniel   I, 430, 496
  Dieboldt   I, 761
  Dorothea   I, 109; II, 150
  Elizabeth   I, 108, 109; II, 5
  Frantz (Frans)   I, 563, 565, 566
  Fried[r]   II, 178
  Georg (Jerg, Jurg)   I, 122, 125, 126
          205, 206, 208
          II, 44
  Georg Friedrich   I, 500, 655, 657, 658
  Giedrut   II, 102
  Hans Georg (Jorg)   I, 358, 459, 750
  Hans Michael
    (Hans Mickel)   I, 370
  Hans Nicklas
    (Johann Nickell)   I, 266, 269, 272
  Hans Philip
    (Johan Philip)   I, 585, 587, 588
  Hector   II, 122
  Heinrich (Hendrick,
    Henry)   I, 80, 96, 97, 98
          499, 621, 623, 625
          727; II, 92
  Henry Adam
    (Hendrick Adam)   I, 266, 269, 272

Jacob   I, 96, 97, 98
304, 305, 306
308, 328, 403
405, 406, 425
437, 459, 483
II, 53, 150
Jacobina   II, 150
Joel   I, 761
Johann Adam   I, 257, 259, 262
508, 726
Johann Andreas
(Jnº And.)   I, 589, 590, 591
Johann Balthas   I, 731
Johan Bardtram
(Bertrum)   I, 280, 281, 282
Joh. Carl Philip   II, 138
Johann Casber   I, 425
Johann Christ   I, 401
Johann Diel   I, 419
Johann Fridig   I, 311, 312, 313
Johann Georg
(Jerg)   I, 403, 430, 532
533, 535
Johann Gerlach   I, 577, 579, 580
Johann Heinrich
(Henrich)   I, 169, 171, 172
415, 443, 754
Johan Jacob   I, 438
Johann Jost   I, 729
Johann Ludwig   I, 466
Johan Martin   I, 698; II, 45
Johann Michael   I, 357, 697
Johan Nicklas
(John Nichlas)   I, 310, 311, 312
422, 502, 536
537, 538
J. Peter   II, 102
Johan Philip
(John Philips)   I, 257, 260, 262
564, 566, 567
667, 669, 671
Johan Teobald   I, 702
Johan Willem
(John Wm)   I, 280, 281, 282
Johannes (Hannes,
Jonas)   I, 78, 81, 82, 258
260, 263, 355, 387
388, 389, 394, 425
462, 609, 610, 612
666, 668, 670, 751
Johannes Gerhard   I, 700
Johannes Michel   I, 304, 305, 306
Johannes Petter   I, 426
Johannes Vallentinus   I, 727
Johannes Wilhelm   I, 700
John   I, 705; II, 156
John Adam   I, 356
Jnº Henry   I, 761
Juliana   I, 108

Katharina   II, 150
Lawrence   I, 226
Lenhart (Lenhard,
Nickolor)   I, 293, 294, 295
Ludewich
(Ludowick)   I, 323; II, 150
Luwisa   II, 102
Marks (Marx)   I, 107, 109, 111, 112
Martin   I, 372, 451
Mary   II, 144
Mathew   II, 150
Mathias   I, 80
Michael   I, 246, 247, 248
637, 639, 641
652, 654, 715, 759
Moritz   I, 405
Nicholas
(Niglaus)   I, 307, 308, 309
666, 669, 671
Peter   I, 323, 325, 326
419, 451, 522
524, 643, 645
II, 102
Peter Michael   I, 716
Philips (Philibs, Philipp
Wilhem)   I, 147, 150, 151
419, 581, 582
584, 759
Philips Wendel   I, 355
Soffie   I, 241
Susana Maria   I, 241
Theobalt (Thiebalt)   I, 355, 739
Uriah Carle   I, 241
Vallentin (Valentine)   I, 48, 52, 53
Wilhelmina   II, 102
(*See also* CLAIN, CLIEN, CLINE
and KLEYN)
KLEINBEHL (KLINBELL)
Johannes   I, 621, 623, 625
KLEINBUB
Johann Jacob   I, 545, 547, 549
KLEINFELD (KLEYNFELT, KLY-
FELT)
Johanes (John,
Johannes)   I, 597, 598, 600
KLEINFELTER (KLEINFELLER)
Gerg   I, 459
Hans Petter   I, 459
Johannes
(Johanes)   I, 459, 717
Melchior   I, 444
KLEINHANS (KLINHAS)
Johann Görg (Georg)   I, 59, 63, 65
Thoredea   I, 61
KLEINHOUSE
Charlotte   II, 198
KLEINJENY   (KLEINGENNY,
GLYNGAN)
Johanes (Johanan)   I, 240, 242, 243

KLEINJUNG
  Anna   II, 192
  Catharina Carolina
    Sophia   II, 190
  Clara Anna Sophia   II, 190
  Johann Chr.   II, 190
  Joh. Fried.   II, 192
KLEINKNECHT
  George E.   II, 41
KLEINMAN (KLYNMAN)
  Johann Diehl
    (Johan)   I, 609, 610, 612
  Joseph   I, 677, 678, 680
KLEINPETER   (KLEYNPETER,
    KLEINPETTER)
  Hans Georg (Hans
    Geo.)   I, 667, 669, 671
  Rudolph   I, 332, 333, 334
KLEINRATH
  Christ. Aug.   II, 160
KLEINSCHMIEDT   (KLEIN-
    SCHMIT, KLEINSMITH)
  Andreas   I, 746
  Johann Baltzar   I, 501
  Lewis   II, 197
  Sebastian   I, 746
KLEINSCHROTH (CLENSHROD)
  Johann Michael
    (John Michael) I, 652, 653
KLEINWORTH
  Hinrich   II, 23
KLEISINGER
  Ludwig   I, 466
KLEISS (GLEITZ)
  Friedrich   II, 110
  Jacob (Jacobin)   I, 384, 386
  Johann Philips
    (Johan Philip) I, 656, 657, 659
KLEIST
  Joh. W.   II, 125
KLEIZ
  Johannis   I, 497
KLEMANN
  Johann Wilhelm   I, 722
KLEMM (KLEM, CLEM, KLEYM,
    KLYM)
  Andreas   I, 122, 124, 126
  Caspar   I, 123
  Fraunek   I, 123
  Georg Christian   I, 505
  Georg Philip (Philip) I, 292
  Gottlob (Goetloop) I, 121, 124, 125
  Hans Adam   I, 328
  Henrick   I, 123
  Jacob   I, 411
  Jacob Friedrich (Jacob
    Friderich)   I, 99, 100, 101
  Johann (Johan) I, 121, 124, 125
  Johan Daniehl I, 509, 510, 511

Johann Davidt   I, 366
Johan Henry   I, 505
Johan Konrat   I, 366
Magdalena   I, 122
KLEMMER (CLEMER)
  Hennrich (Henerich,
    Henrick)   I, 35, 36
  Johan Andres
    (Johannes)   I, 35, 36, 37
  John   I, 722
  Ludewig   I, 469
KLENCK (KLINK)
  Michael   I, 591, 593, 594
KLENCKE
  Joh. Wilhelm   I, 517
KLENÉE
  Thomas   I, 762
KLENTER (GLANTER)
  Conrad   I, 521, 524
KLEPPER
  Johann Valenthin   I, 709
KLEPPERT
  Johannes   I, 755
KLER
  Joh. Geo.   II, 118
KLERMUNDT
  W^m II, 155
KLES
  Erhardt (Dewalt) I, 204, 206, 207
KLETLE (CITLE)
  Hans Adam
    (Hance Adam) I, 194, 195, 196
KLETT
  Gotlb.   II, 179
  Hans Jacob   I, 462
KLETTE
  Friederich   I, 743
KLETTER (KLETER)
  Valentin   I, 341, 342, 343
KLEVE
  Lamerdje, van   II, 92
KLEY
  Felix   I, 406
KLEYN
  Heinrich (Hendrich)   I, 755
                 II, 118
KLEYWER
  Ludw^k II, 16
KLIBERG
  Joh. And.   II, 125
KLIEBENSTEINN
  Johann Henrich   I, 731
KLIEDNUS
  David   I, 423
KLIEF
  William   II, 121
KLIGENBURG
  H.   II, 142

KLINBACH
Jurg   I, 468
KLING (CLING)
Anthony (Andhon)   I, 661, 662, 664
Christian   I, 93, 94, 95
Georg (Hanc Erick)   I, 93, 95
KLINGEL
Hans Jerg   I, 365
Jerg Friderich   I, 365
KLINGELHOVER
Michael   II, 148
KLINGEMEYER
Conrad   I, 476
KLINGENSCHMIT   (KLIENGEN-
SCHMITT,   CLINGESMITH
KLINGENSCHMITT, KLINGE-
SMITH)
Daniel (Daniell)   I, 213, 215
Frantz (Daniell)   I, 212, 214, 215
Georg (Georg
Klingen)   I, 678, 679, 681
KLINGER
Alexander   I, 396
Fieliepp   I, 468
Henry (Henrich, John
Henrick)   I, 199, 201, 203
Johanes   I, 395
Joseph Friederich
(Jos. Ferdt)   I, 605, 607, 608
Maria Sophia   II, 16
Peter   I, 468
KLINGKANN
Jorg Philip   I, 346
KLINGLER
Debalt (Dewald)   I, 225, 228, 230
KLINGMANN   (KLINGEMANN,
KLINGMAN)
Hans Georg   I, 59, 63, 64
Jorich (Georg)   I, 60, 64, 65
Kathrina   I, 61
Petter   I, 62
Thoredea   I, 60
KLINKEL
Sophia   II, 70
KLINKER
Ernst   I, 425
KLINSMITH
Edward   II, 169
KLINTOP (CLANTOP)
Christopher   I, 527, 528, 530
Johannes   I, 527, 528, 530
KLIPPEL
Jacob   I, 415
Johannes   I, 415
KLIPPERT
C. Aeric   II, 120
Chrisn   II, 120
Henry Christn   II, 120
Johannes   II, 120

KLIPSEGEL
Hans Jerick   I, 119
Migel   I, 119
Rosina   I, 118
KLOBLY
Hans George   I, 453
KLOCKMANN
Anna Dorothea   II, 107
KLÖCKNER   (KLÖCKENER,
KLEKNER)
Anthon (Andon)   I, 577, 579, 580
Caspar (Gaspar)   I, 289, 290, 291
Cathrina   I, 144
Clara   I, 144
Joanis Gerard   I, 144
Johan Henrich
(Hendrick)   I, 143, 145, 146
Johannes Steffan
(John Steven)   I, 568, 570, 571
Magdelina   I, 144
Maria Eliza   I, 144
KLONINGER
Johann Philippus   I, 367, 368
Johan Vallentin
(Phalten)   I, 324, 325, 326
KLOPERT
Lenhart   I, 358
KLÖPFER (KLOPFER)
Johan Max   I, 492
Joseph   I, 449
Lorentz   I, 449
KLÖPPER
Johann Heinrich   I, 683
Johann Wilhelm   I, 709
KLOPPEYN
Friedrich   I, 466
KLOSS (KLOS)
Elisebeth   II, 77
Henrich   I, 430
Johann Emanuel   I, 748
Johannes   I, 507
KLOSSE
Thomas   I, 430
KLÖTI
Jacob   I, 442
KLOTZ
Hans Leonhardt   I, 393
Jacob   I, 227, 229
                               231, 393
Jno Chr.   II, 202
Johan George   I, 505
John Phillip   II, 159
KLUBEN
Elizabeth   II, 205
KLUGE (KLUG)
Carl   I, 490
Georg Daniel   II, 67
Nicklas
(Nicholas)   I, 246, 247, 248

KLUMP (KLUMTH)
Johann Peder   I, 469
Peter (Better)   I, 539, 541, 543
KLUNCK (KLUNG)
Alberth (Albert)   I, 667, 669, 671
Joha. Andreas   I, 683
Johann Peter   I, 683
KLUND (KLUNT)
Johan Jacob (Jan
Jacob)   I, 212, 214, 215
KLYMAR
J. Eberhard   II, 122
KLYNE (KLYN)
John   II, 72
Lawrence   II, 103
Nicolaus   II, 125
KNAARS
Matheas   I, 419
KNABE (KNAB, KNAAB, KNAAP)
Friedrich Heinrich
(Fredrick)   I, 551, 553, 554
Hance George   I, 163
Hans Michael   I, 459
Johan Michael
(Michael)   I, 199, 201, 203
Johann Nickelaus   I, 698
Johannes   I, 615, 617, 620
Peter   I, 448
KNABELOCH
Johann Georg   I, 743
KNABENSCHU
Johann Jacob   I, 763
KNABSCHNEIDER (KNAPSCHNY-
DER)
Johannes   I, 531, 532, 534
KNAPP (KNAP)
Jacob   I, 522, 524
  II, 53
Philipp Henrich   I, 734
KNAPPENBERGER
Johan Erhard   I, 400
KNAPPER
Barbary   II, 152
Gottlieb   II, 152
J. Gottfried   I, 532, 533, 535
Jacob   I, 490
Margaret   II, 152
KNAPPING
Luisa Francisca   I, 73
KNAPSCHNEIDE
J. D.   II, 32
KNARTSH (KIGHER, KIGTS)
Sebastian   I, 527, 528, 530
KNATEL (KNOWDEL)
Johan Georg (Johannes
George)   I, 360, 361
KNAUER
Andreas   I, 458
Hans   I, 458

Hans Petter   I, 458
Joh. Christoph
(Christopher)   I, 55, 56, 57
KNAUFF (KNOIF)
Anthon   I, 349, 350, 351
Ernst Fred.   II, 161
Johan Heinrich   I, 349, 350, 351
Nicolaas   II, 24
KNAUSS
Christian Friederich   I, 429
Johannes   I, 448, 449
  II, 41
KNEBEL
Anna Elisabeth   II, 29
Anna Gertrut   II, 29
Christian   I, 448
Hans   I, 448
Johan Henrich   II, 29
Johannes   I, 396
Susanna   II, 29
KNEBLER
Elias   I, 523, 525
KNECHEL
Friederig   I, 471
KNECHT (KNIGHT, KNEIGHT)
Anna Cath.   II, 41
Georg Peter
(Jurig Peter)   I, 78. 81, 82
Gottfried   II, 190
Jacob   I, 276
Joh. G.   II, 41
Johan Jacob (John
Jacob)   I, 28, 30
Joh. God.   II, 41
Johannes   I, 365, 378, 379, 381
John Daniel   II, 41
John Georg   II, 191
Philipp Georg   I, 687
KNECKY
Hans Jacob   I, 234
KNEESER (NYSYNG)
Nicklas (Nicholas)   I, 257, 260, 262
KNEFELI (KNEFELY)
Philipp Valentin   I, 576, 578, 580
KNEIDE (NYDY, NIDY)
Hans Leonhard   I, 84, 86, 87
Margreate   I, 85
KNEILING (KNEELING, KNAEL-
ING)
George   I, 589, 590
KNEIP (KNIPE)
Christian   I, 411
Friedrich   I, 728
KNEISEL
Conrad   II, 112
Michael   II, 112
Stephan   I, 438
KNEIST (KNEP)
Johannes   I, 386, 388, 389

KNEPLY (KNIPLE)
Christoffel
(Christopher) I, 575, 576
KNEPPER (KNIPPER)
Conrad I, 403
Ferina I, 28
Peter I, 180, 182, 184
Wilhelmens (William) I, 27, 29, 30
KNEPPERT
Friedrich I, 476
KNERR
Hans I, 447
Henrich Jacob I, 487
KNES
Adam Karl I, 460
KNESIUS
Anthon II, 94
KNEY
Hans Adam I, 445
KNIE
Carel II, 184
Charlotte II, 184
Christina II, 184
Leopold II, 184
KNIEHL (KNIHLL, NILL)
Michl (Michael) I, 596, 598, 599
KNIERIEMEN (KNIEREAM,
KNEARIEM, KNIREM, NEARA-
MAN)
Chⁿ II, 186
Elfrie (Elfreth) I, 596, 598, 600
Johanes (Hans) I, 573, 574, 575
KNIESS (KNIES, KNEES, KNISS)
Abram (Abraham) I, 300, 301, 303
Carl II, 70
Jacob I, 421
Johan Christian
(Johan) I, 531, 532, 534
Johannes I, 430
KNIEST
Carolina II, 70
Dorothea II, 70
Johanna Christiana II, 70
John George II, 70
Wilhelmina II, 70
KNIPER
R. F. II, 123
KNIPP
Gisbertus Ignatius I, 410
Mathias I, 373
KNIPPING
Anna Eliz. II, 92
Anna Mary II, 92
Jacob II, 92
KNIRNSCHILDT
Johann Christoph I, 457
KNISSEL
Thomas I, 489

KNITTEL (NEEDLE)
Joseph I, 526, 528, 529
KNNODBEL
Christoff I, 442
KNOBEL (KNOBELL, KNOBLE)
Anna Maria I, 108
Christian I, 733
Johan Peter
(Peter) I, 107, 111, 112
Philip I, 382
Ursula I, 108
KNOBLAUCH (KNOBLOCH,
KNOBELACH, KNOBELIG,
KNOBELICK)
Adam I, 605, 606, 607, 714
Caspar I, 683
Henry (Hendrick) I, 386, 387, 389
Jnᵒ Martin I, 695
Jorg Friederich I, 716
Joseph II, 52
KNOCH (KNOCK)
Conraad II, 29
Herman II, 29
Johᵃ Elisabeth II, 29
Joh. Georg I, 485
KNÖCHELL (KNECHELL,
KNOCHEL, KNOCKELL)
Jacob I, 59, 64, 65
Johan I, 234
Laurents (Lorents) I, 59, 63, 64
KNOCHEN
John Andereas (John
Andreas) I, 671, 673, 674
KNOCK (KNOBE)
Peter I, 573, 574, 575
KNODEL
Christop II, 173
Conrad II, 150
Elizabeth II, 150
Hans Jerg I, 439
Jacob I, 523, 525
II, 179
Jacobina II, 179
Johann Georg
(Yerrick) I, 526, 527, 529
Theophilus II, 150
Thierry II, 151
Ulrich I, 526, 528, 530
KNÖDLER
Andereas I, 446
Hans Jerg I, 328
Jacob I, 648, 650
KNODT (KNODH, KNOTH)
Johann Henrich I, 576, 578, 579
KNOERY
Charles Frederic I, 742
KNOES
Jacob II, 203

KNOLL (NOLL)
Ann Mary   I, 766
Anna Maria   II, 170
Elizabeth   I, 767
Johann (Johannes)   I, 113, 114,
                          115, 765
  Ludwig   I, 468
  Margaret   I, 767
KNOPFF (KNOPF)
Dewald   I, 367, 369
KNOPP (KNOOP, KNOB)
Anna (Ann)   I, 40, 123
Caspar (Casper)   I, 610, 613
George   I, 40
Jacob   I, 122, 125, 126
Johan Henrich   I, 39, 41, 42
Katrena   I, 40
Menea   I, 40
Peter   I, 40
Philip (Villips)   I, 39, 41, 42
KNÖRI
Lorentz   I, 685
KNORN
Jane F.   II, 151
KNORR (KNOR, KNORRE)
Durst   I, 447
Friederich   II, 76
Heinr.   II, 108
Johann Melchior   I, 458
KNORR
Johannes   I, 458
Leonhart   I, 716
KNORTZER (KRITZER)
Johann Baldas
  (Baltzer)   I, 246, 247, 248
Johan Georg
  (George)   I, 569, 570, 572
KNÖSS
Johan Hennrich   I, 418
KNOSTRICH   (KNASTRICH,
  KNASTERIG)
Johannes (John) I, 297, 298, 300
KNUBEL (CREBLE, ABEL)
Christoff
  (Christophr)   I, 246, 247, 248
KNUPPEL
Frederich   II, 120
L.   II, 141
KNURRING
Eva   I, 210
KNUTZ
Chr. F.   II, 186
KÖBEL (KOBEL)
David   I, 365
Hans   I, 14
Jacob   I, 48, 52, 53
Johann Philibbus
  (John Philip) I, 577, 578, 580
John Henrich   II, 19

Jost   I, 365
Maria   I, 49
KOBELENTZ (COBLENTZ)
Niclaus   I, 349, 350, 352
KOBER
Adam   I, 461
Bernhart   I, 327, 329
Christian   I, 461
Daniel   I, 378, 380, 381
Dieterich (Titrick) I, 32, 33, 34
Hans Adam   I, 461
Paul   I, 696
———   II, 162
KÖBERLING (KEPERLING)
Caspar (Casper) I, 373, 374, 376
Conradt   I, 582, 583, 584
KOBERSTEIN
Hans Gorg   I, 446
KÖBRICH
Johann Peter   I, 748
KOCH (KOCK)
A. Catharina   II, 69
A. Marg.   II, 105
Adam   I, 458
Albertus (Albertos) I, 205, 207, 208
Andrew   I, 537
Anthon   I, 419
Catharine   II, 24, 106
Christian   I, 498, 629, 632
                           635, 721
Christoph   I, 250, 251
Died.[rich]   II, 114
Elisabeth   II, 24, 85
Filbs Jacob   I, 372
Friederich
  (Fredrick)   I, 637, 639, 640
George   II, 10, 85, 161
                           184, 205
George Adam (Jerg Adam,
  Jurgh Adam)   I, 122, 125
                          126, 292
Georg Henry   I, 508
Hans (Martin)   I, 250, 251
Hans Georg (Hans
  Jorg)   I, 12, 27, 29, 30, 292
Heinrich (Henrich) I, 217, 218, 220
                          421, 434
                          II, 24
J. Conrad   I, 466
J. Henry   I, 503
J. Michael   I, 458
J. Nichs   II, 4
Jacob   I, 250, 251, 430, 720
                          II, 184
Johann   I, 732
Johan Casper
  (Casper)   I, 551, 552, 554
                 560, 561, 563, 742

Johann Frantz
(Frans) I, 564, 565, 567
Johann Friederich I, 693
Johan Georg (Johan
George) I, 40, 41, 42
307, 308, 309, 506
Johann Henrich
(Johanes) I, 217, 218, 220
Johann Jacob (Joan
Jacob) I, 79, 81, 82
283, 284, 285, 450
Johan Jost I, 653, 654
Johan Jurgen (Geo.) I, 681, 682
Johann Michel (John
Michael) I, 330, 652, 654
Johann Nicolaus I, 400
Johan Peter
(Petter) I, 536, 537, 538
564, 565, 567
Johan Stats
(John) I, 536, 537, 538
Johannes I, 258, 260, 263
340, 422, 428
436, 449, 499
642, 644, 649
651, 653, 654, 755
John II, 122, 161
John Conrad II, 69
Jost Henry II, 85
Ludwig II, 53
Marcus (Mark) I, 250, 251
Martin I, 251
Mary Lienda II, 85
Michel I, 84, 86, 87, 458
Nicolaus (Nicklaus) I, 179, 181, 183
Peter I, 204, 206, 208
369, 370
II, 45
Phillip (Phillips) I, 373, 374, 376
Thomas I, 371
(*See also* COCH)
KÖCHEL (KEELER)
Jerg (Jorg, George) I, 637, 638, 640
KOCHENDORFF (COCHENDERFF,
COCHENDERFER)
Andreas (Hants
Andreas) I, 89, 90, 92
Jerg Peter (Pet[r]) I, 638, 639, 641
Johan Georg I, 457
Johan Lenhart
(Leonard) I, 653, 655
KOCHER
Claus (Laus) I, 179, 181, 183
Georg (Jorg, Görg) I, 179, 181, 183
John George II, 99
Martin I, 179, 181, 183
KOCHGES
Laux I, 759

KÖCHLEIN
Johann Peter I, 328
KOCHNAUER (KOCHNOUR,
COCHENAUER)
Jacob I, 156, 159, 161
KOCK (GOCK)
Hans Michael (Michael,
Johannes Mich[1]) I, 559, 561, 562
J. F. II, 202
KOCKERT (COOKHART, KUCK-
HART, KOCKHART)
Daniell (Daniel) I, 256, 259, 261
Johann Jacob
(Jacob) I, 257, 259, 262
KOCKS
Anna II, 23
KODER
A. Conrad I, 462
Conrad I, 462
Hans Jerg I, 463
KOEHL
Bastian II, 199
KOELLING
Johann II, 79
KOENER
Lamb II, 136
KOENINGSFELD
Adam I, 759
KOENTZ *see* KUNTZ
KOEPPER
Moritz Henry II, 94
KOESTEYN
J. H. II, 134
KOETS
Wilhelm I, 676
KOFFER (KUFER, KOSER)
Fredrick I, 142
Jacob I, 142, 145, 146
KOFFMAN
Christian II, 126
Christopher II, 126
Hans I, 175, 176, 177
Isaac I, 175, 176, 177
KOFTLER (KOFFLER)
Florian Peter I, 473
KOGEL
Christoph II, 173
Martin I, 469
KOGER
Jacob I, 105, 106
Nick I, 105
KOGHILL
Michael I, 503
KOHDE (GODEE)
Johan Henrich (Johan
Henrick) I, 266, 269, 272
KOHL (KÖHL)
Christ I, 705

Conradt
(Conrad)   I, 340, 342, 343, 421
David (Davit)   I, 604, 606, 607
Davit (David)
Georg Dietrich   I, 48, 52, 53
Hans Georg   I, 50
Henrich   I, 698
Jacob (Joh. Jacob) I, 564, 566, 568
                        II, 127
Johan (Hans
    Hannes)   I, 564, 566, 568
Johan Christ (Joh.
    Christ)   I, 352, 354
Joh. Georg (Hance
    Jereck)   I, 93, 95, 609
                        610, 612
Johan Ludwig (Johann
    Ludwig Ludwick) I, 293, 294, 296
Katherina Margerita   I, 49
Maria Ursela   I, 49
Peter   I, 167, 168
Philip Christoph   I, 50
William   I, 376, 377
                        II, 162
——
(*See also* COALE)
KOHLASS
Johann Adam (Johan
    Ad^m)   I, 600, 602, 603
KÖHLER (KOLLER, KOHLLER,
    KOHLER, COLLER, KEHLER,
    KEELER)
Abraham   I, 742
Anna Maria   I, 131
Cath^n   II, 161
Cath. W.   II, 161
Conrad   I, 378, 379, 381
Elizabeth   I, 131
Eva Maria   I, 191
Friedrich   I, 88, 90, 91
                346, 576, 578, 580
                        II, 171
Gabriel   I, 327, 329
Georg (Geo.)   I, 601, 602, 603
George Christ   II, 70
Hans (H. K.)   I, 152, 153, 154
Hans Jerig
    (Jurick)   I, 116, 120, 121
Hans Petter   I, 373, 374, 375
Hans Philip (Hans
    Phipp)   I, 199, 201, 203
Henrich Wilhelm   I, 461
Jacob   I, 153, 471
Johann Albrecht   I, 20
Johann Baltzer   I, 357
Johann Christoph
    Friedrich   I, 478
Johan Elbreat   I, 18

Johann Jacob
    (Jacob)   I, 236, 238, 239
Johann Jost   I, 346
Johann Jurg   I, 379, 380, 382
Johann Marthin   I, 353, 354
Johann Peter   I, 327, 329
Johannes
    (Johanes)   I, 180, 182, 184
                189, 192, 194
                378, 379, 381, 463
                596, 598, 599, 717
Jonas   I, 18, 19
Jorg Friedrich
    (Frederick) I, 131, 133, 134
Joseb (Joseph) I, 282, 284, 285
Maria   I, 117
Matteus (Matthäs)   I, 717, 762
Michael   I, 717
Nickolas (Nichlaus) I, 482, 736
Peter   I, 660, 761
Susanna   I, 153
Susanna Margerita   I, 49
Wilhelm   II, 52
KOHLHAUER
Anna Elis.   II, 158
Cath. Eliz.   II, 158
Conrad   II, 158
Henry   II, 158
John   II, 158
Mar. Cath.   II, 158
Peter   II, 158
KOHLI
Hans   I, 470
Jacob   I, 470
Jorg   I, 470
KOHLMAN (COLEMAN, COLMAN,
    KOHLMANN)
J. Adam   I, 564, 565, 567
Jacob   I, 762
Johann Phillip   I, 762
Sebastian   I, 232, 233
Vallentin   I, 522, 524
KOHLSLATES
Johanna Sophia   II, 69
KOHLWEIN
Jacob   I, 719
KOHN
A. H.   II, 71
Levy   II, 139
KOHN (KUN)
Mächel (Mich^l)   I, 649, 650
KOLB (COLB, COLP)
A. M.   II, 5
Adam   II, 5
Andreas   I, 459
Anna B.   II, 5
Anna Phillis   I, 28
Catharina   II, 5

Christian (Johan
  Christ)   I, 569, 570, 572
Christiana   II, 5
Conrath (Connard)   I, 99, 100, 101
Dielman (Dilman)   I, 23, 25, 26
Dorothea   II, 5
Elizabeth   II, 5
Eva   II, 5
Georg Michel (Jurich
  Michell)   I, 212, 214, 215
Hans Caspar (Hans Kaspar
  Hance Gasper)   I, 27, 29, 30
J. B.   II, 5
Johann   II, 29
Johann Andreas   I, 696
Johann Graff   I, 512, 514, 515
Johann Jacob   I, 169, 170, 172
Johann Ludwig
  (Ludwig)   I, 179, 181, 183
Johan Peter
  (Peter)   I, 356, 568, 570, 572
Johann Philipps
  (Philip)   I, 621, 623, 625
Johann Willhelm   I, 438
Johannes   I, 694
John Adam   II, 5
John Hend^k   II, 5
Judith   I, 23
Leonhart   I, 38, 39
Mardi   I, 355
Mattheis   I, 355
Mattias (Mathias)   I, 316, 317
Melchior (Michell) I, 212, 214, 215
Michel (Michael)   I, 328, 532
                             533, 535
Peter (Peiter)   I, 212, 214, 215
                        569, 570, 572
Philip   I, 367, 369
(*See also* COLP)
KOLBE
  Christoph   I, 357
  Joh. Casp.   II, 108
  Paulus   I, 731
KOLEN (read prob. KOHL)
  Marus   II, 135
KÖLHOFFER
  Friedrich   I, 759
KOLL
  Abraham   I, 459
  John H.   II, 98
KOLLE (COLLE)
  Johanes (Johannes) I, 559, 560, 562
KOLLEBERN
  Anthony   II, 68
KOLLEN
  Anna Sophia   II, 140

KÖLLER (COOLIAR, COOLER,
  KOLLER)
Andreas (Andrias,
  Andrices)   I, 286, 287, 288
Erhard   II, 98
Georg Jacob   I, 733
Hans Michael   I, 540, 542, 544
Jacob   I, 417, 656, 657, 658
Johan Carl   II, 29
Michael (Mich^1)   I, 638, 639, 641
KOLLHAGEN
Peter   II, 110
KÖLLIN (KELLIE)
Joh. Wilhelm (Willem) I, 71, 75, 77
Margeritta   I, 73
KOLLMER (KÖLLMER, KILLMER)
Hans Martin   I, 438
Henrich Peter (Henry
  Peter)   I, 643, 645
KOLLNER
Maria Eliz^th   II, 23
KOLLREN (read prob. KOLLER)
Elizabeth   I, 108
KOLMAN (KOLEMAN)
Abraham   I, 327, 329
Ar.   II, 147
Michael   II, 67
KOLMER (COLLMERE, COLEMER)
Daniel   I, 84, 86, 87
Mattelena   I, 85
KÖLSCH (KELSCH)
Johann Georg (Joh.
  Diterich)   I, 178, 180, 182
KOLTER
Johann Adam   I, 458
KOMMER (COMER, COMMER)
Daniel (Dannill)   I, 163, 165, 166
Jan (Hance)   I, 163, 165, 166
KONDER
Hans Geo.   I, 175, 176, 178
Peter   I, 175, 176, 178
KONDEY
Anna E.   II, 158
John Geo.   II, 158
Maria C.   II, 158
——   II, 158
KONFLEUR
Fredrick   II, 76
KÖNIG
Abraham   I, 474
Ann Gertrout   II, 84
Balzar   I, 472
Cath^a Marg^a   II, 23
Christel   I, 692
Christian   I, 358, 573, 574, 575
Christian Ludewig I, 677, 678, 680
Conrad   I, 698
David   I, 698
                                 II, 177

Franz II, 126
Gabriel I, 67, 69, 70
Georg Heinrich I, 492
Gottfried I, 497
Hans I, 448
Hans Georg
  (Jurg) I, 226, 229, 231
Henrich Anthon I, 391
Henry II, 94
J. Chrˢ II, 17
Jacob I, 266, 269, 272
  358, 474
  II, 192
Johann (John) I, 289, 290, 291
Johann August (John
  Argus) I, 672, 673, 674
Joh. Daniel I, 690
Johan Frid. I, 489
Johann Michel I, 404
Johannes I, 340, 341, 343
  465, 488
  II, 169
Joseph I, 479
Ludwig I, 394
Matheus I, 474
Michael I, 376, 377
Nicklaus I, 497
Peter I, 289, 497
Samuel I, 358
KÖNIGSFELDT (KENIGSFELDT)
Johan Wendel I, 667, 669, 671
KONING
Matthias, de II, 73
KÖNNE (KÄNNE, KÖNNEN)
Balthaser, von I, 414
Jacob, von I, 471
Johann Peter, von I, 371
Martin, von I, 414
KONRIN
Agnes II, 119
KONTS, COUNTS *see* KUNTZ
KONZELMAN
Dorothy II, 150
Frederik II, 150
John II, 150
John George II, 150
KOOBLER *see* KUBLER
KOOG (read prob. KOCH)
Johannes I, 44
Julian I, 44
KOOGE
Wilhelm I, 477
KOOGER (read prob. KOCHER)
Jacob I, 102
Nicholaus I, 102
KOOGH (read prob. KOCH)
Conrad I, 43, 46, 47
KOOKES
John Henry I, 322

KOOLER (read prob. KOHLER)
Dorothy I, 103
Elizabeth I, 103
Hans Jacob I, 173, 176, 177
KOONIG (read prob. KÖNIG)
David II, 68
KOOP
Johann Georg I, 437
KOOTS
Andereas I, 508
KOOTSON
Anna I, 104
KOPENHÖFFER (KOPPENHÖFFER,
  KOPPENHEFFER, KOPPEN-
  HÄFFER, KAPPENHEFFER)
Hans Michˡ (Hans
  Michel) I, 610, 611, 613
Jacob (Jan Jacob) I, 212, 214, 216
Thomas I, 21, 22
(*See also* COPENHAVER)
KOPF
Jerg I, 496
KOPINS (CAPPIAS, CAPPIES)
Johannes I, 615, 617, 619
KOPLIN
Matthias I, 21
KÖPLY (KEPLEY, KIPPILY)
Johan Henry (John
  Hendrich) I, 246, 247, 248
KOPP (KOP, KOB)
Adam Friedrich II, 190
Charlet Margretta I, 241
Christina Magdalena II, 190
Daniel I, 463
Friederic I, 358
Georg Henrich I, 508
Georg Leonthart I, 508
George I, 440
Jacob I, 463
Johann Conradt I, 506
Joh. Friedrich II, 190
Johann Heinrich
  (Henry) I, 614, 616, 619
Johann Jacob I, 404
Jorg (Jerg Heinrich) I, 614, 616, 619
Justina Margaret II, 190
Kattarina I, 241
Loadwick I, 241
Mareline I, 241
Margrat I, 242
Philip Cristopher I, 241
Samuel Eberhart (Sam.
  Overhard) I, 240, 242, 243
KOPPE (COBIE)
Erdmann (Edmund) I, 383, 385
Mertje II, 123
KOPPEBERGER
Friederich Christian I, 432

KÖPPEL (KEPPEL, KÖPPELL)
Andröas   I, 702
Henrich   I, 405
Jacob   I, 405
Johan Nickel   I, 405
Michel   I, 405
Paulus   I, 405
Petter   I, 405
KOPPELBERGER
Henrich   I, 357
KOPPELGER
Mich.   I, 328
KOPPER
Fred. Wilch.   II, 118
KOPPING
Christian   II, 73
KOPPMAN
Claus   II, 50
KORB
Catharina   II, 70
KÖRBER (KARBER, KIRBER, KORBER)
Dorothea   II, 69
Johann Michael (John Mich.)   I, 185, 186, 187
(*See also* CÖRBER and KORPER)
KORFES
Ch.   II, 108
KORFF
Joseph   II, 139
KORFMANN
Conrath   I, 701
KORN
Carl   I, 480
J. Friederich (Hans Fred[k])   I, 642, 644
Philip   II, 9
Valentin (Veltin)   I, 513, 514, 516
Valentin Simon   I, 698
(*See also* CORN)
KORNBUSCH
Ab[rm]   II, 101
KORNDÖRFER (CORONDORPH, KORNDÖRFFER)
Johann Nicolas (John Nicholas)   I, 386, 387, 389
KÖRNER
Johann Adam   I, 437, 533, 534
Johann Anthonius   I, 450
Johann Peter   I, 683
Johann Wilhel (Wilhelm)   I, 677, 679, 680
KORNMANN (KORNMAN)
Ludwig   I, 169, 170, 172
KORNSCHEUER
Justus   I, 733
KORPER (KERPER, KORBER, KÖRBER)
Abraham   I, 198, 200, 202

Anna   I, 108
Anna Eve   I, 108
Barbara   I, 109
Elizabeth   I, 109
Eve   I, 109
Johan Caspar (Gasper)   I, 107, 111, 112
Maria   I, 108
Niklas (Nicholas)   I, 59, 63, 64
KÖRPERT
Johann Phillip   I, 449
KORR
Michl   I, 21
KORREL
Petan   II, 61
KORRICH
Alida   II, 58
KÖRSCHNER
Johann Daniel   I, 684
KÖRSCHNOCK (KAARSCHNOCK)
Gottfried (Codfery)   I, 560, 561, 563
KÖRTH (KORTH, KORTT)
Johann Bernhardt   I, 711
Matheus (Matteas)   I, 296, 298, 299
KORTOREL
Friederich   II, 59
KORTSON
Maria   I, 44
KORTZ
Barbara   II, 167
Christian   I, 188, 191, 193
Jacob   II, 167
Johan   II, 167
Johannas   II, 167
(*See also* KURTZ)
KOSSER
Hans Michal   I, 423
KOST (COIST)
Hendrich (John Henry)   I, 297, 298, 299
Ulrich   I, 605, 606, 607
KOSTENBADER
Johann Heinrich   I, 490
KÖSTER (KOSTER)
Christian   II, 147
Jerg   I, 409
Johan Dietrich   I, 709
Johannes   I, 695
Michael (Mich[l])   I, 637, 639, 641
(*See also* COSTER)
KOSTERMAN
R. C.   II, 99
KOSTERS
Anne Catherine   II, 57
KÖTH
Andreas   I, 432
Johann Georg (Georg)   I, 376, 377

KOUTGE
Anna II, 191
Anna Carolina II, 191
Anna Rachel II, 191
Eleonora Constantina II, 191
Johann Gotlieb II, 191
KOUTZ
John Necklos II, 77
KOWLER
John I, 227; II, 104
KRÄBER (GRAVER)
Jacob I, 595, 597, 599
KRÄCHMANN
Jacob I, 503
KRAFF
Johan Gerg I, 394
KRAFFTHORN
Johan I, 484
KRAFT (KRAFFT, CRAFFT)
Andreas (Andries) I, 21, 22, 683
Fridrich
(Frederik) I, 199, 201, 203, 454
George II, 8, 107
Gottfried (Gottsmitt) I, 48, 52, 53
Hans Georg I, 417
Hans Michael I, 327, 329
Heinrich (Henrich) I, 454, 688
Jacob I, 358, 705
Jasper II, 73
Jerg Ludwig I, 605, 607, 608
Johann Friedrich I, 169, 170, 172
Johan Henrich I, 714
Johann Jacob
(Jacob) I, 199, 201, 203
Joh. Ludwig I, 348, 350, 351
Johan Niclos
(Johaniclos) I, 212, 214, 216
Johann Rudolff I, 509
Maria Epha I, 49
Peter I, 686
Valentin I, 322
(*See also* CRAFT)
KRAGHBERGER
Uhlerick I, 490
KRAH (KRA, KRAA)
Hans George
(George) I, 615, 617, 620
KRAHL (KRÄHL)
Joh. Fried II, 108
Michael (Mich¹) I, 628, 631, 634
Theodorus I, 357
KRAIL
James II, 152
John G. II, 152
John Gotlieb II, 200
Margaret II, 152
Mary II, 152
KRALL
John Jacob II, 70

KRAM (KLAM, CRAM)
Clara I, 49
Cornelius I, 66, 69, 70
Elizabeth I, 67
Fredk II, 11
Henrich I, 48, 52, 53
Johannes I, 743
Susannah II, 42
KRÄMER (KREMER, KRAMER,
CRAMER, KRAMMER,
KREAMER)
Adam I, 44
Andreas
(Anderras) I, 79, 82, 83
307, 308, 309, 458
Anna II, 188
Arnold I, 396
Casper I, 89, 91, 92, 478
Catharine II, 156, 188
Christian I, 44, 605, 607, 608
666, 668, 670
II, 188
Christina I, 45
Conrad I, 435
II, 122
Elizabeth I, 43, 80
Ernst I, 676
Eve I, 44
Frantz I, 699
Friedrich I, 62, 340, 522, 524
George I, 62
Gottfrith I, 62
Hans Adam (Adam) I, 43, 45, 46
Hans Gorg (Hans
Jerig) I, 8, 9
Heinrich (Henrich,
Hendrick) I, 43, 46, 253
254, 255, 378
II, 128, 136
Henry I, 418
Isabella Agnes I, 55
Jacob II, 188
Johann II, 50
Johann Adam I, 750
Johann Baldasar I, 750
Johann Caspar I, 378, 379, 381
Johan Georg I, 750
Johann Henrich I, 725
Johann Martin I, 750
Johann Matthias I, 54, 56
Johann Michel I, 310, 312, 313
Johann Petter
(Peter) I, 397, 437
569, 571, 573
Johann Sebalt
(Sebaldt) I, 59, 63, 65
Johannes (John) I, 335, 336, 338, 425
II, 186
Johannes Antonius I, 478

Johannes Ernst I, 401
Ludwig I, 750
Margaretta
(Margretha) I, 55, 61
Maria (Mary) I, 44
II, 188
Martin I, 750
Mathias (Mattias) I, 79, 82, 83, 372
Michael II, 171
Peter I, 310, 312, 313
Sofia I, 61
William II, 188
(*See also* CRAMER, CREMER *and* KREMER)
KRAMERS
Christina II, 11
KRAMLICH (GRAMLICH)
Friedrich II, 134
Matheas (Mathias) I, 560, 561, 563
KRANCK
Hans I, 503
KRANENBURG
Mattheus II, 193
KRANTZ (KRANS, KRANSS, KRANZ)
Georg Fred. II, 44
George Michiel (Johan Mich[1]) I, 221, 223, 224
Johann Henrich (Henry) I, 622, 624, 626
Johann Petter I, 721
Vallendin (Valentine) I, 204, 206, 207
KRAPFF (KRAPF, CRAFT)
Henrich (Hend[k]) I, 387, 388, 389
Peter I, 689
KRAPP (KRAPE)
Heinrich I, 509, 510, 511
Johannes I, 331
KRÄSS
Johann Valentin I, 485
KRASSLE
Peter I, 715
KRATER (CREDER)
Jacob I, 107, 111, 112
KRATSINGER
Peter I, 422
KRATZ (CRATZ)
Albertus I, 735
Andreas (Andries) I, 155, 158, 161
581, 583, 584
Charles Ph. II, 160
Conrad II, 78
Vallentin I, 17
(*See also* KRAZ)
KRATZENBERGEN
Anna Elizabeth II, 170
KRATZER (KRÄTZER)
Johann Philipp I, 173, 174

Johannes I, 686
Joseph I, 162, 164, 166
(*See also* CRATSAR)
KRAUL (KRAUEL)
Johann Georg II, 130
Johan Heinrich I, 757
KRAUN
Johannes I, 398
KRAUSAM
Anna I, 122
Maria I, 122
Susanna I, 122
KRAUSE (KRAUSEN)
Christoph (Christof-fel) I, 180, 182, 184
KRAUSER (KRAUSSER)
Georg Sebastian I, 431
Jn[o] Adam I, 752
KRAUSHAAR
Jacob II, 8
Johannes I, 444, 499
Johannis Claus I, 499
Philip Christian II, 67
KRAUSKOB (KRAUSSKOB, KRAUSZKEEP)
Johann Gorg (Johannes Jerick) I, 559, 561, 563
KRAUSS (KRAUS, KROUS, KRAUTS, KRAWS)
Carl II, 140
Ernst Lutwig I, 577, 579, 580
G. Michael I, 433
Georg Davit I, 459
Hans Georg (Hans Jer-rick) I, 184, 186, 187
609, 611, 613
637, 638, 640
Hans Michael (Hans Mich[1]) I, 677, 678, 680
Jacob I, 71, 75, 77
297, 414, 498
Joh. David (Johan David) I, 645, 647
Joh. Georg I, 414, 661, 662, 664
Johann Henrich I, 585, 586, 588
Johann Jacob I, 39, 41, 42
Johann Michel I, 513, 514, 515
Johan Peter I, 661, 663, 664
Johann Valentin I, 722
Johannes (Hans) I, 13, 360, 361, 503
595, 597, 599
Matthias I, 661, 663, 664, 738
Melchior (Michel, Malchi) I, 264, 268, 271
Mich[1] I, 719
Rosina I, 72
Simon I, 416
Stefan (Stepen) I, 637, 639, 641

Wilhelm (William) I, 117, 120, 121
(*See also* CROUSE *and* GROWS)
KRAUT (KRAUTH, CRAUT,
  KRAUTT
Christoph
  (Christophel) I, 189, 192, 194
George II, 54
Jacob II, 61
Jacob Adam I, 425
Johannes I, 188, 191, 193
Matheis I, 508
Petter I, 419
William II, 198
KRÄUTER (KRAUTER, KRAUT-
  TER)
David II, 172
George II, 197
Johann Melchior (John
  Melchior) I, 387, 388, 389
Melcher I, 474
KRAUTHAMEL (KRAWTHAMEL,
  GRAUTHAMEL)
Andreas (Anderas) I, 615, 617, 619
KRAUTMAN
Johannes II, 113
Valentin II, 113
KRAUTWORST
Anna Maria II, 3
Peter II, 3
KRAYSEMAN
Catrina I, 118
KRAZ (read KRATZ)
Mr. II, 74
KREBER (CRABER)
Henrich (Henrick) I, 290, 291
Philip (Philib) I, 290, 291
KREBIEHL (KREBIELL, KREBIHL,
  KREHBÜHL, KREHBIEHL,
  KRAYEBILL)
Christian I, 17, 358
Henrich I, 14
Johannes I, 708
Michael I, 14
Peter I, 698, 700
Ulrich I, 348, 349, 351
(*See also* CREBIL)
KREBS (KREPS, GREPS)
Adam I, 225, 228, 230
Bernard II, 113
Christian I, 459
Elisab. II, 137
Fillibs I, 355
Geo. I, 705
Hans Georg I, 310, 311, 313, 492
Helena II, 137
Henrich Jacob I, 357
Jacob I, 445
Johan Burck I, 706
Johann Christian I, 546, 548, 550

Johann Henrich I, 458
Johan Jerg
  (George) I, 234, 235, 236
Johann Paulls I, 352, 354
Johannes I, 412
Ludwig (Ludewig) I, 415
Martin I, 665, 668, 670
Michael I, 637, 639, 641
Philip I, 546, 548, 550
Thomas I, 754
KREBSER
Magdelena I, 148
Verena I, 147
KRECH
Jacob I, 88
KREGELO (KREGELOH, KRE-
  GILO)
Johannes I, 569, 571, 572
  577, 579, 581
KREGER
J. Conrad I, 465
Jacob II, 145
Jerick I, 290
KREHL
Johanes II, 171
KREIDERER (KREITER)
Michel I, 59, 63, 65
KREIDLER (KREYTLER)
Georg Martin
  (Yerrick) I, 526, 528, 529
Jerg I, 454
Johann Merden (John
  Martin) I, 551, 552, 554
Philipp Jacob I, 551, 552, 554
Steffann (Stafann,
  Stephen) I, 551, 553, 554
KREIL (KREYL, CRYLE)
Johann Adam I, 72, 76, 78
Tomas (Thomas) I, 72, 76, 78
KREILING
Ewerhart I, 474
KREININGER (KRENINGER)
Jacob I, 546, 548, 550
KREINS
John Herm. II, 160
KREIS (GRIES)
Hans Jerg I, 531, 533, 535
Johan Henrich I, 467
Johan Jacob I, 416
Wilhelm II, 114
KREISCHER
Johan Adam I, 521, 523
Johann Sebastian I, 521, 524
John Nicklas I, 390
Michel (Michal) I, 293, 294, 295
Philibs I, 390
KREISER
Christoff I, 491

KREISSEL (GRYSIL, GRESIL)
Andreas   I, 596, 597, 599
KREISSEMANN (KREISSMAN, KRAYSMAN)
Jerg (Gerg, Jurick) I, 116, 120, 121
KREITER (GREYTER)
Caspar   I, 586, 587, 588
Henrick (Henrich) I, 179, 181, 183
Johannes   I, 723
KREITH (KRITE)
Bernhardt (Bernhard)   I, 652, 654
KREIVE
Johannes   I, 236
KREMER (CRAEMER)
Jost (Joost)   I, 280, 281, 282
Konnrath   I, 425
Nicolaus (Nicholas) I, 560, 561, 563
Nolchen   I, 478
KRENER
Jacob   II, 26
KRESCH
——   II, 162
KRESLER (CRASLER)
Philip (Hans Philip) I, 99, 100, 101
KRESMEN
Magratha   I, 61
KRESS (KROSS, CRIST)
Anna   I, 60
Anna Catrina   I, 28
Carls   I, 493
Caspar   I, 493
Christian   I, 500
Henry   I, 493
Jacob   I, 59, 63, 64
Johann   I, 493
Johan Christoph   I, 417
Johann Fillip   I, 755
Johann Heinrich   I, 485
Johan Jorg (Hans Jurg)   I, 638, 639, 641
Johann Mardin (John Martin)   I, 27, 29, 30
Mattheis   I, 498
Stophel   I, 638
KRESSMANN
Balthas   I, 467
KRETCHER
Anna Cath[r]   II, 147
Anna Schob   II, 147
Anto.   II, 147
Catherine   II, 147
Christane   II, 147
KRETZ
Andreas   II, 135
Michael   I, 539, 541, 543
Peter   I, 372
KREUDER
Johann Martin   I, 466

KREUILICH
Andrew   II, 56
KREUL (CRYDLE)
Thomas, Senr.   I, 72, 76, 78
KREUSCHER
Johan Jost   I, 390
KREUSER (KREUSSER)
Conrad   II, 78
Johann   I, 729
KREUTTER (KREUNTTER, KREITER)
Abraham   I, 117, 120, 121
Johan Wilhelm   I, 340, 342, 343
Ludwig Henrich (Ludwig Kenrick)   I, 655, 657, 658
(*See also* CROYTER)
KREUTZBURG
Joh. Hinr.   II, 140
KREUTZWISSER
Johannes   I, 438
KREUZER
Johann Christoph   I, 696
KREYDER (KRITER)
Jacob (Johannes Jacob)   I, 559, 561, 563
KREYER (FRIOR, FREIR)
Johan Gerge (John George)   I, 638, 639, 641
KREYEVELLER
Heinrick   II, 124
KREYL
Conrad   I, 723
KREYN
Johann Adam   II, 79
KREYS
Marys   I, 731
KREYSER
Ulrich   I, 483
KREYSH
Phil. Jacob   I, 395
KRIBLY (GREEBEL)
Johan Christian (John Kres)   I, 568, 570, 572
KRICK
Friedr.   II, 107
KRICKEL
Joach. Friedr.   II, 106
KRIDEL
J. F.   II, 5
KRIEBEL (KRIBEL, KRIEBLE, KREEBEL, GRIBEL, KREMBELER)
Anna   I, 137, 138
Casper   I, 136, 140, 141
Christopher   I, 136, 137
Georg (George) I, 136, 138, 140, 141
Georg Frederich   I, 336, 337, 339
Johan George (John George)   I, 622, 624, 626

Maria   I, 137, 138
Melchior   I, 136, 140, 141
Rosina   I, 137
Susannah   I, 137, 138
KRIECHBAUM (KRICHBAUM)
Hann Philip   I, 395
Johann Adam   I, 396
Johan Conradt   I, 481
Johan Wilhelm   I, 396
KRIEDELBACH
Johannes   I, 762
KRIEG (KRIECH)
August   I, 643, 644
Jacob   I, 507
Philips (Philip)   I, 677, 678, 679
Valtin   I, 733
KRIEGENMEYER
Johann Georg   I, 494
KRIEGER (KRIGER, CRIGER,
KRUGER, KRYGER)
Benedick   I, 437
Caspar (Casper) I, 31, 33, 34, 506
Christ. Ludw.   II, 107
Hans Adam   I, 400
Hans Jerg   I, 435
Hans Michael   I, 88, 90, 92
Heine   I, 276
Jacob   I, 232, 705
Johann Andreas   I, 318, 319, 320
Johann Henrich   I, 318, 319, 320
Johann Peter   I, 318, 319, 320
Lorrentz (Lorentz) I, 237, 238, 240
Michael   I, 232, 233
Ursela   II, 75
KRIENG
Johann Gottfried   I, 478
KRIESING
Arent   I, 692
KRIESTMAN
Johannes   I, 466
KRIGLER
Anthony   II, 68
KRIGNER
Joseph   II, 20
KRILLER
Hans Jacob   II, 124
KRIM (KRAEM, KREM)
Wendal (Wendel)   I, 628, 631, 635
KRIMMEL
Philibus   I, 714
KRINCKHORN
J. L.   II, 107
KRING
Anna Catharina   II, 172
Anna Margretha   II, 173
Anna Maria   II, 173
Catharina   II, 173
Christian   II, 172, 173
Elisabeth   II, 172

Johan Heinrich   II, 172, 173
Johan Jost   I, 465
Ludwig   II, 172
KRISFELLER (CHRISTFELLEN)
Johan Christ
(John Christ.)   I, 279, 280, 281
KRISTER
C. F.   II, 107
KROB (CROUP)
Johann Georg
(Haneriagh)   I, 240, 242, 243
Jorg Conrad   I, 357
KRÖBER
Anthon   I, 433
Jerg Adolph   I, 404
Johann Adam   I, 367, 368
Johann Gabriel   I, 709
KROBS (KRAPTS)
Anna Percy   I, 108
Christian (Christen) I, 106, 110, 112
Christina   I, 107
Maria Crete   I, 108
KROCKER
Philip   II, 199
KROELLE (KRAYLY, KROELLER)
Johanes (John)   I, 622, 624, 626
KROESEN
Maria Wilh.   II, 193
KROGER (KRAGER)
Johan Christ (John
Christian)   I, 672, 673, 674
KROH
Christian   II, 121
Friedrich (Fred^k) I, 564, 566, 567
Georg Phillippus   I, 367, 368
Henrich (Henrig, J.
Henry)   I, 297, 299, 300
Johann Balthaser
(Baltes)   I, 336, 337, 339, 721
Johann Gottfried   I, 461
(*See also* CROO *and* CROW)
KROHNMEYER
Martin   I, 749
KROLL (CROLL)
Anna   II, 140
Christ (Jno Christ.) I, 23, 25, 26
Fried. Karl   II, 196
Friederica Carol. Christ. II, 140
Johann Martin   I, 453
Johannes   I, 437
Maria   II, 140
Sam. Hinrich   II, 139
Ulrich (Ulderick,
Uldrich)   I, 24, 25, 26
KROM (CROM)
Henrich   I, 699
Jacob (Jacb)   I, 194, 196, 197
Johan Henrich
(John Hend^k)   I, 373, 374, 376

KROMER (KROMAR, CROMER)
Johann Gorg
  (Hans Wright) I, 286, 287, 288
Johann Wilhelm (Jn°
  Willhelm) I, 555, 556, 558
Leonhart I, 717
Michel I, 762
KROMROM
Cathrina II, 50
KRON
Mattheus I, 500
  (See also CRON)
KRONEBURGER
Peter II, 134
KRÖNER
Hans Michel I, 483
KRONING
Catharina II, 56
KRÖNINGER (CRENIGOR)
Johan Daniel
  (Daniel) I, 293, 294, 295
KRONSTUBER
Joach. Carl II, 140
KROON
Naatge II, 123
KROPF (KROPP)
Andreas (Andries) I, 27, 29, 30
Christian (Christen,
  Kristen) I, 27, 29, 30
Daniel I, 28
Jacob I, 27
Joseph I, 485
KROS
Hans Nicolaus II, 138
KRÖTHER
Johan I, 505
KROUSENBURGER
P. II, 186
KRÜCK (KRICK, KRUK, KROOK,
  KRYKE)
Andreas I, 273, 274
Frantz (Frans) I, 43, 46
Johan Jacob (Jacob) I, 43, 46
Johannes I, 154, 157, 160
KRUG (KROEG, GRUGH, KRUGH)
Anna Webern II, 205
Elisabeth II, 205
Fredᵏ II, 29
Gerhard I, 724
Gerret II, 125
J. Christian II, 200
Johann Daniel
  (Daniel) I, 614, 616, 619
Johannes II, 205
Michel (Mich¹) I, 666, 669, 671
  (See also GRUG)
KRÜGELE (KRUGELI)
Conrad II, 170
Johan Conrad I, 470

KRÜGER (KRUGER, KRÖGER)
Anna Christina II, 28
Anna Elisabeth II, 28
Anna Margretha II, 28
Bernhᵈ II, 139
Caston (Clas
  Casten) I, 509, 510, 511
Cathᵃ Elisabeth II, 28
H. II, 141
Joh. Herm. II, 140
Johann Ludᵏ II, 28
Johann Willhelm I, 753
Johan Wolraht
  (Jean Wolf) I, 649, 650
Maria Madelaina II, 28
Martin II, 28
KRUGMAN
Joh. W. II, 137
P. Wilch. II, 119
KRUIN
H. Cath. II, 92
KRUMBACH
Conradt I, 423
KRUMBEIN (CROMBIE)
Leonhart (Leonard) I, 610, 611, 613
KRUMBEL
Hans Adam I, 408
KRUMBHARR
Ludewig II, 83
KRUMHOLTZ (KROMPOLS)
John Carol (John Charles,
  John George) I, 636, 638, 640
KRUMM (KRUM)
Anthon I, 577, 579, 580
Gottfried (God-
  fried) I, 576, 578, 580
John Adam (Johann
  Adam) I, 577, 578, 580
Johann Peter I, 715
Johan Philips I, 467
Philip II, 125
Wilhelm I, 448
  (See also CRUM)
KRUMMLAUF
Johann Görg I, 423
KRUMREIN
Gerg Lenhart I, 371
Hans Michael I, 66, 69, 70
KRÜSS
Georg Christop I, 490
KRUXXE
Ditᶜʰ II, 184
Johann II, 184
KRYBACH
Johan Girg I, 482
KRYNER
Andreas I, 649
KÜBELLER
Johann Wendel I, 706

KUBER (KUBLER)
Elizabeth I, 148
Hans I, 147, 150
Hans Peter I, 456
Jacob I, 148, 480
KÜBLER (KUBLER, KIEBLER, KIEVLER)
Eva Dorothea I, 190
Hans Jorg
(Hans Georg) I, 189, 192, 194
Jacob I, 113, 114, 115, 765
Maria Eve I, 190
Philipp I, 394
KÜBLINGER
Johann Daniel I, 396
Johan Henrich I, 448
Johann Jacob I, 396
KÜBORTZ (KEIPORT)
Jacob I, 265, 268, 271
Johan Gorg Daniel I, 305, 306
KUCH
Burckhardt
(Burghart) I, 627, 630, 633
Christ. Heinr. II, 107
Johann Michael I, 710
Johann Peter I, 738
KUCHE (QUA)
Fridrich I, 531, 533, 534
KUCHER (COOKER)
Johann Peter I, 88, 90, 92
KÜCHERER
Johann Friederich I, 691
KUCHES
Hans Gerg I, 492
KUCHLE (KUCHLI, KUHLE)
Hans Cunrad I, 471
Johannes (Johans) I, 194, 196, 197
KÜCHLER
Christoph I, 470
KUCKEN
Elizb. I, 80
KUDER (CONDER)
Hannes Peter
(Hans Pieter) I, 188, 191, 193
KUELER
Henrich I, 676
KUENTHLEIN (KINSLEY)
Jacob I, 274
Rudolf (Ruduf) I, 274, 276
KUESSLING
Anna Eliz. F. II, 157
Frederica II, 157
Henry II, 157
J. C. Charles II, 157
—— II, 157
KÜFER (KIFFER, KIFER, KÜFFER)
Henrich (Henrick) I, 265, 269, 272
Jacob I, 714

John George I, 485
KÜGEL (KUKEL, KUGELL)
Hans Max I, 498
Jacob I, 472
Leonard I, 185, 186, 187
KUGELBERGER (COWCKLE-BERGH, COUKLEBERGH)
Johannes I, 277, 278, 279
Wilhelm I, 277
KUGELE
Fred II, 188
John II, 188
KUGELLWERTH
Johannes I, 698
KUGERLE (GORLE)
Johann Jacob
(Jacob) I, 212, 214, 216
KUGLER (KUGHLER, KYGLER)
Fillib I, 400
Jacob I, 738
Johan Nickell I, 205
Johanes I, 498
KUGLEY
Hendrick I, 303
KUHBACH (KÜHBAUCH)
Christof I, 508
Matheus I, 489
KUHL (KÜHL, KOOL)
Frantz Jacob I, 405
Han Philip (Johann
Philipp) I, 661, 663, 664
J. C. II, 32
Jacob I, 373, 374, 375
Johannes I, 323, 325, 326
(*See also* COOLL)
KUHLEMANN
Christoph I, 503
(*See also* COOLMAN)
KUHLENKAMPFF
Nicolaus II, 134
KUHLER (KÜHLER)
Gottlieb II, 101
Henrich (Henry) I, 244, 245
KÜHLEWEIN
Franz I, 443
KÜHLMAN
Frederick I, 696
KÜHMLE (KEMELIE)
Conradt (Conrad) I, 221, 223, 224
KUHN (KÜHN, KOEN, KOON, KUOHN)
Abraham I, 106, 110, 112
Andereas I, 454
Anna Crete I, 108
Anthony II, 13
Catharine I, 107
Christian I, 751
Christoff I, 501
Daniel (Danil) I, 509; II, 101

Eve	I, 107
Frantz	I, 695
Friederich	
(Friderich)	I, 106, 110, 112
Georg Marthin	I, 437
Gerg	I, 692
H.	II, 143
Hans	I, 332, 333, 334, 417
Hans Jerick	I, 108
J. Thomas	I, 504
Jacob	I, 22, 23, 493
Johann Georg	I, 521, 523
Johann Heinrich	I, 713
Johan Jacob (Johann	
Jacob, Jacob)	I, 293, 294, 295
Johann Nickel	I, 683
Johan Philip	I, 692
Johannes (Joanis)	I, 225, 228, 230
	293, 294, 296, 327
	329, 355, 424, 447
	531, 533, 535
Lud. C.	II, 41
Michel	I, 513, 514, 516
Mr.	II, 177
Peter (Petter)	I, 293, 294, 295, 692
(*See also* CUHN)	
KUHNEL	
Johannes	II, 193
Margareth	II, 193
KÜHNEMAN (KUNEMAN)	
Johan Henrich	
(John Henry)	I, 569, 571, 572
Johann Theis	
(Matthias)	I, 569, 571, 572
KÜHNER (KUHNER, KIENAR)	
Caspar (Casper)	I, 221, 223, 224
Hans Jerg	I, 442
Joh. Georg	I, 365
Johann Wendel	I, 418
Philip	II, 122
KÜHNERT (KENAR, KINAR)	
Jacob	I, 221, 222, 224
KÜHNLE	
Georg	I, 687
KUHNMAN (KUNEMAN, KENNE-MAN)	
J. Christian	
(Christian)	I, 673, 675, 676
KUHR	
Johann George	I, 740
KUK	
Michael, van	II, 78
KÜLCKRET (KILKERE)	
Lorentz	I, 551, 552, 554
KULLENBERG	
Isack	II, 102
Wilhelmina	II, 102
KULLENTHAL	
Jacob	I, 427

KULLER	
Johanna	II, 136
Johannes	II, 136
Philipina	II, 136
Rosina W.	II, 136
KULLING	
David	I, 469
KULLMER (KILMIERE)	
Burkhart (Borket)	I, 43, 46, 47
KULMAN	
Jacob	I, 404, 720
Johan Nickel	I, 715
Nicklas	I, 720
KULP	
John Christ.	II, 159
P.	II, 185
Wilhelmina	II, 159
KUM (KÜM)	
Chr.	II, 118
Johannes	I, 402
(*See also* CUMM)	
KÜMMEL (KUMEL, KÜMELL)	
Joh. Jacob	I, 722
Michell	I, 479
——	II, 197
KUMMELMAN	
Franz	II, 21
KUMMER	
Charlotte	II, 157
Dorothy Elis.	II, 157
Hannah M.	II, 157
John Christ.	II, 157
John Dan.	II, 157
John F.	II, 157
John Geo.	II, 157
Sam¹ Wm	II, 157
KUMMERER	
G.	II, 144
KÜMMERLE (KEMMWLIE, KIM-MERLY)	
Albrecht	I, 741
Hans Jacob	I, 531, 533, 534
KUMMERLIN (KAEMMERLIN, KIMMERLING, KÜMMER-LYN)	
Hans Jacob (Jacob)	I, 106, 111, 112
Jacob Friederich	I, 446
KÜMPEL	
Philip Jacob	I, 433
KUMPF	
J. W.	II, 24
Wilhelm	I, 737
KUMREIN (KUMEREIN, CINNER-LEY)	
Hans Jacob (Jacob)	I, 236, 238, 239
KUN (KUNN)	
Christoph	I, 371
Johan Christ	I, 425
Johannes	I, 31, 32, 33

KUNCKEL (CUNKEL, KUNGEL, KUNKEL)
Hans   I, 383, 385
Hans Adam (Senior)   I, 383, 385
Henrich   I, 717
Johan, Junior   I, 383, 385
Johann Christian   I, 709
Johannes   I, 383, 385, 717, 721
Lorentz   I, 459
(*See also* CUNCKEL *and* GUN-KEL)
KUND (KÜND, KIND)
Joseph   I, 719
Michal   I, 509, 510, 511
KUNEKE
Frieder.   II, 182
KUNEL (KENNEL, KENEL)
Katherina Elizabeth   I, 49
Nicklaus (Nicholaus)   I, 48, 52, 53
KUNER
Peter   I, 759
KUNGOLDT
Freidrich Willhelm   II, 48
KUNICHE (KUNSHE, KINIGE)
Jobst (Jobst Henrich) I, 517, 518, 520
KUNIG
Godfred   I, 231
KUNKELMANN
Johannes   I, 698
KÜNLE (KUNHLE, KÜNLEN)
Janichl (Johannes) I, 596, 598, 600
Philipp Jacob   I, 475
KUNRAD (KUNRATH)
Hans   I, 415
Ully   I, 415
(*See also* CONRAD)
KÜNSINGER
Johannes   I, 761
KUNSMAN (KUNTSMAN)
August Heinrich   I, 143, 145, 146
Maria   II, 198
KUNSO
Johan C.   II, 136
KUNST (KUNS, KUNSS, KONST)
George   II, 8
Heinrich   I, 398
Johan Jost (Johan Joost)   I, 188, 192, 193
Johannes (Joanis)   I, 204, 206, 208
KUNSTMANN (HONTSMAN)
Johann Gottfried (Johan Godfried)   I, 383, 385
KUNTEL (KUNDELL)
Adam   I, 610, 611, 613
KUNTENTWINE
CHᵣ   II, 186
KUNTER
Melchior   I, 416

KUNTRELL
Jacob   II, 136
KUNTZ (KUNZ, KOENTZ, COONTS, KUHNS, KUNTS, KUHNTZ)
Anthon   II, 198
Barbara   I, 74
Barnard (Hans Bern, Barnet)   I, 99, 100, 101
Catharine   II, 198
Christian (Christe)   II, 127, 198
Dewald   I, 440
F. Jacob   I, 494
Georg   I, 693
Gertrudt   I, 74
Hans Hennerich   I, 356
Hans Jacob   I, 245, 247, 248
Hans Jerick (Jerg) I, 10, 11, 88, 90, 92, 109
Hans Michael   I, 10, 11, 363, 451
Henry (Henri) I, 317, 318, 319 483
   II, 198
J. Gustavus   I, 504
J. Henry   I, 486
Jacob   I, 169, 170, 172, 252, 253 255, 398, 729
   II, 28
Johann (Johannes, Johanis)   I, 40, 41, 42
Johann Arnolt   I, 445
Johann Christoff   I, 427
Johann Georg (Georg)   I, 179, 181, 183, 747
Johann Henrich   I, 366, 368, 745
Johan Jacob (Jacob)   I, 71, 75, 77
Johan Peter   I, 366, 368, 733
Johannes (Johanes) I, 73, 356, 559, 561, 562 701
Johannes Henrich   I, 577, 578, 580
Joost   I, 711
Jos.   II, 119
Jurg Michael   I, 10, 11
Lorentz (Lawrence) I, 72, 76, 77
Margt.   I, 74
Maria   I, 73, 74   II, 198
Maria Barbella   I, 107
Maria Catharina   I, 109
Maria Crete   I, 109
Michel (Michall)   I, 108, 429
Nicklas (Nicolaus) I, 289, 290, 291, 378, 380, 381
Peter   I, 106, 110, 112, 521, 524
Philipp (Philip)   I, 293, 294, 295
Rudy   I, 398
Theobald   I, 405

Wilhelm I, 701
(*See also* COUNTS *and* CUNTZ)
KUNTZE
Friedrich II, 128
Johann Gorg I, 482
KÜNTZEL (KUNTZEL)
David I, 360, 362
Henrich I, 758
Jacob (John Jacob) I, 88, 90, 91
Johann Michael I, 495
KUNTZELMAN (KÜNTZEL-
MANN)
Hans Jerg I, 426
Johan Gottlob (John
Godlop) I, 672, 673, 674
KUNTZER
J. Michael I, 484
Johan Jacob I, 233, 235
KÜNTZI
Hans I, 494
KÜNTZLER
Friedrich (Fredrick) I, 551, 553, 554
Migel I, 717
KUNTZLY (KUNZLY)
Conrad I, 434
Mr. II, 176
KUNTZMAN
Lorence I, 460
Martin I, 480
(*See also* CUNTZMAN)
KÜNY
Henrich I, 708
Johannes I, 609, 611, 612
KUNZIGH (KUHNZICK,
KUNTZY)
Abraham (Hunter) I, 246, 247, 248
Ann II, 51
Casp. II, 51
Cethnet II, 51
KÜPER (KUPER)
George Friederich I, 391
Otto II, 95
KÜPFEL (RUPPELL)
Ludwig David I, 378, 380, 381
KÜPFER
Rudolf I, 708
KUPFERSCHMIT (COOPER-
SMIDT, KOPERSCHMITT,
KUPFERSCHMID)
Caspar (Casper) I, 156, 159, 161
Wilhelm I, 460
KUPPER
Jacob II, 33
Johann Gorg I, 485
KURBECKER
Echart I, 480
KURCHT (CORT)
Johanes Gurg (Johann
Jurg) I, 620, 622, 624

KURFES
Hans Marttin I, 437
KÜRMANN
Michael I, 451
KURR (KORR, KUR)
Georg Phillipp I, 348, 349, 351
Hans Thomas I, 162, 164, 165
Michel I, 23
KURRLIN
Johann I, 479
KÜRRMANN
Marx I, 451
Matthias I, 451
KURSNER
John Gottlob II, 69
KURST
Johannes II, 59
KÜRSTNER
Durs I, 370
KURT
Henry II, 123
KURTER
Anna II, 77
KURTZ (CURTS, CORTES, KURZ,
KORTS)
A. (Abraham) I, 287, 288, 289, 407
Arnd (Arndt) I, 155, 158, 160
Aⁿ Elizabeth I, 157
Christian I, 407, 446
Christina II, 192
Christoph I, 506
Conrad I, 502
Daniel I, 409
Fabian I, 759
Hans I, 358
Hans George (Hans
Jerg) I, 446, 492, 695
Hans Jacob I, 459
Heinrich (Henrich) I, 695, 734
J. George II, 156
J. Michael I, 468
Jacob I, 327, 329, 649
Johann Adam I, 426
Johann Christophel I, 705
Johan Ernst I, 366, 368
Johan Paullus (Jan
Paul) I, 213, 215, 728
Johann Petter I, 760
Johannes (John) I, 14, 15, 489, 526
528, 530, 564
565, 567; II, 99
John William (Jo. Wil-
liam) I, 622, 624, 626
Lorentz I, 502
M. II, 32
Michael I, 178, 180, 182
Peter I, 419, 734
Reinhard I, 643, 644
Siep I, 501

Stephan I, 358
Wiegand II, 202
KUSCHE
Wilhelm I, 401
KUSETT
Joseph II, 113
KUSIG (CUSIK)
Johan Peter I, 357
Niclaus Nich. I, 357
KUSMAUL
John Ulrich II, 84
KUSNER
Michael II, 138
KUSSMAN
Gottlieb II, 193
KÜSTER (KUSTER)
Christian Friederich Ludwig II, 75
Jacob I, 745
Jerg Phillips I, 493
John Geo. II, 118
Johann Phillibes I, 462
Ludwig I, 493
KÜSTERLE (KÜSTERLEN)
Jeremias I, 522, 525
KÜSTNER
Johann Ludwig I, 398
Johann Philipps I, 398
Johannes I, 488
KUTER
Bernhart (Bernhard) I, 383, 385
KUTRER
Engelhardt I, 416
KUTSCHER
Christian II, 46
KUTZ
Michael I, 500
KUTZNER
Michael I, 493
KÜWIT (KÜWITZ)
Jacob I, 507
Peter I, 402
Vallentin I, 372
(*See also* CIEWITS *and* KIE-
WITT)
KUYL
Hendrich (Hend^k) I, 384, 386
KUYPER
Jan. II, 41
Johann II, 68
KUYSER (KYSER read KEYSER)
Barbara I, 103
Hans Philip I, 189
Johan David I, 103
Maris Savina I, 103

LAABER (LAHBER, LAABOUR)
Hans Wendel (Wendel) I, 96, 97, 98
Peter I, 328

LAAMSEN
Julian I, 43
LAAR
Barthold II, 125
LA BEAUME
J. De I, 731
LABENGYGER
Christor I, 8
LABHAHAN
Jacob II, 14
LABORDE
—— II, 81
LACH
Johann Peter II, 97
Johannes II, 97
Maria Eliz. II, 97
LACHENMEYER
G. C. II, 97
LACK (LAK, LÄCK)
Eliz. I, 44
J. Hinrich I, 684
Johann Engelbertt (Engel-
bert) I, 43, 46, 47
Magdalena I, 44
LADEMACHER
Johannes I, 495
LADEMAN
Caspar I, 488
LADENBERGER
Lorens I, 711
LADERT (BLADDELL)
Filibus (Philip) I, 648, 650
LADING (LATINK, LATINCK)
Christian I, 509, 510, 511
Johan Casper I, 509, 510, 511
Wilhelm I, 509, 510, 511
LADSHER (LATCHER)
Johanes (Joanis) I, 293, 294, 295
LÄDTEY
Samuell I, 435
LAF
Gerlach II, 79
LAFAVA
Fred II, 135
LA FEVE
—— II, 81
LAFFER
Johannes I, 521, 524
LAFFERSSWILER (LAFFERS-
WILER, LEBERSWEILLER)
Bernhard I, 335, 336, 338
LAFFERT
Mr. II, 58
LA FLEUR
—— II, 81
LAFORM
—— II, 196
LAGAM
Philip II, 75

LAGEAU
  Pierre   I, 489
LAGENER
  Marrea   I, 84
LAGEROM
  John   I, 18
LA GNEAU (MILLIONEAU)
  Barthelemi
    (Barthold)   I, 666, 668, 670
LAGNI
  Mich.   II, 108
LAHM (LAAM, LAHN)
  Johann Konradt
    (Conradt)   I, 317, 318, 319
  Johann Michael   I, 735
  Johann Nicklaus (John
    Nicholas)   I, 301, 302, 303
  Johans   I, 711
  Peter   I, 277, 278, 279
LAHNEN
  Jacob, von   I, 752
LÄHR (LAHR, LAR)
  Johan George   I, 484
  Wilhelmina   II, 41
  Yerg Henrich   I, 17
LAHRS
  Joh. Conrad   II, 205
LAHRWIND
  Johaneis   I, 732
LAIB
  Johann Peter   I, 430
LÄIBLE (LIBLE)
  Johann Friderich   I, 489
  Simon   I, 649, 650
LAICHINGER (LYKINGER)
  Christoph (Christ[n])   I, 596, 598, 600
LAITENBERGER
  Lewis   II, 200
LALE
  Hans George   I, 169, 170, 172
LALLEMAND
  Jacob   I, 459
LAM (read LAMM)
  Peter   I, 329
LAMAN
  Joseph   II, 195
LAMB
  H. Friederik   I, 505
  Johannes   I, 444
LAMBACH
  Joh. Philipp   I, 710
LAMBE (read LAMPE)
  Adam   I, 402
  Christian   II, 103
LAMBERT (LAMBERDT)
  Andreas   I, 741
  Casper   I, 167, 168
  Christian   I, 755
  Christoph   I, 402

  Frantz   I, 702
  George   I, 421
  Henrich   I, 705
  Jacob   I, 715
  Peter   I, 741
LAMBRECHT
  Jacob   I, 358
LAMBRECHTS
  Matth[s]   II, 122
LAMEER
  Joseph   I, 143
LA MERA (MAER)
  Franc (Francis)   I, 592, 593, 594
LAMERCK (LAMENICH)
  Jacob   I, 256, 259, 261
LÄMLE
  Johann Gabriel   I, 162, 164, 165
LÄMMER (LEMAR, LEAMOR)
  Lenhart (Leonard)   I, 310, 312, 313
LAMOT
  Johannes   I, 406
LAMOTTE
  ——   II, 81
LAMOUROUT
  ——   II, 81
LAMP
  Eliza   II, 159
  Martin   I, 308
LAMPART (LAMPARD)
  Adam   I, 702
  Gottfried   I, 692
  Hans Michal   I, 693
  John   I, 702
LAMPAS
  W. J.   II, 123
LAMPATER (LAMPARTER,
  LAMPADER, LAMPEDER)
  Conrad   I, 531, 532, 534
  Johannes   I, 531, 533, 534
  Joseph   I, 531, 533, 534
LAMPE
  Conrad   II, 134
LAMPERT (LAMBERT)
  Baltzer (Baltzaser) I, 234, 235, 236
  (*See also* LAMBERT)
LAMPRECHT
  Antonias   I, 469
  (*See also* LAMBRECHT)
LANBE
  Martin   II, 119
LANBLENÈ
  Jean Michel   I, 508
LANCE
  Philip   I, 406
LANCK
  Jacob   I, 498
LANCKAU
  Joh. Christ. H.   II, 139

LAND (LANDT, LANT)
Jan II, 135
Reimer (Reymer) I, 678, 679
LANDER
Friederik I, 473
LANDES (LANDIS, LANDIG)
Christian I, 156, 159, 161
Henrich I, 415
Jacob I, 700
Johannes (Johanis) I, 79, 82, 83, 700
Peter I, 527, 528, 530
Rodulf (Rutdolf) I, 13, 14, 415
Samuel I, 347
LANDGRAFF (LANDERAF, LAND-
GRAFF, LANDGRAVE)
Henrich (Henrick) I, 199, 201, 203
Jacob I, 416
Johann Friederich I, 589, 590
Johannes I, 412
LANDMANN (LANDMAN)
Johannes I, 411
Maria II, 135
LANE *see* LEHN
LANG (LANGE, LONG)
Abraham I, 531, 533, 534
Adam I, 432
Anna I, 135
Appellonia I, 109
Barbara I, 135
Catherine (Catharina) I, 108, 135
Christian I, 109, 358, 690
Christoff Albrecht I, 79, 82, 83
Conrath I, 84, 86, 87, 234
Daniel I, 323, 324, 326, 536, 537, 538
Felix I, 250, 251
Fredᵏ II, 83
Hannah Boble I, 84
Hans Adam I, 107, 111, 112
Hans Jerg I, 502
Hans Martin I, 498
Henry I, 250, 251
J. Adam I, 564, 566, 567
Jacob I, 169, 171, 173, 490, 653, 655
Johan I, 135, 136
Johan, Junʳ, I, 135, 136
Johann Adam I, 755
Johann Christophel (Johan
Christoph) I, 642, 643, 655, 657, 658
Johan Conrath I, 707
Johann Georg I, 135, 136, 399
Johan Henrich I, 402, 460
Johan Jacob I, 490, 719
Johann Martin I, 462
Johann Michael I, 513, 514, 515
Johann Nickel I, 390
Johann Peter I, 485
Johann Valting (Joan
Valanteᵉ) I, 169, 170, 172
Johanes I, 169, 170, 172, 420

John I, 250, 251; II, 83
Jost I, 277, 278, 279
Kunrad I, 483
Lenhart I, 424
Lutwig (Ludwig) I, 646, 647
Maria I, 135, 157
Martin I, 498, 726
Matheas I, 498
Michel (Michal,
Michell) I, 234, 235, 236
500, 521, 523, 724
Nicklaus (Nicholas,
Nickel) I, 155, 158, 160
665, 668, 670
Peter I, 402, 461
Philip (Philipp,
Phillip) I, 293, 294, 295
Stephan (Stephen) I, 79, 82, 83
199, 201, 203
Theobald (Tepolt) I, 195, 196, 197
Thomas (Thos) I, 248, 249, 250
Ursula (Ossel) I, 80, 109
Willhelm (Wilhelm) I, 277, 278, 279
LANGBEIN (LANGBANE)
Godfrey I, 317
Johannes Zacharias I, 744
LANGE (LANGEN)
A. L. II, 108
Andreas Hendrich
(Andreas Henry) I, 589, 590, 591
Casper II, 100
Christian Frederick II, 100
Christian Ludwk. II, 100
Daniel II, 97
Frederic Gottlieb II, 58
Gerhᵈ Hinr. II, 107
Jacob I, 428
Jochim II, 139
Johann Christopher II, 48
Johann Godfried II, 184
Joh. Henr. II, 107, 108
Johⁿ Philip II, 128
Maria Gertrude II, 128
Sophia St. Emelia II, 100
LANGEBARTH
Augustus II, 11
Henry II, 11
Sofia II, 11
LANGENBACH (LANGEBACH)
Conrad I, 745
Georg Paul I, 531, 533, 535
John Jost I, 743
LANGENBACHER
Catharine II, 150
George Jacob II, 150
Gottlieb II, 150
John II, 150
Katharine II, 150

LANGENBERGER
Johann Caspar I, 415
Johann Petter I, 363
LANGENEKKER (LONGENACRE, LONGINACRE)
Anna Barbary I, 24
Christian (Christ) I, 24, 26, 27
LANGENFELDER (LINGAVELT, LINGEFELT)
George Michal (Jurich) I, 287, 289
LANGENHAGEN
Peter Andre II, 49
LANGER (LONGER)
Richart (Richard, Reighart) I, 386, 388, 389
LANGERFELDT (LONGERFIELD)
Christ. Eliz. I, 144
Johann Albert I, 143, 145, 146
LANGHAAR (LANKHAER, LANCKHAER, LONGHAAR)
Balser (Balter, Waldes) I, 35, 36
Willhelm I, 406
LÄNGLE (LENGLIE)
Johannes (Joanis) I, 226, 228, 230
LANGLOH
Anna Cath^a II, 23
LANGNECKER (LONINACRE)
Hans I, 10, 11
Jacob (Jackop) I, 116, 119, 120
Ulrich (Olrige) I, 116, 119, 120
LANGS
Jacob I, 450
LANGSDORFF (LANGSDORF, LANGSTER, LANGSTORF)
Conrath (Conrad) I, 643, 645
Henry (J. Henry) I, 614, 616, 618
Johann Conrath (Conrad) I, 615, 617, 619
Johann Danigel (Daniel) I, 615, 617, 619
LANGSPECH
Christian I, 758
LÄNHART see LEONHARD
LANIUS
Jacob I, 43, 45, 46
LANKUS (LAENCUS, LOUKS)
Peter I, 226, 228, 230
LANNERT
Jno Henry I, 699
LANS
Johannes I, 407
LANSISCUS (LENSENNS, LANSENESS)
Hans (Hantz) I, 34, 35, 36
Johan Henrich (Johan Frederick) I, 35, 36
LANTHAN
Christ^n I, 517

LANTZ (LANTS, LANSZ, LANS)
Andres I, 473
Baltzer I, 503
Elizebeth II, 76
Hans I, 234
Hans Jorg I, 369, 370
Hans Nicoll I, 241
Hans Peter I, 240, 242, 243
J. Jacob I, 504
Jacob I, 240, 242, 243
258, 260, 263
387, 388, 389
Johannes I, 386, 388, 389
Martin I, 709
Michel I, 240, 242, 243
Niclaus I, 369, 370
Philips I, 521, 523
Yoghan Poul I, 241
LANTZER
Hans Gerg I, 506
LANTZINGER
Johan I, 234
LAPIERRE (LAPER)
Jean Jaque (Johan) I, 574, 575, 576
LAPLACE
Philipp Peter I, 707
LAPP (LAP)
Anna Catharina I, 132
Anna Maria I, 132
Hanna Christina I, 131
Joh. Henr. II, 108
Johann Jacob I, 474
Johann Jost (Johannes) I, 592, 593, 594
Johannes I, 131, 133, 134, 474
Michel I, 482
Rudolph I, 132
LAR see LAHR
LARBER
Caspar II, 157
Elisabeth II, 157
Gertrude II, 157
Melchior II, 157
Theodor I, 475
——— II, 157
LARIER
Lydia II, 192
Matthias II, 192
Noa II, 192
LAROCHE
Denois II, 198
LAROS (LAROSCH)
Christian I, 761
Johannes I, 666, 669, 671
LÄRTGES
Christoffel I, 735
LASCH (LASH)
Friedr. II, 116
Jacob I, 482

Johann Georg I, 458
LASCHET (LAASCHET,
LAESCHET, LATSEN, LAT-
SIN)
Cathrina I, 156
Christian, von I, 154, 157, 160
Johann (Johannes) I, 154, 157, 160
Johann Wendel (John
Wintell) I, 198, 200, 202
Johannes Peter (J.
Peter) I, 154, 157, 160
LASHER
Leonhart I, 415
LASSALL (LASSAUL)
Jacob I, 227, 229, 231
II, 103
LÄSSIG
Johann Christian I, 705
LÄSSLE
Jacob I, 697
LATCH
Nichs I, 721
LATOUCHE
Mr Alexander II, 109
LATRINE
Anna Maria I, 28
LATSHOW
Frans I, 18
LATTERCHE
Hans Michael I, 393
LATUR
Herman I, 405
Jacob I, 406
LAU
John Henry I, 757
LAUB (LAUP)
Baltes I, 469
Dewalt I, 355
Eliz. II, 4
Johan Michel (Johan
Michael), I, 265, 268, 271
Johannes I, 560, 561, 563
Johannes Michl
(Michael) I, 560, 561, 563
Jorg (Jurg) I, 266, 269, 273
Peter I, 402
LAUBACH (LABACK, LAWBACH)
Christian I, 216, 218, 220
Johan Carl I, 690
Johannes I, 378, 379, 381
John Christoffel I, 449
Renhard (Renhart) I, 216, 218, 220
LAUBE (LAUBIE)
Anna II, 119
Peter A. II, 193
LAUBENGAYER
Hans G. II, 41
LAUBENHAUER
Jacob I, 441

LAUBENSTEIN
Johann Peter I, 701
Peter I, 701
LAUBER
G. II, 141
LAUBINGER
Georg Michael I, 417
Johann Georg I, 506
LAUBSHER
Conrat I, 447
Johan Jacob I, 447
LAUCH
Johannes Adam I, 427
LAUCK (LAUK, LUCK)
Andreas (Andrias) I, 116, 119, 121
David II, 25
John II, 52
Slutik I, 117
LAUCKS
Jacob I, 337
LAUDENBERGER
Jacob I, 384, 386
Joh. Georg I, 346
LAUDENSCHLAGER
Johann Peter I, 437
Johannes I, 403
LAUDERMILCH
Jacob I, 406
LAUDERT
Johannes I, 415
LAUER (LAUR, LOUER, LOWER)
Adam I, 66, 69, 70
Anna Margaretha II, 59
Christian I, 122, 125, 126
II, 59
Elisabeth I, 67
Georg Ludwig II, 59
George (Görg) I, 751
II, 10, 122
Hartmann I, 66, 69, 70
Henrich (Henry) I, 569, 571, 572
II, 59
Henrich Ludwig Baltser II, 59
Jacob I, 169, 171, 172
592, 593, 594
Johann Christian
(Christian) I, 581, 583, 584
Johann Michael I, 710
Johann Nickel I, 712
Johann Philips I, 413
Johanes (Johannes) I, 605, 607, 608
Maria Sophia II, 59
Matthias (Theis) I, 569, 571, 572
Michael I, 169, 171, 172, 488
Philip I, 290, 291
Tobias I, 414
Ullrich Michael I, 490
LAUFANOR
Christian I, 470

LAUFER (LAUFFER)
Conradt I, 417
J. Michael I, 467
Jacob Frediderich I, 741
Michell I, 467
LAUFFERSWEILER (LAUFFERS-
WEBER)
Bernhard I, 335, 336, 338
LAUFFLENTER (LOUFFLYN,
LOUFLIMER)
Reymound
(Reymund) I, 323, 324, 326
LAUMAN (LOWMAN)
Hans Jerig I, 17
Jerg Bernhart (Jurigh
Bernard) I, 237, 238, 239
Johann Georg
(Henrich) I, 573, 574, 575
Johan Ludwig I, 360, 361
Martin I, 360, 361
Steffan (Stephen) I, 113, 114, 115, 765
Tomas Simon I, 498
LAUNAY
Romaine II, 80
LAURENT
Francois II, 80
—— II, 81
LAURER
Gottfried I, 366
LAUSER
Jacob I, 452
LAUSS
Anna II, 105
LAUTENBAGH (LOUDINBACK,
LAUDENBACK)
Johan David (Davit) I, 256, 259, 261
LAUTENSCHLEGER (LAUDEN-
SCHLAGER, LAWTEN-
SCHLAGER)
Adam I, 395
George I, 493
Henrich I, 468
Johann I, 736
Johann Georg I, 737
Johann Henrich I, 736, 737
Mary E. II, 151
Matthias I, 394
Michel I, 470
Philip (Philipp) I, 395, 693
Vallentin I, 494
LAUTER
Linhard I, 480
LAUTERBACH (LAUDERBACH,
LAWTERBACH)
Conrad
(Conrade) I, 184, 185, 187, 411
Francis II, 147
Peter I, 184, 185, 187
Philip I, 411

Philipp Ullrich I, 485
LAUTERMAN
Johan Peter (John
Peter) I, 227, 229, 231
LAUTERMILCH (LAUTHER-
MILCH, LOUDERMILCH)
Georg William (William,
Wendel) I, 48, 52, 53
Gottfried I, 162, 164, 165
Jacob I, 741
Johann I, 93, 94, 95
Magdelena I, 49
LAUTH
Danniell I, 714
Jacob I, 714
Johann Adam I, 733
Michell I, 691
LAUTIERE
Charles II, 122
Maria Iannphe II, 122
LAUTINGER
Jean F. II, 68
LAUTZENHÄUSER (LAUTZEN-
HEISER)
Henrich I, 703
Jacob I, 703
Peter I, 703
LAUX (LAUTZ, LOUCKS)
Friedrich Jacob I, 744
Henrich I, 718
Jacob I, 734
Johann Jacob (Han
Jacob) I, 642, 644
Johan Peter (Peter) I, 383, 385
Johann Wendel
(Wendel) I, 667, 669, 671
LAVASCH
Jacob I, 430
LAVENFORT
Henry II, 126
LAVER
Michael I, 471
LA VOCHE
—— II, 80
LAWALL
Daniel I, 508
Johann Lutwig I, 508
Johann Michel I, 403
Melchior I, 454
LAWDERBRUN
Frederic I, 428
LAWMEISTER
Wendel I, 444
LAX
Christian Ernst II, 54
LAY (LAYE, LEY, LEEY, LYE)
Andreas (Anderas) I, 512, 514, 515
Friderich (Fredrick) I, 551, 553, 554
Georg Christoph I, 88, 90, 92

Hans I, 366
Ludwig (Ludtwig) I, 155, 158, 160
Martin I, 297, 298, 300
Stephen (Stephfan) I, 512, 514, 515
LAYBOLT *see* LEIBOLD
LAYE (LEY)
Johanes (Johan) I, 283, 284, 286
LAYER
Adam I, 410
Eva Schalin II, 192
Johannes II, 192
LAZARUS (LAZRUS, LAZURUS)
Jacob I, 428
Peter I, 429
LAZER
Catharina II, 70
Peter II, 70
LE——
Johan Filibus I, 401
LEA (LEE, LEEA)
Felix I, 332, 333, 334
Hans Petter I, 332
LEABER (LAPER, LÄWER)
Philip I, 290, 291
LEABO
Andrew II, 195
LEADERER *see* LEDERER
LEAMEN *see* LEHMANN
LEAMFORD
William II, 90
LEANDER
John II, 123
LEAP
Anna Christina I, 127
Anna Margaretha I, 128
Anna Maria I, 128
Catherina I, 127
Georg (George) I, 126, 129
Hans Conrad
(Johan Conrad) I, 126, 129
Maria Esther I, 128
LEASEMAN
Jan Hendrick I, 437
LEAVY
Michael I, 346
LEAZER
Matthias II, 104
LEBANK
Geo. I, 756
LEBEGUT * (LEBEGOOD, LEBE-
GOOT, LEEBEGOOT)
Adam I, 135
Anna I, 135
Anna Catherina I, 128
Anna Gretha I, 128
Hans Jacob I, 127, 129, 130
Jacob I, 135
Johan (Pieter) I, 134, 136
Johan Jacob I, 128

Margaretha I, 127
Maria I, 135
Susanna I, 135
Ulrich I, 134, 136
LEBER
Jacob I, 413
Johann Adam I, 760
LEBERGER (LOCHBERGHER)
Barbara I, 73
Johann Adam I, 72, 76, 77
LEBERMAN (AUSLEBERMAN)
Hanicle (Nickolas) I, 661, 662, 664
LEBKUCHER (LEPKUCHER, LEIP-
KIGER)
Henrich I, 340, 342, 343
LEBLE
Lorentz I, 451
LEBOLDT (LEEBOLT, LEOBOLD)
Albert I, 176, 177, 178
Michel (Michael) I, 605, 606, 607
LE CENE (LISSEN, LESSEN)
Jean (Jno.) I, 84, 86, 87
Johan Maria I, 85
Johanna Luiss I, 85
Larrance I, 85
Luiss I, 85
Marrea Katterine I, 85
Paul I, 84, 86, 87
LECH (LEG)
Barbara Cath. II, 11
Maria Elis. II, 93
LECHLEITER (LECHLETER,
LECHLEIDER, LECHLEITNER)
Johann Conrad I, 307, 309, 310
Johannes I, 754
Justus I, 693
LECHLER (LEGLER)
Jacob I, 344, 345
Johann Adam I, 714
LECHNER (LEHNER, LICHTNER)
Anna M. II, 159
Christian II, 159
Hans Jerig I, 84, 86, 87
LECKE (LUIG)
Christian I, 517, 519, 520
LECKROMME (LUKEROW)
Lenhardt (Lehardt,
Leonard) I, 551, 553, 554
LEDER (LEEDER)
Fredrick I, 18, 19
Johan I, 542
John II, 121
Melchior I, 398
LEDERER (LEADERER)
Andereas I, 475
Bartholomaeus I, 480
Johann Paullus
(Paulus) I, 72, 76, 78

LEDERHOLT (LETHERHOLTZ)
Johan Caspar
  (Casper)   I, 373, 374, 376
LEDERMANN (LEDERMAN,
  LEATHERMAN)
Anna   I, 117
Hans Depelt (Tewalt)   I, 10, 11
Hans Peter
  (Hans Petter)   I, 48, 52, 53
Jacob   I, 156, 159, 161
    301, 302, 303
Madlena   I, 117
Matthias (Mattias,
  Matthys)   I, 179, 181, 183
Michael   I, 441
LEDIG
Casper   I, 428
LEE
Eliza   I, 766
LEEB
William   I, 646, 647
LEEBER *see* LIEBER
LEEBY
Henry   I, 392
LEED (LEID)
Martin
  (Johan Marte)   I, 265, 268, 271
LEEGERHOEN
Johannes   I, 19
LEEMER
Uldrich   I, 16
LEENHUYS
Hans Simon   I, 264
LEER (LEAR)
Henry
  (Henderick)   I, 331, 332, 334
Henry   I, 16
Jnº Peter   I, 734
Johan Herman   I, 276, 277, 278
Maria   II, 108
(*See also* LEHR)
LEES
George   I, 429
Johannes   I, 339
LEESENBERG
F.   II, 123
LEESER
Matheus   I, 409
LEESHER
Jacob   I, 363
LEFART
Jnº   II, 75
LEFEVER (LEFIEBER)
Alexander Joseph   II, 90
Catharina   II, 54
Kaatje   II, 54
LEFFLER
J. F.   II, 112

LEGER
———   II, 81
LEFRAN
Joseph   I, 756
LEGNOR
Jacob   II, 160
LEGRARD
———   II, 81
LEGWIN
Gaspar   II, 183
LEHLE
John   II, 156
LEHMANN (LEEMAN, LEHMAN,
  LEMAN, LEYMAN)
Barbara   I, 50, 190
Benedict   I, 188, 190, 192
    193, 406
Catrina
  (Katherina)   I, 50, 190; II, 34
Christian (Christ)   I, 31, 32, 33
    54; II, 193
Christoph (Christ.)   I, 48, 52, 53
Daniel   II, 193
Earnst   II, 77
Eva   I, 73
Ferona   I, 190
Feronica   I, 49
Godfried
  (Gottfried)   I, 56, 589, 590
Hans (Hannes)   I, 10, 11, 190
J. Christoff (John
  Christopher)   I, 573, 574, 575
Jacob   I, 464; II, 15
Johann Christian   I, 54, 56
    II, 110
Johann Daniel   I, 746
Johann Petter   I, 508
Johanna   II, 83
Johanes   I, 448
Johannes
  (Johanes, Johanis)   I, 14, 15, 50
John Godfrey   I, 55
Joseph   I, 469, 610, 611, 613
Ludwig (Lodawick)   I, 72, 76, 77
Michael   I, 440
Nicholas   II, 193
Peter   I, 16, 17
Theobald   I, 691
Vallentin (Valentine,
  Valentin)   I, 605, 607, 608
Wilhelm   I, 743
LEHMBACHER
Daniel   I, 462
LEHMER (LEMER)
Jochem (Jocham)   I, 628, 631, 635
Nicholas   I, 628, 631, 635
LEHMIG
Johann Philipp   I, 412

LEHMKIELS
  Hanna II, 59
LEHN (LANE)
  C. Hind., von II, 101
  Johannes I, 323, 325, 326
  Mich[1] I, 661, 662, 663
  Timothy II, 160
LEHNER (LEONARD)
  Georg I, 693
  Georg Balthas I, 513, 514, 516
  Hans Jerick I, 109
  Hans Leonhartt
    (Leonard) I, 106, 110, 112
  Sabina I, 107
  Wolfgang I, 490
LEHNIG
  Valtin Christian I, 749
LEHR (LAEHR, LEER, LEHER)
  Hans Adam I, 482
  Henrich I, 744
  Jacob I, 760
  Johan Christofel I, 367, 369
  Johann Henrich I, 412
  Johan Michael II, 78
  Johann Nikl.
    (Hanicle) I, 661, 662, 664
  Johannerrich (Johanerich,
    Hendrick) I, 300, 301, 302
  John Peter I, 577, 578, 580
  Philip I, 643, 645
LEHRER (LARER)
  Johann Ferdinand I, 555, 556, 558
  Philipp I, 523, 525
LEHRING
  Adam Christoph I, 480
LEHRS
  Johann Henrich II, 59
LEIB (LEIP, LEYB)
  Hersch II, 189
  Johan Ludwig I, 492
  Johannes I, 8, 10, 498
  Ulrich I, 13, 14
LEIBACHER (LAYBAGGER)
  Heinrich I, 89, 91, 92
LEIBBRAND
  Jo. Conrad I, 476
LEIBE
  Jean II, 87
LEIBENGUT
  Hartman I, 429
LEIBENZETER
  Jacob I, 760
LEIBERICH
  Michael I, 502
LEIBERTH
  Michael I, 12
LEIBHARD
  Fredericka II, 162

LEIBHEIM
  Jacob I, 446
LEIBINGER
  Jost I, 759
LEIBLE
  Matthew II, 202
LEIBLING
  Johann Heinrich I, 438
LEIBOLD (LAYBOLT, LEYBOLDT,
    LIEBOLT)
  Adam II, 126
  Anna Cathar. II, 115
  Jacob I, 648, 650
  Johann Georg II, 115
  Nicolaus II, 115
  Sebastian I, 503
LEIBROCK
  Balzar I, 428
  Jacob I, 456
  Johann Christian I, 363
  Theobalt I, 734
LEIBY (LEYBY)
  Catharina I, 109
  Friedrich
    (Frederick) I, 106, 110, 112
  Hans Michael I, 429
  Jacob I, 109
  Maria Mettlina I, 107
  Michall I, 109
  Wolrick I, 109
LEICHT
  Andreas II, 151
  Christopher II, 151
  Dorothea II, 151
  Dorothy II, 151
  Ewerhardus I, 693
  Gottlieb II, 151
  Ludowig II, 151
  Magdalen II, 151
LEICKLE
  A. II, 142
LEIDENBERGER (LEITEN-
    BERGER, LEYDERBERGER)
  Philib Jacob I, 243, 244, 245
LEIFFER
  Jn° I, 730
LEIGHMAN
  Maria I, 74
LEIGLE
  Nic. II, 47
LEIGUES
  Carl Alexander II, 93
  Catharina II, 93
  Elizabeth II, 93
  Johann G. II, 93
  Johann W. II, 93
  Johanna Elizabetha II, 93
  Johannes II, 93

LEIHER
 Johannes   I, 660
LEIM
 Johann Friederich   I, 410
LEIMAN
 Johann Jacob   I, 698
LEIN
 Andres   I, 503
LEINAU (LEYNAW)
 Andreas Erdman   I, 576, 578, 580
LEINBACH (LINEBACK, LINE-
    BAH)
 Henry (Henderick)   I, 331, 333, 334
LEINBACKER (LINEBAKER, LIM-
    BAKER)
 Felix   I, 252, 254, 255
 Henry (Henrich)   I, 252, 254, 255
LEINBERGER (LENBERGER)
 Johannes   I, 463
 Nicklaus (Nicholas,
    Nickellaus)   I, 257, 260, 262
LEINE
 Balsar   I, 15
LEINER (LEYNART)
 Henrich   I, 585, 586, 588
 Ludwick   II, 136
LEINEWEBER (LEINWEBER)
 Johan Henrich   I, 426
 Wilhelm Henrich
    (Wm Henry)   I, 643, 644
LEININGER
 Hans Thomas   I, 429
 Heinrich   I, 428
 Johan Conrad   I, 383, 385
 Johan Jacob   I, 441
 John George   I, 699
 Martin   I, 622, 624, 626
 Sebastian
    (Sebastin)   I, 383, 385
LEINKUHL
 Anna L.   II, 121
LEIPERSBERGER   (LYPERS-
    BERGER, LYPERSBURGER)
 Hans Georg   I, 98
 Jacob   I, 96, 97
LEIS (LICE)
 Christoffel (Chris.) I, 237, 238, 239
 Johann Ferdinandus   I, 503
 Johan Peter
    (Peter)   I, 569, 571, 573
 Johannes   I, 709
LEISCHERR
 Johannrich   I, 452
LEISER (LEISSER, LESSER, LIS-
    SER)
 Andreas   I, 481
 Benedict   I, 264, 267, 271
 Hans Michael   I, 264, 268, 271
 Johannes   I, 690

Jost (Joost)   I, 266, 269, 272
Nicholas (Nicklas,
    Nicklaus)   I, 240, 242, 243
                        264, 268, 271
LEISTER (LEYSTER)
 Nicklas   I, 448
 Philieb   I, 448
LEISTWITZ
 Alessius, de   II, 54
LEITENBERGER
 Eberhard   I, 718
LEITERT
 Carolina   II, 157
 J. C. F.   II, 157
 Wilhelmina   II, 157
 ———   II, 157
LEITHAUSER   (LEITHEUSER,
    LEITHEISER)
 Joh. Conrad   I, 418
 Johann Gebhart
    (Gebhard)   I, 665, 668, 670
LEITZ
 Casimir   I, 749
LEITZEL
 Johann Wolfgang   I, 546, 548, 550
LE JEUNES
 Jacob   I, 416
LELING
 Johann Conradt   I, 417
 Paul   I, 417
LEMBACH (LEMBACK)
 Anthon
    (Anthony, Ant.) I, 601, 602, 603
LEMBERTY
 Johann Peter   I, 449
LEMBGEN (LAMLEY)
 Jerg (Yerick)   I, 373, 374, 376
LEMEL
 Andres   I, 457
LEMER
 Johan   I, 745
 Wilhelm   I, 430
LEMLE
 Johanes   I, 498
LEMMLEIN
 Johann Frans   I, 366
LEMP
 Johannes   I, 713
LEMPERT *see* LIMPERT
LENARD
 Hanse   I, 660
 Michael   I, 414
LENDEL
 Jacob   I, 427
LENDEN
 Gerrit A.   II, 135
LENGER
 John   II, 186

LENGGENHAG
Joseph   I, 434
LENHART (LENHARD, LEN-
HARDT)
Christoff   I, 402
Johann Jost   I, 753
Johann Nickel   I, 752
Johann
   Petter (Peter)   I, 379, 380, 382
Nicolaus   I, 372
Wilhelm   I, 496
LENN
Johanes   I, 457
LENNENSCHIDT
Johannes   I, 507
LENNER
Cunradt   I, 390
LENNERT (LEMERD)
Johann Vallentin
   (Valentine)   I, 199, 201, 203
LENNIG (LENNICH, LENNICK,
LINNICK)
Jerg   I, 539, 541, 543
Johann Thomas   I, 539, 541, 543
Peiter (Better)   I, 539, 541, 543
LENSHY
Johanes   I, 507
LENTZ (LENZ, LINCE, LINTZ)
Bastian   I, 522, 524
Christian   I, 360, 361
Christian Ulrich   I, 427
Christina   I, 60
Christoph   I, 360, 361
George   I, 481
Hans David
   (John David)   I, 88, 90, 92
Henry   II, 154
Jacob   I, 179, 180, 183
Johan Christian   I, 459
Johann Christophel   I, 436
Johan Jacob
   (John Jacob)   I, 360, 361, 712, 726
   II, 76
Johan Peter   I, 478
Johan Wilhelm   I, 352, 354
Johannes (Johan
   John)   I, 59, 61, 63, 65, 545, 547
   549, 621, 623, 625, 659
Joseph   I, 498
Maria   I, 60
Mathias   I, 340, 342, 343
Philip (Philipus)   I, 256, 259, 261
   II, 148
Wendell (Vindle)   I, 222, 223, 225
LEON
Gabriel   I, 714
LEONHARD (LEONHARDT, LEON-
HART, LEONARD)
Anna   I, 210

Caspar   II, 199
Christian   I, 210
Hans   I, 210
Jacob   I, 420
Johann Adam   I, 735
Joh. Conrad   I, 754
Johan Georg   I, 752
Michael   I, 474, 720
P.   II, 32
Stoffel   I, 676
Vallandin   I, 362
Wilhelm   II, 70
LEONIE
P. E.   I, 716
LEPART (LABORT)
Adam   I, 556, 557, 558
LEPERT
Adam   I, 16
LEPINE
Louis Cr. Houssage   II, 74
LEPOLD (read LEOPOLD)
Anne Marie   II, 86
Charles   II, 87
Chrétienne   II, 87
George   II, 87
Jaques   II, 87
Jean   II, 87
Jean Philipp   II, 87
Louise   II, 87
Marie Elisabeth   II, 86
Valentin   II, 86, 87
LE PORT
John   I, 736
LEPPICH
Johann Henrich   I, 412
LERCH (LERGE, LERICH, LERICK)
Anderas (Andres)   I, 216, 218, 220
Anthon   I, 216, 218, 220
Martin   I, 418
Peter   I, 216, 218, 220
LERCHENZEILER
Joh Michael   I, 470
LEREN
Urdow   I, 191
LERISTEYN (LERINSTEY)
Hans Mart   I, 7
Jan Barned   I, 7
LERMON
George   II, 188
LERNN
Maria, de   II, 136
LERO
Claus   II, 16
LE ROY (LURWALD)
Abraham (Abram)   I, 591, 592, 594
   631, 634
Adam   I, 508, 591, 592, 594
Anton   I, 746
Jean Jaques   I, 507

LERSCH
  Hans Jacob   I, 491
LERSEL
  Francois   II, 80
LERTSCHTLE
  Joerg   I, 365
LERTZ
  Dibolt   I, 702
LESCH (LEESH, LESH)
  Christian   I, 244, 245
  Heronimus   II, 49
  Martin   I, 365
LESHER
  Bastian   I, 144
  Joanis   I, 144
  Maria   I, 143
LESHONG
  Jacob   I, 747
LESIG
  John M.   II, 187
LESLE (LISLEY)
  Anna Caterina   I, 28
  Christina   I, 28
  David   I, 28
  Elizabeth   I, 28
  Jacob   I, 27, 29, 30
  Marilis   I, 28
  Pieter (Peter)   I, 27, 29, 30
LESS (LES)
  Catharina   II, 53
  Christen   II, 82
LESSIE
  Jacob   II, 108
LESSIG
  Johan Georg Phillip   I, 705
LETHAR
  Barbera   II, 102
LETTEN
  Johan Christen   I, 754
LETZBEYER (LESBERGER, LIZA-
    BERBEGER)
  Christian (Christ[1],
    Christ[n])   I, 601, 602, 603
LEUBOLT * (LEUPHOLT, LEOP-
    HOLT, LEOBOLD, LEUBBEL)
  Adam   I, 614, 616, 619
  Conradt   I, 384, 385
LEUCKEL (LEUKEL, LEICKEL)
  Daniel (Dan[1])   I, 666, 668, 670
LEUFFER
  Mr. Thomas   II, 73
LEÜR
  Johan Peter   I, 675
  Philip   I, 675
LEUSER
  Konrad   I, 472
LEUTHÄUSER
  Joh. Henrich   I, 710

LEUTHE
  Christian   I, 748
LEUTHENGER
  George   I, 372
LEUTHOLD
  Heinrich   I, 436
LEUTTEL
  Michel   I, 472
LEUVEL
  Elsi, van   II, 76
LEUZE (LEUTZI)
  George   II, 154
  Johannes   I, 449
LEVAN
  Daniel   I, 7
LEVER
  Adam   II, 29
  Magdalena   II, 29
LEVERN
  George   II, 169
LEVI (LEVY, LEWY)
  Abraham   II, 92
  Alexander   II, 160
  Frederick   I, 395
  Hertzog   II, 93
  Isaac   I, 678, 680, 748
  Johan Peter   I, 277, 278, 279
  Juda Bair   II, 156
  Mich[1]   I, 722
  Moses   II, 139
LEWIS
  Jean   II, 80
  John E.   II, 183
  Lawrence   II, 152
LEWISOHN
  Mr.   II, 176
LEX
  George Diederich   II, 28
  Jacob   II, 28
  Ph. C.   II, 179
LEY
  Anna Maria   I, 107
  Dan. Fred.   II, 44
  Hans Georg (Hans George,
    Hans Jurigh, Hans Yer-
    rick)   I, 113, 551, 552, 554
  Johan Henrich   I, 765, 767
  Matthew
    (Mattes, Matt.) I, 106, 110, 112
  Stephan (Step[n]) I, 585, 586, 587
LEYDECKER (LEYTECKER, LEY-
    DICKER, LEYENDECKER)
  Caspar (Casper)   I, 266, 269, 272
  Jn[o] Jost   I, 753
  Johan Michael   I, 455
  Joseph   II, 26
  Nickolas   I, 486
  Simon   I, 432

LEYDICH (LEIDICH, LEIDIGH, LEIDYG, LEYTICH)
Christian   I, 750
Friederich (Fred)   I, 681, 682
J. Michel   I, 427
Jacob   I, 397
Johann Adam   I, 382
Jurg   I, 714
Phillipp (Philip)   I, 416, 681
LEYDY (LEYTY, LEYTEY)
Gabriel   I, 445
Hans Dewald   I, 370
Jacob   I, 15
LEYENBERGER (LEYBERGER, LYBERG)
Frantz (Frans)   I, 263, 267, 270
Nicklas (Nicholas, Nicolaes)   I, 258, 260, 263
LEYER
Fred.   II, 202
Jacob   I, 540, 542, 544
John Bernard   I, 737
Martin   I, 454
LEYERIGH
Thomas   I, 508
LEYMEISTER (LYMESTER)
Johann Wilhelm (Willhelm)   I, 373, 374, 376
LEYNOLDT
Johannes   I, 734
LEYPOLE
Israel   I, 760
LEYRLE
Johann Christoph (G. Christophel)   I, 605, 606, 608
LEYSS
Johann Georg   I, 439
LEYTMAN
Johann George   II, 76
LIAMUR
Georg   II, 44
LIBELY (LIBELIE)
Christian   II, 163
Jacob   II, 167
Joseph   II, 163
Louisa   II, 163
Maria   II, 163
Michael   II, 163
LIBENTRAUT (LIEBENDRAUT)
Johanes (Johannes)   I, 672, 673, 674
LIBER
Gutman   II, 134
LIBERT (LIBBERT, LIPPERT)
Anna Maria   I, 157
Anna Wilhelmina   II, 93
Jacob   I, 155, 158, 161
Johann Gottlieb   II, 93
Peter   II, 93

LIBERTE
——   II, 81
LIBHART (LIBHARD)
Adam   I, 17
Carel   II, 184
LIBLE
Christina   II, 164
Jacob   II, 164
Johannas   II, 164
LIBMANN
Caspar   II, 148
LIBRANT
Adam   II, 164
Andras   II, 163
Edward   II, 163
Frederica   II, 163
J. A.   II, 163
Jacob   II, 163
Ludwic   II, 163
Rosina   II, 163
LICH (LICK)
Christoph   I, 471
Johann Filib (Hans Philip)   I, 655, 657, 658
Johann Friederich   I, 724
Wilhelm   I, 685
LICHER
Frentz   I, 724
LICHT (LEIGHT, LIGHT)
Anna   I, 80
Catarin   I, 80
Daniel   I, 495
Hans   I, 79, 82, 83
Hans Peter (Peter)   I, 236, 238, 239
Jacob   I, 707
Jnᵒ Godfrey   II, 6
Johann Jacob   I, 707
Johann Nickel   I, 707
Johann Peter   I, 170, 171, 173
Johanes (Joanes, Hannis)   I, 198, 200, 202
LICHTE (LICHTIE, LIGTE)
Catrina   I, 190
Christian   I, 188, 191, 193
Magdaline   II, 61
LICHTENBERGER
Caspar   I, 479
Johan Gerog   I, 711
LICHTENECKER
Frederika   II, 169
Gottlieb Johan   II, 169
LICHTENFELDT
Johann   I, 691
LICHTENWALLNER (WALTER)
Johann (Listen)   I, 106, 110, 111
LICHTY (LIGHTY)
Alexander   I, 731
Jacob   I, 448

LICK *see* LICH
LICKER
  George   I, 472
LIDDI
  Hans   I, 358
LIDERITZ
  Hendrick   II, 187
LIEB
  Johan Michel   I, 427
LIEBENER
  Philip   I, 459
LIEBENGUT (LIEBENGUTT, LIVENGUTH)
  Beder [Peter]   I, 441
  Hanes Fritz
    (Hans Fight)   I, 652, 654
  Hans Jacob   I, 441
  Philip   I, 178, 180, 182
LIEBENSTEIN
  Hans Martin   I, 9
  Johann Georg   I, 57, 58
LIEBER (LEEBER)
  Adam   I, 729
  Jacob   II, 122
  Johann Wil-
    helm (William)   I, 655, 657, 658
LIEBERKNECHT
  Frederick   I, 684
LIEBRICH (LIEBERICH)
  Johannes (Johan)   I, 601, 602, 603
LIECHTENTHÄLLER
  Johannes Christianus   I, 479
LIEN
  Heinrich   I, 398
LIENAU
  Joh. H.   II, 107
LIENENBERGER (LÜNBERGER, LENKENBERGER)
  Friederich (Fredrick)   I, 32, 33, 34
LIES
  Andreas   I, 347
  Hennrich   I, 356
  Jacob   I, 307, 308, 309
  Peter   I, 675
LIESE
  Anna Catrut   II, 28
LIESMAN
  Adam   II, 5
LIEST
  Philipus   I, 510, 676
LIETTEL
  Abraham   I, 322
LIFFT
  John Godfried   I, 509
LIGTMÜLLER
  Johan   I, 694
LIKWILDER (LICKWILDER)
  Henry (Hans)   I, 370

LILIE (LEELLY, LILLIE)
  John George (George, Hundrick)   I, 240, 242, 243
LILIGENTHAL (read LILIEN-THAL)
  Mich[1]   I, 758
LILLICH
  Gottlieb   II, 156
  Jacob   II, 179
LILLY
  Johann Christoph   II, 20
LIMBACH (LIMBACK)
  Friederich
    (Frederick)   I, 551, 553, 554
  Johanes
    (Johannes)   I, 551, 553, 554
LIMBACHER
  Christian   I, 400
  Johann Georg   I, 400
LIMBECK
  Joh. David   I, 428
LIMBERGER
  Johannes   I, 521, 524
LIMBERT
  Carolina Friderica   II, 114
  George   I, 393
LIME
  Mannes   II, 97
LIMP (LIMB)
  Filb Ludwig (Philip Ludwig)   673, 674, 675
  Johannes   I, 564, 565, 567
LIMPER
  Hermanus   I, 484
LIMPERT (LEMPERT)
  Catharine   II, 204, 205
  George   II, 205
  Johannes   II, 204
  Peter   II, 205
  (*See also* LIMBERT)
LIMTICH
  Francis   II, 119
LINAMENS
  Margaret   I, 67
LINAU
  Mr. Vincent   II, 149
LINCK (LINCKH, LINK)
  Andres   I, 415
  Anna Madlena   I, 117
  Friederich   I, 741
  Hans Adam   I, 118
  Hans Peter   I, 500
  Jacob (Jacobes)   I, 117, 470; II, 170
  Johan Friederich
    (Fredrick)   I, 637, 639, 640
  Johann Georg Conrath   I, 539, 541, 544
  Johann Gorg   I, 750

Johann Jost I, 706
Johann Simon I, 750
Johanes (Johannes) I, 655, 657
658, 711
Jonathan I, 741
Joseph I, 156
Konrad II, 196
Maria Aug^e^ II, 196
Marttin I, 335, 336, 338
Michael I, 468
Peter II, 107
Resina I, 118
LINCKARDT (LICKHARDT, LICK-
HART)
Johann Bernhard
(Bernhard) I, 655, 657, 658
LINCKE (LINKE)
Andreas II, 183
Jacob I, 396
LINCKER
Johanes I, 500, 614, 616, 618
LINCKSWEILER
Michel I, 485
LIND (LINDT)
Conrath Thomas I, 496
Georg Philips I, 496
Johann Michel I, 496
Wilhelm II, 184
LINDBERGER
George II, 121
LINDE
Frantz II, 112
LINDEMAN (LINDAMAN, LINDE-
MANN, LINTEMAN)
Bruckhard (Burckhardt) I, 551
552, 554
C. II, 199
Christaan I, 742
George I, 440
Henrich I, 282, 284, 285
Jacob I, 282, 284, 285
Joh. II, 101
Justus I, 282, 284, 285
Nicholas I, 461
——— II, 50
LINDEMUTH (LINDENMUTH)
Georg I, 408
Gottfried II, 190
Hans George I, 409
Johann Michael I, 481
Ludwig I, 408
LINDEN
Abraham, Van der II, 196
LINDENBERGER
Georg Ernst I, 489
LINDENSCHMITT
Johan Daniel I, 372
Ludwig I, 372

LINDER (LINTER)
Gorg Anton
(Jerick Anthony) I, 545, 547, 549
Jacob I, 720
Johannes I, 585, 587, 588
Luis II, 168
Michael I, 159, 161
Philipp II, 46
Simon I, 113, 114, 115, 765
LINDERMEYR
Mattheus I, 741
LINDESTIEGEL
Johan II, 134
LINDGUIST
Casper II, 205
LINDLER
Anna II, 169
Hendrich II, 169
Johannas II, 169
LINDNER
Andreas I, 510, 512
Christian I, 456
LINDÖHMER
Johannes I, 452
LINDOR
Catrina I, 766
Elizabeth I, 767
Hance Jerck I, 767
Larance I, 767
Margret I, 766
LINDORFF (LINTORFF)
Johann Christ I, 467, 699
LINDROT
Johanna Jacoba II, 125
LINENBERGH
Conrad I, 479
Nickolas I, 479
LING (LIN)
Peter I, 179, 181, 183
LINGEL
Johann Jacob
(Jacob) I, 179, 181, 183
Paulus I, 179, 181, 183
LINGENFELDER (LINGENFEL-
TER)
George I, 638
Jacob II, 102
Johan Jacob
(Jacob) I, 569, 570, 572
Johannes (Johanis) I, 200, 202, 204
LINKSWEILER
Anna Cath^a^ II, 3, 4
George II, 3
Johann George II, 3
Johann Jacob II, 4
LINN (LIN, LYNN, LINT)
Jacob I, 714
Johann Nickel
(Nicholas) I, 556, 557, 558

Johanes (Johannes)   I, 629, 632, 635
Philip Henry   I, 522, 524
Valentin   I, 734
LINNEKAM
Peter   II, 112
LINNER
Loisa   II, 44
LINNS (LINSS)
Johann Georg   I, 762
Konnerat   I, 421
LINSENBIGLER (LINSENBEGLER,
   LYNTSENBEGLER)
Paulus (Palus)   I, 66, 69, 70
LINTTOS
Henery Schaub   II, 146
LINTZ (LYNSE)
Andereas   I, 485
Bernhart (Bernard)   I, 217, 219, 220
Daniel   II, 184
Georg Friedrich   I, 440
Jerg   I, 408
Joh. Adam   I, 648
Johan Nickel   I, 724
   (*See also* LENTZ)
LIPKIP (LIPEKIPP)
Christina   I, 28
Paul   I, 27, 29, 30
LIPP
Jacob   II, 179
Johannes   I, 709
LIPPENKAN
Jn° Herman Frid.   I, 726
LIPPER
Henry   II, 73
LIPPERT (LEPARD)
Conrad   I, 217, 219, 221
Peter Nicol.   II, 139
Wilhelm   I, 217, 219, 221
LIPPOLDT
Mr.   II, 176
LIPPOTH
Mattheus   I, 466
LIPS (LIPPS)
Barbara   I, 148
Henrich   I, 84, 86, 87
Henry   I, 493
Jacob   I, 479
Johanes   I, 441
Welly Hannah   I, 85
LISCH
Johannes   I, 339
LISCHER (LISCHIRE, LISHIRE)
Jacob   I, 88, 90, 91
LISCHY
Jacob   I, 320, 321, 322
LISE
Johan   II, 168

LISMAN
Elizabeth   II, 4
Peter   II, 4
LISMANNHAUSEN
Maria   II, 148
LISS (LEES)
Lorentz   I, 297, 298, 299
LIST
Carl Christian Friedrich   I, 755
J. Philip   I, 457
Johann Georg (Hans
   Jurg)   I, 627, 630, 634
John Gat.   II, 118
LITCHTEMBERGER
Theobald   II, 119
LITESS
Elizabeth   I, 241
LITMAN
Valdin   I, 492
LITZ
Johan Wilhelm   I, 456
LITZEMBERGER
Joh.   II, 118
LIVINGSTON
Mr   II, 103
LIYE
Philip   II, 183
LOADIG
George   I, 427
LÖB
Andrew   I, 750
LOBACH (LOOBACH)
Isack   I, 357
Peter   I, 139
LÖBE (LOBE, LEAP)
Caspar (Casper)   I, 217, 219, 220
Jacoba   II, 135
LOBEZ
Ignace   II, 95
LÖBLE
Gorg Aadam   I, 421
Wilhelm   I, 422
LÖBS (LEEPS)
Johannes   I, 585, 586, 588
LOBSTEIN
Johann Erhard   I, 481
LOBWASSER
Joseph   I, 365
LOCH
Jacob   I, 265, 268, 271
Johannes (Johanis)   I, 265, 268, 271
LOCHBAUM (LUGHBOOM)
Jacob (Jackop)   I, 116, 119, 121
LOCHER
Fridrich   I, 709
Hennrich   I, 709
LOCHMAN
Johann Willhelm   I, 431

LOCHMILLER (LOCHILLER,
LOCKMILLER)
George Michael
(Jurig) I, 199, 201, 203
LOCHNER (LÖCHNER, LAGNER,
LEGENER, LOCKNER)
Christoff I, 720
Egieties I, 711
Hans Georg I, 304, 305, 306
Johannes Michl. I, 71, 75, 77
Maria I, 72
Mathes (Mathias) I, 685, 695
LOCKMIR
Johan I, 498
LOCKNILL
Joh. Christ. Ehrenfreid II, 125
LOEBEL
Andreas Gotthard I, 723
LOEFFLER
Aug. Carl Frederick II, 33
LOEHR (LOER)
Friederich Peter II, 191
Johann Christian II, 48
Johan Herber I, 478
Peter Jacob II, 191
LOESCH
Jacob II, 60
LOESER (LOESSER, LÖSER)
Frederick (J. George
Friederich) I, 576, 578, 580
Johann Jacob
(Jacob) I, 317, 318, 319
Johann Christian I, 317, 318, 319
Lemmill I, 739
LOETS
Pieter I, 18
LOEY
Johann II, 61
LÖFFEL (LAFELL)
Christian I, 106, 111, 112
LÖFFLER (LOFLER, LÖFFNER)
Balsazar I, 438
Dietrich I, 471
Gottlieb I, 390
Gottlob Jacob I, 706
Jacob I, 387, 388, 389
Johann Adam
(Adam) I, 170, 171, 173
Johannes I, 365
Ulrich II, 13
LOFINCK
Friedrich I, 699
LOFTLER
J. II, 33
LOGIRE (LESHIRE)
Johan Henry
(Jon Henry) I, 282, 284, 285

LOH (LOOH)
Christoph II, 20
Peter I, 359
LOHMANN (LOHMAN, LOOMAN)
Andrew II, 122
Hans II, 102
Johann Heinrich I, 457
Johann Niclos I, 346
LOHMILLER (LOHMÖLLER)
J. Henry I, 493
Johannes I, 494
LÖHNER (LOHNER, LOONER)
Conrad II, 178
Paullus (Paulus) I, 279, 280, 281
LOHNERT
Johan Georg (Jörg) I, 159, 161
LOHNES (LONES)
Johan Nicklaus (Joh.
Nicholas) I, 564, 565, 567
LÖHR (LOHR, LEHR, LOWER,
LEER, LÖRE)
Andreas (Antreas) I, 71, 75, 77
Carl I, 465
Christianna I, 73
Conrad I, 614, 616, 618
Elizabeth I, 74
George (Jurg) I, 440, 614, 616, 618
Georg Michel (Jerg
Michel) I, 620, 622, 624
Godhart (Godhard) I, 353, 354
Hans Peter I, 401
Heinr. II, 140
Johann Daniel I, 692
Johann Haubrich I, 401
Johann Henrich I, 750
Johan Peter I, 401
Johannes I, 73
Johannes Herman I, 73
Philibbus I, 401
LOHRET
Zachrias I, 747
LOHRMAN (LOHRMANN, LOR-
MAN, LOREMAN)
Barbary I, 40
Catrina I, 190
Elizabeth I, 40
Georg Caspar I, 479
Hans Jerg
(George) I, 39, 40, 41, 42
Johann Andreas
(Andreas) I, 585, 586, 588
Katrena I, 40
Margreta I, 190
Maria Hannah I, 190
Mary I, 40
Peter I, 189, 192, 194
LOHS *see* LOOS

LOLIGER
  John   II, 145
LOMBARTH
  Jerg   I, 693
LOMBERG
  Christofel   I, 683
LÖMLE
  Michel   I, 498
LONAUN
  Johan   II, 50
LONG *see* LANG
LONGBLOOD
  Andᵂ   II, 15
LONGENATTO
  J. B.   II, 108
LONGER
  Hans Zacharias   I, 504
LONGJEAR
  Peter   I, 660
LONGLOCH
  A. Cath.   II, 105
LONIGER
  Johann Phillips   I, 715
LOOBACKER (read LOBACHER)
  Maria   I, 73
LOOMYER (read LOHMEYER)
  Wilm   I, 452
LOORER (read LÖHRER)
  Georg   II, 178
LOOS (LOHS, LOOSS, LOSS)
  Anna Abel   II, 23
  Barbara   II, 56
  Jacob   I, 577, 578, 580
  Johan Christoffer I, 341, 342, 343
  Johann George (Johann
    Jorg)   I, 276, 277, 278
                         577, 578, 580
  Johann Heinrich   I, 756
  John Jacob   II, 3
LOOSE
  Franz   II, 55
LOOSER
  Hans Gerg   I, 490
LOOSKY
  Fredᵏ   II, 16
LOPFFER
  J. W.   I, 743
  Johann Dangel   I, 743
LORAY (LOREY, LORA, LORRA,
    LORY)
  Conrad   I, 656, 657, 658
  Georg (Jeorick)   I, 217, 218, 220
  Johann Caspar
    (Johann Gaspar) I, 656, 657, 658
  Johan Henrich   I, 412, 717
  Johan Michel
    (Michell)   I, 217, 218, 220
  Johann Melcher   I, 412
  Johannes   I, 656, 657, 658

  Matthes   I, 705
LÖRCH (LERICK, LORCH)
  Caspar (Casper)   I, 217, 218, 220
  Christian (Christr) I, 527, 528, 530
  Johan Jacob   I, 495
  Johannes   I, 217, 219, 220
  Martin   I, 414
LORENZ (LORENTZ, LOWRENTZ,
    LOWRENCE, LORENCE)
  Caspʳ   II, 130
  Barbara   I, 103
  F. Michael (Fredᵏ M.)   I, 589
                         590, 591
  Frantz Peter   I, 367, 368
  George Michˡ   II, 118
  Henry   I, 204, 206, 208
  J. Nicklas
    (Nicholas)   I, 629, 632, 635
  Jacob   I, 103, 481
  Johann (Johannes)   I, 154, 158
                    160, 371, 453
  Johann Casper   I, 737
  Johann Friedrich (Johann
    Fridrich, Fredrick)   I, 283
                         284, 286
  Johan Jacob   I, 724
  Johan Nichl.   I, 398
  Johann Philip   I, 371
  Johan Velten   I, 371
  Johannes (Jonnas) I, 323, 325, 326
  Mathias   I, 411
  Moritz (Morris)   I, 102, 104, 105
  Nicklaus (Nichl.)   I, 363, 449
  Peter   I, 277, 278, 279
LÖRER (LÖHRER, LORER)
  Jochamus (Jochmus,
    Asihmes)   I, 335, 336, 338
  Jorg   I, 492
LORESCH
  Nicholas   II, 55
LORIE (LORRIE)
  Johann Petter
    (Peter)   I, 586, 587, 588
LORIG (LERICK)
  Anna Maria   I, 108
  Hans Jerick   I, 109
  Johan (Johanes)   I, 107, 111, 112
LORMAN
  Tick   II, 16
LORO
  Bapᵗ   II, 108
LÖRSCH
  Vallentin   I, 340
LÖSCH (LASCH, LESCH)
  Better   I, 749
  Johann Jacob   I, 448
  Johann Martin   I, 666, 669, 671
  Johannes   I, 744
  Steffan (Stephen) I, 265, 268, 271

LOSCHENKOHL
Frederick II, 160
LÖSCHER (LESER)
Barbara I, 132
Catherina I, 131, 132
Hans Georg I, 132
Jacob I, 131, 133, 134
Margaretha I, 132
LOSHEART
Kattarina I, 241
LOSHORN (LOSHOEN, LESHORN)
Paulus (Paul) I, 614, 616, 618
LOSS
Madam II, 89
Mr II, 88
LOSSING
Luwis I, 157
LOSTÄTTER
Jacob I, 434
Nicolas I, 434
LOTER
Chr II, 186
LOTMAN
Wm II, 32
LOTS see LOTZ
LOTSHARING
Cathrina I, 67
Maria I, 67
LOTSPEICH
Joh. Christoph I, 742
LOTTER (LODDER)
Christian I, 222, 223, 224
Eberhardina Christiana II, 20
LOTZ (LOTS, LOATS, LUTTS)
Adam I, 422, 716
Anna M. II, 158
Annette II, 158
Balthasar I, 497
Catherine II, 158
Henrich I, 444
Johan Adam I, 507
Johan Henrich I, 429
Johann Wilhelm I, 494
Johanes (Johannes) I, 113, 114
115, 387, 388
389, 500, 765
John F. II, 158
Lenhart I, 89, 91, 92
Nicolas I, 494
Peter Henry II, 158
Stephannus I, 500
Susanna II, 20
LOTZE
Elisabeth II, 124
Heinrich II, 124
LOUDIWICK (read LUDWIG)
Christian Hendrich II, 49
LOUGH (LOCKE)
Johan Peter (Peter) I, 265, 269, 272

LOUGHY (LOCHEY)
G. Peter (Yerrick
Peter) I, 595, 597, 599
LOUIS
Carl Christian I, 760
Caroline II, 182
Nicol. II, 182
LOUSEY
Joh. II, 168
LOUTVITH
Carell I, 316
LOUVAT
Joseph I, 757
LOVENHAGEN
Dorothy II, 12
Jno II, 12
Sarah II, 12
Thomas II, 12
William II, 12
LÖVER (LEAZER, LEARER)
Matteus (Mathias) I, 227, 229, 231
LÖW (LAU, LAW, LOW)
Christian I, 102, 104, 105
Conraed I, 102, 105
Johann Adam I, 737
Johan Peter I, 709
Johannes I, 443
LÖWE (LOWE, LEVY)
Anna Gluf I, 103
Barbara I, 103
Christian I, 103
David (Davit) I, 661, 663, 664
Margaret I, 103
Philip I, 103
Samuel I, 661, 663, 664
LÖWENBERG (LOUWENBORG,
LUWENBORG)
Barberry I, 153
Friedrich I, 761
Hannah I, 153
Hans I, 153, 154
Lizarberth I, 153
Peter I, 153, 761
Philipp I, 761
LÖUWENSTEIN (LEWESTEYN)
David I, 162, 164, 166
Michel I, 706
LOWENSTERN
Ferdinant II, 53
LOWIERY
—— II, 121
LOWMAN
Elizabeth II, 194
Henry II, 194
Jeremiah I, 16
Powell II, 194
LOWRER (LOWRA)
Johannes I, 185, 186, 187

LUBECK (LUBEK, LEBECK)
Frederick II, 160
Jacob I, 275, 276
Thomas I, 416
LUBCKEN
George I, 143, 145, 146
LUCAS
Daniel I, 277, 278, 279
J. Adam I, 437
LÜCK (LUCK, LIKE)
Georg I, 730
Jacob I, 730
Johan Henrich (John
Hendrick) I, 300, 301, 302
Johann Philippus I, 750
LUCKEL
W. G. II, 141
LUCKENBACH (LOUKENBACK)
Johann Adam
(John Adam) I, 279, 280, 282
Johan Henerich
(John Henerich,
John Henry) I, 279, 281, 282
John Gerhart
(John Gerradt) I, 279, 281, 282
LUCKENBILL (LUKENBILL,
LÜCKENBILL)
Henrich (Hendrik) I, 31, 33, 34
Johan Ekel I, 31, 33, 34
LUCKER (LICHER, LICKER)
J. George (Gerge,
John Jerrick) I, 609, 610, 612
LÜCKHAUB
Conradt I, 721
LUCKLER
Johs. Jas. II, 118
LÜDE
Georg Wilhelm, von I, 517, 519, 520
LÜDER
Johann Heinrich I, 446
LÜDERACHER
Niclaus I, 745
LÜDERITZ
Friderick I, 709
LUDERS
Christian II, 72
LÜDI (LUDI)
Christof I, 750
Daniel I, 432
Dorothea I, 135
Elizabeth I, 135
Jacob I, 750
Maria I, 135
Martin I, 470
Nicklaus I, 705
Samuel I, 134, 136
LUDICA
Liena II, 76

LÜDIN
Daniel I, 392
LUDWIG (LUDEWIG, LUTWIG,
LUTWICK, LEWDWIG)
Casp. Coenr. II, 118
Catharina II, 53
Christof I, 399, 453
Conrad I, 614, 616, 618
Daniel I, 122, 125, 126
Engelwird
(Engelbert) I, 614, 616, 618
Francis Joseph II, 17
George I, 486; II, 53
Godfried (Godfrey) I, 649, 651
Hans Adam I, 408
Hans Jerg I, 442
Hein. Vinct. II, 118
J. I, 405
Jacob I, 408, 464, 614, 616, 618
Johan (Joh.) I, 449, 757
Johann Conradt
(Joh. Conrad) I, 586, 587, 588
Johann George I, 414, 446
Johann Martin Roettger I, 505
Joh. Nicolaus I, 714
Johann Peter I, 408
Johann Philip I, 433
Johannes (John) I, 484, 614,
616, 618, 697
Lorentz I, 454
Magdalena II, 53
Mathias (Matheas) I, 615, 617, 619
Michael (Michel) I, 122, 125, 126
Mr. II, 74
Philip I, 614, 616, 618
LUDY
Adam I, 691
Johannes I, 685
LUEKE (LÜKE)
A. II, 141
Hans I, 392
LUER
Hobrick I, 675
LUERS
G. H. II, 73
LUFT (LUFFT)
Georg I, 751
Johann Henrich I, 444
Johannes I, 732
LUGEBÜEL (LUGENBIEHL)
Nicklaus I, 690
Peter I, 448
LUGER
Christof I, 710
Johannes I, 710
LUGETBOM, (LUGTBOM)
Anna I, 118
Cristina I, 117

LUGGINS
Anna II, 68
LUHNE
—— II, 206
LUKENBERG
Caroline II, 123
LUKENS
Jacob II, 25
LULL
John II, 185
LULLICH
Jacob II, 155
LUMM (LUM, LANN)
Andreas I, 317, 319
LUMMEL
Friedrich I, 459
LUNCK
Adam I, 395
LUNENMACHER
Gotlieb I, 471
LUNG
Adam I, 465
Joh. Michael I, 465
Simon I, 466
LUNGER (PLUMMER)
Jacob I, 318, 319
LUNGWITZ
Joh. Gottl. II, 140
LUNTZ
Conrad I, 495
LUPACH
Christoph II, 78
LÜPFER (LUPFFER)
Jacob I, 509
Johann Gerlach I, 743
LUPP (LOUB, LUP, LUPE)
Gerlach I, 465
Henrich (Henry) I, 615, 617, 619
Johann Christian I, 465
Johan Peter I, 401
Johan Tunges I, 712
Johannes I, 465, 737
Ludwig
(Ludowick) I, 568, 570, 572
Peter I, 676
LÜPPERT
Melchior I, 416
LUPPOLDT (LEOPOLD)
Hans Martin
(Johans) I, 637, 639, 640
Johanes I, 637, 639, 640
John Caspar
(Johan Caspar) I, 637, 639, 640
LUPRIAN (LUPREAM)
Johann Christian
(Joh. Chris.) I, 564, 566, 567
LURBER
Johan Jacob I, 427

LUSTE
Friedrick II, 183
LUTA
Henrich I, 404
LUTENECKER
Heinrich II, 124
LÜTERS (LURTERS)
C. Wilhilmina II, 101
Carl II, 101
Dorth. II, 101
Jana II, 101
Wilhelmina II, 101
LUTES
Lennard I, 99
LUTHER (LUTTER)
Andreas I, 711
Christian I, 461
Coem II, 45
Henrich I, 406
Ludwig (Lodowick) I, 559, 560, 562
Petter I, 711
LUTHI
Mr. II, 177
LUTJOHAN
Jurgen Mich. II, 139
LUTKENS
Dorᵃ II, 23
LUTSCH (LÜTSCH)
Johann Henrich
(Joh. Hendᵏ) I, 563, 565, 567
Johannes Peter I, 733
LÜTSCHY
Caspar I, 723
LUTSINGER (LUZINGER)
Michael (Michel) I, 205, 207, 208
LUTTERMANN (LUTTERMAN)
Christian Henrich
(Henry) I, 589, 590
LUTTICH (LÜTTIG)
Andreas I, 477
Eberhard I, 705
LUTTMAN
Michael I, 432
Philip Jacob I, 348, 349, 351
LUTZ (LUTS, LOTZ, LOTS)
Andreas Adam I, 754
Barbara I, 62
Caspar (Casper) I, 221, 223, 224
555, 557, 558
Casp. Frederik I, 504
Catrina I, 767
Christian (Christ) I, 221, 223, 224
412, 485, 497
Elizabeth I, 767
Hance Martin I, 767
Hans Conradt
(Hs. Conrad) I, 366, 412
Hans Jacob I, 412

Hans Jerg
  (Jnº George)   I, 555, 557, 558
Henrich   I, 426
Jacob   I, 485; II, 135
Jerg Heinrich   I, 443
Johan Connrad   I, 402
Johann Georg
  (Johan Gorg) I, 221, 222, 224, 422
Johan Henrich   I, 698
Johann Michael   I, 502
Johann Nickel
  (Nicholas)   I, 300, 301, 303
Johann Peter   I, 365
Johann Philipp
  (Philip)   I, 48, 52, 53, 714
Johannes (Johanes)   I, 479, 490
                        638, 639, 641
Jorg Michel   I, 508
Margret   I, 766
Mariradell   I, 767
Marten   I, 412
Mattheis   I, 467
Susanna   I, 62
Thomas   I, 677, 678, 680
Wibbertus (Webbertus,
  Wiepertus)   I, 296, 298, 299
LUTZE
  Georg Wilch.   II, 117
LUTZENS
  Christiana Wilhelmina   II, 72
  Francis Gothilf   II, 72
  Gothilf Nicolas   II, 72
  Susana Barbery   II, 72
LUTZER
  J. Friederich   I, 505
LÜTZING (LESSING)
  Conrad   I, 563, 565, 567
  Leonhart (Leonard) I, 563, 565, 567
LÜTZLER (LITZER)
  Rutolf (Rudolph) I, 175, 176, 177
LUWIG
  Adam   II, 184
LUX
  G. C.   II, 45
LUY (LOUIA)
  Henrich (Henry) I, 614, 616, 619
LYBERT
  Michael   I, 10
LYDIE
  Jacob   I, 14
LYDY (LIGHTIE)
  Hans Adam   I, 221, 223, 224
LYHN
  Frantz Arnold   I, 704
LYME
  Jacob   I, 436
  Palzer   I, 14
LYMP
  Jnº N.   II, 6

LYNTER
  Hans   I, 358
LYS
  Jnº Henry   I, 723
LYSINGA
  Conradt   II, 45
LYSSEY (LEYSIG)
  Hans George   I, 546, 547, 549
LYTZLER
  Friter   I, 392
LYX
  Johannes   I, 498
  Michael   I, 498

MAAG (MAACK, MAG, MOAG)
  Frantz Heinrich I, 336, 337, 339
  Friderich   I, 498
  Heinrich (Hendrich)   I, 335, 336
                        338, 464, 483
  Jacob   I, 335, 336, 338
  Joachim Heinr.   II, 128
  Johann Jacob I, 169, 171, 172, 447
MAAN
  Uhllerich (Ullerick) I, 367, 369
MAANKE
  Frantz Peter   II, 111
MAAS
  Carl Andon   I, 750
  Christina   II, 68
  Lenard   I, 453
MACH (MOAGE, MACHE)
  C. Frederich (Christopher
    Fredrick)   I, 559, 560, 562
MACHLE
  J. H.   II, 205
MACHLEIT
  Daniel   I, 500
MACHLY
  George   II, 104
MACHOL
  Herman   II, 116
MACHOLT (MAKHOLD)
  Johannes Nicolaus   I, 393
  Nicklas   I, 393
MACK (MÄCK, MACKH, MAK)
  Allexander (Alixander) I, 27, 29, 30
  Andereas   I, 496
  Anna   I, 67
  Anna Margaret   I, 28
  Barbara   I, 67; II, 119
  Christian   II, 173
  Georg Michael   I, 84, 86, 87
  George   II, 19
  Hans Martin   I, 487
  Johan George   II, 173
  Johannes I, 27, 29, 30, 383, 385, 485

Peiter I, 485
Philipps Jacob I, 496
Phillipina I, 28
Velten (Felte) I, 27, 29, 30
MÄCKELBURG
Carl Ludwig I, 502
MACKIE
George II, 12
M. II, 138
MACKLY
Davit I, 331
George I, 227
MADDOX
Joshua I, 345
MADENFIND
Andrew II, 200
MADER (MÄDER)
Jeorg I, 464
Johann Mardin I, 699
Ludwig I, 701
MADERY
Hans I, 392
MADICH
Hans Jerg I, 439
MADINGER (MERDINGER)
Elizabeth I, 40
George Tebald (Geo.
Sebald) I, 39, 41, 42
Margreta I, 40
MADLER (METLER)
Jacob I, 147, 150
MADLUNG (MADLONG)
Johannes I, 194, 195, 196
MADORI (MADARI, MADERY)
Hans Jacob I, 266, 270, 273
MADZEN
Niels II, 183
MAELER
Wilhelm I, 676
MAERGLE
J. F. II, 162
—— II, 162
MAERTENS
August II, 205
Friedr. II, 205
MAGASCH
Heinrich I, 408
MAGEL (MAGHELE, MAGELL)
Christoff
(Christopher) I, 286, 287, 288
MÄGLI
Felix I, 415
Hans Jacob I, 415
MAGMER (MAGEMER)
Johann Philip I, 355
Johannes I, 355
MAGNUS
Heinrich I, 505

MAHL
Christopher I, 531, 533, 535
MAHLE
Christian II, 192
Dorothea II, 192
Elizabeth II, 192
Hans George II, 192
MAHLER
Conrad I, 716
Friederich I, 724
Hans George
(Jurg) I, 226, 228, 230
MÄHLICH
Henrich Wilhelm I, 405
MAHN
Johann Davidt I, 700
MAHON
Caspr II, 6
MAHRT (MARTH)
Carl I, 378, 380, 381
MAIDINGER (MEIDINGER, MY-
TINGER)
Daniel I, 348, 350, 351
MAIER see MAYER
MAILLARD
—— II, 81
MAILLE
Catharina Barbara II, 171
Friederika II, 171
Johanes II, 171
Maria Magdelina II, 171
Mathias Friederich II, 171
Walburga II, 171
MAIN (MAIM)
Peter I, 318, 319, 320
MAINSULT
John II, 195
MAINTZER
Johanes I, 464
Martin I, 464
MÄINTZGER
Ludwig I, 399
MAIRE (MEAR)
Adam I, 591, 593, 594
MAISCH
Johann Georg I, 475, 531, 533, 534
Steffe I, 420
MAISHELLER
David I, 468
MAISON
Pr. I, 761
MAITLIN
Vallentin I, 436
MAJER
Fillab II, 134
MAKTER
Bernhart I, 346
MALAMBRE
Jacob II, 59

MALCHIOR
Johannes Michael   I, 398
MALCHOWFF
Christian Heinrich   II, 79
MALCOLM
J.   II, 144
MALL (MAILES)
Christ Ludwig   I, 531, 533, 535
Philipp   I, 491
MALLE
Johan Georg   I, 441
MALLEBERGER
Michael   I, 441
MALLERCHON
Balth   II, 119
MALLERIVE
——   II, 80
MALLERT
Johann Wilhelm   I, 401
MALLESIE
Anna Maria   II, 21
Henrich Pieter   II, 20, 21
Johannes   II, 21
Willem Pieter   II, 21
MALLHERT
Jol   II, 61
MALLO
Hanns Georg   I, 730
Johann Adam   I, 734
Johann Michael   I, 405
MALLYCOAT
Philip   I, 469
MALOW
Allexander   II, 103
Peter   II, 103
MALTHER (MALTTHANER)
Johannes   I, 677, 679, 680
MAMME
Elizabeth   II, 91
MANAR
J.   II, 16
MANCKELL (MANCKER)
Johannes   I, 642, 644
MANDEL (MÄNDEL, MANTEL)
Georg Adam
(Yerrick Adam)   I, 581, 583, 584
Georg Carl   I, 720
Johann Christian
(Christian)   I, 581, 583, 584
MANDELER
Johann David   I, 748
MANDERBACH
Johann Hennrich   I, 726, 727
Johannes   I, 466
MANDERFELTH
Johannes   I, 701
MANENBACH (MANNEBACH,
MANERBACH)
Nicolas   I, 336, 337, 339

MANERBACH
J. Henry   I, 465
MANEUVRE
Manette   II, 193
MANFREZ
Johanna   II, 113
MANG
Gothfrid
(Godfriek)   I, 265, 269, 272
Johann Adam   I, 435
Nikolaus   II, 134
MANGEL (MANGAL)
Lorentz (Lorents)   I, 627, 630, 633
MANGER
Wilhelm   I, 423
MANGOLD (MANGOLT)
Barbara   II, 146
Christian   I, 686
Hannah   II, 146
Heinrich   II, 133
Henery   II, 146
J. Adam (John
Adam)   I, 621, 623, 625
Martin   II, 146
MANGUZER
Jos A.   II, 116
MANHART
Mr.   II, 177
MANHIM
Israel   I, 678
MANI (MANY, MANIE)
Hans Adam   I, 300, 301, 302
Jacob   I, 300, 301, 302
Jost   I, 300, 301, 302
MANIERIK
Charles, v.   II, 57
H., v.   II, 57
MANN (MAN)
Christian   I, 568, 569, 570
571, 572, 573
Hans George (Hanns
Jerg)   I, 551, 552, 553, 554
Jacob (John Jacob) I, 204, 206, 208
407, 551, 553, 554
Johann Georg (John
George)   I, 555, 556, 558
Johann Jacob   I, 690
Johann Phillip (Joh.
Philip)   I, 297, 298, 300
Johannes   I, 552, 553, 554
John   II, 60
Jonas   I, 568, 570, 572
Maria   II, 105
Peter   I, 432
Wilhelm Hanns   I, 372
MANNALTHER
Johann Friedrig   I, 755
MANNBAR
Jerg Michael   I, 452

MANNBEKH
Johann Berndt I, 704
Rudolph I, 704
MANNCHER(?)
Johann Jacob I, 57, 58
MÄNNIG (MINSE, MENICH)
Johan Adam I, 666, 668, 670
Johannes I, 666, 669, 671
MANNSPERGER (MANSBERGER)
Marti (Martin) I, 222, 223, 224
MANNWILLER
Johann Matheus I, 724
Tomas I, 724
MANSER
Jacob Mattheus I, 105, 106
MANTE
Mich¹ II, 68
MANTZ (MANS, MANZ, MENTS)
Casper (J. Casper) I, 227, 229, 231
II, 104
Hans Michel I, 93, 95, 96
Magdel I, 148
Petter I, 449
MANTZINGER (MANSINGER)
Davit (David) I, 248, 249, 250
Jacob I, 248, 249, 250
Melcher (Jnº) I, 248, 249, 250
MANY
Jacob I, 413
MARBACHER
Anna Maria II, 148
Carl II, 148
Carolina II, 148
Christina II, 148
Francisca II, 148
Johan Georg II, 148
Johannes II, 148
Valentine II, 148
MARBES
John I, 685
MARBURG (MARBOOK)
Johann Caspar (John
Casper) I, 551, 553, 554
MARBURGER
Danniel I, 425
George Ludwig I, 484
MARCEL
Mr. II, 175
Mrs. II, 175
MARCHAND (MERCHAN)
Abram Capitaine II, 31
David I, 592, 593, 594
MARCK (MARK)
Eva Cath. II, 9
Eva Margᵗ II, 8
Geo. II, 9
Geo. Adam II, 9
Johan Deest (Johan
Ties) I, 277, 278, 279

Johan Diterig (Johan
Diedrick) I, 277, 278, 279
John II, 195
Mary Cath. II, 9
Michell I, 317, 318, 319
Philip I, 372
II, 9
MARCKBACH
Johann Diether I, 496
MARCKELL (MARKEL, MERCKEL,
MORCKELL, MORGEL)
Abm II, 75
Anthony (Andon) I, 614, 617, 619
Martin I, 638, 639, 641
MÄRCKER (MARCKER)
Johann Jorg I, 523, 525
Matias (Mattisias) I, 137, 141, 142
Sebastian I, 734
MARCKERT
Peter I, 391
MARCUS
Fredᵏ Willem II, 4
Peter I, 430
Simon I, 504
MARDOFF
Conrad I, 753
Wilhelm II, 126
MAREKEI
Jean Christophel I, 495
MARETE
Dominico II, 205
MARGEL (MERGEL, MORTEL)
Fridrich (Fredᵏ) I, 666, 669, 671
Jacob I, 384, 386
MARGGRANDER
Georg Adam I, 760
MARHEFFEN
Johan Niclaus I, 462
MARIENER
Anthʸ II, 15
MARIENG
Maria I, 117
MARK *see* MARCK
MARKEY
Hans Davit (Hance
David) I, 163, 165, 167
Marcus I, 163, 165, 167
MARKHART
Peter I, 415
MARKLY
Conrath II, 147
Hans I, 391
Hans George I, 391
Hans Jacob I, 391
MARKS (MARCS)
Jacob I, 737
John Godfreedom II, 42
John Jost II, 160
Peter I, 690

MARKWARD (MARKWART, MARKWORT)
H. George   I, 482
Hans George   I, 344, 345
Marty (Mart.)   I, 344, 345
MARLACK
John Andrew   II, 123
MÄRLICH
Stephan   I, 432
MARLIER
Etienne   I, 746
MARON (MARUM)
Hans Jacob   I, 257, 260, 262
MARONETTE
Jaques   I, 234
MAROT (MARROT)
Ann Judit   I, 122
Benjamin   I, 123
Daniel   I, 123
Guiliam   I, 123
Jean   I, 123
Marian   I, 122, 123
Philip   I, 123
Pierre (Pieter)   I, 122, 124, 126
Sarah   I, 123
Susan   I, 123
MARPEL
Nathan   II, 26
MARQUARD (MARQUART)
Friedr.   II, 107
Gerick   I, 660
Hans Georg   I, 488
Joh.   II, 107
Johannes   I, 436
MARQUEDANDT
Lorentz   I, 445
MARQUET
——   II, 81
MARRET (MARRETT)
Nichs (Michl)   I, 168, 170, 172
MARSCH (MARSH)
Frederick   I, 24
Henry   I, 404
Jacob   II, 139
Johann   I, 741
MARSCHALL (MARSHALL)
Diderich   I, 162
Francis   II, 75
Frantz   I, 407
MARSTALLER (MARSTELLER, MARRSTALLER)
An Catharina   I, 157
Friederich   I, 26, 27
Hans Jerg (Hans (Yerrick)   I, 551, 552, 554
Johann Petter (Peter)   I, 156, 159, 161
Peter (Petter)   I, 184, 186, 187

MART
John   II, 17
MARTA
Martin   I, 80
MARTANDER
Henry Louis   II, 79
MARTATOR
Hans   I, 14
MARTE (MARTEN)
Christ (Christopher)   I, 27, 29, 30
David   I, 12
Hennrich (Henrick, Henerich)   I, 35, 36
Hennricus   I, 748
Jacob   I, 12
Maria Agnis   I, 28
Mattheus   I, 439
Michal   II, 51
MARTENS
Dora Marga   II, 23
Johannes (Hannes)   I, 323, 324, 326
MARTERSECK (MARDESTECK, MATTERSTEEK, MATTERSTACK, MARDERSTECK, MATTERSTEK)
Johan Martin (Martin)   I, 601, 602, 604
Johannes   I, 601, 602, 604
MARTI (MARTY, MARTEY, MORTY)
Ells   I, 80
Hans Imber   I, 163, 165, 166
Hans Jerg   I, 446
Johannes   I, 392
Johannes (Hans)   I, 153, 154
Lorentz   I, 392
MARTIN (MARTHIN, MARTTIN)
Andw   I, 689
   II, 27
Angau (?)   I, 50
Anna   I, 49, 103
Anna M.   II, 6
Baltzer   I, 472; II, 30
Barbara   I, 50; II, 187
Caspar (Gasper)   I, 107, 111, 113
Christian   I, 78, 81, 82
David   I, 14; II, 73
Ditrich (Derrick, Dieterich)   I, 155, 158, 160
Eberhardt   I, 476
Elizabeth   I, 50; II, 187
Fravin   I, 80
Fronik   I, 81
Georg   I, 521, 524
H. J.   II, 198
Hans   I, 212, 214, 216
Hans C.   II, 6
Hans Caspr   II, 6

Hans Gorg (Hans
  Jorg)   I, 102, 104, 105, 408, 472
Hans Henrich (Hans
  Hendrik)   I, 48, 52, 53
Hans Steffan   I, 454
Heinrich   II, 133
Henry   II, 185
Henry Christ.   II, 121
Jacob   I, 14, 347, 456
    II, 133, 187
J. Jacob (Jacob)   I, 556, 557, 558
Johann Friedrich   I, 402
Johan Jacob (John
  Jacob)   I, 383, 385
Johan Martin (John
  Martin)   I, 672, 673, 674
Johann Nicklaus
  (Nickel)   I, 596, 598, 600, 709, 737
Johannes   I, 258, 260, 262, 347, 472
    II, 128, 187
John   I, 735, 756; II, 19
John Carl   II, 69
Joseph   I, 756
Jost   I, 655, 657, 658
Maria   I, 103; II, 187
Marilis   I, 139
Martin   II, 187
Mary   II, 187
Michael   I, 103
Mr.   II, 176
Mrs.   II, 176
Nicklas (Nickolas)   I, 293, 294, 295
Peter   I, 439, 456
Rudolf   I, 50
Salamy   II, 187
Samuel   II, 178
Veronica   I, 49
Yarah Emmanuel   I, 344
MARTINENGO
Valentine   II, 13
MARTINI (MARTINE)
Johann Theodorus (John
  Theodore)   I, 574, 575
Justus Carl Wilhelm (Jost
  Carols)   I, 574, 575
MARTINS (MARTENS, MARKINS)
Gerhart (George)   I, 629, 632, 635
Jnᵒ Henry   II, 12
Johannes   II, 125
MARTINSSEN
Herman Wilh.   II, 140
MARTTER   (MARTGER,
  MARKER)
Peter   I, 266, 269, 272
MÄRTZ, MARTZ see MERTZ
MARTZLOF   (MARTZHAF,
  MARSTLOFF)
Fullibs (Fillibs,
  Phillip)   I, 264, 268, 271

MARUSE
Johan Hendrick   II, 71
MARX
Adolph   II, 70
Andreas   II, 70
Catharina   II, 70
Christiana   II, 70
Conrad   II, 92
Georg Wilhelm   I, 443
Gerhardus   II, 92
Gertruth   II, 70
Jacob   I, 729; II, 70
Johann Georg   I, 443
Johann Henrich   I, 724
Wilhelm (William)   I, 289, 290, 291
MASAN
Leon   II, 89
MASBECK (MASPECK)
Caspar (Gasper)   I, 240, 242, 243
MASCARD
Nicholas   II, 90
MASCHBERGER (MASHBERGER)
Jacob   I, 396
MASER
Johann Jacob   I, 499
Matheus   I, 499
MASMER
Peter   II, 104
MÄSNER
Jacob   I, 426
MASON
George Michel   II, 47
John   II, 47
Joseph   II, 47
Mary   II, 47
MASS (MÖS)
Anna Maria   I, 23
Jacob   I, 498
Johannes   I, 713
MASSCHERT
H.   II, 32
MASSENER
Hans Jacob   I, 392
MASSENGER
Godfried   II, 114
MASSER
Friderich   I, 489
MASSERLEY
Michael   I, 346
MASSHOLDER (MASOHLDER)
Jacob   I, 693
John   I, 718
MAST (MASHT)
Barbara   I, 190
Christoph   I, 492
Jacob   I, 8, 188, 192, 193
MASTER
Moritz   I, 692

MATERNUS
  Johan David   II, 20
MATHERWATSON
  Hannah   II, 194
MATHERY
  Martin   II, 133
MATHEW
  Louis   II, 57
MATHIAT   (MATCHAIT,
  MACKYO)
  Jean (John)   I, 592, 593, 594
MATSH
  Herman   I, 492
MATT
  Gorg Lutwig   I, 455
MATTER
  Antony   II, 147
  Christopher Gotlip   I, 28
  Diewalt   I, 475
  Georg   I, 460
  Hans   I, 460
  Hans Adtam   I, 460
  Jacob   I, 460
  Stanislaus   I, 727
  Valtin   I, 464
MATTERKUNS
  Henrich   I, 734
MATTERMAN
  Wynlen   II, 196
MATTERN   (MATERN,   MOT-
  TERN)
  Elizabeth   I, 74
  Margereta   I, 72
  Niclaus   I, 716
  Peter   I, 96, 97, 98, 426
  Thomas (Tomas)   I, 71, 75, 77
MATTHÄUS   (MATTHEUS,
  MATHEUS,   MATTHES,
  MATHES,   MATTHEIS,
  MATHEIS, MATTES, MATES)
  Bernhard
    (Bernhardt)   I, 614, 616, 618
  Christian   I, 438
  Hans Jacob
    (Jacob)   I, 106, 110, 112
  Johann Jacob   I, 701
  Johan Miechell
    (Johan)   I, 199, 202, 203
  Johann Philip (Johann
    Filp)   I, 420, 694
  Johannes   I, 310, 311, 313
     614, 616, 618
     709
  Juliana   II, 8
  Maria Crete   I, 108
  Martin   I, 461
  Nicholaus   II, 205
  Stephen   I, 104, 105

MATTHEY   (MATTEY)
  Jacob   I, 296, 298 299
  Joh.   I, 757
MATTHIAS   (MATHIAS,
  MATHEAS,   MATTHIES,
  MATHIES, MATTIS, MODES)
  Casper (Caspar,
    Gosber)   I, 294, 295, 296
  Christopher   I, 703
  Dorothea   II, 69
  Friederich Christian   II, 69
  Hans Jurg   I, 714
  Henry   I, 466
  Herman   I, 615, 617, 619
  Joh.   I, 725
  Johan Carl   I, 753
  Johann Diterich
    (Diedrick)   I, 373, 374, 375
  Johann Jacob
    (Jacob)   I, 386, 388, 389
  Johannes   I, 461
  John Caspar   II, 69
  John George   I, 505
  Mick.   I, 498
  Nicholas   I, 461
  Philip Godfried   I, 706
  Philipp Heinrich   II, 69
MATTHIESEN   (MATHIESON,
  MATTHESEN)
  Christopher (Chr.)   I, 589, 590, 591
  Henrich   II, 79
MATTINGER   (MATINGER)
  Johan Henry   I, 355
  Michael   I, 430
MATTLER
  George   I, 441
MATZ (MATTS, MÄTZ)
  Cathrina   I, 102
  Johann Fred.   I, 758
  Johann Jost   I, 755
  Stephen   I, 102
MATZENBACHER
  Johann Adam   I, 743
  Johan Jacob   I, 709
MATZER   (MATZON)
  George (Jerick)   I, 546, 547, 549
MATZGAR, MATZGER *see* METZ-
  GER
MATZINGER
  Jacob (Felix)   I, 147, 149
MAUBER
  Willm   II, 111
MAUCK
  Johann Phlippes   I, 355
MAUD
  Jacob   I, 450
MAUDER
  Jo. Friedrich   I, 435

MAUER (MAUR, MAWER, MAURER, MOURER, MOWRER)
Bernhart I, 499
Hans Michael I, 455
Herman I, 402
Jacob I, 318, 398
Johann Adam I, 419
Johan Michell I, 485
Johan Nicolaus (Nichol) I, 265, 268, 272
John George I, 700
Jorg Michel I, 403
Peter I, 582, 583, 584
Philips I, 419
Rudy I, 398
MAUERER
Hans I, 297, 298, 300, 458
Jacob I, 420
Ludwig I, 156, 159, 161
Michael I, 403, 722
Paulus I, 480
MAUERLE
Balthasar I, 393
MAUERSHAGEN (MAUSNSHAG, MAUENSHAGEN)
J. Daniel (Joh. Daniel) I, 577, 578, 580
MAUFSIN
Wm. II, 93
MAUG
Tobias I, 424
MAUL (MAULL)
Bartel I, 104, 105
Conradt I, 373, 374, 375
J. II, 141
J. Jacob I, 464
Johan George (John George) I, 653, 654
Johann Anthon (Anthy) I, 373, 374, 375
MÄULE (MEYLY)
Caspar I, 545, 547, 549
MAURER (MAUERER, MOWRER, MOUERE, MOURER)
Adam I, 283, 284, 285
615, 617, 619
Adam Jacob I, 359
Anna Marg. I, 148
Baltas I, 365
Christian I, 704
Christoph I, 488
Conrad I, 749
Elizabeth I, 148
Georg Ernst I, 412
Georg Heinrich I, 730, 741
George I, 162
Hans Adam I, 415
Hans Jerg I, 348, 349, 351

Hans Philip (Philip) I, 245, 246, 247
Jacob I, 147, 150, 151
289, 290, 291
Johann Albert (John Albright) I, 581, 583, 584
Joh. Andr. II, 106
Joh. Christian I, 412
Johan Christof I, 521, 524
Johann Henrich (Johan Hend. Joh. Henry) I, 147, 297, 298, 300
Johan Michael I, 246, 247, 248
Johannes I, 194, 195, 197, 393
Lorentz (Lawrence) I, 661, 662, 664
Margueret I, 148
Martin I, 470
Michal (Michgel) I, 205, 207, 208
Petter I, 460
Phielib Jacob I, 427
Phillippus I, 339
Regula I, 148
Rüdi I, 434
MAURLE
Conradt I, 462
Davidt I, 462
Hans Jerg I, 462
MAUSER (MOUSER)
H. George I, 483
Johans I, 463
Michel I, 463
T. Nicklas I, 483
MÄUSLIN (MEESELEY)
Abraham (Abram) I, 153, 154
MAUSORN
John, van II, 136
MAUSS (MAUS, MOUS, MUYS)
Bernhart (Barent) I, 122, 125, 126
Cathrina I, 123
Daniel I, 346
Friedrich (Fredk) I, 387, 388, 389
Georg (Jerick) I, 290, 291
Hans Georg I, 481
Jacob I, 720
Johans I, 444
Ludwig (Ludwick) I, 266, 269, 273
Peter I, 331
Samuel I, 521, 523
MAUT
Matheis I, 366
MAUTE
Balthas I, 486, 494
MAUTZ
Hans Jacob I, 48, 52, 53
MAXSEINER
Henrich Adam I, 745
Johannes Ludwig I, 745
MAY (MAY, MEY)
Adolff I, 367, 369
Casimir I, 754

Daniel   I, 335, 336, 338
Emanuel   II, 169
Frantz   I, 509
Frantz Peter   I, 371
Gorg   I, 509
Jacob   II, 169
Johann Georg   I, 709
Johann Henrich   I, 336, 337, 339
Johann Leonhard   I, 371
Johann Michael   I, 494
Johannes   I, 704
Kilian   I, 509
Michael   I, 696
Mr.   II, 74
Peter (Petter)   I, 289, 290, 291
Philipp Jacob   I, 734
Philip Wilh.   I, 739
Phillippus Friederich I, 347
Rolandt   I, 450
Traugott Gottfried   I, 757
MAYER (MAIER, MAAYER, MEYER, MOYER)
A. Cath.   II, 105
Adam   I, 62, 373, 374, 375
Andreas   I, 43
Anna   II, 105
Baltas   I, 394
Caspar   I, 156, 159, 161, 450
Christian
 (Cristian)   I, 16, 237, 238, 240
Christoph
 (Christophell) I, 237, 677, 679 680
Conrat   I, 417
Daniel   I, 155, 158, 161
Eleonora   II, 105
Elias   I, 463
Elisabeth   I, 157
Elisaus (Eliseaus)   I, 60, 64, 65
Friederich   I, 478, 761
Georg (Hans
 Georg)   I, 137, 141, 142, 687
Georg Nicolaus (Jurig
 Mich¹)   I, 237, 238, 240
Gottlieb   I, 751
H. Adam   I, 198, 200, 203
Hans   I, 463
Hans Jacob (Joh. Jacob) I, 649, 651
Hans Jerg (Hans
 George)   I, 221, 223, 224, 718
Hans Ulrich   I, 38, 39
Henrich   I, 14
Hs. Barnhardt   I, 718
Jacob   I, 420, 724
Jacob Friederich (Jacob
 Fredrick)   I, 636, 638, 640
Johann Andreas   I, 475
Johann Bernhardt
 (Bernhard)   I, 662, 663, 664

Johann Georg
 (Gerich)   I, 43, 45, 46, 475
Johann Gerhardt   I, 510, 511, 512
Johann Michael   I, 399
Johann Nickel
 (Nicklas)   I, 371, 420, 689
Johan Peter   I, 722
Johannes   I, 156, 159, 161, 243
                 244, 245, 358, 373
                 374, 375, 476, 560
                       561, 563
Johannis Martin
 (Marten)   I, 560, 561, 563
John George   II, 26
Joseph   I, 358, 486
Kathrina   I, 61, 62
Ludwig   I, 156, 159, 161
Maria Ann   I, 139
Maria Urcella   I, 139
Martin   I, 231
Matteus (Maties) I, 311, 312, 313
Michael (Michiel) I, 62, 472, 696
Philip   II, 84
Philipp Henrich   I, 705
Philipp Jacob   I, 366
Susanna   I, 61
Vinsent   I, 16
MAYERHOFF (MAYERHOOF)
Francies   II, 103
Henry   II, 89
MAYRET
Abraham   I, 733
MAYSENHOLDER
Charles   II, 188
Johannes   II, 190
MAYWEG
Isack   II, 101
Johannes   II, 101
Wilhelm   II, 101
McCALLY
Norman   II, 27
McKINLEY
Alexander   II, 27
MEALBURY
Ann   I, 41
John   I, 41
MEAT
John H.   II, 186
MEBALDT
Hans Jerg   I, 365
MEBUS (MAYBUS)
Johannes   I, 643, 645
MECHELE
Joh.   II, 102
MECHLING (MECKLING, MEK-
 ELING)
Jacob   I, 22, 23
Teobald   I, 22, 23

MECK (MECKH)
Hans   I, 400
Hans Jerg   I, 486
Johann Nicolaus   I, 447
Michael   I, 486
MECKE
Georg   II, 110
Johannes   II, 76
MECKEL (MECKELL)
Christian   I, 415, 615, 617, 620
Johann Christophel   I, 169, 170, 172
MECKELEIN (MACKLIN)
Hans   I, 540, 542, 544
Johan Heinrich   I, 540, 542, 544
MECKES
Conrat   I, 359
MECKLE
Johann Adam   I, 475
MECKLING
Johann Georg   I, 508
MEDART (MEDTART)
Henrich   I, 716
Johann Jacob   I, 760
MEDER
Anna Gertroud   I, 108
Catherine   I, 108
George   I, 110
Henry (Hendrick)   I, 107, 111, 113
Johannes   I, 296, 298, 299
Philipp Jacob   I, 475
MEDLELEN
Evens   I, 84
MEEKE
Rudolph   I, 358
MEEMARD
Anna   I, 157
MEERBOGH
Daniel   I, 430
MEES (MEASE, MEESS)
Philip   I, 296, 298, 299
MEFFERT
Andreas   I, 412
Egidius   I, 378, 380, 381
Gorg Conrad   I, 464
Johann Hennrich   I, 745
Johann Peter (Peter) I, 378, 380, 381
Johannes   I, 412
MEFFS
Catherina Eliz.   II, 105
MEGEL
Johann Adam   I, 355
MEGERT (BERK, MOEHERLY)
Georg Michael (Georg Mächer,
Johannis Mich[1]   I, 559, 560, 562
MEGIE
Bernhard   I, 143
MEHELARS
J.   II, 108

MEHIA
M[r]   II, 109
MEHL
Friedrich   I, 461
Johann Nicklaus   I, 461
MEHRENHOLTZ
Jans Pieliep   I, 684
MEHRKAM (MARCOM)
Conrath (Connered) I, 240, 242, 243
Hannah Maria   I, 241
MEHRLING
Johann Petter   I, 709
MEICHLER
Melchior   I, 665, 668, 670
MEIDORF
Anton   I, 710
MEIER (MAIER, MAYER, MEYER,
MEIR, MIRE)
Carl   I, 743
Casper   I, 344, 345
Christian   I, 427
Hans   I, 406
Hans Adam   I, 20
Hans Heinrich   I, 483
Hans Jacob   I, 740
Heinrich   I, 738
Jacob   I, 274 275, 304
   306, 307, 453
Johann Vallentin
(Walledine)   I, 636, 638, 640
Johannes   I, 418
Jorg Karl (Gorg Karle,
Yergeorall)   I, 283, 284, 286
Mattheis   I, 347
Peder   I, 689
Simon   I, 465
(*See also* MEYER)
MEIERHOFER
Mardi   I, 391
MEIGER (MAYER)
Johanes   I, 476
Johann Conrahd
(Conrad)   I, 622, 624, 626
MEIN (MINE)
A[n] Elisabeth   I, 157
Johan Jorg (Hans Jerig, J.
Georg)   I, 155, 158, 160
MEINERSEN (MAYNERS)
Johannes Josephus   I, 509, 510, 511
MEINGÄSSNER
Johannes   I, 363
MEININGER (MYENGER)
Johannes (Johanes) I, 387, 388, 389
MEINTZER (MAYNTZER, MEN-
ZER)
Georg   I, 464
Hans Georg (Hans
Geo)   I, 185, 186, 187

Hans Gerg (Hance
  George) I, 194, 195, 197
Martin I, 464
MEISCH
  Antreas I, 689
  Friedrich I, 433
  Joh. Friedᶜʰ II, 138
  Johannes I, 433
MEISENHEIM
  Joh. George I, 356
  Johannes I, 433
MEISNER
  Henrich I, 739
  Nicolaus (Nicholas) I, 383, 385
MEISSEL
  Jacob I, 700
  Nicklaus I, 700
MEISSEN
  Johann Petter I, 367, 368
MEISSNER (MEISNER, MEIS-
  SENER)
  Georg (Jurg) I, 665, 668, 670
  Hans Joachim I, 573, 574, 575
  Johann Jacob I, 340, 342
MEISSON
  Francis II, 96
MEISTER (MEISHTER, MESCH-
  TER, MEYSTER, MESTER
  Anna I, 138, 139
  Christopher I, 138
  David I, 137, 141, 142
  Eva I, 139
  Gregorius I, 137, 140, 142
  Hans Adam
    (J. Adam) I, 661, 663, 664
  Johann I, 359
  Johannis (Johannes) I, 243, 244, 245
    666, 668, 670, 709
  John Jacob I, 364
  Maria I, 138
  Melchior (Melcher) I, 137, 141, 142
  Peter I, 646, 647
  Veit I, 454
MEITLER
  John II, 196
MEITTINGER (MITINGER)
  Georg Ludwig (Jurig
    Lodwᵏ) I, 609, 611, 612
MEITZEL
  Henrich II, 79
MEITZLER
  Peter I, 372
MEKHEL
  Hans Jerg I, 446
MELBER
  Hans Michel I, 427
MELCH
  Johan Pieter I, 18

MELCHART
  Christian I, 419
MELCHER (MILLGER)
  Friederich I, 538, 540, 543
  Hans I, 473
  Nicklaus (Nicolaus) I, 155, 158, 161
MELCHIONAR
  Ludwick I, 102, 103
  Philip I, 102
MELCHIOR (MELCHIER)
  Johannes I, 307, 309, 310
MELHINGER
  Isach II, 32
  J. G. II, 32
MELHORN
  George I, 660
  Geᵒ Simon I, 660
  Simon I, 660
MELI
  Mr. I, 25
MELIG
  Louvise Charlote II, 71
MELIUS
  William II, 122
MELL
  Michael I, 438
MELLINGER (ELINGER)
  Abraham
    (Abⁿ) I, 609, 611, 612, 727
  Benedick I, 396
  Davidt I, 506
  Johannes I, 397
MELLMAN
  Joseph II, 122
MELTER
  Johan Philib I, 705
MEMMINGER (MEYMINGER,
  MEYMENGER)
  Johannes (John) I, 227, 229, 231
MENCHEN (MINEGAN, MIN-
  CHAM)
  Maria I, 67
  Matthes (Mathias) I, 66, 69, 70
MENCKEL
  Anna I, 117
MENDONG (MINTS)
  Andreas I, 221, 223, 224
MENEIR
  David I, 100
MENG
  Johan Christoph
    (Xtophel) I, 17, 19
  Michel I, 497
  Peter II, 123
MENGE (MENGIN)
  Ernst I, 615, 617, 619
  Henry I, 615
  Johannes I, 615, 617, 619

MENGEL
Catharine II, 180
Christoffel
(Christophel) I, 666, 668, 670
Frietz (Frik) I, 323, 325, 326
Johan Wilhelm I, 545, 547, 549
John Chr. II, 180
MENGEN
Joh. Peter I, 460
Johannes I, 719
MENGER
J. L. II, 71
MENGERLING
Ernst I, 748
MENGES
Adam I, 661, 662, 664
Carl (Carol) I, 661, 662, 663
Conrath
(J. Conrad) I, 396, 661, 662, 664
Hans Peter
(Peter) I, 661, 662, 664
Henrich I, 686
Johann Georg (Johann
Gerg, Han Geo.) I, 661, 662, 664
Johan Jacob I, 737
Johann Jerg
(John George) I, 395, 694
Peter I, 661, 662, 664
MENGS
Gerg I, 729
MENHART (MEMART, MEN-
NARDT)
Friederich
(Frederick) I, 155, 158, 160
MENN
Ann Catharine II, 84
Ann Mary II, 84
Elisabeth II, 84
George William II, 84
John George II, 84
John Henry II, 84
John Jost II, 84
Jost Henry II, 84
Philip II, 84
MENNECKE (MENNIKE)
H. Michael I, 505
Johann Carel I, 505
MENNEL
Peter I, 724
MENNER
David I, 99
MENSCH (MENCH, MENSH)
Adam I, 437
Johannes I, 696
John Nicklas (Joh.
Nicklas, Nickel) I, 296, 298, 299
Nicklas (Nicholas) I, 556, 557, 558
MENSEBACH
Mich¹ I, 705

MENSER
Conrad I, 464
Mathias I, 102
MENSING
John F. II, 99
MENTGER
Frans I, 745
MENTZ
Eva Margareta (2) I, 189
Georg I, 188
Maria Margareta I, 189
MENTZEL (MENTZLE)
Anna I, 138
Barbara I, 138
George I, 137, 140, 142
Melchior I, 137, 140, 142
Urcilla I, 138
MENTZER
Johann Fridrich I, 473
MENTZINGER (MINTZINGER)
Conrad I, 522, 525
Leonhart I, 468
MERCHANT
Jno. Ludwick I, 55
Jno. Yerke I, 55
Maria Katharina I, 55
MERCHEL
Francis II, 60
MERCHER
Johanes I, 660
MERCIER
Carl Friedr. II, 107
MERCIER
—— I, 746
MERCK
Hans I, 148
Henry (Hendryk) I, 147, 149, 150
Hs. Conrad I, 148
Johann Christian I, 749
Johann Jodocus I, 749
Johann Mertin I, 688
Killian I, 147
MERCKEL MERCKELL, MER-
KHEL, MERKEL)
Hans Jacob I, 482
Henrich I, 372
Johann Nicolaus I, 464
Johann Peter I, 721
Johann Theobald I, 740
Johannes (Johanˢ) I, 209, 211, 212
Matteis I, 732
Peder I, 428
MERCKER (MERKER, MERCKEN)
Jacob II, 9
Johanes (Johannes) I, 237, 239, 240
Paul I, 463
MERCKI
Heinrich I, 483

MERCKLE (MERGEL, MERKELL)
Conrad   I, 476
Georg Paulus   I, 758
Hans   I, 707
Hans Jerg   I, 460
Jacob   I, 430
Johan   I, 348, 350, 351
Lenhardt   I, 476
Paul   II, 13
Simon   I, 430
MERCKLIN
Nicklaus   I, 429
MERCKLY (MERKLEY)
Friederich
(Fredrick)   I, 551, 552, 554
Hans Jerg   I, 400
MERGENSCHONERL (MERGEN-
TCHOERLER, MIRGENDAL,
read MERGENTHALER)
Lorentz
(Lawrence)   I, 637, 639, 641
MERGETHER
Philip   II, 122
MERICH
Frederich   II, 160
MERKI (MERKE)
Heinrich
(Hennrick)   I, 559, 560, 562
MERKLEIN
Henry   II, 198
MERKY
Hans   I, 398
MERLE
John   II, 152
MERLING (MERLIN)
Hans George
(Yerrick)   I, 652, 653
MERREE
Bastian   I, 10
MERSCHRATH (MERSCHROTH,
MEERSCHROOT)
Liworius
(Lyborius)   I, 155, 158, 161
MERSTELEN
Gretha   I, 60
MERTEL
Christian   I, 755
MERTEN
Johann Friederich   I, 473
MERTZ (MARTS, MÄRTZ
MERTS)
Andreas   I, 685
Bertholmea   I, 420
Christina   I, 128
David   I, 126, 129
Dorothy   I, 68
Elizabeth   I, 68
Fridrich   I, 426
Georg (Jerich)   I, 66, 69, 70

Georg Henrich (Jurigh
Hendirck)   I, 113, 114, 115, 766
Hans   I, 450
Hans Nickel
(Johan Nicholas)   I, 126, 129
Johan Hennrich
(Henrich)   I, 180, 182, 184, 340
Johan Jacob   I, 359, 390
Johann Jost (Joseph)   I, 383, 385
Johan Peter   I, 127
Johann Wilh.   I, 751
Johannes   I, 416, 750
Margaret   I, 68
Philip   I, 402
Rudolf   I, 331, 332, 334
Veronica   I, 127
Yerick   I, 451
MESENKOB (MISACOP)
Johannes   I, 323, 325, 326
MESLING
Nicklaus
(Nichlos)   I, 163, 165, 167
MESMER (MESEMER, MEESMER)
Hans   I, 392
Jacob   II, 46
Peter   I, 227, 229, 231
MESNER (MESSNAR, MESSNER,
MESSENER, MESNOR)
Caspar (Casper)   I, 225, 228, 230
Hans   I, 392
Johann Michael   I, 419
Johannes   I, 475
John   II, 76
Michael (Michal)   I, 225, 228, 230
MESORE
Daniel   I, 748
MESS
Jerig
(Georg, Jarrick)   I, 100, 101
MESSA
Lucca   II, 108
MESSEN
A. C. E.   II, 23
MESSER
Abraham   I, 693
Conrad   I, 615, 617, 619
Johan Jacob   I, 421
Michael (Mich[1])   I, 237, 238, 239
MESSERLY (MESSERLI)
Daniel   I, 392
Jacob   I, 405
MESSERSCHMID (MESSER-
SCHMIDT)
Andreas   I, 463
Anna Barbara   II, 149
Anna E.   II, 149
Catharine   II, 149
Christina   II, 149
Elizabeth Henerick   I, 73

Fried[k] II, 129
Hans Bernhart I, 463
Hans Henry
 (J. Henry) I, 509, 510, 511
Henrich (Henry) I, 628, 631, 634
Jer[s] II, 129
Johann II, 110
Johann Frederic II, 149
Joh. Hinrich II, 129
Johan Jorg
 (Johan Gorg) I, 378, 379, 381
Johann Just II, 149
Johan Nicolaus I, 355
Johannes II, 129
Johannes Heinrich I, 72, 76, 78
Maria Elisa II, 129
Rudolff (Rudolph) I, 35, 36
MESSING (MASSING)
Johan Henrich I, 576, 578, 579
MESSINGER (MÖSSINGER)
Elizabeth I, 72
Jacob I, 73
Johannes I, 71, 75, 77
Jos. Michael (Joh. Michael,
 Johan Mich[1]) I, 605, 606, 608
Maria I, 74
Michale I, 73
Paule I, 73
MESTENBACH
Johann Jacob I, 405
METCHAR
Everhard I, 648
METGER
Anne Cath. II, 72
METH (MEAD)
Caspar (Casper) I, 256, 258, 261
Johanes
 (Johannes) I, 256, 259, 261
METHE
Johan Gaspar II, 170
METILMOLSKE
Bartel I, 748
METSCH
Joh. Ludw. II, 107
METSEIR
Michael I, 660
METTAUER (MATTEUR)
Johannes I, 301, 302, 303
METTLER
Hans Jerg (Hans George) I, 22, 23
Jacob I, 486
METZ (METS, MEZ, MIXT)
Balser
 (Malster) I, 114, 115, 766
Caspar I, 459
Christof (Christoph) I, 435, 462
H. Michael I, 453
Hans I, 453
Hans Jacob I, 114, 115, 766

Henrich (Henry) I, 677, 678, 680
Jacob I, 696
Johan Carel I, 295, 296
Johann Conrad I, 523, 525
Johan Gerg
 (John George) I, 297, 298, 300
Johann Herrmann I, 419
Johann Jacob I, 419
Johannes Henrich I, 478
Peter I, 314, 315
Peter, von II, 116
METZEM
Johanes I, 479
METZGER (MATZGAR, MATZ-
 GER, METSKER, METZER,
 METZIGER, MEZGER)
Abraham II, 189
Christian I, 499
Conrad II, 87
Daniel II, 87
David I, 438
Dorotha II, 189
Fred. II, 189
George (Gerg) I, 324, 326
 614, 617, 619
 II, 189
Hans Jacob
 (Hans) I, 297, 298, 300, 438
 II, 189
Jacob I, 394, 431; II, 189
Jaques II, 87
Jno. II, 90
Johan Gotllieb I, 752
Johann Jerg I, 479, 531, 533, 535
Johan Jacob I, 330
Johann Mathias II, 60
Johannes (Johanis) I, 39, 41, 42
 II, 189
Jonas I, 328
Josua I, 707
Ludwig I, 324, 325, 327
Mich. I, 692
Philip (Filip) I, 403, 610, 611, 613
Simon I, 423
Valentine (Valetin) I, 688, 705
Wilhelm
 (Wilhelem) I, 628, 631, 634
METZLER
J. Daniel I, 504
Johann Thomas I, 708
Johann Wendel I, 355
Johannes I, 314, 315
Joseph II, 83
Jost (Joob) I, 204, 206, 208
Melchior I, 708
MEULIMAN
Mich[1] II, 122
MEUNDEL
Johann Jorg I, 402

MEURER
Johann Philip   I, 320, 321, 322
MEUSER (MESSER)
   Conrad   I, 615, 617, 619
MEVIUS
   Johannes (Joh.)   I, 179, 181, 183
MEWES
   Goerg   I, 492
MEY
   Christoph
   (Christophel)   I, 667, 669, 671
   Friederich   I, 419, 521, 524
   Hans Simon   I, 33, 34
   Johan Willm   I, 7
   Joseph   I, 496
MEYER (MAYER, MEIER, MEIR,
   MIRE, MYER, MYRE)
   Adam
   (H. Adam)   I, 198, 200, 202, 698
   Adolf   I, 522, 524
   Anderas
   (Andries)   I, 212, 214, 215
   Ann Eva   I, 157
   Anna   I, 81; II, 23
   Anna Christ^a   II, 23
   Anna Maria   II, 52
   Anna Mire   I, 80
   Anton   II, 197
   Barbara   I, 67, 148
   Bastian   I, 393
   Berdolt
   (Bertho.)   I, 237, 239, 240
   Carolina   II, 92
   Caspar (Casparus)   I, 68, 93, 94
     95, 252, 253
     254, 476
   Catharine   II, 47
   Cecilia   II, 92
   Ch. Charlotte   II, 77
   Charl.   I, 103
   Christian (Christon)   I, 17, 80, 179
     181, 183, 225
     228, 230, 656
     657, 658, 691
     755
   Christian Shwaiger (Chris-
   tian Swegle)   I, 276, 277, 278
   Christina Ludwig   II, 92
   Christn. Diterich   I, 505
   Christoph   I, 410, 439, 505
   Christopher
   (Christoffel)   I, 48, 52, 53, 227
     229, 231
   Conrad (Conradt)   I, 147, 150, 151
     687, 737
   Daniel   I, 472, 705, 755
     II, 159
   Eberhardt
   (Bernhard)   I, 35, 36, 754

Egidi
   (Johan Riedy)   I, 264, 268, 271
Elias   I, 8, 9
Elizabeth   II, 62
Eliz^th Magd^a   II, 23
Franick   I, 80
Friederich (Fried-
   rich, Frederick)   I, 35, 36, 72, 76
     78, 293, 294,
     295, 329, 416
     II, 122, 197
Friederich Wilhelm   I, 704
     II, 79
Georg (George)   I, 162, 164, 165
     426, 493, 494
     620, 622, 624
     II, 52, 130
George Christian   I, 504
Georg Ernst
   (Geo. Adam)   I, 243, 244, 245
Gerhard   I, 746
Gottlieb   I, 751
H.   II, 121
H. Michael   I, 458
Hanickel   I, 67
Hans (Hance, John,
   Johannes)   I, 17, 85, 222
     223, 225, 252
     253, 255, 331
     333, 334, 638
     639, 641
Hans Adam   I, 477
Hans Ehwalt
   (Dewaldt)   I, 317, 318, 319
Hans Georg
   (Hans Jurg)   I, 176, 177, 178
     425, 434, 446
     605, 606, 607
     608
Hans Jacob
   (Hs. Jacob)   I, 66, 69, 70
     148, 332, 333
     334, 398, 434
     470
Hans (Hance) Lennord   I, 85
Hans Martin   I, 741
Hans Michael
   (Michal)   I, 227, 229, 231
Hans Nickel   I, 407
Hans Peter   I, 502
Hans Uhllerik   I, 252, 254, 255
Heinrich (Hen-
   rich, Henry)   I, 7, 10, 12, 162
     164, 165, 227
     229, 231, 252
     254, 255, 340
     346, 399, 440
     483, 510, 512
     753

Helena II, 87, 119, 122
II, 92
Hinrich Andreas I, 751
J. Leonhart I, 395
J. Peter
(John Peter) I, 577, 579, 580
Jacob I, 8, 10, 14, 35
36, 48, 52, 53, 80
147, 148, 150, 162
164, 165, 173, 174
227, 229, 231, 234
252, 253, 255, 304
305, 306, 562, 704
707; II, 134, 140
Jacob Fred^k II, 104, 122
Johan (John) I, 227, 229, 231, 505
Johan Adam
(John Adam) I, 279, 280, 281
352, 353, 382
564, 565, 567
721
Johann Adolph I, 320, 321, 322
Johann Andreas I, 536, 537, 538
Johann Christ I, 479
Johan Diedrich I, 544
Johann Friedrich I, 762
Johann Georg I, 506, 739
Johann Gerlach I, 479
Johan Gottfrit I, 699
Joh. Gotthardt II, 111
Johann Henrich I, 209, 211, 212
Johann Herman I, 689
Johan Martin
(Martin) I, 198, 200, 202
Johann Mattheus I, 513, 514, 515
Johann Nickel I, 371, 689, 762
Johan Peter (Peter) I, 258, 260, 263
568, 570, 571, 722
Johan Philipp I, 468, 540, 542, 544
Johann Simon I, 683
Johan Thomas
(Thomas) I, 48, 52, 53
Johann Vincens I, 17
Johann Wil-
helm (Willm) I, 198, 200, 202
478, 743
Johannes (Joh.,
Hans) I, 93, 94, 95, 147, 179
181, 183, 264, 268
271, 293, 294, 295
331, 332, 333, 334
349, 350, 351, 369
370, 382, 393, 440
444, 467, 483, 484
495, 506, 711, 740
II, 168
Johannes Adolph I, 320, 321, 322
Johannes Müchel I, 708

John I, 712
II, 52, 104, 121
John Adam II, 52
John Christian II, 22
John Jacob I, 359
John Jost
(Hans Jost) I, 656, 657, 658
John Peter I, 722
Joseph I, 227, 229, 231, 448
II, 104, 195
Jost I, 407, 697
Katherina I, 49
Leonhardt
(Leonard) I, 148, 420, 596
598, 600
Losker I, 393
Ludewig (Ludwich,
Loadwick) I, 198, 200, 202
240, 242, 243
M. II, 61
Magdalena I, 148
Margaret (Margrat) I, 67, 242
Martin
(Marti) I, 78, 80, 81, 82, 198, 328
Martin Piter
(Martin) I, 227, 229, 231
Matheas I, 446
Matteus (Mathias,
Matheas) I, 331, 353, 354
Melchior
(Michael) I, 147, 250, 251
Michael (Michel) I, 48, 52, 53, 359
364, 366, 410
425, 470, 473
Mr. II, 74
Nichol (Nichol^s,
Nicklas) I, 169, 171, 172
353, 354
Peter I, 314, 315, 359
437, 734
Philipp Friedrich I, 461
Philip Henrich I, 705
Philipp Jacob I, 546, 548, 550
Philip Melchior I, 102, 105, 106
Rudolph I, 559, 561, 562
Samuel I, 78, 81, 82, 397
Simon I, 84, 86, 87
Sophia I, 49
Steffan I, 485
Susanna I, 67
Tonicus I, 7
Ulrich I, 506
Vallentin I, 473
Wolmer Julius Heinr. II, 138
Wm. Nycius I, 740
MEYERHOFF
Franz II, 70

MEYERHOFFER (MEYENHOF-
FEN, MAYERHOUSEN,
MEYERHOVER)
Rudolff
(Rodolph, Ralph)   I, 249, 250
Rudy   I, 331
MEYERING
Anna   I, 49
Elizabeth   I, 49
MEYERLE
Anton   II, 173
MEYERS (MYERS, MYRS)
Elisa   II, 22
J. G.   II, 42
Max   I, 405
MEYLAND
Simeon   I, 746
MEYLÄNDER (MEYLANDER, MY-
LANDER)
Johann Daniel
(Daniel)   I, 591, 592, 594
Johan Yerg
(Johan George)   I, 313, 314, 315
MEYLY
Catherin   I, 148
Hans George   I, 508
MEYMANN
Teodor   II, 102
MEYMINGER (MEMMINGER,
MEYMENGER)
Johannes (John)   I, 227, 229, 231
    II, 104
MEYNERS
Helena   II, 92
Johannes   II, 92
MEYREISS (MEYERHEIS)
Johan Georg
(Hans Georg)   I, 643, 645
MEYS
Johan Wilhelm   I, 353, 354
MEYSEL
Jacob   I, 480
MICH
Jacob   II, 119
MICHAEL (MICHEL, MICHELL)
Adam   I, 690, 755
Andreas   I, 698
Anna Maria   II, 9
Catharina (Cath.)   I, 55; II, 9
Cath. Eliz.   II, 9
Christian Samuel   II, 78
Christoff
(Christopher)   I, 573, 574, 575
Conrad   I, 609, 610, 612
David M.   II, 78
Friederich   I, 355
Hans   I, 13
Hans George
(Joh. Jurg)   I, 586, 587, 588

Jacob   I, 54, 56, 431, 513
    514, 515, 743
Johann   I, 446
Johann Con-
rad (Conrad)   I, 296, 298, 299
Johann Eberth   I, 712
Johann Fridrich
(Frederick)   I, 205, 207, 208
Johann Georg
(Geo.)   I, 662, 663, 664
Johann Michell   I, 694
Johann Nickel   I, 205, 207, 208
    521, 524
Johann Peter   I, 372
Johan Philipp   I, 723
Johanes (Johan)   I, 353, 354
    484, 750
John Adam
(Joh. Adam)   I, 620, 622, 624
Lorentz   I, 501
Margret   I, 55
Maria Margaretta   I, 55
Martin   II, 9
Paulus (Paul)   I, 256, 259, 262
Philibs (Philibus,
Phillip)   I, 373, 374, 376
    601, 602, 603
Philip Jacob   I, 728
Philip Lawrence   I, 55
Querinus   I, 717
Ulrich (Ulrick)   I, 55, 56, 57
MICHAELER
Daniel   I, 317
MICHAELIS
John Died.   II, 160
MICHAELS (MICHELL, MICHELS)
Carle Vallen-
thien (Valantine)   I, 32, 33, 34
Jno P.   II, 186
Margareth   II, 199
MICHAND
——   II, 81
MICHELE (MICHLE)
Catherine   II, 147
Daniel   II, 147
Hans Jerg   I, 399
Jacob   II, 147
Leonard   II, 167
Magrete   II, 147
Nicole   II, 147
Regina   II, 147
MICHELFELDER
Albrecht   I, 506
MICHENER
Absalom   II, 25
MICHER
Philip   I, 724
MICHLER
Johanes   I, 413

MICHTE
  Fried.   II, 114
MICKEL
  John Ludwig   I, 508
MICKINTURFER (McINTERFER)
  Johannes   I, 27, 29, 30
  Phronick   I, 28
MICKSCH
  Anna Johanna   I, 320
  Michel   I, 320, 321, 322
MIDDEL (MIDDLE)
  Johannes   I, 24, 26, 27
MIDDELCALF
  Peter   I, 17
MIDDELDORFF (MIDDELDORF,
    MIDDLEDORF)
  Henrich Peter
    (Henderick Peter)   I, 28, 30
MIDDELERCHER
  Michel   I, 303
MIDEIER
  Han Yarch   I, 323
MIECHELEN
  Christian   II, 56
  John   II, 56
MIEDER
  Hans Jorg   I, 408
MIERMAN
  Fried. Wilh.   II, 193
MIESANDER
  Johanna   II, 59
MIESEMER
  Johannes   I, 709
MIESSE
  Jean   II, 87
MIESTERRER
  Emanuel   I, 687
MIHM (MIEM)
  Johannes   I, 122, 125, 126
MIK
  Tobias   I, 497
MIKT
  Anna   I, 766
MILBERGER (MELBERCHAR)
  Michel (Michael) I, 556, 557, 558
MILBURGER (ULBERGER, MEL-
    BURGER)
  Barbary   I, 40
  Easter   I, 40
  Hendrick   I, 41
  Johannes (Johanes) I, 40, 41, 42
MILCHSACK (MISSACH)
  Adam   I, 560, 562, 563
  Augustus   I, 453
MILDEBERGER
  Nickolas   I, 454
MILDER (MILLDAY, MILDY)
  Cha:les
    (Caral, Charell) I, 540, 542, 544

Christo^r   I, 8
Hans Adam   I, 7
Hans Jerig   I, 8
Hieronimus   I, 7
Jacob   I, 7
Maria   I, 44
MILHAUS (MILLHISER)
  Moritz (Morris)   I, 274, 276
MILL (MILH)
  Hanns Martin   I, 8, 9
  Johann
    Georg (Jurg)   I, 205, 206, 208
  Johan Melchior   I, 470
  Ludwig   I, 740
MILLANT
  Joseph Dominick   II, 93
MILLEFELT
  Erhart   I, 463
  Friederich   I, 463
MILLENDICK
  Peter   I, 447
MILLER   (MILLAR,   MILER,
    MÜLLER)
  A. Eliz.   II, 105
  Abraham (Abram) I, 16, 116, 120
                        121, 188, 192
                        193, 521, 523
  Adam   I, 627, 630, 634, 693
                             II, 114
  Albrecht (Albrick)   I, 642, 644
  Alloys   II, 100
  Andres
    (Andereas)   I, 310, 312, 468
  Anna Cathrina   II, 12, 36
  Anna Maria   II, 36
  Barbara   I, 74, 190
  Bardel   I, 348
  Bernhart   I, 421
  Carl (Carel,
    Charles)   I, 301, 302, 303, 444
  Casper (Casber)   I, 103, 761
  Casper Gabriel   I, 505
  Catherina (Cathrina,
    Katharine)   I, 74, 103; II, 194
  Cath. Marg   II, 105
  Ch.   II, 71
  Christian   I, 10, 14, 188, 192, 193
                      194, 196, 197, 246, 247
                      248, 329, 406; II, 194
  Christoph
    (Christopfer)   I, 14, 15, 436
  Conrad   I, 8, 88, 218, 219
                      221, 404, 456, 488
  Cornelius   I, 330
  Cronomus (Hieronymus)   I, 88
  Daniel (Daniell)   I, 426, 453
  David (Davit) I, 406, 622, 624, 626
  Eleanor   II, 194
  Elizabeth

(Elisabeth) I, 75; II, 85
Erhart I, 382
Everhard I, 246
Even I, 84
Felix (Felicks) I, 99, 100, 101
559, 561, 562
Francis II, 194
Francis Jacobus
(Frances Jacob) I, 655, 657, 658
Friederich (Fredrik) I, 71, 76, 77
346, 437
II, 29, 164
George (Gerg, Gerick,
Jereg) I, 453, 659, 688, 733
750; II, 19, 164, 194
Geo. Adam II, 9
Geo. Andreas I, 348
George Frederick II, 111
George Michael I, 478, 741
Gregorius (Corise) I, 344, 345
H. Georg (Hans
Geo.) I, 667, 669, 671
H. Jacob I, 481
H. Matheas I, 457
Hanna Sofie I, 242
Hans (Hannes) I, 10, 12, 13, 20
21, 103, 344
345, 406, 441
Hans Adam I, 9, 205, 207
208, 429, 460
II, 75
Hans George I, 16, 17, 459
Hans Jacob I, 18, 71, 75
77, 246, 247
248, 467, 509
Hans Leendert I, 18
Hans Martin I, 18, 344, 345
Hans Michael
(Hans Mich¹) I, 83, 86, 347
645, 647
Hennrich (Henrick,
Henry) I, 327, 329, 344
345, 362, 421
441, 456, 754
Henrick Ludwick II, 12
J. C. II, 112
J. Michael I, 486
Jacob I, 71, 75, 77, 188, 191
193, 365, 406, 410
413, 447, 452, 487
521, 523, 525, 545
547, 549, 659, 767
James I, 13
Jeremya I, 17, 310
Jnᵒ I, 700, 718, 743
Jnᵒ Admᵐ I, 700
Jnᵒ Henry I, 686, 688
Johan I, 436
Johan Bastian I, 353, 354

Johann Bernhart
(Bernard) I, 653, 655
Johann Carl I, 745
Johann Daniel I, 391
Johan George
(Jeorg) I, 71, 75, 77, 339
435, 714
Johan Henrich I, 72, 76, 78
Johan Jacob I, 495, 547, 549
Johann Jost I, 710
Johann Peter I, 401, 402, 503
Johan Rotger I, 710
Johan Wolfgang I, 548
Johannes (John) I, 10, 12, 24, 59, 63
65, 195, 196, 197
204, 206, 208, 398
415, 428, 498, 503
521, 523, 609, 610
612, 643, 645, 718
726, 746
II, 36, 76, 194
John Erich I, 517, 519, 520
John George II, 196
John Lenard I, 436
John Nicklas I, 405
Joseph I, 10, 12, 596, 597, 599
Jurgen (Yerg) I, 10, 11
Ludwig I, 330
Margaret (Margret,
Margt.) I, 73, 766
II, 111
Maria I, 74
Maria Madlena I, 118
Mariles Sofie I, 241
Markes (Mathes) I, 198, 201, 202
Martin I, 425
Matheus (Mattheis,
Matheas) I, 413, 437, 446
483, 495, 500
Michael (Michel) I, 14, 15, 17, 102
103, 205, 207, 208
212, 214, 216, 310
311, 312, 417, 621
623, 625, 714, 760
Nicolaus (Nicholas) I, 212, 214, 215
365, 448, 499
551, 553, 554
II, 54
Paulus (Baulus) I, 88, 307, 308
309, 339
Peter (Petter) I, 406, 420, 488
521, 523, 714
729, 730
Philip
(Phillipp) I, 688; II, 85
Philipbena I, 103
Philipp Henerich I, 693
Rudolph (Rutolph) I, 331, 732
Salomon (Solomon) I, 106, 110, 112

Uhllerich I, 500
Valentine (Valtin) I, 100, 101
Waltter I, 358
Weigan [d] II, 83
William I, 175
—— II, 161
(*See also* MÒLLER *and* MÜLLER)
MILLICH
Johann II, 178
MILLING
Maddeus I, 408
MILO
Pierre I, 754
MILTENBERGER
Johann Georg I, 308, 309
MINAN
P. H. II, 141
MINCA (MINCE)
Anna Allhight II, 12
Christian Fredᵏ Carl II, 12
Gottlip Herman II, 12
MINCH, MINNICH *see* MÜNCH
MINDEL
Henrich I, 402
MINDEN
Anna II, 168
George II, 168
MINER (MINEER, MINIER)
Christian I, 93, 95
Hans Georg
(Hance Jerreck) I, 93, 95
MINGEL (MINGALE)
Christopher I, 748
Jasper I, 14
Paul I, 731
MINGER (MEINKEN)
Andreas (Ands.
Christoff) I, 536, 537, 538
Conrad I, 696
Mark I, 37
MINION
Jacob II, 196
MINJAN
Jacob I, 453
MINLER
Friederich I, 413
MINNE
Barand II, 125
MINNER
John II, 147
Magret II, 147
MINOLT (FINHOLD)
Melcher (Melchior) I, 551, 552, 554
MINTZ (MINZ)
Johan Michael I, 422
Ludwig II, 54
MIPERS
Hanna II, 57
MIRBACH *see* WERBACH

MIRCH
Johann II, 184
MIRE (read prob. MEYER)
Anna Margaretha I, 127
Appalona I, 85
Christopher II, 104
Henry II, 103
Jacob II, 104, 183
John II, 104
Joseph II, 104
Marrea I, 84
Martin II, 104
Michael II, 104
Philip I, 127, 129, 130
MIRTORUM
Adam I, 646, 647
MISCHLE (MISCHILE)
Josep I, 406
Nicholas II, 146
MISCHLER (MESLER)
Ann I, 153
Lizarberth I, 153
Peter I, 683
Ullrich (Uldrick) I, 153, 154, 407
MISCHOT
Abraham I, 357
MISE
Daniel I, 732
Henrich I, 424
MISLER (MISSELER)
Daniell I, 241
Jacob I, 406
MISSEN
Anna Maria II, 190
Georg II, 190
John George II, 190
MISSER
Johann Paulus I, 365
MITSCHLER
Johannes I, 399
MITSHIT
Henry I, 405
John Jacob I, 405
MITTELBERGER
Gottlieb I, 445
Samson I, 472
MITTELBURGER
Nickolas I, 455
MITTELKAUFF
Peter I, 19
MITTELSTAEDT
Joh. Dav. Peter II, 139
MITTMAN (MITTMANN)
Conrad I, 445
Phillip I, 701
MITZ
Joh. Andr. II, 106
MITZEL
Johannes I, 737

MIX
Jürgen II, 102
MÖBS
Friedrich I, 456
MOCHEL
Valentin I, 441
MOCK (MAACK, MAAK, MOAK,
MOOK, MOCH, MOKE)
Hans Jorg I, 500
Hans Peter I, 107, 111, 113
Henrich I, 416
Johann Bernhart
(Bernhard) I, 620, 622, 625
Johan Conrat
(Conradt) I, 595, 597, 599
Johannes I, 99, 101, 348
349, 351
Nicholas (Nickel) I, 204, 206, 207
Peter I, 204, 207
Samuel I, 199, 201, 203
MÖCKLI (MEAKLE, MECKLE)
Catherina I, 135
Heinrich (Henry) I, 134, 136
Maria I, 135
Susanna I, 135
MODAT
Mane II, 80
MODE (MOOD, MOOT)
Han Jacob I, 646, 647
Philip I, 646, 647
MODER
Johan Jacob I, 734
MODWEIL
Abraham I, 724
MOEDINE
Eliza II, 56
MOEHLIN
—— II, 196
MOELIEN
Charles II, 78
MOELLER
Carel II, 28
John David II, 93
MOELLINGER
Henry II, 90
MOERCHEL
—— II, 162
MOESER
Martin I, 21
MÖGAN
Michael I, 449
MOHL (MOHLE)
Christoph II, 155
J. G. II, 143
Joachim Diterich
(Jn° D.) I, 589, 590, 591
Johannes I, 430
MOHLER (MAHLER, MOLER)
Henry I, 419

Lutwig (Loudwick) I, 32, 33, 34
MOHMEYER (MOMOYR)
Johan Christoffel I, 574, 575
MOHN (MAN, MOON)
Anna Margrit I, 79
Baltzer I, 367, 369
Catrin I, 79
Jacob I, 80
Jerg Bernhart
(Jurrig Banhart) I, 79, 82, 83
Johannes I, 113, 114, 115, 765
Uhllerich I, 367, 369
MÖHNER (MÜNNER)
Jacob I, 335, 337, 339
MOHR (MOR, MOORE)
Andereas I, 423, 464
Christoph (Christophel) I, 430, 741
Cunrad (Kunrad,
Conradt) I, 301, 302, 303
Hans Martin I, 463
J. C. II, 203
Jacob I, 234, 404
Johan Adam I, 335, 336, 338
Johann Hermann I, 355
Johann Jacob I, 642, 644, 704
Johann Jost I, 167, 168
Johann Michael I, 464
Johann Peter I, 283, 284, 286
Johann Tobias I, 722
Johann Wilhelm
(William) I, 642, 644
Johannes I, 507, 721
Joseph II, 170
Peter I, 464
Philip Henrich
(Phillip Hend*) I, 373, 375, 376
MÖHRING (MERING)
Johann Wolfgang
(Johan Wolfgan) I, 609, 611, 612
MOHRLOCK
Michael I, 738
MOHRMANN
Peter I, 742
MOINE
Augustin Le II, 153
MOIRE
Gerhard I, 660
MOKE see MOCK
MOLAC
Jaque I, 491
MOLENDEL
Mariea II, 77
MÖLICH (MÄHLICH, MÖLIG,
MOELIG)
Andreas I, 149
Ennreich I, 149
Gottfried I, 149
Henrich Wilhelm I, 405
Johann Georg I, 405

Johann Peter   I, 20
Johannes   I, 147, 150, 151
Marie Cath.   I, 149
Veronica Gertrut   I, 149
MOLIN
A. Matheas   I, 505
MOLITOR
Adam   I, 734
MOLL
Anlyas   I, 44
Anthony   II, 9
Bartel   I, 102
Christoffel (Christophel)   I, 43, 46
Clara   II, 70
Conrad   I, 44
Elizab.   II, 9
Fred^k   II, 8
Gerard   II, 9
Johann Henrich   I, 170, 171, 173
   708
Johan Michael
(Michel)   I, 43, 45, 46
Johann Peter   I, 26, 27
Johann Phillips   I, 436
Johannes   I, 51, 357
Joseph   I, 660
Katrina   I, 103
Magdalen   II, 9
Margarite   I, 44
Mattes   I, 366
Melger (Melchior)   I, 360, 362
Nich.   II, 9
Peter   I, 24
Rosina   I, 44
Thomas   I, 449, 740
MOLLE
Hans Jacob   I, 740
MÖLLER (MOLLER, MÖLER, MÜLLER)
Anna Catharina   II, 205
Anna Eliz^th   II, 23, 148
C. Louise   II, 148
Cath^a Marg^t   II, 23
Charles   I, 40
Christian   II, 78
Christina   II, 148
Christoffel   I, 431
Cl. Gottlieb   II, 205
Conrad   I, 39, 41, 42
Elisabeth   I, 40; II, 205
Friedrich (Fredrick)   II, 82, 124
G. Henrich   II, 148
Hinrich   II, 205
J. H.   II, 71
Jacob   I, 430
Johann Brasilius   II, 79
Joh. Henr.   II, 108
Johannes   I, 431, 444, 501
Joseph   I, 320, 321, 322

Jost Henrich   I, 501, 568, 570, 572
Maria Magdalena   II, 148
Marten   I, 720
Motley   I, 40
Peter   II, 120
——   II, 100
MÖLLINGER (MOLLINGER)
Friderich   I, 716
Hein.   II, 61
Jacob   I, 741
Martin   I, 741
MOLLWITZ
Henry   I, 746
MÖLOTH
Nicklaus   I, 422
MOLSBACH
Peder   I, 493
(*See also* MOSSBACH)
MOLSBERGER (MOLSBURGER)
Johan Jacob   I, 466
Johannes   I, 466
MOLTER
——   II, 58
MOLTZ (MOLES)
Johann Jacob   I, 310, 311, 312
MOLTZBERGEF
William   I, 465
MOMBAUER (MOUMBAUR, MOMBOUR)
Johan Nicklas
(John)   I, 257, 259, 262
Michael (Nichel)   I, 257, 259, 262
Peter   I, 257, 260, 262
William (Wm.)   I, 204, 206, 208
MOMMA
Johann Lorentz   I, 367, 368
Julian   I, 74
MOMMATON
Guillaume   I, 731
MÖNCH
Johan Henrich   I, 503
Michael   I, 455
MONDSHAUER (MUNDSCHAU)
Johannes   I, 335, 337, 339
MONGOLT
Bastian   I, 473
MÖNICH (MINNICH, MINECH, MONICK)
Jn° Phil.   I, 716
Lorentz (Laurince)   I, 256, 259, 262
Peter   I, 169, 171, 172
Simon   I, 169, 171, 172
MONIE
Jaque   I, 729
MÖNINGS
Maria   II, 23
MONNIN (MONIE)
Jean Pierre
(Johan Piree)   I, 592, 593, 594

MONSIEUR
Agnes II, 68
MONTANDON
David I, 24, 25, 26
MONTELIUS
Friedrich Marcus I, 748
MONTFORT
Carl II, 174
MONTMOLLING
Fridrich II, 96
MONTZ (MUNS)
Peter I, 310, 311, 313
MOODE (MOOD)
Johan Jacob
(Han Jacob) I, 646, 647
MOOG (MOOGH, MOOK)
Hans I, 252, 253, 255
Jacob I, 439
Jan Christoff I, 454
MOOLEKAMP
Catherina II, 96
Elisabeth II, 96
Maria II, 96
MOON (read MOHN)
Conen Lutwick I, 766
Margret I, 766
Maria I, 766
Matiles I, 766
Vernor I, 766
MOOR (MOORE, read MOHR)
Anthony I, 413
Bastian I, 521, 523
Francis II, 18
Hendk. I, 331
Jno. Adam I, 24
John Wilhelm I, 357
Peter I, 256, 259, 261, 729
Rudolph (Roedolp) I, 23, 25, 26
MOOSELBACK (read MOSEL-
BACH
Anna Margarett I, 24
Corol Arant I, 24
Mary Eliza. I, 24
MOPPS
Johann Friedrich I, 693
MORAND
——— II, 80
MORAS (MORASH)
George Philip I, 540, 542, 544
MORAUBLEY
Joas I, 760
MORCE
James I, 31
MORET
Etienne I, 746
Jean Diedier I, 471
Mathieu I, 455
MORGEDALLER
Hans I, 410

MORGEN
Johan Adam I, 355
MORGENSTERN
Johann Engelbert I, 397
Johannes I, 18, 19
MORGENTHAEL
John II, 47
MORGEWEGG
Jacob I, 234
MORHARDT
Jacob I, 498
MORI
Catharine II, 43
George II, 43
George Henry II, 43
Peter II, 43
MORIA
Anna II, 146
Barbara II, 146
Jacob II, 146
Salem II, 146
MORIAN
Bastian I, 356
J. A. II, 178
MORITZ (MORETZ, MORRIS,
MAURITZ)
Christian I, 217, 219, 220
Jaques I, 393
Johann Henrich I, 559, 561, 563
Johannes I, 445
Lutwig I, 446
Michael I, 451
Nicklaus (Nicholas) I, 131, 133, 134
MORLOCK
Michael I, 715
MORONRUTH
J. Christian I, 504
MORRIN
Nathaniel I, 143
MORSCHHEIMER
Henrich I, 693
MÖRSEN
Davit I, 505
MORTEL
Catharine II, 44
George Henry II, 44
MORTH (MORTI, MOORHEAD)
Bartholomeus
(Bartholomay) I, 72, 76, 77
MORTLEN
Susan II, 44
MORVONT
Nic. van II, 136
MÖS (MYS, MAYES)
Andres (Andrew) I, 23, 25, 26
Anna Maria I, 23
MOSCHIZER
Anna II, 146
Martin II, 146

Sucor II, 146
MÖSCHLER (NESSEL)
Johann Conrad
  (Conrad) I, 637, 639, 641
MOSCK
Jacob I, 747
MOSE
Johann George II, 168
MOSEMANN (MOSMAN, MOSI-
MAN)
Andreas I, 121, 124, 125
Christian I, 121, 124, 125
Johann II, 50
MOSEN
Jette II, 108
Margeretta I, 74
MOSER (MOSSER, MOSSHER)
Andreas (Anders) I, 93, 94, 95
Anna Marea I, 85
Anna Margareatte I, 85
Bas(t)ion I, 85
Christane I, 12
Christian I, 84
Dowid (Tobies) I, 84, 86, 87
Even I, 84
Even Barber I, 84
George (Jorich) I, 84, 86, 87
Hance Jerack I, 85
Hanna Margrett I, 85
Hans I, 12, 14
Hans Adam I, 22, 23
Hans Jacob I, 629, 632, 636
Hans Jerach I, 25
Hans Michel I, 476
Henrich I, 488
Jacob I, 365, 744
Johann Heinrich
  (Joh. Henrik) I, 677, 678, 680, 758
Johannes I, 217, 219, 220, 711
Jost I, 12
Leonhard (Leonart) I, 84, 86, 87
Ludewig I, 410
Martin I, 23
Mattlena I, 84
Michel I, 84, 86, 87
Nicllaus I, 629, 632, 636
Paulus I, 84, 86, 87
Peter (Petter) I, 365
Samuel I, 400
Simon I, 85
Susanah Barber I, 84
Tobies I, 84
Wilhelmus I, 690
MOSES
Jacob II, 135
Johann Adam I, 335, 336, 338
Phillip I, 727
MOSIMAN (MOSSELMAN)
Andereas I, 359

Johann I, 359
Matheus I, 327, 330
MÖSINGER
Jacob I, 448
MÖSMER
Hans Ullrich I, 392
MOSOCK (MUSCHQUE, MOSOKE)
Henry (Hendryk) I, 147, 150, 151
MOSS
Anna II, 165
Philip I, 307
MOSSBACH (MOLSBAH, MOLS-
BOH)
George I, 556, 557, 558
MOSSER (MASSER, MOSER)
Christian I, 359, 435
Johan Philipp I, 446
Michael I, 421
Paulus (Paul) I, 212, 214, 215
MÖSSNER (MÄSSNER, MESNER)
Andres (Anderas) I, 677, 679, 680
MOST
Elias I, 500
Henri II, 197
MOTHERÖ
Niclaus I, 417
MOTHS (MOTHES)
Anna Maria I, 49
Michel I, 48, 52, 54
MOTIG
Ellinger II, 127
MOTTE
Johannes I, 736
MOTTER
George II, 196
MÖTTHS
Johan Henrich I, 394
MOTZ (MOATS, MOOTS)
Bernhart
  (Bernherd) I, 226, 228, 230
Dewald I, 410
Hans Gerg I, 21
Hans Jacob I, 712
Jacob I, 382, 724
Jerik I, 20
Johann Michael I, 685
Paul I, 750
MOTZER
Johann Martin I, 718
MOTZFELD (MOTSFEL)
Israel I, 564, 566, 567
MOUTERMANN
Pierre II, 122
MOYAL
Barbra I, 38
Hans Jedrick I, 37
Lareunce I, 37
Mathew I, 37

MÖZEL
  Anton   II, 156
MOZER
  John   II, 202
MÜCK (MOOG, MOOK, MUCH)
  Georg Christoph   I, 504
  Hans Michel   I, 66, 69, 70
  Johannes (Johanes,
    Conas)   I, 297, 298, 300
MUCKENBERGER
  Georg   I, 366
MUCKENFUS
  Carl Friedrich   I, 489
MÜCKLI (MIKLE)
  Johann Jacob
    (Jackop)   I, 116, 120, 121
MUFFLER (MOSSLEAGER)
  Sebastian   I, 596, 598, 600
MUFLI (MUFFLI)
  Nicklaus
    (Necklows)   I, 194, 196, 197
MUG
  Caspar   I, 431
MUGLER
  Peter   I, 454
MÜH
  Peter   I, 480
MÜHL (MUHL, MILL)
  Georg   I, 721
  Georg Eberhart
    (Jurg Eberhard)   I, 613, 616, 618
  Johann Samuel
    (Joh. Samuel)   I, 297, 298, 300
MUHLBERG (MILLBERG)
  Johan Peter
    (Peter)   I, 509, 510, 511
MÜHLBERGER
  Frantz   II, 160
MUHLEISEN
  Chrisopp   I, 366
  Christian   I, 366
MÜHLENBACH
  Sabilla   II, 59
MUHLER
  J. V. D.   II, 49
MÜHLEYSEN
  Jacob   I, 427
  Nicklas   I, 427
MÜHLHAHN
  Johan Bartolt   I, 505
MÜHLHAUS (MILLHOUSE,
    MEELHUS)
  Caspar (Gasper)   I, 107, 111, 112
  Peter   I, 256, 259, 261
MÜHLHEIM
  Christian   I, 491
  Johann Georg   I, 686
MÜHLHOFF (MÜLHOFF)
  Johann Philiphs   I, 398

John Peter   I, 398
Philipp Jacob   I, 521, 523
Philips   I, 521, 523
MÜHLMICHEL
  Johann Philip   I, 695
MÜHLSCHLÄGEL
  Johann Andreas   I, 427
MUHLSEISEN
  Christ   I, 702
MUILBERGER
  Henrich   I, 737
MULBERGER
  Hendrick   I, 41
MULDER
  Balthasar   II, 24
MULINARI
  B.   II, 108
MÜLL
  Michael   I, 741
MÜLLDALER (MÜLLIDALER,
    MILLTOUR)
  Hans   I, 609, 611, 612
MULLEN
  D. B.   II, 197
MÜLLER (MILLER, MULLER)
  A. Dorothea   II, 69
  Adam   I, 629, 632, 635
                           672, 673, 674
                           714
  Albrecht   I, 357
  Andreas (Andris,
    Andrew)   I, 37, 59, 63, 65
                           169, 171, 172, 290
                           291, 373, 375, 376
                           408, 409, 426, 429
                           741; II, 53, 172
  Anlis   I, 37
  Anna   I, 61, 74
  Anna Barbra   I, 38
  Anna Catharina   II, 127, 170
  Anna Cath. Maria   II, 140
  Anna Franziska   II, 170
  Anna Kattarina   I, 242
  Anna Mar.   II, 115
  Anna Mare   I, 80
  Anna Margaretha
    (Anna Margret)   I, 37
                           II, 115, 158
  Anna Maria   II, 7, 115, 133
  Anne Elisabeth   II, 87
  Anthony (Antony,
    Antonius)   I, 34, 35, 36
                           414, 481, 728
  Arnold   II, 101
  August   II, 139, 206
  Balthas (Baltus)   I, 646, 647
  Barbara   I, 74
  Bernhardt
    (Bernard)   I, 408; II, 203

Burkhart
  (Burkardt)   I, 347; II, 172
C.   II, 130
Carl Friederich   I, 758
Caspar (Casper)   I, 459, 685
    II, 160
Cath. Elis. (Catharine
  Lise)   II, 158, 180
Catharina
  (Katharine)   I, 74; II, 7
    52, 115, 148
Catharina Margretha   II, 170
Charlis   I, 40
Charlotta   I, 72
Christian   I, 37, 38, 48, 52
    54, 67, 80, 168
    170, 171, 327, 330
    347, 419, 577, 579
    581, 761; II, 107
Christiana   II, 14
Christiana Sophia
  Eleanora   II, 160
Christina   II, 172
Christoph Phillip   II, 171
Christopher (Chris-
  toffel, Christoph)   I, 80, 252, 253
    255, 551, 552
    554, 628, 632
    635, 646, 648
    714, 731
Conrad (Conrath)   I, 93, 94, 95
    483, 677, 679
    680; II, 110
Daniel
  (Dangel, Daniele)   I, 66, 69, 70
    240, 242, 243
Dorethea Elisabeth   II, 171
Eckard   II, 160
Elizabeth (Elisabeth)   I, 23, 72, 75
    II, 96
Ernst   II, 139
Ernst Christian
  (Christian)   I, 577, 579, 581
Felix (Felicks)   I, 99, 100, 101
Ferdinand   II, 160
Friederich Casimir   I, 355
Friedrich (Frederick)   I, 72, 76, 77
    240, 242, 243
    330, 486, 497
    551, 552, 554
    629, 632, 635
    755
    II, 70, 139
Friedrich Danniel   I, 464
Georg (George, Gerg,
  Jurg Jurigh)   I, 89, 91, 92
    225, 228, 230
    240, 242, 243
    420, 502, 729

    II, 127
Georg Adam
  (Jorg Adam)   I, 327, 329; II, 9
Georg Christoph   I, 422
Georg Michael   I, 507
Georg Wilhelm   I, 484, 705
Gerhard (Gerrard   I, 23, 25, 26
    II, 173
Gerritje   II, 60
Gotleib   II, 197
Gottlob Jacob   II, 192
Gustavus   I, 736
Hans (Jno.)   I, 23, 25, 26, 147, 150
    151, 263, 267, 270
    410
Hans Adam   I, 93, 94, 95, 724
Hans Georg (Hans
  Görg, Hans Jerick)   I, 48, 52, 54
    304, 347, 384, 386
Hans Henrich
  (Hans Henry)   I, 279, 281, 282
Hans Jacob   I, 71, 75, 77, 304
    II, 133
Hans Jerg   I, 439
Hans Lodwk.   I, 304
Hans Martin   I, 344, 345, 446
    605, 606, 607
Hans Michel
  (Jno Mich1)   I, 249, 250, 483
    582, 583, 584
Hans Peter (Petter)   I, 265, 268, 271
    304, 437
Hans Ulrich
  (H. Ulrich)   I, 80, 252, 253, 254
Heinrich (Henrich,
  Hendryk, Henry)   I, 147, 168, 170
    171, 331, 332
    334, 360, 361
    398, 432, 496
    721; II, 7, 11
    106, 122, 173
Henrich Adam
  (Hendk)   I, 384, 386
Henrich Wilhelm   I, 642, 644
Herman
  (Herrmanes)   I, 48, 52, 54, 466
Hieronimus
  (Cronomus)   I, 88, 90, 92
Isaac   I, 546, 548, 550
Jacob (Jacobus)   I, 35, 36, 71, 75, 77
    88, 90, 91, 113, 114
    115, 162, 164, 166
    199, 201, 203, 252
    253, 254, 359, 384
    386, 452, 478, 480
    483, 490, 521, 523
    551, 552, 554, 591
    593, 594, 628, 632
    635, 667, 669, 671

704, 705, 727, 762
II, 53, 115, 158
Jacob Friederich II, 174
Jacobina II, 134
Jean II, 87
Jeremias I, 310, 311, 313
Jerg I, 405
Johann (John) I, 198, 200, 202, 755
II, 115, 205
Johann Adam
(John Adam) I, 257, 259, 262
279, 280, 281
373, 374, 375
760; II, 115
Johann Andreas I, 143, 145, 146
Johann Benedictus I, 487
Johan Carel II, 58
Johann Christoph
(Christoffel, Chris-
topher) I, 366, 368, 601
602, 604; II, 170
Johan Conrad
(Johann Cunrath) I, 169, 171, 172
II, 171
Johann Daniel I, 258, 260, 263, 706
II, 100
Joh. Erhardt I, 410
Johann Friederich I, 688, 709
Johan Georg (Johan
Jorg, John George) I, 335, 336, 338
352, 353, 437
576, 578, 580
730, 755, 760
II, 115
Johan Georg Antony I, 143, 145, 146
Joh. Georg Gottf^d II, 107
Joh. Gottl. II, 140
Johann Heinrich
(Johann Henrich,
John Henry) I, 258, 260, 263
296, 298, 299
532, 533, 535
627, 631, 634
646, 648, 712
II, 171
Johan Jacob (Jacob) I, 73, 199, 200
201, 203, 246
247, 248, 383
385, 428, 461
484, 496, 552
553, 554, 687
748
Johan Jorg I, 430
Johann Just I, 536, 537, 538
Johan Klaus
(Nicholas) I, 66, 69, 70
Johan Leonhart
(Joh^s Leonard) I, 221, 223, 224
564, 565, 567

Johann Ludwig
(Lodowick) I, 222, 223, 225
Johan Martin II, 171
Johann Mathias
(Joh. Matthias) I, 601, 602, 604
722
Johann Michel I, 410
Johan Nicklaus
(Johann Nickel) I, 96, 98, 420, 426
724
Johann Paullus I, 438
Johann Peter (Peter) I, 198, 200, 202
283, 285, 286
398, 456, 494
675, 720
II, 28
Johann Philip
(John Philip) I, 78, 81, 82, 494
696, 706, 707, 744
Johan Theis
(John Tys) I, 280, 281, 282
Johan Wilhelm
(Wilhelmus) I, 379, 380, 382
469, 564, 565, 567, 759
Johannes (John) I, 24, 25, 26, 59, 63
65, 78, 81, 82, 264
268, 271, 283, 284
286, 378, 380, 381
383, 385, 395, 420
423, 483, 499, 564
565, 567, 569, 570
572, 577, 579, 581
582, 583, 584, 610
611, 613, 642, 644
646, 648, 704, 709
714
Johannes Gerhardus I, 564, 565, 567
I, 736, 737
II, 118, 180
Johannes Heinerich II, 20
Johannes Jorig I, 71, 75, 77
Johannes Theis I, 721
John II, 7, 10, 47, 53
68, 116, 158
John Adam II, 69
John Christoph II, 160
John Frederick II, 160
John H. II, 180
John Nicklaus I, 405
Jonas II, 158
Jost II, 158
Jost Henrich I, 723
Katherine I, 49
Leonhard (Leonhart) I, 96, 97, 98
359, 367, 369, 742
Leopold II, 127
Lorentz I, 336, 337, 339
Louis II, 160

Margareta (Margarita,
   Margt.)   I, 23, 49
                   II, 7, 112
Maria (Marie)   I, 62, 74, 148
Martha Wilhelmina   II, 127
Marthin (Martin)   I, 35, 36, 442
                 459, 487, 720
Matthias (Mathias,
   Matthes)   I, 79, 81, 82, 198
                 201, 202, 422
                 629, 632, 635
                      724
Michael (Michell,
   Michle)   I, 67, 256, 257, 259
                 262, 383, 385
                 408, 471, 546
                 547, 549, 622
                 683, 705, 756
               759; II, 172
Nicolaus (Nickel)   I, 372, 719
Paul (Paulus, Baulus)   I, 88, 90, 92
            307, 308, 309, 425
Peter (Petter)   I, 32, 33, 34, 305
            307, 335, 337, 339
            503, 569, 570, 572
            627, 630, 633, 696
            697, 712, 719, 724
                732; II, 127
Philip (Phillipp, Filib,
   Filip)   I, 80, 405, 414
                 471, 472, 477
                   733, 759
Philipp Friedrich   I, 696
Phillibs Peter   I, 763
Pips Gorg   I, 393
Samuel   I, 686
Simon   I, 93, 94, 95
Sophia   II, 158
Tobias   I, 439
Valtin   I, 371
Veit (Fight)   I, 265, 268, 271
Wilhelm (William)   I, 296, 298, 299
                 414, 433, 728
                   II, 99, 197
Wolfgang
  (Wolffgang Wolfcon)   I, 113, 114
                    115, 765
   ———   II, 58
MULLI
Hans Yacob   I, 483
MULSCHLEGEL (MULCHSLAGER)
Frederick   I, 59, 63, 65
MULTZ
Frantz   I, 684
MUMBAUER   (MONNBOUER,
   MUMBAUHERR)
Johannes Ernst
  (Johanes, Erns)   I, 559, 561, 563

MUMM (MUM)
  John   II, 56, 118
MUMMA (MOMMA, MUMME)
  Anthony   I, 74
  Christian   I, 74
  David   I, 74
  Frederick   I, 45
  Jacob   I, 43 45, 46, 47
  Julian   I, 73, 74
  Katharina   I, 75
  Leonhardt (Lanhart)   I, 72, 76, 77
  Margaret   I, 45
  Peter   I, 383, 385
  ———   II, 98
MUMSEN
  Albrecht Burghard   II, 191
  Sophia Hedewig   II, 191
MUN
  Jacob   II, 193
MÜNCH (MINCH, MINICH, MIN-
   NIG, MINCK, MINK, MÜNCK)
  Christian Ludewig   I, 505
  Conrad   I, 704
  Gottfried (Godfry)   I, 704
                    II, 187
  Hans   I, 31, 32, 33
  Hans (Hannes)   I, 667, 669, 671
  Hans Henrich   I, 479
  Johan   I, 504
  Johann Lenhard
   (Leonard)   I, 646, 648
  Johann Nickel
   (Hanicle)   I, 646, 648
  Lewdwight   II, 36
  Simon   I, 447
  Wendel   I, 454
MÜNCHINGER (MINCHINAR)
  Andreas   I, 526, 528, 529
MÜNCHLER
  Nicolas, van   I, 460
MUNCKEL
  Ernst   I, 399
MÜNCKER (MEENKER)
  Johann Henrich (John
   Henry)   I, 296, 298, 299
MÜNDEL
  Johan Valdin   I, 762
MÜNDEN
  Asmus Hein. v.   II, 139
MÜNDER
  Nicklas   I, 458
MUNDHENK (MUNDHENKE)
  Dorothea   II, 203
  Henry   II, 200
  L.   II, 200
  Lewis   II, 200
MUNDWEYLER
  Mr.   II, 175

MUNGER
  Deitrick I, 739
MUNI
  Andreas I, 440
  Christian I, 440
  Conrad I, 440
  Jacob I, 440
MÜNIG
  Hans Georg I, 418
MÜNNER
  Johannes Peter I, 686
MUNSCH
  Philliphs I, 724
MUNSENHEIMER
  Anna II, 140
  Hinr. II, 139
  Joh. Hinr. II, 140
MUNSTER
  Balsatzar I, 439
  Johanes I, 464
MUNTHAU
  Ephraim II, 139
MÜNTZ (MUNTZ)
  Andreas I, 449
  Georg (Jerg) I, 191, 193
  Johan Caspar I, 48, 52, 54
  Johann Philipp I, 156, 159, 161
  Philip Gotfried I, 173, 174
MUOR
  Augustin I, 487
MÜRI
  Bastian I, 12
MURKENFUSS
  Anna II, 152
  Anna B. II, 152
  Jacob II, 152
  Regina II, 152
MURR
  Hans Jerg I, 446
  Heinrich Gottfrid I, 556, 557, 558
MUSCHCAT (MUSCOTE)
  George Christoph I, 672, 673, 674
MUSCHELL
  Samuel II, 18
MUSCHILTZ (MUSCHLITZ, MOS-
  LETTS)
  Gottfrid (Jacob) I, 585, 587, 588
MUSCULUS
  J. C. II, 71
  Johann Peter I, 546, 548, 550
MUSI (MUSE)
  Ludwig (Ludtwig) I, 604, 606, 607
MÜSLIN
  Mr. II, 174
MUSSE
  H. II, 99
  Johan Georg I, 442
  Samuel I, 491

MUSSELBACH
  Carl Ernst I, 25, 26
MUSSELLMANN (MUSELMAN,
  MOSIMAN, MOSIEMAN)
  Anna I, 60, 191
  Barbara II, 14
  Catarina II, 14
  Christiana II, 14
  Eva Barbara II, 14
  Hans (John) I, 59, 63, 64, 527
  528, 530
  Jacob I, 727; II, 14
  Michael II, 14
MÜSSEMER
  Henrich I, 488
MUSSGENUG (MUSSGNUG)
  Davit I, 464
  Jacob I, 491, 761
MUSSINA
  Lion II, 75
MUST
  Johs Jerg I, 469
MUTCHLER (MUSSELER,
  MUTSELER)
  Christine K. II, 152
  Johannes (Johannes) I, 605, 606, 608
  John II, 152
  John G. II, 152
MUTH
  Dorothia II, 68
  Johann Georg I, 702
  Johann Heinrich I, 503
  Johann Peter I, 444
  Johanes I, 701
  Juliana II, 59
  Maria II, 59
  Michael I, 486
MUTHHART (MUTHHADT,
  MUTHART)
  Johann Friederich
  (Johan Friek) I, 194, 195, 197
MUTLER
  Maria II, 47
MUTSCHLER
  Frantz I, 749
  Friedrich I, 459
  Johann Danniel I, 496
  Jonas I, 436
  Vallentin I, 459
MUTTERSBACH (MUTTER-
  SPACH)
  Johann Gerlach
  (John Gerlach) I, 577, 579, 580
MUTZ
  Georg I, 724
  Joh. Nich. II, 5
MÜTZENBERG
  Catharina II, 133
  Christen II, 133

MYER *see* MEYER
MYNHARD (MINDHARD)
  Hans Jorig   I, 67, 69, 70
MYRING
  Maria Crete   I, 107
MYRS *see* MEYERS
MYRTETUS
  Christoph Gedeon   I, 403

NAAB
  Philip   I, 661, 663, 664
NAALL
  Christian   I, 505
NAAS (NAASS, NAASE, NAZE)
  Anna Maria   II, 10
  Cath.   II, 10
  Conrad   II, 9
  Elizabeth   I, 122
  Eva Maria   II, 10
  Jacob Wilhelm
    (William)   I, 153, 154
  Johann Philip   I, 724
  Johannes   I, 122, 124, 126
  Margaret   I, 122
  Mary   I, 153
  Michael   II, 10
NABINGER (NOVENAR)
  Theobald   I, 323, 325, 326
NACHBAR (NACHBER, NOCH-
  PER)
  Leonhart (Leonard) I, 212, 214, 216
NACHTIGALL
  Johan Pilibus   I, 367, 368
NACHTRUP
  Barbara   II, 192
  Chatharina   II, 192
  Dorothea   II, 192
  Fried.   II, 192
  Joh. Adam   II, 192
  Joshua Fried.   II, 192
NACKE (SCHOLL, SOCKEL)
  George Davit
    (G. David)   I, 258, 260, 263
NADDERMAN (HOTREMAN)
  Johan Georg (John
    Jurgh)   I, 88, 90, 92
NADEM
  Johann   I, 476
NAERYES
  Anthon   I, 687
NAEWISS (NOAWAYS, NOAWYS)
  George (Yerrick) I, 596, 598, 599
NÄFF (NAFF, NAF, NEAFF, NEAF,
  NAFFE)
  Anna   I, 147, 148
  Bernhart   I, 508

  Conrad   I, 147, 150
  Elizabeth   I, 148
  Hans Henrich I, 331, 332, 334
  Hans Jacob
  (Hans)   I, 149, 331, 333, 334
  Hans Ulrich I, 252, 254, 255
  Henry (Hendrick) I, 331, 333, 334
  Jacob   I, 146, 147, 149, 150
      151, 398, 414
  Jacob Conrad
    (Conrad)   I, 147, 150, 151
  Rudolf   I, 398
  Uhllerich   I, 331, 332, 334
NAFFLIGER
  Johann   I, 595
NAFFZER (NAFZER)
  Ulrich   I, 294, 295
NAFTZIGER (NAFZGER)
  Jacob   I, 448
  Matheis   I, 407
  Peter   I, 407
  Rudolf   I, 407
NAGEL
  Anthoni (Anthony) I, 464; II, 122
  Carl (Henrick) I, 217, 219, 220
  Christian   I, 463, 505
  Christoffel   I, 395
  Conrad (Conradt) I, 236, 238, 239
  Dewalt   I, 441
  Fillip   I, 476
  Friedrich Wilhelm I, 283, 284, 286
  Gottlieb (Gotleip) I, 596, 598, 599
  Hans George   I, 395
  Hans Heinrich   I, 441
  Hans Jerg   I, 427
  Heinrich Andreas   I, 505
  Henry Rudolph   I, 505
  Jacob   I, 31, 32, 34, 469
      546, 548, 550
  Joachim   I, 412, 464
  Johan Christian   II, 78
  Johann Ernst I, 531, 533, 535
  Joh. Gottfried I, 601, 602, 603
  Johann Jacob   I, 699
  Johann Leonhard   I, 737
  Johann Michael   I, 699
  Johan Willhelm   I, 461
  Johannes   I, 102, 104, 105
      II, 24, 174
  Joseph   I, 437
  Maria   I, 103
  Matthäus Wend.   I, 328
  Sebastian   I, 464
  Simon   I, 476
NÄGELE (NAGLE, NEGLE, NAGLI)
  David   I, 212, 214, 215
  Heinrich (Henry) I, 605, 608
  Jacob   I, 322, 704

Jan Nichol (Johan
  Michel)   I, 213, 215, 216
Joseph   II, 141
NAGELER
  Anna B.   II, 30
NÄH (NOHE)
  Anna Cathrine   I, 144
  Gerderuth   I, 144
  Johannes (Johanis)   I, 143, 145, 146
  John Jacob   I, 144
  Maria Clara   I, 144
NÄHLIG
  Nickel   I, 492
NAIR (NAAR, NEAR)
  Philip   I, 318, 319, 320
NAMEN
  Van der   II, 137
NANEIKER
  Jnº Jacob   I, 745
NANGESSER
  George William   I, 286
NARGANG (NARGAR, NARR-
  GANG, MERGANG)
  Andreas   I, 155, 158, 160
  Aⁿ Maria   I, 156
  Catharina   I, 157
  Daniel   I, 155, 158, 160
  Johan Peter (Peder)   I, 155, 158, 160
NARGEN (NERGEN)
  Jacob   I, 253, 254, 255
NASCHI
  Jacob   I, 724
NASE
  Andr   II, 113
NASEMANN
  Johan Conrad   I, 748
NASGIGT
  Sebastjan   II, 184
NASS
  Adam   I, 697
  Matheas   I, 474
  Peter   I, 532, 533, 535
  Philipp Jacob   I, 490
NAST
  Daniel   II, 52
  Jacob   I, 490
  Johannes   I, 448
NATCHEM
  Caspar   II, 184
NATHAN
  Moses   II, 41, 107
NÄTTER (NEETER)
  Hendry (Hendᵏ)   I, 384, 386
NAUÄTTER
  Peter   I, 745
NAUER
  Barbara   II, 53
  Charlotta   II, 53
  Christina   II, 53

  George   II, 52
  Jacob   II, 53
NAUMAN
  Christgan   I, 448
  Daniel   I, 727
  Jeremiah   I, 718
  Johann   I, 436
  Johann Gottlieb   I, 436
  Johannes   I, 718
NAUS (NAIS)
  Baltsar (Balthas)   I, 360, 361
NAVINGER (NABINGER)
  Andereas (Andreas,
    Andrias)   I, 252, 253, 255
NAYCOMMET
  Johannes   I, 18
NAYE (NAY)
  Anthony   I, 317
  Johan Peter (John
    Peter)   I, 386, 388, 389
NAZURUS
  Martin   I, 450
NEAS *see* NEES
NEBE (NEB, NEVE)
  Bernard   II, 181
  Gottfried (Godfrid)   I, 589, 590
  Johann Martin   I, 699
  Philip   II, 181
NEBEL (NIEBEL)
  J. Friederich
    (Fredrick)   I, 656, 657, 659
NEBELING (NEBLING)
  Anne Cath.   II, 117
  Georg   I, 508
  Henrich   II, 117
  Jansey   II, 123
  Samuel   II, 117
NEBLINGER
  Jacob   I, 690
NECHTI
  Johannes   I, 731
NED
  Hans Rudolph   I, 310
NEDERHOOD (NEETROTOCK)
  J. Henry (Henry)   I, 573, 574, 575
NEEB
  Christ   II, 173
  Joost   II, 173
NEEREMAN
  Johan Hendᵏ   II, 29
NEES (NES, NEESS, NEAS, NESSE)
  H. Jerge   I, 346
  Hans   I, 417
  Hans Adam   I, 417
  J. Adam   II, 29
  Johan Adam (John
    Adam)   I, 667, 669, 671
  Johan Michel   I, 195, 196, 197
  Johannes (Hannes)   I, 665, 668, 670

Peter I, 430
Richard (Reichard) I, 667, 669, 671
Sebastian I, 226, 228, 230
NEFF (NEEFF)
Christoph Friederich II, 171
Hartman II, 121
Jacob II, 12
Johan Christian I, 341, 342, 343
Johann Jacob I, 462
Michael (Michel) I, 21, 22, 727
Oswalt I, 347
NEGELE (NEGLE, NEGELIE)
Johann Christian II, 191
Johann Leonhart I, 367, 368
Johannes (Joanis) I, 225, 228, 230
NEHER
Johan Martin I, 445
NEHRBASS (NARBAS, NÄHRBASS, NERBASS)
Johann Jacob I, 335, 336, 338
Johannes Frantz I, 335, 336, 338
NEHRLICH (NERLICH)
Christian (Christ[n]) I, 601, 602, 603
NEIDER (NEYDAGH, NYDAGH)
Conrad (Conrath) I, 243, 244, 245
NEIDERMAN (NEDERMAN, NADERMAN)
J. Henry (John Hendrick) I, 573, 574, 575
NEIDHART (NIGHTHART)
Christian I, 217, 219, 220
NEIDIG (NEIDICH, NEIDICK NEYDIG, NYDIG)
Adam I, 661, 663, 664
Daniel I, 661, 663, 664
Görg Adam (Yerick Adam) I, 383, 385
Hans Adam (Adam) I, 59, 63, 65
Hans Leonard (J. Leonhart) I, 661, 663, 664
Johanes (Johannes) I, 564, 566, 567
Margreth I, 61
Philip I, 61
NEIDLEIN
Christof I, 403
NEIDLINGER (NITLINGER)
Benedictus (Benedict) I, 581, 582, 584
NEIEMAN
Daniel II, 159
NEIF
Catharin II, 188
Christian II, 188
Dorothy II, 188
Jacob II, 188
Michael (Mich[1]) I, 666, 668, 670
NEIG (NEIGH)
Ann I, 61
Joseph I, 289

NEIHART (NIEHART, NEI-HARTT)
Georg I, 179, 181, 183
Jerg Fridrich (Frederich) I, 179, 181, 183
Michel I, 178, 180, 182
NEIL
Johan Henrick II, 97
NEIMAN
Andreas I, 717
Johann Gerhart I, 419
Maria II, 60
NEIMRICH
Johann Gottfried I, 749
NEINIGER (LEININGER)
Martin I, 622, 624, 626
NEIPP (NIEB)
Johannes I, 648, 650
NEISER
Hans Martin I, 495
NEISS
Johann Georg I, 458
NEISSEL
Valentin I, 720
NEISWANGER (NYSSWANGER NEYSCHWANGER)
Jacob I, 179, 181, 183
NEITH
Johanna, de II, 122
NEITHMAN
Dorothea II, 119
NEITLINGER
Samuel I, 404
NEITZ
Ludwig I, 492
NEITZERT (NEIZART)
Henry I, 371
Johann Iacop I, 719
Maximilian I, 721
Paulus I, 303, 305, 306
NELL
Jacob II, 113
NELLING
Anna Marg[ta] II, 23
Marg. II, 105
P. II, 144
NENNINGER (MENDINGHAM)
Simon I, 268, 271
NENSTIEL
Andreas II, 106
Joh. Diedr. II, 106
NEOTVOGEL
W. II, 123
NERACHER
Hans Jacob I, 434
NERLINGER
Stephan I, 480
NERN (NEER)
Johann Philip I, 539, 541, 543

NERNER
Hanna II, 17
NERTHWEIN
Henric II, 52
NERTWIG
Joh. G. II, 46
NESSELROTH
J. Christian I, 504
NESSER
Hans Nichelas I, 492
NESTER (NESSTER, NISTER)
Christian II, 159
Elias I, 526, 528, 529
NESTLE
Jacob II, 126
NESTLER
F. II, 125
Johann Gottfried I, 749
NETSCHER
Johann Conrad I, 750
NETTEN
Jochen, van II, 50
NETZ
Adam II, 159
Anna Eliz. II, 159
J. G. II, 142
Lud. II, 142
NETZLY (NETZLJI, NOTZLY)
Caspar I, 147, 149, 150
NEU
Abraham I, 687
An Catharine I, 157
Fallendin (Vallentin) I, 155, 158, 161
Jacob I, 722, 751
Johan Adam I, 398
Johannes Nicolaus (Johan
Nickel) I, 398, 735
Stofel I, 751
(*See also* NOY)
NEUBAUER
Joachim I, 757
NEUBECKER
Johann Martin I, 404
NEUBERTH (NEUBECKER)
Adam I, 642, 643
Christopher (Christo) I, 55, 56, 57
NEUCOMER
Christian I, 448
(*See also* NEWCOMER)
NEUENDORFF (NEUENDORF,
NEYENDORPH)
Jacob I, 582, 583, 584
NEUES (NEY)
Christ (Christn) I, 585, 586, 588
Otto Daniel I, 437
NEUESCHWANDER
Samuel I, 391
(*See also* NEUSCHWANDER)

NEUFANG
Nicol I, 763
NEUFFER
Christian I, 471
NEUGEBRAN
Susana M. II, 15
NEUHART (NEUHARD, NEY-
HART)
Conrad I, 614, 616, 618
NEUHAUS (NIGHOUSE, NEW-
HOUSE)
Johannes I, 378, 380, 381
Mr. II, 175
NEUHOFF (NEUHOFT)
Friederig I, 397
Philipp II, 92
NEUKAMP
Gerrit II, 95
Henrica II, 95
NEUMAN (NAYMAN, NEYMAN,
NEIMAN, NEUMANN)
Andreas I, 221, 223, 224
Carl (Carel) I, 204, 206, 208
Christoph
(Christopher) I, 137, 140, 142
David I, 138
Ernst II, 90
George II, 94
Hermanus I, 366
Johann Christoffel
(Christofer) I, 205, 207, 208
Johann David I, 428
Johann Friedrich Wilhelm II, 74
Johan George
(Hans Geo.) I, 649, 650
Johan Henrich (John
Hendrick) I, 286, 287, 288
601, 602, 603
Johann Jacob
(Jacob) I, 582, 583, 584
John II, 56
Maria I, 138
Melchior I, 137, 140, 142
Michael (Michel) I, 295, 296, 428
Mr. II, 74
Nickel (Nicholas) I, 628, 632, 635
Pieter II, 24
Susannah I, 138
NEUMAUER
Hans Michel I, 267, 270
NEUMEISTER
Christoph (Christian
Erhard) I, 147, 150, 151
NEUMEYER
Johann Jacob I, 496
NEUN (NAYN, NEU)
Johann Casper I, 184, 185, 187
Johannes I, 378, 379, 381

NEUNHOESSURE
Christopher II, 162
NEUSCHWANDER (NEUEN-
SCHWANDER, NEY-
SWANDER)
Christian I, 629, 632, 636
Isaac (Ysach) I, 629, 632, 636
Maria II, 31
NEUSCHWANGER (NEW-
SWANGE)
Ullrich I, 328
Xstian I, 17
NEUSCHWENDER (NEUSCWEN-
TER)
Peter I, 716
NEUSER
Charlotte II, 156
NEUSTERDT
Hans Jacob I, 491
NEUZEHÖLTZER (NEYTHELZER)
Johan Jacob
(Jacob) I , 72, 76, 78
Margt. I, 75
Maria Susanna I, 75
Seville I, 73
NEUZENHOEFFER
George II, 52
NEVELING
Johans I, 237
NEWART (NEWARTEN)
Christian II, 159
M. C. II, 159
——— II, 159
NEWBERT
Joseph II, 192
NEWCOMER (NEUCOM, NEW-
COMMER, NEYCOMER)
Christian I, 328, 629, 633, 636
Uhllerich (Ulrich,
Oulreck) I, 629, 632, 636
NEWDE
Goerg Fridrick II, 71
NEWENHART
Adrianus II, 196
NEWHAUSER
Hans Michael I, 360, 362
NEWMAN (NEWMANN, read
NEUMANN)
Felton II, 75
H. II, 75
Jno II, 75
John Gottfd II, 129
John Jacob I, 444
Martin II, 75
Mary II, 75
Mr. II, 74
Simon II, 75
NEWMEYER
Conrad I, 468

NEY (NAY, NEYE, read NEU)
Andtreas (Andreas) I, 130, 133, 134
Anna Barbara I, 132
Casber (Jasper) I, 14, 15
H. George I, 454
Hans Michel I, 132
Jean Bartholmeus I, 759
Johanes I, 454
Maria Elizabeth I, 131
Otto I, 346
Peter I, 628, 631, 635
NEYKOMET
Johannes I, 19
NEYMAN (NIMAND)
Harm (Herman) I, 661, 662, 664
NEYMEYER (NEMEYR)
Henry (Henning) I, 536, 537, 538
NEYSINGER
George II, 126
NEYTHÖFFER (NEYDERFER)
Johan Markus (Markus) I, 642, 644
NEYTZER
Johann Wilhelm I, 705
NEYTZERT (NEYZART, NEITZER)
Bernhart I, 353, 354
Johan Peter I, 352, 354
NIBLING
Johannes I, 395
NICE (NEICE)
Christian I, 517, 518, 520
NICHOLAS (NICOLAUS, NICOLAS,
NICOLA, NICKLAS, NICKU-
LUS)
Adam II, 58
Georg II, 68
J. George I, 493
Jacob II, 54
Johann Jacob
(Jacob) I, 293, 294, 295
Johann Michel II, 58
Johannes I, 493
Ludwig (Lodwick) I, 243, 244, 245
Peter I, 697
Vallentin I, 234, 235, 236
NICHT (NESH)
Adam I, 198, 200, 202
Carl Christoph I, 758
NICK
Wilhelm I, 372
NICKANS
Stephan I, 492
NICKEL (NICHOL)
Bernard I, 745
Casper I, 763
Johan II, 78
Johann Georg
(Jurig) I, 256, 259, 261
Johann Jacob I, 577 579, 581
Johann Peter (Peter) I, 582, 583, 584

Johannes (Johan) I, 265, 268, 271
Wilhelm I, 753
NICKOM (NICKUM, NECUM)
Friederich I, 257, 260, 262
Nicklas I, 390
Peter I, 257, 260, 262, 390
NICODEMUS
Johann Adam
(Adam) I, 577, 578, 580
Johann Henrich I, 465
Valentin I, 686
NICOLAHR
Johann I, 760
NICOLL
Jacob I, 500
NICOLY
Uhllerik I, 507
NICULAI
Carl Fried^ch II, 140
NIEBEL
Johannes I, 737
NIEBERGALL
Jacob I, 745
Johann Peter I, 310, 312, 313
NIECKE (NICKER)
Johann Jacob
(Jacob) I, 573, 574, 575
NIED
Matthias I, 564, 566, 567
NIEDA
Daniel Dau II, 53
Johann Philipp, von I, 693
NIEDENTHAL
Johann Peter I, 496
NIEDER
Jn° Jacob I, 733
Jn° Martin I, 733
Johann Georg, von I, 733
NIEDERAUER
Michel I, 367, 368
NIEDERHAUS
Daniel I, 735
NIEDT
Johann Christoph I, 446
NIEHANS
Mr. II, 177
NIEL
—— II, 80
NIELER
Johann Daniel I, 760
NIEMANDT (NIEMAN, NIMAN)
Christian Ernst I, 540, 542, 544
Jacob II, 195
Johannes I, 340
John II, 195
John Frederick Gerhard II, 160
NIEMEYER (NEMEIR)
Peter Friederich I, 517, 519, 520

NIENABER
Christ. II, 160
NIERMEYER
Valentine I, 536
NIERSTEDT (NIESTEDT, NEIN-
STED)
Christian Andreas I, 536, 537, 538
NIESER (NISER, NEEZER)
Georg Christop I, 507
Nicholas I, 304, 305, 306
NIESS (NIES, NIESSE, NIESE,
NYCE)
David I, 753
Jacob I, 378, 380, 381
Johann Heinrich I, 493
Johann Henrich I, 684
Johan Herman I, 675
Johan Willem (John
William) I, 655, 656, 657
658, 659
Johannes I, 724
NIETH
Michel I, 698
NIETZEL (SNITZER)
Bongrad (Bengrad) I, 652, 653
NIEVE
Anthony I, 406
NIEVÜHRE
Johann II, 184
NIEWILL
Peter II, 77
NIEWINHUZEN
(NEWINGHUZEN)
Arnoldes II, 77
Jan II, 77
NIKE
Jacob I, 405
Michael I, 405
NIKERICK
Hendrick I, 227; II, 104
NILL
Anna Margratin I, 241
Johan Caspar I, 545, 547, 549
Sebastian I, 707
NIMAN see NIEMANDT
NION
Jean Botis I, 508
NIPMAN
Anna II, 95
Engel II, 95
Peeter II, 95
NIPPES
Abram II, 91
Anna Catharina II, 91
Anna Christina II, 91
Daniel II, 91
Wilhelm II, 91
NISCHWITZ
Joh. Heinrich II, 28

NISS (NIS)
Jacob   I, 178, 180, 182
Johann Herman   I, 401
NISTUCHER
Hans   I, 394
NITH (NIET)
Gottlieb   I, 698
Johann Christoph   I, 513, 514, 515
NITSCHER
Christ.   II, 138
NITSCKO
Gottlieb   II, 128
NITZ (NITZEN)
Johann   II, 184
Marx   I, 38, 39
NIWATEL
Joseph   II, 127
NOBEL (NOBLE)
Antony (Anthony)   I, 143, 145, 146
Catharine (Cathrine)   I, 144
Gerhard Henry   I, 748
NOCHTERN (NICKTON)
Johann Friederich
(Fredrick)   I, 217, 219, 220
NODHARDT (NODHART, NOT-HART)
Jerg (Georg)   I, 248, 249, 250
NOEL (NOWELL, NEWELL)
Eneas (Enoas,
Ennos)   I, 163, 165, 167
Joseph   I, 163, 165, 167
Pierre (Peter)   I, 163, 165, 167
NOFFENEYER
Barbara   II, 134
Franz   II, 134
Magdalena   II, 134
NOLD (NOLDT, NULT)
Johann Philip
(Philip)   I, 621, 623, 625
Johannes   I, 643, 645
Karl   I, 399
Philip   I, 19
Valentin
(Valentine)   I, 609, 610, 612
NOLFF (NOLF)
Anna Maria   I, 190
Elizabetha   I, 190
Lorentz   I, 189, 192, 194
Margareta   I, 190
NOLL
Anton   I, 353, 354
Christian   I, 750
Georg Justavus   I, 461
Hans Hendrech   I, 460
Hans Jerig
(John Jurgh)   I, 88, 90, 91
Henry Jacob   I, 589, 590, 591
Jacob   I, 695

Johann Frantz
(John Frans)   I, 373, 374, 375
Johann Henrich
(John Hend^k)   I, 373, 374, 375
Johann Martin   I, 503
Johan Michel
(Michael)   I, 130, 133, 134
156, 159, 161
Mattias (Matthis)   I, 353, 354
Peter   II, 119
Philips Henrich   I, 466
(*See also* NOOL)
NONN
Jno Bap.   I, 755
Johann   II, 61
NONNENMACHER (NONNE-MACHER, NONNAMAKER, NUNMAKER, NUNNNEN-MACHER)
Abraham   I, 405
Daniel   I, 486
Hans Emerich
(Hans Emric)   I, 301, 302, 303
Henry   I, 301, 302, 303
Jacob Adam   I, 438
Johan Ludwig   I, 462
Ludwig
(Georg Ludwig)   I, 661, 663, 664
Matheus   I, 395
Michael   I, 729
Reinhart (Rey-nard, Rinhard)   I, 301, 302, 303
NONYUS
Johann Jorg   I, 494
NOOL (read NOLL)
Christian   II, 205
NORDHHEIMER (NORTH-HEIMER, NOTHYMER)
Johannes   I, 615, 617, 620
NORDT (NORT)
Hans Jerg
(Jurigh)   I, 113, 114, 115, 766
NORFFKOH
Hans   I, 425
NORHEIMER (read NORDHEIMER)
Charles   I, 701
NORTH (NORT)
Daniel (Danill)   I, 286, 287, 288
Hans Nicl   I, 329
Lavanna   I, 767
Maria Barbara   I, 766
Maria Kret   I, 766
Sibila   I, 60
Tobias   I, 767
NORTMEYER (NORTMEYRE, NORMEYER)
Valentine
(J. Ballentin)   I, 517, 518, 519

NOSCHANG
Anthon I, 690
NÖSS (NEHS, NEAHS, NESS, NOSS)
Anna Katherina I, 49
Dewald I, 48, 52, 54
Dorothea I, 49
Hans Georg
(Hans Jerg) I, 48, 52, 54
Hans Jacob I, 50
Jacob I, 48, 52, 54
Johan I, 48, 52, 54
John Peter I, 357
Katherina I, 50
Magdalena I, 50
Maria Barbara I, 49
Matthias (Mattdes) I, 48, 52, 54
Michael (Michel) I, 48, 50, 52, 54
NOTENIUS (NOTTENIUS)
F. II, 32
Frederica II, 53
Gottliebe II, 53
Maria II, 53
NOTHENGSIELER
Chr. II, 123
NOTHSTEIN
Hans Michel I, 440
Jonas I, 742
NOTHTURFFT
Henry I, 505
NOTNAGEL (NOTHNAGEL)
Christopf Lud^w II, 117
Johann Philip II, 58
Ludwig II, 58
NÖTTERLE
Johannes I, 547, 549
NOTTING
George II, 47
NOTWIG
Elisabeth II, 46
NOTZ (NOTS)
Catharina I, 210
Conradt I, 359
Dorothy I, 210
Friederich
(Fridrick) I, 99, 101
Jacob I, 495
Johannes I, 475
Lenhart (Leonard) I, 209, 211
NOULAND
John I, 143
NOY (read NEU)
John I, 737
Lewis I, 737
NUCKELL
Christian II, 117
Jacob II, 117
John II, 117
John Friedr. II, 117
Maria Cath. II, 117

NUDELL
George Jacob I, 364
NUEL
Benetick I, 15
NUESLI (NUSSLI, NEUSLEY)
Ulrich I, 253, 254, 255
NULL (NOEL)
Killian (Gelian) I, 205, 206, 208
NUM
Hans Yerick I, 451
NUMER
Johan II, 168
NÜMRICH
Johannes I, 340
NUMSEN
——— II, 206
NUNGESSER (NUNGESER)
Johan George
(Johann Georg) I, 59, 63, 64
NURENBERG
Johann Heinr. II, 76
NUSBAUM
Bendickt I, 346
Johannes I, 347
NUSHAGEN
Weybrecht I, 458
NÜSLE (NÜSLI, NEUSLEY)
Hans I, 252, 253, 255
NUSLOCH
Michael I, 97
NÜSS (NUSS, NUS)
David I, 443
Georg Michael I, 715
Jacob I, 716
Johan Georg II, 21
Johann Jacob
(Jacob) I, 156, 159, 161
169, 170, 172
NUSSBUECKEL
Lutwig Hennrich I, 507
NUSSER
Jacob I, 745
NUSWANGER
Christ I, 19
NUTS (NUTTS)
Christoph I, 395
Georg (Yerick) I, 383, 385
NUTTLES
John I, 728
Mich[1] I, 728
NUYNE
Casper I, 759
NYZEL
Joseph II, 24

OAKLY
Philip II, 15

OARE
Eliza I, 766
OARN
Carieliena II, 77
OARTAN
Johan Wilhelm II, 77
OADT (OATS) *see* OTT
OB *see* OPP
OBEL (STOVELL, OVEL)
Christoffel
(Christophel) I, 264, 267, 270
OBELHART
Elias I, 185, 186, 187
OBELMANN (OBELMAN)
Johann Michel
(Michael) I, 652, 653
OBENHEYSER
Johannes I, 347
OBER
Clemence I, 486
Hennrich I, 755
OBERBÄCK (OVERBACK)
Johannes (Hans) I, 37, 38, 39
OBERDORF (OBERDORFF, OVER-
DORFF, OBERTORF)
Adam I, 531, 533, 535
Andreas (Andterreas) I, 444, 753
Baltser (Baltz) I, 540, 542, 544
Jacob I, 502, 539, 541, 543
Johan Gorg I, 539, 542, 544
Johann Michel I, 753
John Simon I, 444
Kasper
(Casper) I, 444, 627, 630, 634
Vallentin I, 542, 544
OBERE (OVER)
Anna Marye I, 24
Jacob I, 24, 25, 26
OBERFEHL (OBERGSALL)
Matthaus
(Maths) I, 677, 679, 680
OBERFELD
Matheas I, 421
OBERHÄNSLE
Marx I, 473
OBERHEUSER
Johan Michel I, 412
OBERHOLTZ (OBERHOLTS, OVER-
HOLDS, OVERHOLTZ)
Hans Jacob I, 35, 36
Henry
(Hendrick) I, 252, 254, 255
Samuel I, 14
OBERHOLTZER (OBERHOLTSER,
OVERHOLSOR)
Elisabeth I, 61
Jacob I, 59, 63, 64
Jno. I, 16
Saml. I, 61

OBERKEHR (OBERKEER)
Johann Peter
(Hans Peter) I, 205, 206, 208
OBERKIRCHER
Henrich I, 761
OBERKIRSH
J. Adam I, 456
Matheas I, 427
OBERKOGLER (OVERCOGLER)
Johan Georg
(Johan Jerig) I, 72, 76, 78
OBERKUHN
Maria Magdelena I, 49
OBERLÄNDER (OBERLAENDER)
Ch. Friedrich I, 746
Pedro I, 711
OBERLE (OBERLY)
Friederich I, 757
Johann Peter I, 421
Johannes I, 421
Michael I, 464
OBERLENDTER (OVERLENDER)
Johann Henrich I, 531, 533, 535
OBERMEY
Maximilliam II, 192
OBERMEYER
Georg I, 464
Jnº Herman I, 723
OBERMÜLLER (OBREMILER)
Johan Georg I, 88, 90, 92
Johann Martin I, 704
OBERNHAUSER
Agata II, 68
Friederik II, 68
Jan II, 68
John F. II, 68
Maria Elizabeth II, 68
Simon II, 68
Willem II, 68
OBERSCHEIMER (OBERSHEIMER)
Johannes I, 762
Peter I, 722
OBERSTÄCH
Abraham, im I, 434
OBERSTEG
Martin I, 407
Peter I, 407
OBERTHÜER
Philipp I, 750
OBERWINTER (OBERWINDER)
Johann Adam I, 545, 547, 549
OBISAU
Scintje II, 46
OBLINGER
Barbara II, 53
Carle II, 53
Christian II, 53
Jacob II, 53
John II, 53

OBMANN
  Anderas   I, 688
  Lorentz   I, 688
OBRIST
  Michel   I, 486
OBUSSIEUR
  Mr.   II, 175
OCHS
  Hans George   I, 706
OCHSA
  Johanes   I, 700
OCHSENBACHER   (AXEBAKER,
  AXELBAKER)
  H. Bernhardt
    (Hans Bernard)   I, 596, 598, 599
OCHSENBECHER
  Henrich   I, 691
OCHSENREITER (OXERYTER)
  Jacob   I, 526, 528, 530
  Johan Friederich I, 526, 528, 530
OCHSNER
  Johann Peter   I, 741
ODENKIRCHEN
  Johann Jacob   I, 735
ODENWALT
  Johann Philipp   I, 506
ODERN
  Peter   I, 737
ODERNHEIMER
  Johann Balthasar   I, 725
  Johannes   I, 323, 324, 326
ODEWALT
  H. George   I, 474
ODEWELDER (ODENWELLER)
  Jann Philipps   I, 335, 336, 338
OECHSLEN
  Georg Christoff   I, 15
OEHME
  J. Edmon   II, 17
OELLEN (OELEN, ELEY, ILLER)
  Caterina   I, 28
  Conrat (Cun-
    rad, Cunrath)   I, 27, 29, 30
  Elizabeth   I, 28
  Hans Ulrich   I, 30
  Jacob   I, 258, 260, 263
  Margaret   I, 28
  Maria   I, 28
  Uldrich   I, 27, 29
OELLENSCHLÄGER (ILESLEGER)
  Nicholas   I, 661, 662, 663
OELLGARDEN
  Jacob   I, 479
OERTEL
  Phillip Heinrich   II, 190
OERTER   (ERTER,   OERDTER,
  OERTTER)
  Johan Ebert   I, 706
  Johann Eckart   I, 686

Johannes Engel   I, 686
Michael (Mich[1])   I, 596, 598, 600
Willhelm (Willhellm)   I, 460, 735
OESSLINGER (ETSLINGHER, EST-
  LINGER)
  Conrad   I, 199, 202, 203
OEST
  Georg   I, 450
OESTERLE
  Bernhard   I, 432
OESTERLEIN
  Jeremias   I, 502
OESTERLIN, (EASTERLY)
  Hans Michael
    (Michael)   I, 209, 211
  Jacob   I, 227, 229, 231
  Johann Daniel   I, 260, 262
OESTERLING
  William   II, 200
OESTREICH
  Johan Conrad   I, 496
OETTINGER
  Georg Michael   I, 693
OETZEL
  Andreas   I, 444
OFFEN
  ——, van   II, 61
OFFENBACH
  Anderras   I, 730
  Jacob   I, 730
OFFENBACHER
  Jacob   I, 169, 170, 172
OFFENHAUSER (OFFENHEISSER)
  Johannes
    (Johannis)   I, 672, 673, 674
OFFENSTEIN
  Henry   II, 9
OFFMAN
  Christian   II, 195
OFFNER
  Johann Martin   I, 424
OGER
  Johannes   I, 300, 301, 303
OGG
  Carl   II, 196
OHL (OLE, ÖHL, OLL)
  Johann Adam   I, 709
  Johann Eberhart   I, 754
  Johan Henrich   I, 329
  Johann Nickel
    (Nickle)   I, 293, 294, 295
  Johannes Ernst   I, 304
  Wilhelm (Willm) I, 282, 284, 285
OHLBACH (AHLBACH)
  Anna Dumat   I, 144
  Anna Eliz[a]   I, 144
  Anna Margaret   I, 144
  Gerderuth Margaretha   I, 144
  Joanis Gerard   I, 144

Joanis Peter I, 144
Johann Wilhelm I, 143, 144, 145, 146
Zacharias I, 143
ÖHLER (ELER, EYLER, OHLLER, OLER, OLLER)
Anthonius (Anthoni) I, 294, 295, 296, 414
Hans Jerg I, 349, 350, 351
Jacob I, 649, 651
Johann Petter (Johan Petter, Peter) I, 31, 32, 33
Lenhard I, 372
Phillipp Jacob I, 721
Willhelm (Wilhm) I, 179, 181, 183
OHLIGER (OHLLIGER)
Carl (Carle) I, 67, 69, 70
Johannes I, 421
ÖHLWEILER
Johan Philib I, 422
OHLWEIN (OHLWEINNY, OLWYN)
Carle I, 744
Johan Just I, 122, 125, 126
Johannes I, 744
OHM
Joh. Hinr. II, 205
OHMS (HOMES)
Christoffel I, 573, 574, 575
OHNSHILD
Johan I, 505
OHRIG (ORIG)
Johan Michel (Michael) I, 373, 374, 375
OHRLE
Johannes I, 436
OHRNDORF (OHRNDORFF, OH-RENDORF, ORENDORFF, ORRENTORFF)
Anna Marga I, 190
Christian I, 297, 299, 300
Hermanus I, 188, 191, 193
Joes [Johannes] I, 705
Johann Chris-tian (Johan) I, 299, 300
Johann Con-rad (Conrad) I, 577, 579, 580
Johannes Henrich I, 706
Johannes Peter I, 577, 579, 581
OHSER
S. II, 32
OKELY
John I, 321
William I, 321
OKHER
Michal I, 409
OLBERS (OLBERTS)
Nicolaus I, 672, 673, 674
OLDENBURG
Christian Martin II, 82

Christiana II, 82
Henrich II, 82
Maria Elizabeth II, 82
OLDHOUSE
Yost I, 753
OLENTHIN
Jacob I, 482
OLEVER
Margeratte I, 85
OLGAATE
Gievan Gaeome II, 121
Peter R. II, 121
OLHI
Elizabeth II, 169
Joseph II, 169
OLIER
Johan Peter I, 234
OLINGER (OLLINGER, OLIGER, OLIGAR)
Hans Jurg (Hans Gorg) I, 307, 309, 310
Philip (Joh Philip) I, 307, 309, 310
OLIVIER
—— II, 81
ÖLLICH
Joh. II, 114
OLPON
Creet I, 242
Meriat I, 242
OLSEN
Johan Hendrik II, 50
OLSTER (HOLSTER)
Joh. Cord I, 536, 537, 538
OLT
Johann Georg I, 710
OLYSLAGE
Herm. II, 137
OMBONY
Martin II, 122
OMMEL (OMMELL)
Isaac I, 221, 222, 224
OMMERTH
Johannes I, 444, 500
ONANGST
John Sebastian I, 479
ONAS (LONES)
Nicklas (Nicholas) I, 227, 229, 231
Nicholas II, 104
ONDER
Ignacio I, 711
ONZINGER
Matheas I, 410
OORD see ORTH
OPFER
Johannes Jerg I, 718
OPFERTUCH
Johann Jakop I, 426

OPITZ
  Carl   II, 137
OPLIGUER
  Jean   II, 31
OPMAN
  Maria   II, 71
OPP (OB, OP, UP)
  Anthony   I, 703
  Fridrich   I, 314, 315
  George   I, 314
  Jacob   II, 19, 60
  Johann Philipp   I, 724
  Johann Valentin I, 371
  Johannes   I, 366, 368
  Leonhart   I, 759
  Martin   I, 486
  Michel   I, 687
  Peter   I, 687
  Phillip Wendel   I, 433
OPPELT
  ——   II, 58
OPPENHEIMER *   (OPPER-
  HEIMER, OPPENHEINER)
  Johan Detrich I, 545, 547, 549
OPPERMANN (OPERMAN)
  Cath.   II, 116
  Christ.   II, 116
  Conrad   II, 116
  Elisabeth   II, 116
  Johan Caspar   I, 504
  Maria   II, 116
OPPLINGER
  Hans   I, 683
OPRINGEN
  Eliz.   II, 157
ÖRDER (read ÖRTHER)
  Johannes Engel I, 686
ORE (OARE)
  Johannes   I, 113, 765
  Jurich
    (Jurigh) I, 113, 114, 115, 765
ORELLIG
  Peter   II, 117
ORF
  Johannes (Henrich) I, 642
ORLEANS
  L. C. B.   II, 90
ORN
  Eliseabeth, Van II, 77
ORONA
  Margret   I, 84
ORRON
  Bart^w   II, 90
ORTH (OORD, OORDT, ORD, ORT,
  OORT)
  Adam   I, 25, 26
  Aug^t   II, 118
  Baltes   I, 26
  Brigita   II, 91

  Catharina   II, 91
  Christian   I, 542, 544
  Christoffel (Christop^l) I, 540, 750
  Dirck   I, 18
  Georg Daniel   I, 448
  Hans Hendk.   I, 348
  Hans Ullrich I, 348, 350, 351
  Jacob   I, 484
  Jno Geo.   I, 696
  Johan Heinrich I, 540, 542, 544
  Johann Melchior I, 444
  Johannes   I, 24, 26, 27
              461, 465, 655
             657, 658, 701
  Ludwig   I, 721
  Peter   II, 91
  Ph. Ernst   II, 41
  Stephen   II, 91
ORTLEY
  Henry   I, 250, 251
ORTMANN
  Johann Henrich I, 735
  Johannes   I, 735
ORTNER
  Casimir   I, 367, 368
ORTTS
  Susannah   I, 85
ORTZER (OETZER, HERTZER)
  Johon Philib
    (Philip) I, 188, 191, 193
ÖRY (OREE, ORE, ORIE)
  Francois
    (Francis) I, 163, 165, 167
  Jacob   I, 384, 386
  Nicolas
    (Nicholas) I, 163, 165, 167
OSELER
  Johannes   I, 401
OSRAM
  Alexander   I, 734
OSSER
  Casper   I, 734
  Hans Adam   I, 14, 15
OST
  Johann Philipp I, 427
OSTENDORFF
  Wilhelmina   II, 71
OSTER
  Anthony   I, 413
  Conrath   I, 734
  Johann Wilhelm
    (Joan Willm) I, 282, 284, 285
ÖSTERLE
  Christoph   I, 489
ÖSTERLEN (ÖSTERLEN, OESTER-
  LIN)
  Christoff   I, 347
  Conrat   I, 347
  Hans Jerg   I, 347

Johann Daniel
(John Daniel)   I, 258, 260, 263
OSTERLOH
Albri   II, 188
Charles   II, 188
Fred   II, 188
Julian   II, 188
Louisa   II, 188
Mary   II, 188
OSTERMAN (OASTERMAN,
HOUSTERMAN)
Barthol. (Bartelma,
Partellmay)   I, 290, 291
Hans Jacob   I, 373, 375, 376
OSTEROTH (OSTEROODT)
Justus   I, 122, 125, 126
OSTERTAG (OSTERDAG, OSTER-
STACH)
Christian   I, 400
Jnᵒ Geo.   I, 743
Martin   I, 707
Matheas (Matdes)   I, 400
Thomas   I, 457
OSTREITH
John   II, 47
OSWALD (OSSWALD, OSTWALD,
OSTWALT, OSWALDT)
Friederich   I, 527, 529, 530
Hans Jacob   I, 532, 533, 535
Henry (Henrich,
Hendryk)   I, 72, 76, 77, 147, 150
Johan Jacob
(Jacob)   I, 556, 557, 558
Johannes   I, 232
OTENHEIMER
Christina   II, 54
ÖTHER (EADER)
Johann (John)   I, 286, 287, 288
Johan Cass-
par (John)   I, 287, 288, 289
OTHO
Jacob   I, 685
OTMANSDORFF
Johan   I, 441
OTT (OADT, ODT, OTH, OOT,
UTT)
Adam   I, 329
Andereas   I, 481, 750
C.   II, 161
Caspar   I, 20
Catharine   II, 162
Conrad   I, 329
Daniel   I, 609, 611, 613
David   I, 729
Gertrouy   I, 123
Hans (Johannes)   I, 147, 150, 151
Hans Michael   I, 347, 454
Hans Nickel   I, 404
Hans Ullrich   I, 404

Heinrich (Henry)   I, 332, 333, 334
627, 630, 633
Jacob   I, 122, 125, 126
332, 471, 523, 525
Johan Bernhart   I, 693
Johann Georg   I, 428, 498
Johan Henrich   I, 329; II, 119
Johann Martin   I, 693
Johan Michel
(Michael)   I, 122, 125, 126
Johann Nickolaus   I, 502
Johannes   I, 329, 360, 361, 694
Johannes Pedter   I, 329
John   II, 145
John Adolph   I, 539, 541, 544
John Frederick   I, 428
Leonard (Linhardt)   I, 627, 630, 633
Martin
(Marti)   I, 246, 247, 248, 471
Nicholas   I, 698
Philip (Fillip)   I, 79, 82, 83
Uhllerig   I, 508
OTTE
Ludoff   II, 135
OTTEHERDENDORP
Conrad   II, 159
Eliz.   II, 159
John   II, 159
OTTEN
Carl   II, 178
OTTENWALDT
Johann Georg   I, 495
OTTERBACH (OTTERPACH,
OTERPACH, OUTERBACH)
Johan Henrich   I, 143, 145, 146
Johan Jost   I, 734
Johannes   I, 88, 90, 91
OTTERSHOLT
Johan Petter   I, 692
OTTERSTE
Hend.   II, 114
OTTIGEN
J. Christian   I, 478
OTTINER (ODERING)
Jacob   I, 237, 238, 239
OTTING
Barbara   I, 210
OTTINGER (ÖTTINGER)
Heinrich   I, 480
Johan Christoph   I, 408
OTTMER
Peter Hinr.   II, 107
OTTO (OTTE)
Alexander   I, 759
Barbara Elisab.   II, 140
Bodo (Potto)   I, 677, 678, 679
C. A. F.   II, 77
Fredk. Wm.   II, 93
Henry (Henrich)   I, 252, 253, 255

Johann David II, 60
Johann Hen-
rich (Henrich) I, 576, 578, 579
Johan Matteus
(Matthias) I, 378, 379, 381
Johannes (John) II, 83, 147
Justus I, 371
Lorenz II, 70
Nicolaus Christian I, 517, 519, 520
Peter II, 129
Ulrich I, 742
OTTWALT
Johann Adam Fried. I, 704
OTZ
Hans Baltes I, 445
Willhelm I, 364
ÖTZEL
Hans Michel I, 501
OUBOLT
Joseph I, 264
Matheus I, 264
OUER (read AUER)
Hans Erick I, 12
OUT
John Nicklas I, 500
OVEN
Barbary I, 40
OVERBECK
Andreas I, 71, 75, 77
Elizabeth I, 72
Johannes I, 73
Matelina I, 74
Philips I, 73
OVERHOLSOR *see* OBERHOLTZER
OVERKIRSH (OVERKISH, ORI-
KER)
Jacob I, 387, 388, 389
Michael I, 387, 388, 389
OVERZELLER (OVERSELER)
Hans I, 652, 654
Hans George
(Hans Yerrick) I, 652, 653
OWANS
Melgert II, 50
OWERHOULSTER (read OBER-
HOLTZER)
Samuell I, 12
OXEMAN
Johanes I, 472
ÖXLI
Johannes I, 467
OXNER
Petter II, 53

PAAP (BAB, PAB)
Conradt (Hann) I, 156, 159, 161

Helena II, 68
Johannes I, 481
PABANE
Fransisco I, 760
PABST (BABST, PAPST)
Christopher I, 504
George Fredk II, 122
Henrich I, 88, 90, 91
Johann Adam I, 564, 565, 567
Joh. David II, 107
PACTOLL
Kongur I, 80
PAETZ
John Andrew II, 22
PAFF
Friedrich I, 433
Georg Gottlieb I, 504
Johan Martin I, 754
Martin I, 723
PAFLITZ (PAVILIEATS)
Jacob I, 227, 229, 231
PAGMAN (read BACHMAN)
Hans Mich¹ I, 7
PAHNKE
Friedrich II, 184
PAINTER (PAYNTER, read prob.
BENDER)
George II, 104
Regina I, 139
PAIR (read BAER)
Michal I, 293
PALIN (BALIEN)
Lars (Lorance) I, 199, 201, 203
PALM
Hans Adam I, 714
Johanes I, 427
PALMER
Mattheas II, 192
PALS (read PALTZ)
Henrich I, 452
PALTZGRAFF (PALSGRAVE)
Jörg (Jerich) I, 67, 69, 70
(*See also* PFALTZGRAFF)
PALTZLY
Peter I, 490
PALYETSO
Abraham Gometz II, 122
PAMPUS
Johannes I, 473
PANCHSON (PAUSHON)
Andreas I, 103
Eve I, 103
Hendrich I, 103
Magdalena I, 103
Maria I, 103
Nicholas I, 102
PANGERT
Bernhart I, 409

PANSER (BANSER, PANSE)
Christian Friedrich I, 545, 547, 549
PANZER
Johann Valentin I, 683
PAPE
Carell Henrich I, 316
PAPPENHEIMER
Elias Salomon II, 139
PAPPLER
Georg II, 139
PAPST *see* PABST
PAQUOT
—— II, 80
PARAET
Corneelis
(Cornelis) I, 143, 145, 146
PARIS
Isa I, 454
Isaac I, 447
Pierre I, 447
PARISIEN (PARISUM)
Daniel I, 585, 587, 588
PARIT
Pierre I, 729
PARITS
Wm. Peter II, 93
PARRENT
Hans Ouer I, 12
PARTE
Zeck. I, 37
PARTEMER
Friederich I, 355
PARTTS
Johanes I, 414
PARVENT
Michell I, 660
PARY
George I, 729
Nicola I, 729
PASCH
Christoph I, 727
Michael II, 108
PASSAGE
Georg (George) I, 48, 52, 54
J. George I, 100
PASSAVANT
—— II, 197
PASSLER
Johannes I, 433
PAST
Joh. Henry I, 464
PASTORIUS
Fred. Carl II, 3
PATIER
Lewis I, 729
PATT
Johannes I, 484
PATZ
Jacob I, 439

PAUL (BAUL, BAAL, BALL)
Gottfried I, 452
John II, 122
Matthias I, 743
Nicklas (Nickles,
Nicholas) I, 629, 632, 635
Peter (Petter) I, 307, 309, 614
617, 619, 742
Tobias I, 96, 98, 99
Valtin I, 330
PAULCHER
Thomas II, 103
PAULI (PAULE, PAULY)
Charlota II, 171
Christian I, 683
Dorothea Helena II, 171
Johann Caspar I, 727
Johan Christoph II, 171
Johan Daniel II, 103
Johan George I, 234
Johan Magnus I, 683
Johanes (Johs) I, 564, 566, 567
Nicklas I, 683
P. I, 684
Paulus I, 698
PAULS
Anna Maria II, 24
Dorethie II, 24
Joh. II, 24
Joh. Adam II, 24
Joh. Georg II, 24
Joh. Hend. II, 24
PAULTEREN
Katterena I, 85
PAULUS (BAULUS)
Christian Gottlob II, 78
Daniel I, 685
George I, 482
Jacob I, 301, 302, 303, 730
Johan Henrich I, 685
Johann Michel
(Michel) I, 323, 325, 326
Johann Wilhelm I, 722
Johanes I, 482
Johannes Henrich I, 685
Nickel I, 743
Philip Adam I, 628, 631, 634
Willm (Wilhelm) I, 301, 302, 303
PAUS (PAUSS)
An Catharina I, 157
Barbara II, 7
Christoff
(Christoph) I, 137, 141, 142
Eva II, 7
Gertrude II, 8
John II, 7
Kunigunda II, 7
Nichs II, 7

PAUSCH
Christophel   I, 363
PAUSE
Jacob   I, 7
PAUSER
Samuel   I, 455
PAVELICH
Jacob   II, 104
PAYSEL (read prob. BEISEL)
George   II, 18
PEALER (read prob. BIELER)
Johannes   I, 13
PEATER (read prob. PETER)
Danil   I, 632
Henery   I, 632
PEBLER
Charlotte   II, 148
George   II, 148
PECHENET
Francois   I, 757
PECHIN (BECHIN, POUSHIN)
J. N.   I, 593, 594
Jean Christofle
(John)   I, 592, 593, 595
Pierre
(Piree)   I, 592, 593, 594
PECK
Hans Jurg (Jerig,
Jerick)   I, 106, 110, 112
Joseph   I, 301, 302, 303
PEDELO
Michaelo   I, 421
PEEKELL (read prob. BICKEL)
Johanes Michl   I, 8
PEEL (read prob. BIEHL)
Thomas   I, 489
PEETSH
Hans Adam   I, 395
PEFFELL (PEFFEL)
Barbara   I, 23
Nicolaas (Nicolas,
Nicho.)   I, 23, 25, 26
PEFFER (PFEFFER, PIFFER)
Barbara   I, 73
Bernhardt   I, 71, 75, 77
Julian   I, 72
Margeretta   I, 74
PEFFERLE
Martin   I, 425
PEGY
Otto   I, 483
PEIER (BOYER)
Carollus (Carlos)   I, 383, 385
PEIETRS (read PIETERS)
Jan   I, 748
PEIFER (PEIFFER, PIPER)
Christ   I, 474
Frederick (Fredrick)   I, 31, 33, 34
Hans   I, 364

Johan Jacob   I, 684
Johann Ludwig   I, 501
Johannes Henrich   I, 467
Johannes Philips   I, 391
Joseph   I, 383, 385
Matheas   I, 474
Philip   I, 474
Wilhelm   I, 676
PEIFFLY
Christian   I, 489
PEIL (PEIHL, PEYL, read prob.
BEIL)
Heinrich   II, 20
Johan Peter   I, 382
Johannes   I, 303
PEIN (PEYN)
Theobald   I, 666, 668, 670
PEIROT
Jaque   I, 491
PEITER (read PETER)
Johan Mathys   I, 18
PEITLEY
Michael   I, 7
PELER
Johans Michl   I, 304
PELMAN (BELLMANN)
John Jurgh
(Hans Georg)   I, 88, 90, 91
PELTZ (BELTZ, PELSS)
Johan Friederich
(Jn° Fred^k)   I, 589, 590, 591
Johannes   I, 341, 342, 343; II, 148
PEMELLER (PINNELE)
Balsazar   I, 521, 524
PENCE (BENCE, BENZ)
Adam   I, 225, 228, 230, 492
Vallentin
(Valatine)   I, 226, 228, 230
PENDER (read BENDER)
Jacob   I, 465
PENHARD (PENHORT)
Henrich   I, 12
Thomas   I, 592
PENS (read BENTZ)
Magdalene   II, 11
Michel   I, 403
PEPPEL
John Peter   I, 412
PEPPER
Joseph   II, 26
PER (read prob. BÄR)
Johannes Ulrick
(Johannis Ulrich)   I, 559, 561
PERCKES (BAGOS)
Willem (Wilhelm)   I, 297, 299, 300
PERGER (PERGE, PORGER, read
prob. BERGER)
Anna Ursella   I, 28

Han Yerech   I, 114, 115, 765
Johannes   I, 27, 29, 30
PERING (PERRING)
Johanes   I, 535
Leonard   II, 15
PERKENS
Edward   II, 71
George   II, 71
Martha   II, 71
PERLET
Johann Friterich   I, 466
PERQUY
Samuel   I, 406
PERRET
Henri   I, 740
PERSONS (PERSONZ, BÖSENTZ)
Gerard   II, 77
John Jacob
(Jacob)   I, 294, 295, 296
PERT
Jacob   I, 293
PERTSCH
Johannes   II, 192
Michael   II, 192
PERTSCHINGER (BERTSCH-
INGER)
Jacob   I, 147, 150
PESCHALETT
John   II, 193
PESSER
John   I, 757
PESSINGER
Michael   I, 730
(*See also* BESSINGER)
PESTEL
——   II, 80
PETER (BETER, BETHER, BET-
TER, PETTER, PEDER)
Abraham   I, 508, 697, 699
Benedick   I, 429
Cathrine   I, 108
Christian   I, 464
Conrad   I, 653
Elizabeth   I, 147
Hance Micall   I, 85
Hans Jerg
(Hs. Jerg)   I, 605, 606, 607
Heinrich (Henrich, Hen-
drich, Henry)   I, 107, 109, 111
112, 252, 253, 255, 429
Jacob   I, 300, 301, 303
Jacob Berent
(Jacob Barn)   I, 323, 324, 326
Jeorg   I, 9
Johan Jacob   I, 440
Johann Melch.   I, 502
Johannes   I, 439, 605, 606, 607
John   II, 103
Joseph   II, 181

Jost   I, 586, 587, 588
Luterich   I, 12
Mattes   I, 697
Michael (Michel)   I, 439, 508
Nicklas   I, 355
Philip   I, 438
Simon   I, 439
PETERLY
Hans   I, 210
PETERMAN (PEDERMAN)
Hans Baltzer   I, 734
Jacob   I, 469
Jnº Henry   I, 734
Johann Jacob   I, 413
Johannes   I, 756
John   II, 188
Michael   I, 445
Mˢ Johanna   II, 99
Peter   I, 383, 385
Welten (Valentin)   I, 445
PETERS (PEDERS, PETTERS)
Arnold   I, 744
Carl   II, 61
Christjan Heinrich   II, 184
Hans   II, 16
Hans Peter   I, 429
Heinrich   II, 184
Jerg Henri (Jarrick
Henrich)   I, 99, 100, 101
Klaas   II, 78
Nick.   II, 118
Ulrich   I, 99, 100, 101
PETERSEN (PETERSSEN)
Friedrich   II, 184
John Chriⁿ   II, 22
Martⁿ Ph.   II, 22
Paridon   I, 732
PETERSHALL
George   II, 149
PETERSON (PETERSOHN)
Anna   II, 79
Charles   II, 117
Henry   I, 617, 619
Johan   II, 126
Johan Christian   I, 369, 370
PETRI (PETERY, PETRY, PET-
TRY)
Andon (Anndon,
Anthony)   I, 614, 616, 618
Andres   I, 488
Cath.   II, 157
Christan   I, 741
Ernst Paul   I, 749
Georg   II, 87
Gorg Philb   I, 698
Hans George (Hans
Gorg)   I, 243, 244, 245, 712
Jacob   I, 701

Johann Georg
  (Jurgh)   I, 113, 114, 115
               765; II, 134
Johann Jacob   I, 335, 337, 338
Johannes Peter   I, 700
John Wᵐ   I, 748
Leonhart (Leonard) I, 665, 668, 670
Lorentz   I, 517, 518, 520
Nickel   I, 398
Philip   I, 277, 278, 279
Stephan   I, 700
Vallentin (Valtin)   I, 403, 419
Wilhelm   I, 700
PETRYGANDT
  Johann   I, 714
PETSCH
  Joh. Christ.   II, 108
PETTENKOFFER (PETTICKHO-
  VER)
  Anna Lisbet   I, 28
  Johannes (Johanes,
    Johannis)   I, 27, 29, 30
  Ketruid   I, 28
  Maeta Lina   I, 28
PETTERSHEIMER
  Anthoni   I, 419
PETTS (read PETZ)
  Died.   II, 47
PETZOLD (PEZOLD)
  Gottlieb   I, 321, 322
PEUCKERT
  Gottfried   I, 441
PEUSER (RISER)
  Johannes (Johˢ)   I, 564, 566, 567
PEZEL
  Anna   II, 110
  Johan   II, 110
PFADT (BAAT)
  Daneil (Daniel)   I, 667, 669, 671
PFAFF
  Anna M.   II, 158
  Cath. Elis.   II, 158
  Catherina (Caterina)   II, 158
  Christian   II, 158
  Henry   II, 158
  Theobalt   I, 724
PFAFFENBERGER (PAPPEN-
  BERGER)
  Adam   I, 132
  Catherina   I, 131
  Christina   I, 132
  Elisabeth   I, 132
  Georg (Jurg)   I, 130, 133, 134
PFAFLIN (read PFÄFFLE)
  George   II, 3
PFAHL
  Lorens   I, 733
PFALTZGRAFF
  George   I, 297

PFANNENBECKER
  Lotharus   I, 403
PFANNER (FONNER)
  Johann Matheus I, 532, 534, 535
PFANNKUCHEN (PFANKUGEN,
  PAHNKUCH)
  Jacob   I, 403
  Johann Bernhard I, 539, 541, 543
  Johan Peter   I, 487
  Johann Peter   I, 508
PFANTZLER (FANSLER)
  Ludwig (Lodowick)   I, 244, 245
PFARR
  Hans Jacob (Johan
    Jacob)   I, 221, 223, 224
PFATTEICH
  Johann   I, 754
PFATTEICHER (PHATEICHEN)
  Martin (Mardin) I, 185, 186, 187
PFAU
  Johannes   I, 725
PFAUTZ
  David   I, 399
  Hans Michel   I, 10
  Johann Jacob   I, 744
PFAWTY (prob. FAUT, VOGT)
  Hans Georg   I, 410
PFEAU (read PFAU)
  Johannes   II, 119
PFEFFER
  Henr.   II, 113
PFEIFFER (PFEIFER, PHEIFER,
  PFIFFER, PIPER)
  Adam   I, 468
  Bernhart (Bernard) I, 568, 570, 572
  Christian   I, 470, 747
  Christoph (Chris-
    topher)   I, 605, 606, 608, 688
  Frantz Joseph   I, 507
  Georg Leonhardt   I, 479
  Hans Jacob   I, 462
  Heinrich (Henrich,
    Henry)   I, 460, 461, 688, 706
  Jacob   I, 303, 305, 306, 470
  Johann Adam   I, 719
  Johⁿ Danˡ   II, 129
  Joh. Emanuel   I, 391
  Johann Henrich
    (Joh. Henr.) I, 613, 616, 618, 727
  Johann Jacob   I, 745
  Johan Martin   I, 490
  Johann Philipus Daniel   I, 467
  Johannes I, 661, 663, 664, 752
  Jorg Leonhard   I, 696
  Magdalena   II, 53
  Martin   I, 653, 655
  Matheas   I, 474
  Peter   I, 371, 461

Philip I, 474
Wilhelm I, 401
PFEIL (PHEIL, PHEYL, PHIEL, PFEILL)
Anne Elisabeth II, 87
Catherine II, 87
Catherine Elisabeth II, 87
Chrétien II, 87
Conrad II, 87
Daniel II, 87
Elisabeth Gertrude II, 87
Fried. II, 192
Friederich I, 323, 325, 326
Gotefried II, 192
Guillaumette II, 87
Hans Matthais I, 185, 186, 187
Henrich I, 313, 314, 315
Jean II, 87
Jean Henry II, 87
Jean Josse II, 87
Joh. Claus II, 139
Johann Daniel (Daniel) I, 628, 632, 635
Johann Fridrich I, 427
Johan Peter I, 213, 215
Johann Wilhelm I, 404
Johannes I, 305, 306, 419, 425
Ludwig II, 192
Madelon II, 87
Marie II, 88
Marie Elisabeth II, 87
Marie Gertrude II, 87
Marie Margarethe II, 87
Peter I, 494
Pièrre II, 87
PFESTERER
Hans Adam I, 438
PFINGSTAG (PHINGTAAG)
Christianus I, 426
Martin I, 365
Michael I, 169, 170, 172
PFIRSICH
Fred. II, 187
PFISTER (FISTER, FIESTAR, PHISTER, PFISTERR)
Caspar I, 398
Hans Adam I, 438
Hans Jacob I, 332, 333, 334
Henrich (Hendrick) I, 555, 556, 558
Jacob I, 609, 611, 613
Johan Jacob I, 362
Johannes (Johanis, Jno.) I, 250, 251, 340, 341, 343
Jurg Hans (Jno) I, 250, 251
Magdalena I, 147
Peter I, 609, 611, 613
Tores I, 434

PFISTERER (FESTERER)
Johann Adam (Jno Adam) I, 637, 639, 641
Martin I, 551, 552, 554
PFLADDERMILLER
Michael I, 490
PFLAG
Johan Godfried II, 78
PFLAUGNER
Leonhardt I, 345
PFLAUM (PFLAUME)
Johan Frans II, 78
Johannes I, 702
PFLEIDERER
Johan Georg I, 744
PFLUEGER (PFLÜGER, PFLIEGER, FLEGER, FLIGER)
Eve I, 40
Georg Friderich I, 531, 533, 534
Hans Georg I, 40, 42
Johann Philip I, 750
Katrena I, 41
Ludwig (Ludwick) I, 386, 387, 389
Mary I, 40
Tobias I, 365
PFLUG (FLUG)
F. Gottl. II, 107
Jeremias (Jeremiah) I, 573, 574, 575
PFÖRSCHING
Friedrich I, 417
PFOSTADECKER
Valentin Sasla I, 734
PFOTZER (PFÖTZER, PFITZER)
Georg I, 451, 747
Johan Adam (Joh. Adam) I, 564, 565, 567
PFRANG
Michael I, 394
PFREMMER
Anne II, 31
Catherine II, 31
Jean George II, 31
PFUDER (FODRY)
Leonhardt (Leonard) I, 37, 38, 39
PFUGFELDER (PHLUGFELDER)
Johann Caspar I, 546, 548, 550
PFUHL* (PFUL, PFÜLL, PHUL, POOLE)
Christian I, 721
Johann Henrich (Hendrick) I, 386, 387, 389
John Georg I, 730
PFULLER
Christoph I, 441
PFUNDER (PENDER)
Fridricht (Frederick) I, 226, 228, 230

PHÄLER
  C. Godfrey   II, 156
PHANINGER (BANNINGER)
  Rudolf (Rudolph)   I, 555, 556, 557
PHAUTS (read PFAUTZ)
  Hans Michl   I, 8
PHEIL *see* PFEIL
PHEMOLER
  Christian Nicolas   II, 103
PHILIBAHR
  Johann Henrich   I, 748
PHILIP (PHILIPP)
  Carl   II, 138
  Gottfried Wilhelm   II, 138
  Hans   I, 19
  Johann   I, 305, 306
  Johannes   I, 441
  Lambrecht   I, 504
  Salomon   II, 122
  Sauter   II, 93
PHILIPI (PHILIPY)
  Adam   I, 697
  Andares   I, 441
  Christian   I, 441
  Johannes   I, 441
  Jorg Frantz   I, 404
  Michael   I, 697
PHILIPOM (PHILIPIEN)
  Johan Conrad   I, 272
PHILIPS (PHILLIBS, PHILLIPS,
  FILLIPPS, VÖLB)
  Aaron   II, 135
  Casper (Chasper)   I, 300, 301, 302
  Conrad (Conerath)   I, 564, 566
       567, 615, 617, 619
  Elizabeth   II, 97
  Hans Nicholas
    (Hans Nicklas,
    Hans Nich)   I, 300, 301, 302
  Jacob   II, 97
  Johann Jacob
    (Jacob)   I, 591, 592, 594
  Johannes   I, 430
  Solomon   I, 440
PHILIPSON
  Joh. F.   II, 125
  Miss   II, 97
  Mr   II, 97
PHILPLE
  Johan Adam   I, 10
PHROPHETER
  Anna Louisa   II, 8
  Anna Rosina   II, 8
  Conrad   II, 8
PHY (VEY, PHEAY)
  Pastion (Bastian, Past)   I, 290, 291
PICK (PIK)
  Johan Nickel   I, 205, 206, 208, 715

Johan Philippus
  (Philip)   I, 556, 557, 558
Johannes   I, 731
PICKEL
  John   II, 201
  John Henry   II, 122
PICKELMANN
  George   II, 75
PICKERING
  Barbara   I, 210
PICKLEATHER
  Hans   I, 80
PICKTLEN
  Soffia Catarina   I, 81
PIECKERT
  Johann Friedrich   I, 757
PIEL
  Peter   I, 488
PIELLER (PILER, BEILER)
  Vincent   I, 248, 249, 250
PIEN
  Peter   II, 50
PIEPER
  Daniel   II, 68
PIER (PEAR, BEER)
  Georg Philip   I, 93, 94, 95
  Johann Daniel (John
    Dan[1])   I, 648, 650
  Johanes (Johannes)   I, 648, 650
  Peter Henry   I, 648, 650
PIERE
  Nicolas   I, 17
PIERMAN (PERMAN, PIRMAN)
  Christoph
    (Christr)   I, 595, 597, 599
PIESH
  Hans George   I, 486
PIETERS (PIETERSZ)
  Christina   II, 59
  Elizabeth Maria   II, 59
  Jan   II, 59
  Joh.   I, 468
  Laurens   II, 59
PIETERSE
  John   II, 136
PIETSCH
  Johann Gottfried   II, 78
PIETZ
  Friederich   II, 22
PIGER
  Christian   I, 15
PIGNOT
  Louis   II, 57
PIKELL
  Henry   II, 16
PILANUS
  Simon   I, 371
PILEPI (read PHILIPPI)
  Adam   I, 697

PILGRAM (read PILGRIM)
Fridrich   I, 430
PILLAB
Krafft   I, 476
PILLER (BILLER)
Phillipp Carl (Phillip Carel)   I, 373, 374, 376
PILREGE
Michael   I, 734
PINARD
Jean Frans   II, 139
PINCKLEY (PINCKLY, PINKELIE, BINGLY, BINCKLY)
Hans (Hance)   I, 163, 165, 167
Peter (Petter)   I, 163, 165, 166
PINER
Christ[n]   I, 176, 177, 178
PINGEL
Jochim   II, 50
PINSEL
Christian   II, 93, 95
Engelina   II, 93
Englia   II, 95
PINTZEL (BINZEL, BINDSEL)
J. Henry   I, 522, 524
Johannes   I, 522, 524
PISCH
Albert   II, 117
PISELL
Jerrick   I, 99
PISTER
Adam   I, 14
Johan Christoffell   I, 330
PISTOIR
Conrath   I, 466
PISTOR (PISTON, BISTOL)
Andries   II, 59
Davit (Johannes David)   I, 560, 561, 563
Jan   II, 59
Johannes   I, 431
PITCHA
Ulrich   I, 14
PITSHER
Abraham   II, 53
Barbara   II, 53
Frederic   II, 53
Maria Margretha   II, 53
Rudolph   II, 53
PITSTÄCH
And.   II, 79
PIXELER
Peter   I, 17
PLACE
Cristefoal   324, 325, 326
Lorentz (Lawrence)   I, 324, 325, 326
PLADE
Anna Juliana   II, 92

Anna Maria   II, 92
Arnoldus   II, 92
Gertruth   II, 92
Johann Christophel   II, 92
Joh. Geo.   II, 92
Joh. H.   II, 92
Joh. Heinrich   II, 92
PLANCK
David   I, 652
Friederich   I, 485
PLANCKENHORN
Georg Heinrich   I, 686
PLANKMAN
Jan   II, 135
PLANNET
Carl   II, 5
PLANTZ (PLACE)
Christohf   I, 324, 325, 326
Georg Jacob   I, 424
Jacob   I, 424
Johann Matteis   I, 328
Leonhardt   I, 424
Lorrance   I, 324, 325, 326
PLAT
Jacob   I, 717
PLÄTSCHER
Michel   I, 328
PLATT (PLAD)
Henrich (Henry)   I, 355, 356
PLATTNER
Hans   I, 740
PLATZ (BLATZ)
Adam Nicolaus   I, 540, 542, 544
Johann Paulus   I, 540, 542, 544
Peter   II, 71
PLAUSER
Finchent   I, 20
PLEBB
Adam   II, 195
PLEESTERY (BLEISTIRE, BLESTRE)
Henry (Hendrick)   I, 265, 268, 271
PLEISZ
Mathew   II, 201
PLENNINGER
Matheas   I, 426
PLESS
Stephan   I, 741
PLESSE
Andreas   I, 490
Johan Hinrich (John Heinrich)   I, 672, 673, 674
PLESSING
Anna Margretha   II, 174
Anna Maria Catharina   II, 174
George Michael   II, 174
Jacob   I, 489
Johana Cristina   II, 174

Johan Daniel II, 174
Maria Magdalena II, 174
PLETZ (PLETTS, PLOTZ, BLAETZ)
Conrad I, 227; II, 104
Johann Friederich (Frid^k) I, 373, 375, 376
Johann Georg I, 706
M^r II, 130
PLOCHER see BLOCHER
PLÖHGER (PLEHER)
Johan Jost (Jost) I, 277, 278, 279
PLOTT
Garret I, 293
PLUMBOK
Hans Fred^k II, 16
PLUMENSTEIN see BLUMENSCHEIN
PLUMSTOCK
George II, 82
POCK (POKE, POK)
Christoffer I, 573, 574, 575
PODMANN
Anthony Henry II, 98
PODUM (PODOM)
Jacob I, 99, 100, 101
POGENER
Catrina I, 766
Johan Tobias I, 767
POGERT
Joh. Phil. II, 178
POGGI
Ant° II, 108
POHL (POHLL, WOLL)
Hans Henry (Hans Henrich) I, 246, 247, 248
J. H., von der II, 102
Johann II, 107
POHN
John Henry II, 122
POIES
Jacob II, 126
POINTZ (PUNCH)
Hans Michael I, 188, 191, 193
POLAND
Peter I, 427
Stephen I, 427
POLANDER
Jacob II, 11
POLCH (POLIGH)
Johan Nicol (John Nicholas) I, 387, 388, 389
POLE
Johan Adam I, 460
POLHANS
Thomas I, 701
POLIER
Sophia II, 80

POLLEN
Lorrentz I, 495
POLLER
Fred^k II, 11
POLLINGER
Peter I, 717
POLMIESER
Johan I, 741
POLO
Peter I, 712
POLWELLER
Jacob I, 523, 525
POMMER
H. George I, 481
POMPIES
Dirk II, 135
POMPLIER
Joseph II, 135
PONCE
Johan Gotlip I, 708
Johannes Gotlip I, 708
PONCELLY
Hipolito I, 761
PONDER
Henry II, 196
PONS
Abraham I, 468
PONTES (PONTEUS)
Johannes (Johanis) I, 204, 206, 208
PONTGEBEAU
Colonel More de II, 90
PONTZIUS
David I, 720
Mart. I, 720
POOFF
Conrad I, 330
POOL (BOOL, read prob. BUHL)
J. Jacob I, 467
Jonas I, 479
Philips (Philip) I, 569, 570, 572
POORBALT
Christian II, 126
Jacob II, 126
POP (PAPE, BUB)
Conrad I, 314
Matheas (Mathas, Mathias) I, 628, 631, 634
Philip I, 436
POPIE
Jacob G. II, 45
POPLAK
Usyer II, 136
POPPE
Henrich II, 79
POPPEL
Elizabeth II, 147
PORCH
H. G. II, 141

PORKER
  Hanah Barbara   I, 241
  Hannah Crett   I, 241
  Marelina Kattrin   I, 241
  Meriles   I, 241
PORKHOLDER
  Eliz.   I, 44
PORT
  Casper   II, 9
  Jnº   II, 9
  Johan Jacob   I, 509, 510, 511
  Maria Magdal.   II, 9
PORTEUR
  Pierre Jos.   II, 61
POSS (BOSS)
  Frantz Joseph (Frans
    Joseph)   I, 552, 554
POSSART *see* BOSSERDT
POSSERT
  Johanes   I, 473
POST
  Friedrich (Christopher
    Frederic)   I, 321, 322
  Nicholas (Niclas,
    Nickel)   I, 155, 158, 160, 396
POTH (POTT, BOTT)
  Barthold Henry
    (Bartle)   I, 665, 668, 670
  Cartrout (Gertrude)   I, 139
  Catrina Gadrout   I, 139
  Christoph   I, 457
  Degenhart   I, 137, 141, 142
  George   I, 643, 645
  Hans Peth.   I, 476
  Johann Heinrich   I, 589, 590, 591
  Johann Wilhelm   I, 139
  Johannes   I, 139
  Michael   I, 751
  Wilhelm (Wil-
    helmus)   I, 137, 141, 142
POTHOFF
  Henrick   II, 135
POTT
  Cath.   II, 125
  Frants   II, 125
POTTS
  John Ludwig
    (Lodowich)   I, 244, 245
POUPONNOT
  Pier Carle   I, 746
POURIOT
  Jean Daniel   I, 746
POUSS
  Johanes   I, 499
POUTIN
  Peter   I, 593
POUTMONT
  Philip   I, 472

POWELL
  Joseph   I, 320
  Martha   I, 320
  Samuel   I, 320
POZ
  Franco   I, 761
PRACH (BRAKE)
  Johann Casper   I, 387, 388, 389
PRACHT (BRACHT)
  Daniel   I, 454
  Vallentin
    (Valentine)   I, 277, 278, 279
PRACK (BRACK)
  Paul   I, 200, 202, 204
PRALL
  Gerg   I, 434
PRASBART (DRASBART)
  Collas (Nicollas)   I, 163, 165, 166
PRÄSTER (PREASTER)
  Johann Henrich   I, 559, 561, 563
PRATT
  Thos H.   II, 90
PRAUEL
  Johann Friedrich   I, 754
PRÄUNER (BRINER)
  Johann Georg   I, 83, 86
PRECHTEL *see* BRECHTEL
PREDIGER
  Mr   II, 130
  Mrs   II, 130
PREEGLY
  Jacob   I, 359
PREICE (PRICE)
  Hans George   I, 582, 583, 585
PREINS
  Henrich   I, 675
PREIS (PREISS, PREYSS, PREICE,
    PRICE, PRYSS)
  Conrad   I, 185, 186, 187
  Friederich (Fred-
    erich)   I, 621, 623, 625
  Hans Jerg   I, 741
  Johannes   I, 390, 526, 528, 529
                        581, 582, 584
  John Nicolas   I, 390
  Philip   I, 522, 524
PREISACH
  George   II, 52
PREISGÄRTNER (PREYS)
  Mathias (Maths)   I, 677, 679, 680
PREISING
  Johan Philip   I, 517, 518, 520
PREISSEMAN
  Philip   I, 730
PREMAUER (BREMHOVER)
  Gottfried (Godfret) I, 387, 388, 389
PREMICH
  Matheus   I, 689

PRENTLER
Jn⁰ Chrs. II, 196
PRENTZ
Adam Hennrich I, 401
(*See also* BRENTZ)
PRENTZEL
Carl Sam. II, 107
PREPPERNAU
Wilhelm II, 107
PRESLER
Heinrich I, 441
PRESSEL (PRESEL, PRESSELL)
Henry II, 140
Vallentin
(Valentine) I, 122, 125, 126
PRESSER
Johan Peter I, 432
Magnus
(Dominicus) I, 378, 380, 381
PRESTET
—— II, 80
PRETRE
Catherine II, 31
David II, 31
PREUSCH (PREISCH, SPREIS,
BRUSH)
August (Haugh,
Augusteen) I, 199, 201, 203
Johann Michel
(Michel) I, 199, 201, 203
PREUSCHER (PREISSER)
Johannes I, 577, 578, 580
PREVOST (PREVOT)
André II, 74
Henry II, 74
Jeanne Elizabeth Malet II, 74
Muller, Jnʳ II, 71
PREYRA
John II, 95
PREZ
Mathieu, de II, 89
PRICKER (read BRUCKER)
Jacob I, 212, 214, 215
Johannes I, 212, 214, 215
PRIE
Michel Antony II, 77
PRIEHL
Johan Valntin I, 722
PRIEM
Johan Martin I, 234
PRIESDECKE
Anthony II, 186
PRIESTER
Henrich I, 727
Jacob II, 136
John II, 136
Maria C. II, 136
Wilhelm H. II, 136

PRIESTERBACK
P. J. II, 108
PRIETSCHLER
Johan Nicolas I, 25, 26
PRIKE
Hans I, 432
Philip I, 432
PRILL *see* BRILL
PRIM (BRIME)
Loui (Lodwick) I, 526, 527, 529
Peter I, 461
PRINCE *see* PRINTZ
PRINCEKOFFER
Christopher II, 126
PRINFINGER
John II, 93
PRINING (read prob. BRÜNING)
Maria Catrina I, 139
Maria Elizabet I, 139
PRINTLY
Peter I, 477
PRINTZ (PRINCE, BRIENTZ)
Hans Georg I, 707
J. Daniel I, 439
Jacob I, 706
Johann Henrich I, 412
Johans (John) I, 226, 229, 231
John II, 103
PRINTZEL
Johann Leohnhard I, 727
PRINTZHOLTZ
F. Adam I, 429
PRISERMAN
Lodwick I, 527
PRISTORE
David II, 77
PRIT
John Joderm II, 93
PRITZ
Johan Peter I, 167, 168
PRITZIUS (BRITZUSE)
Wendel (Wendal) I, 665, 668, 670
PRIZER
Matthews II, 126
PROBE (PROBY)
Johan Hen. I, 536, 537, 538
PROBST (BROBST)
Adam I, 506
Barbara I, 108, 109
Frederick I, 684
Johann I, 107, 111, 112
Johann Jacob I, 684
Johan Lutwig I, 684
Johan Nic. II, 29
Michael I, 107, 111, 112
PROEBSTER
Joh. Adam II, 139
PROEDNIER
John I, 712

PROOPS
 Cathrina I, 103
 Felder I, 103
 Michael I, 102, 103
 Philip Jacob I, 102
PROPHET
 Frederik I, 438
PROS
 Franc^s I, 739
PROSKEY
 George II, 17
PROST
 Johann Gorg (Johannes Jerick) I, 559, 561, 563
PROTZ (RATS)
 Jacob I, 89, 91, 92
PROTZMANN (PROTZMAN)
 Johann Christoph I, 367, 368
 Johan Conrad I, 439
 Lorentz I, 346
 Ludwig I, 430
PROUVA (BRUAW, BRUA)
 Dieble (Debalt) I, 301, 302, 303
 Jacob I, 301
PSOH
 Konradh I, 506
PUCKSPEAR
 Peter I, 16
PUFF
 Vallendin (Valentine) I, 301, 302, 303
PÜGNER (PICKNER)
 Johan Peter I, 574, 575, 576
PULFERICH
 J. II, 181
PULLIG
 Antoni II, 20
PULS
 Jochim II, 50
PUNNEKACH
 Wilhelmina II, 113
PUNTZIUS (read PONTIUS)
 Johan I, 367, 369
PURGAZER
 Otto I, 597
PURPUR
 Carl I, 759
PURSELL
 William I, 143
PURTSCH
 Erasmus I, 734
PURY
 Joachim I, 483
PUSCH
 Gottfriedt I, 393
PÜTH
 Philipp Samuel I, 490
PUTSCHER
 Heinrich Casper I, 505

PUTTERBACH
 Johan Petter I, 479
PUTZ (POTTS, POTS)
 Margret (Margerate) I, 84, 85
 Michel I, 84, 86, 87
PYNNE
 Wilhelm I, 720
PYROTH
 Wendel II, 20
PYTHAN
 Joannes Guilielmus I, 725

QUANDEL
 Johannes Jacob I, 696
QUAST
 Johann Nicolaus I, 760
 Johannes I, 742
QUATTELBAUM
 Petter I, 167, 168
QUEDENFELDT
 Georg Fried^{ch} II, 140
QUERNE
 Lewis II, 178
QUESTRO
 Ary II, 91
 Helena II, 91
QUICK
 Anna Catharine II, 149
 Anna E. II, 149
 George II, 149
 Johann II, 149
 Martha II, 149
QUICKEL (QUICHEL, QUICKELL, QUICKLE, QUICKER)
 Hans Gorg (Georg) I, 60, 64, 65
 Johan George I, 167, 168
 Johan Michel I, 167, 168
 Johan Philippus I, 167, 168
 Maria I, 61, 62
QUIERIN
 Hans Nickel I, 484
QUILMAN
 John II, 55
QUIN
 Moses II, 75

RAAB (RAB, RAP, RAAP)
 Balsatzor (Baltzer) I, 601, 602, 603
 Edmer II, 24
 Johann Georg I, 512, 514, 515
 Michael I, 513
 Nigelas (Nicholas) I, 643, 644

RAAN (RAENS)
Hendk (John Henry)　　　I, 18, 19
RABANUS
Balthasar (Baltzer)　I, 627, 631, 634
RABE (RABIE)
Caspar (Casper)　　I, 180, 182, 184
Christoff (Christo-
pher)　　　　　I, 143, 145, 146
Johan Gorg　　　　　　I, 429
Johann Gottlieb　　　　　I, 430
RABENAU
Meinh^d Matth.　　　　　II, 22
RABENNALT (RABENHOLTS)
Wilhelm　　　I, 170, 171, 173
RABENSTEIN
Albrecht (Albright)　　I, 652, 653
RÄBER (RABER)
Conrad　　　　　　I, 359, 361
Johanes　　　　　　　I, 411
RACHEL
Georg Fred.　　　　　II, 118
RACHUSSER
Henrich　　　　　　　I, 482
RÄCK (RECK, RECH)
Christian (Chris-
tianus)　　　I, 637, 639, 641
Gorg　　　　　　　I, 355
Jerg Migel　　　I, 637, 639, 641
RACKE
Henrich Caspar　　　　I, 397
Johann Phillipp　　　　I, 693
RADDEMAUS
Engel　　　　　　　II, 136
RADEBACH
Christopher　　　　　I, 697
Henrich (Henry)　I, 205, 206, 208
Leid　　　　　　　II, 144
RADEBUSH
Johan Adam　　　　　I, 356
RADECKER * (RAETACKER,
RAERTIGER, RATIKER,
REDACKER)
Heinrich　　　　I, 510, 512
Jacob　　　　I, 596, 598, 599
RÄDELMEYER
Johann Martin　　　　I, 492
RADERMACHER (RADEN-
MACHER)
Hub.　　　　　　　II, 108
Johan Peter　　　I, 645, 647
RADGE (RATGER)
Johann Jacob (John
Jacob)　　　I, 286, 287, 288
RADMACHER
Joh. Michael　　　　I, 727
RADMAN
Conrad　　　　　　I, 737
RÄDTER
Johann Heinrich　　　I, 356

RADTGÄB see RATHGEB
RAFER
Anna Maria Barbara　　　I, 28
Felten (Feltin)　　　I, 28, 30
RAFF (RÄFF)
Christoph　　　　　II, 84
Joseph　　　　　　I, 447
RAFFSCHNEIDER
Johan Philipp　　I, 349, 350, 352
RAHDEN
Johann Heinrich, von　　I, 489
RAHL
George　　　　　　II, 4
RAHM
Jacob　　　　　　I, 723
Marti　　　　　　I, 723
RAHMER
Johann Reinhardt　　I, 521, 524
RAHN (ROHN)
F. J.　　　　　　II, 73
Georg (Gorg)　I, 179, 181, 183
　　　　　　　　　II, 119
Johann Henrich　　　I, 418
Johann Jacob　　　　I, 421
Johannes　　　　I, 418, 465
Konrad (Conrath)　I, 179, 181, 183
RAHNFELTER
Matdeis　　　　　　I, 443
RAIBLE
Hans Marti　　　　I, 498
RAICHERT
Bernhardt　　　　　I, 686
RAICHOET
John　　　　　　　II, 14
RAIGUEL
Abram　　　　　　II, 31
Frederick　　　　　II, 31
RAINARD (RANHARD, RINEHED)
Catrina　　　　　　I, 766
Michael (Michiel,
Mich.)　　I, 114, 115, 766
RAINTRAS
Pärre　　　　　　　I, 363
RAIQUET (GRAGEY)
Jean Jaque (Jacob)　I, 627, 630, 634
RAISCH (REYS, RYS)
Agnes　　　　　　I, 190
Christian　　　　　II, 188
Goodly　　　　　　II, 188
Jacob　　　I, 189, 192, 194
Johan Conrad　　　　I, 442
Johan Michel　　　　I, 467
RAITH
Jacob　　　　　　II, 44
RALFURE
Connard　　　　　　I, 99
Peter　　　　　　I, 99
RALL
Casper　　　　　　II, 193

Christ. II, 179
RAMBACH
Anna Elizabeth I, 132
Asimus I, 131, 133, 134
David I, 132
Hans Jacob I, 132
Johan Phillib I, 436
Maria Catherina I, 131
Sibylla I, 132
RAMBAHAR
David I, 660
RAMBERG
J. Christian I, 536, 537, 538
RAMBLEN (RAMBLER)
Christopher (Christr) I, 536, 537
RAME
Catharine II, 43
Francis II, 43
Frederick II, 43
John Daniel II, 43
RAMEL
George I, 465
RAMER
Katherine I, 24
RAMINGER (RAMMINGER)
Friderick (Fred^k) I, 605, 607, 608
RÄMLANDER
Phillipp Colman I, 710
RAMLER
Godfried II, 184
RAMLY (GRAMLY)
Jurg (H. George) I, 532, 534, 535
RAMM (RAM)
Conrad I, 475
Johann II, 107
Melchior I, 425
RAMON
Mars^e II, 50
RAMP
Rudolph (Roedolph) I, 252, 254, 255
RAMPPENDAHL
Frieterich I, 714
RAMSAUER
Ann I, 61
Henrich I, 59, 63, 65
John I, 61
RAMSKART
Christian II, 82
RAMSPERGER
Hans Jerg (Hans
Jurg) I, 605, 606, 608
Jacob I, 605, 606, 608
RAMSPOTT
Fredrick II, 199
RAMSTER
Johann Georg I, 429
RAMSYER (RANSIER)
Johann Gorg (Jan
Jerick) I, 265, 269, 272

RANBERG
Daniel I, 517
RANCK (RANK)
Anna Barbara I, 23
Johann Michael (Michl) I, 18, 19
Johan Philip (John
Philip) I, 23, 25, 26
Jorg I, 404
RANER
F. II, 123
RANG
Heinrich II, 110
Johan II, 110
Jost II, 110
Maria II, 110
RANGER (RONGER)
Hans Martin (Martine) I, 83, 86
RANGOREE
Louis Marquis II, 83
RÄNNINGER
Adam I, 750
RANTENBERG (RONTENBERG,
RANBERG)
Friederich I, 509, 510, 511
RAPER
Stephannus I, 12
RAPMAN
Christian I, 489
RAPP (TRAP, RAP)
Bernhard
(Parinhorn) I, 293, 294, 295
Christina II, 151
Christopher II, 25
G^o II, 130
Jacob I, 707
Johan George
(Jurg) I, 539, 541, 544; II, 44
Johann Migel
(Michael) I, 622, 624, 626
Johannas II, 165
Jon. II, 130
Maria Catharine II, 165
Maria Juliana II, 165
Martin II, 44
Oswald I, 692
Peter (Petter) I, 178, 180, 182, 421
Rosina II, 151
RAPPERT (RAPER, EBER)
Peter I, 286, 287, 288
RÄPPLE
Christian I, 393
RAPPOLDT
Johann Jacob I, 427
RAQUE
Hans Chris^n I, 692
Henrich Nickel I, 692
RASBACH
Peter I, 701

RASCH (RÄSCH, RASH)
Anton II, 139
Henrick I, 50
Jacob I, 47, 51, 53
Jeanette II, 140
Katherina I, 49
Magdelina I, 50
Michael (Mich¹) I, 609, 610, 612
Peter I, 50, 390
(*See also* RESCH)
RASHAUR (RASHAHR, RAFF-
GARN)
Ludwig I, 516, 518, 519
RASHPAKER
Conrad II, 195
RASSENBERGER (ROUSEN-
BERGER, RODBERGER)
Hans Peter I, 225, 228, 230
RASTLEIN
Friederik I, 480
RATCHMON
Fredᵏ I, 293
RATENMACHER
Clasina II, 93
RATGEN (RATHEN, RÄGENT)
Elias I, 179, 181, 183
RATH (RAT, RAAD)
Anna I, 117
Anne Marie II, 87
Anthoni II, 120
Bernard II, 87
Daniel I, 116, 119, 121
George Henry II, 87
Hans I, 116, 119, 120
Hans Jorg I, 436
Johann Georg
(Jurg) I, 627, 630, 634
Johan Peter I, 402
Johannes I, 500
Johannes Hindrig, von I, 119, 121
Margrita I, 117
Marie (Maria) II, 87, 95
Marie Elisabeth II, 87
Michel I, 710
Nicolas II, 87
Wilhelmus II, 95
RATHEBACH (RADABACK,
BREDENBACH)
Jacob I, 629, 632, 635
RATHGEB (RADTGÄB)
Hans Jacob
(Jacob) I, 146, 149, 150
Johannes I, 471
RATHGEBER (ROTGAVER,
RATTHGER)
Johan Balthas I, 195, 196, 197
RÄTHLEIN (RATHLINE)
Johann Jacob I, 601, 602, 603

RATHMACHER
Ulrich I, 382
RATSCHLAG (RAHTSCHLAG)
Johann Henrich
(Henry) I, 643, 644
RATTENAUER
Conrad I, 394
Gottfrid I, 366
RATTEZ (RATITY)
Jean Frans (Fran-
ciscus) I, 545, 547, 549
RATTGE (RÄGENT)
Nicolaus (Nicklaus) I, 180, 182, 184
RATZ
Henrich I, 460
RÄTZER (REYSTER)
Hans Jerg (Hans
Jurg) I, 637, 639, 641
RAU (RAUGH, RAW, ROUGH,
ROW)
Achilles I, 582, 583, 584
Anna II, 92
Christian II, 126
Conrath I, 716
Georg Adam I, 721
George (Gorge,
Jurg) I, 628, 631, 635
Hans Jerg I, 422
Hans Michael I, 531, 532, 534
Jacob I, 355
Joh. II, 61
Johann Adam I, 693
Johan Bernhardt (Johann
Bernd) I, 753; II, 28
Johann Conrad I, 721
Johann Jacob I, 486
Johann Michael I, 527, 528, 530
Johannes I, 422
Joseph Philip I, 531
Maria Dorothea II, 28
RAUB (CROUB, ROUGH, ROUP)
George (Derick,
Jerick) I, 290, 291
Hans Jerg I, 89, 91, 92
Jacob I, 463
Jonas I, 443
Michael I, 88, 90, 91, 464
Philip I, 88, 90, 91
RAUBENHEIMER
Henrich Jacob I, 736
RAUCH
Adam I, 371
Geo. Jnº I, 749
Jacob I, 362
Johann Bernhardt
(Bernherd) I, 204, 206, 208
Johann Christoffel I, 701
Johan Conradt
(Conrad) I, 378, 379, 381

Johann Georg (John
  Jurich) I, 287, 289
Johan Peter (Peter) I, 376, 377
Johan Stephen (Steffen) I, 233, 235
Johannis I, 481
Martin I, 692
Peter I, 88, 90, 91
RAUDENBUSCH (ROWDENBOSH,
  ROUDENBUSH, ROUDDEBUS)
Heinrich I, 96, 97, 98
Isaac (Isich) I, 99, 100, 101
Peter I, 96, 97, 98
Ullrig (Ulrich) I, 244, 245
RAUFF (ROUF)
Conrad I, 116, 119, 121
RAUFFBEM (BEYM)
Johan I, 522, 524
RAUFFT (RAUFT)
Marthin (Martin) I, 275, 276
RAUH
Nicklas I, 403
RAUHER * (RAWHER)
Conrad I, 468
RAUHMAN
Fridrich Wilhelm I, 716
Johann George I, 755
RAUHZAHN
Johann Ludwig I, 437
RAUL
Christian II, 192
RAUM
Mich¹ I, 725
RÄUMANN
Jacob I, 708
RAUMBERGER (REMBINGER)
Bartel (Baltzer) I, 539, 541, 543
RAUSCH (RAUS, RAUSH, ROUSE)
Anthon I, 744
Clara I, 72
Hartman (John
  Hartman) I, 649, 650
Jacob I, 71, 75, 77
Johan Adam I, 167, 168, 396
Johan Georg (Johan
  Johan Geo.) I, 601, 602, 604
Johann Nicklaus I, 204, 206, 208
Johann Vallentin I, 517, 518, 520
Johannes Peter I, 737
Jorg Casper I, 330
Mardin I, 395
Michael I, 176, 177, 178
Peter I, 184, 186, 187
RAUSCHENBACH (RAUSEN-
  BACH)
Joh. Paul I, 517, 518, 520
Peter II, 196

RAUSCHENBERGER (ROUSEN-
  BURG)
Johan Friederich (John
  Frederick) I, 93, 94, 95
RAUSCHKOBB
Johann Philip I, 694
RAUSHER (RUSHER)
Anna Barball I, 108
Anna Crete I, 108
Anna Maria I, 107
Catharina I, 107
Christina I, 107
Jacob I, 106, 110, 112
Maria Psalma I, 108
Metelina I, 107
Nicklaus I, 724
RAVERE
Geo. I, 756
RAYMON (RAYMAN, REYMAN,
  RAMMAN, RAMON)
Hans Jacob (Jacob) I, 212, 214, 216
Hans Michel I, 212, 214, 216
RAYSER (RAYZOR, RAUSER,
  REISER, RAZOUR)
Daniell I, 241
Gorg Adam (Geo.
  Adam) I, 661, 662, 664
Hannah Maria I, 242
REACH
Cristiana II, 68
Frederick II, 68
Philipina II, 68
READ
Elias I, 359
REAMER
Henry II, 116
John II, 116
Mrs. II, 116
REAP (RAPE, REEP)
Christian I, 88, 90, 91
Johannes I, 89, 91, 92
READ
Mʳ Pierre II, 108
REAVER
Philip II, 26
REB (REBB)
Catrina I, 117
Jacob I, 440
Johann Adam I, 714
Johannes I, 620, 622, 625, 710
REBER
Hans Michel I, 429
Johann Leonhardt
  (Leonard) I, 209, 211, 212
Johanes I, 407
REBERG (REBURG)
George Wilhelm I, 517, 518, 520

REBHOON (RAPOON, read REB-
HUHN)
J. Bernhart
(Bernard)   I, 596, 598, 599
REBLE (RABLE, REHBLE)
Christoph   I, 614, 617, 619
Jacob   I, 438, 614, 617, 619
REBLET (RIBLET)
Christian (Christian) I, 116, 119, 121
REBMAN (RABPMAN, REPMAN)
Agguth   II, 189
Anna   II, 189
Barbara   II, 189
Casper   II, 189
Catharin   II, 189
Christena   II, 189
Conrad   I, 204, 206, 208
Dorothy   II, 189
Johannes   I, 89, 91, 92
John   II, 189
Joseph   II, 189
Magdalena   II, 189
Simeon   II, 189
REBSCHLEGER
Jerg   I, 448
REBSTOCK
Martin   II, 179
RECH
Adam   II, 30
Christianus   I, 637, 639, 641
(*See also* RÄCK *and* RECK)
RECHER
Fritz (Frederick) I, 248, 249, 250
Johann (Jn⁰)   I, 248, 249, 250
Peter   I, 472
RECHNER
C. Rudolff   I, 538
RECHTER (RIGHTER)
Hans Michael
(Johan)   I, 538, 541, 543
RECK (RICK)
Christian   I, 637, 639, 641
Johann   I, 712
Jerg Migel   I, 637, 639, 641
RECKARD
N.   II, 186
RECKMAN
Jan Hendrik   I, 407
REDACKER (REATACKER)
Jacob   I, 596, 598, 599
REDER
Jacob   I, 715
REDIG
Johanes   I, 468
REDIKEN
Ludwig   II, 16
REDLINGER
Henry   I, 434

REDMAN
Hans   I, 395
REEB (REIF)
Gustavus   I, 652, 654
Petter   I, 482
REEBEL
Joseph   I, 483
REEBEMILLER
Johanes   I, 494
REEBY
Michael   I, 451
REECE
Jacob   II, 104
Matthew   II, 104
REED
Anna Maria   I, 107
Ferdinand   I, 409
REEDER
Jacob   I, 322
REEG
Catha   II, 5
George   II, 5
Johann Peter   I, 502
REEGE (RIGA)
Bernhart (Bernard) I, 252, 254, 255
REEL
Johannes   I, 450
REELY
John George   I, 455
REEPE (RIED, ROOSS)
Christoph
(Christopher) I, 217, 219, 220
REEPER
Mathias   II, 105
REER
G.   II, 4
REES
Catherina   II, 95
Johanes   II, 95
Peter   II, 134
REESBACH
Johannes   I, 443
REESE
Conrad   I, 418
Hans   I, 406
Johan Jost (John
Yost)   I, 367, 369
REEST
J. George   I, 489
REEVE
J. J.   II, 206
REFF
Michael   I, 698
REFI (REFFIE, REFY)
Johan Konrath   I, 401, 675
Teys   I, 401, 675
REGAL
——   II, 80

REGEL
  Anthony   II, 49
  Johan Adam   I, 431
REGELE
  Georg Martin   II, 20
REGELMAN
  Martin (Marte)   I, 310, 312, 313
REGENNAS
  Jacob   I, 472
REGENSBERGER
  John Steven   I, 24
REGENSTEIN
  Henry   II, 30
  Johanna   II, 30
  Magdᵃ Christᵃ   II, 30
REGNIER
  Maria N.   II, 136
REGTERS
  ——   I, 748
REGUEL
  Geᵒ Frederick   II, 82
REHBOCK (REABOCH)
  Michael (Andreas
    Mich¹)   I, 656, 657, 658
REHFELD
  Georg   I, 742
REHKOPF
  Johan Christian   I, 358
REHKOPP (REGKOP)
  Johann Nicolaus   I, 509, 510, 511
REHLMANN
  Aug. Friedᶜʰ   II, 140
REHORHN
  Conrad   II, 148
  Elisabeth   II, 148
  Frederic   II, 148
REHVAY (REVY, REHVEY)
  Hans Peter (Peter,
    Hˢ Peter)   I, 600, 602, 603
REHWALT (REWALD)
  Johannes   I, 297, 298, 300
REIBER
  Abraham   I, 423
  Jacob   I, 423
REIBLEN
  Johannis   I, 498
REIBOLT (REYBOLT)
  Adam (H. Adam)   I, 661, 662, 664
REICH
  Anna Maria   I, 131
  Baltasar   I, 131
  Conrath   I, 179, 181, 183
  David   I, 755
  Gottfried (Godfrey)   I, 130, 133, 134
  Johan Jacob   I, 412, 440
  Joh. Math.   II, 108
  Maria Dorothea   I, 132
  Mattheus   I, 475

  Thomas (Thoˢ)   I, 221, 222, 224
  (*See also* REICK)
REICHARD (REICHART, REICH-
  ERT, REIGER)
  Adam   II, 179
  G.   II, 153
  Georg   I, 622, 624, 626
     I, 755
  Hans Jorg   I, 429
  Jacob   I, 378, 380, 381, 417, 427
  Johann Adam   I, 752
  Johan Carl
    (Charles)   I, 217, 218, 220
  Johann Michael
    (Michel)   I, 387, 388, 389, 643, 644
  Johannes (John)   I, 258, 260, 263
     II, 151
  John Frederich   II, 151
  John Henry   I, 706
  Joseph   I, 628, 631, 634
  Michael   I, 276, 277, 278
  Rudolff (Rudolf)   I, 79, 81, 82
  Uhllerich (Ulrick)   I, 234, 235, 236
  Wilhelm   I, 638, 639, 641
REICHEL
  Henry   II, 145
  Johan Deys   I, 495
  Johann Jorg (John
    George)   I, 577, 579, 580
  Johannes   I, 731
REICHENÄCHSER
  Hans Georg   I, 463
REICHENBACH
  Anna Maria   I, 132
  Catherina   I, 131, 132
  Johannes   I, 130, 133, 134
  Maria Barbara   I, 132
  (*See also* RICHENBACH)
REICHENEKER   (REICHENECK-
  HER, REICHENOCKER)
  Fredᵏ   II, 20
  Fridrich   I, 486
  Jacob   II, 197
  Jan   II, 197
REICHHELD
  Pancratius   I, 441
REICHLE
  Georg Christoph   I, 475
REICHLY (REYCHER, REICHER)
  Wilhelm (Wᵐ)   I, 638, 639, 641
REICHMANN   (REICHMAN,
  REICKMAN)
  Eberhardt
    (Eberhard)   I, 621, 623, 625
  Georg   II, 125
  Johan   I, 517, 519, 520
  Johann Geörg   I, 435
  (*See also* RICHMAN)

REICHWEIN
Johan Georg   I, 453
REICK (read REICH)
George   II, 196
REIDBROCK
Rud.   II, 125
REIDEBACH
Mich[1]   I, 696
REIDENAUER   (REIDENAR,
REUDNAUER)
Jerg   I, 702
Johannes   I, 347
Nickolaus   I, 702
Peter   I, 702
(*See also* REITENAUER)
REIDENBACH   (REIDENBECK,
REYDERCACK)
Christian   I, 286, 287, 288
Johann Michel   I, 340, 342, 343
Johann Nickel   I, 340, 342, 343, 696
Peter   I, 696
REIDER
Christopher   II, 161
REIDT (REIT)
Georg   II, 134
Joh. Geo.   I, 649
REIFENAAR
Michael   I, 675
Peiter   I, 675
REIFF (REIF, RIEF)
Anna M.   II, 152
Anna Maria   II, 152
David   I, 532, 533, 535
Freenick   I, 24
Freiderich   I, 445
Hans Jacob
(Jacob)   I, 263, 267, 270
Jacob   I, 24, 734
    II, 152
Johann Christ   I, 687
Jnº Geo.   I, 693
John   II, 152
John George   II, 152
Maria Agnes   II, 152
Maria M.   II, 152
Martin   II, 99
Matthew   II, 152
REIFFEL (RAYFEL, RYFFEL)
Barbra   I, 117
Frederick (Friederich)   I, 173, 174
Hans Jonas   I, 173, 174
Johan Adam
(Adam)   I, 116, 120, 121
Sabina   I, 117
REIFFNER (REYFFENER)
Michael   I, 401
Petter   I, 401

REIFFSCHNEIDER   (REIFF-
SCHNEYDER)
Andreas   I, 284, 357
J. Ernst   I, 346
Johann Conrat
(Conrad)   I, 217, 218, 220
Johann Wilhelm
(Wilhelm)   I, 217, 218, 220
Johannes   I, 217, 218, 220
Michael
(Michel)   I, 378, 379, 381, 412
REIGENBAEHER
Jacob   I, 470
REIHLE
Johann   I, 427
REIHM (REIM, REEM)
Henrich   I, 701
Johannes (Johan)   I, 601, 602, 603
Niclaus (Nicholas)   I, 677, 678, 680
REIHT
Simon   I, 485
REILAND
Aberham   I, 427
REIMAN (REYMAN)
Johannes Ludwig   I, 353, 354
John Jacob   I, 353, 354
REIMEL (REMEL, REIMMEL, REY-
MEL)
Hans Gorg (Geoᵉ)   I, 175, 176, 177
Jacob   I, 175, 176, 177
Johann Nicklaus
(Nicholas)   I, 43, 45
REIMER (RIMER, REEMER, REH-
MER, REMER, REIMOR)
Abraham   II, 182
Balthaser (Baltzar)   I, 609, 611, 613
Jacob   II, 182
Johan Adam (Adam)   I, 266, 269, 272
Johann Jorg   I, 475
John Nicklas
(Nicholl)   I, 266, 269, 272
Matteas (Mathew,
Mathias)   I, 266, 269, 272
Phillip   I, 16, 17
Valtin   I, 372
REIMSCHNEIDER
George Wᵐ   II, 127
REIMSLACH
Anna   II, 50
REIN (REYN, REINN, RHEYN,
RHINE)
Anthony   I, 704
Bernhardt   I, 304, 305, 306
Hans Jerg
(Hans Jurg)   I, 637, 639, 640
Hans Martin   I, 232, 233
Hans Michael   I, 245, 246, 247
Jacob   II, 150
Johan Christoph   I, 555, 556, 558

Johannes Jacob
  (Jacob)   I, 559, 561, 562
  Katharine   II, 150
  Lucina   II, 150
  Maria   I, 67
  Martin   I, 231, 232, 233
  Matthew   II, 150
  Michel   I, 66, 69, 70
REINALDT
  Claudt   I, 418
REINBEIN
  Jacob   II, 159
REINBRACHT (REYNBRACK)
  Rubert (Robert)   I, 287, 288, 289
REINCKE
  Christop   I, 746
REINDELL (REINDEL)
  Erhart   I, 517, 519, 520
REINECK (REINEKH, REINCK)
  Daniel Friedrich
    (Fredrich)   I, 226, 229, 231
  Johan Jacob   I, 601, 602, 603
  Ludwig   I, 745
REINEKE
  F. L.   II, 125
REINEL
  Frederich   I, 715
REINER
  Christian   I, 424, 425
  Friederich
    (Friedrich)   I, 31, 32, 33
  Georg   I, 424
  Johan Dieterich   I, 425
  Johann Gerg   I, 751
  Michael   I, 695
  Steven (Stefen)   I, 31, 32, 33
REINFELD
  Henry   I, 436
REINHARDT (REINHARD, REIN-
  HART, REYNHART, RIEN-
  HARDT)
  Albrecht   I, 457
  Andreas   I, 363, 747
  Anna   II, 159
  Anna Elis.   II, 159
  Barbra   I, 117
  Conrad   I, 185, 186, 187
  Daniel (Dan) I, 265, 268, 271
  Dietdrich (Diedrick) I, 386, 387, 389
  Elisabeth Charlotte   II, 57
  Eliz.   II, 159
  Franz   I, 363
  Friederich   I, 363
  George   I, 441
  George David   I, 459
  George Frederic I, 551, 552, 554
  George Henry   II, 159
  Georg Valthain I, 526, 527, 529
  Godfred   II, 73

  Heinrich (Hendery) I, 422, 427
  Jean   II, 87
  Johan Arnolt   I, 427
  Johann Daniel   I, 435
  Johann Georg   I, 506
  Johan Henry   I, 467
  Johann Jacob   I, 709
  Johann Martinus   I, 435
  Johann Philippus I, 104, 105, 363
  Johans Thomas
    (Johanes)   I, 274, 275
  Johannes   I, 480
  Lorentz   I, 484
  Ludwig   I, 747
  Marie Charlotte   II, 57
  Martin   I, 665, 668, 670
  Matheis (Maths) I, 627, 631, 634
  Nicholas   I, 540, 542, 544
  Peter   II, 159
  Ulrich (Ulrig) I, 116, 119, 120
REINHEIMMER
  Johann Jorg   I, 461
REINHOLD (REINHOLDT, REIN-
  HOLT, RYNHOLT)
  Christoph Heinrich   I, 485
  Ernst Ludwig   I, 694
  Friedrich   I, 526, 528, 529
  Georg Christoph I, 546, 548, 550
  Jacob   I, 426
REINIB (REINEB, REMP)
  Johan Jacob I, 585, 587, 588
REINIG
  Johannes   II, 115
  Maria E.   II, 115
  Sebastian   II, 115
REININGER
  Hans Georg   I, 392
REINKNECHT
  Godfried   I, 505
REINMAN (RAINMANN, RINE-
  MAN)
  Aug. Ferdinand   II, 203
  Christoffei
    (Christopher) I, 574, 575, 576
REINÖHL
  Georg Heinrich   I, 426
REINSCHMIT (REIN SCHMIT)
  Johannes   I, 577, 579, 580
REINSTEIN
  Henrich Anthon   I, 435
REINTHALER (REYNTHALLER)
  Hans George (Hans Jerg) I, 462
  Jacob   I, 394
REINTZEL (RINESILL)
  Valentin
    (Valatin)   I, 226, 228, 230
REINWALD (REYNALD)
  Barbara   I, 138

Christoph
(Christopher) I, 137, 138, 140, 142
George (Georg) I, 136, 140, 141
Susannah I, 138
REISDORFF
Peter I, 724
REISEL (RISELL, RYZER)
Martin I, 290, 291, 292
REISER
Jacob I, 489
Johann Martin I, 425
REISH (RISH, RIEST)
Hans (Hance,
Hannes) I, 627, 630, 633
REISING (REYSING, RISEINGER)
Christian I, 539, 541, 543
REISINGER (RISIGER)
Gottlieb (Godlieb) I, 188, 191, 193
Hans Martin I, 188, 191, 193
Johann Nickelaus I, 413
Johannes Peter I, 413
Maria I, 189
Martin I, 189
Michel I, 446
REISLER (RÖSLER, RÖSSLER)
Johanes (Hans Jerg) I, 292
REISNER (RYSNER)
Hans Michell
(Michael) I, 96, 98
Johann Caspar I, 502
REISS (REIS, REISCH, RICE,
RISE)
Christian I, 712
Daniel II, 146
Frederich I, 429, 622
Fredk Martin II, 118
Hans Jerg I, 506
Hans Michel (Hans
Michael) I, 209, 211, 212
J. Leonhart I, 437
Jacob I, 257, 259, 262
429, 449, 556
557, 558
Johann Christ I, 495
Johan Georg I, 735
Johann Heinrich
(Johan Hend.) I, 236, 238, 239
Johannes (John) I, 24, 25, 26
Katherine I, 24
Philip I, 556, 557, 558
Saml Peter I, 743
Simon I, 556, 557, 558
Wilhelm I, 743
REISSENDORFF
Johannes II, 54
Peter II, 54
REISSER (REYSER, GEISSER)
Hans Georg
(Joseph) I, 245, 246, 247

REISSNER (RISNAR)
Tobias I, 595, 597, 599
REIST
Hans Uli
(Ulrick) I, 629, 632, 636
Marth. Elis. II, 108
REISWINAR
Catharine II, 15
Cathart II, 15
Chria II, 15
Christian II, 15
REITENAUER (REITENHOWER,
REITHNAUER, REITNAUER)
Baltzer I, 213, 214, 216
Caspar I, 346
Hans Henrich
(Hendrick) I, 213, 214, 216
Hans Peder (Peiter) I, 213, 215, 216
Johannes I, 273, 274
Nicholas (Nickelaus) I, 264, 702
(See also REIDENAUER)
REITER
E. II, 142
Henrich II, 97
J. II, 142
Jacob I, 485
Magdalen II, 135
Susanna II, 97
Wilhelm I, 485
(See also REYTER)
REITH (REYD, REED)
Johan Adam I, 335, 337, 338
Johann Goerg
(Johann Geo.) I, 648, 650
REITHLINGER
Jacob I, 473
REITZ (RIETZ)
Gorg Henrich I, 714
Henrich (Henry) I, 615, 617, 619
Johann Philipp I, 714
REITZENBOHN
Joseph II, 107
REITZMANN (RYTZMAN)
Johannes (John) I, 173, 174, 175
REIZER
Hans I, 473
RELING
Friederich I, 573, 574, 575
RELLEI (ROLLEI, ROLEY)
Jan Peirre (Hans
Peter) I, 595, 597, 599
REM (REHM)
Peter (Petter) I, 266, 269, 272
REMELY
Ambros I, 421
REMICHING
Daniel I, 304
Philip Jacob I, 304

REMINGER (REMIGER, REMENGER, REMEINGAR
Elizabeth I, 241
Marcus (Markes) I, 240, 242, 243
REMMANN
Frantz Petter II, 54
REMMICH
Christopher II, 8
REMMLER
Joseph I, 748
REMY (REIMIE, REME, RIMY, REMIE)
Bartel I, 175, 176, 177
Jacob I, 175, 176, 177
RENAN
Frantz I, 479
Joseph I, 698
Petter I, 479
RENCHLER (RENSHLAR)
Matheus (Mathias) I, 596, 597, 599
RENCK
Anna Elis. II, 157
Henry II, 157
J. J. II, 157
John II, 157
Margaret II, 157
Maria II, 157
RENE
Isaac I, 455
—— II, 81
RENECKER
G. Adam I, 432
RENER (RENHART, RENART)
Adam (H. Adam, Hans Adam) I, 297, 298, 299
RENIT
John II, 136
RENN (REN)
Bernhard (Bernard) I, 32, 33, 34
RENNE
Joh. Lud. II, 113
RENNER (REYNHER, RENER, RENDER)
Christoffel I, 522, 524
Georg (Johann Georg) I, 615, 617, 620
George II, 52
Jacob I, 615, 617, 620
Johan Philleps (Philip) I, 665, 668, 670
Johann Tobias I, 501
Katharina I, 74
Margaretta I, 72
Michel I, 472
Nickel I, 403
Valentine (Hans Valentine) I, 71, 75, 77
RENNINGER (RENINGER)
Christian I, 57, 58

Conrad I, 416
Wendel I, 430
RENOLD
Daniel I, 485
RENSCHLER
Micklaus I, 489
RENSHAW
Christoff I, 447
RENTGERS
Catharina II, 59
Christian II, 59
Clement II, 59
Peter II, 59
Wilhelm II, 59
RENTNER
Johann Gottlable II, 83
RENTSCH (RENSCH)
Margreth I, 157
Petter (Peter) I, 155, 158, 160
RENTSCHLER (RENSHLAR)
Matheus I, 596, 597, 599
Michael (Mich[1]) I, 596, 598, 599
(*See also* RENCHLER)
RENTZ (RENZ)
Anna Barbara II, 152
Anna Maria II, 152
Jacob II, 179
Stephen II, 152
RENTZEL
Johann Henrich I, 425
Jost Wilhelm I, 425
RENTZHEIMER
Johann Carl I, 755, 759
Johannes I, 762
Thomas I, 762
REPPERT (REPERT, REPART, RIPPER)
Conrad I, 185, 186, 187
Daniel (Tallyo) I, 559, 561, 563
Stevus I, 14
RESBELL
Elizabeth I, 241
RESCH (ROESCH, RESH)
Christian I, 458
Hans Gerg I, 460
Johannes I, 510, 512
Maddies (Matthias) I, 127, 129, 130
(*See also* RÖSCH)
RESER
Hans I, 16
Johannes I, 218, 219, 221
John Geo. I, 698
RESHEEK (RESHEK)
Margaret II, 158
Peter II, 158
Sophia II, 158
RESHER
Philip I, 694

RESLER (RESLE, RESLAAR)
Jacob (Hans
 Jacob) I, 237, 238, 240
RESSELER
Daniel I, 444
RESSENER (RESNOR)
Joseph I, 399
Leonard I, 188
RESSER
Hans Nickel I, 694
RESSING
Ludwick II, 145
RETELSBERGER
Christian I, 131, 133, 134
RETH (REET)
Johan Henrich
 (Henry) I, 280, 281, 282
RETTER (RETER)
Hans Jerig I, 8
Johanes I, 496
Tobias I, 503
RETTIG
Johan Gorg I, 396
RETTINGER (REDLINGER)
Antony (Anthony) I, 636, 638, 640
Conrad II, 4
Jacob II, 4
RETZ
Magdalena II, 178
REUB
Marg. Eliz. II, 105
REUBER (REIBER)
Johannes I, 642, 644
REUCHERT
Johan Leonhart I, 485
REUDENAUER *see* REIDENAUER
REUDT
Johann Jacob I, 690
REUEL
Johann Wilhelm I, 357
REUK
Jacob II, 156
REUL
Johann Valtin I, 346
REUS
Anna Maria Elisabeth II, 89
Antonius II, 89
Betramus Josephus II, 89
Hermanus Josephus II, 89
Maria Dorothea II, 89
REUSCH (RESCH, REISH)
Anthohn (Anthon) I, 576, 578, 580
Johannes I, 737
Johannes Görg I, 700
Johannes Petter I, 467
Tobias (Dowies) I, 232, 233
REUSCHLING
Johann Melchior I, 716

REUSSE
Christian I, 743
REUSSER (REUSER, RYSNER)
Christ.
 (Christopher) I, 277, 278, 279
REUSSWIG
Johannes I, 329
REUTENBACH (RATHABACK)
Jorg (Jerick) I, 290, 291
REUTER (REUTTER, REYTER,
 REUTHER, REUDER)
Anna II, 110
Catharina II, 148
Christian I, 677, 678, 680
Christoph Friderich I, 439
Conrad II, 107
Daniel I, 488
Henry II, 121
Johann Erich I, 510, 511, 512
Johann Paulus I, 331
Johan Valtin (Falten) I, 681, 682
Johannes I, 400, 712
John Hinr. II, 205
Jost I, 699
Lorentz
 (Lorents) I, 627, 631, 634
Mattheus I, 453; II, 110
Michel (Mekell) I, 194, 195, 196
Philib Jacob
 (Phill Joel) I, 194, 195, 196
Wilhelm I, 714
REUTHNAUER
Johann Nickel I, 750
REUTZEL (REITZEL)
Christian I, 443
Johan Georg I, 310, 312, 313
Johan Wilhelm I, 443
REVENOOCH
Johan I, 103
REVENTLAU (RAVENTLAU)
Johann Hen-
 rich (Jn° Hin.) I, 589, 590
REWOLD
Jacob I, 459
REX
George II, 48
Maria II, 48
REXRODT
Johann Zacharias I, 752
REY
John Adam I, 481
Jurigh Mickel I, 88, 90, 92
REYBOLD (REYBOLT)
Andreas I, 468
J. Jacob I, 437
Nicolas I, 467
Stephan
 (Stephen) I, 551, 553, 554

REYDE
  Casper   I, 688
REYDENAUER (RENHOWSER)
  Baltzer
    (Baltser)   I, 213, 214, 216
REYDER
  Lenert   I, 371
REYDMEYER
  Henry   I, 346
REYEL (REIL)
  Hans Jacob   I, 105
  Henry Henrich
    (Henrick)   I, 642, 644
REYENHAUSE
  Magdalena   II, 124
  Rummeyer   II, 124
REYER (RAYER)
  Christoffel   I, 406
  Hans Michael   I, 88, 90, 91
  Jacob   I, 393
  Johann Carl   I, 88, 90, 91
  Nicolaus   I, 393
REYGINAAS (REYGENAAS)
  Barbara   II, 124
  Christoffel   II, 124
  Elisabeth   II, 124
  Hans Jacob   II, 124
  Trina   II, 124
REYL
  Cathrina   I, 103
  Hans   I, 102
  Hans Jacob   I, 102
  Maria   I, 103
  Michael   I, 103
REYLANDT
  Paulus   I, 427
REYLEN
  Eve   I, 103
  Jerick   I, 103
REYLENDER
  Philip Jacob   I, 8
REYLING (REHLING)
  Vallentin (Valentine)   I, 589, 590
REYMANN (REYMAN)
  Johan George
    (Jürg)   I, 700; II, 120
  Johann Wilhelm   I, 700
REYMENE
  Medelin   I, 24
REYMERS
  Johan   II, 50
REYMERT (RYMERT, RYBERT)
  Anganias   I, 43
  Johannes (Joannes)   I, 43, 46, 47
REYMOND
  Abram David   I, 733
REYN
  Anna Hugel   I, 103

REYNHART (REYNARD)
  Ant   II, 15
  Philip   I, 102
REYNINGER
  Georg   I, 748
REYNOLDS
  Jonathan   II, 78
REYNTZER
  G.   II, 122
REYS (REYSS)
  Friederich   I, 429
  Johan   I, 462
  Johann Conradt   I, 716
  Johannes   I, 454
  Zachary   I, 462
REYSER (RESSER)
  Eliza.   I, 24
  George   I, 452
  Jacob   I, 24
  Ulrich   I, 81, 82, 83
REYSNER
  Phyt (read Veit)   I, 349
REYT
  Peter   I, 711
REYTENAR (REITTENAR)
  Johannes (Joannes)   I, 273, 274
REYTER (read REITER)
  Adam   I, 715
  Christoph   I, 499
  Jacob   I, 715
REYVAL
  Melchior   I, 455
REZER
  Johan   I, 237
  Tewwis   I, 237
RHAN *see* RAHN
RHEIN (REIN)
  Catharina   I, 156
  Conrath   I, 382
  David   I, 461
  Johann Henrich   I, 461
  Peter   I, 461
  Vallendien
    (Valentine)   I, 552, 553, 555
RHEINERT
  Johann Daniel   I, 435
RHEINLENDER
  Philibs Jacob   I, 9
RHIMHARE
  Johannes   II, 92
RHOADE (RHODE)
  Geo. Mich[l]   I, 715
  Jeremiah   II, 104
  Johan Christoph   II, 78
  John Israel   I, 653
RIAN
  John L.   II, 186

RIBELLET (RIBELED, RIBELET)
Abraham	I, 400
Hans Beder	I, 400
Jacob	I, 400

RICART (RIGARD)
Hester	I, 79
Maria Gotliven	I, 80

RICE
Elizabeth	I, 320
Owen	I, 320

RICH
Godfried	II, 166

RICHARD (RICHART, RICHER)
Abraham	I, 745
Barbara	I, 190
Bernhart (Bernhartus)	I, 142, 145, 146
Eva Margareta	I, 190
Henry	I, 456
J. Henry	I, 408
Jacob	I, 408, 698
Lotharius (Lutherus)	I, 582, 583, 584
Matthias	I, 189, 192, 193
Wilhelm	I, 190

RICHARDON
Jean (John)	I, 526, 527, 529

RICHARDS
Henry	II, 42
Ronyard	I, 80

RICHENBACH (read REICHEN-BACH)
George	II, 167
Johannes	II, 167
Magdalene	II, 167

RICHER (read REICHER)
A. B.	II, 161

RICHMAN (read REICHMAN)
H. Adam	I, 346
Hans	I, 304
Henry	II, 136

RICHSTEIN (read REICHSTEIN)
Elizabeth	II, 97
Johann Philip	II, 97
Ludwig	II, 128

RICHTER (RIGHTER)
Ann	II, 56
Carel	II, 184
Catharina	II, 24
Georg (George)	I, 652, 654; II, 205
Gertrud	II, 202
Gregorius	I, 465
Jan Hend[k]	II, 178
J[n] Jacob	II, 28
Johan	II, 28
Johann Gottfried	I, 446
Johan Gottlieb	II, 57
Johann Peter	I, 532, 533, 535

Johannes (Joanis)	I, 143, 145, 146 248, 249, 250
Simon	I, 413

RICHTY (LIGHT)
Uhlrich (Ulrich, Olerick)	I, 629, 632, 636

RICK (RIECK, RECK)
Christianus	I, 637
George Michael	I, 637
Henry	I, 660
Jochim	I, 505
Johann Christ	I, 435
Johannes (Hannes)	I, 643, 645, 689

RICKARD
Jo[n]	II, 19

RICKELL (RICKER)
Frederick	II, 126
George (Jerg)	I, 730; II, 126
Ulrich (Ullerich)	I, 169, 171, 172

RICKENBACHER (RICKEMBAC-KER)
Heinrich (Henry)	I, 275, 276

RICKER
Catherine	II, 157
Dan[1]	II, 185
Hannah Eliz.	II, 157
Henry	II, 157
Johann Fridrich	I, 322
Johannes (Jn[o] Fredrick)	I, 637, 639, 641
Peter	II, 157

RICKERS
Johan Henrych	II, 135

RICKERT (RIGHART, RICKHART)
Johann (Johan)	I, 652, 654
Philip	I, 403

RICKETTS
Johannas	II, 11

RICKNER
Jacob	I, 275
Samuell	I, 275

RICKOS
Henrich	I, 737

RIDEL
Dominicus	I, 372

RIDELSBERG
Michael	I, 407

RIDER
Hans Mich.	I, 23
W[m]	II, 186

RIDERBAND
Fred[k]	II, 18

RIDLE (RIDDLE, read RIEDEL)
Geo.	I, 694
Johan	II, 126

RIEB
Mich[1]	I, 649

RIEBCHLER
Jurg   I, 436
RIEBEL (RIBBLE, RIEBELL)
Anna Eva   I, 131
C. Maria   II, 69
George   I, 484
Jn° Conrad   I, 753
Johann Georg
(Jeorg)   I, 130, 133, 134
John   II, 69, 114
Joseph   I, 451
Maria Barbara   I, 132
RIEBER
Jerg Philipp   I, 425
RIEBMAN
Andres   I, 408
RIED (RIEDT, REED, RIDT, RIET,
RIETH, RIT)
Adam   I, 696
Anna Eve   I, 108
Anna Lydia   I, 109
Anna Maria   I, 197
Casper   I, 21
Catharina   I, 108, 109
Christophel   I, 219
Conrad   I, 19
Hans Jacob   I, 106, 109, 110, 112
Hans Jerick   I, 123
Hendrick   I, 122
Jerick   I, 109
Johan   II, 169
Johan Peter   I, 415
Johann Philb (Philip)   I, 16, 17
Johannes   II, 134
Maria Dorothy   I, 109
William   I, 109
RIEDE
Johan Bernhardt   I, 442
RIEDEL   (RIEDLE,   RIDDLE,
REIDEL, RIETEL)
Andreas (And.)   I, 681, 682
Georg Heinrich   I, 736
Johann Conrath   I, 411
Johann Heinrich   I, 485
Johan Jost   I, 411
Johan Peder
(Johan Peter)   I, 677, 679, 680
RIEDER
Michael   I, 442
RIEDESHEIMER
Jacob (Jacob
Rudolph)   I, 301, 302, 303
RIEDY (REIDY, RIEDI, RIEDIG,
RIETIG)
Johann Jacob
(Jacob)   I, 257, 259, 262
Johan Otto (Otto)   I, 257, 259, 262
Johannes Peter   I, 257, 260, 262
Ludwig   II, 52

RIEFFENACH
Dorothea   II, 52
Johann Philipp   I, 746
RIEFFWEY
J. Adam   I, 396
RIEGEL (RIGEL, RIGELL)
Abraham   I, 123
Caspar (Casper)   I, 592, 593, 594
Christopher   I, 747
Daniel   I, 122, 125, 126
Gertrouy   I, 123
George (Jerg)   I, 84, 86, 87
Johann Jorg   I, 307, 309, 310
Johannes   I, 122, 125, 126
Madteis (Mathias)   I, 84, 86, 87
Marreas   I, 85
Sarah   I, 123
RIEGELMAN REAGLEMAN, REA-
GELMEN)
Conrath   I, 311, 312, 313
Hans George   I, 311, 312, 313
RIEGER (RIGER, RIEGHER, RIG-
GER, RIGHER, RIECKHER)
Casper (Cas-
par, Gosper)   I, 194, 195, 197
Christian   I, 454
Hans Jerick   I, 20, 21
Jacob   I, 470
Jacob Friedrich   I, 137, 141, 142
Johannes   I, 349, 350, 351
Johannes Bartholomay (Johanas
Bathelomus)   I, 47, 51, 53
John Godfried   I, 328
Jorg Simon   I, 699
Lorence
(Lawrence)   I, 252, 254, 255
Melchior   I, 551, 552, 554
Peter   I, 688
RIEGERT (RIGERD)
Jerg   I, 488
Ludwig   I, 127
RIEGLER (KEYLER)
Johann Andreas
(Andreas)   I, 373, 374, 375
Johann Stephan   I, 513, 514, 515
RIEHL (RIELL, RIEL, REEL)
Adolph   I, 428
Catherine   II, 87
Conrad   II, 87
George Adam   II, 87
Jean   II, 87
Johanes (Hannes)   I, 643, 644
Johann Philips   I, 204, 206, 207
Stephan (Stephen) I, 582, 583, 584
RIELMAN
Casper   II, 70
RIEM (RIHM, REEM)
Adam   I, 372

Johannes   I, 372, 707
(*See also* RIHM)

RIEMANN (RIEMAN, REMAN)
Jacob   I, 574, 575, 576

RIEMENSCHNEIDER * (RIEMEN-
SCHEIDER, RIEMENSHIDER)
Johann Henrich
(Johan Henry)   I, 222, 223, 224
——   II, 144

RIEPENHAUSEN
Georg Ludwig   II, 59

RIEPER
Mathias   II, 23

RIESS (RISS, REISS, RIES, REIS)
Adam   II, 8
Andreas   I, 365
Christof   I, 71, 75, 77
Conraht (Conradt)   I, 383, 385
Daniel   I, 180, 182, 184
Elizabeth   I, 73; II, 8
Fridrich (Frederiok)   I, 71, 75, 77
George   II, 8
Hans   I, 17
Hinrich   I, 425
Jacob   I, 227, 229, 231
Johann Dieterich   I, 495
Johann Georg
(John Yerrick)   I, 330, 652, 654
Johann Jacob   I, 330
Johann Peter   I, 539, 541, 543
Johannes
(Joannes, Johans)   I, 169, 170, 172
    501, 539, 541
    543
John Christ.   II, 160
Katherine   I, 24
Lorentz   I, 330
Margeritta (Marg^t)   I, 74; II, 8
Maria Katharine   I, 73
Martin   I, 74, 409
Matthew   I, 227
Michel (Michael)   I, 297, 298, 299
Nicolaus (Nick-
laus, Nich^s)   I, 180, 182, 184
    II, 15
Philip (Philib)   I, 614, 616, 619
Sebastian   I, 539, 541, 544

RIESCH (RIESH)
Christian   II, 154
Godfrey   II, 179
J. Michael   II, 156

RIESER (RIESSER)
Johanes   I, 292, 698
Ulrich   I, 15

RIESTNER
Henry Fred.   I, 749

RIET, RIETH *see* RIED

RIETHMÜLLER (RACKMILLER)
Johann Martin
(John Martin)   I, 555, 556, 557

RIETTERSHAN (TREETERSHAN)
Arnolt   I, 93, 94, 95

RIETWEILL (READWILE)
Johann Michel   I, 445
Ludwig   I, 445

RIETZ (READS)
Christian
(Gristian)   I, 621, 623, 625

RIEVET (RIFFARD)
Conradt
(Johan Conrath)   I, 303, 305, 306
Johannes   I, 340

RIFF
Johannes   I, 690

RIFFEL
Jacob   I, 440

RIFFNACH
Kasper   I, 450

RIGHART
J. Henry   I, 408

RIGHER (read RIEGER)
Henry   I, 366

RIGHT
George   I, 487
Jacob   I, 508
Jeneck Hennick   I, 94

RIGHTER (RIGTAR, RIGTER)
Anna   I, 117
George   I, 317
Jourge (Jerick)   I, 116, 119, 121

RIGLER
Stefan   I, 458

RIGONY
Jean   I, 486

RIGSEGER (RICHSINGER)
Peter   I, 323, 325, 326

RIHL (RIEGEL)
Anndreas
(Andreas)   I, 621, 623, 626
Hans   I, 105, 106

RIHM (REEHM)
Johan Georg   I, 486
Johann Julius   I, 372
Johannes   I, 372

RIHMER
Henrich   I, 742

RIKSAKER
Nicklas   I, 404

RILEY
Johan   II, 126

RIM (RINN)
Conraht
(Conrad)   I, 621, 623, 625

RIMBI (RUMPEA)
Jacob   I, 310, 311, 312
Johann Christopfel   I, 311, 312, 313

RIMBLE (REAMMY)
Peter   I, 591, 592, 594
RIMMEL
Lutwig   I, 456
Nicolaus   I, 456
RINCKER
Jacob   I, 480
RIND (RINDT)
David   II, 41
Johan Bastian   I, 494
RINDERLUST
Jonas   I, 496
RINDLAUB
Johan Georg   II, 21
RINECKER
Georg   I, 728
RINEHED
Catrina   I, 766
RINETROP
Carolina   II, 77
Elisabeth   II, 77
Fredrick   II, 77
Hendrick   II, 77
RING (RINCK)
Daniel   I, 692
Johannes (Hans)   I, 12, 14, 697
Joseph   II, 147
RINGELER
Johannes   I, 483
RINGER
Andreas (Andrew)   I, 227; II, 104
Fred.   I, 689
Hans Ullrich   I, 332, 333, 334
Johan Jacob   I, 348, 350, 351
RINGOLD
Antoni   II, 122
RINGS
Micl   II, 61
RINGWALD (RINGOLT)
Jacob   I, 560, 561, 563
RINHART
Abraham   I, 451
RINHOLD
Melchior   I, 425
RINK
Christ (Christopher)   I, 39, 41, 42
RINKER
Hans Jacob   I, 332
Jacob   I, 434
RINKLE
Laurence   I, 707
RINLEIN (RHINLEN)
Johan Wolfgang   I, 546, 550
RINPFENTHALL
Jacob   I, 747
RINTELMAN (RINDELMAN)
Christoffer
(Christoph)   I, 671, 673, 674
Johann Friederich   I, 746

RIPPART
Catharine   II, 43
Catharine Margt   II, 43
Christian   II, 43
Elizabeth   II, 43
George   II, 43
Jacob   II, 43
Lewis   II, 43
Margaret   II, 43
Martin   II, 43
Sophia   II, 43
RIPPASS
Hans Jacob   I, 721
RIPPE
Anna   II, 95
RIPPEL
J. Nicklas   I, 473
Philipp   I, 725
RISCH (REESH, RISCHIE, RISH)
Carl   I, 363
George Ernst   I, 444
Johann Friedrich   I, 439
Nicklas (John
Nicholas)   I, 656, 657, 658
RISCHEL (RUSHER, RUSHELL)
Johan Michael
(Hans Michell)   I, 199, 201, 203
RISCHERD
Johann   I, 481
RISCHSTEIN
Catharina Elisa   II, 129
Christiana   II, 129
Johann Christ   I, 340, 341, 343
Johannes   II, 129
John Jacob   II, 129
John Jost   II, 129
Louise   II, 129
RISER (RESER, REISER)
Gorg Adam   I, 88, 90, 91
Hans Jerg   I, 88, 90, 91
Jacob   I, 15
Ulrick   I, 15
Wilhelm
(William)   I, 236, 238, 239
RISHT (REEST)
Johannes   I, 662, 663, 664
RISINGER
Adam   II, 137
RISLING
Mathias   I, 14
RISS
Mr.   II, 175
Mrs.   II, 175
Philipp (Filipp)   I, 266, 269, 273
RISSER (RISER, REESER)
G. Willhelm   I, 530
Philip   I, 527, 528
RISSLER
George Henry   I, 403

RISSTEIN
Catherine II, 87
Christine II, 87
Jaques II, 87
Jean Jost II, 87
RISTERHOLTZ
Jacob I, 400
RITBERT
J. II, 24
RITCHER
Johanes I, 419
RITHELBERGER
Casper II, 11
RITHMÜLLER
Abraham I, 441
RITICHER
Catharine II, 56
John II, 56
RITKAR
Jnᵒ II, 75
RITLINGER
Leo I, 648
RITSCHART (RIGHART)
Johannes I, 609, 611, 612
Ullrich I, 407
RITSEKKY
Joseph II, 178
RITTELMEYER
Georg Michael I, 713
RITTENBACH
Joh. Michel I, 408
RITTER (RITER, RITTAR, RETTER)
Adam I, 226, 228, 230
Antonius Henricus I, 749
Barbary II, 162
Carl I, 762
Christopher (Christ.) I, 39, 41, 42
Crates I, 40
Daniel II, 197
Dorotha II, 162
Elizabeth I, 108
Fredᵏ II, 162
George I, 653
Godfrey II, 162
Hans I, 40, 41, 42, 451
Jacob I, 464
Jochim II, 50
Johann Conrad II, 121
Johann Gorg
(George) I, 162, 164, 165
Johann Gottfried
(John Godfred) I, 672, 673, 674
Johann Ludwig I, 436
Joseph I, 417
Jurigh I, 88
Maria (Mary) I, 40; II, 162
Martin I, 406
Michel (Michael) I, 489, 706

Motley I, 40
Wilhelm I, 688
Wilhelm Henrich I, 743
—— II, 162
RITTES
Anna Katrina I, 117
Anna Klara I, 117
Barbra I, 117
RITTESHEIM
Johannes I, 689
RITTNER
Heinrich II, 79
Philip II, 70
RITZ (RITS)
Christian I, 453
Johan George I, 458
John II, 72
RITZEL
John Henry I, 443
RITZEMA
Margᵃ II, 32
RIVER
Catharine (Cath.) II, 146
Elizabeth II, 146
RIVISARD
Jean Richard I, 708
RIZER
Yerrick I, 387
ROAD (read ROTH)
Ana Elizabeth II, 36
Hancrist II, 37
Honer II, 37
Lamburgh II, 36
Nicklas I, 404
ROBB
Michael I, 227; II, 104
RÖBER (RIVER)
Johann Wilhelm
(Johan William) I, 574, 575, 576
ROBERSON
Lamber II, 47
ROBERT
Louis I, 711
ROBERTS
Henry II, 71
Mʳ II, 130
ROBERTUS (ROBETES, ROBERTS)
Hans Adam I, 93, 95
Nicklas (Nicholas) I, 227, 229, 231
II, 104
ROBESON
John I, 143
Joseph II, 135
ROBREACHT
Julian II, 89
ROCH (RUCH)
Johann Peter
(Peter) I, 569, 570, 572

ROCHE
Anna Maria, la — II, 115
Jost Heinrich, la — II, 115
Nicolaus, la — II, 115
ROCHIA
Adam — I, 502
ROCHKENDORF
Mr. — II, 144
ROCKENBAUCH
Jacob — I, 707
Matheus — I, 721
ROCKENBROD
William — I, 751
ROCKENSTIHL
Bernhardt — I, 442
ROCKHOLT
John — II, 126
RODE (RODT)
Daniel — I, 194, 195, 196
Heinrich
(Hendreck) — I, 194, 195, 196
Johannes — I, 286
RODEBAGH
John Peter — I, 478
RODEBURGER (RODEBERGER)
Nicklas
(Nicholas) — I, 266, 269, 273
RODEL (RODELL)
Fred. — II, 3
George Jacob — II, 29
Handerick — II, 3
John Mich. — II, 3
John Nich. — II, 3
Philip Jac. — II, 3
Yohan, de — II, 3
RODELSBERGER
Adam — II, 117
RODENBACH (PRODENBAER)
Christian — I, 257, 260, 262
RODENNILL
Leonard — I, 15
RODENSTEIN
Erhard — I, 693
RODEPILLER
Anna Elise — II, 128
Catharina — II, 128
John Jost. — II, 128
Maria Elisa — II, 128
RÖDER
Conrad — I, 743
Jacob — I, 365
Johan Engel — I, 495
Martin Christofel — I, 466
RÖDHELE
Matthias — I, 459
RODRIGUE
Manuel — I, 760
RÖDTLER
Peter — I, 521, 524

ROEBACK
Valentine — I, 706
ROEDE
Diederich — I, 8
Ernest — I, 8
ROEDEBAS
Hans Jerig — I, 8
ROEDEL
Jno Leond — I, 753
ROEDEULL
Philip — I, 8
ROEHM
Joh. Barth. — I, 733
ROELOFS
Johanna Elisab. — II, 193
ROEMER (ROEMMER)
Antonie — II, 122
Friedrig
(Fredrick) — I, 591, 592, 594
Gertruth — II, 91
Wilhelm — II, 91
ROENES
Maria — II, 76
ROER
Baltzar (Baltsar) — I, 24, 26
Johannes — I, 20
ROESCH
Georg Henrich — I, 457
ROESHER
Philip — I, 346
ROESSER
Hans Petter — I, 404
RÖGER (ROGER)
Conrath — I, 408
H. — II, 184
ROHDE
Carolina
Christina Elisabette — II, 67
Ehrgott Ferdinand Wilhelm — II, 67
Georg Friedrich Heinrich — II, 67
Georg Ludwig Theodor — II, 67
Heinrich
Friederich Segnerus — II, 67
Johann Dietrich
Ernst Valentin — II, 67
Johann Friederich — II, 67
Johannette
Catharina Elisabette — II, 67
Maria Sophia — II, 67
Mariane
Friederike Henriette — II, 67
ROHER
Jacob — I, 392
ROHKOP (ROKOOP, ROUKOP)
Henry
(Hendrich) — I, 252, 254, 255
ROHLANDT (ROELAND)
Jno Adam
(Johan Adam) — I, 649, 650

ROHLEDER (ROLETER)
Johan Philipp   I, 513, 514, 515
ROHL (REEL)
Simon   I, 24, 26
ROHLEBER (ROLEVER)
Vallentine   I, 173, 174, 175
RÖHLING
Johann Henrich   I, 466
RÖHM
Dietrich   I, 454
ROHN (ROAN, RÖHN, RON, RONH)
Henrich
(Johannes Jerick)   I, 560, 561, 563
Johan Friedrich   I, 440
Johan Henrich   I, 418
Johan Moritz
(John Morris)   I, 279, 281, 282
Leonard   II, 26
(*See also* RAHN)
RÖHNISCH
Johan   II, 173
ROHR (ROWER, ROWERS)
Christian   I, 465
Jacob   I, 48, 52, 71
75, 77, 396
Johann Andreas   I, 441
Johann Friedrich, von   I, 441
Johannes   I, 18, 169, 170
172, 396, 433
Martin   I, 652, 654
Ulrich   I, 365
Wynant   I, 743
ROHRBACH (ROERBACH, ROHR-
BACHER, ROARBACH, ROR-
BACH)
Christian
(Christeyan)   I, 266, 269, 272, 347
560, 561, 563
Hans Jerick
(Jerig, Georg)   I, 102, 105
Jacob   I, 266, 269, 272
Johann Reinhart   I, 412
Peter (Peater)   I, 628, 631, 635
ROHRBACHER
Christian   I, 492
RÖHRER   ROHRER,   RORER,
RORRER)
Anthony   I, 661, 662, 664
Fridrich   I, 365
Georg Friderich   I, 683
Heinrich (Henry)   I, 275, 276
Jacob   I, 434, 732
Jann Georg   I, 507
Johann Gott-
fried (Godfry)   I, 212, 214, 215
Johannes   I, 212, 214, 215, 448
Joseph   I, 661, 662, 664
Ludwig   I, 733
Samuel   I, 365

ROHRIG (RÖHRIG, RÖRIG, RÖR-
ICH, ROEHRIG, RÖRRICH)
Anna Margar.   II, 115
Carl   I, 717
Conrad   I, 352, 354
Hans Conradt   I, 395
Henrich Just   I, 687
Johann   II, 115
Johan Adam   I, 280, 281, 282
Johan Henrich   I, 352, 353
Johann Ernst
(John Ernst)   I, 279, 281, 282
Johannes Gorg
(John George)   I, 279, 281, 282
John Casper
(J. Caspar)   I, 672, 673, 674
Lorrentz   I, 503
Niclaus   I, 329
Philip   I, 615, 617, 619
ROHRMAN (ROHRMANN, ROER-
MAN)
Johann Conrad
(John Conrad)   I, 601, 602, 604
Johann Heinrich
(Johan Hen^k)   I, 601, 602, 603
RÖHRSCHEID
Dorothea   II, 53
ROIER (RAYER, ROIR)
Frantz   II, 122
Johann Martin   I, 88, 90, 91
ROISCH (RIESH)
Henrich Willhelm   I, 144
Johann Arnolt
(Arent)   I, 143, 145, 146
Maria   I, 144
ROISLER
George   II, 104
ROKIR
John   II, 22
ROLANDT (ROLAND)
Henrich   I, 743
John   II, 147
ROLFF
Mark   I, 749
ROLL (ROL, ROLE)
Gottlieb   I, 687
Hannes (Johannes) I, 661, 662, 664
Johannes (Joh.)   I, 305, 306; II, 61
ROLLE
Jacob   II, 124
Jeronimus   II, 124
Johannes   II, 124
RÖLLER (ROLLER, ROLER)
Christopher   II, 82
Conrad Sebastian   I, 730
Hans George
(Yerrick)   I, 526, 528, 530
Jacob   I, 438
Jacob Friederich   II, 46

Johann Daniel I, 402
Johan Michael
(Michael) I, 585, 586, 587
Johann Peter I, 487
Johan Theis I, 353, 354
Johanes I, 427
RÖM (RIEM)
Michel I, 527, 529, 530
ROMBURGER (LOMBERGER)
Nicklas (God-
fret Nicholas) I, 652, 654
ROME
Christiana II, 192
Nickolas I, 437
RÖMER (ROMER, REMER, REY-
MER, RÖMMER)
George (Georg) I, 452; II, 113
Hans Peter I, 740
Johann Fridrich
(Friederich) I, 296, 298, 299
Johann Michael
(John Michell) I, 198, 200, 202
Johan Nicklaus I, 89, 91, 92
Peter I, 487, 701
ROMICH (ROMIG, ROMMIGH)
Christian I, 399
G. Michael I, 437
Hans George I, 437
Johann Adam
(Adam) I, 96, 97, 98
Johann Fried-
rich (Frederich) I, 96, 97, 98
Johanes I, 506
ROMMEL (ROMEL, ROMMELL,
RUMMEL)
Christianus I, 761
Gottfriedt I, 420
Hans Jerick
(Johan Yerick) I, 383, 385
Vallentin (Valatine) I, 383, 385
RÖMMELE
Hieronymus I, 459
ROMSHOWER
Derrick I, 14
ROMSTEIN
Berhart I, 392
RONDE
Frunje, de II, 58
RONINGER
Hans Georg I, 430
RONNER (RONER, RUNNER)
Johann Reinhard I, 321, 322
Johanes
(Johannes) I, 586, 587, 588
ROODE
Jurien II, 77
Mielie II, 77

ROODLYS (ROATSLIE, ROAT-
SLICE)
Hans Jacob (Hans Jac.,
Hance Jacob) I, 23, 25, 26
ROODSMAN
Johannes I, 344, 345
ROOGHEL
Johannes I, 364
ROOK
Anton K. II, 122
ROON
John II, 47
ROORIG
Donius I, 406
Johanes I, 406
Simon I, 406
(*See also* ROHRIG)
ROOS (ROOSS)
Andrew Peter II, 22
Anna Maria II, 22
Charles II, 11
Conrad I, 501
Elizab. II, 11
Jnº II, 11
Johann Friderich I, 462
ROOSEN (ROSE)
Albertus I, 649, 650
Herman I, 744
ROPS
Jnº Phillip II, 6
RORBAGH *see* ROHRBACH
RORER, RORRER *see* ROHRER
RORICH, RORRICH *see* ROHRIG
RORR *see* ROHR
ROSAR
Dorothy I, 102
RÖSCH (ROSCH, RESH)
Abraham I, 360, 362
Barbara II, 173
Conradt I, 493
Georg Henrich I, 444
Hanns (Hannes,
Johannes) I, 55, 56, 57
Henrich I, 365
Jacob I, 366, 438; II, 173
Johan Georg II, 173
Johannes Georg I, 462
Michael I, 477
Peter I, 362
Regina II, 173
Thomas (Tomas) I, 227, 229, 231
RÖSCHER (ROSCHER, ROSHER)
Elizabeth Margerite I, 50
Gabriel I, 48, 52, 54
Johannes I, 703, 752
ROSDANNEN
Magdalen II, 151
Margaret II, 151
Maria II, 151

Peter II, 151
Susanna II, 151
ROSDORFF (ROSTDORFF)
J. George (John
Jost) I, 577, 578, 580
ROSE (ROSSE)
Adolph Gottfried
Carl I, 748
Frantz Arend I, 510, 512
Johann Jorg
(George) I, 643, 645
Johannes I, 539, 541, 543
William II, 138
ROSENBERGER
Erasmus I, 412
ROSENBLATT
Johan Hermann I, 506
ROSENBURG
John H. II, 47
ROSENBUSCH
Dora II, 23
ROSENKRANTZ (ROZENKRANS)
Johann Carl I, 749
John Jacob II, 3
ROSENMANN (ROSEMANN)
Johan Jacob
(Jacob) I, 179, 181, 183
ROSENMÜLLER (ROSEMILLER)
Georg Ludtwig I, 513, 514, 516
ROSENSTEEL
Johannes I, 127, 129, 130
ROSENSTELLNER
Johann II, 134
ROSENTHAL (ROSENDAL)
Fredrick II, 73, 188
Maria II, 188
RÖSER (ROSER)
Adam I, 523, 525
Friederich I, 754
Johann Kraft I, 239, 240
Mattheus
(Matheis) I, 156, 159, 161
ROSIER
Laurence I, 102
RÖSLI (RUSELEY)
Hans Conradt
(Conraat) I, 252, 253, 254
Leonhart I, 480
ROSMEISSEL
Adam I, 753
ROSPER (ROSBER)
Petter (Peter) I, 656, 657, 659
ROSS
Casper II, 123
Georg I, 411
Gerret II, 123
Hans Jacob I, 411
Johann Casber I, 521, 524
Johanes I, 414
Peter I, 502
ROSSBACH (ROSEBACH)
Johann Peter
(Peter) I, 642, 644
ROSSBURGER
Peter I, 473
RÖSSEL (ROSSEL, KREISEL, KRIE-
SEL)
Catharine I, 110
Hans George (George,
Hans Jurg) I, 605, 607, 608
Jerick I, 110
Johann Christoph I, 484
Maria Crete I, 110
ROSSELER
George II, 28
ROSSEN
Christian I, 759
ROSSINBERGEN (read ROSEN-
BERG)
C. II, 161
RÖSSLER (ROSZLER)
Conrad I, 444
Gabriel I, 455
Johann Georg I, 444
Johann Henrich I, 444
Matheis I, 439
Michael I, 526, 527, 529
ROSSMAN (RYSSMANN, RISE-
MANN)
Johanes I, 155, 159, 161
ROSSMOYER
Michel I, 699
ROSSNAGEL (ROSNAEGLE)
Michael I, 637, 639, 641
ROST (RUST)
Andreas I, 427
Balthaser (Johan
Baltzar) I, 655, 657, 658
Jacob I, 225, 228, 230
Johann Leonhart (Johan
Leonard) I, 655, 657, 658
Johann Valentin I, 474
Mathias (Matheas) I, 432, 450
RÖSTLIN (ROSTLIN, RIESLY)
Matheis (Mathais,
Mathias) I, 551, 553, 554
ROSTWEILER
Jan Peter I, 756
ROTENBERGER
Johs I, 451
ROTENBURG
Jörg I, 422
ROTENBURGER
Andreas I, 482
RÖTER
Jacob I, 435

ROTH (ROHT, RATH, ROD,
ROODT, ROOT, ROAT, ROTT)
Andreas I, 470, 473, 507
Anna Catharina I, 50; II, 92
Anna Charlotta II, 92
Anna Gertruth II, 92
Anna Margreta I, 50; II, 24
Anna Maria II, 24, 92
Anthony I, 492
Casber I, 705
Catharina I, 44; II, 128
Christian I, 508, 545, 547, 549
700, 726; II, 24
Christina I, 123
Conrad I, 423
Daniel (Daniell) I, 116, 119, 121
Elisa II, 24
Elizabeth I, 44
Friedrich I, 698
Friedrich I, 480, 725
Fritz II, 128
Greta II, 24
Hans Dirk I, 18
Hans Georg
(Earick) I, 96, 97, 98
213, 214, 216
Hans Jacob I, 50, 480
Hans Ludwig I, 476
Hans Michael I, 429
Heinrich (Henrich) I, 99, 100, 101
107, 111, 112
II, 24, 139
Herman II, 128
Jacob I, 54, 66, 69, 70, 123
414, 464, 480, 482
Joannes Josephus I, 482
Johan I, 123
Johan Adam I, 418, 444
Johan Bernhart
(Barnet) I, 216, 218, 219
Johann Christian I, 720
Johann Conrad I, 734
Johan Daniel I, 750
Johann Georg (John
Gorg) I, 19, 169, 170
172, 367, 368, 508
Johann Gottlieb II, 92
Johann Henrich Stophel I, 725
Johann Jacob I, 323, 325, 326
652, 654, 760
Johann Michael I, 258, 260, 263
Johan Philip I, 356, 476
Johannes (Johan) I, 18, 19, 48, 52
54, 198, 200, 202
341, 342, 343, 418
480, 507, 666, 668
670; II, 92
Johannes Adam I, 418

John Geo. I, 734
John Hinrich II, 128
John Jost II, 128
John Willhm II, 128
Jost Mich.
(Jeremiah) I, 227, 229, 231
Laurence I, 43, 46, 47
Louise Rodepiller II, 128
Lucy I, 23
Ludwig II, 128
Margarite (Mar-
greta) I, 44, 117; II, 24
Maria Margerita I, 49, 50
Marti (Martian) I, 348, 350, 351
Matheas I, 483
Mattheus I, 689
Michael I, 444, 487; II, 24
Nicolaas (Nic.) II, 24, 25
Paul I, 449
Peter (Pieter) I, 122, 125, 126
Philip Jacob I, 492
Rahel II, 92
Sarah II, 92
Sophia I, 123
Susanna II, 24
Theobald I, 692
Ulrich (Uldric, Uldry,
Uhllerich) I, 23, 25, 26
301, 302, 303
Vallentin I, 341, 342, 343
Wilhelm II, 178
ROTHAAR
Joh. Coenrad II, 41
ROTHACKER
Christof I, 489
Johannes I, 704
ROTHAM (RUDCAP)
Franc (Frank) I, 596, 598, 599
ROTHBAUS (ROTHBAUST)
Bernhart I, 438
Christoph I, 491
ROTHE (ROTHDE)
Godlieb I, 453
Johan Andreas I, 491
Johan August II, 97
ROTHEHEFFER (ROHTENEFFER,
RODENHAUSER)
Andreas (Andereas) I, 244, 245
Davith I, 327, 330
ROTHENBERG
Peter I, 743
ROTHENBURGER (ROTE-
BURGER)
Johannes (Johan) I, 649, 650
ROTHENHEUSER
Johannes I, 727
Philip Peter I, 727

ROTHENMILK
 John Adam   II, 113
ROTHER (RODHAR)
 Henery   I, 522, 525
ROTHERMEL (ROTDERMAN)
 Georg Michael (Yerick
   Mich[1])   I, 383, 385
ROTHHAAS
 Adam   II, 41
ROTHROCK
 A[n] Margreth   I, 157
 Johannes   I, 130, 133, 134
                        155, 158, 160
 Peter   I, 715
 Philip Jacob   I, 130, 133, 134
ROTHSMITH (ROTSMITH,
   ROTCHMICK)
 Fredrick Bals. (Frederick
   Baltzar, Fred[k]) I, 293, 294, 296
RÖTING
 Joh. Wilhelm   II, 138
ROTJEROTH
 Heinr.   II, 140
 Henrietta   II, 140
 Maria Cath. Lena   II, 140
 Maria Elisabeth   II, 140
ROTT
 Petter   I, 406
ROTTE
 Catherine A.   II, 157
 Henry   II, 157
 Johannes   II, 157
 William   II, 157
ROTTENBURGER
 Peter   I, 448
RÖTTER (ROTTER)
 Catharina   II, 52
 Johan Casber   I, 430
 Johannes
   (John)   I, 672, 673, 674, 686
 Valthin (Valantine)   I, 383, 385
ROTTMANN
 Phillipp   I, 715
ROUCHON (ROSHON, ROCHON)
 Henri
   (Hendrick)   I, 526, 527, 529
 Philippe (Philip)   I, 646, 647
 Pierre (Peter)   I, 526, 527, 529
ROULAND (ROWLAND, CROW-
   LAND)
 Casper   I, 307, 308, 309
ROULETT
 Henrich   II, 53
ROUP (ROUPE, ROWP)
 Conrad (Connar)   I, 100, 101
ROUS
 Lorentz
   (Laurentz)   I, 243, 244, 245

ROUSH
 Andreas   II, 3
ROUSHENBACHT
 Johan Bawl   I, 517
ROUST
 Jacob   I, 12
ROUWER
 M.   II, 94
ROWER
 Johannis   I, 73
 Margeretta   I, 73
ROWLAND
 Katherine   I, 15
ROWLER
 George   I, 227
ROY
 John   II, 182
ROYEN
 Soren   II, 75
ROYER
 Jerck Michel   I, 408
RÜB (RUB)
 Christian   I, 448
 Johan Christ   I, 401
 Johan Deys   I, 401
 Johanes   I, 448
 Mary   II, 12
 Sebastian   II, 12
 Stephan   I, 314, 315
RÜBEL (REBEL, REBELL, RUB-
   BEL, RUPEL, RUPPELE)
 A[n] Catharina   I, 156
 Fredrica   II, 77
 Hans (Johannes)   I, 155, 158, 160
 Jacob   II, 77
 Johan Fridrig   I, 499
 Johann Georg   I, 743
 Julius (Nicholas) I, 199, 201, 203
 Nicolaus
   (Nicklas)   I, 155, 158, 160
 Peter (Johan
   Peter)   I, 328, 621, 623, 625
 Wilhelm   I, 416
RÜBELANDT
 Johannes   I, 700
RUBELIE
 Madlena   I, 117
RUBENTHAL
 Andreas   II, 70
 Christiana   II, 70
 Johannes   II, 70
 Martha Helena   II, 70
RUBER
 Jacob   I, 391
RUBERT (RUBBERT)
 Georg Carl   I, 418
 Henry   I, 418
 Jno Casper   II, 6
 Martin   I, 433

RUBI (RUBY, RUBIE, RUPY)
Bernhart   I, 357
Casper   I, 373, 375, 376
Hans   I, 330
Peter   I, 213, 214, 216
RUBICON (RUBICHON)
Mathias   I, 102, 105, 106
RUBIN
Mr.   II, 176
RUBINS
Fred[k]   II, 185
RUBLY
Jacob   I, 346
RUBRECHT (ROEPERECH)
Henry (Hendrick)   I, 637, 638, 640
RÜBSAMEN (RIEBSOMEN, RÜB-
    SAAMEN)
Christian (John
    Christian)   I, 569, 670, 572
Frantz   I, 699
Johann Gorg   I, 493
Johan Theis (John
    Matthias)   I, 569, 571, 573
RUCHSTEIN (RICKSTEIN)
Johan Philib
    (Philip)   I, 672, 673, 674
RUCHTY
Christen (Christian) I, 162, 164, 166
RÜCK (RUCK, ROOK, ROUK,
    RUCH, RÜCKE)
Andreas   I, 460
Catharina   I, 107
Georg Friedrich   I, 727
Hans Gerg (Hans
    Jurg)   I, 106, 110, 112
Hans Jacob   I, 106, 110, 112
Johann Georg   I, 88, 90, 92
Johan Henrich
    Christoph   I, 573, 574, 575
Johann Wilhelm
    (Wilhelm)   I, 581, 583, 584
Maria Eve   I, 108
Michael   I, 108
RÜCKENBRODT
David   II, 154
RÜCKER
Peter   I, 689
RUCKERT
Christophel   II, 29
Hartman   II, 29
Magdalena   II, 29
Maria   II, 8
Martin   II, 5
Paulus   II, 8
RUCKSTUL (RÜCKSTUL, RUCK-
    STOOL, RUCKSTOLL, ROOK-
    STOOL)
Barbara   I, 151
Hyndrick   I, 151

Olive   I, 151
Solomon   I, 151, 152
Solomon, Junr
    (Sallamon)   I, 151, 152
RUDDISS
Johann   I, 312, 313
RUDE
Barbara   II, 124
Dorcas   II, 124
Dorus   II, 124
Elisabeth   II, 124
Friederick   II, 124
Fritz   II, 124
H.   II, 112
Heinrich   II, 124
Johann Jacob   II, 124
Johannes   II, 54, 124
Maria   II, 124
RUDEL
Johannes   I, 545, 547, 549
RUDELMOS
Michael   I, 415
RUDI (RUDEY)
Bastian (Basston)   I, 78, 81, 82
Hans Ernst   I, 9
Jacob   II, 187
Johan Tiderich   I, 10
Johannes   I, 720
Yoch.   I, 392
    (*See also* RUDY and RUTHI)
RÜDIGER (RÜDINGER, RUTT-
    GER)
Johannes   I, 402, 601, 602, 603
    (*See also* RÜTIGER)
RUDISIELIE (read RUDSLIELE)
Johan Jacob   I, 481
RUDOLPH (RUDOLFF)
Abraham   II, 85
Andreas (Andereas)   I, 383, 385
Ann Mary   II, 85
Anna Catharina   II, 127
Anna Elisabeth   II, 127
Anna Maria   II, 127
Caspar   II, 127
Christian   II, 85
Christoph   I, 156, 159, 161
Francis   II, 85
Hendrick   I, 331, 332, 334
J. Andreas   I, 517, 518, 519
Jacob   II, 85
Johann (Jan)   I, 222, 223, 225
Johann Adam   I, 697
Johann Lutwig   I, 340, 341, 343
Johan Thobias   I, 442
Johannes   I, 483
John Herman   I, 749
Leopold   II, 127
Maria Catharina   II, 127
Mary Ann   II, 85

Mary Catharine II, 85
Peter I, 705
RUDOLPHI
Johann Friedr II, 78
RUDRAUFF (RUHTRAUFF)
Johannes I, 576, 578, 580
RUDT
Hans Jacob I, 14
RÜDTSCHI (RICKIE)
Heinrich (Henry) I, 384, 386
RUDY (RUTHI)
Anna II, 132, 134
Durs II, 132, 133
H. II, 146
Jakob II, 132
Johannes II, 134
Martin I, 740
Nicholas I, 762
RUEB (RÜEB)
Christ I, 676
Michael (Mich1) I, 595, 597, 599
Theis I, 676
RUEGG
Catherine I, 148
RUESS
Michel I, 490
RUFF (ROOFF, ROOF)
Albrecht II, 179
Andreas I, 304
Bastian (Bertran,
Bestian) I, 596, 597, 599
Catrina I, 118
Christian I, 506
Darius I, 169, 170, 172
Elisbat I, 118
Gottlob II, 151
Hans I, 118
Jacob I, 258, 260, 263, 733
Johan Conrat I, 436
Linhart, von I, 434
Madlena I, 117
Michael I, 750
Willhelm I, 328
RUFFENER (RUFFNER)
Simon I, 335, 337, 339
RUGEN
Maria Elizth II, 23
RÜGER (REÜGER, RIEGER, RUG-
GER)
Antoni I, 175, 176, 177
Burckhart I, 175, 176, 177
Carl Ernst I, 440
Christian I, 480
Jacob I, 738
Johan Gottfried I, 440
Samuehl Heinerich
(Saml Fredrick) I, 656, 657, 659
RUGH
Melchior I, 210

RUGHTY
Hans I, 429
RÜGNER
Christian I, 329
Leonhardt Michael I, 329
RUHDE
Adam II, 148
RÜHL (REEL, RIEL, ROOL, RUHL,
RULE)
Conrad (Conradt) I, 581, 582, 584
Jerg Philb
(Yournexfiel) I, 311, 312, 313
Johann Anthon I, 759
Johann Georg I, 454
Johannes I, 324, 325, 327
Peter I, 14, 15, 256, 259, 261
—— II, 58
RUHLE (RÜHLE)
Christ. II, 139
Georg Friedrich I, 736
Johan Michael I, 462
Johann Siegmundt I, 471
RÜHM (RING)
Johann Tobias
(Tobias) I, 293, 294, 296
RUHMONT (RUCHMONT)
Verner I, 536, 537
RUHS
G. II, 142
RUIL
Michael II, 184
RUITER
Anna II, 7
Geo. Casper II, 7
Godfrey II, 7
Hans Michl I, 21
John Bartholomew II, 7
Martin II, 7
RUITZ (ROOTS)
Georg Hendk I, 139
Johann Jorg
(Georg) I, 137, 141, 142
RUKHEN
Johan Jacob I, 506
RUKUCK
Johann Fridrich I, 748
RULER
J. C. II, 67
RÜLLMANN (RÄLLMAN, RIEHL-
MAN)
Johann Georg
(Johan Geo.) I, 666, 669, 671
RULLY
Johan Henry I, 444
RULMAN (ROLLEMAN, ROLL-
MAN)
Aplon I, 118
Hans Jan I, 118

Jacob (Jacobes) I, 117, 120, 121
Maria I, 118
RÜMER (RUMER)
Johann Stephen I, 25, 26
RUMETSCH (ROMETCH)
Johann Casper I, 546, 548, 550
RUMMEL (RUMEL)
Bernard II, 14
Eva II, 3
George I, 759
Jacob I, 400, 449, 715
Jörg Fillips I, 449
Maria Magdᵃ II, 3
Michael I, 400
RUMMEN
Hans Jacob I, 483
RUMMERTH
Johan Pilip I, 697
RUMP
Johann Henrich
(Hendrich) I, 265, 268, 272
RUMPFELLT (RUMPFIELD, ROM-
FIELD, ROMFIEL)
Catrina I, 139
Catrina Margᵗ I, 139
Henrich
(Hendrick) I, 137, 141, 142
Jacob I, 137, 141, 142
RUMPPEL
Johannes I, 423
RUMPTH
Christᶠᵉʳ II, 108
Sophia II, 108
RUNCK (RUNK)
Jacob I, 199, 201, 203
John Crey II, 123
RUNCKEL (RUNKELL, RUNKEL)
George Heinrick II, 134
Jacob I, 373, 374, 375
Jermias (Jeremias) I, 379, 380, 382
Jnᵒ I, 745
Johann Jacob I, 335, 336, 338
Johann Jost
(Joost) I, 379, 380, 382
Johannes I, 330, 396
Mich. I, 750
Nicolaus I, 335, 336, 338
Philip I, 750
Wendel I, 695
RUNE
Joseph II, 122
RUNG (ROM)
George Henry
(Jurg Henry) I, 614, 616, 618
RUNKHORST
Herman II, 122
RUOFF
Johann Georg I, 456

RUOSS (RUOS, RUST)
Friderich I, 445
Hans Georg
(Hans Geo.) I, 646, 647
Hans Jacob I, 646, 647
RUPERT (RUBERT, RUPPERT)
Caspar I, 317, 318, 319
Anna Barbara I, 49
Johann Adam I, 48, 52, 54
Johann Daniel
(John Daniel) I, 577, 578, 580
Johann Martin I, 695
Johannes I, 695
Valentayn I, 89
RUPP (RUP)
Christian I, 366, 694
Jacob I, 407, 418, 741
Johannes I, 407, 615, 617, 619
Jonas I, 471
Peter I, 156, 159, 161
Weybegt I, 399
Wilhelm Henrich I, 701
RUPPEL (RUPLE, RÜPPEL)
Johann Heinrich
(Henrᵏ) I, 601, 602, 604
Johann Jakob I, 428
RUPPERTER (RUPERTER)
Jacob I, 289
Johannes (Johannis) I, 266, 269, 272
Leonhard I, 449
Philipus (Philip) I, 289, 290, 291
RURY
William P. II, 183
RUSH
Anthony I, 483
Thomas II, 104
RUSING see RUSS
RUSPAG
Johannes I, 22, 23
RUSS (RUSE, RUSSE, ROUSE, RUS-
ING)
Anthon (Antone) I, 642, 644
Carl I, 444
Clara I, 72
Johann Bernhardt
(Bernhard) I, 648, 650
Johan Frantz
(Johan Frans) I, 72, 76, 78
John I, 706
RUSSEL (RISSEL, RISSELL)
Henry Uhllerik I, 589, 590, 591
RUSSENBROD (RUSSONBROD)
George II, 151
John II, 151
Mary A. II, 151
Mary M. II, 151
Michael II, 151
RÜSSER (RISSER)
Peter I, 263, 267, 270

RUST
  Christian   I, 433
  Danniel   I, 743
  Joanes
    (Johannes)   I, 456, 551, 552, 554
RÜTELI * (ROOTELEE, ROOTE-
  LIE, RUDLER)
  Hans   I, 66, 69, 70
RUTER
  J. Christian   II, 148
  J. Ludewig   II, 148
  Louise   II, 148
RUTH (RUHT, RUT)
  Adam   I, 699
  Anna Margret   I, 766
  Christian   I, 170, 171, 173
  Georg (George,
    Jeare)   I, 293, 294, 296, 360, 362
  Hans   I, 249, 250
  Johann Christoffel
    (Christophel)   I, 257, 259, 262
  Johan Conrad   I, 496
  Johann Wilhelm   I, 513, 514, 516
  John Fridrich
    (Fred^k)   I, 373, 374, 375
  Melchior   I, 452
  Michel (Mich.,
    Micoll)   I, 113, 114, 115, 765
  Nickolas   I, 494
RUTHARDT
  Chris. Wilh.   I, 759
RUTHE
  Anna   II, 132
RUTHER
  Conrad   II, 187
RUTHI (RUTHY)
  Anna   II, 134
  Friederik   I, 473
  Hans George   I, 328
  Heinrich   II, 134
  Johannes   II, 134
RÜTIGER (REIDECKER)
  Johannes (John,
    Junr)   I, 601, 602, 604
  Matheus Andonius
    (Anthony)   I, 601, 602, 604
RUTSCHI (RUTSCHY)
  Cunrath (Conrad)   I, 147, 150, 151
  Henrich (Hendryk)   I, 149, 398
  Hs. Jacob   I, 149
  Jacob   I, 149
RUTSCHLY
  Philib   I, 9
RUTSCHMAN
  Hans   I, 306, 307
RUTSIELE
  Andres   I, 406
RUTTECHELL
  Wolfgang   I, 466

RUTTENWALDER (ROTENWA-
  TERS, ROTTENWALDER)
  J. Georg (Jno,
    Gorge, Jurg)   I, 627, 630, 633
RUTTER
  John George   I, 760
  Valentin   II, 185
RÜTTGER (RÜTTIGER)
  Michal   I, 499
  ——   I, 759
RUTTINGER (RUTINGER)
  Johann Linhart   I, 539, 541, 543
RÜTTLINGER   (RÜTLINGER,
  REIDLINGER)
  Hans Jacob   I, 332, 333, 334
RUTZ (RUTS, ROOTS)
  Bastion   I, 80
  Jacob   I, 79, 82, 83
  Johannes   I, 485
  Katharina   I, 80
RUYTER (REYTER, RYTER)
  Anna   I, 68
  Barbel   I, 68
  Caspart   I, 68
  Elizabeth   I, 68
  Henrich (Hendrick)   I, 66, 70
  Johan   I, 124
  Martin   I, 68
  Paul   I, 66, 68, 69, 70
RYDEMEYER
  Deterick   I, 718
RYER
  Elizabeth   II, 194
RYGEN
  Anna Maria   I, 43
RYMISNUS
  John George   I, 390
RYNDERS
  John   II, 193
RYNHARDT (RYNHART)
  John Chr^s.   II, 196
  Sophia   I, 104
RYNOLLE
  Daniel   I, 407
RYSLING
  Mathias   I, 15
RYSSMANN *see* ROSSMAN

SAAL
  Anna Barbara   II, 10
  Anna Marg^t   II, 10
  Geo.   II, 10
  Hans Jerg   I, 439
  Leonard   II, 10
  Maria Cath.   II, 10
  Michael   II, 10

SAALER
  Abraham   I, 155
SAALIG
  —— Frederic   II, 58
SAAM
  Johann Steffan   I, 689
SABER
  Jacob   I, 439
SABERNRICK
  Matheus   I, 476
SABLE
  Leonhart   I, 93
SABLES
  Peter   II, 53
SACHS (SACKS, SAX)
  Georg   I, 698
  Johann Heinr. Georg II, 76
  Johan Henrich
    (Henry) I, 628, 631, 635
  Johann Jacob   I, 404
SACHSE (SAXE)
  Cristina   II, 54
  Harmon   II, 91
  Johan Christian I, 509, 510, 511
  Joh. Dottler   II, 206
  Johan George I, 509, 510, 511
  Johan Friedrich I, 510, 511, 512
  Johan Henry I, 510, 511, 512
SACHSMAN
  Christian   I, 694
  Fridrich   I, 694
SACK (SCHICK)
  Johann   I, 683
  Johannes I, 531, 533, 535
  Simon   I, 532, 533, 535
SACKMAN
  Johan Heinrich   I, 505
SACKREIDER (SAKREITER)
  Johann Christian
    (Johan Martin) I, 48, 52, 54
SADELLOR *see* SATTLER
SAEFRIED
  Jacob   II, 197
SAEMANSHAUS
  P.   II, 141
SAGA
  Henry   II, 186
SAGER
  Johan   I, 401
  Patricius Abt   II, 125
SAHL
  Philip   I, 722
SAHLER (SALER, SÄHLER)
  Abraham   I, 43, 45, 46
  Johannes   I, 763
SAHM (SAM, ZAAM)
  Andreas I, 540, 542, 544
  Christian   I, 744

SAHME
  Johann Michael   I, 502
SAHN
  Chris. Wᵐ   II, 22
  J. J.   II, 141
SAHNER
  Johan   II, 28
SAILOR (read SAHLER)
  Felix   I, 407
  Gottfried   II, 117
  Sᵗ ROSIN
  ——   II, 81
SAIM *see* SEIM
SAIPELL
  Michel   I, 19
SALADE (SALLATE, SALLETE, SALATHE, SALLADI)
  Anna Barbara   II, 124
  Anna Maria   II, 124
  Elisabeth   II, 124
  Frederick   II, 124
  Friedlie   I, 472
  Hans Adam   II, 124
  Heinrich   II, 124
  Jacob   I, 416
  Johannes   I, 694
  Lorrens   II, 134
  Migel   I, 694
  Mr.   II, 177
  Nickolas   I, 497
  Peter   I, 449
  Ursula   II, 124
SALBEIN
  C. A.   II, 158
SALCON
  Peter   II, 18
SALDRET
  Samuel   I, 723
SALING
  Catrina   I, 123
  Elizabeth   I, 123
  George   I, 439
  Johan Peter I, 122, 125, 126
  Maria   I, 123
SALION
  M. C.   II, 108
SALLER (SALLEM, SALER)
  Conrad I, 341, 342, 343
  Jonnas   I, 323
SÄLLI (SALLY)
  Hans   I, 406
  Jacob   I, 391
SALOMON (SALOMOND)
  Abraham I, 257, 260, 262
  Johan   I, 441
  Johann Ernst   I, 357
SALTER
  John Junʳ   II, 27
  Joseph   I, 711

SALTSGERRER
  Andrew   I, 7
SALTZER (SALSER)
  Jacob   I, 604, 606, 607
SALTZMANN (SALTZMAN)
  Anne Marie   II, 87
  Frantz   I, 491
  Jaques   II, 88
  Johann Christ.   II, 107
  Willm   I, 460
SALVEYLER
  Christiana   II, 135
SÄMAN (SAMAN, SAMMANN)
  Johan Georg   I, 476
  Johann Hinrich
    (John Henry)   I, 589, 590, 591
SAMANT
  Frantz   I, 722
SAMHARD
  Amalia   II, 116
  Henrich   II, 116
  Louise   II, 116
  Siemon   II, 116
SAMLER (SAMMLER)
  Anthony   I, 433
  Hermann   II, 130
SAMM (SAAMM)
  Adam   I, 488
  Frederik   I, 488
  Nicolas   I, 488
SAMMET (SAMMETT, SAMMIT)
  Jacob   I, 513, 514, 516
SAMPEL
  Adam   I, 686
  Conrad   I, 454
SAMPSON
  Joseph   II, 192
SAMSEL
  Paul   I, 257, 260, 262
SAMUEL (SAMOEL)
  Benjamin   II, 139
  Meirs   II, 189
SAND
  Christian   I, 496
  John Adam   I, 709
SANDAY
  Francis   II, 96
SANDEL
  Valentin   I, 721
SANDER (SANTHER, SAUNDER)
  August   II, 88
  C. W.   II, 24
  Daniel   I, 609, 610, 612
  Gourt (Cord)   I, 509, 510, 511
  H. Jacob   I, 428
  J. F.   II, 97
  Johannes   I, 751
  Peder   I, 494

SANDERS
  Catharina   II, 91
  Joh. Basen   I, 517
  John Matthys   II, 33
SANDERSON
  George   II, 196
SANDMAN (AMBTMAN)
  Lorentz   I, 627, 631, 634
SANDMEIER
  Nicolaus   I, 762
SANDOZ
  P. F. Courvoisier   II, 138
SANDSENBACHER
  Godfrey   II, 201
SÄNGER (SANGER)
  Dorothy   II, 188
  George   II, 188
  J. Nickolaus   I, 433
  Johann Henrich   I, 506
  Johannes Friedrich I, 341, 342, 343
  Sander   I, 433
SANITTE
  ———   II, 80
SANN
  Adam   II, 110
  Barnendina   II, 110
  George   II, 110
  Hendrik   II, 110
  Jacoba   II, 110
  Johan Pieter   II, 110
  Johanna   II, 110
  Maria   II, 110
SANNER
  Georg Ludwig   I, 408
  Jacob   I, 737
SANTON
  J. Philip   I, 355
SANTZ (SANS)
  Johan   I, 411
  Johann Ludwig   I, 754
SAP
  Jowel   II, 11
SARBACH
  Davit   I, 347
  Jacob   I, 327, 329
SARIER
  Gille   I, 729
SARTON
  Herinrith   II, 91
SARTORIUS (SARDORIUS)
  John Balthaser (Bal-
    thasar)   I, 199, 201, 203
  Philipp Jacob   I, 741
SARYOUS (SAVIUS)
  Philip (Phylype)   I, 646, 647
SASSMANN
  Chrétien   II, 87
  Elisabeth   II, 87
  George   II, 87

Gertrude II, 87
Josse II, 87
Marie II, 87
SASSMANNHAUS (SASMANHAU-
SEN, SASSMANNSHAUSZ,
SASEMANSHAUSE, SASMAN-
SHAUS)
Anne Marie II, 87
Davit I, 482
Frederic II, 87
George II, 84
George Guill^me II, 87
Johann Friederich I, 753
Johann Henrich I, 754
Johann Jost I, 731
Johannes I, 367, 369
Jost I, 424
Jus^n II, 143
Mannes (Mainus,
Manus) I, 236, 238, 239
SASTRA
Corlina II, 105
SATORIUS (read SARTORIUS)
Carl II, 72
SATSON
Johan Adam I, 427
SATT
Johann I, 479
SÄTTELE (SATTLE, SETTLE,
SHETTLE)
Heinrich (Hen-
drick) I, 555, 557, 558
Samuel (Sama-
wiele I, 555, 557, 558
SATTELTHALER (STATTELDAL-
LER)
Johann Ernst I, 513, 515, 516
SATTLER (SADDLER, SADLER,
SADELLOR)
Alexr. I, 74
Catharina I, 74
Conrad (Conradt) I, 72, 76, 77
Friedrich I, 715
Henerick I, 74
Jacob I, 199, 201, 203
Johannes (Joanes) I, 74; II, 34
Katharina I, 74
Matelina I, 73
Michael I, 469
Steffen I, 410
SÄTZLER
Daniel I, 696
SAUBEL
Peter I, 727
SAUBER (SOWBER)
Jacob II, 14
Philip I, 226, 228, 230

SÄUBERLICH (SEUBERLICH, ZUY-
BERLIG
Michel I, 310, 312, 313
Ulrich I, 531, 532, 534
SAUDER
Margaretta I, 73,74
Thomas I, 71, 76, 77
SAUER (SAUR, SOUR, SOUER,
SOWER)
Adam I, 43, 46, 47
Catherina Barbara I, 131
Christofel I, 383
Cor. Gott. II, 47
Elizabeth I, 132
Hans Adam I, 627, 630, 633
Hans Michel I, 627, 630, 633
Heinrich (Henrich,
Henry) I, 130, 133, 134, 237
238, 239
Herman I, 310, 312, 313
Jno. I, 14
Johann Adam I, 539, 541, 543
Johann Dietrich I, 458
Johann Friederich I, 356
Johann Jacob I, 185, 186, 187
Johann Leonhardt I, 539, 541, 544
Johan Nickel I, 341, 342, 343
Johan Philb Henrich I, 399
Johan Phillippus I, 401
Johan Reinhard (Ryn-
hard) I, 648, 650
Johan Wilhelm I, 311, 312, 313
Johannes I, 627, 630, 633
John Peter II, 93
Maria Eleonora I, 131
Philip (Philipus) I, 676; II, 113
Wilhelm (William) I, 282, 284, 285
323, 325, 326
SAUERBIER (SOWERBIER)
Johann Georg I, 169, 171, 172
SAUERBREY
Hans Jerg I, 438
SAUERHEBER (SAUERHEBEN)
Jacob I, 697; II, 68
SAUERKAMP
Sophia II, 186
SAUERLAND
Casper II, 95
Maria II, 95
SAUERMANN
Christ. Peter I, 382
Philipphs Anton I, 382
SAUERMILCH (SOURMILG)
Ann I, 40
Catrena I, 40
Ludwig I, 40, 41, 42
Mary I, 40
Neals I, 40

SAUERWALT
Daniel   I, 367, 368
SAUERWEIN
Jacob   I, 412
SAUERZAPFF
Johannes   I, 409
SAUL (SOUL, SAULL)
Johan Adam
(Johan)   I, 539, 541, 544
Johan Lenhart   I, 540, 542, 544
Johan Nicklas   I, 539, 541, 543
SAUM
Johannes   I, 468
SAUPI
Abram   II, 31
SAUR see SAUER
SAURAIN
Abraham   I, 723
SAURE
Anna Catharine   II, 129
Anna Maria   II, 129
Elisabeth   II, 129
Henrietta Friderica   II, 129
Wilhelm   II, 129
SAUREAM
Dan   II, 80
SAUSELIN
Johann Georg   I, 502
SAUTEN
C.   II, 135
Joh. Gerh.   II, 135
SAUTER (SAUTTER, SAUTHER, SOUTER, SODER, SOWTER)
Anna Barbara   I, 131
Anna Margaretha   I, 132
Christoph   I, 649, 650
Felix   I, 371
Georg   I, 692
Hans Henry   I, 131
Hans Martin   I, 122, 125, 126
Jno Wm   I, 758
Johan   I, 234
Johann Frider   I, 445
Johann Georg   I, 546, 548, 550
Johann Filb   I, 88, 90, 92
Johannes   I, 423, 741
John   I, 758
Michel (Mich[1])   I, 250, 251, 741
Nicklaus   I, 130, 133, 134
Pedter   I, 88, 90, 92
Philip   II, 98
SAUVAGE (SAVATSH)
Johan (John)   I, 198, 200, 202
——   II, 80
SAUVAIN
Abram   II, 31
Catherine   II, 31
David   II, 31
Jean Pierre   II, 31

SAVELKOEL (SAVENKOELL, SEVENKOEL, SAVELKOWL)
Jacob   I, 47, 51, 53
Wilhelmus   I, 422
SAVOYE
J.   II, 80
——   II, 81
SAXIE
——   II, 81
SAXER
Jacob   I, 248, 249, 250
SAY
Johan Mar.   I, 349
SAYLER (SELAR)
Peter (Pitter)   I, 116, 120, 121
SAYN
Johan Wilhelm   I, 352, 354
SAYNISCH (SAEYNISH)
Joh. Henri (Joh.
Hendk)   I, 565, 566, 568
SCHAAD (SCHAADT, SHAAD)
Augustus (Agustus)   I, 609, 611, 612
Jacob   I, 67, 69, 70
(See also SCHADT)
Johann   I, 473
Johann Davidt   I, 699
SCHAAF (SHAAFF)
Carl   II, 110
Christian Friedr   II, 78
Frederick   I, 483
Henry   I, 405
Jacob   I, 483
Joh. Georg   I, 358
Johann Jacob
(Jacob)   I, 173, 174, 175
Johann Peter   I, 402, 467
Johannes   I, 687
Jonathan   II, 41
Madame   II, 78
Michel   I, 267
Philipp Jacob   I, 173, 174, 175
SCHAAK (SHAAK)
Johannes (Joannes)   I, 43, 46, 47
Joseph   I, 750
SCHAAL
Friederick   II, 192
Gottfried   II, 192
Hans George
(Jerg)   I, 486; II, 192
Jacob   II, 192
Rosina   II, 192
SCHABBERT
Filb   I, 686
SCHABEL* (SHABEL)
Cathrena   I, 103
SCHÄBELLER
Johann Reinhardt   I, 742

SCHABER (SHABER)
Johann Christoph   I, 503
Ludwig   II, 178
Sebastian   I, 585, 586, 588
SCHABERGER
Philip   I, 10
SCHACHAMAYR
Franz   II, 107
SCHACHT
Abraham   II, 196
SCHACK (SHAAK, SHACK)
Jacob   I, 421, 454
Johannes   I, 43, 46, 47
Michel   I, 421
William   I, 421
SCHACKE (SCHACKI, SCHACKEN, SHAKEY)
J. Georg   I, 155
Johan Christoffel   I, 173, 174, 175
M^{ar} Christina   I, 156
Vincentz (Vincents)   I, 155, 158, 160
SCHAD (SCHADT)
Jacob   I, 686
Johann   I, 690
Johann Andreas   I, 697
Johann Georg (Yerrick)   I, 387, 388, 389
Johanes   I, 508
Ludwig   I, 689
Peter (Peder)   I, 184, 185, 187
Philips Andres   I, 752
SCHADE
Andereas   I, 436
Ant.   II, 99
Hans Adam   I, 205, 207, 208
Johann Georg   I, 718
SCHADEL (SCHÄDEL, SCHODELL)
Joh. Carl   II, 114
Johan Georg   I, 357
Johannes   I, 609, 610, 612
Urbann   I, 576, 578, 580
SCHAEKRER
——   II, 162
SCHAFBERGER
Philip   I, 11
SCHAFF (SCHAF)
A. Marg.   II, 102
Anna Catrina   II, 102
Johann Casper   I, 435
Johann Jacob   I, 366
SCHÄFER (SCHÄFFER, SHAEFFER, SHAFER, SHEAFER, SHAFFER, SHAVER, SHAFFER, SCHEFFER)
Abraham   I, 703
Alexander   I, 213, 215
Andonny (Andon)   I, 709, 745; II, 194

Andrew (Andries)   II, 13, 112
Anlies   I, 123
Anna   I, 123
Anna Margret   I, 38
Anna Maria   I, 37; II, 24
Barbra   I, 37
Bernhart (Bernard)   I, 222, 223, 224
Carol   I, 460
Caspar (Casper, Casber)   I, 218, 219, 221
   263, 267, 270
Catharina (Catrina)   II, 13, 70, 179, 194
Charles   II, 13
Christian   I, 503, 600, 602, 603
Christian Ludwig   I, 693
Christine (Christina)   II, 151, 194
Christop   I, 394
Conradt (Conrad)   I, 469, 504, 692; II, 116
Daniel George   II, 78
David (Davit, Daviet)   I, 263, 264, 267, 270
   II, 151
Elizabeth   I, 123; II, 13, 116
Ernst   I, 401
Franz (Frans)   II, 24, 190
Friedrich (Frederick)   I, 89, 91, 92, 585, 587
   588; II, 13
Fritz   I, 404
Georg (George)   I, 577, 579, 580, 701
   II, 5
George Friederich (Fredrik)   I, 258, 260, 263
George Jacob   I, 414
George Leonh.   II, 118
Gerhardt   I, 355
Gottf^d II, 107
Hans   I, 451
Hans Adam   I, 503, 527, 528, 530
Hans Baltasar   I, 395
Hans Georg   I, 324, 325, 326, 475
Hans Jacob   I, 736
Hans Leonard   I, 37
Hans Martin   I, 605, 606, 608
Hans Michael (Hans Mich^1)   I, 237, 238, 239, 458
Hans Peter   I, 88, 90, 91
Heinrich (Henrich, Henry)   I, 37, 38, 39, 357, 421, 493
   621, 623, 625, 689, 734
   II, 36
Henry Bartholome   I, 222, 223, 225
J. Frederic   II, 156
J. Paulus (Joh. Paul)   I, 564, 566, 567
Jacob   I, 429, 430, 475, 476, 485

540, 542, 544, 693, 710
736; II, 13
Jacob Friederich I, 706
Jerich I, 24
Jnᵒ Geo. I, 752
Johan (Joh.) I, 124; II, 118
Johann Adam (Jan
Adam) I, 199, 201, 203, 256, 259
261, 661, 662, 663
Johann Baltzer (Balt-
zer) I, 324, 325, 326
378, 379, 381
Johann Georg (Johann
Jorg) I, 346, 355, 395, 457, 468
517, 718
Johann Heinrich (Johann
Henrich Heinrich) I, 540, 542
544, 569, 571, 572
672, 673, 674
Johann Herman (Joh.
Herrman) I, 222, 223, 224
II, 139
Johann Jacob (Hans
Jacob) I, 384, 386, 437, 438, 700
Johan Jost I, 401
Johann Lenhard I, 469
Johann Martin I, 430
Johann Mattheis I, 437
Johann Michael I, 493, 711
Johann Nicolaus (Johann
Nickel, Johanickel) I, 404, 414, 415
447, 726
Johan Peter (Johan
Petter) I, 373, 374, 375, 449
Johann Philipp I, 693
Johan Willem (John
Wm.) I, 564, 566, 567, 569
571, 572
Johanna II, 194
Johannes (Hannes,
John) I, 217, 219, 220, 329, 399
447, 459, 493, 503, 569
571, 572, 627, 630, 633
722, 753, 761; II, 117
Johannes Gerlach
(John) I, 569, 571, 572
Johannes Jacob I, 402
Johannes Wilhelm I, 705
Jorg (Jurg) I, 369, 370, 627
630, 634
Jorg Barthel (Jerick
B.) I, 122, 125, 126
Joseph I, 348
Jost I, 430
Katharine II, 151
Louise II, 116
Lucas I, 438
Magdalena II, 4

Margareta (Margaret) I, 124
II, 4, 151
Maria (Mary) II, 194
Martin I, 396
Maudlin I, 37
Michael (Mickell,
Mich¹) I, 37, 38, 406, 480, 509
698, 730, 736; II, 13, 112
Nicolaus (Nicklaus,
Niclaus) I, 421, 444, 517, 518,
520, 715
Paltzer I, 660
Paul (Paulus) I, 122, 124, 125, 126
222, 223, 224, 225, 483
Peter (Petter) I, 194, 195, 196
256, 259, 262, 352, 354
372, 395, 627, 630, 634
Philip I, 357, 496, 660
Philipp Friedrich
(Fredᵏ) I, 628, 631, 635
Phillips Jacob (Ja-
cob) I, 379, 380, 382
Rosina II, 13
Sabina II, 13
Severinus I, 431
Teobalt (Theo-
beld) I, 212, 214, 215
Vallentin I, 459, 546, 548 550
Wilhelm I, 706
—— II, 33
SCHÄFFLE
Johann Adam I, 691
SCHAFFNER (SCHAFNER, SCHÄF-
NER, SHAFNER, SCHAF-
FENER)
Anna II, 185
Casper II, 145
Georg Heinrich I, 513, 514, 516
Hans Jacob I, 610, 611, 613
Hans Rudi I, 417
Henry I, 392
Jacob I, 417, 431; II, 134
Johan Caspar (Cas-
per) I, 107, 111, 112
Johan Jacob I, 722
Johannes I, 95, 96
M. II, 199
Martin (Martyn) I, 17, 266, 270
273, 685
SCHAFFSTEIN (SHAFFSTALL)
Johanes (Johannes) I, 643, 645
SCHAIBLEN
Jacob I, 497
SCHAILLY (SHALLY)
Christian I, 347
Hans Adam I, 347
Johann Ludwig I, 347
Johannes I, 347

SCHALCK (SCHALK, SHALT)
Johan Thobald (Johans
Tebald) I, 194, 196, 197
SCHALKE
Hinrich Gerhard II, 22
SCHALL (SHALL)
Andereas I, 493
Martin I, 486
Nickolas I, 493
Tobias I, 373, 374, 375
Vitus I, 314
SCHÄLLENBERG
Hans I, 473
SCHALLENMILLER
J. G. II, 193
SCHALLER (SHALLER)
Catharina II, 52
Georg I, 513, 514, 516
Hans Peter I, 382
Johann Albrecht (Al-
bert) I, 173, 174
Johann Georg (John
George) I, 173, 174
Johannes (Joanis) I, 225, 228, 230
Simon I, 20, 21
Valentin (Valatine) I, 225, 228, 230
SCHALLIN (SHALLE)
Carl I, 263, 267, 270
Fredᵏ I, 649
SCHALLUS (SHALLES)
Bastian I, 422
Vallendin I, 422
SCHALTER (SHALTER)
Frantz Baltzer
(Frans) I, 615, 617, 620
Johan Alfred I, 411
SCHALTZER (SCHALTSER, SELT-
ZER)
Balser (Baltzar) I, 643, 645
Charles II, 93
SCHAM
Martin II, 118
SCHAMBACH * (SHAMBACH,
SHAMBACK)
Adam I, 24
Anna Dorothy I, 24
Eliza. I, 24
George I, 397
SCHAMBACHER
Catharine II, 165
George II, 165
Jacob II, 165
Johannas II, 165
John George II, 165
Margaret II, 165
SCHAMBERGER * (SHAMBER-
GER)
Henrich (Henrᵏ) I, 175, 177, 178

SCHANCK (SHANCK, SHANK)
Dewalt (Dieble) I, 317, 318, 319
Wendel I, 706
SCHANCKWEILER
Jacob I, 701
Johann Adam I, 757
SCHANDE
Nicklaus I, 450
SCHANG
Johan Petter I, 474
SCHÄNIKE (SHANECK, SHIN-
GELL)
Christian I, 660
Johan Henrich (Hen-
drick) I, 212, 214, 216
SCHÄNKEL
Martin I, 469
SCHANNO
Philipp I, 724
SCHANTZ (SCHANS, SHANTZ)
Abraham I, 698
Barbara I, 190
Carol I, 421
Catrina I, 190
Christian I, 190
Davit I, 423
Elizabetha I, 190
Ferona I, 190
Hans I, 188, 191, 193, 263
264, 267, 270
Jacob I, 185, 186, 187, 188
191, 193, 421, 691
Johan I, 730
Johan Adam I, 540, 542, 544
Johannes I, 194, 195, 196
Magdalena I, 190
SCHÄPHLER
Friderich I, 447
SCHÄPPELER (SCHÖPPELER,
SHIBLER)
Johann Conrad (Joh.
Conrad) I, 613, 616, 618
SCHAPPERT (SCHABERT, SCHAP-
PERDT, SHAPPERT, SHA-
BERT)
Albrecht I, 677, 678, 680
Johan Nickel (Nich-
olas) I, 304, 305, 306
Nicolaus I, 686
SCHARCAUM
John II, 32
SCHARFER
A. Margretha II, 32
Angnita II, 32
Anna Mad. II, 32
Anna Susana II, 32
SCHARFF (SCHARF, SCHERFF)
Conrath (Conrad) I, 78, 81, 82
Henrich I, 367, 369

Jacob I, 358
Johan Christophell I, 430
Johannes I, 367, 369
SCHARFFENBERGER (SCHAR-
FENBERGER)
Nicolaus I, 335, 336, 338
SCHARFFNAT
Martin II, 50
SCHARLLE
Christoff I, 594
SCHARMANN
Carl I, 412
Joh. Daniel I, 469
SCHARP (SHARP, SHARPE)
Ernst I, 217, 218, 220
George (Jnº
Georick) I, 217, 218, 219, 220
Isaac I, 217, 219, 220
Louise II, 36
Pieter II, 110
SCHÄRRER
Michel I, 82, 83
SCHÄRTHLE
Johanes I, 490
SCHÄRTHLEIN (SCHERTLIN)
Johann Michael I, 538, 540, 543
SCHASTLER
George II, 193
SCHÄTTEL
Gorg I, 712
Michel I, 712
SCHATTO (CHATEAU)
Johann Nicklaus (Jan
Nichol) I, 266, 269, 272
SCHATZ (SHATS, SHÄTZ)
David I, 344, 345
Hans Michael I, 498
Henrich I, 372
Johann II, 28
Johann Atam
(Hans) I, 540, 542, 544
John Michael I, 542, 544
Wilhelm I, 425
SCHATZIG
Johan Fredᵏ II, 30
SCHÄTZLEIN
Barthel I, 503
SCHATZMAN * (SHATSMAN,
SHEATSMAN)
Hans Adam
(Adam) I, 555, 557, 558
SCHAU (SHAW)
Hans George I, 434
Joseph I, 321
William II, 117
SCHAUB (SCHAUP, SHAUB,
SHAUP, SCAUB, SHOUB,
SHOUP)
Adam I, 352; II, 133

Andreas I, 84, 86
Anna (Anne) II, 133, 147
Barbara II, 133, 146, 147
Cathⁿ II, 146
Christopher (Chris-
toffel) I, 179, 181, 183
Daniel I, 684
David II, 146
Elisabeth II, 146
Hans (Hanns) I, 433; II, 146
Hans Beter I, 453
Hans Jacob I, 252, 254, 255
II, 133
Hans Jerick I, 8
Hans Ulrich I, 352
Heinz II, 146
Henrich (Henry,
Henery) I, 720, 732
II, 145, 146
Jacob I, 175, 176, 177, 473
740; II, 146
Jan Hendᵏ I, 7
Johann II, 190
Johann Andreas II, 205
Johan Henrich I, 691
Marie (Maria) I, 210; II, 146
Martin I, 18, 19, 433
II, 31, 133, 146
Mathias I, 67, 69, 70
Mr. II, 176
Nicolaus II, 204
Rudolph I, 486
Sebastian (Bosche) I, 275, 276
Susan II, 204
Tidrick (Dietrich) I, 210
Widow II, 146
SCHAUBERGEN
John II, 55
SCHAUBERT
Mr. Charles II, 55
SCHÄUBLIN
Heinrich I, 740
SCHAUCH
Johannes I, 365
SCHAUER (SHAWER)
Adam II, 13
Catarina II, 13
Christoph David I, 486
Elizabeth II, 13
Jacob I, 466; II, 13
John II, 13
Petter I, 697
Philipp I, 486
Rosina II, 13
Susanna II, 13
SCHAUFBERK (SCHAUFBENK,
SHOUFFBON)
Jacob I, 560, 561, 563

SCHAUFELE (SCHÄUFFELE)
Georg Friderich II, 134
Jacob I, 344, 345
SCHAUFLER (SCHAUFFLER)
Hs. Georg I, 447
Jacob I, 750
SCHAUG (SHALK)
Martin (Mathew) I, 275, 276
SCHAUL
Joh. Conrᵈ II, 129
SCHAULLING
Adam I, 416
SCHAUM
Johannes I, 759
SCHAUMAN (SHAUMAN, SHOO-MAN)
Johan (Hans) I, 89, 91, 92, 455
SCHAUMENKESSEL
Fridrich I, 760
SCHAUN (SHOUN)
Johannes I, 297, 298, 300
SCHAURER
Johanes I, 436
SCHAUSS (SCHAUS, SHOUS)
Johann Adam I, 156, 159, 161
Johan Jorg
(Jurig) I, 257, 259, 262
SCHAUWECKER
Hans Cunrad I, 393
Martin I, 393
SCHAZEL
John Peter II, 69
SCHAZENHUBER
Vincent II, 159
SCHE
Johan Henrich I, 734
SCHECHTER
Andreas I, 521, 524
SCHECK (SCHEK)
Caspar I, 213, 215
Michael (Michel) I, 666, 668, 670
SCHECKLER
Philipp I, 722
SCHEDEL (SHEDEL)
Johan Jacob II, 136
Simon I, 194, 196, 197
SCHEDLER
Anna Barbra I, 189
Henrich I, 628, 632, 635
Simon I, 628, 632, 635
SCHEEL (SHEEL, SHIELD)
A. II, 73
Daniel II, 182
Jacob I, 439
Johan Nicklas I, 266, 271, 272
Nicolaus (Nicholas) I, 266, 269, 272
II, 115
SCHEELMANN
Johan Georg I, 456

SCHEER (SCHEAR, SHEER, SHAR, SHERR)
Elizabeth I, 55
Hartmann II, 52
J. Diterich I, 536, 537, 538
Jacob I, 373, 374, 376
Johan Jacob
(Jacob) I, 323, 324, 326
Matelin I, 80
SCHEERTEL (SHERTLE, SHIRTLE)
Bernhard I, 84, 86, 87
SCHEERMESSER
Uhllerich I, 498
SCHEFFER (SCHEFER)
Bernhardt (Bernhard) I, 643, 644
Christ. Peter I, 279
Conrad I, 722
Daniel I, 727
Hans I, 451
Hans Gorg (Hans
Jurg) I, 677, 679, 680
Henrich (Henry) I, 357, 702
Johan Conrad I, 432
Johan Peter I, 495
Jost I, 676
Ludwig I, 702
SCHEFFERS
Henrich II, 53
SCHEFFLER
Johannes I, 367, 368
Mart. E. Gottfᵈ II, 107
Wilhelm (Wilhm) I, 178, 180, 182
SCHEFFNER
Anne II, 31
Catherine II, 31
Jean II, 31
SCHEHLMAN
Lutwig I, 707
SCHEIB (SHEIB)
Andereas I, 286, 287, 288
Anna Catharine I, 107
Anna Maria I, 107
Catharina I, 109
Christian I, 461
Fallendin (Fellting) I, 84, 86, 87
Hans Jacob I, 109
Hans Jerick I, 109
Johann Adam I, 310, 311, 312
Johannes I, 730
Martin I, 106, 110, 112
SCHEIBE
Jacob II, 121
Johann Christoph I, 741
Johann Jacob
(Jacob) I, 39, 41, 42
SCHEIBLE (SCHLBLEY)
Jacob I, 462
Michael I, 526, 528, 529

SCHEIBLING
Andreas   I, 489
SCHEIBLY (SHEWBLY)
Bartholomäus (Barthol-
ome)   I, 383, 385
SCHEID * (SHYD)
Conrad   I, 423
Georg   I, 423
Georg Henry   I, 423
SCHEIDE (SHEIDE)
E.   II, 142
Peter   I, 697
SCHEIDEL
Johann Erhart   I, 723
SCHEIDLER (SCHEIDELER,
SCHEYDELER)
Eve   II, 162
Johann Jerg (J.
Gorg)   I, 156, 159, 161
John   II, 162
———   II, 162
SCHEIDT (SCHIED)
Christian   I, 656, 657, 659
Johann Christigann   I, 684
Johann Conrad   I, 761
Johann Henrich   I, 425
Johanes   I, 462
Mattheus (Mathias)   I, 591, 592, 594
SCHEIER (SHEYER, SHIRE)
Hans   I, 369, 370
Jacob   I, 468
Johann Klaus (Johannis
Nicklaus)   I, 283, 284, 286
SCHEIFFELE
Matthias   I, 422
Michael (Michel)   I, 237, 238, 239
SCHEIFFLEN
Hans Gerch   I, 419
SCHEIMER (SCHYMER)
Andon   I, 403
Anna   I, 74
Daniel   I, 402
Fritrich   I, 402
Johann Conrad (Con-
radt)   I, 71, 75, 77
Johannes   I, 403
Maria   I, 73
Michell   I, 402
SCHEIN * (SHINE)
Jacob   II, 126
SCHEINER (SHRYDER)
Mathes (Mathias)   I, 596, 598, 599
SCHEIP * (SHEIPPEN)
John Conrad   I, 712
SCHEIRER
Hans Henrich   I, 756
Johannis   I, 494
SCHELBERGER (SHILABERGER)
Johan Simon (Simon)   I, 652, 654

SCHELCKHLE
Joseph Antony   I, 480
SCHELEREN
Martin   I, 16
SCHELES
Gosse   II, 58
SCHELFER
G. L.   II, 125
SCHELIGS
Johan   II, 136
SCHELL (SHELL, SCHEL)
A. Diterich   I, 504
Carl   I, 461
Henrich   I, 694
Jacob   I, 717
Johann Caspar   I, 330
Johann Heinrich   I, 690
Joh. Jacob   II, 41
Johann Peter   I, 695
Johannes   I, 495, 729
Lutwig   I, 694
Philips Jacob (Phillip)
    I, 256, 259, 262
Reichart   I, 720
SCHELLENBERG (SHELBERG,
SHELLBERG SHELLEBERG
SHELLEBECHER)
Abraham   I, 290, 291
Hans Jergh   I, 12, 14
Heinrich   I, 252, 253, 255
J. Jacob   I, 501
Jacob   I, 147, 150, 151
Ulrick   I, 12, 14
SCHELLENBERGER (SCHELLEN-
BURGER, SHELLENBERGER)
Georg   I, 62
Johannes   I, 685
Magdlina   I, 62
Maria   I, 61
Martin   I, 147, 150, 151
Peter (Petter)   I, 60, 64, 65
Ursula   I, 148
SCHELLER (SHELLER)
Frederik Albrecht   I, 505
Johann George Friderich   I, 734
Johan Rudolph   I, 198, 200, 202
SCHELLERD
Johann Jurgen   II, 49
John Valentine   II, 49
Martha Eliz[b]   II, 49
SCHELLING (SHELLING)
Georg Baltzer   I, 506
John Jacob   I, 508
Julian   I, 73
Michael   I, 489
SCHELLMAN (SHELLMAN, SHILL-
MAN)
Christian   I, 693
Johannes   I, 344, 345

SCHELVIECK
Anna II, 122
SCHENCK (SHANK, SHENK)
Andreas I, 88, 90, 92
Anna I, 209
Christian I, 210
Christof
(Christopher) I, 551, 553, 554
Friederich (Fredᵏ) I, 595, 597, 599
Geo. I, 478, 749
Hans Georg
(Hans Jorg) I, 246, 247, 248, 328
586, 587, 588
Hans Jacob I, 246, 247, 248
Henrich I, 485
Jacob I, 328
Jacob Fridrich
(Jacob) I, 586, 587, 588
Joh. Jacob
(Jacob) I, 532, 534, 535
Michel
(Michael) I, 12, 14, 637, 638, 640
Samuell I, 758, 759
SCHENCKEL (SCHENKEL, SHEN-
KELL)
Anna Catharina II, 52
Anna Elisabeth II, 52
Cleovea I, 147
Friderich I, 450
Hans Georg I, 429
Henrich I, 497
Jacob I, 146, 149, 150
Johan I, 236
Johann Philipp I, 734
Johannes (Johan) I, 43, 46, 47
Lorentz I, 442
Ludwig I, 752; II, 52
Philipps I, 497
Philipps Carl I, 496
SCHENCKEN (read prob.
SCHENCK)
Johannes I, 490
SCHENEFELT (read SCHÖNE-
FELD)
Johanes I, 20
SCHENELL (read prob. SCHNELL)
John II, 17
SCHENHOLTS (read SCHÖN-
HOLTZ)
Henry I, 16
SCHENSEMA
Annatje II, 70
SCHEP * (SHEP)
George I, 441
SCHEPFLING
Johan I, 702
SCHEPFNIT
Conrad I, 468

SCHEPHELER (read SCHEFFELER)
Augustin I, 447
SCHEPPACH
Johann Jacob I, 708
SCHEPPLEIN
William II, 198
SCHER
J. Jo. Henrig I, 487
Johann Georg I, 722
SCHERDLE (SHERTLY)
Anna Barbara I, 209
Anna Maria I, 209
Melcher (Melchior) I, 209, 211
SCHERDRONG
Abraham I, 405
SCHEREN
Ulrich I, 16
SCHERER (SCHEERER, SHERER,
SCHERRER, SCHERE, SHARER)
Adam I, 417
Bernhart I, 403
Conradt I, 622, 624, 626, 687
Feliep I, 754
Geo. I, 689, 691
Georg Jacob I, 691
Georg Michael I, 711
Hans I, 79, 82, 83
Hans Caspar I, 434
Heinrich Adam I, 461
Henrich I, 372, 643, 645
Jacob (Jan Jacob,
Johan) I, 14, 78, 81, 82, 102,
105, 106, 378, 379
381, 476, 741
Jacob Bart I, 694
Jacob Daniel I, 487
Johan Augustus
(Johannes) I, 31, 33, 34
Joh. Christoffel I, 727
Johan Conradt
(Conrad) I, 576, 578, 579
Johan Georg I, 257, 260, 262
Johan Mattes (Johan
Matthias) I, 234, 235, 236
Johan Nickel (Johan
Nicholas) I, 234, 258, 260, 263
Johann Vallentin I, 156, 159, 161
Johannes I, 421; II, 4
Justice I, 31
Lienhart I, 398
Lorens I, 403
Magdelin I, 80
Mich. II, 179
Nicolaus (Nicklaus,
Niclas) I, 179, 181, 183, 694
Rufinus I, 372
Samuel I, 59, 63, 64
Rudolph I, 434
Ulrich (Ulrick) I, 31, 32, 34

Vallentin   I, 371, 402
Veronica   I, 60
SCHERFFIG
Casper   I, 458
SCHERGER
Andreas   II, 8
Barbara   II, 8
Cath.   II, 8
Kilian   II, 8
Magdalene   II, 8
SCHERGH (SCHERKH, SHERGH)
Dafid   I, 365
Uhllerich   I, 484
SCHERR
Ulrich   I, 485
SCHERRATZ (SCHERATZ, SCHER-
HARTZ)
Arnholt (Arnoltz)   I, 622, 624, 626
SCHERT
Eberhart Christoph   I, 486
SCHERTEL (SHERTEL, SHERTLE)
Johan Jacob
(Jacob)   I, 283, 284, 286
Johanes   I, 412
SCHERTHLEN
Jerg Friedrich   I, 490
SCHERTLEIN
M. Jacob Friderich   I, 489
SCHERTZ
Johann Henrich   I, 327, 329
SCHERTZER (SCHERZER, SHART-
ZER)
Caspar   I, 359
Filipp (Philip)   I, 596, 598, 600
Hans Jacob
(Jacob)   I, 237, 238, 239
Stephan   I, 454
SCHETERLY
Jacob   I, 452
SCHETTLER * (SHETLER, SHIT-
TLER, SCHITTLER)
Andreas   I, 60, 64, 65
Margretha   I, 61
Maria   I, 62
SCHETZEL
Adam   II, 52
SCHEUBER
Louise Frederike   II, 67
SCHEUBLEIN (SCHIBLIEN, SHEY-
BLY, SHEIBLY)
Christian
(Christen)   I, 162, 164, 166
Jacob   I, 417
SCHEÜBLY
Daniel   I, 416
SCHEUCHZER
Hendri (Hendryk)   I, 147, 150, 151
SCHEUER
Otto   I, 475

SCHEUERMAN (SCHEUERMANN,
SCHEURMAN, SHEWERMAN,
SHIREMAN)
Johann Georg   I, 722, 737
Johann Petter
(Peter)   I, 622, 624, 626
Martin   I, 472
Mathias   I, 730
Nicholas   I, 736
SCHEUFELEN (SCHEUFFLEN)
Gerg   I, 445
Jacob   I, 445
SCHEUFLER
Jacob   I, 393
SCHEURBERGER
Johan George   I, 437
SCHEURER (SCHEIR)
Hans   I, 434
Hans Georg   I, 335, 337, 338
Johan Henrich   I, 335, 337, 338
SCHEURICH
Hans Marthin   I, 508
Jacob   I, 507
Johann Matthes   I, 507
Valentin   I, 507
SCHEURMEYER
Hs. Jacob   I, 331
SCHEUSSLER
Michael   I, 721
SCHEWETZER
F.   II, 142
SCHEYDECKER * (SHEYDECKER,
SHYDEAKER)
David   II, 104
Felten (Feltich)   I, 104, 105
Hans   II, 104
Ulrich   II, 104
SCHEY
Nickelaus   I, 468
SCHEYER
Jacob   I, 353, 354
Nicolaus (Nicklaus)   I, 179, 181, 183
SCHEYFLE
Joseph   I, 482
SCHEYHING
Johann David   I, 360, 361
SCHEYVER
Fredrik   II, 50
SCHIAURER
Johann Peter   I, 752
SCHIBB
Jacob   I, 697
SCHIBELEY
Jacob   I, 737
SCHIBLE
Frederich   II, 168
SCHIBLI (SCHEWBLY, SHEEBLY,
SHIBLY)
Casper   I, 384, 386

Henry (Hendrich) I, 253, 254, 255
Johannes I, 252, 254, 255
SCHICK
Christian I, 512, 514, 515
Erhardt I, 513, 514, 515
Johann Adam I, 459
Joh. Fred. II, 119
Johann Jullus I, 402
Johannes I, 360, 361
Ludwig I, 513, 514, 515
Peter I, 700
Veltin I, 307, 308, 309
SCHICKEL (SHICKEL)
Johann Michael I, 646, 647
SCHIDENHELM (SHITTERHELM)
Adam I, 266, 269, 273
SCHIEBE
Christian II, 59
SCHIEBEL (SHIEBEL)
Friedrich
(Johan Fred^k) I, 646, 647
SCHIEBELHUTH
George II, 54
SCHIEBERLE
Christian Gottlieb I, 476
SCHIEBERSTEIN
Johannes I, 743
SCHIEDÖRFER
Hans Georg I, 743
SCHIEDT
Hans Jacob I, 410
Johann Balthasar I, 401
Johann Henrich I, 402
SCHIEF * (SHEAF, SHEEFF)
Johan Peter
(Johannes Peter) I, 352, 353
SCHIEFER
Arnold I, 676
SCHIEFERDECKER (SHIEFFER-
DECKER, SHIFFERDECKER)
Hans Gerg I, 693
Jacob I, 648, 650
SCHIFFERT * (SHIPHERD)
Tobias II, 18
SCHIEFFLER (SHEFFLER, SCHEF-
LER)
Henrich I, 180, 182, 184
Joh. II, 3
SCHIEFT
Madthes I, 472
SCHIEKENDANTZ
Philip Hend^k II, 30
SCHIELE (SHIEL)
A. D. II, 141
Henry Christ^n I, 688
Johann Wilhelm I, 517, 518, 520
SCHIELIN
Martin Matthias I, 459

SCHIERBAUM
Engelbrecht II, 123
SCHIERCHER
Simon I, 444
SCHIERG (SHIRK)
Hans Martin I, 653, 654
SCHIERMAN * (SHIERMAN)
Gorg Jacob I, 422
SCHIERWAGEN (SHEERWAGEN)
Godtfried
(Gottfriedt) I, 143, 145, 146
SCHIESSLE (SCHIESLE)
Johanns
(Johannes) I, 604, 606, 607
SCHIETTINGER (SHITTINGER)
Hanns Jerg (George,
Hans Jorg) I, 638, 639, 641
SCHIEVER
George II, 55
SCHIFF (SHIFF)
George I, 707
Hans I, 451
Senf Mois. II, 135
SCHIFFELD
Joh. II, 119
SCHIFFELIN
Andreas II, 192
George II, 192
Johannes II, 192
Margareth II, 192
SCHIFFER (SHIFFERER, SCHIF-
FERER)
Johann Adam I, 688
Johann Jacob I, 689
Johannes I, 339
Philip I, 688
SCHIKER
Jerg I, 471
SCHILACK
Albertus I, 748
Johann Wilhelm I, 762
SCHILD (SHILLD)
Christina II, 52
George I, 480
P. S. II, 76
SCHILDBACH
Carl Enoch I, 749
SCHILDENRAD (SCHILDENN-
RAD)
Johannes I, 333, 334
SCHILDKNECHT (SCHILT-
KNECHT, SHILKNECHT)
Jacob I, 243, 244, 245
Willhelm I, 721
SCHILL
Carl I, 366
Hans Gerg I, 729
SCHILLER (SHILLER)
Johann Christian I, 415

Johann Ludwig Ernst I, 609, 610, 612
Martin I, 660
SCHILLGER
Johann Jerg I, 489
SCHILLING (SHILLIN)
Anna II, 95
Fillip Joseph I, 446
Hans Adam I, 99, 101
Hein. II, 71
Jan II, 95
Johann Martin
(Johannes) I, 71, 75, 77
Johanna II, 95
Johannes I, 424, 470, 592, 593, 595
Margarite I, 43
Michael (Michel) I, 760; II, 183
Peter I, 14, 15
Philip I, 99, 100, 101
SCHILLINGER
Elizabeth II, 164
Johan George II, 164
Johannas II, 164
Maria Barbara II, 164
Martin I, 490
SCHILPP
Joseph I, 532, 534
SCHILTWÄCHTER
Gerg I, 710
SCHIMMEL (SCHIMEL, SHIMEL)
Beter I, 759
Jerch I, 513, 514, 516
Johannes I, 217, 218, 220
SCHIMPER
Philip II, 46
SCHIMPF
Fridrich (Fredᵏ) I, 614, 616, 618
Johann Jacob
(Jacob) I, 614, 616, 618
Johannes I, 394
Melchior I, 614, 616, 618
SCHINCKEL
Eliz. II, 5
Jacob II, 29
SCHINCKH
Hans Jerg I, 477
SCHINDEL (SCHINTEL)
Johann Peter I, 468
Michgel (Michˡ) I, 677, 678, 680
SCHINDELDEKER (SCHENDEL-
DEKER, SHINDELDECKER)
John. Jacob I, 178, 180, 185
SCHINDLER
Andreas
(John George) I, 671, 673, 674
Conradt I, 506

SCHINDTELMAN (SCHENTEL-
MAN, SCHINDTELMANN,
SCHINDELMANN)
Johann Philip I, 627, 631, 634
Nicolaus (Nichˢ) I, 627, 631, 634
SCHING
Balte I, 683
SCHIPP (read prob. SCHÖPP)
John Frederick I, 310, 311, 313
SCHIPPER
Niclaas II, 122
SCHIPPERT * (SHIPERT)
Christo. I, 349
SCHIRAB
Johann Peter II, 20
SCHIRARDIN
Paulus I, 522, 524
SCHIRCH
Casper (Kasper) I, 57, 58
SCHIREN
Johannes I, 712
SCHIRM
Johann Foglin I, 495
Johann Henrich I, 454
SCHIRMAN (SHEARMAN, SHER-
MAN)
Jorg (Jurigh) I, 113, 114, 115
Simon I, 113, 114, 115, 765
SCHIRMER
Anna II, 52
Conrad II, 52
Georg Jacob I, 474
John II, 52
Peter I, 441
SCHISER
Joh. Jac. II, 118
SCHISLER (SCHISSLER, SCHLIS-
LOR, SHEESLER)
George (Georg) I, 178, 180, 183
J. Peter I, 464
Johan Adam
(Jan Adam) I, 217, 218, 220, 494
Johann Georg I, 330
John I, 691
SCHIT
Jonna Peter II, 36
SCHITTENHELM (SHITTEN-
HELM, SCHATTENHELM)
Friderich I, 711
Jacob I, 711
Johannis I, 688
Martin I, 551, 552, 553
Michael I, 551, 552, 553
SCHIUMAN (read prob. SCHUMAN)
Peter I, 676
SCHLACHENHAUFF
Martin I, 399

SCHLÄCHTER * (SCHLACHTER, SHLEGHTER)
Christian
(Christiane)   I, 163, 165, 166
Henry   I, 492
Jacob   I, 531, 533, 535
SCHLAG
Anne Marg.   II, 106
Anne Savine   II, 106
Barthel   II, 115
Georg Friedrich   II, 115
Henry   II, 106
Johannes   II, 115
Mariane   II, 115
Mich[1]   II, 106
SCHLAGBAUER * (SHLAGBOUER)
Hans Georg   I, 429
SCHLAGEL
Erhard   I, 711
SCHLANG
Gottfried   I, 722
SCHLAPPIG (SCHLAPIG, SHLAPPY)
Adam   I, 300, 301, 302
Johan Daniel
(Danniel)   I, 577, 579, 580
Johann Jost
(John Jost)   I, 577, 579, 581
SCHLARBST
Johann Peter   I, 414
SCHLARP
Johan Simon   I, 763
SCHLATTER (SCHLATER)
Hans Casper   I, 483
Jacob   I, 754
Johanes   I, 461
Martin   I, 451
SCHLATTERER (SLATTERER)
Georg Wilhelm   I, 585, 586, 588
Johannes   I, 418
SCHLAUCH (SHLOWCH, SHLAUGH, SLOUGH)
Andreas   I, 96, 98
Bender   II, 56
Christian   I, 741
Hans Jacob   I, 22, 23
Hans Michel   I, 366
J. Michael
(Mich[1])   I, 661, 662, 664
Johann Philip   I, 96, 98
John   II, 56
John William   II, 56
SCHLAYER
Michael   I, 487
SCHLEBER
Johan Ludwig   I, 439
SCHLEEWEISS (LEWEYS)
Gottlib   I, 348, 350, 351

SCHLEGEL (SHLEGEL)
Christoph   I, 475
Ernst (Johanes)   I, 217, 219, 220
George Adam   I, 475
Johannes
(Johanis, Hans)   I, 185, 186, 187
378, 379, 380, 381
SCHLEICH (SHLEIG)
Jacob   I, 221, 222, 224, 445
Johann Christoph[r] Gottlieb   II, 134
Johann Henrich   I, 501
Johannes   I, 462
SCHLEICHER (SHLIGER, SLYGER)
Johan (John)   I, 185, 186, 187
Johann Georg   I, 731
John Philip   I, 722
SCHLEICHERD
F.   II, 73
SCHLEIDER
Gustav Friederich   I, 432
Hironymus   I, 432
SCHLEIFF
Friederich   I, 747
Johan Jacob   I, 307, 309, 310
SCHLEIFFER (SCHLEYPFER, SLIFFER, SHLEIFFER)
Heinrich   I, 332, 333, 334
Johannes (Johanis)   I, 213, 214, 216
273, 274
SCHLEISING
Law[s]   II, 51
SCHLEISS
Jacob   II, 189
SCHLEMB
Geo.   I, 694
Johann Fridrich   I, 715
Johan Peter
(Peter)   I, 638, 639, 641
SCHLEMILCH
Willhelm   I, 730
SCHLEMMER (SHLEMER SLEMER)
Christian   I, 536, 537, 538
Conrad   I, 649, 650
SCHLENCKER (SCHLENCKHER, SHLENCKER, SCHLENKER)
Andreas   I, 475
Christoffel   I, 536, 537, 538
Frantz Henry   I, 536, 538
Friedrich Wilhelm   I, 536, 537, 538
Hans   I, 410
Hendrick   I, 537
John Wm.   I, 536
SCHLENGELUF (SCHLENGEUFF, SLIGLOFF)
Analis   I, 23
Anna Christian   I, 23
Henrich (Hendrick)   I, 23, 25, 26

SCHLEPPI (SHLEPPY)
Albrecht I, 469
Hans Ulrich I, 440
SCHLER
Johannes I, 167, 168
SCHLESSMANN
Hans Christoph I, 501
Johan Heinrich I, 502
SCHLETZER
Hans Jacob I, 470
Johannes I, 737
SCHLEUCHER (SLIGER)
Heinrich (Henrick) I, 217, 219, 220
SCHLEY * (SHLEY)
H. Georg ┌ I, 487
SCHLEYGER
Nicholas II, 55
SCHLETZ * (SHLETZ)
J. Christopher I, 505
SCHLICHT
Gen. II, 47
SCHLICHTER (SHLIGHTER)
Gallus I, 471
Godlieb I, 743
Henrich I, 359
Johan I, 755
Nicklaus I, 442
Thomas I, 442
SCHLICHTEWEG
Joh. Gottlieb II, 129
SCHLICHTING
Cristian II, 57
SCHLICK
Jacob I, 686
SCHLIEGEL
John II, 196
Nich II, 196
SCHLIEPER
Biniamin II, 101
SCHLIGTER (SLIGHTER)
Johannes I, 221, 222, 224
SCHLIMMER
Carl II, 107
SCHLITZ * (SHLITZ)
Johan Jost I, 662, 663, 664
SCHLÖCHER (SLIGER)
Georg Caspar
(Georick) I, 216, 218, 219
Hans Otto I, 216, 218, 219
Johan Gorg I, 216, 218, 220
Johann Jost I, 216, 218, 219
SCHLOCKMANN
Christopher I, 748
SCHLÖGEL * (SHLOGEL)
Johann I, 357
SCHLÖR
Michael I, 408

SCHLORSER (read prob. SCHLOS-
SER)
Johannes II, 135
SCHLOSSER (SCHLOSSER, SHLOS-
SER, SCHLOSER, SLOSSER)
Gorg I, 415
Gustavus I, 697
Hans Thomas
(H. Thomas) I, 652, 654
Jacob II, 8
Johann Jacob I, 371
Joseph I, 716
Leonhard I, 96, 97, 98
Peter I, 96, 98, 461
SCHLOSSMAN
Johann Niclaus I, 503
SCHLOTER * (SHLODER)
Henry I, 459
SCHLOTERBECK
Hans Gorg I, 470
SCHLOTKE
Joh. Hen. II, 107
SCHLOTSMAN
John Henry II, 93
SCHLOTT (SCHLOT)
Johan Adam I, 759
Johan Michal I, 717
Johannes I, 444
SCHLOTTER (SLOTTERS)
Jacob I, 614, 616, 618
SCHLOTTERER
Jacob I, 393
Johann Conradt I, 394
Martin I, 393
Mathies I, 394
SCHLOTZ (SLOLTZ)
Johannes I, 605, 607, 608
SCHLOTZER (SCHLESSER)
J. Jacob (Jacob) I, 666, 669, 671
Johann Jacob
(Jacob) I, 666, 669, 671
SCHLOUGH
John H. II, 55
SCHLÜCKER
Lutwig I, 464
SCHLUHEIS
Johannes I, 724
SCHLUHTER (read SCHLÜTER)
Nich[1] I, 690
SCHLUMBER
Christian I, 719
SCHLUPP
Johann Conrad I, 716
SCHLÜTER (SCHLIETER SHLÜ-
TER)
Johann I, 504
Johan Jacob I, 234
Lorentz I, 509, 510, 511

SCHLÜTT
Karll I, 724
SCHLUTZ
Johannes I, 467
Philip Henry I, 467
SCHMÄCK (SMICK)
Johann Philips
(John Philip) I, 387, 388, 389
SCHMADTAHN
Carl Hend^k II, 44
SCHMAHL (SCHMAL, SHMALL, SHMELL)
Adam I, 335, 336, 337 338, 339
Johan Adam
(Adam) I, 296, 298, 299
Johan Nick. I, 502
John II, 199
John Adam I, 266, 269, 272
Lorentz I, 335, 337, 338
Nicholas (Nicklas) I, 266, 269, 272
Wentz I, 336, 337, 339
SCHMALTZ (SHMALTZ)
Johan Gorg
(George) I, 297, 298, 299
Johann Henrich I, 733
Johan Michaell I, 412
SCHMALTZHAFT (SMALLSHAFFT, SHMALTZHAFT)
Ludwig I, 327, 329
SCHMALTZRIDT
Georg I, 761
SCHMAUS (SMOUS, SHMAUS)
Conrad I, 564, 566, 567
Henrich
(Joh. Hand^k) I, 564, 566, 567
Johann Nickel I, 753
Johannes I, 564, 565, 567
SCHMEH (SMEE)
Johannes (John) I, 615, 616, 620
SCHMEL
Adam I, 751
SCHMELGER
Johann Gottfried I, 470
SCHMELSEN
Johan II, 50
SCHMELTZER (SCHMELZER, SHMELTZER, SMELZER)
Andereas I, 455
Anna Maria II, 134
Catharine II, 44
Christian II, 44
Conrad II, 43
Johann Adam I, 433
Johan Phillib
(Philip) I, 222, 223, 225
Johannes I, 89, 91, 92
Maretia II, 44
Margaret II, 43

Regina II, 44
Valltin I, 43
Wendal I, 419
SCHMELTZLE
Friederich I, 498
SCHMERBER
Johannes I, 400
SCHMERHAM
Christopher II, 196
SCHMETZER (WOLFSMETSER)
Hans Wolf I, 552, 553, 554
Johann Peter I, 457
SCHMEULL
Joseph I, 726
SCHMICK
Georg Ernst I, 412
Johann Caspar I, 412
SCHMIDER
Joseph II, 160
SCHMIDT (SCHMID, SCHMIT, SCHMITT, SCHMITH, SMITH, SHMIT, SCMIEDT, SCHMIED)
Adam I, 369, 370, 376 377, 628, 632 635, 683, 686 II, 115
Agnes I, 109, 117
Andreas (Andereas, Anderas) I, 179, 181, 183 283, 284, 286 340, 342, 343 627, 630, 634 725
Anna I, 43, 44, 103, 117 II, 110
Anna Catharina
(Anne Cath.) II, 117, 129
Anna Christina I, 144
Anna Christjana II, 184
Anna Elis^h II, 128, 159
A^n Margreth I, 156
Anna Maria I, 109; II, 28
Anna Maria Elisa II, 129
Anna Ursula I, 107
Anthony
(Anthonyus) I, 40, 605, 606, 608 II, 117, 159
August H. II, 75
Balser (Baltzer) I, 419, 676 II, 34
Barbara (Barb.) I, 148, 149
Bastian I, 8
Benedich I, 707
Bernhard
(Bernart, Barent) I, 221, 223, 224 409, 559, 561 562, 750 II, 129, 184

Carl (Carle
  Charles)   I, 461, 503, 690
Carl Friederich   II, 22
Carl Ludwig   II, 78
Casper (Caspar)   I, 432, 442
Catharina (Catherine)   I, 108
     II, 87, 110, 129
     137, 149, 159
Cath^a Corn^a
  (Cornalia)   II, 23, 105
Charles   I, 369, 370, 739
     II, 18, 117
Charles Frederich   II, 160
Child   II, 23
Christian (Christ)   I, 43, 45, 46, 234
     235, 236, 382
     403, 427, 467
     472, 492, 517
     527, 528, 530
     739, 743
Christ. Gottl.   II, 138
Christ. Jacobus   I, 737
Christoph
  (Christoffel, Christopher,
    Stophel)   I, 266, 269, 273,
     445, 490, 561
     701, 728
     II, 53
Christoph Fruht   I, 328
Christoph Philip   I, 649
Conrad (Conradt)   I, 198, 200, 202
     283, 284, 285
     468, 536, 537
     538, 642, 644
     II, 184
Daniel   I, 500, 628, 631, 635
     II, 184
David   I, 330, 427, 522, 524
Dirk   I, 18
Dorothea (Dorothy)   I, 766
     II, 129, 203
Eberhart   I, 522, 524
Elizabeth (Elisabethe)   I, 123
     II, 47, 105
     117, 149
Eliz^a Magdelen   I, 144
Ernst   I, 712
F. C.   II, 71
Felix   I, 149
Ferdinand   II, 98
Frank   II, 50
Frann   I, 754
Fransiscus (Frans,
  Francis)   I, 564, 566, 567, 751
     II, 3, 195
Frantz   I, 506
Friederich
  (Frederick)   I, 179, 181, 183, 234
     331, 498, 676

Friederich Gottfried   I, 401
G. L.   II, 186
G. M.   II, 33
Georg
  (George)   I, 20, 409, 420, 595, 597
     599, 701
     II, 88, 117, 151
Geo. Fred^k   II, 179
Georg Heinrich
  (Jeorg Henrich)   I, 465, 693
George M.   II, 153
Georg Michael   I, 88, 90, 92
     506, 692
George T.   II, 188
Georg Wilhelm   I, 693
Gertruy   I, 104
Godfrey   II, 94
Gottfried Lebrecht   I, 735
Guillaumette   II, 87
Hans (Hannes)   I, 432, 752
Hanns Adam
  (Adam)   I, 438, 652, 654
Hans Frederick
  (H. Friederich)   I, 652, 654
Hans Georg (Hans Jerig,
  Hance Errick)   I, 66, 69, 70, 93
     200, 202, 204
     465, 499, 700
Hans Michael (Hans
  Michäll)   I, 12, 499, 507, 636
     637, 638, 639
     640, 641
Hans Nicholas (Hans Nickel,
  Johan Nicklas)   I, 162, 164, 166
     293, 295, 296
     364
Hans Peder   I, 421
Hans Philip   I, 237
Heinrich (Henrich,
  Henry)   I, 15, 18, 116, 119, 121
     122, 125, 126
     179, 181, 183
     332, 333, 334
     403, 413, 434
     449, 581, 582
     583, 584, 649
     II, 36
Henry Joseph   II, 88
Hinz (Heinz)   II, 61
J.   II, 130, 142
J. A.   II, 32
J. Christian
  (Christian)   I, 577, 579, 580
J. Conrad
  (John Conrad)   I, 577, 579, 581
J. Henry   I, 467
J. Martin   II, 159
J. Reinh^d   II, 178
J^a Judith   I, 156

Jacob I, 14, 147, 150, 151
263, 267, 270
313, 314, 315
347, 373, 374
376, 406, 432
450, 491, 546
547, 549, 661
662, 664, 722
730, 742, 752
II, 110, 149, 203
Jacobina II, 152
James (Janes) I, 118; II, 152
Jan II, 108
Jaques II, 87
Jeremis
(Jerome, James) I, 175, 176, 178
Jnº Dieterich I, 700
Jnº Nichs I, 716
Johann (Johan) I, 746
II, 110, 205
Johan Adam I, 401, 466, 559
560, 562, 564
566, 567, 749
Johann Andreas
(Joh. Andr.) I, 693, 747
II, 107
Johann Balthasar
(John Baltzer) I, 401, 435, 609
610, 612
Johann Carl I, 692
Johann Caspar
(Jan Casper) I, 31, 32, 34
167, 168
Johann Christian (Joh.
Christ., Christian) I, 279, 280, 281
467, 577, 579
581, 643, 645
II, 110
Johann Christophel I, 690
Johann Conrad
(Konrath) I, 292, 609, 610
612, 643, 644
Johann Daniel I, 340
Johan David I, 440
Johann Dieterich
(Dedrich) I, 367, 368
II, 48
Johan Donis
(Joh. Dennis) I, 353, 354
Johann Georg I, 43, 46, 47, 88
90, 91, 286, 287
288, 357, 373
374, 375, 601
602, 604, 683
690
Johann Henrich (Joh. Heinch,
Johan Hendrick) I, 31, 32, 33, 43
46, 167, 168
217, 218, 220

310, 312, 313
581, 583, 584
629, 632, 635
643, 645, 646
665, 668, 670
II, 129, 139
Johan Jacob
(Joh. Jacob) I, 330, 366, 368
463, 585, 586
588, 693, 762
Johann Jost I, 18, 20, 560
561, 563
Johan Mathias
(Mathias) I, 527, 528, 530
Johann Michael I, 102, 493, 734
Johann Nicklaus
(Johan Nickel) I, 55, 56, 57, 105
289, 290, 291
462, 474
Johan Peter
(Joh. Peter) I, 72, 76, 78, 143
145, 146, 217
218, 220, 479
494, 503, 582
583, 584, 589
590, 591, 688
722, 752
II, 102
Johann Philippus
(Philip, Filib) I, 113, 114, 115
371, 459, 766
Johann Theis
(Matthias) I, 436, 569, 571, 572
Johann Thomas I, 412
Johann Wilhelm I, 402
Johann Yorg
(John George) I, 555, 556, 558
Johanna (Johanne) II, 117, 152
Johannes (John) I, 48, 52, 54, 72, 76
78, 210, 217
218, 220, 283
284, 357, 384
385, 402, 421
423, 431, 435
463, 464, 472
485, 490, 499
501, 523, 525
532, 534, 535
621, 623, 625
628, 632, 635
642, 644, 676
687, 704, 710
719, 721, 731
738, 739, 741
II, 53, 110, 129
159, 184, 189
Johannes Bartolome (Johannes
Bartelmi) I, 609, 610, 612

Johannes Fillipus
(Philip)   I, 428, 568, 570, 571
Johannes Henrich   I, 401
Johannes Laurenzius   I, 468
Johannes S.   II, 135
John Christ   II, 129
John Conrad   I, 577, 579, 581
John F.   II, 152
John George (John,
Johan Jurgen)   I, 600, 602, 603
                        642, 644
John Henry   II, 159
John Wᵐ   II, 160
Joseph (Jos.)   I, 400, 559, 561, 563
                        649, 650, 710
Josse   II, 87
Jost   I, 143, 145, 146
Jost Henrich   I, 686
Juliana   II, 23
Justine   II, 87
Justus   I, 732
Katarina
(Katherina)   I, 44, 49
Kilian (Gillian)   I, 106, 111, 112
L.   I, 741
Leonhard (Yer-
rick Leonard)   I, 652, 653, 754
Lorentz   I, 471, 717
Lucia Elizᵗʰ   II, 23
Ludwig (Ludewig)   I, 444, 488, 527
                        536, 537, 538
                   II, 129, 148, 159
Ludwig, von der   I, 432
M. E.   II, 147
Magdalena   II, 110
Margaret (Margarite)   I, 43, 123
Maria (Marie)   I, 103, 210
                   II, 58, 87, 110, 117
Maria Catharina   II, 184
Maria Crete   I, 108
Maria Magdalena   II, 120
Marie Elisabeth   II, 87
Martinus (Mardin,
Martin)   I, 279, 280, 281
                        322, 432, 605
                        606, 607, 707
Marx (Marks)   I, 226, 228, 230
Mary   I, 40
Matheus Friederich   II, 171
Matthes (Mattheis,
Mathias)   I, 88, 90, 91, 195
                        196, 197, 283
                        284, 285
Medestus   II, 119
Melchior (Merchior)   I, 221, 223,
                        224, 722
Michael (Michel,
Michˡ)   I, 13, 106, 110, 112
                        423, 445, 463

                        489, 667, 669
                        671, 686, 729
Mr.   II, 109, 176
Mrs.   II, 23
Nickolaus (Nicklas,
Nickel)   I, 449, 460, 692, 734
                        II, 54
Paulus (Paul)   I, 480; II, 47
Peter (Petter,
Pieter)   I, 43, 45, 46, 102
                        104, 105, 122
                        125, 126, 314
                        315, 387, 388
                        389, 431, 440
                        450, 591, 593
                        594, 705, 730
                   II, 110, 126, 149
                        173, 204
Philip (Philipus,
Fillib)   I, 72, 76, 78, 179
                        181, 183, 209
                        211, 218, 219
                        221, 357, 391
                        430, 568, 570
                        571, 676, 686
                        700, 715, 767
                        II, 47, 149
Philip Jacob
(Filb Jacob)   I, 413, 414
Philipp Wilhelm   I, 744
Regina   II, 152
Reinhard (Reinhart) I, 643, 644
Rosina   I, 45
Rudolph   I, 331, 333, 334
Sarah   II, 108
Sebastian   I, 677, 678, 680
Simon   I, 394, 493
Theobald (Teobalt) I, 217, 219, 220
                        II, 44
Thommas   I, 462
Ulrich (Uhllerich,
Ulrick)   I, 252, 253, 255
                        II, 133
Valentin   I, 341, 342, 343, 487
Walter   I, 402
Wilhelm (Wilm,
Willem)   I, 282, 284, 285, 359
                        361, 676, 737
                        II, 99

SCHMIDTEKNECHT
Johann Michel   I, 405
SCHMIEG (SMICK)
Johann Andreas   I, 513, 515, 516
Johann Simon   I, 512, 514, 515
SCHMIERER (SMIERER)
Johannes   I, 678, 679, 680
SCHMIET (read prob. SCHMIDT)
Joachim   I, 482

SCHMIG
  Henrickes   I, 402
SCHMING
  Abram   I, 706
SCHMITGEN
  Johann Adam   I, 401
  Johan Martin   I, 401
SCHMITLEY * (SHMITLEY)
  Lunzy   I, 450
SCHMITTER
  A. M.   II, 144
SCHMITZER
  Dietherich   I, 485
SCHMOCH
  Joh. Christ.   II, 139
  Maria Dorothea   II, 140
SCHMÖLL (SCHMÖHL)
  Johan Diel   I, 456
  Johannes   I, 446
  Michael (Mich.)   I, 256, 258, 261
SCHMOLLER
  Christian   I, 446
SCHMOLTZ
  George   II, 123
  Johann Daniel   I, 719
  Johann Georg   I, 481
SCHMOYER * (SHMEYER)
  Michael   I, 419
SCHMUCK   (SHMUCK,
  SCHMUKE)
  Hans Jacob
    (Johan)   I, 234, 235, 236
  Johann Peter   I, 437
  Johannes   I, 459
  Peter (Pitter)   I, 116, 120, 121, 735
SCHMUCKER (SMUCKER)
  Appilunia   II, 4
  Christen   I, 485
  Ferdinand   II, 3
  Hend^k   II, 4
  Hend^k Jacob   II, 4
  Joh. Ch.   II, 3
  Johanes Jerg   I, 391
  Peter   II, 5
SCHMUCKHEYDE (SMUKHYD)
  Johann Christoph   I, 308, 309, 310
SCHMÜHL
  Dewalt   I, 403
SCHMUKE *see* SCHMUCK
SCHMUTZ (SMUTZ)
  Abraham   I, 327, 329; II, 30
  Jn°   II, 11
  Johannes   II, 54
SCHMYER (SMEYER, SMYER)
  Elizabeth   I, 123
  Johan   I, 123
  Maira   I, 123
  Philip   I, 122, 125, 126

SCHNABEL (SHNABEL, SCHNAB-
  BEL)
  Andereas
    (Andreas)   I, 586, 587, 588
  Johann Conrad   I, 723
  Johann Görg   I, 415
  Jo. Henrich   I, 723
  Johannes   I, 710
  Martin   I, 723
SCHNÄBELE (SHNABELY, SHNA-
  BLE, SNEVELEY, SNEVELY,
  SNEPPELEY, SNEPPELY)
  Hans Adam   I, 482
  Henry   I, 16
  Jacob   I, 16, 17, 55, 56, 57
    398, 609, 611, 612
  (*See also* SCHNEBELI)
SCHNALL
  Johannes   I, 382
SCHNAP
  Johanna   II, 136
SCHNARRENBERGER (SCHNUR-
  RENBERGER, SNARENBER-
  GER)
  Johannes   I, 596, 597, 599
SCHNATTERLY (SNATHERLY)
  Hans Michel (Hance
    Michael)   I, 100, 101
  Jerg Filib (Filp, Jar-
    rick Phillip)   I, 100, 101
SCHNATZ * (SNATZ)
  Sebastian   II, 148
SCHNAUBER
  Johannes (Joh.)   I, 179, 180, 183
  Wilh.   II, 196
SCHNAUFFER
  Hans Georg   I, 446
  Hans Michael   I, 462
SCHNEARLEY
  John   II, 185
SCHNEBELI (SCHNEBLI, SNA-
  BLEY, SNEABLEY, SNEABELI)
  Anna Barbra   I, 118
  Anna Katrina   I, 118
  Barbra   I, 117
  Casper   I, 332, 333, 334
  Elisbat   I, 117
  Hans (Hanes)   I, 116, 118, 119, 121
  Henrich   I, 17
  Isac   I, 396
  Jacob   I, 364
  Kasper   I, 118
  Katrina   I, 118
  Linnhart   I, 332, 333, 334
  Rudolff   I, 117, 120, 121
SCHNEBERGER
  Hans   I, 473
SCHNECK (SCHNEKH, SNECK)
  Albert   I, 470

Andoni   I, 399
B. G.   II, 51
Georg   I, 426
Hans Georg   I, 704
Jacob   I, 317, 704
Johan Philibus   I, 463
Michal (Michael)   I, 652, 653
SCHNECKENBURGER (SHNEKEN-
    BURGER)
Christian   I, 495
Frantz Fidelis   I, 742
SCHNEDER
Jacob   II, 145
SCHNEE * (SCHNE, SCHNEH,
    SHNEE)
Johan   I, 540
Johannes   I, 346
Jost Schümblin   I, 417
SCHNEEBERG (SNIBER)
Johann Erich
    (John)   I, 573, 574, 575
SCHNEEGANTZ
Johann Georg   I, 758
SCHNEERING (SHNEERING)
George   I, 360, 362
SCHNEFUHES (read SCHNEE-
    FUSS)
Adam   I, 435
SCHNEIBLY
Hans   I, 398
SCHNEIDER (SCHNEDER,
    SCHNEYDER, SCHNYDER,
    SNEIDER, SNYDER, SCHNEI-
    TER, SCHNIDER, SCHNITER)
Abraham (Abia)   I, 376, 377, 437
                                II, 102
Adam   I, 289, 290, 291, 418, 751
Adolph Carl   I, 693
Andreas (Andres,
    Andrew)   I, 282, 284, 285
                                577, 579, 580, 702
                                735; II, 47
Anna   II, 146
Anna Catharina   II, 120, 148
Anna Elisabeth   II, 128
Anna M.   II, 159
Anna Margaretha   II, 128
Anna Maria   II, 97
Anthon (Andon)   I, 316, 317
                                339, 356, 446
Arnold (Arnoldus)   I, 276, 277
                                278; II, 102
Balthas   I, 423
Baltzer (Palzer)   I, 627, 631, 634
Barbara   I, 43
Bastian (Jno.
    Bastian)   I, 569, 571, 573
Bernhardt (Bernard)   I, 471, 551
                                553, 554, 695

Borchart (Burgart,
    Burchard)   I, 622, 624, 626
C. G.   II, 138
Charles   II, 166
Carl (Charles)   I, 307, 308, 309
Casper (Caspar   I, 355, 360, 362
Catherina Elis.   I, 157
Catherine   II, 88, 120, 128
Chrétien   II, 88
Chrétienne   II, 88
Christian (Christ) I, 8, 27, 29, 30, 72
                                73, 76, 78, 366, 420
                                471, 480, 676, 708
                                II, 54, 166, 171
Christianna   II, 166
Christine   II, 88
Christoffel
    (Christoph)   I, 209, 211, 425
Clara   II, 28
Conradt (Conrad)   I, 72, 76, 78, 282
                                284, 285, 473
                                478, 493, 615
                                617, 619, 718
Daniel   I, 204, 206, 208, 221, 222
            224, 277, 278, 279, 443
David   I 693; II, 41
Dewald   I, 414
Elisabeth   I, 62, 190; II, 88, 120
Elisabeth Marie   II, 88
Felix (Phalick)   I, 555, 556, 557
Frederica   II, 53
Frena   II, 146
Friederich (Fred-
    erick)   I, 444, 620, 622
                        625; II, 15, 47
Georg (George)   I, 256, 259, 261
                        321, 322, 480, 496
                        II, 88, 162
Georg David   I, 442
George Jacob   I, 487
George Wilhelm   I, 666, 668, 670
Gerdruth   II, 128
Gottlieb   II, 122
Guillaume   II, 88
Guillaumette   II, 88
Hans   I, 197, 198, 507
Hans Georg (Hans
    Gorg, Jorg)   I, 275, 276, 317
                        319, 322, 359, 451
                        477, 677, 679, 680
Hans Henry   I, 473
Hans Jacob (Hanes
    Jac.)   I, 263, 267, 270
                        301, 302, 303
                        II, 146
Hans Jost   I, 301, 302, 303
Hans Peter   I, 301, 302, 303
Hartmann   I, 716

Heinrich (Henrich,
  Henry)   I, 363, 392, 463, 621, 623
                625, 666, 669, 671, 699
Hermanus   I, 408
Hieart   I, 277
Hieronimus   I, 484, 577, 579, 580
J. Simon   I, 508
Jacob   I, 16, 27, 30, 318, 319
                362, 405, 424, 445, 452
                585, 587, 588, 626, 628
                630, 631, 633, 634, 716
                738, 751; II, 102, 128
                                   159
Jacob Friedrich   I, 507
Jaques   II, 88
Jean   II, 88
Jean Henry   II, 88
Jean Josse   II, 88
Johann (Johan,
  Hans)   I, 212, 214, 216
                488; II, 120, 166
Johann Adam (Hans
  Adam)   I, 169, 171, 172, 204
                206, 207, 221, 222
                224, 256, 259, 261
                277, 278, 279, 280
                281, 387, 388, 389
                                706
Johann Benedick   I, 709
Johann Bernharth   I, 366, 368
Johann Casper   I, 307, 308, 309, 715
Johann
  Christian   I, 517, 518, 520, 675
Johann Conrad
  (Conrad)   I, 577, 578, 580
                615, 617, 619, 734
Johann Daniel
  (Daniel)   I, 378, 380, 381
Johann Deis   I, 400
Johann
  Friedrich I, 212, 214, 216, 280, 281
Johan Georg
  (Georg, Jorg)   I, 179, 181
                183, 283, 284, 285, 424
                490, 577, 578, 579, 580
                581, 649, 650, 706, 756
Johann Gerhard
  (Johann Gerhart)   I, 278, 400, 675
Johann Henrich
  (Henry)   I, 234, 235, 236
                435, 589, 590, 621
                623, 625; II, 120
Johann Jacob   I, 424, 469
Johann Jost (J. Jost)   I, 297, 298
                300, 735; II, 120
Johann Mahtheis
  (Joh. Matthais)   I, 564, 565
                567; II, 120
Johan Michel   I, 418

Johann Nicolaus
  (Nicholas)   I, 212, 214
                216, 414, 701
Johann Peter (Petter)   I, 222, 223
                225, 280, 281, 282
                400, 433, 675, 743
Johan Phillipp
  (Phillips)   I, 266, 269, 272, 496
                564, 566, 567, 707
Johan Ralph   I, 282
Johann Valtin   I, 701
Johann Wendel (Hans
  Wendel)   I, 642, 644
Johann Wilhelm   I, 493, 661
                662, 663, 737
Johannes   I, 12, 155, 158, 161
                217, 218, 220, 256, 258
                261, 301, 302, 303, 355
                403, 411, 435, 442, 448
                462, 506, 564, 565, 567
                577, 579, 581, 628, 631
                634, 684, 688, 716, 727
                737; II, 36, 120, 128
Johannes Henrich   I, 684
Johannes Peter   I, 684, 735, 743
Johannes Philip   I, 576, 578, 580
John   I, 701; II, 138
John Fredrick   I, 280; II, 166
John Georg   I, 404
John Gotlieb   II, 166
John Henry   I, 369, 370
John Nicklas   I, 482
John P.   II, 158
Josse   II, 87
Jost (Johs.)   I, 297, 298, 300, 430
Jost Henrich   I, 723
Jurgen   II, 128, 148
Justine   II, 88
K. Luise   II, 148
Kathrina   I, 62
Krafft   II, 87
Kreiman (Crymon)   I, 280, 281, 282
Louis (Lewis)   II, 15, 88
Louise   II, 88, 128
Ludwig   I, 735, 736; II, 120, 158
Ludwig Konrad   I, 486
M.   II, 44
Magdelin   I, 28
Margarethe
  (Margreta   II, 88, 102, 121
Maria (Marie)   II, 88, 146, 181
Marie Elisabeth   II, 87, 121
Martin (Marte)   I, 227, 392, 425
                546, 548, 550
                551, 554, 642
                644, 687
                II, 29, 104
Marx   I, 741
Mathias (Mattdes)   I, 27, 29, 30

Michael (Michel,
  Michal)   I, 414, 453, 455
               551, 553, 554
Nicholas
  (Nicolaus)   II, 124, 146, 159
Paul   I, 355
Peter (Petter)   I, 60, 64, 65, 493
              494, 706, 735
               II, 158
Philip (Philipus)   I, 294, 295, 296
Philip Peter   I, 743
Susanah   I, 28
Theis (Tys)   I, 280, 281, 282
Thomas (Tho⁸)   I, 204, 206, 207
             280, 281, 282
Vallentin
  (Valentine)   I, 43, 46, 47, 107
             111, 113, 283
             284, 285
Weigand   I, 400
Wilhelm   I, 490, 666, 668, 670
Wyant   I, 675
———   II, 159
  (See also SCHNEYDER)
SCHNEIDMAN
Sebastian   I, 417
SCHNEISS (SCHNEIS, SNUS)
Conrath (Conorod) I, 289, 290, 291
SCHNEITER *see* SCHNEIDER
SCHNELL (SCHNEL, SNELL)
Abraham   I, 461
Anna Elizabeth   II, 120
Anna Sophia   II, 116
Catharine   II, 43
Frantz   I, 724
Hans Jerg   I, 463
Hans Mary   II, 43
Jacob   I, 417, 731
             II, 43
Johan Adam
  (Jan Adam)   I, 212, 214, 215
Johan Georg   I, 461, 711
Joh. Henry   II, 43
Johann Jost   II, 120
Johan Leonhardt   I, 321, 322
Johan Miller   I, 433
Johan Nickel   I, 339
Johann Philipp I, 339; II, 120
Johann Theis   I, 743
Johannes   I, 701, 736
Johst   II, 116
Lewis   II, 116
Mrs.   II, 116
Sebastian   I, 463
Sophia   II, 43
SCHNELLBACHER
Adam   II, 9
Anna Margaret   II, 9
Barbara   II, 9

Christina   II, 9
Geo.   II, 9
Jost Phillipp   I, 501
Maria Eliz.   II, 9
Philip   II, 9
SCHNELLE
Andreas   I, 425
SCHNELLENBERGER (SHNELLEN-
  BERGER)
Hans   I, 662, 664
Johann Adam
  (Adam)   I, 637, 638, 640
SCHNEPP (SNAP, SHNAP)
Barbara   I, 108, 109
Hans Jerg   I, 709
Johann Georg   I, 729
Johann Martin   I, 479
Johannes (Johanes) I, 107, 109,
               111, 112
Lorentz (Lawrence) I, 107, 109, 111,
               112
Mathes   I, 445
SCHNEPPER (SNIPER, SNEPER)
Andreas   I, 539, 541, 543
Catharine   II, 165
Hans Adam
  (Hanns)   I, 540, 542, 544
SCHNERR (SCHNER, SNER)
Hans Michel
  (John Mich¹)   I, 649, 650
Jacob   I, 649, 651
SCHNERTZEL (SNIRTZEL, SNERT-
  ZEL)
Henry (Henrich) I, 256, 259, 261
SCHNERTZINGER
Michel   II, 53
SCHNEYDER   (SHNEYDER,
  SCHNYDER, SHNYDER)
Adam   I, 436
Andereas   I, 434
Casper   I, 473
Georg   I, 496
Jacob   I, 348, 696, 731
Johann Adam   I, 706
Johann Christ   I, 402
Johann Georg
  (Joh. Jörg)   I, 435, 711
Johann Jost   I, 735
Johann Wilhelm   I, 438
Johannes Peter   I, 400
Niclaus   I, 405
Wilhelm   I, 755
Wolfgang   II, 184
  (See also SCHNEIDER)
SCHNEYDERS
Samuel   I, 411
SCHNEYNOW
Andrew   I, 759

SCHNIELL
Johann II, 92
SCHNIEVLY
Leon^d II, 186
SCHNIRINGER
Lorentz I, 469
SCHNITTER
Frantz II, 118
SCHNITZ
Joh. George II, 41
SCHNITZEL (SHNITZEL)
Christian II, 118
J. Jacob I, 428
Joh. II, 118
SCHNITZER (SHNITZER)
Friederich I, 431
Hans Georg I, 366
Johannes I, 425
SCHNOLLER
Niclaus I, 711
SCHNORR (SNER)
Johann Casper I, 539, 541, 544
Wendel I, 395
SCHNORSS (SHNORS)
Joh. Jacob I, 686
Johannes I, 686
SCHNOUDY
Jacob I, 462
SCHNÜBLI
Johannes I, 433
SCHNUG (SCHNUCK, SHNOOK,
    SHNOG, SCHNUK)
Friedrich
    (Friederich) I, 577, 578, 580
Johan Adam I, 352, 353
Johan Dhies (Johan
    Theis, John Tys) I, 279, 280, 281
Margaritha II, 45
Maria Magdalina II, 45
Simon I, 750
SCHNUR (SHNURR)
J. Henry I, 522, 524
Peter I, 661, 663, 664
SCHNURENBERGER (SCHNUR-
    RENBERGER, SCHNURRNBER-
    GER, SCHNURNBERGER, SNUR-
    ENBERGER)
Jacob I, 604, 606, 607
Johannes I, 604, 606, 607
SCHNURER
Jacob Christoph II, 79
SCHNÜRINGER
Johannes I, 469
SCHOBER (SHOBART, SHOBER,
    SHOVER)
Andreas I, 652, 654
Carl II, 198
Christian I, 555, 556, 558
Elisabeth II, 198

Georg Adam I, 531, 532, 534
Jacob I, 168, 170, 172
Johann Simon I, 474
Johannes
    (Johanes) I, 621, 623, 625
John Fred^k II, 118
Leonard II, 198
Maria II, 198
Peter II, 198
Samuel I, 698
Simon Friederich I, 691
SCHOBIG (SCHOPER)
John Georg I, 500
Vallentin I, 532, 533, 535
SCHOCH
Anthony I, 718
Georg Christoph I, 343, 345
Hans Jacob I, 454
Jacob I, 441
Samuel I, 741
Sam. Fried. II, 41
SCHOCK (SCHÖCKH, SCHAUCK,
    SHACK, SHOCK)
Baltzer I, 688
Casper I, 545, 547, 549
Jacob I, 347
Johann Adam I, 546, 548, 550
Johann Jacob
    (Jacob) I, 677, 678, 680
Johan Peter I, 478
Johannes I, 447
Michael I, 410
Peter I, 478
SCHOEFFER
Simon II, 191
SCHOELER
Herrmanus I, 750
SCHOENLEBER
Friederich I, 684
SCHÖFF (SCHOFF, SHOFF)
Friedrich I, 683
Jacob I, 621, 624, 626
Rudolph I, 486
SCHÖFFER (SCHEFFER, SCHAF-
    FER)
Andreas I, 458, 655, 657, 658
Geo. (Jerog) I, 662, 663, 664
Johann Jacob
    (Jacobus) I, 655, 657, 658
SCHOFFLER (SCHEFFLER)
Johannes (Joan^s) I, 168, 170, 172
SCHOFNER
Hans I, 275
SCHOHEN
Anna Maria II, 168
SCHOIT (SHEYTT)
Jerch (Jerick) I, 122, 125, 126
Julian I, 123

SCHOLDER
Andrew II, 136
Eva II, 136
George II, 136
John II, 136
Martin I, 688
SCHÖLER
Wilhelm I, 756
SCHÖLHORN
Johann Balthas I, 470
SCHÖLKOPF (SCHOLKOPF)
Adam I, 357
Anna Maria II, 192
Joh. George II, 192
Margarethe II, 192
Michael II, 192
Rosina II, 192
SCHOLL (SHOLL, SHOLE)
Andreas (Andräs) I, 416, 689
Balsatzor I, 506
Carol (Arnald) I, 266, 269, 273
Christian I, 454
Christoph II, 155
Friedrich (Frederik) I, 21, 23
Georg I, 469
George Davit (G.
Davit) I, 258, 260, 263
George Friedrich I, 513, 514, 516
Hanna Mirea I, 85
Jacob I, 540, 542, 544, 725
Johann I, 84, 86, 87
Johan Fillibs Jacob I, 429
Johann Michel
(Hans Mich[1]) I, 661, 663, 664
Johann Nicel I, 724
Johann Petter
(Johan Peder) I, 506, 702
Johan Thomas I, 684
Johannes Friedrich I, 576, 578, 580
Joseph I, 395
Katterene I, 85
Michel I, 227, 229, 231
II, 104
Peter I, 257, 259, 262
Regina II, 156
SCHOLLE
Elizabeth II, 150
Gottlieb II, 150
Jacob II, 150
Margarette II, 150
Matthew II, 150
Salome II, 150
SCHOLLENBERGER (SHULEM-
BURGER)
Friedrich I, 323, 324, 326
SCHÖLLHAMMER (SCHÖLLHEI-
MER, SCHELHAMMER)
Johan Georg
(Hans Jerg) I, 532, 533, 535

SCHÖLLHORN
Mathas I, 459
SCHOLLS (SCHOLS, SHAOLLS)
Catherina II, 95
Godfrey I, 37
Hermanus II, 95
SCHOLMEYER (SHALLMAYER,
SHULLMYER)
Johan I, 72, 76, 78
Katharina I, 73
Michael (Gerhard
Michel) I, 72, 76, 78
SCHOLTEN
Wid[w] II, 29
Wilhelm II, 29
SCHOLTER * (SHOLTER)
Hans George I, 526, 527, 529
SCHOLTES (SHOLTES)
George I, 392
Hans I, 392
J. Henry I, 501
Johannes I, 503
John Henry I, 503
SCHOLTMANN
Carolina II, 123
SCHOLTZ (SCHOLZ, SHOLTZE,
SHOUTS, SHULTS)
Anna I, 122, 138
Anthony II, 199
Barbara I, 138
Christian II, 83
Christoph
(Christopher) I, 137, 141, 142
David I, 121, 124, 125
George
(Gorg, Jerick) I, 55, 56, 57, 121,
124, 125, 137
141, 142
Gregorius I, 137, 141, 142
Jacob I, 123
Maria I, 138
Melchior I, 137, 141, 142,
151, 152
Rosina I, 138, 139
Susannah I, 138, 139
SCHOMBACH (SHAMBACK)
Adam I, 24
Adolph (Atolph) I, 25, 26
Anna Dorothy I, 24
Elizabeth I, 24
SCHOMERMEL
Johann II, 79
SCHÖMIG
Ullrich I, 305, 306
SCHÖMPERLEN
Hans Jerg I, 416
SCHÖN (SCHÖNN)
George (Gorg) I, 355, 699

Johan Thomas
(Thos) I, 217, 218, 220
Peter Casper I, 546, 548, 550
SCHÖNAU (SHEENAU, SHINAN, SHENAW)
Lorentz (Lorents) I, 596, 597, 599
SCHÖNAUER * (SHOENOWER, SHONHOUR)
Jost (Joost) I, 627, 630, 633
SCHONBACH
Jeremias I, 405
SCHÖNBERGER (SCHÖNENBERGER, SCHÖNEBERGER)
Appalona II, 4
Balthaser I, 79, 82, 83
Cath[a] II, 4
Elizabeth II, 4
Eliz. Cath. II, 4
George II, 4
Hans I, 714
Johann Henrich I, 699
Johann Nich[s] II, 4
Johann Philipp
(Philip) I, 642, 644
Johanes (Hans) I, 642, 644
 II, 4
Peter II, 4
SCHÖNBRUCK
Jasper I, 703
SCHÖNECK (SCHÖNECKH, SCHENICK, SHONICK)
Carel (Charles) I, 526, 528, 529
Johann Michal I, 585, 586, 588
SCHÖNEFELD * (SCHONEFELLDT, SCHONEFIELD, SHONFELDT)
Christian I, 754
Johan I, 122, 124, 126
Johannes I, 21
(See also SCHENEFELT)
SCHÖNEMAN * (SHEANEMAN)
Christoff I, 347
SCHÖNER (SCHONER)
Daniel II, 79
Melcher I, 327, 329
SCHÖNEWALD * (SHOENWALT)
Jost I, 488
SCHÖNFELDER (SCHONFELTER, SHOENVELDEN)
Elizabeth I, 122
Frederick
(Friederich) I, 180, 182, 184
Jn° Christopher I, 708
Johan Peter I, 494
Johannes Peter I, 494
SCHÖNHOLTZ (SCHONHALS)
Friedrich (Fred[k]) I, 763; II, 8
SCHÖNHOLTZER
Johannes I, 17

SCHÖNIG (SHENIGH)
Conradt (Conrad) I, 66, 69, 70
SCHÖNLEIN
Michill I, 502
SCHÖNMAN
Johan Peder I, 401
SCHÖNMANSGRUBER (SCHENEMANSGRUBER)
Georg I, 127, 129, 130
Margaretha I, 127
SCHÖPF (SCHÖPFF, SCHOP)
Catrina I, 190
Christophel
(Christian) I, 581, 583, 584
Jacob I, 189, 192, 194
SCHOPFER (SHOPFER, SHOPFFER, SCHOPFELE)
Abraham I, 440
Christian I, 256, 259, 262
Johan Martin I, 105, 106
SCHOPP (SHOEP, SHOP, SCHOP, SHOPE)
Andreas I, 652, 654
Anna II, 124
Bernard I, 539, 541, 544
Cathrina II, 133
Christoph
(Christophel) I, 266; II, 124
Heinrich II, 124
Jacob II, 124
Johans II, 134
John Jerick I, 266
Ursula II, 124
Veronica I, 139
Wernard II, 124
SCHOPPENMEYER
Herman Adolff I, 467
SCHOPPERT
Nicolaus I, 461
SCHÖPPI
Rudolph I, 457
SCHÖPS (SCHEPS)
Friedrich
(Frederick) I, 137, 141, 142
SCHOR
Fried I, 450
Michel I, 450
SCHORB (SHURP)
Friederich I, 398
Johanes I, 398
Paulus I, 398
SCHORCH
Dobias I, 14
Jacob I, 366
SCHÖRCK (SCHORKH, SHARK, SCHURCH)
Gorg I, 454
Hans Jacob I, 96, 97, 98
Johannes I, 20

Philip
(Philip Jacob)   I, 661, 663, 664
SCHORF
Johann Friederich   I, 495
SCHORI (SCHÖRI, SHORY)
Hans Adam   I, 725
Jacob   I, 556, 557, 558
Johannes   I, 609, 611, 612
SCHORITZER
Johannes   I, 701
SCHORR
Hans Gorg   I, 364
SCHORS
Hans Marden   I, 466
SCHÖSTER
Hans Phpp   I, 418
SCHOTT (SHOTT)
Andreas   I, 504
Anna Catrina   I, 766
Anna Clara   I, 766
Cath.   II, 9
Christian   I, 416, 437
Conhenas   I, 766
Conrad   I, 113, 114, 115, 765
                               II, 9
Dorothy   II, 9
Fridrich   I, 419
Gottfried   I, 695
Hans   I, 451
Hans Peter (Peter) I, 628, 631, 635
Jacob   I, 392, 504, 521, 524
                  637, 638, 640, 750
James   I, 540
Johan Henrich   I, 508
Johann Paul
(John Paulus)   I, 551, 552, 554
Johann Peter   I, 750
Johanes (Johannes) I, 475, 685, 737
Jurg Henrich   I, 417
Ludwig (Lutwig)   I, 323, 325, 326
                       628, 631, 635
Mich[1]   II, 9
SCHÖTTE (SHETTY, SHOTTEY)
Johann Henrich
(John Hendrick) I, 113, 114, 115
                               765
Joseph Michael   I, 453
SCHOTTER
Johannes   I, 179, 181, 183
Peter   I, 711
SCHOUR
Johann Christian   I, 452
SCHOWALDER (SCHOWALTER,
SHAWALTER)
Christian   I, 407, 448, 698
Hannes   I, 448
Jacob   I, 448
John   I, 359

Joseph   I, 448
Peter   I, 448
SCHÖYRER
Johannes   I, 495
SCHRAAG
Johan Henrich   I, 710
SCHRACK (SCHRACH, SHRACK,
SHRECK, SCHRICK)
J. Ludewig (Johs.) I, 564, 566, 567
Nicholas   I, 545, 547, 549
Uli   I, 726
SCHRADE
Fridrich   I, 507
SCHRADER (SCHRATER)
Heinr. Conrd. Her[n].   II, 127
Jerona   II, 7
Johann Christian
(John Christian) I, 673, 674, 675
Nich[s]   II, 7
Philipp Christian   I, 716
SCHRAG
Hanes   I, 712
SCHRAIDT (SHROUD)
Engelberd   I, 39, 41, 42
Fred[k]   II, 19
Hannah   I, 40
John   I, 40
SCHRAMM (SCHRAM, SHRAM)
Christian   I, 31, 33, 34
                               II, 59
Georg (George)   I, 235, 236
George Adam
(Jerg Adam)   I, 552, 553, 555
Georg Bernhard   II, 79
Gorg Simon   I, 457
Jacob   I, 234, 235, 236
Johan Henry   I, 495
Theobald   I, 727
SCHRANCK (SHRANK)
Hans Gerg   I, 454
Johan (John)   I, 596, 598, 599
John Barnhard   I, 454
Martin   I, 596, 598, 599
SCHRANCKWEILER
Jacob   I, 701
SCHRANDEMAN
Johannes   I, 407
SCHRANTZ
Hans   I, 407
Hans Peter   I, 428
SCHREAD (SCHREA, READ)
Philip   I, 656, 657, 659
SCHREB
Nicholas   II, 78
SCHRECK (SHRICK)
Adam   I, 539, 541, 542, 544
Hans   I, 542, 544
Johannes   I, 541, 544
Paul   I, 694

SCHRECKA
Johann   I, 751
SCHRECKEGAST   (SCHRECKEN-
   GAST)
Daniel   II, 87
Floriane   II, 87
George   II, 87
George Henry   II, 87
Johann Jost   I, 690
Marie Elisabeth   II, 87
Sophia (Sophie)   II, 84, 87
SCHREFFEL
Johann Jacob   I, 704
SCHREHER
Andreas   II, 119
SCHREIBER   (SHREIBER, SCHRI-
   BER, SCHRYBER, SCHRIVER)
Adam   I, 297, 299, 300
Baltus   I, 415
Carolina   II, 92
Caspar (Casper)   I, 601, 602, 603
Elias   I, 188, 192, 193
Hans Jacob
   (Jackop)   I, 117, 120, 121
Heneretta   I, 190
Henrich (Hendryk)   I, 147, 150, 151
J. Friedrich   I, 467
Johan Adam   I, 415
Johann Caspar
   (Casper)   I, 217, 219, 220
Johann Christian
   (John Christian)   I, 582, 583
                584, 688
Johann Georg   I, 421
Johann Peter   I, 318, 319, 320
Johannes (Johanis)   I, 225, 228, 230
                289, 290, 291
                484, 532, 533
                535
Johannes Peter   II, 79
Jos.   II, 41
Lohrentz (Lorens)   I, 169, 171, 172
Maria Catriena   II, 79
Maria Eliza   I, 190
Nicolaus
   (Nicholas)   I, 188, 192, 193, 347
Philip   I, 190
Theodor   II, 92
SCHREIDT (SCHREID)
Johann Philip
   (Philip)   I, 642, 644
SCHREIER (SRYER)
Jerg Conrath
   (Conrad)   I, 236, 238, 239
SCHREIK
Anna Cleophe   I, 148
SCHREINER   (SCHREYNER,
   SHRYNER)
Abraham   I, 257, 259, 262

Anselmus (Hans
   Ellmus)   I, 373, 375, 376
Daniel   I, 621, 624, 626
Hans Adam   I, 198, 200, 202
Henrich   I, 692
Johann Georg   I, 416, 487
Johann Jacob   I, 712
Johann Martin
   (Martin)   I, 199, 201, 203
Johann Michael   I, 198, 200, 202
Johan Philipus   I, 712
Johan Wilhelm   I, 403
Johannes   I, 539, 541, 544
Johanes Peder   I, 281
Johannes Silvius   I, 415
Ludwig   I, 431
Wilhelm   I, 431
SCHREMMAN
Henrich Christ   II, 192
SCHRENCK (SHRENCK)
Joh. Jacob   I, 462
Martin   I, 432
SCHREY
Johannes   II, 79
SCHREYACK   (SCHEYACKH,
   SCHREYIACKH, SCHEYECK,
   SCHRYACKH, SCRAYACK)
Barbra   I, 117
Christian   I, 155, 158, 161
Hans Jerg
   (Hans Jarick)   I, 117, 119, 121
Hans Michael   I, 117, 120, 121
Jacob (Jackop)   I, 117, 120, 121
Johannes   I, 96, 98
Susana   I, 118
SCHREYER   (SCHREINER,
   SHREYER, SHRIAR)
Frederick   I, 505
Geo.   I, 752
Johan Adam   I, 234, 235, 236
Johann Leonhardt   I, 495
Johann Simon   I, 495
Johannes   I, 335, 337, 338
Martin   I, 628, 631, 634
SCHROCKHAUS
Hans George   II, 13
SCHRÖDER (SCHRODER, SCHRE-
   DER, SCHRETER, SCHROA-
   DER, SCHROTER, SCHREU-
   DER, SCHRODTER, SHRÖDER)
Andreas (Andries)   II, 30, 148
Anna Elizabeth   II, 92
Anna Maria   I, 49
Anton   II, 113
Anton Christ.   II, 139
August Heinrich   I, 503
Bastian   I, 661, 663, 664
Christian   II, 50
David   I, 629, 632, 635

Friederich I, 742
Gertruth II, 92
Hans Georg I, 51
Henrich
(Henry) I, 469, 536, 537, 538
II, 18, 78, 117
Jacob Fridrich I, 673, 675, 676
Johan (Johannes) I, 360, 362
Johann Adam I, 48, 52, 54
Johann Anton II, 125
Johann Arnoltt
(Arn.) I, 237, 238, 239
Johann Daniel I, 733
Johann Engel I, 495
Johann Friederith II, 92
Johan Michel I, 51
Magnus I, 504
Martin I, 423
Matthias II, 196
Nicholas II, 206
Simon I, 573, 574, 575
Wilhelmine II, 198
SCHRÖDLIN (SHREDLIN)
Johann Andreas I, 545, 547, 549
SCHROFF (SHROOF)
Johann
(Johann Adam) I, 143, 145, 146
Margreta Susanna I, 144
Maria Cathrine I, 144
SCHROLL
Johannes I, 304
SCHRONY
Hans Marten I, 490
SCHROPP
Christoph I, 469
SCHROTH (SHROUT)
Daniel I, 167, 168
Johannes I, 466, 721
Matheis I, 307, 308, 309
SCHROTNER (SHROATNER,
SHAETNER)
Johan Michel I, 48, 52, 54
SCHROTT (SHROTTE, SROTT,
SHROT)
J. Johann Michel
(Joh. Michael) I, 621, 623, 625
J. Peter (Peter) I, 621, 623, 625
SCHRUNTZ
Charlotta II, 166
Johan G. II, 166
SCHRUTT
Matheus I, 410
SCHRYBER (SCHRYVER)
Johann Jorg I, 712
M^r II, 130
SCHUB
Mich^l I, 697

SCHUBERT (SHOEBART, SHU-
BART, SCHUBART)
Anna Maria I, 138
Barbara I, 138
Christoff
(Christopher) I, 136, 140, 141
David I, 137, 138, 139, 141, 142
Johann Michael I, 531, 532, 534
Johann Nicolaus I, 531, 532, 534
Susannah I, 138, 139
SCHUCH (SHUGH)
Anna Eliz. I, 766, 767
Ever Eliza I, 766
Johan Conrad I, 487
Johann Petter I, 460
Martin I, 461
Peter I, 521, 523
Philipp (Philip) I, 628, 631, 634
SCHUCHEN (SHEWHAN, read prob.
SCHUCH)
Henrich (Henry) I, 376, 377
SCHUCK (SCHÜCK, SHOOK)
Cathrina I, 103
Filib Adam I, 754
Hans I, 103
Johann Jerg I, 466
Johann Martin I, 395
Johannes I, 102, 105
Maria I, 103
Peter Henry (Peter
Hendrick) I, 276, 277, 278
Valtin I, 395
SCHUCKMAN
Jacob I, 487
SCHUCKS
Eliz. II, 105
SCHUDE
Jacob II, 145
Johannes II, 124
Mardin I, 742
SCHUDER
Nicolaus I, 489
SCHUDT
Dewalt I, 411
SCHUDY
Elizabeth II, 146
Martin (Marthi) II, 146
SCHUE
Johann Jacob I, 452
Johannes I, 371
SCHUFFERD (SHUFFARD)
Gertrud I, 127
Johan Jerg
(George) I, 127, 129, 130
Johannes I, 127
SCHUH (SCHU, SHUE, SHOE)
Auguste II, 197
David II, 197
Emanuel II, 197

Frederick II, 197
Gottleib II, 197
Jacob (John
Jacob) I, 113, 114, 115, 765
Joh. George II, 193
Johann Wilhelm I, 727
Rosina II, 197
Ulrich I, 113, 114, 115, 765
(*See also* SCHUE)
SCHUHLING
Lampertus I, 358
SCHUHMANN (SCHUHMAN,
SCHUCHMANN)
Hans Georg I, 409
Johann Jacob
(Jacob) I, 221, 223, 224
Stofel I, 403
SCHUHRIEM
Johann Nicolaus I, 743
SCHÜL
Johann Michel I, 432
SCHULD
Lena II, 197
SCHULE
Anna M. II, 152
Anna Maria II, 152
Ferdinand F. II, 152
George II, 152
John Adam II, 152
John G. II, 152
John Jacob II, 152
Maria Agnes II, 152
Mary A. II, 152
SCHULENBERG (SCHULENBURG)
Hinr. Andr. II, 139
Maria II, 173
SCHULER (SCHÜLER, SCHUHLER,
SCHULLER, SHEWLER,
SHOOLER)
Adam I, 35, 36
Bernhardt II, 46
Christian I, 445
Conrad I, 707
Frantz (Francis) I, 126, 129
George I, 227; II, 104
Gottfriedt I, 323, 324, 326
Hans I, 637, 639, 641
Henrich I, 744
Jacob I, 323, 324, 326, 498
Jacob F. II, 152
Johann Bernhardt II, 46
Johann Philipp I, 437
Maria I, 127
Martin I, 393
Michael II, 192
Theophilus II, 152
—— II, 162

SCHÜLPP (SCHILP, SCHIP)
Hans Petter
(Hans Philipp) I, 188, 191, 193
SCHULTE
Johann Friderich I, 408
SCHULTES (SHULTES)
Georg Peter I, 88, 90, 92
SCHULTHEIS (SCHULTHEISS)
Carolin II, 198
Christiana II, 198
Jacob I, 724
Jan II, 198
Johannes I, 476
SCHULTZ (SHOLTZ, SHULTS,
SHULTZ)
Anna Barball I, 242
Anna Cath^a II, 23
Carl Friedrich (Hans
Fred^k) I, 665, 668, 670
Carl Philip I, 327, 329
Cath. II, 105
Christ. II, 107
Christian Otto I, 143, 145, 146
Conrath II, 44
Daniell I, 241
Emanuel Friederich II, 59
Erdman I, 439
Frantz Peter
(Anthony) I, 655, 656, 658
Fried. Augt II, 108
George II, 54
Gorg Michel
(Michel) I, 609, 611, 612
Gottlob II, 87
Gottl. Fried^ch Conrad II, 140
Hans II, 50
Hans Martin I, 43, 46, 47
Henrich (Hendrick) I, 11, 12, 240
242, 243
J. Henry I, 505
Jacob I, 44, 704
James II, 60
Jerg I, 327, 329, 676
Jno Chris^r I, 749
Joh. Christ. II, 139
Johan I, 717
Johan Christoph I, 708
Johan Conrad I, 437
Johan Georg I, 401, 412
Johannes I, 323, 324, 326
Johannes Christian I, 88, 89, 91
John Henry II, 122
Juliana II, 140
Jurg. Hein^ch II, 139
Lorentz I, 750
Marcus Anthony
(Mark Anthony) I, 655, 657, 658
Margaretha II, 54
Nickelaus I, 459

Peter I, 688
Samuel I, 493
Sirach I, 442
Vallentin
(Valentine) I, 43, 46, 212
214, 215
SCHULTZE
A. G. I, 38, 39
Heinrich Conrat Hyronimus I, 749
SCHUM (SHUM)
Christophel (Christoffel,
Christian) I, 627, 630, 633
Jacob II, 9
Joh. Nich^s II, 97
SCHUMACHER (SCHUHMACHER,
SCHUMACKER, SCHUMAKER,
SHOEMAKER, SHUMACHER)
Adam II, 8
Albrecht I, 698
Allecsander I, 735
Anna Maria I, 189
Carol II, 48
Christ (Crist.) I, 280, 281, 282
D. II, 61
Georg
(George, Jerg) I, 22, 23, 189
Godf. II, 137
Hans Casper II, 105
Hans Casp^r E. II, 23
Hans Jacob
(Hans) I, 188, 191, 193, 421
Hans Jerg
(Jerrick) I, 7, 9, 399
Hans Martain I, 7
Henry I, 339
Herbert I, 478
Hs. Jacob I, 399
Jacob I, 48, 52, 54, 371, 738
Johan Adam I, 353, 354
Johann Georg I, 453
Johann Henrich I, 755
Johann Jacob
(Jan Jacob) I, 212, 214, 216
Johann Michael I, 470, 545, 547
549
Johann Nicklaus (Johan-
nes Niclaus) I, 294, 295, 296
Johan Peter
(Peter) I, 280, 281, 282
568, 570, 572, 622
Johan Thomas I, 479
Johannes (John) I, 212, 214, 216
324, 325, 327
637, 639, 641
666, 668, 670
720
Johannes Gerhardus I, 466
Johannes Peter I, 718
Joseph I, 127, 129, 130

Jost (Johan) I, 236, 238, 239
Luise II, 148
Maria I, 127
Michael (Michel) I, 170, 171, 173
213, 214, 216, 399
Paul I, 189
Peter I, 137, 141, 142, 718
Simon I, 488
Wilhelm I, 738
SCHUMANN (SCHUMAN, SCHUH-
MAN, SHOEMANN, SHUH-
MAN)
Anna Cath. II, 158
Arnold
(Arnoldus) I, 277, 278, 279
Christ. II, 158
Christina II, 158
Ernst Friedr. II, 107
Friedrich II, 110
Geo. I, 741
Herman I, 758
Johann E. E. II, 158
Johan Matheas I, 406
Johan Peter I, 277, 278, 279
Johannes I, 444, 620, 622, 624
John I, 697
Michael II, 10
Philibus
(Philip) I, 569, 570, 572
Rudolph I, 697
Wilhelm Fridrich I, 489
—— II, 136
SCHUMBERT (SHUMBERT,
SCHUBERT, SHUMBER)
J. Jacob I, 457
Jacob I, 661, 662, 663
SCHUME
J. II, 144
SCHUMMARY
Adam I, 715
SCHUNCK (SHONK, SHOENK)
Matheas I, 395
Simon I, 175, 176, 177
SCHUNTZ (SHUNTZ)
Johann Henry I, 686
Johannes I, 684
SCHUPP (SHUPP)
Georg Michel I, 438
Henrich I, 521, 523
Jacob I, 226, 228, 230
417, 735
Johan Jacob I, 307, 308, 309
John George I, 269, 272
Martin I, 698
SCHUPPERT
Johann Jacob I, 500
SCHURCH (SHURK)
Johan I, 18
Mr. II, 175

Mrs. II, 175
Sebastian I, 737
Uldrick (Udry) I, 18, 19
Uli I, 19
SCHURER (SHERER)
Eva Catherina I, 128
Hans I, 127, 129, 130
Maria Magdalena I, 127
Veronica I, 128
SCHURG (SCHURGH)
Georg I, 692
Joseph I, 10, 11
SCHURLE
Eliza II, 150
Gottlieb (Gotlief) II, 150
SCHÜRLING
Valentin I, 711
SCHURMANN (SCHURMAN)
Johann Petter I, 412
Peter II, 95
SCHURTZ
Gorg Michel I, 416
Johannes Simeon I, 718
SCHUSLER (SCHUSSLER, SCHÜS-
LER, SCHÜSSLER)
Andrew II, 55
Ann Margarett II, 55
Anna Barbara II, 115
Anna Martha II, 115
C. F. II, 125
Elisa II, 55
Hans Jacob I, 93, 94, 95
Henrich (Henry) I, 93, 94, 95
Jerg I, 93, 94, 95
Johann II, 115
Johann Geörg I, 329
Johannes I, 705
Margarat Elis. II, 115
Margarett II, 55
Valentine II, 55
SCHUST (SHUST)
Stephen (Stefan) I, 162, 164, 165
SCHUSTER (SHUSTER, SHOOS-
TER SCHUOSTER)
Andreas I, 353, 354, 444
Carolina II, 59
Catharina Margaritha II, 59
Christian II, 59
Daniell I, 660
Dorothea Catharina II, 59
Friederich II, 59
Georg II, 110
Hans Michel I, 417
Henrich II, 59
Jacob I, 289, 290, 291, 497
II, 53
Johann Adam I, 371
Johan George I, 353, 354

Johann Henrich
(Han Henrich) I, 667, 669, 671
Johann Marthin I, 687
Johann Nickel I, 307, 308, 309
Johannes
(Johanes, John) I, 637, 639, 641
666, 668, 670
722
Johannes Henrich I, 435
Lorentz I, 717
Louisa II, 59
Ludwich (Lodwᵏ) I, 596, 597, 599
Peter I, 717
Vallentin I, 700
SCHUTT (SCHÜTT)
Anna Maria II, 97
Cathrina II, 97
Frans II, 97
Jacob II, 50
SCHUTTE * (SHUTTY)
Hans I, 417
Johanes I, 473
SCHÜTTEL (SHUTLE, SHITTELL,
SHUTELY)
David II, 6
Elizabeth I, 766
Johann (Johanes,
Johannes) I, 605, 607, 608
SCHUTTER
Elizabeth II, 127
Heinr. (Henry) I, 349, 350, 352
II, 119
Maria II, 127
Valentine I, 349, 350, 352
SCHÜTTERLI (SCHUTTERLIN,
SCHÜTTÜLERLIN)
Andreas I, 452
Georg I, 411
Hans I, 481
Johannes I, 451
SCHÜTTLER
Lutwig I, 454
SCHÜTZ (SCHUTZ, SCHUTTS,
SCHITZ, SHEETS, SHUTES)
Adolph I, 752
Albert I, 415
Christian I, 730, 750
Conrad (Conrade) I, 169, 171, 172
Daniel I, 751
Ditrich (Dirk) I, 167, 168
Felix I, 252, 254, 255
Frans I, 505
Friedrich I, 414
Georg (George) I, 185, 186, 187
Georg Adam I, 484
Gerhard Henrich
(Heinrice) I, 257, 260, 262
Gottfrid I, 499; II, 37
Hans I, 304, 629, 632, 636

Hans George I, 653, 655
Hans Peter I, 456
Hennerotia II, 36
J. Willhelm
(William) I, 564, 566, 567
Jacob I, 569, 571, 572
Jerg Ludwig I, 96, 98
Johan I, 684, 723
Johann Adam I, 696
Johann Allexander I, 466
Johann Conrad I, 335, 336, 338
Johann Friedrich
(Friderick) I, 59, 63, 65
Johann Jorg
(Hans Geo.) I, 667, 669, 671
Johan Peder I, 427
Johann Philip
(John) I, 59, 63, 65
Johann Theis
(Joh. Thys) I, 563, 565, 567
Joh. Wilhelm
(J. Wm.) I, 563, 565, 567
Johannes I, 347
Johannes Christopher
(Christoph) I, 559, 563
John William II, 37
Mathäus I, 88, 90, 91
Matthias I, 569, 571, 572
Peter I, 282, 284, 285
Rudolph
(Roedolph) I, 252, 253, 254, 255
Tilemannus I, 340, 341, 342
Wendel I, 692
Willemenia II, 36
—— II, 33
SCHÜTZER * (SHITZER)
Johanes I, 392
SCHUY (SCHUG, SHOOK)
Cathrina I, 103
Christian I, 257, 259, 262
Hans I, 740
Johan Friedrich
(Joh. Fredᵏ) I, 563, 565, 566
Johannes
(Johˢ, Hans) I, 102, 103, 105, 382
564, 566, 567
Maria I, 103
SCHWAB (SHWAB, SWOP)
Balzar (Baltzer) I, 387, 388, 389
G. Michael
(Jurg Mich¹) I, 678, 679, 681
Hans Michael I, 417
Heinrich I, 497
Jacob Bernhardt I, 497
Johan Adam I, 497
Johann Christian I, 686
Johann Georg (John
George) I, 9, 541, 543, 690

Johann Paul
(Paulus) I, 539, 541, 543
Johan Philipus
(Philip) I, 379, 380, 382
Johannes (Johanes,
Jnᵒ) I, 445, 653, 654, 700
Peter
(Pieter) I, 151, 152, 691
SCHWABELAND
Christian I, 760
Ludwich I, 760
Peter I, 759
SCHWAGER
Bernhard II, 178
Johan Peter I, 339
SCHWÄGLER
Elizabeth II, 156
SCHWALB
Johannes I, 521, 524
John Jost I, 447
SCHWALBACH (SWALBACH)
Johan Henrich (Heny) I, 649, 650
SCHWALDER
Jacob I, 448
SCHWAMM
Hermann I, 431
SCHWAN
Georg Heinerich II, 21
SCHWANFELDER
Johann Daniel I, 736
SCHWANGER
Jacob I, 369, 370
SCHWANNER (SWANER)
Johannes (Joanis) I, 226, 228, 230
SCHWARBACH * (SHWARBACH)
Johannes I, 456
SCHWARBER * (SHWARBER,
SWARBER, SWERBER)
Jacob I, 252, 253, 255
SCHWARM (SHWARM, SWARM)
Johannes I, 702
Wilhelm I, 310, 311, 312
SCHWARTZ (SWARTZ,
SCHWARTS, SWARTS)
Abraham (Abram) I, 16, 17
Adam II, 24
Andreas
(Andrew) I, 16, 17, 490, 627
630, 633, 667
669, 671
Carl II, 24
Carl Gottlob I, 723
Christian I, 629, 632, 636
Christⁿ Elizᵗʰ I, 210
Conrath
(Conrade) I, 265, 268, 271
Daniel I, 346
Frantz I, 689

Friedrich
(Frederik) I, 454, 522, 524
Georg (Jeorg) I, 394, 745
Georg Friederich I, 492
Georg Wilhelm
(Görg Willhelm) I, 48, 52, 54
Gottlieb
(Godleip) I, 390; II, 126
Hans I, 629, 632, 636
Hans Gorg
(Jerg) I, 175, 176, 177, 487
Hans Michel I, 310, 312, 313
Henrich (Henry) I, 340, 342, 343
448, 686
II, 179
Henrich Lutwig I, 48, 52, 54
Hs. Adam I, 480
J. Adam
(Johan Adam) I, 564, 566, 567
Jacob I, 8, 175, 176, 177
476, 492, 740
II, 24, 119
Johann Anthon I, 450
Johan Christian I, 495
Johan George (John
George) I, 341, 342, 343
347, 450, 577
579, 580
Johann Gottlob II, 79
Johan Jacob I, 495
Johann Martin I, 432
Johann Peter I, 481
Johann Philipp I, 450
Johannes
(Johanes) I, 51, 480, 498, 560
561, 563
Justus Rupertus I, 51
Karl I, 347
Maria Elizabeth I, 49
Martin I, 236, 238, 239, 760
Michael I, 487
Nicklaus
(Nicholas) I, 265, 268, 271
591, 592, 594
629, 632, 635
Peter (Petter) I, 629, 632, 636
Philipp Leonhard I, 545, 547, 549
Tobias I, 243
SCHWARTZBACH
Johann Andon I, 416
SCHWARTZENBACH (SWÄRT-
ZENBACH, SWARTABACH)
Henry (Henrich) I, 667, 669, 671
Uhllerik
(Ulrich) I, 252, 253, 255
SCHWARTZHAUBT
Johannes I, 436

SCHWARTZLÄNDER
Johan Philipp I, 506
SCHWARTZSTRAUBER
Daniel II, 100
Jacob II, 100
SCHWARTZWELDER
(SCHWARTZWALD, SWARTS-
WELDER)
Christian (Chris[n]) I, 648, 650
Johann Adam
(Adam) I, 226, 228, 230
Johannes
(Joanis) I, 225, 228, 230, 497
Matthias I, 453
SCHWATTER
Heinrith II, 92
SCHWATZ
Henry II, 93
SCHWATZER
Johanes I, 494
SCHWE (SCHEW, SCHUHL)
Daniel I, 71, 75, 77
Lodawick I, 73
Margeretta I, 74
Maria I, 72
SCHWEBEL (SHWÄBEL)
Hans Adam I, 661, 662, 664
SCHWEDENER (SWEEDNEN)
Joh. Mardin (Mar-
tin) I, 217, 219, 220
SCHWEDINGER
Johann I, 559
SCHWEGLER * (SHWEGLER)
John II, 201
SCHWEICKHART (SCHWEICH-
ART, SCHWEICKART,
SCHWEICKERT, SCHWEIK-
HARDT)
Bernhart I, 400
Friedrich I, 414
Georg (Jerig) I, 539, 541, 543
Georg Conrad I, 454
Hans Phillip I, 9
J. George (Jerick) I, 546, 548, 550
Jacob I, 454
Johann Martin I, 759
Johan Peter I, 367, 368
Peter I, 336, 337, 339
SCHWEIGERT (SWEIGERT,
SCHWEIGERTH, SCHWEIGER,
SWIGER)
Adam I, 552, 553, 554
Hans Georg (Hans
Geo.) I, 446, 637, 638, 640
J. Jost I, 474
Philip I, 296, 298, 299
SCHWEIGERTS
Johan Christoph I, 746

SCHWEIGHOUSER (SCHVEIG-
HOUSER, SWETTOWSER)
Conrad
(Conrade) I, 287, 288, 289
SCHWEIN * (SHWEIN)
Joh. Reinhart I, 391
SCHWEINFURTH (SCHWEIN-
FORTH)
Allbrecht (Albertus) I, 649, 650
Jacob I, 421
SCHWEINHART (SWYNHART)
Andreas I, 67
Barbara I, 67
Eva I, 67
Georg Michael (Jerich
Michael) I, 66, 69, 70
Johan I, 67
Magdalena I, 67
SCHWEINITZ
—— II, 87
SCHWEISHELM (SHWEISHELM,
SCHWEESHELM)
Andreas I, 509, 510, 511
SCHWEISSFURTH
Johan Jacob I, 756
SCHWEISSGUTH
Lorentz I, 461
SCHWEITZER (SWEITZER,
SWITZER)
Bernhart II, 133
Caspar I, 147, 149, 150
Catrina II, 133
Christian I, 227; II, 104
Conrath I, 403
F. I, 445
Frans Stephanus I, 454
Frantz I, 694
Georg Heinrich I, 513, 514, 515
Henrich
(Henry) I, 331, 332, 334, 740
Jacob I, 79, 82, 83, 227, 391
500, 552, 553, 555, 751
II, 104, 145
Johann Daniel I, 756
Johann Jacob I, 688
Johann Martin I, 488
Johannes I, 526, 528, 530
Johannes Jacob (John
Jacob) I, 577, 578, 580
Johannes Ludwig I, 577, 578, 580
Joseph I, 500
Leonhard I, 500
Mathes (Matthew) I, 16, 17
Matthias I, 194, 195, 196
Nicolaus I, 684
Peter I, 715
Vallentin I, 422
SCHWELE
Jacob I, 740

SCHWELGER
Christian II, 97
Fredrick II, 97
SCHWELLER
Jacob I, 481
SCHWEMMLIN
Johannes I, 365
SCHWENCK (SCHWEINCK,
SWENCK, SCHWENCKE,
SHWENK)
Adam I, 252, 253, 255
Christian I, 761
Christoff[el] I, 180, 181, 184
Diebolt I, 429
Friederich I, 490
Hans Jacob I, 301, 302, 303
Hans Michael
(Michael) I, 252, 253, 255, 301,
302, 303, 653, 654
Hartman I, 256, 259, 261
Johann I, 490
Johannes I, 758
L. Henry I, 358
Lorentz (Law-
rence) I, 304, 305, 306
Martin I, 419
Michael I, 283, 294, 295
Nicholas I, 304
Peter (Petter) I, 256, 259, 261
SCHWENCKEL
Uhllerich I, 469
SCHWENS
Johan Ludwig I, 754
SCHWENTZEL
Andres Friederich I, 752
SCHWENTZER
Johan Jacob I, 739
SCHWEPPENHAÜSER
Niclaus I, 759
SCHWERBER * (SHWERBER)
Stephan I, 403
Wilhelm I, 403
SCHWERDLE
Johannes I, 740
SCHWERDT
Baltzer I, 347
Georg I, 694
Henrich I, 175, 177, 178, 697
Johann Nicolaus I, 694
SCHWESTERÜMLLER
Conrad I, 738
SCHWEUDE
Jacob I, 491
SCHWEYER
Georg I, 418
Johannes I, 724
SCHWEYLER
Gorg I, 473

SCHWICKERT
Mr. II, 177
SCHWICKES
Balthas I, 472
SCHWIG
Francis Wm. I, 717
SCHWINDT (SCHWIND)
Johannes I, 335, 337, 338
SCHWING (SWING, SHWING)
Bernard I, 759
Caspar (Gaspar) I, 655, 657, 658
Henrich I, 760
Johanes (Johans) I, 195, 196, 197
Michael I, 447
Samuel I, 447
SCHWINGEL (SWENGEL)
Georg (Jerick) I, 289, 290, 291
Johan George II, 3
Johann Nickel
(Nickel) I, 289, 290, 291
Mickel I, 289
SCHWITGEN
Jnº Henry I, 748
SCHWITTE
George II, 179
SCHWITZER (SHWITZER)
Anna Margaᵗ II, 145
Frantz I, 393
Hance Jacob II, 145
Hannah II, 145
Jacob II, 145
Johan I, 416
Johannes I, 491; II, 145
Margret II, 145
Nicholas II, 145
Ursele II, 145
SCHWOB (read SCHWAB)
Fridrich I, 403
Henrich (Hendᵏ) I, 383, 385
J. Wendal I, 458
Jacob I, 427
Johann Walther I, 404
Martin I, 457
Peter I, 499
SCHWORER
Nicholas II, 44
SCHWÖRTZEL (SCHWERTZEL, TEITZWORTZEL)
Johan Henrich
(Henry) I, 656, 657, 658
Johan Jost I, 656, 657, 658
Johan Teis (John Ties) I, 656, 657, 658
SCHWYER
Nicklaus I, 493
SCHWYZER (read SCHWEIZER)
Mrs. II, 175
SCHYDNER
Anthony I, 451

SCHYRE
Hans Georg I, 691
SCKIERER (read prob. SCHÜRER)
Jan. Fredrick II, 77
SCLIFFER (read SCHLIEFER)
Johan II, 61
SCRAYBR (read SCHREIBER)
Anna I, 117
SCRIBA
Wilh. Heinr. II, 118
SCRIVERS
Catarin I, 80
SCUTESEN
Anna I, 117
Maria I, 117
SCUTTS
Eva Maria II, 77
Jacob II, 77
Jacob Frederick II, 77
SEACRIST (read prob. SIGRISᴦ)
Hans Georg I, 438
SEAFREDT (SEEFRIDT, read SIGFRIED)
Hans Michael I, 451
Hans Yerick I, 451
Johann Michael I, 382
SEAGER see SEEGER
SEAM
Jacob I, 236
SEAMON see SEEMAN
SEBALD
John Michael II, 122
SEBASTIAN * (SEBASTYAN)
Michel I, 12, 13
SEBEINGER
Jnº Adam I, 695
SEBELIE (ZEBERLY)
Martin (Mathyas) I, 266, 269, 272
SEBO
Johan Henrich I, 713
SEBOLDT (SEBOLTT, SEEBOLT, ZEBALT, ZEBOLT)
Jacob I, 715
Johann Peter I, 288, 289
Johann Philip I, 198, 200, 202
Lenhart I, 436
SECK (SACK)
Johannes (Johs.) I, 564, 566, 567
SECKEL (SEKEL)
Johann Georg I, 466
Johan Michael I, 360, 362
Michael I, 360, 362
SECKERING
Eva I, 117
SEE (SAYE)
Johann Bernhard
(Bernet) I, 283, 284, 285

SEEBERGER (SEBERGEN)
Johann Henrich
(Hendrick)   I, 582, 583, 584
SEEGER (SAGER, SEAGER)
Anna Barbara   I, 127, 128
Anna Maria   I, 128
Charles   II, 138
Christine Barbara   I, 128
Johan Christian   I, 128
Johan Conrath   I, 683
Johan Henrich   I, 128
Johan Nickel (Nicho-
las)   I, 127, 129, 130
Johann Wilhelm   I, 683
Maria Louisa   I, 128
Samuel   I, 128
Wilh. Fried.   I, 733
SEEGERIST
Hans   I, 448
SEEL (SEELE, SEELL)
Frantz (Frans)   I, 198, 201, 203
Piper   II, 136
SEELHEIMER
Wilhelm   I, 709
SEELIG (SELIG)
Johann Jacob   I, 457
Johann Michael   I, 540, 542, 544
SEEMAN (SEAMAN, SEAMON,
SEMANN)
Anna Cathᵃ   II, 23
Henry (Hendᵏ)   I, 386, 388, 389
Johann Ludwig (Lod-
wick)   I, 386, 388, 389
Johann Wilhelm   I, 753
Lafel   II, 195
SEEMISCH
Anthonius   I, 466
SEEMULLER
Elizabeth   II, 166
Gotlope   II, 166
Henrica   II, 166
Magdalena   II, 166
Mathew   II, 166
Sarah   II, 166
SEES (SEESS, SEYS, read prob.
SEETZ, SEITZ)
Henry   I, 497
John Ludwig
(Johann)   I, 122, 125, 126
SEETZ (SEEDS)
Hendrick (Henry)   I, 273, 274
SEFUES (SEIEFUES, SEIKEFUES,
ZIFUS)
Andreus   I, 241
Anelies   I, 241
Anna Maria   I, 241
Hanen Christophele   I, 241
Haneriagh   I, 241

Hans Jacob (Hanen
Jacob)   I, 240, 241, 242, 243
Kattarin   I, 241
Powell (Paul)   I, 241
SEGEL
Friederich Gottlieb   II, 76
SEGELER
Adam   II, 24
SEGER (SEEGER, SEYGER)
Gabriel   I, 592, 593, 595
Hans Tamus   I, 503
Jacob Fredk
(Jacob)   I, 304, 305, 306
Johann Gorg   I, 185, 186, 187
Johann Peter   I, 436
Johan Philip
(Philip)   I, 179, 181, 183
Uhlerich (Ulrigh)   I, 222, 223, 225
SEGMAN
George   I, 462
SEGNITZ
Christian   I, 683
SEHL (SEEHL)
Dietrich (Diederick)   I, 383, 385
Johann Paulus   I, 479
SEHM (SAMM)
Johann Gorg (Hans
Jorig)   I, 72, 76, 78
SEHN see SENN
SEIB (SYPE, SIPE, SYP)
Frantz (Frans)   I, 97, 98, 99
Georg   I, 97, 98, 99
Johann Georg   I, 709
Johan Ludwig   I, 167, 168
Ludwig   I, 97, 98, 99
Meliger (Melchior)   I, 457
SEIBALD
Fredᵏ Wilh.   II, 119
SEIBEL (SEIBLE, SYBLE)
Elizabeth   II, 77
Henrich (Henry)   I, 225, 228, 230
Phillib   I, 359
SEIBERT (SEUBERT, SEUBER, SI-
BERT, SEYBERT)
Adam   I, 328, 759
George (Jurig)   I, 199, 201, 203
Johann Bernt (Bern-
ard)   I, 235, 236
Johan Jacob   I, 204, 206, 208, 235
236
Johann Wendel   I, 234, 235, 236
SEIBT (SEIBB)
Caspar   I, 138
Christoph (Christo-
pher)   I, 137, 140, 142
David   I, 137, 140, 142
Judith   I, 138
SEIDEL (SEYDEL)
Johann   II, 107

Johann Georg I, 754
Johann Jacob II, 76
Johann Michel I, 754
Johann Nicolaus (Han-
icle) I, 667, 669, 671
Johann Valentin I, 486
Nathaniel I, 321, 322
SEIDEMAN (ZYDERMAN, SEY-
DEMANN)
Johan Jacob I, 155, 158, 160
SEIDENSPINNER (SYDENSPIN-
DER)
Jorg (Yerick) I, 384, 386
SEIDENSTICKER (SEIDEN-
STRICKER, SEIDEN-
STREICHER)
Henry I, 693
J. Henry I, 443
Johann Philip I, 693
Ott Philipp I, 694
SEIDER (SEYDER)
Adam I, 155, 158, 160
Georg I, 488
SEIDLER
Andereas
(Andreas) I, 559, 560, 562
SEIER
Theis I, 676
SEIFENBACHER
Adam I, 442
SEIFERT
Adam I, 424
Casimer Heinrich II, 191
Conrad I, 758
Philip I, 410
SEIGENDALLER
Peter I, 439
Ulrich I, 439
SEIGLER
Philip I, 8
SEIGMULLER
Friedrich I, 734
SEIL
George Jos. II, 118
Henrich I, 391
SEILER (SAILER, SEYLER, SILER)
Barbara II, 168
Christoffel (Chris-
toph) I, 392, 716
Daniel I, 359
Hans I, 197, 198
Jacob I, 392, 406
Johan Ludwig I, 491
Johanes (Hans) I, 275, 276, 392
Matheas I, 392
Thomas II, 168
Ulrich (Ulrick) I, 197, 198
(*See also* SEYLER)

SEIM (SAIM, SEUM)
Andreas (Andres) I, 199, 201, 203
SEIN
Peter I, 676
SEIP (SEIPP)
Adam II, 127
Albertus II, 127
Anna Catharina II, 127
Anna Elis II, 159
Bernhart I, 731
Conrad II, 159
Georg Conrad I, 709
Jacobine II, 127
Johann Peter II, 127
Johann Wilhelm I, 709
Johannes (John) II, 127, 159
John Friedk II, 127
Maria E. II, 159
Paulus I, 493
Peter I, 481
Philip I, 493
SEIPEL (SIBEL)
Johann Ludwig (Lud-
wick) I, 216, 218, 219
Valentine I, 688
SEIPEN (read prob. SEIP)
John Peter II, 127
Margaretha C. II, 127
Maria E. II, 159
SEIPERT (CIVER)
Michael (Michel) I, 293, 294, 295
SEIRIEUX
Jean I, 729
SEISERAM
Christina Barbara II, 171
SEISLER (SEESLER, SIZLER)
John Lenhart I, 311, 312, 313
John Peter I, 311, 312, 313
SEISS
John I, 763
SEITLE
Andreas I, 365
SEITLER
John Christ. II, 160
SEITLING (SEYDLING)
Heinrich I, 509, 510, 511
SEITNER (SYTNER, SIETTNER,
SIETNER)
Martin I, 627, 630, 634
Michael (Michel) I, 627, 631, 634
SEITZ (SEITZS, SEIZ, SEYTZ,
ZEITS)
Adam I, 526, 527, 529
Carl Adolph I, 732
Catharine II, 203
Christian II, 205
Friederich (Fried-
rice) I, 257, 260, 262
Hans Gorg I, 539, 541, 543

Hans Michael	I, 421
Heinerich	I, 473
Jacob	I, 414, 698
Jean Louis	I, 688
Jn° Adam	I, 752
Johann Henrich	I, 216, 218, 220
Johann Michael	I, 327, 329
Johann Nicklaus (Nicholas)	I, 585, 587, 588, 709
Johann Peter	I, 9
Johannes	I, 498, 500, 610, 611 613, 696; II, 25, 30
Joseph	I, 394
Lorentz (Law.)	I, 681, 682
Ludwig	I, 414
Michael	I, 719
SEITZER	
John Michael	I, 706
SEIVERT	
Johannes	I, 322
SEKATZ	
Peetter	I, 716
SEKLER	
Johans Hendrech	I, 194
SELB	
Johanes	II, 77
SELBACH	
Jacob	I, 479
Johann Thiel	I, 352, 354
Johannes (John)	I, 568, 570, 572
SELBERT	
Adam	II, 106
Barbara	II, 106
Caspar	II, 106
John Georg	II, 106
Maria	II, 106
SELEBERGER (CELEBERGER)	
Johan	I, 66, 69, 70
SELEK	
Anna	I, 80
SELERN	
Barbel	I, 43
SELHOFF	
Conrat	I, 469
SELIA	
John	II, 195
SELIG *see* SEELIG	
SELIGMAN (SELEGMAN, SELLIGMAN, SILIGMAN)	
A.	II, 141
J. Henry (Jost Henry)	I, 573, 574, 575
SELIRIEG	
Anna	I, 118
SELL	
Andres	I, 503
Hans Jorg	I, 503
Jacob	I, 283, 285, 286
Peter	I, 283, 285, 286

SELLER (SELLIER)	
Charles	II, 116
Eliza.	I, 24
Frederick	II, 126
Henderick Philip	I, 21
Jacob	I, 24, 471
Johann Friedrich	I, 484
Peter (Pierre)	I, 384, 386
SELLHEIM	
Johannes	I, 698
SELMAN	
Abraham	I, 400
SELPERT	
Hanne Eve	II, 115
Jacob	II, 115
Peter	II, 115
Rosina	II, 115
SELTENREICH	
Hans Dewalt	I, 356
Johan	II, 137
Leonart	I, 7
SELTZ	
Ludwig	I, 761
SELVERK	
Andrew	II, 56
SELZER (SELTZER, SELLSER)	
Anne Marie	II, 189
Carl	II, 190
Catharina	II, 190
Charlotte	II, 190
Christina	II, 190
Hans Jacob	I, 481
Jacob	I, 24, 481, 722; II, 61 189, 190
Joh. Adam	II, 190
Johannes	I, 439
Ludwig	II, 190
Mattheus (Mathias)	I, 35, 36, 37
Nickolas	I, 403
Ulerich	I, 406
SEMMEL	
Martin	I, 540, 542, 544
SENABLE	
Frederich	II, 163
Johann	II, 163
Regina	II, 163
SENCK	
Johann Georg (Jarrick)	I, 99, 100, 101
SENCLER (DINNLAR)	
Lorentz	I, 652, 654
SENDEL	
Johann Georg	I, 476
SENDERLING	
Johan Nicolas	I, 415
SENFEN (read SENF)	
Rosina	II, 107
SENFFELDER	
Hannes	I, 402

SENFT
Johann Philipp I, 460
John M. II, 51
SENFTLEBER (SENFFTLEBER,
SENFTLEYDER)
Hans I, 627, 630, 634
SENG
Philip Henrich I, 369, 370
SENGER (SENGAR, SINGER)
Carl II, 180
Catharine (Ça-
trina) I, 139; II, 180
Conrad II, 180
Hermann I, 666, 668, 670
Johanes (Johannes) I, 137, 141, 142
SENGEYSEN
Johann Ludwig I, 420
SENGHAAS
Johann Kaspar I, 408
SENN (SEHN, SEN)
Anna II, 134
Anne Marie II, 31
Elisabeth II, 31
Hans Jorg I, 458
Jacob II, 31
Jean Henri II, 31
Johannes I, 341
SENNER (SENNAR)
Abraham I, 688
Baldt I, 695
Gabriel II, 181
Hans Jacob I, 411
SENSEMAN
Ann Catherine I, 320
Heinrich Joachim I, 320, 321, 322
SENSOWKE
Mich. II, 99
SERB
Wentzel I, 726
SEREROS
Andrew II, 47
SERK
Daniell I, 659
SERMATT
George I, 727
SERONI
Maro I, 757
SERRURIER
François II, 129
SERT
Jerg Christian I, 452
SERVAI (ZERWAY)
Jean Jaques
(Jacob) I, 526, 527, 529
SERVAS (SERFAS, SERVEAS)
Johan Philibs (Phil-
ipus) I, 257, 259, 262
Johs Tobs I, 8
SERVER *see* SORBER

SERWIN
Wendel II, 54
SETZER
Johann Adam I, 428
SETZLER (SITZLER)
Johan George I, 465
Zacharias (Zach-
rias) I, 156, 159, 161
SEUBERLICH *see* SÄUBERLICH
SEUBERTH (SEUBERT, SUYBERT,
SYBERT)
Andreas (An-
dereas) I, 502, 540, 542, 544
Baltas (Baltzer) I, 540, 542, 544
Hans I, 501
Johan Georg I, 713
Michael I, 540, 542, 544
Petter (Peiter) I, 212, 214, 215
SEUCKE
Friedr. Wilhelm II, 205
Johann Friedr. II, 205
SEÜFFERT
David I, 346
Leonhardt I, 496
SEUFRIED (SEUFRID, read SEY-
FRIED)
Hans Wendel I, 439
Joseph I, 439
Matheis I, 439
SEULING
Johannes Andreas I, 714
SEUSTERDITZ
Carl I, 440
SEUTER
Hans Jacob I, 440
SEVENBAGGS
Jnº Jacob II, 12
SEVON
Henry I, 708
SEVONBOOM
Fredrick II, 76
SEWALT (SEEWALD)
Johann Ludwig I, 697
Martin I, 697
Nicholas I, 661, 662, 664
SEWENING
John E. II, 122
SEYB
Carl I, 60, 64, 65
Kathrina I, 61
SEYBEL (SEYPELL, SIBEL)
Johann Conradt I, 397
Johann Marx I, 217, 218, 220
Johan Ulrich (Ul-
lerik) I, 217, 218, 220
Michiel I, 18
SEYBERT (SEYPERT, SEYBERTH,
SIBER)
Benedict I, 110

Conrad   II, 54
Jeorg Henrich   I, 721
Johann Adam   I, 697
Lorentz (Laurence)   I, 107, 111, 112
Maria Crete   I, 108
Martin   I, 701
Sebastian   I, 689
Thomas   I, 721
SEYBOLD (SEYBOLDT, SEYBOLT,
    SEIBOLT)
Carl Fried.   II, 192
Jacob   II, 69
Johannes (John)   I, 642, 644
Philip   I, 642, 644
SEYBOT (SEYBOTH)
Christina Friederica   II, 79
Johann Wolfgang   I, 721
SEYDEL (SEIDEL, SEYTEL,
    SIDLE)
Ernst   I, 180, 182, 184
Henrich   I, 463
Johann (Johannes)   I, 286, 287, 288
Johann Michel   I, 754
Johann Nicolaus (Johan
    Nickell)   I, 286, 287, 288
SEYDELMAN
Philip   I, 482
SEYDELMAYER   (SEYTELMIER,
    SEYTELMAN)
Hans George
    (Jurg)   I, 532, 533, 535
SEYDENBENDER
Hennrich   I, 457
Michael   I, 122, 125, 126
SEYDENSTIKER see SEIDEN-
    STICKER)
SEYDER
Christian   I, 422
Henry   I, 426
SEYDLER
Friderik   I, 418
Hans Adam   I, 435
Melchior   I, 346
SEYDS
Peter   I, 418
SEYFERT (SEYFERTH, SYPHERT,
    SEYFARTH)
Christian   I, 256, 259, 261, 724
Joh. Peter   I, 429
Johanes   I, 452, 464
Joseph   I, 685
(See also CEYFERT)
SEYFRID (SEYFRIEDT, SEYFREE,
    SEAFRET, SEYFRIT)
Hans Mardin   I, 453
J. Michael (John
    Mich[1])   I, 596, 598, 600
Johann Jacob   I, 487
Lorentz   I, 409

Phillip   I, 727
(See also SEUFRIED)
SEYGOR
Matheas   I, 407
SEYHAM
John   I, 14, 15
SEYL (SAILLOR)
Johannes   I, 445
Peter   I, 532, 533, 535
SEYLER (SELER)
Baltzer (Balser)   I, 43, 46
Barbel   I, 43
Catharina Elisabeth   I, 157
Hans George
    (Jerik)   I, 22, 23
Henrich   I, 716
Johann Christ   I, 478
Martha   I, 75
Martin   I, 392
Matelina (Mate-
    line)   I, 73, 75
Michael   I, 74
Peter   I, 72, 76, 78, 418
Valentine   I, 74
SEYN (SEG)
Johann Philip
    (Philip)   I, 568, 570, 572
Johannes Petter   I, 402
Johannes Wilhelm   I, 466
SEYNY
Johana Catharina   II, 57
SEYSEN (SYCE)
Johann Adam   I, 307, 309, 310
Joh. Andreas   I, 431
SEYSER (SISET)
Hanns (Henry)   I, 591, 592, 594
SEYSS
Andreas Justus   I, 413
SEYT
Han   I, 19
SEYTER (SEIDEN)
Jan Georg (Jon Georg,
    John Yurg)   I, 283, 285, 286
SEYTFERT (read SEYFERT)
Peter   II, 196
SEYTTER
Friech   I, 394
Jacob   I, 366
SEYTZ (SEYTS, SICKS)
Johann Jacob
    (Jacob)   I, 597, 598, 600
Peter   I, 8
SEYVERT
Jacob   I, 382
SHADIGH (read SCHADIG)
Morritz   I, 499
SHAEFFER see SCHÄFFER
SHAETNER
Hester Maegerita   I, 49

SHAETTER
Jo. Geo. II, 203
SHAFNER, SHAFFNER *see*
SCHAFFNER
SHAINY
Ulrich I, 304
SHALLOBACK (SHALLOBAK,
YELONARK)
Johanes (Hans) I, 592, 593, 595
SHAMAKER
Hans Ubruk I, 12
SHAMAR (SHAMMER, SCHOW-
MACKER)
Peter I, 622, 624, 626
SHAMBACH, SHAMBACK *see*
SCHAMBACH
SHANDZEY
Edward II, 26
SHANECK *see* SCHÄNIKE
SHANGER
Rebecca II, 188
William II, 188
SHANIEMBAR
Elderick II, 195
SHANK *see* SCHENCK
SHANKER
Hans Jacob I, 446
SHANKS
Samuell I, 660
SHAPEN
Aploney I, 80
SHAPPERT, SHABERT *see* SCHAP-
PERT
SHAPPY
Hans Jacob I, 364
Jacob I, 364
SHAPUE
Dan¹ I, 756
SHARE (read prob. SCHEER)
Michael I, 81
SHARPNAGH
Peter I, 277
SHARTZ
Tebalt I, 493
SHARTZER *see* SCHERZER
SHATTINGER
Hans Georg (Yer-
rick) I, 527, 528, 530
SHATTLER
Diterigh I, 357
George II, 202
John II, 202
SHAWDE (read prob. SCHADE)
Christoph I, 503
SHEDEICHER
Helflick I, 102
SHEEYHOUFF
Philip I, 328

SHENNAB
Joseph I, 481
SHEOMAN (SHOMAN)
Johan Henry I, 431
Johanes (Johannes) I, 596, 598, 600
SHERHULT
John II, 195
SHERLY
Paulus I, 459
SHERMAN (read prob. SCHEER-
MAN)
Catrina (Catrine) I, 766, 767
Conradt I, 304
Daniel I, 767
Jerick I, 767
Maria I, 766
Marilis I, 766
Philip I, 767
SHERMILL
John I, 404
SHERNOCK
Kathrine I, 38
SHERTLER
John II, 154
SHETLER, SHITTLER *see* SCHET-
TLER
SHETZ
Friederik I, 454
SHETZGER
Josias I, 507
SHEUD
George I, 475
SHEULE
Passions I, 85
SHEY (SHAVE)
Vallentin (Valen-
tine) I, 266, 269, 272
SHEYBETHAL
Jacob I, 416
SHEYDER
Dewald I, 363
Jacob I, 455
SHEYED
Anthon I, 479
SHEYRISH
Jacob I, 509
SHIAN
Joseph II, 67
SHIDERMANDEL
Nichol I, 308
SHIMFASSEL
Lewis I, 702
SHINEY
Adam I, 499
Lorentos I, 451
SHIPP (TREADELSCHIP, FRE-
DELSCHIP)
John Frederik I, 310, 311, 313

SHIR
 Jacob   I, 12
SHIRRA
 Nicolas   I, 724
SHITERTZ
 Christ[1]   I, 716
SHMERTZKA (SMOTSKA)
 Jacob   I, 586, 587, 588
SHNEAS (read prob. SCHNEE)
 Henry   I, 313
SHOEMAKER see SCHUMACHER
SHOEMAN see SCHUMANN
SHOMONY
 Joseph   I, 434
SHÖN see SCHÖN
SHONFELDT see SCHÖNEFELD
SHONICK see SCHÖNECK
SHONK see SCHUNCK
SHONOWER see SCHÖNAUER
SHÖNHEIT
 Toby   II, 200
SHOOK see SCHUCK
SHOPPFIELD
 Johan Martin   I, 102
SHOUFFMAN
 John Martin   I, 449
SHOUTZ (read prob. SCHATZ)
 Johannes   I, 498
SHOWA (SHOWAY, read prob.
   SCHAUER)
 Friederik (Fred-
   rick)   I, 591, 592, 594
SHREFFLER
 J. Henry   I, 412
SHUE, SHOE see SCHUH
SHULLICUS
 Arns   I, 755
SHULTSONE (read prob.
   SCHULTZ)
 Cathrine   I, 44
 Eliz.   I, 44
SHUNBURG (read prob. SCHÖN-
   BURG)
 Anna Maree   I, 80
SHUREDT
 Jacob   I, 434
SHWANIGEL
 Carrel Henry   II, 19
SHWEYART (read prob.
   SCHWEICKHART)
 Hans Samuel   I, 454
SHYNDECH (read prob. SCHEY-
   DECKER)
 Marilas   I, 102
SIBERBERG
 Johan Christoph   I, 366
SIBIRIT
 Guillaumme   I, 507

SICHER
 Jacob   I, 447
 Peter   I, 447
SICHMUND see SIGMUND
SICKENBERGER
 Peter   I, 430
SIEBENLIST
 Michel   II, 59
SIEBER (SIBER, SIVER, SEWER)
 Fridrich   I, 432
 Hans   I, 163, 165, 166
 Hans Dewald   I, 314, 315
 Peter   I, 724
SIEBERS (SEYVER)
 Conradt (Conrath)   I, 72, 74, 76, 78
 Elizabeth   I, 73
 Lawrence   I, 74
 Matelina   I, 73
SIEBERT
 Carl Frich   I, 491
 Dan[1]   II, 6
 G. A.   II, 141
 J. H.   II, 72
SIEBOLD
 Peter   II, 134
SIEDEL (SIDLER, EADLER)
 Mattias (Mathias) I, 290, 291, 292
SIEFFERT (SIVERT)
 Johann Georg (John
   Georg)   I, 565, 566, 568
 Johann Peter   I, 722
SIEFFNER
 Johann Theis   I, 756
SIEGEL (SEGEL, SIGLE, SIGELL)
 Adam   I, 761
 Eva Elisabeth   I, 157
 Jacob   I, 10, 12
 Johan Albrecht   I, 159, 161
 Johann Carl
   (Carell)   I, 531, 532, 534
 Johannes   I, 167, 168, 360, 362, 736
SIEGENITZ (SEGENITZ)
 Andreas (Adn[x])   I, 589, 590, 591
SIEGENTHAHLER
 Georg   I, 440
 (See also SEIGENDALLER)
SIEGER (SIGER)
 Johann Georg   I, 442
 Johannes   I, 526, 528, 529
SIEGLER
 Hans Heri[k]   I, 7
 (See also ZIEGLER)
SIEGMAN (SIEGEMANN, SIG-
   MAN)
 Bernhart (Bernard) I, 246, 247, 248
 Catarina   II, 14
 Chartar   II, 14
 Christopher   I, 246, 247, 248
 Elisabeth   II, 170

Frederick II, 14
George II, 14
Hans (Johannes) I, 246, 247, 248
Hans Georg (Hans
Jerick) I, 246, 247, 248
Johanes Bernhard II, 170
John (Johannes) I, 246, 247, 248
Peter II, 14
SIEGRIST (SIGRIST, SIGERIST)
Barthol. I, 10, 11
Gorg Adam I, 546, 548, 550
Johann Lorentz I, 585, 587, 588
Michael I, 10, 11
SIEGWALD
Georg II, 19
SIEGWORTH
John II, 188
SIEL
Jurg Friederich I, 403
SIELE (SHEYLIGH)
Hans Georg (Yerrᵏ) I, 526, 528, 530
SIELER (ZIELLER)
Han Titer (J.
Diterich) I, 661, 662, 664
SIELI (SILIA)
Weyrich Ruti I, 169, 170, 172
SIEMEZING
Johann Henrich II, 59
SIEMONSEN
Cathᵃ Elizᵗʰ II, 23
SIEPPERT
Johan Henr. II, 28
SIER
Martin I, 413
SIES *see* SÜSZ
SIEUR
Philip I, 503
SIEVERT (SEIBAS, SEYMER)
Caspar Ludwig I, 536, 537, 538
Johann Henrich I, 536, 537, 538
SIEWER
Jacob I, 346
SIFRY
Henry I, 434
SIGER *see* SIEGER
SIGFRID (SEGFRIED, SIFRIDT,
SIGFRIT)
Frederic II, 84
Georg I, 451
Louis II, 60
Peter I, 704
SIGLE *see* SIEGEL
SIGLER *see* ZIGLER
SIGLIN (ZIEGLIN)
Johannes I, 531, 532, 534
SIGMUND (SIGMUNDT, SIGH-
MOND, SIEGMUND)
Bernhardt I, 31, 32, 33
Chatarina II, 125

Hans Pieter (Hance
Petter) I, 99, 100, 101
Johann II, 125
Johann Michael I, 57, 58
Peter II, 125
Valentine (Valentin) I, 48, 52, 54
SIGWALT
Johann I, 762
SILBER
George I, 411
Tobias II, 179
SILER *see* SEILER
SILHART
Catharine II, 166
David II, 166
Elizabeth II, 166
Gotfry Maga II, 166
SILIGMAN *see* SELIGMAN
SILKS
Anna Maria I, 241
SILLER *see* ZELLER
SILOZ
Benjamin II, 119
SILTZEL
Jacob Ulrich I, 723
SILVIN
Darbie I, 143
SILVIUS (SILICUS)
Caspar I, 716
Johann Hennrich I, 217, 218, 220
SIM (SAEN, SIN)
Anna I, 74
Georg Christian I, 407
Henrich I, 71, 75, 77
Hermann I, 93, 94, 95
Katharine I, 72
SIMBERMAN *see* ZIMMERMANN
SIMER *see* ZIMMER
SIMMERING
Joseph II, 178
SIMON (SIMMON)
A. Carolina II, 105
Andreas I, 234; II, 119
Balsatzer (Baltzar) I, 444, 500
Cath. Eliz. II, 105
Christian I, 162, 164, 166
Conrad II, 191
Dangel (Daniel) I, 293, 294, 295
G. A. II, 141
Hans Nicklas I, 204, 206, 207
Heinrich I, 500
J. Ernst I, 505
Jacob I, 246, 247, 248
307, 308, 309
449; II, 119
Johan Adam (John
Adam) I, 246, 247, 248
Johan Anthon I, 390
Johann Casper I, 526, 528, 530

Johann Christoph   I, 710
Joh. Matthias   II, 44
Johannes   I, 500
Kunigunda   II, 52
Leonhart   I, 474
Lorentz (Lorance)   I, 162, 164, 166
Michael (Michel)   I, 256, 259, 262
                         310, 312, 313
Nickolas   I, 421
Peter   I, 314, 315, 500
Philip·   I, 730; II, 168
Wolf   II, 107
SIMONS (SIMMONS)
Catharine   II, 56
Eve   II, 56
Gabriel   II, 56
Gerhard   II, 161
John   II, 24, 56
Ludwig (Ludwick)   II, 56
Maria   II, 91
Melchior   II, 56
Peter   II, 56
SIMOULT
Jacque   I, 15
SIMS
Charles   I, 531
SIMSON (SIMPSON)
Isaac   II, 148
Mr.   II, 6
Noel   II, 89
SINCLAIR
Anthony   I, 756
SINDER
Jacob   I, 418
SINER (SYNER, SEINIER)
Peter   I, 316, 317
SING
Hans Jerg   I, 427
SINGELE
Andres   I, 443
SINGER
Christian   I, 498
Joseph   I, 710
Michael   I, 435
SINGHAWSE
Michell   I, 660
SINGLY (SINGLEY)
Andreas   I, 452
Margaret   II, 185
Michael   II, 185
Rosina   II, 185
SINGQUET (SYLKET)
Jacob   I, 526, 529
SINGROVE
Folentine (Valentine)   I, 289
SINK see ZINCK
SINN (SIN)
Andreas   I, 236, 238, 239
Frieterich   I, 454

Johann Georg   I, 417
Johann Jacob   I, 400, 417
SINSER
Lodwich   I, 582
SINTZ
Petter   I, 760
SIP see ZIEPF
SIPART
Michel   I, 293
SIPE see SEIB
SIPPEN
Henry   I, 10
SIRACH
Daniel Ernst   I, 719
SISZ (read prob. SÜSZ)
Anna Elizabeth   II, 44
Catharine Eliza   II, 44
George   II, 44
Hans Jacob   II, 44
Hans Jerry   II, 44
Maria Magdalena   II, 44
SITES see SEITZ
SITZER (SETZER)
Johann Martin   I, 454
Michael (Jacob)   I, 551, 553, 554
Peter   I, 426
SIVER
Carl   I, 403
SIVERT (SEEBERT, SEVERT)
J. Joachim (Joh.
    Jacob)   I, 564, 565, 567
SIX (SIXE)
Diterich (Jerich)   I, 222, 223, 225
SLABACH
Dorothea   I, 132
Henry   I, 132
Johan Henrich (Jn.
    Henry)   I, 131, 133, 134
Johannes   I, 131, 133, 134
Maria Elizabeth   I, 131
Tewalt   I, 132
SLATER
Joseph   I, 451
SLAUCH
Anna Katherina   I, 49
John   II, 56
John William   II, 56
SLAUGHTER (SLAUTER)
Caterina   I, 28
Hance (Hanes)   I, 27, 29, 30
Michael   I, 451
SLEEMANN
Jan Matthys   I, 718
SLEGEL see SCHLEGEL
SLEIFENBAUM
Anthon   II, 37
Louisa   II, 36
Maria   II, 36
Wilhelm   II, 37

SLEIG
Geo. I, 689
SLEKMEYER
Blassius II, 135
SLEYDT
Anlies I, 123
SLEYGER
Catharine II, 56
Jacob II, 56
John II, 56
Valentine II, 56
SLIGLOFF (SCHLENGELUF, SCHLENGEUFF)
Analis I, 23
Anna Christian I, 23
Hendrik I, 23, 25, 26
SLINAGER (SLINAGUR, SLYNEGAR, SLINEGAR)
Maria I, 68
Michael I, 66, 68, 69, 70
(See also SLUNACKER)
SLINKER see SCHLENCKER
SLISELL
John II, 186
SLOTHWEILER (ROTHERWITHER)
Jacob I, 248, 249, 250
SLUMMER
Johan Nic. I, 233
SLUNACKER (SLUNAKER, LUNNEKER)
Steven (Stephen, Stifan) I, 117, 120, 121
SLY (SLAY)
Nicholas I, 113, 766
SLYPHER
Phillip I, 660
SMEISSER
Barbara I, 49
Georg I, 50
Margerita I, 49
Mathias I, 48
SMEL
Barbara I, 190
SMELTZ
Clementz II, 113
SMITH see SCHMIDT
SMITTEN (SMITEN, read prob. SCHMIDT)
Adam I, 676
Agnis I, 117
Martin I, 676
SMOKE (read prob. SCHMUCK)
Catharine II, 199
SMYETCH
Lamberth I, 507
SNAVELL (read prob. SCHNABEL)
Henry II, 19

SNEBLER (read prob. SCHNÄBELE)
Ultimer (Ultiner) I, 23, 26
SNEEVLER (SNEEVELER)
Apalone I, 24
Hendrick I, 24
SNESMAN
Joler I, 316
SNOLT
Philip I, 17
SNOW
John I, 556
SNOWFER
Abram I, 660
SNYDER see SCHNEYDER
SNYDING
Ursula I, 107
SOAL
Frantz I, 406
SOAST
Peter I, 753
SOERBER see SORBER
SOETER
Geertruyde II, 70
SÖFFNER
Johannes I, 721
SÖFFRENS (SUFRANCE)
Johanes I, 72, 76, 77
Maria I, 73
SÖFFTEL (SAFFTEL)
Johannes I, 360, 362
Vallentin
(Valentine) I, 360, 362, 429
SOHMITHS (read SCHMITHS)
Rulophs II, 91
SOHN (SOEHN, SOON)
Jacob Friedrich I, 437
Johann Petter
(Joh. Peter) I, 564, 565, 567
Johannes I, 340
SOHNER
Gottlieb I, 424
SOLBRIG
Joh. Gottlieb II, 58
SOLDERMAN
Christane I, 13
SOLDNER
Hans Georg
(Hans Gerg) I, 97, 98, 99
SOLINGER see ZOLLINGER
SOLINUS
Jorgen Henrich I, 465
SOLLBERG
John I, 685
SOLLBERGER (ZOLBERGER, ZOLLBERGER)
Joseph I, 180, 182, 184
Ullrich (Ulrich) I, 180, 181, 184
SÖLLER
Philips Henrich I, 23

SOLMAN *see* ZOLLMANN
SOLOMON (SALLOMON, SOLLO-
MON)
Eberhart
(Everhard) I, 551, 553, 554
Israel II, 153
Joseph I, 729
Levi II, 144
SOLOMONS
Isaac II, 29
SOLT *see* ZOLL
SOLTAN (SOLTANG, SOLT-
HOUGH)
Jerome Diederich (Hironi-
mus Dieterich) I, 672, 673, 674
SOLTZER
John Peter Alls. II, 121
SOMBERO
Johanes I, 683
SOMBERTY
Andreas II, 97
SOMER *see* SOMMER
SOMEY (SOWMY, SOMI)
Hance Jacob I, 127, 129, 130
Hance Michael I, 128
Hance Peter I, 127, 129, 130
Johannes I, 128
Maria Magdalena I, 128
Nicklas I, 82, 83
Otto Frederick I, 127, 129, 130
SOMMER (SOMER, SUMMER, SUM-
ER)
Adam I, 22, 23
Andreas I, 410, 642, 644
Catrina Eliza I, 189
Christian I, 407
Conrad Nic⁸ II, 22
Daniel I, 438
Dieterson II, 121
Hans Adam I, 348, 350, 351
Hans Georg
(Hans) I, 236, 238, 239, 482
Hans Heinrich I, 252, 253, 255
Hans Martin I, 482
Hennrich I, 750
Herman I, 614, 616, 618
Jacob I, 468
Joh. Ernst I, 517
Johan Henrich I, 689
Johann Ludwig I, 513, 514, 516
Johann Michael I, 400, 454, 629
632, 635
Johann Philibus
(Philip) I, 568, 570, 571
Johan Vallenthin I, 474
Johannes I, 482, 615 714
John Jacob I, 357
Johns I, 407
Joseph I, 503

Lenhart I, 454
Matthias I, 451
Michael
(Michel) I, 188, 191, 193, 451
656, 657, 659
Philip I, 614, 616, 618
661, 662, 664
Wilhelmine II, 121
SOMMERFELT
Johan II, 50
SOMMERLAD (SOMERLINE, SOM-
ERLAND, SOMERLADE, SOME-
LADE, SUMERLAUTER)
Johann Gottfried
(Godfrey) I, 376, 377
Johannes (Jones,
Jonas) I, 379, 381
Philip Jacob I, 376, 377
SOMMERS (SUMMER, SOMERS)
J. George
(George) I, 556, 557, 558
SONDERGYSR
Hans Ullrich I, 434
SONLEIDER (SUNLEYDER)
Sebastian I, 677, 679, 680
SONNEBORN (SONEBORN)
Johann Gorg (Johan-
nes Jerich) I, 560, 561, 563
SONNTAG (SONTAG, SONDAGH,
SONTAGH)
Abraham I, 497
Catrina I, 189
Hans Adam I, 314, 315
Hendk. I, 303
Jacob I, 155, 158, 160, 188
191, 193
Johann Jacob I, 686
Johan Ludwig I, 189
SOOPER (read prob. SUPER)
Jacob Fredrich I, 462
SOPEN
Jacob I, 304
SORBER (SOERBER, SORVER, SUR-
BER)
Barbara I, 766
Casper I, 194, 195, 196
Fronegh I, 766
Hans I, 304, 306, 307, 398
Henry
(Hennery) I, 147, 150, 151, 331
Jacob I, 113, 114, 115
331, 765
Johannis I, 483
Rudolff
(Rodolph) I, 113, 114, 115, 765
Verena I, 149
Yak. I, 483
SORG
Adam I, 490

Dewald
  (Diebolt)   I, 546, 547, 549
  Johan Michael   I, 546, 547, 549
SORGE (SURG, SORG, ZORGE)
  George (Jurg)   I, 615, 617, 619
  Johann Julius
    (John Julius)   I, 672, 673, 674
  Philip   I, 546, 548, 550
SÖRGER
  Andreas   I, 356
SOUCHET
  ——   II, 80
SOUCHVRIDT
  Hendrick   I, 123
SOUDER (read SAUTER or SUTER)
  Chris.   I, 237
  Elenor   II, 187
  Feronaga   II, 187
  Fidela   II, 187
  Frena   I, 189
  Henry   I, 660
  J. Frederick   I, 531, 533, 535
  Jacob   II, 187
  Johannes   I, 359
  Joseph   II, 187
  Mary   II, 187
  Werner   I, 394
SOULDER
  Hans Adam   I, 12
SOUS
  John Yerrick   I, 652
SOUST
  Henry   II, 26
SOUTLING
  Johana Maria   II, 58
SOVER (SEVER)
  Philip   I, 113, 765
SOWER *see* SAUER
SOY (ZOHAM)
  Jan Gottfried
    (Godfred)   I, 387, 388, 389
SPAAR
  Hans Michael   I, 331
SPACH (SPAG)
  Adam   I, 134, 135, 136
  Stephanus   I, 762
SPAEL
  Dolly   II, 151
SPAHN (SPAAN, SPANN, SPOAN,
  SPOHN, SPOON)
  Adam   I, 127, 129, 130
  Anna Margaretha   I, 127
  Caspar   I, 468
  George Michael   I, 545, 547, 549
  Hans Jerg   I, 468
  Hans Matis   I, 446
  J. Caspar   I, 486
  Johan Henrich   I, 127
  Petter   I, 408

Uhllerik   I, 486
SPAHNKUCH *see* PFANNKUCHEN
SPAMMANN
  Johannes   I, 752
SPANGENBERG
  Joh. Aug.   I, 517, 518, 519
  Johann Conrad (Johan
    Conr^d)   I, 601, 602, 603, 736
SPÄNGLER (SPANGLER)
  Georg Christian   I, 417
  Michael   I, 169, 171, 172
SPANHAUER (SPAINEHOWER)
  Heinrich (Henrick)   I, 275, 276
  Jacob   I, 275, 276
  Niglaus (Cloyce)   I, 275, 276
SPANHOOFT
  E.   II, 206
SPANLER (read SPANGLER)
  Christoph   I, 406
SPANNAGEL
  Gabriel   I, 485
  Johan Michel   I, 532, 533, 535
  Ludwig   I, 431, 485
SPANSAILER (SPANSEULLER)
  Hans Filipp   I, 88, 90, 91
  Jacob   I, 88, 90, 91
SPANY
  Margaret   I, 123
SPARES
  Johan   II, 50
SPÄTH (SPATE, SPEDT, SPETH,
  SPET, SPED)
  Carl   I, 430
  Fillippus (Fillippus Jacob,
    Philip)   I, 609, 610, 612
  Henry   II, 200
  Joh. Bernhardt   I, 480
  Johan Henrich
    (Henry)   I, 569, 570, 572
  Johan Michael   I, 507
  Johannes   I, 563, 565, 566, 689
  Johannes Philippus
    (Philip)   I, 569, 570, 572
  Margaret   I, 123
  Regina Barbera   I, 144
SPATZ (SPATS)
  George Michael   I, 491
  Lorentz   I, 439
  Michael   I, 494
  Willhelm   I, 348
SPECHT (SPEGT)
  Abraham   II, 164
  Catharine   II, 164
  David   II, 164
  Friedrich   I, 435
  Gotlieb   II, 164
  Jacob   I, 695
  Johann Adam   I, 759
  Johan G.   II, 164

Johann Georg I, 692
Johann Martin (John
Martin) I, 296, 298, 299
Johann Peter
(Peter) I, 217, 218, 220
K. Margaret II, 164
Margaret II, 164
SPECK (SPACK, SPAK)
Adam II, 15
Bernhard I, 649, 651
Carl II, 180
Christian II, 180
Christina I, 157
Christoph I, 621, 623, 625
Daniel I, 555, 556, 558
Dewald I, 357
Fredᵏ II, 180
Frederica II, 180
Johann Adam I, 508
Johannes II, 134
Katrin II, 134
Martin I, 226, 229, 231
Niedarth II, 134
Wilhelmina II, 180
SPEIDEL
Hans Jorg I, 393
Johan Georg I, 445
Joseph I, 393
Matthias II, 179
Maximilianus I, 393
SPEIKER, SPIKER *see* SPIECKER
SPEISER (SPICER)
Elizabeth II, 166
Johan Jeorg I, 757
Joseph II, 166
SPEISS *see* SPIESS
SPEITZEL
Margaret II, 75
Peter II, 75
SPELSHUS
Jan Philip II, 28
SPENGEL
Jerg (George) I, 184, 186, 187
SPENGLER (SPINGLER)
Balser (Balzer,
Balster) I, 99, 100, 101
Hans Caspar I, 9
Hans George I, 457
Henrich (Henry) I, 99, 100, 101
J. George I, 486
Johannis
(Johanis) I, 40, 41, 42, 696
Johenrich I, 413
Jorg (Jerg,
Jerrich) I, 99, 100, 101
Jost I, 759
Michael I, 457

Peter
(Petter) I, 289, 290, 291
431, 486
Wilhelm I, 696
SPENHOVER
Stephen I, 392
SPENNER (SPELLER)
Conrath (Conrad) I, 642, 644
SPENSCHELD
Johan Daniel II, 28
SPERGER (read WOLFERSBER-
GER)
Wolfer I, 31, 33, 34
SPERLING
Andreas I, 714
SPERRY (SPERY, PARREY)
Casper
(Gaspar) I, 331, 332, 334
Melchior I, 456
SPESSARTH (SPESSERTH)
Hans Peter I, 459
Michel I, 458
SPETZIUS (SPITIUS)
Philippus
(Philip) I, 614, 616, 618
SPEYER
Johannes
(John) I, 637, 639, 641
SPICKWALL
William II, 105
SPIECKER * (SPICKER, SPIKER,
SPIGHER, SPEIKER)
Hannes I, 402
Julius I, 402
Maria I, 190
Ulrich
(Ullerik) I, 188, 192, 193
SPIEGEL (SPEAGEL, SPIGELL)
Christoph Friedrich I, 585, 586, 588
Johann Michel I, 195, 196, 197
Johan Remigius I, 459
Michael I, 310, 311, 313
Philip I, 346
Samuel I, 310, 312, 313
SPIELER (SPILLER, SPELER)
Andereas
(Andreas) I, 386, 388, 389
SPIELMAN (SPEELMAN, SPILL-
MAN)
Andereas I, 430
Conrad I, 582, 583, 585
Jacob I, 686
Jnᵒ Theobᵈ I, 691
Johann Peter (John
Peter) I, 581, 582, 584
Johannes I, 691
Lorentz (Lawrence) I, 384, 386
Michael I, 687

SPIER
Bernard   II, 54
Christiana   II, 135
SPIERI (SPIRI, SPIRA)
Nicolas   I, 431
Tomas (Doms,
    Thomas)   I, 189, 192, 194
Wilhelm   I, 522, 524
SPIES (SPIESS, SPIS, SPEISS)
Adam   I, 425
Anna   II, 110
Anna Cath^a   II, 181
Balthaser   II, 69
Caspar   I, 715;   II, 84
Catherine   I, 103;   II, 88
Conradt   I, 415
Daniel   I, 723, 750;   II, 110
Elisabeth   II, 84
François   II, 88
George   II, 84, 88
Hans Jacob   I, 139
Henrich
    (Hendrick)   I, 246, 247, 248, 733
Herrman   I, 752
Hieronimues   I, 484
Jacob   II, 129
Johan   II, 110
Johann Georg (Hans
    Yerrick)   I, 479, 609, 610, 612
                                     II, 205
Johan Jost   II, 110
Johann Ludwig   I, 401
Johan Victtor
    (Victor)   I, 236, 238, 239
John T.   II, 99
Krafft   II, 88
Ludwig   I, 676
Maria   II, 110
Maria Barbara   I, 139
Maria Dorothea   I, 139
Maria Elizabeth   I, 139
P.   II, 142
Philip   II, 84
Susanna   I, 103
Thebus   I, 382
Uhlerich
    (Uldrich)   I, 137, 141, 142
Wilhelm   I, 752; III, 110, 113
SPIGER (read prob. SPEIKER)
Samuel   I, 406
SPILLNER
Lorenz   II, 116
SPINDLER
Johan Philip Davidt   I, 502
SPINGLER (read SPENGLER)
Agnes   II, 165
Barbara   II, 165
David   II, 165
Godfried   II, 165

Gotliep   II, 165
Jacob   I, 130, 133, 134; II, 165
Maria Elizabeth   I, 131, 132
Petter   I, 8
Stophel   I, 131
SPINNER (SPINDER)
Ullrich (Ulrick).   I, 273, 274
SPIRI *see* SPIERI
SPITTELMAYER *   (SPITEL-
    MAYER, SPITTLENMAYER)
Anna Madlena   I, 118
Anna Maria   I, 118
Hans Adam   I, 116, 120, 121
Maria   I, 118
Martin (Marti)   I, 116, 120, 121
SPITTLER (SPITELER, SPITLLER,
    SPITLER, SPIETTELER)
Hans (Hance)   I, 162, 164, 166
Hans Jacob   I, 392
Jacob   I, 450
Jan Georg   I, 432
Johanes   I, 416
Martin   I, 392
Matheas, Senior   I, 392
Wernhar   II, 133
SPITZ
Johannes (Joh.
    Mich^1)   I, 677, 679, 680
SPITZER
Ernestus, de   I, 367, 369
Franz   II, 107
Johan Anderas   I, 693
Johann Henrich   I, 693
SPITZFADEM
Benedict   I, 486
SPITZNAGEL
Baltazar   I, 371
SPONG (read SPANG)
Leonhart   I, 500
SPONHEIMER
Friedrich (Fred^k)   I, 386, 388, 389
Johann Henrich   I, 487
SPONKNÖBEL
Johannes   I, 703
SPONTLER   (WANLER,   WANT-
    LER)
Philip   I, 592, 593, 594
SPOON *see* SPAHN
SPOR (read SPAHR)
Henry   I, 702
SPOTSON
Anna Maria   I, 55
SPOWNER
Michael   I, 12
SPRAHER
Christofour   I, 100
SPRECHER (SPREAKER,
    SPREICKER, SPRECKER)
Cathrina   I, 103

Hans Jerick (Jerig,
Georg) I, 102, 104, 105, 475
Jacob I, 474
Jacob Andreas
(Jacob) I, 638, 639, 641
Johann Christoph (John
Christopher) I, 384, 386
Johann Philipp (Hans
Philips) I, 551, 552, 554
SPRENG
Martin I, 397
SPRENGEL
Adam I, 423
SPRING
Andreas (Androw) I, 343, 345
Hans Gorg I, 453
Jacob I, 369, 370
Johann Casper I, 453
Johan Christoph
(Christ[n]) I, 648, 650
Mardling I, 153
Nicklas I, 430
SPRINGEL
Marx I, 406
SPRINGENKLEE (SPRINGLEY)
Martin I, 227, 229, 231
SPRINGER
Beter I, 405
George (Earak) I, 344, 345
Hans George (Hans
Jerg) I, 405, 406
Jacob I, 176, 177, 178
Johann Friederich I, 486
Johan Gabriel I, 486
Johann Phillip, I, 336, 337, 339
Michael I, 482
SPRINGLER
Caspar I, 7
SPRINGLEY
Martin II, 104
SPRÖTH
Johannes I, 730
SPRUCHMANN
Peter I, 759
SPÜCKER (SPÜKER, SPICKER)
Johann Henrich
(Henrich) I, 379, 380, 382
SPUR
Johan Fridrich I, 489
SPYCKER (same as SPIECKER)
Joh. I, 179, 181, 183
Joh. Peter I, 179, 181, 183
Johannes I, 179, 181, 183
STAAF
Adam II, 24
STÄBLER (STABLER)
Christian I, 485
Christiana II, 187
Johan (John) II, 187

Magdalena II, 187
STACHER
Jacob II, 120
STACKS
Anna Cath[a] II, 23
STADEL
Jacob I, 694
Johann Peter
(Peter) I, 581, 583, 584
STADELLMANN (STADELLMAN)
Johan Willhelm (John
Willm) I, 286, 287, 288
STADELMAYER
David I, 428
STADTLER (STADLER, STATT-
LER, STATLER, STETLER,
STAETLER)
Casper I, 428
Catrina I, 44
Charlote I, 44
Christian I, 213, 215, 216
Daniel I, 492
Georg I, 696, 704
Jacob I, 422
Johann I, 760
Johan Adam (Johann
Adam) I, 35, 36
Johann Georg I, 703
Johanes I, 508
Ludwig Steadler, von I, 167, 168
Maria I, 44
STAEGLICH
Auguste II, 185
Carolina II, 185
Charlotte II, 184
Harms II, 184
STAFF
John II, 55
STAFFEL
Christoph I, 495
STAFFERS
Anna II, 12
Henry II, 12
STAFFON
Uldrich I, 8
STAHD
G. II, 141
STAHL (STAAL, STAHLL, STALL)
Adam I, 531, 533, 534
Andreas II, 170
Augustin I, 498
Christian I, 499
Fredrick I, 344, 345
Frederick Hemming II, 98
Friedrich Wilhelm I, 686
Georg I, 61
Gottfried I, 59, 63, 64
Hans Adam I, 506
Henrich (Henry) I, 297, 298, 300

Jacob   I, 198, 200, 202
    457, 642, 644
Johann Christ.
(Christian)   I, 569, 571, 573
Johann Gorg (Hans
Geo.)   I, 642, 644
Johan Henrich   I, 328
Johann Michael (Hans
Mich¹)   I, 642, 644
Johann Wilhelm   I, 438
Johannes   I, 289, 290, 291, 438
Johanes Peter   I, 755
John   II, 159
John Henry   II, 159
John Jacob (John Cabug,
Jacob)   I, 266, 269, 272
John Wolfgang   II, 121
Katrina   I, 60
Maria E.   II, 159
Maria Elizabetha   II, 69
Matheus   I, 498
Melchior
(Melichor)   I, 199, 201, 203
Michel   I, 505
Tobias   I, 506
Valtin   I, 719
——   II, 159
STÄHLE (STÄHLI, STAELY,
STÄLLY, STALLEY)
Ernst Henri
(Ernest)   I, 536, 537, 538
Hans Jacob   I, 391
Henry (Henrich,
Hans)   I, 252, 254, 255
Joseph   I, 442
Uhllerich (Wilrigh)   I, 327, 329
STÄHLER (STAHLER, STALLER,
STAYLOR)
Johan Adam   I, 397
Johann Nickolas
(Mich¹.)   I, 237, 238, 239
Nichˢ   I, 694
Nicolaus   I, 93, 94, 95
STÄHLIN
Johann Georg   I, 464
STAHLMANN (STOHLMAN,
STALMON)
Jacob   I, 476
Melchior (Milkor)   I, 293, 294, 296
STAHLSMIT (STAALL)
Johan George (John
Georg)   I, 577, 578, 580
STÄHR (STAHR)
Heinrich   I, 391
Michael   I, 497
STAIGER (STEIGER, STEYGER)
Conrad   I, 463
Hans Conrad   I, 463
Leonhard   II, 155

Michael (Mich¹)   I, 604, 606, 607
Sebastian   I, 585, 586, 587
(See also STEIGER)
STAITMAN
Chrisᵗ   II, 153
STALP (STALB)
Johann Gerlach
(Gerlock)   I, 569, 571, 573
STALTON
Hans Martinn   I, 486
STALTZFUS see STOLTZFUS
STAMAN see STAMMANN
STAMBACH (STAMBAGH, STAM-
BOGH, STOMPACH)
Hans Gerg   I, 423
Hans Jacob (Hans,
Jacob)   I, 88, 90, 92, 296
    298, 299, 470
Jacob   I, 263, 267, 270
Pillibs (Philip)   I, 265, 268, 271
Ulrich   I, 305, 306
STAMGAST
Balsazhar   I, 358
Fredrick   I, 660
STAMLER
Jacob   I, 226, 228, 230
Johann Michael   I, 461
STAMM (STAM)
Adam (Johan
Adam)   I, 289, 290, 291, 759
Anna Barbara   I, 127
Conrad   I, 36
Johann Adam   I, 329
Johann Jacob
(Jacob)   I, 340, 609, 610, 612
Johannes   I, 346
Petter (Peter)   I, 143, 145, 146
STAMMANN (STAMMAN, STA-
MAN)
Heinrich Friedrich (Heinrich Fred-
erick)   I, 672, 673, 674
STAMPLIN (read prob. STEMPEL)
Matlina   I, 80
STANCE (read prob. STANTZ)
Anna Maria   I, 767
Hance Jacob   I, 767
Maria   I, 766
Maria Catrina   I, 767
Maria Dorotea   I, 767
STANDEMEYER
Jacob   I, 708
STANG
Johan Philipp   I, 431
Johannes   I, 444
Philip   I, 622, 624, 626
STANGER
Christian Fred.   II, 118
Josse   II, 88
Ludwig (Lodwᵏ)   I, 596, 598, 599

STANTZE
Johann Sigmund   I, 461
STAPF
Friederich   I, 721
STARCK (STARK)
Carl   I, 701
Hannes   I, 695
Jacob   I, 447
Jacob Friederich   II, 171
Johan Goerg
(George)   I, 568, 570, 571
Johann Ludwig   I, 737
Johannes   I, 701
Joseph   II, 93
Ludwig   I, 516, 518, 519
Margretha   II, 171
Michael   II, 171
Pieter   II, 24
Tobias   I, 517
STARR
Johan Donis   I, 479
Johannes   I, 217, 219, 220
STARRFINGER (STAARFINGER)
Johann (John)   I, 296, 298, 299
STARTZ * (STARTS)
Johann   I, 649
STARZMAN (STARTZMAN, STER-
SINGER)
Hans Mardin (Hans
Martin)   I, 213, 214, 216
Henrich   I, 363
STATILY
Hans Uhli   I, 433
Henry Ully   I, 433
STÄTZEL (HETZEL)
Petter (Peter)   I, 621, 623, 625
STAUB (STAUP, STUPE, STOOP)
Adam (Jan Adam)   I, 199, 204, 203
Anderes (Andreas) I, 559, 560, 562
Johannes   I, 717
Matthias (Mathias) I, 656, 657, 658
Michel (Mich¹)   I, 666, 668, 670
Peter   I, 656, 657, 658
STAUBE
Johannes   I, 358
STAUBER (STOUBE)
Peter   I, 564, 565, 567
STAUCH
Andreas   I, 597, 598, 600
Hans Jerg (Yerg) I, 407, 437, 596
                         598, 599
Jacob   I, 407
Johann Jacob (John
Jacob)   I, 596, 598, 600
Joseph   I, 710
Michael (Nich⁸)   I, 596, 598, 600
Wilhelm   I, 493
STAUCKI
Johan Jacob   I, 415

STAUDEHAUER
Carll Ludwig   I, 722
STAUDINGER
Mr. Carl Reinhard
Gottfried   II, 67
STAUDT (STAUD,   STAUT,
STOUT)
Abraham   I, 266, 269 273
Daniel   I, 204, 206, 207
Johann Adam   I, 723
Johan Jerg   I, 266, 269, 273
Johan Michel
(Michael)   I, 122, 125, 126
Johann Nickel   I, 750
Jorg Wilhelm   I, 355
Ludwig Daniel   I, 731
Peter   I, 204, 206, 207
                  293, 294, 295
Wilhelm (William) I, 609, 610, 612
STAUDTER
Johannes   I, 390
STAUFFER (STAUFER, STAU-
FERT, STAWFFER)
Christian   I, 175, 176, 177, 358
                  396, 406, 699
Christob   I, 759
Daniel   I, 78, 81, 82, 397, 732
Henry (Henrich)   I, 397; II, 204
Jacob   I, 59, 63, 65, 79, 82, 83
Johannes (Hans,
John)   I, 175, 176, 177, 465
                         II, 204
Martin   I, 330
Samuel   I, 695
Uhly   I, 11
Ullrich (Uhllerich) I, 397, 486
STAUSS
Eliz.   II, 157
John P.   II, 157
STAUT see STAUDT
STÄUTZEBERGER   (STAUTSEN-
BERGER)
Andreas   I, 59, 63, 65
Silige   I, 61
STAUWER (read prob. STAUFER)
Joh. Wilhelm   I, 465
STAWE
Henry   I, 330
STAY (STEY)
Eva   I, 62
Margretta   I, 62
STEARAG
John Wilm   II, 47
STEB (STEP)
Michael   I, 394
Peter   I, 621, 624, 626
STECHER
Hans Melcher   I, 84, 86, 87
Joseph   I, 704

STECKBEK
Michael   I, 346
STECKEL (STEKKEL)
Johannes   I, 442, 754
Simeon   I, 407
STECKER (STECKEN, STEKER)
Dewald   I, 405
Henry   I, 615, 617, 620
Johan Albert   I, 401
STECKMAR
Gottf^d M.   II, 107
STEDEL (STEEDEL)
Andaris (Andreas)   I, 80
Francis (Frantz)   I, 79, 82, 83
Sharlot   I, 80
STEDLER
Christofel   I, 66, 69, 70
John W. Friedr.   II, 116
STEDTEKORN
John Siegesmund   I, 755
STEEB
Elias   I, 393
STEEBLY
Jacob   I, 432
STEEDOT
John   II, 25
STEERE
Ulrich   I, 7
STEFFAN, STEFFEN *see* STEPHAN
STEFFENS *see* STEPHANS
STEG (STEEG, STEGH)
Albert Otto   I, 591, 593, 594
Johann Arnold (Johann
  Arnoldt)   I, 297, 299
Johann Niclaus (Johann
  Nicolaus)   I, 297, 299
STEGEL (STICKLE)
Caspar   I, 241
Friedrich   I, 717
Henry   I, 448
Johan Peter
  (Petter)   I, 240, 242, 243
Maria Barball   I, 242
Urian   I, 241
STEGER (STEGGER)
Eva   I, 62
Hans Jerig (Hanns) I, 13, 60, 64, 65
Kathrina   I, 61
STEGMANN (STACKMAN)
Elias Conrath   I, 565, 566, 568
Jacob   I, 652, 654
STEGMULLER
Adam   II, 88
Anne   II, 88
Johann Valtin   I, 752
STEGNER
Daniel   I, 621, 622, 625
Lutwig   I, 734

STEHLERT
Johannes   I, 501
STEHLI (STEHLE, STEHELI,
  STEELY, STEELEY, STEILY,
  STELEY, STELLEY)
Anna   I, 80
Hans Jeorg   I, 469
Hans Peter   I, 80
Henrich (Hennerich)   I, 473
Jacob   I, 398, 498
Melcher   I, 332, 333, 334
Ulrich   I, 79, 82, 83
STEHR
Jacob   I, 432
STEIBEL
Joseph   II, 172, 174
STEIDELMULLER
George And^r   II, 128
STEIDGENER (STILLINGER)
Jerg Fridrich
  (Fredrick)   I, 556, 557, 558
STEIDINGER
Hans Jerg   I, 500
STEIDLE (STEITLY)
Johannes (Hans)   I, 552, 553, 554
STEIDLING
Gottlieb   II, 148
STEIGELMAN
Daniel   II, 19
Georg Bernhard   II, 20
Ludwick   II, 19
STEIGER (STEYGER, STEGER,
  STEGGER, STIGER, STYGER)
Anna M.   II, 153
Credle   I, 84
Hannah   I, 84
Hans Peter   I, 84, 86, 87
Henrich (Hendrick)   I, 84, 86, 87
Jerack Adam   I, 85
Johanna   II, 189
John G.   II, 189
Margaret
  (Margerate)   I, 85; II, 189
Michael   II, 189
(*See also* STAIGER)
STEIGERWALD (STEIGERWALT,
  STEICHERWALD)
Friedrich   I, 717
Johann Petter   I, 412
Johannes   I, 717
Joseph   II, 148
(*See also* STEYGERWALT)
STEIGLEDER
Johann Jerg   I, 417
STEIGNER (ZIGANER, STEG-
  GENS, TIGANER)
Hans Bernhart (Hanse
  Barns)   I, 240, 242, 243
Marelis   I, 241

STEILER
Fridrich I, 507
Johan Petter I, 692
STEIN (STEYN, STAIN)
Abraham I, 372, 626, 630, 633
Adam I, 589, 590, 591
Andreas I, 403
Caspar Joseph von II, 190
Christian I, 424
Elias Gottlieb (Elias
Godlif) I, 277, 278, 279
Filibus I, 703
Francis I, 731
Frederik (Fred^k) I, 643, 645
Hans Ludwieg I, 446
Henry I, 372
Jacob I, 330, 438; II, 119
Johan Adam I, 205, 206, 208
430, 464
Johan Casper I, 234, 235, 236
Johan Ebert I, 408
Johann Georg I, 418
Johann Henrich I, 460
Johann Leonhart (Hans
Lenar) I, 116, 120, 121
Johann Philipp I, 531, 533, 535
Johannes I, 217, 219, 220
Leonhardt (Leonhard,
Lenhart) I, 162, 164, 166
348, 349, 351
Nickolas I, 474
Peter I, 256, 259, 261
372, 643, 645
Philip
(Philippus) I, 358, 378, 379, 381
Sebastian I, 318, 372
Simon I, 720
Susanna II, 119
Wilhelm I, 521, 524
STEINBACH (STEINBACK, STEN-
BACH, STENBACK)
Bernhardt
(Bernard) I, 137, 141, 142
Christian I, 66, 69, 70
Dorothy I, 67
Jacob I, 488
Johann Adam I, 760
Johann Elias
(Philip) I, 568, 570, 572
STEINBECKER
Johann Gerg I, 346
John Gotlip I, 737
STEINBERG (STEINBERK)
Robt II, 75
William II, 68
STEINBERGER
Friederich I, 444
STEINBOCK
Johann Georg I, 522, 525

STEINBORN
Michal I, 421
STEINBRECH
Johann Vallentin I, 415
STEINBRECHER (STEIN-
BRECKER)
Gerhart I, 693
J. Diterich I, 527, 528, 530
STEINBRENNER
Jacob I, 485
Marte I, 485
STEINBRINK
Henry I, 753
STEINBRÜCHEL
Jacob I, 364
STEINDORF
Johan Fridrich I, 476
STEINENBACH
Johannes Peter I, 495
STEINER (STEYNER)
Abraham I, 358
Adam I, 736
Anna Cath. II, 4
Bernard I, 698
Christian I, 363, 716
Christoff I, 436
Fred^k II, 4
Georg (George) I, 642, 644
II, 200
Georg Valt I, 712
Gorg Friedig I, 712
Hend^k Philip II, 4
Henrich (Hendrik,
Henry) I, 263, 267, 270, 286
287, 288, 363
Isac I, 363
Jacob I, 43, 45, 46, 263, 267
270, 363; II, 4
Jno Geo. I, 755
Johan Ebert I, 467
Johan Fridrich I, 473
Johan George I, 486
Johanna II, 122
Johannes
(Hannis) I, 263, 267, 270, 363
Johannes Jorg I, 403
Ulrick (Uhlerich) I, 31, 33, 34, 428
STEINERT (STEINERTH, STEIN-
NERT)
Georg Christoph I, 501
Johan Ludwig (Johan Lutwig,
John Lodwik) I, 301, 302, 303
Johan Nickel (Joh, Nickel, John
Nicklas) I, 297, 298, 299
STEINEY (STEILICH, STEYNLL)
Johanes (Johannes) I, 677, 679, 680
STEINGÖTTER
Lewis II, 199

STEINHAUER
Fridrich I, 744
STEINHEUSER
Jonas (Johann) I, 649, 650
STEINIGER (STEINIEGER,
STEININGER)
Jerg (Jurgh) I, 10, 11
Leonhart (Johan
Leonard) I, 48, 52, 54
Magdalena I, 147
STEINKÖNIG
Jacob I, 363
STEINLE
Fridrich I, 489
STEINLEIN
Christoff (Christian) I, 35, 36, 37
STEINMAN (STEINMANN, STEI-
MAN, STEYMAN)
Agnes I, 72
Barbara I, 72
Elizabeth I, 72
Hans I, 116, 119, 120
Hans Conradt I, 434
Johan David I, 755
Johann Jorg I, 71, 75, 77
Johannes (Johans) I, 71, 75, 77
545, 547, 549
Katharine I, 72
Madelen I, 117
Michael (Mickel) I, 595, 597, 599
Peter I, 116, 119, 120
Rudolff (Rudolph) I, 304, 305, 306
STEINMETZ
Bouchardt II, 111
Carl I, 759
Caspar I, 465, 759; II, 8
Cath. II, 8
Christian II, 185
Daniel I, 96
Friedrich I, 169, 170, 172
Henry (Henrich) I, 404, 759
Jacob II, 14
Johann Conrad I, 531, 533, 535
Johann Jacob I, 465
Johann Nicklaus (John
Nicholas) I, 43, 46
Johan Philip I, 694
John I, 465
Marg^t II, 8
Niclas I, 358
Peter I, 366, 368
Simon II, 8
Valdin (Valtin) I, 178, 180, 182
STEINROCK
Johan Georg I, 406
STEINSEIFFER (STEINSAYFER,
STEINSIEFFER)
Johann Danniel I, 484
Johannes I, 408

Johannes Henrich I, 577, 579, 580
STEINWEG
Gorg (George) I, 601, 602, 604
John Yerrick (George,
Junr) I, 601, 604
STEINWEHN (STUNBEAR)
Joachim Behrnt
(Bearns) I, 573, 574, 575
STEINWEIS
John Adam I, 700
STEINWYK
Dominica II, 68
STEISS (STYS)
Carl (Charles) I, 591, 593, 594
STEITZ
Johan Heinrich (Johan
Hendrick) I, 591, 593, 594
Johan Heinrich I, 739
Michel I, 335, 336, 338
Peter II, 20
STELFELT (STELLFELT)
Henry I, 20, 21
STELI (STEALY)
Anna Barbra I, 81
Henrich I, 473
Jacob I, 87, 89, 91, 473
STELL
Katrina I, 61
STELLER
Hennrich (Henrich) I, 642, 644
Leonhart I, 507
STELLEY (STELLY)
Jacob I, 153, 154
STELLEY
Joseph I, 332
STELLING (STOLLING)
Caspar (Casper) I, 156, 159, 161
STELLWAGEN (STELWAG)
Friedrich I, 356
Jacob I, 715
Quardt (Quard) I, 296, 297, 299
STELMERS
E. M. Dorothea II, 23
STELTING
Andrew I, 745
STELTZ (STELS)
Balthser (Baltzar) I, 642, 644
Christian I, 401, 676
STELTZEL (STULTZELL)
Henrich (Henry) I, 586, 587, 588
STEM
Ulrich I, 489
STEMPEL (STEMPLE, STEMBEL)
Jacob I, 93, 94, 95
Johann Frietrich
(Frederick) I, 234, 235, 236
Johann Peter I, 169, 171, 172
Nicholas I, 93, 94, 95
Valentin I, 234

STENG
Johann Michael   I, 407
STENGER
Adam   I, 724
Anna Sophia   II, 103
Catrina   II, 103
Christian   I, 725
Conrad   I, 425
Daniel   I, 724; II, 103
Fritz   II, 103
George (Görge)   I, 425; II, 103
Jacob   I, 724
Johann Adam, Sr.   I, 725
Johannes   II, 103
Salomon   I, 724
STENTZ (STENCE, STANCE)
Henrich
(Henrick)   I, 113, 114, 115, 765
STENZENBERCH
Friedrich   II, 206
STEP *see* STEB
STEPHAN (STEFFAN, STEPHEN,
STEFFEN, STEFFE)
Adam   I, 428
Anna   I, 80
Barba   I, 80
Frieterich   I, 523, 525
Hanns Mates   I, 687
Jacob   I, 356
Johann Anton   I, 721
Johan Jacob   I, 233
Johann Philip
(Philip)   I, 378, 379, 381
Johannes   I, 382
John Michael   II, 105
John Philip (Philip)   I, 180, 182, 184
Mardin   I, 688
Nicolaus Henrich   I, 753
Peter   I, 703, 758
Theobald   I, 749
STEPHANS (STEFFENS)
Catharina   II, 92
Hans Mich[1]   II, 23
STEPHANUS (STEVANUS,
STEFFHANNES)
Johannes   I, 656, 657, 659
STEPHANY
Francis   I, 742
STERB (STERP)
Adam Thomas   I, 569
Andrew   I, 293
STERCHI (STERCHY)
Christian   I, 494
Heinrich   I, 442
Ulrich (Ulrig)   I, 494
STERENFELS
Jacob   I, 391
STERHELD
——   II, 161

STERN (STERNE, STERNN)
Friedrich Heinrich   I, 510, 512
Jacob   I, 237, 238, 239
Johann Michel   I, 323, 325, 326
Paul   I, 660
STERNBERGER
Johann Theobold   I, 546, 547, 549
STERNEMAN
Peter   I, 396
STERTZING
Johann Geo.   II, 120
Jost Henrich   II, 120
STETTELBAUER
Hans Geo.   I, 751
STETTLER (STETLER)
Abraham
(Aberham)   I, 221, 222, 224
Christian   I, 221, 222, 224
Christopher (Chrisofel)   I, 642, 644
Vallentin   I, 693
STETTLY
Christian   II, 75
STETZEL
Andres   I, 712
STETZLER
Peter   I, 409
STEUBESANT (STIVESTAN)
Johann Georg (Hans
Yerick)   I, 591, 592, 594
STEÜDEL
Joseph   I, 491
STEUDTLE (STEIDTLE, STEY-
DLE)
Jacob   I, 605, 606, 608
STEUER
Johann Adam   I, 727
Tobias   I, 212, 214, 215
STEUERNAGEL
Gottlieb   II, 58
STEVERONG
Sante   II, 26
STEY
Eva   I, 62
Margretha (Mergretha)   I, 61, 62
Peter   I, 60, 64, 65
STEYB (STEIPE, STAUP)
J. George (John
George)   I, 560, 561, 563
STEYGER
Andereas   I, 467
STEYGERWALT (STEYERWALD,
STYERWALD)
Christian   I, 462
Eberhard   I, 444
Friederich   I, 717
Georg (George,
Yerick)   I, 373, 374, 375
Johannes   I, 412

STEYL (STYEL)
Hans Jerg (Hans
Yerr^k) I, 596, 598, 599
STEYMANN
Johann Christiann I, 721,
STEYNMUTCH (read prob. STEIN-
METZ)
Catharina I, 44
Johannes I, 44
Lenard I, 44
STEYSEMANN
John Fred^k II, 121
STICHEL (STEGELL)
Johan Conrath
(Conrad) I, 217, 219, 220
STICHET
Adam Charles II, 93
John II, 93
STICHLING (STIGLIN, STICK-
LING)
Frantz (Francis) I, 636, 638, 640
Johannes I, 540, 542, 544
STICHTER (STITTER)
Conradt I, 397
Vallentin I, 397
STICK
Emanuel II, 195
STICKELER (STRICKEL)
Andries (Andreas) I, 22, 23
STIEBEL
John Con^d I, 700
STIEBLER
Johann Adam I, 423
Johannes I, 423
STIEF (STHIEFF)
Gerg Fridrich I, 531, 533, 534
STIEFERS
Anna Chathrina II, 50
STIEFFEL (STIFFEL)
Hans Adam I, 502
Hans Melchior I, 502
Jacob I, 31, 33, 34
STIEFFELMEYER
Stephan I, 422
STIEFLIN
Juliana II, 201
STIEGEKHEL
Jacob I, 498
STIEGEL
Henderick Willem I, 443
STIEGER (STEYGER)
Jacob I, 232, 233
STIEGLER (STIGELER, STEE-
GLER)
Johan Christoff I, 352, 354
Johannes Gorg I, 353, 354
STIEHL
Johann Abraham I, 428

STIELE
Catharina II, 33
Elizabeth Catharina II, 33
Joh^n Henrich II, 33
STIER
Catharine II, 43
Daniel II, 43
Jacob I, 424
Mathes I, 424
Niclaus I, 752
Sebastian I, 695
STIERLE
Jacob I, 677, 678, 680
Johan Georg I, 734
STIERLEIN (STIERLEN)
Michal I, 394
Ulrich I, 585, 586, 588
STIERNKORB
Johann Wilhelm I, 683
STIESS (STIES, STIS)
Hans Adam I, 105
Jerig Adam I, 102
Johann Friedrich I, 476
Johann Jacob I, 689
STIEVER
Jon Henrick II, 76
STIEZEL
Michael II, 122
STIGELMAN (STEIGELMAN)
Johan Jacob I, 545, 547, 549
Peter I, 690
STIGEN
Even Christian I, 84
STIGLITZ (STIGLIEN)
Johan Georg Bern-
hardt (Barnard) I, 384, 386
STIGMAN
John II, 60
STILEY
Jacob I, 660
Ludwick I, 659
Peter I, 660
STILL
Henrich I, 113, 114, 115, 765
STILLCHERD
Johannes I, 304
STILLING
Constantinus I, 322
STIMMEL
Friderich I, 716
Johann Albrecht I, 628, 632, 635
Johann Isaac
(Isaac) I, 373, 374, 375
Johann Petter
(Peter) I, 419, 628, 632, 635
STINDLER
Johann Lorentz I, 459
STINEBROFF
Jacob I, 226; II, 103

STINEFIELD
M^r II, 109
STING
Johann Friedrich I, 425
STINGLIE (STINGLY)
Johannes I, 226, 228, 230
STINTZ
Jacob I, 236
STIPPER
David II, 150
Rosina II, 150
STIRN (STEHRN)
Antoni I, 470
Georg I, 470
STOB
Samuel II, 121
STOBER
Christian I, 447
Jacob I, 173, 174
Joachim (Jockem) I, 231, 232, 233
Valentine (Veltin) I, 173, 174
STOCK (STOK)
Adam I, 480
Anthon I, 700
Conradt I, 74
Eliesa II, 186
Gottfried I, 700
Hans Adam I, 304
Johan I, 18
Johan Adam I, 460, 727, 760
Johann Philipp I, 366
Philip I, 700
Tonina II, 186
W^m II, 95
STÖCKEL (STOCKEL, STÖKEL, STECKEL)
Heinrich I, 700
J. Zacharias (John) I, 601, 602, 603
Johann Baltzer I, 444
Philip Jacob I, 707
STÖCKER (STOCKER, STECHER)
Anna I, 135
Barbara I, 135
Johann Georg
(Johannes Jerick) I, 559, 561, 563
Johann Vallendin
(Valentine) I, 199, 201, 203
Johannes I, 500
Margerite I, 49
Maria I, 135
Michel I, 48, 52, 54
Peter I, 134, 136
STOCKHALERN (STOCKHALERN)
Elizabath I, 241
Michall I, 241
William I, 241
STOCKI (STOCKIE)
Elias I, 471
Hans (Hance) I, 163, 165, 166

STOCKIUS
Erasmus I, 403
STÖCKLY (STECKEL)
Christian I, 156, 159, 161
STOCKMANN (STOKMAN)
J. Engel I, 425
Johann Philipps I, 425
Johannes Peter I, 712
Justus Christ II, 70
STOCKS
A. Cath. Maria II, 105
STOCKSCHLÄGER (STOCK-SCHELDER, STOCKSLEGER, STOCKSCHLEGER, STOCH-SLEGR)
Allexander I, 310, 312, 313
Johannes I, 310, 311, 312
STOEHR, STOER *see* STOHR
STOEL
Anthony II, 183
STOERTZEMEYER
Jno Geo. I, 752
STOFER (read prob. STAUFER)
Anna I, 117
STOFF
Jacob I, 761
STOFFEL (STOPHEL, STOFFLE)
J. Henry (Henry, Johannes Henr^k) I, 559, 561, 562
Johan Michael I, 444
Johan Michel I, 696
Michel I, 686
STOFFLET
Johannes I, 759
STOHL
Hans I, 447
STOHLER
Hans I, 392
Henrich I, 472
Marty I, 720
(*See also* STOLER *and* STOLLER)
STÖHR (STOEHR, STOER, STER, STERR)
Christian I, 677, 679, 680
Conradt I, 477
Friederich I, 497
Gorg (George) I, 648, 650
Henrich I, 178, 180, 183
Jacob I, 456; II, 45
Johann Adam I, 448
Johan Henrich I, 328, 456
Johan Peter I, 752
Johann Wilhelm
(John Wilhelm) I, 576, 578, 580
Johannes I, 178, 180, 183
379, 380, 382
John Engel I, 700
Jost Peter I, 503
Philip (Fillibs) I, 178, 180, 183

STOHS
Carl II, 192
Hans George II, 192
Maria Agnes II, 192
STOKIE
Jacob I, 175, 176, 177
Simon I, 175, 176, 177
STOKINGER
Jean Andree I, 688
STOLER (STOHLER)
Bernhart (Leonard) I, 205, 207, 209
Gerg (Jurg) I, 205, 207, 209
Hans I, 392
Mattias I, 205, 207, 208
STOLL (STALL, STOLLE)
Friederich I, 348, 349, 351
Godfrey I, 738
Hans Adam I, 8
Johann Adam I, 745
Johann Geo. II, 99
Johann Jacob I, 507
Johann Wilhelm I, 438, 728
John Martin I, 690
Matheas (Matthys) I, 585, 587, 588
Valentin I, 500
STOLLBERGER
Daniell I, 716
STOLLER (STOLER)
Bastian I, 162, 164, 166
Uhllerik I, 405
STOLOYN
Andreas I, 123
Anna I, 123
Johan I, 123
Marilis I, 123
STOLTZ (STOLZ)
Carrelle I, 701
Conrad I, 297, 298, 300
Georg (George) I, 234, 235, 236
Henrich I, 143, 145, 146
Johann Adam I, 471
Johann Conrad I, 701
Johan Henrich I, 577, 579, 581
Johann Jacob I, 357
Johannes Michel I, 408
Johannes Peter I, 577, 579, 581
Michael II, 188
Nicolaus I, 466
Regula I, 148
Simon I, 234
STOLTZE
Hein. Rudolff I, 505
Johan Adam I, 504
Joh. Joachim II, 139
STOLTZEL
Geo. Jacob I, 733
STOLTZFUS
Christian I, 712
Nickel I, 712

STOLTZNER
Joh Bernhd II, 139
STÖMFLY (STEMPHLEY, STEM-
FLY)
Hans I, 79, 82, 83
STOMMER (TOMER)
Marcus (Mark) I, 555, 556, 557
STONE
Betsey II, 75
John II, 75
STONER (STOHONER)
Fredrich II, 77
Hans Ullrich (Hans
Ulrich I, 585, 586, 588
STONFIELD
Corn. II, 24
STONING
Susanna I, 766
STONS (STIZHOUS)
Jacob I, 384, 386
STOP
Joseph II, 125
STOPPEL
Philip II, 134
STOPPELBEIN (STOPPELBEINN,
STOPPBEIN)
Jacob I, 297, 298, 300
Johan Balt (Johann
Valtin, Vallentin) I, 297, 298, 300
STOPSTER
Johanna II, 189
STORCH (STORCK, STORICH,
STORK)
Adam I, 452
Dewalt I, 475
George II, 52
Joachim Wilhelm I, 432
Johan Wilhelm II, 49
STÖRCKELL
Conradt I, 709
STORGER
Henrich Valten I, 752
STORICH (STÖRY)
John George I, 336, 337, 339
Lud. Henrick Von II, 72
STORLEIG
Hugh I, 609
STORLL
Charles II, 122
STÖRLLER (STANNER)
Catrina I, 139
Johan Caspar
(Caspar) I, 137, 141, 142
Johan Jacob I, 139
John Nicholas I, 139
Maria Magdalena I, 139
STORM
Jacob I, 18, 19
II, 119

Johannes   I, 8, 415, 422
Philip   I, 417
STORMER
Christoph   I, 410
STÖRNER (STORMER, STORNNER,
    STURNER)
Christoph   I, 737
Deobald (Tewald) I, 225, 228, 230
Hans Jorg   I, 343, 345
Jacob   I, 661, 662, 663
Johann Görg   I, 418
STÖRR
Gorg Adam   I, 453
STORTZ
Johann   II, 125
STÖS
Hans   I, 492
STÖSSER
Johannes   I, 452
STOT
Cath^a   II, 3
STOTENBECKER see STUTEN-
    BECKER
STOTER (STÖTHER)
Han Nich.   I, 236
J. M.   II, 193
STOTTERMAN
Johan Ludewig   I, 505
STOTZ
Christian   I, 446
Johann Georg   I, 459
Ludwig   I, 445
Petter   I, 445
STÖTZEL
Johannes   I, 522, 525
STOUDER (STODER, STODEN)
Christian
    (Cristian) I, 116, 118, 119, 120
STOUDT   (STOUD,   STOUT,
    STAUT, STAUDT)
Andreas   I, 371
Catherina   I, 44
Hans Adam   I, 169, 170, 172
Johann Jacob   I, 170, 171, 173
Johannes   I, 170, 171, 173
John   II, 185
Magdalena   I, 44
Peter   I, 175, 176, 178
STOUGH
Godfried   I, 490
STOUGHER
Vincent   I, 18
STOUPE
Frances   I, 12
STOUPHER (read STAUFER)
Ulrich   I, 10
STOUS
J. Nicklas   I, 500
STOUTSMAN see STUTZMAN

STÖVER (STOVER, STOUVER)
Johann Caspar   I, 22
Johann Caspar
    Ss. Theol. Stud.   I, 22
Martin   I, 327, 330
Philip   I, 225, 228, 230
Uhllerich   I, 397
STOWBACK
J. Henry   I, 501
STOWFER (STOWPER, STRAW-
    BER)
Daniel   I, 526, 528, 530
STRABE
Daniel Godlob   II, 100
STRACK
Henrich   I, 523, 525
Johan Jost   I, 692
Johann Peter
    (Jan Pieter)   I, 66, 69, 70
STRACKBEIN (STRACHBEIN)
A. E.   II, 143
Ann Elisabeth   II, 84
Ann Gertrout   II, 84
Ann Mary   II, 84
Catharine   II, 84
Christian   II, 84
Christina   II, 190
Daniel   II, 84
Elisabeth   II, 84
G.   II, 143
Johann Jost   I, 755
Johannes   I, 754
John Henry   II, 84
John Jost   II, 84
John Philip   II, 190
Jost   II, 84
Jost Henry   II, 84
Ludwick   II, 84
Mary Elisabeth   II, 84
Philip   II, 84, 190
Valentine   II, 84
STRÄCKER (STRECKER)
Johann Lorentz   I, 365
Mardin   I, 365
STRADTER
Johann Henrich   I, 411
John Henry   I, 411
STRAHLHEIMER
Gottl.   II, 139
STRAHLING
Christian   I, 411
STRAMANN
Anna   II, 93
STRASER
Margretha Carolina
    Elisabetha   II, 79
STRASINSKY
Carl   II, 170

Johana Eilhelmina
　Constanz II, 170
　Michael Friederich II, 170
STRASS (STRAS)
　Johann Conradt I, 690
　Johann Friedrich I, 690
　Johann Nicol (Nicolas) I, 59, 63, 65
　Johannes I, 487
STRASSBURGER (STRASBURGER)
　Johann Andreas I, 323, 325, 326, 727
STRATSBURG
　Fredrick II, 77
STRÄTTER
　Johannes I, 488
STRATZ
　Hans Jacob I, 399
STRATZER
　Antoni I, 406
STRAUB (STRAUP)
　Andreas (Andereas) I, 322, 451
　Charles II, 126
　Hans I, 453
　Henry I, 508
　Jacob I, 124
　Jerg I, 466
　Johan Mattheus II, 30
　Johann Philipp I, 509
　Johann Wilhelm
　　(John Wm.) I, 79, 82, 83
　Johannes I, 738
　Maria I, 123
　Michael I, 440
　Peter (Pieter) I, 122, 125, 126
　Thomas I, 493
STRAUBE (STRAUBLE)
　Johann August
　　(Johan Augᵗ) I, 601, 602, 603
　Johann Gottfried I, 258, 260, 263
　Johann Peter I, 452
　Michael I, 234
STRAUBEL (STRAUBLE)
　Johan II, 72
　Zacharias I, 505
STRAUCH (STRUNCH,
　STRANTCH)
　Adam I, 180, 182, 184
　Johann Friedrich I, 759
　Johann Henrich I, 687
　Simon Peter
　　(Simon) I, 556, 557, 558
STRAULL (STRAUEL, STROLE)
　Johanes (Johan) I, 642, 644
　John Hein. II, 47
STRAUMAN
　Heinerich I, 721
　Sebastian I, 738
STRAUSS (STRAUS, STROUS)
　Adolph II, 169
　Albrecht (Albright) I, 93, 94, 95

David I, 707
　Docktour II, 102
　George Niklas
　　(Nicholas) I, 531, 533, 535
　Jacob I, 420
　Johann Fridrich I, 409
　Johann Georg I, 503
　Johann Ludwig I, 404
　Nicklas (Nicholas) I, 226, 228, 230
STRAUWMAN
　Johanes I, 416
STREADER
　Caspar I, 411
　John Henry I, 411
STREAMER
　Charles II, 186
STREB
　Catarina II, 14
　Christiana II, 14
　Jacob II, 14
　Magdalena II, 14
STREBECK
　Christian I, 124
　Jerich I, 124
STREBIG
　Julius Caspar I, 672, 673, 674
STRECK
　Alexander Magnus II, 191
　Carolina Blandina II, 191
　Carolus Magnus II, 191
　Ferdinand Mowritz II, 191
　Helena Clarissa II, 191
　Louisa Wilhelmina II, 191
　Maria II, 191
　Maria Amelia II, 191
　Thomas Magnus II, 191
STRECKER
　Johann Georg Michel I, 721
　Johann Michael I, 485
STREDER (STRETER)
　Hans Wellem I, 352, 353
　Jacob I, 559, 561, 563
STREEMCHILD (STRIEMSHIELD,
　STREMSHILD)
　Jacob I, 545, 547, 549
STREHM (STRAM)
　Adam I, 614, 616, 619
　Johann Heinrich I, 614, 616, 619
STREICHLE
　Mattheis I, 360, 362
STREIDTZ (STRIETE)
　Gottfried (Godfrey) I, 559, 561, 563
STREIGNAGLE
　Johannes II, 135
STREIN
　Adam II, 10
　Hans Martin I, 395
　Hans Petter I, 457
　Jacob II, 10

Johann Gorg I, 689
STREITER (STREIDER, STREID-
 TER)
Hannah II, 83
Henry II, 83
Johann Philipp I, 179, 181, 183
STREITHOFF
Jost I, 396
STRELE (STRELY)
Andreas I, 344, 345
Jacob I, 345
STREMMEL
Ann Catharine II, 84
Ann Gertrout II, 84
Elisa Gertrout II, 84
Joachim I, 756
Richard II, 84
STREMPEL
Johann Wilhelm I, 496
STRENGER
Johanes I, 688
STRENT
Nich^s II, 22
STREUBER
Johann Conradt I, 493
STREVEN
Carolina Dan II, 91
STRIBER
Adereas I, 483
STRICH
Gerlach I, 404
STRICKEM
Mr. I, 20
STRICKER (STRIKER)
Allbright II, 12
George II, 126
Henrich (Henry) I, 113, 115, 766
Johann Wilhellem I, 488
STRICKERT (STRECKIES)
Hendrich (Henry) I, 258, 260, 263
STRICKHAUSCHEN
Wilhelmus I, 401
STRICKLER
Aberham (Ab^m) I, 610, 611, 613
Adam I, 131
Anna I, 191
Anna Catrina I, 191
Barbara I, 191
Christina II, 54
Daniel I, 697
Elias I, 130, 133, 134
George II, 54
Hans Jacob I, 189, 192, 194
Henry (Henrich) I, 16, 17, 131
Johannes I, 130, 133, 134
Margaret I, 67
Maria Catharina I, 131
Philip I, 131
Ulrich I. 189, 192, 194

STRIEBEL
Wilhelm II, 20
STRIEBY (STRIBY, STREVEY)
Hans Michel I, 348, 349, 351
Jacob I, 348, 349, 351
Johan Jacob
 (Jacob) I, 556, 557, 558
STRIEGEL (STRIGEL)
Balthazar II, 199
Christoph I, 704
STRIEL
David I, 331
STRIETZEL
Johann Gottfried I, 749
STRIKHAUSEN
Wilhelm I, 676
STRILY
David I, 344
STRITTENBERG
Gaspar I, 637
STROBANCK
John I, 721
STRÖBEL (STROBEL, STREBEL,
 STRUBEL)
Christoph I, 490
Hans Jerg (Hans
 Gorg) I, 246, 247, 248
Johan Michael I, 605, 606, 607
Leonhart I, 344, 345
Ludwig I, 605, 606, 607
Michael I, 222, 223, 225
STROCH (read prob. STROH)
Wilhelm II, 113
STRÖDER (STREDTER, STRETER,
 STRÖDER, STRÖDTER)
Christoph
 (Christopher) I, 217, 218, 220
Johann Conrad I, 503
Johann Henrich I, 411
Johannes I, 411
John Henry I, 411
STROEMBERG
Ulf. II, 119
STROH (STRO, STROHE)
Carel II, 30
Daniel II, 30
Friederich
 (Frederic) I, 398; II, 155
Jacob I, 652, 654
Jost I, 451
Mad^a II, 30
Peter I, 649, 650
Philipp I, 408; II, 52
Philips Jacob II, 30
STROHAUER (STROHAVER)
Barbara I, 108
Catharina I, 108
Hans Jerg (Jerick) I, 106, 110, 111
Hans Peter I, 108

Maria Catharina I, 107
STRÖHER (STRÖHR, STROHER)
Hans Adam I, 379, 380, 382
Henrich I, 703
Johann Mattes
(Mattys) I, 379, 380, 382
Johan Peter I, 456
Johannes Mattes
(Mathias) I, 379, 380, 382, 398
STROHL (STRAUL, STRALL,
STROHLE)
Adolph I, 746
Caspar I, 430
Johannes I, 217, 219, 220
Joseph I, 450
Peter I, 387, 388, 389
STROHM (STROM, STROME,
STRUM)
Barbara II, 49
Benedice I, 7
Christian I, 79, 82, 83
362; II, 49
Elizabeth II, 49
Evrard II, 184
Henrich I, 694
Jerg I, 360, 362
Johann Henrich I, 723
Johannes I, 551, 552, 554
John II, 49
Kasber I, 347
Margarite Eliz. II, 105
STROHMENGER (STROMINGER)
Johann Jacob
(John Jacob) I, 596, 598, 599
STROHN
Cristina Gertraut II, 34
Henrich II, 30
Johann Jacob II, 34
STROHPETER
Hartman I, 452
STROHSHNEIDER (STROHSCH-
NEYDTER)
Johann I, 390
Johannes I, 455
Johannes Friderich I, 455
STROLM
David II, 61
STROOMS
Mar. II, 47
STROP
John Barnats I, 80
STROTT (STROT)
Johan Konrath
(Conradt) I, 581, 583, 584
STROUBLEN
Clove I, 43
STRÖVER
Joachim I, 501

STROWMA
Baltzar I, 392
STRUB (STRUBB)
Adam I, 432
Jacob II, 146
Johannes I, 473
William I, 169, 170, 172
STRUBEL (STROUBEL, STRU-
BELL)
Dietrich I, 371
Friedrich (Frederick) I, 43, 45, 46
STRUBHAR
Hans I, 406
STRUCKMEYER
Hinrich Jacob I, 505
STRUDTER
Hans Caspar I, 451
STRUM *see* STROHM
STRUMBER (STENBRAND, STEN-
BRANDER)
Barbra I, 118
Hans Michel
(Migel) I, 117, 120, 121
Sibela I, 117, 118
STRUMFER
Charlotta II, 188
John II, 188
William II, 188
STRUNCK (STRUNK)
Johan Engell
(Engle) I, 568, 570, 572
Johan Henrich (John
Henry) I, 569, 571, 572
Johann Peter I, 353, 354
Johann Wilhelm I, 699
Johannes Gerlach I, 699
Weymar I, 356
STRÜVE
Marg^a Eliz^th II, 23
STRUWEL
Casper I, 167, 168
STRYSSKAP
Friederich Christoph, van I, 21
STUBACHER
Susanna II, 177
STÜBBE
——— II, 50
STUBE (STUBBE)
Nicolas (Nicklas) I, 167, 168
STUBENITZKE
Philip II, 47
STÜBER (STEVER, STIVER,
STUBER)
Balthas (Baltzar) I, 84, 86, 87
Eve Crispin I, 84
George Friedrich I, 649, 650
Görg Mölchior I, 383
Hans (Hanse) I, 12, 447
Johann Friederich I, 488

Peter I, 300, 301, 302
SUCHER
Johanes I, 417
SUCHNITZ
Henry II, 122
SUCK
Eliz^th II, 23
Nicol. Adolph II, 138
SUDER
Anthony I, 434
Philip Jacob I, 694
SUDTNE
Marti I, 739
SUER
J. D. II, 108
Rich^d II, 108
SÜHN
Peter I, 413
SUHRER (ZURER)
Martin I, 531, 532, 534
SUINDENER
Thomas II, 183
SULGER
Hans Jerg I, 495
Jacob I, 727
Johann Stephan I, 738
SULION
Johann Bastian II, 4
SULLER
Hanns Uhllerik I, 393
SULLINGER (SULLENGER)
Christopher I, 18
Frederik I, 469
SULTER
C. T. Hannibal II, 107
SULTZBACH (SULSBACK, SULS-
PACK)
Johan Jost (Johan) I, 217, 219, 220
Philips I, 412
SULTZBERGER (SOULTZBERGER,
SOUSBERGER)
Jacob (Jac.) I, 303, 306, 307, 500
SULZER (SULTZER)
Anthoni (Anthony) I, 652, 654
Rudolph I, 741
SUMGER
Geo. I, 31
SUMMERAUER (SUMERAUER,
SOMEROWER)
Heinrich (Hend^k) I, 384, 385
Johannes (Hans) I, 383, 385
SUMWALD (SUMWOLD, SUN-
WOLD)
Andreas I, 175, 176, 178
SUNCKEL
Johann Jacob I, 761
SUNDBERG
Hinrich Willm II, 22

SÜNDEL (read ZÜNDEL)
Christoff I, 475
SUNDER
Jacob II, 151
SUNDLE (read SÜNDEL)
Abraham II, 168
Catharine II, 168
Henrica II, 168
Jacob II, 168
Johann II, 168
Julianne II, 168
SÜNTZEI (SINZEL)
Friedrich I, 656, 657, 659
SUPINING
Christian I, 304
SUPPER
Andreas I, 420
Johann Jacob I, 462
Johann Philipp I, 420
SUPPERT
Philip I, 745
SÜRBI
Christian I, 731
SURERUS
Andreas I, 732
SURTER (SHOOTLER)
Jacob I, 344, 345
SÜS (SIES, SÜS, SÜSZ, SÜSSE)
Balthasar I, 184, 186, 187
Christoph I, 496
Gorg Jacob I, 716
Henry I, 473
Johann Georg I, 429, 734
Johann Jost (Jost) I, 666, 668, 670
Johannes (Joanes) I, 275, 276
Johenrich I, 413
Mathaus (Mathias) I, 605, 606, 608
Valentine I, 304, 305, 307
Wolfgang I, 357
(*See also* SISZ)
SÜSSHOLTZ (SÜSHOLTZ, SUS-
HOLTZ
David I, 35, 36
SÜSTER
Johan Willem I, 395
SUTER (SOOTER, SOUTER, SU-
DER, SUTHER, SUTTER,
SUTOR)
Anna Barbara I, 131
Caspar I, 362
Christian I, 130, 133, 134
156, 159, 161
Christina I, 131
Davit (David) I, 376, 377
Hans (Hannes) I, 331, 472
Hans Georg I, 700
Hans Jacob I, 331
Heinrich
(Hendrick) I, 23, 332, 333, 334

Maria Margaretha I, 132
Mr. II, 175
Mrs. II, 175
Nicol I, 759
Peter I, 362
SUTZ
Johan Jacob I, 416
SUVERMANN
Johann Christoph II, 79
SUVERS
Jo^n II, 18
SWAAL
Bernard I, 585
SWAALZ
Bernard I, 586
SWABBER
Solomon II, 195
SWAEP (read prob. SCHWAB)
Hans Jerrick I, 7
SWALLA
Anna I, 190
SWARTZ (dial. form of
SCHWARTZ)
Balsathar I, 493
Carl II, 24
Hans George I, 493
Joal II, 12
Johan Adam I, 564, 566, 567
Johannes I, 301, 302, 303
Joseph II, 188
Michell I, 660
SWARZENTRUBER
John II, 198
SWEGER (SCHWEAGER)
Philip I, 642, 644
SWERBER
Philip I, 318
SWEREN (SWERIN)
Johann I, 532, 533
Margaret I, 67
SWERER
J. Melchior I, 463
SWETMAN
John II, 69
SWEVER
Jacob II, 118
SWEYELL
Jerig I, 539
SWICKER
Jacob I, 7
SWIDER
Oniri I, 293
SWIERS
John II, 72
SWINDEL
William I, 463
SWINK (read prob. SCHWENCK)
Tobias II, 126

SWISER (SWISAR, read prob.
SCHWITZER)
Andrew I, 99
Maria Catrin I, 80
SWITZ
Magdalen I, 210
SWITZER, SWIZER *see* SCHWEIT-
ZER
SWOB (SWOAP, dial. form of
SCHWAB)
Albert I, 8
Jacob I, 416
Johannes I, 55, 434
SWONDER (read SWANDER)
Friederick I, 392
SWORT
Bevel I, 37
Christian I, 37
Daniel I, 37, 38
Hans I, 37
Jacob I, 37
Nicolas (Nicholas) I, 37, 38
SWYGER
Phillip I, 8
SWYN
Anthony I, 318
SWYNG (SHWENCK, SWINTE)
Michael (Mickel) I, 293, 294, 296
SYBERT (SYPERT, SUYVERT)
Anlies (Anlias) I, 44, 45
Cathrina I, 44
Conrad I, 43, 46, 47
Fredrick I, 660
Gerich I, 44
Marilis I, 44
Peter I, 660
SYBRAND
Anna Maria Christiana II, 58
SYDER (ZIDER)
Michael (Mich^l) I, 237, 238, 239
SYGRIST
Michael I, 11
SYLVA
Hermanus Josephus II, 89
Maria Christina II, 89
Maria Thereza II, 89
Rochus II, 89
SYMAN
John William I, 210
SYMONE
Jaque I, 14
SYMONS
Adam II, 18
SYRUTSCHECK
Johannes I, 426

TAARTS
Christ II, 113

Philip II, 113
TABAS
Johan Hendrich I, 113, 765
TABEL (DABEL)
Johan (Jn°) I, 589, 590
TACE
Henrich I, 116, 120, 121
TACK
Johann Christopher II, 59
TAFELMEYER (TAFFELMEYER, TABLEMIER)
Johanes (Johannes) I, 100, 101
TALLAM
Christina II, 193
Frederika II, 193
Louisa II, 193
Rosina II, 193
TALLEBACH (DALABAACK, DE LA BOUGH, TALLEBAUGH)
Sammuel (Samuel) I, 595, 597, 599
Vallentin I, 358
TAMERUS
Peter I, 403
TAMESI
Hans Jacob I, 403
TAMLONG
John II, 118
TAMNACH
Eliz. II, 105
TAMOOROON
Anna Barbara I, 107
Hans Jacob I, 106
Hans Michael I, 109
TANDY
Napper II, 89
TANNENBERGER
Ann Rosina I, 320
Michael I, 320, 321, 322
TANNER (DANNER, DANER)
Christian I, 107, 111, 113
Michael I, 10, 11
Samuel (Samuell) I, 289, 290, 291
TANNHÖFFER (DANHEBER)
J. Philip (John, Johan Phill.) I, 601, 602, 603
TANTS (read TANTZ or DANTZ)
Erich II, 120
TANY (DANNY, THANIE)
Hance Henrick I, 95
Johann Jacob I, 266, 269, 272
TAPILOTS
Frederick II, 165
TARR (STAIRE)
Matheas (Mathias) I, 652, 654
TARRISMAN
Philip I, 128
TASCH (TARSH)
Michael I, 577, 579, 580

TASHER (TASKER)
Joannes (Joans) I, 176, 177, 178
TATHOWER
Christian I, 406
TATTWEILLER (DOODWILER)
Hans Jacob I, 199, 201, 203
TAUB
Georg I, 695
Johann Dietherich I, 684
TAUBEFISHEL (TOWBILISHELL, TOWIENDICEL)
Jacob I, 323, 324, 326
TAUBENHEIM
Jeremias I, 453
TAUBERMAN (TOWERMAN)
Philip (Philib) I, 614, 616, 619
TAUBERT (TAUBER, TABERTON)
Johannes I, 517, 518, 520
TAUBNER
Chulur II, 13
TAUPHÄUS
Peter I, 355
TAUSCH (TAUTZ)
G. II, 141
Jacob I, 638, 639, 641
TÄXIS (FAXIS)
Georg Friederich (Fredrick) I, 585, 587, 588
TAXLER
Hans Atam I, 694
TAYLOR (TAYLER)
Anna Barbara I, 107
Christina I, 108
Elias (Casper Elias) I, 106, 110, 111
Hans Martin I, 108
Philip Adam I, 108
Rosina I, 108
TCHOP
Martin I, 392
TEACE
George II, 26
TEALE (read prob. THIEL)
Weyan I, 12
TEANY (TEANEY)
Hans Henrich I, 93, 95
TEASEL (TISTEL)
J. Wilhelm (William) I, 556, 557, 558
TEBOY
Conraat I, 20
TECKER (read prob. DECKER)
Ludwick (Ludwig) I, 369, 370
TECKLER
Valantin II, 195
TEDRIN
El^r II, 4

TEELZE (PEITS, PHIETS)
Hans Adam   I, 266, 269, 272
TEETSLER (CALER, TIELER)
Frantz (France,
Frans)   I, 629, 632, 636
TEGARDEN (DECKART,
TIEGARDEN)
Abraham   I, 154, 157, 158, 160
An Margreth   I, 156
TEICH (TIECH, TIESHE)
Henry (Henrich)   I, 198, 200, 202
TEICHGRÄBER
Joh. Paul Thomas   I, 761
TEICHMANN
Gertrude   II, 7
TEICHMULLER
Christoph   II, 116
TEININGER
Frederic   II, 197
TEISSIER
Etienne   I, 735
TEITZ
Johan Fredik   I, 454
TEKLENBURG
Amalia   II, 20
Anna Magdalena   II, 20
TELCHER
Johanes   I, 430
TELEKEN
Mr   II, 130
TELLAGE
Grutge, Van   II, 136
TELTON
Mathias   I, 266
TEMME (DEMME, TEMMY)
Ferdinand   II, 204
George   I, 516, 518, 519
Johann Christian I, 517, 518, 519
Joh. Jurgen   I, 517
TEMPEL (TEMPLE)
Christina   II, 50
John Lorentz   I, 748
Magdalena   II, 187
TENDELSPECH *see* DINTELSBECK
TENI
Nicholis   I, 79
TENKERNEY
Frederic   II, 197
TEOOMET
Hans Michel   I, 268, 271
TEPO (read TIEBO)
Johann   II, 68
TERA (CALLY)
Christian   I, 591, 593, 594
TERASCOU
Mons   II, 72
TERKONIG
Abraham   I, 627

TERMAATEN
Maria   II, 68
TERMEL (TERMELL)
Christopher   I, 536, 537, 538
TERNER
Jon. Jos.   II, 22
TERNOS
Anton   II, 119
TERR *see* DERR
TERRY
Benjamin   II, 121
TESCH
Adam   I, 499
Henrich Peter   I, 499
TESCHE
Catrina   II, 101
Engel   II, 101
TESTHE (read prob. TESCHE)
Anna Catharina   II, 91
Anna Gertruth   II, 91
Daniel   II, 91
Isaac   II, 91
Johannes   II, 91
Wilhelmima   II, 91
TETNER
Hans Erick   I, 12
TEUBEL (DIVEL, DIEFEL, TEW-
BEL)
J. Michael
(Michael)   I, 627, 630, 633
TEUBER (DEUBER)
Christoph
(Christoffel)   I, 48, 52, 54
Maria Katherine   I, 49
TEUFEL (TEUFFEL, TEUFELL)
Georg   I, 471
Ludwig   I, 470
TEUL
Jorg Pilus   I, 449
TEUNISSEN
Mary   II, 199
TEUSFER
Hartmann   II, 92
TEVENTAL (read TIEFENTHAL)
Andereas   I, 404
TEVIS
Johan   I, 676
TEXTUR
Hieronimus   I, 461
TEYEN
Hen.   II, 99
TEYER
Andrew   I, 686
TEYGER
Hans   I, 12
THALMAN
Charles Andrew   II, 58
THEEMAN
Margaret   I, 139

THEIL (TEYLE, THEYL)
Dewald   I, 440
Garret Hienrich   II, 125
P. Peter   I, 432
Simon Jacob   I, 330
THEIMSER
Joh. Jac.   II, 125
THEISEN
Johannes   I, 689
THEISS (THEIS, TEIS, THEYS, DEYS, THAIS)
Geo. Adam   I, 704
Jacob   I, 313, 314, 315, 743
Johan Georg   I, 689, 755
Johann Henrich   I, 423
Johann Mattheis
(Johann Matheus)   I, 33, 34
Johan Nickel   I, 233, 235, 236
Johannes   I, 560, 562, 563, 689
Mathias   I, 31
Michel   I, 372
THEISSINGER (THEISINGER, TISSINGER)
Jacob   I, 629, 632, 635
THEOBALD (THEBALD, THEO-BALTH, TEOBALT, THEO-BALD)
Johann Friedrich
(Fred^k)   I, 665, 668, 670
Johann Jacob
(Jacob)   I, 282, 284, 285
Johan Michel   I, 420
Mattis (Michel)   I, 264, 267, 270
P.   II, 24
THESSER
Michael   I, 328
THIEBAUT
Philipp   I, 759
THIEL (TIEL, DIHL, TIELL, TILL)
Abraham   I, 137, 141, 142
Christiana   II, 4
Hans Michl   I, 7
Hendrik   II, 50
Henrich Gottfried   I, 577, 579, 580
Herman (Frans Herman)   I, 236, 238, 239
Jacob   I, 205, 206, 208
Johann   II, 4
Johann Christian   I, 695
Johann Christoph   I, 754
Johann Ernst   I, 686
Johann Gerhart   I, 724
Johann Jacob   I, 706
Joh. Philip   II, 140
Jost Henrich   I, 728
Kathrina   I, 60
Martin (Martien)   II, 4, 50
Michael   I, 221, 223, 224
Peter   I, 423

Vallentin
(Valentine)   I, 137, 141, 142
THIELBON (DEALBONE, DIEL-BOEN)
Henry (Henrich)   I, 282, 284, 285
THIELE (TEELE)
Cornelius   I, 93, 94, 95
Gottfried   I, 441
Johann Heinrich   I, 748
John D.   II, 197
Mary   II, 12
THIELEMANN
Christoff Gottlieb   I, 738
THIERMAN
John   II, 185
THIFFORT (TOFORT, TOFFER)
Jacob (Junr)   I, 212, 214, 216
Philip (Phylip)   I, 212, 214, 216
THIMAN
Hans Jacob   II, 71
THIMM
David   II, 121
THIRINGER (DEERINGER, read THÜRINGER)
Philip (Phil.)   I, 601, 602, 604
THOM (TOMM. THUM, THYM, abbr. of THOMAS)
Anne Elisabeth   II, 88
Christian   I, 487
Elias   I, 649, 650
Fred   II, 146
Geo. Fredric   II, 201
Hans George
(Georg)   I, 637, 639, 641
Jacob   I, 637, 639, 641; II, 146
Jean   II, 88
Joh^n Heinr. Fried.   II, 127
Johannes   II, 146
Michael   I, 649, 650
Peter   II, 146
Velten (Felte)   I, 596, 598, 599
THOMAN
Christof   I, 366
Mr.   II, 175
Mrs.   II, 175
Philip   I, 20, 21
THOMAS (TOMAS, THOMMAS)
Adam   I, 365
Benedict   I, 169, 170, 172
Christian   I, 32
Eberhart   I, 467
Elisabeth   II, 172
Fallentin   I, 735
Gerhardt (Gerhart)   I, 628, 631, 634
Henrich (Henry, Hendrick)   I, 359, 421; II, 3, 147
J. Adam (Adam)   I, 621, 623, 625
J. Peter   I, 456

Johan Attam   I, 570, 572
Johan Engel   I, 569, 570, 572
Johann Friedrich   I, 438
Johann Nickel   I, 755
Johan Phillippus   I, 366, 368
Johannes (John)   I, 250, 251, 467, 556, 557, 558
Ludwig (Ludwick)   I, 217, 218, 220
Margretha   II, 172
Mathias   II, 119
Michel   I, 31, 33
Peter   I, 250, 251, 456 628, 631, 634
Philipp   I, 466
Wishard   II, 15
THOMME (THOMMEN, THOMEN, THOME, TOMA, TOMEN, DOMME, DOMEN)
Adam   I, 392
Anna   II, 133
Christian   II, 178
Durst   I, 162, 164, 166
Elisabeth   II, 133
Frederick   II, 31
Hans Georg   II, 133
Hans Jacob   I, 162, 164, 166
Henrich (Hendrick)   I, 212, 214, 216, 392
Jacob   I, 162
Johann Michael   I, 751
Johann Phillipp   I, 688
Johannes   II, 133
Martin (Marthin)   I, 162, 164, 166, 738
Nicklas (Nicholas)   I, 162, 164, 166
THÖNER (DHENNE)
Friedrich (Heinrich)   I, 559, 560, 562
THOR
Johan Friederich   I, 339
THORMYER
Beter   I, 690
THORN (read prob. DORN)
Peter   I, 728
THORREN
——   II, 81
THORTER
Philip   II, 114
THORWARTH (THORWART, DORWART, TOORWARD)
Christopher   II, 13
Elizabeth   II, 179
Henrich   I, 256, 259, 261
Jacob   I, 704; II, 179
Martin (Matthew)   I, 646, 647
Philip   II, 14
Samuel   II, 13

THOULOUZAN
Jean   I, 416
THOWE (TOBY)
Johann Jost (Hans Jost)   I, 317, 318, 319
THRAN (TRAAN, STRIAN)
Hans Georg   I, 89, 91, 92
Johan Migel   I, 691
THREHR, THRER, THREER see DREHER
THREIBOS
Johann   I, 719
THREIN (THREYN)
Jacob   I, 522, 524
Johann Gorg   I, 724
THRON (TRON)
Johann Christian (Christian)   I, 179, 181, 183
THUMANN
Jacob   II, 184
THUNGES (DIRGRIS)
Nicklas (Nickel, Nicholas)   I, 376, 377
THUP
Joseph   II, 121
THÜRIG
Jacob   I, 459
THÜRINGER (TIERINGER, TURRINGER)
Baltzar (Baltes)   I, 480, 649, 650
Jacob   I, 453
Lutwig   I, 491
THURM
Gottlieb   I, 441
THÜRWÄCHTER
Ehrhardt   I, 474
THUSSING (TUSSING)
Peter   I, 301, 302, 303
THUY (DOUEY)
Conradt (Conrade)   I, 283, 285, 286
Johann Philipp   I, 701
TIBBER
Lorentz   I, 348
TIEBENDERF
Johannes   I, 8
TIEFENTHAL see TEVENTAL
TIEGER (TIGER)
Efferen   II, 75
Joh. Henr.   II, 107
TIELMAN (TILLMAN, TILMAN)
J. Henry   I, 467
Johanes   I, 495
Nickolas (Nicholas)   I, 656, 657, 658
Peter   I, 35
TIEN
Daniel   I, 455
Jean Henri   I, 455

TIER (DEAR)
Jacob   I, 526, 527
Matieu (Mathias)   I, 526, 527, 529
TIERKING
Fried^k   II, 127
TIETJENS
P. A.   II, 71
TIEZE
Johannes   I, 357
TILBREY
Frans   II, 114
TILHAS
Francis, Van   II, 73
TILIWAHESS
Frents   I, 60
TILLICH
Henry   II, 13
TILLIGER
Jacob   I, 495
TILLINGER* (TILLINGOR)
Johan Fredrick   I, 767
Maria Barbra   I, 766
TILLSHOFFER (TILZIEFFER)
Hans Michael   I, 234, 235, 236
TILLY
Johanes   I, 400
TILSOVER
Jacob   I, 43
TILWITS
Jerg   I, 744
TIMANUS (TIMMANES)
Johan Jacob (Johannes
Jacob)   I, 99, 100, 101
TIMMER (DEIMER)
Gerick   I, 659
Hans (Johannes)   I, 234, 235, 236
TIMMERMANN   (TIMERMAN,
TIMBERMAN, TIMBERMON)
Anna   I, 117, 241
Anna Marelina   I, 241
Anna Maria   I, 241
Barbra   I, 117
Christian   I, 116
Dorothy   II, 7
Hanah Mariats   I, 241
Hans   I, 116, 119, 120
Nicholas   I, 119, 120
TIMOTHEE
Charles   I, 50
Elizabeth   I, 49
Louis   I, 47, 50, 51, 53
Mary   I, 50
Peter   I, 50
TIMPE (TIMBER)
Conraht (Conrad)   I, 681, 682
TING
Wesselman   II, 61
TINICK
Anna Barbara   I, 767

Anna Margret   I, 766, 767
Johan Hendrick   I, 113, 765
Michel   I, 767
TIPPENHOUER
Geo.   II, 160
TISCHER
Johann Christian   I, 689
TITSHLER
J. Philip   I, 500
TITUS
Wendel   II, 178
TIZLER
Johan Jost   I, 355
TOCHTERMAN
Conrad   II, 204
Frederika   II, 204
Godfry   II, 204
R. Frederika   II, 204
TODT
Jœs Franciscus   I, 726
TOGEND (DOGENT)
Jacob   I, 667, 669, 671
TOKING
Henry   II, 122
TÖLCKER
Johann Joachim   I, 496
TOLDER (SOLDER)
Barbara   I, 209
Johannes (Johans)   I, 209, 211
TOLL (DILL, THOLL)
Christian Wilhelm
(Willhelm)   I, 510, 511, 512
Christop^r (Christ^n)   I, 175, 177, 178
Conrad   I, 348, 445
Edmundus   I, 422
Philip   II, 123
TOLLE
Johann Chrystian
(Christian)   I, 517, 518, 520
TOLLER
Daniel   II, 118
TÖLLY
Michael Vogelfanger   I, 364
TOLMAN (TALMON)
Jaques (Jacob)   I, 646, 647
Piere   I, 646, 648
TOMPPRÄTZ
Mich.   I, 394
TONDT
Johannes   I, 689
TONKELBERG (TONCKELBERG)
Clements   I, 18
Fredrick   I, 18
Peiter   I, 18
TONNER
Jacob   I, 422
TOOLAT
Lewdwight   II, 37

TOON
Mathias   II, 122
TÖPPER
Ludewig   I, 511
TORBANN
——   II, 51
TÖRENTZ
Johim   II, 50
TÖRREBERGER (DURNBERCHER,
    TORENBERGER)
Hans Jacob   I, 212, 214, 215
Hans Michael   I, 212, 214, 215
Stephan (Stephen)   I, 213, 214, 216
TORSON
F. Christopher   I, 505
TOUNNEN
Anna   II, 124
Hans Jacob   II, 124
Martin   II, 124
Trina   II, 124
TOUNNER
Fredrick   II, 124
TOUTENHOOFD
Cath.   II, 136
Magdel.   II, 136
Roger   II, 136
TRABER
Johan Ludwig   I, 443
TRACHSALL
Hans   I, 322
TRACKTEHENGST
Johannes   I, 18
TRAEN
Mathias   I, 676
TRAGER (TRAGHER)
Christian   I, 366
Jnº Anton   I, 731
(*See also* TREGER)
TRAGH
Andereas   I, 502
TRAM (DRAM)
Hans Jorg   I, 637, 638, 640
Hans Martin   I, 637, 638, 640
Johann George (Hans
    George)   I, 637, 638, 640
TRAN
Peter (Diedrick)   I, 582, 583, 584
TRANBERG (THRONBERG)
Fridrich Ambrossius   I, 199, 201, 203
TRANCK (TRANCH)
Joh. Fred.   II, 119
Johannes   I, 444
TRÄNCKNER
J. Nicklas   I, 504
TRANSU
Abraham   I, 31, 33, 34
TRAPP (TRAP)
Margritha   II, 77
Philip   II, 104

TRASHER (read prob. DRESCHER)
Hans George   I, 360, 362
TRAUB
Hans Adam (J.
    Adam)   I, 595, 597, 599
Jacob   I, 449, 595, 597, 599
Johann Georg   I, 489
Johann Michael   I, 734
Johann Paul   I, 416
TRAUT   (TRAUDT,   TRAUTH,
    TRAUTT, TROUD)
Anna Crate   I, 766
Carolina   II, 196
Cuglick   I, 766
Hans Martin   I, 113, 765
Jacob   I, 418
Johan Debalt
    (Taball)   I, 113, 114, 115, 765
Johann Gerlach   I, 699
Marg. Apell.   I, 766
Peter   II, 118
Wenel (Wintell)   I, 198, 200, 202
TRAUTMANN   (TRAUTTMANN,
    TRAUTMAN, TROUTMAN)
Christian   I, 743
Hyronimus   I, 348, 350, 351
Johan Leonhart   I, 469
Johann Petter   I, 468
Johannes (Hans)   I, 213, 215
Melchior   I, 468
Willhelm   I, 493
TRAUTWEIN
Johann Wilhelm   I, 480
Mathias   II, 179
Nicolass   I, 743
TRAUTZ (TRAUTS, TROUTS)
Christoph   I, 545, 547, 549
Joh.   II, 113
TRAWIENER (TRAVINGER)
Peter   I, 32, 33, 34
TRAWN
Mattheas   I, 401
TRAXEL
Bernard   I, 405
George   I, 405
Johann Georg
    (Jerge)   I, 620, 622, 624
Michael   I, 405
TRAY (TREY, read prob. TREU)
Hans Jerig (Hans
    Yerich)   I, 72, 76, 78
Johan Conradt   I, 74
Johan Jacob (Jacob)   I, 72, 76, 78
Johannes   I, 72
Margaretta   I, 73
Susanna   I, 73
TREADELSCHIP *see* SHIP
TREBER (TREWER)
Catharina   I, 156

Johan Christoffel I, 155, 158, 160
Mᵃʳ Anna I, 156
Mᵃʳ Engel I, 156
Niclaus (Nikolaus) I, 155, 158, 160
TREBERT
—— II, 81
TREFFENSTÄTT
Christian I, 564, 565, 567
TREGER
Hans Peter I, 426
TREIBEL
Martin I, 418
TREICH
Martin I, 437
TREICHEL
Christian II, 34
TREIER (TRYER, read DREIER)
Peter I, 626, 630, 633
(*See also* TRYER)
TREIN
Jacob I, 692
Johann Peter I, 690
TREITTER (DRAYTER)
Georg Michael
(Migel) I, 116, 120, 121
TRESBACH
Anna Margᵗ II, 97
Anna Maria II, 97
Cathrina II, 97
Maria Cath. II, 97
TRESCHUM (TURSCHUM, WIRSHON)
Casper I, 531, 533, 534
TRESENREUTHER
Conradt I, 762
TRESSLER
Johann Peter I, 391
TRESZ
G. Adam II, 156
Ulrich I, 348
TREUPEL
Johanes V. II, 173
TREUTTLE
Jacob I, 704
Jonathan I, 741
TREVETT
Chris. I, 237
TREWER *see* TREBER
TREWILL
Carl Wilh. II, 139
TREWITZ (TRIEWITZ)
Jacob I, 755
Johann Conrath I, 755
TREXLER
Michael I, 737
Peter I, 737
TREYSH
J. Jacob I, 437

TREYSTER
Fredrick I, 137
Hans Martin I, 137
TRIBER (read prob. TREIBER)
Ludewig I, 424
TRIEBEL (TRIBLE)
Casper I, 739
Christian II, 190
TRIEBIG (TRIEBIEG)
Andreas I, 539, 541, 544
TRIES (read prob. DRIES)
Johan Jacob I, 493
TRIMBACH
Cath. Marg. II, 105
TRIMPLE
Joh. Melch. II, 117
TRINKELS
Elizabeth II, 59
TRIPPEL
Conrad I, 751
Daniel II, 155
TRIPPNER
Johan Georg I, 412
TRISSLER (DRESSER)
Joseph Davidt I, 246, 247, 248
TRITE
G. H. II, 143
Just II, 143
TRITSCH
Jacob I, 468
TRITT (THRITT, TREIT, TRETT)
Christian
(Christaen) I, 264, 267, 271
Hans Peter I, 264, 267, 271
TROCK
Anna Elisab. II, 135
TROCKENMILLER (TROOKMILLER)
Bastian
(Sebastian) I, 102, 105, 106
Cathrina I, 103
Johann Ludwig I, 347
Johann Martin
(John Martin) I, 555, 557, 558
Johann Michell I, 327, 329
TROESTER (TROSTEL)
Abraham (Abram) I, 637, 639, 640
TROLL
Elizabeth II, 99
Jacobina II, 99
Maria II, 99
Wilhelm II, 29
TRÖLLER
Johan Wilhelm I, 352, 354
TROMPER
Hendᵏ II, 5
TROMPETER
Johan II, 178

TROOTMEN (read perhaps TRAUT-
MAN)
Catharina   I, 108
TROSSENBERG
Christiana   II, 91
TRÖSTERS (DRESER)
Johan Michal (John
Michael)   I, 652, 653
TROTT (DRUTT)
Herman   I, 156, 159, 161
Johann Conrad   II, 4
TROTZ
Carl de Man   II, 58
TROUD (read prob. TRAUT)
Anna Crate   I, 766
Cughlick   I, 766
Johanes   I, 767
Marg. Apell   I, 766
TRUCHÄUSER
Johann Georg   I, 739
TRUCKEL
Matheus   I, 346
TRUKE
Georg   I, 395
TRUMMANER
Ewald   I, 469
TRUMP (TRUMPF)
Anna Barberer   I, 85
Georg   I, 710
Hance Adam   I, 85
Johann Caspar   I, 712
Johan Christian (John
Chris)   I, 609, 611, 612
Johann Michael   I, 762
Johan Peter   I, 710
Johannes   I, 539, 541, 543
Ossell (Ursula)   I, 84
Philip Thomas   I, 130, 133, 134
Susanna Ossell   I, 85
TRÜMPER
Johannes   I, 432
TRUMPETER
Felix   II, 156
TRUMPHELLER
Peter   I, 736
TRUNCKEL
Michael   II, 14
TRÜNCKHLER
Johann Conradt   I, 501
TRUNKING
Catherine Margarett   II, 55
TRUPPERT
Anton   II, 56
TRUSSLER
Michael   I, 734
TRYCLER
Jacob   I, 16
TRYER (read prob. DREIER)
Frederick   I, 226; II, 103

TRYSTER (SCYSTER)
Bastian   I, 116, 120, 121
TSAWN
Gaspar   I, 290
TSCHANTZ
Joseph   I, 726
TSCHIFFELY
David Fred   II, 175
Mr.   II, 174
TSCHOPP (CHOAPE)
Durs (Theoars)   I, 275, 276
Hans   I, 720
Jacob   I, 392
TSHAKKY
Conrad   I, 434
TSHUDI (TSCHUDY, TSCHUTI)
Adam   II, 133
Jacob   I, 416
Johannes   I, 391, 392, 720
Martin (Mardin)   I, 249, 250
                             391, 720
Martin Nicolaus   I, 720
Weinbert   I, 473, 507
TSHUMY
Jacob   I, 434
TSOBER
Georg   I, 97
TUCHMANN (DUCHMAN)
Christman   I, 423
Peter   I, 423
Stephan   I, 714
TUCHTER
Martin   II, 124
TUCKERMANN
Johannes   I, 410
TULIPAN
Frantz   I, 490
TUNECE
Tuniss   II, 48
TUNGENT
Anne Lusarye   II, 51
Barbry   II, 51
Catha.   II, 51
John   II, 51
Niclos   II, 51
Susana   II, 51
TUNISSE
Frederick   II, 183
TÜNTE (DONTE)
Gottlieb   I, 604, 606, 607
TUPPEL
Joh. Gottl.   II, 139
TUPS *see* DUBS
TURCHING
Johann   II, 149
TÜRENBERGER (TORENBERGER)
Hans Jacob
(Johannis)   I, 212, 214, 215
Hans Michael   I, 212, 214, 215

TURICHER
Conrad   I, 269
TURINGER (TEREINGER)
John Adam
  (Hanadan)   I, 323, 325, 326
TURMER
W.   II, 144
TURN* (TURNN)
Johanes   I, 500
TURNER
Elizabeth   I, 320
John   I, 320
William Francis   I, 745
TURNI (TURNY, TURNEE,
  DURRNY)
Johanes   I, 435
Peter   I, 307, 309
TÜRNIES (DÖRRNIS, TURNIS,
  TURNAS, TURNUS)
Johann Gerg (Jurg) I, 628, 632, 635
Peter   I, 628, 632, 635
TURRINGER *see* THURINGER
TUSSING (TUSCHING, DUSING)
Jacob   I, 693
Paullus (Paul)   I, 652, 654
TUSTADO
——   II, 57
TUTTERBERG (STEEDEBERGER)
Hans Henry   I, 573, 574, 575
TUXLY
Uhllerich   I, 450
TYBLY
Michael   I, 439
TYSEN (TISEN)
Barent   I, 40, 42
Wilhelmina   II, 58

ÜBEL (UEBEL)
Johann Friederich I, 546, 548, 550
UBER
Hans Jacob   I, 400
Johann Ludwig   I, 497
UBERER
Jacob   I, 740
UBERHOFF
Heinr.   II, 138
UBERNESSER
Jur. Fredk.   I, 304
ÜBERROTH
Nickolaus   I, 699
UBLOND
Joseph   II, 139
UBUNG
William   I, 748
UDER (ODER)
Jurgen (Jurg)   I, 666, 668, 670

UFFERMAN
John C.   II, 186
UHL (UHLL, UEL, OOL)
Carl   I, 701
Casper   I, 760
G. Davit (David)   I, 646, 647
Johann Peter I, 340, 341, 343, 717
Johan Reinhardt   I, 398
Michael (Miel)   I, 536, 537, 538
UHLAND (UHLANDT, ULLAND)
Catrina   I, 28
Johann Friderich   I, 491
Johannes   I, 28
Matthue (Matheus,
  Mathias)   I, 27, 29, 30
UHLE
Andrew   II, 79
Dietrich   I, 194, 195, 196
Friedrich   II, 79
Johann Christoph   I, 453
Johan Ditrich   I, 194, 195, 196
ÜHLEIN (UEHLEIN, ELY)
Bernhard   I, 683
Frantz Lutwig (Frans
  Lodw[k])   I, 596, 597, 599
UHLER (ULLER, OULER)
Anastasius   I, 60, 64, 65
Andrew   II, 13
Dieterich (Titrich) I, 189, 192, 194
Hanns Martin   I, 408
Johannes   I, 372
Vallentin
  (Fredrick)   I, 189, 192, 194
UHRICH (URICH, URRICH,
  ORICH, URRY, dial. forms of
  ULRICH)
Christoph (Stoffel) I, 199, 201, 203
Hans Jerg   I, 457
Henrich
  (Henr[k])   I, 601, 602, 603
Johannes (John)   I, 59, 63, 65
John Christoff (John
  Christoph)   I, 672, 673, 674
Jorg Petter   I, 408
Peter   I, 494
Valentinus   I, 322
UHRRER
Henry   I, 453
UHTING (UTING)
Johan Michael (Hans
  Mich[l])   I, 667, 669, 671
ULGERSH
John   II, 145
ULICK
Johan Jost   I, 610, 612
ULIGER
Maria   I, 210
UHLMANN (ULLMANN)
Friederich Engelhart   I, 97

Michael I, 508
ULMER (ULLMER, OLMER)
Hans Adam (Adam) I, 232, 233
Jacob I, 422
Johann Fridrich I, 740
Johannes I, 506
Leonhard II, 155
Martin I, 437
Peter I, 474
Philip
(Philibb) I, 304, 305, 306
II, 137
Thomas II, 155
William II, 189
Wolfgang I, 605, 606, 608
ULRICH (ULLRICH, UHLRICH,
ULLERICH, ULRICK, OLD-
RICH, UHLLERIK, ULRIK,
ULERICH)
Adam I, 231, 232, 233
Caspar (Casper) I, 677, 679, 680
Caspar (Joseph) I, 66, 69, 70
Christopher
(Christo.) I, 15
Dorothea II, 130
Elizabeth II, 4
Ernst I, 517
Eva I, 67
Fridrich
(Frederick) I, 265, 268, 271
Georg* (Gerch) I, 445
Georg Christian II, 59
Gorg Jacob I, 472
Hans Görg I, 451, 464
Hans Michael (Hans
Mich¹) I, 175, 176, 178
Hans Philip
(Philip) I, 55, 56, 57, 67
Jacob I, 418, 446
Johan Christoph I, 401
Joh. Fried. II, 113
Johann Henrich I, 709
Johann Jacob II, 59
Johann Peter I, 745
Johannes (John) I, 14, 15, 55, 56, 57
349, 350, 351
421, 758
Louisa II, 59
M. II, 30
Maria Margretha II, 59
Mathaus (Matehys) I, 199, 201, 203
Michell I, 175, 177, 178
Nicholas I, 517
Paul I, 372
Peter
(Pieter) I, 67, 727; II, 5, 30, 162
Susanna I, 67
Vallentin I, 614, 616, 619
Zacharias II, 116

ULTSCH
Andereas I, 504
UMBERGER (UMBERIGER, HUM-
BERG)
Hans I, 118
Hans Leonhardt (Leonhart,
Lenart) I, 116, 120, 121
Henrich (Henrick) I, 116, 120, 121
Julian I, 117, 118
Lisbat I, 118
Micgel I, 116
UMENSETTER (UMENSÄTTER)
Jacob I, 475
Michael I, 475
UMRADT
Johannes I, 340
UMSTATT (UMSTADT)
Jacob I, 74
Johan Veltin
(Valentine) I, 72, 76, 77
Peter I, 701
UNANGST (UNANCKS, UNANKS,
UNONGST, ONANGST)
Andreas I, 408
Burckhardt I, 479
George Wolff (Yerrick
Wolff) I, 596, 597, 599
H. Michael (Hams) I, 596, 597, 599
Hans Georg I, 400
Jeorg Henerich I, 408
Johann Andreas I, 699
Johann Martin (John
Martin) I, 596, 598, 599
Johann Sebastian I, 479
UNBEHAND (UNBEHEND, UN-
BEHENDT, UNBEHEN)
Bastian (Sebastian) I, 257, 260, 262
Conrath (Conrad) I, 258, 260, 263
Jacob I, 258, 260, 263
Vallentin (Valentine,
Velten) I, 258, 260, 263, 652, 654
UNCKEL (UNKEL)
Christopher Frederick II, 193
George I, 493
Joh. Adam II, 193
UNCKELBACH (ANGELBACH,
UNGELBACH)
J. Henry (John
Henry) I, 627, 630, 633
UNDERKOFFLER (UNDERKAUF-
FER, UNDERKOFLER)
Jacob I, 188, 192, 193
Michal (Mich¹) I, 221, 223, 224
UNDERSEEL
Conrad I, 745
UNDERTENERD
Geo. I, 32

UNDERWEG (UNDERWEGH, ONDERWEG)
Casper   I, 492
Hans George (Hans Yerrick)   I, 551, 552, 554
UNFUG
Adolph   I, 749
UNGER (UNGUER, UNGAR)
Andereas   I, 310, 312, 313
Christopher   I, 710
Frederick   II, 122
Jacob   I, 122
Johann   II, 68
Johan Friederich (Joh. Fred., John Frederich)   I, 516, 517 518, 519
Joh. Valt.   II, 107
Johannes   I, 346
John Georg   II, 205
Michael   I, 382
UNGERER (UNGRER, UNGER)
Jerg Baldas (Jorg Baldas, Jerick Pattus)   I, 559, 560, 562
Johan Michel   I, 513, 514, 515
Johann Wolfgang (Woolf)   I, 209, 211, 212
Nicodemus   I, 718
UNGEWICKELL
John Henrich   II, 111
UNGRA (read prob. UNGER)
Martin   I, 660
UNRATH
Johan Friedrich   I, 443
UNRUH (ONRU, UNRUINE)
Hannah   I, 85
Jerg   I, 84, 86, 87
Johannes   I, 481
Maria Catrina   I, 139
Valetin (Valentine)   I, 137, 141, 142
UNSELT (UNSELDT, ONSELT, ONESELF)
Georg Friederich (Fredrick)   I, 113, 114, 115, 765
Michael   I, 719
UNVERZAGT (UNDERSIGHT)
Johannes   I, 387, 388, 389
UPHOLD (KUBHOLD)
Joseph   I, 267, 270
UPPER
Jno Geo.   I, 700
URBACH (OURBACH, OVER-BEECK)
Adolph   I, 601, 602, 604
URBAN
Augustus   I, 483
Jacob   I, 560, 561, 563
Johan Lewis   II, 44

URBICH (URBECH, ORBIG)
Godfret (Godfried)   I, 304, 305, 306
URCKHAUS (URDANS)
Hendrich Ludewig (Fredk Lodwk)   I, 137, 141, 142
URFFER
Jorg   I, 704
URING
Catherine   II, 55
URJENBACHER
Abraham   I, 461
URLETTIG (ORLEDIG)
Valentin (Valentine)   I, 609, 611, 613
URMI
Andrew   I, 16
URSBURG
Hendrick   II, 187
URY see UHRICH
USBECK (USBEAK)
Johann Beter (John Peter)   I, 672, 673, 674
USENBERG
Christian   II, 118
USENER (USSENER, USNER)
Andw   I, 722
Johannes   I, 367, 368
Wilhelm   I, 725
USTER
Am   I, 372
UTHE
David Gottfried   I, 503
UTT
Jacob   I, 732
UTTER
Friederich   I, 509, 510, 511
UTZ (UTS)
Daniel   I, 481
Gottlieb   I, 432
Hans Jacob   I, 127, 129, 130
Hans Jurk (Georg)   I, 127, 129, 130
Johann Georg   I, 432
Maria Catherina   I, 127
UTZMAN (HOOTSMAN)
Johannes   I, 237, 238, 239

VADEL
Johan Peter   I, 694
VAHLL, VAL see WAHL
VAIBEL (read prob. WEIBEL)
Barbe   II, 31
Catherine   II, 31
Frederick   II, 31
Jacob   II, 31
Jean   II, 31
Jean Jacques   II, 31

Jean Noe II, 31
Martin II, 31
Ursule II, 31
Villiame II, 31
VAIHINGER
Joshua II, 155
VAL
Nicola, de II, 119
VALCK
Hans Martin I, 21, 22
VALENTIN (VALENTINE, VAL-
LENTINE, VALLENDIN)
Conrad I, 419
Hans Michael I, 396
Henry I, 486
Jacob I, 428
Johan Georg I, 396
John (Jan) II, 24, 42
VALET
Jacob II, 114
VALIER
Gab. I, 747
VALLEN
Hans Jerg I, 229, 231
VALTH
Peter II, 92
VAN
Hans Jacob I, 499
Matheas I, 499
VAN BAUKE
Francis I, 749
VAN BERG
Johann Georg I, 748
VANDALIN
H. Martin I, 453
VANDELL
Christian II, 126
VANDENBURG
—— II, 123
VANDER
J. S. II, 162
VANDERHUYST
John I, 749
VAN ENST
Mr II, 130
VAN GEMITA
Conrat I, 387
VAN HOKMEL
—— I, 20
VAN KOUTEN
Gerret I, 322
VAN NUWENHUYS
Carl I, 748
VANSETTEL
Cathrina I, 103
Johan Jerich I, 102
VAN STAVEREN
Cornelis I, 421

VANTERBOURG
Christoph I, 469
VAREFFEN
Evart I, 747
VARINGER
Martin I, 483
VARLET
C. I, 753
VARON
P. 'H. II, 71
VASAR
Jacob I, 459
VASHOLD
Casper II, 56
Dorothy II, 56
Maria II, 56
Valentine II, 56
VASPAR
Just. H. II, 83
VASS
Johann Melchior I, 739
VASSEM (WASOM)
Johann Michael I, 540, 542, 544
VATER
Paulus I, 328
VAUCKER
Henry II, 70
VAUTIE (VOTIE)
Pierre (Berrie) I, 592, 593, 594
VAYE
Friedk Albert II, 23
VECHER (VEEKER)
Friederich I, 536, 537, 538
VEDET
Godlieb II, 184
VEEN
Wm., van der II, 156
VEIGNER (read prob. WIEGNER)
Catharina II, 161
Christiana II, 161
Frederich II, 161
Michael II, 161
—— II, 161
VEIL (read prob. WEIL)
Joh. II, 119
VEIOCK
Jacob I, 716
VEIT (FAYT, VIT)
Anna Maria II, 69
Diebolt I, 167, 168
Godlieb I, 340
Hans (Johannes) I, 246, 247, 248
Johan Jörg I, 328
Johan Nicklas
(Micheal) I, 283, 284, 285
Johann Peter (John
Peter) I, 386, 387, 389
Johannes I, 629, 632, 635
Jorg I, 369, 370

Xav.   II, 3
VEITEL (FIDLE)
  Wilhelm Moritz (Willm
    Morris)   I, 287, 289
VEITZHANS
  Fridrich   I, 471
VEIZAPFF
  John   II, 22
VELCKEL see VÖLCKEL
VELDO
  Lamberdus   II, 95
  Susanna   II, 95
VELLIN
  Franck   II, 119
VELTE (dial. form of VALENTIN)
  Christian   I, 14; II, 151
  E. Katharine   II, 150
  E. Katy   II, 150
  Frederica   II, 151
  George   II, 150
  Katharine   II, 151
  (See also WELTHE)
VELTEN (FELTER)
  Conradt   I, 427
  Hans Georg (Hans
    Elrich)   I, 232, 233
  Joh. Alberth   I, 428
VELTES
  Mary Katy   II, 151
  Widow   II, 151
VELVERISS
  Rebecca   II, 76
VENAN
  Jence   II, 75
VENBLECK
  Mr Johan   II, 90
VENNIL
  Barbara   II, 148
  George   II, 148
VENUSBAKER
  Johan   I, 401
VERBER (read prob. FÄRBER)
  Abraham   II, 5
VERDAL
  Gasper   II, 100
VERLY
  Hans Peter   I, 93, 95
VERNER see WERNER
VERNIKE see WERNICKE
VERNIN
  Adam   II, 167
  Anna Maria   II, 167
  Daniel   II, 167
  Louisa   II, 167
  Margaret   II, 167
VERSBACH
  Johan Wilhelm   II, 45
  Wilhelm   II, 45

VERYLIE (VERYLY)
  Maria Anna (Mari-
    anna)   II, 68, 94
VETTER (FETTER, VÄTTER)
  Caspar   I, 449
  Christoph   I, 605, 606, 608
  David   I, 47, 51, 53
  George (Jorg)   I, 649, 650
  Isaac   I, 411
  Jacob   I, 763
  Johann Georg   I, 686
  Johann Heinrich   I, 466
  Johannes   I, 467, 469
  Lucas (Lucka)   I, 47, 51, 53
  Margerita   I, 49
  Philip   I, 359
  Sophia   I, 50
  Wendel (Windel)   I, 323, 324, 326
  Xtian   I, 763
VETTERMAN (VATERMAN)
  Balthasar   I, 427
  Georg Michael (Jerick
    Mich^1)   I, 559, 560, 562
VETZBERGER (FETSBERGER)
  Daniel   I, 614, 616, 618
VEY
  Andereas   I, 500
  Jacob   II, 15
VIAL (VIALL)
  Isaac (Isack)   I, 199, 201, 203
VIAUD
  Augustino Doinique   II, 35
VICK
  John   II, 17
VIDEBANT
  Jac. Lud.   I, 751
VIDRING
  Eliz^t   II, 5
VIEBEL
  Johann Nicolaus   I, 710
VIEGE
  Catharina   II, 68
VIEGLE
  Hans Jerig   I, 8
VIEHMAN (VIEMAN, FIEMAN)
  Conrad   I, 423
VIEHMAN (FIEMAN)
  Johann Connradt   I, 378, 379, 381
VIELARD see WILGAR
VIERLING
  Jacob   I, 372
VIET
  Georg   I, 442
VIETOR
  Gertraud Elisabette   II, 67
  Henriette Maria   II, 67
VIGAL
  Zwanan   II, 72

VIGELIE
Johannes I, 102
VILEMAN
Hans I, 304
VILLARD
Elisabeth II, 31
Jacob II, 31
Jean Henri II, 31
Jean Jacques II, 31
Louis II, 31
Marie II, 31
Marieanne II, 31
Susane II, 31
Susanne Marie II, 31
VILLE
Elizabeth, de II, 129
Victor, de II, 129
VILLENEAVE
Francis I, 757
VILLGENTZ
Michel I, 721
VILLIB
Velten I, 418
VILLINGER (read prob. WILLIN-
GER)
David II, 156
Godfrey II, 154
VILLIOT
Jean Geofroid II, 31
Jean Henry II, 31
Jean Pierre II, 31
Marie Anne II, 31
Marie Salome II, 31
VILSOVER (VELSOVER)
Anna I, 44
Katrina I, 44
VINCENT (VINSENT)
An Margreth I, 156
Lewis I, 236
VINETTIER
Jean I, 731
VINK
Sebastian I, 7
VINNINGER (read prob. WIN-
NINGER)
Christopher II, 13
Juliana II, 13
VINTENHELVER
Johan I, 102
VINTZ (read prob. WENTZ)
Caspar I, 740
VISANANT
Allena I, 55
Jno. Adam I, 55
Jno. Peter I, 55
Philip Peter I, 54, 56, 57
VISARD
Abram Louis II, 31
Jean Henry II, 31

Madelaine II, 31
Marguerithe II, 31
Marie Anne II, 31
VISHEHING
Caritas I, 123
Christian I, 124
Elizabeth I, 124
Sophia I, 124
VISSER (Dt. form of FISCHER)
Jacob I, 661, 662, 663
John L. II, 24
VISTERMYER
John I, 716
VITZ (VIZ)
George II, 121
Jannett, de II, 119
VITZTHUM (FITZCOM)
Georg Michael (Jerg
Michael) I, 620, 622, 624
VIUNT
Rudolph I, 416
VIVEL
Lewick I, 289
VIVENT
James II, 177
VIX
Lorentz I, 729
VLAG (read prob. FLACH)
——— II, 24
VOBEL (VOBELL)
Anthony II, 181
Elizabeth II, 181
George II, 99
John II, 181
Justina II, 181
VOCART
——— II, 81
VOCK (VOLCK)
Fillib I, 442
John Peter (Peter) I, 264, 267, 271
VOEGT
J. G. II, 137
VOEHLE
Christian II, 152
VOELKEL see VÖLCKEL
VOGEL (VOGELL, VOGALL, VOGL,
VOOGEL)
Alida Maria II, 92
Andreas I, 399
Anna Maria II, 92
Ar., de II, 71
Burkh. F. II, 202
Catrena I, 40
Dorothee II, 88
Filibs Friedrich (Phillip,
Villibs) I, 39, 41, 42
Fridrich Adam
(Adam) I, 677, 679, 680
Friederich I, 741

Georg Henrich (Geo.
  Henrick)   I, 656, 657, 658
Gottfried   I, 749
Guillaume   II, 88
Jacob   I, 184, 185, 187
Johann   II, 68, 188
Johann Friederich   I, 693, 754
Johann Gabriel
  (Gabriel)   I, 217, 218, 220
Johann Georg   I, 755
Johann Lorentz (John
  Henry)   I, 589, 590, 591
Johannes (Johanis,
  Johan Peter) I, 88, 90, 92, 286, 287
                288, 364, 656, 657, 658
Martin   II, 20, 145
Michael   I, 586, 587, 588
Paser   I, 40
VÖGELE   (VÖGLE,   VOGELEY,
  VOGELLE, VOGHLEY)
Caspar   I, 453
Chr. Emanuel   II, 122
Hans Jerg   I, 9
Johann Georg   I, 747
Johannes   I, 105, 106
Mr.   II, 175
Mrs.   II, 175
(See also FÖGLE)
VOGELER (VÖGLER)
Andereas   I, 421
Görg   I, 422
Hans   I, 48, 52, 54
Johann Friderich   I, 521, 524
Johann Jacob   I, 709
Johann Simon   I, 498
Katherin   I, 49
Nicklas (Nichs)   I, 296, 298, 299
                     II, 7
Susanna   II, 7
VOGELGESANG
Geo. Adam   I, 750
Georg   I, 684
Johan Nickel   I, 439
Johann Philipp   I, 585, 587, 588
John Jacob   I, 684
Simon (Simmon)   I, 293, 294, 295
VOGELHOVE
Martin   I, 18
VÖGELIN (FAGLEY)
Johanns (Johannes),
  John   I, 113, 115, 766
VOGELMAN (FOGLEMAN)
Conradt (Hans Conrad) I, 244, 245
Hans Georg   I, 454
Mellicher   I, 418
Michael   I, 454
VOGHT see VOGT
VOGLHUTTER
Martin   I, 20

VOGNIET
J. Fredk   II, 16
VOGT (VOGHT, VOIGT, FOCH)
Andreas   I, 135, 693
Antoni   I, 689
Caspar   I, 135
Catherine   I, 135
Christ.   II, 179
Conrad   II, 174
Fred   II, 119
Hans   I, 727
Hans Jacob   I, 416
Heini   I, 417
Ignatius   I, 545, 547, 549
Johann Jacob
  (Jacob)   I, 451, 517, 518, 520
Johan Paul (Johan)   I, 135, 136
Johan Sebastian   I, 505
Johannes   I, 417, 421, 643, 644, 709
Jonas   I, 432
Jorg Peter   I, 408
Maria   I, 135
Peter   I, 732
Valtin   I, 356
VOIGT
Beder (Peter)   I, 305, 306
Johann Heinrich   I, 739
Johann Mathias
  (Mathes)   I, 158, 160
Johann Valtin
  (Valentin)   I, 154, 158, 160
VOISIN (VOYZIN, NAGBAR, read
  NACHBAR)
Abram   I, 723
Jean Pierre (Peter) I, 627, 630, 634
John Peter (Johan
  Peter)   I, 237, 238, 240
VOITEN (read prob. VOISIN)
Margaret   II, 151
VOLANDT see VOLLANDT
VÖLBEL (PHILEPLY, PHILPEL)
Johan Carle (Carl) I, 581, 583, 584
Johann Wilhelm (John
  Wilhelm)   I, 582, 583, 584
VOLCAMPE
Jac. Baltsatzer   I, 506
VOLCK (FOLK, VOLCH, WOLG,
  FOLCK, VOLK)
Daniel   I, 738
Friederich   I, 661, 663, 664
Godlib   I, 395
Hans George Carl I, 539, 541, 543
J. George (Joh.
  Jurg)   I, 564, 565, 567
J. William   I, 457
Jerg Friedrich   I, 512, 514, 515
Johan Burkhart   I, 169, 171, 172
Johann Christophel   I, 496

Johan Friederich (Joh.
Fred.) I, 502; II, 118
Johann Gerg (Hans
Jurg) I, 678, 679, 681
Johann Willhelm I, 395
Johannes (John) I, 418, 622, 624, 626
700; II, 70
Joseph I, 418
Peter I, 661, 662, 663
Uhlerich I, 488
Valentin I, 699
VOLCKEL (VÖLCKEL, VOLKEL,
VELCKELVOELKEL)
Anne Elisabeth II, 88
Florentine II, 88
Fred. I, 753
George II, 88
Jacob II, 28
Johan Friedrich I, 754
Johannes II, 28, 120
John Jost II, 84
Jost (Joos) I, 754; II, 28
Krafft II, 88
Louis II, 107
Lud^g II, 28
Maria II, 28
Maria Catherine (Mary) II, 84, 88
Maria Elisabeth II, 28
Philipp II, 88
Valentin II, 107
VÖLCKER (FELKER)
Georg Christian I, 731
Gorg Gottfriedt (Got-
fried) I, 615, 617, 620
Johan Henrich I, 692
Joseph II, 113
VOLCKERTH (VOLCKARTH,
FOLGART)
Christofel (Chris-
toffel) I, 610, 611, 613
VOLCKMANN (WOLDMAN)
Johannes (Johanes) I, 35, 36, 37
VÖLCKNER
Johann Hentrich I, 460
Johan Jacob I, 460
VOLCKS (FOLKES)
Johan (Jno) I, 589, 590
VOLEY
Jacob II, 167
VOLKEMEYER (FOLKAMAYER)
Martin I, 652, 654
VOLKMAN
Diterich I, 506
VOLKMAR
Godf. Henry II, 203
VOLL
C. Henry II, 201
Eliz. II, 201
Hans Jorg I, 411

Henrietta II, 201
Jn. Fred. II, 201
Jn. Godlieb II, 201
Jn. Henry II, 201
Sophy Eliz. II, 201
VOLLANTE (VOLLANDT, VO-
LANDT)
Carel I, 428
Jullius Fridrich I, 429
Philip Jacob I, 440
VOLLBERTH
George II, 160
VOLLERT
Johann Georg I, 469
VOLLKLE
Johann Heinrich I, 730
VOLLMAN
A^n Barbara I, 157
VOLLMER (FOLMER, VOLMAR,
VOLMER)
Adam I, 122, 125, 126
Anna Marg^t II, 97
C. II, 161
Christ. II, 107
Daniel I, 731
J. II, 161
J. G. II, 201
Jacob I, 225, 228, 230, 531, 649, 650
Johann Gerge I, 710
Johannes I, 442, 731
Jost Henry I, 710
Michael I, 533, 534
Philip Jacob II, 79
Willhelm I, 685
—— II, 161
VÖLPEL
Johann Adam I, 12
VOLPP
Georg I, 470
VOLLPRECHT (VOLPRECHT)
Andreas I, 691
Johann Wilhelm (John
W^m) I, 286, 287, 288
VOLTZ
Anna Liese II, 30
Anna Maria II, 3, 30
Barbara II, 30
Conrad I, 751
Engelica II, 30
Georg (Yerrick) I, 595, 597, 599
Heinrich (Hendrick) I, 188, 191, 193
Jacob I, 759; II, 30
Jerg I, 441
Johan Peter (Jan Peter) I, 383, 385
Johannes I, 704
Joseph I, 451
Martin II, 3
Michael I, 545, 547, 549
Nicolaas II, 30

Wilhelm I, 751
VOM BERG (VON BERG, VON BERGE)
Johann Michael (John Leonhard (Lenhart) I, 297, 298, 300
Michael) I, 652, 654
VOM HOFF
Johann Christ I, 732
VON BESTEN BOSTEL (VON BESTENBOST)
Hinrich Graven (Heinrich) I, 673, 674, 675
VON DER BORG (VAN DER BORG, FOUNDERBURGH)
Peter I, 221, 222, 224
Walter I, 221, 222, 224
VON DER LIND (VANDERLINT)
Albert I, 264, 268, 271
VON DER LINDT
Johannes I, 403
VON DER WEYT (WERDT)
Hans Jacob (Jn⁰ Jacob) I, 248, 249, 250
VONHOLT
Cunrath I, 737
VORBACH (FORTHBACK)
Balthaser (Baltzer) I, 581, 582, 584
Mattheus I, 390
Philipp I, 390
VORLENDER
Ludwig II, 20
VORM WALT
Jacob I, 431
VORMAN
Isaac II, 118
VORNEY
Jacob I, 485
VOSS (VOS)
Anna II, 96
Anna Christina II, 28
Friederich II, 22
Johann Henrich (Johan Henrick) I, 643, 645
Joh. Rudolf II, 28
Lorrentz I, 456
Nickolas Daniel I, 504
VOSSELLER
Jacob I, 415
VOSSELMAN
Hans Earhart I, 102, 104, 105
VOTRIN (VOTRING, WATERING)
Johannes (Johannis) I, 264, 267, 270
Samuel I, 404
VÖTT
Georg Martin I, 495
VOTTLER
Jacob I, 439
VOUBEL (FAUBEL, FAURBEL)
Johanes (John) I, 638, 639, 641

VOUGT (VOUGHT, read VOGT)
Johan Andreas I, 509, 510, 511
VOUNER
Elias II, 184
VUILLE (WILD)
Abram I, 593, 594
Alexandre (Alexander) I, 592, 593, 594
VULGARN
Johann II, 127
VUNBERT
Philippe I, 746
VÜSEL
Michael I, 406
VYBERTON
Maria I, 104
Susan I, 104
VYL
Jacob II, 203

WAAG (WAGG)
Carl Fridrich I, 545, 547, 549
Paul I, 492
WAAGENAER see WAGENAAR
WAALL see WAHL
WAAS
Sebastian I, 480
WAASSER see WASSER
WABER see WEBER
WACHDEL
Georg I, 444
WÄCHNISEN
Nicolas I, 452
WACHS (WAX)
Johann Philippus (Philipus) I, 582, 583, 584
WÄCHTER (WACHTER, WAGHTER)
Catharine II, 177
Gabriel I, 472
Georg I, 720
Hans Jorg I, 500
Jacob I, 41c
Martin I, 393
Martin P. II, 121
WACHTERHOLT
Wilhelm II, 108
WÄCHTLER
Christoph (Christ) I, 589, 590
WACK
Joh. II, 5
Johann Conradh I, 495
Johan Gorg (Johan Yerick) I, 383, 385
Julianna I, 156

WACKENHUT
Jacob I, 719
WACKER
Bernhart I, 413
Georg I, 403
John II, 202
John G. II, 189
Michel I, 403
WACKERLY *see* WEKERLY
WADTLI (WATTLEE)
Hans I, 88, 90, 92
WAGE
Johanes I, 697
WAGELY
George Chr. II, 121
WAGEMAN (WAGEMANN, WAG-
HEMAN)
Johann Philipp (J.
Philip) I, 154, 157, 160
Tobias I, 363
WAGENAAR (WAAGENAER)
Andreas II, 124
Conraet I, 367, 369
Hendrick I, 675
Johan Henrich I, 675
Martin II, 94
Ulrich II, 124
WAGENER (WAGGENER, WAG-
GONER)
Andrew I, 749
Carel II, 36
Caspar I, 472
Catha Ma II, 23
Hendrick II, 3
Herman (Harman) I, 601, 602, 603
Jacob I, 666, 668, 670, 736
Jno II, 6
Johann II, 50
Johann Henrich I, 323, 325, 326
Joh. Jacob I, 437
Johannes (Johans) I, 564, 565, 567
II, 36
Peter I, 736
WAGENHORST
Johann Carl I, 741
Johann Heinrich I, 741
WAGENMANN
Michel I, 435
WAGENTBOTTEN
John Albertus I, 373
WAGER
Mardin I, 730
Nicolaus I, 480
WAGHMER (read prob. WAGNER)
Philip I, 357
WAGMAN
Gotlieb I, 460

WAGNER WAGENER, VAGNER,
VAUGHNER)
Abraham I, 180, 182, 184
Adam I, 734
Anna II, 152
Anna Mary II, 152
Bastian I, 66, 69, 70
Carl I, 79, 81, 83, 474
Carl Jacob I, 279, 281, 282
Caspar I, 424, 472, 609, 611, 612
Catherine I, 108; II, 44
Cath. Margaretha II, 105
Chris. I, 236
Christian I, 360, 362
Christoph I, 365
Conrad I, 407, 413, 521, 524, 609
610, 612, 621, 623, 625, 716
Danjel II, 132
David II, 165
Elias I, 79, 82, 83
Engelhart I, 437
Georg (George) I, 421; II, 152, 179
Georg Andreas I, 731
George F. II, 165
Georg Jacob I, 421
Georg Lutwich (Gorg)
Ludwig) I, 189, 192, 194
Hans I, 442
Hans Adam I, 431, 463
Hans Görg (John Jurge,
Jurrig) I, 78, 81, 82, 88
90, 91, 209, 211
Hans Jacob I, 395
Heinr Georg II, 107
Heinrich (Hendrick,
Henry) I, 268, 282, 284, 285, 349
350, 351, 401, 453, 685, 716
Hiney (Heini) I, 275
Jacob I, 226, 228, 230
356, 711
II, 146, 152, 160, 193
Jacob Walter I, 468
James II, 123
Jann Ulrich I, 79, 82, 83
Jchoh Georg I, 450
Jean II, 88
Jean Chrétien II, 88
Jean Conrad II, 88
Jgl. Adam I, 450
Johan Adam (Adam) I, 352, 353
591, 593, 594
Johann Andreas I, 423, 461
Johann Christof (Christophel)
I, 199, 201, 203
318, 319
Johann Georg (Gerg) I, 293, 294
295, 490
Johann Georg Friederich I, 762

Johann Henrich (Johan Henry)
I, 346, 401
Johan Jacob   I, 237, 330, 495
II, 135
Johan Leonhard   I, 721
Johann Ludwig (Lodwick)   I, 373
374, 375
Johan Michael I, 348, 349, 351, 454
Johann Nicolaus (Johann Nickel)
I, 355, 683, 694
Johann Philip (Johan
Phil.)   I, 198, 200, 202
453, 600, 602 603
Johanna Catharine   II, 165
Johannes (Johanes,
Hanes)   I, 198, 200, 202
283, 284, 285
409, 413, 431
472, 559, 561, 562
Joseph   I, 757
Jusdus Simonius
(Augustus)   I, 106, 111, 112
Magdalana   II, 165
Margrett (Margareta)   I, 81, 190
Marie   II, 88
Marie Gertrude   II, 88
Mari Marlin   I, 79
Martha   I, 108
Martin   I, 470
Mathias (Matheas, Mat-
teis)   I, 84, 86, 87, 413
596, 598, 599
Melcker (Malcker,
Meliker)   I, 106, 111, 112
Michael   I, 365, 372, 396
Nicolaus   I, 318, 319, 320
Orsell   I, 80
Peter (Petter)   I, 185, 186, 187
198, 200, 202
Philip   I, 576, 578, 580
628, 631, 634, 660
Philipp Ernst   I, 470
Philipps Otto   I, 420
Philipus Jacob   I, 460, 759
Sebastian   I, 497
Thomas   I, 693
Ullreich   I, 434
Wilhelm (William) I, 387, 388, 389
Yorick   II, 160
WAGONER see WAGENER
WAGSHITER
Johanna   I, 190
WAHL (WALL, WAALL, VAHLL)
Adam   I, 199, 201, 203
Anna Clara   II, 205
Friderich   I, 689
G.   II, 144
Heinrich   II, 205

J. H.   II, 142
Johan Caspar (Casper)   I, 652, 654
Johanes (Johs, John)   I, 423, 425
II, 83, 142
Jost   I, 688
Kunigunte   II, 205
Martin   I, 205, 207, 208
Martin Gerg   I, 486
Matthias   I, 753
Melchior   II, 205
Wendel   I, 419
WAHM
Valtin   II, 121
WAHNERT
David   I, 320, 321, 322
Mary Elizabeth   I, 320
WAHNSIDEL
Johan Jorg (Philip)   I, 105, 106
WAHRLICH
Michael   I, 474
WAIBEL
Johannes   I, 693
WAIBLINGER
Johann Jacob   I, 750
WAIDELE
Johann Michel   I, 328
WAISSER (read prob. WEISER)
Johann L. (Lodwich)   I, 583, 584
WALATEIN (read prob. VALEN-
TIN)
Filipp   I, 442
WALB (WALD)
Conrath   I, 179, 181, 183
WALBER (WULLER)
Johan Peter   I, 35, 36
WALBERT
Johann Christoph   I, 409
WALCH (WALCK, WALK)
Hans Michel   I, 93, 94, 95
Johann Jacob (John
Adam)   I, 297, 299, 300
Stephann Fridrich   I, 512, 514, 515
WALCKER (WALCHER, WALCK-
HER, WALKER)
Jerg Michel   I, 454
Johanes (John)   I, 637, 639, 641
Joseph   I, 757
Peter   I, 456
WÄLCKLY
Jacob   I, 400
WALD (WALDT)
Anna Barbara   I, 50
Hagen   I, 660
Hans Henrich   I, 51
Johann Henrich
(Hend.)   I, 237, 238, 239
Johannes   I, 363

Oswald (Ostwald,
  Ohswald)   I, 48, 52, 54
Roselva   I, 51
WALDBERG
  Augusta   II, 70
WALDER *see* WALTER
WALDMAN   (WALTMAN,
  WALDTMANN, WALTMANN)
  Conrad   I, 234, 235, 236
  David   I, 711
  Emanuel   I, 723
  Gorg Jacob   I, 723
  Hannes   I, 709
  Henrich Adam   I, 759
  Johann Wilhelm   I, 723
  Johannes   I, 736
  Nich[s]   I, 734
WALDMER
  Uhllerich   I, 434
WALDY
  Caspar   I, 434
WALKER (WACKER)
  Andreas (Adrius)   I, 237, 238, 239
  C.   II, 130
  Christopher   II, 56
  F.   II, 130
  Gorg   I, 462
  Johann Michael   I, 407
WALL *see* WAHL
WALLACE
  James   II, 26
WALLER (WÄLLER)
  Johan Fredrick   I, 35
  Johann Georg (John
    Georg)   I, 577, 579, 580
  Johann Peter   I, 328
  Johannes   I, 473
  Lenard   I, 414
  Paulus   I, 480
  Rubertus   I, 702
WALLES
  Fredich   I, 417
  Wilhelmus Peter   I, 478
WALLESET
  Martin   I, 392
WALLEYSEN
  Paul   I, 508
WALLHAUER (WALHOWER)
  Georg Stephanus (Georg
    Stafon)   I, 555, 556, 558
WALLHEYER (WALHYSER)
  Anthony   I, 637, 639, 641
WALLMAN
  Peter   I, 759
WALLSENER
  Jacob   I, 392
WALLTONE
  Christane   I, 12

WALMER
  Peter   I, 317, 318, 319
WALPER
  Gottfried Samuel   I, 418
WALSCH (WALSH)
  George   II, 83
  John   II, 83
  Michael   II, 134
WALSER
  Casper   I, 395
WALSPAN
  Gunther   II, 83
WALTAICH
  Andreas   I, 328
WALTE (WALDI, WALTI)
  Andereas (Joseph) I, 258, 260, 263
WALTER   (WALDER, WALDOR,
  WALDTER, WALTHER)
  Albrecht   I, 498
  Alida   II, 91
  Anna Clara   II, 5
  Antoni (Andony)   I, 335, 337, 338
  Antonius   I, 488
  Barbara   I, 107
  Bernhard   I, 88, 90, 91
  Caspar   I, 716
  Catharina   II, 5
  Christopher   I, 8, 10
  Conrad   I, 89, 91, 92
  Dhomas   II, 134
  Elizabeth   II, 5
  Ely   I, 333, 334
  Engell   II, 137
  Eva   II, 5
  Felix   I, 331
  Friederich   I, 683; II, 54
  George   II, 84, 91
  Gottfried (Godfritt) I, 289, 290, 291
  Gottlieb   I, 417
  Hannah Barbary   I, 24
  Hans Casper   I, 364
  Hans Henrich   I, 364
  Hans Jacob   I, 364; II, 146
  Heinrich (Henrich, Henderick,
    Hinrich, Henry) I, 331, 614, 616
     618, 716
     II, 114, 160
  Isaac   II, 136
  J. Jost   I, 467
  Jacob   I, 10, 12, 93, 94, 95
     149, 236, 348
     349, 351, 406
     431, 471, 474
     498; II, 51
  John Adam   I, 406
  Johann Antoni   I, 395
  Johann Jacob (Joh.
    Jac.)   I, 10, 12, 398
     420, 546, 548

550, 722, 727
II, 107
Johan Martin   I, 495
Johan Michel   I, 697
Johann Nickolaus   I, 731
Johan Peter   I, 749
Johan Valltin   I, 492
Joh. Wilh.   II, 107
Johannes (Johanes) I, 327, 329, 364
                     397, 437, 546
                     548, 550, 702
                     II, 51
Johannes Christian   I, 340, 341, 342
Johannes Henrich   I, 305, 306, 307
John Fred.   II, 201
Joseph   I, 286, 287, 288
Justus   II, 137
Kunrad   II, 5
Margret   II, 51
Maria   II, 5
Maria Sophia   II, 5
Martin   I, 406
Matheus   I, 471
Matthias (Mathias)   I, 84, 86, 87
                     II, 91
Michael   I, 122, 125, 126, 698
Nicolaus (Nicklaus, Nicholas,
  Nicola)   I, 198, 201, 202
                     328, 456, 488
Peter   II, 5, 51, 91
Philipp   I, 712
Philipp Jacob   I, 396
Rudolff (Rudolph) I, 24, 25, 147
                     150, 151
Sebastian   I, 314
Simon   I, 404, 514, 515
Susana   II, 51
Velte   I, 236
Walter   II, 191
Wilhelm (Wil-
  liam)   I, 677, 679, 680, 756
                     II, 51
WALTERSCHEE (read WALTER-
  SEE)
Johannes Henrich   I, 723
WALTHORN
Johann Adam   I, 460
WALTMAIER
Johan Lutwig   I, 709
WALTMAN *see* WALDMAN
WALTON
Margeratt   I, 84
WALTZ (WALZ, WALTS)
Catharena   II, 188
Christiana   II, 189
Christoff (Christoph) I, 503, 532
                     533, 535
Elizabeth   II, 188
Friedrig   I, 757

George   II, 155
Hans   I, 482
Hans Martin (Hans
  Marte)   I, 237, 239, 240, 446
Hans Wolff   I, 335, 337, 339
Jacob   I, 237, 471
Joan   II, 188
Joel   I, 498
Joh.   II, 179
Johann Jacob I, 477
Johan Reinhart I, 355
Johannes   I, 378, 380, 381, 489
John Peter (Geo.
  Peter)   I, 246, 247, 248
Joseph   I, 440
Mart.   I, 486
Michael   I, 438; II, 189
Regena   II, 189
William   II, 188
WALTZER
Friederich   I, 427
WALY (WALLEY)
Hans Adam   I, 513, 514, 516
WAMBECK (WAMBECHT)
Johan Friederich I, 517, 519, 520
WAMBOLD (WAMBOLDT, WAM-
  BOLT)
Adam   I, 159, 161
An Maria   I, 157
Catharina   I, 157
George   I, 179, 181, 183
Georg Heinrich (Georg
  Frist Friedrich) I, 178, 180, 182
Johann Gorg   I, 156, 159, 161
Johann Peter I, 159, 161
WAMPFLER,   (WAMPFFLER,
  WAMBLER, WAMLER)
Christian   I, 364
Hans Michael (Hans
  Mich.)   I, 300, 301, 302
Hans Peter (Hans
  Petr)   I, 300, 301, 302
Johann Christian I, 364
Johann Lutwich I, 364
Jorg   I, 364
WAMSER (WOMSER)
Nicklas (Nich1) I, 384, 386
WANAMAKER   *see*   WANNE-
  MACHER
WANDEL (WANDELL)
Jacob Adam   I, 605, 606, 607
Tobias   I, 585, 587, 588
WANDERBURG
Henrich Jacob I, 429
WANGER (WENGER, WENGAR)
Christian   I, 386
Hans (Johannes) I, 384, 386
Joseph   I, 629, 632, 636
Stephan   I, 386

WANKEL
Carl II, 172
WANKMILLER
Christiana II, 187
Christopher II, 187
Rachel II, 187
WANN
Jacob I, 499
Joh. Casper (Casper) I, 531, 532, 534
Johan Wilhelm I, 427
Peter I, 701
WANNBOLT (read WAMBOLT)
Andʷ II, 144
WANNEBACH
Michel I, 715
WANNEMACHER (WANNEN-
MACHER, WANEMACHER,
WANNAMAKER, WANMA-
CHER, WANAMACHER)
Bernd (Bernard) I, 243, 244, 245
Georg (Jorg, Jurg) I, 48, 52, 54, 404
Jacob I, 246, 247, 248
Margerite I, 50
Samuel I, 404
WANNER (WONNER, WANER)
Adam I, 394
Anna Maria I, 109
Christian I, 109
Elizabeth I, 108
Ferdend (Ferdinand) I, 689
Franz I, 683
Hans Adam I, 652, 654
Jacob I, 13, 14
Maria Crete I, 109
Martin (Marten) I, 107, 111, 112
WANSTHER
Martin II, 91
WANTHER (WARNTHER, WAR-
INKEN)
Christopher I, 509, 510, 511
WANTLIN
Dewald I, 429
WANTZ (read WENTZ)
Michel I, 483
WARMER
Andreas I, 137
WARMKESSEL
Georg Michel I, 382
WARNER
Anna I, 138
Christian I, 509, 510, 511
Johanes I, 439
Joseph, junʳ II, 26
Wendel (Wendal) I, 636, 638, 640
WARNICK
M. II, 136
WARTH (WAERTH)
Bern (Barnet) I, 266, 269, 272
Philipp Friderich I, 582, 583, 584

WARTMAN (WARDMAN,
WARTHMAN)
Abraham I, 40
Caspar I, 60, 64, 65
Elizabeth I, 40
Greda I, 61
Hans Adam (Hand
Adam) I, 40, 41, 42
Mary I, 40
Michael I, 741
WASHER
Johanes I, 489
WASLING
Johannes I, 740
WÄSPY
Jacob I, 435
Johannes I, 435
WASS
Leonhart I, 687
WASSER (WAASSER)
Jacob I, 434
Johann Ludwig I, 727
Peter I, 736
WASSERMANN (WASSERMAN,
WATERMAN)
Joh. II, 99
Matthias I, 637, 638, 640
WASSUM (WASSOM)
Johann Conrad I, 501
Joh. George I, 501
Johanes I, 501
Leonhart I, 501
WAST (read prob. WEST)
Jacop II, 36
WÄSTENHABER (WISTHAFER)
Henry I, 569, 571, 572
WASTGAU
Heinrich II, 69
WASTS (read prob. WATZ)
Fredrik II, 34
WATINBURG
John II, 195
WATTENBERG (VALTENBERG)
Johann Heinrich I, 516, 518, 519
WATZIN
Johan I, 540
WAULKE
Carel II, 184
WÄYDMANN
Johann Henrich I, 449
WAYER see WEYER
WAYMAN see WEIMANN
WAYS see WEISS
WEASTE (read prob. WIEST)
Rodlafe I, 344
WEAVER see WEBER
WEBEL (WEABEL, read WAIBEL)
Johann Valentin (Valen-
tine) I, 610, 611, 613

WEBER (WEABER, WEBBER, WEAVER, WEBHER, WEVER)
Adam   I, 307, 308, 309, 436
Albreck   I, 760
Alexander   II, 110
Andreas   I, 189, 192, 194
Anna (Anne, Ann)   I, 153
                      II, 88, 110
Anna Christiana   II, 180
Anne Elisabeth (Anna
  Lise)   II, 88, 180
Anthony   I, 750, 761
Barbara   II, 124
Bernard   I, 750
Burgart (Burgat)   I, 250, 251
Carl   I, 695
Carrolinia   II, 36
Caspar   I, 356, 434
Caterrinia Maria   II, 36
Catherina (Catherine,
  Cathe)   II, 8, 36, 88
Christian   I, 10, 11, 153, 154
              276, 277, 278, 581
              583, 584, 694, 735
                      II, 133
Christoph (Christof, Christof-
  fel)   I, 358, 372, 397
              463, 609, 695
Conrad   II, 110
Daniel   I, 721
David   II, 8
Debalt (Deobald) I, 205, 207, 208
Elisabeth   II, 147, 148
Enoch   I, 474
Erhart (Erhard) I, 614, 616, 619
Eve   II, 148
Everhard   II, 147
Frederich Henerich   II, 37
Friederich Earl   II, 37
Gabriel (Gaberiel) I, 642, 643
Georg (Gorg,
  George)   I, 353, 354, 363, 376
           377, 637, 638, 640
                   II, 180, 181
Georg Friederich (Fred-
  rick)   I, 681, 682
Gerdrudt   I, 73
Gottfriedt   I, 320
Hans   I, 153, 391, 450
Hans Adam   I, 450, 493
Hans Georg (Hans
  Jorg)   I, 237, 470, 609
Hans Michael   I, 502
Hans Ullerik (Hans
  Ulrick)   I, 273, 274
Hans Yerrick   I, 609
Henerita   II, 36
Henrich (Henrick,
  Henry)   I, 73, 414, 714

Herman   I, 356, 424
Heronimus   I, 340, 341, 342
Jacob   I, 105, 330, 384
                386, 413, 714
                   II, 133, 147
Jean   II, 88
Jno Maths   I, 755
Johann Adam   I, 357, 376, 377
                661, 663, 664, 696
Johann Best   I, 699
Joh. Christ   II, 129
Johann Daniel   I, 415
Johann David   I, 762
Johan Engel   I, 467
Johann Friederich
  (Fritz)   I, 378, 379, 381
                      II, 29
Johann George I, 237, 239, 240
                357, 373, 374
                375, 483, 709
Johann Henrich   I, 36, 217, 218
                220, 414, 752
           II, 29, 37, 107, 148
Johan Herberd (Her-
  bert)   I, 143, 145, 146
Johann Herman (Her-
  mann)   I, 180, 182, 184
Johann Jacob (Han
  Jacob)   I, 646, 647
                      II, 107
Johan Jost   II, 36
Johan Jurgen   II, 128
Johann Ludwig   I, 698
Johan Martin   I, 747
Johann Nickel   I, 461
Johan Peter (J. Peter) I, 646, 648
                683, 699, 753
Johann Philip I, 57, 58, 416, 761
Johan Ullrich   I, 522, 525
Johan Volandin (Valentin) I, 414
Johann Wilhelm (Johan
  Willem)   I, 522, 525, 692
Johannes (John) I, 66, 69, 70, 127
                129, 130, 273, 274
                329, 357, 412, 413
                416, 452, 459, 489
              614, 616, 619, 643, 645
          646, 647, 648, 692, 710, 727
                   II, 29, 124, 133, 148
Johanes Leonhart   I, 502
Johannes Petter   I, 372
John   II, 84
John Georg I, 248, 249, 250, 493
John Peter   I, 691
Joseph (Jocip)   I, 496, 694
Josse   II, 88
Jost   I, 425
Juliana   II, 29
Justus Henrich   I, 522, 525

Kraft (Graft) I, 559, 561, 562
645, 647
II, 29, 88
Leonhart (Leonard) I, 646, 648
Lorens I, 71, 75, 77
Margaretha (Mar-
gareth) I, 127; II, 36, 180
Maria (Marie) I, 147; II, 133, 146
Maria Anneleese II, 180
Maria Cath^a II, 180
Marie Elisabeth II, 88, 128
Maria Gert^de II, 128
Maria Magdalene II, 128
Martin (Mardin) I, 391, 435, 437, 705
Mathews II, 96
Mathias I, 57, 58, 729
Mattheis (Matthys) I, 180, 181, 184
Mattheis Koch I, 695
Michael (Michel,
Michell) I, 24, 25, 26, 301
302, 303, 461, 464
Mr. II, 176
Nickelas (Nich^s, Nickel) I, 461, 727
II, 9
Paul I, 441
Peter I, 314, 315, 420
453, 459, 710
II, 29
Phillip I, 198, 200, 202
522, 525, 762
II, 112
Phillis I, 24
Pierre II, 88
Sebastian (John
Bastian) I, 569, 571, 572
Steffan (Christopal) I, 609, 611, 612
T. II, 129
Theobald (Dewald) I, 314, 315, 691
Tobias I, 266, 269, 273
Valentin I, 413, 414
Wilh. Christian II, 128
Wilhelm (William) I, 356; II, 180
Willeminia II, 36
WEBERT (WEPPERT)
Melchior (Melchor) I, 627, 630, 634
WEBNER (read prob. WEBER)
Theodor II, 190
WECHTERLING
Hans I, 441
WECK
Johan Nichol I, 702
Mich^l I, 702
WECKER
Görg Balthes I, 458
Johann Gottlieb (Got-
leap) I, 574, 575
WECKERLE (WECKERLY, WEK-
ERLY)
Abraham I, 147, 150, 151

Johannes II, 20
Verena I, 149
WECKERLIN
Immanuel Friderich I, 497
WECKESSER
Hans Michael I, 366
Johann Anderas I, 399
WECKFORT
Marcus (Markus) I, 636, 638, 640
WEDEL (WEEDLE)
Georg Adam (dirick
Adam) I, 24, 25, 26
Johan Peter (Johan
Peere) I, 591, 593, 594
Johannes I, 441
Petter I, 697; II, 41
WEDER
Augustin I, 12, 13
WEDERTZ
Johannes Nicklaus I, 398
WEDLEBERGER
Jurgen I, 307
WEEGENAAR
Maria II, 68
WEEGER see WEGER
WEESLIN
Christoff I, 392
WEESSIG (WIESICH, WIESICK)
George (Jurg) I, 614, 616, 618
WEG
Andras I, 489
WEGER (WEEGER, WEEGAR)
Johan Friderich I, 688
Peter I, 23, 25, 26
163, 165, 167
WEGERLEIN (WEGERLINE)
Anna Clara I, 74
Jacob I, 73
Katharine I, 74
Otilia I, 72, 74
Paulus I, 71, 75, 77
WEGFALLER
David I, 489
WEGMANN (WAGMAN)
Jacob I, 332, 333, 334
WEGNER (WEGENER)
Christoph I, 509, 510, 511
Henrich I, 693
Johann Ignatz II, 205
WEHHAGEN
Cath. Margar. II, 140
Joh. Eberhard II, 139
Joh. Fried^ch H. II, 140
Joh. Hinr. II, 140
Johanna Maria Christ. II, 140
WEHLER (WELLER)
Hans Henrich I, 408
Johannes I, 297, 298, 300
Jost Henrich I, 443

WEHLSPACH
G. II, 32
WEHMEYER (WETHERMEIR)
Johann Ledolff I, 536, 537, 538
Valten I, 537, 538
WEHNER
Johann Gottlieb I, 360, 361
WEHNIG
Johannes I, 497
WEHR
Christjan I, 707
Hans Jorg I, 476
Simmon (Simon) I, 282, 284, 285
WEIAND (WYANDT)
Johannes I, 378, 380, 381
WEIBEL (WEIBELL, WEYBOL, WIBEL)
Adam I, 392
Daniel I, 754
Fridrich I, 476
Jacob I, 392
Johannes I, 258, 260, 263
Samuel II, 160
Steph[n] I, 693
WEIBRECHT (WEYBRICH, WIBRECHT)
Georg Christoff (Christoph) I, 677, 679, 680
WEICHEL
Dan[l] I, 695
John II, 9
Johann Georg (George) I, 168, 170, 172
Johan Petter I, 502
Marg[t] II, 9
WEICHENBACHER
Paul I, 721
WEICHSTIER
Johan Wendel I, 459
WEICK (WEYCKH)
Johann Georg I, 490
Johann Gerhardt I, 340, 341, 343
WEICKEL (WEYGEL, WEYGELL)
A[n] Elisabeth I, 157
Gorg Adam I, 697
Johan Michell I, 155, 158, 161
WEICKER (WEYCKER, WYKER)
Johann Ludwig I, 155, 158, 161
Johan Michael I, 311, 312, 313
Johann Nicolaus (Johan Nicol) I, 383, 385
Yergen Zemen [Georg Simon] I, 310
WEICKERT (WIGER, WEIGHELT)
Hannes I, 723
Hans Dries (Johan) I, 539, 541, 543
Johann Georg (Jerig) I, 538, 540, 543
WEID (WEIDT)
Hans I, 494

Michael I, 452
WEIDBRECHT (WEYBRICH)
Andreas I, 335, 337, 339
WEIDEBACH (WYDEBACH)
Henrich I, 156, 159, 161
WEIDEMANN *see* WEIDMANN
WEIDEMER
Christoffer I, 520
Peter I, 517
WEIDENAUER
Hans Goerg I, 404
WEIDENMEIER
Urban I, 697
WEIDER (WEITER)
Hans Michl I, 7
Lutwig I, 364
WEIDINGER (WIDENGER, WHITHINGAR)
Frantz (Frans) I, 627, 630, 633
Marcus (Marks) I, 627, 630, 633
WEIDKNECHT (WYTKNECHT)
Martin I, 96, 97, 98
WEIDLER (WEITLER)
Jacob I, 414
Lawrence II, 3
Rudoff Vallen I, 328
WEIDMANN (WEIDMAN, WEIDEMANN, WIDEMAN, WEIDTMAN)
Abraham I, 146, 149, 150
Barbara I, 147, 148
Caspar I, 253, 254, 255
Christofel (Christopher) I, 252, 253, 255
Georg II, 139
Hans Jerg I, 730
Hendrick (Henry) I, 331, 332, 334
609, 610, 612
J. C. II, 32
Jacob I, 147, 148, 150
Jacob Heinrich I, 195, 196, 197
Johannes (Johans) I, 195, 196, 197, 434
Judith I, 148
Lennert I, 483
Magdalene I, 148
Matheus (Matheis, Mathias) I, 113, 114, 115, 765
Rudolff (Rodolph) I, 146, 149, 150
(*See also* WAYDMAN *and* WEYDMAN)
WEIDNER (WEITTNER, WIEDNAR)
Gott. II, 99
Hans Georg (Jerick) I, 116, 119, 121
Hans Willhellm I, 364
Henrich I, 496

Johann Heinrich (John
Heinrich)   I, 672, 673, 674
(*See also* WEYDNER)
WEIDY (WEYDY, WYTIGH)
Jeremias   I, 341, 342, 343
WEIEL *see* WEIL
WEIER (WEIR)
Geo.   I, 730
Johann Adam   I, 423
Johan Peter   I, 404
WEIFFERT (WEIFFER)
Johann Jorg (Hans
George)   I, 642, 644
WEIG
Jorg Matias   I, 470
WEIGAND (WEYGAND, WEY-
GANDT, WEYGANT, WY-
GANT)
Conrad (Conrat)   I, 382; II, 52
Cornelius   I, 155, 158, 160
Fredrick (Peter)   I, 661, 663, 664
Hanna   II, 13
Jacob   II, 13, 119
Johann Albert   I, 374, 375
Johan Jost   I, 448
Johann Lorentz   I, 382
Johan Nicolaus   I, 714
Johan Philip   I, 411
Johannes (Hannes)   I, 666, 668, 670
Nicolaus   I, 503
Paulus (Johannes
Paul)   I, 559, 561, 562
WEIGELE
Johan Wendel   I, 742
WEIGELL (WEIGGELL)
Mardin (Merdin)   I, 59, 63, 65
Torothea   I, 60
WEIGHART
Caspar   I, 457
WEIGHER (WEYCHELL)
Niclas (Jan Nickell)   I, 266, 272
WEIGHLER
Hans   I, 348
WEIL (WEYL, WEILL, WEIEL,
WEILE)
Aⁿ Catharine   I, 157
Anna M.   II, 158
Cath. Elis.   II, 158
Conradt (Conrad)   I, 621, 624, 626
Henrich (Henry)   I, 613, 616, 618
J. G.   II, 158
Jacob   II, 129
Johann Christoph   I, 721
Johann Georg (John
Yerick)   I, 373, 374, 376
Johan Jacob (Hans,
Jacob)   I, 155, 158, 160
Johann Petter   I, 737

Johannes (Johanns)   I, 488, 591
593, 594
Magdalena   II, 129
Maria Cath.   II, 158
William   II, 158
(*See also* WEYL)
WEILAND
Conradt   I, 249
Friedʳ   II, 178
(*See also* WEYLAND)
WEILER
And.   I, 507
Lorentz   I, 422
WEILTZ
Adam   II, 118
WEIMANN (WEIMAN, WAY-
MAN)
George   II, 53
Gerg Mich.   I, 471
Johann George (Jörg) I, 323, 324, 326
II, 134
(*See also* WEYMANN)
WEIMER (WEIMMER)
Anthoni   I, 466
Caspar   I, 458
Hans   I, 149, 150
Jacob   I, 474, 475
Martin   I, 759
(*See also* WEYMER)
WEIN (WYN)
Fredʳ, de   II, 22
Hans Jurig   I, 304
Jacob   I, 513, 514, 515
WEINANDT
Johannes Wilhelm   I, 466
WEINBERG (WINBERG)
J. Martin (John Martin) I, 574, 575
WEINBERGER
Balser   I, 397
Martin   I, 449
WEINBRENNER (WINEBRENER,
WEINBRENER)
Anthon   I, 509
Johann Christ (Chris-
tian)   I, 568, 570, 571
Wolfgang   I, 509
WEINDLING (read prob. WEN-
DLING)
Barbara   II, 44
Valentine   II, 44
WEINEL (WINEL)
Jan   II, 197
Wilh.   II, 118
WEINERT
Ernestine   II, 119
Nicolas   II, 119
WEINGAND (read prob. WEI-
GAND)
Joseph   I, 483

WEINGART (WEINGARD)
Catharina II, 69
Jacob I, 455, 667, 669, 671
Johan Peder I, 352, 354
Peter I, 371
WEINGARTEN (WINEGARDEN)
Conrad I, 478
Matthew J. II, 92
WEINGÄRTNER (WINEGARDEN, WYNGARTNER)
Car. Fred^k II, 5
Christina II, 151
Friderich II, 151
George II, 151
Georg Nicolaus I, 538, 540, 543
Godfrey II, 151
Jacob II, 151
Jacob F. II, 151
Johann Michael I, 709
Margaretta II, 151
Michael II, 151
WEINHEIMER (WYNHAMER, WYNHEYMER)
Catharine I, 73
Henrick I, 74
Jacob I, 74
Paulus (Paul) I, 71, 76, 77
Philip I, 74
Wendel (Vindael) I, 67, 69, 70
WEINIG
Johann Gorg I, 683
WEINIGER (WEYNINGER, WEININGER)
Jacob I, 586, 587, 588
Nicolaus I, 444
WEINKOTEN (WINEGAT)
Anthoni (Anthony) I, 383, 385
WEINMAN (WEIMAN)
Friederick II, 20
Johan Jacob I, 600, 602, 603
WEINMÜLLER (WYMULLER, WEYMILLER, WEGMILLER)
Conrad (Conradt) I, 221, 223, 224
Johannes I, 221, 223, 224
WEIPERT
Johan Stephan II, 174
WEIR *see* WEIER
WEIRICH
Johann Jacob I, 427
WEIRMULLER
Joh. Christ^n II, 44
WEIRTZ (read prob. WIRTZ)
Hans Adam II, 124
Heinrich II, 124
Margareth II, 124
WEISÄCKER
Friederich II, 45

WEISBACHER
Johanes (Johans, Johannes) I, 551, 552, 554
WEISBECK
Fried. II, 193
WEISBORRN (WEISBORN)
Barbara II, 43
Christina II, 43
Daniel II, 43
Laurens II, 43
Margaret II, 43
WEISE
Johann Christ. II, 107
WEISEBURGER
Jacob I, 483
WEISENBERGER
Johann Daniel I, 496
WEISENER
Freiderich II, 160
Jacob I, 392
WEISER (WEYSER, WEISSER)
Adam I, 466
Christian I, 43, 45, 46
Davidt (David) I, 266, 269, 273
Johan Gorg I, 475
WEISHART (WEYSHART)
Henry (Henrich) I, 198, 200, 202
WEISIGER (VESSINGER)
Daniel I, 55, 56, 57
WEISKOB (read prob. WEISSKOPF)
Johan Esaias I, 382
WEISMEYER
H. Michael I, 480
WEISNER (WEISSNER, WYSNER, WASENER)
Conrad I, 390
Johann Peter I, 15
Michael I, 551, 552, 553
Philip I, 363
WEISON
Katy II, 151
WEISS (WEIS, WEES, WISE, WICE, WEYES, WYS)
Abraham I, 175, 176, 178
Adam I, 175, 176, 178, 441
Adam Friedrich I, 491
Andreas (And^w) I, 84, 86, 87, 600, 602, 603, 709
Anna I, 138, 148
Anna Barbara I, 190
Augustus I, 692
Barbara (Barbra) I, 61, 118, 147, 190, 766
Bastian I, 406
Benedict (Benedick, Benedicus) I, 116, 120, 121, 412
Casper I, 48, 52, 54
Catherine (Kathrina) I, 62, 148
Charles I, 660

Christ. Gottl. II, 139
Christian I, 335, 337, 338
555, 556, 558
Christina II, 129
Christoffel (Chris-
toph) I, 226, 228, 230
Cunrad (Konradt) I, 473, 491
Daniel I, 595, 597, 599
Elizabeth I, 147
Felix I, 364
Frans Philip (Francis
Philips) I, 592, 593, 595
Frantz (France) I, 113, 114, 115, 765
Friderich I, 443
Fridrich Salomon I, 505
G. M. I, 9
Georg (George) I, 137, 140, 142, 365
449
Georg Jacob I, 758
H. Hansen (Johannes) I, 147, 149, 150
Hans Adam I, 751
Hans Jacob (Johan
Jacob) I, 276, 277, 278, 473
Hans Jerg I, 438
Hans Rudi I, 364
Heinrich (Hendreck) I, 434; II, 34
Heronomus I, 660
Jacob I, 20, 21, 60, 64, 65, 397
438, 718, 734; II, 36
Jacob Wilhelm I, 189, 192, 193
Jerg Michael I, 736
Johan I, 46
Johann Adam
(Adam) I, 373, 375, 376
Johann Carl II, 79
Johan F. II, 168
Johan Georg I, 234, 394, 437
Johann Gottfried I, 698
Johan Henrich (Hen-
rick) I, 217, 218, 220
Johan Jacob I, 443
Johann Leonharth
(Leonard) I, 106, 111, 112
Johann Melcher
(Melchior) I, 199, 201, 203
Johann Michael (Johan
Mich¹) I, 601, 602, 603
677, 679, 680
Johann Peter I, 436
Johan Philipps
(Phylip) I, 212, 214, 216
Johann Wilhelm I, 440, 689
Johannes (Joansˢ,
John) I, 176, 177, 178, 410, 422
600, 602, 603, 697, 716
II, 53, 129
Johannes Casper (J.
Caspar) I, 559, 561, 563
John Peter I, 301, 302, 303

Jorg I, 539, 541, 543
Joseph II, 184
Kiliana I, 62
Lewis II, 153
Ludwig I, 763
Maria Greta (Maria
Creta) I, 108, 118
Martin I, 438
Mathias (Matheas,
Matheis) I, 397, 400, 678, 679, 680
Michael
(Michel) I, 127, 129, 130, 330
453, 711; II, 3
Nicklas I, 473
Peter I, 359
Peter Jacob I, 457
Philip I, 526, 528, 530, 539, 541, 543
Phillipp Henrich I, 462
Philipp Jacob I, 733
Reinhart I, 615, 617, 619
Rosina I, 62
Ruthy I, 434
Samuel I, 458
Sicilia I, 50
Susanna I, 148
Torethea (Dorothea) I, 61
Ullerich (Uhllerich,
Ueldrick) I, 296, 298, 299
Wilhelm I, 628, 631, 635
WEISSBACH
Christian I, 763
WEISSBAHRT
Adam I, 489
WEISSEL (WYSEL, WYSELL)
Albonia I, 103
Barbara I, 103
Frederick I, 102, 104, 105
Michael I, 102, 104, 105
Susanna I, 103
WEISSENBACH
George II, 52
WEISSERT
Andreas I, 741
Jacob I, 687
WEISSGERBER
Dilmanus I, 443
Johannes I, 503, 701
WEISSHARDT
Martin I, 724
WEISSKOPF
Christoffel I, 335, 337, 338
WEISSMAN (WEISMAN, WIES-
MAN)
Johann David I, 463
Johann Georg
(Yerick) I, 373, 374, 376
Johannes I, 366
Michael I, 448
Nicklas I, 448

Peter   I, 614, 616, 619
WEISSMANTEL
Catharina   II, 114
WEISSMÜLLER   (WISEMILLER,
   WEYSMILLER)
Andrew   I, 304
Heinrich   I, 306, 307, 741
Jorg Michel   I, 348, 349, 351
WEISSMUTH
John Daniel   I, 749
WEITHARD
Maria   II, 136
WEITZEL (WEISELL, WEISSELL,
   WEITSAL, WITSELL)
Adam (Anthony)   I, 609, 611, 612
Friedrich   I, 411
George   I, 615
Hans Adam   I, 754
Henrich   I, 217, 219, 220
Jacob   I, 709
Johann Friederich   I, 577, 578, 580
Johann Georg (Jurg) I, 614, 617, 619
Johann Hennrich   I, 411, 456
Johann Wernner
   (Weinard)   I, 217, 218, 220
John Henry   II, 116
Martin   I, 217, 219, 220
Peter   I, 609, 611, 612
Sebastian   I, 411
WEITZEN (read prob. WEITZEL)
Johan Diterich   I, 456
WEITZENHÖLLER
Nickles   I, 502
WEITZLER
Henrich   I, 747
WELCH *see* WELSCH
WELCHEL (VELHELL, WELLICK)
Frantz (Frans)   I, 258, 260, 263
WELCHHANS   (WELCHANTS,
   WELSHANS
Abraham (Abram) I, 264, 267, 271
Joseph   I, 264, 268, 271
WELCK
Johann Andres   I, 693
Johann Jacob   II, 107
WELCKER   (WELKER,   WEL-
   LECKER)
Andereas   I, 395
Carl   I, 734
Hans Görg   I, 9
Jacob   I, 723, 734
Johann Jacob   I, 761
Johan William   II, 68
Johannes   I, 723
Michael   I, 723
Rutolff   I, 9
Vallentin   I, 382, 740
WELDEN (WELDE)
Cathⁿ   II, 28

Georg   I, 497
Jacob   I, 496
Johan Philipp   I, 691
Peter   I, 16, 17
Philip * (Phipps)   I, 433
WELDENBERG
Cornelius Van den   II, 72
WELDER
Conrat   I, 479
WELDGRAU
Hans   I, 19
WELFLING (WILFLINGER, WIL-
   FLINGEN)
Henry   I, 665, 668, 670
WELHAN
Johan Peter   I, 317
John Christian   I, 317
WELHAUSEN
Christo   I, 516
WELLE
Jean Pierre   I, 723
WELLEN
Jacob   I, 480
WELLER (WILLER)
Georg Mattas
   (Geo. Mathˢ)   I, 222, 223, 225
Hans Mart.   I, 9
Hans Michael   I, 492
Henry   I, 401
Johann Adam   I, 726
Johann Filibus   I, 495
Johann Georg   I, 577, 579, 580
Johan Jacob
   (Jacob)   I, 179, 181, 184
Johan Ruben   I, 707
Johann Wilhelm
   (John Wilhelm) I, 577, 579, 580
Johannes   I, 340, 341, 342, 406, 686
Philipp Christian   I, 493
Thomas   I, 700
WELNAGLE
M. A.   II, 136
WELPER
Jacob   II, 186
WELSCH (WELCH, WELSH)
David   I, 496
Jacob   I, 735
Johann Jacob
   (Jacob)   I, 170, 171, 173
Johan Michael
   (Mical)   I, 293, 294, 295
Johann Nickel   I, 735
Johann Wilhelm   I, 170, 171, 173
   293, 294, 295
Johannes   I, 697
John Philip   I, 506
Peter   I, 322
WELSCHANS (WELCHHANS)
Jacob   I, 300, 301, 302

WELSNACK
Johann Joachim   I, 749
WELSS (read prob. WELSCH)
Hans Michael   I, 696
WELTE (WELDE, WELTHE)
Anthoni   I, 690
Hans Jerg
(Hans Jurg)   I, 605, 606, 607
Jacob   I, 605, 606, 607
Johann Bernharth   I, 719
Johan Philip   I, 691
Johannes   I, 469, 691
Michael (Michel)   I, 605, 606, 607
WELTER
Anton   I, 495
Georg   I, 474
Johann Jacob
(Jacob)   I, 559, 561, 563
Johan Willm   I, 479
WELTESCHEIDT
Johannes   I, 471
WELTNER
Jacob   I, 745
Ludwig   I, 464
WELTZ (WELTS)
Anderes (Andrews) I, 107, 111, 112
Anna Maria   I, 108
Johann Jacob   I, 474
Johann Ludwig
(Ludwick)   I, 551, 552, 554
WELTZHEIMMER
Johan Philib   I, 712
WELZET
Johndre   II, 119
WENCH
Johannes   I, 689
WENDEL (WENDELL, WERBEL,
WENDLE, WENDAL)
Abraham   I, 226, 228, 230
Augustinus   I, 60, 64, 65
Caspar (Caspar)   I, 185, 186, 187
Conrad   I, 430
Geo. Adam   I, 752
J. Henry   I, 505
Johann   I, 687
Johann Georg
(John George)   I, 365, 499
Philip   I, 60, 64, 65
Samuel   I, 366
WENDELING see WENDLING
WENDER (WINDER)
Andreas   I, 139
Anna Margaret   I, 139
Anna Maria   I, 139
Carl (Caral)   I, 642, 644
Maria Catrina   I, 139
Marilis   I, 139
Nicklas (Nicholas) I, 137, 141, 142

WENDLING (WENDLIN, WEN-
DELING)
George (Görg)   I, 367, 369, 725
Hans Dewald   I, 483
Jacob   I, 414
Johann Nickel   I, 762
Petter   I, 483
Wendel   I, 629, 632, 635
WENGER (WENGEN, WINGER)
Ann   I, 153
Casper   I, 690
Christian   I, 14, 369, 370, 386, 397
                        745
Hans (Hannes)   I, 188, 191,
                    193, 384, 397
Jacob   I, 690
Joh. Jacob
(Jacob)   I, 107, 111, 112
Johannes   I, 369, 370, 384, 386
Joseph   I, 190; II, 9
Lazarus
(Lazerus)   I, 152, 153, 154
Nicholas (Nicholaus)   I, 370
Stephan   I, 386
WENGERT
Hans   I, 458
WENHOLT (WINHOLDT, VEN-
HOLT)
Nicklas
(Nicholas)   I, 217, 218, 220
WENIG (WEINIG, WENIGH)
Bastian   I, 404
Dietrich   I, 628, 631, 635
George   I, 491
Jacob   I, 199, 201, 203
Johann Henricus   I, 396
WENIGER (WENIG)
Adam   I, 677, 678, 680
Daniel   I, 689
Gotlip   I, 439
WENNER
Jacob   I, 751
Joh. Georg   I, 750
Wilhelm   I, 761
WENNERT
Michael   I, 466
WENSELL see WENTZEL
WENT
———   II, 206
WENTEROTT (WINTEROUT)
Johan Casper
(Gasper)   I, 100, 101
WENTZ (WENST)
Andreas   I, 438
Ann   I, 40
Christian   I, 496
Christina   II, 50
Fritrich   I, 410

Gorg   I, 698
Jacob   I, 430, 734
Joest   I, 39, 41, 42
Johann Diel
  (John Till)   I, 387, 388, 389
Johann Georg
  (Jacob)   I, 621, 623, 625
Johann Nickel   I, 413
Johann Philipp   I, 335, 337, 338, 487
Johannes   I, 702
Jörg Balser (George)   I, 40, 42
Michael   I, 614, 617, 619
Peter   I, 702
Valentin   I, 335, 337, 338
WENTZEL (WENSEL, WENSSEL, WENTZELL, WENZEL)
Johan Adam   I, 428
Johan Adolph
  (Han; Adolph)   I, 162, 164, 166
Johann Andreas   I, 700
Johann Carl   I, 750
Johan Caspar   II, 115
Joh. Henrich   I, 685, 754
Johann Willm
  (Hans W^m)   I, 209, 211
Lorentz   I, 373, 375, 376
Philip   I, 493
WERBACH (MIRBACH, WIRA-BAACK)
Bernhart (Bernard)   I, 596, 597, 599
WERBEL
Johannes
  (Johanes)   I, 283, 284, 285
Philip   I, 319
(*See also* WÖRBEL)
WERBER (WEAVER)
Georg Michael   I, 458
Jacob   II, 187
Johann Valentin
  (Valentine)   I, 564, 566, 568
WERBUNG
Johannes   I, 466
WERCKHÄUSSER (WERKYSER, WERCKHEISER)
Carl Hennrich
  (Henry)   I, 626, 630, 633
Nicol   I, 433
Reinhard   I, 642, 644
WERCKING (WERCKIN, WERKING)
Jacob   I, 433
Joh. Nicolaus   I, 433
Peter   I, 688
WERFFEL (WERFLE)
Hans Melchior (Hans Melker)   I, 79, 82, 83
WERGER
John   I, 734

WERKENTIN
Heinr.   II, 140
WERLE (WERLIE, WERLY, WERLLY, WERLLE, WIRLEY)
Diterich (Diderick, Diederich)   I, 163, 165, 166
Heinrich (Henerich)   I, 168, 170, 171
Jacob   I, 440
Widow   II, 178
WERLEIN (WERLINE, WEYRLIN)
Johann Michael   I, 539, 541, 543
Sebastian   I, 539, 541, 543
WERLIN
John Balth.   II, 118
WERLISCH (WERLICK)
Johann Christian
  (John Christian)   I, 672, 673, 674
WERNBERGER
Johannes   I, 689
WERNER (WARNER, VERNER)
Adam   I, 74
Carl   II, 181
Caspar   II, 52
Catharine   II, 168
Christian   I, 321, 322
Conrad   II, 52
Daniel   I, 427
Debalt   I, 357
Diedrich   I, 304
Dietmar   I, 452
Dorothy   II, 168
Elias   I, 704
G. F.   II, 186
Georg   I, 304
Gotlieb   II, 168
Hans Adam   I, 72, 76, 77, 495
Hans Jorg   I, 456
Hans Martin   I, 364
Hendrick (Henry)   I, 23, 25, 26, 538
Jacob   I, 364, 440, 605, 606, 608
Jerg Adam
  (Geo. Adam)   I, 156, 159, 161
Johan Friederich
  (Fredk)   I, 526, 528, 530
Johann George   I, 481, 492
Johann Henrich   I, 330
Johannes (Johanis, John, Hans)   I, 265, 268, 272
   469; II, 52
Katharina   I, 73, 74
Ludwich   I, 450
Margaretha   II, 52
Michael   I, 304, 477
Peter (Johann Peter)   I, 290, 291, 349
   350, 351, 364
   451; II, 52
Philip Jacob   I, 476

Philip Christian
(Philipp Christoph) I, 265, 268, 272
Phillipp I, 685
Sarah I, 23
Sebastian I, 438
Wilhelm (Wᵐ) I, 265, 268, 272, 448
WERNESS *see* WERNTZ
WERNI (VARNI)
Heinerich (Henry) I, 653, 654
WERNICKE* (VERNIKE, WER-
NICK)
Johan Andreas II, 103
Lois II, 82
WERNING
Johan Jost (Joh.
Jobst) I, 517, 518, 520
WERNLEY
Henry I, 731
WERNTZ (WERNS, WERNESS,
WÖRNTZ)
Connard I, 23
Jacob I, 700
Johans Adam I, 359
Katherine I, 23
Philipp Bendt I, 359
WERNWAG
Johⁿ Ludwig II, 33
WERRY
Jacob I, 179, 181, 183
WERS
Johan Deis I, 478
WERSCHIEDE
Johann Caspar II, 68
WERSS (WERT, WERSCH)
Johahnn Petter (Johann
Petter) I, 609, 610, 612
Johann Tiel
(John Deal) I, 609, 610, 612
WERSUM (WINSCHUM, WIRSUM)
Johannes (John) I, 637, 639, 641
WERTH (WORTH)
Jerrig I, 676
Johann Wielhem I, 328
Johannes I, 93, 95
Jureg Kilian I, 714
WERTHES
Lorentz I, 371
WERTHMANN (WERTMAN,
WIRTMAN, WÄRTHMANN)
Gorg (George) I, 646, 648
John George I, 741
Juliana II, 71
WERTHMÜLLER (WIRTMILLER)
Jacob I, 666, 669, 671
WERTHWEIN
Johann Christoph I, 424
WERTZ (WERTS)
Frantz I, 742
Kathrina I, 62

WERVEL (WEVEL, WERVELL)
Elizabeth I, 107
Hans I, 106, 110, 112
Hans Jurg (Hans
Jerick) I, 106, 110, 112
Leonard I, 109
Maria Lydia I, 107
WESCH
John I, 144
WESCHENBACH (WESHBACH,
WESPACH)
Johan Henrich I, 143, 145, 146
Maria Margret I, 144
Thiellmannus
(Tielman) I, 188, 191, 193
WESNER (WESENER, WESSNER,
WESSENER)
Andereas I, 498
Christina Frederika II, 170
Jacob I, 498
Johan Adam I, 346
Johanes I, 419
Lorentz I, 476
Matthes I, 498
WESSEL (WESEL, WESELL,
WEISELL, WESSELLS)
Cassimir I, 307, 308, 309
Francis II, 135
Godfret I, 303
Samuel II, 139
WESSELMANN
Henderietta II, 203
WESSNER, WESSENER *see* WES-
NER
WEST (WEIST)
Gibbs II, 162
H. Georg (George) I, 637, 638, 640
Jacob Friedrich I, 441
William II, 25
WESTENBERGER (WASTEN-
BURGER)
Paulus I, 323, 325, 326
Peter I, 323
WESTENS
Gerardus I, 735
WESTER
Johannes (Johan) I, 7
WESTERBERGER
Christoffel I, 355
Johan George I, 355
WESTERMAN
Peter I, 702
WESTFAL (WESTFAHLEN, WEST-
FALLEN, WESTPALEN)
Carl Wilhelm II, 97
Christian II, 77
Fridrik Oldrich II, 50
WESTFALLEN
—— II, 50

WESTHEBER
Valentine   I, 57, 58
WESTHOFF
A. Margreta   II, 102
Frantz   II, 102
Frantzcisca   II, 102
Geronimus   II, 102
Wilhelm   II, 102
WESTLE
Salomon   I, 490
WETEKIND
Gustaf   II, 73
WETTER
Johan Jost   I, 346
Johannes   II, 128
WETTERHOLD   (WETERHOLD,
WERTHERHOLT)
J. Jacob (Jacob)   I, 652, 654
Johan Nickel
(John Nichol)   I, 652, 654
WETTERICH (WEDERIGH)
Johann Christoph
(Christopher)   I, 212, 214, 216
WETTSTEIN
Elizabeth   I, 147
WETZEL   (WETZAL,   WETZELL,
WETSELL)
Christoff   I, 443
George   I, 489
Hans Georg   I, 429
Hans Martin   I, 48, 51, 52, 54
Jacob   I, 360, 361
Johann Georg
(Johann Jorg)   I, 692, 697
Johann Jacob   I, 189, 192, 193, 501
Johannes   I, 605, 606, 608
Katherina   I, 51
Maria Barbara   I, 50
Nicholaus   I, 51
Philip   I, 234
WETZGER
Filib   I, 630, 633
WETZLER   (WETZLAR,
WETZELER)
Herman   I, 643, 644
Jacob   I, 365
Maria Barbara   I, 50
WETZSTEIN (WETTSTEIN)
Elisabeth   I, 60
Magratha   I, 61
Peter   I, 59, 63, 64
WEUHRMAN *see* WOERMAN
WEXLER
Matthias   I, 753
WEYAND (WEYANDT, WEYANT,
WYANT)
George (Jorge,
Jurg)   I, 282, 284, 285
Jacob   I, 424

Johan Henrich   I, 731
Johann Jost   I, 731, 732
Johann Peter   I, 413
Johanes   I, 487, 732
Krafft   I, 753
Mary Cath.   II, 84
Wendel   I, 24
WEYBER   (WYPERT,   VYPERT,
VYBERT)
Jacob   I, 102
Jerich   I, 102, 105, 106
WEYBRECHT (WAYBRIGHT,
WAYBRICK)
Hans Martin   I, 89, 91, 92
Marthin   I, 88, 90, 92
WEYDA
Godlib   I, 431
WEYDEMEYER (WEYDEN-
MEYER, WEYDEMYER)
Eberhardt   I, 697
Johann Georg   I, 697
Melchior   I, 698
Urban   I, 697
WEYDEN
Johann Jacob   I, 422
WEYDENHAUER
Johannes   I, 371
WEYDIGH
John Henry   I, 439
WEYDMAN
Conrad   I, 434
WEYDNER (WEDENER, WI-
DENER, WEYNER)
Johan G.   I, 410
Johann Henrich   I, 311, 312, 313
John Christoph   I, 502
Philipp Conrath   I, 310, 311, 312
WEYEL *see* WEYL
WEYER (WAYER)
Anna   I, 75
Elizbt.   I, 75
Johan Diedrich   I, 540
Jnº   I, 730
Johann Kunrad   I, 352, 354
Johann Peter   I, 352, 354
Johann Wilhelm   I, 353, 354
Leonardt (Leonart)   I, 72, 76, 77
Margt.   I, 73
Paul   I, 234
WEYERBACHER
Isaac   I, 461
Joh. Nicklaus   I, 461
Johannes   I, 461, 551, 553, 554
WEYERICH
Wilhelm   I, 461
WEYERSHAUSSEN (WEYERS-
HAUSEN)
Jost Hennrich   I, 576, 578, 580

WEYGEL (WHIGEL)
Adam   I, 449
Johannes   I, 449
Jacob   I, 637
WEYHINGER (WAYHINGER)
Johanes   I, 449, 475
Michael   I, 475
WEYL (WEYELL, WEYEL, WEYLL, WYLL)
Andräas (Andreas)   I, 614, 616, 618
Conrad   II, 107
Hans Joreg   I, 750
Johann Gorg   I, 762
Johann Jacob   I, 456
Johanes   I, 689
Johannes Petter
(Peter)   I, 568, 570, 571
WEYLAND (WEYLLAND, WY-LAND)
Godfried   I, 501
Hans Leonhart   I, 344, 345
J. F.   II, 15
Michael   I, 344, 345
Peter   I, 179, 181, 183
Teobalt   I, 447
WEYLER
Christopf Friederich   I, 471
Friedrich   I, 759
Michael   I, 422
WEYMANN (WEYNEMAN, WIGHTMAN)
Charles   II, 123
George   I, 621, 623, 625
John   II, 188
John Georg
(Jerrie)   I, 316, 317
WEYMAYER (WEMEYER, WEY-MAER)
J. Hendrick
(J. Henry)   I, 582, 583, 584
WEYMER (WYMER)
Bernard (Bernhard)   I, 102, 104, 105
Johann Georg   I, 697
Matheas   I, 436
Peter (Petter)   I, 742
WEYMERT * (VEYMERT)
Barbara   I, 103
Johannes   I, 103
WEYN
Jacob   I, 498
WEYNANDT (WEYNAND, WY-NAND, WYNANT)
Jacob   I, 621, 623, 625
Johann Jacob   I, 48, 52, 54
Johann Philip   I, 122, 125, 126
Johannes Wilhelm   I, 465
WEYNLAND
J. F.   II, 16

WEYRICH (WEYRIGG, WEY-RICK)
Andonius   I, 355
G. F.   II, 141
Görg (Jörg, Geoe)   I, 169, 171, 173
WEYS (WEYSS, WEYSZ)
Adam   I, 469
Georg Adam   I, 469
Hans Jacob   I, 397
Henry   I, 434
Johan George   II, 28
Ruthy   I, 434
WEYSBACH
J. Christoph   I, 474
WEYSHAAR
Johann Georg   I, 522, 525
WEYSHIT (WEYSHIRK)
Herman   I, 532, 533, 535
WEYSPERGER
Casper   I, 212
WEYTS
Jacob Urban   II, 121
WEYTTMAN (WYDMAN)
Johannes   I, 564, 566, 567
WEYTZEL (WYTZEL, WISIEL)
Conrad   II, 56
Harolt   I, 508
Johann Paul
(Johanpol)   I, 323, 324, 326
Johann Philipps   I, 702
Johannes (John)   I, 683; II, 56
WEYZER
Francisco   I, 728
WHEELER
——   II, 161
WHIGEL *see* WEIGEL
WHILIMACK
G. A.   II, 141
WHITCOMB
Jacob   II, 42
WHITE (read prob. WITTE)
Baltz   I, 463
Christopher   II, 26
Taylor   II, 109
WHITEMAN (WHITMAN, read prob. WITTMAN)
Christoffer   I, 767
Elizabeth (Eliza)   I, 767
Godfrey   I, 741
Hans Adam   I, 316
Henrich   I, 316
Johanes   I, 767
John George   I, 316, 317
Margret   I, 766
Maria Catrina   I, 766
Maria Phillis   I, 28
Mathias   I, 767
Matthew   I, 113
Wendell   I, 767

WHITMER (WITMAN)
Anna   I, 117
Hans   I, 116
Michiel (Michl.,
   Migiel)   I, 116, 119, 120
Peter (Pitter)   I, 116, 119, 120
Ulrich (Ulrick,
   Ulrige)   I, 116, 119, 120
WHOLGEMUTH   *see*   WOHLGE-
   MUTH
WIBBELING
Jacob   II, 54
WIBEL *see* WEIBEL
WICE *see* WEISS
WICHEL (WHICKEL, WYCHEL)
Hans   I, 37, 38, 39
John   I, 745
Lewis   I, 37
Lodwick   I, 37
Margret   I, 37
WICHLER
——   II, 161
WICK
Johann Philipp
   (J. Philip)   I, 154, 157, 160
WICKEL (WYCKEL)
Johan Georgen   I, 690
Johannes   I, 685, 752
WICKER (WIKER, WEIKER)
Jacob   II, 126
Johann Philibus
   (Johan Philip)   I, 199, 201, 203
WICKERSHEIM
Georg Adam   I, 451
WICKERT (WICKER)
Christian   I, 694
Johann Paul   I, 419
Johann Peter   I, 419
Johann Phillips
   (Philip)   I, 234, 235, 236
Melchior   I, 759
Sem.   I, 694
WICKLEIN
Johan Georg   I, 167, 168
WIDA
Herman   II, 22
WIDEABACK (read prob. WEIDE-
   BACH)
Henrich   I, 176, 177, 178
WIDELING
Joh. Joah   II, 118
John Diet.   II, 118
WIDEMAN *see* WEIDMAN
WIDENER *see* WEYDNER
WIDENMEYER
Balthas   I, 470
WIDERHOLT
Louis   II, 60

WIDERICH (WIDERICK)
Christoff (Christian) I, 629, 632, 636
Michael   I, 704
WIDERSTEIN
Johann Adam   I, 712
WIDLE
Johannes   I, 592
WIDMANN (WIDMAN, same as
   WITTMANN)
Christian   I, 435
Franz Carl   I, 741
Hendrick   I, 303
Johann Fridrich   I, 414
Johannes   I, 349, 350, 351
Michal (Michael)   I, 373, 374, 375
Philip   II, 84
WIDMER (WIDMAR, WIEDMER)
Andreas   I, 151, 152
Anna   I, 151
Elizabeth   I, 151
Hans Rudolff   I, 434
Isach   I, 433
Jacob   I, 151, 406
Marget   I, 151
Mathias   I, 730
Susannah   I, 151
WIDMEYER (WIDMAYER)
Friederich   I, 522, 525
Simon   I, 470
WIDTEN (WITTEN)
Wilhelmus   I, 137, 141, 142
WIDTER (WEIDER)
Caspar   I, 250, 251
WIDTMANN *see* WITTMANN
WIED
Chrétien   II, 88
François   II, 88
George   II, 88
Justine   II, 88
Krafft   II, 88
Sophie   II, 88
WIEDACH (WEYDON)
Carl Fredk
   (Frederick)   I, 531, 533, 534
WIEDEMANN
Daniel   II, 116
Philipp   II, 134
WIEDENSAHL (WITHESALE)
Friedrich (Frederick) I, 672, 673, 674
WIEDER
Johann Christoph   I, 456
Michael   I, 455
WIEDERHOLT
Carle   I, 452
WIEDERSPRECHER
Jean Henry   II, 88
WIEDMAN
Barbara   II, 166
Catha Maria   II, 4

Johan II, 168
Johannes II, 166
Leonard (Lanard) II, 134, 166
Michael II, 168
Philip II, 134
WIEDMAYER
Georg Friederich I, 720
WIEDNER (WIDNER, VERDUS, VITNER)
Hans Michel (Hans Michael) I, 35, 36, 37
Johannes I, 35, 36
WIEG
Johann Michael I, 466
WIEGAND (WIGAND, WIGANDT, WIGANT)
Catharina II, 111
Elias I, 704
Henrich II, 79
Johann Friedrich I, 441
Johann Wilhelm I, 441
Joseph I, 642, 644
WIEGNER (WIGNER, WEIGNER, WEGENER)
Abraham I, 138
Andreas (Andres, Andrews) I, 107, 111, 112
Anna I, 138
Christoph (Christopher) I, 136, 137, 140 141, 142
George (Georg) I, 137, 138, 140, 141
Hans I, 136, 140, 141
Maria I, 138
Melchior I, 137, 138, 140, 142
Rosina I, 137, 138
Susannah I, 137, 138
WIEL
Johan Justus II, 78
WIELAND (WIELANDT, WIL-LAND)
Bernhard I, 741
Christane I, 13
Friedrich I, 454
Marte I, 741
Peter I, 427
Wm Mart. II, 25
WIELDINAR
Wm II, 15
WIELE
Anna Elisabeth II, 148
Catharine Elisabeth II, 148
Kraft II, 148
WIELER
Gerhard II, 121
WIELING
Julina II, 76
WIEN
Johann Gorg I, 390

Johannes I, 430
WIENER (WINER)
Christiana II, 13
Christopher II, 13
Jacob II, 13
Paulus I, 353, 354
WIER
Andreas I, 461
WIERD (VEARTE)
Martin I, 344, 345
WIERDEMAN
Jacob I, 480
WIES
Heinr II, 178
WIESE
Peter I, 505
WIESENBACH (WISSENBACH, WIESENBACK)
Johannes Christjan (John Christian) I, 621, 623, 625
——— II, 121
WIESER (WEESER, WIESSER, WISSER, WISER)
Jacob I, 416
John Gerlach (J. Gerlach) I, 577, 579, 581
John Joachim (J. Jacob) I, 577, 578, 580
John Wilhelm (J. Wilhelm) I, 577, 579, 581
Peter I, 14
WIESINGER
Johan Jacob I, 521, 523
WIESNER (WIESSENER, WISLER)
George I, 321, 322
WIEST (WÜST, WYST)
Christian I, 730
George (Jerg) I, 646, 647
Hanns Henrich I, 473
Jacob I, 147, 150, 151
Johan Andreas I, 721
Johannes I, 222, 223, 225
WIESTEIN
Johan Henrich I, 495
WIETH (WIETT)
Christian II, 109
Christina II, 29
Peter II, 29
WIETTERSTEIN
Henrich I, 731
WIGAND see WIEGAND
WIGGERDT (WIGARDT)
Jacob I, 11
Johann Wilhelm I, 11
WIGHAM
Conrad II, 148
Veit II, 148
WIGHTERMAN
George J. II, 41

WIGHTMAN (WEIGHTMAN)
Johannes (John) I, 27, 30
WIGLER
Hans Jerrick I, 7
WIGMAN (WIGGMAN)
H. Andereas
(Henry Andreas) I, 573, 574, 575
WIGMORE
Felex I, 344
Hance Felex I, 344
WIGOLD
Johannis I, 498
WIGTHORN
Andereas I, 477
WIKE
Catharina II, 148
Christian II, 148
J. Frederic II, 148
J. H. II, 148
Johann Christn II, 148
WIKER *see* WICKER
WILBER
Henry I, 736
WILD (WILDT, WILT, WIELT, WELT)
Abraham I, 455
Adam I, 102, 105
Elizabeth I, 73, 74
George I, 490; II, 150
Jacob I, 490
Johan Peter
(Johan) I, 184, 185, 187
Johannes (John) I, 357; II, 126
John Adam I, 493
John Jac. II, 24
John M. II, 188
Josias (Joseph) I, 531, 533, 534
Margt. I, 73
Maria II, 150
Matthias I, 759
Michel II, 191
Nicolas I, 71, 76, 77
Paul I, 74
Philip (Fillib) I, 621, 623, 625, 751
Valentine I, 71, 76, 77, 222
223, 225, 712
WILDANGER (WILLDANGER, WILTANGER)
Johannes I, 449
Ludowig (Ludwig) I, 179, 181, 183
Matheas I, 449
WILDE
Elizabeth, de II, 41
WILDENMANN
Jacob I, 477
WILDER
Hans Martin I, 8
WILDERMUTH
Johann David I, 484

Johannes (Johs) I, 209, 211
WILDFANG (WOOLFANG)
Elizabeth I, 139
George Mich. I, 139
Johanes
(Johannes) I, 137, 139, 141, 142
WILDHENGST
Johannes I, 19
WILDHEYDT
Barbara I, 43
Eliz. I, 45
Frederich I, 45
Lucretia I, 43
Magdalena I, 43
WILDSCHUTZ
Jacob I, 234
WILEMAN
Hans Geo. I, 304
WILEN
J. F. II, 5
WILGAR (VILGAR, VIELARD)
Casperrias I, 102, 104, 105
Magdalena I, 103
WILGENSON
Christn I, 505
WILGER (WILLGER, WILCHART)
Jacob I, 540, 542, 544
WILHAUSEN
Anna Marg. II, 157
Caroline II, 157
Frederick II, 157
George F. II, 157
Henry W. II, 157
John Christ II, 157
Marg. Charles II, 157
William II, 157
—— II, 157
WILHEISER
Johannes I, 753
WILHELM (WILLHELM, WILLIAM)
Adam (Fredrik
Adam) I, 264, 268, 271
An. Catrina II, 101
Andreas II, 101
Christian Frederick II, 150
Christoph II, 191
Elias II, 150
Elisabeta II, 101
Frantz I, 714
Friedrich I, 754
Georg I, 698
Georg Peter
(Peter) I, 551, 553, 554
Gottlieb II, 150
Hans Adam I, 373, 374, 375
Hans Michel I, 48, 52, 53
Henrich (Henrick) I, 217, 219, 220
Jacob Henrich I, 735

Johann Daniel   I, 719
Johann Frantz
  (Frantz)   I, 185, 186, 187
Johan Jacob   I, 335, 337, 338, 481
Johann Jorg
  (Jurg)   I, 614, 616, 618
Johan Lorenz   I, 463
Johanna   II, 150
Johannes (John)   I, 18
                        II, 102, 203
John Jacob   II, 150
Maria   I, 139
Michael (Michel)   I, 500, 689, 725
                            II, 75
Nicholas (Nick⁸)   I, 317; II, 11
Peter   I, 397
Regina   II, 150
WILHELMI (WILLHELM)
Anna Catrina   I, 139
Jacob   I, 137, 139, 141, 142
Valantine   I, 139
———   I, 139
WILHELMUS
Jacob   I, 14, 15
Johannes   I, 478
WILHERTZBACH
Philip   I, 432
WILKE
Franz Adolph   II, 107
WILKES
Rudolph   I, 8
WILKING
Heinr Wilhelm   II, 107
WILL (WILD)
Beder (Peter)   I, 441
Gerhart   I, 356
Johann Daniel   I, 466
Johann Jost
  (John Joost)   I, 601, 602, 603
Johannes (Johanes) I, 503, 601, 602
                        603, 697
Jost   I, 662, 664
Michael   I, 304, 305, 306
Philib   I, 689
WILLAR
Anthonius   I, 356
Johannes   I, 433
WILLE
Isaac   I, 346
Johan Fredk.   II, 93
Sebastian   I, 736
WILLEM
Peter   I, 363
WILLEMANN
Christoph   I, 711
WILLEMIN (WILMER)
Alphonse Louis
  (Alphonso Lewis) I, 592, 593, 595
WILLEMS *see* WILMS

WILLER
Abraham   I, 592
Henrich   I, 676
Johan Jacob
  (Hans Jacob)   I, 592, 593, 594
WILLERICH (WILLERICK, WIL-
  RICH, WILRICK)
Barbry   I, 153
Christian   I, 153
Johannes (John)   I, 376, 377
Peter   I, 714
Ulrich (Ulrech,
  Uldrick)   I, 153, 154
WILLERS
John   II, 116
WILLERT
Christian Gottlieb   I, 763
WILLET (WILT)
Christoph   I, 424
Hans Jorg   I, 513, 514, 516
WILLFIELD
H. Christian   I, 504
WILLFOOT
Jnᵒ Fredᵏ   II, 12
WILLGER *see* WILGER
WILLHAN (WULLHAN)
Frantz   I, 367, 369
WILLIAM *see* WILHELM
WILLIAMS (read WILHELMS)
Hend.   II, 136
Jacob   II, 77
WILLIAMSON
Joseph   II, 18
WILLIAR
Peter   I, 357
WILLIGMANN
C. H.   II, 149
WILLJAHR
Johann Elias   I, 447
WILLMAN
Christⁿ   II, 4
Conrad   II, 4
Elizabeth   II, 4
Hendᵏ   II, 4
Joh. Adam   II, 4
Johann Conrᵈ   II, 4
Johannes   I, 736
Maria   II, 4
Wilhelm   II, 4
WILLMANS
Louis   II, 83
WILLMER
Cyprian   II, 103
WILLSON
Alexander   II, 26
WILLY
Christian   I, 452
WILMS (WILLEMS, WILLMS)
Aⁿ Margreth   I, 157

Gerrit II, 197
Johan Christian I, 760
Johan Peter
  (Johans Petter) I, 195, 196, 197
Johannes I, 155, 158, 160
WILPLEY
  Christian II, 126
  Conrad II, 126
  Martin II, 126
WILRICH *see* WILLERICH
WILSCHÜTT
  Johann II, 138
WILSENLEHR
  Phlyppus I, 391
WILSHEYT *see* WULHEIT
WILSTACH
  Charles II, 25
WILT *see* WILD
WILTENSIN (WILTENSINN,
  WILDERSON)
  Johannes I, 252, 253, 254
WILTRAUT
  Johann Jacob I, 494
WIMMER (WIMER)
  Christoffel I, 425
  Johann Georg I, 502
WINCHINS
  J. L. II, 96
  J. Maria Sara II, 96
WINCKAUS
  Johannes Adam I, 468
WINCKELBLECH (WINGLE-
  PLECH, WINCLEPLANK)
  Alizabeath I, 85
  Credleless I, 85
  Hance Felter I, 85
  Hannah Boble I, 85
  Johannes I, 84, 86, 87
  Mr. II, 176
WINCKELMAN (WINKELMAN)
  Melcher I, 434
  Oswald I, 234
WINCKLER (WINKLER, WIN-
  CLEAR)
  Christian II, 99
  Conradt I, 539, 541, 543
  Elizabeth I, 147
  Hans Domas (Thos) I, 539, 541, 543
  Hans Jacob I, 539, 541, 543
  Henrich (Henry) I, 614, 616, 619
  Jacob I, 447
  Johann Adolph II, 21
  Johann Peter I, 395
  John II, 60, 204
  L. Ludewig I, 504
  Ludwig I, 614, 616, 618
WINCKUR
  Caspar I, 483

WIND (WINT)
  Andrices I, 286
  John II, 7
WINDEMUTH (WINDERMUTH,
  WINDMUTH)
  Georg Philip I, 59, 63, 64
  Joh. Christoph I, 155, 159, 161
  Johann Georg
    (Jörg) I, 159, 161
WINDER *see* WINTER
WINDERBAUER *see* WINTER-
  BAUER
WINDERHAMER *see* WINTER-
  EHLER
WINDERMEYER
  Anthon I, 391
  Philip I, 391
WINDERS (read WINTERS)
  Pauel II, 3
WINDISCH (WINDESCH)
  Joh. Caspar I, 489
  Johann Friedrich I, 457
WINDLANDT
  Hinrich I, 734
WINDLINGER (WINDLINGE)
  Hanns Jerg
    (Hans Geo.) I, 244, 245
WINDMILLER (WEINMILLER)
  Carl (Carol) I, 545, 547, 549
WINDMYER
  Eberhardt I, 418
WINEL *see* WEINEL
WINEMAN
  Christ I, 715
WINER *see* WIENER
WINESHEIM
  Vallentin I, 355
WINGAARDE
  Otto, Van II, 136
WINGER (MATZINGER)
  Felix I, 149
  Jacob I, 147, 150, 151
WINGERT (WINGART)
  Frin
    (Fredrach) I, 323, 325, 326
  Johan Herbert I, 479
  Polis I, 344
WINGERTMANN (WINGERMAN,
  WENGERMAN)
  Anna Margaretha I, 132
  Catherina I, 131
  Hanna Felicia I, 132
  Johannes
    (Philip) I, 130, 131, 133, 134
  Maria Madgalena I, 132
WINHART (WINHARD, WYN-
  HARD, WENHART)
  Adam I, 527, 528, 530
  Mich[l] I, 661, 662, 663

WINHOLT
  Johanes
    (Hannes)   I, 665, 668, 670
WINK
  Hartman   I, 759
WINKEBAH
  Joh. Jacob   II, 118
WINKEL (WINKLE)
  Frederich   II, 26
  M. H.   II, 203
WINKELGRIET
  Johann   I, 696
WINKELMEYER
  Margaretha Elisab. II, 140
WINOHT
  Johann Frich   I, 362
WINSCHER
  Christgan   I, 716
WINSH see WÜNSCH
WINSHIP
  Mrs.   II, 32
WINTER (WINDER, WINTHER)
  Christophel   I, 738
  Ehric   II, 136
  Friedrich   I, 745
  Gerhard (Gerrard) I, 595, 597, 599
  Hans   I, 123
  Hans Jerg
    (Jerick)   I, 122, 125, 126, 476
  J. George
    (Joh. Jurg)   I, 564, 565, 567
  J. Jacob   I, 481, 507
  Jacob   II, 97
  Jerick   I, 123
  Johan Christoph   I, 506
  Johannes (John)   I, 173, 174, 476
                    II, 153, 172
  John Ab.   II, 138
  Maria Cath.   II, 97
  Philip Friedrich I, 441
  Samuel Fridrich   I, 741
WINTERBAUER   (WINDER-
  BAUER)
  Gorg Adam   I, 718
  Sebastian   I, 195, 196, 197
WINTERBERGER
  Henry   I, 127, 129, 130
  Maria Madalena   I, 127
WINTEREHLER   (WINDER-
  HAMER)
  Johan Jacob
    (Jacob)   I, 323, 324, 326
WINTERGRESS
  Leonhard   I, 346
WINTERRADT
  Johanes   II, 170
  Phillip   II, 170
WINTERSTEIN (VINTERSTEEN)
  Vallentin (Valentine) I, 316, 317

WINTRINGER   (WINTERMAN)
  Bernart   I, 545, 547, 549
WINTZBERGER
  J. Jacob   I, 487
WIRBEL (WERBALL)
  Philip   I, 319
WIRDEBERGER
  Johann Adam   I, 468
WIRHEIMER
  Hans   I, 439
WIRTH (WERT, WIRD, WIRDT,
  WIRT, WÜRTH)
  Caspar   I, 277, 278, 279
  Catharina   II, 115
  Conrad
    (Konradt)   I, 340, 341, 343, 347
  Daniel   II, 173
  Eva   II, 115
  Friederich   I, 460
  Hans Conrad   I, 483
  Hans Jacob   I, 93, 94, 95
  Hendrich
    (Henry)   I, 253, 254, 255, 418
  Jacob   I, 93, 94, 95, 403
                          II, 173
  Jeorge Jacob   I, 401
  Johann Adam   I, 564, 565, 567
  Joh. Christ   I, 352, 353
  Johann Henrich   I, 479
  Johann Jacob   I, 424
  John Georg   II, 98
  Ludewig
    (Lodewick)   I, 629, 632, 635
  Michael (Mich¹) I, 661, 663, 664
                          II, 115
  Ulrich   I, 378, 379, 381
WIRTMAN
  Jacob   II, 136
WIRTZ   (WEERTZ,   WIRZ,
  WUERTZ,   WURTS,   WURTZ,
  WURZ)
  Barbara   II, 53
  Cath.   II, 10
  Conrad   I, 146, 149, 150
  Dorothy   II, 10
  Eva   II, 10
  Eva Eliz.   II, 10
  Ferdinandt   I, 526, 528, 529
  Friederich   I, 364
  Geo.   II, 10
  Hans   I, 432
  Hans Martin   I, 432
  Henry   I, 432
  Jacob   I, 48, 52, 54
                   392, 443, 677
                      678, 680
  Johann Georg   I, 720
  Johanes   I, 508

Lutwig
(Lodwick)   I, 560, 561, 563
Matthias   II, 10
Mr.   II, 175
Mrs.   II, 175
Ottilia   II, 10
Peter   I, 539
Philip   II, 10
Wilhelm   I, 539, 541, 544
WISCHAN (WISHAN, WISHANG)
  WISHONG)
Conradt (Con-
  rad, Conrade)   I, 283, 284, 285
Philip   I, 283, 285, 286
Simon   I, 323, 324, 326, 448
WISCHNESKE
Carl Ludw.   II, 119
WISE see WEISS
WISEL see WISSEL
WISEMAN
John   I, 747
Philipine   II, 96
Wernart   II, 96
WISEN
Magdalena   I, 127
WISER see WIESER
WISHT
Jerik   I, 445
WISLER see WISSLER
WISMAN (WISMANN)
Johann Philipps
  (Philip)   I, 179, 181, 183
WISMATT
Christian   II, 199
WISNER (WISSNER)
Hans Michael   I, 444
Johan Gorg   I, 444
WISS (WIS, WYS)
Hans Rudi   I, 364
Jacob   I, 27, 29, 30
                   652, 654
Johannes   I, 398
WISSEL (WISEL)
Fridrich   I, 102
Jacob   I, 19
WISSELS
Debora   II, 191
WISSER (VISSERER, WISER)
Balsazar
  (Baltzer)   I, 636, 638, 640
Casper   I, 460
Peter   I, 693
WISSICH
Heini   I, 740
WISSINGER (WISINGER)
Ludwig (Ludiwick) I, 275, 276
WISSLER (WISLER)
Hans   I, 237, 238, 239

Henrich   I, 179, 181, 183
Jacob   I, 708
Johan Casper   I, 501
Johan Michael   I, 501
Johan Wolf   I, 501
Philip   I, 485
Ulrich
  (Ulrig)   I, 116, 119, 120, 708
WISSMAN
Jacob   I, 115
WISSNER see WISNER
WIST (read prob. WÜST)
Jacob   I, 348, 350, 352, 445
Jerg Adam
  (Adam)   I, 526, 528, 530
WISTADIUS
Nicolaus   I, 687
WISTHOLTZ (WILSTEYTS)
Melcher (Melchier) I, 43, 46, 47
WITHMAN see WITTMANN
WITMER see WITTMER
WITMEYER
G.   II, 147
WITSCHIEF (WITTSCHIF)
Danniel   II, 50
Johann   II, 50
WITSELL (read prob. WITZEL)
Hans Michel   I, 237
Jacob   I, 18
WITSTACH
Gerhard Benjn   II, 200
WITT
Catherine   II, 72
Gustavus   II, 72
Johan   II, 72
WITTE (WITTEE, WITTY)
Carl   II, 79
Joh. Diderich I, 517, 518, 520
WITTEL
Jacob   II, 179
WITTEMER see WITTMER
WITTENMEYER
Andreas   I, 441
Gorg   I, 718
Ludwig   I, 442
WITTER
Görg Heinrich   I, 423
WITTERSPOR
Dewalt   I, 493
WITTERSTEIN
Gerlach   I, 688
WITTIG
Johannes   I, 698
WITTKE (WITTGEE, WITTGIE)
Matthew (Mathias) I, 321, 322
WITTLER
Michael   II, 179

WITTMANN (WITHMAN, WIT-
MAN, WITTMAN, WIDT-
MANN)
Alexander
(Alecksantter)   I, 672, 673, 674
Frantz   I, 414
Georg Adam   I, 532, 533, 535
Jacob   I, 532, 533, 535
Jacob Carl W.
(Carel)   I, 221, 223, 224
Johann Georg   I, 349, 350, 351
Johann Ludwig   I, 431
Johannes
(Johanns)   I, 96, 97, 98, 328
Michael   I, 66, 69, 70
WITTMER (WITMER, WITTE-
MER, WITTMORE)
Bastian   I, 645, 647
Christian   I, 759
Christopher (Christoffel) I, 8, 482
Georg (George)   I, 645, 647
Hans Jacob   I, 405
Jacob   II, 5
Johan Christian   I, 610, 611, 613
Joh. Jacob   I, 610, 611, 613
Josep   I, 453
Peter (Petter)   I, 359, 365
Samuel   I, 363
WITTSCHER
Herrman   I, 699
WITTSER
Hendrick   I, 7
WITZ (WERTS)
Carl Philipp
(Carel Philip)   I, 303, 305, 306
Lenard (Lonert)   I, 275, 276
WIZER
Hans Jacob   I, 463
WÖBER (read prob. WEBER)
Christoffel   I, 695
Moritz   I, 450
WOELSCHLAEGER (read WOLL-
SCHLÄGER)
Johannes   I, 430
WÖERMAN (WEUHRMAN,
WUHRMAN)
Anna   I, 151
Barbara   I, 151
Elizabeth   I, 151
Heinrich (Heyn-
drick, Hyndrick)   I, 151, 152
Johanns
(Johannes, Johnis) I, 151, 152
Magdalena   I, 151
Orsula   I, 151
Rede   I, 151
WOHAND
Johan Joachim   I, 507

WOHL
David   I, 708
WOHLER
Christoph   I, 739
WOHLERS
Anna Maria   II, 23
WOHLFARTH (WOHLFAHRT,
WOLFART)
Conrad   I, 406
Friedrich   I, 407
Johann Adam   I, 437
Johannes   I, 522, 525
Ludwig   I, 442
Melchior   I, 418
Niclas   I, 340
WOHLFEEL
John   II, 160
WOHLGEMUTH (WOHLGEMUT,
WOLLGEMUHT,   WOLGE-
MUTH)
Abraham   I, 156, 159, 161
Christian   II, 150
Henrich   I, 156, 159, 161
Jacob   II, 150
John Jacob   II, 150
Joseph   I, 156, 159, 161
Margaret   II, 150
Samuel   I, 328
WOHLLEBEN (WOLLEBEN)
Johann   I, 357
John Friedr.   II, 116
WOHNER
Johann Peter   I, 427
WOHNFIEDT
Cath.   II, 119
WOHNLE
Anna Mary   II, 152
Jacob   II, 152
John G.   II, 152
Katy   II, 152
WOHNSITLER
Johan Jerg   I, 355
WOLCKENER
Johann Jacob   I, 447
WOLDER see WOLTER
WOLDI (WOOTEL)
Rudolph   I, 522, 524
WOLETE
Isaac Wilch.   II, 119
WOLF (WOLFF, WOLFE, WOOLF,
WULFF)
A.   II, 136
Abraham (Abram)   I, 17, 19
                            II, 188, 189
Adam   I, 729
Andreas
(Andris)   I, 79, 82, 83, 391, 697
                            II, 3
Anna Dority   I, 80

Anne II, 88
Anthon I, 390
Barbara II, 189
Christian I, 711
Christiana II, 189
Christoph
(Christopher) I, 591, 593, 594
II, 193
Conrad
(Conratt) I, 204, 206, 207
394, 685
Daniel I, 473, 738, 760
David I, 605, 606, 608
Elizabeth II, 88, 163, 189
Eve II, 188
Fridrich (Fredrick) I, 433, 471
II, 188
Georg (Gerg,
Jurg, George) I, 472, 473, 540
542, 544, 748
II, 44, 163, 187
Georg Michael
(Jurig Mich.) I, 265, 268, 271
Hans Bernhart
(Bernard) I, 106, 110, 112
Hans Jerg (Hans Jerrick,
Hans Jurg) I, 7, 9, 585, 586, 588
Hans Peter I, 96, 97, 98
Henrich (Henrick,
Henry) I, 10, 11, 289, 290
291, 433, 464
II, 88
Isaac II, 188
J. C. II, 148
J. Jacob I, 257, 259, 262
Jacob I, 170, 171, 173, 175
177, 178, 283, 284
286, 423, 455, 472
502, 604, 606, 607
II, 59, 181, 188, 199
Jan Bernard I, 7, 9
Jean II, 88
Johann Adam I, 415, 495, 531, 533
535
Johan Carls I, 495
Johan Conrad
(Conrade) I, 265, 268, 271
621, 623, 625
Johann Henrich I, 329
Johan Jacob
(Jacob) I, 492, 646, 647
Johan Nickel
(Jo. Nicklas) I, 204, 206, 207, 474
Johan Peter
(Jn° Peter, Peter) I, 170, 171, 173
266, 269, 272
283, 284, 286
614, 616, 618
646, 647

Johannes I, 282, 284, 285
415, 495, 707
II, 163
Johannes Paulus
(Paulus) I, 559, 561, 562
John Christ Fried I, 465
Jonas (Jones) I, 89, 91, 92
Magdalena
(Magdaleina) II, 149, 163
Martin I, 464
Mary Elis^th II, 84
Michael (Michel) I, 330, 477, 604
605, 606, 607
608, 721
II, 172, 188
Moses II, 113
Nickolas
(Nicholas) I, 367, 368, 376
377, 430, 456
Paul II, 172
Peter (Peterus) I, 433, 686
Philip (Phillip) I, 383, 385
[Philip Jacob]
Fielieb Jacob I, 502
Reinhart (Reichart,
Richard) I, 628, 632, 635
Samuel I, 344, 345
Solomon II, 163
Soph. Dor. II, 24
Wilhelm II, 126
Wilhelm Adam I, 461
Wolfgang
(Wolffgang) I, 373, 375, 376
605, 606, 608
WOLFANGER (WOLFANGEL)
Fredk. I, 317
Mich. II, 179
WOLFART see WOHLFARTH
WOLFE
Benjamin II, 75
Conrad I, 419
WOLFER (WOLFFER)
Frederic II, 155
Georg Friederich (George
Fredrick) I, 656, 657, 658
Hans Martin I, 445
Johannis I, 446
Simon I, 360, 361
WOLFERS
Ab^rm II, 101
WOLFERSBERGER
— I, 31, 33, 34
WOLFERT (WOOLFERT)
Johannes
(Johanes) I, 265, 268, 271
WÖLFFLE (WÖLFLE, WOLFLEY,
WOLFELL)
Christof I, 585, 587, 588
George II, 165

Joh. Conradt I, 427
WOLFFSKEHL (WOLFKEHL,
WOLFFS KEHL, WOFKIL)
Henrich I, 323, 325, 326
Johann George I, 336, 337, 339
Johannes I, 323, 325, 326
Just I, 336
WOLFGANG (WOLFFGANG,
WOLFGONG)
Albrecht I, 70
Michael I, 349, 350, 351
WOLFINGER (WOLFFINGER,
WOOLFINGER)
Bernhart (Barent) I, 66, 69, 70
Bustnip I, 68
Jacob I, 652, 654
Johannes I, 68
Odels I, 68
Pieter I, 68
WOLFRAM * (WOLFROM, WOLF-
RUM)
Hans Adam I, 266, 269, 272
Henrich
(Henrick) I, 266, 269, 272
WOLFS see WOLF
WOLLEBEN see WOHLLEBEN
WOLLENWEBER (WOLWEBER,
WOLLOWEBER, WULLE-
WEBER, WULLENWEBER)
Georg Friederich I, 173, 174
Gottfriedt I, 318, 319
Johann Conrad I, 466
Johan Wil-
helm (Wilhelm) I, 577, 579, 580
WOLLENWEIDER
Heinrich I, 398
WOLLETT (WOLLET)
Anna Margaretha I, 127
Johannes (Hannes) I, 127, 129, 130
WOLLHUTER
H. George I, 475
WOLLINGER (WOLINGER)
Andreas I, 348, 349, 351
Georg Mich[1] I, 188
WOLLMILLER
George I, 365
WOLM
Carl Fried. II, 107
WOLMER
Adam I, 421
Johan II, 168
WÖLPERT
Johann Davidt I, 422
WOLSEY
Phil. Jacob II, 118
WOLTER (WALTER, WOLDER)
Jacob I, 451
Johann Hen-
rich (Henry) I, 204, 206, 208

John II, 16
WOLTERS
Fried. W. II, 193
John II, 122
WOLTZ (WALTZ, WOLST,
WOLTS)
Catharine II, 43
Christian I, 609, 611, 612
II, 43
WÖLTZHOFFER (WOLTZHOF-
FER)
Johann Jakob (Jacob) I, 46
WOLWEBER see WOLLENWEBER
WOMBACH
Hans Gerg I, 423
WOMMER (WOMER)
Jacob I, 419
Michael I, 419
WOMSER see WAMSER
WOOD
Phillip Carrel II, 19
WOODSAND
Elinora II, 73
Elizabeth II, 73
Thos II, 73
WOOLF see WOLF
WOOLMAKER (read WOLLEN-
MACHER)
Dolly II, 55
WOOMER
Barnard
(Bernard) I, 169, 171, 172
WOOSER
Anna II, 187
WOOSING
Johanes I, 396
WOOST see WUST
WÖRBEL (WERBEL)
Gretha I, 60
Johanes I, 62
Sara I, 61
Wendel I, 60, 64, 65
WORHY
Hendrich II, 58
WORKMAN
Hendrick I, 411
WORLEIN
John Godf. II, 202
WORLEY
Jno. Danl I, 24
WORM
J. Henry
(John Henderick) I, 573, 574, 575
WORMER
Cath. II, 162
Mag. II, 162
—— II. 162

WÖRN (WENN)
Henrich Ludwig
(Henry Lodowick)   I, 637, 639, 641
WÖRNER (WERNER, WORNNER,
WARRNER)
Barbara   I, 131
Jacob   I, 470
Johann Adam   I, 131, 133, 134
Joh. Jacob   I, 472
Johann Michel   I, 472
Johannes   I, 378, 379, 381
Michael
(Michel)   I, 472, 677, 679, 680
WÖRNTZ (WERNESS)
Katherine   I, 23
Kunradt
(Konradt, Connard)   I, 23, 25, 26
WORRELL
Isaiah   II, 25
Robert   II, 25
WORSCHELER (WELSLOR)
Johannes (Joanis)   I, 293, 294, 295
WORST
Jacob   I, 304, 305, 306
WORTHLIN
Hans   I, 455
Hans George   I, 455
WORTMANN
Hinrich Burchard Gabriel   I, 504
WÖSENER
Martin   I, 419
WOTRING (WOOTRING)
Abraham   I, 127, 129, 130
Anna Louisa   I, 128
Anna Margaretha   I, 127, 128
Hance Peter   I, 128
Maria Magdalena   I, 128
WRIGHT
John   II, 26
WUCHBOHR
Marie Catherine   II, 88
WÜCHEL
Nicklaus   I, 487
WUCHER
Barbara   II, 53
WUCHERER
Johannes   I, 736
WUCHTER
Hans   I, 463
WUERTZ, WURTS see WIRTZ
WUHEIT see WULHEIT
WUHRMAN see WOERMAN
WULFF see WOLF
WÜLFFART (WILLFORT)
Johann Lenhart
(John Leonard)   I, 173, 174
WULHAUER (FILHAWER)
Jerg Pilipps (Phillip)   I, 383, 385

WULHEIT   (WUHEIT,   WILS-
HEYT)
Friedrich (Frid-
rich, Fredrick)   I, 43, 45, 46
WÜLL (WILL)
Michel (Michael)   I, 66, 69, 70
WULSHLEG (read WOLLSCHLAG)
Abrah.   I, 61
Christian   I, 61
WUND (WEIDENER)
Petter (Peter)   I, 637, 639, 640
WUNDEND
Calfing   I, 594
WUNDER (WONDER)
Christian   I, 704
Jacob   I, 704
Johann Gorg   I, 539, 541, 543, 725
Philipp Jacob   I, 491
Steffan   I, 476
WUNDERLICH   (WONDERLICH)
Anna Liese   II, 29
Cath. Elisabeth   II, 140
Cathᵃ Liese   II, 29
Daniel   I, 551, 552, 554
George (Görg)   I, 753; II, 88
Jean   II, 88
Johann   II, 29
Johann Georg   I, 500
Johann Joost   II, 29
Joh. Krafft   II, 139
Johannes   I, 476
Joost   II, 29
Maria Annetta   II, 29
John Henry   I, 522, 525
WÜNGER (WINEYARD)
Philip Fried-
rich (Ph. Fred.)   I, 620, 622, 625
WUNNING
Georg Diederich   II, 61
WÜNSCH (WINSH)
Hans Uhlerik   I, 447
Johann Bernhard   I, 442
WÜNST (WEIST)
Hans Jacob   I, 332, 333, 334
WURFEL (WURFFEL)
Christian   II, 149
Martin   I, 410
WURM
Michael   I, 448
WÜRMLE (WORMLEY)
Johannes   I, 526, 528, 529
WURSTER (WOUSTER)
Fred   II, 189
Johan Friedrich   I, 462
Michael   I, 637, 639, 641
WURTENBERGER
H. Georg   I, 454
H. Michael   I, 454

WURTS, WURTZ, WURZ *see* WIRTZ

WURTZBACHER
Friederich   I, 699

WÜRTZER
Johan Jorg   I, 714

WÜST (WOOST, WUST)
Bernhart   I, 446
Hans Jerg (Hans)   I, 232, 233
Hans Peter   I, 331
Herman   I, 367, 369
Jacob   I, 445
Johann Nickel
(Nickel)   I, 290, 291, 367, 369
Johannes   I, 711
Jorg Heinrich   I, 421
Laurentius   I, 445
Martin   I, 417

WÜSTER
Hans Jerg   I, 439

WYANT *see* WEYAND

WYBERTON
Anna   I, 104

WYCHEL *see* WICHEL
WYCKEL *see* WICKEL
WYDMAN *see* WIDMANN
WYES *see* WEISS
WYGART (read WEIGART)
Jacob   I, 10
Wm.   I, 10

WYKERDING
Hanes Christ   I, 495

WYLL *see* WEYL
WYNAND *see* WEYNANDT
WYNER
Johan Nicklas   I, 423

WYNGARDE
Peter   II, 108
T., van   II, 108

WYNGARTNER *see* WEINGÄRT-NER
WYS *see* WEISS
WYSEL, WYSELL *see* WEISSEL

XANDER
David   I, 491

YAGER *see* JÄGER
YAKLEY *see* JACKLE
YARRELL
Ann   I, 320
Thomas   I, 320

YAUBLE
Anthony   I, 451

YAUCH *see* JAUCH

YAUSE *see* JAUSS
YAYA
——   II, 80
YBACH *see* IBACH
YEAGER *see* JÄGER
YEAL
Henry   I, 439
YEATER, YETTER *see* JETTER
YEATZ (YEITES)
John (Johannes)   I, 244, 245
YEGE (read prob. JÄGI)
Johannes   I, 102
Paulina   I, 103
YEGOLD (EGOLD)
Georg Adam
(Geo. Adam)   I, 244, 245
YEISER *see* JAYSER
YEISLY
Nicklaus   I, 440
YENNY
Johannes   II, 34
YET
Johan Wilhelm   I, 370
YODER *see* JODER
YONER (JONER)
Hance   I, 163
Jacob
(H. Jacob)   I, 163, 165, 166
Jonas   I, 163, 165, 166
YONGMAN *see* JUNGMAN
YONILY (YONILEY, JONLIEY)
Christian
(Christian)   I, 116, 120, 121
Elisbat   I, 118
Froneck   I, 118
Hans Raynart   I, 118
Johanes   I, 118
YORDEN, YORDE *see* JORDAN
YORIGH *see* JÖRG
YORTS (read prob. GÖRTZ)
John   I, 737
YOSEY (read JOSE)
Peter   I, 237
YOST *see* JOST
YOUGHLEY (JOOGHLY)
Johannes   I, 344, 345
YOUNG *see* JUNG
YOUNGBLOOD *see* JUNGBLUD
YOUNGE *see* JUNGE
YOW
Hans   I, 12
YOWCH (read prob. JAUCH)
Johannes   I, 410
YSERLOH, YSERLOCH *see* ISER-LOH
YTT (EATIE)
Hans   I, 176, 177, 178
YUCHLI *see* JOCHLIE
YUNDT *see* JUND

YUNG *see* JUNG
YURE
George   I, 439

ZABERER
Johannes   I, 551, 553, 554
ZABERN
David   I, 762
ZABORY
Friederich   I, 458
Jacob   I, 458
ZACHARIAS (ZACHARIS, ZACH-
ARIES, ZACHRISS, ZACHRIAS)
Daniel (Dan[1])   I, 179, 181, 184
     188, 192, 193
     559, 561, 562
     II, 181
Johan Christoff
   (John Christoph)   I, 672, 673, 674
Johann Gerge   I, 425
Johannes   I, 155, 158, 161
Matheis (Mathias)   I, 559, 561, 562
     II, 130
ZADLER *see* SATTLER
ZAHN (ZAHAN, TSAWN)
Joh. Fried.   II, 139
Peter (Petter,
   Peter)   I, 289, 290, 291
ZAHNER *see* ZEHNER
ZAHNLE
Andreas   I, 755
ZAHNLEYTER (SANDLYTER)
Gorg (Gorg,
   Wright)   I, 286, 287, 288
ZALLER *see* ZELLER
ZÄMER (ZEMIER, SEMER)
Jerimias
   (Jeremiah)   I, 245, 246, 247
ZANEICHEL (SAYNHISIN, SAYN-
HAYSEN)
Vallentin
   (Felte)   I, 595, 597, 599
ZÄNER *see* ZEHNER
ZANGMEISTER (read SANGMEIS-
TER)
Georg Friederich   I, 408
Johann Adam   I, 408
ZANTZINGER (SONGSINGER)
Hans Paulus (Paul)   I, 83, 86
ZARBURGER (SERBURGER, AR-
BURGHER)
Lenhart (Leonard)   I, 316, 317
ZARINGER
Hans Jörg   I, 508
ZÄRLIN
Mr.   II, 176
Mrs.   II, 176

ZARTMANN   (ZAARTMAN,
ZARTTMANN)
Alexander   I, 20, 21
ZAUERLING
Christian   II, 69
ZEB *see* ZEPP
ZEBALT, ZEBOLT *see* SEBOLDT
ZEBERLY *see* SEBELIE
ZECH
Jacob   I, 476
ZECHIEL
Johan Jacob   I, 718
ZEEGELE *see* SIEGEL
ZEEKENDOFF
Gustav   II, 83
ZEELER *see* ZELLER
ZEELIE
Johanna   I, 45
Margarite   I, 45
ZEG
P.   II, 32
ZEGLER *see* ZIEGLER
ZEH (SEE)
Philippus
   (Philip)   I, 581, 582, 584
ZEHENBAUER *see* ZEHNTBAUER
ZEHERMAN
Simon   I, 397
ZEHN
Andrew   II, 55
ZEHNER (ZENER, ZAHNER, ZÄH-
NER, ZÄNER)
Ann Margaret   II, 56
Anton   I, 340
Catherine   II, 56, 115
Eberhard   II, 56
Elisabeth   II, 115
Jacob   I, 706
Johann Adam
   (Johan Adam)   I, 666, 668, 670
Johannes (John)   I, 347; II, 56
John   II, 56
John Philip   II, 56
Michael   I, 707
Zigmond (Sigmund)   II, 56
ZEHNTBAUER   (ZEHENBAUER)
Johann Michael   I, 476
Martin   I, 509
ZEHRING (ZEHRUNG, SARING)
Johannes (John)   I, 568, 570, 572
ZEIBIG
John. Benj.   II, 127
ZEIDLER (ZEITLER)
G. Carl   II, 205
Jacob   I, 498
John   II, 123
ZEIFS
Andrew   II, 82

ZEIGENER (ZEIGNER)
Gorg Caspar   I, 179, 181, 183
ZEIGER (ZIEGER, ZIGER)
  Christina   I, 61
  Jacob   I, 62
  Johan   I, 60, 64, 65
  Margretha   I, 61
  Matheas   I, 497
  Susanna   I, 62
ZEIGLER see ZIEGLER
ZEILER (ZEILLER)
  Frantz (Francis)   I, 568, 570, 572
  Peter   I, 704
  Philips Conradt   I, 456
ZEIMER
  Andrew   II, 89
ZEINER
  Hans George   I, 686
  Michael   I, 686
  Simon   I, 486
ZEISE (SEISE)
  Johann Christian
    (Jnº Chr.)   I, 589, 590, 591
ZEISELER
  Adam   II, 101
ZEISER * (ZISER)
  Johannes   I, 592
ZEISIGER
  Johan Godfried   I, 505
ZEISINGER (REYTRINGER)
  Johann Nicklas   I, 348, 349, 351
ZEISLOFF (ZEISSLOFF, SYSLOOF)
  Aⁿ Catharina   I, 156
  Balthasar
    (Johan Baltzar) I, 155, 158, 160
  Georg (Jorg)   I, 155, 158, 160
  Hˢ Nickel
    (Johan Nickolas) I, 155, 158, 160
ZEISTER
  Johan Michgel   I, 322
ZEISZLER
  Johannes   I, 464
ZEITLER see ZEIDLER
ZEITZ see SEITZ
ZELINGER
  Gabriel   II, 75
ZELL
  Erick Lutwich   I, 12
ZELLER (ZEELER, ZALLER, SEL-
    LER)
  Anne   II, 31
  Anne Marie   II, 31
  Barbe   II, 31
  Casper   II, 55
  Conrad   I, 425
  Frena   II, 31
  Hans Jacob   I, 392
  Hans Mardin   I, 484
  Hennrich   I, 217, 219, 220

  Jacob   I, 425
  Jean   II, 31
  Johann Friedrich   I, 484
  Johannes (Johanes) I, 425, 642, 643
                             II, 92
  Regina   II, 151
ZELLMAN (SELMAN)
  Johannes   I, 311, 313
  Mical   I, 310
ZELLNER see ZÖLLNER
ZEMBA
  Andreas   II, 118
ZEMBSCH
  Johann Leonhardt   I, 533, 534
ZEMMER see ZIMMER
ZENBERGE (read prob. ZUM-
    BERGE)
  Adem   I, 701
ZENCK see ZINCK
ZENDMEYER
  Bernhard   I, 507
ZENG (ZENGH)
  Jerg (Jurg)   I, 11, 12
ZENGERLE
  Ignatzius   I, 723
ZENORE
  Geo. Balista   II, 205
ZENTLER
  Georg Petter   I, 699
ZEPERNICK
  Gottfried   I, 740
ZEPP (ZEB, ZEP)
  Georg Adam   I, 693
  George (Jerg,
    Jurg)   I, 605, 606, 608
                             II, 30
  Henry   I, 314
  Johan Peter   I, 460
  Johannes Sim.   I, 692
  Philipp (Philip) I, 629, 632, 635
ZEPPERFELD
  Johannes Peter   I, 707
ZEPPRICH
  Friedrich   II, 184
ZEPTER (SEPTER)
  Johannes   I, 340, 341, 342
ZERBINGER (SERBINGER, SEL-
    WINGER)
  Jacob   I, 546, 547, 549
ZERCHER
  Henrich   I, 741
ZEREL
  Jacob   I, 403
ZERFASS (ZERFAS, SURFAS)
  Friederich   I, 404
  Gottfrit (Gotfriet) I, 204, 206, 207
  Nicol (Nickel,
    Johann Nickel)   I, 290, 291
  Thiels   I, 763

ZERGIEBEL (ZWIGEBUL)
Gottfried I, 677, 678, 680
ZERN see ZÜRN
ZERR
Johann Georg I, 437
ZERVIN
John Jacob I, 331
ZERWICK
Christian II, 165
ZERWINNA
Philippine II, 54
ZESH (read ZESCH)
Georg Frederik I, 504
ZESSELER
Caspar I, 425
ZETTEL (SHITTLE, SHITTEL)
Jacob I, 113, 114, 115, 766
ZETTELMEYER (SEDELMEYER)
Georg I, 468
Jacob I, 468
Sebastian (Sebasting) I, 198, 200, 202
ZETY
Abraham I, 484
ZEULLER
Conrad I, 425
ZEY
John Adam I, 499
ZEYLER (read prob. SEILER)
Adam I, 67, 69, 70
Hans Peter I, 210
Michael Frederick
(Bliker Tidrick,
Blenhart Dit.) I, 209, 211
ZEYLEY
Michel II, 53
ZEYLIN
Conrad II, 5
ZHÜR (SYRRO)
Adam (Johannes
Adam) I, 559, 560, 562
ZIB (ZWIB, SMIT)
J. Wilhelm
(Wilhelm, Leonard) I, 628, 631, 634
ZIBIG
Henrich I, 725
ZICHELHARDT
Johann Gottfriedt I, 442
ZIEBLI see ZÜBLY
ZIEFUS (read prob. ZEHFUSS)
Peter I, 699
ZIEGELER see ZIEGLER
ZIEGER
Christoph I, 459
ZIEGET
Jacob I, 493
ZIEGLER (ZIGLER, ZIEGELER,
ZEIGLER)
Andres (Andreas) I, 188, 191, 193
Anna Margaretha I, 210; II, 114

Caspar (Casper) I, 615, 617, 619
Catharina II, 114
Christian I, 498
Christoph Gotthart I, 672, 673, 674
Conrat (Conrad) I, 393, 484
Dewald I, 715
Durs I, 330
Frantz I, 399
Friedrich (Fried.) I, 349, 350, 351
II, 114
Georg (Gorg) I, 471, 497
Georg Heinrich I, 727
Georg Philipp
(Jerick) I, 545, 547, 549
Hans Adam I, 209, 211
Hans Georg I, 10, 445
Hans Marti I, 711
Hans Wilhelm I, 96, 98
Jacob I, 360, 361
Jacobina II, 14
Johann II, 114
Joh. A. II, 198
Johann Conraht
(Conradt) I, 222, 223, 225
Joh. David I, 741
Johann Ernst
(John Ernst) I, 672, 673, 674, 739
Johann Georg
(Hans Georg) I, 169, 170, 172
513, 514, 515
Johan Heinrich
(Henrick) I, 573, 574, 575
Joh. Jacob I, 458
Johan Leonhardt
(Leonhard) I, 59, 63, 65
Johann Ludwig I, 457
Johannes I, 330
Martin I, 470
Melchior I, 472
Mr. II, 175
Mrs. II, 175
Nicklas
(Nicholas) I, 218, 219, 221, 462
Peter I, 393
Philip I, 9, 360, 361
Thomas I, 365
ZIEGLY (SIEGLE)
Jacob I, 360, 362
Johannes I, 360, 362
ZIELER
Hannes I, 715
ZIELING
Ludwig II, 4
ZIEMERMAN see ZIMMERMAN
ZIEPF (SIP, ZEIBF)
Hans Gorg
(Hans Jerg,
John Jorick) I, 609, 611, 612
Joseph I, 609, 611, 612

ZIESERSON
Peter II, 122
ZIFFE
Leonhart I, 411
ZIFFEL
Johan David I, 440
ZIGENFUSS
Johann Jacob I, 463
ZILCHART
Jacob I, 461
ZILLING
Hans Conradt I, 454
Michel I, 409
ZILLS
Wm I, 719
ZIMDECKER
Andreas II, 93
ZIMMELMAN (read prob. ZIMMER-MAN)
Jacob I, 721
ZIMMER (ZEMMER, ZIEHMER, ZIMER, ZUMMER, ZÜMMER)
Charles I, 757
Christian I, 700
Christopher I, 234
Claudius II, 184
Friederich I, 506
Georg Amelius II, 148
Heinrich I, 410
Johan Conrath
(Conradt) I, 591, 593, 594
Johann Danniel
(Daniel) I, 591, 593, 594
Johan Jacob
(Hans Jacob) I, 106, 110, 112
Johan Martin I, 740
Johannes I, 451
M. II, 147
Melchior I, 234
Michall I, 725
Nickollaus I, 763
Philip (Phillip) I, 386, 387, 389
Rudolph I, 307
Wilhelm I, 307, 308, 309
ZIMMERLE (ZIMERLY, SEMERLY)
Hans Georg
(Garrick) I, 232, 233
Philipp Lorentz I, 424
Wilhelm I, 424
ZIMMERMANN (ZIMMERMAN, ZIMERMAN)
Abraham I, 360, 362
Adolph I, 563, 565, 566
Andony I, 481
And* I, 7
Anna I, 190
Anna Marga II, 23
Anna Maria II, 36
Balthas I, 393

Barbara (Barbil) I, 73, 80, 190
Bastian I, 80
Christian I, 80, 408
Conrad (Conrat) I, 199, 201, 203
Daniel I, 710
David I, 507
Elizabeth (Eliz.) I, 80; II, 36
Friederick I, 441, 468
G. Godlob II, 156
George
(George, Jarig) I, 363, 480; II, 126
Geo. Wendel I, 689
Gerhard (Gerhartt) I, 290, 291
H. Michael I, 416
Hans I, 78, 80, 81, 82
188, 192, 193
Hans Adam I, 349, 350, 351
Hans Heinnrich I, 737
Hans Jacob Serber I, 483
Hans Ludwig I, 446
Hans Michael I, 9
Hans Philip (Filb) I, 71, 76, 77
Hendrich Wilhelm II, 36
Henry I, 467
Hermannus (Manuel) I, 569, 571, 573
J. Gerhart I, 466
J. Jacob (Jacob) I, 621, 623, 625
Jacob I, 738; II, 150
Jno Geo. I, 730
Johann I, 759
Johann Christ. I, 466, 467
Johann Christoffel
(Christoffel) I, 256, 259, 261
Johan Friedrich I, 416, 690
Johann Georg I, 710
Johann Gottfr. Paul I, 759
Johann Jacob
(John Jacob) I, 286, 287, 289
Johan Jost I, 408
Johan Nickel
(Hans Nichel) I, 290, 291, 683
Johann Peter I, 409
Johann Tobias I, 441
Johannes
(Johanis, Jno) I, 416, 418, 684, 752
John Adam
(Adam) I, 79, 82, 83
John Henry I, 741
Juliana I, 74
Kilian I, 407
Ludwig I, 605, 606, 608
Margaretha (Marg.) II, 105, 116
Maria I, 74, 81
Matheas (Matthias) I, 569, 571, 573
Michel I, 360, 362, 521, 523
Nicklos I, 79, 82, 83
Peter (Better) I, 265, 268, 271
Salome I, 79
Simm I, 489

Susanna   I, 144
Ulrich   I, 79, 82, 83
Wilke   II, 191
ZIN *see* ZINN
ZINCK (ZINCKH)
Andreas (Anderas)   I, 604, 606, 607
Anthony   I, 482
Christan (Christianus,
  Christianes)   I, 605, 606, 608
Christopher
  (Christophel)   I, 604, 606, 607
Conrad   I, 460
Daniel   I, 310, 312, 313
Gottlieb   I, 499
Jacob   I, 22, 23, 604
                                 606, 607
Johann Gottlieb   I, 459
Learmer   I, 232
Martin   II, 119
ZINCKE (ZINKE, ZINCKER)
Johann Caspar   I, 677, 678, 680
ZINCKWINTZ
Joachim Friederich   I, 757
ZINLAUB *see* ZUMBAUB
ZINN (ZIN)
Casber   I, 357
Gerhart (Gerard)   I, 31, 32, 33
Jacob   I, 403
Johannes (Johanis) I, 204, 206, 207
ZINSER
Hans   I, 448
Johannes   I, 498
ZINTEL (SHINDEL, LINTHELL)
George Ernst
  (Geo. Erd)   I, 199, 201, 203
ZIRCHER
Balthes   I, 366
ZIRN *see* ZÜRN
ZISSLER
Gorg Philib   I, 755
ZITTEL (ZITTLE)
Barbry   II, 51
Daniel   I, 761
Eliz^t   II, 51
Gartrute   II, 51
Geo.   II, 51
Johann   II, 51
John Geo.   II, 51
Nicholas   II, 51
ZLUHAN (SLUHAN)
Jacob Fridrich
  (Fredrick)   I, 637, 639, 640
ZOBEL
Gorg Adam   I, 431
ZOBELI, ZÖBLI *see* ZUBLY
ZOBINGER (SOUPINGER)
Johannes   I, 384, 385
ZÖFNER
Johans   I, 434

ZOLFERS
Doctor Heinrich   II, 74
ZOLL (ZOL)
Jacob   I, 722
Hadolf   I, 483
Henry   I, 404
Johann Nickel
  (Nicholas)   I, 282, 284, 285
Johann Peter
  (Peter)   I, 656, 657, 658
ZÖLLER (ZELLER, ZOLLER, SOL-
LER)
Bartel   I, 335, 336, 338
Daniel   I, 464
Elias   I, 221, 223, 224
Fridrich   I, 475
Geo. Leon^d   I, 715
Hans Jerg
  (Jeick)   I, 107, 111, 112
Mr.   II, 174
Nichlas (Nicklas,
  Nickel)   I, 289, 290, 291
ZOLLICKER
Jacob   I, 405
ZOLLIKOFFER (ZOLLICOFER)
Casper   II, 41
Matthias   I, 66, 69, 70
ZOLLINGER (SOLLINGER)
Caspar   II, 49
Felix   I, 348
Hans   I, 252, 254, 255
ZOLLMANN (ZOLLMAN, SOL-
MAN)
Anthon (Anthony) I, 656, 657, 658
Johan Adam   I, 656, 657, 658
ZÖLLNER (ZELLNER)
Conrad   I, 439
Friederich (Fredrick) I, 293, 294, 295
ZOMBRO
Jacob   I, 522, 524
Joseph   I, 460
Peter   I, 432
ZONGER
Simmon   I, 347
ZÖNGRIG
Peter   I, 494
ZONY
Mr. A.   II, 74
ZOPFF (ZAB)
Daniel   I, 179, 181, 184
ZOPSE
Jacob   II, 197
ZÖRLEN
Johannes   I, 358
ZORN
Andres   I, 485
Caspar   I, 614, 616, 618
Conrad   I, 672, 673, 674
Jacob   I, 225, 228, 230

ZORR
Hans I, 448
ZOTZEL (SUTZILL)
Wilhelm I, 596, 598, 600
ZOWCK (read prob. ZAUCK)
Henrich I, 97
ZUBLER
Hans I, 399
ZUBLY * (ZUBLEY, ZÖBELI,
ZÖBLI, ZIEBLY)
Hans I, 331, 332, 334
384, 386
Hans Jacob I, 434
Heinrich (Henry) I, 384, 386, 483
Joseph I, 347
ZUCH
Jacob I, 197, 198
ZUCHER
Henry II, 204
ZUCKER
Heinrich Siegmon II, 76
Johann Jacob I, 545, 547, 549
Ludwig I, 649, 650
ZUEGRI
Christian I, 197, 198
ZÜFFLE
Jacob I, 452
ZUG
Christian I, 327, 329
Johannes I, 327, 329
Moritz I, 327, 329
Peter I, 10, 11
Ulrich I, 10, 11
ZÜGEL (ZIEGELL, ZIGEL, SEIGEL,
ZUGEL)
Gottlieb (Godliph) I, 349, 350, 351
Jerg Friedrich
(Fredk) I, 348, 350, 351
John Wm iI, 200
ZUGMEYR
Joseph I, 469
ZULTZ
A. II, 32
ZUMBOTT
Johannes I, 730
ZUMLAUB (ZENLAUB, ZINLAUB)
Frederick I, 582, 583, 585
Johan Gorg
(Daniel) I, 582, 583, 584
Johann Philip
(Johan Philip) I, 581, 583, 584
ZUMOST (SMOUS)
Hans (Johannes) I, 222, 223, 225
ZUMSTAIN
Phillip I, 686
ZÜND
Johanes I, 434
ZUNDEL
Johann Georg I, 727

ZUNEIN
Joh Th. II, 125
ZUNFT (ZUNFFT)
John Casper
(Johann Caspar) I, 195, 196, 197
ZUPMANN
Isaac Christian II, 183
ZUPPINGER (ZUPINGER)
Conrad I, 147
Hendryk I, 148
Hs. Ulric I, 148
Marguerit I, 148
ZURBRÜCK
Johannes I, 440
ZURBÜCHEN
Heindrich I, 494
ZÜRCH (ZURG, ZORGE)
Anthony I, 423
Philip I, 546, 548, 550
ZURCHER (ZEREHART, SIRGIER)
Jacob I, 264, 267, 270
ZURDIOGH
——, van II, 122
ZURFLIE
Johannes I, 494
ZURGER (ZURCHEN)
Justina I, 190
Michael I, 188, 192, 193
Uhllerigh I, 485
ZÜRN (ZIRN, ZERN, ZUERN)
Casper I, 413
Christian I, 497
F. Wilhelm I, 531, 532, 534
Friederich I, 512, 514, 515
Johannes I, 480
Peter I, 689
ZUTHEIMER
Nicholas I, 754
ZUTTER
Balthaser I, 686
Daniel I, 686
ZUTZ (SUTZ)
George I, 234, 235, 236
ZWALLE
Hans (Hance) I, 163, 165, 166
Johannes I, 413
ZWALLEN (SWALLER)
Christen (Christan) I, 153, 154
ZWANZGER (ZWANSIGER)
Andreas I, 655, 657, 658
ZWEIG (ZWEYK, SWICK, SCHWY)
Baltus I, 513, 514, 515
Christoph I, 513, 514, 515
ZWEIGELE (ZWEIGLE)
Caspar II, 121
Johannis I, 442
ZWEISIG (SWITZICK, SHWEY-
ZIG, SWITZIG)
Bernhart I, 311, 312, 313

Diterich
  (Jno Fredrick)   I, 311, 312, 313
  Valdin   I, 310, 311, 312
ZWEYER
  H. George   I, 474
  Stephen   I, 474
ZWICK
  Heinrich   I, 348
ZWICKEL
  Johann George   II, 79
  Johannes   I, 480
ZWICKER (ZWEKSEER)
  Wendel   I, 185, 186, 187
ZWIEBELLER
  Johan   I, 504
ZWIECRANTZ
  Ludwig   I, 426
ZWIER
  Daniel   I, 360, 361

ZWIGART (read prob. SCHWEICK-
  HART)
  Daniel   I, 706
ZWINGER
  Johan   I, 32, 34
ZWINGLER
  J. P.   II, 3
ZWIRNER
  Johan Adam   I, 545, 547, 549
  Lorenz (Lawrence)   I, 84, 86, 87
ZWIRSKY
  Joseph   I, 521, 524
ZWISSLER (SWITZLER)
  Ludwig Bernhard
    (Loder[k] Bernard)   I, 596, 598, 600
ZYNDELBACH (read prob. ZÜND-
  ELBACH)
  Michael   I, 414
ZYPHER
  Philip, van   II, 122